# Credits

**Product Director**
Stephanie Gould

**Product Development Specialists**
Kurt D. Hampe
Robin Drake

**Acquisitions Editors**
Cheryl D. Willoughby
Fred Slone

**Acquisitions Coordinators**
Angela C. Kozlowski
Ruth Slates

**Production Editors**
Linda Seifert
Nanci Sears Perry

**Copy Editors**
Geneil Breeze
Charles K. Bowles
Kelli M. Brooks
Keith Davenport
Noelle Gasco
Lisa M. Gebken
Theresa Mathias
Julie A. McNamee
Lynn Northrup
Maureen Schneeberger

**Editorial Assistant**
Andrea Duvall

**Technical Editors**
Randall A. Maxey
Rob Fassberg
Jeff Hester
Allen Smith
Scott Taylor
LeAnne Thurmond
Warren Wolf

**Technical Specialist**
Cari Ohm

**Book Designer**
Sandra Schroeder

**Cover Designer**
Jean Bisesi

**Cover Art**
Brad Kelley

**Graphic Image Specialists**
Becky Beheler
Steve Carlin
Brad Dixon
Teresa Forrester
Jason Hand
Denny Hager

Clint Lahnen
Cheri Laughner
Michael Reynolds
Laura Robbins
Dennis Sheehan
Craig Small
Jeff Yesh

**Production Team**
Steve Adams
Claudia Bell
Maxine Dillingham
Chad Dressler
DiMonique Ford
Aren Howell
Barry Jorden
Daryl Kessler
Bob LaRoche
Darcy Meyers
G. Alan Palmore
Kaylene Riemen
Clair Schweinler
Kris Simmons
Mike Thomas
Scott Tullis
Elaine Voci-Reed

**Indexer**
Rebecca Mayfield

Composed in *Stone Serif* and *MCPdigital* by Que Corporation

# About the Authors

**Jay H. Zirbel** is an associate professor at Murray State University in Murray, Kentucky in the department of Industrial Engineering and Technology. He received his Ph.D from Texas A&M University, and M.S. and B.S. degrees from the University of Wisconsin–Stout. Dr. Zirbel's professional experience spans over 15 years, teaching manufacturing courses at the university and community college levels. He has been using AutoCAD extensively for the past seven years and instructs industrial workshops in AutoCAD on a regular basis. His hobbies include working with computers and studying Tae Kwon Do.

**Steven B. Combs** is on the faculty of IVY Tech State College in Evansville, Indiana. He teaches mechanical and architectural design for the Design Technology Department and is also an Autodesk Training Center trainer. He has used and taught courses in AutoCAD and 3D Studio since 1991. After graduating from high school in 1983, he received his bachelor's and master's degrees in Industrial Education from Murray State University in Murray, Kentucky. He is a Certified Industrial Technologist as well as a commissioned officer in the United States Army Reserves. He currently resides with his wife, Elizabeth, in Evansville, IN. He can be reached through e-mail at stevecombs@aol.com.

**Ashim Guha** is a free-lance writer, based in Silicon Valley, California. Mr. Guha has a Master's Degree in Mechanical Engineering. He has an extensive background in CAD products and has coauthored and edited several AutoCAD books.

**Robert L. Knight** is a registered architect and partner with Architectural Alliance, an architectural firm in Indianapolis, Indiana. He also is a partner in Computer Projects Unlimited, a consulting group that specializes in AutoCAD consulting. Bob's background includes training, support, customizing, and application development for AutoCAD systems in architecture and engineering industry. He has coauthored and edited several books on AutoCAD Releases 10, 11, and 12. His project list includes Que's *Using AutoCAD,* 2nd and 3rd Editions, and *AutoCAD Quick Reference,* 2nd Edition. Bob can be reached via CompuServe at 72002,2071.

**Heather Krause** is the CAD Coordinator for Smith & Loveless, Inc. in Lenexa, Kansas, and has been using AutoCAD for over 11 years. She has taught both credit and non-credit CAD classes at Longview Community College in Lee's Summit, Missouri. She wrote an article for *CADalyst* about her experiences teaching AutoCAD. *PC World* also published an article regarding her computer work at Smith & Loveless. She is presently working on an office automation project using the Microsoft Access database and other associated software. She also is studying to become a Certified Netware Engineer. You can reach Heather via CompuServe at 75106,1662, or on the Internet at 75106.1662@compuserve.com.

**Jeffrey Pike** spent five years working at Autodesk, Inc. in the Product Support department, where he provided technical support for Autodesk customers, dealers, and developers as Primary Sysop for the Autodesk Forums on CompuServe. He has installed, trained, supported, and used AutoCAD since 1986. He holds a bachelor's degree in Rangeland Resources Management and a bachelor's degree in Economics from Oregon State University.

**Ranjit S. Sahai**, a licensed Professional Engineer, is a Senior Engineer with Alpha Corporation, a consulting engineering firm based in Sterling, Virginia. He is passionately interested in CAD and writes for several computer magazines, including *CADalyst* and *MicroStation Manager*. He recognized early on the benefits of working in the Windows graphical environment and has written several articles on writing custom applications that interface a spreadsheet with AutoCAD for Windows using the operating system's Dynamic Data Exchange inter-application communication facility. He can be reached via CompuServe at 70621,3147.

**Scott Sawdy** currently works in the Technical Support Group of Electro-Matic Products, Inc. of Farmington Hills, Michigan. He is in charge of AutoCAD development and support and is the Windows NT Network Administrator. Formerly a contributing writer of product reviews for *CADENCE,* he has written or rewritten software manuals and corporate CAD standards. As a user of AutoCAD since 1987, he has specialized in menu customization and written several hundred specialized LISP and Script routines. He can be reached via CompuServe at 71726,503.

**Mark Scott** currently works as a freelance consultant. He has devoted the past 10 years to learning as much about AutoCAD as he can, and then passing that knowledge on to others. Mark most recently worked for an AutoCAD dealership where he was responsible for custom programming, support, and training. He also has worked for a large multidiscipline AEC firm where he was in charge of supporting an AutoCAD operator base of various disciplines. During this same period, Mark was an ATC instructor at a community college. He has written for *CADalyst*, and enjoys using visualization applications such as 3D Studio and AutoVision. A frequent user of CompuServe, Mark can be reached at 71501,2622.

**Craig Spaid** has a Master's Degree in Landscape Architecture from Ball State University, in Muncie, Indiana. He also has undergraduate degrees in Urban Planning, Natural Resources, and Geography. Since 1983, he has been involved with AutoCAD as an end-user, reseller, instructor, and developer. Craig continues to help AutoCAD users capture its potential in the areas of GIS and Digital Document Management through his employment at Alco Marbaugh in Indianapolis, Indiana. He has a very patient (especially when it comes to writing books) wife of 15 years, Marcia, and two junior software developers, Melissa, 12 and Daniel, 10 years old.

**Gene Straka** is the AutoCAD support specialist at Hudson Engineering in Houston, Texas. He also has served as an AutoLISP instructor at the University of Houston—Downtown. Working with various CAD packages since 1983, Gene has used AutoCAD since version 2.18. He has worn many hats including AutoCAD instructor, software and hardware troubleshooter, AutoLISP programmer, AutoCAD designer, custom menu developer, and author of *AutoLISP Programming by Example*. Gene resides in Katy, Texas with his wife Debbie and sons Jacob and Zachary. A frequent traveler on the information highway, Gene can be reached on CompuServe at 73627,1443, on America Online at GSTRAKA, and on Prodigy at NARA06A.

**Dennis Strieter** is a Systems Designer at Zenon Municipal Systems Inc., a manufacturer of on-site wastewater treatment and recycling systems in Ann Arbor, Michigan. Dennis has been using AutoCAD since 1985, starting with Version 2.17. As Systems Designer and CADD System Manager he provides company support for installation, training, software integration and supervising the company's Workgroup for Windows network. He has developed custom software and menus to aid in the design of wastewater treatment facilities, programming in AutoLISP.

**William Valaski** graduated from the University of Cincinnati with a degree in Architectural Engineering. He works for CDS Associates, Inc., an A/E firm in Cincinnati, Ohio, where he practices architecture and manages computer operations. Bill also is a partner in Computer Projects Unlimited, a computer consulting firm, and a sysop for the Cincinnati Freenet, Tristate Online. Bill has been an author for Que and New Riders Publishing for over five years, working on projects such as *Using AutoCAD*, 2nd Edition, *The AutoCAD Quick Reference, AutoCAD: The Professional Reference, Killer AutoCAD Utilities*, and *Inside AutoCAD LT for Windows*.

**Brad Winsor** has been using AutoCAD since 1986 and is the owner of Winsor CAD Consulting, a CAD instruction and production firm in Atlanta, Georgia. He teaches all levels of AutoCAD and 3D Studio for the Office of Continuing Education at the Southern College of Technology in Marietta, Georgia. Brad also is an expert in the customization and use of AutoCAD for mechanical and civil engineering applications. He holds an Industrial Design degree from Auburn University.

## Trademark Acknowledgments

# Contents at a Glance

Getting Started

Basic Drawing Techniques

Editing a Drawing

Viewing and Plotting

Advanced Drawing

Advanced Editing

# Contents

## 2 Creating Your First Drawing     45

## III Editing a Drawing      209

### 9 Understanding Selection Sets      211

## 10 Editing Techniques                                          239

# IV Viewing and Plotting a Drawing 329

## 12 Viewing a Drawing 331

# V Advanced Drawing and Annotation    425

## 15 Advanced Drawing Techniques    427

## 24 Working with Attributes                                              713

# VIII Isometrics and 3D Drafting                 745

## 25 Creating Isometric Drawings                 747

## 26 Introduction to 3D Modeling                 759

## 27  Understanding 3D Coordinate Systems    **785**

# IX  Solid Modeling and Rendering                899

## 32  Introduction to Solid Modeling Concepts          901

# X Using and Managing Drawing Data    975

## 35 Converting AutoCAD Drawings to Other Formats 977

## C System Variables Reference            1147

# Introduction

Welcome to *Special Edition Using AutoCAD Release 13 for Windows*. AutoCAD Release 13 for Windows is truly a milestone upgrade for the industry's standard and most popular computer-aided drafting program. Autodesk put significant effort into the Windows product, giving it many new and exciting features.

## Who Should Read This Book

*Special Edition Using AutoCAD Release 13 for Windows* is written and designed to help both first-time and experienced AutoCAD users become more proficient with this significant upgrade. If you are a first-time AutoCAD user, you will appreciate the concise steps and clear descriptions of commands and procedures. You will get up and running quickly, creating your first drawing in Chapter 2. By starting with Chapter 1, "Introducing AutoCAD," and continuing through each chapter, you will create an entire apartment complex, complete with furniture and a hot tub! The On Your Own exercises at the end of the chapters are provided to help you review what you have learned.

Near the end of each chapter, the From Here section gives a brief explanation of what topics are ahead. The chapters mentioned in the From Here section are related to material just covered.

Experienced AutoCAD users can use this book to learn about the new features in Release 13 and master more advanced drawing techniques. New features found in Release 13 are identified by an icon found in the margin. This book also serves as a reference for your day-to-day questions and problems about commands.

# What to Expect in This Book

*Special Edition Using AutoCAD Release 13 for Windows* is divided into twelve parts, each containing a new set of AutoCAD commands. Along with the commands, associated options and system variables are discussed. Each chapter also contains notes, tips, and cautions that will help you become more productive.

Whether you are a new or experienced AutoCAD user, *Special Edition Using AutoCAD Release 13 for Windows* shows you how to use the updated interface and to get the most out of AutoCAD. Here is an overview of the book with a short description of each part:

- **Part I. Getting Started.** Whether you are a new or experienced user, this section has you creating your first drawing very quickly. You are introduced to the updated Windows interface and the toolbars. In this part, you also work with coordinates and units, and create a prototype drawing.

- **Part II. Basic Drawing Techniques.** Creating accurate geometry and working with layers are two essential elements needed to generate your drawings. This section covers object snaps, a technique used to ensure precise geometry creation. Chapter 8, "Understanding Linetypes," explains the different methods available in Release 13 to load and use linetypes, and the new ISO linetypes.

- **Part III. Editing a Drawing.** After you have created a drawing in AutoCAD, you should never have to redraw it; this part shows you how to copy, move, rotate, stretch, and edit your drawing. You also learn several different methods of selecting objects for editing. Grips, another method for selecting and editing objects, is also covered.

- **Part IV. Viewing and Plotting a Drawing.** This part introduces you to the different ways to view a 2D drawing on-screen. You learn how to magnify or shrink the drawing to show more detail or more of the drawing. You also learn how to use the aerial view window, and store views and slides for later use. You also are guided through the steps required to produce a copy of the drawing on paper using your printer or plotter.

- **Part V. Advanced Drawing and Annotation.** After you have mastered the basics, you can begin to explore some of AutoCAD's more advanced features. You start by using several advanced drawing techniques, including the new XLINE, RAY, and MLINE commands.

You also are shown how to add details to any drawing with text, dimensions, and hatching.

- **Part VI. Advanced Editing Techniques.** In this part, you learn AutoCAD's more involved editing commands that enable you to change the properties of an object. You also learn how to get information from your drawing, calculate area, and keep track of your drawing and editing time.

- **Part VII. Using Symbols and Attributes.** You complete the apartment complex tutorial, and in the process learn how to integrate everything you have learned. In this part, you are shown how to put together a library of commonly used parts, drawings, and find out how to attach information to drawing objects.

- **Part VIII. Isometrics and 3D Drafting.** AutoCAD's 3D capabilities give you a chance to expand your ideas and look at them from a different perspective. You create 3D objects, view them from different angles, and make them look more realistic. This part also shows you how to draw revolved and meshed surfaces.

- **Part IX. Solid Modeling and Rendering.** A *solid model* contains a complete representation of the shape of a physical object. AutoCAD Release 13 includes ACIS technology to create solid objects. This technology allows for more accurate and exact representations of objects than was possible using the Advanced Modeling Extension in AutoCAD Release 12. You learn how to use this new technology to create solid objects, and how to create realistic shadings and renderings to produce life-like representations of your model.

- **Part X. Using and Managing Drawing Data.** One advantage of working in the Windows environment is the ability of AutoCAD to interact with other Windows applications, such as spreadsheets, databases, and desktop publishing programs. In this part, you practice extracting and exchanging information with other programs from your drawing.

- **Part XI. Customizing and Expanding AutoCAD Resources.** One of the great benefits of using AutoCAD is the ability to adapt AutoCAD to your own work style. AutoCAD is now more flexible than ever with Release 13 for Windows. In this part, you learn how to customize the toolbars, menus, and linetypes. You also are shown how to tap the power of AutoLISP, ADS, and ARX.

■ **Appendixes.** The five appendixes address new features in Release 13 for Windows. They also tell you how to install and configure Release 13, how to work with digitizers, and how to trace an existing drawing. Appendix C is a system variables reference.

# Conventions Used in This Book

This book uses conventions designed to make it easy to use. You can learn AutoCAD's commands and capabilities quickly and easily.

With AutoCAD, you use the keyboard and pointing device to perform operations. The keyboard procedures include shortcut key combinations and mnemonic keys. In this book, key combinations are joined with a plus sign (+). For example, Ctrl+B means hold down the Control key, press the B key, and then release both keys.

Some menu and dialog box options will have underlined characters that indicate mnemonic keys. To choose a pull-down menu or dialog box option using the mnemonic key, press and hold the Alt key, press the indicated mnemonic key, then release both keys. To choose an option from a displayed pull-down menu using the option's mnemonic, simply type the mnemonic key. In this book, mnemonic keys are underlined; for example, File.

Words printed in uppercase include AutoCAD commands (LINE) and system variables (BLIPMODE). Information and commands you type appear in **boldface**.

The special typefaces used in *Special Edition Using AutoCAD Release 13 for Windows* to indicate special text are as follows:

| Typeface | Meaning |
| --- | --- |
| *italic* | Used to indicate new terms or phrases when they are defined. |
| **boldface** | Information you need to type. |
| `special typeface` | Direct quotations of words that appear on-screen as part of a command. |
| | Toolbar buttons appear in the margin next to the steps in which they are used. |

**Note**

A note is used to provide additional information that may help you avoid problems, or offers advice that relates to the topic.

**Caution**

A caution warns the reader of potentially hazardous procedures (for example, an activity that would delete all files).

**Tip**

A tip suggests easier or alternate methods of executing a procedure, or shortcuts to simplify the process described in the text.

**Troubleshooting**

*Troubleshooting sections anticipate common problems in the form of a question.*

The response provides you with practical suggestions for solving these problems.

## Tutorials

Tutorials are used throughout this book to give you hands-on practice in the use of AutoCAD commands and practices. Each tutorial begins with an introductory paragraph, such as this, containing a brief explanation of what will be accomplished, followed by a numbered list of steps.

**1.** Select the New button from the Standard toolbar. Enter a path and name for the drawing if you desire.

   *Most tutorials begin by starting a new drawing or loading a prototype from the work disk, as shown in step 1.*

**2.** Choose File, Import to access the Import File dialog box.

   *Pull-down menus will be referenced as shown in step 2. Hot keys will be underlined as shown.*

**3.** After the file finishes loading, AutoCAD asks for the insertion base point.

```
Insertion point <0,0,0>: 2,2
```

   *As shown in step 3, you should type what appears in bold, and then press Enter.*

**4.** Use the default scale factor.

    Scale factor<4>:

*If an AutoCAD command is shown during one of the tutorial steps and does not indicate that you should do anything, press Enter. As an example, look at step 4. The explanation says you are to use the default scale factor. On the next line, the AutoCAD command is given, showing the default scale factor. When a situation like this appears in a tutorial, press Enter.*

# Making AutoCAD Easy—Your Free Companion Disk

To help you gain more productivity from *Special Edition Using AutoCAD Release 13 for Windows,* a companion 3 1/2-inch disk is included. If you turn to the inside back cover of the book, you will find the disk in a sleeve. The disk is designed to provide you with all the drawings and documentation needed to get started with *Special Edition Using AutoCAD Release 13 for Windows.* Whether you are a new or experienced AutoCAD user, you can do all of the tutorials because the disk provides you with complete prototype drawings used in the tutorials.

# New Features of Release 13 for Windows

AutoCAD Release 13 for Windows offers an updated interface that contains 17 toolbars that can be moved to any convenient location on-screen. Besides the interface, other new features include:

- A resizable drawing and command window that can be moved.

- A drawing previewer used with the FILE OPEN and BLOCK INSERT commands.

- A text editor and integrated spell checking.

- A new multiline text object featuring word wrapping.

- TrueType and PostScript Type 1 Font support including 3D-filled TrueType fonts.

- Electronic online documentation and improved online Help.

- Improved support for external databases, covering more brands of databases. ASE has also been improved, requiring fewer commands and streamlined dialog boxes.

- New construction objects allowing you to create infinite lines, rays, and multilines.

- Integrated Geometric Dimensioning and Tolerancing symbol generation.

- Improved editing commands including TRIM, EXTEND, FILLET, and CHAMPHER. Also the new editing command LENGTHEN.

- Enhanced dimensioning features presented in a reworked and less complex set of dialog boxes.

- Enhanced hatching features, including associative hatching and island detection, presented in a reworked and less complex set of dialog boxes.

- Ability to group objects as part of a named selection set.

- New object snaps.

- Ability to change the linetype scale by object.

- Ability to PURGE the drawing at any time.

- ACIS technology for solid modeling and other new object types such as true ellipses and splines.

- Updated library of materials that can be assigned to the surfaces of 3D models for rendering purposes.

Let's get started!

# Part I

# Getting Started

YER

FENCELINE2 ——□——□——□——

BATTING

GAS_LINE ——— GAS ——— GAS ——— GAS ——— GAS ——— GAS ——— G

## Button Icon

Edit...

nu Groups

Menu Bar

ups:

Unload

☐ Replace All

Load

File Name:

File  Edit  View  Data  Options  Tools  Help

# Chapter 1

# Introducing AutoCAD

Welcome to the world of Computer Aided Design (CAD) as implemented in AutoCAD, the world's most popular CAD software. From its humble beginnings in 1982—when it started life on Zilog Z-80-based CP/M microcomputers as an affordable, though underpowered, alternative to high-priced turnkey systems—it now runs on a wide range of computers with capabilities to match the best in the business.

> **Note**
>
> Throughout this book you will see the acronyms CADD and CAD. CADD stands for Computer Aided Design and Drafting, while CAD is simply Computer Aided Design. Both refer to using the computer as a drafting tool. The latter term, however, is more common and is used in this book.

The brainchild of 16 programmer friends who founded Autodesk over 10 years ago with only $60,000 in capital, AutoCAD, the company's flagship product, grosses over $400 million in revenues annually. It is used worldwide not only by architectural, engineering, and construction companies, but also by manufacturing facilities and the aerospace, naval, and transportation industries. Anyone who needs precision drafting and design capabilities can benefit from AutoCAD.

Every new release of AutoCAD has added significant new features, helping its users perform design and drafting more flexibly and easily. Release 13 for Windows is no exception. It marks the introduction of a modern, multiwindow graphical interface with multiple floating toolbars as its primary means of command selection. Of course, there are scores of other enhancements as well.

This chapter introduces you to AutoCAD and covers the following basics:

- Starting AutoCAD

- Understanding the opening display

- Interacting with AutoCAD

- Getting help

- Saving drawings and quitting AutoCAD

Whether you are new to AutoCAD or just new to Release 13 for Windows, you should become familiar with the concepts presented in this chapter.

# Starting AutoCAD

▶ See "Installing and Configuring AutoCAD," p. 1095

When you install AutoCAD, the Install program copies all relevant program and support files into a directory on your computer's hard disk or your network file server's hard disk. The Install program also creates the AutoCAD R13 program group in Program Manager, as shown in figure 1.1.

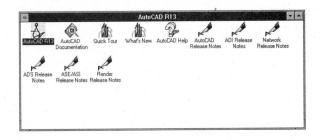

**Fig. 1.1**
Double-click the AutoCAD icon in the AutoCAD group window in Windows Program Manager to start AutoCAD.

To start AutoCAD, activate the AutoCAD group window in Program Manager and double-click the AutoCAD icon. Alternatively, you can click the AutoCAD icon in the group window and press Enter.

**Tip**
Windows also maintains an association between the DWG file name extension and AutoCAD. Double-clicking a drawing file with the DWG extension starts AutoCAD with the drawing already loaded.

> **Note**
>
> AutoCAD Release 13 for Windows is a Win32s application. This means that AutoCAD runs under Windows as a 32-bit application and also runs under Windows NT in native mode.

You also can start AutoCAD from Windows File Manager (see fig. 1.2). Navigate the contents of your hard disk to locate the AutoCAD executable file ACAD.EXE in the program's base directory, and double-click that file to start AutoCAD.

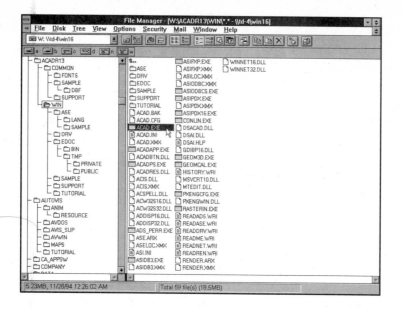

**Getting Started**

**Fig. 1.2**
To start AutoCAD
from File Manager,
double-click
ACAD.EXE or a
drawing with the
DWG file name
extension.

If you are running AutoCAD under Windows NT, you also can start
the CAD software from the MS-DOS command prompt by typing **start
c:\acadwin\acad**. If you installed AutoCAD in a directory other than
the C:\ACADWIN directory, use that path instead of the one shown.

> **Note**
>
> Although you can invoke AutoCAD from the Windows NT command line by simply
> typing the executable file name **c:\acadwin\acad**, you will want to precede it with
> the START command as just shown. This initiates a separate process in which to run
> AutoCAD. Otherwise, the MS-DOS command window from which you invoke
> AutoCAD will be unavailable until you exit the software.

On starting AutoCAD for the first time on a given computer, you are taken
through a configuration process to identify various hardware-specific choices.
These are not discussed here. For the purposes of this chapter, it is assumed
that AutoCAD has already been installed and configured to run properly on
your computer. (For details on installing and configuring AutoCAD for your
system, see Appendix B.)

# Understanding the Display

On starting AutoCAD, you are presented with an application window similar to that shown in figure 1.3. Take a moment to study this window and identify its various interface elements. All these elements will become familiar to you in this section.

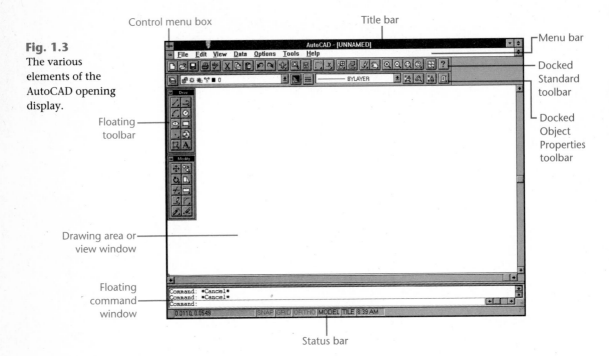

**Fig. 1.3**
The various elements of the AutoCAD opening display.

Control menu box

Title bar

Menu bar

Docked Standard toolbar

Docked Object Properties toolbar

Floating toolbar

Drawing area or view window

Floating command window

Status bar

The AutoCAD display is highly configurable, as you will discover in the course of reading this book. Thus, if the display on your computer screen does not match the one shown, your preferences settings are different from those used to create these images. The default AutoCAD settings are used here, and to follow along in this chapter, you too may want to maintain AutoCAD's "factory" settings.

Some components of the screen are meant to convey information; some are meant to accept command and data input. The various methods of invoking commands and interacting with AutoCAD are reviewed later in this chapter. For now, you should spend some time examining each of the screen components.

## Title Bar

At the top of the screen is the *title bar*. It displays the name of the software, AutoCAD, followed by the name of the currently open drawing file. If no drawing is open or you just started AutoCAD, the word UNNAMED appears instead. To the left of the title bar is the standard Windows application Control menu. To the right of the title bar are two buttons: Minimize and Maximize/Restore. The Control menu, the Minimize button, and the Maximize/Restore button have the same functions as in any other Windows application.

You can run only one session of AutoCAD 13 for Windows at a time, and that session has only one drawing area. If you attempt to run multiple sessions, you will get an error message and may lock up your system. It is likely that future versions of Windows will allow Autodesk to create a version of AutoCAD for Windows that can run multiple sessions.

Directly under the title bar is the *menu bar*, which provides access to AutoCAD's pull-down menus. To display a pull-down menu, choose one of the menu options. Figure 1.4 shows the View pull-down menu.

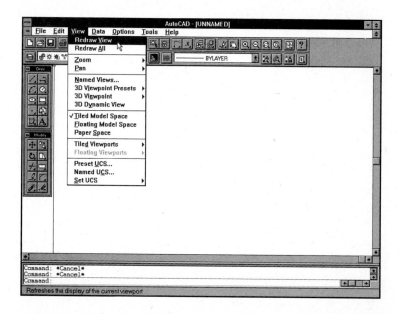

**Fig. 1.4**
Choosing an option on the menu bar pulls down AutoCAD's menus.

---

**Note**

AutoCAD's pull-down menus are customizable; you can change them to suit your needs. If you've used AutoCAD before, you probably know that AutoCAD's standard menu file is maintained in the text file ACAD.MNU.

▶ See "Customizing AutoCAD," p. 1019

AutoCAD Release 13 for Windows comes bundled with two sets of pull-down menus. Type **menu** at the Command: prompt and select the file ACADFULL.MNU from the list in the Select Menu File dialog box to switch from the standard menu to the full menu.

## Standard Toolbar

The *toolbar* introduced in Release 12 for Windows has been completely re-vamped. With Release 13, the toolbar is now similar to most Windows applications in that the most commonly used commands are included there. Figure 1.5 shows the Standard toolbar located directly under the menu bar.

**Fig. 1.5**
AutoCAD's
Standard toolbar
contains com-
monly used
commands.

Table 1.1 lists the commands and actions associated with icons in the Standard toolbar.

| Table 1.1 | Standard Toolbar Commands | |
|---|---|---|
| **Icon** | **Name** | **Use** |
| | New | Creates new drawings |
| | Open | Opens existing drawings |
| | Save | Saves active drawings |
| | Print | Prints or previews the current drawing |
| | Spelling | Checks the spelling of selected words or the entire drawing |
| | Cut | Cuts the selected elements from a drawing and places them on the Windows Clipboard |
| | Copy | Copies the selected elements from a drawing and places them on the Windows Clipboard |
| | Paste | Pastes the contents of the Windows Clipboard in your current drawing |
| | Undo | Sequentially undoes drawing, editing, and viewing commands since the last time you issued a save |

| Icon | Name | Use |
|------|------|-----|
|  | Redo | Sequentially redoes commands from the undo buffer |
|  | Aerial View | Accesses the Aerial View window or invokes any of the other toolbars |
|  | Select Window | Creates a selection set of objects for performing an editing task on them |
|  | Object Group | Creates groups from a selection set |
|  | Snap From | Invokes a snap mode |
|  | _.X_ | Invokes the point filtering commands |
|  | Preset UCS | Configures the User Coordinate System |
|  | Named View | Provides access to viewpoint commands |
|  | Redraw View | Repaints the screen to clear it of temporary "blips" or other objects that clutter up your display |
|  | Pan Point | Scrolls the drawing along a distance and angle that you specify, or along any of the preset directions, without changing its display scale |
|  | Zoom In | Zooms in on a drawing so its display scale is twice what it was before |
|  | Zoom Out | Zooms out from a drawing so its display scale is one half what it was before |
|  | Zoom Window | Zooms in on a drawing area specified by a rectangular window |
|  | Zoom All | Accesses various Zoom commands |
|  | Tiled Model Space | Switches between paper space and model space |
|  | Help | Accesses the on-line Help system |

The purpose of the Standard toolbar is to let you access the most frequently used commands quickly and easily. Some icons stand by themselves, whereas others are *nested* and offer a choice of related commands. Each nested icon has a little black arrow on the lower-right corner; if you click and hold down the left mouse button on one of these icons, additional icon(s) will "fly out."

---

**Note**

If you do not like the Standard toolbar along the top under the menu bar, you can drag the toolbar to "float" on the screen. Or you can place it along the left, right, or bottom edge of AutoCAD's application window. To drag the toolbar and make it float, place the cursor on it at any location not covered by an icon, click the mouse button and, while keeping the button pressed, move the pointer. You will see a gray outline of the toolbar following your cursor. When you release the mouse button, the toolbar will float at that location.

---

### Floating Toolbars

Instead of relying on the use of pull-down menus or the Command prompt as a primary means of invoking commands, Release 13 marks a fundamental shift in how it expects you to select commands. There are no drawing or editing commands available on the standard pull-down menus! These commands must be selected from one of several *toolbars* organized by category (or must be typed at the command line, as in earlier AutoCAD versions). See figure 1.6 for the variety of floating toolbars available.

**Fig. 1.6**
The comprehensive set of floating toolbars offered by Release 13 provides a quick means of invoking commands.

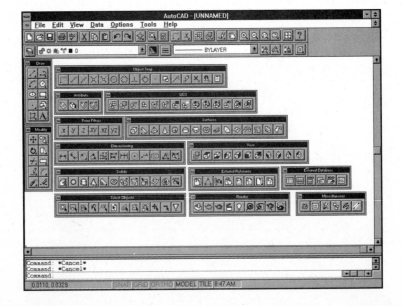

**Note**

Depending on your experience with AutoCAD and your work preferences, you may want to use commands rather than icons. This book includes a variety of options for working with AutoCAD: commands typed at the command line, items chosen from menus, and icons. Whenever possible, the text shows multiple options for executing the command.

Only the Draw and Modify toolbars are displayed initially when you start AutoCAD. To display additional floating toolbars, choose Tools, Toolbars to display the cascading menu that provides access to all available toolbars.

## Command Window

At the bottom of the screen is the *command window*. It is made up of two components: the command line and the command history window. The command line displays what you type from the keyboard. The command history window is a scrollable list of the commands you have previously entered. The command window also displays prompts that AutoCAD uses to communicate with you. Figure 1.7 shows the command window.

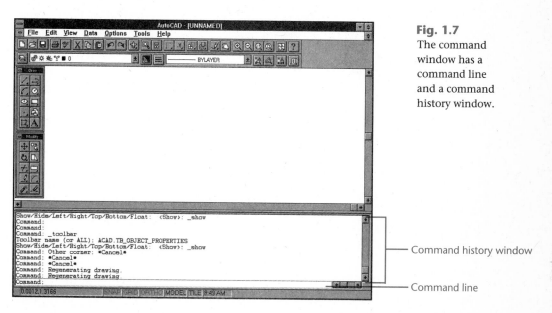

**Fig. 1.7**
The command window has a command line and a command history window.

Command history window

Command line

AutoCAD displays the following prompt when the program is waiting for you to provide input:

    Command:

After you enter a command, additional commands or prompts appear, as well as the results of many of your actions. Always watch this area closely because AutoCAD uses it to communicate with you. Error messages, command options, and other prompts are all displayed here.

> **Note**
>
> The command window reserves one line for the command line and a configurable number of lines for the command history window. To change the size of the command window, choose Options, Preferences from the pull-down menu. The Text Window section in the Misc tab of the Preferences dialog box provides an option field in which you type the size of the command window.

The command line has traditionally been along the bottom of the AutoCAD screen. With Release 13, that remains the default location for the command window, but now it can be made to float, as shown in figure 1.8. Simply click an edge of the command window and drag it to the location you want.

**Fig. 1.8**
You can float the command window by simply dragging it with a mouse.

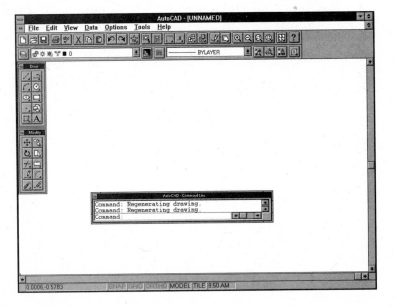

## Status Bar

The status line that appeared in earlier AutoCAD versions along the top of the screen has been relocated with this release to the bottom of the screen and is now called the *status bar*. It displays the current layer name, cursor coordinates, status of various AutoCAD operational states (such as ortho, paper space, snap), and help messages.

The coordinate readout area and the ortho, snap, and paper space mode display areas are also toggle buttons. Double-click them to toggle their status on and off. Don't worry if ortho, snap, and space concepts are unfamiliar. These are discussed later in the book.

▶ See "Using AutoCAD Drafting Tools," p. 55

## Drawing Area/View Window

The large blank window on the screen is the *drawing area*, also referred to as the *view window*. The drawing area is analogous to the drawing sheet on which you manually draw except that in AutoCAD, this area is infinite in its extents. You control how much of your drawing is displayed in the view window by using the Zoom commands.

▶ See "Using ZOOM to Control the Display," p. 336

Like most windows, you can also resize, minimize, or maximize a view window (see fig. 1.9). When you start a new drawing, the view window is displayed maximized in the AutoCAD application window. To resize it, click the restore button (the button with up and down arrowheads) along the right of the menu bar.

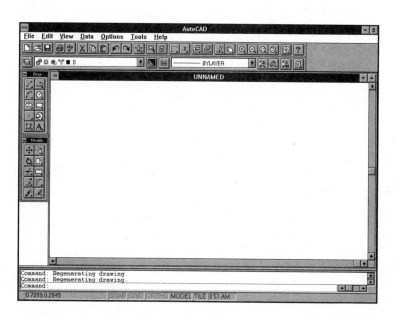

**Fig. 1.9**
You can resize the AutoCAD view window.

## Screen Menu

The screen menu is also called a sidebar menu. Because of the ease with which this menu can be customized, it has been used extensively by third-party application developers. However, it is no longer considered necessary, and support for it is retained in Release 13 only for compatibility reasons. The default configuration has screen menus turned off. To turn on screen menus, choose <u>O</u>ptions, <u>P</u>references to invoke the Preferences dialog box, and click the Screen <u>M</u>enu check box as shown in figure 1.10.

**Fig. 1.10**
Screen menus are turned off as a default; if you want to use the screen menus, use the Preferences dialog box to turn them on.

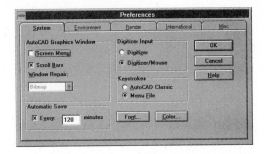

When turned on, the screen menu hugs the right edge of a view window, as seen in figure 1.11. For those of you who have used earlier versions of AutoCAD, the screen menu will seem familiar. But as you get used to the ease of use and one-click efficiency offered by the new toolbars, you will probably want to keep the screen menu turned off.

**Fig. 1.11**
The screen menu at the right edge of a view window.

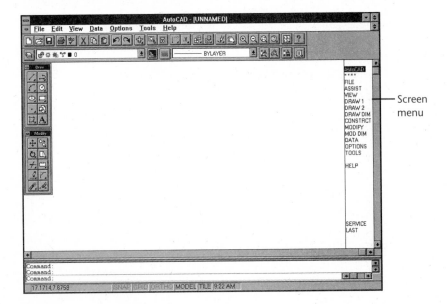

## Crosshairs, Pickbox, and Cursor

Depending on your activity in AutoCAD, you see the *crosshairs*, representing two of the coordinate axes; the *pickbox*, a square used for selecting objects; or the *cursor*, a small arrow used to access menus and toolbars. The cursor can also change its shape to become a double-headed arrow when resizing windows. Figures 1.12, 1.13, and 1.14 show examples of the crosshairs, the pickbox, and the cursor.

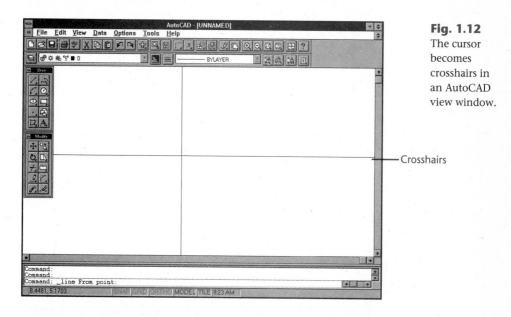

**Fig. 1.12**
The cursor becomes crosshairs in an AutoCAD view window.

Crosshairs

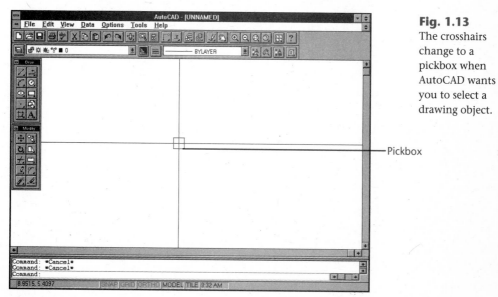

**Fig. 1.13**
The crosshairs change to a pickbox when AutoCAD wants you to select a drawing object.

Pickbox

**Fig. 1.14**
When the cursor is moved to the menu bar or a tool palette, the cursor's shape changes to a small arrow.

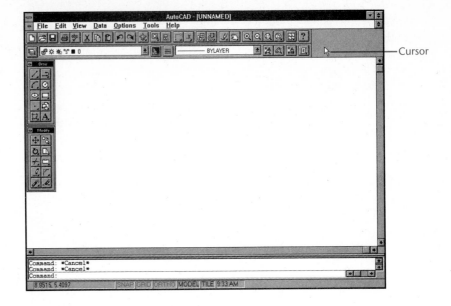

Cursor

AutoCAD displays the crosshairs to help you visualize what you are doing in the drawing area in relation to the coordinate system. The crosshairs therefore define any two components of the three-dimensional space: *x,y*, *x,z*, or *y,z*. The current coordinate of the crosshairs is known as the *crosshairs position*; AutoCAD displays this position in the status bar.

The third component of the crosshairs position is defined by setting AutoCAD to a particular elevation. To understand crosshairs position, picture yourself in the elevator of a high-rise building. When you get off the elevator, the *elevation* of your position is the current floor level. The other components of your position are based on the distance you have traveled, measured in two directions from the elevator doors.

▶ See "Understanding the User Coordinate System (UCS)," p. 788

When working with AutoCAD, you can use this building analogy to visualize your work. Just as when you are in a building, you first need to know which floor you are on; then you can start looking for the room you want to visit. The "universe" in which you operate when using AutoCAD is known as the *World Coordinate System (WCS)*. You learn more about the WCS and how the position of the crosshairs can be oriented to match an object for convenience by using a *User Coordinate System (UCS)* later in this book.

# Interacting with AutoCAD

AutoCAD is a precision drafting system, but if needed, you also can draw freehand without regard to accuracy. To place objects in a drawing, you can select their location interactively with a mouse, or you can type the exact coordinates of points. AutoCAD has a wide range of commands for creating, altering, enhancing, or viewing your drawing. AutoCAD also offers commands to display and extract information from objects in your drawing.

You can invoke any of AutoCAD's commands by selecting them from toolbars, pull-down menus, or other menus such as screen menus and tablet menus. You also can enter the commands at the command line. With the earlier releases of AutoCAD, command entry from the keyboard was the most popular method of interaction, especially for learning the software. With Release 13, however, Autodesk has added an extensive set of floating toolbars that offers a more efficient method of interaction than the keyboard provides.

When using the keyboard, you must answer a series of prompts about many commands before they are executed. But toolbars and menu options are designed to answer many of these prompts automatically, making command entry more efficient. Dialog boxes are also extensively used in AutoCAD to ease significantly the process of selecting various environment settings.

Although using menus and floating toolbars is likely to be more efficient for most of your drawing needs, the importance of learning AutoCAD the old-fashioned way—by entering commands at the keyboard—cannot be ignored. The primary benefit of the keyboard approach becomes apparent when you reach a stage when you want to write your own AutoLISP routines to automate repetitive tasks.

▶ See "What Are AutoLISP, ADS, and ARX?" p. 1049

This book uses a combined approach to teaching you the use of AutoCAD. You will use the keyboard to invoke some commands, and you will use the toolbars, menus, and dialog boxes to invoke other commands.

## Issuing Commands

The command window and the status bar along the bottom of the screen are the primary interface elements that AutoCAD uses to communicate with you. AutoCAD is ready to accept a command from you when the command line is empty, as shown here:

```
Command:
```

Getting Started

If a command is in progress, AutoCAD displays a prompt requesting input from you, as in the following example:

```
Command: line
From point:
```

In this example, AutoCAD expects you to provide a point to start the LINE command. You can enter the LINE command or the point in several ways: the keyboard, the toolbars, the screen menu, or a digitizing tablet menu.

> **Note**
>
> In this book, responses to command prompts appear in **boldface**. AutoCAD commands appear in lowercase in command lines, but you can type the command in uppercase, lowercase, or any combination. After typing the response (if any) as shown in the text, press Enter unless instructed otherwise.

## Using Transparent Commands

When AutoCAD prompts you for data, as with the From point: prompt when you type the **line** command, you can invoke—without canceling the active command—commands known as *transparent* commands. Note the following example (see fig. 1.15):

```
Command: line
From Point: (pick a point in the drawing area)
To point: (pick another point in the drawing area)
To point: 'zoom
>>Center/Dynamic/Left/Previous/Vmax/Window/<Scale(X/XP)>:.5x
Resuming LINE command.
To point:
```

You must issue a transparent command with an apostrophe preceding it. And when a transparent command is completed, the command it was invoked from resumes. The transparent command feature is handy as it lets you adjust AutoCAD environment variables, the display, or even invoke help from within another command.

You can transparently issue most of AutoCAD's commands that do not select or create new objects. Some of the commands you are likely to use transparently on a regular basis are: ZOOM, PAN, REDRAW, SNAP, GRID, ORTHO, DDLMODES, DDRMODES, and DDOSNAP. When you select these commands from the pull-down menus, they are automatically issued transparently.

The following sections review the two methods of invoking commands in AutoCAD: with the keyboard and with menus.

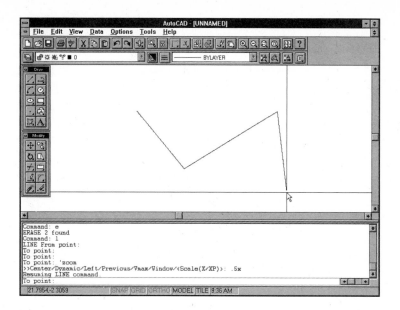

**Fig. 1.15**
By using an apostrophe before them, several commands, such as ZOOM, can be issued transparently from within another command.

## Typing Commands

The keyboard is the most basic command-entry method. You first type the command, and then you press Enter or the space bar to execute the command or to reply to a query.

Various command-entry keyboard techniques are available for editing what you type at the keyboard, for correcting errors, and for replying to subcommand prompts. These techniques aren't necessarily shortcuts, but rather alternative ways of using the keyboard. Following is a list of these options and practices:

**Tip**
If you press the Enter key at an empty command prompt, AutoCAD repeats the last command.

- To signify to AutoCAD that you have completed a command entry (except when entering text), you can press the space bar instead of the Enter key.

- To delete a character typed at the Command: prompt, press the Backspace key or Ctrl+H before pressing Enter.

- To delete a line of a command entry (before pressing Enter), press Ctrl+X and then type the new entry.

- To cancel a command or to cancel everything typed at the keyboard, press the Esc key. AutoCAD responds with a *CANCEL* prompt and returns the Command: prompt to its empty state. (Note that the keystroke to cancel a command is Esc, not Ctrl+C as DOS users have grown accustomed to over the years. In AutoCAD Release 13 for Windows, like other Windows applications, Ctrl+C is used to copy a selection set to the Windows Clipboard.)

■ To move the cursor around the screen, use the arrow keys instead of the pointing device. The cursor moves in the direction of the arrow key you use. To increase the cursor-movement step size, press PgUp before using the arrow keys. To reduce the step size, press PgDn.

■ Use the Esc key to cancel dialog boxes and back out of pull-down menus.

Many AutoCAD commands have *subcommands*—after you enter the command, AutoCAD prompts you with options for using the command. Instead of typing the complete subcommand name, you can type the characters in the subcommand name; AutoCAD recognizes those characters as a shortcut for the complete entry. Here is an example of the subcommand prompt for the ZOOM command:

```
Command: zoom
All/Center/Dynamic/Extents/Left/Previous/Vmax/Window/
    <Scale(X/XP)>:
```

To reply to the subcommand prompt in this example, you can type **a** for All, **c** for Center, and so on. Notice that the Scale(X/XP) option is enclosed in angle brackets. Options enclosed in angle brackets are default options that are selected by default if you do not make a choice.

AutoCAD also uses function keys and other special keys for quick access of a few of its important settings and frequently used commands. Table 1.2 describes the default settings of the function keys; Table 1.3 describes accelerator key combinations you can use.

**Table 1.2   Standard Function Key Assignments**

| Key | Action |
| --- | --- |
| F1 | Invokes Help |
| F2 | Calls up the AutoCAD Text window |
| F4 | Toggles tablet mode |
| F5 | Cycles between isoplane modes |
| F6 | Toggles the coordinate display mode |
| F7 | Toggles grid display |

| Key | Action |
|-----|--------|
| F8 | Toggles ortho mode |
| F9 | Toggles snap mode |
| F10 | Activates the menu bar |

**Table 1.3    Standard Accelerator Key Assignments**

| Accelerator Key | Action |
|-----------------|--------|
| Ctrl+Z | Undoes the last command sequentially since the last time the file was saved |
| Ctrl+X | Cuts the selection set from the drawing and places it on the Windows Clipboard |
| Ctrl+C | Copies the selection set in the drawing and places it on the Windows Clipboard |
| Ctrl+V | Pastes the contents of the Windows Clipboard in the current drawing |
| Ctrl+O | Invokes the OPEN command |
| Ctrl+P | Invokes the PLOT command |
| Ctrl+N | Invokes the NEW command |
| Ctrl+S | Invokes the QSAVE command |

## Using the Toolbars and Menus

Each type of AutoCAD menu (toolbar, pull-down menu, screen menu, and icon menu) uses macros to execute AutoCAD commands. A *macro* is a sequence of commands and prompt responses, assigned to a menu option in a menu file called ACAD.MNU. Because toolbar actions are also defined with macros in the menu definition file, toolbars are considered menus. You can customize the menu file or purchase third-party custom menu files. You learn more about menu files in Chapter 37.

▶ See "Customizing Toolbars and Menus," p. 1020

Whenever you select an option from a menu, AutoCAD executes one of the macros contained in the menu file—the macro keyed to the selected menu item. With this system, you don't have to type the command; the macro enters the command for you. In addition to issuing single commands, the menu file included with AutoCAD can execute multiple commands, display other menus, display a dialog box, or issue automatic repeating commands.

Getting Started

Menu selections can display any type of menu required for the results you want. A screen menu selection, for example, can cause a pull-down menu to appear; when you select from the pull-down menu, an icon menu may appear. Any time you make a selection from a menu item, you can use Esc to cancel your selection. The following sections show you how to make a selection from each type of menu.

### Using the Toolbars

The addition of multiple toolbars is the most significant user interface enhancement in AutoCAD Release 13. Toolbars make it easier for you to get familiar with this sophisticated drafting and design software. Toolbars were mentioned earlier in this chapter, and several were shown in figure 1.6. Here you take a more detailed look at them.

The Tools, Toolbars submenu on the menu bar lists all available toolbars. You probably will keep the following four toolbars open most of the time, as they provide quick access to the most frequently used set of drawing, editing, and display control commands:

- *Standard toolbar.* Provides access to file, print, Clipboard, snap, view control, and other commands.

- *Object Properties.* Provides access to layer management, color, linetype, and other object property commands.

- *Draw.* Provides access to drawing commands such as line, arc, ellipse, and so on.

- *Edit.* Provides access to editing commands such as explode, trim, erase, and so on.

You will open and dispose of other toolbars, such as Dimensioning, Render, and Inquiry, as the need arises.

> **Note**
>
> The Tool Windows icon on the standard toolbar offers access to additional toolbars, such as View, Select, and others. These are not listed under the Toolbars submenu.

**Tip**
You can change the size of the toolbars to your liking. Simply select an edge of the palette and drag the mouse till the gray outline that appears is the size you want.

Toolbars contain icons that can be either simple buttons or *fly-out* buttons. You can distinguish a fly-out button by the small black arrow in the lower-right corner of the button. If you click and hold down the cursor on a fly-out button, an additional set of buttons will "fly out" to offer a choice of related commands.

AutoCAD also implements cursor help for buttons on the toolbars. Simply hold the cursor over a button, and a yellow box will pop out under the cursor with the name of the command associated with the button in it.

To invoke a command from a toolbar, simply click the command's icon.

### Using the Menu Bar

Pull-down menus are a standard feature of all Windows applications. To activate the menu bar, you simply choose a menu option with the mouse, or you press and release the Alt key and move through the menus with the arrow keys. You also can pull down a menu by pressing the Alt key in combination with the menu item's underlined letter in the menu bar.

Many pull-down menu items have accelerator keys displayed next to them, such as Ctrl+C beside the Copy option on the Edit menu. To invoke a command from a pull-down menu, you can use the accelerator key, choose the command with the cursor, or first activate the menu bar and then press the underlined letter in the menu item's name.

In a pull-down menu, the items that have three dots (an ellipsis) after them activate a dialog box in which you can select additional command options. When you click a menu item that has a right-pointing arrow beside it, a cascading submenu appears.

The term *icon menu* was used earlier in this chapter. Icon menus are simply menus that offer command choices in the form of pictures rather than text—providing a graphic interface for menu selection. Icon menus appear as submenus to selections made from pull-down or screen menus. Figure 1.16 shows an icon menu.

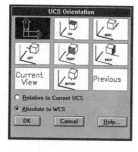

**Fig. 1.16**
Icon menus appear as submenus to selections made from pull-down menus.

### Using the Screen Menus

Screen menus were discussed earlier in the chapter (refer to figs. 1.10 and 1.11). Because you sometimes have to navigate several screens to find the required command, screen menus have fallen out of favor. By default, they are not turned on. You must use the Preferences dialog box to turn them on.

To invoke a command from a screen menu, you simply click the name of the command. Alternatively, you can press the Ins key to activate the screen menu, use the arrow keys to highlight the command you want, and then press Enter to activate it.

Screen menus follow these conventions: subcommands and options appear in a combination of lowercase and uppercase letters, a menu item in all upper-case calls up subcommands and options, and a menu item that ends in a colon directly invokes a command when you select the item.

The first item on the screen menu is the word AutoCAD. If after navigating the screen menus you seem to have gotten lost, don't despair. Just click the first item, the word AutoCAD, and you will be transported back to the main screen menu. The second line of a screen menu is a line of asterisks (****). If you select this line, a screen menu of Object Snap options appears, as shown in figure 1.17.

**Fig. 1.17**
Selecting the asterisks under the word AutoCAD on the screen menu calls up a submenu of Object Snap options.

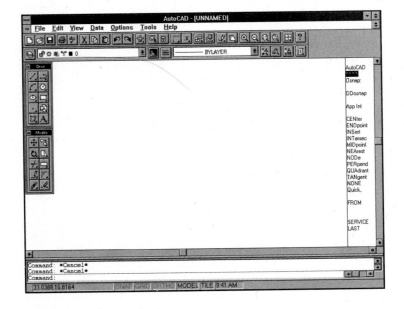

## Working with Dialog Boxes

Whereas Release 12 introduced dialog boxes to AutoCAD, Release 13 improves their usability by incorporating functions that were previously found in several dialog boxes into a single, more functional dialog box. Dialog boxes have a number of enclosed areas, known as *tiles,* that perform a variety of functions.

Any dialog box tile that contains a string of characters can have a single-key option assigned to it. If the displayed string has an underlined letter, you can select the string by typing that letter on the keyboard. If the current field is editable, you can press Alt and the letter key.

The following sections explain the components of a dialog box.

### Scroll Bars

Scroll bars contain an up arrow at the top, a down arrow at the bottom, and a *slider box* (or scroll box) on the scroll bar. Clicking the arrows increments the displayed information, one line at a time. You also can click the scroll bar above or below the slider box to scroll the display one page up or down, respectively. You can drag the slider box to scroll the display. Figure 1.18 shows a dialog box with a scroll bar in use. Though vertical scroll bars are implied in the discussion above, scroll bars also can be horizontal.

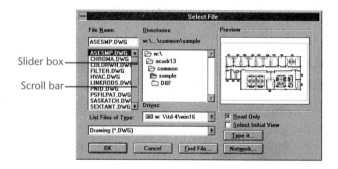

**Fig. 1.18**
A scroll bar in a dialog box lets you move the displayed information up or down.

Scroll bars work in association with list boxes, described next.

### List Boxes

List boxes display a group of items in a box. You can select an item from the list box by clicking it with the cursor. Selecting the item usually causes an action, such as moving the selected item to an edit box for possible changes. List boxes can be fixed, as shown in figure 1.19, or they can pop up when you click a pop-up arrow, as shown in figure 1.20.

**Fig. 1.19**

A list box that is fixed in size.

List box

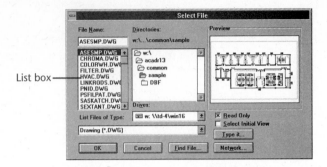

**Fig. 1.20**

A pop-up list box that "pops up" when you click the drop-down arrow next to a selection field.

Pop-up list box

Pop-up arrow

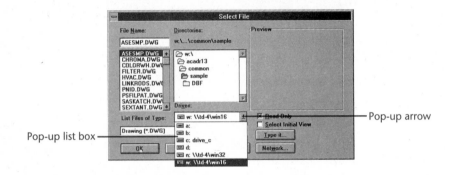

### Buttons and Radio Buttons

Buttons (also called command buttons) are common items in dialog boxes. The OK and Cancel functions appear as buttons in almost all dialog boxes. A button containing an ellipsis displays an additional dialog box; a button containing an arrow requires that you provide input on the graphics screen. Buttons that aren't available for selection have grayed or dimmed text labels.

Radio buttons are a group of buttons from which you can select only one button. Selecting a radio button highlights it and simultaneously removes the highlight from another previously highlighted button. Figure 1.21 shows examples of command buttons and radio buttons.

**Fig. 1.21**

Command buttons and radio buttons in a dialog box.

Radio buttons

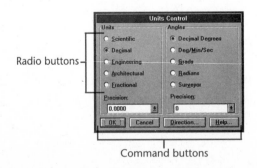

Command buttons

## Check Boxes

Check boxes are toggle buttons. Toggle buttons have only two states: on or
off. When you want to turn on an option, you click its check box so an X
appears in it. Figure 1.22 shows examples of check boxes.

Check boxes →

**Fig. 1.22**
Check boxes in
a dialog box.

## Edit Boxes

Dialog boxes that require a reply provide an edit box or text box in which
you type your characters. Figure 1.23 shows an edit box.

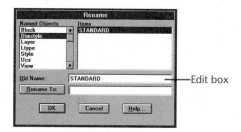
—Edit box

**Fig. 1.23**
An edit box in
a dialog box.

While the cursor is in an edit box, you follow standard Windows conventions for editing text. Ctrl+arrow keys move the cursor one word at a time,
Shift+arrow keys highlight letters, and double-clicking on a word will highlight it. You can highlight any sized area by picking at the start point and
dragging the cursor over the text to highlight and then releasing the pick
button. You can highlight the text in an edit box and then anything you type
will replace the highlighted text.

## Image Tiles

Dialog boxes can contain a picture that represents a drawing or image for use
with the dialog box. Some of these image tiles are for display only; others can
be used for making selections—by pointing and clicking some portion of the
image tile. Figure 1.24 shows an image tile in a dialog box.

**Fig. 1.24**
An image tile in
a dialog box.

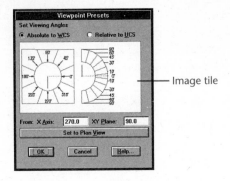

Image tile

# Getting Help

AutoCAD implements a very good Help system that exploits the native Windows Help engine, as shown in figure 1.25. AutoCAD's Help also implements figures to clarify concepts. Even if you have been using AutoCAD for a while, and you feel comfortable with its many features, there probably are aspects of the software you have never explored before. For instance, you may be using AutoCAD primarily to create 2D drawings and only occasionally get involved in 3D work. At times like these, when you are in relatively new territory, knowing the functionality of the Help system can mean the difference between looking up an answer to your problem quickly and efficiently on-line without leaving your drawing, or pulling away from the computer system to open the printed manual and thumb through the pages.

**Fig. 1.25**
AutoCAD takes
advantage of the
Windows Help
engine.

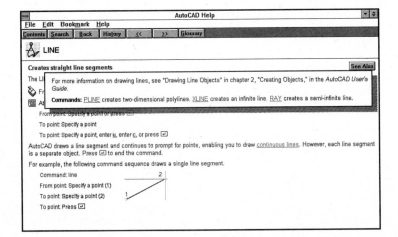

You choose Help, Contents from the AutoCAD menu bar to display the Help window shown in figure 1.25. The Contents screen of the Help system is organized in two major sections. The first gives you access to the use of menus and toolbars; the second gives you access to AutoCAD's commands and environment variables that are usually typed at the command line. Note that the button bar in the Help window has several navigational commands.

You use the Contents button to come back to the initial screen from anywhere in the Help system. You use the Search button to locate information by keyword, as shown in figure 1.26.

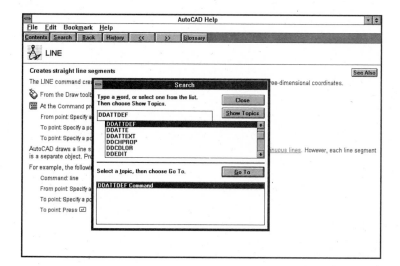

**Fig. 1.26**
The Search button lets you locate information by keyword.

The Back button is provided to trace your path back to a previous screen. The History button displays a list of topics you have visited thus far, as shown in figure 1.27. Double-clicking an item in the History list takes you back to that topic.

The Glossary button in the Help window opens up yet another window, as shown in figure 1.28. This window displays an alphabetical list of important concepts. When you click a term for which you want information, its definition pops up on-screen. Many terms also include a figure to explain the concept better.

As you read the Help text, you will notice that several words are underlined in green. These words are linked to additional help screens, making access to related information just a click away. Help also implements the concept of bookmarks so that you can return to a specific location easily. When you are at a location to which you may want to return, choose Bookmark from the menu bar to mark that location. To move to this location later, you simply choose Book**m**ark again and click that bookmark from the displayed list (it is possible to maintain several bookmarks).

This completes a basic introduction to the AutoCAD interface and how to communicate with it. Next, you turn to some basic file operations.

**Fig. 1.27**

The History window is a convenient way to jump back to a topic of interest you visited before.

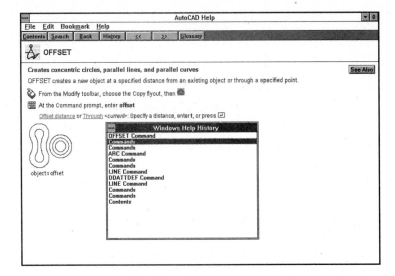

**Fig. 1.28**

The Glossary button provides access to an alphabetical list of important concepts and their definitions.

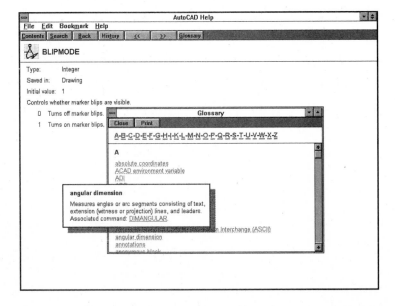

# Introduction to File Operations

While you are still in the process of learning AutoCAD, you may find it wasteful of disk space to save your scratch file. But once you begin doing serious work with AutoCAD, the importance of saving your drawings for later use will be obvious. AutoCAD offers all the basic file input/output operations, such as open, save, and save as. It also enables you to open drawings in read-only mode and to activate a timed autosave feature. The following sections examine each of these operations.

## Creating a New Drawing (NEW)

Choose File, New from the menu bar (or enter **new** at the command line) to activate the Create New Drawing dialog box shown in figure 1.29. You use this dialog box to specify a name for the new drawing file you want to create. Additionally, you can choose to specify whether a prototype drawing is to be used when creating the new drawing.

**Fig. 1.29**
The Create New Drawing dialog box.

A prototype drawing is nothing more than a regular drawing file that has been configured for environment settings you normally use. The prototype edit field lists the factory default drawing name, ACAD.DWG, but you can access your local or network hard drive by pressing the Prototype button in the dialog box to select any drawing you choose.

It is common practice to maintain several prototype drawings, each for a different purpose. For instance, a survey prototype drawing may be configured for decimal units, but the architectural drawing may be configured for feet-inch units.

To create a drawing without using a prototype, turn on the No Prototype check box in the dialog box. A new drawing is created with all default settings.

▶ See "Understanding Prototypes" p. 79

**Getting Started**

## Opening an Existing Drawing

Choose File, Open from the menu bar (or enter **open** at the command line)
to activate the Select File dialog box, as shown earlier in figure 1.18. This
dialog box displays drives, directories, and file names in a scrollable list format. It also displays a thumbnail preview of the drawing you highlight. To
search for files based on a date or directory location criteria, you can choose
the Find File button, located along the bottom of the dialog box. Choosing
the Find File button brings up the Browse/Search dialog box, as shown in
figure 1.30. The Size list box in this dialog box offers a choice of small,
medium, or large for the size of the thumbnail views shown in the File
Name list box.

**Fig. 1.30**
The Browse/Search
dialog box lets you
view a thumbnail
sketch of your
drawings.

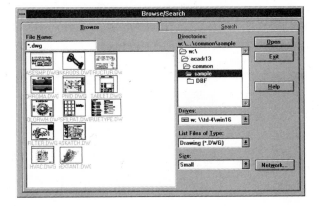

As figure 1.30 shows, in addition to the Browse tab in the dialog box, there is
a Search tab. You use this tab to specify a drawing search criterion by date
and directory location. After a list of files that match your criteria has been
generated, you can either double-click the file name to open it, or you can
highlight the file name and choose the Open button.

## Using Read-Only Mode

In the Select File dialog box there is a check box labeled Read Only. If you
want to open a drawing just for the sake of viewing but not modifying, you
can select this check box to turn it on.

After you open a drawing in read-only mode, obviously you cannot save it
back under the same name. You can, however, use the Save As command to
save it under a new name.

## Saving a Drawing

Choose File, Save from the menu bar (or enter **qsave** at the command line) to save the current drawing. Any drawing and editing operations you perform during an AutoCAD session take place either in the computer's RAM or in virtual memory, which also is temporary. Thus, using the Save command frequently is simple protection against possible data loss due to an electrical surge or other unrecoverable error.

If the current drawing on which you are working has already been named, the Save command saves the drawing. However, if the drawing has not yet been named and you invoke the Save command, the Save As dialog box opens to let you assign a name under which to save it.

## Renaming an Existing Drawing

Choose File, Save As from the menu bar (or enter **saveas** at the command line) to open the Save As dialog box. Use this command to save a drawing that has not yet been named, or to save the current drawing at a new location or under a new name.

As noted in the preceding section, the Save As command is also automatically invoked if you issue the Save command for a drawing that has not already been named.

## Using SAVETIME

As noted in the discussion under the "Saving a Drawing" section, it is a good idea to save your work frequently. AutoCAD provides a means to save your drawings automatically after a fixed time interval.

Choose Options, Preferences to display the Preferences dialog box. The Automatic Save tile in the System tab of the dialog box provides a text field where you can type the frequency in minutes you want your drawing saved. See figure 1.31.

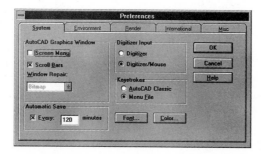

**Fig. 1.31**

The Automatic Save tile in the System tab of the Preferences dialog box lets you type a time interval, in minutes, for autosaving drawings.

You also can change the automatic-save time interval by typing SAVETIME at the command prompt.

```
Command: savetime
New value for SAVETIME <120>: 15
```

In the example shown above, you have specified a time interval of 15, in minutes, when you would like to perform an automatic save of your current drawing.

It should be pointed out that, when performing an automatic timed save, AutoCAD does not save the drawing with its original name. It uses the file name extension SV$ instead. The file name is Auto. SV$ by default.

## Closing AutoCAD

The last of the file operations discussed in this chapter is closing AutoCAD. Choose File, Exit from the menu bar (or enter **quit** at the command line) to display the AutoCAD dialog box shown in figure 1.32. This dialog box offers three buttons to let you save your most recent modifications before closing AutoCAD, discard the changes from the time you last saved the drawing, or cancel the command and return to AutoCAD.

**Fig. 1.32**

The AutoCAD dialog box lets you save or discard your most recent changes before you close AutoCAD.

If you save the drawing just before choosing the Exit command, the AutoCAD dialog box shown in figure 1.32 will not appear, and your AutoCAD session will be terminated immediately.

In addition to the command QUIT, AutoCAD offers the END command. This command combines the function of the SAVE and QUIT commands. Thus, if you make modifications to your current drawing and wanted to save them and close your AutoCAD session at the same time, you would enter **end** at the Command: prompt. Again, the AutoCAD dialog box shown in figure 1.32 would not be displayed in this case. It should be noted that using the END command also creates a backup of your drawing file that has the extension BAK.

# From Here...

This completes the introduction to the interface elements of AutoCAD, along with information on the various ways of interacting with the software. You learned how to open existing files, save new drawings, and perform other related file operations. You also learned how to close your AutoCAD session. You are now ready to move to the next step of actually creating drawings with AutoCAD.

For more information about drawing and editing objects, and controlling the content displayed in your drawing area, see the following chapters:

- Chapter 5, "Creating Basic Geometry," shows you how to draw basic geometric objects such as an arc, circle, and a rectangle.

- Chapter 10, "Editing Techniques," introduces you to basic editing commands that let you erase, move, copy, and mirror existing objects in your drawing.

- Chapter 12, "Viewing a Drawing," explains the use of display manipulation commands that let you zoom or pan around your drawing area.

Getting Started

# Chapter 2

# Creating Your First Drawing

In manual drafting, a pen or pencil is used to draw lines, arcs, text, dimensions, and other geometry. A manual drafter may use a straight edge, scale, triangle, and other standard drafting equipment. To complete the finished drawing, each geometric object is created one at a time. Templates of standard parts are used in certain cases to speed up the drawing process. Even the use of templates, however, is unsuccessful in speeding up the labored task of dimensioning and adding notes.

AutoCAD provides tools similar to those used in manual drafting for the creation of geometry. AutoCAD imitates many standard drafting tools with a variety of functions. To draw a straight line, for example, AutoCAD provides a function that imitates a straight edge. When this command is invoked, straight horizontal and vertical lines are drawn.

In this chapter, several of AutoCAD's basic functions are introduced. You start by creating a new drawing and setting up the drawing environment. Several of AutoCAD's drafting tools are then introduced. These tools help speed up the drawing process.

As you go through this chapter, keep in mind that there is no right or wrong way to use AutoCAD. Many of the commands can be accessed differently, just as geometry can be created by following diversified procedures. This resourceful feature of AutoCAD is due to the fact that AutoCAD was designed to meet the needs of a wide variety of users.

In this chapter, you learn to do the following:

- Create a new drawing
- Set the display format and units

- Set the drawing size

- Use AutoCAD drafting tools

- Draw lines

- Clean up the display

- Save and exit your drawing

The tutorials in this chapter are designed to be completed as individual exercises or as part of a chapter project. They have been divided so that you can explore the concepts of each section without spending time to complete the entire project. In this chapter, you create a new drawing of the apartment roof. The drawing you create is named ROOF.DWG. If you skip this chapter's tutorials, rename the ROOFB.DWG file in C:\UAW13 to ROOF.DWG.

## Starting a New Drawing

◄ See "Understanding the Display," p. 14

When you first start AutoCAD, the standard AutoCAD window is displayed along with a new blank drawing. This is called the *drawing editor* (see fig. 2.1). You can begin creating geometry immediately.

**Fig. 2.1**
The standard drawing editor in AutoCAD 13 for Windows.

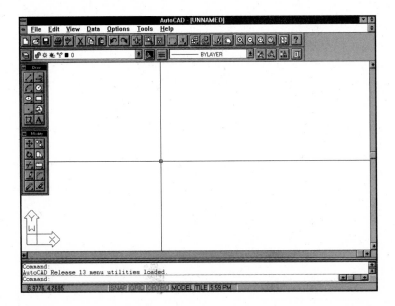

**Note**

You can create and edit a drawing within the drawing editor without giving the drawing a name. You are prompted for a name and have the opportunity to change the drive and/or path the first time you save the drawing.

While you can create and edit a drawing within the drawing editor without giving it a name, the drawing is not saved until you store it in a file. DOS stores the drawing information on the disk in a file. The contents of a file can be any number of things, such as a word processing document, a spreadsheet, or an AutoCAD drawing. When you give the drawing a name and save it, DOS creates a file using that name. This named file contains all important information regarding the drawing. When you later open the file, the drawing appears exactly the same on-screen as when you last saved it to the file.

### Tutorial: Starting the Example Drawing

By the time you finish this chapter, you will have drawn the roof plan shown in figure 2.2. To complete this project, you should begin here and advance through the chapter. The roof plan that you are drawing is the actual roof plan of the apartment complex that you draw if you complete all of the tutorials through Chapter 18.

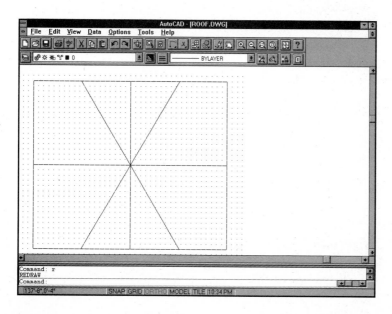

**Fig. 2.2**
The roof plan created by completing the tutorials in this chapter.

To begin your new drawing and assign a name to it, select the New button on the Standard toolbar. The Create New Drawing dialog box is displayed, as shown in figure 2.3. You also can access this dialog box by entering **new** or pressing **Ctrl+N** at the Command: prompt.

**Fig. 2.3**
The Create New
Drawing dialog
box is used to start
a new drawing.

---

### Caution

It's important that you know the exact location of your drawings. If your drawings are not placed on the proper disk or in the proper directory, they may be difficult to find later. Proper file management techniques are an essential part of working with AutoCAD.

---

Notice that the cursor appears in the New Drawing Name edit box. Select the New Drawing Name button and change to the appropriate drive and subdirectory where your data is stored. If you followed the default installation procedures for your data disk, this will be C:\UAW13. For the name of the drawing, enter **roof** in the file name edit box. Select OK. Your screen should now look like figure 2.4. To continue, click OK or press the Enter key to return to the drawing editor.

**Fig. 2.4**
Creating the new
drawing named
"roof."

## Saving Your Work

 Remember to save your work every 10 to 15 minutes as you go through the tutorials. This is extremely important in the event of a power failure or some other unforeseen problem. By saving your work regularly, all the work saved before the problem is most likely usable. You can invoke the SAVE command by entering **save** at the Command: prompt. The SAVE command displays the Save Drawing As dialog box.

You also can use the QSAVE command to save your drawing. The QSAVE command (Quick SAVE) does not display a dialog box and therefore is a quicker way to save your drawing. When you issue the QSAVE command a drawing file already exists with the same drawing name and it is renamed as a backup file with a BAD extension. The current drawing file is written to disk. If your drawing is unnamed, the Save Drawing As dialog box appears. When you press Ctrl+S or select the Save button on the Standard toolbar, the QSAVE command is issued. You also can select File, Save from the pull-down menu.

> **Note**
>
> If you want to stop working on the tutorial and continue later, you can end your drawing session, exit the drawing editor, save your work, and return to Program Manager all at once by entering **end** at the Command: prompt.

When you enter **end** or **save**, your drawing is saved with the drawing name and a DWG file extension. The old version is saved as a backup with a BAK file extension. For example, when you work on the drawing ROOF and enter **end**, the drawing is saved as ROOF.DWG. If you have a previous version of ROOF on your disk, that old version is saved as ROOF.BAK. The extension is automatically added by AutoCAD. You enter only the file name.

If you do stop working on the ROOF drawing and exit AutoCAD, you need to restart AutoCAD and open the ROOF drawing when you are ready to continue with the tutorial. To restart AutoCAD, double-click the AutoCAD icon in the AutoCAD program group. To open the ROOF drawing, select the Open icon, choose File, Open, or enter Ctrl+O at the Command: prompt. When you select the File pull-down menu, you are given a list of the most recent drawings you have worked on toward the bottom of the pull-down menu. To open a drawing from this list, select the drawing name from the list or enter the number preceding its name.

At this point, you should be able to open AutoCAD successfully, begin a new drawing, and understand how to use dialog boxes. You also should know how to save a drawing, properly end a drawing, and open an existing drawing.

## Setting Display Format and Units (DDUNITS)

Through careful planning before beginning a drawing, you can greatly reduce the time it takes to complete it. Setting up the drawing correctly involves several factors that affect the final accuracy and quality of the drawing. Some decisions that you should make before beginning the drawing are:

- Name and storage location of the drawing file

- Units with which the drawing is created

- Paper size on which the drawing fits

The AutoCAD system of *units* lets you use real-world units of measure in your drawing such as architectural and decimal units. By default, decimal units are used for numeric display and input within AutoCAD. These units, however, can represent anything you want. One unit on-screen can represent one inch, millimeter, or mile. The first task is to determine the appropriate type of measurement for your drawing.

Most drawings use a variety of sizes and scales. For example, you may want to create a drawing of a floor plan. In that case, it would be advantageous to specify feet, inches, and fractions of an inch. The easiest way to set units in AutoCAD is with the Units Control dialog box. You access this dialog box when you choose Data, Units. You can also enter **ddunits** at the Command: prompt. Figure 2.5 shows the Units Control dialog box.

**Fig. 2.5**
With the Units Control dialog box, you can set the units and precision.

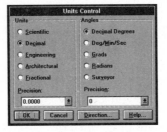

### Tutorial: Setting the Display Format and Units

In the first tutorial, you set the name and storage location of the drawing. In this section, you set the drawing units used by the roof plan. When you change the drawing units, the coordinate display format also changes to reflect the current units. For this project, you use architectural units with a precision of 0'-0". Follow these steps:

◄ See "Using the Toolbars and Menus," p. 29

1. When you initially load AutoCAD, you see the standard drawing editor. For this tutorial, you only need the Standard and Object Properties toolbars displayed. Any other toolbars should be closed at this time. Before continuing, check to make sure your screen looks like figure 2.6.

2. From the pull-down menu, choose Data, Units. The Units Control dialog box appears (see fig. 2.7).

3. Select Architectural in the Units section of the dialog box.

4. Click the down-arrow button for the <u>P</u>recision option. In the pop-up list, select 0'-0".

5. Click the OK button to accept the changes.

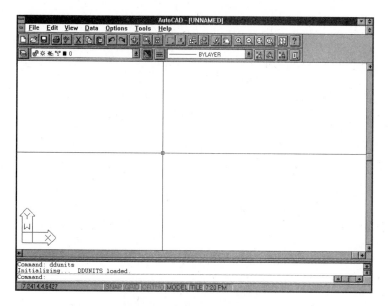

**Fig. 2.6**
The standard drawing display used for this tutorial.

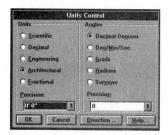

**Fig. 2.7**
Setting the Units to Architectural in the Units Control dialog box.

Notice that the coordinate display format in the status bar now includes both feet and inch measurements for both the X and Y axes. In the next section, you choose the size of your drawing area with the LIMITS command.

## Setting the Drawing Size (LIMITS)

The first task in creating a new drawing is to determine the name and storage location of the drawing. The second task is to determine and set the units with which the drawing is created. The third task is to determine the paper size on which the drawing fits. When you compare the paper size selected to the overall geometry of the object, in most cases the geometry can't be represented at true size on standard-size paper. When you use manual drafting methods, the geometry itself is scaled accordingly to fit on the paper size selected. When working with AutoCAD, however, never scale the geometry itself.

Lines, arcs, circles, and other geometric objects should always be drawn full size within AutoCAD. If the length of a floor plan is 52', it is drawn 624 units (inches) within AutoCAD. Consequently, the size of the product determines the size of the drawing. The command that AutoCAD uses to specify the drawing area is LIMITS.

A drawing's *limits* help designate your working area. Limits can be thought of as representing the perimeter of the paper on which you create the drawing. The primary use of setting the limits is to provide a boundary to help contain the drawing within a set sheet size. When the limits are set properly, AutoCAD prevents you from drawing geometric objects outside the limits. This is similar to preventing you from drawing off the edges of a sheet of paper.

Because geometry should always be created full scale, the limits must be modified. The limits of the AutoCAD drawing area are determined by the following:

- The actual size of the geometry

- The extra space allowed for dimensions and notes

- A border and a title block

- The actual size of the paper on which the drawing will be plotted

To determine the minimum amount of space needed for a drawing, first determine the actual size of the geometry. For example, suppose that a house plan measures 46 feet by 24 feet. Next, add any additional space needed for dimensions, notes, a border, and a title block. For this example, an additional 20 feet is needed (10 feet on each side) all around the plan for dimensions, notes, and a border. Thus, this drawing needs a minimum space of 66 feet by 44 feet.

After you determine the minimum space that the drawing requires, you need to decide the actual size of the paper on which the drawing will be plotted. For the preceding example, you'll use a C-size sheet of paper. A C-size sheet of paper is 22" × 17". Most architectural floor plans are drawn at 1/4"=1'-0". If you multiply 4' (4 units/inch) × 22 = 88' and 4' × 17' = 62', using a C-size paper with a 1/4"=1'-0" scale, you will have a space of 88' × 62'. Since the drawing needs a minimum space of 66 feet by 44 feet, it will easily fit in this 88' × 62' space. The drawing limits for this example should be set at 88' × 62'.

You access the LIMITS command by choosing Data, Drawing Limits or by entering **limits** at the Command: prompt.

The following command sequence is used to set the limits:

```
From the Data pull-down menu, choose Drawing Limits.
Reset Model Space Limits:
ON/OFF<Lower left corner>< 0'-0",0'-0">: 0'-0",0'-0"
```

Your value displayed in the <0'-0",0'-0"> section may indicate something different. The numbers in this section display the current value. Depending on what has been done in AutoCAD prior to beginning this tutorial, your value may be different.

This prompt sets the lower-left corner of the designated sheet size to the lower-left corner of the display screen. Responding with 0'-0",0'-0" places the lower-left corner at 0'-0",0'-0". The horizontal distance is entered first, followed by a comma, then the vertical distance. The value of 0'-0",0'-0" refers to the Cartesian coordinate (X and Y) values of the lower-left corner of the drawing area. Using these values places the lower-left corner of the drawing area at 0'-0",0'-0". The lower-left corner may be set at any location other than 0'-0",0'-0", however. Setting the lower-left corner to 0'-0",0'-0" is the most common and recommended setting.

The LIMITS command continues with a request for the upper-right corner. The AutoCAD default for the upper-right corner is 1'-0",0'-9" This is a standard A-size sheet. The values entered determine the upper-right corner of the sheet size. The horizontal distance (X value) is entered first, followed by a comma, then the vertical distance (Y value). Note that in figure 2.8, the drawing limits 1'-0",0'-9" do not extend all the way to the right side of the screen. This is because the computer monitor differs from the aspect ratio of standard drawing sheet sizes.

You can change the limits at any time by executing the LIMITS command. The first section of the LIMITS command, ON/OFF, refers to a limits check. Using the LIMITS command helps you designate your working area and avoid drawing off the paper. It is possible, however, to draw outside the limits, either deliberately or accidentally. With the limits check turned on, drawing outside the limits results in an ** Outside limits error message. With the limits check turned off, the error is not given.

**Tip**
When setting the lower-left corner, technically you should enter 0'-0",0'-0". In this case, typing 0,0 works the same as typing 0'-0", 0'-0".

### Tutorial: Setting the Drawing Size

In the first tutorial, you set the drawing name and storage location. In the second tutorial, you set the units in which the drawing is created. The next task is to define the size of the work area with the LIMITS command. The roof plan is plotted at a scale of 1/8"=1' For this project, you set limits to be proportional to the size of an 8.5" × 11" A-size sheet of paper. Because the majority of printers available for the consumer today do not print on 9" × 12" paper, you have to set the limits to the more common 8.5" × 11": A-size paper. The limits are set to 0'-0",0'-0" for the lower-left corner and 88'-0",68'-0" for the upper-right corner. The upper-right limits were determined by taking the size of the A-size sheet of paper and multiplying it by 4.

**Fig. 2.8**

Use of the LIMITS command, with the AutoCAD default lower-left limit set to 0'-0",0'-0", and the upper-right limit set to 1'0",0',9".

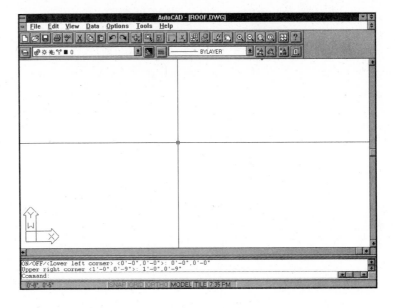

To define the size of the drawing area, follow these steps:

1. Start the LIMITS command.

   Command: **limits**

   Alternatively, choose <u>D</u>ata, Dr<u>a</u>wing Limits.

2. Specify the limits.

   ```
   Reset Model space limits:
   ON/OFF/<Lower left corner><0'-0",0'-0">:
   Upper right corner<1'-0",0"-9">: 88',68'
   ```

3. Move the cursor to the upper-right corner of the drawing area.

   Notice that the coordinate display on the toolbar indicates the upper-right corner to be smaller than the upper-right limit you just entered.

4. Issue the ZOOM ALL command, which enables you to view the limits of your drawing area on-screen:

```
Command: zoom
All/Center/Dynamic/Extents/Left/Previous/Vmax/Window/
    <Scale(X/XP)>: a
```

Alternatively, choose View, Zoom, All from the pull-down menu or choose the Zoom All button on the Standard toolbar.

5. Move the cursor back to the upper-right corner of the drawing area. You should see that the coordinate display on the toolbar now indicates the upper-right corner to be greater than the default upper-right limits set for 9" × 12" paper.

▶ See "ZOOM All," p. 337

In the next section, you set up and use several AutoCAD drafting tools. The first command is GRID, which assists you in viewing the actual drawing limits.

# Using AutoCAD Drafting Tools

AutoCAD provides a variety of drawing aids that help in laying out the drawing and increasing speed and efficiency. These drawing aids include:

- Grid

- Snap

- Coords

- Ortho

Grid, snap, and ortho can be selected and changed through the Drawing Aids dialog box. You access this dialog box by choosing Options, Drawing Aids. You also can display the Drawing Aids dialog box by entering **ddrmodes** at the Command: prompt. You can enter the GRID, SNAP, COORDS, and ORTHO commands directly at the Command: prompt. Figure 2.9 shows the Drawing Aids dialog box.

**Fig. 2.9**
The Drawing Aids dialog box can be used to set many of the AutoCAD drafting tools.

## Using the Drawing Aids Dialog Box (DDRMODES)

The Ortho, Snap, and Grid functions can be activated by single-clicking the appropriate box. The snap and grid spacing can also be set by typing the values in the boxes after X Spacing and Y Spacing (under Snap), and after X Spacing and Y Spacing (under Grid).

> **Note**
>
> To set the same snap values for the X and Y spacing, type the value in the box after X Spacing and press Enter. The Y Spacing is automatically set to the same value as the X Spacing. The same procedure works for setting the grid.

The BLIPMODE system variable can also be set in the Drawing Aids dialog box by clicking the Blips check box. Blips are temporary markers displayed on-screen whenever you designate a point. These marks are not printed, plotted, or saved as a part of the drawing. When Blips is off, the marker blips are not displayed. The Blips setting can be changed at any time during the drawing session.

▶ See "Picking Objects," p. 212

▶ See "Hiding Text (QTEXT)," p. 479

The HIGHLIGHT variable can be set as well in the Drawing Aids dialog box. The Highlight variable is covered in Chapter 9, "Understanding Selection Sets." Quick Text determines how text is displayed on-screen, as covered in Chapter 16, "Working with Text."

Certain geometric objects, such as solids, have filled interiors. The Solid Fill option controls the FILLMODE variable, which can be set as well in the Drawing Aids dialog box. When the Solid Fill mode is off, only the outlines of filled objects are displayed. Objects with filled interiors include traces, solids, and wide polylines. Creation and manipulation of these objects are discussed in upcoming chapters.

## Using the Grid (GRID)

Certain types of drafting paper used for manual drafting are printed with a grid to assist the drafter in laying out the drawing. A similar type of grid can be used in AutoCAD. Invoking the GRID command places a pattern of dots on-screen at any spacing, as shown in figure 2.10. The grid pattern appears only within the drawing limits and helps define the drawing area. The grid is for visual reference only and is not considered part of the drawing. It does not appear in print or on any plot of the drawing.

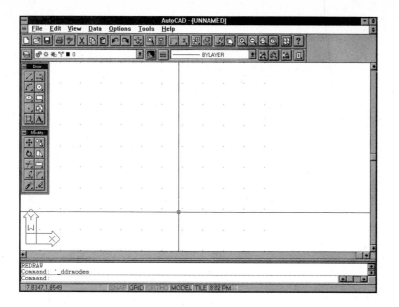

**Fig. 2.10**
The default grid
shown in the
standard drawing
editor.

Getting Started

### Setting Up the Grid

The grid can be changed through the Drawing Aids dialog box by typing
**ddrmodes** at the Command: prompt. Alternatively, you can type **grid** directly
at the Command: prompt. When you enter the GRID command, a prompt appears that shows the default grid spacing and several other options:

```
Command: grid
Grid Spacing(X) or ON/OFF/Snap/Aspect <Current Value>:
```

You can press Enter to accept the default values or enter a new value. You set
the dot spacing of the grid by entering a specific measure. If the grid spacing
you enter is too small to display on-screen, a Grid too dense to display message appears. If this happens, enter a larger grid spacing.

---

**Caution**

In many cases, the screen can display a very dense grid pattern. This can significantly
slow down the computer when certain operations are performed. A very dense grid
also lessens the usefulness of the grid.

---

### Toggling the Grid

If you have a dense grid pattern on the screen, it may be advantageous to
turn it off to increase the speed of your computer. Alternatively, you can
toggle the grid on and off to redraw the screen. This removes any blips when

you create geometry. You can turn the grid on and off using any of the following methods:

- On the status bar, double-click GRID.

- Press the F7 key.

- Press Ctrl+G.

- Type **grid** at the Command: prompt and then type **on** or **off**.

- Access the Drawing Aids dialog box by choosing Options, Drawing Aids. Select or deselect the On check box under Grid to turn the grid on or off.

### Setting the Aspect Ratio

The Aspect option at the grid prompt line enables you to set different values for horizontal and vertical spacing. For example, if you want to set the horizontal grid spacing at .25 and the vertical grid spacing at 1 while in the standard drawing editor, enter the following:

```
Command: grid
Grid Spacing(X) or ON/OFF/Snap/Aspect<Current Value>: A
Horizontal Spacing(X)<Current Value>: .25
Vertical Spacing(X)<Current Value>: 1
```

Setting this aspect ratio provides the dot spacing shown in figure 2.11. You also can set the aspect ratio by entering the appropriate values for the X and Y spacing in the Drawing Aids dialog box.

### Selecting the Grid Style

By invoking the Aspect option of the grid, you can display different horizontal and vertical spacing. The grid also can be rotated and aligned to geometry, and set up to define an isometric grid.

Using a grid does not ensure accurate point selection, but instead enables you to estimate distances quickly. The grid provides only a frame of reference by which you can estimate distances in the drawing. For you to accurately pick a grid point, the grid must be used with another command called SNAP. The SNAP command causes the crosshairs to snap to specific intervals. If the snap spacing is set to the grid spacing, you can accurately pick a grid point. Snap is discussed later in this chapter in the section "Using Snap." Grid points by themselves, however, are useful only as a visual estimating mechanism.

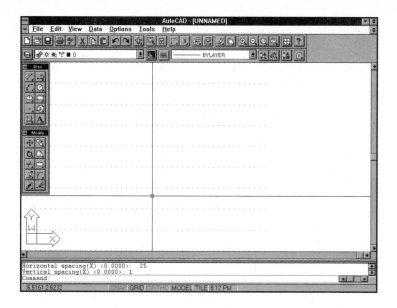

Getting Started

**Fig. 2.11**
The grid can act
as a drawing aid.
Note the greater
spacing in the
vertical direction
invoked with the
Aspect option, as
compared with
figure 2.10.

## Tutorial: Setting the Grid

Continuing with the roof plan project, you are now ready to get visual feed-
back of the limits, as well as define the grid increment. For this project, you
set the grid equal to 2'. Follow these steps:

1. Open the Drawing Aids dialog box.

   Choose Options, Drawing Aids.

2. Define the grid increment.

   > Enter **2'** for the X and Y spacing, and check the Grid
   > On box.

3. Select OK in the Drawing Aids dialog box.

   You should now see the grid displayed in the drawing area (see
   fig. 2.12).

You may have noticed that the grid does not extend all the way to the right
of the drawing area. That area is outside the limits settings established in the
preceding exercise. The grid is constrained within the limits and can be
toggled on and off with the F7 key.

**Fig. 2.12**

The drawing area after the limits have been set and the grid displayed.

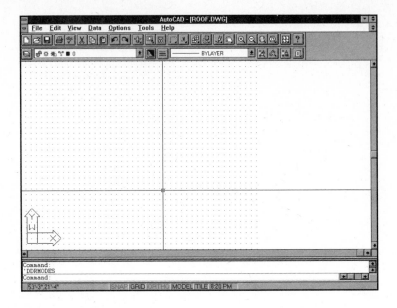

## Using Snap (SNAP)

In the earlier section, "Setting Display Format and Units (DDUNITS)," you learned how to display coordinates, distances, and angles to the precision selected. The GRID command enabled you to display a reference pattern of dots on-screen. Even with the correct display and the grid activated, however, you can't easily move the crosshairs to an exact location on-screen.

One drafting tool that AutoCAD uses to make creating precision drawing easier is the SNAP command. When the SNAP command is invoked, the cursor moves only in specific increments. For example, if snap is set to 6", you could quickly draw a line that is 1'-6" long. You do this by picking a point on-screen and moving the crosshairs three snap increments, and then picking another point.

### Setting the Snap Increment

The SNAP command enables you to set the snap increment and control the snap in other ways. When you enter **snap** at the Command: prompt, the following information is displayed:

```
Command: snap
Snap Spacing or ON/OFF/Aspect/Rotate/Style <Current Value>:
```

At the SNAP command prompt, enter the snap spacing or increment. If the snap spacing is set to one foot, for example, the crosshairs move only in one-foot increments. Setting the snap properly for the drawing you are working on can greatly increase your drawing speed and accuracy.

When beginning a new drawing, examine the overall distances and points involved in the drawing. Set the snap to a distance that enables you to easily lay out the main features of the drawing. As you continue to work on the drawing, you can change the snap increment at any time to suit your current needs without affecting the drawing.

> **Note**
>
> It's important to understand that the snap increment and grid have no relationship. The snap spacing can be set to match the grid points, but the snap increment also can be set so that the crosshairs snap to points other than the grid. If the grid is displayed but the snap is turned off, picking a grid point does not place the crosshairs exactly at that grid point's coordinate.

> **Note**
>
> If the snap increment does not seem to be affecting the movement of the crosshairs, check the snap setting. If snap is turned on and the snap increment is set too small, the incremental movement of the crosshairs may not be evident. To remedy this, increase the snap increment.

### Toggling Snap

At times you may want to turn the snap off. If you need to erase an object that doesn't fall on the snap increment, for example, toggling the snap off makes it much easier to select it. You can turn the snap function on and off with one of these methods:

- On the status bar, double-click SNAP.

- Press the F9 key.

- Press Ctrl+B.

- Type **snap** at the Command: prompt and then type **on** or **off**.

- Access the Drawing Aids dialog box by choosing Options, Drawing Aids. Select or deselect the on check box under Snap to turn the snap on or off.

Unlike the grid, the snap increment is invisible. Toggling the snap on or off only forces the crosshairs to move to the specified increment.

Getting Started

**Tip**
To set the grid at the same increment as the snap, use the Snap option after entering the GRID command at the Command: prompt.

### Setting the Aspect Ratio

The normal application of the SNAP command sets equal horizontal and vertical spacing. The Aspect option at the Snap prompt line enables you to set different values for horizontal and vertical spacing. Note an example:

```
Command: snap
Snap Spacing or ON/OFF?Aspect/Rotate/Style <Current Value>: a
Horizontal Spacing <Current Value>: .75
Vertical Spacing <Current Value>: 1
```

You also can change the aspect ratio by entering different values for the X and Y spacing in the Drawing Aids dialog box.

### Rotating the Snap

The normal pattern for snap is horizontal rows and vertical columns. Circumstances arise, however, when it would be beneficial to align the snap and grid to an angle other than horizontal and vertical. Changing the angle of the snap and grid can be very beneficial when drawing an auxiliary view that is at an angle to another view in the drawing. When the snap is rotated, you are given the option of setting a new base point. The base point is the pivot about which the snap is rotated. The base point of the normal snap is 0,0, or where the lower-left corner of the limits are usually set. When drawing an auxiliary view, for example, you may want to set the base point at the location where the view begins. After the base point is located, the rotation angle is set. The angle may range from 0 to 90 or 0 to –90 degrees. You do this with the Rotate option:

```
Command: snap
Snap Spacing or ON/OFF?Aspect/Rotate/
    Style <Current Value>: r
Base point <0,0>: Press Enter or pick a new base point.
Rotation Angle <0>: 30
```

The grid automatically rotates counterclockwise when a positive value is given and clockwise when a negative value is given. Figure 2.13 shows a rotated snap and grid used in the construction of an auxiliary view. Remember that the snap is invisible. The grid is shown only for illustrative purposes. You can also rotate the snap and enter a new base point in the Drawing Aids dialog box.

▶ See "Setting SNAP for Isometric Drawing," p. 749

The SNAP Style option can set two different grid styles. The standard option is the one used up to this point. The SNAP Style also can be set to isometric, which aids in the creation of isometric drawings.

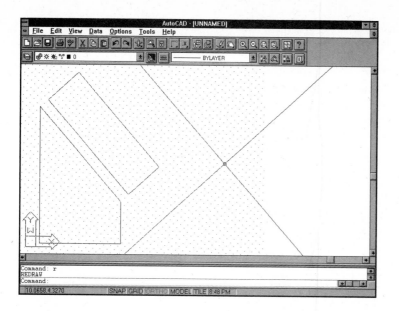

**Fig. 2.13**
The SNAP Rotate
command rotates
the grid to aid in
the drawing of
auxiliary views.

### Tutorial: Setting the Snap

The SNAP command is used to constrain the movement of the cursor. For the
roof framing plan, it is beneficial to have the snap set to 1'. Follow these
steps:

**1.** Open the Drawing Aids dialog box.

From the pull-down menu, choose Options, Drawing Aids.

**2.** Set the snap increment in the Drawing Aids dialog box to 1'. Additionally, select the Snap check box to turn snap on. The Drawing Aids dialog box should now look like figure 2.14

Moving the crosshairs around the screen, you now notice that the coordinate
display changes in increments of 1" and the crosshairs appear to snap to specific points. To notice the change, use the F9 key to toggle snap on and off
and continue to move the crosshairs.

## Using the Coordinate Display (COORDS)

The coordinate display is located at the bottom of the screen in the status bar.
By default, the coordinate display is on. AutoCAD dynamically displays the
current location of the crosshairs in the current unit of measure. You can
toggle the coordinate display on and off with one of these methods:

■ On the status bar, double-click the coordinate display.

■ Press the F6 key.

■ Press Ctrl+D.

When the unit of measure changes, the coordinate display changes accordingly. Figure 2.15 shows the coordinate display in the status bar.

**Fig. 2.14**
The Drawing Aids dialog box, with the snap spacing set to 1'0" and the grid set to 2'0".

**Fig. 2.15**
The coordinate display in the status bar showing decimal units.

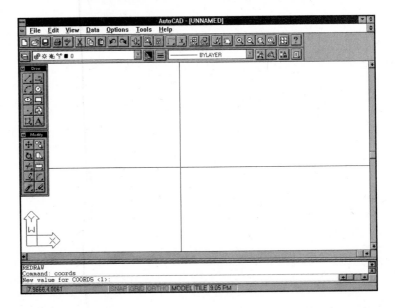

▶ See "Using Coordinates in AutoCAD," p. 89

Two modes are offered with the coordinate display. The default mode shows the *absolute* coordinate of the current crosshairs location. Absolute refers to the distance the crosshairs is from the origin, or 0,0. As you move the crosshairs, the coordinate display dynamically changes to show the current crosshairs' location. The second mode that the coordinate display can use is *relative*. In the relative mode, the coordinate display shows the current crosshairs' position *in relation* to the last point. The display is given in a relative polar mode, as discussed in Chapter 4,"Understanding Coordinates and Units."

You can use the coordinate display as a display guide to aid in locating points and specific coordinates. When used in combination with the SNAP and GRID commands, the coordinate display can speed up drawing time considerably.

## Using Ortho Mode (ORTHO)

While snap is a useful tool for drawing horizontal and vertical lines, AutoCAD provides another tool to help you draw straight lines. With AutoCAD's ortho mode, you can draw lines that are perpendicular or parallel to one another. The term *ortho* comes from *orthogonal*, which means "at right angles." The advantage of using the ortho mode when drawing rectangular shapes is that all corners are guaranteed to be square. You can toggle ortho mode on and off with these methods:

- On the status bar, double-click ORTHO.

- Press the F8 key.

- Press Ctrl+L.

When ortho mode is activated, it's impossible to draw a line at an angle using the crosshairs. When used with the SNAP and GRID commands, it makes geometry significantly faster.

## Drawing Lines (LINE)

One of the most common geometric objects created in any form of drafting is the line. Lines are used in many areas of drafting—from object lines to construction lines. Since lines are involved in almost every aspect of drafting, the line is the first AutoCAD object introduced.

You access the LINE command by choosing the Line icon from the Draw toolbar. Alternatively, you could enter **line** at the Command: prompt.

Selecting the Line button from the Draw toolbar will bring up a fly-out menu. The first button is Line. If the Draw toolbar is not displayed, you can access it by selecting Dra<u>w</u> from the <u>T</u>ools, <u>T</u>oolbars pull-down menu.

### Drawing Line Segments

After you enter the LINE command, you are prompted for two pieces of information. The first is the beginning of the line, and second is the end of the line. After you select the first point at the From point: prompt, AutoCAD responds with To point:, and you select the second point. When the second

**Tip**

You also can type **l** (the letter *l*) at the Command: prompt as a shortcut to begin the LINE command.

To point: prompt is given, you may stop adding lines by pressing Enter or the space bar. If you want to draw a series of connected lines, continue selecting as many additional points as you like. When you are drawing a series of lines, you are repeatedly prompted for the end point of the line. When finished, press the Enter key or space bar to return to the Command: prompt. The following command sequence for drawing a series of lines is illustrated in figure 2.16.

 Select the Line button on the Draw toolbar.

> From point: *Enter POINT 1.*
> To point: *Enter POINT 2.*
> To point: *Enter POINT 3.*
> To point: *Enter POINT 4.*
> To point:

**Fig. 2.16**

The LINE command is used to draw a series of connected lines.

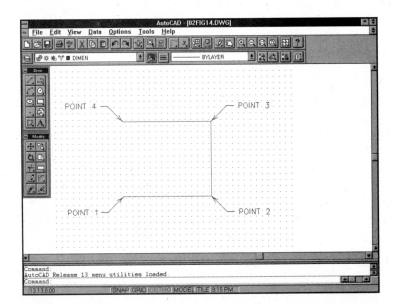

---

### Note

Even if you are drawing a series of connected lines, each line remains a separate object.

---

Choosing the Line button enables you to draw one or more line segments, as described earlier. The From point: prompt is issued, and then To point: is automatically issued until you press Enter or the space bar.

### Using the Close and Undo Options

In many instances when you draw a polygon, the last line drawn ends at the beginning location of the polygon. The definition of a *polygon* is a series of lines which enclose an area. The Close option within the AutoCAD LINE command makes this happen. Close sets the To point: to the same value as the From point: in the group of line segments making up the polygon. The Close option also ends the LINE command. To use this option, type **c** or **close** at the To point: prompt. Here is the command sequence for the Close option, as illustrated in figure 2.17:

Select the Line button from the Draw toolbar.

```
From point: Enter POINT 1.
To point: Enter POINT 2.
To point: Enter POINT 3.
To point: c
```

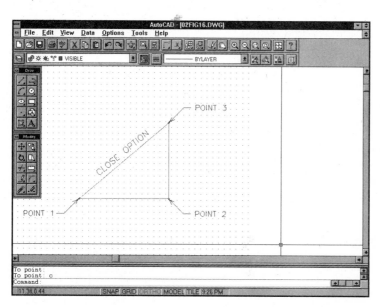

**Fig. 2.17**
The Close option draws a line back to the From point: of the polygon.

In case you make an error in selecting a point location for a line, the Undo option removes the last point picked and the associated line segment. You are still in the LINE command, and can reselect the point. Undo can be used after picking any To point: if you don't like the last line segment drawn. You can use Undo also after picking the first From point: if you don't like the starting point for the line. Once you are back to the Command: prompt, the UNDO command will remove all the lines drawn by the LINE command.

### Drawing Continued Line Segments

The LINE command also allows you to continue a line from the last point picked. If you press the space bar or Enter at the From point: prompt, the line segment continues from the last point picked. This option allows you to create adjoining line segments without drawing all the segments within a single LINE command.

### Cleaning Up the Display (REDRAW)

When you use an option such as Undo within the LINE command, blips may still appear on the display where points were picked. If the grid was activated when you used the Undo option, the section of the grid under the line may also appear missing. Issuing the REDRAW command when the screen has become filled with blips and missing objects cleans up the computer display. REDRAW restores the image on-screen and removes the blips and any missing parts of the grid. You use the REDRAW command with one of these methods:

■ Enter **redraw** or **r** at the Command: prompt.

■ Choose View, Redraw View.

**Tip**

To redraw the screen quickly, press F7 or double-click GRID in the status bar. This toggles the grid on or off, which causes the screen to redraw. The grid must be set to a value that is visible on-screen.

You can issue the REDRAW command at any time when the Command: prompt is displayed. To redraw the screen in the middle of a command, precede REDRAW with an apostrophe ('). The REDRAW command is transparent, which means that you can use it while another command is active. The Redraw View function in the View pull-down menu is also a transparent command.

### Quitting AutoCAD

To complete your AutoCAD drawing session, type **end** at the Command: prompt. This exits the drawing editor, saves your drawing, and returns you to Program Manager. Other options for ending your drawing session are:

■ Type **quit** at the Command: prompt.

■ Choose File, Exit.

If either of these commands is entered before you have saved your work, AutoCAD gives you a chance to decide what to do with your work. The AutoCAD dialog box is displayed, as shown in figure 2.18.

You also can begin a new drawing or open an existing drawing without having to exit AutoCAD. To begin a new drawing while in the drawing editor, choose New from the File pull-down menu. If this is done before you have saved your work, the AutoCAD dialog box will appear on the screen. To open an existing drawing while in the drawing editor, choose <u>O</u>pen from the <u>F</u>ile pull-down menu. You will again be prompted with the AutoCAD dialog box if you have not saved your work.

**Fig. 2.18**
The AutoCAD dialog box enables you either to save or discard any changes you made to the drawing.

Pressing Enter when the AutoCAD dialog box is displayed activates the high-lighted <u>Y</u>es button. This saves the drawing as it was previously named. If the drawing has not been named, the Save Drawing As dialog box is displayed. You also can choose <u>N</u>o if you don't want to save any changes made to the drawing since the previous save was issued. Choose Cancel if you decide that you don't want to quit and want to return to the drawing editor.

### Tutorial: Using the LINE Command to Create the Roof Plan

After setting the units, limits, grid, and snap as shown in the previous sections, you are ready to create the roof plan, as shown in figure 2.19.

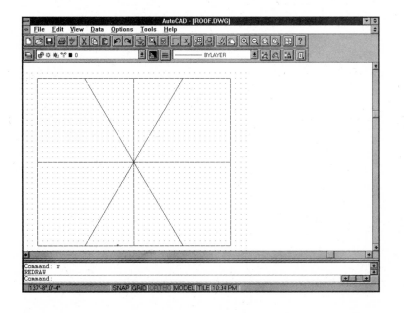

**Fig. 2.19**
The completed roof plan.

In this tutorial, you first draw the perimeter of the roof plan as shown in figure 2.20. You begin by using the LINE command. Next, you move the crosshairs and select locations at points A, B, C, D, and back to A. You will be moving in a counterclockwise direction. Before you begin, ensure that the snap, ortho, and coordinate display options are toggled on. The snap will allow you to select specific locations in the increments established, making it possible to choose exactly the required location. The ortho option will constrain your lines to be vertical and horizontal only.

As you work on this tutorial, if you make a mistake in selecting a point location, type **u** at the To point: prompt. This removes the last line segment, enabling you to pick another point location and continue.

**Fig. 2.20**

Completing the roof plan perimeter.

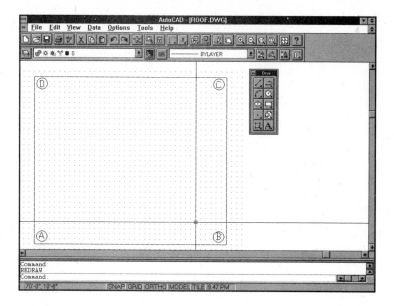

To draw the roof perimeter, follow these steps:

1. Check to make sure the snap and grid are on, and they are set properly. This can be done with the Drawing Aids dialog box. To invoke the Drawing Aids dialog box, select Drawing Aids from the Options pull-down menu. Make sure the Snap and Grid check boxes are on, and the snap spacing is set to 0'4" increments and the grid is set to 2'0" increments.

2. Ensure that the ortho option is toggled on.

   This can be done by checking the status bar at the bottom of the screen to see if ortho is bold. If it is not, double-click in the ORTHO box.

3. Next, ensure that the coordinate display is turned on.

Check the status bar for coordinates. If it is bold, the coordinates are turned on. If it is not bold, double-click in the COORDS box.

**4.** Start the LINE command.

Select the Line button from the Draw toolbar.

**5.** Moving the crosshairs, select points A, B, C, and D at the prompts that appear.

> From point: *Move your crosshairs to point A.*

The coordinate display in the status bar indicates the coordinates 6'-0",2'-0". Select that location for point A.

> To point: *Move your crosshairs toward point B.*

Notice that because ortho has been turned on, the line being created is forced to be horizontal and only the X coordinate value in the status bar is changing. The coordinate display in the status bar indicates the coordinates 82'-0",2'-0". Select that location for point B.

> To point: *Move your crosshairs toward point C.*

The line is now forced to be vertical and only the Y coordinate value is changing. The coordinate display in the status bar indicates the coordinates 82'-0",66'-0". Select that location for point C.

> To point: *Move your crosshairs to point D.*

The coordinate display in the status bar indicates the coordinates 6'-0",66'-0". Select that location for point D.

**6.** Connect point D to point A, completing the perimeter.

> To point: **c**

The Close option automatically connects point D to point A and ends the line command.

Next, you create the ridge lines for the roof plan (refer to fig. 2.19). Notice that the ridge lines are composed not only of vertical and horizontal lines, but also of diagonal lines. You begin by drawing the vertical and horizontal lines as shown in figure 2.21. You first draw the vertical line from point E to point F.

To draw the vertical and horizontal lines, follow these steps:

**1.** Choose the Line button from the Draw toolbar.

**Fig. 2.21**
Drawing the vertical and horizontal lines for the roof plan.

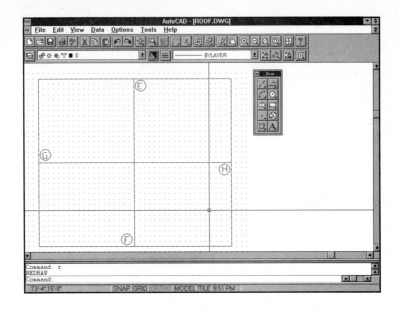

2. Moving the crosshairs, select points E and F at the prompts that appear.

> From point: *Move your crosshairs to point E.*

The coordinate display in the status bar should indicate the coordinates 44'-0",66'-0". Select that location for point E.

> To point: *Move your crosshairs to point F.*

The coordinate display in the status bar should indicate the coordinates 44'-0",2'-0". Select that location for point F.

3. At the next To point: prompt, press Enter. This exits the command and returns you to the Command: prompt.

4. You are now ready to draw the horizontal line from point G to point H. Select the Line button from the Draw toolbar.

5. Moving the crosshairs, select points G and H at the prompts that appear.

> From point: *Move your crosshairs to point G.*

The coordinate display in the status bar should indicate the coordinates 6'-0",34'-0". Select that location for point G.

> To point: *Move your crosshairs to point H.*

The coordinate display in the status bar should indicate the coordinates 82'-0",34'-0". Select that location for point H.

**6.** At the next To point: prompt, press Enter. This exits the command and returns you to the Command: prompt.

To finish the roof plan, you must add the diagonal ridge lines as shown in figure 2.22. You first draw the diagonal line from point J to point K. Because these lines are diagonal, it is important that the Ortho option be turned off.

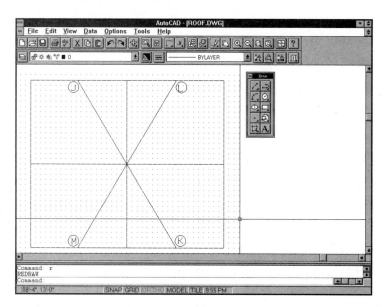

**Fig. 2.22**

Drawing the diagonal ridge lines to complete the tutorial.

To draw the diagonal lines, follow these steps:

**1.** Toggle the ortho off by pressing the F8 key once or double-clicking the word ORTHO on the status bar. The ORTHO button on the status bar should no longer be bold, indicating ortho is turned off. Toggle snap off as well.

**2.** Select the Line button from the Draw toolbar.

**3.** Moving the crosshairs, select points J and K at the prompts that appear.

> From point: *Move your crosshairs to point J.*

The coordinate display in the status bar should indicate the coordinates 24'-8",66'-0". Select that location for point J.

> To point: *Move your crosshairs to point K.*

The coordinate display in the status bar should indicate the coordinates 63'-4",2'-0". Select that location for point K.

4. At the next To point: prompt, press Enter. This exits the command and returns you to the Command: prompt.

To complete the roof plan, you draw the diagonal line from point L to point M. Since the Ortho option was turned off previously, it isn't necessary to alter its setting. Follow these steps:

1. Select the Line button from the Draw toolbar.

2. Moving the crosshairs, select points L and M at the prompts.

> From point: *Move your crosshairs to point L.*

The coordinate display in the status bar should indicate the coordinates 63'-4",66'-0". Select that location for point L.

> To point: *Move your crosshairs to point M.*

The coordinate display in the status bar should indicate the coordinates 24'-8",2'-0". Select that location for point M.

At the next To point: prompt, press Enter. This exits the command and returns you to the Command: prompt.

 3. Save your drawing by selecting the Save button from the Standard toolbar.

Congratulations! You have created your first AutoCAD drawing. If you are finished drawing for now and want to leave the drawing editor, type **end** or **quit** at the Command: prompt.

# Understanding Objects

The smallest part of an AutoCAD drawing is called an *object*. An example of an object is a line. When you select the different buttons from the Draw toolbar, you create objects. The buttons on the Draw toolbar and corresponding command names refer to the objects they create.

## What Is an Object?

Some examples of objects are lines, circles, and arcs. The rectangle created in the previous tutorial for the outline of the roof plan contained four objects.

Complex objects are defined as geometry that is created with one command. Although the objects appear to consist of several segments, they are considered by AutoCAD to be one object. Examples of complex objects created by a single command are polygon, polyline, and donut as shown in figure 2.23.

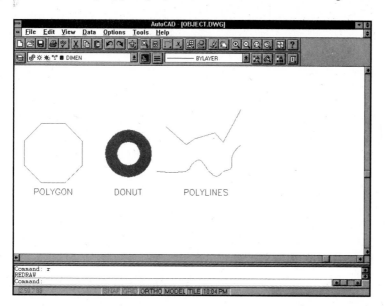

**Fig. 2.23**
The polygon, donut, and polyline appear to have several segments but are considered by AutoCAD to be one object.

As shown from the preceding example, it isn't always apparent whether a shape is composed of one or more objects. One way to find out is to select the object with the pickbox. Highlighting the form will reveal if it consists of one or more objects, as shown in figure 2.24.

## Understanding the Drawing Database

A database is a collection of information. When you create a drawing in AutoCAD, you are, in effect, creating a database. All the information for your drawing is stored in a file. The AutoCAD drawing file contains the electronically stored version of the drawing. This information is kept in binary digital form. These digits describe the coordinate values for all objects in the drawing, such as endpoints, center points, radii, etc. Additionally, the file contains codes that describe the kinds of objects in the drawing (line, arc, circle, polyline, and so on).

Understanding how AutoCAD stores the drawings by keeping the coordinate data can help you better understand how to use AutoCAD. The types of input required to create objects and the different prompts that appear on the screen are directly related to how this information is stored in the drawing file.

**Fig. 2.24**

Highlighting a form will show if it's composed of one or several objects.

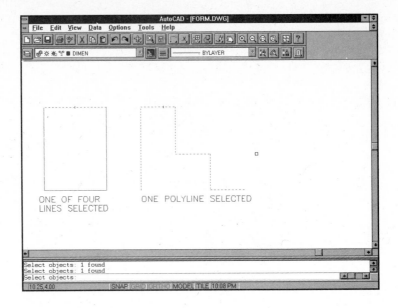

## From Here...

Before beginning any actual geometry creation, you must make several decisions regarding the drawing. The name and storage location should be determined before you begin, as well as the units the drawing uses. Next, you must decide the paper size on which the drawing is output. After you make these decisions, you can begin a new drawing and enter the path and name. Then you set the units. Finally, you set the limits based on the paper size and the size of the drawing. Remember to include extra space in the actual size of the drawing to account for dimensions, notes, border, and title block.

After you have made these preliminary decisions, you can set up the AutoCAD drafting tools. You use the Drawing Aids dialog box to set the snap, grid, and ortho. As you begin drawing, it's very important to save your work often. In Chapter 3, "Understanding Prototypes," you learn additional methods of entering point locations into the drawing other than using the snap, grid, and coordinates.

For more information about working with files, managing your database, and creating basic geometry, see the following chapters:

- Chapter 1, "Introducing AutoCAD," explains how to begin new drawings and open existing drawings.

- Chapter 5, "Creating Basic Geometry," shows you how to create other objects, including rectangles, circles, arcs, and polygons.

# On Your Own

Sketch the remaining six views of the Angle Plate as shown in figure 2.25.

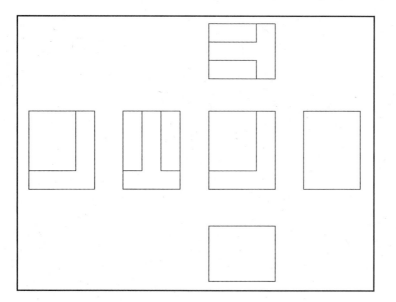

**Fig. 2.25**
Before beginning
the Angle Plate
drawing, sketch
the remaining
views first.

Hints:

1. Sketch the remaining six views on paper first. To determine the size of the object and location, count the grid spacing, which is .25 inches.

2. Determine where you want to store the drawing and what you want to call it.

3. Begin a new drawing, type the storage location (such as C:\UAW13) and name the drawing ANGPLATE.

4. Leave the limits set to 12,9. Set the drafting aids by using the Drawing Aids dialog box to change the grid, snap, and ortho. The grid spacing on the drawing is .25 inches.

5. Using the crosshairs and the coordinate display, use the LINE command to draw the remaining views. Remember to make sure that the snap and ortho are turned on.

6. Your completed drawing should look like figure 2.26.

**Fig. 2.26**
The completed
Angle Plate
drawing.

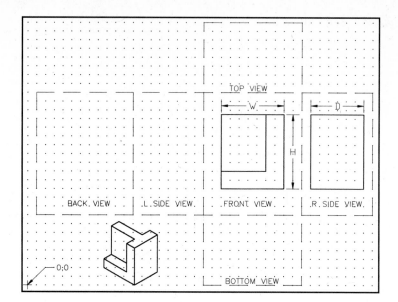

# Chapter 3

# Understanding Prototypes

The manual drafter normally begins with a sheet of drafting paper. In many cases, the sheet of paper has a preprinted border and title block. The title block is frequently labeled with the company name and address and has a place for the drawing title, part number, scale, material, and drafter's name, as well as an area for revisions. The manual drafter tapes down the sheet of paper and adds the necessary views, dimensions, and so on. Using drafting paper with a preprinted border and title block ensures standardization within the company. This approach also saves time because the manual drafter doesn't have to draw the border and title block with each new drawing.

AutoCAD has a feature called a *prototype drawing*, providing a similar function to that of the preprinted border and title block used in manual drafting. A simple prototype drawing may contain values for limits, grid, and snap. A complex prototype may contain a border and title block, established text styles, and other drawing variables.

In this chapter, you examine the prototype drawing and its uses by creating a site plan for use with an apartment complex. The following tasks are covered:

- Creating a prototype drawing
- Setting the prototype drawing options
- Beginning a new drawing by using a prototype drawing

## Working with Prototype Drawings

AutoCAD comes with a standard prototype drawing named ACAD.DWG. By default, this prototype drawing is used every time you begin a new drawing. If you continually use the default ACAD prototype drawing, you will soon discover that you frequently make the same drawing aids adjustments over and over. Units, limits, grid, and snap are drawing tools that need to be set every time you begin a new drawing that is at a different size than the prototype.

A *prototype drawing* may be defined as any drawing file that you want to use as the template for the new drawing you are creating. The prototype drawing can contain settings for such variables as the limits, snap increment, and grid spacing. After the prototype drawing is loaded, you create geometry as before. The advantage of using a prototype drawing is that it frees you from having to change the same settings every time you start a new drawing.

> **Note**
>
> There is nothing different about a drawing that is used as a prototype. Any AutoCAD drawing can be used as a prototype for any other drawing.

When you initially create a prototype drawing in AutoCAD, you set the limits, units, snap, and grid variables to your current specifications. In time, you may want to set up a prototype for each drawing size and type. For example, you might establish different prototype drawings that set the AutoCAD drafting tools and contain a border and title block for A-, B-, and C-size drawings.

You may set up different prototypes for mechanical, electrical, and architectural drawings. Whenever you create several drawings that contain similar settings, consider making and using a prototype drawing. You can select any drawing to be your prototype drawing when you choose New from the File menu.

# Creating a New Drawing from a Prototype

When AutoCAD starts, the standard AutoCAD graphics window is displayed. As discussed in the preceding chapter, you can begin creating geometry immediately, without giving your drawing a name. If you want to use a prototype drawing, it must be assigned before you begin working on the new drawing. You can begin a new drawing using one of these methods:

■ Select New from the Standard toolbar.

■ Enter **new** at the Command: prompt.

■ Choose File, New .

Any of these methods accesses the Create New Drawing dialog box (see fig. 3.1). The text box to the right of the Prototype button is already filled in with the file name ACAD.DWG. This is AutoCAD's default prototype drawing.

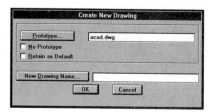

**Fig. 3.1**

The Create New Drawing dialog box with the AutoCAD prototype drawing, ACAD, already provided.

When you click the Prototype button, a list of possible prototype drawings appears in the Prototype Drawing File dialog box (see fig. 3.2). AutoCAD displays the contents of the c:\acad13\common\support subdirectory because this is where the default ACAD.DWG prototype drawing is located. If you change directories and choose a different prototype drawing, that directory becomes the default directory automatically displayed in the Create New Drawing and Prototype Drawing File dialog boxes. The List Files of Type list box at the bottom of the Prototype Drawing File dialog box filters out all file names that do not have the DWG extension.

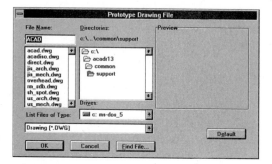

**Fig. 3.2**

In the Prototype Drawing File dialog box, you can select a different prototype drawing.

After you select a new prototype drawing, you're ready to begin working on the drawing. All settings that were part of the prototype drawing are now part of your new drawing. The prototype drawing file will not be changed in any way when you begin creating geometry in the new drawing.

> **Note**
>
> After you select a prototype drawing, you do not have to enter a drawing name in the Create New Drawing dialog box. If you press Enter after selecting a prototype drawing, you can create and edit your drawing without giving it a name. You are prompted for a name the first time you save the drawing. Although this is fine for experimental drawings, you should get into the habit of naming your drawings from the beginning.

# Setting Prototype Drawing Options

The Create New Drawing dialog box contains two options that can be set regarding prototype drawings. They are the No Prototype and Retain As Default check boxes. The ACAD.DWG drawing remains as the default prototype drawing unless you select the Retain As Default check box and then select a different prototype.

Occasionally, you may need to start a new drawing with AutoCAD's default settings but without any prototype drawing. You usually do this when you import into the drawing editor a DXF or IGES file made by AutoCAD or another graphics program. In this case, you use the No Prototype option. When you use No Prototype, you only get AutoCAD's default settings; any settings or objects you may have in your own prototype will not be set or drawn. The next time you create a new drawing, your prototype will load as usual.

Proper use of prototype drawings can increase considerably the speed at which drawings are created. Many repetitive setup tasks can be stored in prototype drawings. Remember, a prototype drawing is created like any other drawing. Consequently, any drawing can be used as a prototype drawing.

## Tutorial: Creating a Prototype Drawing

▶ See "Understanding Linetypes," p. 193

In this tutorial, you create a prototype drawing to help you draw the site plan. In the prototype drawing, you set units, limits, grid, and snap; load a phantom linetype; and set the linetype scale. You begin by creating a new drawing. Follow these steps:

1. Select New from the Standard toolbar. The Create New Drawing dialog box appears.

2. Enter **C:\UAW13\APROTO** in the New Drawing Name text box (see fig. 3.3). Because you are creating a prototype drawing and not actually using one, the AutoCAD default ACAD.DWG prototype is used.

You should now see the standard AutoCAD graphics window. First, you need to set the units. For this exercise, you will be using architectural units with a precision of 0'-0" and surveyor angles with a precision of N 0d E. Follow these steps:

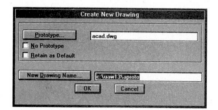

**Fig. 3.3**
Using the Create New Drawing dialog box to create the prototype file.

1. Choose Un<u>i</u>ts from the <u>D</u>ata menu. The Units Control dialog box appears.

2. Using the pointing device, adjust the dialog box to reflect the settings shown in figure 3.4. Select OK.

▶ See "Setting Display Format and Precision (UNITS and DDUNITS)," p. 97

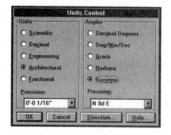

**Fig. 3.4**
Setting Units to <u>A</u>rchitectural, <u>P</u>recision to 1/16", and Angles to <u>S</u>urveyor.

Next, you set the limits for the prototype drawing. The lower-left limits will remain 0'-0",0'-0" and the upper-right limits will be 144'-0",96'-0". Follow these steps:

◀ See "Setting the Drawing Size (LIMITS)," p. 51

1. Choose D<u>r</u>awing Limits from the <u>D</u>ata menu.

2. At the `ON/OFF/<Lower left corner><0'-0",0'-0">:` prompt, press Enter.

3. At the `Upper right corner <1'-0",0'-9">:` prompt, type **144'-0",96'-0"** and press Enter.

To show the entire limits within the view window, you issue the Zoom All option:

1. From the Standard toolbar, choose the Zoom All icon or type **z** at the `Command:` prompt.

▶ See "Using
ZOOM to
Control the
Display
(ZOOM),"
p. 336

2. Enter **a** at the `All/Center/Dynamic/Extents/Left/Previous/Vmax/`
   `Window/<Scale(X/XP)>:` prompt. This shows the entire limits within
   the viewport.

After the limits are established, you set the grid to 5' and the snap to 1':

1. Choose Options, Drawings Aids.

2. Enter **5'** for the grid X and Y spacing.

3. Enter **1'** for the snap X and Y spacing.

4. Check the Snap On and Grid On check boxes.

You next load a phantom line. Up to this point, the only linetypes you have
drawn have been continuous lines. To create the site plan, you will need to
use a phantom linetype. Although this procedure is introduced here, an in-
depth discussion of loading linetypes and modifying linetype scales can be
found in Chapter 8, "Understanding Linetypes." Follow these steps:

1. From the Object Properties toolbar, choose the Linetype icon.
   This displays the Select Linetype dialog box.

2. To load the PHANTOM linetype, select Load. The Load or Reload
   Linetype dialog box is displayed. If the linetype has been previously
   loaded, the Reload Linetype dialog box will appear.

3. Use the scroll bar to display PHANTOM in the Available Linetype list
   box, and then select PHANTOM.

4. Press Enter or choose OK to accept the Load or Reload Linetypes dialog
   box and return to the Select Linetype dialog box.

5. In the Select Linetype dialog box, pick PHANTOM Linetype from the
   Loaded Linetypes list box to set it as the current linetype.

   The next task is to set the linetype scale to 96 so that the line will be
   scaled correctly when displayed or plotted. A full description of linetype
   scaling is covered in Chapter 8, "Understanding Linetypes."

6. In the Select Linetype dialog box, select the Linetype Scale edit box.

7. For the new scale factor, enter **96**.

8. Choose OK to accept the Select Linetype dialog box. The PHANTOM
   linetype is now loaded and set, and the linetype scale is set.

9. The APROTO.DWG prototype file is now ready to be saved for use later.
   To save the drawing, click the Save icon on the Standard toolbar.

# From Here...

Prototype drawings, if properly used, can save you a considerable amount of time. Including common settings, title blocks, and even geometry in a prototype drawing not only improves drawing standardization but also increases productivity. The AutoCAD drafting tools (grid, snap, coords, and ortho), if properly used, can increase the speed and accuracy of geometry creation.

For more information about Units and Linetypes, see the following chapters:

- Chapter 4, "Understanding Coordinates and Units," shows you how to create geometry using the coordinate system and how to standardize drawings using prototypes.

- Chapter 8, "Understanding Linetypes," explains how to load and use various linetypes.

# On Your Own

1. Create a prototype file with the following drawing variables:

   Limits=0,0 and 10.5,8

   Units=Decimal with 0.00 precision

   Grid=.5 units

   Snap=.25 units

2. When you have finished with the above settings, use the LINE command to create a unique title block of your choosing.

3. After you have finished, save the drawing.

4. Now begin a new drawing using the prototype drawing that you just created.

If you begin the new file correctly, you should see all of your settings, as well as your title block, appear in your new drawing.

Getting Started

# Chapter 4

# Understanding Coordinates and Units

In Chapter 2, "Creating Your First Drawing," you learned how to set up AutoCAD to use the snap increment and grid to accurately locate points in the drawing. Another way to specify exact points and create accurate drawings is to use coordinates. AutoCAD uses the Cartesian coordinate system for specifying exact points in a drawing. The second part of this chapter discusses the two-dimensional coordinate system for locating points and lines. Four different coordinate entry methods are discussed: absolute, relative, absolute polar, and relative polar.

In this chapter you will explore the different coordinate methods used in drawing. The following tasks are covered:

- Creating geometry using absolute coordinates

- Creating geometry using relative coordinates

- Creating geometry using absolute polar coordinates

- Creating geometry using relative polar coordinates

## Coordinate System Basics

One of the historic landmarks of science and mathematics was the introduction of coordinates into geometry. The key idea behind the coordinate system is how a given set of points is represented. Points are represented as an ordered pair of real numbers, written in such a way that you can distinguish one number as the "first" and the other as the "second." The usual notation is $(x,y)$, where $x$ and $y$ are real numbers.

Ordered pairs of real numbers may be associated with points of a *coordinate plane*. For example, suppose that an ordered pair of numbers (*x,y*) is given. The first number of the pair is located on horizontal line L1, with the positive direction to the right (the *x* axis). The second number of the pair is located on vertical line L2 (the *y* axis), with the positive direction upward and the origin the same as that of the *x* axis. The point (*P*) where the two lines intersect is labeled (*x,y*). The numbers *x* and *y* are called the *Cartesian coordinates* of the point *P* (see fig. 4.1). Cartesian is named in honor of Descartes, a French philosopher who introduced the concept in the 17th century.

**Fig. 4.1**

The Cartesian coordinate system used to locate point P.

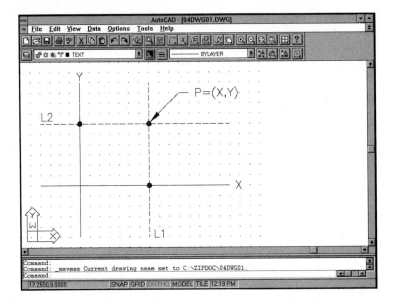

When both the *x* and *y* values are 0, forming a coordinate of 0,0, that point is called the *origin*. The origin can be displaced and relocated to assist in the creation of geometry, but with the ability to use relative coordinates, it is often unnecessary to do so.

AutoCAD uses the same Cartesian coordinate system to designate points within a drawing. When you create a two-dimensional drawing, you can enter points for geometry creation with either the pointing device or the keyboard. The coordinate display in the status bar at the bottom of the screen shows the current location of the crosshairs in the present unit of measure. Note that the readout uses the Cartesian coordinate system. It should also be noted that AutoCAD has full 3D potential by adding the distance from the origin along the *z* axis to the Cartesian coordinates, as in (X,Y,Z). This concept is discussed in detail in Chapter 27, "Understanding 3D Coordinate Systems."

# Using Coordinates in AutoCAD

At this point, you should be familiar with the standard AutoCAD graphics window. Notice that an icon is shown in the lower-left corner, consisting of two perpendicular arrows. These arrows are directional indicators for the *user coordinate system,* or *UCS.* While creating 2D drawings, the UCS icon shows the direction of the positive values for the X and Y axes. In later chapters, you will find the UCS icon an invaluable tool in creating 3D models. The UCS is based on the Cartesian coordinate system and divides space into four quadrants. Figure 4.2 shows the UCS icon and the division of space based on Cartesian coordinates. You locate points in these quadrants by specifying their location in horizontal (*x*) and vertical (*y*) directions along the plane. Points are always specified with the *X* coordinate first, the *Y* coordinate second, and the Z coordinate (if needed) third. The + symbol represents the origin point of the current UCS.

▶ See "Changing the UCS Origin," p. 793

**Getting Started**

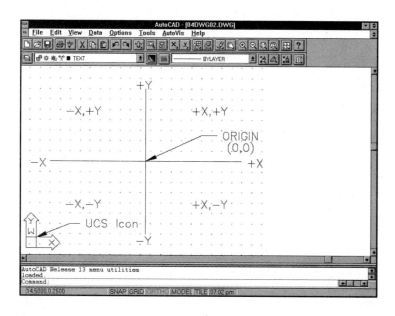

**Fig. 4.2**
The division of space, using the Cartesian coordinate system, with the UCS icon displayed.

The AutoCAD screen has a direct relationship to the Cartesian coordinate system (see fig. 4.3). As you begin creating lines, AutoCAD asks you to specify the `From point:`. In Chapter 2, you entered this information, using the pointing device, in association with the snap and grid. You did that by moving the crosshairs to a point on-screen and pressing the pick button on the pointing device.

**Tip**
To remove the UCS icon, choose <u>O</u>ptions from the menu bar, then <u>U</u>CS, then <u>I</u>con. If Icon has a checkmark next to it, the UCS icon is displayed.

**Fig. 4.3**

The relationship of the drawing screen to the Cartesian coordinate system. Limits are set with the lower-left corner at 0,0 and the upper-right corner at two positive values.

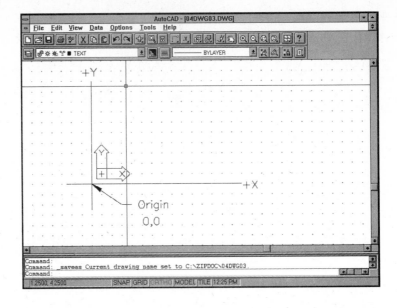

**Tip**

You can switch the coordinate entry method at any time during a command sequence. The first coordinate may be absolute, followed by a relative move, an absolute polar coordinate and then using the pointing device.

Using the pointing device with the snap and grid is excellent for creating certain types of geometry. Because of constraints imposed by the snap and grid, however, very specific locations cannot be made. In an attempt to locate more specific points, you could change the snap and grid settings to smaller values. When the grid spacing is too small, AutoCAD responds with the message `Grid too dense to display`. When the snap increment is set very small, it becomes difficult, if not impossible, to pick exact locations. Because the fields of architecture and engineering often deal with very specific locations, a more exact means of controlling the "to point" is needed. You can control this point by using absolute, relative, absolute polar, and relative polar coordinates.

> **Note**
>
> Even though the grid, snap, and ortho modes may be activated, any coordinate entered through the keyboard overrides any of these settings. This is true even if the desired point location does not fall on the grid or cannot be snapped to, or if the To point: location is at an angle to the previous location with ortho mode turned on.

## Entering Absolute Coordinates

The absolute coordinate system locates all points from an origin presumed to be 0,0. The origin point is understood to be the same point on which the limits, snap, and grid are based. The origin is presumed to be 0,0 because the lower-left corner of the display screen may be set at any location other than 0,0. Setting the lower-left corner at 0,0 is the most common and recommended setting, however.

The axes for the *x* and *y* coordinates intersect at 0,0 (refer to fig. 4.3). Each point on the screen is located by a numeric coordinate based on the intersection of the *x* and *y* axes at 0,0. You define points by entering the coordinates of *x* and *y*, separated by a comma.

---

**Caution**

Point locations can be entered in architectural units as well as decimal units. When you indicate architectural units, use hyphens only to distinguish fractions from whole inches. Additionally, do not use spaces while giving a dimension. For example, you can specify 6 feet, 5 1/4 inches as 6'5-1/4" or 6'5.25", but not as 6'-5 1/4".

---

## Tutorial: Using Absolute Coordinates to Create a Side Elevation Profile

In this tutorial, you create a side elevation profile (see fig. 4.4) using the LINE command and absolute coordinates. Follow these steps:

1. Choose the New button from the Standard toolbar. If prompted with the Save Changes dialog box, choose No if you do not want to save your drawing. Enter a name for the drawing and select OK.

2. Choose the Line button from the Draw toolbar. Draw the side elevation profile. Draw all five lines continuously, starting at point A and moving counterclockwise to points B, C, D, E, and finally back to point A. All points in this exercise are specified using absolute coordinates.

3. At the From point: prompt, type **2,2** and press Enter.

   The line starts at point A. Continue using absolute coordinates to complete the drawing.

---

**Troubleshooting**

*I entered the wrong ending coordinates for a line. How can I easily correct my mistake?*

When you enter the ending coordinates and notice a mistake, simply type **u** at the To point: prompt and press Enter. This will undo the last coordinate and allow you to reenter the correct coordinates.

---

4. To locate point B, enter **8,2** at the To point: prompt.

5. To locate point C, enter **8,5.5** at the To point: prompt.

6. To locate point D, enter **5,7** at the To point: prompt.

7. To locate point E, enter **2,5.5** at the To point: prompt.

8. To close the line on starting point A, enter **c** at the To point: prompt.

**Fig. 4.4**

Creating the side elevation profile, using absolute coordinates.

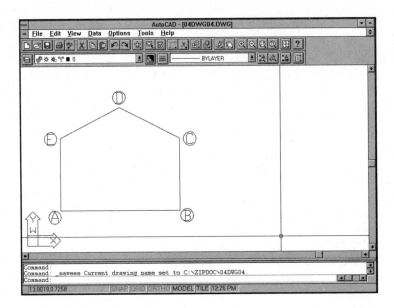

## Entering Relative Coordinates

Relative coordinates are used to locate "to points" *in relation* to the previous point, rather than the origin. You enter relative coordinates in a manner similar to the way you enter absolute coordinates. When you enter relative coordinates, the @ (at symbol) must precede your entry. You select this symbol by holding down the Shift key and pressing the number 2 key on the keyboard. For example, if the last point specified was 6,4, then entering **@3,4** is equivalent to specifying the absolute coordinates 6+3 and 4+4, or 9,8.

---

### Note

To draw an object from a previous data point, you enter @ for the relative specification. This stipulates a zero offset. For example, if the last point entered was 5,7, entering just the @ specifies 5,7 again.

## Tutorial: Using Relative Coordinates to Create a Side Elevation Profile

In this tutorial, you create the side elevation profile found in figure 4.4, using the LINE command and relative coordinates. Follow these steps:

1. Choose the New button from the Standard toolbar.

2. If prompted with the Save Changes dialog box, choose Yes or No as desired.

3. You will draw all five lines continuously, starting at point A and moving counterclockwise to points B, C, D, E, and finally back to point A. All points in this exercise are specified using relative coordinates except point A, which will be specified using absolute coordinates.

4. Choose the Line button from the Draw toolbar.

5. At the From point: prompt, enter **2,2** for point A.

6. To locate point B, type **@6,0** at the To point: prompt.

7. To locate point C, type **@0,3.5** at the To point: prompt.

8. To locate point D, type **@-3,1.5** at the To point: prompt.

9. To locate point E, type **@-3,-1.5** at the To point: prompt.

10. To close the line on starting point A, enter **c** at the To point: prompt.

# Understanding Polar Coordinates

Polar coordinates can be defined as a distance and angle from a specified point. By default, AutoCAD measures angles in a counterclockwise manner. Zero degrees is toward the positive *x* axis, to the right of the point being referenced. This means that 90 degrees is straight up, toward the positive *y* axis; 180 degrees is to the left, toward the negative *x* axis; and 270 degrees is straight down, toward the negative *y* axis. Figure 4.5 shows the default AutoCAD angle measurement in a two-dimensional coordinate system. This direction can be changed using the units command if so desired. If your AutoCAD is not measuring angles counterclockwise you may want to use the units command to correct this problem.

## Using Absolute Polar Coordinates

You designate an absolute polar coordinate by entering first the distance, then the < sign, and then the angle. For example, to specify a 6-unit-long line at an angle of 45 degrees, you would enter **6<45** as the coordinate at the To

◀ See "Setting Display Format and Units," p. 49

**Tip**
When units are set to architectural and you are inputting distances in feet and inches, you do not need to type the inch sign ("). This saves typing and speeds up the drawing process.

Getting Started

point: prompt. AutoCAD locates the end point of the line 6 units away from the *origin* 0,0 point at an angle of 45 degrees. All absolute polar coordinates are measured from the *origin*.

**Fig. 4.5**

The default AutoCAD angle measurement system in a two-dimensional coordinate system.

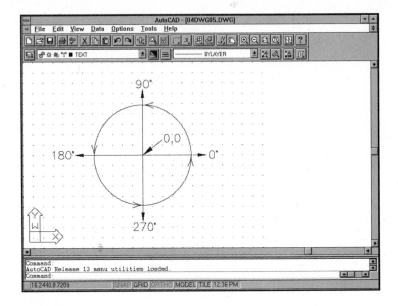

## Using Relative Polar Coordinates

Relative polar coordinates are measured from the last point entered as a distance followed by an angle. To specify a relative polar coordinate, precede the distance and angle with the @ symbol. To specify a line of 3 units at an angle of 60 degrees from the last point picked, you would enter **@3<60** at the To point: prompt. AutoCAD locates the end point of the line 3 units away from the *last point* entered at an angle of 60 degrees.

## Tutorial: Using Relative and Absolute Polar Coordinates to Create the Side Elevation Profile

In this tutorial, you create the side elevation profile found in figure 4.4. You use the LINE command and relative and absolute polar coordinates. Follow these steps:

1. Choose the New button from the Standard toolbar.

2. If prompted with the Save Changes dialog box, choose No.

3. Issue the LINE command and draw the side elevation profile. As in the preceding tutorials, you draw all five lines continuously, starting at

point A and moving counterclockwise to points B, C, D, E, and finally back to point A. Point A is located using absolute polar coordinates. All subsequent points are located using relative polar coordinates.

    From point: **2.8284<45**

The line begins at point A.

4. To locate point B, enter **@6<0** at the To point: prompt.

5. To locate point C, enter **@3.5<90** at the To point: prompt.

6. To locate point D, enter **@3.3541<153** at the To point: prompt.

7. To locate point E, enter **@3.3541<207** at the To point: prompt.

8. To close the line on starting point A, enter **c** at the To point: prompt.

You may notice that the last line segment does not appear perfectly vertical. This is because the values for the distance and the angle were rounded off.

In the next tutorial, you load the prototype drawing you created in the previous chapter and create a site plan, using several of the coordinate entry methods previously discussed.

## Tutorial: Creating Property Lines with Coordinates and a Prototype Drawing

In this tutorial, you create the property lines shown in figure 4.6. To begin this drawing, you will need to have completed the prototype drawing exercise at the beginning of the previous chapter. That file is used to load default settings for this drawing. After loading this prototype and beginning a new drawing, you will be ready to create the property lines, using a phantom linetype.

You begin by starting a new drawing, using the C:\UAW13\APROTO.DWG prototype file created in the previous chapter's On Your Own section or open 04DWG02. Follow these steps:

1. Choose the New button from the Standard toolbar.

2. If prompted with the Save Changes dialog box, choose No.

3. When the Create New Drawing dialog box appears, adjust your settings to reflect those found in figure 4.7.

**Fig. 4.6**
The completed
property lines
drawing.

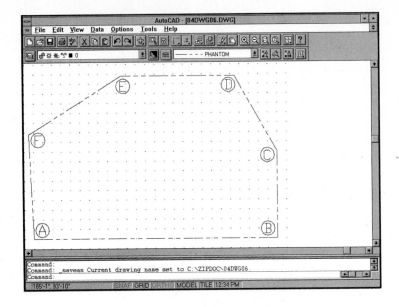

**Fig. 4.7**
Use the Create
New Drawing
dialog box to
begin the property
line drawing.

Now you begin the drawing, using the LINE command and absolute coordinates to specify point A at 5',5':

1. Choose the Line button from the Draw toolbar.

2. The line begins at point A. At the From point: prompt, enter **5',5'**.

   To continue the line to points B, C, and D, you use relative polar coordinates. Note that you will be using architectural units and the surveyor's units of angle measurements.

3. To locate point B, enter **@130'<N90E** at the To point: prompt.

4. To locate point C, enter **@45'<N0E** at the To point: prompt.

5. To locate point D, enter **@45'<N30W** at the To point: prompt.

   To continue the line to points E and F, you use relative coordinates, absolute coordinates, and the Close option to complete the property lines. Although you are using different coordinate entry methods in this tutorial, it should be apparent that any method could be used to place the points. You should not limit yourself to only one coordinate entry method. An efficient AutoCAD user will know which coordinate method to use and when to use it.

6. To locate point E, you use relative move. At the `To point:` prompt, enter **@-60',0'**.

7. To locate point F, you use a relative move. At the `To point:` prompt. enter @-**50',-30'**.

8. To close the line on starting point A, enter **c** at the `To point:` prompt.

9. Save your drawing by choosing the Save button from the Standard toolbar.

# Setting Display Format and Precision (UNITS and DDUNITS)

The AutoCAD UNITS command and the Units Control dialog box enable you to set the type and precision of units you will use in the drawing. Options within the UNITS command and Units Control dialog box control two types of unit display: linear and angular. Other options enable you to control the precision with which the unit values appear for linear and angular measurement.

The unit settings affect the following:

- The display of the coordinates on the status bar

- The appearance of the values when dimensioning

- The format of the values when you examine the drawing for an area or distance

- The format for entering coordinates, distances and angles at the `Command:` line

You can set the type of units and the precision with the Units command, which flips to the AutoCAD text box. Access the text box by entering `units` at the Command: prompt. You can also set the units and precision through the Units Control dialog box. To access this dialog box:

- Enter **ddunits** at the `Command:` prompt.

- Choose Units from Data on the menu bar.

> **Note**
>
> Most AutoCAD commands have a default response. It appears in angle brackets at the end of the command prompt, like this : `<default response>`. Default responses help increase work speed because they decrease the amount of typing. AutoCAD remembers how you last responded to a command prompt and gives you the option of responding the same way.
>
> Your last response to a command prompt appears in the angle brackets as the default response the next time the command is issued. If the default response is the same as the action you want to take, press Enter or the space bar.

## Report Formats

AutoCAD has five different measurement report formats: scientific, decimal, engineering, architectural, and fractional. The examples shown in table 4.1 show how the value of 15.5 drawing units appears in each format.

**Table 4.1   Units of Measurement**

| Report Format | Example |
| --- | --- |
| Scientific | 1.55E+01 |
| Decimal | 15.50 |
| Engineering | 1'–3.50" |
| Architectural | 1'–3 1/2" |
| Fractional | 15 1/2 |

Each type is designed for a specific purpose. You must determine the units in which to create the drawing. Note the five types:

- *Scientific units.* Dimensions are given as a real number raised to a power of 10, such as 125E+02. You can use scientific notation to represent any system of measure. You use scientific notation primarily when working with very large numbers.

- *Decimal units.* Dimensions are given in units, such as 1.75 or 3.625. Decimal units are generally used in mechanical drafting, because ANSI Y14.5M *Dimensioning and Tolerancing* standards specify that decimal inch or metric units in millimeters be used in engineering drawings. AutoCAD can display a maximum of eight decimal places. Decimal is the default type of unit in AutoCAD.

**Getting Started**

> **Note**
>
> A generic unit can be declared as anything: an inch, a mile, a millimeter, a kilometer.

- *Engineering units.* Dimensions are given in feet, inches, and decimal parts of an inch, such as 6'–5.25". AutoCAD automatically converts and displays 12 inches as one foot. It is important to note that inches is the default unit. If 6 is entered it is assumed to be 6 inches. To enter feet, you must include the ' symbol. Each engineering unit in AutoCAD represents one inch. Engineering units are used primarily in civil drafting. Detailed construction drawings and topographic maps for planning and constructing highways and harbors are examples of typical civil drafting projects.

- *Architectural units.* Dimensions are given in feet, inches, and fractional parts of an inch, such as 6'–11 1/4". Twelve inches is automatically converted to one foot. Architectural units are used for residential and commercial planning and construction drawings. The smallest fraction that AutoCAD can display is 1/256". It is important to note that inches is the default unit. If 6 is entered, it is assumed to be 6 inches. To enter feet, you must include the ' symbol.

- *Fractional units.* Dimensions are given in whole units and parts of a unit as a fraction, such as 26 5/8. Fractional units may be any value, such as inches, feet, or miles. You can use fractional representation with any system of measure. As with architectural units, the smallest fraction that AutoCAD can display is 1/256".

## Display Precision

The display format and entry format of the units selected is determined by the number of decimal places or the smallest fraction. The easiest method of selecting the units and setting the display precision is with the Units Control dialog box (see fig. 4.8). You can access this dialog box in one of two ways:

- Choose Units from Data on the menu bar.

- Enter **ddunits** at the Command: prompt.

The default precision value is shown in the dialog box. After you have determined the type of units you will use, you must decide on the accuracy of the drawing display. For example, if you are using decimal units, two digits may be shown as 2.88, three digits as 2.875, and four digits as 2.8751. As shown in this example for decimal units, AutoCAD rounds the value of the display.

**Fig. 4.8**

You can use the Units Control dialog box to set the type of units and the precision.

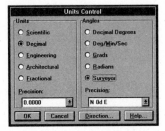

> **Note**
>
> Regardless of the display precision setting, AutoCAD is accurate to 14 places for all types of units. The only values affected by changing the precision are the display of the coordinates on the status bar, the appearance of the values when dimensioning, and the format of the values when you examine the drawing for an area or distance.

When you are working on mechanical drawings, three to four digits are normally used for inch drawings. For metric drawings, one- or two-place decimals are generally used, such as 16.5 or 16.50. This difference is due to the greater distance represented by inches as opposed to millimeters.

With architectural and fractional units, the precision is determined by the size of the fraction's denominator. Selecting 1/8 results in the values being displayed in 1/8-inch increments (or their least common denominator). For example, the display may read 6'–5 1/8". If 1/4 was chosen as the precision, the same dimension would be rounded off to the nearest 1/4-inch increment, or 6'–5 1/4".

## Angular Measurement

AutoCAD also has five different angular measurement options. The examples in table 4.2 show how the value of 42.5 degrees appears in each format.

| Table 4.2  **Units of Angular Measurement** | |
|---|---|
| **Report Format** | **Example** |
| Decimal degrees | 42.5000 |
| Deg/min/sec | 42d30'0" |
| Grads | 47.2222g |
| Radians | 0.7418r |
| Surveyor's units | N 47d30'0"E |

Here are descriptions of the angular measurement options for AutoCAD:

- *Decimal degrees.* Displays angular measurement as real numbers with up to eight decimal places. This is the default type of angular measurement in AutoCAD.

- *Deg/Min/Sec.* Displays angular measurement in degrees, minutes, and seconds. This representation uses ASCII characters, such as 30d12'38". Measurements of less than one second are displayed as decimal places.

- *Grads.* Displays angular measurement as grads. A lowercase *g* appears after the value, such as 37g. Ninety degrees equals 100 grads.

- *Radians.* Displays angular measurement as radians. A lowercase *r* appears after the value, such as 6.2832r. A radian is 180/pi degrees.

- *Surveyor's units.* Displays angular measurement in degrees, minutes, and seconds together with quadrant bearings. An example is N45d12'25"E. Surveyor's units are based on a circle divided into four quadrants, so no angular value can be greater than 90 degrees.

> **Note**
>
> If the status bar doesn't have enough room to display the coordinates normally, AutoCAD sometimes displays them in scientific units. This does not mean that the units have changed, only that AutoCAD must use scientific units to display them.

Getting Started

## Angle Display Precision

The degree of accuracy for angles is determined by the drawing requirements. Two-place decimal degrees or degrees and minutes are normally used for mechanical drawings. Mapmaking with civil drawings often requires degrees, minutes, and seconds.

You can easily change the angle display precision in the Units Control dialog box. As noted, you access the Units Control dialog box by entering **ddunits** at the Command: prompt or choosing Data, Units. To change the precision, select the arrow at the right of the Precision text box. The Precision list box appears, as shown in figure 4.9. Use your pointing device to select the precision you want.

**Fig. 4.9**

You can use the Units Control dialog box to set the precision for angles.

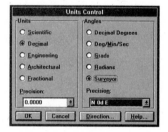

## Angle Direction

By default, AutoCAD assumes that 0 degrees is toward the right (east, or three o'clock). Also by default, angles increase in the counterclockwise direction, as shown in figure 4.5.

You can change the location of 0 degrees and the direction of angular measurement with the Direction Control dialog box. Surveyors often change these defaults because typically they measure angles clockwise from north rather than counterclockwise from east. To change the angle direction and location of 0 degrees, choose Direction in the Units Control dialog box. The Direction Control dialog box appears, as shown in figure 4.10.

To change the angle 0 direction, select the appropriate location with the corresponding radio button. If you choose Other, you can enter an angle value into the box, which becomes the new angle 0 direction, or you can choose Pick, which allows you to "show" AutoCAD the direction for angle 0 by picking two points in the drawing window.

**Fig. 4.10**
You can change the angle 0 location and direction of angular measurement in the Direction Control dialog box.

## Tutorial: Drawing Lines Using the Five Different Units

In this tutorial you will create five parallel lines using the different units discussed in the chapter. Once all five lines are created you'll be able to compare them.

1. Choose the New button from the Standard toolbar.

2. If prompted with the Save Changes dialog box, choose Yes or No as desired.

3. Choose Data, Units.

   Change the units to Scientific and choose OK.

4. Choose the Line button from the Draw toolbar.

   At the `From point:` prompt, enter **2e00,2e00** and press Enter.

   At the `To point:` prompt, enter **1.45e01,2e00** and press Enter.

   At the `To point:` prompt, press Enter.

   A line is drawn that may extend beyond the drawing area. Do not be concerned with this now. Continue on to the next step.

5. Choose Data, Units.

   Change the units to Decimal and choose OK.

6. Choose the Line button from the Draw toolbar.

   At the `_line From point:` prompt, type **2,3** and press Enter.

   At the `To point:` prompt, type **14.5,3** and press Enter.

   At the `To point:` prompt, press Enter.

7. Choose <u>D</u>ata, Un<u>i</u>ts.

8. Choose the Line button from the Draw toolbar.

   At the From point: prompt, type **0'2 ",04** and press Enter.

   For this example, we'll use the polar coordinate method to describe the line length.

   At the To point: prompt, type **@1.45e01,4e00** and press Enter.

   At the To point: prompt, press Enter.

9. Choose <u>D</u>ata, Un<u>i</u>ts.

   Change the units to <u>A</u>rchitectural and choose OK.

10. Choose the Line button from the Draw toolbar.

    At the _line From point: prompt, type **2,6** and press Enter.

    For this example we'll use the polar coordinate method to describe the line length.

    At the To point: prompt, type **@12-1/2<0** and press Enter.

    At the To point: prompt, press Enter.

11. Choose the Zoom All button from the Standard toolbar. All lines are now displayed for your inspection.

# From Here...

It is important that you become proficient with the coordinate entry methods introduced in this chapter. Without a mastery of these concepts it is impossible to create many difficult drawings accurately. It's very important that the AutoCAD user never "guess" the appropriate points. What may look fine on the AutoCAD screen will probably result in an inaccurate drawing when plotted. Likewise, it's important that you be familiar with the various types of units. Although you may only have a use for one or two of the types on a regular basis, you should know what is available should the need arise for another type of unit.

For more information about drawing, see the following chapters:

- Chapter 5, "Creating Basic Geometry," shows you how to begin using basic drawing commands.

- Chapter 15, "Advanced Drawing Techniques," continues to introduce advanced drawing commands.

# On Your Own

With keyboard entry only, use the absolute, relative, absolute polar, and relative polar coordinate entry methods to draw the shape shown in figure 4.11.

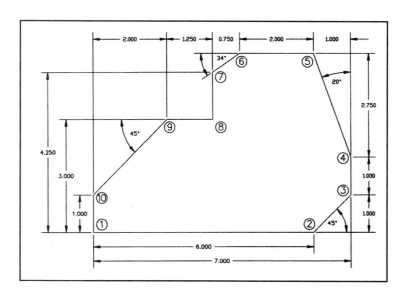

**Fig. 4.11**
Using coordinates to draw.

Hints:

1. Begin by loading APROTO.DWG created in Chapter 3 or load 04DWG02. This sets the limits and other drawing variables that you use for this exercise. This drawing also includes a border and title block.

2. Point 1 is located at 2,2.

3. Remember, you can work in any direction and start at any location. You can also change your coordinate entry method from point location to point location.

# Part II

# Basic Drawing Techniques

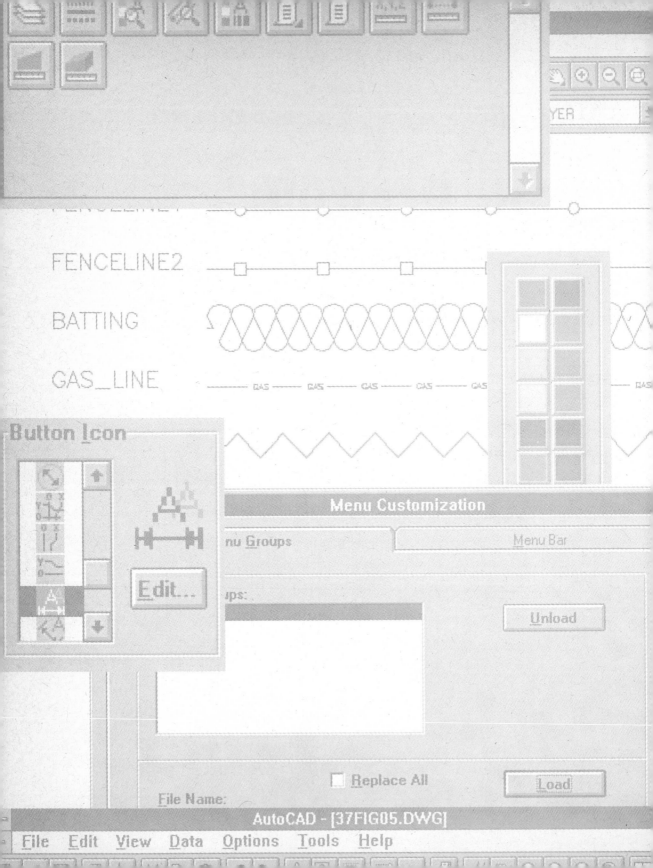

FENCELINE2

BATTING

GAS_LINE — GAS — GAS — GAS — GAS — GAS — GAS

Button Icon

Edit...

Menu Customization

nu Groups

Menu Bar

ups:

Unload

Replace All

Load

File Name:

AutoCAD - [37FIG05.DWG]

File   Edit   View   Data   Options   Tools   Help

YER

# Chapter 5

# Creating Basic Geometry

This chapter describes some very basic AutoCAD commands. These commands cast the foundation for almost any geometry you create. The LINE command draws lines, the CIRCLE command draws circles, and the ARC command draws arcs. (Most AutoCAD commands have names that describe their functions.) Lines, circles, and arcs make up the majority of most objects.

In this chapter, you learn how to use circles, arcs, rectangles, and polygons to create architectural symbols. For creating specialized geometry, this chapter also discusses the RECTANG and POLYGON commands. You use these architectural symbols in a final apartment complex drawing that includes a stove, breakfast bar, and hot tub. To complete this drawing, you learn how to do these tasks:

- ■ Draw a rectangle

- ■ Draw circles with the CIRCLE command options

- ■ Draw arcs with the most common ARC commands

- ■ Draw polygons with the POLYGON command options

## Drawing Rectangles (RECTANG)

With the RECTANG command, you can draw rectangles easily. AutoCAD asks you to locate the first corner and then the opposite corner, as shown in figure 5.1. You mark corner locations with the crosshairs or keyboard coordinate entry. The corners of the rectangle don't have to be selected from left to right or top to bottom—you can pick any two diagonally opposing corners. To locate the corners, you can use any combination of coordinate entry methods, including absolute, relative, absolute polar, and relative polar.

◄ See "Standard Toolbar," p. 16

You access the RECTANG command in one of two ways:

■ Enter **rectang** at the Command: prompt.

■ Choose the Rectangle button on the Draw floating toolbar. To access the Draw floating toolbar, select Tools, Toolbars, Draw from the pull-down menu bar.

**Fig. 5.1**
Use the mouse or keyboard coordinate entry to locate the first corner and then the opposite corner of a rectangle.

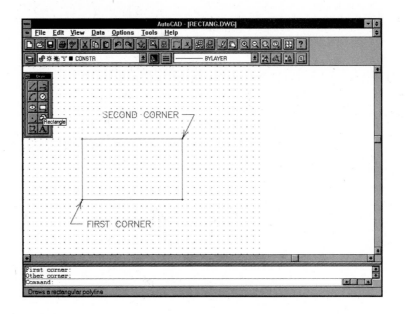

▶ See "Using Polylines," p. 573

When you create a rectangle, AutoCAD treats it as one object, called a *polyline*. To edit the individual sides, you must explode the rectangle.

▶ See "Breaking Blocks Apart (EXPLODE)," p. 697

## Tutorial: Creating a Rectangle

In this tutorial, you create the simple 3-unit by 5-unit rectangle shown in figure 5.2. Follow these steps:

1. Choose New from the Standard toolbar. In the New Drawing dialog box, click OK or press Enter.

2. Choose Rectangle from the Draw toolbar.

3. Specify the coordinates for the two corners of the rectangle:

```
First corner: 1,1
Other corner: @3,5
```

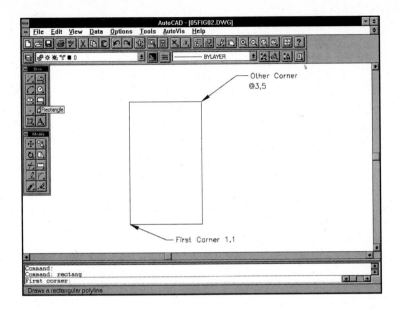

**Fig. 5.2**
You can easily
create this 3-unit
by 5-unit rectangle.

**II**

**Basic Drawing Techniques**

# Drawing Circles (CIRCLE)

Circles are as much a part of a typical drawing as lines are. AutoCAD gives
you five options for drawing a circle:

- *Center, Radius*. First specify the center point of the circle and then the
  radius of the circle.

- *Center, Diameter*. First specify the center point of the circle and then the
  diameter of the circle.

- *2 Point*. Specify two points that define the diameter of the circle.

- *3 Point*. Specify three points on the circumference of the circle.

- *Tangent, Tangent, Radius*. Specify two objects that will be tangent to the
  circle and the circle's radius.

You access the CIRCLE command in one of three ways:

- Enter **circle** at the Command: prompt.

- Click the Circle button on the Draw toolbar. This will bring up a
  submenu called a *fly-out menu*, showing the five options for creating a
  circle (see fig. 5.3).

■ You also can enter **c** at the Command: prompt as a shortcut to access the CIRCLE command.

**Fig. 5.3**

The five options for drawing the circle, plus the Donut button, are available on the fly-out menu.

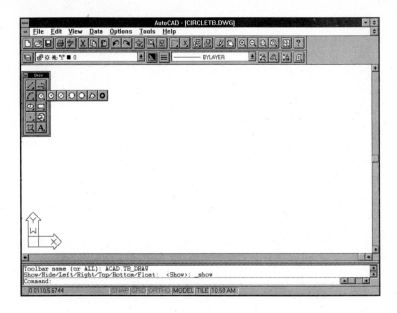

## Drawing Circles with Center Point and Radius

When you select the Circle Center Radius button from the Circle fly-out menu, AutoCAD first asks you to select a center point. You can locate the center point with the crosshairs or coordinate entry. After you select the center point, pick the radius in the drawing window or type the radius value (see fig. 5.4). If you're selecting the center point and radius with the crosshairs, you can set and turn on snap and grid to help locate the center point. Watch the coordinate display window to locate the exact center point and radius. Here's the command sequence for using the Center, Radius option:

```
3P/2P/TTR/<Center point>: Enter the coordinates or pick the
     center point.
Diameter/<Radius>: Drag the circle to the desired radius
     and pick.
Alternately enter the radius size.
```

## Setting the Default Radius

Radius is the CIRCLE command's default option. The radius value of the last circle created becomes the default value the next time you use the CIRCLE command.

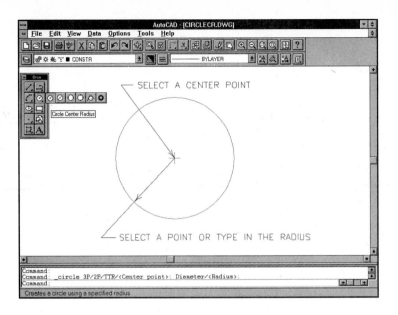

**Fig. 5.4**
First specify a center point, and then specify the radius when drawing a circle.

If you want to set a default radius for the CIRCLE command, use the CIRCLERAD system variable. Then the same default circle radius appears each time you use the CIRCLE command until you use a different value. The following command sequence sets the CIRCLERAD value:

```
Command: circlerad
New value for CIRCLERAD<current value>: Set the value you
    want, such as .25.
```

When you use the CIRCLE command, the sequence now looks like this:

```
Select the Circle Center Radius button from the Circle
    fly-out menu.
3P/2P/TTR/<Center point>: Locate center point.
Diameter/<Radius><.25>:
```

This command draws a circle with a radius of .25 at the center location specified. If you set the CIRCLERAD system variable to a nonzero value and then issue the CIRCLE command, you just need to pick the circle's center point as prompted and then press Enter at the `Diameter/<Radius>:` prompt. You can always enter a different radius or pick a different radius point if you don't want to use the default value you set with CIRCLERAD. Remember, if you override the default value for the radius by picking a new point or entering a new value, the default value is reset to your new entry.

**Tip**
When drawing a series of identical circles, the radius of the first circle is retained as the default by CIRCLERAD. When drawing other identical circles, establish the center point, then press Enter to accept the default radius.

**II**

**Basic Drawing Techniques**

---

**Note**

The value for CIRCLERAD is automatically set to 0 when you first start AutoCAD. When CIRCLERAD is set to 0, AutoCAD prompts you for a radius rather than providing a default value. Once you draw a circle or expressly set a value for CIRCLERAD, the default value is maintained and updated in your current drawing session only. If you save the drawing, quit, and open the drawing again later, CIRCLERAD is set to 0. If you open a new drawing, CIRCLERAD is set to 0.

---

### Tutorial: Creating a Circle with Center Radius

This tutorial and the next show you how to create the series of circles shown in figure 5.5 by using the Center Radius and Center Diameter options. Circles A, B, and C are created using the Radius option. Begin by creating a new drawing:

1. From the Standard toolbar, select the New button. If the AutoCAD dialog box appears, select No unless you want to save the current drawing. If you want to save the current drawing, select Yes and enter a path and drawing name. At the New Drawing dialog box, click OK or press Enter.

**Fig. 5.5**
Drawing circles A, B, and C using the Center Radius and Center Diameter options.

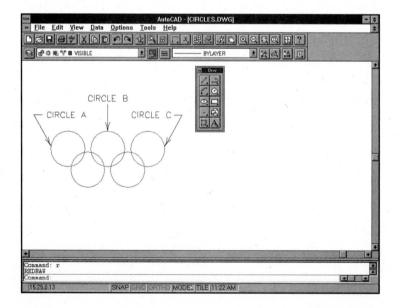

2. Select the Circle Center Radius button from the Circle fly-out menu.

3. Enter the absolute coordinates for the center point for circle A:

   `3P/2P/TTR/<Center point>:` **`2,4.25`**

4. Enter the value for the radius:

   `Diameter/<Radius>:` **`.75`**

5. Next, reenter the Circle Center Radius command.

6. Enter the absolute coordinates for the center point for circle B:

   `3P/2P/TTR/<Center point>:` **`3.75,4.25`**

7. Because the radius value was entered in the previous circle, pressing Enter will accept the default value and draw the circle.

   `Diameter/<Radius><0.7500>:` *`Press Enter.`*

8. Reenter the Circle Center Radius command and draw circle C. Use the absolute values of **5.5** and **4.25** for the center point and use the default radius value of **.75**. The next tutorial on drawing circles with the Center Point and Diameter will continue from here.

> **Tip**
>
> Although you can select the Circle Center Radius button from the Circle fly-out menu, pressing Enter at the Command: prompt repeats the previous command.

## Drawing Circles with Center Point and Diameter

You can select the Center Diameter option of CIRCLE by:

- Selecting the Circle Center Diameter button from the Circle fly-out menu.

- Typing **circle** at the Command: prompt.

If you enter **circle** at the Command: prompt, you must enter **d** for the Diameter option because radius is the default, as shown in the following example:

```
Command: circle
3P/2P/TTR/<Center point>: Locate center point.
Diameter/<Radius>: d
Diameter: Enter the diameter size or drag the circle to the
    desired diameter size and pick.
```

When you use the Circle, Diameter option, notice that as the pointer measures the diameter of the circle, the circle's edge passes midway between the center and crosshairs, as shown in figure 5.6. The Center, Diameter option is frequently used because most circle dimensions are given as diameters.

**Fig. 5.6**
When you draw a circle with the Center, Diameter option, the distance from the center of the circle to the crosshairs represents the diameter of the circle.

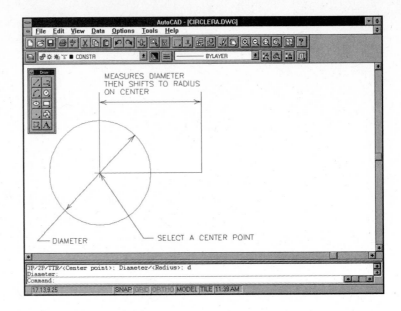

When you choose the Circle Center Diameter button from the Circle fly-out menu, the initial prompt is for the center point of the circle. After you locate the center point, you're automatically prompted for the diameter.

After you draw a circle with the Diameter option, the previous default setting is converted to a diameter. If your next circle is drawn with the Radius option, AutoCAD changes the default to a radius measurement based on the previous diameter. If the CIRCLERAD value is set to .75, for example, the default for a circle drawn with the Diameter option is automatically set to 1.50 (twice the radius).

### Tutorial: Creating a Circle with Center Diameter

For this tutorial, you'll create circles D and E as shown in figure 5.7 by using the Center Diameter option.

1. Continue from the previous tutorial. Select the Circle Center Diameter button from the Circle fly-out menu.

2. Enter the absolute coordinates for the center point for circle D:

   3P/2P/TTR/<Center point>: **2.875,3.375**

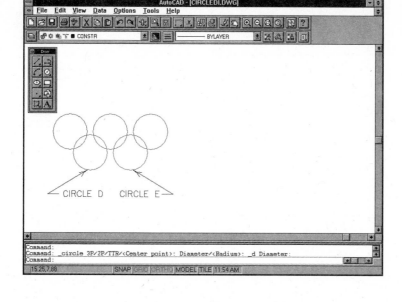

**Fig. 5.7**
Draw circles D and
E using the Center
Diameter option.

3. In the preceding tutorial, you set the circle radius to **.75**. AutoCAD automatically changes this value to the diameter and displays it in the prompt. Press Enter to accept the default diameter for the circle.

   ```
   Diameter <1.5000>:
   ```

4. Reenter the Circle Center Diameter command and draw circle E. Use the absolute values of **4.625** and **3.375** for the center point and use the default diameter value of **1.5000**.

## Drawing Circles with Three Points

When you know three points on the perimeter, the three-point option is the best method to use for drawing a circle. You can select the three points in any order, as shown in figure 5.8. Here's the command sequence for a three-point circle:

Select the Circle 3 Point button on the Circle fly-out menu.

```
3P/2P/TTR/<Center point>:
First point: Select first point.
Second point: Select second point.
Third point: Select third point.
```

AutoCAD automatically calculates the radius of the circle just created and uses this value as the default for the next circle.

**Fig. 5.8**
You can draw a
circle by selecting
three points on
the perimeter.

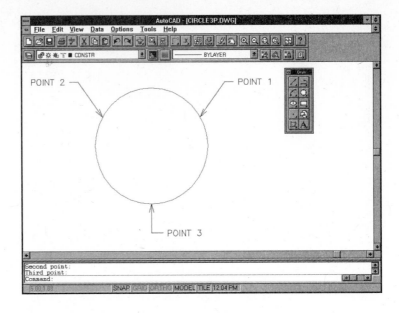

### Tutorial: Creating a Circle with Three Points

This tutorial and the next two show you how to create the series of circles
shown in figure 5.9, using the different methods available in AutoCAD. Circle
A is created using the three-point option. Begin by creating a new drawing:

1. Select the New button from the Standard toolbar. If the AutoCAD dialog box appears, select No unless you want to save the current drawing.
   If you want to save the current drawing, select Yes and enter a path and
   drawing name. In the New Drawing dialog box, click OK or press Enter.

2. Select the Circle 3 Point button from the Circle fly-out menu.

3. Enter the absolute coordinates for all three points:

   ```
   First point: 2,2
   Second point: 3,3
   Third point: 4,2
   ```

You should now have the circle A shown in figure 5.9.

## Drawing Circles with Two Points

You draw a two-point circle by selecting two points that lie on the circle's
perimeter, as shown in figure 5.10. These two points define the circle's diameter. This option can be useful when the diameter of the circle is known but
the center point is difficult to locate. Here's the command sequence for a
two-point circle:

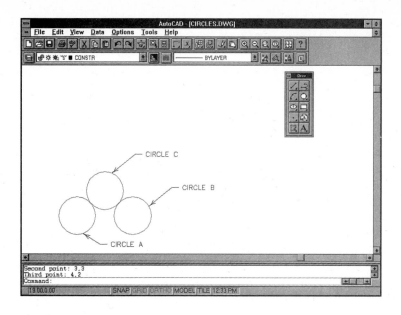

**Fig. 5.9**
Drawing circle A using the 3-point option, circle B using the 2-point option, and circle C using the Tan Tan Radius option.

Select the Circle 2 Point button from the Circle fly-out menu.

> First point on diameter: *Select first point.*
> Second point on diameter: *Select second point.*

AutoCAD will automatically calculate the radius of the circle just created and use this value as the default for the next circle.

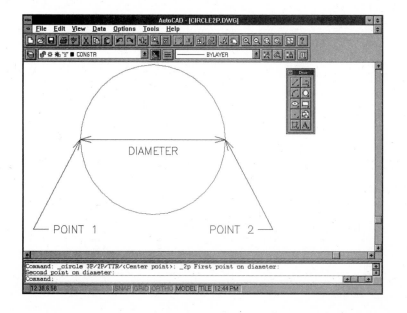

**Fig. 5.10**
You can draw a circle by selecting two points on the perimeter.

**Basic Drawing Techniques**

### Tutorial: Creating a Circle with Two Points

Continuing from the preceding tutorial, you draw circle B with the two-point option. Follow these steps:

1. Select the Circle 2 Point button from the Circle fly-out menu.

2. Enter the absolute coordinates for the first point and the polar coordinates for the second point:

   ```
   First point: 5,2
   Second point: @2<0
   ```

You should now have the two circles labeled A and B, shown in figure 5.9.

## Drawing Circles with Tangent, Tangent, Radius

 The Tangent, Tangent, Radius option (TTR) allows you to draw a circle of a specific radius that has two points of tangency with existing objects. The existing objects may be another circle or a line. After selecting the two tangency points, you specify the circle radius.

> **Note**
>
> The term *tangent* refers to a circle, line, or arc that comes into contact with a circle or arc at one point. The point where the objects touch is called the *point of tangency*. When two circles are tangent, they touch at only one point. A line drawn between the centers passes through the point of tangency.

When you have to draw a circle tangent to two given lines, circles, or arcs, choose the Tangent, Tangent, Radius option. Select the lines or line and arc that the new circle will be tangent to. After you select these objects, give the radius. Here's the command sequence for using the Tangent, Tangent, Radius option:

Select the Circle Tan Tan Radius button from the Circle fly-out menu.

```
Enter Tangent spec: Select the first line, circle, or arc.
Enter second Tangent spec: Select the second line, circle,
    or arc.
Radius <current>: Enter a radius value.
```

> **Note**
>
> If you enter a radius value that's too small, AutoCAD displays the message Circle does not exist.

The radius you enter for the Tangent, Tangent, Radius option becomes the default value for the next circle. Figure 5.11 shows two examples using the Tangent, Tangent, Radius option.

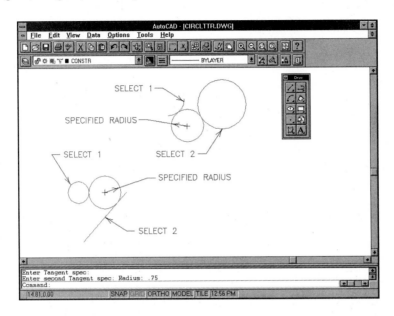

**Fig. 5.11**
You can use Tangent, Tangent, Radius to draw circles tangent to two given objects.

**II**

**Basic Drawing Techniques**

---

### Note

To locate the center of a circle at the same coordinates as the last selected point on the previously created object, use the @ symbol. The @ symbol retrieves the value stored as the AutoCAD LASTPOINT value. For example, if you want to locate the center of a circle at the endpoint of a previously drawn line, enter the @ symbol at the Circle-Center Point prompt, as in the following example:

Select the Line button from the Draw floating toolbar.

```
From point: 2,2
To point: 4,4
To point:
Select the Circle Center Radius button from the Circle fly-out
    menu.
3P/2P/TTR/<Center point>: @
```

Using the @ symbol in this example automatically retrieves the last selected point 4,4 (endpoint of the last drawn line) as the center of the circle.

```
Diameter/<Radius>: Press Enter to accept the default value.
```

### Tutorial: Creating Circles with Tangent, Tangent, Radius

Now create another circle that's tangent to circles A and B drawn in the previous tutorials. The new circle will have a radius of 1 unit. Follow these steps:

1. Select the Circle Tan Tan Radius button from the Circle fly-out menu.

2. Specify the first two circles. Depending on the location where you pick the two circles, the new circle may be below the two existing circles. This is because the Tangent, Tangent, Radius option is *position sensitive*—that is, the position of the crosshairs on the circles you select influences the location of the resulting tangent circle. To create a tangent circle above the two existing circles, be sure to pick the top parts of the circles.

    ```
    Enter Tangent spec: Select circle A.
    Enter second Tangent spec: Select circle B.
    ```

3. At the Radius: prompt, enter **1**.

    You should now have the three circles as shown in figure 5.9.

### Tutorial: Drawing a Stove/Oven Symbol

This tutorial describes how to create a stove/oven symbol to be used when completing the apartment floor plan (see fig. 5.12). The symbol, composed of a rectangle and four circles, enables you to practice the commands you used earlier in the chapter. Because you'll use this symbol in an architectural drawing, you should change the units. After completing the symbol, save it as STOVE in your UAW13 subdirectory.

**Fig. 5.12**
The stove/oven symbol, created with the rectangle and circle commands.

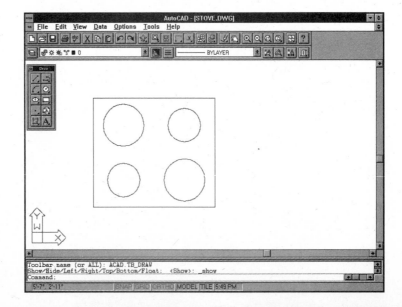

You can draw this stove/oven symbol to use in a floor plan. In creating the stove/oven symbol, you'll use several different methods described in the preceding sections to draw circles. To begin the process, follow these steps:

**1.** Select the New button from the Standard toolbar. In the Create New Drawing dialog box, change to the UAW13 subdirectory and enter **STOVE** for the new drawing name. If the AutoCAD dialog box appears, select No unless you want to save the current drawing. If you want to save the current drawing, select Yes and enter a path and drawing name.

**2.** Choose Data, Units. The Units Control dialog box appears. Change the units to architectural with a precision of 0'-0".

**3.** Now begin drawing the symbol. Start by creating the rectangle shown in figure 5.13. Make sure that the Draw floating toolbar appears on-screen. Select the Rectangle button from the Polygon fly-out menu.

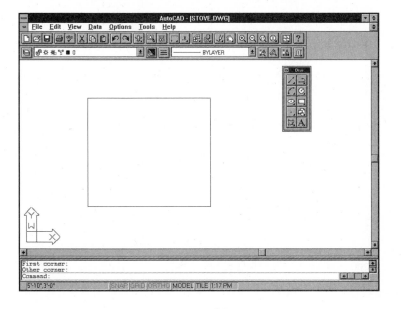

**Fig. 5.13**
Use the RECTANG command to create the stove/oven symbol.

**4.** Locate the corners of the rectangle:

```
First corner: 1,1
Other corner: @30,26
```

> **Note**
>
> When working with architectural units, it's not necessary to type the inch (")
> symbol after a distance value. If a distance value isn't followed by a foot sym-
> bol ('), AutoCAD assumes the value to be in inches.

▶ See "ZOOM
Scale," p. 350

5. Notice that you can't see the complete rectangle. You need to use the
   ZOOM command to display the rectangle within the drawing area.
   Select the Zoom Scale button from the Zoom fly-out menu. For the
   scale factor, enter **.2**.

Now you're ready to create the circles that represent the burners on the stove.
Two burners will be 8" diameters, and the other two will be 10" diameters.
You begin by drawing the 8" diameter burners. Follow these steps:

1. Select the Circle Radius button from the Circle fly-out menu.

2. Specify the absolute coordinates for the center point and give the
   radius.

   ```
   CIRCLE 3P/2P/TTR/<Center point>: 9",8"
   Diameter/<Radius>: 4"
   ```

   You should now have the lower-left burner drawn.

3. Repeat steps 1 and 2 for the upper-right burner. Pressing Enter at the
   Command: prompt reissues the CIRCLE command.

   ```
   Command:
   CIRCLE 3P/2P/TTR/<Center point>: 2',1'-9"
   Diameter/<Radius><0'-4">:
   ```

   Your drawing should now resemble figure 5.14.

4. To complete the stove/oven symbol, create the two remaining 10" diameter burners—first the upper-left burner and then the lower-right
   burner.

   ```
   Command:
   CIRCLE 3P/2P/TTR/<Center point>: 9",1'9"
   Diameter/<Radius><0'-4">: 5"
   Command:
   CIRCLE 3P/2P/TTR/<Center point>: 2',8"
   Diameter/<Radius><0'-5">:
   ```

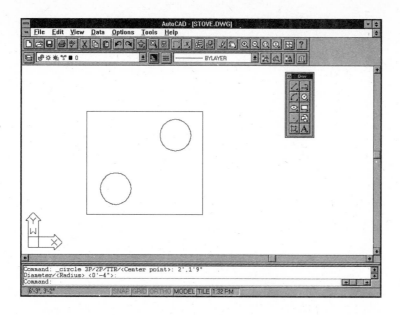

**Fig. 5.14**
The stove/oven symbol with the 8" diameter burners completed.

The stove symbol is now complete and should resemble the symbol in figure 5.12. You can save the drawing for use later by selecting the Save button from the Standard toolbar.

# Drawing Arcs (ARC)

An *arc* may be defined as a partial circle. AutoCAD offers 11 different methods for drawing an arc. These methods are based on start points, start directions, center points, included angles, endpoints, lengths of cord, and radius. You can access the ARC command in one of several ways:

- Enter **arc** at the Command: prompt.

- Choose the 3 Point button on the Draw floating toolbar. A fly-out submenu appears, showing 11 options for creating an arc (see fig. 5.15).

## Note

When you select one of the 11 options for creating an arc on the fly-out submenu, the information needed to create the particular arc appears at the bottom of the AutoCAD display. When you select the first Arc icon 3 Points, for example, it says Creates an arc using three points at the bottom of the AutoCAD display.

**II**

**Basic Drawing Techniques**

**Fig. 5.15**

Eleven different options for creating an arc are available on the Arc fly-out menu.

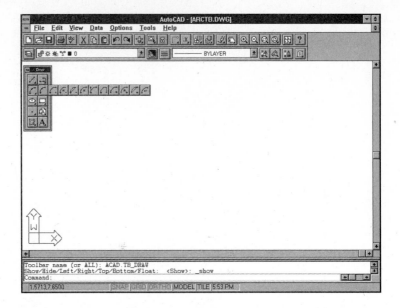

## Drawing Arcs with Three Points

When you draw an arc with the 3 Points option, AutoCAD prompts you for the start point, a second point along the arc, and the endpoint, as shown in figure 5.16. You can draw the arc clockwise or counterclockwise. You drag the arc into position as you locate the endpoint. AutoCAD uses the following command sequence when you click the 3 Points button on the 3 point fly-out from the Draw toolbar:

```
Choose the Arc-3 Points button.
Center/<Start point>: Select the start point (S) on the arc.
Center/End/<Second point>: Select the second point on the
        arc.
End point: Select the endpoint (E) of the arc.
```

**Tutorial: Creating an Arc with the 3 Points Option**

This tutorial describes how to create an arc using the 3 Points option, one of the many options available. Because of the great variety of ways to create arcs, the tutorials provided here cover only three of the most popular methods. Follow these steps:

1. Choose New from the Standard toolbar. In the Create New Drawing dialog box, click OK or press Enter. If the AutoCAD dialog box appears, select No unless you want to save the current drawing. If you want to save the current drawing, select Yes and enter a path and drawing name.

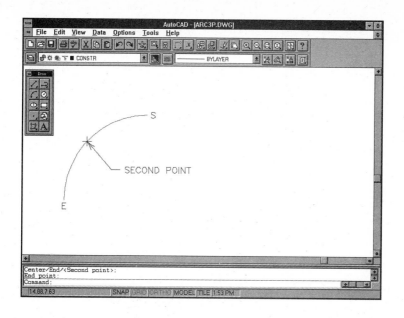

**Fig. 5.16**
Use the 3 Points
option to draw an
arc.

2. Select the 3 Points option from the Arc fly-out on the Draw toolbar.

```
Center/<Start point>: 5,5
Center/End/<Second point>: 3,3
End point: Using the crosshairs, drag the arc into
     place until your arc looks similar to that found
     in figure 5.17.
```

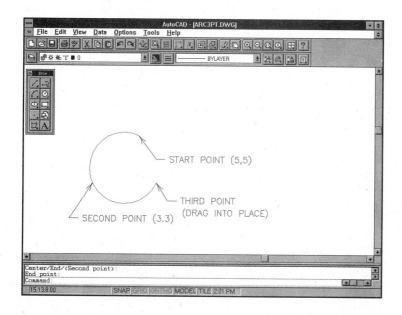

**Fig. 5.17**
Creating an arc
with the 3 Points
option.

II

**Basic Drawing Techniques**

## Drawing Arcs with Start, Center, End (SCE)

You select the Arc Start Center End button when you know the start point, center point, and endpoint of the arc. When you locate the start and center points, you establish the arc's radius. The endpoint furnishes the arc length. Because the endpoint furnishes the arc length, the arc doesn't pass through the endpoint unless this point is also on the radius (see fig. 5.18). AutoCAD uses the following command sequence when you select the Arc Start, Center, End button:

```
Center/<Start point>: Select the start point (S) on the
    arc.
Center/End/<Second point>: _cCenter: Select the arc's
    center point (C).
Angle/Length of chord/<End point>: Select the arc's end-
    point (E).
```

**Fig. 5.18**
Drawing an arc with the Start, Center, End option.

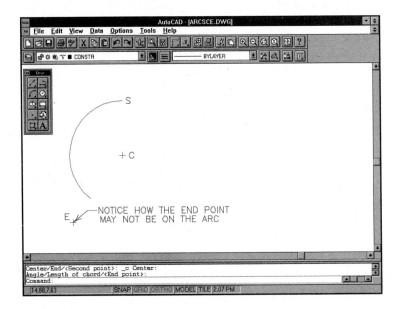

### Tutorial: Creating an Arc with Start, Center, End

This tutorial describes how to create an arc using the Start, Center, End option:

1. Select the New button from the Standard toolbar. In the Create New Drawing dialog box, click OK or press Enter. If the AutoCAD dialog box appears, select No unless you want to save the current drawing. If you want to save the current drawing, select Yes and enter a path and drawing name.

**2.** Select the Arc Start, Center, End button from the Arc fly-out on the Draw toolbar.

**3.** Establish the three points of the arc.

> ARC Center/<Start point>: *Click near the center of the drawing area.*
> Center/End/<Second point>: *Select a point approximately two units to the right of the start point.*
> End point: *Select a point approximately two units above the second point.*

Use your coordinates display to help estimate your movement. You should have an arc similar to that shown in figure 5.19.

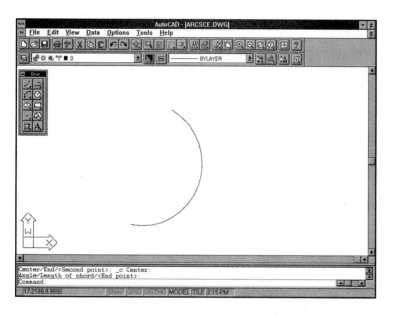

**Fig. 5.19**
Create this arc by using the Start, Center, End option.

## Drawing Arcs with Start, Center, Angle (SCA)

The *included angle* is the angle formed between the two radius lines extending from the center point through the endpoints of the arc (see fig. 5.20). The arc is drawn in a counterclockwise manner if you use a positive angle, and clockwise if you use a negative angle. AutoCAD uses the following command sequence when you choose the Arc Start, Center, Angle button from the Arc fly-out menu:

> Center/<Start point>: *Select the start point (S) on the arc.*
> Center/End/<Second point>: _cCenter: *Select the arc's center point (C).*
> Included Angle: *Enter or select the included angle.*

**Fig. 5.20**

Drawing an arc
with the Start,
Center, Angle
option.

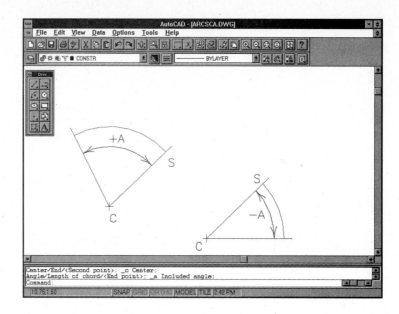

## Drawing Arcs with Start, Center, Length (SCL)

 The Length in Start, Center, Length refers to the chord length. A *chord* is a
line segment joining two points on an arc. Because you draw arcs counterclockwise, a positive chord length gives the smallest arc possible with the
given chord length. Using a negative chord length gives the largest arc possible (see fig. 5.21). AutoCAD uses the following command sequence when
you select the Arc Start, Center, Length button:

```
Center/<Start point>: Select the first point on the arc.
Center/End/<Second point>:_cCenter: Select the arc's center
        point.
Length of chord: Type a positive chord value for the small-
        est arc or a negative chord value for the largest
        possible arc.
```

## Drawing Arcs with Start, End, Angle (SEA)

 The *included angle* refers to the angle the arc occupies. Using a positive included angle draws the arc counterclockwise. A negative angle draws the arc
clockwise (see fig. 5.22). The command sequence when you select the Arc
Start, End, Angle button is as follows:

```
Center/<Start point>: Select the arc's start point.
End point: Select the arc's endpoint.
Angle/Direction/Radius/<Center point>:a Included Angle:
        Enter or select a positive or negative angle.
```

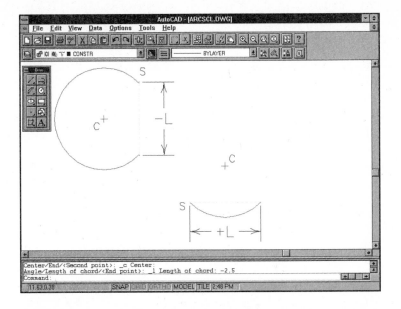

**Fig. 5.21**
Drawing an arc
with the Start,
Center, Length
option.

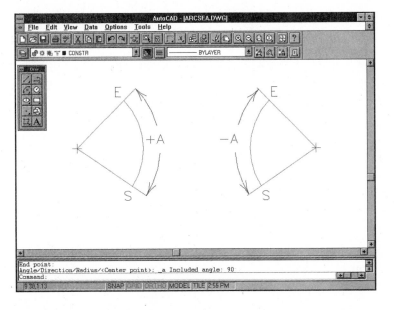

**Fig. 5.22**
Drawing an arc
with the Start,
End, Angle option.

## Drawing Arcs with Start, End, Radius (SER)

When using the Start, End, Radius option, you can draw an arc only in the
counterclockwise direction. A positive radius value results in the shortest arc
possible between the start point and the endpoint. A negative radius value

results in the longest arc possible (see fig. 5.23). The command sequence when you select the Arc Start, End, Radius button is as follows:

```
Center/<Start point>: Select the arc's start point.
End point: Select the arc's endpoint.
Angle/Direction/Radius/<Center point>:_r Radius: Pick or
    type a positive or negative radius.
```

**Fig. 5.23**

Drawing an arc with the Start, End, Radius option.

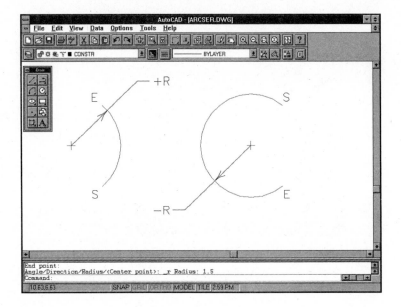

### Tutorial: Creating an Arc with Start, End, Radius

In this tutorial, you create an arc using the Start, End, Radius option. Follow these steps:

1. Select the New button from the Standard toolbar. In the New Drawing dialog box, click OK or press Enter. If the AutoCAD dialog box appears, select No unless you want to save the current drawing. If you want to save the current drawing, select Yes and enter a path and drawing name.

2. Select the Arc Start End Radius button from the Arc fly-out menu on the Draw toolbar.

3. Establish the points of the arc.

```
ARC Center/<Start point>: Click near the center of the
    drawing area.
End point: Select a point approximately six units to
    the right of the second point.
```

**4.** Give the radius.

> Angle/Direction/Radius/<Center point>: r_radius: **5**

You should now have an arc similar to the one shown in figure 5.24.

**Fig. 5.24**
An arc drawn with
the Start, End,
Radius option.

## Drawing Arcs with Start, End, Direction (SED)

*Direction* refers to the direction of rotation in degrees of the arc. The distance between the start point and the endpoint of the arc and the number of degrees determine the arc's location and size. The start direction of the arc is tangent to the direction specified (see fig. 5.25). Here's the command sequence when you select the Arc Start, End, Direction button:

> Center/<Start point>: *Select the arc's start point*
>     (S)Center/End/<Second point>:_e.
> End point: Select the arc's endpoint (E).
> Angle/Direction/Radius/<Center point>: d Direction from
>     start point: *Select the direction from the start point*
>     *or enter the direction in degrees.*

**Fig. 5.25**

Drawing an arc with the Start, End, <u>D</u>irection option.

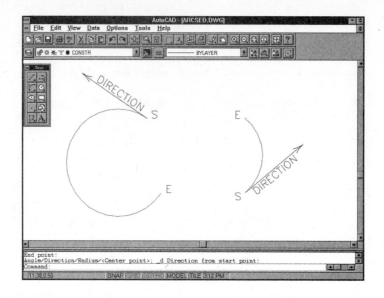

## Drawing Arcs with Center, Start, End (CSE)

The <u>C</u>enter, Start, End option shown in figure 5.26 is a variation of the <u>S</u>tart, Center, End option. Use <u>C</u>enter, Start, End when it's easier to begin the arc by locating the center point. Here's the command sequence when you select the Arc <u>C</u>enter, Start, End button:

```
Center/<Start point>:_c Center: Select the arc's center
    point (C).
Start point: Select the arc's start point (S).
Angle/Length of chord/<End point>: Select the arc's end-
    point (E).
```

**Fig. 5.26**

Drawing an arc with the <u>C</u>enter, Start, End option.

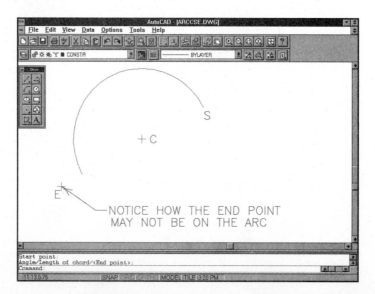

## Drawing Arcs with Center, Start, Angle (CSA)

The Center, Start, Angle option shown in figure 5.27 is a variation of the Start, Center, Angle option. You can use Center, Start, Angle when it's easier to begin the arc by locating the center point. The command sequence when you select the Center, Start, Angle button is as follows:

```
Center/<Start point>:_c Center: Select the arc's center
    point.
Start point: Select the arc's start point.
Angle/Length of chord/<End point>:_a Included angle: Select
    the included angle or enter a positive or negative
    angle.
```

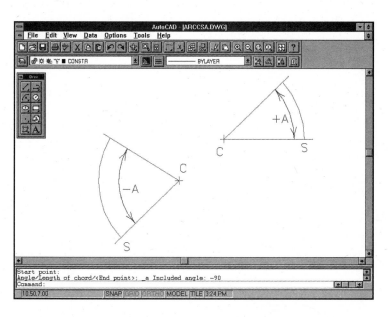

**Fig. 5.27**
Drawing an arc with the Center, Start, Angle option.

## Drawing Arcs with Center, Start, Length (CSL)

The Center, Start, Length option shown in figure 5.28 is a variation of the Start, Center, Length option. Use the Center, Start, Length command when it's easier to begin the arc by locating the center point. Here's AutoCAD's command sequence when you select the Arc Center, Start, Length button:

```
Center/<Start point>:_c Center: Select the arc's center
    point.
Start point: Select the arc's start point.
Angle/Length of chord/<End point>:_l Length of chord:
    Select or type the chord length.
```

**II**

**Basic Drawing Techniques**

**Fig. 5.28**
Drawing an arc
with the Center,
Start, Length
option.

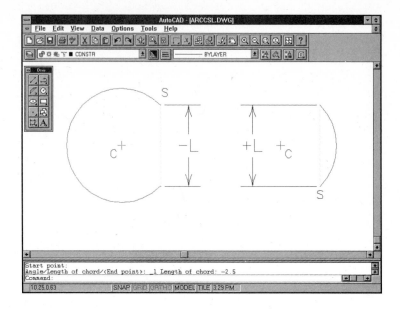

## Continuing an Arc from an Existing Arc

With the Continue option, you can continue an arc from the previous arc.
When you draw arcs with this method, each consecutive arc is tangent to the
previous arc. The start point and direction are taken from the endpoint and
direction of the previous arc or line (see fig. 5.29). Here's the command sequence when you select the Arc Continue button:

> End point: *Select or type the distance from the start point.*

**Fig. 5.29**
Drawing an arc
with the Continue
option.

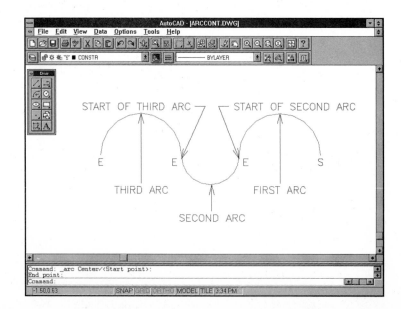

> **Note**
>
> When using the Arc Continue option, if you draw an arc and then press Enter, AutoCAD reissues the ARC command. If you press Enter again (at the first Arc prompt), you accept the last point entered (end of the last arc) as your start point for the next arc. This is equivalent to selecting the Arc Continue option.

### Tutorial: Continuing an Arc from an Existing Arc

In this tutorial, you'll create an arc with the Start Center End method to create arc A, as shown in figure 5.30. You'll then use the Arc Continue option to create arcs B and C. Follow these steps:

1. Select the New button on the Standard toolbar. If the AutoCAD dialog box appears, select No unless you want to save the current drawing. If you want to save the current drawing, select Yes and enter a path and drawing name. In the Create New Drawing dialog box, press Enter.

2. Create arc A by using the Arc Start Center End method. Select the Arc Start Center End button from the Arc fly-out menu and enter the absolute coordinates of 1,2.75 for the start point of the arc.

    ```
    Center/<Start point>: 1,2.75
    ```

3. For the center point, enter the absolute coordinates of 2.50,2.75.

    ```
    Center/End/<Second point>: _c Center: 2.50,2.75
    ```

4. For the endpoint, enter the absolute coordinates of 4,2.75.

    ```
    Angle/Length of chord/<End point>: 4,2.75
    ```

5. Select the Arc Continue button to create arc B. Notice how the next arc begins at the end point of the previous arc, A. Enter the absolute coordinates of 6.75,2.75 for the endpoint of the continued arc.

    ```
    End point: 6.75,2.75
    ```

6. To create the final arc, press Enter twice to reenter the Arc Continue command and use the endpoint of the previous arc B as the start point for the next arc. Use the absolute coordinates of 8,2.75 as the endpoint of the continued arc.

    ```
    Command:
    ARC Center/<Start point>:
    End point: 8,2.75
    ```

**Fig. 5.30**

You can use the Arc Continue option to create several arcs in succession.

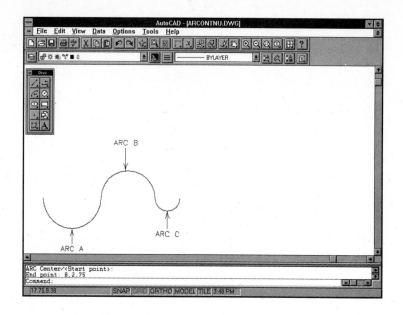

## Tutorial: Drawing a Breakfast Bar Symbol

This tutorial explains how to create the breakfast bar symbol shown in figure 5.31. In later chapters, you use this symbol to complete the plan of a kitchen for an apartment complex. You create this symbol by using the LINE, ARC, and CIRCLE commands. All the commands are available on the Draw floating toolbar.

Because this symbol is for an architectural drawing, you need to change the units. After you complete the drawing, save the file as C:\UAW13\BRKBAR.

To draw this symbol, follow these steps:

1. Select the New button from the Standard toolbar. If the AutoCAD dialog box appears, select No unless you want to save the current drawing. If you want to save the current drawing, select Yes and enter a path and drawing name. In the Create New Drawing dialog box, change the path to the UAW13 subdirectory and use BRKBAR for the drawing name.

2. From the Data pull-down menu, choose Units. The Units Control dialog box appears. Change the units to architectural with a precision of 0'–0".

3. Make sure that the Draw floating toolbar is on-screen. Select the Line button from the Draw floating toolbar.

```
From point: 1',1'
To point: @2'6"<90
To point:
```

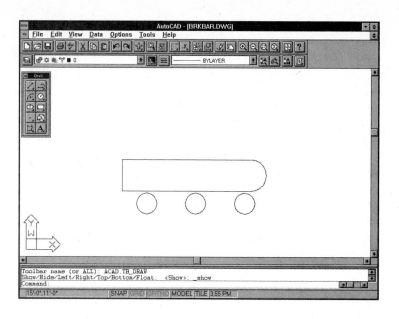

**Fig. 5.31**
The completed
breakfast bar
symbol.

4. At this point, you can't see the line you've just drawn, so use the ZOOM command.

   Select the Zoom All button from the Zoom fly-out menu.

   Your screen should resemble figure 5.32.

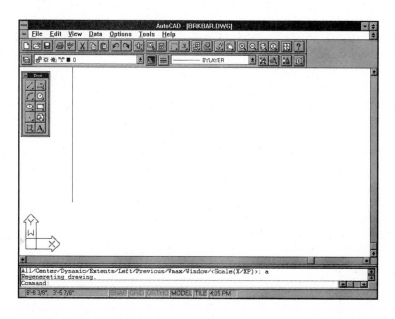

**Fig. 5.32**
Drawing the
first line of the
breakfast bar
symbol.

**5.** Now draw the next line.

```
Select the Line button from the Draw floating toolbar.
From point: 1',1'
To point: @10'6"<0
To point:
```

**6.** Notice that you still can't see the complete drawing, so use ZOOM again. Select the Zoom Scale button from the Zoom fly-out menu.

```
All/Center/Dynamic/Extents/Left/Previous/Vmax/window/
    <Scale(X/XP)>: .05
```

Your screen should now look like figure 5.33.

**Fig. 5.33**
Using the ZOOM command to display the uncompleted breakfast bar symbol.

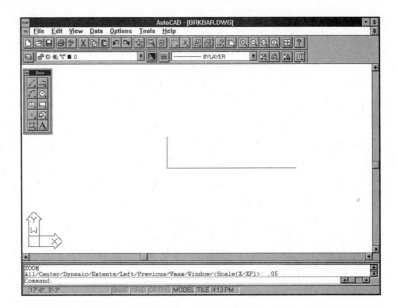

**7.** Now draw the third line.

Select the Line button from the Draw floating toolbar.

```
From point: 1',3'6"
To point: @10'6"<0
To point:
```

**8.** Draw an arc, establishing its three points using the Start Center End option. Select the Arc Start Center End button from the Arc fly-out menu.

```
Center/<Start point>: 11'6",1'
Center/End/<Second point>: _c Center: 11'6",2'3"
Angle/Length of chord/<End point>: 11'6",3'6"
```

You should have the bar itself drawn as shown in figure 5.34.

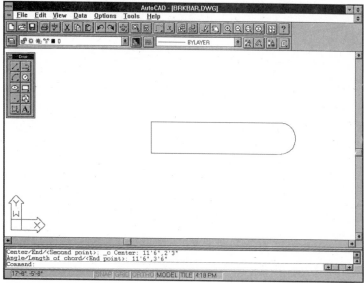

**Fig. 5.34**
The completed
breakfast bar
without chairs.

Basic Drawing Techniques

**9.** You're now ready to add three chairs to the breakfast bar. The chairs are
20" in diameter. Use the CIRCLE command to draw three circles to the
specifications that follow. Select the Circle Center Radius button from
the Circle fly-out menu.

```
3P/2P/TTR/<Center point>: 3',0"
Diameter/<Radius><0'-1">: 10"
```

Select the Circle Center Radius button from the Circle fly-out menu.
Alternatively, you can press Enter. Pressing Enter at the Command:
prompt will automatically recall the last command executed.

```
3P/2P/TTR/<Center point>: 7',0"
Diameter/<Radius><0'-10">: Press Enter to accept the
    default value of 10".
```

At the Command: prompt, press Enter to return to the CIRCLE command.

```
3P/2P/TTR/<Center point>: 11',0'
Diameter/<Radius><0'-10">: Press Enter to accept the
    default value of 10".
```

**10.** Select the Save button from the Standard toolbar.

# Drawing Polygons (POLYGON)

A *polygon* is a closed figure bounded by three or more line segments. Triangles, squares, and hexagons are examples of polygons commonly found in many drawings. Creating polygons in manual drafting can be difficult and time-consuming. Templates are available for some common polygons, such as triangles and hexagons, but templates are limited in the sizes they offer.

With AutoCAD's POLYGON command, you easily can draw *regular* multi-sided polygons. A polygon created in AutoCAD is drawn as a closed polyline object. In other words, the polygon is one object, and you can't edit the individual objects unless you explode the polygon. Chapter 19, "Using Polylines," discusses polylines. You can access the POLYGON command in one of these ways:

- Enter **polygon** at the Command: prompt.

- Choose the Polygon button from the Draw floating toolbar. A fly-out menu appears, displaying the Polygon options (see fig. 5.35).

**Fig. 5.35**
The Polygon button on the Draw floating toolbar.

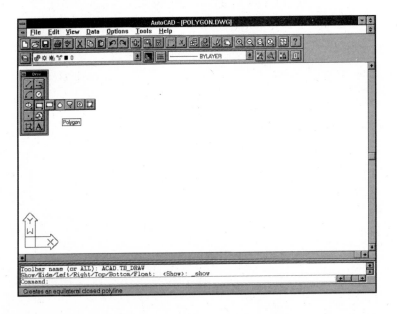

The POLYGON command enables you to create a figure with up to 1,024 sides of the same length. To create a polygon, any of three methods may be used.

## Using Inscribed Polygons

One method for creating a polygon is to create an *inscribed polygon*. In an inscribed polygon, the lines making up the polygon are contained totally within an imaginary circle on which the polygon is based. The endpoints of the polygon sides lie on this circle. The circle itself is never actually drawn. Here's the command sequence for the Inscribed polygon option:

Select the Polygon button from the Draw floating toolbar.

```
Number of sides <4>: Enter the number of sides.
Edge/<Center of polygon>: Enter or Select the polygon's
    center point.
Inscribed in circle/Circumscribed about circle (I/C) <I>:
    Since Inscribed is the default, press Enter.
Radius of circle: Enter or select the polygon's radius.
```

> **Note**
>
> While you're being prompted for the radius, AutoCAD displays a temporary image of the polygon that will be created. You can rotate and resize the polygon at this time by using the crosshairs or by entering a coordinate value.

## Using Circumscribed Polygons

In a *circumscribed polygon*, the polygon's lines are outside the imaginary circle on which the polygon is based. Again, the circle isn't drawn. The Circumscribed option creates a polygon with the polygon edges tangent to an imaginary circle. The following command sequence is used with the Circumscribed polygon option:

Select the Polygon button from the Draw floating toolbar.

```
Number of sides: Enter the number of sides.
Edge/<Center of polygon>: Select the polygon's center
    point.
Inscribed in circle/Circumscribed about circle (I/C)<I>: c
Radius of circle: Enter or select the polygon's radius.
```

> **Note**
>
> The POLYSIDES system variable keeps track of the number of sides specified in the previous POLYGON command. When you reenter the POLYGON command, the default value in the Number of Sides prompt will be the same as the number of sides you specified in the previous polygon command.

## Specifying Polygons by Edge

When you need to draw a polygon with one corner passing through a point, the Edge option is very useful. Occasionally, you may know the length of each of the polygon's sides but not the radius of the polygon. By choosing the Edge option, you can specify the length of one of the polygon's sides by selecting two points (or entering coordinates) to determine the endpoints of a side. AutoCAD draws one edge between these points and constructs the rest of the polygon accordingly. Here's the command sequence for the Edge polygon option:

Select the Polygon button from the Draw floating toolbar.

```
Number of sides: Enter the number of sides.
Edge/ <Center of polygon>: e
First endpoint of edge: Indicate first endpoint of edge.
Second endpoint of edge: Indicate second endpoint of edge.
```

### Tutorial: Drawing an Inscribed Polygon

This tutorial covers the basics of drawing polygons in AutoCAD. You create an eight-sided inscribed polygon with a radius of four units. Before you begin to draw the polygon, you start a new drawing. Follow these steps:

1. Select the New button from the Standard toolbar. In the New Drawing Dialog box, click OK or press Enter. If the AutoCAD dialog box appears, select No unless you want to save the current drawing. If you want to save the current drawing, select Yes and enter a path and drawing name.

2. Select the Polygon button from the Draw floating toolbar.

3. Draw the polygon.

```
Number of sides <4>: 8
Edge/<Center of polygon>: Select a point near the
    center of the drawing.
Inscribed in circle/Circumscribed about circle
    (I/C)<I>: Press Enter to accept the default.
Radius of circle: 4
```

You should now have an eight-sided polygon similar to the one in figure 5.36.

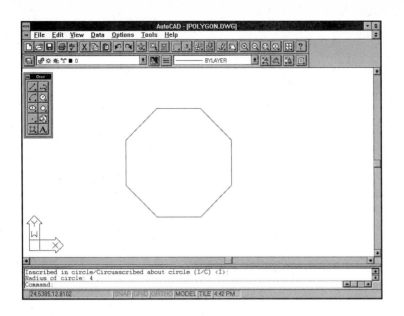

**Fig. 5.36**
Drawing an inscribed polygon.

## Tutorial: Drawing a Hot Tub Symbol with POLYGON, RECTANG, and CIRCLE

This tutorial explains how to create the hot tub symbol shown in figure 5.37. This symbol requires you to use the RECTANG, POLYGON, and CIRCLE commands.

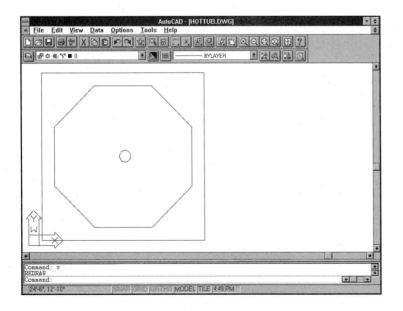

**Fig. 5.37**
The completed hot tub symbol.

II

Basic Drawing Techniques

To create the hot tub symbol, follow these steps:

1. Select the New button from the Standard toolbar. If the AutoCAD dialog box appears, select No unless you want to save the current drawing. If you want to save the current drawing, select Yes and enter a path and drawing name. Change to the UAW13 subdirectory and enter **hottub** as the drawing name.

2. Choose <u>D</u>ata, U<u>n</u>its. In the Units Control dialog box, change units to architectural with a precision of 0'-0".

3. Make sure that the Draw floating toolbar is on-screen before you continue. First, you'll create the rectangle.

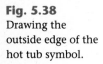 Choose the Rectangle button from the Draw floating toolbar.

        First corner: **2",2"**
        Other corner: **@12',12'**

4. At this point, you can't see the rectangle you've just drawn, so use the ZOOM command.

 Select the Zoom All button from the Zoom fly-out menu.

Your screen should resemble figure 5.38.

**Fig. 5.38**
Drawing the outside edge of the hot tub symbol.

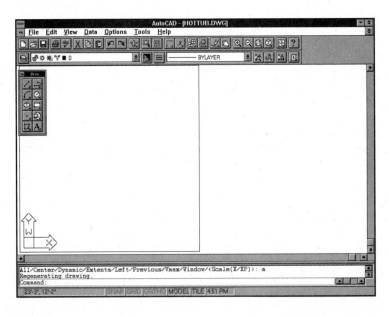

5. Now draw the polygon.

   Choose the Polygon button from the Rectangle fly-out menu.

   ```
   Number of sides:<4>: 8
   Edge/<Center of polygon>: 6'2",6'2"
   Inscribed in circle/Circumscribed about circle(I/C)<I>:
   Radius of circle: 5'6"
   ```

6. Complete the symbol by drawing the drain, using the CIRCLE command.

   Choose the Circle Center Radius button from the Circle fly-out menu.

   ```
   3P/2P/TTR/<Center point>: 6'2",6'2"
   Diameter/<Radius>: 5"
   ```

7. To save the file for use at a later time, select the Save button from the Standard toolbar.

# From Here...

The AutoCAD basic drawing commands—LINE, ARC, and CIRCLE—usually make up most of the geometry in a typical drawing. To speed up the drawing process and help create complicated geometry, AutoCAD offers the RECTANG and POLYGON commands.

For more information about viewing your drawing, making your drawings more accurate, and assigning colors to your objects, see the following chapters:

■ Chapter 6, "Using Object Snaps," explains methods for making your drawings more accurate and for increasing your drawing speed.

■ Chapter 7, "Understanding Layers," presents a method for placing objects on transparent layers and assigning color to your objects.

■ Chapter 12, "Viewing a Drawing," shows you how to make a drawing fill the screen, and zoom in on sections of a drawing.

# On Your Own

Using the commands you learned in this and previous chapters, create the kitchen sink and bathtub symbols shown in figure 5.39. The overall dimensions are given. Estimate dimensions to complete the symbols.

**Fig. 5.39**
The kitchen sink
and bathtub
symbols can be
created using the
line, circle, and arc
commands.

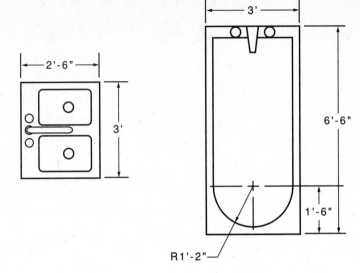

Hints:

1. Save each completed symbol in an individual file.

2. When creating arcs, remember the different methods available.

# Chapter 6

# Using Object Snaps

A competent draftsperson can locate a point on a drawing by using a straight edge and rule with a fair amount of accuracy. Using the point as a reference, the draftsperson can draw more objects. One of the first steps in creating accurate drawings is to locate precise points. One method of locating precise points in AutoCAD is to type the coordinates, as you did in Chapter 4, "Understanding Coordinates and Units." In most cases, however, you do not have such complete information that you can type all the points. Regardless of the information available, typing points is tedious work and prone to typing errors.

When you attempt to pick points on-screen, you may have difficulty locating an exact position without some type of help. Typing the point coordinates is one method. AutoCAD has several other methods to help control the movement of the crosshair. One method is the snap function introduced in Chapter 2, "Creating Your First Drawing." This chapter introduces another method for accurately locating precise points—the object snap, or osnap, function.

Object snap is a very useful tool. The term *object snap* refers to a function in which the crosshair is forced to snap exactly to a specific point or location of an existing object. One of the primary advantages of using object snap is that you don't have to pick an exact point. Suppose you want to draw a line beginning at the exact intersection of two previously created lines. If the intersection point of the lines is not on the snap increment, you may try to guess and pick the intersection point with the crosshair. Unfortunately, you'll probably miss. Using object snap, you just pick somewhere near the intersection of the lines. The crosshair automatically snaps to the exact intersection. AutoCAD offers several object snap modes to help accurately locate specific points on existing geometry.

In this chapter, you use object snap to assist in the creation of a front elevation for an apartment building. After completing this chapter, you will be able to do the following:

- Understand the relationship between object points and object snap

- Draw with the temporary object snap modes

- Draw with the running object snap modes

- Control the aperture size for object snap

# Understanding Object Points and Object Snap

When you create geometry in AutoCAD, vectors are used to display the objects drawn on the graphics screen. A *vector* may be defined as a quantity completely specified by a magnitude and a direction. Using vectors allows AutoCAD to store a great deal of information about each object. A line, for example, has a starting point, ending point, and specific length, and the line points in a certain direction. Different types of objects have different types of information associated with them. A circle, for example, has a center point and radius.

The vector information stored with each object enables AutoCAD to perform calculations on the object. By accessing the information stored with each object, you can locate endpoints, midpoints, intersections, center points, and other geometric information. The object snap function allows you to access this information and select these exact points when creating geometry. It is very important that the new user of AutoCAD understand it is never accurate to just guess or "eyeball" locations and points. What may appear accurate on the screen, will probably be inaccurate when plotted, and will definitely be inaccurate in the drawing database. Generally, the plotting device has a higher level of precision than the computer display and therefore can display mistakes that otherwise seemed fine on the computer display. In later chapters, you will find it is also absolutely necessary that points be placed accurately when creating 3D solid models as well as 2D drawings. Inaccurate geometry can lead to inaccurate analysis of a model.

Before discussing the object snap modes, you should learn about the objects on which you'll use the object snap modes. Figure 6.1 shows the most common graphic objects and their potential snap points.

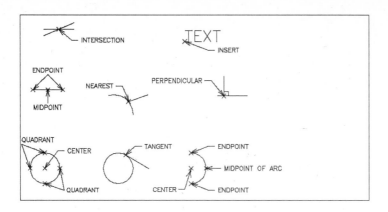

**Fig. 6.1**
Object snap points
on eight common
graphic objects.

AutoCAD has 11 different object snap modes. The next sections explain each object snap and provide examples.

Each object snap can be abbreviated to its first three letters. Notice that the first three letters are capitalized in the following sections. These abbreviations are the only letters you need to enter to access the corresponding object snap mode. The following section explains the service performed by each object snap mode.

> **Note**
>
> Object snaps are not commands but modes used in connection with AutoCAD drawing and editing functions. Entering **int** or **cen** at the Command: prompt displays an error message.

**Tip**

Object snaps can also be picked from the cursor menu, by holding down the Shift key while using the right button on the pointing device. The cursor menu appears at the location of the crosshair.

**II**

**Basic Drawing Techniques**

An alternative to typing the first three letters is to select the corresponding *object snap button.* You can find the object snap buttons by first selecting the Object Snap button in the Standard toolbar. When you select the Object Snap button, a fly-out menu appears, displaying buttons for all the object snap modes. The Object Snap button is shown in figure 6.2.

## ENDpoint

A common task when you are creating geometry is to connect a line, arc, or center point of a circle to the endpoint of an existing line or arc. To select the endpoint, move the aperture box past the midpoint of the line or arc toward the end you want to pick and select. Figure 6.3 snaps a new line to the endpoint of an arc.

**Fig. 6.2**
The Object Snap
button on the
Standard toolbar
shows all the
object snap modes
in a fly-out menu.

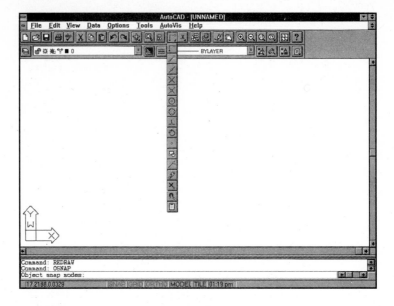

**Fig. 6.3**
Object snap a new
line to the end-
point of an arc.

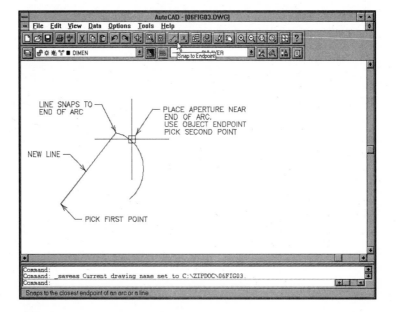

## MIDpoint

To find the midpoint of a line or arc, use the MIDpoint object snap mode.
For example, to connect a line from any point to the midpoint of an arc,
place the aperture anywhere on the arc and pick. The line automatically

snaps to the midpoint of the arc (see fig. 6.4). You can also snap to the midpoint of a line (see fig. 6.4). Notice that you don't need to pick anywhere near the midpoint of the arc or line to snap to the midpoint.

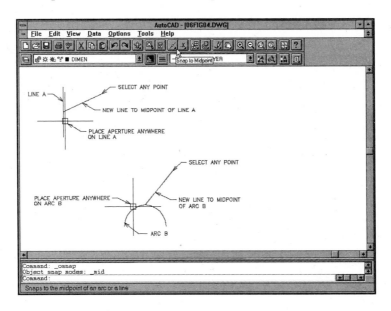

**Fig. 6.4**
Object snap to the midpoint of a line or arc.

## CENter

The CENter option enables you to snap to the center point of an arc, circle, or donut. Figure 6.5 shows a line snapped between the center of circle A and the center of arc B. To select the center point, you must select the arc or circle itself, not the center.

## NODe

In addition to drawing geometry such as lines, circles, and arcs, you can define point objects in AutoCAD. A point object is referred to as a *node.* You can use point objects singularly or with other commands such as DIVIDE and MEASURE. Chapter 15, "Advanced Drawing Techniques," covers point creation and the use of points with the DIVIDE and MEASURE commands. Using the NODe object snap finds a point object (see fig. 6.6).

▶ See "Drawing Rings and Solid Filled Circles (DONUT or DOUGHNUT)," p. 441

## QUAdrant

AutoCAD defines a *quadrant* as a quarter section of a circle, donut, or arc. Using the QUAdrant object snap mode, you can find the 0, 90, 180, and 270 degree positions on a circle, donut, or arc (see fig. 6.7).

**II**

**Basic Drawing Techniques**

When snapping to a quadrant, locate the aperture on the circle, donut, or arc closest to the proposed quadrant. Figure 6.7 shows the endpoint of a line located at one of the quadrants in circle A.

**Fig. 6.5**
Object snap to the center of a circle or arc.

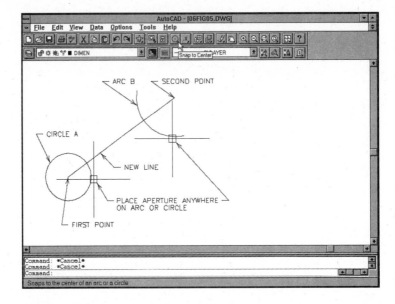

**Fig. 6.6**
Object snap to a point object, referred to as a *node*.

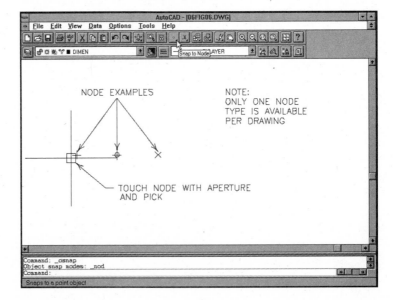

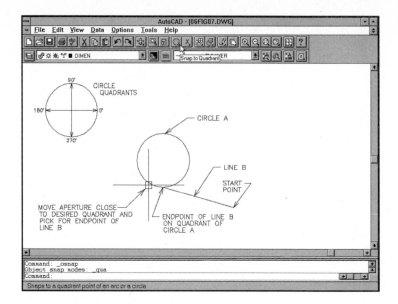

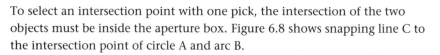

**Fig. 6.7**
Using object snap
QUAdrant to locate
one of the quad-
rants on a circle.

II

Basic Drawing Techniques

## INTersection

The INTersection object snap mode snaps to the point where objects cross each other. The INTersection mode also allows you to snap to the imaginary intersection of two objects that do not actually intersect but would if one or both were extended. The INTersection object snap mode requires that there be a point (real or imaginary) in two- or three-dimensional space where an intersection occurs.

To select an intersection point with one pick, the intersection of the two objects must be inside the aperture box. Figure 6.8 shows snapping line C to the intersection point of circle A and arc B.

You can also select the intersection of objects one at a time. This method works well when geometry is crowded together and snapping to an intersection point is difficult. When you use INTersection and select a single object, AutoCAD prompts you to select the second object. The crosshair will snap to the intersection of the two objects selected or to the point where they would intersect if one or both were extended.

## INSertion

When you create text in AutoCAD, you must first specify its location. The location point where you initially create the text is the *insertion point.* Other AutoCAD objects that have insertion points are shapes, blocks, and attributes. Figure 6.9 shows a snap to the insertion point of text.

**Fig. 6.8**
Using the INTer-
section object
snap mode.

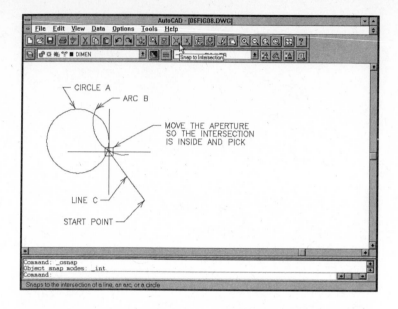

**Fig. 6.9**
Using the
INSertion object
snap mode to
snap to the inser-
tion point of text.

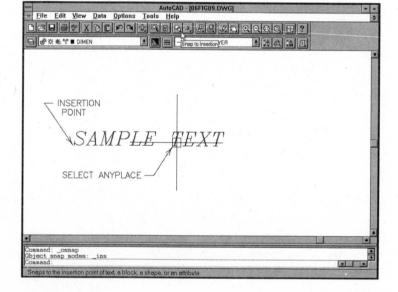

## PERpendicular

A typical geometric construction is to snap a point on a line, arc, or circle
that forms a perpendicular from the current point to the selected object. You
can perform this step easily, using the PERpendicular object snap. Figure 6.10
shows how the PERpendicular object snap mode is used to create a line perpendicular to line B.

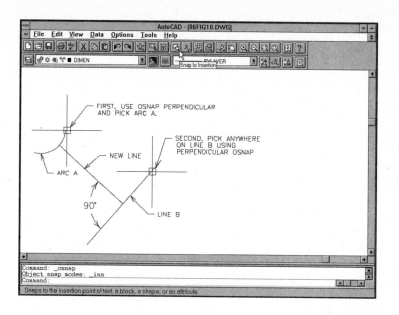

**Fig. 6.10**
Using the PERpen-
dicular object snap
option.

## TANgent

Locating tangent points on arcs and circles can be difficult if you use manual drafting procedures. AutoCAD greatly simplifies this process by providing the TANgent object snap mode. TANgent enables you to snap to a point on an object that forms a tangent between the object and another point. Figure 6.11 shows a new line tangent to arc A and circle B.

> **Note**
>
> AutoCAD sometimes has problems finding a tangent point unless you are zoomed in close to the selected object.

▶ See "Using
ZOOM to
Control the
Display
(ZOOM),"
p. 336

## NEArest

The NEArest object snap mode snaps to a point on a line, circle, arc, or other object that is nearest to the center of the aperture box, where the crosshair intersects. Figure 6.12 shows how NEArest is used to connect a line from a point to a location on an arc.

## FROm

In AutoCAD Release 13, another useful tool for precisely locating points in a drawing is the FROm function. The FROm function allows you to use any position on the screen as a base point for entering relative coordinates. For example, let's say you want to draw an 18-inch diameter circular ceiling light fixture in a floor plan that's five feet in either direction from the corner of a room. You could use the FROm function to select the corner and then enter relative coordinates to locate the center of the circle. The command sequence in this example would be:

**Fig. 6.11**
Using the TANgent object snap to draw a line tangent to a circle and arc.

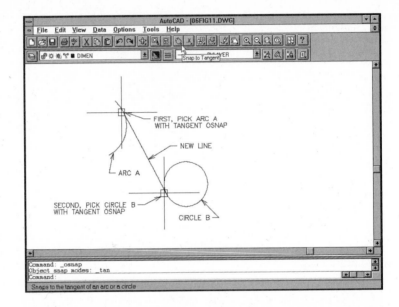

**Fig. 6.12**
Using the NEArest object snap mode to draw a line to an arc.

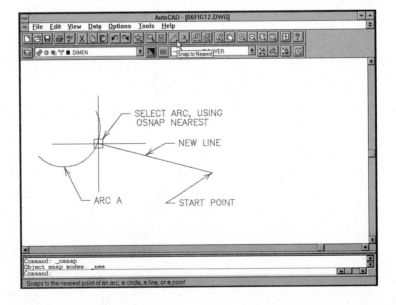

Select Circle from the Draw toolbar.

```
At the CIRCLE  3P/2P/TTR <Center point>:  prompt, type FROM and press Enter.
At the FROM prompt, type INT and press Enter.
At the of prompt, pick the wall corner and type @5',5' and press Enter.
At the Diameter/<Radius> <default>:  prompt, type 18 and press Enter.
```

If you press Enter at the From point: prompt of the LINE command or the Center/<Start point>: prompt of the ARC command, the crosshair snaps to the endpoint of the last object created. You also can type a relative coordinate, which begins a new object relative to the last object.

### APParent Intersection

This object snap snaps to the APParent intersection of two objects which may or may not intersect in 3D space. For APParent intersection to work in 3D space, the objects must appear to intersect from the current viewpoint. To learn more about this object snap, refer to Chapter 29, "3D Editing Essentials."

## Drawing with Temporary Object Snap Modes

A *temporary object snap mode* is effective for one selection only. An alternative to a temporary object snap is the *running object snap mode,* which is discussed in the next section. Use any of the following methods to activate a temporary object snap mode:

- Enter an object snap mode by typing its first three letters at a prompt line. The following command sequence shows the temporary ENDpoint object snap:

Select the Line button from the Draw toolbar.

```
From point: end
of: Select the endpoint of the object you want.
```

Entering **end** at the From point: invokes the object snap END for one command.

> **Note**
>
> Instead of typing **end** as the abbreviation for endpoint, you might want to type **endp**. If you accidentally enter **end** at the Command: prompt rather than at a prompt line, you save your drawing and exit AutoCAD.

> **Note**
>
> Holding down the Shift key and clicking the right mouse button, or the middle button of a three-button mouse activates the cursor menu of osnap commands. The cursor menu appears at the location of the screen crosshair. Select the object snap you want, and the cursor menu disappears. The selected object snap is enabled for one pick (see fig. 6.13).

**Fig. 6.13**
The popup menu displays all available object snap modes.

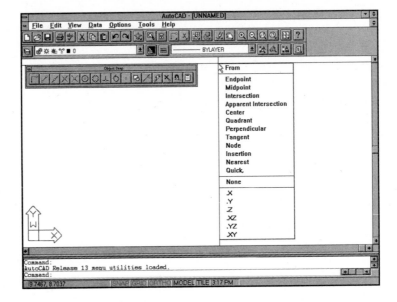

■ From the Standard toolbar, select the Object Snap button. A cursor menu shows all the object snap modes (refer to fig. 6.2). Pick the object snap mode you want.

## Tutorial: Using Temporary Object Snap Modes to Create a Circle-Top Window

In this tutorial, you use temporary object snaps to create the circle-top window shown in figure 6.14.

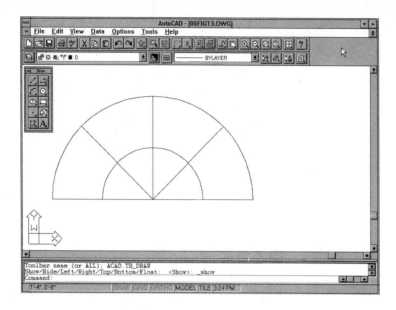

**Fig. 6.14**
Drawing a circle-
top window using
temporary object
snap modes.

1. Choose the New button from the Standard toolbar. If prompted with
   the Save Changes dialog box, choose No. Enter a name for the drawing
   and accept the dialog box.

2. Choose Data, Units.

3. In the Units dialog box that appears, change the units to architectural
   with a precision of 0'–0".

4. Draw the first horizontal line and the vertical line.

   Select the Line button from the Draw toolbar.

   ```
   From point: 2',3'
   To point: 7',3'
   To point: 7',8'
   To point:
   ```

   To exit the command, press Enter at the To point: prompt. Use the
   Zoom command to adjust your display to see the lines.

5. Draw the second horizontal line.

   Select the Line button from the Draw toolbar.

   ```
   From point: 7',3'
   To point: 12',3'
   To point:
   ```

6. Begin drawing the inner arc.

   Select the Arc Start Center End button from the ARC Flyout on the Draw toolbar

   ```
   <Start point>: mid
   ```

   AutoCAD is now waiting for the midpoint of an object.

7. Move the aperture box to the middle of line C,D and click the pick button (see fig. 6.15).

   ```
   Center: int
   ```

8. Now select point C (see fig. 6.15).

   ```
   <End point>: mid
   ```

9. Move the aperture box to pick the middle of line A,C (see fig. 6.15).

   The drawing should now look like that in figure 6.16.

**Fig. 6.15**

Using object snaps to create the inner arc of the circle-top window.

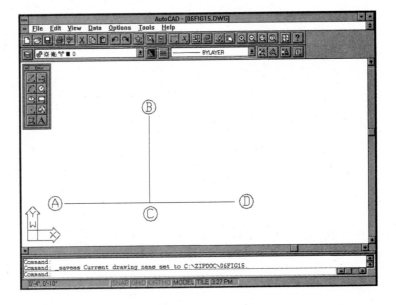

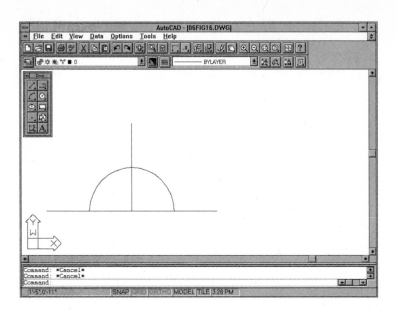

**Fig. 6.16**
The circle-top
window with
the inner arc
complete.

**10.** Begin drawing the outer arc.

Select the Start, Center, End arc from the ARC flyout on the Draw
toolbar.

    <Start point>: **end**

AutoCAD is now waiting for an end of object selection.

**11.** Pick point D, as shown in figure 6.15.

    Center: **int**

**12.** Pick point C (refer to fig. 6.15).

    <End point>: **endp**

Move the aperture box to point B and pick that point (refer to fig. 6.15).

**13.** Continue with the outer arc.

    Command: *Press enter (this repeats the previous command).*
    Center/<Start point>: **endp**

**14.** Move the aperture box to point B and pick that point, as shown in figure
6.15, and click the pick button.

    Center/End/<Second point>: **c**
    Center: **int**

15. Pick point C (refer to fig. 6.15).

    ```
    Angle/Length of chord/<End point>: endp
    ```

16. Move the aperture box to point A and pick that point (refer to fig. 6.15).

    The drawing should now look like figure 6.17.

**Fig. 6.17**
The circle-top window with the outer arc complete.

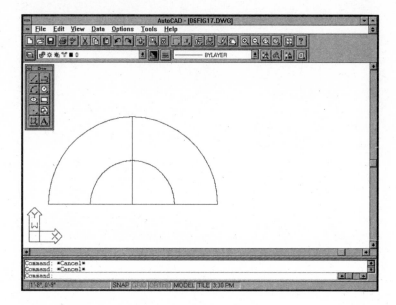

17. Issue the LINE command.

    Select the Line button from the Draw toolbar.

    ```
    From point: int
    ```

18. Move the aperture box to point C, as shown in figure 6.15, and press the pick button.

19. At the To point: prompt, enter **mid** and select the middle of the outer arc at point E (see fig. 6.18).

20. At the next To point: prompt, press Enter to end the command.

21. Issue the LINE command again.

    Choose the Line button from the Draw toolbar.

    ```
    From point: cen
    ```

22. Move the aperture box to point F, and pick that point as shown in figure 6.18.

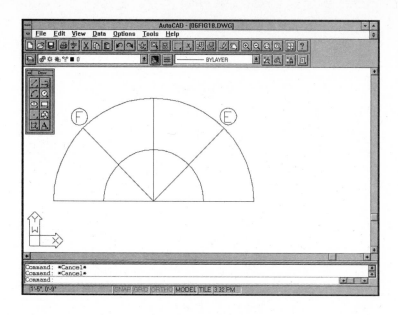

**Fig. 6.18**
Drawing diagonal lines for the circle-top window.

**23.** At the To point: prompt, enter **mid** and then pick point F (refer to fig. 6.18).

**24.** At the next To point: prompt, press Enter to end the command.

You have now completed the circle-top window, as shown in figure 6.14.

# Using Running Object Snap Modes (OSNAP and DDOSNAP)

An earlier section explained the use of temporary object snap modes. You can access these osnaps by entering the first three letters at a prompt line during a command sequence, selecting the options from the pull-down menu, floating cursor menu, or clicking the Object Snap button in the Standard toolbar. When you use one of these methods, the object snap mode is activated for one selection only. When AutoCAD prompts you to indicate a point, you can use a temporary object snap mode to help you locate that point precisely on existing geometry.

The temporary object snap modes work well in many situations. If you plan to use an object snap frequently, you can set up a *running* object snap mode.

When you set up a running object snap mode, the chosen object snap is activated every time you make a selection. Any of the following methods set a running object snap mode:

- At the Command: prompt, enter **osnap**. AutoCAD prompts with Object snap modes:. Enter the first three letters of the object snap you want.

- Access the Running Object Snap dialog box by selecting the Object Snap button from the Standard toolbar. From the fly-out menu that appears, click the Running Object Snap button. The Running Object Snap dialog box appears (see fig. 6.19). Select the object snap you want; then click OK.

- Enter **ddosnap** at the Command: prompt to open the Running Object Snap dialog box.

- Select Running Object Snap from the Options pull-down menu.

**Fig. 6.19**
You can use the Running Object Snap dialog box to set a running object snap.

AutoCAD lets you know that an object snap mode has been selected by automatically displaying the aperture box whenever a command is started. Under normal use the aperture box is not displayed until an object snap has been selected.

To discontinue a running object snap, enter **none** at the Object snap modes: prompt. You can also deselect the object snap mode in the Running Object Snap dialog box.

> **Note**
>
> You can use a temporary object snap to supersede the running object snap mode for a given selection. As with using temporary object snaps, the temporary snap is good for one selection.

## Tutorial: Using Running Object Snap Modes to Create a Divided Octagon

In this tutorial, you use running object snaps to create the divided octagon shown in figure 6.20. To create the octagon, use these steps:

1. Choose the New button from the Standard toolbar. If prompted with the Save Changes dialog box, choose No. Enter a name for the drawing and accept the dialog box.

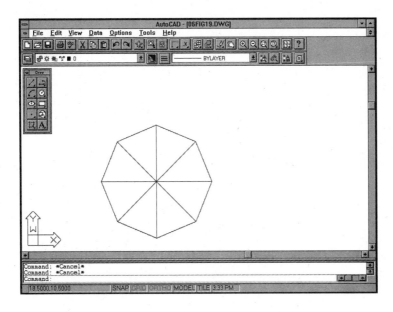

**Fig. 6.20**
Drawing a divided octagon using running object snap modes.

II

**Basic Drawing Techniques**

2. In the File Name text box of the Open Drawing dialog box, type **C:\DWG13\06DWG01** and click OK.

   You should now have the drawing shown in figure 6.21 in your drawing area.

3. From the Options menu, choose Running Object Snap.

4. In the Running Object Snaps dialog box, choose Endpoint.

   This command sets the running object snap to the END of the object snap setting.

5. Choose the Line button from the Draw toolbar.

6. At the From point: prompt, move the aperture box and pick point A (see fig. 6.22).

**Fig. 6.21**
Opening the 06DWG01 drawing in preparation for creating a divided octagon.

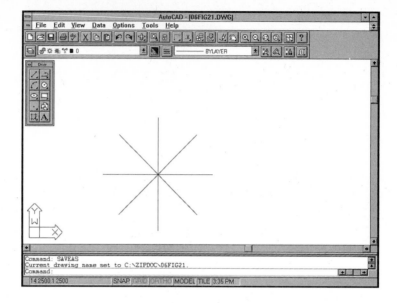

7. At the To point: prompt, move the aperture box and pick point B.

8. Continue responding to the To point: prompts by moving the aperture box and picking each point (see fig. 6.22).

9. After you finish point H, respond to the next To point: prompt by pressing **C**, then Enter.

You now have the divided octagon shown previously in figure 6.20.

**Fig. 6.22**
Selecting the endpoints to create the divided polygon.

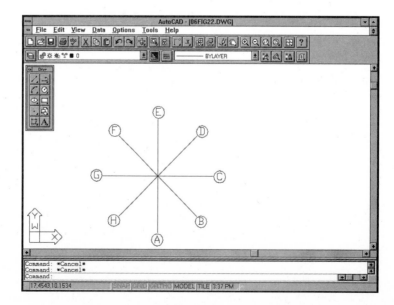

---

**Troubleshooting**

*Every time I try to select a point, it jumps to the end of a line that is close by.*

A running object snap is probably still selected. When you try to select a point, you may have the other line within the aperture box. AutoCAD remembers the running osnap and selects that point. To correct this, turn off the running object snap using the Running Object Snap dialog box.

---

## Using Multiple Running Object Snap Modes

In addition to using single object snap modes, you can direct AutoCAD to use multiple object snap modes. When you use multiple object snap modes, AutoCAD chooses the point closest to the center of the pickbox that meets the criteria of one of the set object snap modes. You can activate multiple object snap modes in one of two ways:

- At the Command: prompt, enter **osnap**. When AutoCAD prompts with Object snap modes:, enter the first three letters of the object snap modes you want, separated by commas.

- Access the Running Object Snap dialog box (DDOSNAP) and select the object snap modes you want.

- Access the Running Object Snap with the Osnap fly-out toolbar.

### Tutorial: Using Multiple Running Object Snap Modes

In this tutorial, you learn how to use multiple running object snap modes. Follow these steps:

1. Choose the New button from the Standard toolbar. If prompted with the Save Changes dialog box, choose No. Enter a name for the drawing and accept the dialog box.

2. Choose the Line button from the Draw toolbar.

3. At the From point: prompt, move the crosshair to the lower-left portion of the screen and pick point A (see fig. 6.23).

4. At the To point: prompt, move the crosshair to the upper-right portion of the drawing area and pick point B.

5. At the To point: prompt, press Enter to exit the command.

   You should now have a line similar to that in figure 6.23.

**II**

**Basic Drawing Techniques**

**Fig. 6.23**

Creating line A,B.

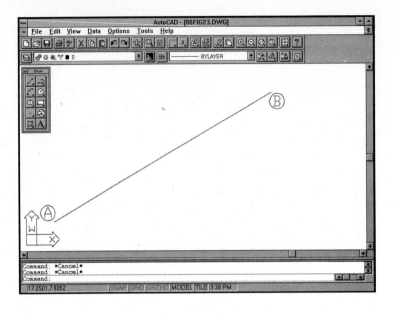

6. From the Options menu, select Running Object Snap.

   The Running Object Snap dialog box appears.

7. Select the Endpoint and Midpoint options and click OK (see fig. 6.24).

**Fig. 6.24**

Selecting Endpoint and Midpoint object snap modes in the Running Object Snap dialog box.

8. Choose the Line button from the Draw toolbar.

   Notice that the aperture box automatically appears on the crosshair and is waiting for a selection.

9. At the From point: prompt, move the crosshair close to point B (see fig. 6.23). When the line is within the aperture box, pick that point.

Now move your crosshairs away from the line. Notice that the line begins at the endpoint of the previous line.

10. At the To point: prompt, enter **u** to undo your last selection.

11. The From point: prompt appears again. This time, instead of selecting the endpoint, move your crosshairs toward the center of the line.

    Notice that the aperture box automatically appears. When the middle of the line is within the aperture box, pick the point. Now move your crosshair away from the line. This time, notice that the line begins at the middle of the previous line.

12. At the To point: prompt, press Enter to exit the LINE command.

## Using QUIck Object Snap Modes

When you select geometry in AutoCAD by using object snap modes, AutoCAD searches for the best solution to your request. In a simple drawing, this process happens very quickly. As drawings become more complex, however, finding the object snap may take some time. You can speed up this process by selecting the Quick modifier for the object snap mode.

When you use the Quick modifier, the method of picking the best point is overridden, and AutoCAD picks the first point that meets the selection criteria set with the running object snap mode. The problem you may find with using Quick object snaps is that the first AutoCAD selection may not be the best choice. In most cases, though, the Quick mode works to your advantage and helps increase productivity. You can access the Quick mode in one of two ways:

- When you enter object snap modes by typing the first three letters at a prompt line, precede them with QUI. The following command sequence shows the Quick temporary object snap END:

    Select the Line button from the Draw toolbar.

    ```
    From point: qui,endp,int
    of: Select the endpoint of the object you want.
    ```

    Entering **qui,end,int** invokes the Quick object snap for whichever criteria is met first, either end or int met first.

- Select the Quick check box in the Running Object Snap dialog box.

### Turning Running Object Snaps Off

When you are finished using a particular set of running object snaps you can change them to another SNAP, set of snaps, or you can turn the running object snaps off. To turn the object snaps off, select Clear All from the Running Object Snap dialog box or select the Snap to None button from the Object Snap flyout on the Standard toolbar or Object Snap toolbar.

### Controlling Aperture Box Size

The aperture box appears on-screen when you enter an object snap mode or use the OSNAP command. You can enlarge or reduce the size of the aperture box. Do not confuse the aperture box with the pickbox. The aperture box appears on-screen only when object snap modes are used. The pickbox appears on-screen when you issue any command that activates the `Select objects:` prompt. The pickbox is displayed in place of the crosshairs.

Enlarging the pickbox makes it cover a wider area, enabling you to place and pick objects more easily. Enlarging the aperture box makes it cover more potential pick points. However, these enlargements can force AutoCAD to process longer before determining the best point.

Reducing the size of the pickbox makes it cover a narrower area. This lessens the potential pick process, speeding up AutoCAD's selection of the best pick point. The disadvantage to a small pickbox is that you must place it more precisely because it covers less area. Try experimenting on your own to see how changing the aperture box size affects point selection. You can change the aperture box size with one of two methods:

- At the `Command:` prompt, enter **aperture**, or at any prompt enter **'aperture**. Enter the aperture box size in pixels. You are limited to a number between 1 and 50 pixels.

- In the Running Object Snap dialog box, move the scroll bar between Min and Max, watching the sample aperture box change size. Choose OK when the aperture box is the size you want.

# From Here...

Proper use of object snaps increases the accuracy of your drawings as well as simplifying the creation of geometry. Object snaps ensure that no points are "guesses"—all points are precise. When used with coordinates, object snaps will help you create drawings that are accurate and useful.

**Tip**
You can use object snaps to help you select a specific object when selecting objects for editing commands.

▶ See "Understanding Selection Sets," p. 221

For more information about using selection sets and editing existing drawings:

- Chapter 9, "Understanding Selection Sets," shows you how to create selections sets.

- Chapter 10, "Editing Techniques," explains how to edit existing geometry.

In the next chapter, you will begin to explore the concept of layers. You'll find layers to be one of the most powerful and useful tools in AutoCAD for grouping of objects. The use of layers will also allow you to automate your linetype and color selections for objects by assigning these attributes by specific layers. A proper use of layers allows you to become a more proficient and expedient AutoCAD user.

## On Your Own

Using the object snap skills you learned in this chapter, draw the layout for the basketball court shown in figure 6.25.

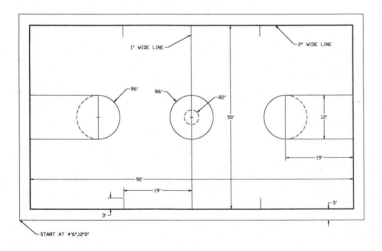

**Fig. 6.25**
Draw this basketball court using object snap functions.

Hints:

**1.** Set Limits appropriately.

**2.** Begin drawing at the given start point.

# Chapter 7

# Understanding Layers

Layers offer you a means of grouping objects together. Layering is done similarly to the way a manual drafter may draw groups of objects on separate transparent sheets of paper. The final product consists of all the transparent sheets combined in a single stack. Under these circumstances, the manual drafter can draw on only one sheet at a time. The same concept is true for AutoCAD. When using layers in AutoCAD, you can place objects only on the current layer. However, AutoCAD enables you to move objects from one layer to another with the CHANGE, CHPROP, and DDCHPROP commands covered in Chapter 21, "Modifying Object Characteristics."

In this chapter, you'll use layers to create a front elevation for an apartment building. After completing this chapter, you'll be able to do the following:

- Use a dialog box to control layers

- Create new layers

- Change the current layer

- Change a layer's color

- Assign a linetype to a layer

- Control the layer visibility

## Working with Layers

In manual drafting, you can separate details of a design by placing them on different sheets of media. This technique is called *pin drafting*, in which accurately spaced holes are punched in the polyester drafting film at the top edge of the sheets. These holes are aligned on pins attached to a metal strip, and the pins match the holes punched in the film. The technique ensures that each overlay is perfectly aligned with the others. To reflect the finished design, the overlays are attached by the alignment pins and run through a reproduction operation to obtain full-size prints.

Using overlays, or *layers*, as they are called in AutoCAD, is much easier in computer-aided design than in the manual pin-drafting technique. Using layers in AutoCAD has many other benefits:

- You can group distinct information on separate layers. In an architectural drawing, the floor plan can be on one layer, the electrical plan on another layer, and the plumbing plan on a third layer.

- Several different drafters can work on a project at the same time to increase productivity. In an architectural project, for example, several drafters may be given the same floor plan. One drafter can complete the electrical plan on one layer, and another drafter can complete the plumbing plan on a different layer. When the different plans come together, they fit because everyone worked from the same floor plan.

- You can assign each layer a different color to improve clarity. A complex floor plan combined with an electrical plan and a plumbing plan can be very difficult to visualize. Separating the different elements by color can greatly improve clarity.

- You can plot each layer in a different color or pen width. Again, this technique can help improve clarity when you visualize the final drawing.

- You can turn off layers, or *freeze* them, to decrease the information on-screen. Turning off the plumbing layer when viewing the electrical plan, for example, can make the electrical plan much easier to see.

- You can reproduce drawing layers individually or combine the layers in any format. You can reproduce the floor plan and plumbing plan together to send to the plumbing contractor. You can reproduce the floor plan and electrical plan together to send to different electrical contractors for a bid.

Layers are commonly used in all fields of CAD drafting. In electronics drafting, for example, each level of a printed circuit board can be placed on a different layer. Interior designs can have a layer for the floor plan and a layer for each article of furniture. Mechanical designs can have separate layers for each of the views, dimensions, sections, notes, and symbols.

AutoCAD allows an unlimited number of layers on which to create a drawing. You can assign each layer its own name, own color, and its own linetype. Properly used, layers can improve the clarity of a drawing and improve productivity.

## Using the Layer Control Dialog Box (DDLMODES)

You can create layers and assign a name, color, and linetype at the Command: prompt by entering **layer**. All the layer options are shown at the Command: prompt if you access the LAYER command in this manner. In practice, however, it's more efficient to set the layer options you want by using the Layer Control dialog box (see fig. 7.1). You access the Layer Control dialog box in one of three ways:

- Enter **ddlmodes** at the Command: prompt.

- Select Layers from the Data menu.

- Choose the Layers button from the Object Properties floating toolbar.

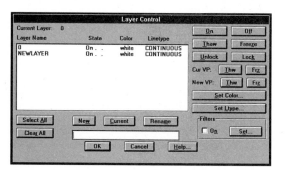

**Fig. 7.1**
You can use the Layer Control dialog box to set all the layer variables.

The features for selecting a layer or layers to set or reset the layer properties are covered later in the section, "Changing the Layer Color."

## Naming Layers

The structure of AutoCAD drawing layers is normally defined in the drafting standards of a firm. These standards should, at a minimum, specify the names of layers and the type of information to be placed on each layer. Many firms follow the ANSII Y-14 standards that define CAD layer naming and content when creating AutoCAD layering standards.

Standardizing layer names and content is an extremely important aspect of CAD drawing. In a typical architectural drawing, you may easily have over 100 layers. You may, for example, have separate layers for the floor, ceiling, foundation, partition layout, electrical, structural, heating, ventilation, air conditioning, and roof drainage.

Without standardization, it becomes virtually impossible to have different people work on a project. Imagine trying to determine which layer contains the plumbing plan from a list containing over 100 layer names. You may even have deviant versions of the same layer names, each created by different people working on the project!

## Adding New Layers

When working on a drawing, you can add new layers at any time with the Layer Control dialog box. To create a new layer, type the name in the edit box. By default, the vertical flashing bar appears in the edit box (see fig. 7.2).

**Fig. 7.2**
To create a new layer, type the new layer name in the edit box and choose New.

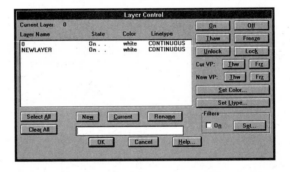

**Tip**
You can create multiple layers in the edit box by typing the layer names, separated by commas and no spaces.

Layer names can consist of 31 characters, including numbers, letters, and the special characters dollar sign ($), hyphen (-), and underscore (_). You can't use spaces within the layer name. After entering the name, choose the New button.

> **Caution**
>
> Make sure you choose New and not the OK button after you type the layer name. If you click OK, the layer just named is not created and saved in the Layer Control dialog box.

When you initially type the layer names, AutoCAD adds the new names to the bottom of the list. When you reenter the Layer Control dialog box,

AutoCAD automatically alphabetizes the layer names. If a layer name doesn't appear on the list, use the scroll bars to move down the list.

> **Note**
>
> The list of layer names in the Layer dialog box is alphabetized provided that the number of layers doesn't exceed the value of the MAXSORT system variable. The default for MAXSORT is 200. This means you can have up to 200 layers and still get the names displayed in order. If you add another layer, AutoCAD stops trying to sort the layers. This keeps AutoCAD from wasting valuable time on potentially trivial pursuits. If you have more layers than the setting for MAXSORT allows, you can increase the value of MAXSORT to a number higher than the current number of layers to get the layers displayed in order. To do this, enter **maxsort** at the Command: prompt or select Options, then System Variable, then Set, and type **maxsort**. At the MAXSORT prompt, enter the new number.

**II**

**Basic Drawing Techniques**

### Tutorial: Adding Layers to a Prototype Drawing

In this tutorial, you will create new layers to add to the apartment complex drawing. Follow these steps:

1. From the Standard toolbar, select Open. If prompted with the Save Changes dialog box, select No. Enter a name for the drawing and accept the dialog box.

2. In the Open Drawing dialog box, enter **C:\UAW13\07DWG01** in the File Name input box. Click OK to load an incomplete prototype drawing.

   You use the file that is displayed to create layers for the completed prototype drawing.

3. Choose Layers from the Object Properties toolbar.

   The Layer Control dialog box appears (see fig. 7.3). Notice in the Layer Name column that three layers are already created, the default 0 layer, the FRONT_ELEV layer, and the HATCH layer. You'll add four more layers to this prototype drawing.

4. In the edit box, enter **windows,doors,vents,constr**, and then choose New. Four new layers are now listed in the Layer Name column. Notice that at this time the names are not alphabetically listed.

> **Note**
>
> Don't close the drawing or dialog box; the next tutorial continues from this point.

**Fig. 7.3**
Using the Layer
Control dialog box
to add new layers.

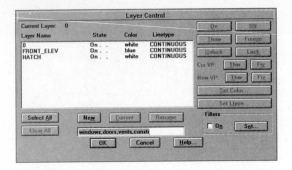

## Changing the Current Layer (CLAYER)

When you set a layer to be current, all geometry created will be on that layer, acquiring all the characteristics assigned to it (color, linetype, state, etc.). The name of the current layer is displayed in the status bar and in the Object Properties toolbar as shown in figure 7.4. Layer 0 is the default current layer.

**Fig. 7.4**
The current layer
name appears in
the Standard
Toolbar.

The current layer is the one on which objects are drawn. To create objects on a layer that is not current, you must first make the layer current and then create the objects. The following options change the current layer:

■ At the Command: prompt, enter **clayer**. AutoCAD displays the prompt New value for CLAYER <"current layer">:. Enter the name of the layer you want to make current. The layer name you type must be an existing layer.

■ In the Layer Control area of the Object Properties floating toolbar, click the down arrow. A list of all available layers appears (see fig. 7.5). Move the pointer to the layer you want to make current and then click. The new current layer appears in the Object Properties floating toolbar.

**Fig. 7.5**
You can use the
Object Properties
floating toolbar
to change the
current layer.

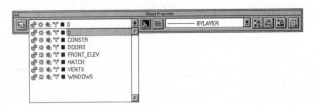

■ Use the Layer Control dialog box and highlight the appropriate layer (see fig. 7.6). Then choose Current. The current layer name appears at the top of the Layer Control dialog box. Choose OK.

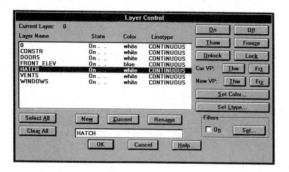

**Fig. 7.6**
To make a layer current by using the Layer Control dialog box, highlight the appropriate layer and choose Current.

## Tutorial: Changing the Current Layer in the Apartment Complex Drawing

This tutorial continues from the preceding tutorial. The Layer Control dialog box should still be displayed. In the Layer Control dialog box, notice that the current layer is the 0 layer. You want to change that setting so that the Windows layer is the current layer. Follow these steps:

1. Move your cursor to the word Windows in the Layer Name column and click it. Notice that many previously dimmed options become available.

2. Click the Current button. Notice that the Current Layer: prompt has now changed to Windows. Now click OK to accept the new layers and the current layer setting.

   The toolbar now shows the current layer as Windows (see fig. 7.7).

**Fig. 7.7**
The current layer name appears in the toolbar.

## Changing the Layer Color

When you change a layer's color, all objects drawn on that layer will display the assigned color. To change a layer's color, use the Layer Control dialog box and highlight the layer name, in the layer name list. If you have multiple layers that are to be the same color, you can select those layers as well. If all layers are to receive the same color, you can use the Select All button. To deselect or clear your group of layers, use the Clear All button in the Layer Control dialog box.

**II**

**Basic Drawing Techniques**

By choosing Set Color, you open the Select Color dialog box (see fig. 7.8). The number of colors displayed depends on your graphics card and monitor. A monochrome monitor usually displays only one color—white, amber, or green. Color systems generally support 16 or 256 colors. Layer colors are coded by name and number. To change the color, you can select any of the colors that appear in the dialog box.

> **Note**
>
> Layer color may not always affect the object color. You can assign colors to individual objects. When this occurs, the object color takes precedence over the layer color. By default, an object's color is Bylayer which means the object takes the color of the layer that the object is drawn on. You should get in the habit of not using the individual object colors. Instead, use the proper layers and layer color.

**Fig. 7.8**
To select a layer color, pick any color displayed on-screen.

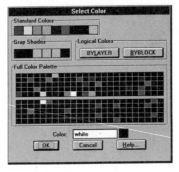

### Tutorial: Controlling Layer Color

In this tutorial, you will learn how to control a layer's color.

1. From the Standard toolbar, select Open. If prompted with the Save Changes dialog box, select Yes and save the previous work. Next, enter a name for the drawing and accept the dialog box.

2. In the Open Drawing dialog box, enter **c:\UAW13\07DWG02\** in the File Name edit box. Choose OK.

   The front elevation of an apartment complex appears (see fig. 7.9). You can use this file to adjust layer colors.

3. Select Layers from the Object Properties toolbar.

4. When the Layer Control dialog box appears, highlight the Doors layer.

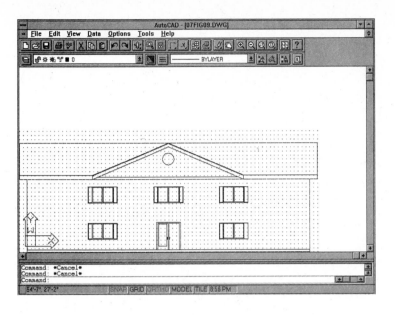

**Fig. 7.9**
You can use
the apartment
complex file to
adjust layer colors.

5. Choose the Set Color button.

   The Select Color dialog box appears (see fig. 7.10).

6. Choose the color Red. Notice that the word Red appears in the Color edit box. To accept the color, choose OK.

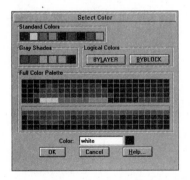

**Fig. 7.10**
You can set the
layer color with
the Select Color
dialog box.

7. You now return to the Layer Control dialog box.

   Notice that the Color column now says Red for the Doors layer. Click OK. Notice also that the front door on the front elevation of the apartment complex turns red. Any new line drawn with the Doors layer set to current will now be red.

II

**Basic Drawing Techniques**

Complete this tutorial by assigning cyan to the Windows layer and blue to the Vents layer.

> **Note**
>
> Don't close the drawing; the next tutorial continues from this point.

## Assigning Linetypes to Layers (LINETYPE)

In addition to changing a layer's color, you can assign a specific linetype to a layer. To do this, you must first load the linetype by entering **linetype** at the `Command:` prompt or by choosing it within the layers dialog box. In practice, however, it is more efficient to set the linetype options you want with the Select Linetype dialog box (see fig. 7.11). You can access the Select Linetype dialog box in one of these ways.

- Enter **ddltype** at the `Command:` prompt.

- Choose the Linetype button from the Object Properties floating toolbar.

- In the Layer Control dialog box, choose Set Ltype. To use this option, you must have a layer highlighted in the Layer Control dialog box.

**Fig. 7.11**
You can use the Select Linetype dialog box to load and set linetypes.

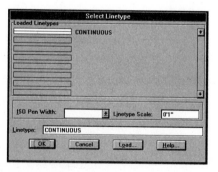

Linetypes are assigned to a given layer so that all objects drawn on that layer will automatically have that linetype. Linetypes are set to a layer for the same reasons that colors are.

> **Note**
>
> AutoCAD Release 13 for Windows is the first AutoCAD version to allow you to load a linetype within the Ltype option in the Layer Control dialog box.

> **Note**
>
> The appearance of a given linetype varies depending on the size of the object, your current view, and the linetype scale (LTSCALE). Without the same size objects, view, and linetype scale, the linetypes may not always plot correctly.

▶ See "Under-standing Linetype Scale," p. 201

## Controlling Layer Visibility

One of the advantages of using layers is the capability to turn them on and off to make viewing the drawing easier. You also can freeze and thaw layer plotting. You control layer visibility from the Layer Control dialog box and from the Object Properties floating toolbar.

### Turning Layers On and Off

When you turn off a layer, it isn't displayed on-screen or plotted. Often, you may need to turn a layer off to decrease the confusion on your screen. Or you may need to turn layers off to hide dimensions, hatching, or other parts of the drawing. To turn layers off, use one of two methods:

- In the Layer Control dialog box, highlight the layer or layers you want to turn off. Then choose Off.

- Click the face icon in the standard toolbar (see fig. 7.12). When you click the face icon, the eyes close, indicating that the layer is off. In figure 7.12, the Center and Cutting layers are turned off.

**Fig. 7.12**
You turn layers off by clicking the face icon in the Object Properties floating toolbar.

> **Note**
>
> Layers that are turned off are not plotted. Although turning off a layer will sometimes increase the visibility of a drawing, turning off a layer won't affect AutoCAD's speed because the objects are still calculated.

> **Caution**
>
> If you try to turn the current layer off, AutoCAD displays the error message shown in figure 7.13. If you turn the current layer off, you cannot see any objects already on it or any new objects you add to it until you turn the layer back on. In most cases, there is no reason to turn the current layer off.

**Fig. 7.13**
AutoCAD displays a warning when you attempt to turn the current layer off.

### Freezing and Thawing Layers

▶ See "Viewing a Drawing," p. 331

Freezing a layer is similar to turning it off. The layer is not displayed on-screen or plotted. When a layer is turned off, however, it's still regenerated during a drawing regeneration. Frozen layers are not regenerated, so freezing layers in a complex drawing is a good way to speed up regeneration time. Freezing a layer makes the objects invisible, the objects are not displayed, regenerated, or plotted. Note that you cannot freeze the current layer.

You can freeze layers in these ways:

■ In the Layer Control dialog box, highlight the layer or layers you want to freeze. Then choose the Freeze button.

■ Choose the sun icon in the Object Properties floating toolbar (see fig. 7.14). When you click this icon, the Sun icon changes to a snowflake, indicating that the layer is frozen. In figure 7.14, the Constr and Hatch layers are frozen.

**Fig. 7.14**
You can freeze layers by clicking the sun icon in the Standard toolbar.

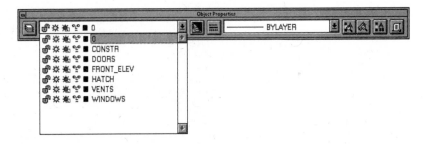

▶ See "Displaying More than One View (VIEWPORTS or VPORTS," p. 876

You may notice the other options in the Layer Control dialog box. These features allow you to control the visibility of layers in multiple viewports. This concept will be discussed in Chapter 30, "Viewing a 3D Model."

### Locking and Unlocking Layers

When different people have access to or are working on a drawing, locking a layer can be beneficial. When a layer is locked, you can't edit or change it. You can lock a layer to make object selection easier. You can see the objects on a locked layer, but you can't select them. That means that you can use the locked layer objects as reference points without selecting them by accident when you're selecting objects in a complex drawing. The layer is still visible and can be plotted. Note that you can't lock the current layer. Use one of these methods to lock a layer:

■ In the Layer Control dialog box, highlight the layer or layers you want to lock. Then click the Lock button.

■ Choose the lock icon in the Object Properties floating tool box (refer to fig. 7.14). When you choose the Lock (the picture of a padlock) icon, the icon changes, indicating that the layer is locked.

### Tutorial: Controlling Visibility of the Layers in the Apartment Complex Drawing

This tutorial continues from the preceding tutorial. Follow these steps:

**1.** Select Layers from the Object Properties toolbar.

The Layer Control dialog box appears.

**2.** Highlight the Doors, Windows, and Vents layers. Now choose the Off button near the upper-right corner of the dialog box.

Notice that the word On disappears from the State column for each entry.

**3.** Now choose OK.

You should notice that the windows, doors, and vents are no longer visible in the drawing (see fig. 7.15).

**Fig. 7.15**
Turning off the Doors, Windows, and Vents layers in the apartment complex front elevation drawing.

**4.** Select Layers from the Object Properties toolbar. The Layer Control dialog box appears.

**5.** Select the Doors, Windows, and Vents layers again. Now select the On button near the upper-right of the dialog box.

Notice that the word On reappears in the State column.

6. Choose OK.

Notice that the windows, doors, and vents are now visible in the drawing.

---

**Note**

Don't close the drawing; the next tutorial continues from this point.

---

## Renaming Layers

To change the name of a layer, select the layer (only one) in the Layer Control dialog box. Then click in the edit box below the Rename button and edit the name. When you have finished typing the new name in the box, click the Rename button. AutoCAD changes the layer's name.

## Using Filters to Limit the Display of Layer Names

Some drawings may contain hundreds of layer names. Because the Layer Control dialog box displays layer names in alphabetical order, you must scroll through all the layer names to find the ones to change. The Filters section of the dialog box enables you to limit the number of layers the Layer Control dialog box displays. Click the Set button under Filters, and the Set Layer Filters dialog box appears (see fig. 7.16).

**Fig. 7.16**
You can use the Set Layer Filters dialog box to limit the layer names displayed.

In the Set Layer Filters dialog box, you can display layers that are on, off, frozen, thawed, locked, or unlocked (or any combination of these). In the Layer Names edit box, you can use wildcards to specify layer names. For example, if you want to display only layers whose names begin with H, type **h\*** in the Layer Names edit box. Only layers whose names begin with H appear in the list of layers. You can also use wildcards to display layers by Colors or Ltypes.

### Tutorial: Completing the Apartment Complex Front Elevation with Layers

This tutorial continues from the preceding tutorial. You may have noticed that the front elevation is incomplete. In this tutorial, you complete the drawing by drawing objects on specific layers. First create the rest of the vent found on the gable of the roof. Use these steps:

1. Use the Object Properties toolbar and select the Vents layer. To do this, select the down arrow on the Layer Control box of the Object Properties toolbar. Now select the Vents layer. The Vents layer is now current.

2. Select Circle from the Draw toolbar.

   ```
   3P/2P/TTR/<Center point>: 37'11",23'1"
   Diameter/<Radius>: 1'4"
   ```

   The inner portion of the vent should be drawn in blue (you chose blue for this object in an earlier tutorial).

3. The door is the next section you need to complete. Using the Object Properties toolbar, make the Doors layer the current layer.

4. Select Rectangle from the Draw toolbar.

   ```
   First corner: 38'4",1'6"
   Other corner: 40'5",7'
   ```

   You should now have the inner glass pane for the right door drawn in red.

5. Now draw the shutter on the lower-right window. Using the Object Properties toolbar, make the Windows layer the current layer.

6. Select Rectangle from the Draw toolbar.

   ```
   First corner: 57'4",3'4"
   Other corner: 58'2",7'2"
   ```

   You should now have the shutter drawn in cyan. Cyan was chosen in a previous tutorial. You also should have the completed front elevation (see fig. 7.17).

7. Select Save from the Standard toolbar.

**Fig. 7.17**

The completed apartment complex front elevation.

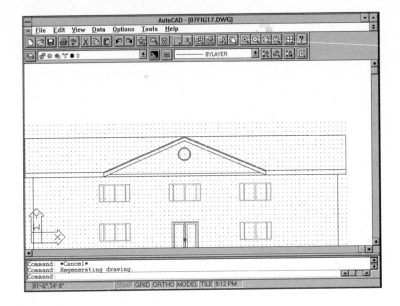

# From Here...

Proper use of layers not only helps organize your drawing's linetypes, colors, and objects, but also helps in visualization and plotting. Standardizing layer names, linetypes, and colors is an essential part of AutoCAD and should be used in all of your drawings.

For more information about linetypes and plotting layer control, see the following chapters:

- Chapter 8, "Understanding Linetypes," introduces you to the use and creation of linetypes and how to assign them by layer.

- Chapter 14, "Plotting a Drawing," shows you how to plot your drawing to a hardcopy device.

In the next chapter, you'll be introduced to the use of linetypes. Drafting requires the proper use of various linetypes such as continuous, hidden, and center. In order for a mechanical or architectural draftsman to properly present his ideas or drawings, it's imperative that he or she know how to properly use linetypes. AutoCAD Release 13 for Windows has made it easier than ever to use linetypes.

# On Your Own

Using the layers you learned in this chapter, draw the layout for the basket-ball court shown in figure 7.18.

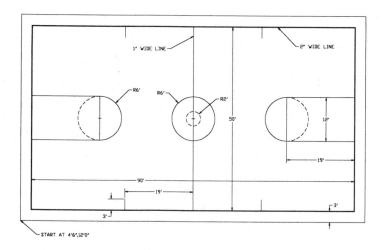

**Fig. 7.18**

A basketball court drawn using layers.

Hints:

1. Group all linetypes by layers.

2. Set limits appropriately.

3. Begin drawing at the given start point.

# Chapter 8

# Understanding Linetypes

In the previous chapter you created layers and assigned colors and existing linetypes to them. You also can assign AutoCAD's wide variety of linetypes to the layers you created. This chapter discusses the use of linetypes in your drawing.

Whether creating a drawing manually or on a CAD system, the basis of the drawing is the line. Each line on a technical drawing has a definite meaning and is drawn in a specific way. This can be a very tedious and time-consuming process in manual drafting. Creating a hidden line, for example, involves drawing a series of dashes and spaces. Each dash and space must be precisely measured.

Using AutoCAD instead of manual drafting procedures frees you from having to draw different linetypes. AutoCAD contains a predefined *alphabet of lines,* including several that conform to ISO (International Organization of Standardization) standard linetypes. An alphabet of lines is a set of conventional symbols covering all the lines needed for different purposes on a drawing.

To use a linetype, it must meet two qualifications. First, its definition must exist. It may be a predefined AutoCAD linetype, or one you created. Second, the existing linetype must be loaded into the drawing.

In this chapter you learn how to:

- ■ Recognize a linetype
- ■ List the available linetypes

- Load a linetype

- Set a linetype

- Understand the linetype scale

# What Are Linetypes?

A *linetype* is simply a repeating pattern of dots, dashes, and blank spaces. The linetype name and its corresponding definition determine the specific sequence and relative lengths of dashes, dots, and blank spaces.

A drawing may contain a variety of different linetypes. A certain type of line may be used on a drawing to represent a hidden surface, for example. Other lines may be used to represent the center point of circles or arcs. Figure 8.1 shows examples of several different linetypes available within AutoCAD.

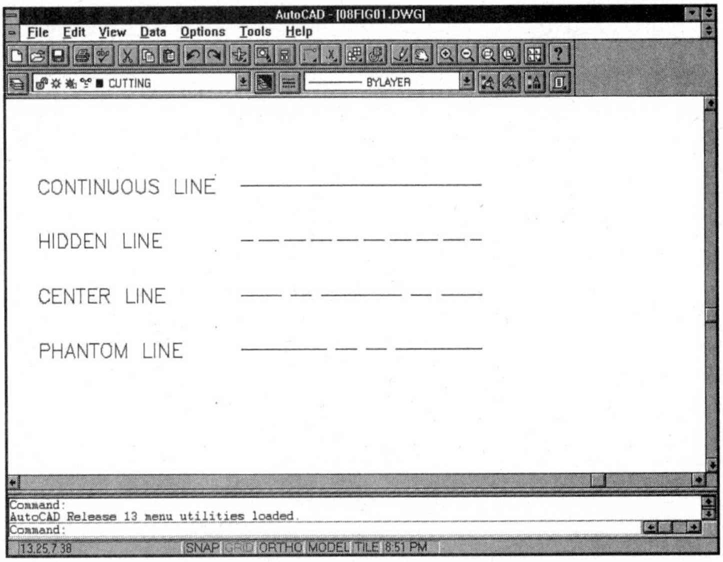

**Fig. 8.1**

The continuous, hidden, center, and phantom lines are examples of linetypes available within AutoCAD.

# Listing Linetypes

AutoCAD has a wide variety of linetypes available for use in a drawing. You can use two methods to obtain a list along with a picture of available linetypes. One method is to type **linetype** at the Command: prompt, and respond with a question mark (**?**) as follows:

```
Command: linetype
?/Create/Load/Set:?
```

This method accesses the Select Linetype File dialog box (see fig. 8.2). Select acad.lin in the File Name column. Choose OK. You see a text window and a list of AutoCAD's predefined linetypes. Press Enter until you see the ?/Create/ Load/Set: prompt. Pressing Enter at this prompt returns you to the Command: prompt. To switch from the text screen to the drawing editor, press F2.

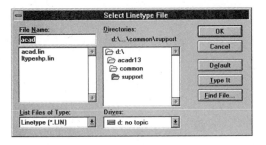

**Fig. 8.2**
Use the Select Linetype File dialog box to choose from the available linetypes.

It's much easier to access the Load or Reload Linetype dialog box by choosing Load in the Select Linetype dialog box. The following procedures first access the Select Linetype dialog box (see fig. 8.3). In the Select Linetype dialog box, choose Load and the Load or Reload Linetypes dialog box appears (see fig. 8.4).

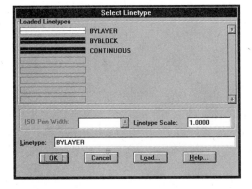

**Fig. 8.3**
Choosing Load in the Select Linetype dialog box causes the Load or Reload Linetypes dialog box to appear.

Each of the following procedures gives you access to the Select Linetype dialog box:

- Choose the Linetype button from the Object Properties toolbar.

- Choose Linetype from the Data pull-down menu. In the Select Linetype dialog box, choose Load to access the Load or Reload Linetypes dialog box.

**II**

**Basic Drawing Techniques**

■ Access the Layer Control dialog box. In the Layer Control dialog box, choose Set Ltype.

When you see the Select Linetype dialog box, choose Load to access the Load or Reload Linetypes dialog box.

> **Note**
>
> To use this option, you must have a layer highlighted in the Layer Control dialog box. This accesses the Select Linetype dialog box.

◄ See "Working with Layers," p. 175

■ Access the Object Creation Modes dialog box by choosing Object Creation from the Data pull-down menu. Choose Linetype to display the Load or Reload Linetypes dialog box (see fig. 8.4).

■ Enter **ddltype** at the Command: prompt.

**Fig. 8.4**
Linetypes available within AutoCAD may be viewed in the Load or Reload Linetypes dialog box.

Notice AutoCAD has several predefined linetypes available that meet the ISO format. To see a complete listing of all available linetypes, use the arrow keys on the right side of the dialog box to scroll through the list.

> **Note**
>
> All linetypes available with AutoCAD are found in the acad.lin file. If you have linetypes stored in a different file or location, choose the File button in the Load or Reload Linetypes dialog box and select the appropriate path and file name.

# Loading a Linetype

Before you can use a linetype, it must be loaded. You can load a linetype from the Load or Reload Linetypes dialog box. To load a linetype, first select any linetype in the Load or Reload Linetype dialog box to highlight it (refer to fig. 8.4). You can select as many different linetypes as you like. You also can use the Select All or Clear All buttons.

> **Note**
>
> By default, AutoCAD has the Continuous linetype loaded.

◀ See "Assigning Linetypes to Layers (LINETYPE)," p. 184

When you have selected all the linetypes you want to load, choose OK. The linetypes selected for loading appear in the Select Linetype dialog box.

▶ See "Using BYBLOCK with Blocks," p. 686

> **Note**
>
> You should limit the number of linetypes loaded to the ones necessary for the current drawing. Limiting the number of linetypes decreases the file size. A convenient alternative is to load all the linetypes and later purge the unneeded ones.

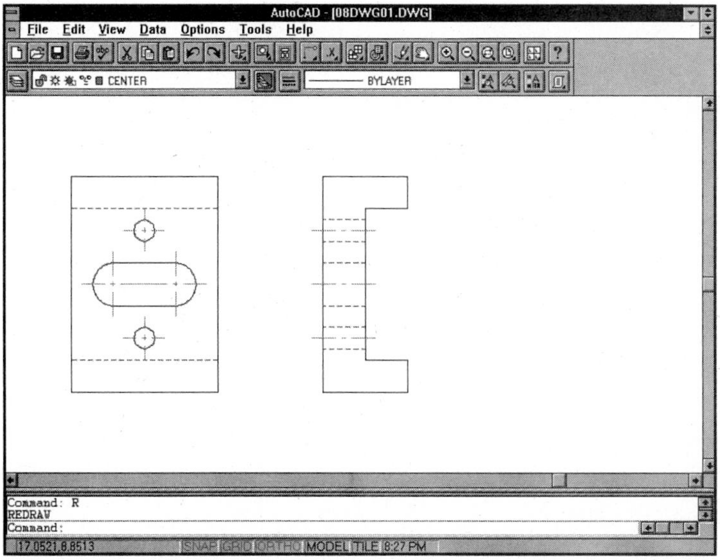

**II**

**Basic Drawing Techniques**

**Fig 8.5**
Using linetypes to complete the clamp bracket drawing.

## Tutorial: Loading a Linetype

In this and the following chapter tutorials, you complete the drawing of the clamp bracket shown in figure 8.5. You start by loading a file from the work disk. Then, you load two linetypes using two different methods. You'll finish the clamp bracket drawing later in the chapter.

1. Choose the Open button from the Standard toolbar to access the Open Drawing dialog box. Change to the UAW13 subdirectory, and load the 08DWG01 file.

   After the file is loaded, your screen should resemble figure 8.6.

**Fig. 8.6**

Loading the clamp bracket work file.

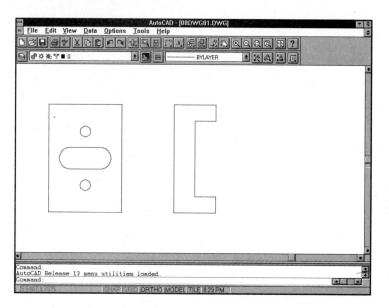

2. Choose the Linetype button from the Object Properties toolbar. Use the Select Linetype dialog box to load the hidden linetype.

   The Select Linetype dialog box appears (refer to fig. 8.3).

3. Choose the Load Button in the Select Linetype dialog box.

   The Load or Reload Linetypes dialog box appears (refer to fig. 8.4).

4. Use the scroll bar to move down the list and select the hidden linetype. Choose OK.

   The hidden linetype now appears in the Select Linetype dialog box under the Loaded Linetypes section.

**5.** Choose OK to accept the new loaded linetype. The next tutorial continues from this point.

# Setting the Linetype

After a linetype has been loaded, it can be assigned to a layer. This is done within the Layer Control dialog box. To assign a linetype to a layer, select the applicable layers and choose Set Ltype. When the Select Linetype dialog box appears, select the linetype you want to assign to the layer and choose OK.

## Tutorial: Setting the Linetype

The Load or Reload Linetype dialog box also can be invoked using the Layer Control dialog box. In this tutorial, you use the Layer Control dialog box to access the Load or Reload Linetype dialog box and load a center line. You also assign the center line and the hidden line you loaded in the previous tutorial to existing layers.

◀ See "Setting the Linetype," p. 199

**1.** Continue from the previous tutorial. Choose the Layers button from the Object Properties toolbar.

The Layer Control dialog box appears (see fig. 8.7).

**Fig. 8.7**
The Layer Control dialog box for the clamp bracket drawing.

**2.** Select the CENTER layer and then choose the Set Ltype button.

The Select Linetype dialog box appears (refer to fig. 8.3).

◀ See "Adding New Layers," p. 178

**3.** Choose the Load button.

When the Load or Reload Linetypes dialog box appears, select the CENTER linetype and choose OK.

4. In the Select Linetype dialog box, select the CENTER linetype, and then choose OK to accept the changes.

   The CENTER linetype is now the current linetype for the center layer.

5. Finish the linetype assignments by selecting the HIDDEN line, loaded previously for the HIDDEN layer.

6. After the selection is made, make the HIDDEN layer the current layer and then choose OK in the Layer Control dialog box to accept the changes. The next tutorial continues from here.

You are now ready to start drawing with the loaded linetypes.

## Setting a Default Linetype

Normally when you assign a linetype to a layer and make it the current layer, any objects you create will have the linetype assigned to that layer. AutoCAD also gives you the option of setting a default linetype for all objects drawn, regardless of what layer you select and what linetype is assigned to it. You can change this setting in the Object Creation Modes dialog box. Access the Object Creation Modes Dialog box by:

■ Choosing the Object Creation button from the Object Properties toolbar.

■ Choosing Object Creation from the Data pull-down menu.

■ Entering **ddemodes** at the Command: prompt.

By default, the setting after Linetype reads BYLAYER (see fig. 8.8). To assign a default linetype, click the Linetype box. This opens the Select Linetypes dialog box. If the desired linetype does not appear, choose the Load button and the appropriate linetype and choose OK to return to the Object Creation Modes dialog box. The setting after Linetype should now show the name of the linetype just selected. Choose OK to return to the drawing editor. From this point on, all objects drawn will have the default linetype unless you modify them with the CHANGE, DDCHPROP, CHPROP, or DDMODIFY commands.

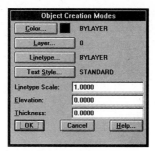

**Fig. 8.8**
Use the Object
Creation Modes
dialog box to
assign a default
linetype to all
objects created.

**II**

**Basic Drawing Techniques**

---

**Troubleshooting**

*Even when I change layers, the lines I draw have the same linetype. I have different*
*linetypes assigned to the layers, but it doesn't seem to matter when I change layers.*

You need to change the default linetypes set in the Object Creation Modes dialog
box. Even though you change to a different layer assigned a new linetype, the default setting in the Object Creation Modes dialog box is overriding any linetype you
select in the new layer.

---

# Understanding Linetype Scale

A linetype in AutoCAD is defined by a series of dashes and spaces. The
LTSCALE command allows you to change the relative scale of the dashes and
spaces that define a linetype. As long as the linetype scale is set to 1.0, the
length of the spaces and dashes are the same as when the linetype was originally defined.

Most drawings created on AutoCAD are drawn full-size. When the drawing is
plotted, it remains full-size while the plot is scaled. Use the LTSCALE command to achieve the correct linetype scale in the finished drawing. Generally,
the linetype scale should be proportional to the working scale of the drawing.
For example, a drawing that is plotted at 1/8'=1'–0" is reduced 96 times its
actual size when plotted on the paper. For this example the linetype scale for
the drawing should be 96.

## Setting the Linetype Scale

The default setting for the linetype scale is 1.0. If the drawing is going to be plotted at full scale (1=1), the default linetype scale setting is fine. If the drawing is going to be plotted at a smaller scale (such as 1=96), you need to increase the size of the linetype by increasing the value of the linetype scale (to 96 if the plot scale is 1=96). You can change the linetype scale by using any of the following methods:

- Choose Object Creation from the Data pull-down menu and enter the new linetype scale in the Linetype Scale edit box.

- Choose the Object Creation button from the Object Properties toolbar. Enter the linetype scale in the Linetype Scale edit box.

- Access the Select Linetype dialog box by choosing the Linetype button on the Object Properties toolbar and enter the new linetype scale in the Linetype Scale edit box.

- From the Options pull-down menu, choose Linetype, and then choose Global Scale.

- Enter **ltscale** at the Command: prompt.

The LTSCALE command displays the following prompt:

```
New scale factor <1.0000>: Enter a positive whole number or
         a decimal, not a fraction.
```

▶ See "Regenerating the Screen (REGEN)," p. 334

This sets the linetype scale for all linetypes in the entire drawing. After you set a new linetype scale factor, AutoCAD automatically regenerates the drawing unless you have the automatic regen turned off.

New in AutoCAD Release 13, you can assign a different linetype scale to individual objects by using the Change Properties dialog box (see fig. 8.9). Access this dialog box by entering **ddchprop** at the Command: prompt.

After entering **ddchprop**, AutoCAD prompts Select objects:. After creating your selection set and pressing Enter, the Change Properties dialog box appears. Enter the new linetype scale and choose OK. The linetype scale is changed only for the objects selected.

You can also change individual linetype scale with the Modify dialog box. To access the Modify dialog box:

- Enter **ddmodify** at the Command: prompt. AutoCAD prompts Select object to modify:

■ Choose the Properties button from the Object Properties toolbar. You are given the option of selecting one or more objects. If you select one object, you see the Modify dialog box. If you select more than one object, you see the Change Properties dialog box.

▶ See "Changing Object Characteristics (DDMODIFY)," p. 629

The Modify dialog box that appears depends upon the object selected. To change the linetype scale for the individual object selected, enter the new value in the Linetype Scale edit box.

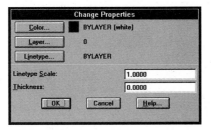

**Fig. 8.9**
The Change Properties dialog box allows you to change the linetype scale of individual objects.

## Tutorial: Adding Hidden and Center Lines to the Clamp Bracket Drawing and Changing the Linetype Scale

In this tutorial, you complete the orthographic projection drawing of the clamp bracket. You add center and hidden lines to the drawing, and change the linetype scale.

1. Continue from the previous tutorial.

2. Begin by drawing the hidden lines. Start with the top hidden line in the right side view.

   The hidden line layer is the current layer, so all lines drawn are hidden.

3. Choose the Line button from the Draw toolbar.

   ```
   From point: 8,6
   To point: 9,6
   To point:
   ```

4. Complete the hidden lines in both views (see fig. 8.10). All pickpoints are on SNAP points. If the SNAP is not active, turn it on by double-clicking the word SNAP in the status bar or by pressing F9.

**Fig. 8.10**
Completing the
hidden lines of the
clamp bracket
orthographic
drawing.

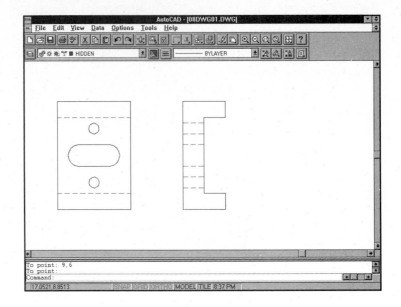

**5.** Change the current layer to the CENTER layer by choosing the Layer
Control button.

**6.** Draw the center line for the slot first.

**7.** Choose the Line button from the Draw toolbar.

```
From point: 2.25,4.5
To point: 3.75,4.5
To point: 5.25,4.5
To point:
```

Notice that the lines don't appear as center lines. You must change the
linetype scale.

**8.** Set the linetype scale using the LTSCALE command. Choose the
Linetype button from the Object Properties toolbar. The Select Linetype
dialog box appears.

In the Select Linetype dialog box, enter **.75** in the Linetype Scale edit
box and choose OK.

The lines now appear as center lines and all linetypes in the drawing are
modified according to the new scale factor.

> **Note**
>
> Linetypes are defined as a series of dash-dot sequences per drawing unit. Depending on the scale of the drawing, the linetype scale may have to be modified to make the linetype look correct.
>
> The HIDDEN linetype is defined as a sequence of visible segments and open spaces with the visible segments 0.25 drawing units long and the spaces 0.125 drawing units long. By setting the LTSCALE to 0.75, objects shown in the HIDDEN linetype appear with visible segments that are 0.1875 (0.25 × 0.75) drawing units long and open spaces that are 0.09375 (0.125 × 0.75) drawing units long.

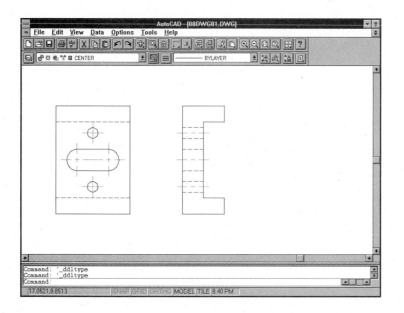

**Fig. 8.11**
Completing the center lines of the clamp bracket orthographic drawing.

**II**

**Basic Drawing Techniques**

**9.** Complete the drawing (see fig. 8.11).

Notice that the center lines on the two small holes do not appear as center lines. Your first reaction may be to change the linetype scale again. Another change may adversely affect the rest of the drawing. The scale only needs to be changed for those center lines.

AutoCAD Release 13 allows you to change the linetype scale for these lines independently.

**13**
**RELEASE**

To change the linetype scale independently follow these steps:

1. Choose the Properties button on the Object Properties toolbar.

2. Select the four center lines that are on the smaller holes on the front view and press Enter.

   The Change Properties dialog box appears.

3. In the Change Properties dialog box, change the linetype scale to .5 and choose OK.

   The center lines change scale and the drawing should now be similar to figure 8.5.

> **Note**
>
> Dashed and dotted linetypes normally take longer to repaint or regenerate. Setting LTSCALE to a large number turns every linetype into a solid line. This can significantly speed up display in large drawings with multiple linetypes. Before plotting, however, set the correct LTSCALE number and regenerate the drawing.

# From Here...

Creating different linetypes (such as hidden or center lines) in manual drafting can be a long and tedious process. One of the major advantages of using AutoCAD over manual drafting procedures is the freedom from having to draw different linetypes. AutoCAD contains many predefined linetypes, including several industry standard ISO linetypes.

To use a linetype in a drawing, its definition must exist in a LIN library file. Once its definition exists, it must be loaded into the drawing. The linetype can then be assigned to layers for use in the drawing.

Most drawings done on AutoCAD are drawn full-size, but when the drawing is plotted, the plot is scaled to enable the drawing to fit on a standard size of paper. You can use the LTSCALE command to achieve the correct linetype scale in the finished drawing. In most cases, you should set the linetype scale proportional to the working scale of the drawing.

In this chapter you have loaded existing linetypes into your drawing, assigned them to layers, and changed the linetype scale. Editing your drawing and plotting the drawing are discussed in two important upcoming chapters.

For more information about editing and adding dimensions to your drawing, see:

- Chapter 10, "Editing Techniques," explains how to edit your existing geometry.

- Chapter 14, "Plotting a Drawing," shows you how to obtain a plot of your drawing.

- Chapter 37, "Customizing AutoCAD," shows how to create your own linetypes.

# On Your Own

Load drawing 08DWG02 from your UAW13 subdirectory. Your drawing should look like figure 8.12. Add the necessary hidden and center lines so your finished drawing looks like figure 8.13.

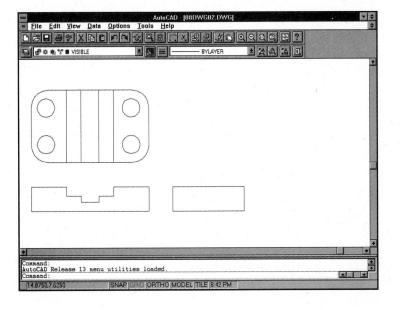

**Fig. 8.12**
Add the necessary hidden and center lines to the base plate.

Here are some helpful hints to help you add the necessary hidden and center lines:

- Create two new layers—one for center lines, and one for hidden lines.

- Load hidden and center linetypes and assign them to the appropriate layers.

■ Add the missing lines to the drawing.

**Fig. 8.13**
The finished base
plate, with the
hidden and center
lines added.

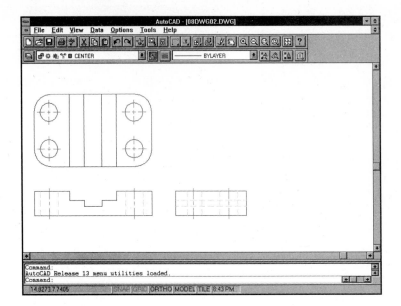

# Part III

# Editing a Drawing

AutoCAD - [37FIG05.DWG]

File   Edit   View   Data   Options   Tools   Help

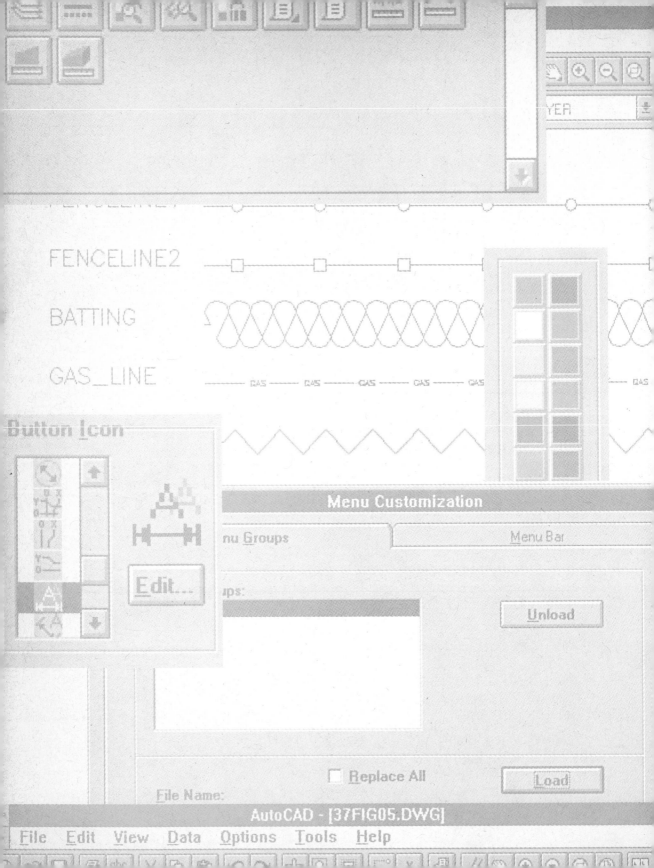

FENCELINE2

BATTING

GAS_LINE ——— GAS ——— GAS ——— GAS ——— GAS ——— GAS ——— GAS

Button Icon

Edit...

## Menu Customization

nu Groups                    Menu Bar

ups:

Unload

☐ Replace All                 Load

File Name:

AutoCAD - [37FIG05.DWG]

File   Edit   View   Data   Options   Tools   Help

# Chapter 9

# Understanding Selection Sets

Creating objects in AutoCAD is only a small part of producing a finished drawing. Many times, you have to *edit* existing objects. Editing objects includes selecting the objects during one of various editing commands. Erasing objects is one example of editing when objects are selected.

When you perform any editing operations, you must tell AutoCAD what objects you want to edit. When you invoke the ERASE command, for example, AutoCAD prompts you to select the objects to erase. When you select one or more objects, you create a *selection set*.

Before you can use many of the editing commands, you need a thorough understanding of selection sets. In this chapter, you use selection sets with the apartment floor plan. In this chapter, you learn the following:

- The purpose of selection sets
- How to create selection sets with the pick-first method
- How to create selection sets with the pick-after method
- How to control the selection set with 16 different methods

When you use an editing command (such as ERASE), `Select objects:` is usually the first prompt you see. AutoCAD uses the term *object* as a general reference to any element that can be seen on-screen. When the `Select objects:` prompt appears, AutoCAD asks you to select the objects that you want to edit. When an object is selected, it becomes highlighted on-screen. When an object is highlighted for selection, it typically changes from a solid color to a dashed outline. When you execute the editing command, it affects only the highlighted objects.

> **Note**
>
> The way objects appear when selected is controlled by the HIGHLIGHT system variable. When this system variable is set to 0, objects do not appear highlighted when selected. When the variable is set to 1, objects appear highlighted when selected. Set this variable by entering **highlight** at the Command: prompt or clicking Highlight in the Drawing Aids dialog box. In most cases, you should leave the HIGHLIGHT system variable set to 1 (on), which is the default.

◀ See "Using the Drawing Aids Dialog Box (DDRMODES)," p. 56

▶ See "System Variables Reference," p. 1147

> **Note**
>
> AutoCAD uses both a Select objects: prompt and a Select object: prompt. AutoCAD displays the Select objects: prompt when the current command works for multiple objects (selection sets). AutoCAD displays the Select object: prompt when the current command works with only one object.

# Methods for Creating a Selection Set

You can use the AutoCAD editing commands on a single object or a group of objects. Editing a single object is simple—just pick the object. Selecting many objects can be tiresome and nonproductive when you pick them one at a time. Fortunately, AutoCAD offers many ways to choose groups of objects to create a selection set. A selection set can consist of anything from a single line to the entire drawing.

## Picking Objects

Whenever you enter a command that requires you to select an object, a small box called the *pickbox* becomes visible where the pointing device is located. The pickbox sometimes appears at the junction of the crosshairs when grips are enabled and always occurs by itself whenever you enter a command that requires you to select objects. Grips are discussed in Chapter 11, "Editing with Grips." Figure 9.1 shows the pickbox by itself as well as at the junction of the crosshairs.

To select objects, place the pickbox on the object and click the pick button on the pointing device. When the object is selected, it appears dashed, as shown in figure 9.2.

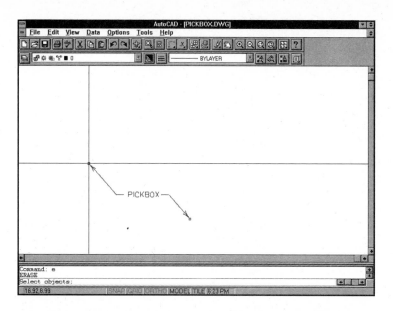

**Fig. 9.1**
The pickbox
indicates when
you can select
objects.

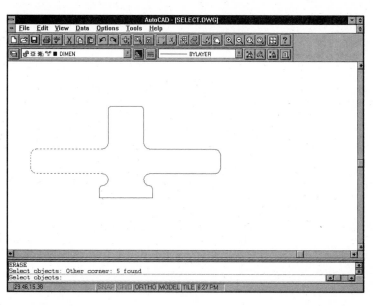

**Fig. 9.2**
Objects in a
selection set
appear dashed.

You can adjust the size of the pickbox in the Object Selection Settings dialog box, as shown in figure 9.3. You can access the Object Selection Settings dialog box by doing either of the following:

■ Enter **ddselect** at the Command: prompt

■ Choose Options, Selection.

To change the size of the pickbox, drag the Pickbox Size slider until the sample pickbox is the size you want to use.

**Fig. 9.3**

You adjust the size of the pickbox in the Object Selection Settings dialog box by dragging the Pickbox Size slider bar.

## Selecting Objects with the Toolbar

Different methods for selecting objects are also available on the Select Objects floating toolbar. The Select Objects toolbar is shown in figure 9.4. You can access the Select Objects floating toolbar by doing either of the following:

- Choose Toolbars, pick Select Objects.

- Select the Select Window button on the Standard toolbar. This will invoke a fly-out menu, showing all of the Select Objects options.

**Fig. 9.4**

The Select Objects floating toolbar contains various buttons for creating selection sets.

## Using the SELECT Command

Besides providing all the editing commands that prompt you to select objects, AutoCAD offers a separate command called SELECT. SELECT does nothing but create a selection set. When using the SELECT command you can select the objects you want to edit *first,* then issue the appropriate editing command. At the editing command's `Select objects:` prompt, you can tell the command to use the selection set you created with SELECT. This is discussed in greater detail in the sections that follow.

All the selection options are available with the SELECT command. The following command sequence is used with this command:

```
Command: select
Select objects: Use any method for creating a selection
          set.
```

You can access the SELECT command by doing either of the following:

- Enter **select** at the Command: prompt.

- From the Standard toolbar, choose the Select Window button. This invokes a fly-out menu, showing the different Select Objects options. You can choose any option to select objects.

# Pick-First Selection versus Pick-After Selection

AutoCAD offers two methods for building a selection set:

- AutoCAD's default is called *pick-first selection*. With pick-first selection enabled, you may build the selection set first and then issue the editing command. The editing command performs the appropriate operation on the selection without prompting for any additional selection information. This method of selection is also called *noun/verb selection*.

> **Note**
>
> When attempting to build a selection set before issuing an editing command, you may notice small blue boxes appearing on the objects selected. These are called *grips,* and are discussed in Chapter 11, "Editing with Grips."

- With *pick-after selection*, you can first issue the command and then select the objects to be edited. If you haven't established a selection set by using pick-first selection, AutoCAD automatically uses pick-after selection. Pick-after selection is also called *verb/noun selection*.

When pick-first selection is enabled and no commands are active, the pickbox appears at the intersection of the crosshairs. With pick-first selection, you may begin selecting objects at any time when you are at the Command: prompt. Objects may be selected before you enter any commands.

The pick-first selection method is governed by the PICKFIRST system variable. To disable pick-first selection, do one of the following:

1. Enter **pickfirst** at the Command: prompt. The default value is 1 (on). To disable PICKFIRST, enter **0** as the New value for PICKFIRST.

2. Enter **ddselect** at the Command: prompt to access the Object Selection Settings dialog box. You can also access the Object Selection Settings dialog box by choosing Options, Selection. Under Selection Modes, check the Noun/Verb Selection box. By default, this box is checked to turn pick-first selection on. To disable pick-first selection, remove the X in Noun/Verb Selection.

Only certain AutoCAD commands may be used with pick-first selection. Some commands, because they need to know exactly where an object is selected, ignore pick-first selection. The following list shows which commands work with pick-first selection and which commands do not:

| Commands That Work with Pick-First Selection | Commands That Don't Work with Pick-First Selection |
| --- | --- |
| ARRAY | BHATCH |
| BLOCK | BREAK |
| CHANGE | CHAMFER |
| COPY | DIVIDE |
| DDCHPROP | EDGESURF |
| DVIEW | EXTEND |
| ERASE | FILLET |
| EXPLODE | MEASURE |
| HATCH | OFFSET |
| LIST | REVSURF |
| MIRROR | RULESURF |
| MOVE | TABSURF |
| ROTATE | TRIM |
| SCALE | |
| STRETCH | |
| WBLOCK | |

# Selecting Objects

AutoCAD offers a variety of ways to select objects, add objects to the selection set, and remove objects from the selection set. Any of the options described in the following sections can be used with the SELECT command, pick-first selection (provided the PICKFIRST system variable is set to 1), or pick-after selection. The different ways of selecting objects are summarized in Table 9.1.

**Table 9.1  Methods Available for Creating a Selection Set**

| Button | Name | Abbreviation | Description |
|---|---|---|---|
| | Window | W | Selects all objects completely enclosed within a defined window. |
| | Crossing | C | Selects all objects completely enclosed or touching a defined window. |
| | Group | G | Selects all objects within a defined group. |
| | Previous | P | Selects the objects included in the most recent selection set. |
| | Last | L | Selects the most recently created visible objects. |
| | All | A | Selects all visible objects on thawed layers. |
| | Window Polygon | WP | Selects all objects completely enclosed within a defined polygon. Similar to a window, but the defined polygon can have more than four sides. |
| | Crossing Polygon | CP | Selects all objects completely enclosed or touching a defined window. Similar to a crossing window, but the defined crossing polygon can have more than four sides. |
| | Fence | F | Selects all objects that cross a selection fence. Creating a selection fence is similar to drawing a line. As the fence is created, any object crossing the fence is selected. |

(continues)

**Table 9.1 Continued**

| Button | Name | Abbreviation | Description |
|--------|------|--------------|-------------|
| | Add | A | Switches the selection set to the add mode. This is normally used after the Remove option to continue adding objects to the selection set. |
| | Remove | R | Switches the selection set to the remove mode. This is used to remove objects that were inadvertently included in the selection set. To continue adding more objects to the selection set, use the Add option. |
| | AUto | | Enables automatic selection. Automatic selection allows you to select objects by picking directly on objects and/or by defining a selection method. AUto and Add are the default selection methods. |
| | BOX | | Allows you to define a window or crossing selection window. AUto enables this feature automatically. |
| | Multiple | | Allows you to select multiple objects without requiring AutoCAD to highlight the selected objects. This speeds up the selection process by reducing AutoCAD's workload, particularly in large drawings. |
| | Undo | | Removes the last object selected from the selection set. |
| | SIngle | | Selects a single object or set of objects and then returns you to the command without prompting for another selection. |

## Tutorial: Picking Points

AutoCAD automatically uses the default method for adding objects to the selection set. Just use the pickbox to select single objects to add to the selection set. Objects added to the selection set appear dashed, provided the HIGHLIGHT system variable is set to 1 (on).

In this tutorial, you use the default selection option, the pickbox, to select specific items found in the apartment floor plan shown in figure 9.5. This drawing will be used for all tutorials in this chapter.

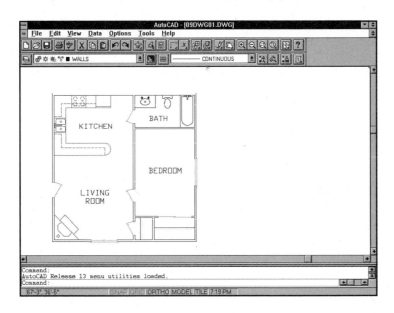

**Fig. 9.5**
Using the apartment floor plan to make selection sets.

To create a selection set using the default method, follow these steps:

1. Select the Open button from the Standard toolbar. If the AutoCAD Save Changes dialog box appears, select No unless you want to save the current drawing. If you want to save the current drawing, select Yes and enter a path and drawing name.

2. In the Select File dialog box, change to the appropriate drive and directory (C:\UAW13) and choose file 09DWG01. Your screen resembles figure 9.5.

3. At the Command: prompt, enter **select**. The Select objects: prompt appears, and you see the default pickbox in the drawing area (see fig. 9.6). Move your pointing device and notice that the crosshairs is no longer available. All selections are made with this pickbox.

4. Click the arc at the end of the breakfast bar. Notice that the end of the breakfast bar becomes highlighted, as shown in figure 9.6. The default selection option allows you to enter one object at a time to the selection set.

5. Press Enter to accept the selection.

## Using the Shift Key to Select Objects

Microsoft Windows uses a standard of pressing the Shift key to add objects in a selection set. By default in AutoCAD, you do not need to use the Shift key to add objects in a selection set. If you feel comfortable using the Windows standard of Shift key for object selection, you can enable AutoCAD to use the Shift key to add objects in a selection set.

By default, you can add objects to the selection set by picking them with the pickbox. If you want to remove an object from the selection set, hold down the Shift key and pick the object with the pickbox. The existing selection set remains intact minus the object you just selected with the pickbox.

Use of the Shift key is governed by the PICKADD system variable. By default, PICKADD is on and AutoCAD behaves as previously described. When PICKADD is turned off, each selection replaces the objects in the current selection set with the object you just selected. You must press the Shift key to add objects to the selection set. To remove an object from the selection set, press the Shift key when selecting it. If you add an object without pressing the Shift key with PICKADD off, any previous objects in the selection set are removed.

You can invoke the PICKADD system variable by typing PICKADD at the Command: line. You can also turn on the PICKADD variable in the Object Selection Settings dialog box. The option is labeled Use Shift to Add in the dialog box.

**Fig. 9.6**

Using the pickbox to select the arc at the end of the breakfast bar.

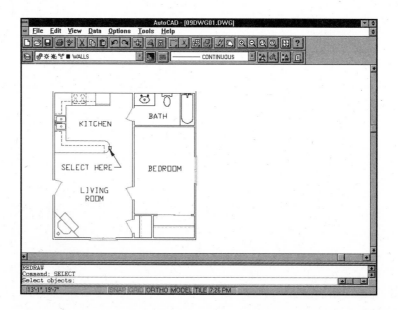

## Tutorial: Selecting Objects with a Window

When you choose to select objects with a window, AutoCAD asks you to pick the two corners of a rectangle that *completely surround* the objects you want to edit. After you pick the second corner point, AutoCAD highlights all objects that are completely enclosed within the window.

In this tutorial, you use the Window selection option to select specific items found in the apartment floor plan in figure 9.5. Follow these steps:

1. Choose the Select Window button in the Select Objects floating toolbar.

2. At the First corner: prompt, move the crosshairs to the upper-left corner of the window and pick the first corner point (see fig. 9.7).

3. At the Other corner: prompt, move the crosshairs to the bottom-right corner to create the window shown in figure 9.7, and pick the second corner point. Notice that all items within the kitchen are now highlighted, as shown in figure 9.8. Notice also that the walls in the kitchen are not highlighted because those objects are not completely within the window.

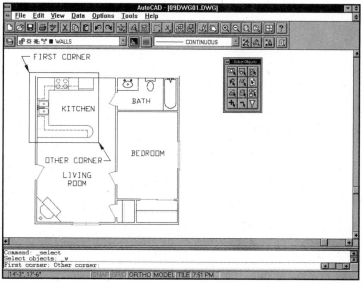

**Fig. 9.7**
Defining the upper-left and bottom-right corners needed to create a window selection.

4. At the Select objects: prompt, press Enter to accept the selection.

**III**

**Editing a Drawing**

**Fig. 9.8**
Use the Window
selection option to
select all items
located in the
kitchen.

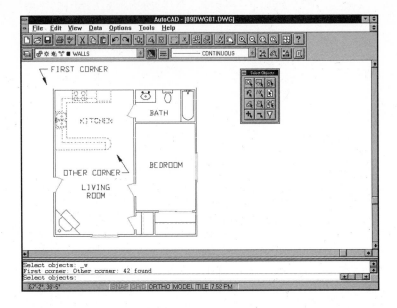

## Note

It is not necessary to select the Window button to use it as the selection mode. In the default selection set mode, move the pickbox directly to the first point of the window on the left side of the objects to be selected and pick the first corner point. Be careful not to pick an object with the pickbox. When using the window selection mode it is important to select the first point on the left side of the objects being selected. Selecting a point on the right side of the objects being selected has a different function. AutoCAD automatically starts the window selection mode as you move the crosshairs to the right.

## Changing the Press and Drag Setting

Certain software packages utilize the click-drag-release method of object selection. This means that a selection window is created by clicking one corner, dragging the window into place, and releasing the pointing device button. If you feel comfortable using the click-drag-release method of object selection, you can enable AutoCAD to use this method also.

The Press and Drag setting governs how boxes are formed. With Press and Drag turned off (default), you create pickboxes by clicking the Pick button once for each corner. When Press and Drag is turned on, you can create boxes by holding down the Pick button and dragging the crosshairs from the first corner to the second corner of the box, and then releasing. You can change the Press and Drag setting in the Object Selection Settings dialog box. The option is labeled Press and Drag.

You can also set Press and Drag with the PICKDRAG system variable. To change the PICKDRAG variable, enter **pickadd** at the Command: prompt.

## Tutorial: Selecting the Last Object Created

The Last option tells AutoCAD to select the last object that was drawn and is visible on-screen. In this tutorial, you use the Last selection option to select specific items found in the apartment floor plan in figure 9.5.

For this example, you must first draw a line on the floor plan. Notice that the top line for the upper exterior wall is missing. You draw that line before you use the last selection option. Follow these steps:

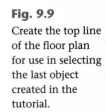

1. Select the Line button from the Draw toolbar.

2. At the From point: prompt, enter **1',31'**.

3. At the To point: prompt, enter **31',31'**.

4. At the To point: prompt, press Enter to exit the LINE command.

You should now have the completed floor plan, as shown in figure 9.9.

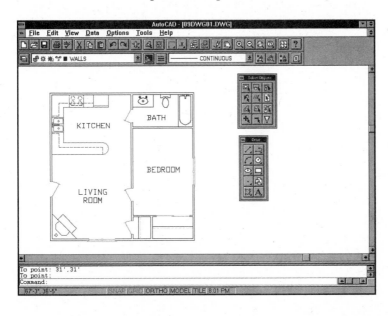

**Fig. 9.9**

Create the top line of the floor plan for use in selecting the last object created in the tutorial.

In this part of the tutorial you use the Select Last option to select specific items found in the apartment floor plan.

1. Choose the Select Last button from the Select Objects floating toolbar.

2. Notice that the line you just created is highlighted. The Last selection option always chooses the object that was drawn last as long as that object is visible on-screen.

3. Press Enter to accept the selection set.

## Tutorial: Selecting with the Crossing Option

The Crossing option is similar to the Window option except that Crossing selects any object that *touches* or *crosses* the window border, as well as any objects contained inside the window. A crossing window can be identified by a highlighted or dashed border on the window.

Figure 9.10 shows the difference between the crossing window and window selection options. The figure on the left shows a window totally enclosing the box and only touching the circle. Notice only the box is selected. The figure on the right shows the same geometry with the same size crossing window. The crossing window is totally enclosing the box and only touching the circle. Notice, with the crossing window, both the box and circle are selected.

**Fig. 9.10**
A crossing window selects all objects totally enclosing or touching it.

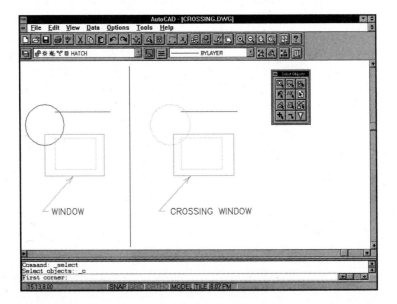

In this tutorial, you use the Crossing selection option to select specific items found in the apartment floor plan. Follow these steps:

1. Choose the Select Crossing button from the Select Objects floating toolbar.

2. At the First corner: prompt, move the cursor to the upper-left corner of the window and pick the first corner point, as shown previously in figure 9.8.

3. At the Other corner: prompt, move the crosshairs to the bottom-right corner to create the window shown earlier in figure 9.8, and pick the other corner point. Notice that all items within the kitchen are now highlighted and include the walls that were not selected when the Window option was used. The Crossing option selects all objects that the window crosses or encloses.

4. At the Select objects: prompt, press Enter to accept the selection set.

> **Note**
>
> It is not necessary to pick the Crossing button to use it as the selection mode. In the default selection set mode, move directly to the first point of the crossing window on the right side of the object and make the selection. Be careful not to pick an object with the pickbox. AutoCAD automatically starts the crossing selection mode as you move the crosshairs to the left.

## Tutorial: Selecting Objects with a Box

The Box option combines the Window and Crossing options. If the second point picked is to the right of the first, the box uses window selection. Only objects completely inside the box are selected. If the second point is to the left of the first, the box uses crossing selection. With the crossing selection, any object that touches or crosses the window border, as well as any objects contained inside the window, is selected. As with the Window and Crossing options, the crossing window is identified by a highlighted or dashed border. To use this option, you must enter **box** at the prompt, without abbreviation.

In this tutorial, you use the Box selection option to select specific items found in the apartment floor plan in figure 9.5. Use these steps:

1. At the Command: prompt, enter **select**.

2. At the Select objects: prompt, enter **box**.

3. At the First corner: prompt, move the crosshairs to the upper-left corner of the window as shown in figure 9.7, and pick the first point.

4. At the Other corner: prompt, move the crosshairs to the bottom-right corner to create the same box shown in figure 9.7, and pick the other corner point. Notice that the selection is identical to the Window option used previously.

**III**

**Editing a Drawing**

5. Press Enter to accept the selection set.

6. At the Command: prompt, press Enter to reissue the SELECT command.

7. At the Select objects: prompt, enter **box**.

8. At the First corner: prompt, move the crosshairs to the lower-right Other Corner of the window as shown in figure 9.8, and pick the first corner point.

9. At the Other corner: prompt, move the crosshairs to the upper-left corner to create the box and make the selection. Notice that the selection is identical to the Crossing option used previously.

10. Press Enter to accept the selection set.

## Tutorial: Selecting All Objects

In this tutorial, you use the All selection option to select specific items in the apartment floor plan in figure 9.5. Follow these steps:

1. Choose the Select All button from the Select Objects floating toolbar.

   Notice that all objects in the drawing are highlighted. The All selection option chooses all objects in the drawing.

2. Press Enter to accept the selection set.

## Tutorial: Using the Window Polygon (WPolygon)

The WPolygon option stands for Window Polygon, and is similar to the Window option in that the polygon you create must totally enclose the objects to be selected. A polygon is defined as a closed plane figure bounded by three or more line segments. You can have any number of sides surrounding the objects you want to include in the selection set. The shape of the polygon is limited to straight line segments that cannot intersect. AutoCAD automatically closes the polygon on the start point after the second point is picked, but you can continue to add sides to it. If you enter an incorrect point on the polygon, enter **u** (for Undo) to remove the last point entered. You can designate the last point by pressing Enter or the space bar.

In this tutorial, you use the WPolygon selection option to select specific items found in the apartment floor plan in figure 9.5. Use these steps:

1. Choose the Select Window Polygon button from the Select Objects floating toolbar.

**2.** At the First polygon point: prompt, move the crosshairs so that it is approximately in the same location as the one found in figure 9.11 and pick the first point.

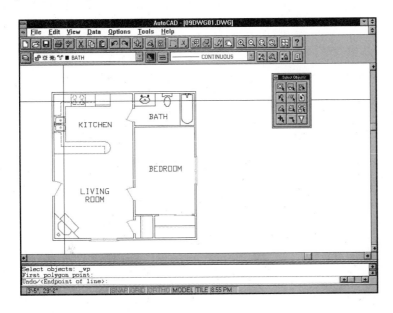

**Fig. 9.11**
Select the first point of the WPolygon selection option.

**3.** At the Undo/<Endpoint of line>: prompt move the crosshairs so that it is approximately in the same location as the one found in figure 9.12. Pick the second point.

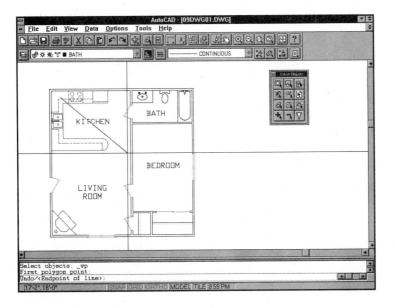

**Fig. 9.12**
When selecting the second point of the WPolygon selection option, remember the completed polygon must totally enclose the objects to be selected.

**III**

**Editing a Drawing**

4. At the `Undo/<Endpoint of line>:` prompt, move the crosshairs so it is approximately in the same location as the one found in figure 9.13 and pick the third point. You now have a triangle as your selection polygon.

**Fig. 9.13**
When you select the third point of the WPolygon selection option and press Enter, all objects totally enclosed in the polygon are selected.

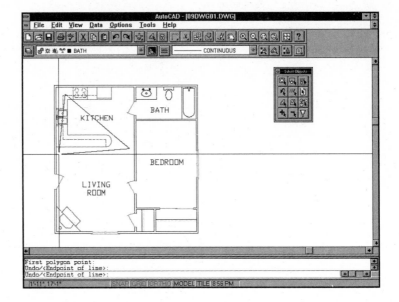

5. At the `Undo/<Endpoint of line>:` press Enter to accept the triangle as the polygon selection. The WPolygon option selects all objects that are completely within the polygon.

6. At the `Select objects:` prompt, press Enter to accept the selection set.

## Tutorial: Using the Crossing Polygon (CPolygon)

The CPolygon option stands for Crossing Polygon and is similar to the Crossing window option in that anything the polygon touches is added to the selection set. As with the WPolygon, the CPolygon can have any number of sides, and the shape of the polygon is limited to straight line segments that cannot cross each other. If you enter an incorrect point on the CPolygon, enter **u** (for Undo) to remove the last point entered. You can designate the last point by pressing Enter or the space bar.

In this tutorial, you use the CPolygon selection option to select specific items found in the apartment floor plan in figure 9.5. Follow these steps:

1. Choose the Select Crossing Polygon button from the Select Objects floating toolbar.

2. At the `First polygon point:` prompt, move the crosshairs so that it is approximately in the same location as the one found previously in figure 9.12, and pick the first point.

3. At the `Undo/<Endpoint of line>:` prompt, move the crosshairs so that it is approximately in the same location as the one found previously in figure 9.13, and pick the second point.

4. At the `Undo/<Endpoint of line>:` prompt, move the crosshairs so that it is approximately in the same location as the one found previously in figure 9.13 and pick the third point. You should now have a triangle as your selection polygon.

5. At the `Undo/<Endpoint of line>:` prompt, press Enter to accept the triangle as the polygon selection. The CPolygon option will select all objects within the polygon as well as those objects that are crossed over by the polygon (see fig. 9.14).

6. At the `Select objects:` prompt, press Enter to accept the selection set.

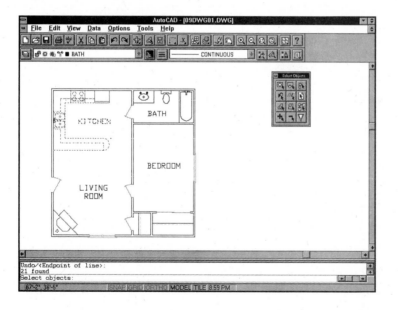

**Fig. 9.14**
The Crossing Polygon selects all objects within the polygon as well as all objects crossed over by the polygon.

## Tutorial: Selecting with a Fence

The Fence option is similar to the CPolygon option, but the polygon is never closed by connecting the first point to the last. Any objects that cross or intersect the fence are included in the selection set. The fence can cross over itself. As with the CPolygon or WPolygon option, you can enter **u** to undo a pick point.

In this tutorial, you use the Fence selection option to select specific items found in the apartment floor plan in figure 9.5. Follow these steps:

1. Choose the Select Fence button from the Select Objects floating toolbar.

2. At the First Fence point: prompt, enter **1'7,16'2**.

3. At the Undo/<Endpoint of Line>: prompt, enter **1'7,28'5**.

4. At the Undo/<Endpoint of Line>: prompt, press Enter.

   Notice that all objects that the fence crossed over were selected, as shown in figure 9.15.

5. At the Select objects: prompt, press Enter to accept the selection set.

**Fig. 9.15**
When using the Fence selection option, any objects that cross or intersect the fence are included in the selection set.

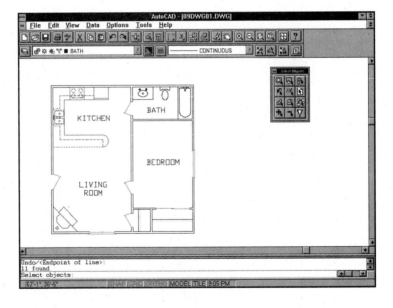

**Tip**
In this example, you typed coordinates to make the selection. It is not necessary to use the crosshairs exclusively when creating selection sets.

## Selecting Multiple Objects from the Drawing Database

Every time you pick an object to be included in a selection set, AutoCAD immediately scans the entire database of the drawing. This process can be very slow in a complex drawing. Using the Multiple option makes AutoCAD scan the drawing database only once to look for the objects to include in the selection set. This allows you to specify multiple pick points without highlighting the objects. This can increase the selection process for complex objects.

To use the Multiple option, enter **m** at the Select objects: prompt. AutoCAD then repeats the Select objects: prompt. Continue adding or removing objects from the selection set. All other selection set methods are disabled until you have individually selected the objects to include in the selection set. When you have completed the selection set, press Enter. AutoCAD scans the drawing once to look for items to include in the selection set.

### Tutorial: Selecting a Single Object

With the Single option, you can select one object only rather than continuing to prompt for further selections. This can speed up the editing process when you need to select only one object or a single group of objects.

In this tutorial, you use the Single selection option to select specific items found in the apartment floor plan in figure 9.5. Follow these steps:

1. At the Command: prompt, enter **select**.

2. At the Select objects: prompt, enter **single**. Single can be abbreviated as **si**.

3. Select any object in the apartment floor plan. Notice that after the object is selected you are automatically taken back to the Command: prompt. The Single selection option allows only one selection for that selection set.

### Completing the Selection Set

Pressing the Enter key or the space bar causes AutoCAD to stop asking you to select objects. AutoCAD continues the editing command based on the current selection set. Pressing the Enter key or space bar is called a *null response,* indicating there is nothing more to add to AutoCAD.

### Tutorial: Reselecting the Previous Selection Set

The Previous option enables you to use the preceding selection set as the current selection set. This option is helpful when you want to use several different commands on the same group of objects.

**III**

**Editing a Drawing**

In this tutorial, you use the Previous selection option to select specific items found in the apartment floor plan in figure 9.5. Follow these steps:

1. Choose the Select Previous button from the Select Objects floating toolbar. Notice that the selection set from the preceding tutorial is selected. The Previous selection option always recalls the last selection set created—for possible additions or removals to the set.

2. At the `Select objects:` prompt, press Enter to accept the selection set.

# Changing the Selection

When using any of the selection methods to select objects, you may occasionally pick unwanted objects or change your mind about a selection. You can cycle through multiple objects in the pickbox area, undo a selection, remove objects from the selected group, or even cancel the entire selection.

### Object Selection Cycling

When working on a complex drawing, it's often difficult to select the correct object by picking. With several objects falling inside the pickbox, AutoCAD is likely to grab the wrong one at any given time. You can always make the pickbox smaller to make it less likely that multiple items are captured, but that also makes it less likely that you'll be able to easily select what you're trying to get. Another option is to zoom in for a closer look, but that takes time and is distracting.

AutoCAD's solution to the problem is object selection cycling. Go ahead and enlarge that pickbox to keep from squinting. Then hold down the Ctrl key when you press the pick button to select an object. If AutoCAD highlights an item that you don't want, press the pick button again to move to the next item within the pickbox range. Repeat until you get the item you want.

### Tutorial: Removing and Adding Objects to the Selection Set

**Tip**

Instead of selecting the Remove icon, you can hold down the Shift key and pick the objects that you want to remove from the selection set.

In certain instances, it may be more beneficial to use a crossing window than to select individual objects. This allows you to save time by selecting a large group of objects at once. You can then go back with the Remove option and remove objects you don't want included.

You can remove objects from the selection set with the Remove option. When you enter **r**, AutoCAD responds with the `Remove objects:` prompt. To remove objects, you can use any selection option to pick objects to remove from the selection set.

When you are in the remove mode, the Add option switches you back to the selection mode. The `Select objects:` prompt returns, and you can continue to add objects to the selection set.

In this tutorial, you use the Remove and Add selection options to select specific items found in the apartment floor plan in figure 9.5. Follow these steps:

1. Choose the Select All button from the Select Objects floating toolbar.

2. At the `Select objects:` prompt, choose the Select Remove button from the Select Objects floating toolbar.

3. At the `Remove object:` prompt, move the crosshairs to any wall line and select it.

   Notice that the object is now no longer highlighted and is no longer included in the selection set.

4. At the `Remove object:` prompt, select any other wall line.

   That object is also no longer part of the selection set.

5. At the `Remove object:` prompt, choose the Select Add button from the Select Objects floating toolbar.

6. Now reselect the wall lines you just removed.

   Notice that they are rehighlighted and added to the selection set.

7. At the `Select objects:` prompt, press Enter to accept the selection set.

## Tutorial: Undoing a Selection

The Undo option enables you to step back through the object selection process and remove objects in the reverse order in which they were chosen.

In this tutorial, you use the Undo selection option to deselect specific items found in the apartment floor plan in figure 9.5. Use these steps:

1. At the `Command:` prompt, enter **select**.

2. At the `Select objects:` prompt, select any wall line object.

   The object is highlighted.

3. At the `Select objects:` prompt, enter **undo**.

   The wall line object is removed from the selection set. The Undo option reverses any selection made in the previous selection attempt.

4. At the `Select objects:` prompt, press Enter.

III

Editing a Drawing

### Tutorial: Canceling the Selection

Using the Escape key is the quickest way to cancel the object selection process. Pressing the Escape key immediately returns you to the Command: prompt. AutoCAD does not remember any selection set created, and you cannot use the set with the next editing command.

In this tutorial, you use the Escape key to cancel a selection option of specific items found in the apartment floor plan in figure 9.5. Follow these steps:

1. Choose the Select All button from the Select Objects floating toolbar.

2. At the Select objects: prompt, press the Escape key. Notice the message Select objects:*Cancel* above the Command: prompt. This message verifies that the previous selection set has been canceled.

# Using the Object Selection Filters

Object selection filters are used to create a list of properties that are required of an object for it to be selected. For example, you could set up an object selection filter for a specific layer. When you used any object selection method, the only objects selected would be the ones included in the selection set and residing on the filtered layer.

You can access the Object Selection Filters dialog box (see fig. 9.16) by choosing the Selection Filters button on the Select Objects floating toolbar. Entering **'filter** at the Command: prompt or at the Select objects: prompt will also access the Object Selection Filters dialog box.

Object selection filters can be useful if you have a complex drawing and want to select specific objects. For example, your drawing contains a large number of 2" diameter circles residing on different layers, and they all need to be changed to a 2.125" diameter. By setting up a filter for a 2" circle, you can use it in conjunction with the Select All option. When the selection process begins, only objects meeting the filter criteria (a 2" circle) are selected.

### Tutorial: Creating an Object Selection Filter

For this tutorial, use the apartment floor plan and set up an object selection filter. After the filter is defined, you select all objects. Only the objects meeting the filter criteria are selected.

1. Choose the Selection Filters button from the Select Objects floating toolbar.

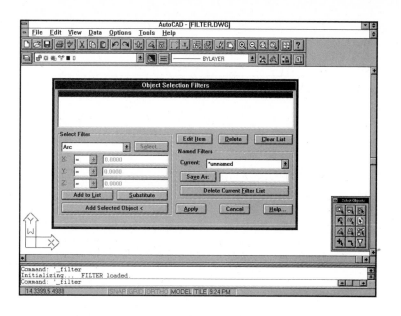

**Fig. 9.16**
The Object Selection Filters dialog box is used to create a list of properties required of an object for it to be selected.

2. Under Select Filter, click the down arrow next to Arc. Use the scroll bars to move down to layer, and select it.

3. Choose the Select button in the Select Filter box. The Select Layer(s) dialog box appears. Choose the Doors layer. Select OK to close the Select Layers dialog box.

4. In the Select Filter box of the Object Selection Filters dialog box, choose Add to List. The Object Selection Filters dialog box now looks like figure 9.17.

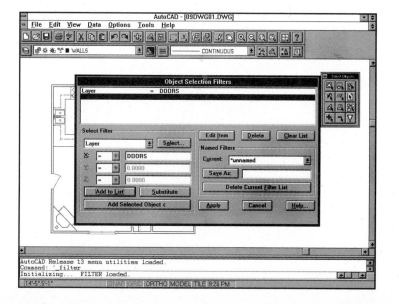

**Fig. 9.17**
The Object Selection Filters dialog box can be used to set a filter to select only objects residing on a specific layer.

III

**Editing a Drawing**

5. Select <u>A</u>pply. The Select Filters dialog box disappears, and you return to the drawing. The `Select Objects:` prompt appears.

6. At the `Select Objects:` prompt, type **all**.

7. AutoCAD responds with 169 found, 155 were filtered out. Notice only the objects on the Doors layer are selected.

8. Press Enter to accept the selection set.

In addition to specifying specific layers, you can also pick objects from your drawing. The Add Selected Object button in the Object Selection Filters dialog box returns you to the drawing, where you can select an object. After the object is selected, you are returned to the Object Selection Filters dialog box. The information captured from the object selected now appears in the box at the top of the dialog box. You can edit this information or delete it as needed.

You can also save object selection filters you defined for later use. Properly used, object selection filters can greatly speed up the selection process in complicated drawings.

## Selecting Groups

AutoCAD Release 13 includes the ability to group a set of objects together in a named selection set. This feature allows you to select a group of objects with one selection.

 After you have defined a group, you can select it by choosing the Select Group icon from the Select Objects floating toolbar. When AutoCAD prompts `Enter group name:`, type the name of a previously defined group. All objects in the defined group are selected.

## System Variables That Affect Selecting Objects

▶ See "Using Groups," p. 678

System variables are used to store information about the current drawing and AutoCAD configuration. Several system variables are used specifically to control AutoCAD's behavior when selecting objects. By changing the settings of certain variables, you can make AutoCAD behave like previous releases or other systems.

## PICKFIRST

The PICKFIRST system variable controls the method of object selection. By default, PICKFIRST is enabled, so that you can select an object first and then use an edit or inquiry command.

## PICKADD

PICKADD is used to control how objects are added or removed from the selection set. By default, PICKADD is enabled. When each object is selected, either by windowing or selected individually, it is added to the current selection set. To remove objects from the selection set with PICKADD enabled, hold down the Shift key while selecting.

▶ See "System Variables Reference," p. 1147

When PICKADD is disabled, only the objects most recently selected, either by windowing or selected individually, become the selection set. Any objects previously selected are removed from the selection set. To add more objects to the selection set, hold down the Shift key while selecting.

## PICKDRAG

PICKDRAG is used to control the method for drawing a selection window. By default, PICKDRAG is set so the selection window is drawn by clicking the pointing device at one corner, and clicking it again at the other corner.

If you set the PICKDRAG system variable to 1, you create the selection window by clicking the selection window at one corner, holding down the button, dragging the window to size, and releasing the button at the other corner.

## PICKAUTO

The PICKAUTO system variable controls automatic windowing any time the Select objects: prompt appears. By default, you can draw a selection window (either window or crossing window) automatically at the Select objects: prompt. Turning PICKAUTO off disables this function.

# From Here...

A thorough understanding of selection sets is important because all editing commands use them. AutoCAD offers a variety of selection methods designed to cover almost any circumstance. Remember, there is no right or wrong way to use selection sets. Use the method or combination of methods best suited to the task at hand.

**III**

Editing a Drawing

For more information about applying selection sets when editing objects, extracting information from your drawing and using them with Symbols and Xrefs, see the following chapters:

- Chapter 10, "Editing Techniques," explains the practical use of selection sets in editing objects.

- Chapter 22, "Getting Information from Your Drawing," shows you another practical use of selection sets in extracting information from your drawing.

- Chapter 23, "Using Symbols and XRefs," introduces you to groups, which can be used in conjunction with selection sets.

## On Your Own

Load the drawing 09DWG02 from your UAW13 subdirectory. Your drawing should look like figure 9.18.

**Fig. 9.18**
Use different selection sets to choose different objects on the Lathe Back Gear.

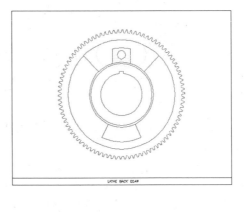

Use any single or a combination of the different selection sets discussed in this chapter to accomplish the following:

1. Select only the outer gear teeth.

2. Select only the hidden lines.

3. Select only the inner circle and key slot.

# Chapter 10

# Editing Techniques

No matter what type of drawings you create, you must go through two basic phases to form your ideas in AutoCAD—creation and editing. AutoCAD provides more commands for editing your drawing than for creating the objects that make up the drawing. There are two reasons for this. First, few drawings are created perfectly the first time—unless you draw only circles or squares—you will be required to edit them. Second, several of the editing commands assist in you in creating objects. In fact, you are likely to spend more time using the editing commands than the drawing commands to create your drawings.

AutoCAD also allows you to recover easily from mistakes you may accidentally make when drawing or editing. The powerful UNDO command can reverse any drawing or editing action you perform in a drawing, back to the point at which you opened the drawing.

In previous chapters, you learned how to use various commands to create drawings. This chapter covers AutoCAD commands you can use to modify those drawings.

In addition to using commands to edit drawings, AutoCAD provides object grips, as discussed in Chapter 11, "Editing with Grips." Object grips adapt many of the editing commands covered in this chapter to work in a manner more typical of other Windows applications, such as desktop publishing or graphic arts.

▶ See "Editing with Grips," p. 301

In this chapter, you learn the major editing commands and features, including these tasks:

- Using the ERASE command to remove objects from the current drawing

- Relocating, duplicating, and stretching objects, using the MOVE, COPY, and STRETCH commands

**III**

**Editing a Drawing**

- Creating offset objects, using the OFFSET command

- Performing additional editing with ROTATE, MIRROR, SCALE, BREAK, TRIM, EXTEND, and other commands

# Using the Editing Commands

The names of most of the editing commands quickly identify the type of actions they perform. The ERASE command, for example, erases objects; the ROTATE command changes an object's orientation; and the FILLET command joins two objects at a point or with an arc. With a few minor exceptions, you simply decide on the type of modification you want and then select the command with that name.

The simplest types of editing you will perform involve moving the elements of your drawing into different positions or copying similar elements to form new details. You also are likely to rotate drawing elements and erase objects no longer needed. To perform these simple types of editing, use the MOVE, COPY, ROTATE, and ERASE commands, respectively.

Editing also can include more complex tasks, such as the following activities:

- Lengthening or shortening a group of objects

- Breaking objects into multiple pieces

- Duplicating complex object shapes parallel to the original shape

- Creating copies of objects in a row/column format

- Joining objects by using arcs or straight line segments

The STRETCH, EXTEND, BREAK, TRIM, OFFSET, ARRAY, FILLET, and CHAMFER commands provide the functions necessary to perform this type of editing.

### Note

In general, the editing commands work with object selection sets. As each command executes, it requests an object (or objects) and performs the required action on the selected objects. AutoCAD provides many methods for properly selecting objects, as discussed in Chapter 9, "Understanding Selection Sets." By familiarizing yourself with these selection methods, you can speed up the process of the edit you are performing.

# Deleting Objects (ERASE)

No matter what type of work you do, some portion always becomes superfluous. It could be a note that no longer applies to the work you are describing, a detail that will not be used, construction lines used to create complex objects, or even the remains of other types of editing. Selecting these elements while using the ERASE command clears them from your drawing. The ERASE command performs one simple function—it removes objects from a drawing.

Access the ERASE command by either of these methods:

- Click the Erase button on the Modify floating toolbar.

- Enter **erase** at the Command: prompt.

The ERASE command has the following prompt, indicating that you select the objects to be removed from the drawing:

- Select objects: Select the objects you want to erase within the drawing. You can use any of the selection methods described in Chapter 9, "Understanding Selection Sets," to choose the objects you want to move.

**Tip**

As a shortcut, you can type **e** and press Enter to start the ERASE command.

After AutoCAD erases the objects, they are not gone permanently until you end the drawing session. You can use commands such as OOPS or UNDO (discussed later in this section) to restore objects that have been erased.

## Tutorial: Erasing Objects

In this tutorial, you erase objects from a sample drawing file. The initial drawing is shown in figure 10.1; figure 10.2 shows how the drawing should look after erasing the objects. Follow these steps:

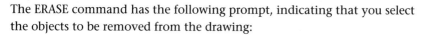

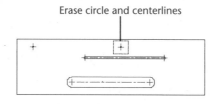

Adjustable Proximity Switch
Bracket Zoom Factor = 1:1

**Fig. 10.1**
Objects to be erased.

III

Editing a Drawing

**Fig. 10.2**
The drawing with
the objects
removed.

Adjustable Proximity Switch
Bracket Zoom Factor = 1:1

1. Open the sample drawing C:\UAW13\10DWG01.

2. Click the Erase button on the Modify floating toolbar.

3. At the Select objects: prompt, select the objects as shown in figure 10.1 and press Enter.

AutoCAD removes the selected objects, as shown in figure 10.2.

Leave this drawing open for the next tutorial. If you don't plan to try the next tutorial (using the OOPS command) immediately, close the drawing file without saving your changes.

> **Note**
>
> You must repeat the preceding tutorial (Erasing Objects), before continuing to the next tutorial (Restoring Objects with the OOPS Command).

# Restoring Accidentally Erased Objects (OOPS)

You may not always remove the proper elements when you use the ERASE command. Also, AutoCAD sometimes removes objects, as part of commands such as creating a block. If you are quick, the simplest method to restore objects removed accidentally is to use the OOPS command.

At times, you might want to intentionally erase objects to see what result it might have on your design. You can experiment like this, knowing that you can bring the objects back using the OOPS command. Also, you may find editing a complex drawing simplified by erasing an object to get it out of the way, performing the edit (such as a move), and then using OOPS to get the *last* erased object set back.

You access the OOPS command by either of these methods:

■ Click the OOPS button on the Miscellaneous toolbar.

■ Enter **oops** at the Command: prompt.

This command has no additional prompts or options. When you use OOPS, AutoCAD restores the *last set* of objects that had been removed from the drawing.

> **Caution**
>
> AutoCAD only retains the last group of removed objects on a temporary basis, where they can be retrieved by using the OOPS command. If you use the ERASE command twice, only the last group of objects erased will be restored by using the OOPS command. To retrieve objects accidentally erased at an earlier point in the drawing session, you may need to use the UNDO command. UNDO is discussed later in this chapter, in the section "Undoing Your Work (UNDO, REDO)."

## Tutorial: Restoring Objects with the OOPS Command

This tutorial is an extension of the earlier tutorial for the ERASE command. In that tutorial, you removed objects from the drawing (C:\UAW13\10DWG01); in this tutorial, you restore the objects you removed.

> **Note**
>
> If you closed the drawing file after the tutorial for the ERASE command, or if you didn't do the earlier exercise, complete the previous tutorial now.

With the drawing file open, type **oops** at the Command: prompt; then press Enter. The objects deleted by the ERASE command are restored, as shown in figure 10.3.

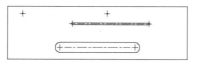

Adjustable Proximity Switch Bracket
Zoom Factor = 1:1

**Fig. 10.3**
The objects, restored to the drawing.

III

Editing a Drawing

Leave this drawing open for the next tutorial. If you don't plan to try the next tutorial (using the MOVE command) immediately, close the drawing file without saving your changes.

# Moving, Copying, and Stretching Objects

The majority of editing you perform on a drawing involves moving, copying, or stretching objects to produce the results you want. These commands are similar in that they relocate objects from one point in the drawing to another. This may sound like a simple concept, but many people fail to use it appropriately and end up more confused about how the commands work than is necessary.

◀ See "Coordinate System Basics," p. 87

The Base point: and To point: prompts that appear when you use these commands require you to define the direction and distance you are using to edit objects. The points you use can be two locations chosen arbitrarily, a relative distance between starting and ending points, or starting and ending points located on other objects within the drawing. These combinations can be mixed and matched to relocate the objects you are editing in the direction you need them to be placed.

## Moving Objects (MOVE)

One of the beauties of using CAD for drafting is the ease of manipulating the elements of your drawing. On a paper drawing, moving a detail may require you to physically erase the image from the paper and redraw it at a new location. The MOVE command performs the same function, but is quicker and easier to use. The command relocates objects from one point in your drawing to another—you simply choose the starting and ending points.

You access the MOVE command by either of these methods:

- Click the Move button on the Modify floating toolbar.

- Enter **move** at the Command: prompt.

**Tip**
As a shortcut, you can type **m** and press Enter to start the MOVE command.

The MOVE command has the following prompts:

- Select objects: Select the objects you want to relocate within the drawing. You can use any of the selection methods described in Chapter 9, "Understanding Selection Sets," to choose the objects you want to move.

- `Base point or displacement:` This point defines where objects will be moved *from*.

- `Second point of displacement:` This point defines where objects will be moved *to*.

You can use relative point entry to define a displacement for the starting and ending points. After choosing a base point, for example, you can enter **@150<90** to move the objects 150 units at 90 degrees.

You aren't limited to relocating objects within the current X,Y plane; the MOVE command can also relocate the selected objects in the direction of the current Z-plane, in one of two ways:

- Use the .Z filter to supply a starting or ending elevation.

- Use the 'DDUCSP command to modify the coordinate system so that it is aligned parallel to the current *z*-axis.

▶ See "Using Point Filters," p. 785

▶ See "Understanding the User Coordinate System (UCS)," p. 788

> **Note**
>
> Moving objects within different construct planes within AutoCAD's three-dimensional drawing space can be cumbersome. The ALIGN command allows you to define a location anywhere in 3D space where the objects you have selected will be moved. See Chapter 27, "Understanding 3D Coordinate Systems," for more details on using ALIGN.

### Tutorial: Moving Objects

This tutorial shows you how to relocate objects with the MOVE command, using an object reference point for the base point and relative distance and angle for the displacement. After you have finished the tutorial, the mounting hole will be located at the horizontal midpoint of the bracket. You can continue using the drawing from the previous tutorials in this chapter, or you can reload the original file (C:\UAW13\10DWG01). Follow these steps:

1. Click the Move button on the Modify floating toolbar.

2. At the `Select objects:` prompt, select the objects highlighted in figure 10.4 and press Enter.

**III**

**Fig. 10.4**
Objects to be
moved.

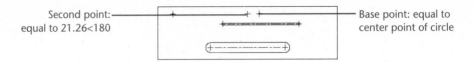

Second point:
equal to 21.26<180

Base point: equal to
center point of circle

Adjustable Proximity Switch Bracket
Zoom Factor = 1:1

3. At the `Base point or displacement:` prompt, use the object snap center point to select the center of the highlighted mounting hole. Type **cen** and press Enter. Pick the circle shown in figure 10.4. This point will serve as the base point, as shown in figure 10.4.

4. At the `Second point of displacement:` prompt, enter **@1.26<180**. This moves the circle and centerlines to the horizontal middle of the bracket, by using a relative displacement point value.

AutoCAD moves the selected objects. Figure 10.5 shows the result.

**Fig. 10.5**
The drawing after
moving the
objects.

Adjustable Proximity Switch Bracket
Zoom Factor = 1:1

### Tutorial: Moving Objects with Point Filters, Relative to Another Object

This tutorial shows you how to move objects relative to other objects in the drawing by using x,y,z filters with the MOVE command. After you have completed this tutorial, the upper mounting slot and the lower switch slot will be vertically aligned with each other.

1. Click the Move button on the Modify floating toolbar.

2. At the `Select objects:` prompt, select the objects highlighted in figure 10.6 and press Enter.

3. At the `Base point or displacement:` prompt, use the object snap MID-point to select the midpoint on any of the horizontal lines that make up the upper mounting slot. This point will serve as the base point, as shown in figure 10.6.

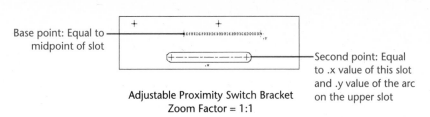

Base point: Equal to midpoint of slot

Second point: Equal to .x value of this slot and .y value of the arc on the upper slot

Adjustable Proximity Switch Bracket
Zoom Factor = 1:1

**Fig. 10.6**
Objects to be moved.

4. At the `Second point of displacement:` prompt, type **.x** and press Enter. You are going to enter x,y,z filters to move the upper slot into vertical alignment with the lower switch slot. Now select a midpoint using the MIDpoint object snap on either of the horizontal lines that make up the lower slot. Refer to figure 10.6.

5. At the `of (need YZ):` prompt, type **.y** and press Enter. Now select the center point on one of the arcs on the upper mounting slot. Refer to figure 10.6. This keeps the y location of the upper slot the same as it was before being moved.

6. At the `of (need Z):` prompt, type **0** and press Enter. Because this is a 2D drawing, you don't need to enter a value for the .Z filter.

**Tip**

Since you are using a relative displacement for the `Second point of displacement:`, any point could be used as a base point.

AutoCAD moves the upper mounting slot into vertical alignment with the lower slot, as shown in figure 10.7.

Adjustable Proximity Switch Bracket
Zoom Factor = 1:1

**Fig. 10.7**
The drawing after moving the objects.

### Tutorial: Moving Objects by Displacement

In this tutorial, you continue to move the slots on the bracket. After you have finished, both slots will be located at the proper distance from the left edge of the bracket. This tutorial uses the Displacement option of the MOVE command.

1. Click the Move button on the Modify floating toolbar.

2. At the `Select objects:` prompt, select the objects highlighted in figure 10.8 and press Enter.

**Fig. 10.8**
Objects to be
moved.

Adjustable Proximity Switch Bracket
Zoom Factor = 1:1

**3.** At the `Base point or displacement:` prompt, enter **-4,0**.

**4.** At the `Second point of displacement:` prompt, press Enter.

AutoCAD moves both the upper and lower slots the specified 4 units to the left, as shown in figure 10.9.

**Fig. 10.9**
The drawing after
moving the
objects.

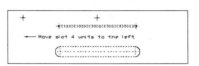

Adjustable Proximity Switch Bracket
Zoom Factor = 1:1

This concludes the tutorials on the MOVE command; leave this drawing open for the next tutorial. If you do not plan to try the next tutorial (using the COPY command) immediately, save your changes and close the drawing file.

## Copying Objects (COPY)

Many drawings are made up of common elements—a hole pattern repeated in a die, a window used in a storefront design, or the beams and columns in a structural plan. When you draw these elements in AutoCAD, the most time-saving method to reuse those objects is to make a copy of the objects at a new location. AutoCAD's COPY command performs this function for you. As your understanding of AutoCAD advances, you may find it more appropriate to use the BLOCK or XREF commands, for more complex object groups, in place of the COPY command. See Chapter 23, "Using Symbols and XRefs," for more details on using BLOCK and XREF.

You access the COPY command by either of these methods:

■ Click the Copy Object button on the Modify floating toolbar. This is the default button when AutoCAD first starts. If it has been replaced by another button, continue holding down the pick button on your digitizer while moving the pointer over to the first button on the fly-out menu, then release the pick button.

- Enter **copy** at the Command: prompt.

The COPY command's prompts are similar to those used by the MOVE command:

- Select objects: Select the objects you want to duplicate. You can use any of the selection options described in Chapter 9, "Understanding Selection Sets."

- <Base point or displacement>/Multiple: This point defines where objects are copied *from*. By default, AutoCAD creates only a single copy of the selected objects, unless you first choose the Multiple option. Choosing Multiple allows you to create several duplicates of the original objects. After you choose Multiple, you must then choose a base point.

- Second point of displacement: This point defines where objects are copied *to*. If you selected the Multiple option, AutoCAD repeats this prompt until you cancel the command by pressing Enter or Esc.

The COPY command is similar to the MOVE command in another way; you are not limited to duplicating objects within the current drawing plane. You can copy the selected objects in the direction of the Z-plane. Try either of these methods when AutoCAD asks you to choose the starting and ending copy locations:

- Use the .Z filter to supply a starting or ending elevation.

- Use the 'DDUCSP command to modify the coordinate system so that it is aligned parallel to the current z-axis.

### Tutorial: Copying Objects
This tutorial shows you how to make a second copy of the bracket by using the COPY command. You can continue using the drawing from the previous tutorials in this chapter. If you are just starting, you can reload the file (C:\UAW13\10DWG01). Follow these steps:

1. Click the Copy Object button on the Modify floating toolbar.

2. At the Select objects: prompt, select the objects highlighted in figure 10.10 and press Enter. These objects will be used to create a second copy of the bracket, to the top of the original part.

3. At the <Base point or displacement>/Multiple: prompt, select the base point indicated in figure 10.10.

**Tip**
As a shortcut, you can enter **cp** at the Command: prompt.

**III**

**Editing a Drawing**

**Fig. 10.10**
Objects to be
copied.

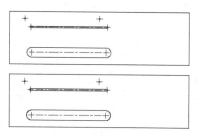

Base point

Adjustable Proximity Switch Bracket
Zoom Factor = 1:1

4. At the Second point of displacement: prompt, type **@8<90** and press Enter. This action creates a copy of the bracket, 8 inches to the top of the original bracket.

After AutoCAD has made a second copy of the bracket, the drawing should look like figure 10.11.

**Fig. 10.11**
The second
bracket, created
with the COPY
command.

Adjustable Proximity Switch Bracket
Zoom Factor = 1:1

### Tutorial: Making Multiple Copies of Objects

This tutorial shows you how to make multiple copies of the mounting holes with the COPY command. Continue using the drawing from the preceding tutorial. If you did not complete the preceding tutorial, go back and do it now. Follow these steps:

1. Click the Copy Object button on the Modify floating toolbar.

2. At the Select objects: prompt, select the objects highlighted in figure 10.12 and press Enter. The objects will be used to create two more sets of mounting holes for each bracket.

3. At the <Base point or displacement>/Multiple: prompt, type **m** and press Enter.

4. At the Base point: prompt, type **cen** and press Enter. This allows you to use the object snap center point to select the center of the mounting hole. This point will serve as the base point, as shown in figure 10.12.

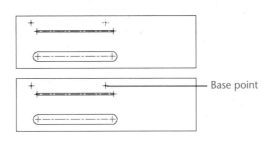

Base point

Adjustable Proximity Switch Bracket
Zoom Factor = 1:1

**Fig. 10.12**
Objects to be copied.

5. At the `Second point of displacement:` prompt, type **@4<0** and press Enter. This action creates another set of mounting holes, 4 inches to the right of the originals.

6. At the next `Second point of displacement:` prompt, type **@9<0** and press Enter. This action creates the second set of mounting holes, 9 inches to the right of the originals. Press Enter again to end the command.

AutoCAD creates two more sets of mounting holes. The drawing should now look like figure 10.13.

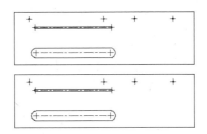

Adjustable Proximity Switch Bracket
Zoom Factor = 1:1

**Fig. 10.13**
The additional sets of mounting holes copied on each bracket.

Leave this drawing open for the next tutorial. If you do not plan to try the next tutorial (using the STRETCH command) immediately, save your changes and close the drawing file.

## Stretching Parts of a Drawing (STRETCH)

How many times have you designed something—perhaps a house or piece of furniture—and then decided that it should be longer, shorter, or maybe taller? When dealing with paper drawings, you must erase the portion of the drawing that you want to modify, and then redraw what you erased at its new position.

AutoCAD's STRETCH command makes these types of modifications much easier. With this command, select the portion of the drawing that needs to be lengthened or shortened, and then choose two points that correspond to the length and direction of the modification.

You access the STRETCH command by either of these methods:

- Click the Stretch button on the Modify floating toolbar. Stretch is the default button when AutoCAD first starts. If it has been replaced by another button, then continue holding down the pick button on your digitizer while moving the pointer over to the first button on the fly-out menu; then release the pick button.

- Enter **stretch** at the Command: prompt.

When you execute the STRETCH command, AutoCAD displays the following prompt:

◀ See "Selecting Objects," p. 217

- Select objects to stretch by crossing-window or -polygon... Select objects: If you enter **stretch** at the Command: prompt, you have the choice of using either a crossing-window or a -polygon for selecting objects. If you pick the Stretch button from the Modify toolbar, STRETCH uses a crossing-window by default. Select the objects you want to stretch.

> **Note**
>
> If you do not use either the crossing-window or -polygon selection method, you will be unable to stretch any of the objects selected.

- At the Base point or displacement: prompt, you indicate where objects will be stretched *from*.

- At the Second point of displacement: prompt, you specify where objects will be stretched *to*.

### Selecting Objects with the STRETCH Command

The process of selecting objects for use by the STRETCH command is somewhat different from other editing commands. STRETCH works by use of an *anchor point* that limits one end of the object to being stretched. You must enclose one endpoint or vertex of an object, by using a crossing selection (either crossing-window or crossing-polygon). The endpoint or vertex not selected serves as the anchor point. The `Base point:` and `To point:` prompts allow you to define the direction and angle at which the objects are stretched.

◀ See "Tutorial: Selecting with the Crossing Option," p. 224

For example, using a crossing-window to select the end of a line object causes the end that you selected to move, while the other end of the line remains fixed. This also means that you cannot modify objects without endpoints. Using the STRETCH command on block, circle, point, and text objects relocates those objects, only if the window completely encloses them. Line, arc, ellipse, and polyline objects all have endpoints or vertices that can be relocated with STRETCH.

▶ See "Tutorial: Hatching an Area of a Drawing," p. 494

> **Note**
>
> The STRETCH command, along with the use of object grips, provides a quick way to relocate dimensions and dimension text.

In addition, the STRETCH command modifies only the *final* selection set you create. If you use a crossing-window selection twice to select all the objects you want to modify, only the objects that are part of the final selection set are changed.

▶ See "Stretching Objects with Grips," p. 312

After you have made your selection, decide how much deformation to apply to the selected objects when choosing your responses for the `Base point:` and `To point:` prompts. Think of deforming objects as stretching a piece of taffy. If you pull the ends of the taffy apart, the middle stretches. If you push the ends together, the middle compresses. This same effect is what happens when you use the STRETCH command.

### Tutorial: Stretching Objects

This tutorial shows you how to deform objects with the STRETCH command. You will modify the slots of the bracket created in the previous tutorial (see fig. 10.14). Follow these steps:

1. Click the Stretch button on the Modify floating toolbar.

2. At the `Select objects:` prompt, select the slots shown by the crossing window in figure 10.14. Select either the bottom or upper-right corner first, to activate the crossing-window option.

3. At the `Base point or displacement:` prompt, enter **quad** to use the QUADrant object snap to pick the arc, as shown in figure 10.14.

**III**

**Editing a Drawing**

4. At the Second point of displacement: prompt, type **@1.5<0** to elongate the slots by 1.5" to the right.

AutoCAD stretches the slots of both brackets. The drawing should look like figure 10.15.

**Fig. 10.14**
The initial part showing the selection window and starting stretch point.

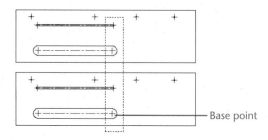

Adjustable Proximity Switch Bracket
Zoom Factor = 1:1

**Fig. 10.15**
The bracket after the slots are lengthened with the STRETCH command.

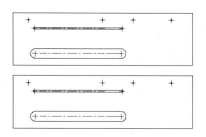

Adjustable Proximity Switch Bracket
Zoom Factor = 1:1

Leave this drawing open for the next tutorial. If you do not plan to try the next tutorial (using the ROTATE command) immediately, save your changes and close the drawing file.

# Rotating, Mirroring, Scaling, and Offsetting Objects

The number of steps required to take an image from a paper drawing and mirror the image's contents can be overwhelming: make a copy of the original image, erase any text on the image, erase the original image, turn the copy over and place the sheet on a light table, redraw the image on the sheet, and re-create any text that was erased. This description may seem somewhat exaggerated, but really is only the *minimum* number of steps to reverse an image manually. How often, in addition to reversing an image, do you also need to rotate and/or scale the image? Generally, rotating an image is a simpler process than mirroring, but you still need to erase the current image, rotate and redraw the image, and re-create the text.

Computer-aided drafting is ideal for performing these types of advanced object editing tasks. No matter how you do it, electronic means always produce a superior result, both in limiting the amount of effort expended to perform the editing and in improved output. AutoCAD excels in the capacity to perform difficult editing, such as image mirroring, scaling, and rotating. The following sections describe the AutoCAD editing commands that provide these capabilities.

## Rotating Objects (ROTATE)

Not everything you draw is composed strictly of horizontal and vertical lines. Often the task is as simple as drawing a piece of furniture that is angled within a room, but what about a house with an angled entry or a plaza shaped like a pentagon? The simple way to work on plans like this is to create your drawing elements with typical horizontal and vertical objects, and then rotate the objects into the proper angled position using the ROTATE command. At times, you also will want to change existing designs with horizontal, vertical, or angled objects. You can use ROTATE to change the angle of all the objects or a selected group. You access the ROTATE command by either of these methods:

- Click the Rotate button on the Modify floating toolbar. This is the default button when AutoCAD first starts. If it has been replaced by another button, continue holding down the pick button on your digitizer while moving the pointer over to the first button on the fly-out menu, then release the pick button.

- Enter **rotate** at the Command: prompt.

The ROTATE command has the following prompts:

- Select objects: Select the objects you want to rotate, using any of the normal selection methods.

- Base point: This point is the center of the imaginary arc that is used to rotate the objects. This is similar to the Base point: prompt of the MOVE or COPY command, except that this is the point around which the selected object is rotated.

■ `<Rotation angle>/Reference`: The default option, `<Rotation angle>`, defines how far from its original position the object will be rotated. To rotate the objects clockwise, use a negative angle value; for counter-clockwise rotation, supply a positive value.

For example, think of a circle. If the selected objects are somewhere on the circle's circumference, the center of the circle is the base point. The angle you supply rotates the objects around the circumference of the circle.

In addition to supplying a single angular value specifying how much rotation must be applied, you also can give a value by reference, as described in the next item.

■ `Reference angle <0>`: When you use the Reference option, you describe the starting and ending angles for the objects. Supply a starting angle. This value is compared with the `New angle`: value that follows, and the objects are rotated by the difference between the two entries. The starting angle can be a number or two points that describe a beginning angle.

▶ See "Editing Commands for 3D Objects," p. 841

■ `New angle`: This is the ending angle to which the objects should rotate. The New angle can be either a specific value or a point selected to describe the New angle.

### Tutorial: Rotating Objects

In this tutorial, you continue modifying the brackets created and edited in earlier tutorials. For this tutorial, both brackets are rotated vertically to represent their assembled position. Follow these steps:

1. Click the Rotate button on the Modify floating toolbar.

2. At the `Select objects`: prompt, select all the objects that make up both brackets and press Enter.

◀ See "Understanding Object Points and Object Snap," p. 150

3. At the `Base point`: prompt, type **mid** to use the MIDpoint object snap to pick the point indicated in figure 10.16.

4. Next at the `<Rotation angle>/Reference`: prompt, type **r** and press Enter to select the Reference option.

5. At the `Reference angle <0>`: prompt, type **@** and press Enter. Entering @ at this prompt creates a vector to define the starting angle. Press the F8 key to turn on the ortho mode. The `Second point`: of the vector will be perpendicular to the object pointed out in figure 10.16.

**6.** At the Second point: prompt, select a point 90 degrees to the base point.

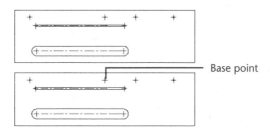

Adjustable Proximity Switch Bracket
Zoom Factor = 1:1

**Fig. 10.16**
Objects to be rotated.

**Tip**
If necessary, use the ZOOM OUT command to reduce the drawing display magnification to .5x so both parts are shown. If the magnification is too small, use ZOOM W to fill the display.

**7.** At the New angle: prompt, type **180** and press Enter or pick a point parallel to the base point. This action rotates the elements of the part so that they are aligned vertically, as shown in figure 10.17.

> **Note**
>
> It is possible to enter the ZOOM command transparently while in the middle of executing another command.

▶ See "Using ZOOM to Control the Display (ZOOM)," p. 336

**Fig. 10.17**
The drawing elements, rotated to vertical and zoomed to fill the screen.

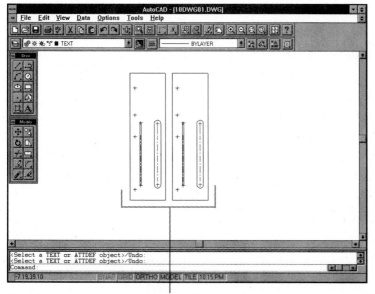

Adjustable Proximity Switch Bracket
Zoom Factor = .5:1

Editing a Drawing

**Tip**
Use the MOVE command to move the drawing title and text to the bottom of the screen.

**Tip**
If you would like to edit the reference text Zoom Factor = 1:1 so it represents the new zoom factor .5:1 use the DDEDIT command.

▶ See "Editing Text (CHANGE, DDEDIT, and DDMODIFY)," p. 476

▶ See "3D Editing Essentials," p. 839

> **Note**
>
> If you are working with 3D objects, the 3DROTATE and ALIGN commands shown in the Rotate fly-out menu will assist you.

Leave this drawing open for the next tutorial. If you don't plan to try the next tutorial (using the MIRROR command) immediately, save the changes and close the drawing file.

## Creating Mirror Images (MIRROR)

Mirror images are a common part of the work you perform, no matter what your discipline. Architects typically use facades that are mirror images of each other at building entrances; mechanical parts typically have slots and holes that are the same on both sides of the part's axis; and so on. Even engineers use parking lot designs that are duplicated along a main driveway entrance. The benefit to this type of design is that you can create it once and then use a function such as AutoCAD's MIRROR command. By selecting objects and specifying the *mirror line*—an imaginary line about which the objects are flipped or mirrored—you can duplicate your work with a minimum of effort.

You access the MIRROR command by either of these methods:

■ Click and hold the Copy Object button on the Modify floating toolbar. While holding down the pick button on your digitizer, move the pointer to the third button on the fly-out menu; then release the pick button.

■ Enter **mirror** at the Command: prompt.

The MIRROR command displays the following prompts:

■ Select objects: Select the objects you want to mirror, using any of the standard selection methods.

■ First point of mirror line: The mirror line determines where the reverse-image of the selected objects will be drawn. At this prompt, specify the beginning point of the mirror line.

You are not limited to using a vertical or horizontal line; you can use a line at any angle.

■ Second point: Specify the ending point of the line that defines where the mirror image is created.

After you have defined the points that make up the mirror line, the objects are duplicated about this line. AutoCAD then asks if you want the original objects to be erased. This is a time-saving option of the MIRROR command. If the mirror image is the only copy of the objects you want as part of the drawing, the original objects can be removed by entering **y** in response to the Delete old objects? <N> prompt. This leaves only the mirrored image after the MIRROR command is completed.

▶ See "System Variables Reference," p. 1147

> **Note**
>
> Before using the MIRROR command to mirror text, find out what the MIRRTEXT system variable is set to. The MIRRTEXT variable defines how mirrored text is treated with MIRROR. If the MIRRTEXT variable is set to 0, text objects are not created as mirrored images—they still read left to right. If the MIRRTEXT variable is set to 1, text objects are reversed, similar to any other objects selected. To change the MIRRTEXT system variable at the Command: prompt, type **mirrtext** and press Enter. Next enter the appropriate value in response to the New value for MIRRTEXT <1>: prompt. The value shown in < > represents the current MIRRTEXT setting.

### Tutorial: Mirroring Objects

This tutorial continues modifying the brackets created and edited in earlier tutorials. In this procedure, you mirror the slots and mounting holes in the left bracket, using the MIRROR command. Follow these steps:

1. Click the Mirror button on the Modify floating toolbar.

2. At the Select objects: prompt, select all the objects that make up the right bracket, as highlighted in figure 10.18 and press Enter.

3. At the First point of mirror line: prompt, enter **mid** to use the MIDpoint object snap. Pick the first point indicated in figure 10.18.

4. At the Second point: prompt, enter **per** to use the PERpendicular object snap to pick the opposite side of the part, as shown in figure 10.18.

◀ See "Understanding Object Points and Object Snap," p. 150

5. At the Delete old objects? <N> prompt, enter **y** to delete the original objects.

AutoCAD mirrors the slots and mounting holes (see fig. 10.19).

**III**

Editing a Drawing

**Fig. 10.18**
Objects to be
mirrored.

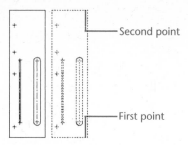

Second point

First point

Adjustable Proximity Switch Bracket
Zoom Factor = .5:1

**Fig. 10.19**
The slots and
mounting holes,
reoriented by
using the MIRROR
command.

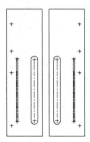

Adjustable Proximity Switch Bracket
Zoom Factor = .5:1

Leave this drawing open for the next tutorial. If you do not plan to try the next tutorial (using the SCALE command) immediately, save your changes and close the drawing file.

## Scaling Parts of a Drawing (SCALE)

When creating a drawing, scaling an object is a requirement everyone takes for granted. If a title is too small, you increase its size; if a detail is unreadable, you draw it at a different scale; if a plan takes too much room, you decrease its size to take up less room. Each of these changes requires the capacity to increase and decrease the size of selected drawing elements. For these tasks, AutoCAD provides the SCALE command.

You access the SCALE command by either of these methods:

- Click the Stretch button on the Modify floating toolbar. While holding down the pick button on your digitizer, move the pointer to the second button on the fly-out menu, Scale; then release the pick button.

- Enter **scale** at the Command: prompt.

The SCALE command has the following prompts:

- `Select objects:` Select the objects you want to scale, using any of the selection methods.

- `Base point:` This is a reference point, away from which or toward which AutoCAD scales the objects. This point can be located anywhere, but it should be close to, if not centered about, the selected objects. This ensures that when the objects are enlarged or reduced, they remain in the general area where they are currently located.

- `<Scale factor>/Reference:` The size of the final objects is based on the scale factor entered after you have chosen the base point. The default option is to enter a value by which AutoCAD scales the objects. Use the Reference option when you want to specify a starting and ending scale factor.

  If the scale is greater than 1, the selected objects are enlarged. If the scale factor is less than 1, the objects are reduced. For example, a scale factor of 2 enlarges the selected objects to twice their initial size.

- `Reference length <1>:` This prompt appears if you used the Reference option at the preceding prompt. Enter a starting scale value, the actual length of an object. This value is used as an absolute value to calculate the actual scaling factor applied to the chosen objects.

- `New length:` This ending scaling factor is compared to the previously entered value. AutoCAD calculates the difference between these two values and uses the result as the scaling factor applied to the selected objects. For example, if you enter a starting value of 3, and an ending value of 2, the selected objects are reduced in scale by 33 percent.

### Tutorial: Scaling Objects

This tutorial uses the SCALE command to enlarge the size of the drawing title that was zoomed out in a preceding tutorial. Follow these steps:

1. Click the Scale button on the Modify floating toolbar.

2. At the `Select objects:` prompt, select the text objects at the bottom of the brackets, highlighted in figure 10.20, and press Enter.

3. At the `Base point:` prompt, enter **ins** to use the INSertion point object snap. Pick the insertion point of the top line of text highlighted in figure 10.20 and press Enter.

4. At the `<Scale factor>/Reference:` prompt, type **r** to select the Reference option and press Enter.

5. At the `Reference length <1>:` prompt, type **0.5**, which represents the text's current height, and press Enter.

6. At the `New length:` prompt, type **0.625**, which represents the new text's height, and press Enter.

AutoCAD calculates the scale factor, and the objects that make up the bracket title are scaled up by 125 percent, as shown in figure 10.21.

**Fig. 10.20**
Objects that will
be enlarged.

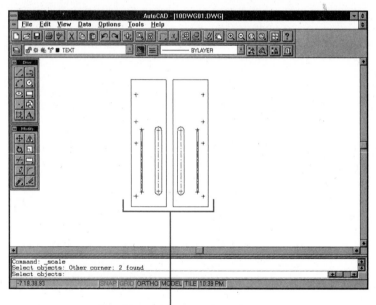

Adjustable Proximity Switch Bracket
Zoom Factor = .5:1

Leave this drawing open for the next tutorial. If you do not plan to try the next tutorial (using the OFFSET command) immediately, save your changes and close the drawing file.

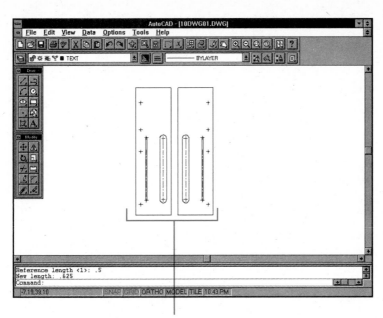

**Fig. 10.21**
The text objects
after being scaled
up.

Adjustable Proximity Switch Bracket
Zoom Factor = .5:1

## Copying Objects with OFFSET (OFFSET)

Offset images are a natural part of the drawings you create. These parallel images can be as simple as two wall lines that make up a courtyard or the edges of a road on a map. In AutoCAD, you create offset copies with the OFFSET command.

You access the OFFSET command by either of these methods:

■ Click the Copy Object button on the Modify floating toolbar. While holding down the pick button on your digitizer, move the pointer to the second button on the fly-out menu, Offset; then release the pick button.

■ Enter **offset** at the Command: prompt.

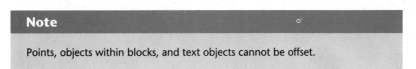

**Note**

Points, objects within blocks, and text objects cannot be offset.

The OFFSET command has the following prompts:

- `Offset distance or Through <Through>:` Enter either a numerical value or select a starting and ending point to serve as an offset distance. By typing **t** at the prompt, you can specify a through point to offset a selected object to. AutoCAD prompts, `Select object to offset:`. After selecting an object, AutoCAD prompts, `Through point:`. Select a point or object to where the selected object will be offset.

> ### Note
>
> The OFFSET command does not work with selection sets in the same manner as the other AutoCAD editing commands. First, you enter an offset distance and then you select the single object for which you want to make offset copies.

- `Select object to offset:` This object must be a line, arc, polyline, circle, or ellipse.

- `Side to offset?` The side you choose is the direction in which the object is duplicated.

  When dealing with circles and arcs, choosing a point towards the center of the object creates an object with a smaller radius, whereas choosing a point outside the object creates an object with a larger radius.

If you use the OFFSET command to duplicate two lines that meet at a corner, you must use a command such as FILLET to re-create the corner intersection for the new lines. Polyline objects composed of line and arc segments automatically adjust the intersection points to compensate for the offset distance.

### Tutorial: Offsetting Objects

This tutorial continues to build on the part created in previous tutorials. Use the OFFSET command to duplicate the top and bottom edges on the brackets. These edges represent a shoulder for tenons on the end of each bracket. Follow these steps:

1. Click the Offset button on the Modify floating toolbar.

2. At the `Offset distance or <Through>:` prompt, enter **0.75** to set the offset distance or through value.

> **Note**
>
> OFFSET remembers the last value entered and uses it as the default offset value the next time you enter the OFFSET command.

**3.** At the Select object to offset: prompt, select one of the objects highlighted in figure 10.22.

> **Note**
>
> OFFSET only allows you to select one object at a time for duplication.

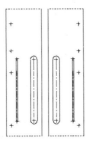

Adjustable Proximity Switch Bracket
Zoom Factor = .5:1

**Fig. 10.22**
Objects to be offset.

**4.** At the Side to offset? prompt, pick a point on the side shown in figure 10.23, which shows the new objects created by AutoCAD using offset.

**5.** The OFFSET command continues to repeat. Continue to offset the other objects shown in figure 10.22 by repeating steps 3 and 4. When you are finished, end the OFFSET command by pressing Enter at the Select object to offset: prompt.

AutoCAD duplicates the shoulder lines, as shown in figure 10.23.

**III**

**Editing a Drawing**

**Fig. 10.23**
Lines created with
the OFFSET
command.

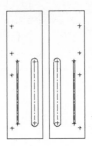

Adjustable Proximity Switch Bracket
Zoom Factor = .5:1

# Editing Edges, Corners, and Lengths of Objects

The commands in this section add fine details to AutoCAD drawings. The TRIM, EXTEND, and LENGTHEN commands shorten and remove sections or lengthen objects within the drawing. The FILLET and CHAMFER commands produce rounded and sharp corners or beveled edges. The BREAK command removes selected portions of objects or can separate them into two or more individual objects.

## Trimming Objects (TRIM)

The TRIM command defines one or more lines to serve as cutting planes—the point to which objects are shortened or have sections removed.

You access the TRIM command by either of these methods:

- Click the Trim button on the Modify floating toolbar. This is the default button when AutoCAD first starts. If it has been replaced by another button, then continue holding down the pick button on your digitizer, while moving the pointer over the first button on the fly-out menu; release the pick button.

- Enter **trim** at the Command: prompt.

The TRIM command has the following prompts:

- Select cutting edges: (Projmode = UCS, Edgemode = No extend)
  Select objects: Select the objects to use as the cutting planes. Most AutoCAD objects except for points, text, blocks, and hatch patterns can serve as cutting planes. Select as many cutting planes as necessary.

- `<Select object to trim>/Project/Edge/Undo`: Select the objects from which you want to shorten or remove a section from. AutoCAD removes the part of the object that extends from the point you select to the cutting plane. If an object crosses more than one cutting plane, the portion of the object selected is removed to the nearest trim border. To trim a circle, a trim border must cross the circle in two locations; this ensures that the arc object created by the TRIM command is less than 360 degrees.

  Choosing the Undo option at this prompt undoes the trimming; the Project and Edge options are discussed later in this section.

- `None/Ucs/View <Ucs>`: If you chose the Project option at the preceding prompt, you are given the option to specify how objects not in the current UCS should be trimmed back to the selected cutting planes. These options are used for 3D editing; see Chapter 29, "3D Editing Essentials," for more details on UCS.

- `Extend/No extend <No extend>`: If you chose the Edge option at the preceding prompt, you are given two options to determine how cutting planes behave. The default option, No extend, forces objects that are to be trimmed to visually cross over a cutting plane. If you select the Extend option, the cutting plane is extended, temporarily, into infinity. An object that crosses this extended plane—anywhere in model or paper space—can be trimmed to that plane.

▶ See "Editing Commands **and** the Current UCS," p. 840

---

### Note

If line objects are strictly horizontal or vertical, the CHANGE command's Point option can be quicker than using the TRIM command. You choose a point to which the closest endpoints of the selected lines will be relocated. In ortho mode, the endpoints are relocated to the specified point and still maintain horizontal or vertical orientation.

---

**Tutorial: Shortening Objects with the TRIM Command**

In this tutorial, you use the TRIM command to shorten one of the adjustment slots to a point even with a centerline. This tutorial uses the drawing (C:\UAW13\10DWG01) as it was last edited in the OFFSET tutorial. Follow these steps:

1. Open the sample drawing C:\UAW13\10DWG01.

2. Click the Trim button on the Modify floating toolbar.

3. At the `Select cutting edges: (Projmode = UCS, Edgemode = No extend)` `Select objects:` prompt, select the object highlighted in figure 10.24 and press Enter.

4. At the `<Select object to trim>/Project/Edge/Undo:` prompt, type **e** and press Enter to select the Edge options.

**Tip**

The same exercise can be completed using the STRETCH. However, commands such as TRIM are more efficient to use when selecting specific objects within a close-knit group of objects.

5. At the `Extend/No extend <No extend>:` prompt, type **e** and press Enter to select the Extend option. Notice in figure 10.24 that the centerline selected as the cutting plane does not cross both objects. Selecting Extend will extend the "implied" cutting plane across both objects.

6. Now back at the `<Select object to Trim>/Project/Edge/Undo:` prompt, select the objects in figure 10.24 at the ends shown. Be sure to select the correct end, or the incorrect end of the object will be trimmed back to the cutting plane. Figure 10.25 shows the revised part.

> **Note**
>
> Use the MOVE command, discussed earlier, to move the arc and centerlines up to the end of the slot. Use ENDpoint object snaps to assist you.

**Fig. 10.24**
Trim border and objects to be shortened.

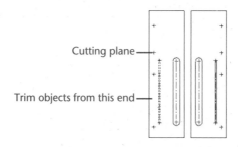

Cutting plane

Trim objects from this end

Adjustable Proximity Switch Bracket
Zoom Factor = .5:1

Leave this drawing open for the next tutorial. If you do not plan to try the next tutorial (using the BREAK command) immediately, save your changes and close the drawing file.

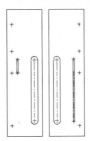

Adjustable Proximity Switch Bracket
Zoom Factor = .5:1

**Fig. 10.25**
Lines shortened
with the TRIM
command.

## Erasing Parts of Objects (BREAK)

It's not always easy to remove part of an object with a command such as
TRIM—setting up trim borders can take time, and after the command is finished, the borders may need to be erased. The BREAK command can be a
handy alternative. This command allows you to define two points on an
object that correspond to the portion of the object you want to remove.

You access the BREAK command by either of these methods:

- Click the Break button on the Modify floating toolbar. There are four
  variations of the Break command in this fly-out menu. If the default
  button when AutoCAD first starts is not the one you want, then continue holding down the pick button on your digitizer, while moving
  the pointer over the button you want to use; then release the pick
  button.

- Enter **break** at the Command: prompt.

You can select the portion of the object to remove in two different ways. The
first method is to select two points on the object that define the section you
want to remove. The second method is to select the object you want to break
and then select the two breakpoints. The second method is particularly useful
when you need to select breakpoints that correspond to other objects in the
drawing. For example, consider a room with a door opening along one wall.
If you want to add another door on the opposite wall, select the wall where
you want to add the new door and then select the endpoints of the existing
door opening. The BREAK command removes the portion of the wall corresponding to the points you selected.

**III**

Editing a Drawing

The BREAK command has the following prompts:

- `Select object:` Select the object you want to break. (This command breaks a single object each time you execute it.) AutoCAD uses the point where you select the object as the starting point for the break, unless you specify that you want to select a new first point at the next prompt.

- `Enter second point (or F for first point):` This point defines the end of the portion you want to remove from the object. If you enter **F**, for first point, in response to this prompt, you can enter a new starting break point. This allows you to bypass the first point where the object was selected as the starting break point.

- `Enter first point:` If you chose the First Point option at the preceding prompt, this prompt appears next; you can now enter a new starting break point.

- `Enter second point:` This is the endpoint where the object break stops. AutoCAD erases the portion of the object between the first and second points. This prompt appears only when you have chosen to bypass the point where the object was first selected as the starting break point.

### Tutorial: Shortening Objects with the BREAK 1 POINT Command

In the preceding tutorial, you used the TRIM command to shorten the adjustment slot on the left bracket. In this tutorial, you use the BREAK command to see another method of shortening objects. You are going to shorten the corresponding adjustment slot on the right bracket.

1. Click the 1 Point button on the Modify floating toolbar.

2. At the `Select object:` prompt, enter **mid** to use the MIDpoint object snap, and select the object as shown in figure 10.26.

   This separates the single line into two lines of equal length.

> **Note**
>
> Use the ERASE command, covered earlier, to erase the bottom object. The result of the BREAK command is shown in figure 10.27.

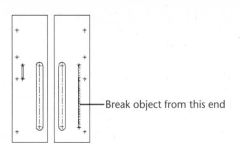

**Fig. 10.26**
Line to be broken
into two segments.

Break object from this end

Adjustable Proximity Switch Bracket
Zoom Factor = .5:1

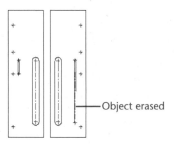

**Fig. 10.27**
Line resulting from
the BREAK 1
POINT command.

Object erased

Adjustable Proximity Switch Bracket
Zoom Factor = .5:1

### Tutorial: Shortening Objects with the BREAK 2 POINTS Command

In the preceding tutorial, you used the BREAK 1 POINT command to shorten
the adjustment slot on the right bracket by separating the object into two
parts and erasing the unwanted section. In this tutorial, you use the BREAK 2
POINTS command to see another method of shortening objects. You are
going to shorten the other side of the adjustment slot on the right bracket
and erase the unwanted section in one command.

1. Click the 2 POINTS button on the Modify floating toolbar.

2. At the `Select object:` prompt, type **mid** and press Enter to use the
   MIDpoint object snap to select the object as shown in figure 10.28.

3. At the `Enter second point (or F for first point):` prompt, select a
   point below the arc at the bottom of the slot. The result is shown in
   figure 10.29.

   This separates and erases the lower half of the object in one command
   sequence, as compared with the BREAK 1 POINT and ERASE commands
   that were used in the previous tutorial, which took two command
   sequences.

**Fig. 10.28**
Line to be
shortened.

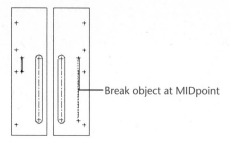

Break object at MIDpoint

Adjustable Proximity Switch Bracket
Zoom Factor = .5:1

**Fig. 10.29**
Line shortened
using the BREAK 2
POINTS com-
mand.

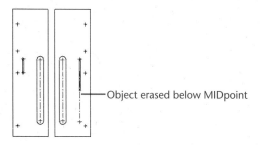

Object erased below MIDpoint

Adjustable Proximity Switch Bracket
Zoom Factor = .5:1

Leave this drawing open for the next tutorial. If you do not plan to try the next tutorial (using the EXTEND command) immediately, save your changes and close the drawing file.

## Extending Objects (EXTEND)

Whereas the TRIM command shortens objects to selected cutting planes, the EXTEND command lengthens objects to selected boundary lines. This command is useful when your initial design is lengthened or enlarged, and linework representing column lines, fenestration, or piping diagrams needs to be extended to reach the new borders you have set.

You access the EXTEND command by either of these methods:

■ Click the Trim button on the Modify floating toolbar. While holding down the pick button on your digitizer, move the pointer to the second button on the fly-out menu, Extend; then release the pick button.

■ Enter **extend** at the Command: prompt.

The EXTEND command has the following prompts:

- `Select boundary edges: (Projmode = UCS, Edgemode = No extend)`
  `Select objects:` The selection process is similar to that of the TRIM command. First, you select the objects to serve as borders for object lengthening. These objects can be lines, arcs, circles, polylines, or ellipses—so long as they are in the path of the object you want to lengthen. If several borders are in the path of the object to be extended, you must choose the object each time you want to extend it to the next border.

- `<Select object to extend>/Project/Edge/Undo:` Select the objects to lengthen. You can only extend line, polyline, and arc objects. The Project and Edge options are described in the next two prompts. The Undo option restores any lengthened object to its original size.

- `None/Ucs/View <Ucs>:` If you chose the Project option at the preceding prompt, you are now given the option to specify how objects not in the current UCS should be extended to the selected border lines.

- `Extend/No extend <No extend>:` If you chose the Edge option at the `<Select object to extend>/Project/Edge /Undo:` prompt, you are given two options to determine how the border lines behave. The default option, No extend, prevents objects from being extended to meet a border line that it does not actually intersect in space. If you select the Extend option, the border line is extended, temporarily, into infinity. An object that would meet this extended plane—anywhere in model or paper space—can be lengthened to that border.

**13**
**RELEASE**

▶ See "Editing Commands and the Current UCS," p. 840

## Tutorial: Extending Objects

In this tutorial, you use the EXTEND command to lengthen the lines shortened in the preceding tutorial. Follow these steps:

1. Click the Extend button on the Modify floating toolbar.

2. At the `Select boundary edges: (Projmode = UCS, Edgemode = No extend) Select objects:` prompt, select the arc highlighted in figure 10.30 and press Enter.

3. At the `<Select object to extend>/Project/Edge /Undo:` prompt, select the lines that were shortened in the preceding tutorial in figures 10.26 and 10.28, at the ends shown; then press Enter to end the command. Make sure that you select the correct end, or the object will not be extended to the border. Figure 10.31 shows the revised slot.

**III**

**Editing a Drawing**

Leave this drawing open for the next tutorial (using the LENGTHEN command). If you do not plan to try the next tutorial immediately, save your changes and close the drawing file.

**Fig. 10.30**
Arc to be used as the border for the EXTEND command.

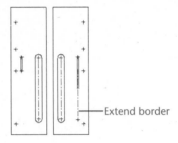

Adjustable Proximity Switch Bracket
Zoom Factor = .5:1

**Fig. 10.31**
Adjustment slot revised with the EXTEND command.

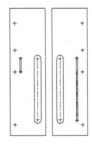

Adjustable Proximity Switch Bracket
Zoom Factor = .5:1

## Changing Object Lengths (LENGTHEN)

◄ See "Interacting with AutoCAD," p. 25

LENGTHEN is a new command added in AutoCAD Release 13. LENGTHEN is used to change the size of objects, both increasing and decreasing their starting or ending points. You can change the size of open lines and polylines, open splines, and the included angle of arcs or ellipses. LENGTHEN does not affect closed objects such as polylines, splines, or ellipses. LENGTHEN is similar to both the TRIM and EXTEND commands. LENGTHEN can be a good alternative to the TRIM and EXTEND commands, especially if you would need to first create construction geometry for cutting planes or border lines, which are required to get the same result using the TRIM or EXTEND commands. Using LENGTHEN, you can change objects by dynamic dragging, specifying a new length as a percentage of the total length or angle, providing an absolute length or angle for an object, or by selecting an incremental length or angle measured from an object's endpoint. LENGTHEN relocates the endpoint closest to the object selection point. To access the LENGTHEN command:

- Click the Resize button on the Modify floating toolbar. While holding down the pick button on your digitizer, move the pointer to the third button on the fly-out menu, Lengthen; then release the pick button.

- At the Command: prompt, type **lengthen** and press Enter.

The LENGTHEN command has the following prompts:

- DElta/Percent/Total/DYnamic/<Select object>: This displays the current length and included angle, if applicable, of the object selected.

  Current length: and Included angle: are the prompts used to report these values. If you choose one of the other options at this prompt, AutoCAD displays additional prompts, no described next.

- Angle/<Enter delta length (0.00)>: Choosing the DElta option at the first prompt displays this prompt. The Delta Length option allows you to change the length of an object by a specified incremental length. If you have used this option before, the previous value will be shown in place of (0.00).

  - Enter delta angle <0.00>: If you chose the Angle option at the preceding prompt, a prompt to enter the delta angle is displayed. The DElta option changes the length of an arc by the angle specified. If you have used this option before, the previous value will be shown in place of <0.00>.

- Enter percent length <100.00>: This prompt is displayed if you chose the Percent option at the first prompt. The Percent option allows you to change the length of a selected object or the angle of a selected arc. By entering a specified percentage, LENGTHEN changes the object's total length or angle. If you have used this option before, the previous percentage will be shown in place of <100.00>.

> **Note**
>
> The value you enter must be positive and nonzero.

**Tip**

The specified length or angle affects the endpoint closest to the point where the object was selected.

**Tip**

If you enter a negative length or angle, the object you select will be reduced in size by the value you entered.

III

■ Angle/<Enter total length (1.00)>: Choosing the Total option at the first prompt displays this prompt. The Total Length option allows you to change the length of an object by entering a total absolute length from the fixed endpoint. If you have used this option before, the previous value will be shown in place of (1.00).

- Enter total angle <57.30>: If you chose the Angle option at the preceding prompt, a prompt to enter the total angle is displayed. The Total option changes the length of an arc to the total angle specified. If you have used this option before, the previous value will be shown in place of <57.30>.

> **Note**
>
> The value you enter must be positive and nonzero.

■ <Select object to change>/Undo: This prompt follows after you have selected one of the previous Lengthen options and entered a value. Selecting an object changes its length by the value you entered. Entering **u** undoes only the most recent change. This prompt continues to repeat until you press Enter to end the command.

■ <Select object to change>/Undo: This prompt also follows if you select the DYnamic option. Selecting an object allows you to enter dynamic dragging mode. The endpoint of the object closest to where you select the object is dragged, while the other endpoint remains fixed. Entering **u** undoes only the most recent change. This prompt continues to repeat until you press Enter to end the command.

### Tutorial: Extending Objects Using LENGTHEN

In this tutorial, you are going to extend the bracket sides to meet the tenon edges made using the OFFSET tutorial; figure 10.32 shows the lines. However, rather than using the EXTEND command to lengthen these lines, use the LENGTHEN command. Follow these steps:

1. Click the Lengthen button on the Modify floating toolbar.

2. At the DElta/Percent/Total/DYnamic/<Select object>: prompt, type **de** and press Enter to select the DElta Lengthen option.

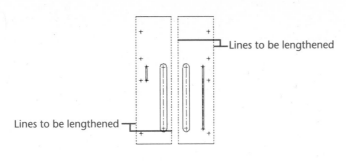

**Fig. 10.32**
Lines to be
lengthened.

Lines to be lengthened

Lines to be lengthened

Adjustable Proximity Switch Bracket
Zoom Factor = .5:1

3. At the `Angle/<Enter delta length (0.00)>:` prompt, type **end** and press Enter to use the endpoint object snap. Select the First point for delta reference, shown in figure 10.33.

4. At the `Second point:` prompt, type **end** and press Enter to use the endpoint object snap again. This time select the Second point for delta reference, shown in figure 10.33. You have now set the delta length value by picking reference points on the drawing.

5. At the `<Select object to change>/Undo:` prompt, select the objects highlighted in figure 10.34. You will have to pick each object twice, at the top and at the bottom. The command repeats until you press Enter.

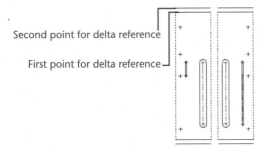

Second point for delta reference

First point for delta reference

**Fig. 10.33**
Reference points
for delta length
value.

Adjustable Proximity Switch Bracket
Zoom Factor = .5:1

6. After you have selected all the objects twice, your drawing should appear like figure 10.34. Then at the prompt `<Select object to change> /Undo:` press Enter to end the command.

Save the drawing file before beginning the next tutorial (using the FILLET command). The changes made during that tutorial will not be saved.

**Fig. 10.34**
The brackets after all the sides have been extended.

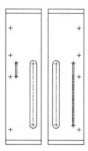

Adjustable Proximity Switch Bracket
Zoom Factor = .5:1

## Filleting Objects (FILLET)

No matter what type of drawing you create, objects must often join at certain points. Wall lines need sharp corners; street designs have curved radii at intersections; and structural drawings have metal assemblies that meet at corners. Each of these applications requires two objects (usually lines, but also arcs, circles, and polylines) to be joined at a corner or using a slight arc. In AutoCAD, the FILLET command performs this function.

To use FILLET, do one of the following:

■ Click and hold the Chamfer button on the Modify floating toolbar. The FILLET command is the second button on the Chamfer fly-out menu; highlight it to execute the command.

■ Enter **fillet** at the Command: prompt.

When you use the FILLET command, you first supply a fillet radius. This value determines how AutoCAD will join the two objects that you select. If you enter a value of zero (0) for the radius, AutoCAD lengthens or shortens the objects to form a sharp corner. If you supply a value larger than zero, the two objects are joined by an arc of the specified radius. If you enter a radius value larger than the distance between the two objects at all points where they might be joined, the FILLET command does not join the selected objects. Figure 10.35 shows examples of objects filleted with different radii.

The FILLET command has the following prompts:

- `Polyline/Radius/Trim/<Select first object>`: Select the first line you want to fillet. If you choose one of the other options at this prompt, AutoCAD displays additional prompts, described shortly.

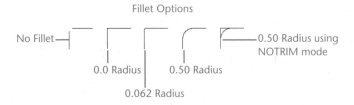

Fillet Options

No Fillet

0.0 Radius

0.062 Radius

0.50 Radius

0.50 Radius using NOTRIM mode

**Fig. 10.35**
Lines edited with different FILLET options.

> **Note**
>
> The default radius value is zero (0). When the default is changed it remains current for all future FILLET commands, until you change the value once again.

> **Note**
>
> If you attempt to fillet two parallel lines, AutoCAD draws a semi-circle to join the two lines at their endpoints. If the endpoints of the lines do not line up, AutoCAD either trims or extends the lines to meet the semi-circle. AutoCAD determines whether to trim or extend based on which object you pick first.

In AutoCAD Release 13, you may fillet a polyline to a line. In previous releases of AutoCAD, you had to explode the polyline before you could fillet it to another object.

**13**
**RELEASE**

**III**

> **Note**
>
> If you use the Polyline option of the FILLET command, the current fillet radius and trim setting are applied to *each* vertex of the selected polyline. If you supply a positive value for the fillet radius, a radius of that size is used at each vertex. If the radius value is too large for some of the vertices, AutoCAD informs you of how many vertices were skipped. To fillet each vertex with different radii, do not select the Polyline option; select each line combination as if they were separate lines.

▶ See "Editing Polyline Vertices (PEDIT Edit Vertices)," p. 592

▶ See "Breaking Blocks Apart (EXPLODE)," p. 697

Editing a Drawing

- ■ `Select second object:` After you select the first object, this prompt appears. Select another object to be joined to the first by an arc.

- ■ `Select polyline:` If you chose the Polyline option at the first prompt, select the polyline object you want to modify. AutoCAD replaces the vertices of the polyline with arcs. Figure 10.36 shows various Fillet options on polylines.

- ■ `Fillet radius <0.0000>:` By choosing the Radius option at the first prompt, this option allows you to define the size of an arc used to join the two objects.

- ■ `Trim/No trim <Trim>:` By choosing the Trim option at the first prompt, this option determines how AutoCAD places the arc between the selected objects. By default, AutoCAD trims the objects back to the starting and ending points of the connecting arc. If you use the No trim option, the objects are not modified; AutoCAD places the arc between them.

**Fig. 10.36**
Polylines filleted with different radius options.

Polyline Fillet Options

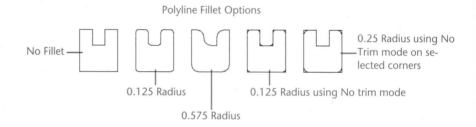

No Fillet

0.25 Radius using No Trim mode on selected corners

0.125 Radius

0.125 Radius using No trim mode

0.575 Radius

> ▶ See "Drawing Polylines (PLINE)," p. 573

---

**Caution**

You can modify the fillet value along a polyline's vertices an infinite number of times, so long as you don't use the BREAK command on the polyline. The fillet arcs along the polyline are temporary, and can be changed or altered at any time. The BREAK command forces the arcs to become permanent parts of the polyline definition, which then cannot be modified by the FILLET command.

---

### Tutorial: Rounding Edges with the FILLET Command

In this tutorial, you use the FILLET command to round the corners of the brackets created and edited in earlier tutorial sections. Follow these steps:

1. Click the Fillet button on the Modify floating toolbar.

**2.** At the `(TRIM mode) Current fillet radius = 0.00 Polyline/Radius/`
`Trim/<Select first object>:` prompt, type **r** to specify the fillet radius.

**3.** At the `Enter fillet radius <0.00>:` prompt, enter **0.375** and press
Enter.

**4.** Press Enter again to reissue the FILLET command. This time at the
`(TRIM mode) Current fillet radius = 0.38 Polyline/Radius/Trim/`
`<Select first object>:` prompt, select one of the lines highlighted in
figure 10.37.

**5.** At the `Select second object:` prompt, select another line that intersects
the first line highlighted in figure 10.37.

**6.** Now repeat steps 4 and 5 for all the other corners highlighted in figure
10.37. The final drawing should appear as shown in figure 10.38.

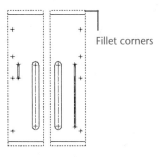

Adjustable Proximity Switch Bracket
Zoom Factor = .5:1

**Fig. 10.37**
The bracket and
selected lines to be
filleted.

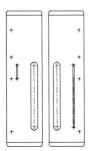

Adjustable Proximity Switch Bracket
Zoom Factor = .5:1

**Fig. 10.38**
The brackets with
rounded corners.

Do not save the changes made to the drawing during this tutorial. If you do not plan to try the next tutorial (using the CHAMFER command) immediately, quit to cancel your changes and close the drawing file. If you are going to continue on to the CHAMFER tutorial, simply reload the drawing 10DWG01 by using the OPEN command. You can also select it from the list of previously opened files, at the bottom of the File pull-down menu. Make sure that you select the No button in response to the Save Changes to C:\UAW13\10DWG01? question dialog box.

## Chamfering Objects (CHAMFER)

Not all objects are joined at corners with arcs. In many disciplines, a line joins two lines, producing a beveled edge. The CHAMFER command produces similar results to the FILLET command, but uses a line rather than an arc to connect two selected objects.

Use either of the following methods to start the CHAMFER command:

- Click the Chamfer button on the Modify floating toolbar. The CHAMFER command is the first button on the Chamfer fly-out menu; highlight it to execute the command.

- Enter **chamfer** at the Command: prompt.

Due to the manner in which it joins two objects, the CHAMFER command needs two distances from the point where the selected objects might meet (see fig. 10.39). AutoCAD uses these distances as the starting and ending points for the bevel used to join the two objects. You also can enter a value of zero to join the selected objects in a sharp corner.

**Fig. 10.39**
The required chamfer distances.

Chamfer Distances

0.500

0.500 ──────Chamfer

The CHAMFER command works with base objects such as lines and arcs as long as the two selected objects meet at a point somewhere in AutoCAD's drawing space. For polylines, the Polyline option in the first CHAMFER prompt applies the chamfer to each vertex along the polyline (where it will fit). Similar to the fillet radii applied to a polyline, the chamfer bevel is a temporary addition to the polyline. You can change the chamfer value at any time, as long as you don't use the BREAK command, and the new bevel value is applied along the polyline.

The CHAMFER command has the following prompts:

- `Polyline/Distances/Angle/Trim/Method/<Select first line>`: This first prompt presents each of the CHAMFER command options. The default method of using the command is to select two objects to be joined by a chamfer line. The following prompts discuss the other options.

- `Enter first chamfer distance <0.0000>`: If you chose the Distances option at the preceding prompt, enter the distance from the joining point to the start of the chamfer line. This prompt is the distance from the joining point to the start of the chamfer for the first selected object.

- `Enter second chamfer distance <0.0000>`: Specify the distance from the joining point to the start of the chamfer for the second selected object.

- `Enter chamfer length on the first line <0.0000>`: If you chose the Angle option at the first prompt, you can define the chamfer line by indicating a starting distance and the angle from the first selected line.

- `Enter chamfer angle from the first line <0.0000>`: This is the angle at which the chamfer line will be drawn, relative to the first selected object. The chamfer line extends to the second selected object at the supplied angle.

- `Trim/No trim <Trim>`: The Trim option defines how AutoCAD places the line between the selected objects. By default, AutoCAD trims the objects back to the starting and ending points of the connecting chamfer line. If you use the No trim option, the objects are not modified, and the line is placed between them.

- `Distance/Angle <Distance>`: If you chose the Method option at the first prompt, you will be able to toggle between the Distance and Angle options. This applies the current chamfer values you have set for either of those options. The default remains set at the last option you used.

**III**

### Tutorial: Creating Chamfers

In this tutorial, you use the CHAMFER command to remove the corners of the brackets that were filleted in the preceding tutorial; figure 10.39 shows the highlighted objects to be chamfered.

1. Open the sample drawing C:\UAW13\10DWG01.

2. Click the Chamfer button on the Modify floating toolbar.

3. At the `(TRIM mode) Current chamfer Dist1 = 0.00, Dist2 = 0.00 Polyline/Distance/Angle/Trim/Method/<Select first object>`: prompt, type **d** to specify the chamfer distances.

4. At the `Enter first chamfer distance <0.00>:` prompt, enter **0.25** and press Enter.

5. At the `Enter second chamfer distance <0.25>:` prompt, press Enter to accept the default value.

6. Press Enter again to reissue the CHAMFER command. This time at the `(TRIM mode) Current chamfer Dist1 = 0.25, Dist2 = 0.25 Polyline/ Distance/Angle/Trim/Method/<Select first object>:` prompt, select one of the lines highlighted in figure 10.40.

7. At the `Select second line:` prompt, select another line that intersects the first line highlighted in figure 10.40 that creates the corner to be chamfered.

8. Now repeat steps 6 and 7 for all the other corners highlighted in figure 10.40. The final drawing should appear as shown in figure 10.41.

**Fig. 10.40**
The starting brackets and the corners to chamfer.

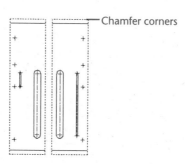

Adjustable Proximity Switch Bracket
Zoom Factor = .5:1

**Fig. 10.41**
The brackets with corners chamfered.

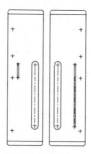

Adjustable Proximity Switch Bracket
Zoom Factor = .5:1

Leave this drawing open for the next tutorial. If you do not plan to try the next tutorial (using the UNDO and REDO commands) immediately, save your changes and close the drawing file.

# Undoing Your Work (UNDO, REDO)

Everyone makes mistakes; it's part of the process of learning. Even if mistakes are costly, they usually teach you a valuable lesson. When using any CAD package, lessons such as "Always have a backup of the file," and "Always save the drawing when you leave your computer" are often learned the hard way—once. But you never forget them after that.

When working in the drawing editor, AutoCAD is forgiving of the mistakes you make. An earlier section of this chapter discussed the OOPS command, which allows you to restore the last set of erased objects. Sometimes, though, even OOPS isn't enough. You may need to reverse the last ten drawing commands because a simple mistake made earlier caused radical changes as you continued drawing. Or the objects you deleted five ERASE commands ago are what you really need now. The OOPS command can't help you in this situation, but the UNDO command can.

As long as you do not quit or end the drawing, UNDO stores information about each type of editing and drawing modification you perform while editing the current drawing. With this command, you can step back through each of the previous commands to a point where you made your initial mistake, even if you have saved the drawing during the current editing session. You then can start editing your drawing again, avoiding the mistake.

> **Note**
>
> Some AutoCAD commands can't be undone. For a complete listing, refer to the online UNDO help file.

In addition to the UNDO command, AutoCAD offers the REDO command. This command allows you to "step forward" in the chain of commands reversed when you used the UNDO command.

To run UNDO and REDO, use these methods:

- In the Standard toolbar, the button with the counterclockwise arrow is Undo, and the button with the clockwise arrow is Redo.

- Enter **undo** at the Command: prompt.

**III**

**Editing a Drawing**

■ Enter **u** at the Command: prompt.

The U command is a single-use version of the UNDO command. It has no command-line options, and it backs up one command at a time in the series of commands used since starting the editing session. The UNDO command, which is the full-featured version, has several options for working back through the commands you've used.

■ Enter **redo** at the Command: prompt.

The REDO command has no options, and only works if the last command executed was U or UNDO; if another command is issued between UNDO and REDO, REDO will not work. Also, if you issue two or more consecutive U or UNDO commands, REDO will only work on the last U or UNDO.

The UNDO command has one prompt:

```
Auto/Control/BEgin/End/Mark/Back/<Number>:
```

The following list describes these options:

■ *Auto.* Menu choices may have several commands that perform an action, all of which can be reversed with a single UNDO command, if Auto is set to ON. If the Auto option is set to OFF, each individual step in a menu choice is recognized by the UNDO command.

■ *Control.* To reverse changes you have made to the drawing, AutoCAD maintains a secondary file with information about the state of the drawing prior to each command you enter. The storage of this information can cause your hard disk to fill up, which precludes you from performing any editing. The Control option allows you to determine how much undo information you want to maintain at any time, All/None/One <All>. By default, the UNDO command maintains information on all operations. Changing the setting to None disables the UNDO command entirely; the One option saves data for a single undo operation at a time.

■ *BEgin.* The BEgin option allows you to define a series of drawing and/or editing actions to be treated as a group by the UNDO command. When the UNDO command encounters this group definition, it reverses all the actions defined by the BEgin and End definition at one time.

■ *End.* The End option works with the BEgin option to define an end to a group of drawing and/or editing commands that will be acted on as a single command by UNDO.

> **Note**
>
> AutoCAD refers to a sequence of commands marked by BEgin and End as a *group*. When one of these sequences is encountered by UNDO, it will be referred to as GROUP at the Command: prompt.

■ *Mark.* The Mark option, which works with the Back option, allows you to define points in the editing session where you may want to return when using the UNDO command. This is often a handy option for testing a series of edits. If the results aren't what you wanted, use UNDO with the Back option to go back to the point where you set the original mark.

■ *Back.* The Back option works together with the Mark option to return the drawing to its original state at a selected point. If the Mark option has not been used, this option undoes all modifications made to the drawing since it was originally opened.

■ *Number.* This option defines how many commands you want to step back through. By default, UNDO steps back a single command at a time. If you know exactly how many commands have elapsed and need to be reversed, you can enter that number.

## Tutorial: Working with UNDO and REDO

In this tutorial, you use the UNDO and REDO commands to work backward and forward through edits you are going to perform in this tutorial. Figure 10.42 shows the drawing that starts this tutorial.

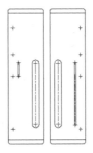

Adjustable Proximity Switch Bracket
Zoom Factor = .5:1

**Fig. 10.42**
The initial drawing.

III

Editing a Drawing

1. At the Command: prompt, type **undo** and press Enter.

2. Now specify the beginning of this exercise by using the Mark option. At the Auto/Control/BEgin/End/Mark/Back/<Number>:prompt, type **M**.

   Now you are ready to do some editing that can be undone.

3. Erase the highlighted objects in figure 10.43.

4. Click the Undo button on the Standard toolbar until all the erased objects have returned.

   The drawing should now look as it did before you started this tutorial.

**Tip**
If you erased the objects by issuing several ERASE commands, you will have to click Undo the same number of times to return all the objects.

5. At the Command: prompt, type **undo** and press Enter.

6. Specify the beginning of a GROUP edit by using the BEgin option. At the Auto/Control/BEgin/End/Mark/Back/<Number>:prompt, type **BE**.

7. Erase each of the highlighted objects in figure 10.43 again, only this time perform an ERASE command for each individual object.

8. Next draw several objects, such as lines or circles.

9. At the Command: prompt, type **undo** and press Enter.

10. At the Auto/Control/BEgin/End/Mark/Back/<Number>: prompt, type **E** to end the group edit.

11. At the Command: prompt, press Enter to reissue the UNDO command.

12. At the Auto/Control/BEgin/End/Mark/Back/<Number>: prompt, type **1** to undo the previous group edit. Your drawing should once again appear as it did in figure 10.42, when you started the tutorial.

13. At the Command: prompt, type **redo** and press Enter.

    This step removes the bracket objects; it also restores the objects that you created.

14. You are now ready to conclude this tutorial, at the Command: prompt, type **undo** and press Enter.

15. At the Auto/Control/BEgin/End/Mark/Back/<Number>: prompt, type **B** and press Enter.

    This step reverses all the editing changes you made in the tutorial, and returns the drawing to its original state at the time you set the undo marker.

> **Note**
>
> Notice the commands listed under the `Auto/Control/BEgin/End/Mark/Back/ <Number>:` prompt. These are all the commands that were issued during this tutorial.

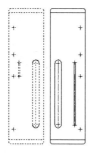

Adjustable Proximity Switch Bracket
Zoom Factor = .5:1

**Fig. 10.43**
Objects to be erased.

End this drawing for now, saving your changes. You will come back to it later in the chapter.

# Removing Unwanted Objects (PURGE)

As you continue working on a drawing, it can become cluttered with extra layers, linetypes, text styles, and block definitions that you created but no longer need. Having extra objects in the drawing enlarges the size of the drawing file and increases the time needed to load the drawing into AutoCAD. The PURGE command can be used to remove unwanted named objects from a drawing.

> **Note**
>
> You can purge the drawing *at any time* during the drawing session. This is a significant drawing management enhancement. It is now possible to keep drawing sizes and REGEN times to a minimum during the current editing session.

The PURGE command can remove the following objects from a drawing:

- Layers (LAyers)
- Linetypes (LTypes)

- Text Styles (STyles)

- Dimension Styles (Dimstyles)

- Shapes (SHapes)

- Blocks

- Application IDs (APpids)

- Mlinestyles

▶ See "Writing
Blocks to a File
(WBLOCK),"
p. 687

To access the PURGE command, type **purge** at the Command: prompt. AutoCAD allows you to specify the type of objects you want to delete. Normally, you should select the All option to clear everything you don't need. PURGE only removes named objects that aren't used in the drawing. Additionally, AutoCAD prompts you for confirmation before deleting any objects.

## Tutorial: Purging Unwanted Objects

In this tutorial, you use the PURGE command to remove unwanted named objects from the sample drawing C:\UAW13\10DWG02. Because PURGE does not have a graphical effect on the drawing screen, this tutorial shows you the text screen, listing the objects AutoCAD removes using the PURGE command. For your reference, figure 10.44 shows the drawing used in the tutorial.

1. Open the sample drawing C:\UAW13\10DWG02.

**Fig. 10.44**
Drawing to be
purged.

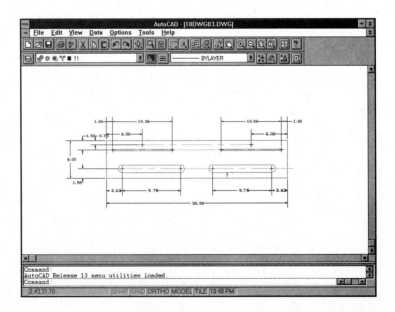

2.  At the `Command:` prompt, type **purge** and press Enter.

3.  At the `Purge unused Blocks/Dimstyles/LAyers/LTypes/SHapes/STyles/APpids/Mlinestyles/All:` prompt, type **a** and press Enter to PURGE All named objects.

4.  When AutoCAD responds with the `Purge block REVOUT? <N>` prompt, type **y**. This is the response AutoCAD provides to inform the user that an unused object has been found. Continue responding with **y** to the remaining prompts. You can see in figure 10.45 how the text screen looks after you have completed purging one level of unused objects.

> **Note**
>
> If AutoCAD does not find any unused named objects, it responds with the prompt `No unreferenced linetypes found`.

```
                        AutoCAD Text Window
 Edit
Purge block *D9? <N> y
Purge block *D10? <N> y
Purge block *D11? <N> y
Purge block *D18? <N> y
Purge block *D20? <N> y
Purge block *D21? <N> y
Purge block *D22? <N> y
Purge block *D23? <N> y
Purge block *D24? <N> y
Purge block *D25? <N> y
Purge block *D26? <N> y
Purge block *D29? <N> y
Purge block *D34? <N> y
Purge layer REPLOT? <N> y
Purge layer MESSAGES? <N> y
Purge layer TEMP? <N> y
Purge layer 31? <N> y
Purge layer 51? <N> y
Purge layer 61? <N> y
Purge layer 71? <N> y
Purge layer 81? <N> y
Purge layer 91? <N> y
Purge layer D1? <N> y
Purge linetype DIVIDE? <N> y

No unreferenced text styles found.
Purge shape file SIMPLEX? <N> y
Purge shape file scriptc? <N> y

No unreferenced views found.

No unreferenced UCSs found.

No unreferenced viewport configurations found.

No unreferenced appids found.

No unreferenced dimension styles found.

No unreferenced mlinestyles found.

Command:
```

**Fig. 10.45**
First level of objects purged from the drawing.

III

Editing a Drawing

> **Note**
>
> Many times unused objects will be *nested* several levels deep in the AutoCAD database. To remove them, you must repeat the PURGE command several times. With AutoCAD Release 13, you now can repeat the PURGE command several times in an editing session, which allows you to remove these levels in one session.

**13**
**RELEASE**

**5.** Repeat steps 1 through 3, until no more unused objects are in the drawing. Refer to figure 10.46 to see how the AutoCAD text screen appears as you remove additional object levels.

**Fig. 10.46**
Second level of
objects purged
from the drawing.

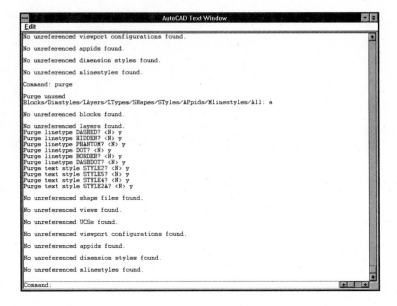

```
                        AutoCAD Text Window
 Edit
No unreferenced viewport configurations found.

No unreferenced appids found.

No unreferenced dimension styles found.

No unreferenced mlinestyles found.

Command: purge

Purge unused
Blocks/Dimstyles/LAyers/LTypes/SHapes/STyles/APpids/Mlinestyles/All: a

No unreferenced blocks found.

No unreferenced layers found.
Purge linetype DASHED? <N> y
Purge linetype HIDDEN? <N> y
Purge linetype PHANTOM? <N> y
Purge linetype DOT? <N> y
Purge linetype BORDER? <N> y
Purge linetype DASHDOT? <N> y
Purge text style STYLE2? <N> y
Purge text style STYLE5? <N> y
Purge text style STYLE4? <N> y
Purge text style STYLE2A? <N> y

No unreferenced shape files found.

No unreferenced views found.

No unreferenced UCSs found.

No unreferenced viewport configurations found.

No unreferenced appids found.

No unreferenced dimension styles found.

No unreferenced mlinestyles found.

Command:
```

This drawing is not used for any other tutorials. You should QUIT, to cancel the changes and save this drawing for future reference.

# Producing Arrays of Objects (ARRAY)

Repetition of drawing elements appears everywhere you look—a series of post-office boxes, the structural column grid for a warehouse, the mounting hole pattern for a part, even a series of columns surrounding a dome. Repetition is one of the reasons that CAD is so beneficial. When you draw an element once and use a command such as COPY to reproduce the element, the subsequent copies of the element are identical. Although the COPY command can make multiple copies of any element, if the copies have an offset in both horizontal and vertical directions, or you need to rotate multiple copies about a central point, the ARRAY command is much faster.

You access the ARRAY command by either of these methods:

   ■ Click the Copy Object button on the Modify floating toolbar. You have the option of selecting either a Rectangular Array or Polar Array from the fly-out menu. While holding down the pick button on your digitizer, move the pointer to the fifth (Rectangular Array) or sixth button (Polar Array) of the fly-out menu and release the pick button.

■ Enter **array** at the Command: prompt.

You can create two types of arrays with the ARRAY command: rectangular arrays and polar arrays. The following sections discuss how to create each type of array.

## Rectangular Arrays

A *rectangular array* duplicates objects along a grid pattern. After selecting the objects you want to duplicate and specifying that you want to create a rectangular array, you indicate how many rows and columns will make up the duplication grid. The currently selected objects are always the first row and column of the array; the number you specify must also provide for the additional rows and columns you require. Then you must supply the offset distances for the rows and columns. These distances can be entered by typing values at the Command: prompt, or graphically selecting points on the screen.

The ARRAY command has the following prompts when creating rectangular arrays:

■ Select objects: Select the objects you want to duplicate.

■ Rectangular or Polar array (R/P) <R>: This option determines whether you will create a rectangular or polar array. Rectangular is the original default. The last type of array you perform will become the new default. If you select Rectangular or Polar specifically off the toolbar, AutoCAD automatically selects the desired option.

■ Number of rows (---) <1>: Specify the number of horizontal grid elements to be used to create the array.

■ Number of columns (¦¦¦) <1>: Indicate the number of vertical grid elements to be used to create the array.

After you define the grid size, AutoCAD asks for the distance between each row and column. Positive values for each of the following prompts duplicates the selected objects above and to the right. If you enter negative values, the duplicates appear below and to the left of the original objects.

■ Unit cell or distance between rows (---): This is the distance between each horizontal grid element. This includes the width of the element being duplicated.

◀ See "Using the Drawing Aids Dialog Box (DDRMODES)," p. 56

■ `Distance between columns (┊┊┊)`: This is the distance between each vertical grid element. This includes the height of the element being duplicated.

> ### Note
>
> You can create rectangular arrays only at right angles to the current coordinate system. To create an array that is rotated, change the snap angle of the crosshairs using the DDRMODES command.

### Tutorial: Duplicating Elements in a Grid Format

In this tutorial, you use the RECTANGULAR ARRAY command to copy the bottom mounting hole on the left bracket. You will copy the hole and centerlines up the outside edge of both brackets. The drawing that you have been editing has been modified to remove the original mounting holes. For this tutorial, use sample drawing C:\UAW13\10DWG03. The initial drawing is shown in figure 10.47; figure 10.48 shows the brackets after the holes have been duplicated.

**Fig. 10.47**
Hole to be duplicated using the RECTANGULAR ARRAY command.

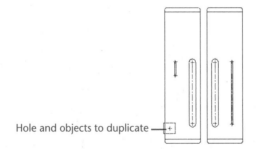

Hole and objects to duplicate ——

Adjustable Proximity Switch Bracket
Zoom Factor = .5:1

1. Open the sample drawing C:\UAW13\10DWG03.

2. Click the Rectangular Array button on the Modify floating toolbar.

3. At the `Select objects:` prompt, select the hole and centerlines highlighted in figure 10.47 and press Enter to end the selection process.

4. The `Rectangular or Polar array (R/P) <R>:` `_r` prompt defaults automatically to Rectangular when you select the Rectangular Array button from the toolbar.

5. At the `Number of rows (---) <1>:` prompt, type **4** and press Enter for the number of rows to copy.

6. At the `Number of columns (¦¦¦) <1>:` prompt, type **2** and press Enter for the number of columns to create.

7. At the `Unit cell or distance between rows (---):` prompt, enter a value of **6.50**. This value is the distance between each row in the grid.

8. At the `Distance between columns (¦¦¦):` prompt, type in **12.91** and press Enter. This value represents the distance between each column in the grid.

AutoCAD duplicates the holes and centerlines, as shown in figure 10.48.

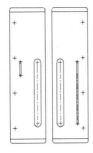

Adjustable Proximity Switch Bracket
Zoom Factor = .5:1

**Fig. 10.48**
Brackets after holes have been copied using a Rectangular Array.

This drawing is not used for any other tutorials. You should QUIT to cancel the changes and save this drawing for future reference.

## Polar Arrays

Whereas rectangular arrays are created in a grid pattern, *polar arrays* duplicate the selected objects in a circular pattern. The ARRAY command has the following prompts when creating polar arrays:

- `Select objects:` Select the objects you want to duplicate in a circular pattern.

- `Rectangular or Polar array (R/P) <R>:` Choose P to create a polar array. If you select the Polar Array tool from the toolbar, AutoCAD automatically selects the Polar option.

- `Center point of array:` This is the center point about which AutoCAD copies the objects. The nearer the point is to the selected objects, the smaller the radius through which the objects are copied.

- ■ `Number of items:` This is the total number of copies you want to create. This number must include the original set of objects you are dupli-cating.

- ■ `Angle to fill (+=ccw, -=cw) <360>:` You determine through how much of the circle the copied objects will be distributed. By default, this is typically a full circle, 360 degrees. You also can supply a smaller angle. If you enter a value of 0, you can supply the amount of separation (in degrees) between each duplicate. You can enter this separation as either a positive angle (+=ccw), which copies the objects counterclockwise; or as a negative angle (-=cw), which copies the objects in a clockwise direction.

  After you specify the angle, AutoCAD calculates where each copy should appear and draws it.

- ■ `Rotate objects as they are copied? <Y>:` Here you indicate whether you want AutoCAD to rotate the duplicates as they are copied around the circle. If you choose **Y**, each copy is rotated so that its features are orientated toward the center of the array at the calculated angular off-set. Answering **N** simply copies the objects around the circle, using the calculated angular offset.

### Tutorial: Duplicating Elements in a Circular Format

In this tutorial, you use the Polar option of the ARRAY command to copy timbers, used to frame a gazebo roof, in a circular array. For this tutorial, you use sample drawing C:\UAW13\10DWG04. The initial drawing is shown in figure 10.49; figure 10.50 shows the timbers copied in the circular format.

**Fig. 10.49**
Timbers to be duplicated using the Polar ARRAY command.

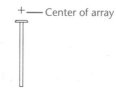

1. Open the sample drawing C:\UAW13\10DWG04.

2. Click the Polar Array button on the Modify floating toolbar.

3. At the `Select objects:` prompt, select the two timbers shown in figure 10.49 and press Enter to end the selection process.

4. The `Rectangular or Polar array (R/P) <R>:` _p prompt defaults auto-matically to Polar when you select the Polar Array button from the toolbar.

5. At the Center point of array: prompt, enter **int** to use the INTersect object snap to pick the intersection of the crosshairs provided as a reference point as shown in figure 10.49.

6. At the Number of items: prompt, type **6** and press Enter for the number of copies to create.

7. At the Angle to fill (+=ccw, -=cw) <360>: prompt, press Enter to accept the default value.

8. At the Rotate objects as they are copied? <Y> prompt, press Enter to accept the default option.

AutoCAD duplicates the timbers around the center point, as shown in figure 10.50.

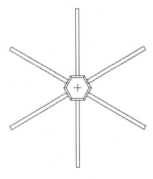

**Fig. 10.50**
Timbers copied using a Polar Array.

This drawing is not used for any other tutorials. You should QUIT to cancel the changes and save this drawing for future reference.

# From Here...

For more information about editing and modifying objects, see the following chapters:

■ Chapter 11, "Editing with Grips," shows you how to use many of the commands covered in this chapter in a manner more typical of other Windows applications.

■ Chapter 16, "Working with Text," presents editing tools and concepts to work with text.

- Chapter 21, "Modifying Object Characteristics," explains how to change the properties of AutoCAD objects.

- Chapter 29, "3D Editing Essentials," explains the commands necessary to edit in the 3D world.

# On Your Own

In this tutorial, you use the commands introduced in this chapter to merge the two separate brackets that you have been editing into one bracket. Space the outside mounting holes 3.0" in from the top and bottom. Space the remaining holes 6.0" apart. Make both sets of slots symmetrical. Figure 10.51 shows the bracket as it was lasted edited and figure 10.52 represents the finished bracket.

**Fig. 10.51**

Individual brackets, as last edited.

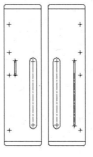

Adjustable Proximity Switch Bracket
Zoom Factor = .5:1

**Fig. 10.52**

Completed Proximity Switch Bracket.

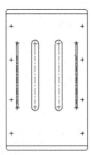

Adjustable Proximity Switch Bracket
Zoom Factor = .5:1

Hints:

1. Use the ERASE command to remove duplicate objects.

2. Use the EXTEND and STRETCH commands to lengthen existing objects.

3. Use the MOVE command to relocate objects.

4. Use the MIRROR command to make the slots and holes symmetrical.

5. Use the ARRAY command to duplicate the holes.

6. Do not forget to use object snaps and point filters to make alignments accurate and easier.

# Chapter 11

# Editing with Grips

Editing a drawing is a very common practice when using AutoCAD. Moving, copying, and rotating objects are just some of the common editing functions you use when working on your drawing. The grips function offers a convenient way to edit objects in AutoCAD. In this chapter, you learn how to

- Turn on grips and set grip options
- Stretch objects with grips
- Move objects with grips
- Rotate objects with grips
- Scale objects with grips
- Mirror objects with grips
- Copy objects with grips

If you use manual drafting techniques, it can take hours or sometimes even days to modify and edit a drawing. Using AutoCAD makes these same editing tasks simpler and quicker. In Chapter 10, "Editing Techniques," you learned how to perform a variety of editing tasks such as move, copy, stretch, rotate, mirror, and scale.

Grips provide one of the quickest methods for performing many of the editing tasks you learned about in Chapter 10. Understanding and using grips is an important skill that you need to develop to become proficient with AutoCAD.

# What Are Grips?

*Grips* are small squares or boxes that appear at specific locations on an object after the object is selected. After an object is selected with grips, you can perform several different grip functions on the object. The grip modes include stretch, move, rotate, scale, and mirror.

By default, grips are turned on in AutoCAD. A simple way to check if grips are turned on is to select an object while the AutoCAD Command: prompt is displayed. If small squares (grips) appear on the object, grips are enabled.

> **Note**
>
> The small pickbox on the AutoCAD crosshairs does not necessarily mean that grips are enabled. The cursor pickbox also indicates that the pick first, or noun/verb, selection is enabled.

◀ See "Pick-First Selection versus Pick-After Selection," p. 215

## Turning on Grips

When using grips, you select the objects first and then issue the appropriate grip mode. This is called *noun/verb*, or *pick first*, *selection*. For more information, see Chapter 9, "Understanding Selection Sets," which discusses two methods for selecting objects in AutoCAD.

In the first method, you issue a command and then select the objects. The objects are selected in response to the command's prompts. This method is called verb/noun, or pick after, selection. It is called verb/noun selection because you specify the verb action or command, such as ERASE, *before* you specify the objects to which you want to apply the action.

In the second method for selecting objects, you select the objects *before* you issue the command. This method is called noun/verb, or pick first, selection. With this selection method, the objects are identified *before* you specify the verb action or command, such as ERASE.

Grips can work in conjunction with noun/verb (pick first) selection. By default, noun/verb selection is enabled in AutoCAD. The PICKFIRST system variable controls the method of object selection. This is saved as part of the configuration, which means that after it's turned off, it will remain turned off for all subsequent drawings until it is turned on again. You can change the PICKFIRST system variable by doing any of the following:

■ Enter **pickfirst** at the Command: prompt and enter the new value.

- Access the Object Selection Settings dialog box shown in figure 11.1. This can be done by entering **ddselect** at the Command: prompt. The Noun/Verb Selection check box will change the setting of the PICKFIRST system variable.

- Access the Object Selection Settings dialog box by choosing Selection from the Options menu and change the setting in the Noun/Verb Selection check box.

▶ See "System Variables Reference," p. 1147

◀ See "Editing Techniques," p. 239

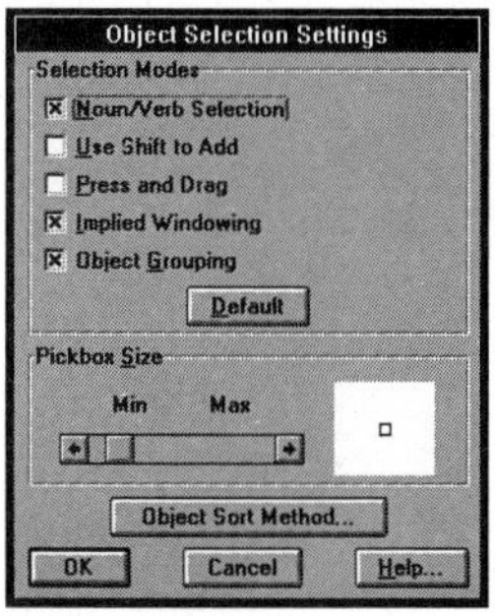

**Fig. 11.1**
The Object Selection Settings dialog box governs the enabling of noun/verb object selection.

## Selecting Objects with Grips

With Grips enabled and the Command: prompt displayed, you can use any object selection method to make grips appear on the object. One method used to select an object is to place the crosshairs directly on the object.

Alternatively, you can invoke the implied selection (AUTO selection) method. As described in Chapter 9, "Understanding Selection Sets," when using the implied selection method you do not pick directly on the object but rather define a window. By specifying the second window point to the left of the first window point, you create a window. Everything *totally enclosed* by the window is selected. By placing the second window point to the right of the first window point, you create a crossing window. Anything *touching* the window is selected.

When an object is selected using grips, boxes appear at specific locations on the object, as shown in figure 11.2. Grips allow the user to modify the selected object by moving one or several grips together, in combination with one of the five grip modes.

◀ See "Selecting Objects," p. 217

Initially, grips appear as hollow blue boxes. This type of grip is called a *warm grip*. Grips are always warm first, with the object's grips displayed in blue (default color) and the object highlighted. After an object is selected and its grips appear, you have two options. One option is to invoke one of the grip

**III**

**Editing a Drawing**

modes. The other option is to select multiple grips on the objects. When a grip is selected for editing with the cursor, the grip becomes a solid red box (default color) and is called a *hot grip*. The blue and red colors are defaults, and can be changed. See "Setting Grips Options" later in this chapter for more information on how to set the grip colors.

**Fig. 11.2**
Grips displayed on several AutoCAD objects.

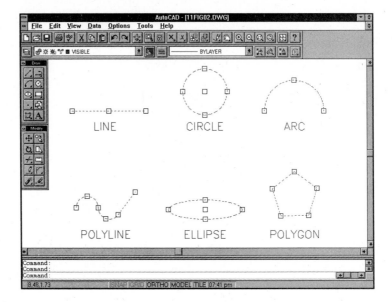

To select a single grip and invoke the grip modes, place the cursor on the grip and click the Pick button. The cursor will automatically snap to the exact center location of the grip and the grip will turn red. The stretch grip mode is the first grip editing mode invoked.

You also can enable multiple objects with grips to create a selection set. Creating a selection set and editing objects with multiple grips is a two-step procedure:

1. Select the objects you need to include in the selection set to enable the warm grips. The grips will appear blue and all of the objects selected will appear highlighted.

2. Select a single grip. The selected grip will be changed to hot (default red color). A hot grip is the default base point used for the editing action. The base point may be defined as the reference point that will be used for subsequent grip modes. When a hot grip exists, a different series of prompts appear in place of the Command: prompt. A grip must be changed to hot before the editing options appear.

You can also select multiple hot grips, each on a different object. Two or more grips can be made hot at the same time by pressing Shift while selecting each grip.

You also can remove an object from the selection set. This is done by pressing the Shift key and selecting a highlighted object that has warm grips. The object's grips are now called *cold grips*. Cold grips are created when you deselect a highlighted object that has warm grips. Even though an object containing cold grips is not included in the selection set, you can still select a grip on the object to use as the base point for the editing action. Selecting a grip on a deselected (unhighlighted) object to use as a base point does not turn red, however. Table 11.1 and figure 11.3 summarize the three grip states:

**Table 11.1   Summary of Hot, Warm, and Cold Grip States**

| Grip State | Grip Color | Object State | Grip Explanation |
|---|---|---|---|
| Cold | Blue Grips | Unhighlighted object | The object is not part of the selection set. A cold grip can be snapped to or used as an alternate base point. A grip is made cold by deselecting a highlighted object that has warm grips. |
| Warm | Blue Grips | Highlighted object | The object is included in the selection set. A grip is always warm first. |
| Hot | Red Grips | Highlighted object | The object is included in the selection set. A hot grip is used as the base point, or control point, for the editing action. A grip is made hot by selecting a warm grip. More than one grip can be hot at one time. This is done by pressing the Shift key while selecting each grip. |

**Note**

You can only select multiple grips when AutoCAD is displaying the Command: prompt and you hold down the Shift key when selecting the first grip. Once the grip mode is active, you can't select any more grips as "hot" grips, although you can select any grip as a response to a grip mode prompt.

III

Editing a Drawing

**Fig. 11.3**

Grips have three
states: warm, hot,
and cold.

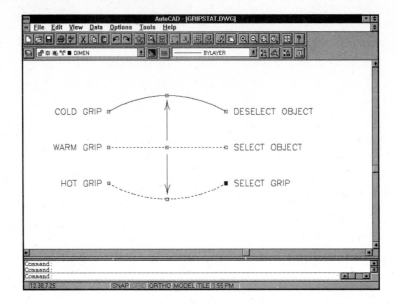

To deselect all objects and remove their grips, press the Esc key twice.
The first press removes the objects from the selection set. The second press
removes all grips. The REDRAW and REGEN commands don't have any effect
on displayed grips.

To change a specific object's grip status (change it from warm/highlighted to
cold/unhighlighted), pick the object while holding down the Shift key. Picking the same object a second time while holding down the Shift key will
remove the object's grips.

---

### Troubleshooting

*Which editing method is best to use, grips or the more traditional verb/noun (pick after)
method?*

Unfortunately, no hard and fast rules exist to help you choose between the two
editing methods. In some situations, grips can provide you with a better editing
method. In other situations, the more traditional verb/noun method (type in the
editing command first, and then select the objects) works best. The more you work
with AutoCAD, the easier it will be to determine which editing method will work best
for each application.

If you start editing with a method that doesn't allow you to modify the objects as you
need, you can always use the UNDO command. You also can deselect the Noun/
Verb Selection check box in the Object Selection dialog box by typing **ddselect** at
the Command: prompt. You can also access the Object Selection dialog box by picking Selection from the Options pull-down menu.

## Tutorial: Selecting Single and Multiple Grips

In this and the following chapter tutorials, you will use grips to modify the drawing of the gear shown in figure 11.4. Begin by opening an existing drawing.

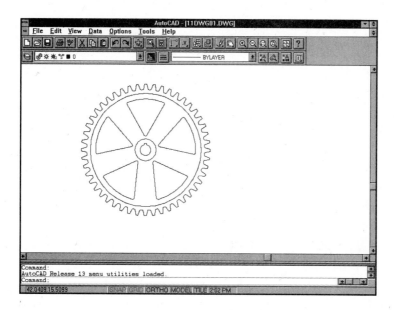

**Fig. 11.4**
The gear drawing to be modified.

In the following tutorial you will use grips to modify the gear drawing.

1. Select the Open button from the Standard toolbar. If the AutoCAD Save Changes dialog box appears, select No unless you want to save the current drawing. If you want to save the current drawing, select Yes and enter a path and drawing name.

   When the Select File dialog box appears, change to the UAW13 subdirectory, and load the 11DWG01 file.

   After the file is loaded, your screen should resemble figure 11.4.

2. Select the circle, as shown in figure 11.5.

   The circle becomes highlighted and the grips appear (see fig. 11.6).

   You have just made a single selection.

   To make a multiple selection, click any other object and notice that the grips will appear on that object as well.

**III**

**Editing a Drawing**

**Fig. 11.5**
Select the inner
circle.

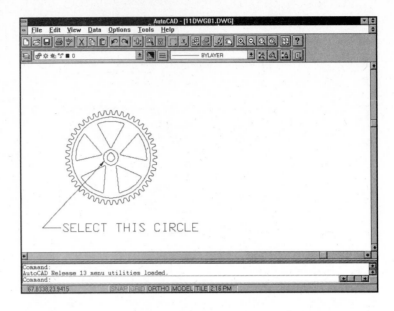

**Fig. 11.6**
The highlighted
circle showing the
grips.

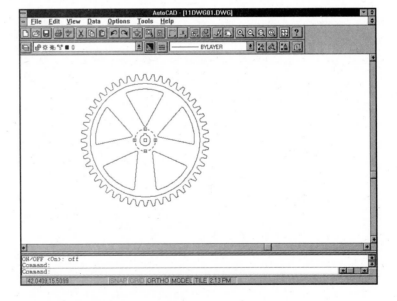

The next tutorial will continue from here.

# Setting Grips Options

The Grips dialog box, shown in figure 11.7, can be used to change several
grip characteristics. In this dialog box, you can turn the grips on and off, set

the grip size, and specify the colors to be used for selected and unselected grips. You can access the Grips dialog box by doing either of the following:

- Enter **ddgrips** at the Command: prompt.

- Choose <u>O</u>ptions, <u>G</u>rips.

**Fig. 11.7**
The Grips dialog box can be used to change many of the grip features.

If you deselect the <u>E</u>nable Grips check box in the Grips dialog box, grips will not appear when you select objects. This can be useful if you do not want to use the grip modes on the selection set.

Grip colors can be changed by selecting the <u>U</u>nselected or <u>S</u>elected buttons. Choosing either box will invoke the Select Color dialog box (see fig. 11.8). This will change the color of the grips on objects.

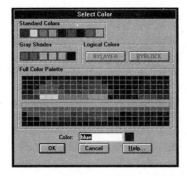

**Fig. 11.8**
The Select Color dialog box can be used to change the unselected and selected grip colors.

You also can change grip size in the <u>G</u>rip Size area of the Grips dialog box. This allows you to change the size of the pickbox located at the intersection of the crosshair. To change the grip size, move the slider bar back and forth. You can also change the size of the pickbox by changing the system variable PICKBOX.

**III**

**Editing a Drawing**

The settings for grips are stored in several system variables. All of these variables are saved in the configuration—not in the individual drawings. Table 11.2 lists the system variables and their corresponding use:

| Table 11.2 Grips System Variables and Their Uses | |
|---|---|
| **System Variable** | **System Variable Settings** |
| GRIPBLOCK | By default (color 0), assigns grips only to the insertion point of blocks |
| GRIPCOLOR | By default, blue (color 5) is assigned to nonselected grips |
| GRIPHOT | By default, red (color 1) is assigned to selected grips |
| GRIPS | By default (1), grips are enabled |
| GRIPSIZE | By default (3), the height of the grip boxes in pixels |

## Tutorial: Setting Grip Options

In this tutorial, which is a continuation of the previous tutorial, you use the Grips dialog box to change the Grip options settings.

1. Choose Options, Grips.

    The Grips dialog box appears (refer to fig. 11.7).

2. Change the unselected grip color to yellow. In the Grip Size area of the Grips dialog box, double-click the right arrow on the slider bar to increase the size of the grips. Choose OK to accept the changes.

3. When bringing up the Grips dialog box, all previously displayed grips are cleared. You must reselect the circle seen earlier in figure 11.6. Notice that the grip colors and sizes have now been changed.

4. Open the Grips dialog box and change the grip settings back to the defaults (refer to fig. 11.7). The Unselected grip color should be blue, and the Grip size should be approximately the same size as shown in figure 11.7.

    The next tutorial continues from here.

## Editing Blocks with Grips

AutoCAD has a command called BLOCK that allows you to define a group of objects as a single object. Once defined, these symbols, or *blocks,* can be inserted into a drawing full-size, scaled, or rotated. Blocks are discussed in Chapter 23, "Using Symbols and XRefs."

AutoCAD recognizes a block as a single object, regardless of the number of objects it contains. For this reason, blocks usually display only one grip. This single grip is located at the block's insertion point.

AutoCAD has the system variable called GRIPBLOCK to control the method of displaying grips within a block. By default, GRIPBLOCK is 0, meaning off. When it is turned on, all objects within the block display grips as if they are individual objects. This is useful when you want to edit a block using a base point other than the block's insertion point. To change the GRIPBLOCK system variable, do either of the following:

■ Enter **gripblock** at the Command: prompt. AutoCAD will respond with New value for GRIPBLOCK <0>:. The default value is 0, for off. Entering **1** will turn GRIPBLOCK on.

■ Invoke the Grips dialog box and select the Enable Grips Within <u>B</u>locks check box.

# Using the Grip Modes

When you pick a grip and it becomes active (hot), the grip changes color. If you pick a grip without pressing the Shift key, AutoCAD enters the *stretch grip mode*. The stretch grip mode can be used to stretch selected objects based on the selected grip. Pressing Shift while selecting your first grip allows you to select multiple grips.

The stretch mode is one of five grip modes. The grip modes include:

■ *Stretch.* This grip mode allows you to stretch objects. It is similar to the STRETCH command.

■ *Move.* With this grip mode, you can move objects from one location to another. This grip mode is similar to the MOVE command.

■ *Rotate.* The rotate grip mode enables you to rotate objects around a hot grip or selected base point. This is similar to the ROTATE command.

■ *Scale.* The scale grip mode allows you to scale objects larger or smaller. It is similar to the SCALE command.

◀ See "Moving Objects (MOVE)," p. 244

◀ See "Rotating Objects (ROTATE)," p. 255

◀ See "Scaling Parts of a Drawing (SCALE)," p. 260

III

Editing a Drawing

◀ See "Creating Mirror Images (MIRROR)," p. 258

■ *Mirror.* Using the mirror grip mode enables you to mirror selected objects about an axis. The mirror grip mode is similar to the MIRROR command.

To cycle through the five grip editing modes in order to select one, use one of the following methods:

■ Press the Enter key.

■ Press the space bar.

■ Enter the first two letters of the command.

## Stretching Objects with Grips

When modifying objects in mechanical drafting, it is common to increase the length of a part. In architectural drafting, room sizes can be stretched to increase the square footage. The STRETCH command will move a selected part of an object without disturbing the connections between the objects.

The stretch mode is very similar to the STRETCH command. The main difference is that the STRETCH command cannot be accessed by selecting a grip and that there is no default base point. While stretching objects generally makes them longer or shorter, the effects of stretching certain objects is somewhat different. When a circle is stretched using the stretch grip mode, its radius becomes larger or smaller.

Stretching objects with grips is a fairly straightforward process. Selecting the grip at the endpoint of a line will change the location of the endpoint, which lengthens or shortens the line. Selecting the grip on the quadrant of a circle will modify its radius. Invoking the stretch mode displays the following `Command:` prompt:

```
** STRETCH **
<Stretch to point>/Base point/Copy/Undo/eXit:
```

■ *Base point.* The Base point option appears with all of the main grip editing options. Typing the letter B allows you to use any point or any other grip (including a cold grip from another object) as the basepoint instead of the hot grip.

■ *Copy.* Copy is another suboption of every choice. Its use is discussed in the section later in this chapter, "Copying Objects with Grips."

■ *Undo.* You can invoke the Undo option by entering **u**. It will undo the last Copy or Base point selection.

■ *Exit.* Entering an **x** will exit the stretch mode.

Attempting to stretch certain objects will result in moving the object rather than stretching it. This will happen when you select a grip that does not have a valid stretch modification. Selecting the midpoint of a line, center of a circle, or insertion point of text will move the object rather than stretch it.

Some objects can't be stretched regardless of which grip is selected. Blocks (discussed in Chapter 23, "Using Symbols and XRefs") are an example of such objects. A block may consist of a number of different objects, but AutoCAD recognizes a block as one single object. The objects are *locked* together and cannot be changed in any way, including stretching. Another example is text. Text can be moved or scaled, but can't be stretched.

### Tutorial: Stretching Objects with Grips

In this tutorial, which is a continuation of the previous tutorial, you use grips to modify the diameter of the hub on the gear.

1. Using the crosshairs, select the circle shown previously in figure 11.5.

   Grips will appear on the center and at the quadrants of the circle.

2. Ensure that the Ortho mode is off by checking the status line at the bottom of the screen. If you see Ortho displayed, double click the word Ortho.

3. Click one of the quadrant grips and move the crosshair left and right.

   Notice that the diameter of the circle changes as you move the crosshairs.

4. Make the diameter of the circle smaller than it was originally and click the pick button.

   Notice that the grips are displayed after the stretch has been performed.

   AutoCAD is ready to perform another operation on that object.

5. Next, stretch the circle using the Base point option.

   First, select the outer circle. You should have grips displayed on both circles (see fig. 11.9).

6. Select one of the quadrant grips on the inner circle. AutoCAD prompts:

   ```
   ** STRETCH **
   <Stretch to point>/Base point/Copy/Undo/eXit:
   ```

**III**

**Editing a Drawing**

**Fig. 11.9**
Using the base
point on the outer
circle to stretch
the diameter of
the inner circle.

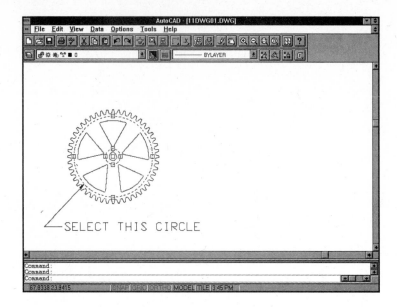

**Fig. 11.9**
Using the base
point on the outer
circle to stretch
the diameter of
the inner circle.

7. Enter **b** in response to the prompt. This will allow you to use any other grip or point as the base point instead of the hot grip.

```
** STRETCH **
<Stretch to point>/Base point/Copy/Undo/eXit: b
Base point:
```

8. Select one of the quadrant grips on the outer circle.

   Notice the diameter of the inner circle changes as you move the crosshairs, using the new base point, but the outer circle does not change because the quadrant grip was not hot.

9. Make the diameter of the circle approximately the same diameter it was originally, and pick a point on the screen.

   The next tutorial will continue from here.

## Moving Objects with Grips

In the previous section on stretching objects with grips it was noted that you can move certain objects to a new location with the stretch mode. If you select the midpoint of a line, center of a circle, or insertion point of text you will move the object rather than stretch it.

Moving objects with the stretch mode does not work in all situations or for all objects. The move mode is explicitly for moving objects.

AutoCAD also provides the MOVE command for pick-first selection. In certain cases the MOVE command is preferred over the move grip mode. If you need to define and move a complex selection set, the MOVE command is generally easier to use. Invoking the move grip mode displays the following command prompt:

◀ See "Moving Objects (MOVE)," p. 244

```
** MOVE **
<Move to point>/Base point/Copy/Undo/eXit:
```

The options for using the Move grip mode are as follows:

■ *Base point.* The Base point option appears with all of the main grip editing options. Typing the letter B allows you to use any point or any other grip (including a cold grip from another object) as the basepoint instead of the hot grip.

■ *Copy.* The Copy option is another option of every choice. Its use is discussed in the section later in the chapter, "Copying Objects with Grips."

■ *Undo.* You can invoke the Undo option by typing the letter **u**. It will undo the last copy or base point selection.

■ *Exit.* Entering **x** will exit the move grip mode.

### Tutorial: Moving Objects with Grips

In this tutorial, which is a continuation of the previous tutorial, you use grips to move the circle that represents the hub on the gear.

**1.** Grips should still be displayed from the previous tutorial on the inner and outer circles.

If grips are not present on the circles, select the circles with the crosshairs.

**2.** Select the grip located in the center of the circles. This will display the ** STRETCH ** prompt and options.

**3.** To change to the ** MOVE ** prompt and options, press the space bar.

The grip mode prompt will indicate that you will now be performing a move function.

As mentioned in the text, it's not necessary to perform this step. If the prompt indicates stretch and the center of a circle is selected, results of the stretch grip mode will be the same as the move grip mode.

**III**

**Editing a Drawing**

4. Move the crosshairs around the screen and notice that the circles move with it.

5. Click anywhere on-screen to place the circle.

6. Undo the previous move. Use the UNDO command to place the circle back in its original position.

   ```
   Command: u
   ```

7. Next, move the circle using the Base point option.

   First, select the inner and outer circles. You should have grips displayed on both circles, as shown earlier in figure 11.9.

8. Remove the outer circle from the selection set.

   Hold the Shift key down and select the outer circle. The outer circle grips are still blue, but the grips are cold and the outer circle object is no longer highlighted.

9. Select one of the quadrant grips on the inner circle. When AutoCAD displays the ** STRETCH ** prompt, press the space bar. AutoCAD will display the ** MOVE ** prompt as follows:

   ```
   ** MOVE **
   <Move to point>/Base point/Copy/Undo/eXit:
   ```

10. Enter **b** in response to the prompt. This will allow you to use any other grip or point as the base point instead of the hot grip.

    ```
    ** MOVE **
    <Move to point>/Base point/Copy/Undo/eXit: b
    Base point:
    ```

11. Select one of the quadrant grips on the outer circle.

    Notice the inner circle moves as you change the location of the crosshairs, using the new base point.

12. Click anywhere on-screen to move the circle.

13. Use the UNDO command to place the circle back in its original position.

    The next tutorial will continue from here.

## Rotating Objects with Grips

With the rotate grip mode, you can rotate existing objects on a drawing. The ROTATE command can be very useful if you need a part drawn at a specific angle. Using the rotate grip mode, you can draw the part in normal *x,y* coordinates and then place it at any angle in the drawing.

For example, if you need to draw the wing of a building at 80 degrees, you can draw the wing at 0 degrees, and then use the rotate grip mode to rotate it into place. Rotating an object using the rotate grip mode is a three-step procedure:

1. Select the objects that you want to rotate. To select more than one object, hold down the Shift key when selecting the first object, or use a window.

2. Select a grip that you want to use for the center of rotation. The selected grip will turn red.

3. Specify the rotation angle. You can either select a point on the screen, or type in the rotation angle.

The rotate grip mode displays the following Command: prompt:

```
** ROTATE **
<Rotation Angle>/Base point/Copy/Undo/Reference/eXit:
```

The following options are listed when using the Rotate grip mode:

- *Base point.* Allows you to use any other grip or point as the base point instead of the hot grip.

- *Copy.* Using copy in combination with rotate is discussed in the "Copying Objects with Grips" section later in the chapter.

- *Undo.* This will undo the last copy or base point selection. It will only function after a Base point or Copy option.

- *Reference.* Allows you to either enter an angle to use as a reference, or select two points on an existing object you want to align it with.

- *Exit.* Entering an **x** will exit the rotate grip mode.

**Tutorial: Rotating Objects with Grips**

In this tutorial, which is a continuation of the previous tutorial, you use grips to rotate the drawing of the gear.

1. Create a window by picking the first point to the upper-left of the gear and the second point to the lower-right of the gear as shown in figure 11.10.

**III**

**Editing a Drawing**

**Fig. 11.10**
Create a window around the gear by selecting the upper-right corner first and the lower-left corner second.

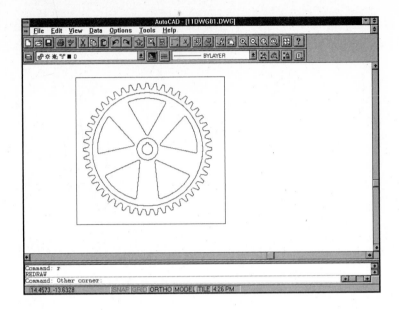

Grips will appear on all objects in the drawing.

**2.** Click the grip located in the center of the gear.

**3.** Press the space bar twice to invoke the Rotate option.

**4.** Rotate the gear 30 degrees, as shown in figure 11.11. AutoCAD will prompt:

```
** ROTATE **
<Rotation Angle>/Base point/Copy/Undo/Reference/eXit:
    30
```

**5.** Rotate the gear again using the Reference option. The Reference option will allow you to either enter an angle to use as a reference, or select two points on an existing object you want to align it with.

Click the grip located in the center of the gear to make it hot.

**6.** Press the space bar twice to invoke the Rotate option. At the ** ROTATE ** prompt, enter **r**.

```
** ROTATE **
<Rotation Angle>/Base point/Copy/Undo/Reference/eXit:
    r
```

**7.** AutoCAD will prompt for the reference angle. Enter **30**, which is the angle you originally rotated the gear to.

```
Reference Angle <0>: 30
```

**8.** You are now prompted for a new angle based on the reference angle you just entered. Entering **0** (zero) will rotate the gear back to its original position.

```
** ROTATE **
<New angle>/Base point/Copy/Undo/Reference/eXit: 0
```

The next tutorial will continue from here.

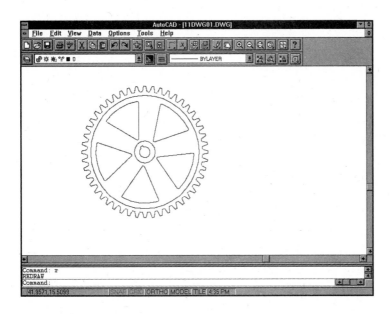

**Fig. 11.11**
Placement of the gear drawing after rotating it 30 degrees.

## Scaling Objects with Grips

The Scale grip mode can be used to adjust the size of the objects proportionally. The grip initially selected will be the base point for the scaling operation. The scale grip mode displays the following Command: prompt:

```
** SCALE **
<Scale factor>/Base point/Copy/Undo/Reference/eXit:
```

The following options are available when using the Scale grip mode:

- *Base point.* You can use any other grip or point as the base point instead of the hot grip.

- *Copy.* Using Copy in combination with Scale is discussed in "Copying Objects with Grips," later in this chapter.

- *Undo.* This undoes the last copy or base point selection.

III

Editing a Drawing

■ *Reference*. Used to calculate a scale factor based on reference units you provide.

■ *Exit*. Entering an **x** will exit the scale grip mode.

Selecting the Reference option will cause AutoCAD to calculate a scale factor based on the reference units you provide. For example, suppose you have a line that is 2.5 units long, and you want it to be 3.375 units long. You can calculate the scale factor on a calculator (1.35), but the scale factor reference allows AutoCAD to do all of the work for you.

When you select the Reference option, the following prompt appears:

```
Reference Length <1.0000>:
```

Enter the current length of the line (**2.5**). When AutoCAD displays the <New length>: grip mode prompt, enter the final distance (**3.375**). AutoCAD will perform the calculation for you.

### Tutorial: Scaling Objects with Grips

In this tutorial, which is a continuation of the previous tutorial, you use grips to scale the size of the gear.

1. Create a window around the gear, as shown previously in figure 11.10.

   Grips will appear on all objects in the drawing.

2. Select the grip located in the center of the gear.

3. Press the space bar until Scale appears on the Command: prompt.

4. Scale the gear to half of its original size by typing **.5**.

   ```
   ** SCALE **
   <Scale factor>/Base point/Copy/Undo/Reference/eXit: .5
   ```

5. Use the UNDO command to return the gear to its original size.

   ```
   Command: u
   ```

   The next tutorial will continue from here.

## Mirroring Objects with Grips

The mirror grip mode allows you to make a mirror image of the objects selected along a mirror line. The *mirror line* is a line that shows where the mirror image reflects the original. When using the mirror grip mode, AutoCAD assumes the most recent active grip is one endpoint of the mirror line unless you specify a different point. The mirror line can be thought of as a pivot point for the objects being mirrored. The mirror grip mode displays the following prompt:

```
** MIRROR **
<Second point>/Base point/Copy/Undo/eXit:
```

The following are Mirror grip mode options:

- *Second point.* The point which defines the other endpoint of the mirror line. The first point is the most recent active grip unless specified otherwise.

- *Base point.* Allows you to use any other grip or point as the first point in the mirror line instead of the hot grip.

- *Copy.* Using Copy in combination with Mirror is discussed in the "Copying Objects with Grips" section later in the chapter.

- *Undo.* This will undo the last copy or base point selection.

- *Exit.* Entering an **x** will exit the Mirror grip mode.

The mirror grip mode is ideal for creating symmetrical objects. Many designs contain parts that are symmetrical. Before you begin drawing, examine the parts carefully and look at the relationships between the different objects. If the parts contain symmetrical objects, mirror greatly reduces the amount of geometry creation you need to do in the drawing.

When using the mirror grip mode, you can leave the original drawing intact and make a mirror duplicate of it, or remove the original object. To leave the original intact, select the Copy option. The Copy option will be fully discussed in "Copying Objects with Grips," later in this chapter.

### Tutorial: Mirroring Objects with Grips

In this tutorial, which is a continuation of the previous tutorial, you use grips to mirror one of the gear splines.

1. Clear all previous grips by pressing the Esc key twice.

2. Erase the line shown in figure 11.12.

3. Select the line and arc shown in figure 11.13.

4. Deselect the arc to remove it from the selection set. Do this by placing the crosshairs directly on the arc and holding down the Shift key while selecting the arc.

**III**

**Editing a Drawing**

**Fig. 11.12**
Erase the line in
the gear drawing.

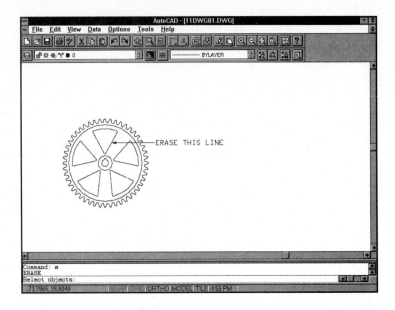

**Fig. 11.13**
Selecting the line
to be mirrored,
and the arc.

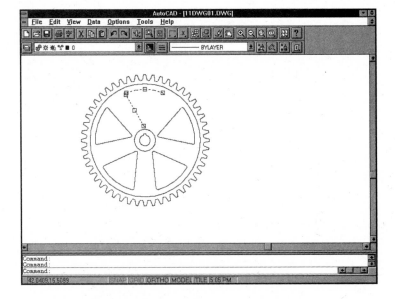

**5.** Select the grip at the bottom of the line.

**6.** Press the space bar until the Mirror option is displayed as shown below:

```
** MIRROR **
<Second point>/Base point/Copy/Undo/eXit:
```

7. Check to make sure the ortho mode is on.

8. At the Mirror: prompt, change the base point by entering a **b**.

   ```
   ** MIRROR **
   <Second point>/Base point/Copy/Undo/eXit: b
   Base point:
   ```

9. Select the grip in the midpoint of the arc.

10. Move the crosshairs up; notice how a ghosted mirrored line will appear.

11. In order to keep the original line, enter **c** at the Mirror: prompt and press the space bar. This will invoke the Copy option, keeping the original line intact.

    ```
    ** MIRROR **
    <Second point>/Base point/Copy/Undo/eXit: c
    ```

12. When you return to the Mirror (multiple): prompt, press the pick button to mirror the line.

    ```
    ** MIRROR (multiple)**
    <Second point>/Base point/Copy/Undo/eXit: Press the
          Selection button.
    ```

13. When you return to the Mirror (multiple): prompt, press Enter or type **x** to exit the mirror grip mode.

14. Press Escape to clear all of the grips.

    The next tutorial will continue from here.

## Copying Objects with Grips

Each of the grip modes contains a Copy option. Copy provides a great deal of flexibility when used to edit objects. The Copy option allows you to combine a copy operation with any of the other grip modes. This capability allows you to copy objects while you also stretch, move, rotate, mirror, or scale the objects.

While each of the grip modes includes the Copy option, its usage differs slightly depending on which grip mode you are using. In all cases, however, the original object remains intact and a copy is made of it. The following list describes how the Copy option affects the different grip modes:

■ *Stretch.* The object originally selected remains intact and is not stretched. All copies of the object are stretched.

**III**

**Editing a Drawing**

- *Move.* The original object remains intact and in its current location. The copy is moved to its new location.

- *Rotate.* The original object is not rotated and remains in its original location. All duplicate objects are rotated around the selected grip point.

- *Mirror.* Using the Copy option with Mirror causes the original object to remain in its original location. All mirrored objects are mirrored about the defined mirror line.

- *Scale.* The original object is not scaled and remains in its same location. All duplicate objects are scaled.

When the Copy option is selected with any of the other grip modes, it also switches to a *multiple mode.* This means you can perform the selected grip mode as many times as needed without having to reselect objects or re-enter the command. For example, say you use the rotate grip mode with the Copy option. With the Copy option you can create as many copies of the original as needed, all rotated around the same center point, but at different rotation angles.

### Tutorial: Copying Objects with Grips

In this tutorial, which is a continuation of the previous tutorial, you use grips to copy the gear.

1.  Create a window around the gear, as shown earlier in figure 11.10.

    Grips appear on all objects in the drawing.

2.  Click the grip located in the center of the gear.

3.  Press the space bar one time until the Move option is selected.

    ```
    ** MOVE **
    <Move to point>/Base point/Copy/Undo/eXit:
    ```

4.  Enter **C** to choose the Copy option and move the cursor to the right of the gear.

    ```
    ** MOVE **
    <Move to point>/Base point/Copy/Undo/eXit: c
    ```

Notice that a gear appearing in dashed lines is attached to the crosshairs.

**5.** Click anywhere to the right of the gear to place a copy of the gear in the drawing area.

This completes the tutorials for this chapter.

> **Note**
>
> Pressing Shift while in the Move option allows you to move the gripped objects. Holding the Shift key down during the Move (multiple) grip mode causes the crosshairs to move based on a grid described by the previous point selected.

You also can switch to the multiple copy mode by entering **c** (for the Copy option).

In figure 11.14, a rectangle was first drawn using the Rectangle icon from the Draw toolbar. Then the grips on the rectangle are activated by selecting it. The upper-right grip is selected as the grip point. Next, the Move grip mode is activated by pressing the space bar. In the Move grip mode, entering **c** from the command line will let you copy and move multiple times. Pressing the Shift key before picking the point to move fixes the distance to copy. You can make multiple copies of the rectangle with the same offset distance, as shown in figure 11.14.

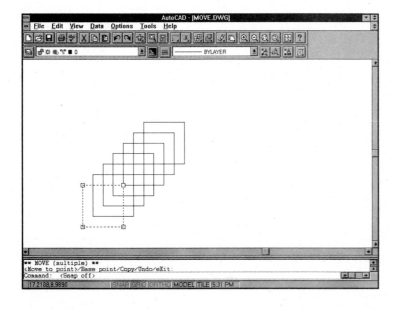

**Fig. 11.14**
Use the multiple copy mode by pressing Shift.

## Implications of Using the Same Grip Point

◀ See "Using Object Snaps," p. 149

As part of your drafting tasks, often you will find that multiple objects will share the same grip point. This can happen when you create objects using Object Snaps. For example, drawing a line from the midpoint of another line means that the midpoint of the first line and the endpoint of the second line are the same point. When grips are activated, by selecting both of these lines, the common grip point helps to maintain the relationship between the lines. Thus, any command executed with the common grip point affects both objects.

In figure 11.15, circle A shares its center point with a quadrant point on circle B. Also, the lines shown connect the centers to the respective quadrant point of each circle. If you rotate both circles and lines about a common grip point (the center of circle A) by 45 degrees, both circles and lines will maintain their respective snap points.

**Fig. 11.15**

Rotating objects with a common grip point maintains their respective snap points.

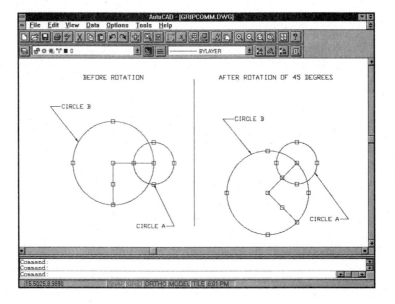

However, there are cases where using the common grip point to affect multiple objects may not be desirable. In such cases, objects that should not be affected need to be removed from the selection set. Layer control also can be used to turn off or freeze layers consisting of objects that you want to remain unaffected. Remember, grip selection only applies to objects on active layers.

# From Here...

When creating a drawing in AutoCAD, editing your geometry is a very common practice. The proper use of grips gives you a fast and efficient method of stretching, moving, rotating, scaling, mirroring, and moving objects.

By default, grips are turned on in AutoCAD. You can change several of the grip settings in the Grips dialog box, including grip size and color. These settings are saved as part of the AutoCAD configuration file, and not with each individual drawing.

After completing this chapter, you have used grips to perform a variety of editing functions. Before continuing, you may want to review the earlier chapter on editing techniques. This will give you a chance to compare editing with grips and the more traditional editing methods. Often, it is difficult to see intricate details on your drawing while attempting to edit it. The next chapter on viewing a drawing will discuss methods for allowing you to see drawing details better. The following chapters will give you more information on editing objects, and better methods of viewing them as you edit.

- Chapter 10, "Editing Techniques," allows you to compare traditional editing techniques with grips.

- Chapter 12, "Viewing a Drawing," shows you how to obtain different views of your drawing, which can be very beneficial when working on complex drawings.

# On Your Own

Load drawing 11DWG02 from your UAW13 subdirectory. Your drawing should look like figure 11.16. In this exercise, you need to re-arrange the furniture for an upcoming piano recital to make it look similar to figure 11.17. Use all of your grip modes, including move, copy, rotate, stretch, scale.

**Fig. 11.16**
Using your grip
modes, rearrange
the furniture for
an upcoming
piano recital.

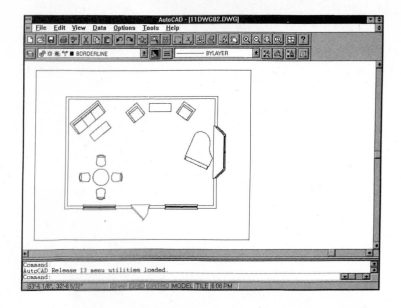

**Fig. 11.17**
The furniture
arrangement
needed for the
piano recital.

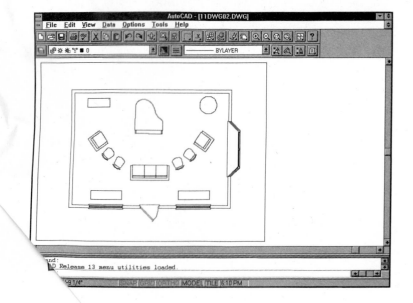

# Part IV

# Viewing and Plotting a Drawing

AutoCAD - [37FIG05.DWG]

File    Edit    View    Data    Options    Tools    Help

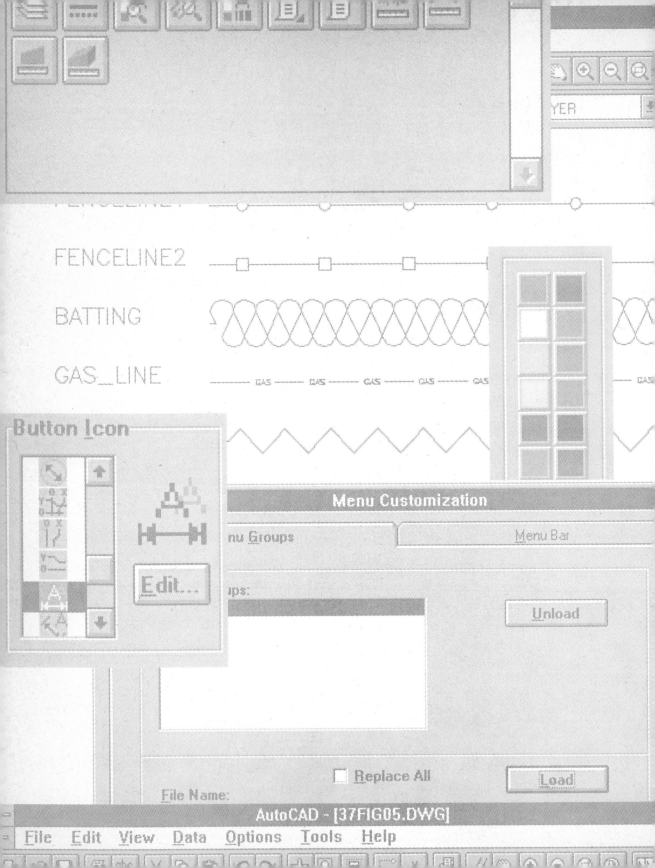

FENCELINE2

BATTING

GAS_LINE     —— GAS —— GAS —— GAS —— GAS —— GAS ——        GAS

**Button Icon**

Edit...

**Menu Customization**

nu Groups          Menu Bar

ups:

Unload

□ Replace All

File Name:

Load

AutoCAD - [37FIG05.DWG]

File    Edit    View    Data    Options    Tools    Help

# Chapter 12

# Viewing a Drawing

CAD drawings present a unique problem absent in manual drafting. Regardless of whether you set your drawing limits to represent $11 \times 17$ inches or $1,500 \times 2,500$ feet, your display screen is not large enough to clearly view the entire drawing. Because you need to draw full size in AutoCAD, you're generally limited to seeing only a portion of your drawing on a typical monitor. In many CAD drawings, you can't see enough detail to work effectively. Even with large monitors and ultra-high-resolution graphics boards, you cannot see all of the details on a drawing that fits on a C-size sheet ($24" \times 17"$).

After reading this chapter, you will be able to do the following:

- Understand the difference between the REDRAW and REGEN commands

- Practice viewing a large drawing on a small screen with the ZOOM command

- Move the display around on-screen with the PAN command

- Create named views that can be recalled instantly with the VIEW command

- Use the Aerial View window

- Create slide presentations with your drawings

The best solution to working on drawings with a high level of detail is to let AutoCAD increase and decrease the magnification of the drawing. AutoCAD allows you to view enlarged portions of the drawing so you can see all the details. When you have a section of the drawing magnified on-screen, you only see that section, but the entire drawing is still intact.

In the creation of drawings, you often can see artifacts left by AutoCAD, such as blips, small dots on the screen, and incomplete lines. You may think that these lines were erased inadvertently. Before you begin to construct missing lines or re-create new lines, try the REGEN or REDRAW commands. You may find that your drawing is not in as bad of shape as you thought. In this chapter, you're shown how these two commands are the most common and useful commands in the viewing of a drawing.

The ZOOM command allows you to enlarge or reduce the amount of the drawing displayed on-screen. You can move the portion of the enlarged drawing back and forth or up and down with the PAN command. In the Windows version of AutoCAD, the DSVIEWER command invokes an Aerial View window that allows you to see the entire drawing in a separate window. When using DSVIEWER, you can locate the part of the drawing you want to view and move to it using the zoom and pan functions.

The VIEW command allows you to create, name, and save specific views of a drawing. When you have to do additional drawing or editing operations in the area of a drawing defined by a saved view, you quickly and easily can recall the view.

Displaying a large drawing on-screen can be a tedious process. It takes time to access the Open menu, find the correct file, and load the drawing from the disk. If you need to zoom in on a specific part of the drawing, the process slows down even more. Fortunately, AutoCAD has a method to display a large drawing quickly and efficiently.

A slide in AutoCAD is similar to a slide in photography. When a slide is created, AutoCAD takes a *snapshot* of the screen. Because it's a snapshot and not an actual drawing, the slide can't be plotted or edited. Slides can be viewed one at a time or as a continuous show; they're an excellent tool for presentations, demonstrations, and displays, or for any situation in which several drawings have to be displayed rapidly.

In this chapter, you learn how to use AutoCAD's display commands. By viewing your drawing in different ways, AutoCAD gives you the ability to create drawings with greater speed, ease, and accuracy than is possible in manual drafting.

# Understanding the Display

AutoCAD uses *vector graphics* to store and display geometry in a drawing. Vector data gives useful information about the geometry, such as endpoints, midpoints, and center points. The advantage of using vector graphics is that they enable you to find points relative to other geometric objects, such as intersections and tangent points. The object snap commands take advantage of the vector data stored for the geometric objects.

◀ See "Using Object Snaps," p. 149

When you create a drawing in AutoCAD, you're really building a database list of the objects in the drawing rather than originating the drawing on-screen. The drawing display serves as a representation of the drawing database to make it easier to work with.

# Understanding the Virtual Screen

When you are working on a drawing, AutoCAD maintains the drawing information in more than one format. One format uses the vector graphics information and stores the information in a database by using *floating-point values*. This format ensures high precision. The drawback, however, is that calculations involving floating-point numbers take longer than those involving integers.

Besides the vector graphics database, AutoCAD maintains information needed for the screen display. The screen display uses integer values to locate screen coordinates. Each coordinate on-screen is called a *pixel*. A pixel is a single point of light on-screen; each pixel is defined separately. The information required to display the pixel are the coordinates of the pixel and its color.

When AutoCAD displays an object on-screen, it converts the floating-point database values to the appropriate integer screen coordinates. Because it takes a great deal of time to convert the coordinates from the floating-point database to the screen pixel integer coordinates, AutoCAD maintains a *virtual screen* between your drawing and the screen.

When the drawing view is changed, AutoCAD refreshes the screen; it reads the virtual screen and changes the physical screen accordingly. The translation from the virtual screen data to the physical screen data is very fast. AutoCAD quickly recalculates changes in the physical screen from the virtual screen.

Refreshing the screen forces AutoCAD to recopy the current drawing area from the virtual screen to the physical screen. Certain display commands, such as ZOOM and PAN, automatically refresh the screen.

> **Note**
>
> Many video card and software developers market display drivers that enhance or alter the display. The drivers usually offer additional display-related commands and options. The display drivers usually offer trade-offs between display speed, the regularity of display refreshing, memory usage, and other display-related items. This chapter discusses the display features that come with AutoCAD. Users running a third-party display list driver need to read this chapter and consult their driver's documentation.

## Refreshing the Screen (REDRAW)

▶ See "Redrawing All Viewports (REDRAWALL, REGENALL)," p. 880

As you continue working on a drawing, the physical screen can become corrupted or "dirty." This can be caused by adding, erasing, or modifying objects. Parts of objects can disappear when an overlapping object is removed. Small crosses, or *blips*, may appear on the display where points were picked. Use any of the following commands to clean up the screen after editing:

- Click the Redraw button on the Standard toolbar.

- Enter **redraw** at the Command: prompt. Or enter **r** or **'r** when within another command.

- Choose <u>V</u>iew, Redraw <u>V</u>iew.

**Tip**
A quick way to redraw the screen is to use the F7 key. This toggles the grid on and off, causing a redraw in the process. The grid spacing must be set to a value you can see for this to work.

> **Note**
>
> You can issue REDRAW as a transparent command by preceding it with an apostrophe ('). Because a transparent command can be used when another command is active, you can clean up the screen whenever you want—even in the middle of another command.

## Regenerating the Screen (REGEN)

When you change the drawing, AutoCAD must update both the drawing database and the virtual screen so that they match one another. However, not every change to the drawing database necessitates a regeneration. For example, when you draw a line, the drawing database, virtual display, and physical screen are updated; when you edit a line, the drawing database and virtual display are updated, but the physical screen must be refreshed with the REDRAW command. A complete regeneration is not required. When a regeneration occurs, the floating-point database values are converted to the appropriate integer which updates the screen coordinates and the entire drawing database is read. This can be a time-consuming process, depending on the configuration of the computer and the size of the drawing.

Several commands described in this chapter move, magnify, or shrink the image on-screen. Occasionally, these operations require that AutoCAD regenerate the entire drawing, recomputing the screen coordinates for all objects. If the display is moved or zoomed to the point where the virtual screen no longer has the necessary information to create the physical screen, then you get a regeneration. In a large drawing, this can take a long time. AutoCAD displays the message Regenerating drawing. . ., whenever a regeneration is performed.

You can force AutoCAD to regenerate the drawing by entering **regen** at the Command: prompt. The advantage of using REGEN is that the regenerated image is the most accurate image AutoCAD can produce. The disadvantage of using REGEN is that it takes time to regenerate.

### Freezing Layers to Control Regeneration Time

Layers that are FROZEN are not included when a drawing regeneration is done; layers that are turned OFF are included. When you work with large drawings, you can freeze layers that are not needed. You avoid unnecessary drawing generations and help speed up your drawing time.

## Regenerating the Drawing Automatically (REGENAUTO)

Certain commands cause AutoCAD to regenerate the drawing automatically. To control the regenerations and help speed up the drawing process, you can ask AutoCAD to warn you before it regenerates the screen. To access the REGENAUTO command enter **regenauto** at the Command: prompt.

At the ON/OFF <ON>: prompt that appears, enter **off**. AutoCAD now asks permission before regenerating the drawing:

    About to regen -- proceed?<Y>

If REGENAUTO is OFF and a regen is required during a transparent command, you get the message ** Requires a regen, cannot be transparent. When a change in a system variable that requires a regeneration to display it is made transparently, you get the message Regen queued. When REGEN is queued, AutoCAD will wait until a regen is forced before regenerating the drawing. REGENAUTO controls the setting of the REGENMODE system variable.

▶ See "System
Variables
Reference,"
p. 1147

▶ See "Redrawing
All Viewports
(REDRAWALL,
REGENALL),"
p. 880

If you answer **n** to this prompt, AutoCAD doesn't regenerate the drawing. Because REGEN goes through the entire drawing's database and redisplays the information on-screen, a REGEN can take a great deal of time.

## Setting Display Options (VIEWRES)

The VIEWRES (VIEW RESolution) command controls drawing regeneration and the appearance of curves in the drawing. The speed of zooms and regenerations are controlled in two ways. First, *fast zooms* can be turned on or off. Fast zoom means that AutoCAD maintains a large virtual screen so that most operations can be done at redraw (fast) speed. If fast zooms are turned off, all pan and zoom operations cause a regen. By default, the fast zoom option is turned on.

Second, VIEWRES determines how fine to generate curves. When circles or arcs are small, AutoCAD uses a few straight vectors to fool your eyes into seeing a smooth curve. When circles and arcs are large, AutoCAD needs more vectors to make a smooth arc. The VIEWRES circle zoom percent tells AutoCAD how smooth you want your circles and arcs to be. The higher the percentage, the more vectors AutoCAD uses to display arcs and circles. VIEWRES only affects the AutoCAD screen; the database is used to plot the drawing, therefore all arcs and circles are plotted as actual curves.

The following command sequence is used to control VIEWRES resolutions:

```
Command: viewres
Do you want fast zooms? <Y>: This is the default setting
    and will enable transparent display commands, so press
    Enter.
Enter circle zoom percent (1-20000) <100>: The higher the
    number, the smoother the arcs and circles will appear.
    As the number increases, regenerations will take longer.
```

You may need a regular regeneration or a regeneration with a higher zoom percent to see the information you need for picking points on curves. For example, if a circle is drawn with a few big lines, you may have a hard time finding a quadrant or tangent point. Sometimes a curve may intersect with another object, but not show the contact on the display if a regen is necessary or the VIEWRES zoom percent is set low. Use REGEN to display the arc or circle as a curve.

# Using ZOOM to Control the Display (ZOOM)

One of the most important functions of AutoCAD is to provide a means to let you see your drawing more clearly. The ZOOM command lets you magnify your drawing to do detailed work. You access the ZOOM command in one of the following ways:

■ Choose the Zoom button on the Standard toolbar. This brings up a fly-out toolbar that shows the different zoom options. (Zoom In, Zoom Out, and Zoom Window are the only zoom tools available on the Standard toolbar.)

■ Choose View, Zoom. A cascading submenu appears, listing the different Zoom options (see fig. 12.1).

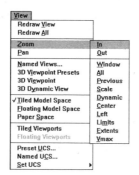

**Fig. 12.1**
The Zoom cascading submenu.

■ Enter **zoom** at the Command: prompt. The following options are then displayed:

```
All/Center/Dynamic/Extents/Left/Previous/Vmax/Window/
    <Scale(X/XP)>:
```

**Note**

You can also enter **z** at the Command: prompt as a shortcut to begin the ZOOM command. Likewise, the ZOOM command options each have a mnemonic that indicates the shortcut you can enter for the option. For example, you can enter **z** for the ZOOM command and **a** for the All option.

**Tip**
You can issue ZOOM transparently as long as a regen is not required to do the zoom.

## ZOOM All

The ZOOM All option displays the drawing to its limits or extents, whichever is greater. The size of the drawing's limits is determined by the LIMITS command, discussed in Chapter 2, "Creating Your First Drawing." If you have geometry outside the limits, ZOOM All zooms beyond the limits to display everything in the drawing file (this is called the drawing's *extents*). ZOOM All always regenerates the drawing.

### Tutorial: Using the ZOOM All Command

In this tutorial, you use the ZOOM All command to view all items found in the apartment floor plan shown in figure 12.2. This apartment floor plan is used for all tutorials in this chapter and each tutorial continues from the one before it.

**Fig. 12.2**

Use ZOOM to view the apartment floor plan.

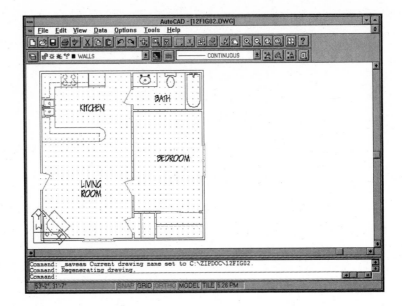

To view the items, follow these steps:

1. Select Open from the Standard toolbar. If prompted by the AutoCAD Save Changes dialog box, select the appropriate response.

   The Open Drawing dialog box appears.

2. In the File Name input box, type **C:\UAW13\12DWG01** and press Enter or click OK.

   After the file is loaded, your screen should resemble figure 12.2.

3. Choose ZOOM All from the Standard toolbar Zoom flyout menu.

   The drawing extends to the edges of the drawing area, as shown in figure 12.3. ZOOM All always makes full use of the drawing area to display the drawing.

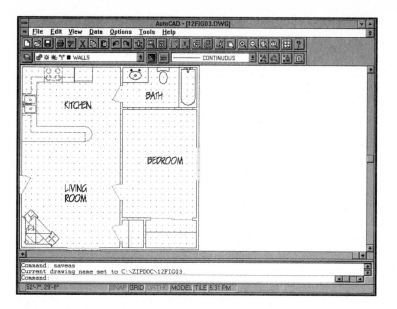

**Fig. 12.3**
Use ZOOM All to
view the apartment
floor plan.

## ZOOM Center

With the ZOOM Center option from the Zoom flyout menu, AutoCAD creates a new view of the drawing based on a new center point. When you select
ZOOM Center, AutoCAD prompts for the center point of the new view. You
can specify exact coordinates or use the cursor to pick a point on-screen. After
specifying the center point, AutoCAD prompts you for the magnification or
height of the new view.

A value followed by an × indicates "times" or the magnification power.
A number larger than one zooms in; a number smaller than 1 will zoom out.
If you supply a number without the ×, AutoCAD reads the number as the
height of the new view in the current units.

### Tutorial: Using the ZOOM Center Command

As a reminder, this tutorial continues from the preceding tutorial. Here you
use the ZOOM Center option to view the bathroom in the apartment floor
plan. Follow these steps:

1.  Choose Center from the Zoom fly-out toolbar.

2.  At the Center point: prompt, pick a point in the center of the
    bathroom.

3.  At the Magnification or Height <30',2">: prompt, enter **2x**.

The bathroom centers in the drawing area at a scale two times larger than the previous scale (see fig. 12.4).

**Fig. 12.4**
Use Zoom Center with magnification to view the apartment bathroom.

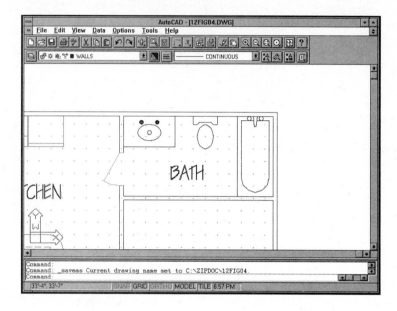

To try a different height, use these steps:

1. Select Center from the Zoom fly-out toolbar.

2. At the Center point: prompt, move the crosshairs to the center of the bathroom and press the pick button.

3. At the Magnification or Height <30',2">: prompt, enter **8'**.

The bathroom is now centered in the drawing area with 8' of height displayed similar to figure 12.5.

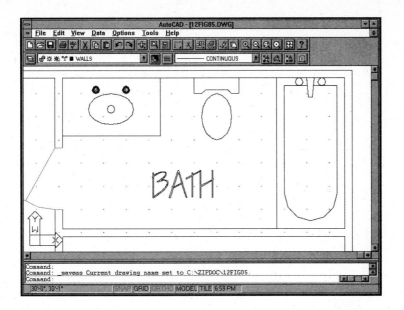

**Fig. 12.5**
Using Zoom
Center to view
the apartment
bathroom.

## ZOOM Dynamic

The ZOOM Dynamic option temporarily displays the whole drawing (as much as possible without causing a regen) and allows you to display any portion of the drawing as your next screen view. AutoCAD does this by constructing a *view box*. When you choose ZOOM dynamic, the screen switches to a temporary display, showing the sum combination of the limits, extents, current display location, future display location, virtual display boundaries, and an icon (described in the following list):

- *Drawing extents*. This box (a white line) displays the drawing's extents or limits, whichever is greater. This is the same area that is displayed when you use the ZOOM Extents option.

- *Current view*. This box (a dotted green line) shows what the view was before you selected ZOOM Dynamic. If the current display is coincident with the drawing extents or limits, the green box may not be visible.

- *Generated area*. This area, indicated by four red corner angles, marks the virtual screen. This is the area you can zoom to without causing a regeneration.

If you select an area inside the four red corner angles, the next display is calculated at the faster redraw speed. If you select an area outside the four red corner angles, a REGEN is performed, slowing the next display. Try to size the view and pan boxes inside the four red corner angles.

- *Panning view box.* This view box (a white box with an X in the center) represents the area that will be drawn next on-screen. An X indicates that this is a panning box. Place the X at the spot you want to be the center point of the next display. The width and height ratio of the view box matches the width and height ration of the drawing area. If you press the pick button, the Zooming view box appears.

- *Zooming view box.* With this box (a white box with an arrow on the right side), you can increase or decrease the zoomed display. Moving the pointer to the right increases the box size. Moving the pointer to the left decreases the box size. You also can pan up or down with the zooming view box. However, you can't move the box to the left.

- *White hourglass.* When the white hourglass appears in the lower-left corner, it is a warning that the current view will cause a regeneration. As you adjust the panning and zooming view boxes, the hourglass may appear and disappear. As long as you stay in the four red corner angles, the hourglass does not appear, and AutoCAD is not forced to regenerate the drawing.

The ZOOM Dynamic command is not completed until you press Enter or click the pick button. You can select between the panning view box and zooming view box by pressing the pick button. By using the different box options and the pick button, you can fine-tune the display you need.

### Tutorial: Using the ZOOM Dynamic Command

This tutorial continues from the preceding tutorial. Here you use the ZOOM Dynamic command to view the kitchen in the apartment floor plan. Follow these steps:

1. Choose Dynamic from the Zoom fly-out toolbar.

   Your screen changes as shown in figure 12.6. Notice the dotted green line around the bathroom. This is the previous zoom setting, allowing you to reference your last ZOOM command.

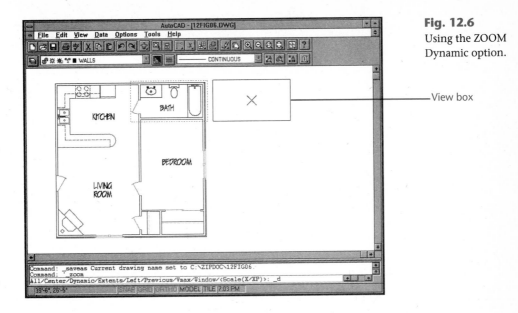

**Fig. 12.6**
Using the ZOOM
Dynamic option.

———View box

2. When you move the cursor, a view box connects to your movements.

   At this time, the view box is the same size as the one for the previous zoom setting from the preceding tutorial.

3. Move the view box so that the upper-left corner is aligned with the upper-left corner of the kitchen, as shown in figure 12.7.

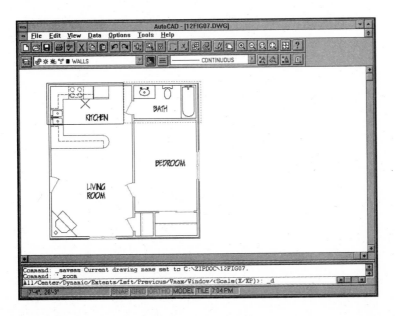

**Fig. 12.7**
Moving the view
box.

The viewing area now has an arrow on the right side. This lets you know that you are ready to adjust the view box size proportionally to the drawing area.

4. Move the cursor to the right, as shown in figure 12.8, and press the pick button.

**Fig. 12.8**
Adjusting the view box size.

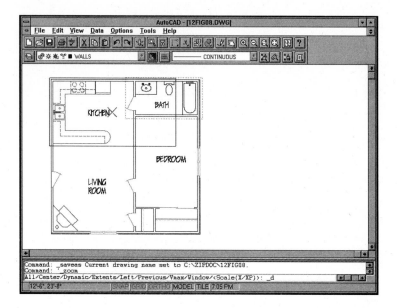

The right arrow is replaced by an X in the middle of the viewbox.

5. Center the view box over the kitchen, as shown in figure 12.9, and press Enter.

Your screen should now resemble figure 12.10.

## ZOOM Extents

The ZOOM Extents option zooms to the portion of the drawing that has objects. This option gives the tightest possible view of all geometry in the drawing file. ZOOM Extents always causes a regeneration.

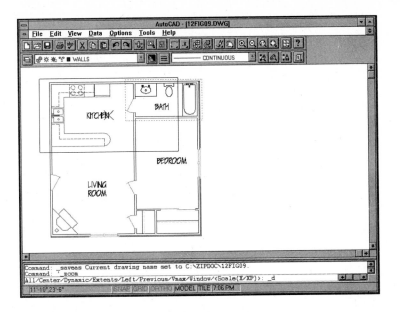

**Fig. 12.9**
Centering the view
box over the
kitchen.

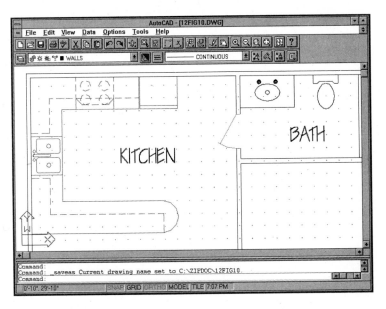

**Fig. 12.10**
Using ZOOM
Dynamic to view
the kitchen.

### Tutorial: Using the ZOOM Extents Option

Again, this tutorial continues from the preceding tutorial. Here you use the ZOOM Extents command to view the apartment floor plan. Choose Extents from the Zoom fly-out toolbar. The apartment extents are placed within the drawing area (refer to fig. 12.3). For this example, the ZOOM Extents option is very similar to ZOOM All.

## ZOOM Left

With the ZOOM Left option, you can create a new zoomed view by specifying the new location of the lower-left corner and the zoom height. The lower-left corner can be specified with coordinates or the screen crosshairs. After you specify the lower-left corner coordinates, AutoCAD prompts for the magnification or height of the new view.

As with the ZOOM Center option, you can enter a value followed by an X. This indicates "times" the current magnification. A number larger than one will zoom in; smaller numbers will zoom out. If you supply a number without the X, AutoCAD reads the number as the height of the new view in the current units. Pressing Enter at the Magnification or Height prompt is the same as panning to the new location because you are accepting the default current height.

### Tutorial: Using the ZOOM Left Command

This tutorial continues from the preceding tutorial. Here you use the ZOOM Left command to display the closets in the apartment floor plan. Follow these steps:

1. Select Left from the Zoom fly-out toolbar.

2. At the Left point: prompt, move the crosshairs to the bottom-left of the closets in the bedroom and press the pick button.

3. At the Magnification or Height <30',2">: prompt, enter **2x**.

   Your screen should resemble figure 12.11. The ZOOM Left Magnification or Height option is identical to the ZOOM Center option. This option always puts the drawing to the right of the point you selected as the left point.

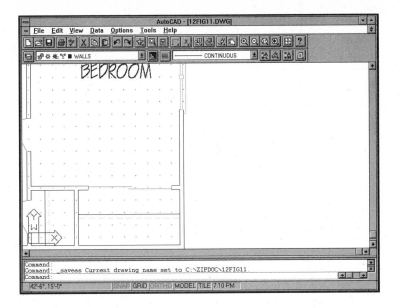

**Fig. 12.11**
Use ZOOM Left to
view the closets in
the apartment
floor plan.

## ZOOM Previous

Every time you zoom in or out of a drawing, AutoCAD keeps track of the
previous display. AutoCAD remembers the last 10 views. Continually entering ZOOM Previous causes AutoCAD to step back through the previous 10
zooms.

### Note

If you erase several objects and issue ZOOM Previous, the previous view is displayed,
but the erased objects do not reappear.

### Tutorial: Using the ZOOM Previous Command

This tutorial continues from the preceding tutorial. In this tutorial, you use
the ZOOM Previous command to view the apartment floor plan. Select Zoom
Previous from the Standard toolbar Zoom flyout.

The screen reverts to how it looked for the ZOOM Extents command (refer to
fig. 12.3), because that was the previous zoom before the Left option was
used. ZOOM Previous always reverts to the last zoom scale factor.

## ZOOM Vmax

ZOOM Vmax zooms out to the drawing's virtual screen limits. The virtual screen is the area to which AutoCAD can zoom out without regenerating the drawing. Usually, the virtual screen is larger than either the drawing's extents or limits.

### Tutorial: Using the ZOOM Vmax Command

This tutorial continues from the preceding tutorial. Here you use the ZOOM Vmax command to view the virtual screen limits of the apartment floor plan. Select Vmax from the Zoom fly-out toolbar.

The drawing area zooms out to the drawing's virtual screen limits, as shown in figure 12.12. This is the largest area to which AutoCAD can zoom or pan without calculating a regeneration.

**Fig. 12.12**
Use ZOOM Vmax to display the virtual screen limits of the apartment floor plan.

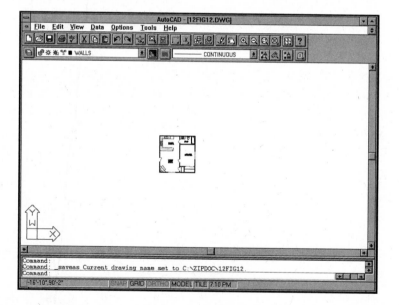

## ZOOM Window

The Zoom Window icon is available directly from the Standard toolbar. A rectangular window is used to select a drawing area to display on-screen. It is similar to the window used to create a selection set of objects. The window grows out of the first point you select. When you press the pick button to pick the second corner, the objects in the box enlarge to fill the screen. To use the zoom window from the ZOOM command's option prompt, it is not necessary to enter **w**. You can just pick a point at the zoom option and AutoCAD assumes you want to define a window. Be sure the point you pick is one of the four corners of the window.

### Tutorial: Using the ZOOM Window Option

As before, this tutorial continues from the preceding tutorial. In this tutorial, you use the ZOOM Window command to view the apartment floor plan. Follow these steps:

1. Select Zoom Window from the Standard toolbar.

2. Create a window by picking two points to define it (see fig. 12.13). When the second point is picked, AutoCAD will automatically zoom.

   Your resulting screen should look similar to figure 12.14.

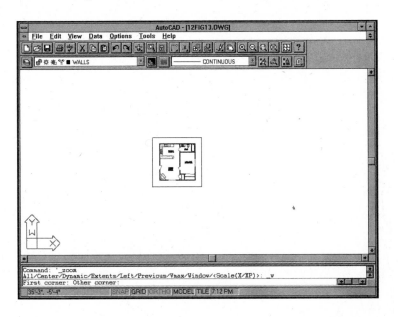

**Fig. 12.13**
Creating a window around the apartment floor plan with the ZOOM Window option.

**Fig. 12.14**
Using ZOOM
Window to display
the apartment
floor plan.

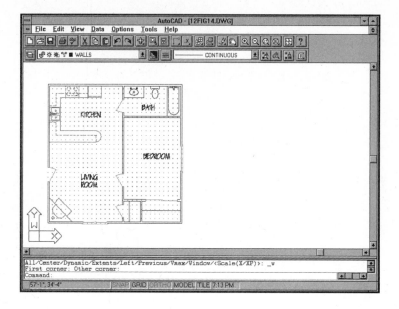

## ZOOM Scale

▶ See "Scaling
Paper Space
Viewports,"
p. 385

The ZOOM Scale option enables you to zoom in and out while maintaining the same center point of the screen. Applying a magnification factor of one displays a view of the drawing limits. A value of less than one zooms out from the limits; a value greater than one zooms in. If you use an X in the scale factor, the image is magnified in relation to the current view. In the next chapter, you learn how to use the XP option to scale a viewport in paper space.

> **Note**
>
> In most cases, you zoom the screen image at a percentage of what the current view is displaying. With no X after a value, the numeric size is an absolute value of the limits size (considered a zoom scale of one). The X is used after the zoom scale value more than the absolute size.

### Tutorial: Using the ZOOM Scale Option

This tutorial continues from the preceding tutorial. Here you use the ZOOM Scale command to view the apartment floor plan at half scale. Follow these steps:

1.  Choose Scale from the Zoom fly-out toolbar.

**2.** At the `All/Center/Dynamic/Extents/Left/Previous/Vmax/Window/` `<Scale(X/XP)>:` prompt, enter **.5**.

The drawing zooms at the absolute half (.5) scale and displays in the drawing area (see fig. 12.15).

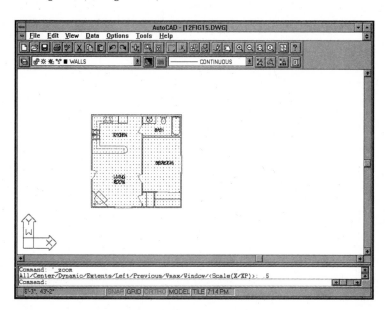

**Fig. 12.15**
Using ZOOM Scale to display the apartment floor plan at half scale.

# Zoom In and Zoom Out

There are two new Standard toolbar buttons available in AutoCAD Release 13: Zoom In and Zoom Out. These two buttons allow you to quickly and easily select a scale factor of two times the relative size (2×) using Zoom In and half the relative size (.5×) using Zoom Out. In normal use, you should find these buttons very useful for quickly zooming in or out to allow for a better view of the overall drawing or of smaller details.

■ Clicking the Zoom In button invokes the ZOOM Scale option with a scale factor of 2×.

■ Clicking the Zoom Out button invokes the ZOOM Scale option with a scale factor of .5×.

# Panning the Display (PAN)

Occasionally, you may want to see a section of the drawing that is outside the current viewing screen. Panning is generally faster than zooming because you don't have to zoom out to a larger view and back in again. However, the ability to use the PAN command is largely dependent on knowing where you want to go in the drawing. If you know you want to see a feature just to the left of the current view, you can easily pan to the left. If, however, you don't know exactly where the view is, relative to the current view, you have no choice but to zoom out and then back in at the new location or use Zoom Dynamic.

Using the PAN command is often faster than using the ZOOM command to change views. The reason is that you often must use the ZOOM command several times to display the necessary view unless you begin with a large initial view. Furthermore, PAN does not cause a drawing regeneration unless you pan outside the virtual screen.

With the PAN command, you can move the current view, as seen in the viewport, very quickly. You move the current area where you are working from an initial point to a second point of displacement, and the view of the drawing changes accordingly. Use the following methods to access the PAN command:

- Click the Pan button on the Standard toolbar. This brings up a fly-out toolbar, showing all the pan options.

- Choose View, Pan. AutoCAD displays a cascading submenu that lists the different pan options, as shown in figure 12.16.

- Enter **pan** or **p** at the Command: prompt or enter **'pan** or **'p** to use the command transparently during another command. AutoCAD then prompts for the pan displacement.

**Fig. 12.16**
The Pan cascading submenu offering several options.

IV

Viewing and Plotting

## Moving the Display

The PAN command can be very useful when you want to see part of a drawing that is just outside the current viewport. AutoCAD shifts the view the distance between the two picked points.

> **Note**
>
> You can issue the PAN command transparently by preceding it with an apostrophe (´). PAN works only if the desired pan does not require a regen. Transparent pans can only be done if VIEWRES Fast Zoom mode is on. You cannot use PAN transparently while in paper space. Also, you cannot use PAN transparently when a VPOINT, DVIEW, ZOOM, PAN, or VIEW command is currently in progress.

## Shifting the View a Specific Distance

At times, you may want to shift the view further than the two points you can pick on-screen. You can also execute a pan displacement by entering a pair of coordinates at the `Displacement:` prompt.

For example, you can enter a coordinate as the initial displacement point and press Enter for the second point. The coordinate specifies a relative distance that the view will move. A negative value in the *x* axis moves the viewport to the left. A negative value in the *y* axis moves the viewport down.

The Pan option on the Standard toolbar and pull-down menu also offers several preset pan distances. When you select a preset pan distance, the drawing pans a set amount and direction. The Pan L button (choose Left in the pull-down menu), for example, pans the drawing to the left. Refer to figure 12.16 for the Pan cascading submenu and its preset options. Each preset option pans the current view in the preset direction by a distance that is approximately half of the value of the VIEWSIZE system variable. VIEWSIZE measures the height of the current view.

### Tutorial: Panning a Drawing

This tutorial continues from the preceding tutorial. In this tutorial, you use the PAN command to shift the view of the apartment floor plan. Follow these steps:

1. Choose Pan from the Standard toolbar.

2. At the `Displacement:` prompt, enter **14',15'**.

3. At the `Second point:` prompt, enter **52',15'**.

The apartment floor plan is shifted to the right 38', as shown in figure 12.17. You can also use the crosshairs to pick the points necessary to accomplish this process.

**Fig. 12.17**
Using the Pan option to shift the view of the apartment floor plan.

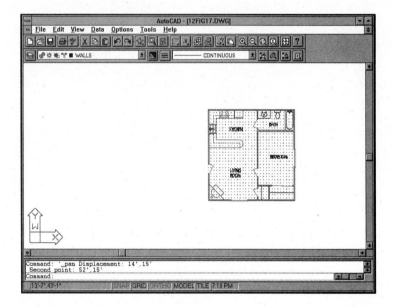

4. Select Previous from the Zoom fly-out toolbar.

   The drawing reverts to that in figure 12.9. Notice that the ZOOM Previous option works not only with the ZOOM command but also with the PAN command.

5. Select Pan from the Standard toolbar.

6. At the `Displacement:` prompt, move the cursor so that the coordinates displayed in the Status bar are approximately 14',15' and press the pick button. Don't worry about being exact.

7. At the `Second point:` prompt, move the cursor so that the absolute coordinates displayed in the Status bar are approximately 52',15'. Then press the pick button.

   Again, don't worry if the coordinates are not exactly right. Your drawing area should now resemble figure 12.10.

8. Select All from the Zoom fly-out toolbar.

IV

# Creating Views (VIEW and DDVIEW)

Panning and zooming a small drawing takes little time, but these operations can slow down considerably when working on a large drawing. Saving *views* of your drawing and accessing them later can greatly increase your drawing speed; this is possible with the VIEW command. A view can be a specific part of your drawing, such as the zoomed view of a room. After creating the view, you can name and save it. You can instruct AutoCAD to display the view at any time. The VIEW command is accessed in the following ways:

■ Choose the Named Views from the View fly-out toolbar.

■ Choose View, Named Views from the pull-down menu. The View Control dialog box is displayed (see fig. 12.18).

■ Enter **ddview** at the Command: prompt. This command also accesses the View Control dialog box.

■ Enter **view** at the Command: prompt. AutoCAD responds with
?/Delete/Restore/Save/Window:.

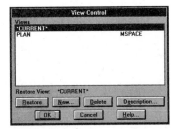

**Fig. 12.18**
The View Control dialog box is used to save and restore views.

> **Note**
>
> The Open File dialog box, used to open existing drawings, includes an option to Select Initial View. This option displays a list of views saved in the drawing and enables you to select the view that you want to see displayed when AutoCAD loads the drawing. This is a very fast way to open a drawing and get to a specific view.

## Listing Views

Entering **?** at the AutoCAD VIEW prompt lists all views you created with the drawing. An alternative is to bring up the View Control dialog box. It also lists all the views saved with the drawing.

## Restoring Views

A saved view can be restored to the screen at any time by highlighting the view in the View Control dialog box and choosing Restore.

## Deleting Views

The best method for listing and deleting views is through the View Control dialog box. To delete a view, highlight it and choose Delete. The view name is immediately removed from the list. If no view name is highlighted, the Delete option is grayed.

## Saving Views

To create a new view, select the New button in the View Control dialog box. This brings up the Define New View dialog box, as shown in figure 12.19. If the view currently on-screen is the view you want to save, enter the name in the text box and click Save View.

**Fig. 12.19**

You can name and define a new view in the Define New View dialog box.

To create a new view, select the Define Window radio button. The Window button is now active. When you click the Window button, you return to the drawing and are asked to define a window. After you name this view and click Save View, it appears in the list as a saved view.

> **Note**
>
> To save on regeneration time, especially with large drawings, you can save a view of the entire drawing. Issue the ZOOM All command and then save the view. You can restore this view at any time without experiencing a drawing regeneration.

### Tutorial: Creating and Saving Views

This tutorial continues from the previous tutorial. Here you use the DDVIEW command to create specific views of the apartment floor plan that can be recalled at any point during the drawing. Follow these steps:

1. Select Zoom Window from the Standard toolbar.

2. Specify the two corners of the window.

        First corner: **16'6",22'5"**
        Other corner: **30'4",30'**

   Your drawing area should look like that in figure 12.20.

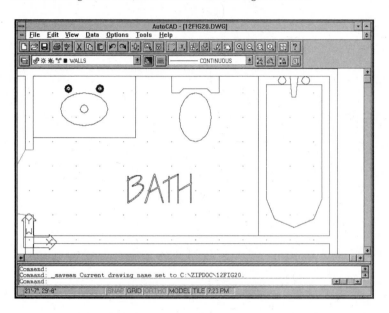

**Fig. 12.20**
ZOOM Window obtains a view of the bathroom in the apartment floor plan.

3. Choose <u>N</u>amed Views from the <u>V</u>iew pull-down menu.

   The View Control dialog box is displayed (see fig. 12.21).

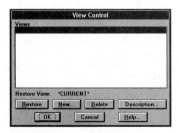

**Fig. 12.21**
Use the View Control dialog box to create a new view.

4. Select the <u>N</u>ew button in the dialog box.

   The Define New View dialog box appears (see fig. 12.22).

**Fig. 12.22**
Use the Define
New View dialog
box to define a
new view of the
bathroom in the
apartment floor
plan.

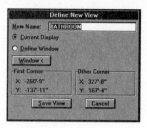

5. Enter **bathroom** in the New Name input box and click Save View.

   The View Control dialog box appears and the view BATHROOM has
   been added to the list.

6. Click OK to close the View Control dialog box.

7. Select All from the Zoom fly-out toolbar.

   The full view of the apartment floor plan returns.

8. To return to the BATHROOM view, choose View, Named Views.

   The View Control dialog box is redisplayed, as shown in figure 12.23.

9. Select the BATHROOM view, click the Restore button, and click OK.

   The BATHROOM view is once again displayed on-screen (refer to
   fig. 12.20).

**Fig. 12.23**
The View Control
dialog box with
the BATHROOM
view listed.

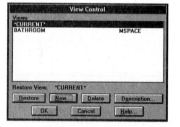

# Using the Aerial View Window

AutoCAD for Windows offers a very powerful feature for zooming and panning a drawing. Aerial View is a tool that allows you to see the entire drawing
in a separate window, as shown in figure 12.24. You can use the Aerial window to quickly locate a view or detail of the drawing. You can change the

magnification, zoom in on an area, and match the view in the graphics window to the one in the Aerial window (or vice versa). You can access the Aerial
window in one of two ways:

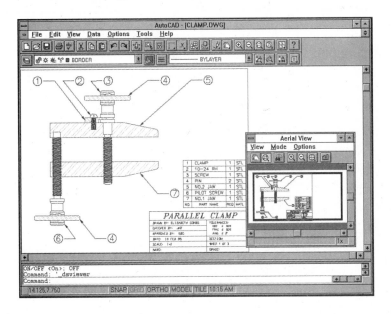

**Fig. 12.24**
The Aerial View
window enables
you to quickly pan
and zoom a
drawing.

- Choose Aerial View from the Tools fly-out toolbar.

- Select Aerial View from the Tools pull-down menu to toggle the Aerial
  View off and on.

- Enter **dsviewer** at the Command: prompt.

You can move the Aerial View window to any location on-screen by clicking
the title bar, holding down the left mouse button, and dragging. You can also
resize this window by moving the cursor to the edge of the window until the
double arrow appears, then hold down the left mouse button and drag the
edge of the window.

## Aerial Window Options

Pan, Zoom Window, Zoom In, Zoom Out, Global, Locator, and Display
Statistics can be directly accessed from the icons in the Aerial View window.
The icon commands are described here:

■ *Pan.* When you press the Pan button, a box outlined in dashes appears. This is the pan box outline, which is the same size as the current zoom box. If there is no zoom box, the pan box is the same as the aerial window. When you move the pan box to a new location and click, the main view displays what was selected in the Aerial View window.

■ *Zoom.* The Zoom option uses crosshairs to create a zoom box in the Aerial View window. The crosshairs are used to select two opposite corners of the zoom box. The zoom box appears as a solid border, and the graphics window displays the area defined in the Aerial View window.

■ *Locator.* Allows you to select the area of the drawing that you wish to have displayed in the Aerial View window. Select Locator from the Aerial View pulldown and drag the target to the drawing area. Let up on the button and the area is displayed in the Aerial View window. The amount of zoom can be changed by selecting Locator Magnification from the Options pull-down menu in the Aerial View window.

■ *Zoom In.* This option automatically doubles the magnification in the Aerial View window.

■ *Zoom Out.* This option reduces the magnification by one-half in the Aerial View window.

■ *Global.* This option redisplays the entire drawing in the Aerial View window.

■ *Statistics.* This option displays information about the display-list driver in the Display Drive Info window (see fig. 12.25). This window shows how many bytes are in the display list and what percentage of the physical memory is being used to maintain the display list. The display list is part of the video driver that controls the display in AutoCAD for your graphics card.

---

**Caution**

It is always good to keep a good account of your memory and system resources. When both of these become low, AutoCAD and other applications may terminate.

---

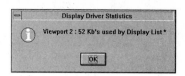

**Fig. 12.25**
The Statistics option.

**IV**

Viewing and Plotting

## Aerial Window Menu Options

The Aerial Window menu bar contains three choices: Ｖiew, Ｍode, and Ｏptions. The following selections are available on the Ｏptions pull-down menu:

■ *Auto Ｖiewport.* The Auto Ｖiewport toggle option is used when multiple viewports are displayed on-screen. The default status of ON displays the active or current viewport in the Aerial View window. When this option is turned off, you must click in the Aerial View title bar to update the window to match the current viewport.

▶ See "Displaying More Than One View (VIEWPORTS or VPORTS)," p. 876

■ *Dynamic Ｕpdate.* When you edit a drawing, the Aerial View window is automatically updated. If the computer begins to slow down during intensive editing operations, you can turn this option off to conserve system resources.

■ *Locator Ｍagnification.* This option enables you to change the magnification. When you choose this option, the Magnification dialog box appears (see fig. 12.26). Choose the + or − button to increase or decrease the magnification.

**Fig. 12.26**
You can change the view magnification in the Magnification dialog box.

■ *Display Ｓtatistics.* This option displays information about the display-list driver in a separate window. It performs the same function as the Statistics button.

The Ｍode pull-down menu contains the following two options:

■ *Ｐan.* This option allows you to pan in the Aerial View. When you move the pan box to a new area and click, the graphics window displays the area you selected in the Aerial View window. This option performs the same function as the Pan button.

■ *Ｚoom.* With this option, you can zoom in on a defined area in the Aerial View window and display it in the graphics window. Ｚoom performs the same function as the Zoom button.

The <u>V</u>iew pull-down menu contains these three options:

- *Zoom <u>I</u>n.* This option controls the magnification of the image in the Aerial View window. Zoom <u>I</u>n doubles the magnification.

- *Zoom <u>O</u>ut.* This option reduces the magnification in the Aerial View window by one-half.

- *<u>G</u>lobal.* With this option, you can redisplay the entire drawing in the Aerial View window.

**Tutorial: Using the Aerial View Window**

This tutorial continues from the preceding tutorial. Here you use the functionality of Aerial View. Follow these steps:

1. If you do not have the Aerial View window displayed, choose <u>T</u>ools, <u>A</u>erial View or choose the Aerial View button from the Standard toolbar.

   The Aerial View window appears over the drawing area (see fig. 12.27).

2. Click <u>P</u>an. Move your cursor within the Aerial View window.

   Notice that a view box similar to the zoom dynamic view box appears in the Aerial View.

3. Move the view box over the kitchen in the Aerial View, as shown in figure 12.28; press the pick button. Notice that not all the kitchen is shown on the main display because the kitchen has a different width to height ratio than the display screen (see fig. 12.29).

**Fig. 12.27**
The Aerial View window.

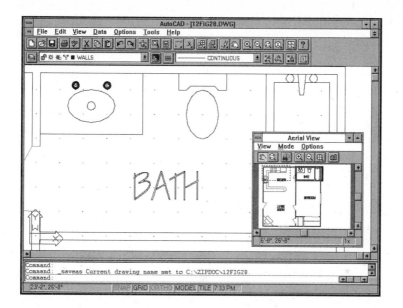

**Fig. 12.28**
Moving the view
box within the
Aerial View
window to display
the kitchen.

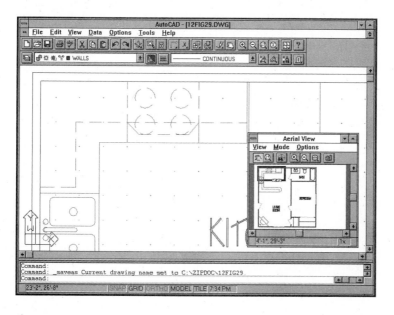

**Fig. 12.29**
The drawing area
after moving the
view box to display
the kitchen.

4. To see a complete view of the kitchen, click Zoom in the Aerial View
   window.

5. Now, still in the Aerial View window, create a window around the
   kitchen, as shown in figure 12.30.

   The resulting drawing area should resemble that in figure 12.31.

**Fig. 12.30**
Creating a window around the kitchen in the Aerial View window.

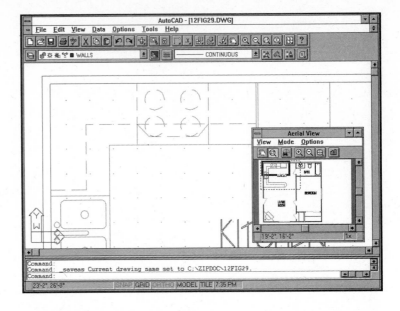

**Fig. 12.31**
The drawing area after you created the window around the kitchen.

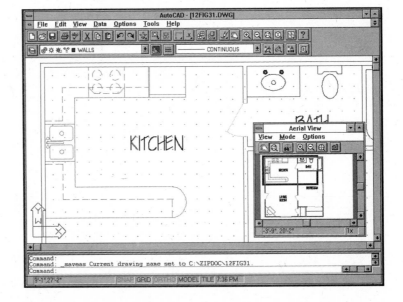

**6.** To perform what is similar to a ZOOM All, select global from the Aerial Window toolbar.

**7.** To close the Aerial View window, click the Minimize button.

# Creating and Viewing Slides (MSLIDE and VSLIDE)

Besides creating geometry with AutoCAD, you can create slides of your drawings. A *slide* is an exact snapshot of your drawing view. You cannot edit, zoom, or modify slides in any way—they are just pictures, not drawings. You can make a slide from any drawing or view of a drawing.

Slides are very useful if you need to give someone an image of your drawing that you don't want edited or changed. Another advantage is that slides appear quickly on-screen. Furthermore, you can create an automated slide show of several drawings to use as a presentation.

When you create a slide of a drawing or a drawing view, a separate file is created. Even if the drawing is changed, the slide remains the same. A slide is an exact *image* of what appears on-screen when the slide is created.

To create a slide, you first display the drawing for which you need a slide. You can display the entire drawing or zoom in to a specific area. You can create as many slides as you like—your only limitation is storage space. The MSLIDE command is used to create a slide.

When you enter **mslide** at the Command: prompt, the Create Slide File dialog box appears. Select the correct path and name the slide. Do not enter a file extension; AutoCAD automatically attaches an SLD file extension.

Viewing a slide is as easy as creating one. You use the VSLIDE command to view slides. When you enter **vslide** at the Command: prompt, the Select Slide File dialog box appears. Select the correct path and pick the slide you want to display. Don't enter the SLD file extension because AutoCAD knows that it's looking for a slide. When the slide is displayed, it doesn't remove your previous drawing. Any attempt to edit the objects on the slide result in editing the objects hidden underneath.

**Tip**

To create a a slide file at its highest resolution, set VIEWRES to its maximum of 20000 before using MSLIDE. When you complete the slides, restore VIEWRES to its previous value.

# Viewing Slides with a Script

A slide-show script file contains three commands:

- *VSLIDE*. This command displays a slide on-screen. You can preload a slide into computer memory for quick display by placing an asterisk (*) before the slide name.

- *DELAY*. This command determines how long the slide file is displayed on-screen. Delays are given in milliseconds. A delay of three seconds is given as DELAY 3000. Any slide can be delayed for a maximum of 33 seconds.

- *RSCRIPT*. This command creates a continuous slide show. You can include the RSCRIPT at the end of the script file to have the slides continually cycle through the show. To stop the show, press the Backspace key.

To create a slide show, you begin with a script file as shown below. The script file can be any text editor, such as Windows Notepad. When naming the script file, include the extension SCR. The following sample script loads four slides, each appearing for two seconds. The show then repeats. The next slide is preloaded while the current one is viewed. Following is a sample script file:

```
VSLIDE C:\UAW13\PLAN1
VSLIDE *C:\UAW13\PLAN2
DELAY 2000
VSLIDE
VSLIDE *C:\UAW13\PLAN3
DELAY 2000
VSLIDE
VSLIDE *C:\UAW13\PLAN4
DELAY 2000
VSLIDE
DELAY 2000
RSCRIPT
```

When creating slide shows on disk, make sure that you include the disk drive and path where the slides appear. In this example, it is assumed that all the slides are located in C:\UAW13\.

To view the slide show, enter **script** at the Command: prompt and select the script file from the Select Script File dialog box. You don't need to enter the *.SCR extension. When the show begins, the commands in the script file are displayed at the Command: prompt as the slides appear. Just press the Backspace key to stop the show.

# From Here...

Zooming and panning a drawing are as common as creating and editing geometry because most drawings don't show enough detail on-screen to work on properly. In a simple drawing, zooming and panning operations are performed very quickly. As the drawing complexity increases, remember to save and restore views to reduce regeneration time.

Take advantage of the Aerial View window. This can greatly increase your productivity because you can always display a full view of the drawing on-screen. The Aerial View window also slows down on complex drawings, so it is not a substitute for saving and restoring views.

Creating and viewing slides can be an effective method for showing others your work or creating CAD presentations. Although slides can't be edited or modified, they can be displayed quickly on-screen. A slide is just a snapshot of a drawing and cannot be affected by any changes to the drawing.

For more information about model space and paper space and viewing 3D models, see the following chapters:

■ Chapter 13, "Understanding Model Space and Paper Space," explains the use of creating viewports with different scales to be plotted on a single sheet of paper.

■ Chapter 30, "Viewing a 3D Model," shows you how to use multiple viewports and dynamically change a viewpoint.

In the next chapter you begin to learn how to create and utilize viewports in paper space. All of the geometry that you created up to this point has been in model space. Using paper space, you can now create geometry without concern for its plotted scale. Paper space and model space are very important topics for both 2D and 3D drawings.

# On Your Own

Load the file C:\UAW13\12DWG01. This is the apartment complex example that you worked with throughout this chapter. Create a slide show of the apartment complex, showing each room.

Hints:

1. Use any combination of the different viewing commands and zoom in on one room. Create a slide of the view with the MSLIDE command.

2. Zoom back to the full view; then zoom in on another room and create a different slide. Save the slides in \UAW13, as C:\UAW13\ROOM1, C:\UAW13\ROOM2, and so on.

3. Continue creating a different slide for each room until you create four different slides.

4. Open Windows Notepad and create a script file. Call it C:\UAW13\APART.SCR. Type the script, following the example earlier in the chapter, substituting C:\UAW13\ROOM1 for C:\UAW13\PLAN1 in this example. Include all four slides you just created. Save your script file and exit Notepad.

5. Return to AutoCAD and enter **script** at the Command: prompt. Select the C:\UAW13\APART file. Then sit back and watch the show.

# Chapter 13

# Understanding Model Space and Paper Space

Understanding model space and paper space is essential in order to become a proficient AutoCAD user. Regardless of the 2D or 3D nature of your drawings, knowing why and how to use paper space is important. Model space and paper space commands are sometimes challenging to learn, but always well worth the effort. Let's get to it!

This chapter discusses the basics of learning why and how paper space can be used to plot a drawing. Topics include the following:

- How model space is different from paper space

- Defining tiled model space

- Creating viewport configurations

- Getting familiar with multiple viewports—tutorial

- How paper space is great for plotting

- Floating model space—a new term, a familiar process

- Planning your plot using paper space

- Using the TILEMODE system variable to control your space

- Creating and arranging paper space viewports

- Making floating viewports ready for plotting

- Unleashing powerful plotting abilities—tutorial using paper space

# What Is Model Space?

There are two spaces in AutoCAD—model space and paper space. *Model space* is where most of the action is. This is a three dimensional environment where sky scrapers are drawn, race car engines are designed, and the cities of the future are evaluated. You can have a lot of fun in model space. *Paper space* is an optional two-dimensional environment that is well-suited for plotting multiple views of your 2D or 3D work.

There are two terms you need to study to begin understanding model space: *model space* and *viewports*. Consider the following:

> In a kitchen there is a chef, and several video cameras and televisions. The cameras film the chef and the televisions display the chef. The televisions are welded together, making it impossible to move them around separately. If you stand in the kitchen you can see the chef, from different angles, displayed on the televisions.

The chef in the kitchen is an object in model space. The chef is displayed through one or more televisions. Objects in model space are displayed through one or more viewports. The televisions are in a nonmovable configuration like the viewports in model space which are always tiled and cannot be moved individually.

Unlike the example with the chef, objects in model space are not only displayed, but also created and edited through viewports. In the model space environment, there is always at least one active viewport displaying the objects in model space. It is possible to create multiple viewports in model space.

When you start a new drawing using the unchanged ACAD.DWG drawing, or by choosing No Prototype in the Create New Drawing dialog box, you are looking at model space through a single viewport. This viewport is in model space and until now, you may not have thought of creating, editing and displaying your drawing through a viewport, but you were.

Sometimes it's important to see several views of your drawing being displayed at once. This is when multiple viewports are used instead of just a single viewport. Figure 13.1 shows a drawing displayed through a single viewport. Figure 13.2 is the same drawing displayed through four viewports.

The advantage of multiple model space viewports is the ability to zoom and pan to show different magnified areas of the drawing while having another viewport show the entire drawing. This arrangement makes it easier to draw large objects from one small area of the drawing to another without having to do transparent zooms and pans, and without losing your global view.

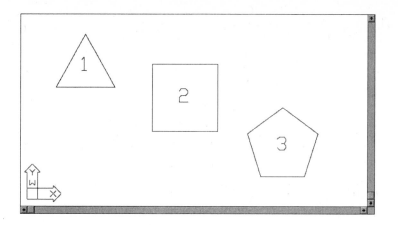

**Fig. 13.1**
A single viewport
in model space.

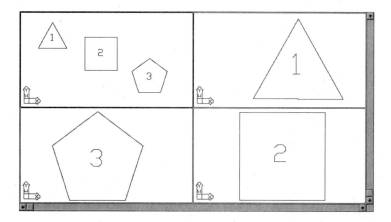

**Fig. 13.2**
Four viewports in
model space.

> **Note**
>
> Although you can display several tiled model space viewports, you can plot only one viewport.

## What Is Tiled Model Space?

Multiple viewports in model space are always tiled. Just like ceramic tiles in a typical bathroom, tiled viewports cannot overlap one another. Tiled model space is a new term used with AutoCAD Release 13. Tiled model space is the environment where viewports are always tiled. Though the term tiled model space is new, the ability to create multiple configurations of tiled viewports is not new.

## Creating Multiple Model Space Viewports (VPORTS)

Setting up multiple viewports in model space or tiled viewports is easy. By using the Tiled Viewport Layout dialog box, you control not only the number of tiled viewports displayed, but also the configuration of these viewports. Using the View pull-down menu, select Tiled Viewports to display the menu options available for controlling tiled viewports (see fig. 13.3). When you choose Tiled Viewports, Layout, the Tiled Viewport Layout dialog box is displayed (see fig. 13.4).

**Fig. 13.3**
The View pull-down menu showing Tiled Viewports menu options.

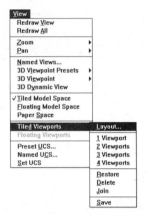

**Fig. 13.4**
The Tiled Viewport Layout dialog box. If the OK button is chosen, AutoCAD will create three viewports where the active viewport is now.

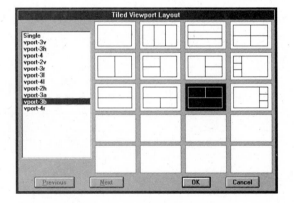

The number and arrangement of tiled viewports can be controlled by using the VPORTS command, or by using the Tiled Viewport Layout dialog box. To access the VPORTS command, do one of following:

■ Select View, Tiled Viewports.

■ Enter **vports** at the Command: prompt.

By default, when multiple viewports are created, the active viewport is the viewport located in the lower-right corner of the previously active viewport. This is true regardless of how many viewports you have created. There probably won't be a need to create more than 12 tiled viewports. Creating more than 12 viewports in tiled model space yields very small viewports that are probably too small for practical use. Depending on your computer hardware, you may be able to create over 40 tiled viewports.

Though several viewports can be created, only one viewport can be active at any given time. The active viewport is indicated by a heavy border around the viewport and is where your screen cursor (or crosshairs) is located. Through the active tiled viewport you create, edit and change the display of your objects in model space. The method of making a different viewport active is simple. The screen cursor is first moved away from the active viewport. When the screen cursor is outside the active viewport, it is displayed as an arrow. Placing this arrow within a viewport border and pressing the pick button makes that viewport active.

---

**Caution**

When selecting objects from multiple viewports, the previously selected objects may not appear to be highlighted in viewports other than the current viewport, even though the objects may be selected and included in the selection set.

---

To access the VPORTS command type **vports** at the `Command:` prompt. You are shown the following response:

```
Command: vports
Save/Restore/Delete/Join/SIngle/?/2/<3>/4:
```

Viewport layouts can be saved, restored and deleted using the VPORTS command options. Saving a viewport layout in model space allows the same layout to be restored if the configuration is changed. The tiled viewport configuration, which has been given a name, also can be restored when creating non-tiled viewports in paper space (see "What is Floating Model Space?" later in this chapter). If you want to delete the name of a viewport configuration, use the Delete option with the VPORTS command.

The SIngle option restores the display to a single viewport regardless of how many viewports are currently being displayed. The 2 option creates two viewports. AutoCAD prompts you to specify whether the viewports will be created with a horizontal or vertical common border.

**Tip**

It is better to save a multiple viewport configuration before changing it. It's quicker to restore the viewport layout rather than to go through the steps to create the viewports and arrange the views. Also, if viewport configurations are saved, they can be restored in paper space using the MVIEW command.

**Tip**
When changing the display from multiple viewports to a single viewport, AutoCAD displays the new single viewport with the same drawing area and zoom scale factor as the previously active viewport. To eliminate unnecessary steps, make the desired viewport active before changing from multiple viewports to a single viewport.

Sometimes two viewports can be joined into one viewport. Joining viewports is accomplished using the Join option with the VPORTS command. When joining tiled viewports, the viewports must share a border of the same size and the joined, or combined, viewport must form a rectangular shape (L shapes aren't possible).

### Caution

If you join two viewports, and then use the UNDO command, the active viewport will be the one closest to the lower-right corner of your display, regardless of which viewport was active before joining the viewports.

The 3 option (default) creates three viewports. The options are Horizontal, Vertical, Above, Below, Left or Right. Horizontal and Vertical options create three parallel viewports where the viewports are parallel vertically or horizontally. The Above, Below, Left or Right options divide the current viewport into three viewports, where the larger of the three viewports are located above, below, to the left or right of the other two smaller viewports.

Choosing the 4 option divides the current viewport into four equally sized viewports, making the lower-right viewport the active viewport.

When you have finished creating the number and arrangement of viewports, create or restore views to each viewport created. To restore views to each of the viewports, make the desired viewport active. Using the VIEW command with the Restore option, specify the view to restore. This method is only possible if views have been saved previously. The alternative to restoring views requires that you create the views within each viewport by making the desired viewport active, then using ZOOM and/or PAN commands to create the desired view within each viewport.

◀ See "Using Zoom to Control the Display (ZOOM)," p. 336

### Note

It's OK to create multiple viewports if names of views have not been saved. You may find it easier to use the ZOOM command with the Dynamic option, and perhaps also the PAN command, to create the desired view of the area of the drawing you want to display in each of the multiple viewports. Using ZOOM with the dynamic option displays the viewport window proportionate to the viewport. If the viewport is wide horizontally and narrow vertically, the dynamic window shown, while using the DYNAMIC ZOOM command option, displays the same shape as the current viewport. This is very helpful when selecting the desired area for each viewport to display.

Model space is a 3D environment where drawing objects are created and edited. The objects in model space are always created, edited and viewed through viewports. AutoCAD can display a single viewport or multiple viewports in the tiled model space environment. Tiled model space is the model space environment where viewports are always tiled. The VPORTS command allows us to create and arrange multiple tiled viewports and save and restore the viewport configurations. When multiple viewports are created, only one viewport can be active at any given time.

## Tutorial: Using Tiled Viewports

In the following tutorial, you examine several of the options available when using the VPORTS command. Using the VPORTS command you learn how to create multiple tiled viewports, how to restore views to desired viewports, and how to draw within viewports. Also, you learn how to join viewports, how to save viewport configurations, and how to restore our display to a single viewport.

**1.** Open the drawing named 13DWG01 (see fig. 13.5).

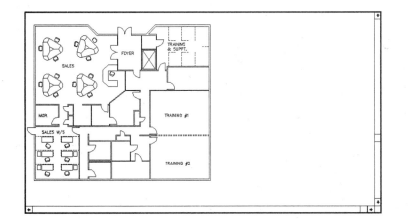

**Tip**
When you are prompted to specify the vertical or horizontal orientation of new viewports, remember AutoCAD wants to know if the common viewport border needs to be horizontal or vertical.

**Fig. 13.5**
The drawing before creating a viewport configuration.

**2.** Choose View, Tiled Viewports, Layout. This displays the Tiled Viewport Layout dialog box. The desired viewport layout for beginning this exercise is described on the right side of the dialog box as Three: Left. Highlight and double click Three: Left, or highlight Three: Left and choose OK. (Refer to fig. 13.4.)

This changes the display from a single viewport to having three viewports—two on the right and one left. Notice the left viewport is active—the screen cursor is within it and this viewport also has a heavier border around it (see fig. 13.6). With the left viewport active, restore a view (the views you'll be restoring were saved before you opened this drawing).

**Fig. 13.6**

The drawing as it looks after using the Tiled Viewport Layout dialog box and selecting the Three: Left configuration. Notice the bottom viewport is active.

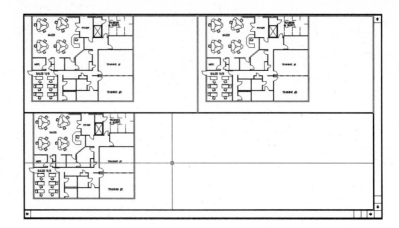

3. To restore the first view, select <u>V</u>iew, <u>N</u>amed Views from the pull-down menu. This displays the View Control dialog box. The view you want to restore is called Overall—choose Overall Restore and OK.

   Notice that a horizontal wall line is missing from the bottom of the drawing. Use the smaller viewports to draw in the missing line. Restore the views to the upper viewports, and then you are able to draw the missing line at the bottom of the building.

4. Before a view can be restored to a viewport, the viewport must be active. To activate the upper-right viewport, move the screen cursor from the left viewport to the upper-right viewport area. Notice that the screen cursor changes from the crosshairs to an arrow when you move it outside of the active viewport. With the screen cursor above the upper-right viewport (now displayed as an arrow), click the pick button. This makes this upper-left viewport active. Now that the upper-left viewport is active, the screen cursor is within this viewport and there is a heavy border around this viewport.

5. To restore the desired view to this upper-left viewport, choose <u>V</u>iew, <u>N</u>amed Views, then pick 1507 as the view name to restore. Choose Restore and OK. You won't need to alter the zoom factor of this viewport. This viewport is now ready for editing.

6. Make the lower-right viewport similar in appearance to the current, upper-left viewport. To do this, make the lower-right viewport active. Move the screen cursor to the lower-right viewport area and click the Pick button.

**7.** Restoring the necessary view to this viewport can be accomplished again by invoking the View Control dialog box. Restore view 1532 to the current viewport.

At this point, the drawing is set up to allow you to draw a long line from one small part of the drawing to another without having to use transparent zooms and pans and without losing the global view.

The next step involves drawing a horizontal line connecting the end points of the vertical lines in the two upper viewports. Notice the objects in these viewports do not "line-up"—that's OK. When setting up these viewports, don't worry about lining up objects in adjacent viewports—focus on displaying the important parts you need for creating and/or editing your drawing.

**8.** Draw a line from the endpoint of the line in the upper-right viewport (see fig.13.7) to the endpoint of the line in the right viewport. Click to make viewports active and use object snap for accuracy.

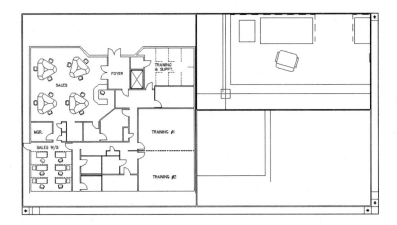

**Fig. 13.7**
Endpoint selections for drawing a line from one small part of a drawing to another, using multiple viewports.

The next steps reviews how to join viewports, how to make multiple viewports within a viewport when multiple viewports are being displayed, how to save viewport configurations for later use, and how to restore the display from multiple viewports to a single viewport.

**9.** To join the two right viewports, select Vi̲ew from the pull-down menu, then T̲iled Viewports, J̲oin. AutoCAD displays the following prompt:

```
Select dominant viewport <current>:
```

Your response should be to pick within the current upper-right viewport, or to press Enter (because the current viewport is the default option, and it is the first of the two viewports you want to join).

After selecting the dominant viewport, the next prompt from Auto-CAD is

```
Select viewport to join:
```

Move the screen cursor to the lower-right viewport area (again, the crosshairs changes to an arrow), and select the Pick button.

10. Restore the view of the overall drawing to the single viewport at the top of your display. Use the ZOOM command to have the objects displayed bigger in the viewport. From the pull-down menu, select View, Named Views. Choose ALL as the view to restore; choose the Restore option, then choose OK.

11. Use the ZOOM command to enlarge the view. At this point, the top and bottom viewports should look identical. Two viewports are displayed, each indicating the same view at the same zoom factor.

   The next step involves creating multiple viewports within the left viewport, while keeping the top viewport unchanged. In this example, the desired result yields two viewports at the bottom where there is currently one. Again, use the VPORTS command from the pull-down menu.

12. Make the left viewport active by moving the screen cursor to that area and then press the Pick button.

13. Create two viewports within the current viewport by using the pull-down menu and picking View, Tiled Viewports, 2 Viewports. AutoCAD prompts you for the following:

```
Horizontal/<Vertical>:
```

Because the viewports have a common horizontal side, choose the horizontal option by pressing Enter. This creates two viewports.

Make one of the newly created viewports active and zoom into a portion of the drawing. Repeat this for the other new viewport to zoom into a different area.

It's easy to restore your display to a single viewport, but it is usually good practice to save the current viewport configuration before doing so. By saving a viewport layout, you have the option of being able to quickly restore the viewport configuration at the time it was saved. The restoration of the saved viewport layout displays the same number and arrangement of viewports. The displayed areas and zoom factors within each viewport are also restored as they were saved.

By saving viewport layouts, you can reuse the layout in the paper space environment when creating floating viewports (see "Setting up Floating Model Space Viewports in Paper Space," later in this chapter).

**14.** To save the viewport settings, select <u>V</u>iew, Tile<u>d</u> Viewports, <u>S</u>ave. AutoCAD displays the following prompt:

```
Name for new viewport configuration:
```

At the prompt, type **1563-1547**. AutoCAD is now able to restore this viewport configuration using the restore option with the VPORTS command in model space, or with the MVIEW command in paper space.

**15.** With the current viewport configuration saved, go back to displaying your drawing through a single viewport. First, click on the top viewport to make it active.

**16.** Change the display from multiple viewports to a single viewport by Selecting <u>V</u>iew, Tile<u>d</u> Viewports, 1 Viewport.

# What Is Paper Space?

Model space and paper space are like outer space—you can't see them, but you can see objects in them. Drawings in paper space appear as 3D images but cannot be manipulated as such. These images are displayed in preparation for printing or plotting. The view you see in the paper space environment is referred to as the paper space view (regardless of how many, if any, paper space viewports have been created).

The main purpose of paper space is the ability to create floating viewports (a new term used in AutoCAD Release 13). *Floating viewports* are viewports created in the paper space environment. These floating viewports have, until now, been referred to as paper space viewports, or non-tiled viewports. There are many advantages of floating viewports compared to tiled model space viewports: the ability to move and overlap floating viewports, and the ability to make viewport edges invisible so only the objects in model space are displayed. Floating viewports also can be turned off so the display within them is invisible.

Viewports in paper space are objects similar to polylines created with the RECTANGLE command. They can be edited many ways: stretched, moved, erased, and so on. The advantages of non-tiled viewports makes paper space well-suited for plotting multiple views of your 2D or 3D objects. You can only select objects that are drawn in the current space.

Plotting from paper space typically involves the following procedure.

**1.** After objects are drawn in model space, the paper space view is displayed, which, when first displayed, looks like a blank sheet of paper.

**2.** A title block is inserted at a scale of 1:1 (full size).

**3.** Floating viewports are created.

**4.** Views of model space are created or restored and zoomed to the proper scale within each of the floating model space viewports being displayed in the paper space environment.

**5.** Viewport borders can be made invisible and titles or other annotations can be added.

The key difference between a viewport in paper space versus in model space is that a paper space or floating viewport is in itself an object like other AutoCAD objects. These ports can be moved or stretched to accommodate your viewing needs. Model space ports cannot be moved or even be plotted.

As Table 13.1 indicates, the TILEMODE system variable controls which space you are in—model space or paper space. To set the value of TILEMODE, choose the Model Space icon on the Standard toolbar. Notice the fly out has icons to switch TILEMODE from model space to floating model space to paper space (see fig. 13.8).

| Table 13.1 | TILEMODE System Variable Controls | | | |
| --- | --- | --- | --- | --- |
| **System Variable** | **Setting** | **Meaning** | **Space Activated** | **Viewport Configuration** |
| TILEMODE | 0 | OFF | Paper Space | Non-Tiled |
| TILEMODE | 1 | ON | Model Space | Tiled |

**Fig. 13.8**
Controlling the TILEMODE system variable using the fly out menu.

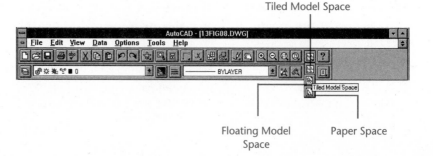

Tiled Model Space

Floating Model Space

Paper Space

In figure 13.9, focus your attention on the Tiled Model Space, Floating Model Space and Paper Space icons. Choosing the Tiled Model Space icon sets the TILEMODE value to 1. This means viewports must be tiled, therefore, you automatically go to model space (there is no change if you're already there). If multiple viewports exist in model space, the active viewport is the same viewport that was active when you left model space. To set TILEMODE to a value of one from the Command: prompt, do the following:

```
Command: tilemode
New value for TILEMODE <1>: 1
```

When you choose the Paper Space icon, TILEMODE is set to a value of zero, making non-tiled viewports available and forcing you into paper space. When first going into paper space, you may be surprised because your drawing disappears (see fig. 13.9). Don't worry; everything is still there in model space. In the next section you will create a few paper space viewports to view your drawing.

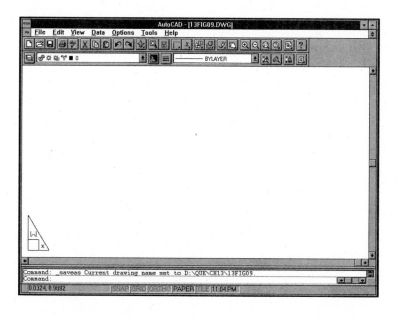

**Fig. 13.9**
The display showing the paper space view before floating viewports are created.

## What Is Floating Model Space?

Floating model space is a new term used with AutoCAD Release 13. Floating model space means that model space is accessed through a floating viewport in paper space. Floating viewports must be created before floating model space is possible.

The flow chart in figure 13.10 illustrates what happens when you select Floating Model Space from the View pull-down menu. First, AutoCAD makes sure you're in paper space by checking and then setting, if necessary, the TILEMODE system variable to zero.

Next unless there are no viewports in the current paper space display, AutoCAD starts the MSPACE command, making a viewport in the current display active (this is floating model space). The flow chart describes in detail which viewports are chosen to be active. If there are no viewports in the current paper space display, AutoCAD starts the MVIEW command so they can be created. The MVIEW command can be canceled if you do not want to create viewports.

**Fig. 13.10**

A chart of what happens when you choose Floating Model Space from the View pull-down menu.

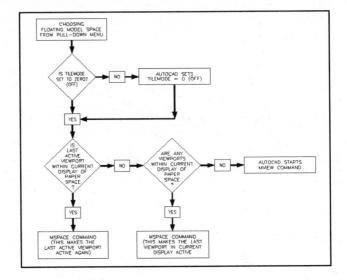

## Setting Up Floating Model Space Viewports in Paper Space (MVIEW)

The MVIEW command allows us to, among other things, create one or more floating viewports. It is the paper space equivalent of the VPORTS command used in model space. The same configuration of predefined viewport configurations available with the VPORTS command is available when creating floating viewports with the MVIEW command. The viewports created with MVIEW are always non-tiled, or floating, and the MVIEW command is only available while you are in paper space when TILEMODE has a value of zero (off). To access the MVIEW command:

- Choose Floating Viewports from the View menu.

- At the Command: prompt enter **mview.**

```
Command: mview
ON/OFF/Hideplot/Fit/2/3/4/Restore/<First Point>:
```

---

**Caution**

Avoid making paper space viewports within other paper space viewports. Also, use caution when creating two paper space viewports with the same size and location (one on top of another). This makes it difficult to select one of the viewports.

---

The MVIEW command also can be used to hide the lines of 3D objects when plotting. This is achieved by choosing the Hideplot option, then selecting Floating Viewports which, when plotted, will have hidden lines removed.

▶ See "Plotting a 3D Model," p. 883

Using MVIEW with the Restore option allows a viewport configuration to be duplicated in paper space if the tiled viewport configuration was previously saved and created in model space. The floating viewports created would have the same layout as the tiled viewports in model space, and the views within each viewport would also be the same.

Finally, the MVIEW command can be used to set floating viewports off or on. When a floating viewport is set to off, the viewport is similar to a rectangle. The display of model space within the viewport is completely invisible, but the viewport border is visible. If floating viewports have been set to off using MVIEW, they cannot be active. Use the MVIEW OFF option to turn off viewports that you don't need while editing your drawing. This will speed up screen regenerations because AutoCAD won't have to regenerate the viewport. You can only turn off viewports that are visible on the screen so that you can select them.

---

**Note**

To hide the floating viewport borders, put the floating viewport on a frozen layer. If a floating viewport is on a frozen layer, the objects displayed within the viewport remain visible. Only the active floating viewport has a temporary border around it—indicating it is active. To hide the display of objects in the viewport, use the MVIEW command with the off option and then select the desired viewport(s). If you don't need the floating viewport, erase it.

> **Note**
>
> Leave the UCS icon on if you put a floating viewport on a frozen layer and there are
> no objects in model space being displayed in the viewport. When paper space is your
> environment, you may not be able to see any indication that a viewport exists unless
> the UCS icon is on, and unless the floating viewport is active, the UCS icon is not
> plotted.

The maximum number of viewports that can be regenerated at one time is
controlled with the MAXACTVP system variable. This can be set from 1 to a
maximum of 48.

## Switching from Paper Space to Floating Model Space and Back (MSPACE and PSPACE)

When you are editing your drawing with TILEMODE=0, you can switch in
and out of floating viewports using the commands MSPACE and PSPACE. The
MSPACE command takes you into the most recently active floating viewport.
You can access the MSPACE command with one of the following methods:

- From the Standard toolbar choose the Floating Model Space button.

- From the pull-down menu select <u>V</u>iew, <u>F</u>loating Model Space.

- At the Command: prompt enter **mspace** or **ms.**

Re-entering paper space can be accomplished through one of the following
methods:

- From the Standard toolbar choose the Paper Space button.

- From the pull-down menu select <u>V</u>iew, Paper <u>S</u>pace.

- At the Command: prompt enter **pspace** or **ps**.

MSPACE and PSPACE are commands that are only available when the paper
space view is displayed (TILEMODE set to zero). MSPACE and PSPACE commands swap the AutoCAD user back and forth from an active Floating Model
Space viewport to the paper space environment. In other words, the paper
space view is still displayed; but MSPACE and PSPACE control whether a
floating viewport is active (making objects in model space accessible), or if
the active drawing environment is paper space.

## Scaling Paper Space Viewports

When you are in floating model space, you use several display commands to observe the objects in model space. The ZOOM and PAN commands are usually used to display the part of your drawing in each viewport. If you have already created the views and saved them with the VIEW command when you were in tiled model space, simply use the VIEW command again in floating model space to restore those views.

Usually, it is easier to consider everything in the paper space environment to be at the full scale of the plotted output. The title block and drawing border are typically inserted as blocks at full scale. After the views have been created or restored to the desired viewports, floating model space should be scaled relative to the scale of the plotted drawing. This is done with the ZOOM command.

If you're plotting a floor plan of a house in paper space, create a floating viewport within a full size border indicating your plot size. Make the floating viewport active using the MSPACE, or MS command. This puts you in floating model space (a floating viewport is active).

With the Floating Model Space viewport displaying the desired objects, issue the ZOOM command to scale the objects in the viewport relative to the area in paper space (which is the size of the plotted drawing). If you plot the drawing at a scale of 1/4"=1', consider this to be a factor of 1:48 between the actual size of the objects drawn and the size of the plotted objects. The plotted scale factor of 1:48 is derived by dividing the actual drawing units (12 inches) by the plotted units (1/4"). For example, (12/.25=48). Remember, always draw your objects at full scale.

While the floating viewport is active (the environment is Floating Model Space), type **zoom** and then press Enter at the Command: prompt followed by **1/48xp**. This will scale the objects in the active floating viewport exactly 48 times smaller than the paper space environment (the paper space environment should always be full size).

The same procedure is used for creating and plotting other floating viewports for the same drawing. If the objects within the viewport aren't lined up within the viewport, use the PAN command to change the location of the objects in model space relative to the floating viewport.

If the viewport turns out to be the wrong size, you can fix it easily. First, go to the paper space environment (PSPACE or PS). Second, resize the viewport (stretch it, scale it, move it, and so on). In paper space you also can move the floating viewports so the objects within them line up properly in the paper space drawing. In paper space, viewports can be moved relative to object snaps in model space. Floating viewports can be scaled, stretched, and mirrored like most any other AutoCAD object. This is perhaps most easily accomplished using grips.

## Tutorial: Creating and Using Floating Viewports in Paper Space

In the following tutorial, you set up a drawing to be plotted in paper space. First, you make paper space the working environment, then create a couple of floating viewports. The viewports display the objects in the drawing at different scales. Notes will be added to the drawing, and the floating viewport borders will be frozen.

1. Open the drawing 13DWG02, supplied on the work disk. The drawing, should look like figure 13.11. The model space of the wrench is displayed through a single tiled viewport. To observe the paper space view, choose Paper Space from the View pull-down menu.

**Fig. 13.11**
The WRENCH drawing as displayed in model space.

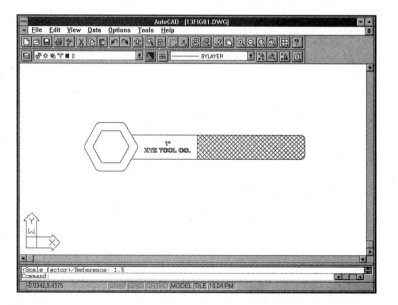

2. Click the Layers icon on the Object Properties toolbar to open the Layer Control dialog box and select Viewport as the current layer.

3. From the Standard toolbar choose the Tile Model Space flyout and select the Floating Model Space button. This will start the MVIEW command.

4. AutoCAD wants to know, by default, where the first corner of a single floating viewport will be. Enter an absolute value of 2,1 for the first corner of the floating viewport. The other corner is entered using a relative coordinate of @5,3. This creates a 5" × 3" floating viewport. Type **ms** to make the new viewport active

5. Choose <u>V</u>iew, <u>N</u>amed Views, and select the view named Stamp.

6. At the Command: prompt type **Z,** Enter followed by **2XP** and Enter. This starts the ZOOM command, then scales the objects in the active floating viewport relative to the paper space scale. This means that the objects in this viewport are plotted to a scale factor of 2:1.

7. To create the other floating viewport choose the Floating Viewport icon from the Tiled Model Space flyout. Similar to the first viewport, specify the first point of the viewport to be 2,4 and the other corner to be @8,4.

8. At the Command: prompt type **z,** and press Enter, followed by **1xp** and Enter. This starts the ZOOM command, then scales the objects in the active floating viewport relative to the paper space scale. This means that the objects in this viewport are plotted to a scale factor of 1:1.

9. Now add a title block. Choose the Insert Block button from the Draw toolbar to insert the TBAF block (this is a block with a border for plotting your drawing on standard 8 1/2" × 11" paper, which was created for the wrench example on the disk). Attributes are used in the title block within the border. Specify the insertion base point to be 1,0; then choose the defaults for the x and y scale factors, and the rotation angle.

▶ See "Working with Attributes," p. 713

10. After you have chosen the three default values, AutoCAD prompts you for attribute information to be automatically placed in the title block. When prompted to enter an attribute value, either choose the default attribute value by pressing Enter, or fill in the attribute values as you like. Now the drawing is ready for a few finishing touches.

11. To add notes, switch from floating model space to paper space. From the Tiled Model Space flyout choose the Paper Space button.

12. Because the floating viewports were created on a layer called VPORTS, you can make their borders "invisible" by freezing that layer. Select the

◀ See "Under-
standing
Layers,"
p. 175

Layers button from the Object Properties toolbar to open the Layer Control Dialog box. Create a current layer NOTES, then freeze layer VIEWPORTS.

**13.** Choose the Rectangle button from the Draw toolbar, specifying the corners to be 2,1 and @5,3.

**14.** Using the Copy icon on the Modify toolbar. Copy this rectangle from the pick points shown in figure 13.13.

**15.** Using the Scale icon on the Modify toolbar, scale the last rectangle to a value of .5 (the base point for the scale is the same endpoint as the second point of displacement (see fig. 13.12) used when copying the rectangle).

**16.** Draw lines connecting the corners of the two rectangles that you just created as shown in figure 13.13. Note that the two bottom lines have been trimmed to give the drawing a 3D effect.

**17.** Finally, label your two views by selecting the Dtext icon from the Draw toolbar, and entering the scale value as shown in figure 13.13.

**Fig. 13.12**
Object snap indications assisting the annotating of the WRENCH drawing in paper space.

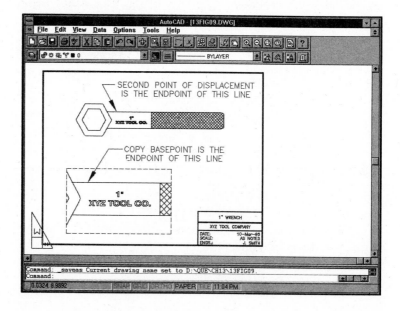

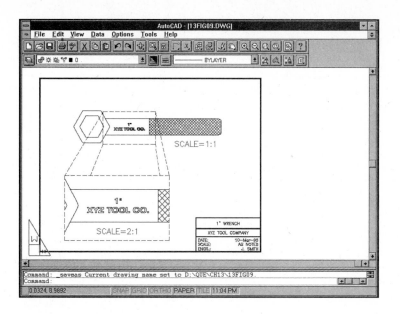

**Fig. 13.13**
The paper space
view of the
WRENCH drawing
ready for plotting.

# From Here...

This chapter discussed the basics of how and why paper space can be used to plot a drawing. For related information, see the following chapters:

- Chapter 14, "Plotting a Drawing," discusses how to use the PLOT command.

- Chapter 30, "Viewing a 3D Model," includes more information on using multiple viewports.

# On Your Own

Using the drawing 13DWG01 used earlier in the chapter, create a 34" × 22" border in paper space for plotting on a D-size sheet. Create a viewport to show the entire floor plan at 1/4"=1'-0" scale. Create another viewport to show an enlarged view of the desk arrangement in the sales department at 1/2"=1'-0".

Hints:

**1.** Draw a 34" × 22" rectangle border in paper space.

**Fig. 13.14**

A viewport showing an office floor plan with another viewport showing a desk arrangement.

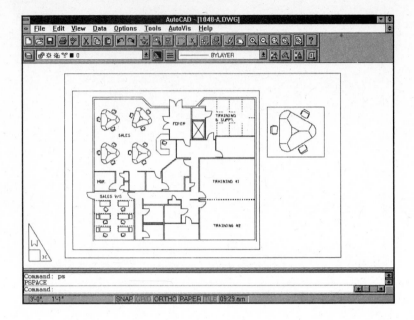

2. Create the larger viewport using coordinates 1",1" and 24",20" as the corner points.

3. Use the XP option of the ZOOM command to zoom to a scale factor of 1/4"=1'–0".

4. Create the smaller viewport at coordinates 25",12", and 32",18".

5. Zoom this viewport to a scale factor of 1/2"=1'–0".

# Chapter 14

# Plotting a Drawing

Plotting an AutoCAD drawing is an essential part of the drafting process. Plotting lets you see the image of the drawing on paper. This "hard copy" image can be used to check for errors, distribute the image, and archive it for later use. To create the desired image on paper, you must understand the PLOT command and plotting configuration parameters. This chapter shows you how to reproduce an AutoCAD drawing on paper.

Before you begin, you first need to understand the plot process. When you create drawing objects such as lines and circles, AutoCAD stores them on the computer hard drive/disk as descriptive parameters (line, style, layer, and so on) and geometric values (coordinates, radius, etc.) They are saved permanently in the drawing database for future use. So, every time a drawing is opened, AutoCAD converts that drawing's database into data in the form of pixels, which then are displayed on-screen. When you execute the PLOT command, AutoCAD uses the configured plotter driver software to convert the drawing's database into commands that the chosen plotter can understand. For pen plotters, this translates into a series of PEN UP and PEN DOWN movements along with the movement of paper or pens in relation to one another.

After you complete this chapter, you'll know how to use the PLOT command. This chapter discusses the plotting process as it relates to two-dimensional drawings. The process to plot a three-dimensional drawing is similar, except for the settings of the drawing. For more information on plotting 3D drawings, refer to Chapter 31, "Plotting a 3D Model."

# Configuring AutoCAD for Plotting

To use the plotter or the printer, you need to configure AutoCAD. AutoCAD could have been configured when it was first loaded. Configuration parameters, including those of the chosen plotter, are stored in the file named ACAD.CFG. Even if a plotter was configured, you should follow the instructions to set up a system printer and a generic C-size plotter. These instructions set all of the default options as the examples in this chapter will use them.

## Tutorial: Configuring Your Plotter

In this tutorial, you can configure your plotter for the other tutorials in this chapter. Follow these steps:

1. To configure a plotter or printer, choose Options, Select Configure.

   AutoCAD lists the existing configuration and gives you the prompt Press RETURN to continue until your entire configuration is displayed.

2. Press Enter until AutoCAD displays the list of options shown in figure 14.1.

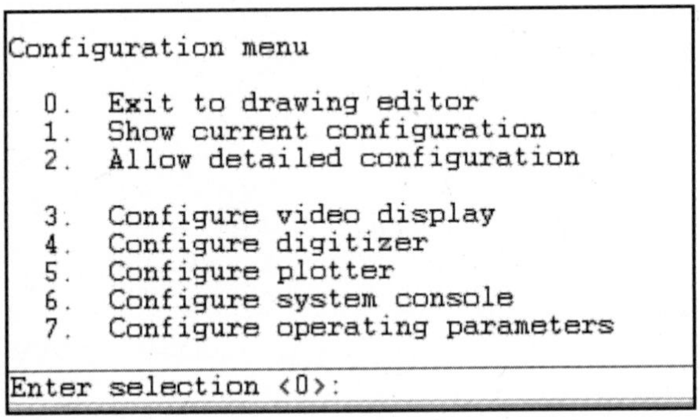

**Fig. 14.1**
The Configuration
menu.

```
Configuration menu

  0.   Exit to drawing editor
  1.   Show current configuration
  2.   Allow detailed configuration

  3.   Configure video display
  4.   Configure digitizer
  5.   Configure plotter
  6.   Configure system console
  7.   Configure operating parameters

Enter selection <0>:
```

3. From the list of options, choose option 5 to configure the plotter. This displays the list of options shown in figure 14.2.

4. Choose option 1 to add a plotter configuration. This displays the list of supported printers and plotters shown in figure 14.3.

IV

```
Plotter Configuration Menu

  0.  Exit to configuration menu
  1.  Add a plotter configuration
  2.  Delete a plotter configuration
  3.  Change a plotter configuration
  4.  Rename a plotter configuration

Enter selection, 0 to 4 <0>:
```

**Fig. 14.2**
The Plotter
Configuration
menu.

```
Available plotter:

   1.  None
   2.  AutoCAD file output formats (pre 4.1) - by Autodesk, Inc
   3.  CalComp ColorMaster Plotters ADI 4.2 V2.8 - by Autodesk
   4.  CalComp DrawingMaster Plotters ADI 4.2 V2.8 - by Autodesk
   5.  CalComp Electrostatic Plotters ADI 4.2 V2.8 - by Autodesk
   6.  CalComp Pen Plotters ADI 4.2 V2.8 - by Autodesk
   7.  Canon Laser Printer ADI 4.2 - by Autodesk, Inc
   8.  Hewlett-Packard (HP-GL) ADI 4.2 - by Autodesk, Inc
   9.  Hewlett-Packard (PCL) LaserJet ADI 4.2 - by Autodesk, Inc
  10.  Hewlett-Packard (PCL) PaintJet/DeskJet ADI 4.2 - by Autodesk, Inc
  11.  Hewlett-Packard HP-GL/2 devices, ADI 4.2 - for Autodesk by HP
  12.  Houston Instrument ADI 4.2 - by Autodesk, Inc
  13.  PostScript device ADI 4.2 - by Autodesk, Inc
  14.  Raster file export ADI 4.2 - by Autodesk, Inc
  15.  System Printer ADI 4.2 - by Autodesk, Inc

Select device number or ? to repeat list <1>:
```

**Fig. 14.3**
The Available
Plotter menu.

### Note

To follow the exercises in this chapter, you have to choose option 11,
Hewlett-Packard HP-GL/2 devices, ADI 4.2, and option 15, System Printer
ADI 4.2. You configure the HP-GL/2 driver for Preview purposes only.
The System printer is used to create an image on paper.

5. Choose option 11 from the Available Plotter menu to select Hewlett-Packard HP-GL/2 devices ADI 4.2 driver.

6. Choose option 1, DesignJet 650C, which is the default. A message is then displayed explaining how to modify the default configurations of this plotter.

7. Press Enter to continue.

8. Accept all other defaults.

9. Enter the name of the plotter as DesignJet.

This brings you back to the Plotter Configuration Menu (refer to fig. 14.2). You can now add another plotter or make changes to existing plotter configurations. You can also accept the default to exit to the Configuration menu. Follow these steps to add another plotter:

1.  Choose option 1, Add a Plotter Configuration. The list shown in figure 14.3 is displayed.

2.  Choose option 15, System Printer ADI 4.2, to add the default printer as it is already configured to the Control Panel group of Window's Operating environment.

3.  Accept all other defaults by pressing Enter.

4.  Enter **system** as the name for the plotter. You return to the Plotter Configuration menu.

5.  Choose 0 to Exit to the Configuration menu.

6.  Choose 0 to Exit to the drawing editor.

7.  Enter Yes to accept configuration changes. You then return to the drawing editor.

You have configured the system printer and a generic plotter. Before you can begin the process of plotting, however, you need to make sure that the plotter or printer is set up properly.

**Tip**
Consult the plotter manufacturer instructions before you make any modifications to plotter setup. Also, read the *AutoCAD Installation Guide* for information on cable pin settings and other communication issues.

> ### Note
>
> AutoCAD provides a standard set of drivers needed to configure plotters and printers. If your plotter is not displayed in the list in figure 14.3, you should consult your plotter manufacturer for ADI drivers or possible emulation modes. ADI drivers are third-party software written to make the plotter work with AutoCAD. Emulation modes allow plotters to imitate the behavior of supported plotters, so standard drivers can then be used to communicate with the plotters.

# Configuring the Plotter

To configure the plotter, you need to understand how the plotter and the computer communicate. At times, you also need to be able to diagnose and correct plotter problems. Given the large number of plotters and printers available, the following discussion is meant to provide only a general understanding of some of these issues. Consult your plotter manufacturer or dealer for specific details.

Some essential tasks that have to be performed before you start to plot, include:

- Connecting the plotter to the power source.

- Connecting the plotter to the computer. This includes checking for the correct port and appropriate pin settings (these are detailed in the *AutoCAD Installation Guide*).

- Running self-tests on the plotter or printer. Always do this on a new plotter or printer; it ensures the basic setup of the plotter or printer.

- Checking for fit, size, and alignment of media to be used for plotting.

## Plotting Considerations

You have completed the first two steps towards your goal of plotting a drawing: AutoCAD is properly configured to interact with the chosen plotter and printer, and the plotter is checked and configured to communicate with AutoCAD. Before you explore the PLOT command and all its options, consider the following aspects of creating the correct plotted image of a drawing:

- *Scale*. AutoCAD drawings are normally created at full scale, meaning that they are drawn at a 1:1 scale. If you plot from model space, you have to plot a specific scale factor for this full-scaled drawing to fit the desired paper size. Plotting from paper space eliminates the need to plot at a specific scale factor other than 1:1, because you scale the images in paper space viewports and then plot from paper space at 1:1. Plotting from model space and paper space are covered in detail in the sections, "Plotting from Model Space and "Plotting from Paper Space" later in this chapter.

- *Paper Size*. Paper size depends on the selected plotter. Consult your plotter documentation for the range of paper size it supports. Plotters can leave a border (normally 1/2") on all sides, as non-plottable area. This margin also varies from plotter to plotter. Plot scale factor, discussed in the previous bulleted item, should be related to the actual plottable area on paper.

■ *Plot Origin.* Plot origin is the starting pen position on your plotter. Usually, plot origins are located at or near the lower-left corner. Consult your plotter documentation to determine the plot origin. You can move the plot origin by specifying an *x,y* displacement at the plot origin prompt of the PLOT command.

> **Note**
>
> With the origin set at 0,0, plot a rectangle the exact size of the limits of the plotter and measure the differences (if any) from the border to the edge of the paper. Any changes to the location of the rectangle can then be measured and monitored as the origin is changed. Usually, 0,0 works as the origin for most plotters.

■ *Pens.* There are different types of plotters, such as pen, thermal, and electrostatic. In most plotters, pen numbers are used to assign colors, line widths, line types, and pen speed. Drawings can be organized by colors by grouping similar items on a layer and assigning a layer color. All such objects plot using the same pen number, plotter line type, and pen speed. AutoCAD supports up to 255 colors at a time.

■ *Configuration Parameters.* Parameters such as plot scaling, clipping, and rotation play an important role in creating the desired plot. Use the PLOT command dialog box to set these parameters as required.

# Plotting from Model Space

In Chapter 13, "Understanding Model Space and Paper Space," you learned about model space and paper space. Model space is used to create geometry at a 1:1 scale. If you plot from model space, depending on the size of paper to be plotted on, your plot has to be scaled by the plot scale factor. If you plot from paper space, you plot at a 1:1 scale. Plotting from paper space is discussed in the section "Plotting from Paper Space," later in this chapter.

In this section, you learn how to plot from model space. First you learn about the different options in the Plot Configuration dialog box, then you use these options to plot the drawing from model space.

## Accessing and Understanding AutoCAD's Plotting Options

This section discusses the PLOT command and shows you how to use it to get a printed image of your AutoCAD drawing on paper. The PLOT command can be accessed by any one of the following methods:

- Choose the Print button on the Standard toolbar.

- Choose File, Print.

- Type **plot** at the Command: prompt.

The PLOT command can be used with two different interfaces. The new graphical interface using dialog boxes is used when the system variable CMDDIA is set to 1. The dialog box interface is easier to use and is used to illustrate examples in this chapter.

When CMDDIA is set to 0, a command-line interface is presented. The option offers a few extra capabilities that are useful in some circumstances. You should familiarize yourself with this interface. Programmers trying to automate the plot process need the command-level version.

> **Note**
>
> If you are attempting to write a program to automate your plotting, remember that AutoCAD gives you different command-line prompts for different plotters. Also, AutoCAD asks you if you want to change plotters if you have more than one plotter configured.

## Tutorial: Using the Plot Configuration Dialog Box

You can now explore the PLOT dialog box interface. First, load the 14DWG01.dwg file from the disk offered with this book. To do this, follow these steps:

**1.** Choose the Open icon from the Standard toolbar or choose File, Open.

The Select File dialog box appears. Choose the UAW13 directory from the A: or B: drive. Then choose 14DWG01 from the file listing. If you do not see the file, use the scroll bar to scroll up or down the file listing to find it. After the drawing loads, it should look like figure 14.4.

**Fig. 14.4**
The apartment
drawing.

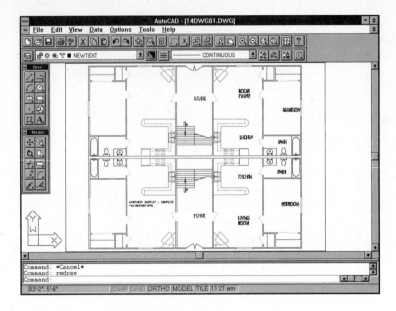

2. Now set the CMDDIA system variable to 1.

   ```
   Command: cmddia
   New value for CMDDIA <1>:
   ```

> **Note**
>
> The default setting for CMDDIA variable is 1. After CMDDIA is set, it is stored
> in the Configuration file, ACAD.CFG, and stays set. You do not need to check
> the value of CMDDIA every time you want to plot.

3. Choose the Print icon from the Standard toolbar or choose File, Print.

   The Plot Configuration dialog box appears (see fig. 14.5), if the plotter
   was correctly configured. AutoCAD displays a message if the plotter is
   unavailable or incorrectly configured.

## Understanding the Plot Configuration Options

The Plot Configuration dialog box is divided into six main areas, three areas
on each side. On the left side, you can see the Device and Default Information section, the Pen Parameters area below that, and the Additional Parameters section.

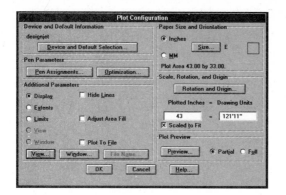

**Fig. 14.5**
The Plot Configuration dialog box.

IV

Viewing and Plotting

The Device and Default Information section lists the name of the configured plotter. In the example, it shows that the HP DesignJet plotter was specified during configuration. Choosing the Device and Default Selection button brings up the Device and Default Selection dialog box shown in figure 14.6.

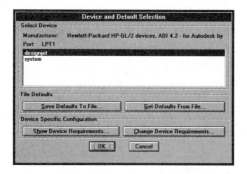

**Fig. 14.6**
AutoCAD's Device and Default Selection dialog box.

The Device and Default Selection dialog box lists the names of all plotting devices that were configured. The HP DesignJet is the selected plotter. If you need to change to a different configured plotter or printer, you can choose it from this list. When you choose the plotter, you specify the driver to be used during plotting. The configured driver listing is shown at the top of the dialog box.

AutoCAD lets you store different plot parameters in an ASCII file, called the Plot Configuration Parameters (PCP) file. You can use multiple PCP files to hold different combinations of plot parameters, such as sheet size, pen assignments, and so on. Storing information in separate PCP files allows for quick reconfiguration of plot parameters, as per requirements. PCP files can also be edited outside of AutoCAD.

> **Note**
>
> Plot parameters are not saved with each drawing. All settings are stored as global system settings. This means that after changing drawing size from a 36 × 24 sheet to a 22 × 16 sheet, the user needs to change paper size settings, among other things, to get the right plot.

### Save Device Requirements

Choosing the Save Defaults To File button in the Device and Default Selection dialog box creates a PCP file with the name to be specified in the Save to File dialog box. Type in a name and then choose OK to accept the name.

### Get Device Requirements

After a PCP file is saved, you can retrieve it later by choosing the Get Defaults From File button. This brings up the Get From File dialog box. Here you can select the name of the PCP file to retrieve (choose OK to accept).

### Show Device Requirements

When you choose the Show Device Requirements button, a dialog box appears that lists pertinent information regarding the configured plotter driver and how to make changes to the default. Because HP DesignJet is the configured plotter in the example, information on the HPCONFIG option is given. HPCONFIG can be executed from the Command: prompt to make any changes to the default settings for this driver.

### Change Device Requirements

You can modify the default settings by choosing the Change Device Requirements button. If the Windows System printer is configured, the Print Setup dialog box is displayed. This allows you to make permanent changes to the printer setup. If the HP DesignJet is configured, you are given a list of steps to change the configuration using HPCONFIG, from the Command: prompt.

Choose OK from an open dialog box to return to the Plot Configuration dialog box shown previously in figure 14.5.

## Specifying Paper Size and Orientation

In the upper-right corner of the Plot Configuration dialog box is an area called Paper Size and Orientation. Here you can set the unit of measure to Inches or Millimeters (MM). You can also set the paper size (Size) and you can see the orientation of paper in the plotter.

## Specifying Paper Size

Paper size is selected in the upper-right corner of the Plot Configuration dialog box. Choosing the Size button in the Paper Size and Orientation section brings up the Paper Size dialog box (see fig. 14.7).

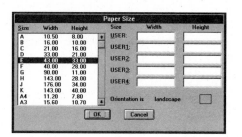

**Fig. 14.7**
The Paper Size dialog box.

On the left side of the Paper Size dialog box is a list of available paper sizes. The width and height numbers refer to the actual plottable area. These numbers are derived by subtracting the margin from the paper size. Select a size from the list that includes any predefined sheet sizes for that plotter and any user-defined sizes already set up.

On the right side of the Paper Size dialog box, you can create five custom plottable areas by entering numbers in the empty cells. Type one set of width and height for each user-defined sheet you want. The sheet will be named USER, USER1, USER2, and so on, according to which set of width and height cells you use. After you press Enter in the second cell (Height), the width and height values are placed in the list of paper sizes.

After you select the desired size, click OK to accept the dialog box.

## Understanding the Plotter Orientation

AutoCAD sets the default orientation for the paper to landscape, which means the width is greater than height. The orientation varies from plotter to plotter; the setting for a given plotter can't be changed from the Plot Configuration dialog box. You may be able to change the setting at the plotter or with the plotter's own software. Consult the plotter documentation for further details.

For the Windows System printer, orientation can be changed from Window's Control Panel or by choosing the Change Device Requirements button in the Device and Default Selection dialog box.

### Specifying the Unit of Measure

Units of paper size can be set to either inches or millimeters. Choose which one by selecting the appropriate radio button in the Plot Configuration dialog box. Changing the units automatically changes the available paper sizes to the predefined Imperial system or the Metric system standard sheet sizes for the current plotter. Any user-defined plot sizes are automatically converted from one system of measure to the other when you change units (the selected size is displayed in the Plot Configuration dialog box and all sizes are shown in the Paper Size dialog box). Changing the units also affects the pen widths in the Pen Assignments dialog box. For more information, see the section "Setting Pen Parameters" later in this chapter.

## Specifying the Plot Scale, Rotation, and Orientation

There is an area in the Plot Configuration dialog box called Scale, Rotation, and Origin. Options in this area allow you to control the scale of the plot, the rotation at which the plot is created, and the orientation of the image to plot.

### Specifying Plot Scale

Plot scale depends on the drawing size and the paper size on which you want to plot. Plot scale is also affected by which space you are plotting from. Generally, you plot 1:1 from paper space because you already scaled the paper space viewport views. If you select the Scaled to Fit check box in the Plot Configuration dialog box, AutoCAD calculates the plot scale required to fit the drawing on the selected paper size. This option makes the plot as large as possible.

Users also have the option to enter the desired plot scale in the Plot Configuration dialog box. Specifying a standard plot scale of 1/4"=1'-0" means that an object specified as 1'-0" in drawing length will plot out as 1/4" on paper.

Plot scale affects text, dimensions, and additional annotations along with drawn objects. You should take care to create text and dimensions at appropriate sizes so they look correct when scaled. If plot scale is set to 1/4"=1'-0", to achieve plotted text at 1/8", text height when created should be 8".

> **Note**
>
> If you have paper space active and you are drawing in model space via a paper space viewport and DIMSCALE is set to 0, AutoCAD automatically scales the dimension and leader text so that your set text height (for example, 1/4") will actually be drawn at the necessary height to plot correctly (8" in the preceding example). AutoCAD determines the scale based on the magnification of the view in the paper space viewport.

## Specifying Plot Rotation

AutoCAD sets the orientation of paper to landscape by default. The default orientation depends on the configured plotter. It can be adjusted from the plotter using its system software. You can choose the Rotation and Origin button in the Plot Configuration dialog box to bring up the Plot Rotation and Origin dialog box as shown in figure 14.8. Options within this dialog box can be used to rotate the image being sent to the plotter. The plotter ends up plotting the image facing the direction you want.

**Fig. 14.8**
The Plot Rotation and Origin dialog box.

You may have to rotate the plot depending on the size of the drawing and the overall width of the plotter. To plot a 24" by 36" drawing on a 36"-wide plotter, the plot needs to be rotated by 90 degrees. This is based on the default orientation being set as landscape.

The Plot Rotation and Origin dialog box is divided into two areas: Plot Rotation and Plot Origin. The Plot Rotation section has four available options to rotate the plot. Choosing a radio button selects the specified degree to rotate the plot. Choose the OK button to confirm your selection.

> **Note**
>
> Generally, printers need the plot rotated 90°, while plotters can plot without any rotation from the default of 0°.

**Tip**
Rotate plots to the maximum available paper width and/or height to save paper. Because some plottable media is quite expensive, this technique can save your resources.

To achieve the desired plot orientation, you can run a few check plots or use the Plot Preview option discussed in "Previewing the Plot" later in this chapter.

## Specifying the Plot Origin

Plot origin corresponds to the position at which the plotter starts plotting. In most pen plotters, the lower-left corner is designated as plot origin. AutoCAD normally places the lower-left corner of the drawing at the plot origin.

Plot origin can be moved by providing *x*- and *y*-coordinate values. Some plotters accept negative values for plot origins. Plotters that set their plot origin in the middle of the page may need such negative translation to get an accurate plot.

Plot origin can be changed from the Plot Rotation and Origin dialog box, as shown in figure 14.8. The Plot Origin section of this dialog box provides input boxes for specifying the *x*- and *y*-coordinates of the origin.

To check the origin of your plotter, you can run a check plot of a simple drawing or use the Plot Preview option discussed in "Previewing the Plot" later in this chapter.

> **Note**
>
> AutoCAD sets the origin of the plot at the lower limits, as specified in your drawing. In the example, the lower limits are set at 0'-0",0'-0".

## Previewing the Plot

Previewing the plotted image on your computer screen before actually plotting it has many benefits. It allows for WYSIWIG (What You See Is What You Get) plotting. Previewing also saves time and resources by allowing you to check the plotted image before it actually appears on the media.

You can see either a Partial or Full preview of your drawing as it will plot. Preview selections are made from the Plot Preview section located in the lower-right area of the Plot Configuration dialog box (refer to fig. 14.5). This section consists of the Preview button and two other radio buttons to specify the type of preview desired—Partial or Full.

Selecting the Partial radio button, then choosing the Preview button, brings up the Preview Effective Plotting Area dialog box shown in figure 14.9. Partial preview displays a dialog box with the plottable area on the paper in red and the effective drawing area in blue.

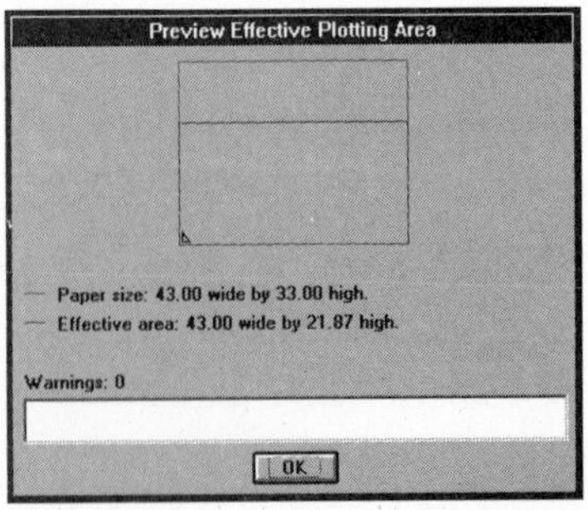

**Fig. 14.9**
The Preview
Effective Plotting
Area dialog box.

> **Note**
>
> The Partial Preview dialog box provides warning messages at the bottom of the dialog box if any part of the desired plot will not fit on the paper.

Selecting the F̲ull radio button, then choosing the P̲review button, displays the Full Preview. Full preview shows the result of the plotted image. A Plot Preview dialog box appears on-screen, allowing Pan and Zoom interactions on the plotted image to check certain areas (see fig. 14.10). The P̲an and Zoom option behaves like the DYNAMIC ZOOM command. For more details on DYNAMIC ZOOM, refer to Chapter 12, "Viewing a Drawing."

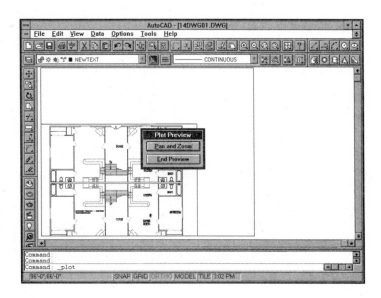

**Fig. 14.10**
The Plot preview.

After you finish previewing the image, choose the E̲nd Preview button to return to the Plot Configuration dialog box.

## Tutorial: Experimenting with Plot Scale, Paper Size, and Preview

In this tutorial, you experiment with changing paper size and plot scale as a continuation from the previous tutorial (steps are provided if you are starting with this tutorial first). You also use the Plot Preview option to see the effect of your changes without creating any paper plots.

**Fig. 14.11**
A zoomed view of
Full preview.

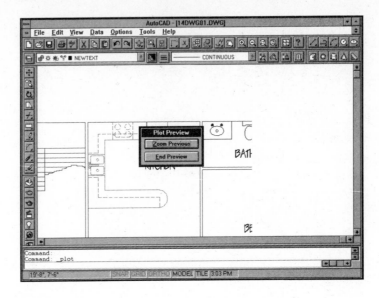

1. If you are starting new, open the drawing 14DWG01 from the UAW13 directory, in the drive specified during installation. Choose File, Print, or choose the Print icon from the Standard toolbar, to bring up the Plot Configuration dialog box.

> **Note**
>
> You use the default option, Display, to plot the displayed portion of the drawing. In a later section "Specifying Plot Area," you'll learn how to change the area to plot.

2. Notice the following:

AutoCAD selects size "E" (43 × 33" ) as the appropriate size for the selected drawing. This is the default size set when the plotter is configured.

Plot scale is set at 43=131'3". This is based on the limits of the drawing, which are (0,0) and (88',62') and paper size selection "E" (43 × 33" of plottable area). Scale to Fit is the default option, unless otherwise specified during the plotter configuration or changed in the dialog box.

> **Note**
>
> In Plot scale factor the drawing units number, 131'3", may be different based on resolution of the graphics window selected or the size of the window. For example, at 640×480 resolution, you may get a different number. It is a relative scale, thus getting a different number does not affect steps taken in this and other tutorials, to follow.

**3.** Preview this plot using the Partial Preview option.

Select the Partial radio button at the lower-right corner, then choose the Preview button.

The Preview Effective Plotting Area dialog box shows the area to be plotted in relation to the paper size. Partial preview provides basic information about form and fit of the drawing to be plotted before it is actually plotted.

**4.** After you preview the plot, choose OK to finish the preview.

**5.** Next, change the paper size to C.

Choose the Size button in the upper-right corner.

Select size C from the Paper Size dialog box, then choose OK. Note that the scale to fit changes to 21=131'3"1.

**6.** Preview the changes made using the Full Preview option.

Select the Full radio button, then choose the Preview button. Full preview displays the drawing on-screen as it will appear when plotted.

The Plot Preview dialog box lets you Pan and Zoom around the Full Preview image to check for spelling and accuracy of small details. When you select the Pan and Zoom box, you see a screen very similar to the Zoom Dynamic window. By picking with your selection device you can pan and define the area to be previewed closely.

**7.** Choose the End Preview button to end the preview.

The Plot preview shows that the drawing can occupy more space on paper. Notice that the image to plot fills up only a portion of the paper available. The available paper size is denoted by the outside border.

You should make full use of the space available on paper. You can do this by changing the plot scale, choosing a smaller paper size, or by changing the plot area. You learn how to change plot area in the next section, "Specifying Plot Area." Changing the plot scale is done in the Plotted Inches box in the Scale, Rotation, and Origin area of the Plot Configuration dialog box. To see how changing the plot scale can give the desired result, follow these steps:

1. Click the Plotted Inches input box and type in **30**. Make sure the Drawing Units value stays the same. Note that the Scale To Fit check box is automatically deselected because you are specifying the scale to use for plotting.

2. Full preview the changes, as shown in step 4 above. The plot now occupies a large portion of the available paper space.

3. Select End Preview when you're done previewing. This returns you to the Plot Configuration dialog box.

## Specifying Plot Area

The Additional Parameters section, located in the lower-left corner of the Plot Configuration dialog box, enables the user to specify the desired portion of the drawing to be plotted. The section consists of radio buttons that specify the area to be plotted (options include Display, Extents, Limits, View, and Window); check boxes for special options such as Plot To File; and three buttons at the bottom for View, Window, and the File Name.

> **Note**
>
> Changes to the area to be plotted significantly impact other settings. By specifying the plot area correctly, you can reduce the number of changes to be made to other settings to achieve the same result.

### Plotting the Display

This option tells AutoCAD to plot what you see on-screen. Everything inside the area of the current viewport is plotted.

Plotting the display is suitable for plotting a certain portion of your drawing without plotting the entire sheet with title block. Remember to PAN or ZOOM into the area to be plotted before using the Display option. The displayed area may change from one computer to the other. The PAN and ZOOM commands are discussed in Chapter 12, "Viewing a Drawing."

### Plotting the Drawing's Extents

This option lets you plot the extents of your drawing regardless of the LIMITS setting. This commonly used option is suitable for plotting everything in the file to fit the paper, if the plot scale factor allows it to fit.

◀ See "Creating Your First Drawing," p. 45

**IV**

*Viewing and Plotting*

### Plotting the Drawing's Limits

The limits of the drawing are set using the LIMITS command. This option plots everything in the set limits of the drawing.

Normally, the limits of a drawing are not prone to frequent changes. Thus, using the LIMITS command to plot gives you the option to plot a consistent plottable area.

**Tip**

If your drawing is plotted with the Extents option, any modification to the lower-left corner of your drawing may cause a shift in the plotted drawing as the Extents are based on the lower-left corner.

### Plotting a View

This option allows you to plot a previously saved view. Named views can be saved using the VIEW command and then plotted using Plot a View. The VIEW command is discussed in Chapter 12, "Viewing a Drawing."

The view saved using the VIEW command stores information in the form of its center, width, and height of the screen image. This may not translate into the same image when plotted on paper, due to the conversion of high-resolution dots (pixels) into plot commands. Thus, to create the view, it's better to use the Window option of the VIEW command. Using this option, the center, width, and height are derived from points picked to create the window. This translates into more accurate plotted images.

The View radio button in the Additional Parameters section of the Plot Configuration dialog box is available only if a view has been saved previously. It is grayed out otherwise. If it is available, selecting the View button lets you choose the desired view from the View Name dialog box. A list of all available views is displayed in this dialog box. To set up a view for plotting, select a view from the View Name dialog box and then choose OK to confirm.

### Plotting a Window

Plotting using the Window option lets you define a rectangular window around the area of the drawing you want to plot. The Window radio button is grayed out until a window is created by picking on-screen coordinates or the default values are accepted. To define a window, choose the <u>W</u>indow button at the bottom of the Additional Parameters section. Creating a selection set using the Windows option is discussed in Chapter 9, "Understanding Selection Sets."

◀ See "Tutorial: Selecting Objects with a Window," p. 221

Choosing the <u>W</u>indow button brings up the Window Selection dialog box, shown in figure 14.12. Choose the <u>P</u>ick button to specify a viewing window by picking on-screen the corners of the window. The coordinates picked are displayed in the Window Selection dialog box after the selection is completed. You can also type in the *x*- and *y*-coordinates of the <u>F</u>irst Corner and <u>O</u>ther Corner by entering values in the input boxes in the Window Selection dialog box.

**Fig. 14.12**
The Window
Selection dialog
box.

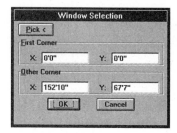

## Tutorial: Using the Plot Area Options

In this tutorial, you use the available plot area options and observe changes between options with the Full Preview capability.

1. Continue from the previous tutorial.

   If you are starting new, open the drawing 14DWG01 from the UAW13 directory on the drive in which it was installed. Use the scroll bar to scroll up or down the file listing to find the file. Choose the Print button from the Standard toolbar to access the Plot Configuration dialog box.

2. In the previous tutorial, you selected the C-size paper on which to plot. For that paper size, the plot scale to fit is 21=118'11". Make sure that the Scaled To Fit check box is selected. This plot scale factor is for the default plot area set to Display, with zoom set to all.

3. <u>F</u>ull preview the plot. The drawing occupies a small area of the actual paper.

4. Choose the <u>E</u>nd Preview button to end the preview process.

Now you can see the change in the plot scale and occupied paper space by changing the plot area to LIMITS. You can now change the Plot display option to LIMITS.

1. Click the Limits radio button. Limits should appear as the selected option. Note that the plot scale changes to 21=88', with the Scaled To Fit option selected.

2. Full preview the plot. End preview when done.

Next, you can observe the change in the plot scale and occupied paper space by changing the plot area to EXTENTS. You now can change the Plot display option to EXTENTS.

1. Click the Extents radio button. Extents should appear as the selected option. Note, the plot scale remains the same, with the Scaled To Fit option selected. In this case, the limits and extents define the same area in the drawing.

2. Full preview the plot. End preview when done.

You can now retrieve a saved view named "KITCHEN" and use this view to create a plot preview. To use this option, views have to be saved previously. For more information on saving and retrieving named views, refer to Chapter 12, "Viewing a Drawing." The View radio button is not available until a view is selected. Follow these steps to select a previously saved view:

1. Select the View button. This displays the View Name dialog box with available views.

2. Select the view named KITCHEN and choose OK to accept it. The View check box is now automatically selected.

3. Full preview the plot by view option. End preview when done.

The last plot area option is WINDOW. This option allows you to plot a selected area by using the familiar WINDOW selection technique. For more information on the Window selection technique, see Chapter 9, "Understanding Selection Sets."

1. Select the Window button.

   This brings up the Window Selection dialog box (refer to fig. 14.12).

2. Click the Pick button and create a window around the foyer area in the middle of the drawing by selecting the opposite corners of the window.

3. Full preview the plot by window option. End preview when you're finished.

## Setting Pen Parameters

Your drawing is now ready to plot. Correctly setting the pen parameters plays an important role in achieving the desired image on paper.

The pen parameters can be set in the Plot Configuration dialog box. The Pen Parameters area contains two buttons. The Pen Assignments button allows you to map each pen to a color, line type, pen speed, and line weight. The Optimization button can increase the efficiency of the plotter by eliminating the travel of the pen across overlapping objects.

### Specifying Pen Assignments

To set assignments to pens, choose the Pen Assignments button from the Plot Configuration dialog box. The Pen Assignments dialog box appears (see fig. 14.13).

**Fig. 14.13**
The Pen Assign-
ments dialog box.

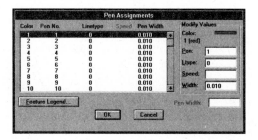

The options displayed in the Pen Assignments dialog box depend on the type of plotter selected. For most pen plotters, you can specify pen speed and pen width. Not all low-end printers support multiple pen widths. AutoCAD can assign up to 255 pens to the 255 AutoCAD colors. In the apartment complex drawing (refer to fig. 14.4), colors were assigned to different objects. AutoCAD normally assigns color 7 to all objects in a drawing unless otherwise specified.

> **Note**
>
> The number of pens your plotter supports determines how many pens AutoCAD allows you to set and use. Only certain types of plotters, such as color ink, electrostatic, and thermal plotters, can create shades of a color. Pen plotters cannot blend colors and intensities.

The Modify Values section of the Pen Assignments dialog box remains empty until a pen number is selected. After a pen number is selected, information regarding that number is displayed. The assigned color is also displayed in the upper-right corner. If more than one pen number is selected, the first selected color is displayed along with the message Color Varies.

Picking a line more than once in the Pen Assignments list box toggles the selection on or off: if you pick a line once, it is selected; if you pick the same line again, it is deselected. A common parameter such as Pen Width can be assigned to multiple pens by selecting all desired pens together, and then changing the <u>W</u>idth value in the Modify Values section.

Assignment of pen widths can result in different actions, depending on the plotter. On pen plotters, width is a guideline that AutoCAD uses to plot wide lines, traces, and so on. Width setting determines how far AutoCAD moves the pen between strokes. While working with multiple line widths and colors, you can usually ignore the pen widths.

Try making changes to pen assignments in the Modify Values section. After you are finished, click the OK button to return to the Plot Configuration dialog box.

> **Note**
>
> Pen numbers cycle every eight colors. Sometimes, geometry assigned to high-color numbers, such as 144, may not plot. Make sure that all colors used are mapped to a pen that is in the pen holder.

### Specifying Pen Optimization

Another pen parameter option is optimizing pen motion. You can access the Optimizing Pen Motion dialog box (see fig. 14.14) by choosing the <u>O</u>ptimization button in the Pen Parameters section of the Plot Configuration dialog box.

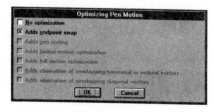

**Fig. 14.14**

The Optimizing Pen Motion dialog box.

Pen optimization helps reduce plot time by minimizing wasted pen motion. Selecting the first check box, <u>N</u>o Optimization, automatically deselects all other check boxes. The list of optimization options is in the order of complexity. Selecting one of the lower check boxes preselects the options above it. For example, selecting the A<u>d</u>ds Elimination of Overlapping Diagonal Vectors check box will automatically select all of the preceding check boxes.

Selecting the <u>N</u>o Optimization option means that AutoCAD plots each object in the order of that object in the drawing database. Selecting the Adds <u>E</u>ndpoint Swap check box plots lines from the end closest to the pen. Selecting Adds <u>P</u>en Sorting causes all similar objects to be grouped and plotted by the same pen. The next two options involve motion optimization. These options are useful if you have a slow plotter and a fast computer. Some plotters have internal motion optimization. Eliminating overlapping lines saves plotting time on three-dimensional drawings.

## Setting the Final Options

This section discusses the options found in the Additional Parameters section in the lower-left corner of the Plot Configuration dialog box (refer to fig. 14.5).

### Hiding Lines

The Hide <u>L</u>ines check box allows you to perform hidden line removal on plotted images. This is useful when plotting 3D drawings. Hidden line removal allows 3D drawings to give an illusion of depth on 2D media, such as paper.

Removing hidden lines is an intense computer process. Though it was significantly enhanced in AutoCAD Release 13, this process can still take a long time to perform on large 3D drawings.

> **Note**
>
> For paper space viewports, the Hideplot option of the MVIEW command has to be used to achieve hidden-line removal during plotting.

### Adjusting Filled Areas

The Adjust Area Fill option provides control over the width and size of plotted polylines and solids.

In order to create wide lines, the plotter may make several passes on the same line. Depending on the width of the pen used, this may result in slightly wider lines than expected or shown in drawing. This option is useful in applications such as PCB layout, where it is critical to hold the width of lines drawn.

When used, this option results in the offset of the outside boundary of the filled region by one-half the pen width.

### Plotting to File

The Plot To File option creates a plot file on the computer disk rather than outputting it directly to the plotter. A created plot file gets the PLT extension. You can also specify the directory in which to save the plot file.

This option is useful when plotting over a network or for plotting images at an outside source. Network plot spooling software programs can be used to queue the created plots on a network drive to plot on a network plotter. AutoCAD can be configured to create an AUTOSPOOL plot file for network plotting.

Plotting directly to the plotter may also result in delays while AutoCAD communicates with the plotter. Plotting to file and later plotting them can result in saving time.

Created plot files get the same name as the drawing with a PLT extension. You can give a different name and extension by clicking the File Name button in the Additional Parameters section of the Plot Configuration dialog box.

## Saving Your Settings

You may want to save the setting changes that you make in a section. These changes are stored in the PCP (Plot Configuration Parameter) file.

To save changes, click the Device and Default Selection button from the Plot Configuration dialog box. From the Device and Default Selection dialog box, click the Save Defaults To File button. This brings up the Save to File dialog box. In the File Name field, type the name of the PCP file, then choose OK to confirm your save to the desired file name.

# Plotting from Paper Space

As mentioned earlier in this chapter, you can plot from both model space and paper space. You have already covered plotting from model space. In this section, you learn to plot from paper space.

In paper space, you always plot at a 1:1 scale. Paper space is designed to simulate the paper on which you plot. WYSIWIG (What You See Is What You Get) plotting became a reality with paper space. Paper space also enhances the capability of plotting multiple viewports at different scales. For example, in a Standard Engineering drawing with four viewports, you can plot each view at different scales. Paper space is covered in detail in Chapter 13, "Understanding Model Space and Paper Space."

In paper space, you can create objects without having to take scale factor into account. Any object or text created in this space is created at a 1:1 scale. For example, if the desired text height after plot is 0.18 inch, then you also create the text in paper space at 0.18 inch. Title block, text, and other annotations needed to complete the drawing are created in paper space at a 1:1 scale. Drawing objects and dimensions are normally created in model space. Then, using the Zoom XP option, these objects are scaled relative to paper space, establishing a consistent scale for that viewport. The XP scale factor represents a ratio between the size of paper space borders and the size of objects displayed in model space.

## Tutorial: Plotting from Paper Space

In this tutorial, you learn how to plot the drawing 14DWG01 from paper space. You also use a C-size title block to set up the drawing. This C-size title block already exists in the paper space environment, from where you will plot at 1:1 scale. In this tutorial, you place the floor-plan drawing inside the title block via an existing floating model space viewport in paper space, and then preview the plot from paper space at a 1:1 scale.

1. Continue from the previous tutorial. If you closed the drawing, open the drawing titled 14DWG01.

    Choose Open from the Standard toolbar or choose File, Open. Select the UAW13 directory on the drive in which it was installed. Then, from the file listing, select 14DWG01. Use the scroll bar to scroll up or down the file listing to find the file.

   Now you switch to paper space, where the title block and paper space viewport are set up. Remember, model objects and dimensions are created in model space.

2. Choose View, Floating Model Space.

   AutoCAD switches to paper space and places the crosshairs in the existing floating model space viewport. The model space UCS icon appears in the lower-left of the viewport, indicating that you are in the floating model space.

**3.** Choose Zoom/All to display the drawing.

**4.** Switch back to paper space before you plot by choosing View, Select Paper Space from the pull-down menu.

**5.** Select the Print icon from the toolbar or choose File, Print. Here, you need to check the plot settings before you preview the drawing. Check your settings and change them as necessary. Remember, you are plotting from paper space at a 1:1 scale.

The Plot Configuration dialog box should appear as follows:

- The Device and Default Information section should list the name of the configured plotter ("DesignJet" in the example).

- The Additional Parameters section should have the Display radio button selected.

- The paper size should be set to C.

- In the Scale, Rotation, and Origin section, the Scaled to Fit check box should be *unchecked*. This sets the plot scale to 1=1 in the Plotted Inches and Drawing Units input boxes.

**6.** Make all necessary changes, if required, and then do a Full Preview.

First select the Full radio button, and then click the Preview button at the lower-right section of the Plot Configuration dialog box. This displays the drawing with the title block as it appears when plotted from paper space.

**7.** Choose Cancel to close the Plot Configuration dialog box.

> **Note**
>
> All tutorials to this point have used the HP DesignJet 650C plotter drive. This was done to give you access to several paper sizes and other options. Because you may not have an HP DesignJet 650C, the steps do not go on to have you actually do a plot. The next section uses your system printer to do an actual plot.

**IV**

Viewing and Plotting

# Making Your First Plot

In this section, you complete the plot process by plotting the 14DWG02 drawing on your system printer, as it was initially configured in this chapter. Make sure this A-size printer is available and properly configured before you attempt to create your final plot.

## Tutorial: Creating a Final Plot on the System Printer

In this tutorial, you create your final plot on the system printer. To do this, follow these steps:

1. Open the drawing titled 14DWG02.

   Choose Open from the Standard toolbar or choose File, Open. Choose the UAW13 directory on the drive in which it was installed. From the file listing, select 14DWG02. Use the scroll bar to scroll up or down the file listing to find the file.

   You are plotting this drawing from paper space at 1:1 scale. You need to switch to paper space and create a viewport.

2. Choose View, Paper Space. You are switched into Paper Space. To create a viewports, Choose View, Floating Viewport, followed by 1 Viewport

   ```
   ON/OFF/Hideplot/Fit/2/3/4/Restore/<First Point:>0,0
   Other Corner:10.5,8
   ```

   The viewport created fits A-size paper (8.5 × 11) in landscape mode, where width is greater than height. You change the paper size to A and orientation to landscape later. Select View, Floating Model Space. This places you within the model view you just created.

   Next, you scale the drawing relative to paper space using the Zoom XP option. This is done in model space (where you already are). The XP value is derived by dividing your paper space borders by your models extents. In the example, if you use the Scaled To Fit option, the scale factor is 10.5"=88'. Thus, dividing 10.5" by 88' gives you .00994318. This is the ZOOM XP value.

3. From the Standard toolbar, choose the Zoom Scale icon.

   AutoCAD displays the zoom prompts and requests a scale factor.

   ```
   All/Center/Dynamic/Extents/Left/Previous/Vmax/Window/
       <Scale(X/XP)>:.00994318xp
   ```

You now are ready to set your plot options. Remember to plot from paper space.

4. Choose View, Paper Space.

5. Choose the Print button from the Standard toolbar or choose File, Print.

6. In the Plot Configuration dialog box, click the Device and Default Selection button.

   Select the System printer in the dialog box.

7. Using the Change Device Requirements button, change the paper orientation to landscape in the Print Setup dialog box.

8. Choose OK to confirm the changes until you get back to the Plot Configuration dialog box.

9. A-size paper may be selected. This depends on the system printer configured in your Windows environment. If A-size is not your default, change the paper size to A.

10. Make sure that the Scaled to Fit check box is *unchecked*, because you're plotting at 1:1 scale. Make sure the scale is set to 1:1.

11. Click the OK button at the bottom of the Plot Configuration dialog box to begin plotting.

The exact message displayed by AutoCAD at this time depends on your plotter. You selected the "A" paper size of 10.5" wide by 8" high (landscape orientation). With a standard printer, AutoCAD displays the following prompt:

```
Effective plotting area:10.43 wide by 7.92 high
Position paper in plotter
Press RETURN to continue or S to Stop for hardware setup
```

By selecting S, AutoCAD sends an initial reset to the plotter. Any final plotter settings can be done at this point by using the front panel of the plotter. When such changes are completed, press the Enter key to begin plotting. AutoCAD displays a message regarding the percentage of regeneration completed, such as the following:

```
Regeneration Done:20%
```

Press Escape to interrupt the plot at any time. AutoCAD displays the following messages:

```
Plot canceled
Press RETURN to continue:
```

When AutoCAD completes the transfer of data to the plotter, it displays this message:

```
Plot complete
```

After AutoCAD finishes the transfer, the plotter has to finish the plot. Depending on the memory available on the plotter, data can be transferred in small packets or as one file. Wait for the plotter to finish plotting.

You have just completed your first plot. Congratulations!

# Understanding Spooling

A large number of organizations currently operate in a networked environment. One of the benefits of operating in a networked environment is the ability to share resources such as plotters, printers, and so on. This allows many users to share a common printer or plotter on the same network.

For resources to be shared effectively, all users on the same network must have equal access. *Spooling* is the process by which files to be printed or plotted are stored in a common location and then routed to the printer queue one at a time. Print-spooling programs available on the network are used to redirect the plot to the appropriate plotter at the right time.

## What Is Autospool?

*Autospool* is the assigned name of plots to be spooled. When AutoCAD finds Autospool to be the default plot name for plotting to file, it places the plot file (*.ac$, ) in the assigned directory.

To assign Autospool as the default plot name, choose Options, Configure. Press Enter until you get to the Configuration menu. From the Configuration menu, choose option 7: Configure Operating Parameters. Next, choose option 3: Default Plot File. Enter Autospool as the default file name. To change the spool file directory location, choose option 4 to direct the plot files. By default, it goes to the \SPFILES directory of your current drive.

## Spooling Your Plot

In the Windows environment, Print Manager acts as a spooler. It can manage both a local and a network printer. A local printer is physically connected to the computer from which a drawing is plotted. A network printer is connected somewhere on the network. Choosing the System Printer from the Configuration menu sets up the printer (local or network) as the one on which to print. You don't need to use Autospool when using the System Printer option in Windows. Print Manager can monitor print queues, pause, and resume if required. For more information on Print Manager, refer to the *Windows Users Guide* or any other Windows-related documentation.

> **Note**
>
> If you are on a network with other DOS and Windows users, you may need the AUTOSPOOL functionality. Network spooling programs can then monitor the print queues. Print Manager's spooling capability is only available to Windows users. The system printer does not work with AUTOSPOOL, so Windows users may not be able to use the system printer driver when sharing plotters with DOS users. You may have to use a standard driver, available with AutoCAD, or obtain an ADI 4.2 driver.

## Third-Party Plotter Drivers

AutoCAD contains a host of standard plotter drivers. These drivers are meant to support the most widely used plotter models. Check your plotter documentation to ensure that the standard driver can be used. In case you have a plotter that doesn't have a standard driver in AutoCAD, contact your plotter manufacturer or ADI developers. Manufacturers often provide you with their own plotter driver. These drivers may have special features or special enhancements that make interfacing with AutoCAD better.

> **Note**
>
> Make sure to use ADI 4.2 plotter drivers when plotting with Release 13. Older plotter drivers may cause problems. Contact the plotter manufacturer or ADI developer if you are using ADI plotter drivers.

**13**
**RELEASE**

If you need a plotter driver for your plotter that is not supplied by Autodesk or the plotter manufacturer, try contacting a third-party developer. For example, at the time of this writing, if you buy an HP 650C DesignJet, it comes with drivers for AutoCAD for DOS and for the Windows System Printer. If you are sharing an Autospool, you cannot use the System Printer. That leaves you with no driver for your plotter for AutoCAD for Windows. You can buy a third-party driver that is a DLL file that loads as a plotter driver and is displayed in the plotter Configuration menu.

The following are two resources for plotter drivers:

Robert McNeel and Associates
3670 Woodland Park Ave. N.
Seattle, WA 98103
1-206-545-7000

Limburg Engineering Associates
3411 227th St. W.
Torrance, CA 90505
1-800-234-2380

For additional information on third-party developers, see your *AutoCAD Resource Guide.*

## From Here...

The PLOT command allows the transfer of created drawings onto any desired media, such as paper. To create the right image successfully, every time, keep the following issues in mind:

- The plotter is correctly configured.

- AutoCAD's printer driver is the appropriate one for your plotter and is correctly configured.

- The chosen media size is supported by your plotter. Also check for proper feed, alignment, and jamming of media on the plotter.

- The chosen plot scale is appropriate for the media size and is the desired one. Check the plot using Plot Preview before you plot.

- Check pen assignments and optimizations requested for the plotter being used.

- Finally, make sure that all connections between the computer and the plotter are OK.

In this chapter, you covered various aspects of plotting a two-dimensional drawing.

For more information on related topics such as text creation, plotting 3D models, and dimensioning, see the following chapters:

- Chapter 16, "Working with Text," shows you how to add notes to your drawings.

- Chapter 18, "Dimensioning a Drawing," shows you how to create dimensions.

- Chapter 31, "Plotting a 3D Model," explains how to plot three-dimensional models.

# On Your Own

Plot the drawing titled 14DWG03. Use the system printer with all default options. Plotting options should be set as follows (see fig. 14.15):

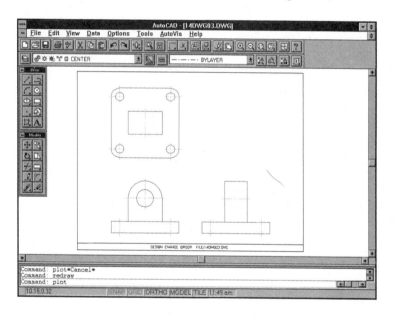

**Fig. 14.15**
Setting plotting options for the drawing.

Hints:

**1.** Set plot area to Display.

**2.** Plot scale set to 1:1.

**3.** Plot rotation set to 90.

**4.** Plot origin set to X=0.2;y=0.2.

Create the plot on A-size paper. Use Plot Preview as needed.

# Part V

# Advanced Drawing and Annotation

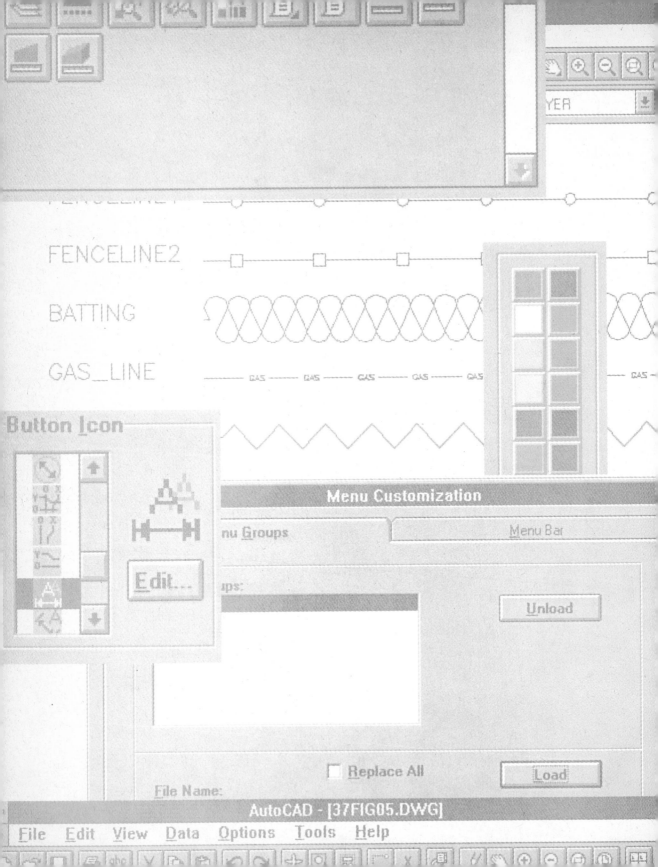

FENCELINE2

BATTING

GAS_LINE — GAS — GAS — GAS — GAS — GAS GAS

## Button Icon

Edit...

## Menu Customization

nu Groups | Menu Bar

ups:

Unload

☐ Replace All

Load

File Name:

AutoCAD - [37FIG05.DWG]

File   Edit   View   Data   Options   Tools   Help

# Chapter 15

# Advanced Drawing Techniques

As you begin creating objects in AutoCAD, information on each object is stored in a database. This information is available in a form that is easily accessed. AutoCAD can calculate the exact length of a given object, regardless of its shape. This greatly simplifies certain procedures, such as dividing an object into an equal number of segments. The DIVIDE command can divide an object, regardless of its shape, into equal segments. (Dividing an object into equal parts in manual drafting can be accomplished with geometric construction but with a limited degree of accuracy.)

Along with dividing an object into equal segments, another common occurrence in drafting is to place objects at equal distances, such as marking a wall to locate studs. By accessing the database, AutoCAD simplifies the process of marking equal distances along an object. The MEASURE command measures equal lengths that you specify along an object, and then places corresponding points on the object.

Certain types of objects, such as ellipses, can be very time-consuming to draw with manual drafting techniques. Geometric construction techniques can be slow and cumbersome. Ellipse templates can help speed up the process, but you are limited to the templates available. The ELLIPSE command makes drawing ellipses simple. AutoCAD provides a wide variety of techniques for creating ellipses. In addition, the DONUT or DOUGHNUT (AutoCAD will accept either spelling) command provides an efficient method for producing rings and solid-filled circles.

New in Release 13 are infinite and semi-infinite lines that can be used as construction lines. A *ray* is a semi-infinite line that has a finite starting point and extends to infinity. An infinite line (XLINE) has no starting or stopping point. In addition to drawing straight line segments, AutoCAD also offers the SKETCH command. SKETCH allows you to create freehand drawings.

In this chapter, you practice different methods used to divide an object into equal segments and a method for laying out equal distances along an object. You also learn how to create filled circles and ellipses, create infinite and semi-infinite construction lines, and create freehand drawings. After completing this chapter, you will be able to:

- Use the POINT command to understand and use permanent points

- Control the display and size of points with DDPTYPE

- Use the DIVIDE command to divide an object into equal segments

- Use the MEASURE command to measure equal distances along an object

- Use the DONUT or DOUGHNUT command to create filled circles

- Use variations of the ELLIPSE command to create ellipses

- Use the RAY and XLINE commands to create construction lines

- Create freehand drawings with the SKETCH command

> **Note**
>
> Besides the advanced techniques shown in this chapter for drawing line-based objects, AutoCAD also provides multilines and complex lines. A *multiline* (MLINE) is a single object made of multiple parallel lines. A *complex line* is a line that consists of lines, spaces, dots, and shapes.

▶ See "Using Multilines," p. 597

▶ See "Customizing Linetypes," p. 1034

# Indicating Locations (POINT)

In a drawing, you can create points as objects, just as you can create lines, circles, and arcs. Points are used for many different purposes in technical drawings. For example, points can be used to represent the following:

- Intersection location of objects

- Center line of structural beams

- Locations of contact for mechanical parts

- Centers of rotation

Although point objects created with the POINT command are referred to as *permanent points*, they are no more permanent than any other AutoCAD object. Points can be copied, moved, or erased just like lines or circles. The term *permanent points* is used to distinguish between POINT objects and points that are picked during the course of a command. When you specify a center point for a circle, for example, you designate a coordinate for the circle. You do not create a point object. When using the POINT command, however, you actually create an object. By default, a point appears as a dot on-screen. When the drawing is saved, any points created with the POINT command are saved with the drawing.

While the point is a permanent object saved with the drawing, in most cases the POINT object is used temporarily until another object is laid over it or references it. After an object is placed over the point or references it, the point is normally removed from the drawing screen. You can remove the point by erasing it or freezing the layer where the point is located.

To access the POINT command, use one of these methods:

■ Click the Point button on the Draw toolbar. A fly-out submenu appears. The Point button displays a fly-out toolbar that has point, divide, and measure on it.

■ Enter **point** at the Command: prompt.

You can enter point locations with a pointing device or any coordinate method (absolute, relative, absolute polar, and relative polar). You can snap to a point location, using temporary or permanent object snap modes. The object snap mode associated with POINT is node.

◄ See "NODe," p. 153

◄ See "Coordinate System Basics," p. 87

## Selecting the Point Style

By default, points appear as dots on-screen. Dots can be difficult to see, especially in a complex drawing. The size and style of the point can be changed by the AutoCAD system variables PDSIZE and PDMODE. You use PDMODE to change the point style at the Command: prompt. However, because it is difficult to remember the value for each point style, it's easier to use the Point Style dialog box to set the point style.

AutoCAD offers the Point Style dialog box with graphic options. As suggested, this dialog box is much easier to use than the PDMODE and PDSIZE commands. To change the point style, select the new style from the Point Style dialog box (see fig. 15.1). You can access the Point Style dialog box by using one of these methods:

**V**

**Advanced Drawing**

■ Enter **ddptype** at the Command: prompt.

■ Choose Options, Display, and Select Point Style.

**Fig. 15.1**
The Point Style
dialog box is used
to change the style
and size of a point.

> **Note**
>
> When the point style is changed in a drawing, *all* current and previously created points are displayed with the current point style. Although all previously created points are changed, they do not appear changed on-screen until after the drawing regenerates. Changing the point style does not automatically cause the drawing to regenerate.

## Setting the Point Size (PDMODE)

Besides changing the point style, you can change the size of the point. AutoCAD offers two options for setting the point size: Set Size Relative to Screen and Set Size in Absolute Units. Both options are available in the Point Style dialog box.

### Setting Point Size Relative to Screen Size

By default, the Set Size Relative to Screen radio button in the Point Style dialog box is selected. The height of the point symbols are a percentage of the screen height. Thus, the point size remains constant as you zoom in and out of the drawing. The size of the symbols changes only during a drawing regeneration, and a drawing does not automatically regenerate when you zoom in and out. For example, say you set the height of a point symbol to a percentage of the screen height and zoom in on the point. Without regenerating the screen, the point will appear much larger. When the screen regenerates, however, the points will appear approximately the same size as before.

> **Note**
>
> When using paper space, the point size still remains constant as you zoom in and out of the drawing if the Set Size Relative to Screen radio button in the Point Style dialog box is selected.

### Setting Point Size to an Absolute Unit

Selecting the Set Size in Absolute Units radio button in the Point Style dialog box gives the points a set unit size. Selecting this option causes the points to change size as you zoom in and out of the drawing. The point size remains proportional to the rest of the drawing, however.

> **Note**
>
> You can also change the point size by entering **pdsize** at the Command: prompt. A zero setting generates a point that is five percent of the screen height. If PDSIZE is positive, the point is given an absolute unit. Using a negative value sets the point size relative-to-screen size.

Setting point size to an absolute unit or to a relative-to-screen size depends on personal preference and whether you will be zooming the display in and out to select points. To keep the points at a constant size, even when zooming in and out, set the point size relative-to-screen size. To keep the points size consistent with the rest of the drawing, set the point size to an absolute unit.

# Dividing an Object (DIVIDE)

In manual drafting, you are often called on to divide an object into equal spaces. The divisions may be used to lay out lines or to reference other geometry. Geometric construction techniques make it possible to divide lines, arcs, and circles into equal distances. Geometric construction techniques are often inaccurate, are always time-consuming, and may not work on curves or other objects.

AutoCAD, however, provides a simple method of dividing an object. Auto-CAD maintains a mathematical model of every object in the database, so it is possible to calculate the exact length of the object, regardless of its shape. Using this information, you can divide the object into an equal number of segments.

**V**

**Advanced Drawing**

The DIVIDE command enables you to partition most types of objects into equal-length segments. DIVIDE works with lines, arcs, circles, donuts, polylines, splines, and ellipses.

Unlike manual methods for dividing objects, AutoCAD's DIVIDE command calculates division points to the same 14-decimal-place accuracy as all other AutoCAD functions. To divide an object into equal spaces, select the object to be divided and specify the number of segments.

You can access the DIVIDE command in one of two ways:

- Select the Point button on the Draw floating toolbar. A fly-out menu is displayed. Then select the Divide button (the second button).

- Enter **divide** at the Command: prompt.

## Dividing Objects into Equal Segments

The DIVIDE command does not actually divide an object into separate segments. The object is unaffected by the division. DIVIDE places point objects on the object at the exact segment divisions, as shown in figure 15.2. The Node object snap can be used to snap to the division marks.

**Fig. 15.2**
The DIVIDE command can be used to place evenly spaced point objects along a line.

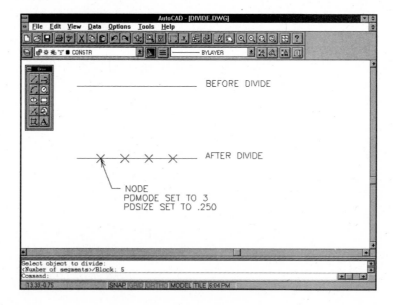

To divide an object into equal spaces, first select the object to divide. When the DIVIDE command is issued, AutoCAD prompts with Select object to divide:. You can select any line, arc, circle, donut, ellipse, polyline, spline, or any other object made using polylines (such as a polygon). After the object to divide is selected, AutoCAD displays the prompt <Number of segments>/ Block:. You specify the number of segments into which the object should be divided. AutoCAD calculates the distance for each segment and places points on the object.

## Using DIVIDE to Insert Objects

The DIVIDE command also enables you to insert a block at each division point, as shown in figure 15.3. A *block* is an object or group of objects that can be used repeatedly in a drawing. For example, you could use the DIVIDE command in combination with a block of electrical outlet symbols to space the outlets evenly along a wall. To use a block with the DIVIDE command, the block must already be defined in the drawing and have a name. To insert a block at each division point, first select the Divide button on the Draw toolbar. The following command sequence appears:

**Tip**

Because DIVIDE uses points to indicate segment divisions, change the point size and style through the Point Style dialog box (DDPTYPE) before issuing DIVIDE. The segment division points are then easier to see.

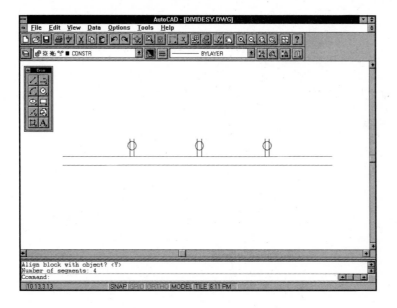

**Fig. 15.3**
The DIVIDE command can also be used to insert a symbol at each division point.

▶ See "Using Blocks to Represent Symbols," p. 680

```
Select Object to Divide: Select the object to divide.
<Number of segments>/Block: b
Block name to insert: Enter the name of the block insert.
Align block with object?<Y>: If you answer y here, AutoCAD
      rotates the block to follow the contour of the object.
      If you answer n, AutoCAD does not rotate the block.
Number of Segments: Specify the number of segments.
```

Using DIVIDE when inserting blocks can save some of the time required to lay out the location manually. Aligning the blocks with the object depends

**V**

**Advanced Drawing**

on the purpose you need to achieve. If all the blocks need to be oriented the same way, do not align them with the object. Figure 15.4 shows a block that is both aligned and not aligned with an object.

**Fig. 15.4**
Blocks can be aligned with an object using divide, saving some of the time required to lay the block out manually.

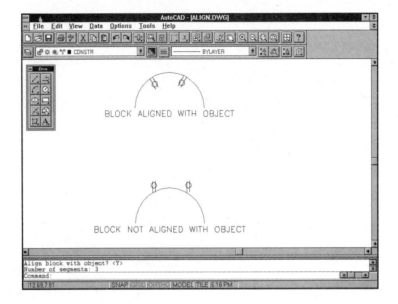

# Measuring an Object (MEASURE)

In addition to dividing an object into equal spaces, you are often called on to lay out fixed distances along an object. AutoCAD provides another command for this purpose. The MEASURE command calibrates equal lengths that you specify. DIVIDE creates equal lengths as well, but MEASURE uses a fixed length. As with the DIVIDE command, MEASURE places points on the object. Figure 15.5 shows the difference between the DIVIDE and MEASURE commands. Notice that the point objects are spaced every 1" with the MEASURE command, even though the line cannot be equally divided into 1" increments.

The MEASURE command can be used to locate outlets along a wall, locate pitch points for a thread, or mark specified graduations for a gauge. You access the MEASURE command using one of these methods:

■ Click the Point button on the Draw floating toolbar. From the fly-out menu that appears, click the Measure button (the third button).

■ Enter **measure** at the Command: prompt.

The MEASURE command is similar to the DIVIDE command. When MEA-SURE is invoked, AutoCAD prompts you to select an object. With MEASURE, you can partition lines, arcs, circles, ellipses, splines, donuts, polylines, or other objects made using polylines (such as a polygon).

MEASURE and DIVIDE work similarly. The difference is in the results. MEA-SURE places points or blocks at a spacing *you* specify. DIVIDE places points or blocks on an object by dividing it into a specific number of equal segments.

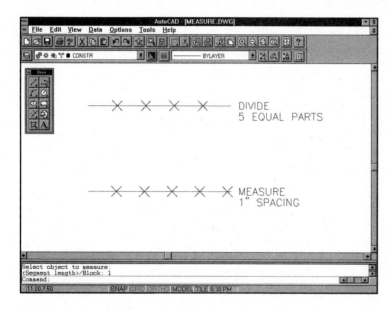

**Fig. 15.5**
The MEASURE command places point objects at 1" increments, even though the object selected cannot be equally divided into 1" increments.

**V**

Advanced Drawing

## Measuring an Object with MEASURE

As with the DIVIDE command, MEASURE does not actually separate the object into individual segments. The object is unaffected by the MEASURE command. MEASURE places point objects at intervals you specify at the exact segment divisions. You can then use the object snap Node to snap to the division marks.

Before using the MEASURE command, change the point size and style through the Point Style dialog box (DDPTYPE). After you have issued the MEASURE command, AutoCAD displays the prompt `Select object to measure:`. After you select the appropriate object, AutoCAD prompts with `<Segment length>/Block:`. Specify the distance at which you want to place points on the object.

> **Note**
>
> The location that you initially select on the object is important when you use the MEASURE command. The endpoint of the object nearest your selection defines the end of the object from which AutoCAD begins measuring.

▶ See "Using Blocks to Represent Symbols," p. 680

## Using MEASURE to Insert Objects

You can also use the MEASURE command to automatically insert a block at each point measured on an object. To use a block with MEASURE, the block must be previously defined in the drawing and have a name.

You first click the Point button on the Draw floating toolbar. From the fly-out menu that appears, click the Measure button (the third button). Then use the following command sequence to insert a block at a specified interval on an existing object:

```
Select object to measure: Select the object to measure.
<Segment length>/Block: b
Block name to insert: Enter the name of the block insert.
Align block with object?<Y>: If you enter y here, AutoCAD
          rotates the block to follow the contour of the object.
          If you enter n, AutoCAD doesn't rotate the block.
Segment length: Specify the segment length.
```

## Tutorial: Drawing a Stair Elevation

In this tutorial, you use the commands covered thus far to draw a stair elevation (see fig. 15.6).

To begin, follow these steps:

1. Click the Open button on the Standard toolbar.

   The Open Drawing dialog box appears.

2. In the File Name text box, enter the appropriate path and drawing name (C:\UAW13\15DWG01), then press enter or click OK.

   This step loads the drawing needed to begin the stair elevation drawing (see fig. 15.7).

3. From the Options menu, select Display, then Point Style.

   The Point Style dialog box appears.

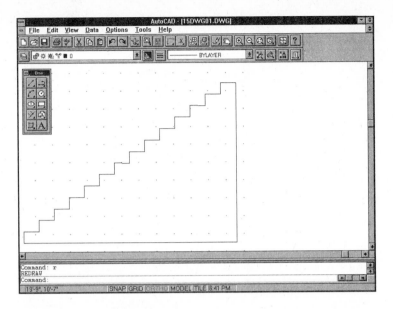

**Fig. 15.6**
Drawing a stair
elevation.

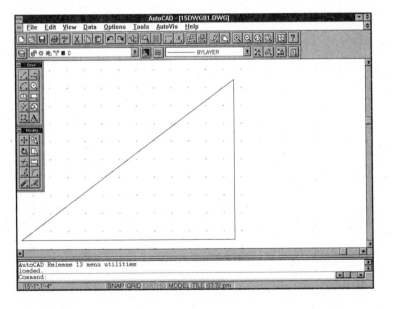

**Fig. 15.7**
Loading the
prototype drawing
to draw the stair
elevation.

**4.** Select the point style that resembles an X, which is found in the first
row (see fig. 15.8), then click OK.

**5.** Divide the diagonal line into 14 equal segments.

```
Select the Divide button from the Draw toolbar.
Select object to divide: Click the diagonal line.
Number of segments>/Block: 14
```

The diagonal line is now divided into 14 equal segments, and those segments are divided using the X point style (see fig. 15.9).

**Fig. 15.8**
Specifying the
point style.

**Fig. 15.9**
The diagonal line
divided into 14
equal segments.

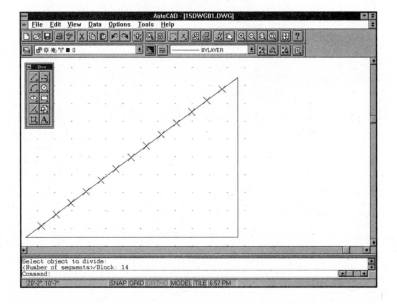

6. Issue the LINE command and draw the first stair, using the Node object snap mode to snap to the division marks.

```
Select the Line button from the Draw toolbar.
From point: 4",6"
To point: @7-11/16"<90
To point: nod
```

7. Select the first X point at the lower-left corner (see fig. 15.10).

The Node object snap always snaps to a point.

```
To point:
```

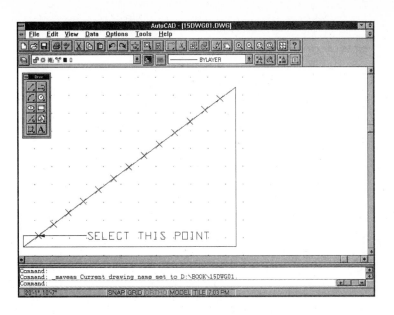

**Fig. 15.10**
Drawing a line to a
point by using the
Node object snap.

Now that you have drawn one step, complete the stairs by copying the point objects to the top of each step's riser. This sets up an object selection filter to easily select all of the point objects.

```
Command: copy
Select objects: At this point you will set up an object
    selection filter.
```

1. Choose the Selection Filters button from the Select Objects fly out on the Standard toolbar.

2. In the Object Selection Filters dialog box, choose the down arrow to the right of Arc. Using the arrows, scroll down until you see Point and select it.

◄ See "Using the
Object Selection
Filters," p. 234

3. Click Add to List. Your Object Selection Filters dialog box should look like figure 15.11.

4. In the Object Selection Filters dialog box, select Apply.

```
Select objects: '_filter
Applying filter to selection.
Select objects: all
18 found
5 were filtered out.
Select objects:
Exiting filtered selection. 13 found
Select objects:
<Base point or displacement>/Multiple: nod
```

**Fig. 15.11**
Creating a point
object selection
filter.

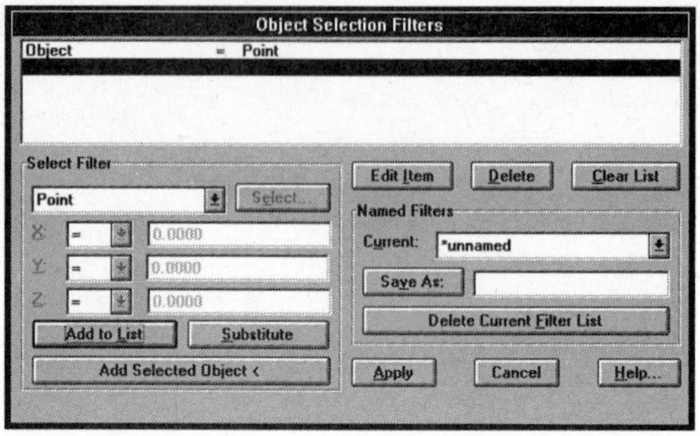

5. Select the first x point at the lower-left corner (refer to fig. 15.10).

   Second point of displacement: `@7-11/16<90`

6. Now you have copied the point objects. To complete the stairs, use the LINE command to connect the point objects, using the Node object snap.

7. Repeat this procedure until you have drawn all 14 steps in the stairs.

You may have noticed that the drawing looks peculiar with each point represented as an x. To correct the situation, follow these steps:

1. Select Options, Display, Point Style.

2. Select the first point style in the first row of the Point Style dialog box. Click OK.

   Notice that no change takes place on the drawing.

◄ See "Regenerating the Screen (REGEN)," p. 334

3. To change the representation of the points, enter **regen** at the Command: prompt.

   The points appear to have been removed. They are still there, but now they are represented as dots that can't be seen because the lines overlap them.

After you have drawn all the stairs, complete the drawing by following these steps:

1. At the Command: prompt, enter **e**.

2. At the Select objects: prompt, select the diagonal line that you divided earlier. Press Enter.

   The diagonal line is erased.

You should now have the completed stair elevation (see fig. 15.6).

Both the DIVIDE and MEASURE commands can insert a block at each division point. In the previous tutorial, you could have made a block out of the first step and then used the DIVIDE command to insert the step along the line. When DIVIDE prompts you for the number of objects, respond with **b** for block and enter the name of the first step block, then specify 14 as the number of segments.

▶ See "Using Blocks to Represent Symbols," p. 680

There are many ways to accomplish tasks in AutoCAD, as shown by the preceding example. For the majority of tasks, there is no right or wrong way. The best method is the one that works best for you.

# Drawing Rings and Solid-Filled Circles (DONUT or DOUGHNUT)

To construct solid circles, AutoCAD offers the DONUT or DOUGHNUT command. When creating the circles, you can specify both inner and outer diameters. The "donuts" are actually circular polylines.

▶ See "Using Polylines," p. 573

The DONUT command allows you to draw thick circles. It can have any inside or outside diameter, or be completely filled in. You access the DONUT command with one of two methods:

- From the Draw floating toolbar, select Circle to access the fly-out menu. The last button is Donut.

- Enter **donut** or **doughnut** at the Command: prompt.

The DONUT command first prompts for the inner and outer diameters and then for the center point. AutoCAD then draws the two circles and fills in the space between them. You use the following command sequence to create a donut:

```
Select Donut from the Circle fly-out menu.
Inside diameter <current>: Specify a new inside diameter or
    press Enter to accept the current value.
Outside diameter <current>: Specify a new inside diameter
    or press Enter to accept the current value.
Center of doughnut: Select the donut center point with the
    crosshair or enter the coordinates.
Center of doughnut: Select the center point for another
    donut or press Enter to return to the Command: prompt.
```

> **Note**
>
> If your drawing contains a lot of donuts, filling them can take a long time. You can temporarily turn off the fill inside the donuts with the FILL command. When the FILL mode is turned off, donuts appear as segmented or concentric circles. You can use FILL transparently by entering '**fill** while inside a command.

With AutoCAD, you can draw three kinds of donuts (see fig. 15.12):

- *Solid-filled.* Set the inside diameter to 0.

- *Regular.* Set the inside diameter to a value greater than 0.

- *Ring.* Set the inside diameter equal to the outside diameter.

**Fig. 15.12**
Donuts with different inside diameters.

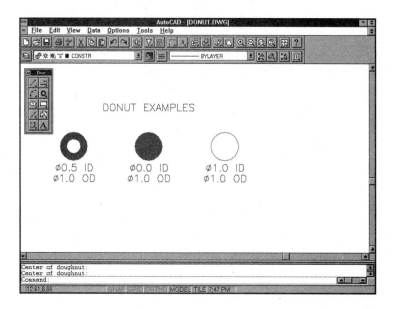

▶ See "System Variables Reference," p. 1147

The DONUTID and DONUTOD system variables control the inside and outside diameters of the donut. These variables are updated whenever you use the DONUT command. These diameters can be set directly when using the DONUT command and remain the same until you change them. Knowing this can save time if you need to draw several donuts with the same inside and outside diameters.

# Drawing Ellipses (ELLIPSE)

Ellipses are used in many forms of drawing. When you view a circle at an angle, you see an elliptical shape. For example, when you rotate a circle 60 degrees from the line of sight, you see a 30-degree ellipse.

▶ See "Creating Isometric Drawings," p. 747

An ellipse consists of a center point, major axis, and minor axis (see fig. 15.13). The ELLIPSE command provides several methods for creating an ellipse based on these three characteristics. You can also create isometric circles with the ELLIPSE command. The method you use to create the ellipse depends on the drawing you are creating. You access the ELLIPSE command in one of these ways:

- Click the Ellipse button on the Draw floating toolbar. This brings up a fly-out menu, offering three options for creating an ellipse.

- Enter **ellipse** at the Command: prompt.

V

Advanced Drawing

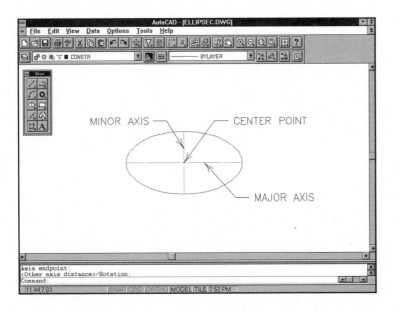

**Fig. 15.13**
The major parts of an ellipse.

## Defining Endpoints and Distances

To create an ellipse, you can define two endpoints to locate one axis of the ellipse, and then define a third point to determine the boundaries of the radius of the second axis.

To create an ellipse by defining two axis endpoints with a third point, you first choose the Ellipse button from the Draw floating toolbar and then choose the Ellipse Axis End button (the second button). Then follow this command sequence:

```
Arc/Center/<Axis endpoint 1>: Specify endpoint 1 with
        coordinates or the cursor, as shown in figure 15.14.
Axis Endpoint 2: Specify endpoint 2.
<Other axis distance>/Rotation: Specify endpoint 3 for the
        second axis.
```

**Fig. 15.14**
Constructing an ellipse by defining the axis endpoints.

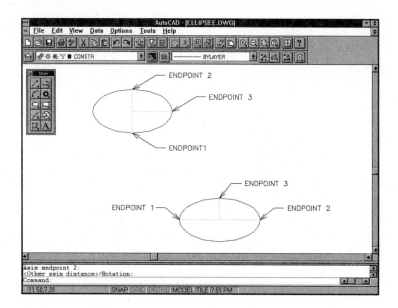

## Defining Endpoints and Rotation

You can also create an ellipse by defining the endpoints of the major axis and the rotation angle of the ellipse. The shape of the ellipse is defined by rotating a circle about the ellipse's axis by the specified angle. A response of 45 draws an ellipse that is 45 degrees from the line of sight. Responding with 0 draws a circle with the circle's diameter equal to both major and minor axes. AutoCAD rejects any angle greater than 89.4 degrees because the ellipse appears as a line. Figure 15.15 shows the relationship between several ellipses having the same major axis length but different angles of rotation.

 To create an ellipse by defining the endpoints of the major axis and a rotation angle of the ellipse, you first choose the Ellipse button on the Draw floating toolbar and then choose the Axis End button. The following command sequence is then given:

```
Arc/Center/<Axis endpoint 1>: Specify endpoint 1 of the
        major axis with coordinates or the cursor.
```

```
Axis Endpoint 2: Specify endpoint 2 of the major axis.
<Other axis distance>/Rotation: r
Rotation around major axis: Enter a rotation angle.
```

Notice that you can create an isometric ellipse by using the Rotation option and an angle of 60 degrees. AutoCAD, however, does not rotate the ellipse along the isometric axis the way it needs to be. To create a true isometric ellipse, use the isometric snap and the ISOCIRCLE option of the ELLIPSE command.

▶ See "Setting Snap for Isometric Drawing," p. 749

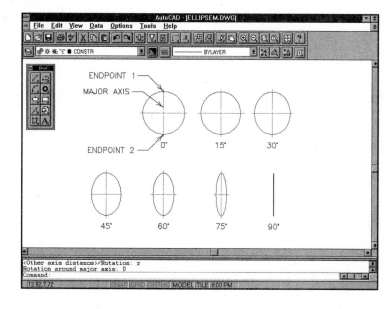

**Fig. 15.15**

Creating an ellipse by defining the major axis length with different angles of rotation.

## Defining Center and Axis Points

Besides locating the axis endpoints to define an ellipse, you can also locate the center point and two axis points (see fig. 15.16).

To create an ellipse by defining the center and two axis points, you first choose the Ellipse button on the Draw floating toolbar and then choose the Center button (the first button). Then use this command sequence:

```
Arc/Center/<Axis endpoint 1>: _c
Center of ellipse: Specify the axis center with coordinates
    or the cursor, as shown in figure 15.16.
Axis endpoint: Specify the endpoint of the first axis.
<Other axis distance>/Rotation: Specify the endpoint of the
    second axis.
```

Notice that you can also specify an axis of rotation after defining the center point and the endpoint of one axis.

**Fig. 15.16**
You can draw an ellipse by specifying the center and two axis endpoints.

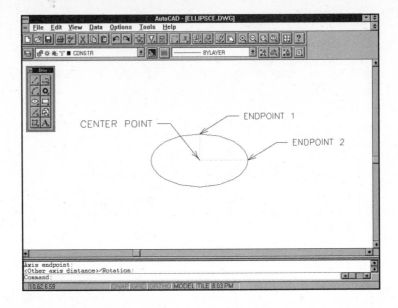

## Defining an Ellipse Arc

In addition to creating a complete ellipse, you can define a partial ellipse (see fig. 15.17). The ELLIPSE ARC command begins by creating an ellipse. By selecting the proper options in the ELLIPSE ARC command, you can use any of the previous methods to create the ellipse. After the ellipse is created, the default prompt asks for start and end angles. These angles determine the start point and endpoint of the ellipse.

**Fig. 15.17**
You use the ELLIPSE ARC command to create a partial ellipse.

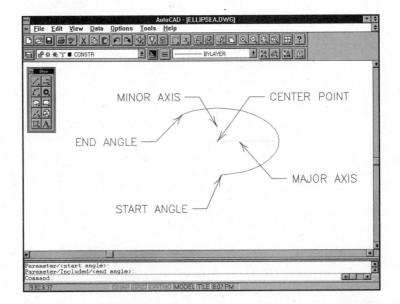

To define an ellipse arc, you first choose the Ellipse button on the Draw floating toolbar and then choose the Ellipse Arc button (the third button). Then follow this command sequence:

```
Arc/Center/<Axis endpoint 1>: _a
<Axis endpoint 1>/Center: Specify the axis center with
     coordinates or the cursor.
Axis endpoint 2: Specify the axis endpoint.
<Other axis distance>/Rotation: Specify the endpoint of the
     second axis.
Parameter/<start angle>: Specify where you want the ellipse
     to begin.
Parameter/Included/<end angle>: Specify where you want the
     ellipse to end.
```

## Tutorial: Creating a Bathroom Sink Symbol

In this tutorial, you create the bathroom sink symbol to be used in completing the apartment floor plan (see fig. 15.18).

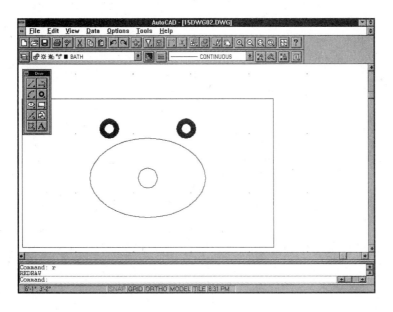

**Fig. 15.18**
Creating a
bathroom sink
symbol.

V

**Advanced Drawing**

To create the bathroom sink symbol, follow these steps:

**1.** Select the Open button from the Standard toolbar.

The Open Drawing dialog box appears.

**2.** In the File Name text box, enter the appropriate path and drawing
name (C:\UAW13\15DWG02), then press enter or click OK.

This loads the prototype drawing needed to begin the bathroom sink symbol drawing (see fig. 15.19).

**Fig. 15.19**
Loading the
prototype drawing
to draw a bath-
room sink symbol.

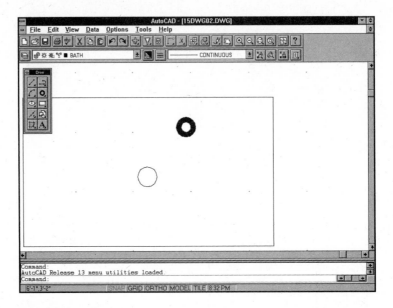

Select the Ellipse Center button from the Ellipse fly-out menu on the Draw floating toolbar.

```
<Axis endpoint 1>/Center: c
Center of ellipse: cen
```

1. Select the circle in the middle of the drawing that represents the drain of the sink.

2. Next, establish first the length of the ellipse's major axis and then the minor axis.

```
Axis endpoint: @1'<0
<Other axis distance>/Rotation: @8"<90
```

Your drawing should now resemble that in figure 15.20.

Complete the bathroom sink symbol by using the DONUT command to draw the left handle.

1. Select the Donut button from the Circle fly-out menu on the Draw toolbar.

```
Inside diameter<0'-1">: 2"
Outside diameter<0'-1">: 4"
```

2. At the Center of doughnut: prompt, enter **1'7",2'1"**. At that same prompt, press Enter to finish the command.

You should now have the symbol shown earlier in figure 15.18.

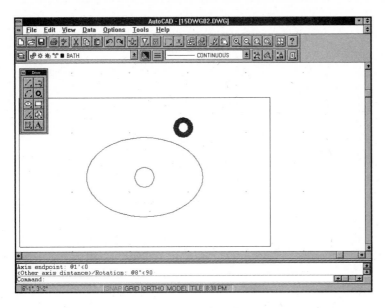

**Fig. 15.20**
Drawing the bowl
of the bathroom
sink symbol with
the ELLIPSE
command.

# Drawing Infinite Lines (XLINE)

The XLINE command creates an infinite construction line. Since the line created by XLINE is infinite, it does not affect the ZOOM command. An infinite line can be useful in geometry construction and the XLINE command is a good way of creating lines that orient you in 2D and 3D space. You can access the XLINE command by using one of these two methods:

■ From the Draw toolbar, choose the Line button. This causes a fly-out menu to appear, showing the Construction Line button.

■ Type **xline** at the Command: prompt.

After invoking the XLINE command, AutoCAD prompts:

    Hor/Ver/Ang/Bisect/Offset<From point>:

The XLINE options are different methods that can be used to create an infinite line. These options are described below.

## From Point

This option is the default that creates an infinite line passing through two points, as shown in figure 15.21.

    Hor/Ver/Ang/Bisect/Offset<From point>: *Specify Point 1.*
        *This will become the first point the XLINE will pass*
        *through.*

> Through point: *Specify Point 2. This will be the second point you want the XLINE to pass through.*
>
> Through point: *Continue to specify points. All XLINEs created will pass through point 1. When you are done selecting points, press Enter to end the command.*

**Fig. 15.21**
An infinite XLINE can be created by specifying two points.

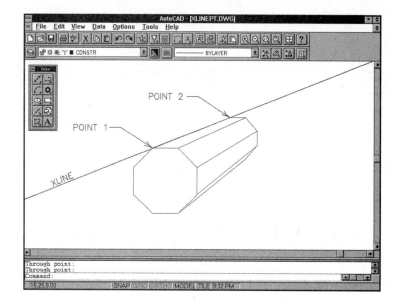

## Hor

This option creates a horizontal XLINE passing through a single point, as shown in figure 15.22.

> Hor/Ver/Ang/Bisect/Offset<From point>: **hor**
>
> Through point: *Specify a point (point 1) through which you want the XLINE to pass. This will create an XLINE parallel to the X axis, passing through the selected point. When you have completed selecting points, press Enter to end the command.*

## Ver

This option creates a vertical XLINE passing through a single point, as shown in figure 15.23.

> Hor/Ver/Ang/Bisect/Offset<From point>: **ver**
>
> Through point: *Specify a point (point 1) through which you want the XLINE to pass. The XLINE created will pass through the selected point and be parallel to the Y axis. When you have completed selecting points, press Enter to end the command.*

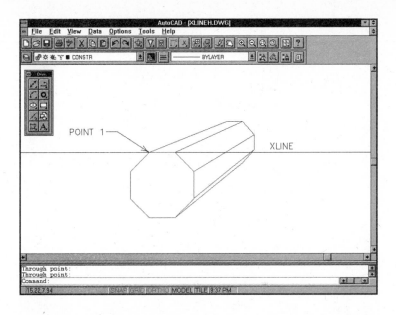

**Fig. 15.22**
The Hor option creates an XLINE parallel to the X axis through a specified point.

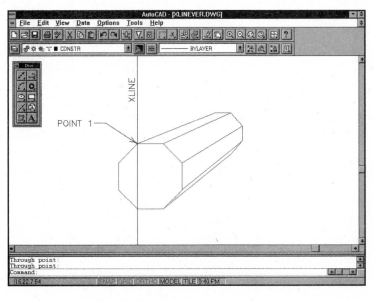

**Fig. 15.23**
Use the Ver option to create an XLINE parallel to the Y axis passing through a selected point.

**V**

**Advanced Drawing**

## Ang

This option creates an XLINE at a specified angle. There are two options when creating an angular XLINE. You can specify the angle of the XLINE and a point the XLINE will pass through, or create the XLINE at a specific angle from a reference line.

### Specifying the Angle of the XLINE and a Point

This option creates an infinite XLINE at the specified angle going through a point, as shown in figure 15.24.

```
Hor/Ver/Ang/Bisect/Offset<From point>: ang
Reference/<Enter angle (0.00)>: Specify the angle of the
      XLINE.
Through point: Specify the point (1) through which you want
      the angular XLINE to pass. When you have completed
selecting points, press Enter to end the command.
```

**Fig. 15.24**

Creating an angular XLINE by specifying the angle and a point it passes through.

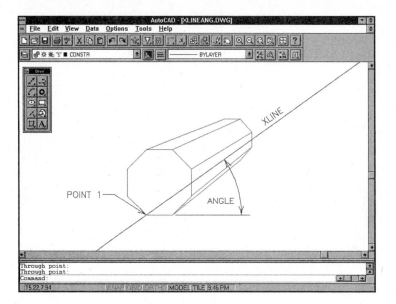

### Specifying the Angle of the XLINE from a Selected Reference Line

This option creates an angled XLINE by referencing an existing object, as shown in figure 15.25. The angle is measured in a counterclockwise direction from the reference line.

```
Hor/Ver/Ang/Bisect/Offset<From point>: ang
Reference/<Enter angle (0.00)>: r
Select a line object: Select another XLINE, ray, line, or
      polyline.
Enter angle: Specify the angle.
Through point: Specify a point (1) through which you want
      the XLINE to pass. When you have completed selecting
      points, press Enter to end the command.
```

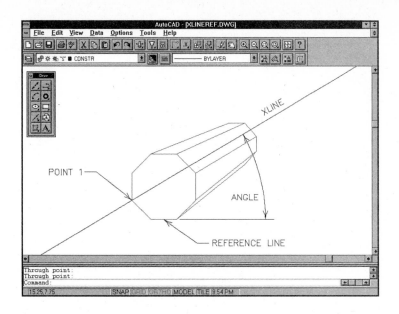

**Fig. 15.25**
Creating an
angular XLINE by
specifying an
angle from a
selected reference
line.

## Bisect

This option creates an XLINE that passes through a selected angle vertex and
bisects the angle between two selected points. The XLINE lies in the plane
determined by the three points. The Bisect option is shown in figure 15.26.

> Hor/Ver/Ang/Bisect/Offset<From point>: **bisect**
> Angle vertex point: *Specify a point (1) that will be the*
> *vertex of the angle. The completed XLINE will pass*
> *through this point.*
> Angle start point: *Specify a point (2) that will form one*
> *side of the angle.*
> Angle end point: *Specify a point (3) that will form the*
> *other side of the angle. When you have completed*
> selecting points, press Enter to end the command.

## Offset

This option creates an XLINE that is parallel to another object, as shown in
figure 15.27. This is similar to the OFFSET command discussed in chapter 10,
except that an infinite XLINE is created.

> Hor/Ver/Ang/Bisect/Offset<From point>: **offset**
> Offset distance or Through <0.00>: *Specify an offset*
> *distance or T.*
> Select a line object: *Select another XLINE, line, polyline,*
> *or ray.*
> Side to offset? *Specify a point (1). When you have com-*
> *pleted selecting points, press Enter to end the command.*

**Fig. 15.26**
Creating an
XLINE that passes
through a selected
angle vertex,
bisecting the angle
between the
second and third
points.

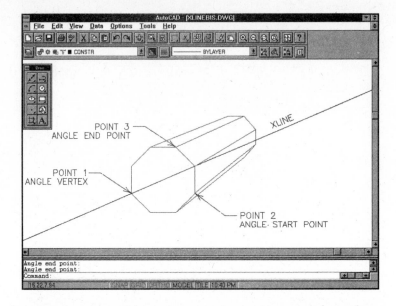

**Fig. 15.27**
Creating an
XLINE parallel to
another object.

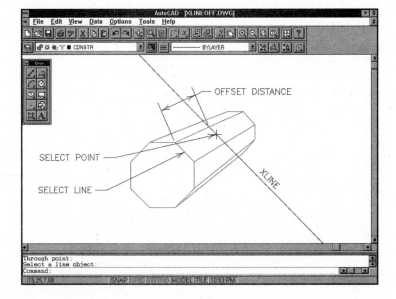

# Drawing Rays (RAY)

The RAY command creates a semi-infinite construction line. As opposed to an infinite line (XLINE), a ray (RAY) has a finite starting point and extends to infinity, as shown in figure 15.28. You can access the RAY command by using one of these two methods:

- From the Draw floating toolbar, choose the Line button. This causes a fly-out menu to appear. The third button is Ray.

- Type **ray** at the Command: prompt.

After invoking the RAY command, AutoCAD prompts:

From point: *Specify a starting point (1) where you want the ray to begin.*
Through point: *Specify a point (2) through which you want the ray to pass. When you have completed selecting points, press Enter to end the command.*

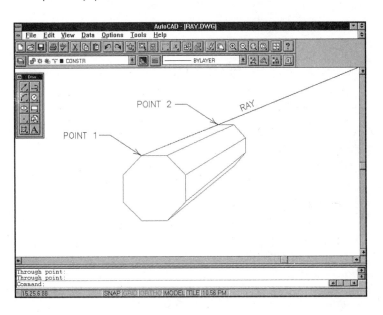

**Fig. 15.28**
A ray is a semi-infinite line, defined by specifying a starting point and a point through which you want the ray to pass.

# Creating Freehand Drawings (SKETCH)

The SKETCH command can be used to create freehand drawings in AutoCAD. Common uses of this command include creating map outlines, entering signatures, or creating short break lines in mechanical drawings. When using the SKETCH command, the sketching is captured as a series of short independent lines. The length of these lines is governed by the record increment. You can access the SKETCH command by using one of these two methods:

■ Choose the Sketch button from the Miscellaneous toolbar.

■ Type **sketch** at the Command: prompt.

After invoking the SKETCH command, AutoCAD prompts:

```
Record increment <0.10>: Specify an increment or accept the
            default.
```

The record increment specifies the distance, in drawing units, that you move your drawing device before AutoCAD draws a line on the drawing. The larger the record increment, the farther the drawing device must be moved before it will generate a line.

---

### Caution

If you use a small record increment, you can quickly add hundreds of lines to your drawing, resulting in very large drawing files. You should use SKETCH conservatively, taking care to choose a record increment appropriate to your task so that you can draw accurately while keeping your drawings to a manageable size.

---

After specifying the record increment, AutoCAD displays the following options on the Command: line:

```
Sketch. Pen eXit Quit Record Erase Connect.
```

At this point you are ready to begin sketching. Select a point on the drawing and begin freehand sketching. The options displayed above apply once you start sketching.

---

### Troubleshooting

*When I attempt to create a sketch, my lines look funny. They seem to be a series of straight lines, even though I am using a small record increment.*

Make sure your Ortho and Snap are turned off. Sketch is intended to create freehand drawings. Using Snap while sketching can cause the freehand lines to "snap" to specific points. Ortho can cause the sketch to appear blocky, since Ortho is intended to create only horizontal and vertical lines.

---

When you are sketching, AutoCAD displays the <Pen down> prompt. As you move your pointing device, freehand geometry begins to appear on-screen. The appearance of the freehand geometry depends on the record increment setting. When you have completed your sketch, type **p** or pick a point with your drawing device. AutoCAD displays the <Pen up> prompt.

At this point, you can select one of the following options shown in Table 15.1, or you can lower the pen (press the pick button or type **P**) and start sketching again. Also, you do not have to pick up the pen (pick button or **P**) before selecting one of the options.

| **Table 15.1** | **Sketch Command Options** |
| --- | --- |
| **Option** | **Use** |
| Pen | This option raises and lowers the sketching pen. You must raise the pen before you can select any menu items with your pointing device. |
| eXit | AutoCAD ends the SKETCH command and makes your sketch part of the drawing. |
| Quit | AutoCAD exits the command without recording anything. |
| Record | AutoCAD records your sketch without exiting the command or changing your pen's position. You can move the cursor to another position and sketch some more. |
| Erase | AutoCAD lets you erase all or part of your *temporary* sketch lines and raises the pen if it is down. |
| Connect | This option lowers the pen and continues the sketch from the endpoint of the last sketched line. |
| . (period) | Draws a straight line segment from the endpoint of the last sketched line to the pen's current location. The pen is automatically lowered at the beginning of the line segment and raised at the end. |

## Tutorial: Sketching Your Initials with the SKETCH Command

Now give SKETCH a try. Use the drawing you've been working on in this chapter—15DWG02, the bathroom sink symbol. Sketch your initials in the lower-right corner of the sink.

1. Choose the Open button on the Standard toolbar. The Select File dialog box appears.

2. Change to the UAW13 subdirectory. In the File Name text box, select the file 15DWG02 and press Enter or click OK.

3. Choose the Aerial button from the Tool Windows toolbar to invoke the Aerial View dialog box. Use the Aerial View to draw a window around the lower-right corner.

◀ See "Using the Aerial View Window," p. 358

V

Advanced Drawing

4. Make sure Snap and Ortho are turned off in the toolbar at the bottom of the screen.

5. Choose Sketch from the Miscellaneous toolbar.

6. Press Enter to accept the default Record increment of 0'–1". AutoCAD displays the SKETCH options on the Command: line:

   Sketch. Pen eXit Quit Record Erase Connect.

7. Move the crosshairs into the lower-right corner of the windowed section and select a point to begin sketching. AutoCAD prompts with <Pen down>.

8. Move your pointing device around (you don't need to hold down the pick button) to get a feel for how SKETCH works. When you want to stop sketching, press the pick button again. AutoCAD prompts with <Pen up>.

9. Now you can take one of two actions. You can enter **q** to exit from the command and not record your sketched lines, or you can enter **e** to access SKETCH erase mode and erase what you've drawn. If you quit, immediately press Enter to start the SKETCH command again.

10. Experiment with sketching lines and erasing or quitting until you feel comfortable with sketching. Then try sketching your initials. When they look good to you, enter **X** to record what you sketched and exit the command.

11. Select the Save button on the Standard toolbar to save your drawing.

# From Here...

Although the POINT command can be used by itself to locate permanent points on a drawing, it is normally used with the DIVIDE and MEASURE commands. Always set the point size and style in the Point Style dialog box before using either the DIVIDE or MEASURE command.

You can also use the DIVIDE and MEASURE commands to insert groups of objects (blocks). Both commands give you the option of aligning the inserted objects with the object. If used properly, these commands can speed up drawing time immensely.

AutoCAD also offers several other commands for creating specific types of objects that can be time-consuming or difficult to draw. The ELLIPSE command makes ellipse creation simple, while the DONUT command provides an excellent method for creating rings and solid filled circles. Additionally, you can use the SKETCH command to create freehand lines on your drawing.

After completing this chapter, you will have covered the majority of two-dimensional drafting commands. Adding text to a drawing and dimensioning the drawing are two important topics that are covered in upcoming chapters. For more information about adding text to a drawing and dimensioning your drawing, see the following chapters:

- Chapter 16, "Working with Text," explains how to add text to your drawing.

- Chapter 18, "Dimensioning a Drawing," explains how you can add dimensions to your geometry.

# On Your Own

Using the ELLIPSE command, create the water closet symbol shown in figure 15.29.

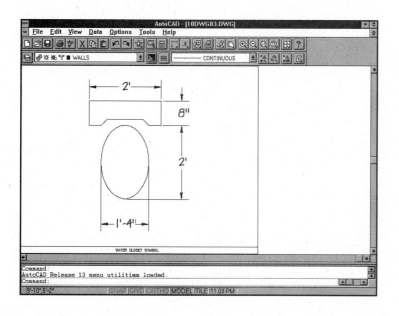

**Fig. 15.29**
Use the ELLIPSE command to create the bottom portion of the water closet symbol.

Hints:

**1.** Use the dimensions found in figure 15.29 to determine the major and minor axes of the ellipse needed to complete the water closet symbol.

Not all dimensions are given. Estimate dimensions to create your own unique symbol.

2. Remember to save the drawing when you have completed it.

3. Your symbol does not have to be exactly like the one shown. Add a handle or other items to increase the detail of the symbol.

# Chapter 16

# Working with Text

V

Advanced Drawing

AutoCAD enables you to communicate your ideas through the use of pictures. You'll find, however, that even the most skillfully drafted concepts can't always completely convey the necessary information. AutoCAD's text tools can help you add and emphasize details about your designs that can't be shown through drawing alone.

In this chapter, you learn how to do the following tasks:

- Use the STYLE command to create and edit your text styles

- Add text to your drawing with the TEXT command

- Add multiple lines of text to your drawing with the DTEXT command

- Create paragraphs with the new MTEXT command

- Utilize the QTEXT command to aid quick regens on text-intensive drawings

- Find and correct any spelling mistakes using the new SPELL command

- Edit text using the DDEDIT command

- Specify object properties and change styles with DDEMODES

- Change the style name with RENAME

## Adding Text to a Drawing

You'll probably never create a drawing without adding text in some form, even if it's only the date the drawing was created. AutoCAD's TEXT, DTEXT, MTEXT, and STYLE commands provide you with powerful, easy-to-use tools for creating text and customizing its appearance. SPELL and DDEDIT help you edit your text quickly, and DDEMODES, DDRENAME, and DDMODIFY help you control and change the text properties.

You use TEXT, DTEXT, and MTEXT to create text in your drawings. These commands evolved as AutoCAD progressed. TEXT was the first text-creation command, included in the earliest versions of the program. It allows you to enter text, one line at a time, on the AutoCAD command line. DTEXT enters characters dynamically on-screen as you type them on the command line. With DTEXT, you can also enter multiple lines of text within one instance of the command.

MTEXT, new to Release 13, provides a full-featured text-editing window within which you can cut and paste, as well as assign properties such as color and height to your text, for as much text as you want to enter. When you're finished creating the text, AutoCAD puts it into your drawing. Additional features unique to MTEXT include the ability to mix height, styles, fonts, and other text properties within your MTEXT object.

You use the STYLE command to create text styles that define the characteristics and appearance of your text, and to modify existing styles. The Object Creation Modes or DDEMODES are useful for changing the current text style and viewing the complete character set for the selected style. With AutoCAD, you can use many styles within a single drawing.

Because this chapter is dealing with all aspects of text, you'll need to use the Modify and Draw toolbars. They are not default toolbars and may need to be turned on if you haven't already done so. Choose Tools, Toolbars and then Modify and Draw to activate them.

## Defining a Text Style

**Tip**
You'll want to define a standard set of text styles and include them in your prototype drawings. That way, all the text on all your drawings will have a consistent look.

Before you begin to add text to any drawing, you must decide how the text will look. What kind of font will it use? How big will it be? Should it be scrunched up or spread out? Should it lean left or right, or even appear backward? Each style has a unique name and is defined by a text font, height, width, obliquing angle, and orientation (backward, upside-down, and/or vertical).

After you determine the kind of style you want, you can set it up with the STYLE command. The following sections describe how to use the STYLE command from the command line and with the AutoCAD menus.

### Creating Styles (STYLE)

Styles are used to customize your text, ensure uniform use of text, and allow for special text requirements like italic to highlight an important note.

The majority of your styles will be the same font with different text size and width factors. You invoke the STYLE command using the following methods:

- At the Command: prompt enter **style**.

- Choose Data, Text Style (see fig. 16.1).

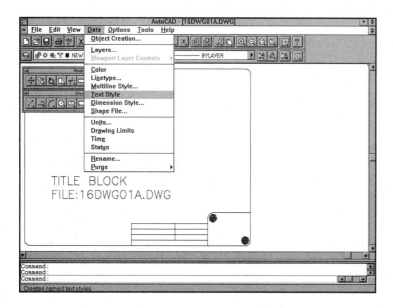

**Fig. 16.1**
The pull-down menu for selecting the Text Style command.

Regardless of which method you use to invoke the Text Style command, following these steps will define a new text style that you'll use in your drawings. You'll always create a new text style at the Command: prompt, so follow these steps:

1. Enter **style** at the AutoCAD Command: prompt or select Data, Text Style.

2. At the Text style name (or ?) <STANDARD>: prompt, enter the name you want to give the style.

3. Select a text font.

   If the system variable FILEDIA is set to 1, AutoCAD displays a File dialog box with a list of available fonts to choose from. If the font you seek isn't here you can change directories, Type the path and font name, or select Find to locate the desired font in the Select Font File dialog box in figure 16.2.

**V**

**Advanced Drawing**

**Fig. 16.2**

The Select Font
File dialog box
with a list of
available fonts
you can select.

Figure 16.3 shows the Browse/Search dialog box. This dialog box can be
used to find fonts and view them for selection. If you still don't see the
font you're looking for, you can select the Search tab and the Search
information will appear (see fig. 16.4). Here you can perform a search
for a specific font or for a font type like *.PFB (PostScript fonts).

**Fig. 16.3**

The Browse
portion of the
Browse/Search
dialog box used
when looking for
fonts.

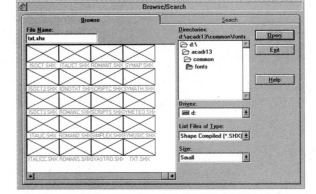

**Fig. 16.4**

The Search portion
of the Browse/
Search dialog box
used when looking
for fonts.

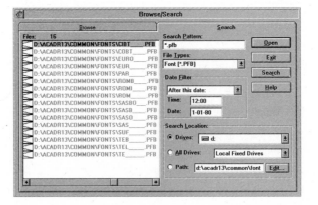

If FILEDIA=0, AutoCAD prompts for a font file name on the command line; type the name of the font you want to use. For more details on system variables, see Appendix C, "System Variables Reference."

4. Supply a text height at the command line prompt.

If you accept the default height of 0, AutoCAD always prompts you for a height when you enter text using this style.

> **Note**
>
> You'll likely end up creating text styles with fixed heights by entering a particular value, instead of accepting the default of zero. By using text styles with predetermined heights, you can avoid the extra step of having to supply a height when entering text with TEXT or DTEXT. Remember to keep your plotting scales in mind, though, as you make these styles. For example, if you want your text to plot 0.25" high at a scale of 1/4"=1', then give your text style a height of 12".

◀ See "Specifying Plot Scale," p. 402

5. At the command line prompt enter a text width factor, default is <1>. This value determines the amount by which AutoCAD compresses or stretches the text along its width. A factor less than 1 compresses your text while a factor more than 1 stretches your text.

6. Enter an obliquing angle if you want the text to lean to the right or left. A negative value causes the text to lean left. This is relative to the face of a clock, 0 equals twelve o'clock and 90 equals three o'clock. See figure 16.5 for an example of text obliquing.

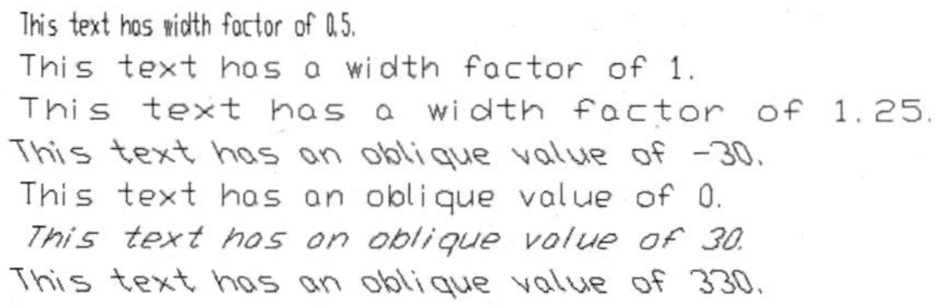

This text has width factor of 0.5.
This text has a width factor of 1.
This text has a width factor of 1.25.
This text has an oblique value of -30.
This text has an oblique value of 0.
*This text has an oblique value of 30.*
This text has an oblique value of 330.

**Fig. 16.5**
A sample of different Obliquing and Width factors in a text style.

7. Answer yes to one, two, or all of the next three questions if you want text that uses this style to appear backward, upside-down, or vertically.

```
Backwards<N>:
Upside-Down<N>:
Vertical <N>:
```

The selected font must support dual orientation for you to make it vertical.

V

Advanced Drawing

After you have answered the prompts, AutoCAD creates the style with the properties you've selected. AutoCAD also makes this style current so you can begin immediately to use it with AutoCAD's text commands.

**Caution**

If AutoCAD can't find the font file used to create a particular style, the text created with that style won't display with that font. You'll be prompted for a substitute font or none. If you select another font, it will display the text using the substituted font.

If you must send your drawings out of the office, you need to send the font files along with the drawings if you want your text to display as you originally created it. Some third-party font publishers may not allow people who haven't purchased their fonts to have access to them. If you use third-party fonts and anticipate having to send them out, you'll want to check the license agreement that came with the fonts to make sure you can freely distribute the font files.

**Note**

If you create text with a particular style and later change that style's parameters, AutoCAD won't automatically update any text already generated using that style. You can use either the CHANGE or DDMODIFY command to update the existing text. You may prefer CHANGE to DDMODIFY if you have to update a lot of text. You can choose more than one piece of text with a single CHANGE command, but DDMODIFY allows you to pick only one piece of text at a time. For instructions on using CHANGE and DDMODIFY, see Chapter 21, "Modifying Object Characteristics."

**Troubleshooting**

*AutoCAD displays an empty list in the File dialog box, or, after I type a font file name, AutoCAD returns a message that it can't find the selected font.*

From the Options menu, choose Preferences, Environment and Support. Here you should see the path to your font files. If you don't see the directory where your font files are stored, you must add it to this line.

*My text isn't displaying in the proper color even when it's on the proper layer.*

Check your Object Create Modes with DDEMODES to make sure your object's Color mode is set to BYLAYER. Select the DDEMODES icon and the Object Creation Modes dialog box, shown in figure 16.6, appears. If color is not BYLAYER, select the Color button and choose BYLAYER.

**Fig. 16.6**
The Object
Creation Modes
dialog box is
used to control
object creation
properties.

## Troubleshooting

*My text is not displaying in the font that I want.*

Select the DDEMODES icon and the Object Creation Modes dialog box shown in figure 16.6 appears. Then select the Text Style button and the Select Text Style dialog box appears with a list of existing text styles (see fig. 16.7). Highlight the font you want to use and select the Show All button. Figure 16.8 shows you the complete character set for the style. The question marks represent ASCII characters that AutoCAD doesn't recognize.

**Fig. 16.7**
The Select Text
Style dialog box
with the list of
existing styles.

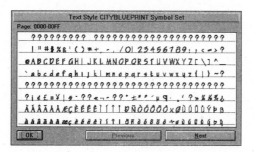

**Fig. 16.8**
The character
set for the
CITYBLUEPRINT
font.

V

Advanced Drawing

**Troubleshooting**

*I made a mistake in naming my style, do I have to re-create it from scratch?*

No, you simply rename the style by selecting Data, Rename as shown in figure 16.9. The Rename dialog box shown in figure 16.10 appears. Highlight Style in the list box and the style you want to rename in the Items list box. The name appears in the Old Name box. Enter the new name in the Rename To box and select OK.

**Fig. 16.9**
Selecting Data, Rename from the pull-down menu.

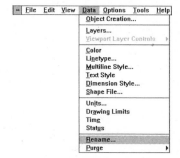

**Fig. 16.10**
The Rename dialog box that you get when you select Data, Rename or enter **ddrename** at the Command: prompt.

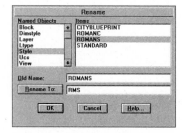

## Tutorial: Creating Your Own Text Style

Now that you've learned how to create a text style, you're ready to try the process in a drawing. In the directory UAW13 created for this book, you should find a drawing called 16DWG01, as shown in figure 16.11. Follow these steps:

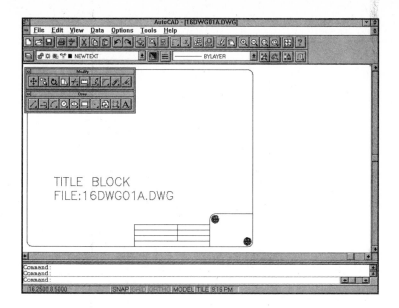

**Fig. 16.11**
The drawing used
in this tutorial.

1. Open 16DWG01 located in the UAW13 directory.

2. Choose <u>D</u>ata, <u>T</u>ext Style.

3. Enter **cityblueprint** for the name of your new font style.

4. You should see the Select Text Font dialog box. Select <u>L</u>ist Files of Type, Font (*.PFB).

5. Select cibt____.pfb from the font list. Click OK. The "_" characters shown in the name are added as a filler to make all of the font names an even eight characters long.

6. On the command line, AutoCAD prompts for the rest of the STYLE command's options. Accept all defaults. The command ends with the message CITYBLUEPRINT is now the current text style. If you choose a different font, that font's name is the name of the current style, instead of CITYBLUEPRINT.

7. Repeat steps 1 through 5 to create another style called ROMANC using the ROMANC.SHX font. Then save the drawing as 16DWG01B for later use. Note that ROMANC is now the current text style.

**V**

**Advanced Drawing**

## Justifying Text

AutoCAD provides you with the ability to accurately place, or justify, text based on a specific point, called the *text insertion point*. When you specify text justification, you're telling AutoCAD where to locate the text's insertion point:

```
Command: text
Justify/Style/<Start point>: j
Align/Fit/Center/Middle/Right/TL/TC/TR/ML/MC/MR/BL/BC/BR:
```

AutoCAD recognizes fifteen positions on text strings that you can use to justify text (T = Top, M = Middle, B = Bottom). See figure 16.12.

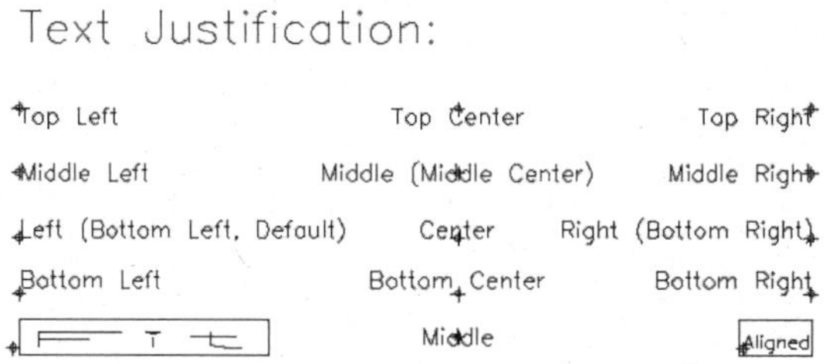

**Fig. 16.12**
The different text justification points.

Text Justification:

Top Left        Top Center        Top Right

Middle Left       Middle (Middle Center)      Middle Right

Left (Bottom Left, Default)    Center    Right (Bottom Right)

Bottom Left       Bottom Center       Bottom Right

Middle     Aligned

Justify is one of the options you'll find in the first prompt after entering the TEXT or DTEXT command. If you already know the justification option you want to choose, you can enter it at the first TEXT or DTEXT prompt without first selecting Justify.

You'll probably use the following four justifications the most. Obviously, left justification will be your primary justification with center or middle a close second. Some possible uses include setting up a table in your drawing, aligning text in your title block, or centering text inside objects.

- *Left justification.* If you don't specify another justification option, AutoCAD justifies text by using the text's lower-left corner as its insertion point.

- *Right justification.* The opposite of left justification, AutoCAD uses the lower-right corner of the text for the insertion point.

- *Center justification.* You may want to center your text at some point on your drawing. The Center justification option uses the text's lower center point as the text insertion point.

- *Middle justification.* The Middle option uses the exact middle of the text for the insertion point. This is very useful for centering text in circles and rectangles.

The other justifications (TL, TC, TR, ML, MC, MR, BL, BC, and BR) are variations on the first three above. The difference is that the insertion point is modified to include both vertical and horizontal alignment at the left, center, or right justification points as shown previously in figure 16.12.

## Aligning Text (Align and Fit)

Sometimes you want text to fill up space between two points that you choose. The Align and Fit options give you that opportunity. Both options operate the same; after you choose either one, you are asked to specify two points between which AutoCAD will generate the text.

The Fit option stretches or compresses the text to fit, while maintaining a constant height (using the height of the last piece of text as the default). Fit text can appear squeezed or stretched. This option is useful for putting the designers last name in the title block when it's a long one like "Kazmierczak" (see fig. 16.13).

The Align option adjusts the text's height to maintain a natural-looking ratio between the text's height and length. This option is good to use in a Bill of Material or drawing change column.

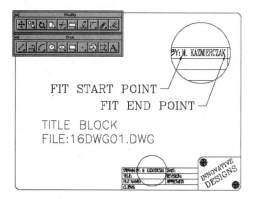

**Fig. 16.13**
An enlarged view of a text string justified to fit in a predefined area.

## Entering Text with TEXT and DTEXT

The two primary text commands you will use are TEXT and DTEXT. With TEXT you enter a quick single line of text. Using DTEXT you can enter multiple lines of text in column alignment and you can backspace to the previous line if needed. To access TEXT and DTEXT do one of the following:

- At the Command: prompt enter **text** or **dtext**.

- From the Draw toolbar select the Text or the Dtext button.

Both the TEXT and DTEXT commands run pretty much the same course until the point when you actually start typing text. For a single line of text or text that you'll be entering randomly around your drawing you should use TEXT. For text that will be entered in a columnar form or as a paragraph you'll need to use DTEXT. With either text command, keep in mind what style you're using and what kind of justification you need to use.

To use either of these commands, follow these steps:

1.  Select the Text or Dtext icons from the Draw toolbar.

2.  At the `Justify/Style/<Start point>:` prompt, enter **j** to see a list of justification options from which to pick. Enter a justification option directly, if you know its name (refer to fig. 16.12); enter **s** to specify a different text style; or pick the point where the text will start (the default).

3.  Enter a text height, if AutoCAD prompts for one, and then a rotation angle or accept the defaults.

    If the current text style doesn't have a predefined height, AutoCAD prompts for a height. If the current style has a predefined height, AutoCAD asks only for a rotation angle.

4.  Finally, AutoCAD asks you to enter the text itself. Begin typing. The following is what your command prompts should look like:

```
Command: _text Justify/Style/<Start point>: j
Align/Fit/Center/Middle/Right/TL/TC/TR/ML/MC/MR/BL/BC/BR: c
Center point:
Height <0.2000>:
Rotation angle <0>:
Text: <your text goes here>
```

**Tip**

To place text at scattered positions around your drawing, use the DTEXT command. At any `Text:` prompt, pick a point where you want text to appear. The edit box jumps to that point and allows you to enter text.

If you're using the TEXT command, your text appears, as you type it, on AutoCAD's command line. When you press Enter, AutoCAD writes the text on your drawing and cycles back to the `Command:` prompt.

If you're using the DTEXT command, a box approximately the size of a single character appears on-screen. As you type the text, it appears, character by character, on the screen as well as on the command line. When you press Enter, AutoCAD again displays the `Text:` prompt, and you can type the next line of text. To end the command, press Enter at a blank `Text:` prompt.

## Tutorial: Creating Text with DTEXT

Now that you've learned how to put text in drawings, try adding to a drawing of your own. You can use the same drawing in which you defined styles earlier—16DWG01B.

1. Open 16DWG01B.

2. Select the Zoom, Window icon in the Standard toolbar and zoom in on the title box in the lower-right corner.

3. Select the Dtext icon on the Draw toolbar.

4. Confirm that CITYBLUEPRINT is the current style. Otherwise, select it:

   ```
   Justify/Style/<Start point>: s
   Style name (or ?) <CITYBLUEPRINT>: cityblueprint or
       press Enter
   ```

5. Choose Middle Left (ML) justification:

   ```
   Justify/Style/<Start point>: j
   Align/Fit/Center/Middle/Right/...ML/MC/MR/BL/BC/BR: ml
   ```

6. Choose the text's start point:

   ```
   Justify/Style/<Start point>: 5.3125,1.125
   ```

7. Choose a text height and rotation angle:

   ```
   Height <0.0000>: .125
   Rotation angle <0>:
   ```

8. Type the first text string:

   ```
   Text: DRAWN BY:
   ```

   Do not press Enter.

9. At the next Text: prompt, pick the point 5.3125,0.875 before you type any text. Then type the next string.

   ```
   Text: TITLE:
   ```

   > **Tip**
   > When you are picking the next point you don't need to press Enter to get the next text prompt.

10. Enter the rest of the CITYBLUEPRINT text by picking points at the Text: prompts. Then type the text shown here.

| At this point: | Enter this text: |
|----------------|------------------|
| 5.3125,0.625 | **FILE NAME:** |
| 5.3125,0.375 | **CLIENT:** |
| 7.3125,1.125 | **DATE:** |
| 7.3125,0.875 | **REVISION:** |
| 7.3125,0.625 | **APPROVED:** |

V

**Advanced Drawing**

11. After typing APPROVED:, press Enter at the `Text:` prompt to end the command.

12. At the `Command:` prompt, press Enter to start the DTEXT command again.

13. Set a different text style:

```
Justify/Style/<Start point>: s
Style name (or ?) <CITYBLUEPRINT>: romanc
```

14. Create the ROMANC text with the settings provided here:

```
Justify/Style/<Start point>: j
Align/Fit/Center/Middle/Right/...ML/MC/MR/BL/BC/BR: m
Middle point: 9.625,1.1875
Height <0.1250>: .1875
Rotation angle <0>: 30
Text: INNOVATIVE
Text:
Command:
DTEXT Justify/Style/<Start point>: j
Align/Fit/Center/Middle/Right/...ML/MC/MR/BL/BC/BR: m
Middle point: 9.8125,.875
Height <0.1250>: .25
Rotation angle <30>:
Text: DESIGNS
```

After entering these last two text strings, your drawing should look similar to figure 16.14.

**Fig. 16.14**
The finished title block.

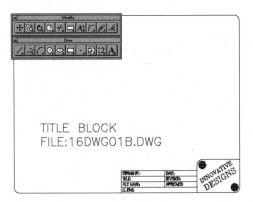

## Repeating Text

When you use the TEXT command, you can enter multiple lines of text, one below the other, with the same justification, style, and height by pressing Enter two times after creating the first line of text.

```
Command: text
Justify/Style/<Start point>:[ENTER]
Height <0.2000>:[ENTER]
Rotation angle <0>:[ENTER]
Text: Repeating text[ENTER][ENTER]
Command:
TEXT Justify/Style/<Start point>:
Text: Second line[ENTER]
```

This method saves you some time because you don't have to enter the TEXT command at the Command: prompt or select the command from a menu. The DTEXT command enables you to do the same without exiting the command.

## Entering Text with MTEXT

MTEXT, a new feature in Release 13, provides an integrated text editor that you use to create and edit text from within AutoCAD. You can invoke the MTEXT command in the following ways:

- Select the MText button from the Draw Toolbar.

- Enter **mtext** at the Command: prompt.

MTEXT is a feature-rich text editor for AutoCAD Release 13. With MTEXT you can create paragraph objects, define a specific area of your drawing for your MTEXT objects, import text, and change properties of your text MTEXT objects. A major improvement is a feature unique to MTEXT that allows you to intermix font styles and sizes within a single MTEXT object (see fig. 16.15).

> **Note**
>
> It's important to note here that MTEXT creates a single text object. Unlike DTEXT which creates multiple lines of text string objects, MTEXT creates one multiple line text string object. This is important because you may wish to move one sentence and move the entire paragraph instead.

## Tutorial: Using MTEXT to Create Text

Regardless of the method used to invoke MTEXT, here's how you use it:

1. Enter **mtext** at the Command: prompt, or pick the MText icon on the Draw toolbar text flyout. You'll see the two prompts that follow:

```
Command: _mtext
Attach/Rotation/Style/Height/Direction/<Insertion
    point>:
Attach/Rotation/Style/Height/Direction/Width/2Points/
    <Other corner>:
```

AutoCAD asks you to specify a region on the drawing by making a window, just like the window you use to select objects. When you've completed the MTEXT command, AutoCAD fits the text within that window.

2. AutoCAD displays the Edit MText window, where you can begin typing or importing text (see fig. 16.15).

**Fig. 16.15**

The Edit MText text entry box allows you to enter and edit text in a standard text-editing environment.

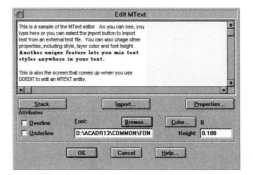

You can mix font type, size, underline, and overline throughout your text and use editing commands like Cut and Paste while in the Edit MText dialog box. You can change almost all aspects of your MText object in the Edit MText dialog box while creating it. "Editing MText Objects" later in this chapter will go into more detail.

If your text disappeared from view while entering it, you can scroll up and down as well as across. Be aware that your text won't go horizontally outside the box you picked, but your text can flow vertically down and outside that box.

## Editing Text (CHANGE, DDEDIT, and DDMODIFY)

Three AutoCAD commands enable you to edit existing text: CHANGE, DDEDIT, and DDMODIFY. The CHANGE command works from the command line; DDEDIT and DDMODIFY use dialog boxes.

### DDEDIT

Of these commands, DDEDIT is the simplest—with it, you can edit a single line of text, and only the text itself (see fig. 16.16). You can't change any of the text's properties. You use DDEDIT to edit an MTEXT object as shown later in "Editing MTEXT Objects." When you select an MTEXT paragraph, DDEDIT opens the Edit MText window and places the selected paragraph inside it. DDEDIT is also used to edit Attribute Definitions.

To use DDEDIT, follow these steps:

1. Select the Edit Text icon from the Modify toolbar. You also can enter DDEDIT at the command line.

2. At the `<Select a TEXT or ATTDEF object>/Undo:` prompt, choose anywhere in the text string to edit.

3. The Edit Text dialog box appears displaying the line of text you chose. Edit the text as you require.

## CHANGE

You can use the CHANGE command to edit both text and its properties. CHANGE allows you to pick any number of text strings and edit them sequentially. To use CHANGE, follow these steps:

1. Select the Change icon or enter **change** at the `Command:` prompt.

2. At the `Select objects:` prompt, select the text to edit.

3. Press Enter three times to get to the `Enter text insertion point:` prompt.

4. From here, drag the selected text to a new location or press Enter to move to the next prompt.

5. At the `Text style:` prompt, enter a new style for the existing text, or press Enter for the next prompt.

6. At the `Text height:` prompt, enter a new height or press Enter to get to the `Text rotation:` prompt.

7. Supply a new rotation or press Enter to move to the `New text:` prompt, where you can edit the text.

## DDMODIFY

DDMODIFY combines the text-editing features of DDEDIT and CHANGE into a single dialog box. When editing MText objects, the DDMODIFY dialog box will pop up the Edit MText dialog box to allow editing of the contents. To use DDMODIFY to edit text, complete these steps:

1. Select the Properties button from the Object properties toolbar or choose <u>E</u>dit, <u>P</u>roperties.

**Fig. 16.16**
The Edit Text dialog box allows you to use standard text editing methods.

▶ See "Editing Attributes in a Block (ATTEDIT, DDATTE, ATTREDEF)," p. 722

**Tip**
If you just need to correct the current text, use DDEDIT. If you need to change or replace scattered text strings and their properties, use CHANGE.

**V**

Advanced Drawing

2. AutoCAD asks you to select an object to modify. Pick the text you want to edit. Select the text DRAWN BY:.

You must pick the object directly; you can't use a window or crossing box, and you can pick only one object or you'll get the Change Properties dialog box instead of the Modify Text dialog box.

3. The Modify Text dialog box appears. As figure 16.17 shows, it contains areas in which you can change every aspect of the drawing's text. Try changing the font style to ROMANC. Look at the change in your drawing. Now, use the change command to change it back to CITYBLUEPRINT.

In "Editing MText Objects," later in this chapter, the Modify Text dialog box will be used again.

**Fig. 16.17**

The Modify Text dialog box allows you to change every aspect of your text object.

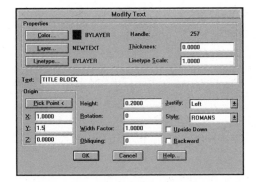

## Using Special Characters in Text

With AutoCAD, you can generate some special characters in text strings by embedding control codes in your text as you type it (see fig. 16.18). These codes are used by dimensioning to show degrees, diameter, and center point. They are also used to display underscore and overscore and can be programmed to display fractions, subscript, and superscript text. The codes that AutoCAD recognizes are these:

| | |
|---|---|
| %%o | Overscore |
| %%u | Underscore |
| %%d | Degree symbol |
| %%p | Plus/minus symbol |
| %%c | Diameter symbol |

%%%        Percent sign

%%*nnn*      ASCII character with decimal code *nnn*

Overscored text
Underscored Text
Degree Symbol — °
Plus/Minus Symbol —
Diameter Symbol — ø
Percent Sign — %

**Fig. 16.18**
Showing the
results of using the
special character
codes.

AutoCAD recognizes codes that you embed in text as you type it. These codes
cause AutoCAD to generate special characters. Because AutoCAD is using the
% symbol here as a place holder and as a switch, you must use the three
%%% symbols in order to display the % sign in your text string. Check your
DOS manual for information on the ASCII character codes.

## Hiding Text (QTEXT)

Sometimes your drawings contain so much text that redrawing and regeneration take a long time because AutoCAD has to redraw all the text to the
screen. You can speed up this process by using the QTEXT command to reduce the text in your drawing to rectangular outlining of the space consumed
by the text. The following list shows how to invoke the QTEXT command:

■ Enter **qtext** at the Command: prompt.

■ Select Options, Display and then Text Frame Only.

■ Select Options, Drawing Aids and select the Quick Text box in the
Drawing Aids dialog box (see fig. 16.19).

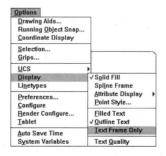

**Fig. 16.19**
To use QTEXT,
you can choose
Options, Display
Text Frame Only.

When AutoCAD redraws or regenerates the screen, it can draw the rectangles
much faster than it can draw the text itself. To activate QTEXT, use this command sequence:

◀ See "Refreshing the Screen (REDRAW)," p. 334

◀ See "Regenerating the Screen (REGEN)," p. 334

1. Choose Options, Display, and then Text Frame Only.

2. At the ON/OFF<Off>: prompt, enter **on**.

   You're now back at the Command: prompt, and nothing has changed.

3. Enter **regen**.

After AutoCAD redraws the screen, you should see rectangles instead of text as shown in figure 16.20. Figure 16.21 shows the text restored to normal after QTEXT is turned off and the drawing is regenerated.

**Fig. 16.20**
The effects of QTEXT after it's turned on and a regen has occurred.

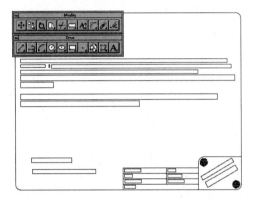

> **Note**
>
> If your regenerations are too slow because of the amount of text on your drawings, but QTEXT rectangles are too annoying to look at, you might want to try another way. Complex fonts regenerate more slowly than simple fonts. The font TXT (defined in TXT.SHX) regenerates the fastest because it's the simplest. While you're working on your drawings, define all your styles—or at least the ones that use complex fonts or get used a lot—to use the TXT font. When the time comes to present your drawings or generate final plots, redefine all your styles to use the permanent fonts, and then edit the text to update it.

> **Caution**
>
> Be sure to turn QTEXT off before you plot your drawing. If QTEXT is on, your text will appear on the plot as rectangles instead of text.

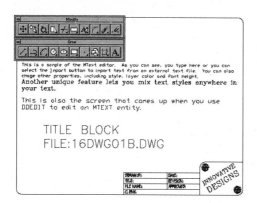

**Fig. 16.21**
The default mode
of QTEXT turned
off.

# Spell Checking a Drawing (SPELL)

A new and long-awaited feature of AutoCAD is the SPELL command. If you're familiar with a word processor, you'll recognize the benefits of this new feature. With SPELL you can spell check a single string, an mtext object, or all text objects at once. It can't spell check attributes or text nested in an unexploded block though.

SPELL is accessed in the following ways:

- Enter **spell** at the Command: prompt.

- Select the Spelling icon from the Standard Toolbar.

- Choose Tools, Spelling.

The following list explains the features of the check spelling dialog box (see fig. 16.22).

- Current dictionary displays the name of the dictionary in use.

- Current word shows the word that isn't recognized.

- Suggestions edit box and list box show the most likely word spelling and a list of any other possible spellings.

- Ignore button tells SPELL to ignore the displayed word this time only.

- Ignore All button tells SPELL to ignore the displayed word every time it sees it in this drawing.

- Change button instructs SPELL to change the existing word to the suggested word this time only.

V

Advanced Drawing

- Change All button instructs SPELL to change the existing word to the suggested word every time it sees it in this drawing.

- Add button will add the displayed word into the custom dictionary for future use.

- Lookup button instructs SPELL to check the spelling of the word in the suggestion box.

- Change Dictionaries button brings up the Change Dictionary dialog box.

### Tutorial: Spell Checking Your Drawing

Start the spelling checker and select all the text in your drawing. When you select your text, try entering **all** at the `Select Objects:` prompt to quickly select all text in your drawing.

**1.** Select the Spelling icon from the standard toolbar.

**2.** At the `Select Objects:` prompt, enter **all**. This will cause SPELL to check all text in your drawing.

**3.** Press Enter again and the Check Spelling dialog box will appear if there are any unrecognized words, otherwise the AutoCAD message `Spelling Check Complete` alert box will appear.

**4.** As each unrecognized word is displayed with the listed suggestion and possible spellings, select the appropriate action button until done. In the Check Spelling dialog box you have several options for dealing with unrecognized words.

The Context box displays the sentence with the suspect word in it. The Check Spelling dialog box is shown in figure 16.22.

**Fig. 16.22**
The Check Spelling dialog box showing a misspelled word.

> **Note**
>
> It's important to note that the spell checker works on the basis of word recognition. You may have spelled the word correctly, but the word may not exist in the dictionary. You can add these words to your own dictionary as you use SPELL.

# Editing MText Objects

In AutoCAD Release 13 you can now create multiline text objects, but how do you edit them once they have been created? There are two ways to edit these MText objects:

■ Use the DDEDIT command.

■ Use the DDMODIFY command.

Both of these commands are briefly mentioned in the "Editing Text (CHANGE, DDEDIT, and DDMODIFY)" section earlier in this chapter. When editing the MText object, use DDEDIT or DDMODIFY. The Edit MText dialog box is the same dialog box you used in the "Entering Text with MText" section earlier.

If you need to edit the contents only, it's quicker to use the DDEDIT command. You would select DDEDIT by selecting the Edit Text icon from the Modify toolbar or by entering **ddedit** at the command line. At the <Select a TEXT or ATTDEF object>/Undo: prompt, select your MTEXT object and the Edit MText dialog box appears (see fig. 16.23). The results of making the changes entered in the Edit MText dialog box are shown in figure 16.24.

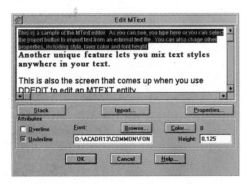

**Fig. 16.23**
The Edit MText dialog box with changes to text size being made to the highlighted text.

**V**

**Advanced Drawing**

**Fig. 16.24**
The results of the changes made to the text by selecting attributes in the Edit MText dialog box.

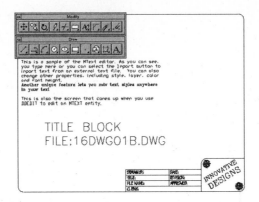

If you need to change just the properties, like layer or insertion point, you can use the DDMODIFY command. Figure 16.25 shows the Modify MText dialog box. Selecting the Edit contents button takes you to the Edit MText dialog box shown earlier in figure 16.23. Clicking the Edit Properties button brings up the MText Properties dialog box shown in figure 16.26.

When editing the MTEXT object, you must select the text you wish to change as shown earlier in figure 16.23. Highlighting text works the same way in the Edit MText dialog box as it does in all Windows text editors. If you're familiar with any other Windows text editor like Notepad or Write you will quickly master the Edit MText dialog box.

**Fig. 16.25**
The Modify MText dialog box allows you to edit every aspect of your MText objects.

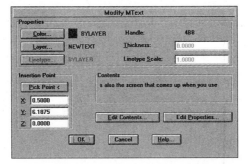

**Caution**

Editing MTEXT objects uses the same interface as creating them. They will spill out of the bottom of the box you originally selected when you created them if you add a lot of text. Of course, if you enter too much text when creating an MTEXT object, it will also extend beyond the box you drew.

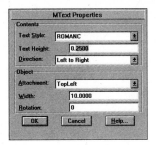

**Fig. 16.26**
The MText
Properties dialog
box that comes up
in DDMODIFY or
is accessed from
the Edit MText
dialog box.

# From Here...

In this chapter, you used a standard set of text styles to give your drawings a uniform look. For more information on text and it's relationship to proto-types, plotting, dimensioning, and the 3D coordinate system, refer to these chapters:

- Chapter 3, "Understanding Prototypes," explains how to use a proto-type drawing—the best location in which to store your text styles. Then, when you begin a new drawing, your defined styles will be available for you to use.

- Chapter 14, "Plotting a Drawing," contains the information you'll need for plotting or printing your drawings that contain text.

- Chapter 18, "Dimensioning a Drawing," covers AutoCAD's other major means of annotating your drawings.

- Chapter 27, "Understanding 3D Coordinate Systems," shows you how to place text in planes other than the one parallel to the XY plane. You need to create these other planes with AutoCAD's UCS command.

# On Your Own

Now that you have explored the text commands, it's time to try them out. The following exercise will provide you the opportunity to test your mastery of text in AutoCAD. In this exercise you'll need to open the drawing 16DWG01B from the earlier tutorials in this chapter.

**1.** Use the TEXT command to fill in the title block with your name, today's date, and file name of your choice.

**2.** For Title, enter **Chapter 16** and for Client, enter your company name.

3. Use MTEXT to import the contents of the file AUTOEXEC.BAT and pick a box starting at 2,8 and ending at 8,2.

4. Use DDMODIFY to make the text TITLE BLOCK and FILE: 16DWG01B.DWG smaller.

5. Use SPELLING to fix any errors in the spelling.

**Fig. 16.27**
The drawing
16DWG01B
created earlier in
this chapter.

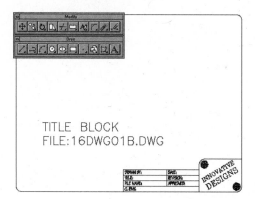

Feel free to explore all the commands discussed in this chapter. Experiment and have fun. You will be honing your text skills and adding words to your dictionary for future use.

# Chapter 17

# Filling Areas with Hatching

The capability to communicate ideas through pictures is only as successful as the clarity of what you draw. AutoCAD provides many tools to enhance the readability of your drawings. One of the most effective two-dimensional tools is AutoCAD's hatching command.

*Hatching*, or *poché*, as it is known in the architectural discipline, provides a way of applying various patterns to certain areas of your drawing. These hatch patterns can be as simple as line patterns representing various forms of materials for a section cut of a mechanical part, or as complex as a wood shaker shingle pattern on an architectural drawing.

Some of the improvements of AutoCAD's hatching abilities in Release 13 include associative hatching and island detection. *Associative hatching* is a powerful new feature that enables you to modify the boundary of your hatch pattern while AutoCAD automatically updates the hatch pattern to the new boundaries. The new hatching capabilities also can detect *island* or boundary regions within a larger boundary that should not have the hatch pattern drawn within them.

The discussion of hatching is not complete without an understanding of the boundaries used to enclose the hatch pattern. A *boundary* is simply an area enclosed by AutoCAD objects. These objects can overlap or intersect one another. There must be no openings or gaps between objects that define the boundary. When you apply a hatch pattern, AutoCAD draws a temporary closed polyline boundary over the objects you select that define the hatch boundary. AutoCAD then applies the hatch pattern. You may optionally choose to leave this polyline boundary for future reference or to use it for area and perimeter calculations of the hatched area.

In this chapter, you learn to:

- Fill in drawing areas using the BHATCH command

- Modify the look of a hatch pattern

- Create a simple or complex boundary from existing objects

- Draw associative hatched areas

- Avoid common hatching problems

# Creating Hatched Areas Using Boundary Hatch (BHATCH)

Before diving into a discussion of the BHATCH command, you need to understand what makes this command different from the old HATCH command. Although Autodesk has chosen to leave the HATCH command in, most users will choose to use the BHATCH command. Most AutoCAD veterans know that the HATCH command requires you to create your own boundary using objects that close perfectly. Any gaps or overlaps in objects can yield unwanted results, as shown in figure 17.1.

**Fig. 17.1**
Comparing the results of HATCH versus BHATCH.

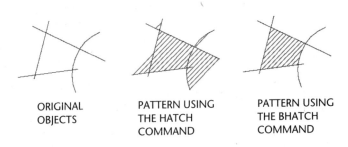

ORIGINAL
OBJECTS

PATTERN USING
THE HATCH
COMMAND

PATTERN USING
THE BHATCH
COMMAND

Unlike the HATCH command, BHATCH can fill any area as long as it can find some kind of bounding object. These objects can be small segments of larger objects, and they do not have to be connected.

New in Release 13 is the associative hatch property. Objects used to define a pattern area can be moved or changed, and the pattern will change to fit the new area. This capability only applies to patterns created with the BHATCH command. These differences make BHATCH much more desirable than the HATCH command.

You can access the BHATCH command by using one of the following methods:

- Choose the Hatch button from the Draw toolbar.

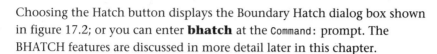

- Type **bhatch** at the Command: prompt.

Choosing the Hatch button displays the Boundary Hatch dialog box shown in figure 17.2; or you can enter **bhatch** at the Command: prompt. The BHATCH features are discussed in more detail later in this chapter.

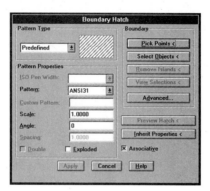

**Fig. 17.2**
Accessing the Boundary Hatch dialog box.

**V**

**Advanced Drawing**

## Pattern Type

Before a hatch can be applied, you must first select and define the pattern you want to use. The three different types of patterns are predefined, user-defined, and custom.

AutoCAD provides a number of predefined hatch patterns stored in the ACAD.PAT file. Choosing a pattern type displays the pattern in the window at the top of the Boundary Hatch dialog box. The name of the pattern is also displayed in the Pattern pull-down list box in the Pattern Properties area. Choosing the down arrow allows you to scroll through the pattern names. The pull-down list box to the left of the pattern image tile allows you to specify a predefined, user-defined, or custom hatch pattern.

> **Note**
>
> You can also scroll through the patterns by repeatedly clicking the pattern image.

A user-defined hatch pattern uses lines based upon the current linetype. These lines are modified based upon the pattern properties discussed in the following section.

▶ See "Custom-
izing Hatch
Patterns "
p. 1040

Custom hatch patterns include those patterns not found in the standard ACAD.PAT file, and may be supplied by third-party software developers or other sources.

## Pattern Properties

Like most AutoCAD objects, hatch patterns have properties that affect the way they are drawn. These properties help define the size angle and pattern of the hatch pattern. Hatch properties can be modified using the HATCHEDIT command, or copied to create a new hatch pattern using the Inherit Properties option in the Boundary Hatch dialog box.

### ISO Pen Width

If a predefined ISO hatch pattern is selected, the ISO Pen Width selection becomes active. The ISO Pen Width sets the pattern scaling with relation to the ISO linetype.

### Pattern

If a predefined hatch pattern is selected under pattern type, the names of the available patterns found in the ACAD.PAT file are displayed in this field. You can scroll through these names by selecting the arrow to access the scrollbar.

### Custom Pattern

This option allows you to access those patterns not found in the ACAD.PAT file. This option is only available if Custom Pattern is chosen under the Pattern Type option.

### Scale

After a predefined or custom pattern has been chosen, you can assign a Scale to the pattern. The default value of 1 is the scale the original pattern was defined as. A value of 2 is twice the original scale and .5 is half the scale.

### Angle

Unlike scale, Angle applies to all three types of patterns. Its purpose is to set the pattern angle relative to the x axis of the current UCS.

### Spacing

This pattern property is unique to user-defined patterns. *Spacing* is the distance between lines of a user-defined hatch pattern and is measured in the current drawing units.

### Double

Like spacing, this property is only used with user-defined patterns. The double property takes the line definition and repeats it perpendicular to or at 90 degrees from the first set of lines. The resulting pattern will be a cross-hatch pattern in the case of a solid linetype.

### Explode

Hatch patterns are a special kind of block that, like blocks, can be exploded. Creating an *exploded* pattern simply means that the pattern will be individual lines and/or dots when drawn. Patterns drawn in this manner have a draw-back. You lose the associativity of the pattern, and it becomes very difficult to edit. Also, because the exploded hatch is no longer a single object (it's many lines), the drawing file size increases tremendously.

▶ See "Breaking Blocks Apart (EXPLODE)," p. 697

> **Note**
>
> AutoCAD stores the pattern properties in the following system variables:
>
> | | |
> |---|---|
> | Predefined or Custom Pattern Name | HPNAME |
> | Scale | HPSCALE |
> | Angle | HPANG |
> | Spacing | HPSPACE |
> | Double | HPDOUBLE |

## Boundary

The Boundary area of the Boundary Hatch dialog box provides the tools to fine-tune the way AutoCAD defines the area to be hatched.

### Pick Points

A powerful feature of BHATCH is AutoCAD's capability to automatically de-tect the boundary by simply pointing inside the area. By default, once you have selected a point on the drawing, AutoCAD looks at every object in your drawing to define a boundary. This process can be very time-consuming if you have a large drawing. When you select the Pick Points option, AutoCAD prompts you to <Select internal point:> (see fig. 17.3).

You may choose a point that does not have a closed boundary based on AutoCAD's search. A Boundary Definition Error occurs in such a case. Choos-ing OK allows you to select another point, or you can have AutoCAD show you the point it thinks you chose.

V

Advanced Drawing

**Fig. 17.3**
Defining a
boundary using
the Pick Point
option.

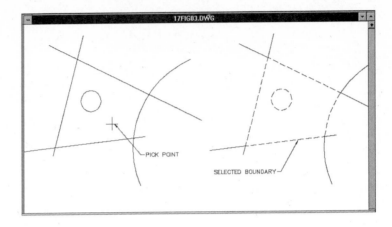

**Select Objects**

The Select Objects option is much like AutoCAD HATCH command. It works best when you want to fill an already closed object, such as a polyline or circle. If the objects overlap or extend beyond each other, you get some undesirable results, as shown in figure 17.4.

**Fig. 17.4**
Selecting objects
instead of a pick
point can be
undesirable.

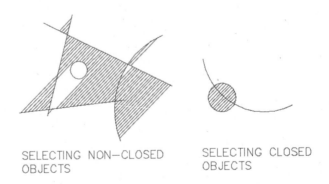

SELECTING NON—CLOSED
OBJECTS

SELECTING CLOSED
OBJECTS

> **Note**
>
> Any text must be part of the selection set if you want the hatch pattern to avoid it.

**Remove Islands**

The Remove Islands option is only active if you define the boundary by picking points. If an island is removed, AutoCAD hatches through the object as if it doesn't exist. To be an island, the object must be entirely within the outer boundary. The exception to this rule is a text object. When you select Remove Islands, AutoCAD prompts `<Select island to remove>/Undo:`.

### View Selections

Sometimes it's difficult to see how AutoCAD has interpreted the selected objects. The View Selections option allows you to see the boundary or selection set AutoCAD has created. If this is not the boundary you expect, you can redefine the boundary using the Advanced options. (See the section "Advanced Options" later in this chapter.)

### Advanced

The preceding section mentions that AutoCAD by default searches every object in the drawing to see if it is part of the boundary. This can be a lengthy process if you have a large drawing. To expedite this process, AutoCAD gives you the option to select specific objects limiting the boundary definition search. For more detail, see the "Advanced Options" section later in this chapter.

## Preview Hatch

Preview Hatch is a quick and easy way to test your hatch pattern selections visually. AutoCAD removes the dialog box and applies your settings to the boundary or objects you have selected. When you are finished, choose Continue to go back to the Boundary Hatch dialog box.

> **Note**
>
> AutoCAD does not always complete the preview hatch pattern. This doesn't mean that your pattern is incorrect. If it looks close, apply it. You can always use HATCHEDIT to change it.

## Inherit Properties

You may have a number of hatch patterns already on your drawing. The Inherit Properties option takes advantage of pre-existing hatch patterns, setting the hatch options by pointing to a hatch pattern already in your drawing. AutoCAD prompts you to <Select hatch object:>.The resulting hatch pattern should look exactly like the one you chose in the drawing. This option will not work on hatch patterns created with the HATCH command or exploded hatch patterns.

## Associative

A hatch pattern that is Associative means that all the objects that make up the pattern are linked to the boundary that defines it. This link allows the hatch pattern to adapt to any changes in that boundary. Figure 17.5 shows a hatched area that is then modified by moving one of the bounding objects.

**V**

**Advanced Drawing**

**Fig. 17.5**
An associative
hatch pattern
conforms to
boundary changes.

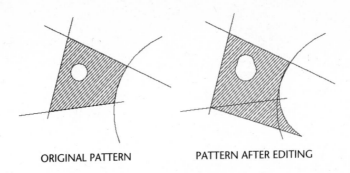

ORIGINAL PATTERN                    PATTERN AFTER EDITING

> **Note**
>
> Associative hatch patterns created with more than one pick point may produce unpredictable results if edited.

## Apply/Cancel/Help

After you have defined your hatch pattern, you create it by choosing Apply. You can also get help at any time by choosing the <u>H</u>elp button. To abort the command, choose Cancel.

## Tutorial: Hatching an Area of a Drawing

This tutorial shows you how to pick a predefined hatch pattern, specify a boundary, preview the hatch pattern, and apply it. Now, it's your turn to try your hand at creating a hatched area. First, you'll try something simple using a predefined hatch pattern.

1.  Begin a new drawing and create four objects, making sure that each object overlaps to create an enclosed area (see fig. 17.6).

**Fig. 17.6**
Creating a
hatched area.

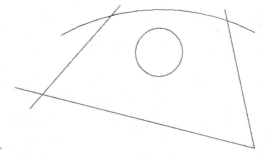

2. Select the Hatch icon from the Draw toolbar or enter **bhatch** at the `Command:` prompt.

3. Choose Predefined pattern type. Under the Patter_n_ name, scroll down to AR-HBONE.

4. Now, set the Sca_le_ to .01, set the _A_ngle to 90, and make sure the Associati_ve_ button is checked.

5. For the first exercise, use the Pick Point method to define a boundary. Choose _P_ick Points from the Boundary Hatch dialog box. AutoCAD prompts you to `<Select internal point:>`. Choose a point inside your objects, but not inside the circle.

6. Press Enter to return to the Boundary Hatch dialog box. Select Preview Ha_t_ch to see what your pattern looks like.

7. Press the _C_ontinue button to return to the dialog box. Your hatch pattern should look something like figure 17.7. Try changing the pattern, scale, and angle; then preview it to see how it changed.

8. To finish your first hatch pattern, select Apply from the dialog box.

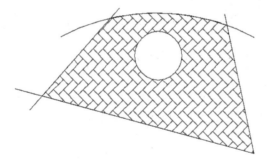

**Fig. 17.7**
The finished hatch pattern.

## Tutorial: Editing a Hatch Boundary

Now let's test the associativity of the hatch pattern you just drew by changing its shape. Figure 17.8 shows the result of an edited boundary.

◀ See "Editing with Grips" p. 301

1. Select the boundary of the hatch pattern using a crossing window and use the grips to modify its shape. Notice how the pattern redraws to fit the new shape.

**Fig. 17.8**
Testing the
associativity of a
hatch pattern.

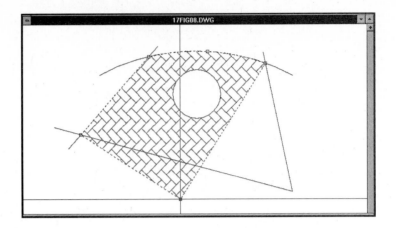

## Advanced Options

Sometimes you have to fine-tune how AutoCAD creates a boundary. The
Advanced Options dialog box allows you to speed up your boundary search
and refine its results (see fig. 17.9).

**Fig. 17.9**
Using the
Advanced Options
dialog box.

### Object Type

▶ See "Extruding
2D Geometry"
p. 907

The two object types used to define boundaries in AutoCAD are *polylines* and
*regions*. The Object Type selection allows you to choose between them.
Polyline is the default and is the most common choice.

### Define Boundary Set

When you use BHATCH to hatch inside a boundary, AutoCAD evaluates
every object currently visible on-screen. In crowded drawings, this search
process can slow AutoCAD. You can avoid this delay by constructing a
boundary set made up of a limited number of objects. To perform this operation, click the Advanced Options button in the Boundary Hatch dialog box.

Then click the Make <u>N</u>ew Boundary Set button. The dialog box disappears so that you can pick the objects on the drawing that you want for composing your boundary set. After you have selected all the objects for the boundary set, press Enter to bring back the Advanced Options dialog box. Notice that the From E<u>x</u>isting Boundary Set button is now active and selected. Now you can use the boundary set you defined by selecting OK, which returns you to the Boundary Hatch dialog box.

### Style

Normal, Outer, and Ignore are the three <u>S</u>tyle types available when defining a hatch pattern. Each defines how AutoCAD evaluates objects within the outer boundary of the hatch pattern. An example showing the result of each style type is shown in the image tile to the right of the <u>S</u>tyle list.

### Ray Casting

Applying a hatch pattern isn't an exact science, and you may sometimes run into errors that keep you from successfully hatching the areas exactly as you want them to be hatched. Most commonly, you see an error message like `Point is outside of boundary`. This message probably indicates that AutoCAD didn't find a suitable boundary element when it began to look for objects within which to construct the hatching. When AutoCAD begins to look for boundary objects, it looks first at the closest object. You can often correct this error by picking a point closer to the object that you prefer AutoCAD to use for a boundary edge. If that doesn't work, you can tell AutoCAD to look in a specific direction. In the Advanced Options dialog box, the <u>R</u>ay Casting list box lets you tell AutoCAD in which direction to look for its first boundary—for example, +*x* (right), -*x* (left), +*y* (up), or -*y* (down), relative to the current UCS.

▶ See "Drawing Boundary Polylines (BOUNDARY)," p. 583

### Island Detection

As AutoCAD defines a boundary, it also looks for island areas within that boundary and adds them to the final boundary definition. When Island Detection is turned off, AutoCAD ignores these objects in its boundary definition.

### Retain Boundaries

If Retain <u>B</u>oundaries is on, AutoCAD draws a polyline or region around the boundary it defined. This is a separate object that can be hard to find because it is on top of your existing objects used to define the original boundary.

## Tutorial: Using Advanced Hatching Options

Now try out a few of the advanced features on another drawing and see what happens.

1. Draw a shape similar to the one in figure 17.10.

**Fig. 17.10**
Objects for creating a hatch pattern.

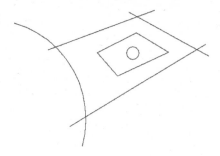

2. Start the BHATCH command. Choose the User-defined Pattern Type. Specify an Angle of **30** degrees and a Spacing of **0.10**.

3. Using the pick point, select a point just inside the outer boundary.

4. Next, preview your hatch pattern and notice how the outer and inner areas are hatched. It should look something like figure 17.11.

**Fig. 17.11**
Preview hatch pattern with normal style.

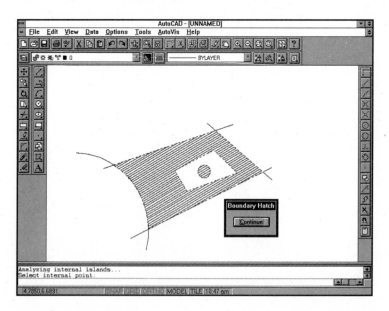

5. Now choose <u>C</u>ontinue to return to the Boundary Hatch dialog box. In the Advanced Options dialog box, choose Outer <u>S</u>tyle and Ignore <u>S</u>tyle, previewing each to see the effect on the hatch pattern.

6. Using the Normal Style, define a boundary with Retain <u>B</u>oundaries on. Apply the hatch pattern.

7. Using the STRETCH command and the Crossing option, grab a corner of the outer boundary and move it to another location. This command can be found on the Modify toolbar, or entered at the Command: prompt.

8. If your original objects overlap each other like the one in figure 17.11, you'll notice that the modified hatch boundary no longer lines up with the original lines or arcs (see fig. 17.12).

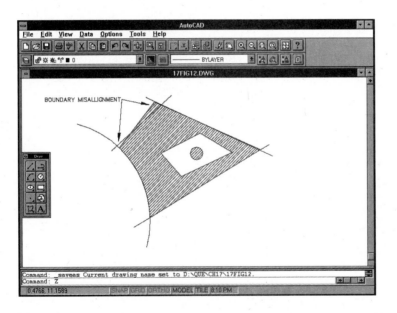

**Fig. 17.12**
Boundary misalignment when editing an associative hatch pattern.

# Common Hatching Problems

Most of the problems related to hatching have to do with not fully understanding the effects of the many variables that control the hatch pattern definition. For instance, the preceding tutorial clearly shows that when Retain <u>B</u>oundaries is on, editing the associative hatch reveals an alignment problem with the original overlapping objects. To resolve this problem, deselect the Retain <u>B</u>oundaries check box in the Advanced Options dialog box.

Another common problem is when the pick point causes an outside boundary error. To overcome this situation, select the Make <u>N</u>ew Boundary Set option in the Advanced Options dialog box to clear out any previous boundaries.

Remember that hatch patterns are always oriented to the x axis of the current UCS. If the hatch angle does not come out the way you expected, check the UCS orientation.

## From Here...

In this chapter, you learned how to apply hatch patterns using the BHATCH command. For more information on hatching, boundaries, and how to edit hatch patterns, refer to the following chapter:

- Chapter 11, "Editing with Grips," shows you how to move, stretch, rotate, scale, and mirror objects using their grips. This is a useful technique for modifying the objects that comprise a hatch boundary.

## On Your Own

Using the skills you've acquired in this chapter, apply a hatch pattern to the section cut of a mechanical part using drawing 17DWG01. On mechanical drawings, hatch patterns are used in section views to indicate the type and location of the material cut to provide the section view.

Hints:

1. Use the ANSI31 predefined hatch pattern with a scale of 1.0.

2. Use the Pick Points button to specify the areas to hatch.

**Fig. 17.13**
The section view
of a mechanical
part.

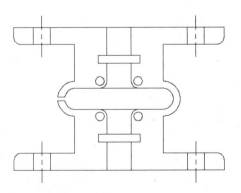

**3.** You can specify several hatch areas at once.

**4.** Preview your hatch before applying it.

**5.** Apply the hatch pattern.

Your drawing should look similar to figure 17.14.

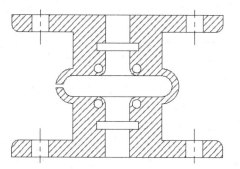

**Fig. 17.14**
Completed hatching of a mechanical section view.

# Chapter 18

# Dimensioning a Drawing

A drawing you create is a tool that informs the viewer how an object is assembled. This is true whether you're creating an isometric exploded view of an engine, a floor plan for a house, or a landscape plan for an office building. However, assembly can imply different things to different people. To the casual viewer, assembly may only mean that tab A fits into slot B. To the person who must actually build or manufacture your drawing, assembly implies quantities and dimensions.

While AutoCAD can't tell you how many 2 × 8s you need to support a floor, with the dimensioning commands you can define the size of the subfloor and then calculate how many pieces of lumber you need. This example may suggest a rectangular area, but you're not limited to just dimensioning rectangles; AutoCAD supports dimensioning for arcs, circles, and lines that are *not* horizontal and vertical. You can even create dimension notes and geometric tolerance symbols—there aren't really any limits to the types of dimensions you can create. In this chapter you learn to:

- Create dimension styles and assign attributes for each of the dimension style families

- Create and edit the contents of associative dimensions

- Use the various types of dimensioning

One basic tenet to remember is that AutoCAD's dimensioning commands are only as accurate as the drawing to which they relate. If you want, AutoCAD can dimension drawing elements to 1/64', to 6 decimal places, or to the nearest 1 second of angular rotation. This kind of accuracy demands that you

◀ See "Setting Display Format and Units (DDUNITS)," p. 49

◀ See "Setting Display Format and Precision (UNITS and DDUNITS)," p. 97

draw your drawings to scale when you create the drawing. If you simply "place" the drawing elements and "eyeball" them into position, your lack of precision shows up when you create your dimensions.

# Dimensioning Basics

Dimensioning a drawing is sometimes as much of an art as the creation of the drawing itself. Dimensions, similar to drawing details, can either confuse or clearly illustrate how to create an element. The purpose of dimensions is to give the reader concrete information about how to construct an element. If the dimensions you create are not clear, or if they don't relate in a useful manner to what you're drawing, then they can hinder the reader's ability to build the element from your drawings.

Everyone who works with AutoCAD uses dimensions differently. You are shown the "correct" way to create dimensions for your drawings. The purpose of this chapter, and this book as a whole, is to show you where the tools are and how to use them correctly. You must rely on past experience and guidance from others in your profession to show you how to correctly use dimensions in your work.

Prior to AutoCAD Release 13, you had to enter a dimension-only command area, represented by the Dim: prompt, to use dimensions. You had to "leave" the normal Command: prompt to work with dimensions and then exit the Dim: prompt when you finished generating dimensions. It was difficult to create dimensions and work with the other drawing and editing commands in a normal manner.

With Release 13, this is no longer a problem. If you want to create a horizontal dimension, type **dimlinear** at the Command: prompt. After you create your dimension, you can, for example, use the MOVE command without going through extra steps. You no longer have to use the DIM or DIM1 commands to access the dimensioning commands.

AutoCAD Release 13 still maintains compatibility with the original DIM commands, such as HOR, VER, and LEA. So if you use SCRIPT, LISP, or ADS routines that make use of original DIM commands, you aren't forced to change them. Also, if you feel more comfortable using the original DIM commands, you can still access them by using the Dim: prompt. You should be aware however that many of the new dimensioning commands, such as DIMLINEAR or LEADER, have new functionality built-in. If you use the VER and LEA commands instead, you can't access those new features.

> **Note**
>
> If you use ADS routines from Release 12 that use the old `Dim:` prompt, you can still use the routines, but you must recompile (and maybe rewrite) them for Release 13. Because you must take the time to make some degree of conversion from Release 12 ADS to Release 13 ADS, consider completely rewriting the routines. At the same time, if you are a registered developer, you should make sure your code meets the Autodesk Interoperability Guidelines for Release 13.

> **Note**
>
> Each version of the dimensioning commands—those accessed at the `Command:` prompt and those accessed at the `Dim:` prompt—offer unique features. Take those differences into consideration while dimensioning. Some of the differences of each command are discussed in this chapter. In general, the new `Command:` prompt dimensioning commands are more powerful and easier to use.

A final note about dimensions is that all of the dimension-related commands are now contained in a single toolbar, called the Dimensioning toolbar (see fig. 18.1). When you create a drawing, you don't initially see this toolbar. To view it, choose <u>T</u>ools, <u>T</u>oolbars, <u>D</u>imensioning. Each button on the Dimensioning toolbar, and the command it invokes, is discussed in the following sections.

**Fig. 18.1**
The Dimensioning toolbar, which allows you to access all the dimensioning commands.

## Associative and Non-Associative Dimensions

The dimensions you can create come in two basic flavors: associative and non-associative. Non-associative dimensions are simply text, lines, arcs, blocks, or solids. They can't adapt to a changing drawing. If you modify the length of a line with the STRETCH command, the dimension relating to that line only reports the length it originally calculated, not its new length.

Associative dimensions, on the other hand, are complex objects, similar to polylines. As complex objects, associative dimensions can respond to changes in the drawing—automatically updating the values they report. If you stretch an associative dimension with the line to which it relates, its value changes. Also, if you base the dimension on a dimension style, that dimension automatically changes when you modify the dimension style.

▶ See "Using Polylines," p. 573

By default, AutoCAD automatically creates associative dimensions. Use this type of dimension object whenever you create dimensions in your drawing. There is *nothing* you can do with non-associative dimensions that cannot be done to associative dimensions. Associative dimensions always accurately reflect your drawing.

▶ See "System Variables Reference," p. 1147

▶ See "Breaking Blocks Apart (EXPLODE)," p. 697

If you don't want to use associative dimensions, you have two options. You can use the DIMASO variable to turn off associative dimensions. Anytime AutoCAD creates a dimension, it simply draws the lines, arcs, and text that make up the dimension. The other option is to use the EXPLODE command on any dimensions you want to be non-associative. This gives you the benefit of using associative dimensions for the majority of your drawing and only reducing them to their component state when necessary.

## Parts of a Dimension

All dimensions are a collection of individual objects such as lines, arcs, text, solids, and blocks. AutoCAD uses the settings for the various dimension styles to arrange these elements into a complete dimension—or dimension string, as it's often called. The elements in a dimension have their own unique names. As you learn how to create dimension styles in the next section, you'll need to know what these names refer to. Figure 18.2 identifies the elements of typical dimension types. These elements are as follows:

■ *Definition Points*. These two points indicate where the dimension begins and ends. AutoCAD uses these points to update associative dimension values as they are edited.

**Fig. 18.2**
The elements which comprise radial and linear dimensions.

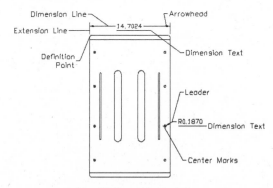

Adjustable Proximity Switch
Bracket Zoom = .5:1

> **Note**
>
> AutoCAD automatically sets up a special layer, DEFPOINTS, with the first associative dimension you create. All definition points appear on this layer. The points are visible only when their associated dimension object's layer is on. Generally, however, you can't see the definition points because of their size.

**Tip**
Objects on the DEFPOINT layer can't plot, even when the layer is on and thawed. If there are objects you don't want to plot, create them on the DEFPOINT layer.

- *Extension Lines.* These are line objects that project from the definition points to the dimension line.

- *Arrowheads.* These symbols appear on either side of a dimension line and mark the beginning and end of the dimension.

- *Dimension Lines.* This line appears between the dimension extension lines. The dimension text is usually placed on or above this line.

- *Dimension Text.* This is a text element that holds the distance, or angle, between the definition points.

- *Center Mark.* When using radial dimensions, this mark is placed at the center of the radius that's being dimensioned.

- *Leader.* When you dimension a radial object, AutoCAD uses a leader to reference the radius or diameter. You also can use the LEADER command to generate a leader with text, a block, a copy of text that is already in the drawing, or a geometric dimensioning and tolerancing control frame annotation.

**V**

**Advanced Drawing**

# Dimensioning with Precision

As mentioned earlier, dimensions done in AutoCAD are only as accurate as the objects they reference. AutoCAD offers several commands to assist the user in drawing and dimensioning precise components. Ideally, you know before starting a drawing what level of accuracy is required for the elements being illustrated. The UNITS and DDUNITS commands set the proper degree of accuracy for the objects you draw.

After you create accurate objects, you need tools to assist you in transferring that accuracy to the dimensions. The object snaps provided in AutoCAD allow you to select precise points on the objects you dimension. Most linear dimensions reference endpoints and intersection points. The OSNAP and

**Tip**
You can snap to definition points using the node object snap.

◀ See "Setting Display Format and Units (DDUNITS)," p. 49

◀ See "Using
Running
Object Snap
Modes
(OSNAP and
DDOSNAP),"
p. 165

**Tip**
Your productivity
improves remark-
ably when you use
object snaps. You
can select objects
much quicker and
you can pick
points at lower
levels of zoom
magnification.

DDOSNAP commands allow you to set running object snaps. By using object snaps, you guarantee that the accuracy of your geometry is transferred to your dimensions.

# Creating Dimension Styles

A *dimension style* is a formatted series of dimensions that achieve a consistent appearance. Styles are concepts borrowed from word processing programs. They allow you to define the appearance of certain paragraphs in a document. For example, there might be a style called "Normal," which states that the paragraph font is 12 point Arial text; that the paragraph has a left and right margin of 1/2"; and that there is one blank space after each paragraph. Any text formatted using the "Normal" style takes on the defined settings.

Dimension styles operate in the same manner. You define how the dimension looks: arrowheads or dots, text above the dimension line or centered between, ROMAN or STANDARD text style, and so on. The dimensions you create reflect these settings. With dimension styles, you can create dimensions at any time in the process of working in a drawing, and can quickly conform to a specific desired appearance.

If your dimensions are associative, making changes to the dimension style changes the appearance of all dimensions formatted with that style. With a single dialog box serving as the focus of working with dimensions, customizing and managing dimension strings becomes a one-step event.

However, this isn't the best reason to use dimension styles. Currently, there are 60 dimension variables that control how a dimension is displayed. As you read through the following sections, notes in the text show the name of the dimensioning variable affected by each dimension style setting. AutoCAD Release 13 improved dimension styles and the DDIM command to simplify the process of setting and tracking each of these variables. The number of dialog boxes required to set dimension variables is reduced to four. The dialog boxes are redesigned to improve user interaction and perform more tasks— making it much easier to manage your dimension styles. You only need to be concerned with whether the settings you choose display the dimension correctly for your uses.

## Dimension Styles and Their Families

The DDIM command controls the creation, management, and editing of dimension styles. You access the command in the following manner:

■ Click the Dimension Styles button on the Dimensioning floating toolbar.

■ At the Command: prompt, type **ddim** and press Enter.

When you invoke the DDIM command, the Dimension Styles dialog box appears (see fig. 18.3). The Dimension Styles dialog box allows you to choose an existing dimension style for continued use, create new dimension styles, and set the formatting for dimension style families. This dialog box allows you to perform the following:

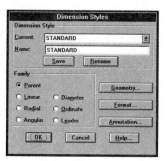

**Fig. 18.3**
The Dimension
Styles dialog box,
opened using the
DDIM command.

**V**

**Advanced Drawing**

■ *Dimension Style Manipulation.* This part of the dialog box displays the name of the dimension style currently in use. If you have not created any dimension styles, the current style is the Standard dimension style. If you have created other dimension styles, you can select one from the Current list box.

To create a new dimension style, type in the name you want to give the style in the Name edit box. The name you supply must follow the same naming guidelines as layer or text style names.

> **Note**
>
> The dimension variable DIMSTYLE stores the name of the currently selected dimension style. The dimension style name can be changed using the DDRENAME dialog box. Refer to Chapter 21, "Modifying Object Characteristics," for further details on the RENAME command.

■ *Dimension Families.* The area of the dialog box labeled Family is for modifying dimension settings for dimension sub-types. Each dimension style is composed of a "parent" style and many "children" styles.

**Tip**
The parent and each of the child dimension sub-types will be covered in more detail throughout the chapter.

The settings used for the parent are general in nature and apply to each of the children. The children's styles can vary from what is used for the parent and enhance what is used by the parent.

For example, the style of the parent is to have arrowheads at each end of the dimension line and split the dimension line with the dimension text. This format can be overridden for each of the children by selecting the child type (Linear, Radial, Angular, Diameter, Ordinate, or Leader) and then modifying its particular settings.

■ *Dimension Settings.* The three buttons labeled Geometry, Format, and Annotation are used to modify individual dimension settings. The effects on dimensions by these options are described in the following sections.

> **Note**
>
> There is no limit to the number of parent styles that can be defined, each with its own unique settings. Also each defined parent style includes the ability to define its own set of "child" sub-styles. This can drastically reduce the number of named dimension styles needed in a complex drawing file.

## Setting Up Dimension Geometry

Selecting the Geometry button from the Dimension Styles dialog box brings up the Geometry dialog box shown in figure 18.4. This area is used to modify each of the settings controlling how dimension lines, extension lines, arrowheads, and center marks are created. The options set by these dialog entries are as follows:

**Fig. 18.4**
The Geometry dimension dialog box, used to set variables that control dimension string elements.

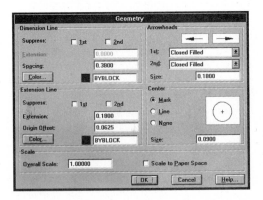

■ *Dimension Line Suppression.* The Suppress 1st and Suppress 2nd check boxes control the suppression of dimension lines.

■ *Dimension Line Extension.* The Extension edit box allows you to define how far past the extension line the dimension line will go. If this value is 0, dimension lines will not be extended. A value greater than zero generates dimension line extensions which may be suppressed by the previous option. This option is only available if you have selected Oblique style arrows for at least one of the Arrowhead styles.

> **Note**
>
> The dimension variable DIMDLE contains the distance which the dimension line will go past the extension line.

■ *Dimension Line Spacing.* The Spacing edit box defines the horizontal and vertical spacing between successive dimension strings. When using the DIMBASELINE command, spacing between the first and second dimension lines are set to this value. This spacing continues with each successive dimension from the selected baseline.

> **Note**
>
> The dimension variable DIMDLI controls the horizontal or vertical distance between the dimensions of successive dimension lines, BASELINE dimensions. A value of zero puts each dimension line on top of one another.

**Tip**

When selecting a value for the DIMDLI variable, consider the amount of room required for your dimension text and annotations such as Alternative Units and Tolerances.

■ *Dimension Line Color.* The Color button brings up the Select Color dialog box. Similar to its effect with the DDEMODES command, you can choose to have the color of the dimension line appear in the current layer or by block color. You can also click the color image button to display the Select Color dialog box. After you display the Select Color dialog you can choose from 255 colors, to represent the dimension line.

> **Note**
>
> The dimension variable DIMCLRD contains the color used to draw the dimension line.

V

**Advanced Drawing**

■ *Suppress Extension Lines.* The Suppress 1st and Suppress 2nd check boxes control the suppression of dimension string extension lines. These lines, sometimes called witness lines, extend from the definition points to the dimension line. Selecting either of these check boxes causes the chosen extension line not to be displayed. You can use these variables to suppress overlapping extension lines, which are common to baseline and continuous dimensions.

> **Note**
>
> Overlapping extension lines are particularly noticeable if you plot with pen or inkjet plotters.

■ *Extension Line Creation.* The Extension edit box defines the distance beyond the dimension line that the extension line is drawn. If this value is 0, the extension lines stop at the dimension line.

> **Note**
>
> The dimension variable DIMEXE contains the distance beyond the dimension line in which the extension line is drawn.

■ *Origin Offset.* This setting defines the distance from the selected definition points to the start of the extension line.

> **Note**
>
> The dimension variable DIMEXO contains the distance from the dimension point to the start of the extension line.

■ *Extension Line Color.* The Color button displays the Select Color dialog box. You can also click the color image tile to display the Select Color dialog box. You can choose to have the color of the extension line appear in the current layer color or by block color. You can also choose any one of the 255 colors, which appear in the palette, to represent the line.

> **Note**
>
> The dimension variable DIMCLRE contains the color used to draw the extension line.

- *First and Second Arrowheads.* These two pop-up list boxes allow you to choose from a variety of arrow styles that can be used for the first and second arrows. Each arrow selected is displayed by a miniature image tile at the top of the Arrowhead section. If you click in the first window, both arrows cycle in unison. Clicking in the second window allows you to select different styles for each arrow. This feature is also true for the pop-up lists.

> **Note**
>
> The dimension variables DIMBLK1 and DIMBLK2 contain the names of the blocks used to draw the first and second dimension arrowheads.

- *Arrowhead Size.* This edit box can be used to define the size of the arrowhead selected in the previous option.

> **Note**
>
> The dimension variable DIMASZ contains the size used to draw the dimension arrowheads.

- *Center Mark Creation.* When creating radius, circular and angular dimensions, you can choose to have a marker placed at the center of the dimension. The Mark option places a cross at the center point, the Line option extends each leg of the center mark, and None suppresses the creation of a center mark. AutoCAD displays your selection in an image tile to show you how it will look as part of your dimension. This image tile works similarly to the arrow image tile, in that you can cycle through the Center options by clicking the tile.

- *Center Mark Size.* This edit box can be used to define the size of the center mark or line selected in the previous option. This size is measured between the endpoints of the center mark. If you selected None at the previous option, the Size option won't be accessible because there are no features to size.

> **Note**
>
> The dimension variable DIMCEN contains the size used to draw the dimension center mark. If this value is zero, no center mark is drawn. If the value is negative, only a single line is drawn.

- *Dimension Scale Factor.* The edit box labeled Overall Scale is used to define the scaling factor applied to each of the dimension elements. This is similar to the scale factor which must be applied to text so that it plots at the correct size.

> **Note**
>
> The dimension variable DIMSCALE contains the scaling factor used to multiply the size of dimension variables that specify sizes, distances, or offsets. It also affects the scale of objects attached to leaders.

- *Scale to Paper Space.* This check box informs AutoCAD to use the scale factor of the current viewport when scaling dimension objects. By using this option you don't have to create a separate dimension style for each differently scaled viewport that you may use in a drawing. Selecting this box automatically sets the DIMSCALE variable to zero and disables the Overall Scale option.

> **Note**
>
> If the dimension variable DIMSCALE is set to zero, AutoCAD calculates a scaling factor based on the scale of the current viewport.

### Tutorial: Changing Dimension Geometry

The tutorial demonstrates how changes made to these settings affect existing dimensions in a drawing. This tutorial uses the Proximity Switch Bracket, drawing 18DWG01, shown in figure 18.5. This drawing has been dimensioned using the Standard dimension style. Notice how small the text is and how close the Baseline dimension strings are to one another. In this tutorial you change the settings that affect these characteristics and others. You then save the settings in a new dimension style, to be used throughout the tutorials in this chapter. Follow the steps below to change the Geometry settings:

1. Open the sample drawing C:\UAW13\18DWG01.

2. Click the Dimension Styles button on the Dimensioning floating toolbar.

3. Select the Geometry button from the Dimension Styles dialog box. Refer to figure 18.4 to see the Geometry dialog box.

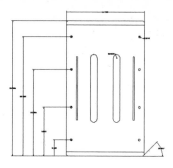

**Fig. 18.5**
The Proximity
Switch Bracket,
dimensioned using
the Standard
dimension style.

Adjustable Proximity Switch Bracket
Zoom Factor = .5:1

Most of the changes required to make the dimensions clearer can be corrected by editing the Overall Scale, located in the Scale area of the dialog box. However, for the purpose of this tutorial, you first modify some of the other settings to show how they affect the existing dimensions.

4. First, change the spacing of the Dimension Lines. Working in the Dimension Line area of the Geometry dialog box, select the Spacing setting. By double-clicking the edit box, you both select the edit box and highlight the existing value of 0.38. Type **0.50** and press Enter. This enters the new value while replacing the original value of 0.38, all in one step.

5. Change the color of the dimension line. By selecting either the Color button or the color image tile, you open the Select Color dialog box. Select the color blue from the Standard Colors area, at the top of the dialog box. Click OK to confirm the choice and return to the Geometry dialog box.

6. Next, you change some of the extension line settings. Working in the Extension Line area of the Geometry dialog box, select the Origin Offset setting. As before, by double-clicking the edit box you both select the edit box and highlight the existing value of 0.06. Type **0.125** and press Enter. This enters the new value, 0.13, and replaces the original value all in one step.

7. Also change the color of the extension line. As with the dimension line, selecting either the Color button or the color image tile, you open the Select Color dialog box. Select the color red from the Standard Colors area, at the top of the dialog box. Click OK to confirm the choice and return to the Geometry dialog box.

**Tip**
By assigning standard colors to dimension objects you can bypass layer color settings. This gives you better control over the line weights assigned to these colors through your plotter settings.

V

**Advanced Drawing**

8. Next change the type of arrowhead AutoCAD uses to terminate the dimension line. Working in the Arrowhead area of the Geometry dialog box, keep picking the left arrowhead image tile until the Open style is displayed. Note how the right tile and both pop-up lists scroll as you pick the left image tile.

   Before you change the Overall Scale factor, the final change in this dialog box, let's see how the changes made up to this point affect the existing dimensions. Follow steps 9 through 14:

9. Click OK to confirm the setting changes and return to the Dimension Styles dialog box.

10. Now, save these settings to a new dimension style. Working in the Dimension Style area of the Dimension Styles dialog box, select the Name setting. As covered in earlier steps, double-clicking the edit box allows you to both select the edit box and highlight the existing style name Standard. Type **18DWG** and select Save. This copies the original settings along with the changes you just made to the Standard style, to the 18DWG dimension style. Selecting Save also sets 18DWG as the Current style.

11. Click OK to confirm the setting changes and return to the AutoCAD drawing editor.

    Note that the dimensions still appear as they had before you made the setting changes. This is because you didn't replace the Standard style with the 18DWG style by renaming the Standard style. Instead you "copied" the Standard style, with the changes, to the 18DWG style by using the Save option. This left the Standard style and existing dimensions unchanged. Renaming the Standard style to 18DWG would have automatically updated the existing dimensions, but it would also have eliminated the Standard style from the drawing database. Saving a new style is the safest way to create a dimension style since it preserves the original dimension style. This allows you to use the original dimension style as a template for new styles.

    AutoCAD provides the DIMSTYLE command to change from one dimension style to another. Before using the DIMSTYLE command you might want to ZOOM in on all, or part of, the dimension string(s) that you are changing using the Window option. You can zoom back to the previous magnification using the Previous option. While not necessary, nor mentioned in the following steps, it allows you to see some of the more subtle changes that take place. If you aren't familiar with the ZOOM command refer to Chapter 12, "Viewing a Drawing."

12. At the `Command:` prompt, type **dimstyle** and press Enter.

13. At the `dimension style:` prompt, type **18DWG**.

   At the `Dimension Style Edit (Save/Restore/STatus/Variables/Apply/?)` `<Restore>:` prompt, type **a** and press Enter to use the Apply option. This option applies the current dimension style, 18DWG, to dimension strings that you select.

14. At the `Select objects:` prompt, select each dimension string on the bracket and press Enter to change the style to 18DWG. As mentioned earlier, use the ZOOM command if you want to see the effects on each dimension string. Figure 18.6 shows the dimensions after they have been changed to the 18DWG dimension style.

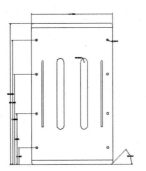

Adjustable Proximity Switch Bracket
Zoom Factor = .5:1

**Fig. 18.6**
The dimensions after changing to the 18DWG dimension style.

You probably noticed right away that the dimension objects changed color. However, unless you zoomed in on different sections of the drawing you probably didn't notice the arrowhead or extension line origin changes. These changes and several others will become more apparent after the Overall Scale is changed. To make that final change follow the steps below.

1. Click the Dimension Styles button on the Dimensioning floating toolbar.

2. Select the Geometry button from the Dimension Styles dialog box. Refer to figure 18.4 to see the Geometry dialog box.

   Most of the changes required to make the dimensions clearer can be corrected by editing the Overall Scale, located in the Scale area of the dialog box. However for the purpose of this tutorial, you first modify some of the other settings to show how they affect the existing dimensions.

3. Change the scale factor used to change the values of the dimension settings. Working in the Scale area of the Geometry dialog box, select the Overall Scale setting. Double-clicking the edit box, type **4.00** and press Enter. This enters a new value of 4.00000, while replacing the original value of 1.00000. This multiplies all the dimension variable settings that are numeric values by a factor of 4.00000.

4. Click OK to confirm the scale factor change and return to the Dimension Styles dialog box.

5. Save these settings to 18DWG dimension style. Working in the Dimension Style area of the Dimension Styles dialog box, select the Save button. This saves the change you just made to the 18DWG dimension style.

6. Click OK to confirm the setting changes and return to the AutoCAD drawing editor. Figure 18.7 shows the results.

---

**Caution**

Early releases of AutoCAD 13 have failed to update dimension strings after revising certain variables. If you witness this symptom use the `Dim: `**update** command to update the dimension string(s).

---

**Fig. 18.7**
The dimensions after the dimension scale factor is changed.

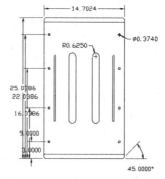

Adjustable Proximity Switch Bracket
Zoom Factor = .5:1

The change in the dimension scale factor should be apparent. Refer to figure 18.7 to compare it with your screen. The change is most obvious when you compare the size differences of the dimension text, leaders, and arrowheads between figures 18.6 and 18.7. It's also worth noting how the changes took effect. This time, the dimension scale factor took effect the moment you entered the drawing editor; you didn't have to use the DIMSTYLE command. This is because the dimension style 18DWG already existed. The dimension scale factor change was made to the dimension style 18DWG rather than to the style STANDARD, which then was saved to a new style, as was done previously.

## Formatting Dimension Lines

Selecting the Format button from the Dimension Styles dialog box brings up the Format dialog box shown in figure 18.8.

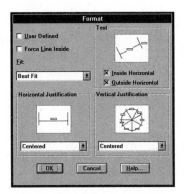

**Fig. 18.8**
The Format dialog box, used to format dimension string text.

Use the Format Styles dialog box to modify each of the values that control how text is positioned with respect to the dimension line. The options set by these dialog entries are as follows:

■ *User Defined.* Generally, dimension text is centered in the dimension line. The settings of the surrounding options each affect the default placement of the dimension text. They set a uniform location, relative to the dimension, every time. When you select this check box, you are asked to supply a location for the dimension text every time you create a dimension. Because you select each dimension text location, selecting this option disables the Horizontal Justification option.

> **Note**
>
> The dimension variable DIMUPT determines whether the user supplies the dimension text position.

■ *Force Line Inside.* If you pick dimension points that are too close to each other, AutoCAD may have a difficult time fitting arrowheads and a dimension line between the extension lines. Many times AutoCAD omits this line entirely. By selecting this check box you force AutoCAD to create a dimension line and place it between the extension lines, no matter what distance is between dimension points.

> **Note**
>
> The dimension variable DIMTOFL determines whether the dimension line is forced to be drawn between the extension lines.

■ *Fit.* Similar to the previous option, if the distance between extension lines is too small there may not be room for arrowheads or text. This pop-up menu allows you to choose which elements you want to "force" to fit between the extension lines.

> **Note**
>
> The dimension variable DIMTIX determines if dimension text is always forced to appear between the extension lines.

■ *Horizontal Justification.* This setting is used to define the horizontal position of the dimension text string, relative to the dimension and extension lines. This setting applies to all dimensions that utilize dimension and extension lines. The options are as follows:

- *Centered.* Places the horizontal middle of the text centered on the dimension line.

- *1st Extension Line.* Places the text near the first extension line.

- *2nd Extension Line.* Places the text near the second extension line.

- *Over 1st Extension.* Places the text over the first extension line.

- *Over 2nd Extension.* Places the text over the second extension line.

Each option you choose displays a small graphic in the image tile above it, which shows the position of the text. With the Center option, for example, you can click this image tile to cycle through the horizontal justification options.

> **Note**
>
> The dimension variable DIMTAD determines the horizontal position of the text in relation to the dimension line.

- *Text.* The Text area in the Format dialog box is used to define the orientation of dimension text both Inside and Outside the extension lines. These settings apply to any dimension that uses extension lines. They describe whether text, placed between or forced outside of the extension lines, is drawn horizontally or parallel to the dimension line. The image tile above these check boxes shows you a preview of each option setting. As with the previous image tile, you can click the tile area to cycle through the available options. The Text orientation settings also affect the Vertical Justification of dimension text.

> **Note**
>
> The dimension variables DIMTIH and DIMTOLJ define whether text placed inside or outside the extension lines is oriented horizontally.

- *Vertical Text Justification.* This setting is used to define the vertical position of the dimension text string relative to the dimension line. This setting applies to all dimensions that utilize dimension lines. The options are as follows:

  - *Centered.* Place the vertical middle of the text centered on the dimension line.

  - *Above.* Place the vertical position of the text above the dimension line.

  - *Below.* Place the vertical position of the text below the dimension line.

  - *JIS.* Place the text to conform with Japanese Industrial Standards (JIS).

**V**

**Advanced Drawing**

Each option you choose displays a small graphic in the image tile above it, which previews the vertical position of the text. As with the previous image tiles, you can click the tile area to cycle through the available options.

> **Note**
>
> The dimension variable DIMTVP defines how vertical text is oriented.

### Tutorial: Changing Dimension Style Formats

This tutorial demonstrates how changes made to these settings affect the text placement in dimension strings that already exist in a drawing. So you can see how all the Format options are best applied, each option is changed on the children's style that is best suited to show the example. This also provides an opportunity to become comfortable with the new Family concept of dimension style management. The tutorial continues to use the Proximity Switch Bracket, drawing 18DWG01, used in the previous tutorial. If you didn't do the previous tutorial, you need to go back and complete it before continuing. Figure 18.9 shows the drawing as it was last modified. Follow these steps to change the Format settings:

1. Open the sample drawing C:\UAW13\18DWG01.

2. Click the Dimension Styles button on the Dimensioning floating toolbar.

3. Select the Linear option in the Family area of the Dimension Styles dialog box.

4. Select the Format button from the Dimension Styles dialog box. Refer to figure 18.8 to see the Format dialog box.

5. Change the settings in the Inside and Outside Horizontal text. Working in the Text area of the Format dialog box, select the Inside Horizontal and Outside Horizontal check boxes to disable these options. You could also continue to select the image tile to cycle through all the possible combinations, until both options are disabled.

6. Click OK to confirm the setting changes and return to the Dimension Styles dialog box.

7. Save these settings to 18DWG dimension style. Working in the Dimension Style area of the Dimension Styles dialog box, select the Save

button. This saves the changes you just made to the 18DWG dimension style settings.

8.  Click OK to confirm the setting changes and return to the AutoCAD drawing editor.

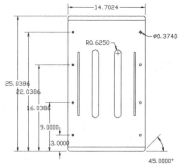

**Fig. 18.9**
The Proximity Switch Bracket, as last modified.

Adjustable Proximity Switch Bracket
Zoom Factor = .5:1

All the LINEAR dimensions should now have dimension text parallel to the dimension line. Figure 18.10 shows the revised linear dimension strings.

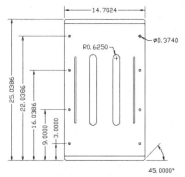

**Fig. 18.10**
Linear dimension strings with parallel dimension text.

Adjustable Proximity Switch Bracket
Zoom Factor = .5:1

---

**Caution**

Early releases of AutoCAD 13 have failed to update dimension strings after revising certain variables. If you witness this symptom use the Dim: **update** command to update the dimension strings.

---

The next Format changes affect the child dimension styles of Radial and Diameter.

V

Advanced Drawing

1. Click the Dimension Styles button on the Dimensioning floating toolbar.

2. Select the Radial option in the Family area of the Dimension Styles dialog box.

3. Select the Format button from the Dimension Styles dialog box. Refer to figure 18.8 to see the Format dialog box.

4. Change the settings in the vertical text justification. Working in the Vertical Justification area of the Format dialog box, select the Above option from the pop-up list. You could also continue to select the image tile to cycle through all the possible choices until the Above option is set.

5. Click OK to confirm the setting changes and return to the Dimension Styles dialog box. Save these settings by selecting the Save button.

6. Select the Diameter option in the Family area of the Dimension Styles dialog box.

7. Repeat steps 3 through 5 for the Diameter dimension child.

8. Save these settings to 18DWG dimension style. Working in the Dimension Style area of the Dimension Styles dialog box, select the Save button. This saves the changes you just made to the 18DWG dimension style settings.

9. Click OK to confirm the setting changes and return to the AutoCAD drawing editor.

All the RADIAL and DIAMETER dimensions should now have dimension text that is above an extended leader leg. Figure 18.11 shows the revised radial and diameter dimension strings.

**Fig. 18.11**
Radial and diameter dimension strings above extended leader legs.

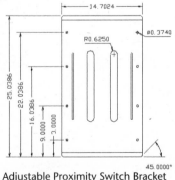

Adjustable Proximity Switch Bracket
Zoom Factor = .5:1

The last Format change affects the Angular child dimension style.

1. Click the Dimension Styles button on the Dimensioning floating toolbar.

2. Select the Angular option in the Family area of the Dimension Styles dialog box.

3. Select the Format button from the Dimension Styles dialog box. Refer to figure 18.8 to see the Format dialog box.

4. Change the settings of the horizontal text placement. Working in the Horizontal Justification area of the Format dialog box, select the Over 1st Extension option from the pop-up list. You could also continue to select the image tile to cycle through all the possible options until the Over 1st Extension is set.

5. Click OK to confirm the setting changes and return to the Dimension Styles dialog box.

6. Save these settings to 18DWG dimension style. Working in the Dimension Style area of the Dimension Styles dialog box, select the Save button. This saves the changes you just made to the 18DWG dimension style settings.

7. Click OK to confirm the setting changes and return to the AutoCAD drawing editor.

All the ANGULAR dimensions should now have dimension text at the end and parallel to the extension line. Figure 18.12 shows the revised angular dimension string.

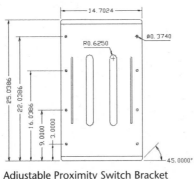

Adjustable Proximity Switch Bracket
Zoom Factor = .5:1

**Fig. 18.12**

Angular dimension string with parallel dimension text, located at the end of the extension line.

V

**Advanced Drawing**

## Establishing Dimension Text Formats

Selecting the Annotation button from the Dimension Styles dialog box displays the Annotation dialog box shown in figure 18.13. This dialog box is used to modify each of the values which control how special text features are handled and text is drawn.

**Fig. 18.13**

The Annotation dialog box used to adjust text size, tolerance options, and alternate units.

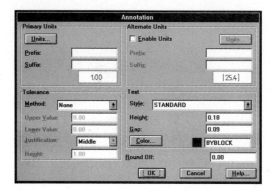

The upper-left area of the Annotation dialog box is used for setting the values for the dimension string Primary Units. This allows you to define how the dimension text will appear in the dimension string which is created. The Units button displays the Primary Units dialog box shown in figure 18.14. This area allows you to define the type of drawing units you want to represent your dimension. You can also choose the level of precision and add special formatting characters to the units.

**Fig. 18.14**

The Primary Units dialog box allows you to set the type of units and level of precision to display.

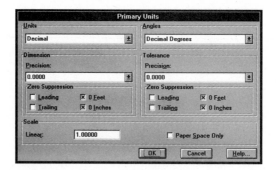

When you click the Units button in the Annotations dialog box, and bring up the Primary Units dialog box, you can change the following options:

- *Units*. This pop-up list allows you to choose a variety of unit formats. The formats available are Scientific, Decimal, Engineering,

Architectural, and Fractional. You can see the format of your selection by referring to the Dimension Precision pop-up list.

> **Note**
>
> The dimension variable DIMUNIT defines the type of format used for the display of dimension units.

■ *Dimension Precision.* This pop-up list allows you to set the level of precision for the units. The format of the list depends on the type of units you previously selected.

> **Note**
>
> The dimension variable DIMDEC defines the precision of the units format.

■ *Dimension Zero Suppression.* You can suppress zeros in the Leading, Trailing, 0 Feet and 0 Inches positions by selecting the appropriate check boxes. The end result depends on the type of unit format currently selected.

> **Note**
>
> The dimension variable DIMZIN defines the zero suppression setting for leading, trailing, feet, and inches.

■ *Angles.* This pop-up list allows you to choose from a variety of angle formats. The format options available include Decimal Degrees, Deg/Min/Sec, Grads, Radians, and Surveyor. You can see the format of your selection by referring to the Tolerance Precision pop-up list.

> **Note**
>
> The dimension variable DIMAUNIT defines the type of angle format used for the display of angular dimensions.

■ *Tolerance Precision.* This pop-up list allows you to set the level of precision for the angle format you previously selected. The format of the list depends on the type of angle format currently selected.

**V**

**Advanced Drawing**

> **Note**
>
> The dimension variable DIMTDEC defines the precision of the angle format.

- *Tolerance Zero Suppression.* You can suppress zeros in the Leading, Trailing, 0 Feet and 0 Inches positions by selecting the appropriate check boxes. The end result depends on the type of angle format currently selected.

> **Note**
>
> The dimension variable DIMTZIN defines the suppression setting zeros in the leading, trailing, feet, and inches positions.

- *Scale Linear.* By providing a value in the linear edit box you can set a global scale factor for all linear dimension measurements.

> **Caution**
>
> The linear scale factor also affects the content of the default text.

> **Note**
>
> The dimension variable DIMLFAC contains the global scale factor for linear dimension measurements.

- *Scale Paper Space Only.* By selecting this check box you tell AutoCAD to apply the zoom scale factor for a model space viewport to dimension objects created in paper space. This scale factor is applied to all linear dimension measurements. Selecting this option also disables the Scale Linear edit box.

> **Note**
>
> The dimension variable DIMLFAC contains the linear value for the Paper Space Only scale factor. This scale factor is stored as a negative value.

Refer to the Annotation dialog box in figure 18.13. The descriptions for the other options in the Primary Units area of the Annotation dialog box are the following:

- The <u>P</u>refix and <u>S</u>uffix options allow you to have text strings added before and after the dimension value.

> **Note**
>
> The dimension variable DIMPOST holds both the prefix and suffix strings.

The lower-left area of the Annotation dialog box, shown previously in figure 18.13, is used for setting the values of dimension tolerances. Tolerances are used in situations where an element must meet a certain dimensional precision. The tolerance value is used to tell the person building the element how much larger or smaller the element may be and still work within the confines of the design.

There are five options available to display tolerance information with a dimension. They are listed in the <u>M</u>ethod pop-up list; each of these options has a different effect on the <u>U</u>pper and Lo<u>w</u>er Value edit boxes. To clarify the effect that each method has on these values, all three areas are covered together, as follows:

- *None.* This method adds no tolerance information to the dimension string. Selecting this method disables all other edit boxes and pop-up lists in this area.

> **Note**
>
> The dimension variable DIMTOL controls the display of tolerance values.

- *Symmetrical.* This method displays a ± symbol followed by a tolerance value. This value represents the amount by which the dimension can either increase or decrease. Since both upper and lower values are identical, the value entered in the <u>U</u>pper Value edit box is displayed, while the Lo<u>w</u>er Value edit box becomes disabled.

> **Note**
>
> The dimension variables DIMTOL and DIMLIM control how dimension tolerances are displayed.

> **Note**
>
> The dimension variable DIMTP holds the upper tolerance value.

- *Deviation.* This method allows you to display different tolerance values for the + and – signs. As with the symmetrical method, these values represent the amounts that the dimension value can either increase or decrease by. You use the Upper and Lower Value edit boxes to enter these values. The upper value is represented by the + sign and the lower value by the – sign.

> **Note**
>
> The dimension variables DIMTOL and DIMLIM control how dimension tolerances are displayed.

> **Note**
>
> The dimension variable DIMTM holds the lower tolerance value.

- *Limits.* This method displays two values in place of the dimension text. The upper dimension is the original dimension with the Upper Value added. The lower dimension is the original dimension with the Lower Value subtracted. Because the limit values replace the original dimension, selecting Limits disables the Justification pop-up list.

> **Note**
>
> The dimension variables DIMTOL and DIMLIM control how dimension tolerances are displayed.

- *Basic.* This method is used to create a basic dimension. The dimension value has a box drawn around it. Selecting this method disables all the other edit boxes and pop-up lists in this area.

> **Note**
>
> The dimension variable DIMGAP controls the distance maintained between the dimension and the box drawn around it.

You can also select the Tolerance Method by clicking the image tiles in the Primary Units or the Alternate Units area, if alternate units are enabled. Both of these tiles cycle through the available options in unison as you click them.

■ The tolerance information added to a dimension may be formatted in several different ways. Selecting a justification setting from the Justification pop-up list lets you place the tolerance text in several different positions. The available settings are Top, Middle, and Bottom. Each location is relative to the dimension string.

■ By using the Height edit box you can also define a scale factor that is applied solely to the tolerance text. This helps distinguish the tolerance from the dimension string.

If you selected None or Basic for the Tolerance Method, the Justification and Height options are disabled.

### Note

The dimension variable DIMTFAC contains the scaling factor for the height of text used to create the tolerance information.

The upper-right area of the Annotation dialog box is used to enable and set the values of alternate dimensioning units. By default, AutoCAD returns lengths in one of the five formats supported by the DDUNITS command (Decimal, Engineering, Architectural, Scientific, or Fractional). Alternate units allow you to define a scaling factor to be applied to the distance calculated for the dimension string and display this new value in addition to the primary units value.

To enable alternate units to be used, you must first select the Enable Units check box. When this is checked, the other controls within this group are enabled, allowing you to change their properties.

### Note

The dimension variable DIMALT determines if alternate units will be used when creating the dimension.

**V**

**Advanced Drawing**

**Note**

The dimension variable DIMAPOST contains any suffix or prefix value which will be used with the alternate dimension value.

**Note**

The Alternate Units area functions very much the same as the Primary Units area. You can refer to the Primary Units area section for discussion on the Units dialog box and the Prefix and Suffix text edit boxes. The only exception to this is the Scale Linear edit box in the Units dialog box which is discussed next.

■ The following option in the Alternate Units dialog area is the scaling factor. This factor is applied to the original dimension length. If you want to display millimeters instead of inches, enter the scaling factor of **25.4** in this edit box.

**Note**

The dimension variable DIMALTF contains the scaling factor used for the creation of the alternate units.

■ The lower-right area of the Annotation dialog box is used for setting the general options for the text used to display the dimension value. The first option, Style, allows you to choose a specific text style to be used for the display of any dimensions created with the current dimension style.

**Note**

The dimension variable DIMTXSTY contains the name of the style currently in use for dimension text.

The Height option is used to define the height of the dimension text. If you have supplied a dimension scaling factor in the Geometry dialog box, as discussed earlier, the height of text is scaled up by that value.

> **Note**
>
> The dimension variable DIMTXT contains the value used to determine the height of dimension text.

The <u>G</u>ap option defines the distance between the dimension line and the dimension text.

> **Note**
>
> The dimension variable DIMGAP contains the value which determines how close the dimension text must be to the dimension line before the line is broken.

The <u>C</u>olor button allows you to define a specific color for all dimension text created using this style. You can choose to have the color of the text appear in the current layer color or by block color. You can also choose any one of the 255 colors, which appear in the palette, to represent the text. The Color image tile shows the current color setting. Click on the image tile to set the color just as you would with the Color button. The default color is BYBLOCK because the dimension itself is a block.

▶ See "Using BYBLOCK with Blocks," p. 686

> **Note**
>
> The dimension variable DIMCLRT stores the color setting for the dimension text.

■ The final option for the Annotation dialog box defines the round-off factor applied to dimensions. The dimension text is shown to whatever precision you specify with the primary units <u>U</u>nits option. The <u>R</u>ound Off option changes the dimension text to match the nearest round-off value which you supply.

> **Note**
>
> The dimension variable DIMRND contains the values which dimension text will be rounded off to.

### Tutorial: Changing Dimension Style Annotations

This tutorial demonstrates how changes made to these settings affect the appearance, values, and tolerances of dimension text that already exist in a drawing. The tutorial guides you through the Annotation dialog box and its supporting dialog boxes. You'll make changes that affect the precision with which the part is manufactured and add alternate units, so the part can be manufactured in foreign markets. The tutorial continues to use the Proximity Switch Bracket, drawing 18DWG01, used in the previous tutorials. If you didn't do the previous tutorials, you need to go back and complete them before continuing.

Figure 18.15 shows the drawing as it was last modified. This concludes the series of tutorials that have focused on changing existing dimensions. Follow the steps below to change the ANNOTATION settings:

**Fig. 18.15**

The Proximity Switch Bracket, as last modified.

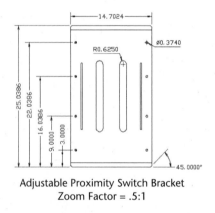

Adjustable Proximity Switch Bracket
Zoom Factor = .5:1

1. Open the sample drawing C:\UAW13\18DWG01.

2. Click the Dimension Styles button on the Dimensioning floating toolbar.

3. Verify that the Parent family member, located in the Family area of the Dimension Styles dialog box, is selected. Each time you open the Dimension Styles dialog box the Parent family member is automatically selected.

4. Select the Annotation button from the Dimension Styles dialog box. Refer to figure 18.13 to see the Annotation dialog box.

5. Select the Units button from the Primary Units area of the Annotation dialog box. Refer to figure 18.14 to see the Primary Units dialog box.

**6.** Working in the Dimension area of the Primary Units dialog box, select the Precision pop-up list. Highlight the 0.00 example, making it the new default. The dimension precision level is now set for two places to the right of the decimal point.

**7.** In the Tolerance area of the Primary Units dialog box, select the Precision pop-up list and highlight the 0.00 example, making it the new default. This sets the tolerance precision level to two places right of the decimal point, identical to the dimension precision.

**8.** Click OK to confirm the setting changes and return to the Annotation dialog box.

**9.** Change the type of tolerancing method used to Symmetrical, by selecting it from the Method pop-up list. The list is located in the Tolerance area of the Annotation dialog box. You could also cycle through the available methods by picking the Method Image Tile, located in the Primary Units area.

**10.** Change the upper tolerance value to 0.06. Highlight the existing value in the Upper Value edit box by double-clicking in the box. Then type **0.06** and press Enter to replace the original value.

**11.** Change the tolerance justification to top, placing the tolerance values at the top of the dimension text. From the Justification pop-up list select Top.

**12.** Enable the use of alternate units by selecting the Enable Units check box, in the Alternate Units area of the Annotation dialog box.

**13.** Once you enable the use of alternate units, the Units button in the Alternate Units area becomes accessible. Select the Units button and verify that steps 6 through 8 have been updated automatically for the Alternate Units dialog box.

**14.** Since the alternate units being used are metric and the units of measure are millimeters, add mm as a suffix by entering **mm** in the Suffix edit box.

**15.** Change the text style to simplex by selecting it from the Style pop-up list in the Text area of the Annotation dialog box.

**16.** Reduce the text height by double-clicking the Height edit box. Type **0.125** and press Enter to change the value.

17. Because adding alternate units increases the length of the dimension text, reduce the gap between the text and the dimension line to 0.06 by double-clicking the Gap edit box. Type **0.06** and press Enter to change the value.

18. Change the color of the text to correspond with the proper plotter line weight. Selecting either the Color button or the Color Image Tile opens the Select Color dialog box. Select the color magenta from the Standard Colors area, at the top of the dialog box. Click OK to confirm the choice and return to the Annotation dialog box.

19. Click OK to confirm the annotation changes and return to the Dimension Styles dialog box.

20. Select the Save button in the Dimension Style area of the Dimension Styles dialog box. This saves the changes you just made to the 18DWG Parent dimension style settings.

21. After you've made a dimension override change to one of the child family members, such as Linear or Leader, it then becomes necessary to duplicate any changes that are made to the Parent settings for the child members that have overrides. Unless you don't want those child settings to be identical to the Parent settings. Since changes were made to the Linear, Radial, Angular, and Diameter child members in an earlier tutorial, it now becomes necessary to duplicate steps 4 through 20 for each of these child family members. Start by duplicating step 3; however, replace the Parent selection with the appropriate child member.

> **Note**
>
> The Angular child member doesn't allow the use of alternate units.

22. Click OK to confirm the setting changes and return to the AutoCAD drawing editor.

Figure 18.16 shows all the dimensions with the characteristics of the new dimension annotation settings. Dimensions should have tolerances and alternate metric units, except for the angular dimension. Text should be the simplex font and a smaller size. Notice how two of the baseline dimensions extend up, crossing other dimensions' extension lines. You'll learn how to correct that in a later tutorial.

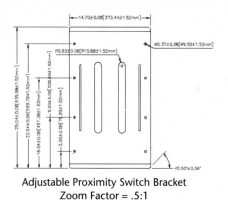

Adjustable Proximity Switch Bracket
Zoom Factor = .5:1

**Fig. 18.16**
Dimension strings
after new Annota-
tion settings.

---

**Caution**

Early releases of AutoCAD 13 have failed to update dimension strings after revising
certain variables. If you witness this symptom, use the `Dim:` **update** command to
update the dimension strings.

---

Be certain that you save the drawing before exiting AutoCAD; this drawing
will be used in later tutorials.

# Linear Dimensioning

Linear dimensions are the most common type of dimensioning used in almost all professions. In your designs you often strive to keep elements limited
to horizontal and vertical surfaces. This keeps production costs for the element to a minimum, and also minimizes the time required to design and
draw the elements.

When dimensions are created, the current style settings are used to display
the dimension information. You can use the Linear dimension family sub-
style to override the current dimension style settings for linear dimensions.

## Horizontal and Vertical Dimensions

AutoCAD provides the DIMLINEAR command, which makes creating linear
dimensions a speedy process. The HORIZONTAL and VERTICAL commands
have been combined in AutoCAD Release 13 into the DIMLINEAR command.
DIMLINEAR creates dimensions parallel and perpendicular to the current
drawing axis. These commands may be accessed by one of the following
methods:

- Select the Linear Dimension button on the Dimensioning floating toolbar.

- At the Command: prompt, type **dimlinear** and press Enter.

When using this dimension command, you can either select the two points which correspond to the starting and ending point of the dimension, or you can select a Line or Arc object. If you do the latter, AutoCAD automatically locates the starting and ending definition points for you, and you only need to accept the value of the current dimension and position the dimension line where you want it.

The type of linear dimension created depends on your two definition points and the dimension line location you pick. Figure 18.17 shows two typical horizontal and vertical dimensions created around a rectangular drawing element. Figure 18.18 shows how the dimension line location you select can affect what type of dimension created on an angular object. Figure 18.18 also shows how to create a dimension by picking an object, rather than picking definition points.

**Fig. 18.17**
Examples of a typical horizontal and vertical dimension string.

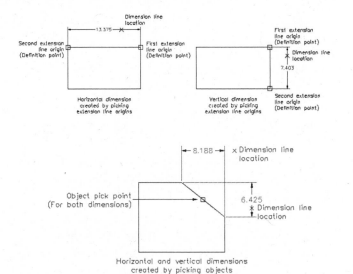

**Fig. 18.18**
Picking horizontal and vertical dimensions on an angular object.

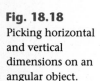

> **Note**
>
> Note in figure 18.18 how the horizontal dimension line pick point wasn't even on the dimension line. Select any point above or below an object to create horizontal dimensions. Select any point left or right of an object to create vertical dimensions. AutoCAD creates perpendicular extension lines, but you don't have to concern yourself with that step.

## Aligned Dimensions

The Aligned dimension is also a part of the Linear sub-style family. AutoCAD provides the DIMALIGNED command which makes it possible to dimension objects that aren't horizontal or vertical. DIMALIGNED creates dimension lines parallel to the angular object and extension lines perpendicular to the object. In fact, you can even use DIMALIGNED to dimension horizontal and vertical objects. To access this command:

- Click the Aligned Dimension button on the Dimensioning floating toolbar.

- At the Command: prompt, type **dimaligned** and press Enter.

The DIMALIGNED command prompt is the same as the DIMLINEAR command. When using this dimension command, you can either select the two points which correspond to the starting and ending point of the dimension, or you can select a Line or Arc object. If you do the latter, AutoCAD automatically locates the starting and ending definition points for you, and you only need to accept the value of the current dimension string and position the dimension line where you want it placed. Figure 18.19 shows an example of an aligned dimension created by selecting an object. The figure also illustrates that the dimension line location you select does not have to be on the dimension line proper.

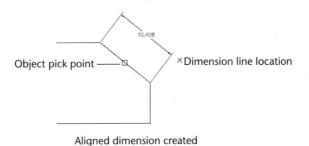

Object pick point —— Dimension line location

Aligned dimension created
by picking object

**Fig. 18.19**
An aligned dimension, created by selecting the object.

V

Advanced Drawing

## Continuing Dimension Strings

A single dimension is useful, but not always typical in drawings you create. Often you see a string of dimensions which locate various elements in the perpendicular and horizontal planes. These dimensions have a common starting point, or use a dimension line which appears uniform across the group of dimensions.

Creating a series of dimensions in AutoCAD can be accomplished using the DIMLINEAR or DIMALIGNED commands which created your first dimension, but locating your first and second dimension points and setting the position of the dimension line can take a lot of time. Instead, you can use the DIMCONTINUE or DIMBASELINE commands to speed up this process.

To create dimensions which start at the ending dimension point of the previous dimension and have dimension lines which line up with each other, do one of the following:

- Select the Continue Dimension button on the Dimensioning floating toolbar.

- At the Command: prompt, type **dimcontinue** to create continuous dimension strings.

To create dimensions with a common baseline and dimension lines which stack alongside each other:

- Select the Baseline Dimension button on the Dimensioning floating toolbar.

- At the Command: prompt, type **dimbaseline** to create baseline dimension strings.

AutoCAD creates these two types of dimensions by using the last dimension, which was created by specifying both a starting and an ending point. For baseline dimensions, the starting point is the baseline for all new dimensions created, and you choose a new second, or ending, dimension point. Each new dimension is spaced aside or above the previous dimension, by the value of the Dimension Lines Spacing option in the Geometry dialog box of the DDIM command.

Continuous dimensions start at the ending, or second, dimension point of the last dimension. This point becomes the starting point for the new dimension. Then you choose a new ending dimension point for the new dimension. These two types of dimensions are shown in figure 18.20.

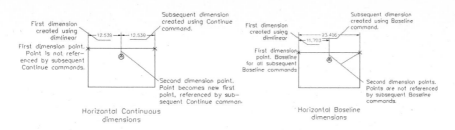

**Fig. 18.20**
Examples of
the continue
and baseline
dimensions.

## Tutorial: Adding Linear Dimensions

This tutorial demonstrates how you can use these tools to add new dimensions to a drawing. The tutorial guides you through examples of each LINEAR command. This tutorial uses a new drawing: 18DWG02. Figure 18.21 shows the drawing and identifies the object points that will be dimensioned. Follow these steps to add the additional dimensions:

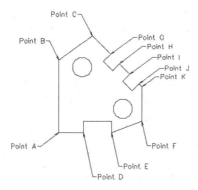

**Fig. 18.21**
Part with
dimension points
identified.

The first seven steps cover creating VERTICAL and BASELINE dimensions:

1. Open the sample drawing C:\UAW13\18DWG02.

2. Click the Linear Dimension button on the Dimensioning floating toolbar.

3. The object snaps ENDpoint and INTersect have been preset for you, using the OSNAP command. At the First extension line origin or RETURN to select: prompt, pick the point identified in figure 18.21 as Point A.

> **Note**
>
> Don't use the select object feature to pick an object when you're planning to follow up the DIMLINEAR command by using the BASELINE or CONTINUE dimension commands. The first definition point that the Select Object option uses might not be the correct reference point for future BASELINE or CONTINUE commands. The Select Object option uses the first endpoint picked when drawing the object selected as the first reference point for future commands.

4. At the `Second extension line origin:` prompt, pick the point identified in figure 18.21 as Point B.

5. At the `Dimension line location (Text/Angle/Horizontal/Vertical/Rotated):` prompt, pick a point to the left of the object being dimensioned. You don't have to be precise; however, leave some extra room for future dimensions. After you've picked the dimension line location the command terminates by itself.

 6. Click the Baseline Dimension button on the Dimensioning floating toolbar.

7. At the `Second extension line origin or RETURN to select:` prompt, pick the point identified in figure 18.21 as Point C. Press Enter twice to terminate the command.

> **Note**
>
> When you're using the BASELINE and CONTINUE dimension commands you can't use the select object feature to pick objects that aren't drawn orthogonally. You must pick the point as you did in step 7.

The vertical dimensions you added should be similar to those in figure 18.22. Again the exact dimension line locations on all the dimensions covered in this tutorial don't have to be precise. The next seven steps, 8 through 14, cover creating Horizontal and Continuous dimensions.

 8. Click the Linear Dimension button on the Dimensioning floating toolbar.

9. At the `First extension line origin or RETURN to select:` prompt, pick the point identified in figure 18.21 as Point A.

10. At the Second extension line origin: prompt, pick the point identified in figure 18.21 as Point D.

11. At the Dimension line location (Text/Angle/Horizontal/Vertical/ Rotated): prompt, pick a point to the bottom of the object being dimensioned.

12. Click the Continue Dimension button on the Dimensioning floating toolbar.

13. At the Second extension line origin or RETURN to select: prompt, pick the point identified in figure 18.21 as Point E.

14. At the next Second extension line origin or RETURN to select: prompt, pick the point identified in figure 18.21 as Point F. Press Enter twice to terminate the command.

The horizontal dimensions you added should be similar to those shown in figure 18.22. As with the other dimensions the dimension line locations can vary. The next seven steps, 15 through 21, cover creating Aligned and Baseline dimensions.

15. Click the Aligned Dimension button on the Dimensioning floating toolbar.

16. At the First extension line origin or RETURN to select: prompt, pick the point identified in figure 18.21 as Point C.

17. At the Second extension line origin: prompt, pick the point identified in figure 18.21 as Point G.

18. At the Dimension line location (Text/Angle): prompt, pick a point above the object being dimensioned.

19. Click the Baseline Dimension button on the Dimensioning floating toolbar.

20. At the Second extension line origin or RETURN to select: prompt, pick the point identified in figure 18.21 as Point H.

21. Repeat step 20 for Points I, J, and K. After you have selected Point K press Enter twice to terminate the command.

Figure 18.22 shows all the dimensions added. This drawing will be used in the next tutorial.

**Fig. 18.22**
Part after linear
dimensions are
added.

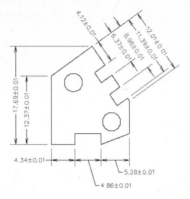

# Radial Dimensioning

Your world is not limited to sharp angles and corners; there are a variety of shapes that help to soften your perception of the environment. Curved walls, tubular handrails on a stair, buildings built around octagons or hexagons, and machine parts with filleted edges all utilize forms of construction which need to be drawn and dimensioned to be built correctly.

AutoCAD provides the DIMRADIUS, DIMDIAMETER, and DIMCENTER dimensioning tools to properly display dimensions for these elements. Each is described in the following sections, and the way each type of dimension is displayed is controlled by the Radial and Diameter dimension families of the current dimension style.

## Radius and Diameter Dimensions

Circular forms are as much a part of the world as sharp corners. To properly construct these elements you often need to supply a value for the radius of the object to be constructed, or if it's a free-standing circle, such as a concrete column or the tapping hole for a machine part, the diameter of the object. AutoCAD provides the DIMRADIUS and DIMDIAMETER commands to supply these values in your dimensions. AutoCAD also provides the DIMCENTER command to serve as a utility for marking the center point of radii and circles.

To create radial dimensions:

- Select the Radius Dimension button on the Dimensioning floating toolbar. This displays a fly-out list of buttons, the first of which is the Radius button.

- At the Command: prompt, type **dimradius** to create radius dimensions.

To create dimensions which measure the diameter of a circle:

- Select the Radius Dimension button on the Dimensioning floating toolbar. Highlight the second button in the fly-out list which is the Diameter Dimension button.

- At the Command: prompt, type **dimdiameter** and press Enter.

To draw centerlines that designate the center of an arc or circle:

- Select the Center Mark button on the Dimensioning floating toolbar.

- At the Command: prompt, type **dimcenter** and press Enter.

To use any of these commands, you must choose an arc or a circle. When you're using one of the dimension commands, the value of the radius or diameter can be edited by choosing the Text option from the Command: prompt. This allows you to make any changes to the value before it's placed in the dimension string. AutoCAD asks you to choose a point for where the text is to be placed. A leader line extends from the text position to the circle or arc. When AutoCAD uses a leader to identify the arc or circle it automatically adds center marks at the center point of the object. If you want to mark the center of arcs or circles, use the center mark command. AutoCAD places crosshairs at the center point of the object. Figure 18.23 shows several different types of radius and diameter dimensions, along with examples of center marks.

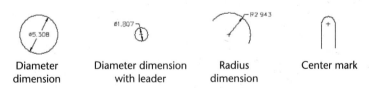

| Diameter dimension | Diameter dimension with leader | Radius dimension | Center mark |

**Fig. 18.23** Dimensions created using the RADIUS, DIAMETER, and CENTER MARK dimensioning commands.

### Tutorial: Adding Radial Dimensions

The tutorial demonstrates how you can use these tools to add new dimensions to a drawing. The tutorial guides you through examples of each the DIMDIAMETER and DIMCENTER commands. This tutorial continues to use the drawing 18DWG02. Figure 18.24 shows the drawing and identifies the objects to be dimensioned. Follow the steps outlined below to add the additional dimensions:

**Fig. 18.24**
Part with
objects to be
dimensioned.

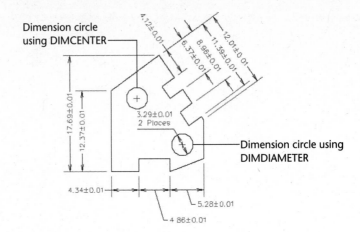

1. Open the sample drawing C:\UAW13\18DWG02.

2. Click the Center Mark button on the Dimensioning floating toolbar.

3. At the `Select arc or circle:` prompt, pick a point on the upper circle, identified in figure 18.24. AutoCAD adds the center marks to the circle and ends the command.

4. Click the Dimension Diameter button on the Dimensioning floating toolbar.

5. At the `Select arc or circle:` prompt, pick a point on the lower circle, identified in figure 18.24.

6. At the `Dimension line location (Text/Angle):` prompt, type **t** and press Enter. This allows you to edit the dimension text using the Edit MText dialog box.

7. The first time you select this option during an AutoCAD edit session you'll probably have to select a font that Windows recognizes. This isn't an AutoCAD font and won't affect your dimension text. Pick one that you like and click OK to enter the Edit MText dialog box.

8. After you're in the Edit MText dialog box, press the End key on your cursor key pad. This moves you to the end of the first line that contains <>. These greater than and less than symbols represent the diameter value of the circle you selected. Press Enter to add a new line. Once you are on the second line type **2 Places** and click OK. AutoCAD closes the MText Edit dialog and returns you to the command line.

**9.** At the `Dimension line location (Text/Angle):` prompt, select a point above and to the left of the circle. AutoCAD adds the center marks, dimension line, and dimension text along with the 2 Places you added in the MText dialog box and ends the command.

Figure 18.25 shows the dimensions that were added. You may want to leave this drawing open for the next tutorial.

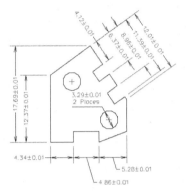

**Fig. 18.25**
Part after radial dimensions are added.

V

Advanced Drawing

# Angular Dimensioning

Because linear dimensions can't fully describe how to construct or manufacture angled elements in a design, AutoCAD offers the DIMANGULAR command. Buildings built around octagons, hexagons or machined parts with chamfered and angled edges, all utilize forms of construction which need to be drawn and dimensioned. AutoCAD provides the DIMANGULAR dimensioning tool to properly display dimensions for these elements. The dimensions DIMANGULAR creates are controlled by the Angular dimension family sub-style of the current dimension style.

## Angular Dimensions

Odd angles are a natural part of anything you create, whether you are designing a school with walls that aren't perpendicular to each other or machine parts which are not rectangular. The DIMANGULAR command allows you to display the interior or exterior dimension for any portion of your drawing where objects don't lie perpendicular to each other. To access this command:

- Click the Angular Dimension button on the Dimensioning floating toolbar.

- At the `Command:` prompt, type **dimangular** and press Enter.

Angles occur differently within a drawing, and AutoCAD provides you with several different ways to define the angle for which the dimension string will be created. These different ways are as follows:

- *Two non-parallel lines.* AutoCAD defines an angular dimension if you select two lines which are not parallel to each other. You must locate where the dimension angle will be placed. If there's enough space, the dimension of the angle is placed between the two lines chosen, otherwise you can choose where the text should be located.

- *An arc.* If you choose an Arc object, AutoCAD uses the starting, ending, and center points of the arc to determine the angle. Similar to the previous option, you must locate where the dimension angle will be placed. If there's enough space, the dimension text of the angle is placed between the endpoints of the arc; otherwise, you can choose where the text should be located outside of the arc.

- *A circle and a user-defined point.* This option allows you to use a circle object as part of an angular dimension. The point where you select the circle becomes the starting angle point for the dimension. The circle's center is the vertex point for the angle. You must then choose a final point through where the angle will be measured. This point can also be located on the circle, or it can correspond to any other location in the drawing except the first point you used to select the circle.

- *Three user-defined points.* This final option to create an angular dimension allows you to select any three points in a drawing which will be used to draw the dimension. When you press Enter at the prompt the first point you select becomes the starting angle vertex for the dimension. The second point chosen is the first endpoint for the angle and the final point is the second angle endpoint through where the angle will be measured. You can use the angle vertex as one of the angle endpoints.

Each of these options can be applied in a variety of situations. You must decide which is most appropriate for the angle you're dimensioning. The angular dimensions shown in figure 18.26 represent each of the previous options for creating angular dimensions.

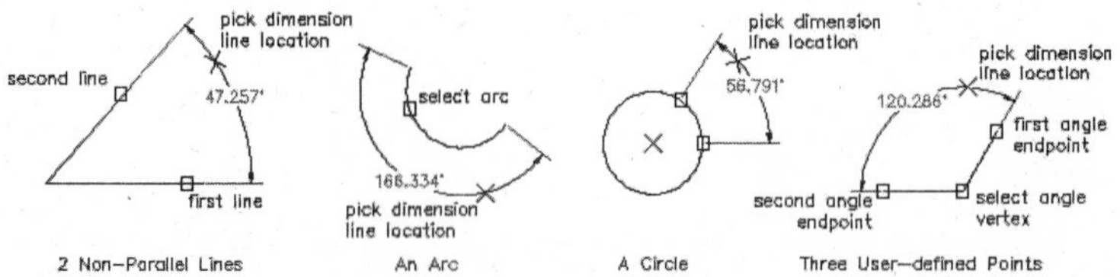

**Fig. 18.26**
Angular dimensions created using a variety of options.

2 Non-Parallel Lines  An Arc  A Circle  Three User—defined Points

### Tutorial: Adding Angular Dimensions

This tutorial demonstrates how you can use these tools to add new dimensions to a drawing. The tutorial guides you through examples of adding two angular dimensions. This tutorial uses drawing 18DWG02, which has been used for the last several tutorials. Figure 18.27 shows the drawing and identifies the object points that will be dimensioned. Figure 18.28 shows the dimension line locations; these are approximate locations. Follow the steps that follow to add the dimensions:

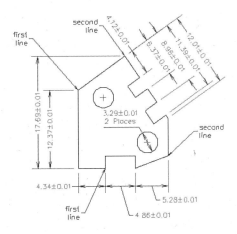

**Fig. 18.27**
Part with
dimension points
identified.

**V**

**Advanced Drawing**

1. Open the sample drawing C:\UAW13\18DWG02.

2. Click the Angular Dimension button on the Dimensioning floating toolbar.

3. At the `Select arc, circle, line, or RETURN:` prompt, pick one of the lines identified in figure 18.27 as "first line."

4. At the `Second line:` prompt, pick the matching line identified in figure 18.27 as "second line."

> **Note**
>
> Be certain to place the top dimension arc close to the vertical edge. This dimension will be used in a future tutorial on editing dimensions.

5. At the `Dimension arc line location:` prompt, select a point near the corresponding dimension line shown in figure 18.28.

6. Repeat steps 3 through 5 for the other angular dimension.

Figure 18.28 shows the dimensions added. Be sure to save the drawing before exiting AutoCAD, because it will be used in later editing tutorials.

**Fig. 18.28**
Part after angular dimensions are added.

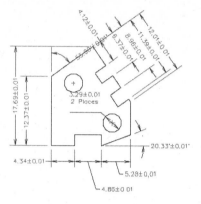

# Ordinate Dimensioning

Ordinate dimensions are usually limited to the machining industries where computer-controlled milling and lathe machines are used to create parts. When using ordinate dimensions, all distances are measured relative to a starting point located at a corner of the part which is to be created. The dimensions which are created then provide the distance from the reference point to the object in the horizontal or vertical plane.

## Establishing a Reference Point

▶ See "Understanding the User Coordinate System (UCS)," p. 788

Ordinate dimensions are always measured from an established reference point. AutoCAD uses the origin point established using the UCS command. If no origin point is established, AutoCAD uses 0,0, which is the default UCS origin point. To establish the origin point, follow these steps:

1. Click the Origin UCS button on the Standard toolbar.

2. Select <u>V</u>iew from the pull-down menu, then <u>S</u>et UCS and then Origin.

3. At the Command: prompt, type **ucs** and press Enter to execute the UCS command. Use the Origin option to choose a new coordinate system origin point.

The location of the reference point is usually determined by how the machinists create the parts. Typically a corner of the part serves as the reference point.

## Creating Ordinate Dimensions

After the reference point has been located, creating the ordinate dimension is a very simple process. First, you must access the DIMORDINATE command by doing the following:

- Click the Automatic button on the Dimensioning floating toolbar.

- At the `Command:` prompt, type **dimordinate** and press Enter.

The Ordinate command displays the following prompts:

- `Select feature:` At the `Select feature:` prompt, select the point you want to dimension.

- `Leader endpoint (Xdatum/Ydatum/Text):` At the `Leader endpoint:` prompt, select the endpoint where you want to create the dimension. AutoCAD calculates the difference between the feature location and this endpoint to determine if the dimension is in the x or y axis. You are able to override this feature by entering **x** or **y** in response to the Leader endpoint prompt.

    To enter a different dimension value at the `Leader endpoint (Xdatum/Ydatum/Text):` prompt, enter **t** and press Enter. The Edit MText dialog box is opened, allowing you to confirm or change the value.

Figure 18.29 shows a simple part with X and Y ordinate dimensions.

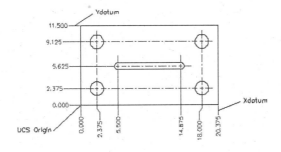

**Fig. 18.29**
An example of X and Y ordinate dimensions along with the UCS origin identified.

### Tutorial: Creating Ordinate Dimensions

This tutorial demonstrates how you can use these tools to create new dimensions to a drawing. The tutorial guides you through examples of the UCS ORIGIN and ORDINATE commands. This tutorial uses a new drawing 18DWG03, the drawing shown in figure 18.29. Figure 18.30 shows the drawing and identifies the features that will be dimensioned. As with the other tutorials the exact location of the leader endpoints is not critical; experiment to see the results.

**Fig. 18.30**
A part with the features to be dimensioned labeled.

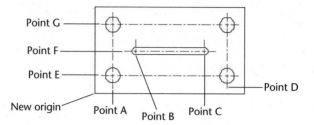

Follow these steps to add the additional dimensions:

1. Open the sample drawing C:\UAW13\18DWG03.

2. Click the Origin UCS button on the Standard toolbar.

3. At the `Origin point <0,0,0>`: prompt, pick the intersect identified in figure 18.30 as "new origin."

4. Click the Automatic button on the Dimensioning floating toolbar.

5. As in the past tutorials, the object snaps ENDpoint and INTersect have been preset for you, using the OSNAP command. At the `Select feature`: prompt, pick the point identified in figure 18.30 as Point A.

6. At the `Leader endpoint (Xdatum/Ydatum/Text)`: prompt, turn on ORTHO mode by pressing the F8 key and pick a point below Point A.

7. Continue to repeat steps 4 and 6 for Points B through D. Experiment with the leader endpoints you select. Try turning off the ORTHO mode key and observe the results.

8. To create a Ydatum dimension, repeat step 4. At the `Select feature`: prompt, pick the point identified in figure 18.30 as Point E. Turn ORTHO mode back on and pick a point to the left of Point E at the `Leader endpoint (Xdatum/Ydatum/Text)`: prompt.

9. Continue to repeat steps 7 and 8 for Points F and G.

10. As the last step, use the steps covered before to identify the X and Y origin points. This provides a good example of how the Leader endpoint location determines whether the dimension is an X or Y value.

Figure 18.31 has all of the ORDINATE dimensions. Your leader endpoints may differ, but the number of dimensions should be the same.

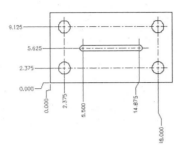

**Fig. 18.31**
A part after dimensioning with ordinates.

# Editing Associative Dimensions

As you know from Chapter 10, "Editing Techniques," editing is as much a part of the drawing creation process as actually creating lines, text, or dimensions. While the normal editing commands work similarly on dimension objects as they do on lines or circles, certain parts of the dimensions need unique commands to alter their values. This section covers these commands, as well as other general commands that also can be used to modify dimensions.

## Modifying Dimension Text

The value of dimension text is derived from the distance or angle between definition points. All dimension commands display the value for the current dimension before the dimension object is actually created. You have the option of accepting the calculated dimension value or entering a value of your own.

In addition to modifying the dimension value as the dimension is created, you can use several other AutoCAD commands to change this value. The first command you can use is DDEDIT, which allows you to supply a new dimension value for selected dimension objects. After you select the dimension, DDEDIT opens the EDIT MTEXT dialog box, shown in figure 18.32. To access this command:

- Click the Edit Polyline button on the Modify floating toolbar. While holding down the pick button on your digitizer, move the pointer to the Edit Text button on the fly-out; release the pick button.

- Enter **ddedit** at the Command: prompt.

**Fig. 18.32**
The Edit MText
dialog box with a
default dimension
value and a second
line of text.

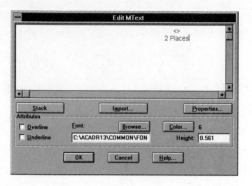

You can enter any type of value to be used for the selected dimensions. You can even add a string of text before or after the dimension value, or on a completely separate line if you want. If you choose to change the supplied value for the dimension, when you modify the dimensioned object at some later time, AutoCAD won't update the value of the dimension. Overriding the default value essentially "locks in" that value until you either override it again, or allow AutoCAD to use the true value of the dimension.

If you decide to restore a dimension value to its original calculated length, use the DDEDIT command and enter the left and right arrows from the keyboard (<>). AutoCAD uses this as a marker in a dimension string for holding the calculated value of the dimension.

The Edit MText dialog box allows you to edit many other text features and add other attributes that may prove beneficial in annotating your drawing. For a complete review of the Edit MText dialog box, refer to Chapter 16, "Working with Text."

## Relocating and Rotating Dimension Text

Generally, you use the settings of the DDIM command Annotation dialog to determine where dimension text should be located and if it should be rotated. Occasionally though, you need to modify only a few dimensions, and setting up a new style for these few exceptions is pointless. AutoCAD provides the DIMTEDIT command which is used to relocate and rotate the dimension text. DIMTEDIT also allows you to relocate dimension lines by moving them closer or farther from the dimensioned object, similar to the STRETCH command.

To access the DIMTEDIT command:

■ Click the Home button on the Dimensioning floating toolbar. This fly-out offers individual buttons for each of the DIMTEDIT options;

the fly-out is shown in figure 18.33. While holding the pick button on your digitizer, move the pointer to the option of your choice, then release the pick button.

■ Enter **dimtedit** at the `Command:` prompt.

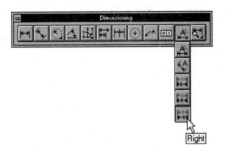

**Fig. 18.33**
Fly-out showing
DIMTEDIT
options, accessed
from the Home
button on the
Dimensioning
toolbar.

The DIMTEDIT command offers several options. Each option has its own button on the Home fly-out of the Dimensioning floating toolbar. Following are the options and command prompts for DIMTEDIT:

■ `Select dimension:` Select the dimension you want to relocate.

■ `Enter text location (Left/Right/Home/Angle):` You are able to drag the text to a new location using the crosshairs. You also are able to drag the dimension and extension lines to a new location. The effect of this varies depending on the dimension type.

■ At the `Enter text location (Left/Right/Home/Angle):` type **l** and press Enter to left-justify the text within the dimension line.

■ At the `Enter text location (Left/Right/Home/Angle):` prompt, type **r**. Press Enter to right-justify the text within the dimension line.

■ At the `Enter text location (Left/Right/Home/Angle):` prompt, type **h**. Press Enter to move the text back to its default position.

■ At the `Enter text location (Left/Right/Home/Angle):` prompt, type **a**. Press Enter to rotate the text in its current horizontal and vertical center point. At the `Enter text angle:` prompt, enter a value for the angle. Press Enter or select two points on the screen to represent the angle.

## Modifying the Dimension Object Using Object Grips

Dimension objects are similar to any other AutoCAD drawing object that you use. They may be moved, copied, rotated, stretched and erased like other objects. Often you need to modify a dimension string by adjusting the location of the dimension line or moving the dimension points to a new position. You can now do this, to some degree, with the DIMTEDIT command. But if you have stacked dimensions or need to change the size of an object and want the dimension string to reflect the new size, using the STRETCH command is your best bet. However, because you must use a crossing window, it is easy to choose objects other than what you wish to stretch. The simplest method to modify dimension objects is to use object grips.

As you discovered in Chapter 11, "Editing with Grips," every object has specific grip points that can be used as base points for performing five types of editing: stretching, moving, rotating, scaling, and mirroring. With respect to dimension objects, the grip points are easily selected and don't need to involve any other objects other than the dimension you are modifying. Figure 18.34 shows drawing 18DWG01, with the five grip points used in all linear associative dimensions and the three grip points used to edit all radial dimensions. The grips are annotated in the order in which the dimension elements were created.

**Fig. 18.34**
The grip points of an associative dimension.

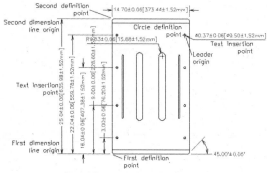

Adjustable Proximity Switch Bracket
Zoom Factor = .5:1

Using the associative dimension grip points and Stretch edit mode, you can quickly edit any dimension location. To move the position of the dimension text, select the text grip point and use the Stretch edit mode to reposition the text. To reposition the dimension line, select one of the grip points at either end of the dimension line and use Stretch edit mode to move the dimension line location. Finally, to change the length of the dimension, you can select either of the grip points at the end of the extension lines and use Stretch edit mode to reposition their definition point location. If the dimension text has not been overridden, the value for the new location is displayed.

### Tutorial: Editing Associative Dimensions

This tutorial covers the editing tools that AutoCAD provides for working with Associative dimensions. The tutorial demonstrates how to use these tools to add new text, change existing text, move dimensions, and dimension text. The tutorial guides you through examples using the commands that were covered in this section. This tutorial uses the drawing 18DWG01, as it was last modified. Figure 18.35 shows the drawing and identifies the dimensions that will be edited.

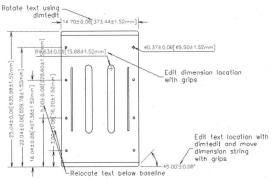

Adjustable Proximity Switch Bracket
Zoom Factor = .5:1

**Fig. 18.35**
Bracket with dimensions to be edited identified.

**V**

**Advanced Drawing**

The first eight steps cover editing and adding dimension text values with DDEDIT and EDIT MTEXT. Steps 11 through 16 show you how to relocate and rotate dimension text within the dimension lines using the DIMTEDIT options. The last seven steps cover moving dimensions and text using Object Grips. Follow these steps to edit the dimensions:

1. Open the sample drawing C:\UAW13\18DWG01.

2. Click the Edit Text button on the Edit Polyline fly-out of the Modify floating toolbar.

3. At the `<Select a TEXT or ATTDEF object>/Undo:` prompt, pick the diameter dimension 0.37, in the upper-right corner of the drawing.

4. AutoCAD opens the Edit MText dialog box. Go to the second line by moving your cursor to the end of the first line and pressing Enter. Once at the second line, type **drill hole through (6 places)**.

5. Click OK on the Edit MText dialog box. AutoCAD adds the new line of text below the original dimension. Refer to figure 18.36 to see the new text.

6. At the `<Select a TEXT or ATTDEF object>/Undo:` prompt, pick the angular dimension 45.00 degrees that is in the lower-right corner of the drawing.

7. AutoCAD once again opens the Edit MText dialog box. This time, delete the origin value represented by <>. Replace it with a value of **30 degrees**, typing over the existing value.

8. Click OK on the Edit MText dialog box. AutoCAD replaces the origin line of text. Press Enter to end the DDEDIT command.

9. Click the Center button on the Home fly-out of the Dimensioning floating toolbar.

10. At the `Select objects:` prompt, pick the angular dimension 30 Degrees again and press Enter. AutoCAD places the dimension between the angle extension lines.

11. Click the Rotate button on the Home fly-out of the Dimensioning floating toolbar.

12. At the `Select dimension:` prompt, pick the horizontal dimension 14.70 at the top of the bracket.

13. At the `Enter text angle:` prompt, type **5** and press Enter. AutoCAD rotates the dimension text 5 degrees between the dimension lines. Type **u** and press Enter to undo this change.

14. At the `Command:` prompt, type **dimtedit** and press Enter.

15. At the `Select dimension:` prompt, pick one of the vertical dimensions at the left of the bracket labeled "Relocate text below baseline."

16. At the `Enter text location (Left/Right/Home/Angle):` prompt, turn on ORTHO mode by pressing the F8 key. Pick a point below the vertical dimension extension baseline. AutoCAD relocates the dimension text below the baseline, spacing it according to the dimension's style settings.

17. This step repeats the previous result, only this time use object grips to accomplish the same dimension text move. Select the other vertical dimension; this should turn on the Object Grips option.

18. Pick the grip that is located in the middle of the text string.

**19.** At the `<Stretch to point>/Base point/Copy/Undo/eXit:` prompt, pick
a point below the baseline, as you did in step 16. Just as with the
DIMTEDIT command, AutoCAD relocates the dimension text below
the baseline, spacing it according to the dimension's style settings.

**20.** Repeat step 19, relocating the angular dimension this time. Pick the
dimension text again and pick a new point to the right of the current
text location. Notice how the extension lines extend as you drag the
text further to the right. Also notice that the object grips remain active
until you press Enter.

**21.** This step relocates the radius dimension R0.63 and its dimension string.
Pick the dimension to activate the object grips.

**22.** Pick the grip that is located in the middle of the text string.

**23.** At the `<Stretch to point>/Base point/Copy/Undo/eXit:` prompt, pick a
point that is to the right of the bracket, where the text will not be on
the part. Turn off the ORTHO mode by pressing the F8 key again. Now
you can select a point that is both to the right of the bracket and below
the other radial dimension (see fig. 18.36).

Use the ZOOM and PAN commands so the entire drawing can be seen. See
figure 18.36 to see the changes you made during the Associative Dimensions
tutorial. Leave this drawing open for the next tutorial. If you don't plan to try
the next tutorial (Adding Leaders and Annotations) save the drawing and exit
AutoCAD.

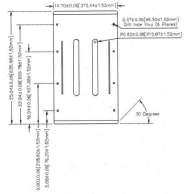

Adjustable Proximity Switch Bracket
Zoom Factor = .5:1

**Fig. 18.36**
Bracket after
dimensions are
edited using
associative
dimension editing
commands.

**V**

**Advanced Drawing**

# Additional Dimensioning Features

In addition to all of the dimensioning commands for finding lengths, angles, diameters, and radii of the elements in your drawing, AutoCAD also includes two commands that provide information for the objects in your drawing. The LEADER command is used to enter notes about drawing elements, and then to place a point used to show to which drawing element the note applies. The TOLERANCE command is used to add a marker indicating geometric tolerances used in the machining of parts. Each of these commands is discussed in the following sections.

## Oblique Dimensions

The OBLIQUE command is an option of the DIMEDIT command, which allows you to change the appearance of a dimension string. By selecting a dimension string you are given the option of specifying an oblique angle. This angle alters the angle of the extension lines on the dimension string you select, making them appear oblique. Figure 18.37 shows an example of a horizontal dimension string before and after using the OBLIQUE command. To access the OBLIQUE command:

- Click the Dimension Styles button on the Dimensioning floating toolbar. Move your digitizer to the second button on the fly-out menu.

- At the Command: prompt, type **dimedit** and press Enter.

The OBLIQUE command only has two prompts, which are described as follows:

- At the Select objects: prompt, select the dimension string that you want to make oblique.

- At the Enter obliquing angle (RETURN for none): prompt, enter a value for the obliquing angle. You can also specify two points that represent the angle you want to apply to the dimension string. AutoCAD considers the angle you enter to be relative to the dimension string you select. So if you select a dimension with extension lines that were drawn at 90 degrees and want them to oblique 3 degrees to the right you would enter an angle of 87 degrees. Figure 18.37 demonstrates this.

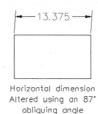

Horizontal dimension

Horizontal dimension
Altered using an 87°
obliquing angle

**Fig. 18.37**

An example of
two horizontal
dimension strings
with one having
a 87 degree
obliquing angle
applied using
the OBLIQUE
command.

## Leaders

Notes are a common part of any drawing you create. Often you use a note to
call out a feature of importance or to remind the fabricator of certain features
that must be field-verified. To create notes in your drawing, use the DTEXT
command to create the Text object. Use lines and solids to create a pointer
to the feature to which you are drawing attention. The preferred method,
though, is to use the LEADER command. In past releases of AutoCAD the
leader elements were all separate objects. In AutoCAD 13 all the elements
that make up a leader, except for the text, are handled as one object. Text
objects are still considered separate objects. To access the LEADER command:

- Click the Leader button on the Dimensioning floating toolbar.

- At the Command: prompt, type **leader** and press Enter.

The options and command prompts for the LEADER command are as follows:

- At the From point: prompt, select the starting point from which the
  leader will be drawn. Typically, this points to the object that is to be
  annotated.

- At the To point: prompt, select a point to serve as the endpoint of the
  first segment of the leader. This point often determines where the text
  is located. It also can serve as a definition point for many of the new
  features available with the LEADER command.

- At the To point (Format/Annotation/Undo)<Annotation>: prompt, continue to add leader vertices, press Enter to accept the default option
  annotation, or select one of the other options shown in parentheses.

The Annotation option and its commands are covered here.

- Pressing Enter at the previous prompt accepts the default option, Annotation. At the Annotation (or RETURN for options): prompt, enter text
  or press Enter for the list of annotation options. If you enter text, the

second line you create will have the prompt `MText:`, which allows you to keep entering additional lines of text. Press Enter twice to end the MText option. AutoCAD draws a "hook" line; if the leader angle is greater than 15 degrees, this line acts as a pointer to the text string. The text is then entered based on current text style and annotation settings. Multiple lines of text are created as paragraphs; they are located vertically centered and horizontally aligned based on the x-axis location of the last two vertices of the leader.

◀ See "Entering Text with MTEXT," p. 475

■ Pressing Enter at the previous prompt displays the `Tolerance/Copy/Block/None/<Mtext>:` prompt. The options for this prompt are as follows.

   • Begin typing text to accept the default MText. This has the same effect as entering text at the previous prompt.

   • Type **n** and press Enter to use the None option. This option draws a leader without any annotation.

   • Type **b** and press Enter to use the Block option. The Block option allows you to *insert* a block at the end of the leader line. This option uses the same prompts as the INSERT command. Refer to Chapter 23, "Using Symbols and XRefs," for information on using the INSERT command and BLOCKS.

■ Type **c** and press Enter to use the Copy option. The Copy option allows you to copy objects such as text, MText, control frames with geometric tolerances, or a block to the end of the leader. The command prompt is `Select an object:`. Picking the object automatically moves it to the end of the leader. How the object is located depends on the object and current dimension variable settings.

■ Type **t** and press Enter to use the Tolerance option. The Tolerance option allows you to create a control frame that contains geometric tolerances. This option uses the Symbol dialog box (see fig. 18.38). See "Geometric Tolerances," later in this chapter for a complete description of the dialog box. Once you have completed the geometric tolerance, the LEADER command ends.

**Fig. 18.38**

The Symbol dialog box, used to add geometric tolerances.

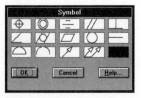

Figure 18.39 shows examples of the Leader Annotation options.

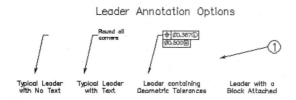

Leader Annotation Options

Typical Leader with No Text    Typical Leader with Text    Leader containing Geometric Tolerances    Leader with a Block Attached

**Fig. 18.39**
Leader Annotation options.

The FORMAT option and its commands are covered below. These commands allow you to format the leader. You can access these options as long as you are drawing leader segments. Once you begin entering text they are no longer available.

- Type **f** and press Enter at the previous `To point (Format/Annotation/ Undo)<Annotation>:` prompt to display the leader format options, `Spline/STraight/Arrow/None/ <Exit>:`. Press Enter to execute the default and return you to the previous prompt.

    Type **n** and press Enter to use the None option. This option draws a leader without any arrowhead.

    Type **a** and press Enter to use the Arrow option. This option draws a leader with an arrowhead at the starting point. The arrowhead set in the current dimension style will be drawn.

    Type **st** and press Enter to use the Straight option. This option draws a leader with straight line segments.

    Type **s** and press Enter to use the Spline option. This option draws a leader using a spline in place of straight line segments. The spline passes through the definition points created at each vertex of the leader lines.

Figure 18.40 shows examples of the Leader Format options.

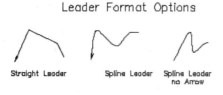

Leader Format Options

Straight Leader    Spline Leader    Spline Leader no Arrow

**Fig. 18.40**
Examples of different Leader Format options.

**V**

**Advanced Drawing**

The UNDO command is the last option on the `To point (Format/Annotation/Undo) <Annotation>:` prompt. Type **u** at the prompt to remove the last vertex point selected for the leader line. After removing the vertex, AutoCAD continues with the `To point (Format/Annotation/Undo) <Annotation>:` prompt.

### Tutorial: Adding Leaders

This tutorial demonstrates how to use the command to add annotations to your drawing. The tutorial also guides you through examples of three Leader options. The tutorial uses drawing 18DWG01. Figure 18.41 shows the drawing with the leaders that are to be added. As with all of the tutorials in this chapter, the exact object locations are not important; focus on the steps used to create the leader. Follow these steps to add the annotations:

**Fig. 18.41**
Bracket
with leader
annotations.

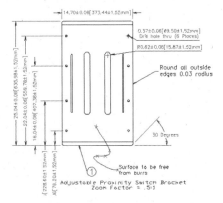

Adjustable Proximity Switch Bracket
Zoom Factor = .5:1

1. Open the sample drawing C:\UAW13\18DWG01.

2. Click the Leader button on the Dimensioning floating toolbar. Begin by drawing the spline leader at the bottom of the bracket.

3. At the `From point:` prompt, pick the start point of the leader.

4. At the `To point:` prompt, pick the first vertex point on the spline leader. The vertices are represented by an x on the spline.

5. At the `To point (Format/Annotation/Undo)<Annotation>:` prompt, type **f** and press Enter to access the Format options.

6. At the `Spline/STraight/Arrow/None/<Exit>:` format prompt, type **s** and press Enter to use a spline leader format. AutoCAD turns the first leader segment to a spline and returns you to the previous prompt.

7. At the `To point (Format/Annotation/Undo)<Annotation>`: prompt, type **f** and press Enter to access the Format options again.

8. At the `Spline/STraight/Arrow/None/<Exit>`: prompt, type **n** and press Enter to use the None option. AutoCAD removes the arrow at the start of the leader and returns you to the previous prompt.

9. At the `To point (Format/Annotation/Undo)<Annotation>`: prompt, pick the second vertex point on the spline leader. Repeat this step three more times, picking the remaining vertices on the leader. Press Enter when you are done picking points.

10. At the `Annotation (or RETURN for options)`: prompt, type **surface to be free** and press Enter to start a new line of text. AutoCAD draws the hook line and adds the text.

11. At the `MText`: prompt, type **from burrs**. and press Enter. AutoCAD adds the last line of text.

12. At the `MText`: prompt, press Enter to end the command. (This is the last step of the spline leader example.)

13. Click the Leader button on the Dimensioning floating toolbar to draw the conventional leader located on the right edge of the bracket.

14. At the `From point`: prompt, pick the start point of the leader. AutoCAD draws an arrow to signify the starting point of the leader.

15. At the `To point`: prompt, pick the first vertex point of the straight leader. This is also the only segment of the leader.

16. At the `To point (Format/Annotation/Undo)<Annotation>`: prompt, press Enter because the previous point was also the last. This forwards you to the annotation options.

17. At the `Annotation (or RETURN for options)`: prompt, type **round all outside** and press Enter to start a new line of text. AutoCAD draws the hook line and adds the text.

18. At the `MText`: prompt, type **edges 0.03 radius** and press Enter. AutoCAD adds the last line of text.

19. At the `MText`: prompt, press Enter to end the command. This concludes the conventional straight leader example.

**20.** Click the Leader button on the Dimensioning floating toolbar to draw a straight leader with a block attached to it. This leader is located at the bottom of the bracket next to the spline leader.

**21.** At the From point: prompt, pick a start point for the leader. AutoCAD draws an arrow to signify the starting point of the leader.

**22.** At the To point: prompt, pick the first vertex point of the straight leader. This also is the only segment for this leader.

**23.** At the To point (Format/Annotation/Undo)<Annotation>: prompt, press Enter because the previous point selected will also serve as the last point. Pressing Enter also forwards you to the default option, Annotation.

**24.** At the Annotation (or RETURN for options): prompt, press Enter to move to the annotation options prompt.

**25.** At the Tolerance/Copy/Block/None/<Mtext>: prompt, type **b** to initiate the Block option. This starts the same series of prompts that the INSERT command uses.

**26.** At the Block name (or ?): prompt, type **item** and press Enter to use a block that has already been created. The block represents an item balloon, often used to identify parts in an assembly.

**27.** At the Insertion point: prompt, type **end** to use the ENDpoint object snap. Select the endpoint of the leader segment.

**28.** At the of X scale factor <1> / Corner / XYZ: prompt, press Enter to accept the default value of 1.

**29.** Do the same at the Y scale factor (default=X): and Rotation angle <0>: prompts. AutoCAD places the block at the endpoint of the leader and ends the command.

Figure 18.41, which you have been referencing, should be similar to the drawing you completed during the Leader Dimensions tutorial. This drawing is not used for the next tutorial. You can save the drawing before the next tutorial or exit AutoCAD to reuse the drawing.

## Geometric Tolerances

Earlier in this chapter you were introduced to tolerance as a simple maximum and or minimum distance that is one of the dimension variables. The TOLER-ANCE command refers to geometric tolerancing. Geometric tolerancing is used to describe the limit that a part's surface, location, orientation, and runout may deviate from an ideal or perfect geometry. This method is useful when describing the relationship between multiple objects, surfaces, or parts.

Unlike the tolerance dimension variable, a geometric tolerance is added to a drawing using a *feature control frame*. The frame is made up of a series of boxes that hold the various geometric symbols and values that describe the material's form, location, or runout. See figure 18.42 for an annotated description of a feature control frame.

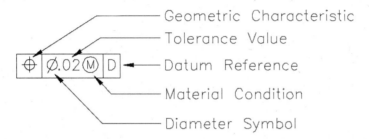

**Fig. 18.42**
The geometric tolerance feature control frame.

> **Note**
>
> You also can place a geometric tolerance into your drawing using the LEADER command.

### Geometric Characteristics

As mentioned in the introduction, geometric tolerances are made up of a variety of symbols and values. This section covers the different elements that make a geometric tolerance control frame.

- Figure 18.43 lists the available geometric characteristic symbols. These symbols appear in the first box of the control frame. They are used to tell the designer to which characteristic the tolerance applies.

**Fig. 18.43**
The available
geometric
tolerance symbols.

| | CHARACTERISTIC | SYMBOL |
|---|---|---|
| FORM | Straightness | —— |
| | Flatness | ▱ |
| | Roundness (Circularity) | ○ |
| | Cylindricity | ⌀ |
| PROFILE | Profile of a line | ⌒ |
| | Profile of a surface | ⌓ |
| ORIENTATION | Angularity | ∠ |
| | Perpendicularity | ⊥ |
| | Parallelism | // |
| LOCATION | Position | ⊕ |
| | Concentricity | ◎ |
| | Symmetry | ⩵ |
| RUNOUT | Circular runout | ⟍ |
| | Total runout | ⟍⟍ |

---

**Note**

The control frame components are set by the following system variables:

| | |
|---|---|
| DIMCLRE | Sets the control frame color |
| DIMCLRT | Sets the color of the tolerance text |
| DIMGAP | Sets the gap between the feature control frame and the text |
| DIMTXT | Controls the size of the tolerance text |
| DIMTXSTY | Sets the style of the tolerance text |

---

■ The second box of the control frame contains the tolerance amount followed by the material condition. AutoCAD offers three different types of material conditions. Maximum Material Condition (the symbol M or MMC) is used to represent the *maximum* amount of material permitted by the tolerance size for the specified characteristic. For holes, slots, and other internal features, it means the *minimum* allowable sizes. For objects like shafts, tabs, and other external features, the Material Condition applies to the maximum allowable sizes. Least Material Condition (the symbol L or LMC) defines the least amount of material permitted by the tolerance size. It affects objects in the opposite manner as MMC. The designation Regardless of Feature Size (RFS), represented by the symbol S, means that a form or positional tolerance must be met irrespective of where the feature lies within its size tolerance.

■ A frame with an enclosed letter identifies a datum (see fig. 18.44). The references are specific points, planes, or axes from which dimensions are verified. AutoCAD allows for as many as three datum references for each material feature. Although all of the datum objects in our example are planes, a datum also can be a point of revolution as in the case of a cylindrical part.

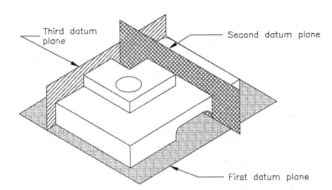

Third datum plane

Second datum plane

First datum plane

**Fig. 18.44**
Datum planes help identify the geometric tolerance.

■ This feature control is noted by the letter P and is inserted in a box just below the primary tolerance information. This type of tolerance is recommended where variations in perpendicularity of threaded holes or press fit holes may cause bolts or pins to interfere with mating parts.

### Tutorial: Creating a Geometric Tolerancing Control Frame

This tutorial shows you how to build a geometric tolerancing control frame. Throughout the tutorial, unless you are told otherwise, you can select symbols and enter values that are used in your application. After you have finished you should have an understanding of how AutoCAD creates control frames and inserts geometric tolerance symbols in them. You can use the sample drawing 18DWG01 for this exercise; the changes you make will not be saved. Follow the steps outlined below to construct the geometric tolerance control frame.

1. Open the sample drawing C:\UAW13\18DWG01.

2. Begin the process of building a geometric tolerance by choosing the Tolerance button from the Dimensioning toolbar. Again, if the Dimensioning toolbar is not currently visible, you can find it in the Tools pulldown menu under the Toolbars cascading menu. You also can enter **tolerance** at the command line.

3. You should now see the Symbol dialog box, as shown in figure 18.45. Choose the appropriate geometric symbol to begin your first tolerance line.

V

Advanced Drawing

**Fig. 18.45**
The Symbol dialog box, used to add geometric tolerances.

4. Now that you have selected a geometric symbol, enter the rest of the tolerance information into the Geometric Tolerance dialog box, shown in figure 18.46.

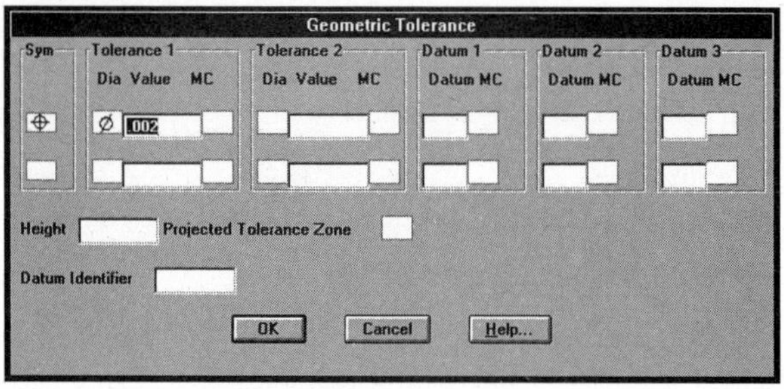

**Fig. 18.46**
The Geometric Tolerance dialog box, used to enter tolerance information.

5. Select the Dia or Diameter box to insert the diameter symbol, if necessary.

6. Enter the first tolerance amount in the Value box.

7. Choose the Material Condition symbol. Figure 18.47 shows the Material Condition dialog box and the symbols from which to select.

**Fig. 18.47**
The Material Condition dialog box displaying the optional symbols.

8. Now you can add an additional tolerance value, and as many as three datum references.

9. The second line of tolerance information is provided for you to create a composite tolerance. Enter all information the same as in the first line.

10. The last three fields allow you to define an optional Projected Tolerance Zone.

**11.** Finally, AutoCAD asks you where to place your completed geometric tolerance control frame. Pick a point on the drawing where AutoCAD can create the control frame. If you created a composite tolerence with three datum references and a projected tolerance zone, it might look like the one in figure 18.48.

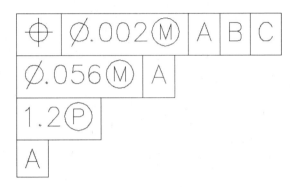

**Fig. 18.48**
A completed geometric tolerance.

V

**Advanced Drawing**

# From Here...

For more details about getting information out of your drawings and sharing that data with other people, see the following chapters:

- Chapter 22, "Getting Information from Your Drawing," shows you how to access other information in your drawing file.

- Chapter 24, "Working with Attributes," explains how to add intelligence to your drawings with attributes and blocks, then pass the data along to others.

- Chapter 36, "Exchanging Data with Windows Applications," shows you how to exchange the AutoCAD with other Windows applications using OLE and DDE.

# On Your Own

In this tutorial, use the commands introduced throughout this chapter. Dimension the proximity switch bracket shown in figure 18.49 (sample drawing C:\UAW13\18DWG04). Figure 18.50 represents the finished bracket.

**Fig. 18.49**
A proximity switch
bracket to be
dimensioned.

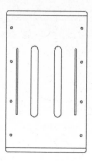

Hints:

1. Use DDIM to set your dimension variables before you start
   dimensioning.

2. Use running object snaps (OSNAP) of ENDpoint and MIDpoint to
   select definition points for dimension strings.

3. Complete the dimensions in the sequence that have been presented
   throughout the chapter.

**Fig. 18.50**
A dimensioned
proximity switch
bracket.

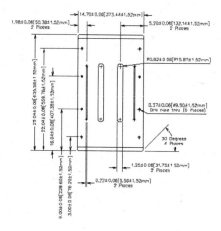

# Chapter 19

# Using Polylines

Polylines are one of AutoCAD's most versatile objects. Polylines can replace some of AutoCAD's more basic objects—lines, arcs, solids, traces—and combine characteristics of all four into a single object. Polylines are so flexible that AutoCAD itself uses them to draw polygons and donuts when you use the POLYGON and DONUT commands. Also, polylines are so complex that they require their own command to edit them.

This chapter shows you how to do the following tasks:

- Draw a polyline with PLINE

- Draw a polyline with BOUNDARY

- Edit a polyline with PEDIT

V

Advanced Drawing

## Drawing Polylines (PLINE)

You use the PLINE command to draw polylines. When you call the PLINE command, AutoCAD presents many different command options and even suboptions. They may seem overwhelming at first, but with the help of this chapter, you'll see that each option, when taken by itself, is easy to understand.

▶ See "Creating 3D Polylines (3DPOLY)," p. 808

A *polyline* is a single object composed of any number of connected straight (line) and curved (arc) segments. You can assign widths to polylines to create wide and tapered segments. You can use polylines in place of lines, traces, solids, and, to a certain extent, arcs. You can also draw lines and arcs and convert them to polylines later. Figure 19.1 shows a polyline that contains line and arc segments.

> **Note**
>
> Polylines are very useful when drawing closed areas or when line width is required. However, these added features do require more space in the drawing database. This additional space may become a factor in large drawings. If this is a concern, polylines can be exploded, returning them to lines and arcs.

**Fig. 19.1**

Polylines can be composed of line and arc segments.

You may use one of the following methods to initiate the PLINE command:

- Type **pline** at the command line.

- Choose the Polyline flyout then the PLINE button from the Draw toolbar.

To draw a polyline, follow these steps:

1. Select the PLINE button from the Draw toolbar.

> **Note**
>
> If the Draw toolbar isn't visible, access it by choosing the Tools menu and selecting the Toolbars option. The PLINE button also has a fly-out bar.

   AutoCAD prompts you to pick a starting point for the polyline.

2. After you pick the starting point, AutoCAD displays a list of command options.

   If you draw in response to the default <Endpoint of line:> prompt, you see that, so far, drawing polylines is just like drawing lines. AutoCAD prompts you to keep picking points and draws straight segments between them. If you press Enter at an <Endpoint of line:> prompt, the command ends, leaving the polyline on-screen and AutoCAD at the Command: prompt.

It is important to know the major difference between lines and polylines.

Single objects such as lines are used together but are not connected. Polylines, on the other hand, are connected, forming one complex object. If you were to draw a box using four lines, the box itself would not be recognized as a group. Any change to the box would require four separate object selections in order to edit it. However, if you draw the box using polylines, it becomes one object and is easily manipulated.

Polylines don't need to contain just straight line segments. To draw a polyline with some curves, use the PLINE command, pick a starting point, and enter **a** at the prompt:

```
Arc/Close/Halfwidth/Length/Undo/Width/<Endpoint of line>:
```

You see a new set of command options—those used to generate polyline arcs:

```
Angle/CEnter/Close/Direction/Halfwidth/Line/Radius/Second
    pt/Undo/Width/<Endpoint of Arc>:
```

As you drag the crosshairs around, AutoCAD displays prospective arc segments on-screen. When you like what you see, pick the point where you want the arc to end. AutoCAD continues to prompt for the next arc endpoint until you enter **l** to begin drawing line segments again, or press Enter to exit the command.

> **Note**
>
> Note that as you draw multiple arc segments, they always remain tangent to each other unless you invoke the Direction option which breaks the string of tangent arcs.

## Polyline Line Options

The PLINE command features options you can use when you make polylines. These features are in the form of quick single letter options you enter on the command line. You can use some of the arc segment options to accurately specify points on the arc. The next sections describe additional options that apply to all polylines, whether created with lines, arcs, or both.

### Close

The Close option automatically completes the polyline by connecting the last endpoint that you selected with the polyline's first point, and then ends the command.

You should always close a polyline that ends where it began, particularly if the polyline is wider than the default of 0. AutoCAD draws a clean corner there. If you leave the polyline open, AutoCAD leaves a notch at the coincident start point and endpoint (see fig. 19.2). AutoCAD also fits curves differently on open and closed polylines.

**Fig. 19.2**

If you don't close polylines that begin and end at the same point, AutoCAD leaves a notch at that point if the polyline has a width greater than 0.

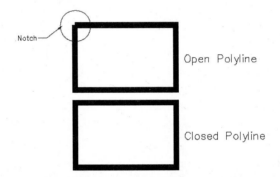

### Halfwidth

Halfwidth lets you specify half the total width of the polyline (default is 0). AutoCAD prompts you for the starting and ending halfwidth. The next polyline segment drawn is double the width you entered. If you entered two different values for beginning and ending halfwidth you get a tapered line or arc segment. Halfwidth can be changed at any time while you draw your polyline.

> **Note**
>
> Polylines with a <u>W</u>idth or <u>H</u>alfwidth greater than zero are filled in solid. The visibility of this solid fill is controlled by the FILLMODE variable. If FILLMODE = 1 solid fills are visible. If FILLMODE = 0 then only the outline of the polyline is visible. If you change this variable you'll have to REGEN the drawing to see the change.

### Length

The Length option prompts you for the length of the next straight polyline segment and draws it in the same direction as the previous segment. If you use the <u>L</u>ength option while drawing polyline arcs, AutoCAD draws a straight segment tangent to the previous arc.

> **Note**
>
> The <u>L</u>ength option doesn't appear when drawing polyline arc segments. You must return to the <u>L</u>ine option and then select <u>L</u>ength to create a line tangent to the previous arc.

### Undo

<u>U</u>ndo removes the last segment that you drew from the polyline. You can use <u>U</u>ndo to remove an entire polyline one segment at a time as long as you don't end the command.

### Width

<u>W</u>idth allows you to draw wide polylines and is another feature that differentiates polylines from lines. For all practical purposes <u>W</u>idth and <u>H</u>alfwidth have the same effect on a polyline. The only difference is that when <u>W</u>idth is selected, the number you entered is not doubled. When you select the <u>W</u>idth option, AutoCAD prompts:

```
Starting width <0.0000>:
```

If you entered .1 for the starting width, the next prompt would read:

```
Ending width <0.1000>:
```

The two don't need to be equal, so you can draw segments that taper. You can apply width to both straight line and arc segments. Figure 19.3 shows a polyline with various widths.

> **Note**
>
> Use the PLINEWID system variable to preset the default polyline width.
>
>     Command: **plinewid**
>
>     New value for PLINEWID <0.0000>;

**Fig. 19.3**

You can assign variable widths to AutoCAD's polylines.

## Polyline Arc Options

Many of the polyline options such as <u>W</u>idth, <u>U</u>ndo, and <u>H</u>alfwidth apply to both line and arc segments. The following options are unique to polyline arcs and are used specifically when drawing arc segments.

### Angle

This option is used to specify the included (inside) angle of an arc segment (see fig. 19.4). The angle begins at the start point of the arc and is completed using one of three methods, Center/Radius/<Endpoint>:. If Radius is chosen to set the second arc point, AutoCAD additionally prompts for Direction of chord <current>:.

> **Note**
>
> If a positive number is entered for the angle, the arc will be drawn counterclockwise. Entering a negative number produces a clockwise arc.

**Fig. 19.4**

A polyline arc can be described using the included angle and the center point.

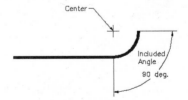

### CEnter

<u>CE</u>nter creates a polyline arc segment by specifying a center point. Once a center point has been specified, AutoCAD prompts Angle/Length/<End

Point>:. If you choose <u>A</u>ngle, AutoCAD prompts you for the included angle. Just like the <u>A</u>ngle option in the previous section, a negative angle produces a clockwise arc and a positive angle (<default>) draws your arc counterclockwise. Choosing the Length option allows you to specify the length of the coordinates.

### Direction
This option allows you to change the starting direction of the arc by choosing a point in the direction you want the arc to go. It's usually used when you don't want a series of tangent arcs. An example would be a scalloped tree line on a Civil Engineering plan.

### Radius
To draw a polyline arc using the <u>R</u>adius option you must first enter a radius distance or choose two points representing that distance. AutoCAD then prompts: `Angle/<End point>:`. Choose the end point and the arc segment will be drawn. If you choose <u>A</u>ngle, AutoCAD prompts: `Direction of chord <current>:`. At this point, you either enter a specific angle or choose a point on the screen and the arc segment is finished.

### Second pt
This method specifies an arc using the three point method similar to the three-point arc described in Chapter 5, "Creating Basic Geometry." Simply choose the second point of the arc and AutoCAD prompts you for the endpoint. The arc passes through both points.

◀ See "Drawing Arcs (ARC)," p. 125

### Tutorial: Drawing Polylines Using the Line and Arc Options
In this tutorial you build a parking lot using a combination of polyline arc and line segments. Open the file 19DWG01 and follow each step. When you are finished, your parking lot should look similar to figure 19.5.

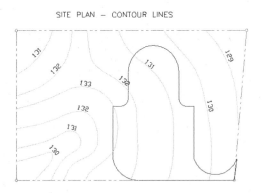

SITE PLAN — CONTOUR LINES

**Fig. 19.5**
Drawing the parking lot using PLINE.

Starting at point 200,50, draw a series of polyline line and arc segments in one continuous stream. Remember, if you get lost or make a wrong selection, you can always <u>U</u>ndo.

**1.** Choose the Polyline tool from the Draw toolbar.

**2.** `From point:` **`200,50`**

This is the absolute coordinate to start from.

Current line width is 0.0.

**3.** `Arc/Close/Halfwidth/Length/Undo/Width/<Endpoint of line>:` **`200,150`**

**4.** `Arc/Close/Halfwidth/Length/Undo/Width/<Endpoint of line>:` `215,150`

**5.** `Arc/Close/Halfwidth/Length/Undo/Width/<Endpoint of line>:` **`a`**

**6.** `Angle/CEnter/CLose/Direction/Halfwidth/Line/Radius/Second pt/Undo/Width/<Endpoint of arc>:`**`ce`**

**7.** `Center point:` **`215,165`**

**8.** `Angle/Length/<End point>:`**`a`**

**9.** `Included angle:` **`90`**

**10.** `Angle/CEnter/CLose/Direction/Halfwidth/Line/Radius/Second pt/Undo/Width/<Endpoint of arc>:`**`l`**

**11.** `Arc/Close/Halfwidth/Length/Undo/Width/<Endpoint of line>:`**`l`**

**12.** `Length of line:` **`50`**

**13.** `Arc/Close/Halfwidth/Length/Undo/Width/<Endpoint of line>:`**`a`**

**14.** `Angle/CEnter/CLose/Direction/Halfwidth/Line/Radius/Second pt/Undo/Width/<Endpoint of arc>:`**`a`**

**15.** `Included angle:` **`-180`**

**16.** `Center/Radius/<Endpoint>`**`r`**

**17.** `Radius:` **`50`**

**18.** `Direction of chord <N>:` **`e`**

**19.** `Angle/CEnter/CLose/Direction/Halfwidth/Line/Radius/Second pt/Undo/Width/<Endpoint of arc>:` **`l`**

**20.** `Arc/Close/Halfwidth/Length/Undo/Width/<Endpoint of line>:` **`l`**

21. Length of line: **50**

22. Arc/Close/Halfwidth/Length/Undo/Width/<Endpoint of line>:**a**

23. Angle/CEnter/CLose/Direction/Halfwidth/Line/Radius/Second pt/Undo/ Width/<Endpoint of arc>:**a**

24. Included angle: **90**

25. Center/Radius/<Endpoint>: **345,150**

26. Angle/CEnter/CLose/Direction/Halfwidth/Line/Radius/Second pt/Undo/ Width/<Endpoint of arc>:**l**

27. Arc/Close/Halfwidth/Length/Undo/Width/<Endpoint of line>:**l**

28. Length of line: **15**

29. Arc/Close/Halfwidth/Length/Undo/Width/<Endpoint of line>: **360,50**

30. Arc/Close/Halfwidth/Length/Undo/Width/<Endpoint of line>:**a**

31. Angle/CEnter/CLose/Direction/Halfwidth/Line/Radius/Second pt/Undo/ Width/<Endpoint of arc>:**s**

32. Second point: **375,30**

33. End point: **445,50**

34. Angle/CEnter/CLose/Direction/Halfwidth/Line/Radius/Second pt/Undo/ Width/<Endpoint of arc>:**l**

35. Arc/Close/Halfwidth/Length/Undo/Width/<Endpoint of line>: **440,10**

36. Arc/Close/Halfwidth/Length/Undo/Width/<Endpoint of line>: **250,10**

37. Arc/Close/Halfwidth/Length/Undo/Width/<Endpoint of line>:**a**

38. Angle/CEnter/CLose/Direction/Halfwidth/Line/Radius/Second pt/Undo/ Width/<Endpoint of arc>:**cl**

Now that you're finished, refer to figure 19.5 to see how you did. Try your own parking lot design using different combinations of the line and arc polylines.

## Tutorial: Drawing Polylines

Now that you're familiar with how to draw polylines and what they can do, add a few to a real drawing. On the disk that accompanies this book is the drawing file 19DWG02, a site drawing. In this tutorial, add some contour lines to the site drawing. Follow these steps:

1. Open 19DWG02. You see a fairly blank drawing with some dashed lines creating a rectangular area.

2. If the layer CONTOUR_LINES is not current, choose Layer Control in the Object Properties toolbar. Click the CONTOUR_LINES layer. If the snap isn't turned on, press the F9 key.

3. Select the Polyline tool button from the Draw toolbar. Then enter your specifications at the prompts that appear.

```
From point: 10,46
Arc/Close/Halfwidth/Length/Undo/Width/<Endpoint of line>: 56,56
Arc/Close/Halfwidth/Length/Undo/Width/<Endpoint of line>: 80,68
Arc/Close/Halfwidth/Length/Undo/Width/<Endpoint of line>: 84,56
Arc/Close/Halfwidth/Length/Undo/Width/<Endpoint of line>: 76,38
Arc/Close/Halfwidth/Length/Undo/Width/<Endpoint of line>: 58,24
Arc/Close/Halfwidth/Length/Undo/Width/<Endpoint of line>: 48,10
Arc/Close/Halfwidth/Length/Undo/Width/<Endpoint of line>:
```

The finished drawing contains nine more polylines. You can draw the rest, using the following list of coordinates. If that gets too tedious, you can skip drawing all the polylines; 19DWG03 is the completed drawing (see fig. 19.6).

**Fig. 19.6**
Drawing site contours with PLINE.

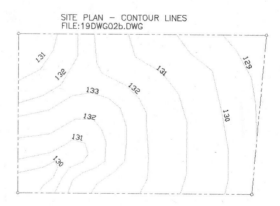

SITE PLAN — CONTOUR LINES
FILE:19DWG02b.DWG

| From point: | Endpoint of line: |
|---|---|
| 10,70 | 70,82; 100,98; 112,106; 134,100; 140,80; 130,66; 106,56; 94,40; 78,10 |
| 10,108 | 70,116; 116,142; 148,142; 164,124; 172,102; 170,68; 154,56; 132,48; 112,34; 104,10 |
| 10,146 | 66,158; 110,184; 144,190; 176,180; 198,162; 210,128; 210,102; 206,68; 188,50; 156,28; 150,18; 146,10 |
| 10,170 | 56,184; 90,204; 120,254; 120,294 |
| 10,210 | 50,230; 74,264; 82,294 |
| 150,294 | 154,244; 164,224; 206,204; 232,180; 246,154; 246,134; 250,76; 248,38; 234,10 |
| 212,294 | 224,254; 274,226; 304,188; 320,138; 320,94; 320,46; 310,14; 308,10 |
| 300,294 | 324,262; 366,230; 384,156; 396,90; 396,36; 390,10 |
| 384,294 | 410,266; 438,218; 446,170; 448,108 |

**V**

**Advanced Drawing**

# Drawing Boundary Polylines (BOUNDARY)

BOUNDARY is a powerful tool that allows you to create a closed polyline or region from a number of unrelated objects. BOUNDARY is very similar to the BHATCH command without the hatching. One use for BOUNDARY is finding the area of irregular objects that may also include curves. Once identified, the resulting polyline can be listed or used with the AREA command to find its area or perimeter.

To access the BOUNDARY command, choose the Boundary tool from the Polygon fly out on the Draw toolbar, or type **boundary** at the command prompt.

Figure 19.7 shows the Boundary Creation dialog box and its options. Object type is the first option that allows you to choose between a polyline or a region.

▶ See "3D Modeling Essentials," p. 807

**Fig. 19.7**

Defining the boundary with the Boundary Creation dialog box.

## Define Boundary Set

AutoCAD, by default, considers all visible objects when evaluating a boundary. This process might become very lengthy on large drawings. To expedite the identification of a boundary, you can specify which objects are to be considered in the boundary analysis. If a boundary set exists, the From Existing Boundary Set option is active.

To define your first boundary set simply accept all the defaults in the dialog box and select the Pick Points button. AutoCAD then prompts you to Select internal point:.

◄ See "Define Boundary Set," p. 496

You may encounter a Boundary Definition Error box that tells you that the point you chose is outside of boundary (see fig. 19.8). This means that you either chose a point outside of any closed geometry or that you have a pre-defined boundary set. The latter possibility can be resolved by selecting the Look at it button to highlight the existing boundary set. To resolve the problem you should choose the From Everything on Screen radio button or Make New Boundary Set.

**Fig. 19.8**

Picking points outside the boundary produces the Boundary selection error message.

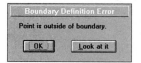

A successful boundary creation process might look something like the third drawing in figure 19.9.

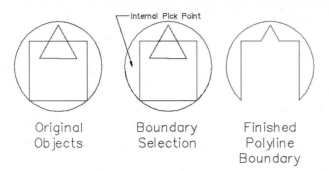

**Fig. 19.9**
Creating a finished
polyline using the
BOUNDARY
command.

## Ray Casting

Sometimes AutoCAD has difficulty specifying the proper boundary because
objects are too close together or too complex. *Ray casting* allows you to
specify the direction in which AutoCAD looks for a boundary. Of the five
options, Nearest is most likely to provide you with the best results. The other
options are shown in figure 19.10. Ray casting is only available when Island
Detection is inactive.

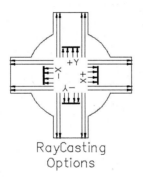

**Fig. 19.10**
Ray casting more
specifically defines
a boundary object.

## Island Detection

Objects that are completely within other bounding objects are considered
islands. When Island Detection is active AutoCAD uses these objects to define
the boundary.

## Boolean Subtract Islands

Using Boolean geometry, AutoCAD deletes or removes areas that are part of
islands from the finished boundary object. It is like taking a piece of dough
and cutting a hole in the center. You actually end up with two objects,
a doughnut and a doughnut hole. But the hole is no longer part of the
doughnut.

### Pick Points

Specifying a point inside the surrounding objects starts the process of defining a boundary. Once AutoCAD has found what it thinks are the edges of the boundary, it highlights those sides so you can evaluate the results. You may choose multiple areas before accepting the final boundary. Remember, boundaries are polylines and can be moved, rotated, and copied just like any other object. This new polyline may be hard to see because it's on top of other objects, so you might want to change them to a different color layer in order to find them.

# Editing Polylines (PEDIT)

Basic AutoCAD editing commands like STRETCH, COPY, and MOVE apply to polylines, but these commands don't give you access to a polyline's unique features. AutoCAD provides a command, PEDIT, specifically designed to edit polylines. With PEDIT, you can fine-tune a polyline, editing down to the vertex level if you want. You can use PEDIT to do the following:

- Convert AutoCAD lines and arcs to polylines

- Open a closed polyline or close an open polyline

- Join lines, arcs, or other polylines to the polyline you are editing

- Change a polyline's width

- Move, add, or remove vertices

- Add or remove curves

To start the PEDIT command, choose the Edit Polyline button on the Modify tool bar. AutoCAD prompts the user to Select polyline:.

You can pick a polyline, line, or arc. If you pick a polyline, AutoCAD displays the PEDIT options:

```
Close/Join/Width/Edit vertex/Fit/Spline/Decurve/
    Ltype gen/Undo/eXit <X>:
```

## Converting a Line or Arc to a Polyline

If you start the PEDIT command and then pick a line or arc, AutoCAD displays this prompt:

```
Object selected is not a polyline.
Do you want to turn it into one? <Y>
```

If you accept the default or type **y**, AutoCAD converts the selected line or arc into a polyline and then displays the PEDIT options.

You can use the PEDIT options to add sections to polylines, open or close them, give the polylines a new width, fit a curve through the polyline's vertices, remove curves, or adjust the polyline's vertices. Each of these operations is discussed in the following sections.

## Joining Polylines (PEDIT Join)

You can join other polylines, lines, and arcs to a polyline with the Join option. The objects that you want to join to the polyline must share the same endpoints before they can be joined to the polyline or to objects already chosen to be joined.

When you enter the Join option on the command line, AutoCAD displays the `Select objects:` prompt. You can continue to select connected objects until you have chosen all that you want to join to the polyline. Press Enter when you're through selecting objects. AutoCAD joins the chosen objects and then reports the number of segments that it added to the polyline. If AutoCAD reports that it added fewer objects than you selected, not all the objects you selected were connected either to the polyline or to one of the other objects that you chose to join to the polyline. Most objects don't join because they have different endpoints, although they may appear to be the same on the screen. Other objects fail to join because they are at a different elevation or plane.

## Closing or Opening a Polyline (PEDIT Close and Open)

If the polyline you're editing is open (that is, it wasn't closed with the PLINE command's Close option when it was created), you can use PEDIT's Close option to close the polyline. Similarly, you can open a closed polyline with PEDIT's Open option.

**V**

**Advanced Drawing**

> **Caution**
>
> If you open a polyline that was closed with the PLINE command's Close option, AutoCAD deletes the last segment of the polyline. This is AutoCAD's normal, though possibly inconvenient, behavior.

**Tip**
If you want to use PEDIT to create tapers or assign variable widths, use the Width option under Edit vertex as discussed in "Editing Polyline Vertices," later in this chapter.

## Setting Polyline Width (PEDIT Width)

With the PEDIT command's Width option, you can assign a constant width to the entire polyline. You can't use this option to make tapering segments or assign variable widths to different parts of the polyline.

## Curving and Decurving Polylines

You have seen how a polyline can contain individual arc segments. AutoCAD also lets you fit mathematically calculated curves across an entire polyline, as well as remove curves and arcs. Figure 19.11 compares a regular straight polyline with the three types of curved polylines you can generate.

**Fig. 19.11**
There are four kinds of polylines: uncurved, fit curved, quadratic, and cubic b-spline.

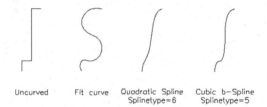

Uncurved    Fit curve    Quadratic Spline    Cubic b-Spline
Splinetype=6    Splinetype=5

### Fitting a Curve (PEDIT Fit)

The PEDIT Fit option draws a smooth curve through all the selected polyline's vertices. At each polyline vertex, Fit creates a new arc segment that is tangent, at its start point, to the endpoint of the previous arc (with the exception of the very first start point, of course, where there is no previous arc to be tangent to). The arc's endpoint is tangent to the next vertex (see fig. 19.12).

You can't directly control how Fit draws the curve; it has no control options of its own. You can, however, use the vertex Move option to move a polyline's vertices and the vertex Tangent option to apply tangent directions to individual vertices, thereby influencing how the curve is drawn. Move and Tangent are discussed in "Editing Polyline Vertices" later in this chapter.

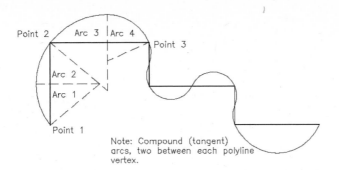

**Fig. 19.12**
Fitting a poly-
line creates two
compound arcs
between each
vertex.

### Unfitting a Curve (PEDIT Decurve)

The Decurve option removes all curves from a polyline, including curves created with PLINE's Arc option, and those that resulted from PEDIT's Fit and Spline options. The curves are replaced with straight line segments. If you accidentally decurve a polyline, you can recover the curves with the PEDIT Undo option.

### Creating a Spline Curve (PEDIT Spline)

Before AutoCAD, when shipbuilders wanted to model the curves of the vessel they were designing, they pounded some pegs into the floor and threaded thin strips of wood around them to generate the required complex curves. By moving the pegs, they could fine-tune their curves, thus perfecting their design. This practice found its way into general mathematical use and, eventually, into computer modeling in the form of spline curves. The pegs came to be called *control points*, which define the curve. AutoCAD can generate splines from polylines with the Spline option, using the vertices of the original, uncurved polyline as the curve's control points. The location of these vertices and their relationship to each other define the path of the resulting curve. This path can be modified by moving the vertices to another location. You can affect the appearance and generation of splines by adjusting the values of three AutoCAD system variables: SPLINESEGS, SPLFRAME, and SPLINETYPE. To get to these variables, type their names at the Command: prompt.

▶ See
"SPLFRAME,"
"SPLINESEGS,"
"SPLINETYPE,"
pp. 1190-1191

The SPLINESEGS variable adjusts the coarseness with which AutoCAD approximates the spline; a lower value means a coarser approximation. A higher value means a better approximation, but it also slows down AutoCAD and makes the drawing file larger. Figure 19.13 shows how three different values—1 (the minimum allowed), 2, and 20—affect the display of the spline. AutoCAD's default value is 8.

**Fig. 19.13**
A higher
Splinesegs value
makes a nicer-
looking curve but
slows performance
and increases file
size.

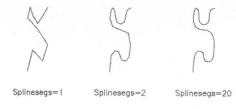

Splinesegs=1      Splinesegs=2      Splinesegs=20

The SPLFRAME setting determines whether the spline frame (that is, the original polyline) displays on-screen. You can change the spline by setting SPLFRAME to 1, regenerating the drawing to see the frame, and then using the STRETCH command or grips to move the frame's vertices. The spline automatically adjusts to the new frame position. Figure 19.14 shows a spline with the frame turned off and turned on.

**Fig. 19.14**
The SPLFRAME
system variable
governs the
display of the
spline frame.

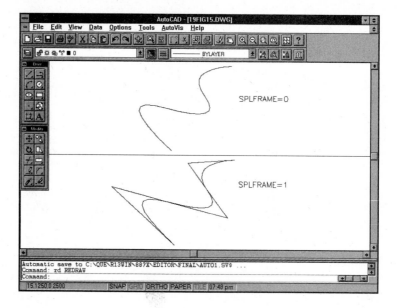

The SPLINETYPE variable accepts only two values, 5 or 6. The default is 6, which causes AutoCAD to generate a cubic b-spline. If you set SPLINETYPE to 5, AutoCAD draws a quadratic b-spline. The practical effect of these settings is that the cubic b-spline is smoother, but the quadratic b-spline more closely follows the frame.

## Adjusting Linetype Generation (PEDIT Ltype gen)

In Chapter 8, "Understanding Linetypes," you learned how to assign different linetypes to objects in your drawings. You saw that if a circle is too small or a line too short, there may not be enough room for AutoCAD to generate the linetype, so the object looks like it's drawn with the continuous linetype. The same can happen with polylines; if the polyline's individual segments are too short, they won't display the linetype. If you draw lines or circles and can't see the linetype, you're pretty much out of luck. If you have drawn a polyline, though, there is a possible remedy. Under default conditions, AutoCAD treats each segment of a polyline as if it were an individual line or arc, applying the linetype to each segment individually. The Ltype gen option lets you override that setting, with AutoCAD applying the linetype to the polyline as a whole rather than to its individual segments. This allows the polyline to display in whatever linetype you have chosen. When you choose Ltype gen, AutoCAD displays the prompt

◀ See "Setting the Linetype," p. 199

```
Full PLINE linetype ON/OFF <Off>:
```

Enter **on** to generate the linetype over the entire polyline. Figure 19.15 shows the difference between Ltype gen OFF and ON for uncurved, fit curved, and splined polylines. You can see that this option is particularly effective with splined polylines.

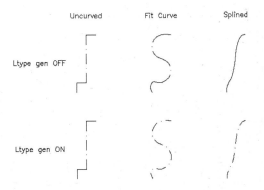

**Fig. 19.15**
If your polyline doesn't look like it was drawn with a continuous linetype, even though you assigned it something else, try turning Ltype gen ON.

## Changing the Last PEDIT (PEDIT Undo)

The PEDIT Undo option allows you to undo your edits to a polyline one step at a time, all the way back to the time you invoked the PEDIT command.

**V**

**Advanced Drawing**

## Tutorial: Creating Splines with PEDIT

Now that you have explored the PEDIT command in some detail, you can put it to use in creating some splines. Use the drawing you began earlier to follow these steps:

1. Open 19DWG02.

2. Choose the Modify toolbar, Edit Polyline fly out.

3. When AutoCAD prompts with `Select polyline:`, select one of the polylines you drew.

4. Enter **s**. AutoCAD fits a spline to the polyline.

5. Press Enter once to exit the PEDIT command and a second time to begin the command again.

   ```
   Repeat steps 2 through 5 for the rest of the polylines in
   the drawing.
   ```

## Editing Polyline Vertices (PEDIT Edit Vertices)

AutoCAD applies the PEDIT options discussed so far to the entire polyline. You also can edit polylines on a vertex-by-vertex basis to apply your edits to individual parts of the polyline. To select these options, pick Edit vertex from the PEDIT options. AutoCAD displays another series of editing options:

```
Next/Previous/Break/Insert/Move/Regen/Straighten/Tangent/
     Width/eXit <N>:
```

Notice a small "x" sitting on the first vertex of the polyline (see fig. 19.16). Press Enter. You should see the "x" move to the next vertex on the polyline. By repeatedly pressing Enter, you can move to any vertex on the polyline and begin editing the polyline anywhere along its length. The rest of this chapter covers the vertex editing options.

**Fig. 19.16**
Recognizing the
current vertex.

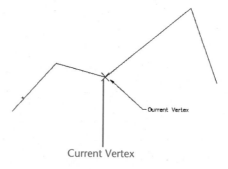

Current Vertex

### Moving the Place Marker (Next and Previous)

As you saw in the preceding section, you can navigate along the polyline by pressing Enter, because the Next option is the default. When you get to the last point on the polyline, you can go back the other direction by selecting the Previous option (of course, in AutoCAD fashion, you just have to type **p**; you don't type the entire word). When you type **n** or **p**, AutoCAD makes that option the default. You can go forward or backward easily by typing **n** or **p** and then pressing Enter repeatedly until you reach the vertex where you want to begin editing.

> **Note**
>
> You may have noticed that, on an open polyline which begins and ends on the same point, Next moves the X all the way to the polyline's starting vertex. On closed polylines, Next stops at the vertex before the starting vertex. What's really happening is that open polylines that start and end at the same place contain coincident vertices at that point. So Next isn't going to the starting vertex; it's going to the ending vertex that lies on top of the starting vertex. Figure 19.17 illustrates the difference.

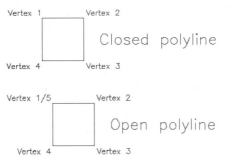

**Fig. 19.17**
Open polylines have one more vertex than closed polylines.

### Breaking a Polyline at a Vertex (Break)

The Break option breaks a polyline at the designated vertex, creating two new endpoints and two new polylines. You can break a polyline at a single vertex, leaving all the original segments of the polyline intact. Or you can break it between two vertices, which removes one or more segments of the polyline.

To use the Break option, start the PEDIT command, pick a polyline, choose Edit vertex, and use Next or Previous to move to the vertex where you want to start the break. Select Break. AutoCAD displays the following options:

```
Next/Previous/Go/eXit <N>:
```

**V**

**Advanced Drawing**

◀ See "Erasing
Parts of Objects
(BREAK),"
p. 269

To break the polyline at the current vertex, select G̲o. To break out a section of the polyline, enter **n** or **p** to move to another vertex, and then enter **g** to break the polyline. You can't break a polyline at its start point or endpoint.

### Moving Vertices (Move)

Sometimes you may want to relocate polyline vertices. The M̲ove option provides that capability. Enter **n** or **p** to get to the vertex you want to move, and then choose the M̲ove option. AutoCAD prompts with

```
Enter new location:
```

Pick the vertex's new location, and AutoCAD moves the vertex there.

### Adding Vertices (Insert)

◀ See "Under-
standing Coor-
dinates and
Units,"
p. 87

With the Insert option, you can add new vertices to the polyline. To add a vertex, use N̲ext or P̲revious to move to a vertex beyond which you want to add a new one. Enter **i** to choose the Insert option. AutoCAD displays the prompt

```
Enter location of new vertex:
```

and stretches a drag line from the current vertex. You can pick a point or use AutoCAD's polar, relative, or absolute point selection methods to specify the location of the new vertex.

### Removing Vertices (Straighten)

The opposite of I̲nsert, S̲traighten removes extra vertices from a polyline. Move the X marker with **n** or **p** to the vertex that marks the beginning of the segment you want to straighten. Enter **s** to select the S̲traighten option. At the prompt

```
Next/Previous/Go/eXit <N>:
```

use N̲ext or P̲revious to move to the vertex that marks the end of the segment you want to straighten. Select G̲o. AutoCAD removes all the vertices that lie between the beginning and ending vertices and draws a single straight segment between them.

### Changing Tangency (Tangent)

The T̲angent option enables you to add a tangent direction, or angle, to a vertex. The PEDIT F̲it option uses the tangent direction when it fits the curve; the curve is tangent to the angle at that point. The tangent angle has no effect on spline-fit curves. You can specify the angle by pointing with your mouse or entering a value with the keyboard.

### Changing Segment Width (Width)

You can use the Width option to assign variable widths to different parts of the polyline. Using <u>N</u>ext or <u>P</u>revious, move to the vertex that begins the segment to which you want to assign width. Enter **w**. AutoCAD asks for a beginning width and then an ending width, just as when you applied widths with the PLINE command. You can see that the <u>E</u>dit vertex <u>W</u>idth option, unlike the PEDIT Width option, allows you to create tapered sections and assign variable widths to different parts of the polyline.

> **Note**
>
> AutoCAD applies the beginning width at the current vertex and the ending width at the next vertex in the direction that you drew the polyline. AutoCAD uses this rule regardless of whether you used Next or Previous to get to the current vertex.

When you finish specifying widths, the polyline doesn't update immediately to show the new widths. You must either exit the <u>E</u>dit vertex mode or use the <u>E</u>dit vertex <u>R</u>egen option to see your new widths.

### Redrawing a Polyline (Regen)

Use the <u>R</u>egen option to update the polyline on-screen, restoring sections of the polyline that appear to be missing. Or use <u>R</u>egen to see new widths that you've applied to the polyline with the <u>E</u>dit vertex <u>W</u>idth option. The <u>R</u>egen option regenerates only the polyline, not the entire drawing.

### Leaving Edit Vertex and PEDIT (eXit)

When you've edited your polyline's vertices, you need to exit from <u>E</u>dit vertex mode. The e<u>X</u>it option serves that purpose, taking you back to the PEDIT options. From there, the PEDIT e<u>X</u>it option (the command's default) lets you end the PEDIT command.

## From Here...

Now that you've learned about polylines, you may want to extend your knowledge by visiting their first cousin, 3D polylines, and their second cousin, polyface meshes. These objects extend the polyline concept into the third dimension and form the foundation for 3D modeling in AutoCAD. You will find more information about these objects and about basic three-dimensional composition in Chapter 28, "3D Modeling Essentials."

V

Advanced Drawing

For more information about lines, arcs, and polyline objects, see the following chapters:

- Chapter 2, "Creating Your First Drawing," shows you how to use the LINE command.

- Chapter 5, "Creating Basic Geometry," presents arcs, rectangles, and polygons.

- Chapter 15, "Advanced Drawing Techniques," shows you how to draw donuts.

## On Your Own

In the following exercise, create the outline of the three views of the fixture shown in figure 19.18 using polylines.

**Fig. 19.18**
Creating a counter bore drawing using polylines.

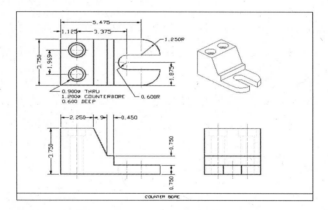

Hints:

1. Create a three-view orthographic sketch of the counter bore, using polylines.

2. Begin by loading a prototype drawing.

3. Center the three views within the border, leaving a 1" space between the views.

# Chapter 20

# Using Multilines

Almost every drafting and design discipline has the need to create multiple lines parallel to one another. Architects represent walls, counters, siding, and trim that are made up of parallel lines. Civil engineers design roadways that show dividing lines, road edges, and curbs. Electrical engineers must draw wiring diagrams and circuit boards made of multiple parallel lines. Multilines are a powerful new feature of AutoCAD Release 13 that addresses these needs. Multilines allow you to create up to 16 parallel lines. These lines are referred to as *elements*. Each element can have its own unique offset, color, and linetype. The MLSTYLE command is used to create different multiline styles and define the properties of each element. To create multilines, based on the style(s) you defined, AutoCAD provides the MLINE command. If you need to edit a multiline, AutoCAD uses the MLEDIT command.

In this chapter, you learn the multiline editing commands and features, including these tasks:

- Using the MLSTYLE command to define a multiline style

- Using the MLINE command to draw multilines

- Using the MLEDIT command to edit multilines

## Defining Multiline Styles (MLSTYLE)

If you do not want to use the default STANDARD multiline style, which consists of two elements, you need to create your own style. It is possible to create a style with up to 16 parallel elements. Each element can be defined with its own color and linetype. Each element of a multiline is located by its own offset distance, which you define. The origin point of the multiline serves as the offset point. The multiline style also controls the background color and end caps of each multiline. The MLSTYLE command allows you to create multiline styles and define their options. You also can display style names; set the current style; load, save, add, and rename styles; or edit their descriptions.

You can access the MLSTYLE command by any of these methods:

- Click the Multiline Style button on the Object Properties toolbar.

- Choose <u>D</u>ata menu, <u>M</u>ultiline Style.

- Enter **mlstyle** at the Command: prompt.

The MLSTYLE command opens a dialog box, as shown in figure 20.1. This dialog box has three areas: Multiline Style, Element Properties, and Multiline Properties. Each of these areas is described in this section.

**Fig. 20.1**
The Multiline Styles dialog box.

The Multiline Style area offers you the capability to work with style names.

- *Current.* This pop-up list displays the current multiline style, along with all the styles currently loaded in the drawing. This allows you to select a new name from the list to make current. If the display contains more than one name, the current style is highlighted.

> **Note**
>
> If you have externally referenced files in your current drawing that include multiline styles, those styles are listed in the pop-up list as well.

- *Name.* Use this edit box to create a new multiline style or rename an existing one. After you have defined the Element and Multiline Properties, enter a style name and then choose the Save button.

> **Note**
>
> AutoCAD stores the multiline style definitions in the multiline library file, ACAD.MLN.

To rename a style, first make it the current style. Next enter the new name in the edit box and choose the Rename button.

> **Note**
>
> You can't rename the default STANDARD multiline style.

You also can use the Name edit box to make a copy of the current style. Make the style you want to copy current, enter a new name, and choose the Save button.

- *Description.* The description edit box allows you to attach up to a 255-character description, including spaces, to the current multiline style.

- *Load.* Choose this button to load a multiline style from the multiline library. Choosing this button opens another dialog box that allows you to specify a library file other than the default ACAD.MLN, if you want. When the library file is opened, select the style you want from those listed on the screen.

- *Save.* Use the Save button to save or copy a multiline style. Refer back to Name.

- *Add.* Choosing this button adds the style name listed in the Name edit box to the Current list of multiline styles available.

- *Rename.* Use this command to rename a multiline style. Refer back to Name.

The Element Properties button opens the Element Properties dialog box, shown in figure 20.2. The options in this dialog box allow you to set the properties of each element in the current multiline style. Set the number of elements and the offset, color, and linetype of each element using this dialog box. Each area is described in more detail:

V

**Advanced Drawing**

**Fig. 20.2**
The Element
Properties dialog
box.

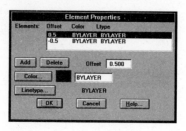

- *Elements.* This window displays all the elements (lines) in the current multiline style. An offset value defines the location of each element, based on this distance, from the multiline origin point. The origin point is considered 0.0. This window also displays the color and linetype properties of each element. Elements in the window are displayed in descending order of their offsets.

- *Add.* Choose this button to add new elements to the current multiline style.

- *Delete.* Choosing this button deletes the highlighted element from the current multiline style.

- *Offset.* In this edit box, you enter the amount of offset desired for the highlighted element. Offset values can be either positive or negative. Refer to figure 20.3 for examples of positive and negative offsets.

**Fig. 20.3**
Negative and
positive element
offsets from the
origin point (0.0).

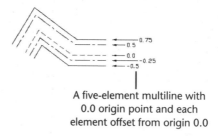

A five-element multiline with
0.0 origin point and each
element offset from origin 0.0

◀ See "Changing
the Layer
Color," p. 181

▶ See "Changing
Color and
Linetype,"
p. 627

- *Color.* Choose this button to assign a color to the highlighted element. When you choose this button or the color swatch, AutoCAD displays the Select Color dialog box.

- *Linetype.* Choosing this button allows you to assign a different linetype to the highlighted element. AutoCAD displays the Select Linetype dialog box. From this dialog box you can select from any of the linetypes currently loaded in the drawing or load the linetype of your choice. For additional information on loading linetypes, refer to Chapter 8, "Understanding Linetypes."

The Multiline Properties button opens the Multiline Properties dialog box, shown in figure 20.4. The options in this dialog box allow you to set properties of the current multiline style. Properties you can set include: display of segment joints, the start and end caps along with their angles, and the background color of the multiline.

**Fig. 20.4**
The Multiline Properties dialog box.

■ *Display joints*. Select this check box to display segment joints at the vertices of each multiline segment. A *joint* is also referred to as a *miter*. See figure 20.5 for examples of a multiline with and without segment joints displayed.

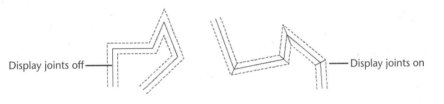

Display joints off

Display joints on

**Fig. 20.5**
Multiline examples of segments with Display joints both off and on.

The Caps area of this dialog box offers several options for controlling and displaying caps at the start and end of multilines. You can select the type of cap you want at those points, as well as specify if you want an arc drawn between pairs of inner elements. These options are described in detail as follows. Refer to figure 20.6 for examples.

■ *Line*. To cap the starting and/or ending segments of a multiline with a line, select these check boxes.

■ *Outer arc*. To cap the starting and/or ending segments of a multiline with an arc, select these check boxes.

■ *Inner arcs*. To create an arc between pairs of inner elements, select these check boxes. If there is an odd number of inner elements, the center element is left unconnected.

**Fig. 20.6**
Multiline cap
examples.

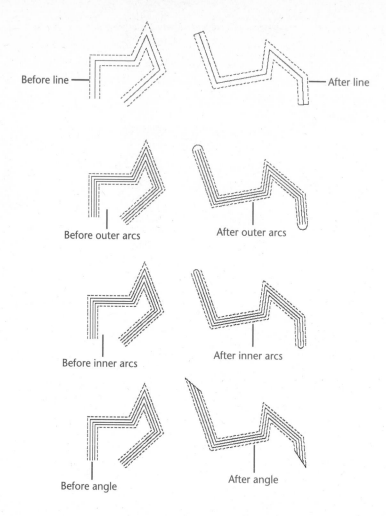

The Fill area of the dialog box allows you to control the background fill of the current multiline and set its color.

- *On.* Select this check box to turn on the background fill option.

- *Color.* When background fill is turned on, use of the Color button is made available; otherwise this option is grayed out. When you select this button or the color swatch, AutoCAD displays the Select Color dialog box.

**Note**

The preview window on the Multiline Style dialog box provides a thumbnail view of the current multiline settings except for color fill.

## Tutorial: Creating Multiline Styles Using the MLSTYLE Command

In this tutorial, you use the MLSTYLE command to create two new multiline styles. The next tutorial uses these styles to expand your understanding of multilines. The tutorials covering multilines use a new sample drawing. Follow these steps:

1. Open the sample drawing C:\UAW13\20DWG01.

2. Click the Mlstyle button on the Object Properties toolbar.

3. Create a new style by first choosing the Element Properties button.

4. Change the offset of the 0.5 highlighted element to **1.00**, by changing the value shown in the Offset edit box.

5. Choose either the Color button or the color swatch to change the color of the highlighted element. Choose the red swatch, from the Standard Colors area or type **red** in the Color edit box. Choose OK to accept your choice.

6. Choose the Linetype button in the Element Properties dialog box to change the linetype of the highlighted element.

7. Set the linetype for this element to CONTINUOUS. Select it from the Loaded Linetypes area of the Select Linetype dialog box or type **continuous** in the Linetype edit box.

   The settings for the first element should now match figure 20.7.

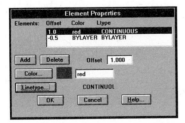

**Fig. 20.7**
The Element Properties dialog box, after the first element properties have been set.

8. Highlight the element –0.5 and repeat steps 4 through 7 to change the properties of this element to 0.00, red, and continuous.

9. This step involves adding a new element to the list. Choose the Add button. A new element should be added to the list and highlighted.

10. Repeat steps 4 through 6 to change the new element's properties to 22.00, red, and hidden. Hidden is not a linetype loaded by default. Follow step 11 to load it into the drawing.

11. Choose the Load button from the Select Linetype dialog box. Choose the linetype HIDDEN from the scrolling window. Hidden should be highlighted after you select it; choose OK to accept your choice.

12. You can now repeat step 7, only select HIDDEN as the linetype.

13. Add one last element for this style, as you did in step 10. This time you can repeat steps 4 through 7 to change the element's properties to 24.0, red, and continuous.

14. Four elements should now be in the list 0.0, 1.0, 22.0, and 24.0. Choose OK to return to the Multiline Styles dialog box.

15. Choose the Multiline Properties button to set properties that are unique to the multiline as a whole. The Multiline Properties dialog box should be displayed on the screen.

16. Select the Display Joints option.

17. In the Caps area of the dialog box, select both the Start and End caps for the Line option.

    Your selections should be the same as in figure 20.8.

**Fig. 20.8**
The Multiline Properties dialog box, after all the options have been set.

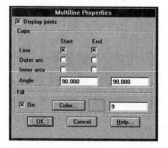

18. Choose OK to return to the Multiline Styles dialog box.

19. Enter the name **COUNTER**, in the Name edit box, replacing STANDARD.

20. Choose the Save button to save the new multiline style you have just defined. The Save multiline style dialog box opens. Choose OK to accept the default ACAD.MLN file name.

21. Choose the Add button to include the new style in the current list of styles loaded in the drawing file.

Your Multiline Styles dialog box should now look like the box displayed in figure 20.9. Notice the new, current style shown in the preview window.

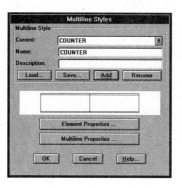

**Fig. 20.9**
The Multiline Styles dialog box, after the new multiline style has been defined.

Now use the commands you have just covered to create another new multiline style. This style is similar to the COUNTER style you just defined.

1. Start by changing the element 1.0 to 2.0 and the linetype from CONTINUOUS to HIDDEN.

2. Next select both the Start and End caps for the Outer arc and Line options.

3. Name the new style ISLAND, save the style (using the Save button), and use the Add button to add it to the current list of loaded multiline styles.

You have now created two new multiline styles that will be used in the following tutorials to create a kitchen layout. Figure 20.10 shows the last style you defined in the preview window.

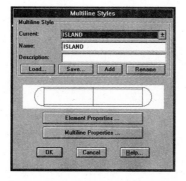

**Fig. 20.10**
The Multiline Styles dialog box, after the ISLAND multiline style has been defined.

If you are going to continue to the next tutorial (Drawing Multilines), leave this drawing open. If you don't plan to try the next tutorial immediately, save this drawing file as you leave AutoCAD. You must complete the preceding tutorial (Creating Multiline Styles), before continuing to the next tutorial.

# Creating Multilines (MLINE)

You are ready to begin using the MLINE command once you have set up a multiline style to represent the objects you are going to draw. As mentioned at the start of this section, multilines have many applications and can be used by practically every design discipline. You can represent walls, counters, siding, trim, roadways with dividing lines, road edges and curbs, or wiring diagrams and circuit boards, just to name a few examples. Multiple parallel lines are part of all these objects.

Access the MLINE command by either of these methods:

- Click the Polyline button on the Draw floating toolbar. While holding down the pick button on your digitizer, move the pointer to the third button on the flyout, Multiline; then release the pick button.

- Enter **mline** at the Command: prompt.

The MLINE command has the following prompts:

- Justification = Top, Scale = 1.00, Style = STANDARD Justification/ Scale/STyle/<From point>: Select the origin point, or starting point, of the multiline or enter an option. The top line of the prompt displays the current multiline's settings.

> **Note**
>
> This command sequence for multiline is similar to the line and polyline command sequences.

- <To point>: Select a To point that will create a multiline segment, using the current multiline style.

- Undo/<To point>: Continue selecting points to create additional multiline segments. Once you have created a multiline segment, you are given the option of undoing it. If the point you just entered is wrong, type **u** at the prompt, to remove the last vertex point on the multiline.

■ `Close/Undo/<To point>`: If you have created more than two segments, the option to close the object is added.

■ `Top/Zero/Bottom <top>`: These are the justification options, accessed at the first prompt by entering **j**. Select one of the justification options or press Enter to accept the default. These options determine where the multiline will be located between the points you specify. See figure 20.11 for examples of these options.

■ *Top*. This is the default setting. Top draws the multiline with the outer most positive offset element at the specified points.

■ *Zero*. Selecting zero draws the multiline with the origin points centered at the specified points.

■ *Bottom*. Bottom draws the multiline with the outermost negative offset element on at the specified points.

Top justification

Bottom justification

Zero justification

**Fig. 20.11**
Multiline justification examples.

■ `Set Mline scale <1.00>`: The multiline scale option is accessed at the first prompt by entering **s**. Enter a new value or press Enter to accept the default. The value is a scale factor that controls the overall width of the current multiline style. The overall width of the style is determined by the element offset values entered when the style was defined. A scale factor of 2 results in the multiline being twice as wide as the style definition. A scale factor of 0 collapses all the multiline elements into a single line. Entering a negative scale factor flips the multiline 180 degrees; the smallest (outermost negative) element is placed at the top. A negative scale factor also alters the scale by the absolute value.

■ `Mstyle name (or ?)`: The multiline style option is accessed by typing **st** at the first prompt. At the prompt, enter a multiline style name, type **?** for a list of styles loaded in the drawing file, or press Enter to retain the current style.

## Tutorial: Drawing Multilines with the MLINE Command

In this tutorial, you use the multiline styles defined in the preceding tutorial (Creating Multiline Styles) to draw a simple kitchen layout. If you did not do the preceding tutorial, go back and complete it now before you continue. Follow these steps:

1. Click the Mline button on the Draw floating toolbar.

2. At the `Justification = Top, Scale = 1.00, Style = ISLAND Justification/Scale/STyle/<From point>:` prompt, type **st** and press Enter to change the multiline style.

3. At the `Mstyle name (or ?):` prompt, type **?** and press Enter. The AutoCAD Text Window opens and a list of loaded multiline styles is displayed that should match figure 20.12.

**Fig. 20.12**
The AutoCAD Text Window displaying the loaded multiline styles.

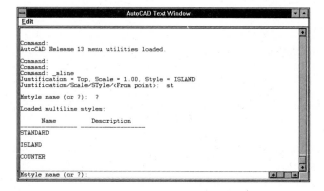

4. At the `Mstyle name (or ?):` prompt, type **counter** and press Enter to set that as the current multiline style.

5. At the `Justification = Top, Scale = 1.00, Style = COUNTER Justification/Scale/STyle/<From point>:` prompt, pick the coordinates **17'0",0'6"**, or type them and press Enter.

6. At the `<To point>:` prompt, pick the coordinates **17'0",6'8"**, or type them and press Enter.

7. At the `Undo/<To point>:` prompt, enter **@2'<135**. This adds a 45-degree angle at the corner of the counter.

8. At the `Close/Undo/<To point>:` prompt, pick the coordinates **5'4",8'1"**, or type them and press Enter.

9. At the next `Close/Undo/<To point>:` prompt, pick the coordinates **5'4",5'6"**, or type them and press Enter.

10. At the `Close/Undo/<To point>:` prompt, press Enter to end the MLINE command.

This completes the first section of the kitchen layout. The layout on your screen should match figure 20.13. Next, you are going to complete the layout by adding an island. Complete the following steps:

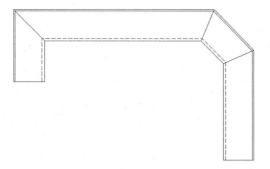

**Fig. 20.13**
The first section of the kitchen layout.

1. At the `Command:` prompt, press Enter to start the MLINE command again.

2. At the `Justification = Top, Scale = 1.00, Style = COUNTER Justification/Scale/STyle/<From point>:` prompt, type **st** and press Enter to change the multiline style.

3. At the `Mstyle name (or ?):` prompt, type **island** and press Enter to set it as the current multiline style.

4. At the `Justification = Top, Scale = 1.00, Style = ISLAND Justification/Scale/STyle/<From point>:` prompt, pick the coordinates **5'4",2'6"**, or type them and press Enter.

5. At the `<To point>:` prompt, pick the coordinates **13'0",2'6"**, or type them and press Enter.

6. At the `Undo/<To point>:` prompt, press Enter to end the MLINE command.

This completes the kitchen layout. Figure 20.14 shows the completed layout. Leave this drawing open for the next tutorial. If you don't plan to try the next tutorial (using the MLEDIT command) immediately, save your changes and close the drawing file.

**V**

**Advanced Drawing**

**Fig. 20.14**
The completed
kitchen layout.

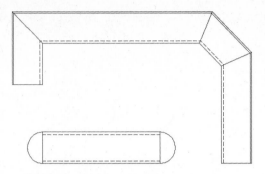

# Editing Multilines (MLEDIT)

AutoCAD requires the use of special editing commands to change the intersections of multilines. Standard AutoCAD commands such as TRIM, EXTEND, FILLET, CHAMFER, OFFSET, and BREAK do not have an effect on multilines. To perform these types of edits, AutoCAD uses the MLEDIT command. MLEDIT has four sets of editing tools. These tools are designed to allow editing on multilines that cross, form a tee, and create corner joints and vertices, and multilines that are to be cut or welded. Each of these four tools has three options. AutoCAD displays all the main editing tools and their options in a dialog box, shown in figure 20.15.

**Fig. 20.15**
The Multiline Edit
Tools dialog box.

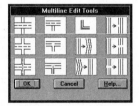

You access the Multiline Edit Tools dialog box by either of these methods:

- Click the Edit Polyline button on the Modify floating toolbar. While holding down the pick button on your digitizer, move the pointer to the second button on the flyout, Edit Multiline; then release the pick button.

- Enter **mledit** at the Command: prompt.

As mentioned in the introduction, the MLEDIT command opens a dialog box, which has four main sets of editing tools. Each main set has three commands, twelve commands in all. To access the editing commands, click the image tile of your choice; this also displays the name of the editing option in the lower left corner of the dialog box. Next, choose the OK button to start the command. It is assumed that you have followed these steps before you get to the following prompts.

> **Note**
>
> You can only access the multiline editing commands from the Multiline Edit Tools dialog box.

The first set of tools, listed in the first column, are for editing crossing multilines. Each of the three commands creates a different type of crossing intersection. The CLOSED CROSS command creates a closed intersection between two multilines. The OPEN CROSS creates an open intersection between two multilines, whereas the MERGED CROSS creates an open intersection between outside multiline elements, and merges inner elements. Figures 20.16 through 20.18 provide examples of each option. The crossing commands work similarly to a combination of the TRIM and FILLET commands, used for editing other AutoCAD object. The prompts for these commands, starting from the top image tile, are as follows:

- ■ Select first mline: Select the first multiline to be edited.

- ■ Select second mline: Select a second multiline that crosses the multiline that you first selected.

- ■ Select first mline (or Undo): You can continue selecting multilines, to create additional closed crosses; type **u** to UNDO the last closed cross edit. Press Enter to end the CLOSED CROSS MLEDIT command.

**Tip**
The first multiline selected will be closed and trimmed at the points where it intersects the second multiline.

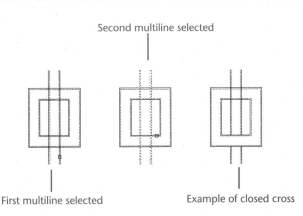

Second multiline selected

First multiline selected

Example of closed cross

**Fig. 20.16**
An example of closed crossing multilines.

- ■ `Select first mline:` Select the first multiline to be edited.

- ■ `Select second mline:` Select a second multiline that crosses the multiline that you first selected.

- ■ `Select first mline (or Undo):` You can continue selecting multilines, to create additional open crosses, or type **u** to UNDO the last open cross edit. Press Enter to end the OPEN CROSS MLEDIT command.

**Fig. 20.17**
An example of open crossing multilines.

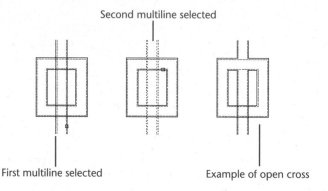

**Tip**
The OPEN CROSS command breaks all elements of the first multiline selected at each point that it intersects the second multiline. Only the outside elements of the second multiline are broken.

- ■ `Select first mline:` Select the first multiline to be edited.

- ■ `Select second mline:` Select a second multiline that crosses the multiline that you first selected.

- ■ `Select first mline (or Undo):` You can continue selecting multilines, to create additional merged crosses, or type **u** to UNDO the last merged cross edit. Press Enter to end the MERGED CROSS MLEDIT command.

**Fig. 20.18**
An example of merged crossing multilines.

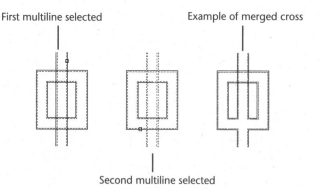

> **Note**
>
> Look back at the three crossing multiline figures, 20.16 through 20.18. Note where the second multiline is selected. This pick point determines where AutoCAD trims and joins the crossing multilines.

The next set of tools, listed in the second column, are for creating tee intersections between two multilines. All the tee commands either trim or extend the first multiline selected to meet the second multiline. The results can vary quite a bit, depending upon the configuration of the two multilines being joined. As with the crossing commands, each command creates a different type of connection. The CLOSED TEE command creates a closed intersection between two multilines, trimming or extending the first multiline selected. The OPEN TEE command creates an open intersection between two multilines, also trimming or extending the first multiline. Whereas the MERGED TEE command creates an open intersection between outside multiline elements and merges inner elements, again either trimming or extending the first multiline. Figures 20.19 through 20.21 provide examples of each command. The prompts for these commands, starting at the top image tile, are as follows:

- `Select first mline:` Select the first multiline to be trimmed or extended.

- `Select second mline:` Select a second multiline that intersects the first multiline, to *trim* the first multiline. To *extend* the first multiline, select a second multiline that *will* intersect the first multiline.

- `Select first mline (or Undo):` You can continue selecting multilines, to create additional closed tees, or type **u** to UNDO the last closed tee edit. Press Enter to end the CLOSED TEE MLEDIT command.

**Tip**

The order in which you select multilines for the MERGED CROSS command has no effect on the command. All the intersecting points will be joined, similar to the FILLET command.

**Tip**

If you are creating a tee that trims the first multiline you selected, then the section of the first multiline that you picked will always be left intact. Refer to figures 20.19 and 20.20; note which ends of the first multilines were selected and remain after AutoCAD trims the multiline.

V

Advanced Drawing

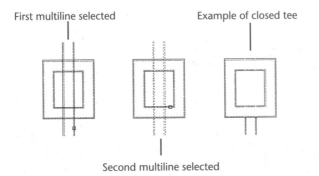

First multiline selected

Example of closed tee

Second multiline selected

**Fig. 20.19**
An example of closed tee multilines.

- `Select first mline:` Select the first multiline to be trimmed or extended.

- `Select second mline:` Select a second multiline that intersects the first multiline, to *trim* the first multiline. To *extend* the first multiline, select a second multiline that *will* intersect the first multiline.

- `Select first mline (or Undo):` You can continue selecting multilines, to create additional open tees, or type **u** to UNDO the last open tee edit. Press Enter to end the OPEN TEE MLEDIT command.

**Fig. 20.20**
An example of open tee multilines.

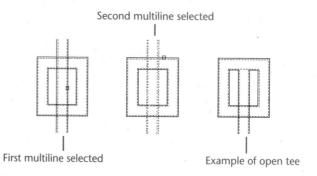

- `Select first mline:` Select the first multiline to be edited.

- `Select second mline:` Select a second multiline that intersects the first multiline, to *trim* the first multiline. To *extend* the first multiline, select a second multiline that *will* intersect the first multiline.

- `Select first mline (or Undo):` You can continue selecting multilines to create additional merged tees, or type **u** to UNDO the last merged tee edit. Press Enter to end the MERGED TEE MLEDIT command.

**Fig. 20.21**
An example of merged tee multilines.

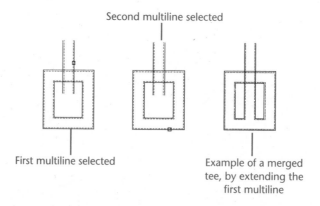

The next set of editing tools, listed in the third column, alters the vertices of one or two multilines. The CORNER JOINT command either trims or extends the first multiline selected to meet the second multiline. The results can vary quite a bit, depending upon how the multilines are selected. The ADD VERTEX command adds a vertex to the selected multiline at the point where it was picked. The DELETE VERTEX command removes the vertex that is selected when picking the multiline. Figures 20.22 through 20.24 provide examples of each command. The prompts for these commands, starting at the top image tile, are as follows:

- `Select first mline`: Select the first multiline to be trimmed or extended.

- `Select second mline`: Select a second multiline that intersects the first multiline to *trim* the first multiline. To *extend* the first multiline, select a second multiline that *will* intersect the first multiline.

- `Select first mline (or Undo)`: You can continue selecting multilines to create additional corners, or type **u** to UNDO the last corner joint edit. Press Enter to end the CORNER JOINT MLEDIT command.

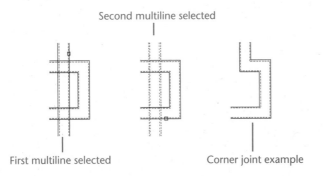

Second multiline selected

First multiline selected          Corner joint example

**Fig. 20.22**
An example of corner joint multilines.

- `Select mline`: Select a multiline to add a vertex to. AutoCAD adds a vertex at the point where you selected the multiline.

- `Select mline (or Undo)`: You can continue selecting multilines to add additional vertices, or type **u** to UNDO the last vertex added. Press Enter to end the ADD VERTEX MLEDIT command.

**Fig. 20.23**
An example of a
vertex added to a
multiline.

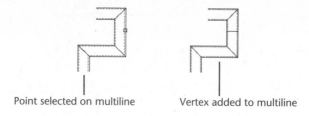

Point selected on multiline        Vertex added to multiline

- `Select mline:` Select a multiline to delete a vertex from. AutoCAD deletes the vertex nearest to the point you selected.

- `Select mline (or Undo):` You can continue selecting multilines to delete other vertices, or type **u** to UNDO and return to the last vertex deleted. Press Enter to end the DELETE VERTEX MLEDIT command.

**Fig. 20.24**
An example of a
vertex deleted
from a multiline.

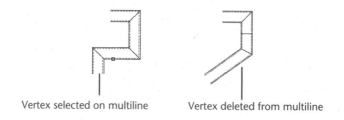

Vertex selected on multiline        Vertex deleted from multiline

The last set of editing tools, listed in the fourth column, is used to cut and join multiline elements. The CUT SINGLE command is similar to the BREAK command. Use it to remove a section from a single element in a multiline. The CUT ALL command removes a section from all the elements in a multiline. Both commands function like the 2 POINT, BREAK command. The point that selects the multiline serves as the first break point, and the second point selected removes the section of the element(s) between the two points. The WELD ALL command repairs, rejoins, sections of multilines that have been removed. Figures 20.25 through 20.27 provide examples of each command. The prompts for these commands, starting at the top image tile, are as follows:

- `Select mline:` Select the multiline to be cut.

- `Select second point:` Select a second point on the multiline to specify the section to be removed from the element selected first. This point does not have to be on the same element, however it must be on the same multiline.

- `Select mline (or Undo):` You can continue selecting multilines to create additional breaks, or type **u** to UNDO the last break edit. Press Enter to end the CUT SINGLE MLEDIT command.

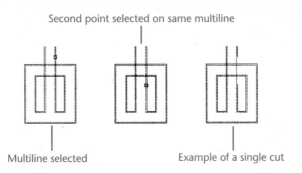

Second point selected on same multiline

Multiline selected        Example of a single cut

**Fig. 20.25**
An example of a section removed from a single element of a multiline.

- `Select mline:` Select the multiline to be cut.

- `Select second point:` Select a second point on the multiline to specify the section to be removed from each element. This point does not have to be on the same element, however it must be on the same multiline.

- `Select mline (or Undo):` You can continue selecting multilines to create additional breaks, or type **u** to UNDO the last break edit. Press Enter to end the CUT ALL MLEDIT command.

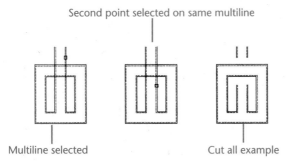

Second point selected on same multiline

Multiline selected        Cut all example

**Fig. 20.26**
An example of a section removed from all the elements of a multiline.

- `Select mline:` Select a multiline to replace—or *weld*—the missing section. AutoCAD rejoins—welds—the two sections back together again.

- `Select mline (or Undo):` You can continue selecting multilines to rejoin, or type **u** to UNDO the repair. Press Enter to end the WELD ALL MLEDIT command.

V

Advanced Drawing

**Fig. 20.27**

An example of a cut multiline repaired using WELD ALL.

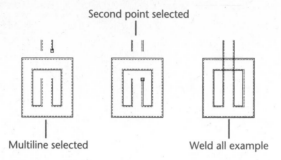

Second point selected

Multiline selected          Weld all example

## Tutorial: Adding Vertices to Multilines with the ADD VERTEX Command

In this series of tutorials, you use the multiline edit commands to change the layout of the kitchen plan. This first tutorial uses the ADD VERTEX command to start creating a new opening in the kitchen floorplan. If you did not do the preceding tutorial, go back and complete it now before you continue. Follow these steps:

1. Click the Edit Multiline button on the Modify floating toolbar.

2. At the Multiline Edit Tools dialog box, select the ADD VERTEX image tile (second row, third tile) and choose OK.

3. At the `Select mline:` prompt, pick the coordinates **8'0",8'1"**, or type them and press Enter. This adds a vertex to the top horizontal section of the original countertop.

4. At the `Select mline(or Undo):` prompt, pick the coordinates **11'0",10'1"**, or type them and press Enter. This adds a second vertex to the same countertop section.

5. At the `Select mline(or Undo):` prompt, press Enter to end the MLEDIT command.

You have now added two vertices to the countertop section. These vertices will represent a new opening into the kitchen, after you complete the next tutorial (using CUT ALL). Figure 20.28 shows the kitchen layout with the vertices added.

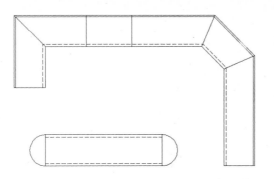

**Fig. 20.28**
Kitchen layout
with vertices
added.

## Tutorial: Removing Multiline Sections with the CUT ALL Command

This tutorial uses the CUT ALL command to "open" the countertop where the new vertices were added in the preceding tutorial. If you did not do the preceding tutorial, go back and complete it now before you continue. Follow these steps:

1. Click the Edit Multiline button on the Modify floating toolbar.

2. At the Multiline Edit Tools dialog box, select the CUT ALL image tile (second row, last tile) and choose OK.

3. At the Select mline: prompt, type **end** and press Enter to use the ENDpoint object snap, and select the endpoint of the first vertex added in the preceding tutorial. Refer to figure 20.29.

4. At the Select second point: prompt, type **end** and press Enter to use the ENDpoint object snap again. This time select the endpoint of the second vertex added in the preceding tutorial. Refer to figure 20.29.

5. At the Select mline(or Undo): prompt, press Enter to end the CUT ALL command.

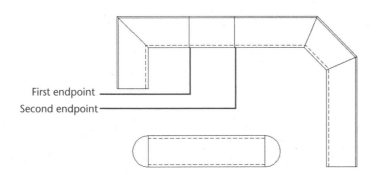

First endpoint
Second endpoint

**Fig. 20.29**
Endpoints to select
for CUT ALL
command.

You have now added two vertices to the countertop section and created a new opening for access into the kitchen. In the next tutorial (using CORNER JOINTS to edit multilines), you eliminate one of the original openings from the kitchen plan. Figure 20.30 shows the kitchen layout with the new opening.

**Fig. 20.30**
Kitchen layout, with new opening.

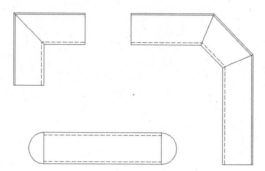

## Tutorial: Making Multiline Corners with the CORNER JOINT Command

This tutorial uses the CORNER JOINT command to eliminate one of the original openings into the kitchen. If you did not do the preceding tutorial, go back and complete it before you continue. Follow these steps:

1. Click the Edit Multiline button on the Modify floating toolbar.

2. At the Multiline Edit Tools dialog select the CORNER JOINT image tile (first row, third tile) and choose OK.

3. At the `Select first mline:` prompt, pick the first multiline shown in figure 20.31.

4. At the `Select second mline:` prompt, pick the second multiline shown in figure 20.31.

5. At the `Select mline(or Undo):` prompt, press Enter to end the CORNER JOINT command.

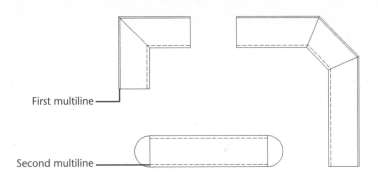

First multiline

Second multiline

**Fig. 20.31**
Multilines to select for CORNER JOINT command.

You have now added two vertices to the countertop section, created a new opening for access into the kitchen, and removed one of the original openings. Figure 20.32 shows the completed kitchen layout. This concludes the tutorials on multilines. You can save this drawing for future reference or QUIT to use the file again.

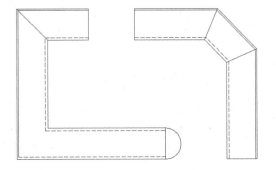

**Fig. 20.32**
Completed kitchen layout.

**V**

**Advanced Drawing**

# From Here...

For more information about object properties, line objects, and modifying objects, see the following chapters:

- Chapter 10, "Editing Techniques," shows you how to edit AutoCAD objects.

- Chapter 19, "Using Polylines," shows you how to draw another of AutoCAD's advanced line objects.

- Chapter 21, "Modifying Object Characteristics," shows you how to set default object properties using the DDEMODES command.

# On Your Own

Test your multiline drawing and editing skills. Define a multiline style and draw a series of multilines so that you can use each editing option once. Try drawing all the lines before you start editing and try not to draw more lines than necessary for using each editing option once.

Hints:

1. Use MLSTYLE to define the multiline style you need before you start drawing.

2. Use MLINE to draw the multilines; think about the editing options you will use before you start to draw.

3. Use MLEDIT to test yourself.

# Part VI

# Advanced Editing Techniques

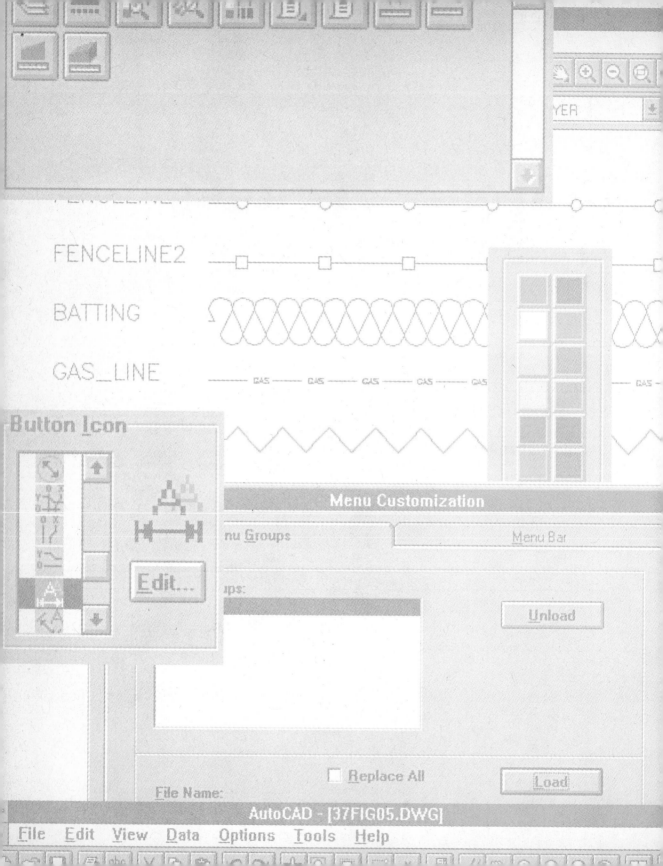

FENCELINE2

BATTING

GAS_LINE ——— GAS ——— GAS ——— GAS ——— GAS ——— GAS ——— GAS

**Button Icon**

Edit...

**Menu Customization**

nu Groups        Menu Bar

ups:

Unload

☐ Replace All

File Name:

Load

AutoCAD - [37FIG05.DWG]

File   Edit   View   Data   Options   Tools   Help

# Chapter 21

# Modifying Object Characteristics

AutoCAD's major advantage over manual drafting techniques is its capacity to change drawings quickly and easily. To change the linetype of a line on a manually created drawing, erase the line and then draw it again. With AutoCAD, simply select the line and assign it a new linetype.

Every time an object is created in a drawing, AutoCAD stores information in a database for that specific object. For example, the information stored for a linetype includes starting point, ending point, specific length, and direction, but isn't limited to just those items. AutoCAD offers several commands that allow you to modify the database information for each particular object.

There are times when it's advantageous to change certain properties. AutoCAD gives you the ability to easily change the layer an object is on, along with the linetype.

Changing text, including dimensions, is another easy task. Instead of retyping a line of text to change one word, you can invoke a dialog box showing the existing text. To edit the text, use the cursor, backspace, and arrow keys to make the necessary changes in the dialog box. When you press enter, the updated text appears on the screen, in the same location with the same style.

You can also rename object traits, such as layer names, linetype names, or text style names through a dialog box. Finally, you can purge or remove unwanted objects, such as layers or linetypes, from your drawing at any time.

◀ See "Removing Unwanted Objects (PURGE)," p. 289

In this chapter you will change and modify several different objects including lines, arcs, circles, text, and dimensions. You'll also learn how to:

- Change the properties of drawing objects

- Change the geometric characteristics of drawing objects

- Set default object properties

- Edit text with a dialog box

- Rename object traits

- Remove unwanted objects

# Modifying Object Properties (CHANGE, CHPROP, and DDCHPROP)

AutoCAD allows you to make a variety of changes to an existing object. The CHANGE and CHPROP commands allow you to change the layer, linetype, color, and thickness properties. Neither of these commands provides a dialog box, however. CHANGE allows you to edit properties or point information. The Properties option of CHANGE includes ELEVATION and LTSCALE in the list of properties. The Change Point option of CHANGE allows you to change start points, endpoints, insertion points, text styles, text wording, and so on. The exact options depend on the type of object selected. CHPROP includes an LTSCALE option. The DDCHPROP command will access the Change Properties dialog box that allows you to modify several object properties (see fig. 21.1). The Change Properties dialog box can be accessed by typing **ddchprop** at the Command: prompt.

**Fig. 21.1**
Use the Change Properties dialog box to modify many object characteristics.

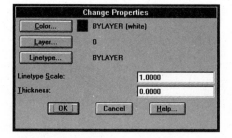

The Change Properties dialog box displays the existing color, layer, linetype, linetype scale, and thickness of the object. The following sections describe how to use the dialog box to change the properties of the selected object. See Chapter 7, "Understanding Layers," Chapter 8, "Understanding Linetypes," and Chapter 28, "3D Modeling Essentials," for more information on the properties themselves.

## Selecting Multiple Objects for Modification

By using the Change Properties dialog box, you can modify object properties of more than one object at a time. When the DDCHPROP command is invoked, AutoCAD prompts Select Objects:. At this point you can use any method for creating a selection set, such as window, fence, and so on. When you have finished creating the selection set, press Enter. The Change Properties dialog box appears.

### Note

You can also use pick-first selection to create the selection set of objects to be changed. If a selection set exists when you invoke the DDCHPROP command, AutoCAD performs the changes specified on the existing selection set.

When selecting more than one object to modify, you can select any combination of objects. A selection set could consist of a line, arc and circle, each on a different layer with a different linetype. When the Change Properties dialog box appears, Varies will appear after the Layer button, indicating the selected objects are on different layers. The DDCHPROP dialog box will give *all* selected objects the same settings. When you click OK, *all* selected objects will be on the same layer with the same LTSCALE.

◀ See "Changing the Layer Color," p. 181

## Changing Color and Linetype

If you want to change the object color from the Change Properties dialog box, pick the Color button. The Select Color dialog box appears. Picking the Linetype button will display the Select Linetype dialog box.

◀ See "Setting the Linetype," p. 199

**VI**

**Advanced Editing**

◀ See "Assigning Linetypes to Layers (LINETYPE)," p. 184

> ## Caution
>
> In the Change Properties dialog box you can change color and linetypes for objects regardless of the layer the object is on. For example, you can have a green object with a hidden linetype on a layer that is red with a continuous linetype. Modifying individual object characteristics (color and linetype) without regard to layer settings can cause confusion in a drawing. It's recommended that you leave the default BYLAYER setting for the color and linetype so it is not always necessary to change color and linetypes before creating new objects.

## Moving the Object to a Different Layer

To change the layer an object is currently on, pick the Layer button from the Change Properties dialog box. This will bring up the Select Layer dialog box as shown in figure 21.2. When a different layer is chosen, either by typing the name of the layer in the edit box or selecting the layer from the list, the setting for the new layer will appear in the Change Properties dialog box. The object selected will now be on the layer selected, and it will have the corresponding color and linetype for that layer.

**Fig. 21.2**
The Select Layer dialog box is used to change the layer the selected objects are on.

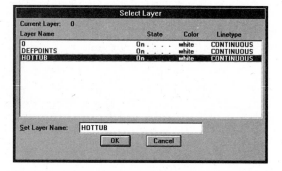

## Adjusting the Linetype Scale

The Change Properties dialog box will also allow you to individually change the Linetype Scale for selected objects. The LTSCALE variable changes the linetype scale for all objects. Proper use of the Change Properties dialog box allows you to have objects with different linetype scales within a drawing.

## Tutorial: Using the Change Properties Dialog Box

In this tutorial you'll use the Change Properties dialog box to change the properties of a circle and a line.

1. Select New from the Standard toolbar. If prompted by the AutoCAD Save Changes dialog box, select the appropriate response.

   When the Create New Drawing dialog box appears press Enter.

2. Select Line from the Draw toolbar.

   At the `Line From point:` prompt, type **2,2** and press Enter.

   At the `To point:` prompt, type **7,7** and press Enter.

3. Select Circle from the Draw toolbar.

   At the `Circle 3P/2P/TTR/<Center point>:` prompt, type **10,4** and press Enter.

   At the `Diameter/<Radius prompt>`, type **2** and press Enter.

4. Select Layers from the Object Properties toolbar and create a new layer called Objects in the Layer Control dialog box.

   Make the color of the layer blue. Select OK.

5. Select the Properties button on the Object Properties toolbar.

   At the `Select objects:` prompt, select the line and the circle and press Enter.

6. Click the Layer button in the Change Properties dialog box. The Select Layer dialog box appears.

7. Select the Objects layer and click OK.

   Select OK at the Change Properties dialog box.

   Both the line and the circle change to blue and are placed on the Objects layer.

# Changing Object Characteristics (DDMODIFY)

AutoCAD allows you to edit an object by modifying the information stored for the object in a dialog box. AutoCAD also lists various properties of the selected object.

The DDMODIFY command displays the Modify dialog box.

**VI**

**Advanced Editing**

> ### Note
>
> The title of the dialog box changes, depending on the object selected. For a line, the title bar displays Modify Line. For an arc, the title bar displays Modify Arc.

The information that appears in the Modify Arc dialog box changes according to the type of object selected (see fig. 21.3). The dialog box may display current properties or object characteristics without giving you the option of changing all of them. The Modify dialog box can be accessed by using any of these methods:

- Click the Properties button on the Object Properties toolbar.

- Select Properties from the Edit pull-down menu.

- Type **ddmodify** at the Command: prompt.

**Fig. 21.3**
The Properties section of the Modify Arc dialog box can be used to edit objects.

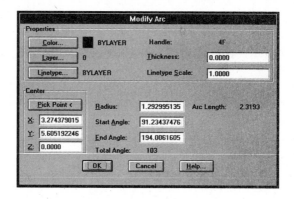

The information that can be changed with the Modify Arc dialog box varies depending on the object selected. See the Table 21.1 for a listing of each object type as well as a cross reference to the section in the book that describes these objects. Regardless of the type of object selected, the top portion of the Modify dialog box will display the same information.

### Table 21.1  DDMODIFY Object Reference

| Object | Reference |
| --- | --- |
| line | Drawing lines (Chapter 12) |
| arc | Drawing arcs (Chapter 5) |
| circle | Drawing circles (Chapter 5) |

| Object | Reference |
| --- | --- |
| ray | Drawing rays (Chapter 15) |
| xline | Drawing infinite lines (Chapter 15) |
| hatch | Creating hatch areas (Chapter 17) |
| dimension | Dimensioning a drawing (Chapter 18) |
| point | Indicating locations (Chapter 15) |
| ellipse | Drawing ellipses (Chapter 15) |
| leader | Additional dimension features (Chapter 18) |
| mtext | Entering text with Mtext (Chapter 16) |
| mline | Drawing and editing (Chapter 10) |
| attributes | Working with attributes (Chapter 23) |
| 3D Face | Creating 3D faces (Chapter 27) |
| 3D Solid | Introduction to solid modeling concepts (Chapter 31) |
| block insert | Creating symbol libraries (Chapter 22) |
| xref | Using external references (Chapter 22) |
| viewpoint | Controlling viewpoints (Chapter 30) |
| polyline | Drawing polylines (Chapter 19) |
| solid | Creating solid areas (Chapter 27) |
| region | Creating solid areas (Chapter 27) |
| shape | |
| spline | Creating a spline curve (Chapter 19) |
| tolerance | Geometric tolerances (Chapter 18) |

**VI**

**Advanced Editing**

In the Properties section of the Modify dialog box, the Color and Linetype should both be set to BYLAYER unless the color or linetype has been changed. Selecting the Layer button will bring up the Select Layer dialog box shown earlier in figure 21.2. Depending upon the type of object selected, you may or may not be able to change the Thickness and Linetype Scale. The Thickness edit box allows you to change the thickness of an object. This is used in 3D drawing, which is discussed in Chapter 18, "Dimensioning a Drawing."

▶ See "Introduction to 3D Modeling," p. 759

> **Note**
>
> The DDMODIFY command allows you to change the layer an object is on, but it won't let you create new layers or rename existing layers.

The Modify dialog box also displays the handle for the object. The *object handle* is a unique identifier that AutoCAD assigns to the object. The handle is permanently assigned throughout the object's lifetime in the drawing. The handle is saved with the object in the drawing file and never changes. If the object is deleted from the drawing, the handle is also deleted and not used again in that drawing.

> **Note**
>
> While the Modify dialog box allows you to change many object characteristics, you can only edit one object at a time. To change layers, Linetype Scale, and Thickness for more than one object at a time, use the Change Properties dialog box (DDCHPROP). The Change Properties dialog box allows you to change several objects at the same time.

## Changing a Line

When a line is selected using DDMODIFY, the following attributes can be modified:

- *From Point and To Point Pick Point.* The dialog box disappears and you return to the drawing editor. The From point or To point option allows you to pick a new endpoint with the cursor, or enter coordinates for a new endpoint.

- *From Point and To Point X, Y, Z.* The edit boxes change the X, Y, and Z coordinates for an endpoint of the line. The endpoints automatically change when you click the OK button.

When a line is picked, the Modify Line dialog box appears as shown in figure 21.4. The Modify Line dialog box contains information about the line from the two endpoints, with edit boxes to change the endpoint coordinates. Selecting the Pick Point< button returns you to the drawing editor. In the drawing editor you can select a new point with the cursor. You can also type a coordinate, using an absolute, relative, absolute polar or relative polar coordinate entry method in response to the To point: prompt.

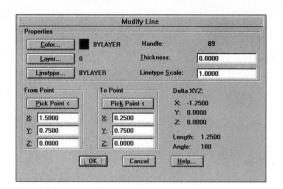

**Fig. 21.4**
The Modify Line dialog box can change the two endpoints of a line.

## Changing an Arc

When an arc is selected using DDMODIFY, the following attributes can be modified (see fig. 21.5):

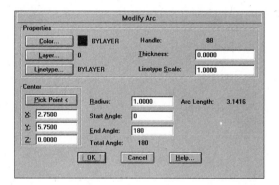

**Fig. 21.5**
The center point, radius, start angle, and end angle of an arc can be edited in the Modify Arc dialog box.

- *Pick Point.* The dialog box disappears and you are returned to the drawing editor. The Center point: prompt appears, where you can pick a new center point with the cursor, or enter coordinates for a new center point.

- *X, Y, Z.* The edit boxes change the X, Y, and Z coordinates for the center point of the arc. The center point automatically changes when you click the OK button.

- *Radius.* To change the radius, double-click the Radius edit box. Enter a new value and the arc will change to the new value as reflected in the Arc Length value edit box.

- *Start Angle.* Double-clicking in the Start Angle edit box changes the start angle of the arc. Arcs are drawn in a counterclockwise manner. Pressing Enter after changing the Start Angle updates the Arc Length and Total Angle values.

**VI**

**Advanced Editing**

■ *End Angle.* The edit box changes the End Angle of the arc. Pressing Enter after changing the End Angle also updates the Arc Length and Total Angle values.

## Changing a Circle

When a circle is selected using DDMODIFY, the following attributes can be modified:

■ *Center Pick Point.* The dialog box disappears and you return to the drawing editor. The Center option allows you to pick a new center point with the cursor, or enter coordinates for a new endpoint.

■ *X, Y, Z.* The edit boxes change the X, Y, and Z coordinates for the center point of the circle. The center point automatically changes when you click the OK button.

■ *Radius.* Changing the value will change the size of the radius of the circle.

When changing circular objects, related information for the Diameter, Circumference, and area appear. Typing a new value in the Radius edit box and pressing Enter updates the Diameter, Circumference, and Area values. You can also change the Center location with the Pick Point< button or by entering coordinates in the X, Y, and Z edit boxes (see fig. 21.6).

**Fig. 21.6**
Use the Modify
Circle dialog box to
change the size of a
circle.

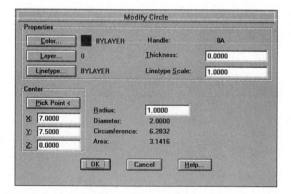

## Changing Text

Use the Modify Text dialog box to easily and quickly change text created with the TEXT or DTEXT command. To open the Modify Text dialog box as shown in figure 21.7, enter the DDMODIFY command and select the text to modify. After selecting the text, the following information is displayed:

- *Text.* To edit the text wording, move the cursor to the Text edit box and remove, add, or change the text as necessary.

- *Origin.* To change the text origin, select the Pick Point< button and select a new point on the screen. You can also enter new coordinates in the X, Y, and Z edit boxes.

- *Height.* To automatically change the text height enter a new value in the Height edit box.

- *Rotation.* Use this to change the Rotation angle of the selected text.

- *Width Factor.* Alters the Width (expansion/compression) factor of the selected text.

- *Obliquing Angle.* The obliquing angle is an offset from 90 degrees. A positive offset results in characters that lean to the right, and a negative value causes the characters to slant to the left. The maximum angle you can enter is 85 degrees.

- *Justify.* Selecting the arrow to the right of the Justify: box brings up the justification pop-up list. Select the desired justification from the list.

- *Style.* To change the text to a new style, select the arrow to the right of the Style box. All text styles that have been previously created appear in the pop-up list. Select the desired style from the list.

- *Upside Down and Backward.* Checking the Upside Down and Backward boxes causes the text to appear upside down or backward.

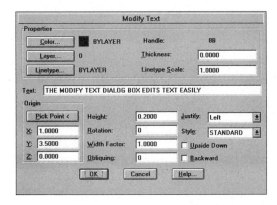

**Fig. 21.7**

The Modify Text dialog box offers a simple means of editing text.

**VI**

**Advanced Editing**

## Changing an Xline

When an xline is selected using DDMODIFY, the following attributes can be modified:

- *RootPoint and Second Point Pick Point.* The dialog box disappears and you are returned to the drawing editor. The From point or To point option allows you to pick a new endpoint by using the cursor, or by entering coordinates.

- *Root Point and Second Point X, Y, Z.* The edit boxes change the X, Y, and Z coordinates for an endpoint of the line. The endpoints automatically change when you click the OK button.

The *Root Point* of an xline is the initial point that was used to define the xline. The Root Point can be changed with the Pick Point< button or by entering the coordinates in the X, Y, or Z edit boxes.

Modifying the Second Point allows you to change the Direction Vector of the Xline. The Modify Xline dialog box is shown in figure 21.8.

**Fig. 21.8**
With the Modify
Xline dialog box,
you can change
the Root Point
and Second Point,
automatically
updating the
Direction Vector.

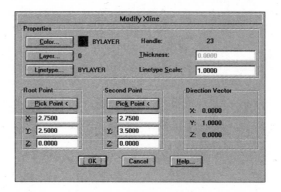

## Changing a Ray

When a ray is selected using DDMODIFY, the following attributes can be modified:

- *Start Point and Second Point Pick Point.* The dialog box disappears and you are returned to the drawing editor. The Start point or Second point options allow you to pick a new endpoint with the cursor, or enter coordinates for a new endpoint.

- *From Point and To Point X, Y, Z.* The edit boxes change the X, Y, and Z coordinates for an endpoint of the line. The endpoints automatically change when you click the OK button.

The Modify Ray dialog box is similar to the Modify Xline dialog box as shown in figure 21.9. The Start Point is the point where the ray begins. As with the Xline, modifying the Second Point allows you to change the Direction Vector of the ray.

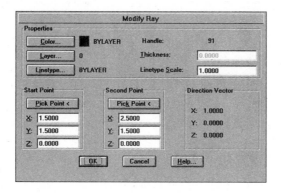

**Fig. 21.9**
In the Modify Ray dialog box, you can change the Start Point and Second Point of a ray.

## Changing an Mline

When an mline is selected using DDMODIFY, no attributes can be changed. The standard selection for the DDCHPROP command are the only changes allowed for this line. For more information about DDCHPROP, see "Modifying Object Properties (CHANGE, CHPROP, and DDCHPROP)," earlier in this chapter.

## Changing a Hatch

If you pick a hatch, you get the Modify Associative Hatch dialog box as shown in figure 21.10. Selecting Hatch Edit from the Modify Associative Hatch dialog box opens the Hatch edit dialog box as shown in figure 21.11. This is the same dialog box that appears when you use the BHATCH command. When editing a hatch, you are limited to certain selections in the Hatch edit dialog box. To learn more about the limitations, see Chapter 17, "Filling Areas with Hatching."

**Fig. 21.10**
To modify a hatch, use DDMODIFY and select the hatch, then select Hatch Edit in the Modify Associative Hatch dialog box.

**VI**

**Advanced Editing**

**Fig. 21.11**
The Hatchedit dialog box is displayed when Hatch Edit is selected from the Modify Associative Hatch dialog box.

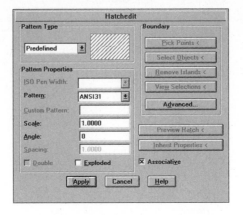

## Changing a Dimension

When a dimension is selected using DDMODIFY, the following attributes can be modified:

- *Edit.* Brings up the Edit Mtext dialog box which allows you to change the text as a paragraph formatted text string.

- *Style.* Allows you to quickly change the style of the Dimension text font.

- *Geometry.* Brings up the Geometry dialog box which allows you to change the dimension geometry attributes.

- *Format.* Brings up the Format dialog box which allows you to change the dimension format attributes.

- *Annotation.* Brings up the Annotation dialog box which allows you to change the dimension annotation attributes.

The Modify Dimension dialog box offers several options to change an existing dimension as shown in figure 21.12. To change the existing text, select the Edit button and enter a new value in the Edit MText dialog box. To change the dimension text to a new style, select the arrow to the right of the Style pop-up box. All text styles previously created appear in the pop-up list. Select the desired style from the list and press Enter.

Selecting the Geometry button in the Modify Dimension dialog box brings up the Geometry dialog box as shown in figure 21.13. You can modify the Dimension Line, Extension Line, Arrowheads, and Center (if applicable to the dimension selected). You can also change the Overall Scale for the dimension selected.

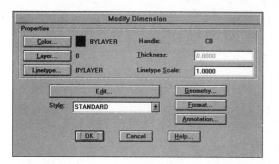

**Fig. 21.12**
In the Modify Dimension dialog box you can change the text and text style.

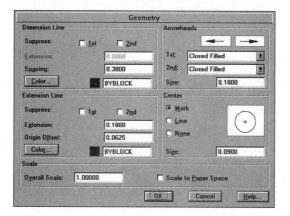

**Fig. 21.13**
Selecting the Geometry button in the Modify Dimension dialog box opens the Geometry dialog box.

The Format button in the Modify Dimension dialog box allows you to change the fit and justification of the text in the selected dimension. This is accomplished with the Format dialog box, as shown in figure 21.14.

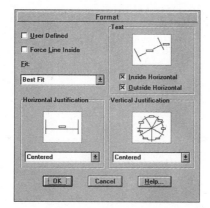

**Fig. 21.14**
Fit and justification changes to the selected dimension text can be made in the Format dialog box.

To change the units and tolerance of the selected dimension, choose the Annotation button. This brings up the Annotation dialog box as shown in figure 21.15. Here you can assign different primary units to the selected dimension as well as alternate units. You can also apply a tolerance to the dimension. While the Modify Dimension dialog box enables you to change the text style, the Annotation dialog box enables you to change the Height and Gap as well.

**Fig. 21.15**

In the Annotation dialog box, a Tolerance can be applied or changed and units can be assigned to the selected dimension.

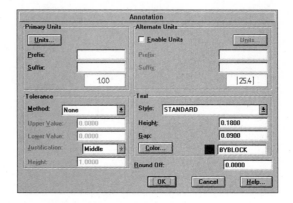

## Tutorial: Using the Modify Dialog Box

In this tutorial you will use the DDMODIFY command to change the attributes of the line and circle you created in the previous tutorial.

1. Continue from the previous tutorial.

2. Select Properties from the Object Properties toolbar.

3. Select the line that you created in the previous tutorial. The Modify Line dialog box appears. Change the From Point X value to 3 and click OK.

   If the change was not apparent and you would like to see the difference, select Undo from the Edit menu. Watch the screen closely to see the change.

4. Select Properties from the Object Properties toolbar.

5. This time select the circle that was created in the previous tutorial. The Modify Circle dialog box appears.

6. Change the Radius from 2 to 3 and click OK. Again, if the changes were not apparent, use Undo to see the changes made.

# Setting Default Object Properties with a Dialog Box (DDEMODES)

Every object created within AutoCAD has color, linetype, thickness, linetype scale, and layer properties. Normally the object receives the current setting at the time the object is created. The Object Creation Modes dialog box allows object creation with specific settings regardless of the layer. It's important to note at this point that the ltscale is independent of the layer.

You can set the default properties when creating objects in the Object Creation Modes dialog box. The dialog box shows settings for color, layer, linetype, linetype scale, text style, elevation, and thickness. The Object Creation Modes dialog box can be accessed by using the following methods:

- Select the Object Creation button on the Object Properties floating toolbar.

- Select Object Creation from the Data pull-down menu.

- Type **ddemodes** at the Command: prompt.

The Object Creation Modes dialog box, shown in figure 21.16, controls the current settings for color, layer, linetype, text style, linetype scale, elevation, and thickness.

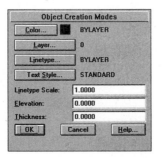

**Fig. 21.16**
The Object Creation Modes dialog box controls current object settings.

**VI**

*Advanced Editing*

## Setting the Default Object Color and Linetype

Selecting the Color button opens the Select Color dialog box. This is the same dialog box displayed when selecting Color from the Layer Control dialog box. Click any of the displayed colors to set the color you want. You can also select the BYLAYER or BYBLOCK buttons under Logical Colors.

The Linetype button opens the Select Linetype dialog box. This dialog box is identical to the one displayed in the Layer Control dialog box. You can also select the BYLAYER or BYBLOCK options.

Selecting a Color or Linetype in the Object Creation Modes dialog box overrides the current layer color and linetype. Selecting a specific color or linetype in the Object Creation Modes dialog box enables objects with various colors or linetypes to reside on the same layer. For example, you could draw a line on one part of the object in yellow with a hidden line. A different line could have a continuous linetype with a red color. Both objects could reside on the same layer, so when the layer is frozen or turned off, neither of the lines appear on screen.

---

### Caution

Changing the color or linetype in the Object Creation Modes dialog box causes all future objects to be drawn in that color or linetype regardless of the layer on which they reside.

---

In certain cases it may be easier to change the current color and linetype setting as you work. Initially this may seem easier than planning ahead and creating a well-organized set of layers, complete with preset colors and linetypes. Creating a prototype drawing involves careful planning, and is more advantageous. It can be very difficult to reset objects to a specific layer at a later time, especially in a complex drawing.

**Tip**

Both the DDMODIFY and DDEDIT commands can be used to edit text. While the DDMODIFY command allows greater flexibility for changing the text, DDEDIT is normally faster for strictly text editing.

---

### Troubleshooting

*When I begin creating new geometry, everything is drawn on the same layer with the same color. I changed layers, and this didn't make any difference.*

Check the Change Properties dialog box (DDCHPROP) and make sure Color and Linetype both say BYLAYER. Also, check the Object Creation Modes dialog box (DDEMODES), making sure Color and Linetype each say BYLAYER. When BYLAYER is selected, objects inherit the linetype and color properties assigned to their respective layer.

---

To avoid problems and confusion, don't use explicit settings for color and linetype in the Object Creation Modes dialog box. Leave the Color and Linetype settings to the default values of BYLAYER unless you need to mix color and linetypes on the same layer.

## Setting Other Default Object Properties

Selecting Layer in the Object Creation Modes dialog box brings up the Layer Control dialog box. You can create new layers, or make an existing layer current. The Text Style button activates the Select Text Style dialog box. Although you can't create a new text style, you can select any existing text style as the current style.

You can also set the default Linetype Scale by entering the value in the edit box. The elevation and thickness commands are discussed further in Chapter 18, "Dimensioning a Drawing." When working on standard 2D drawings, use the following settings in the Object Creation Modes dialog box:

▶ See "Introduction to 3D Modeling," p. 759

> Color: BYLAYER
>
> Linetype: BYLAYER
>
> Elevation: 0.00
>
> Thickness: 0.00

# Editing Text (DDEDIT)

You can use the DDMODIFY command or access the Edit Text dialog box to revise existing text. To open the Edit Text dialog box, type **ddedit** at the Command: prompt.

The DDEDIT command brings up a dialog box that acts as a line editor to edit a single line of text created with the TEXT or DTEXT command. The default prompt asks you to <Select a TEXT or ATTDEF object>/Undo:. The screen cursor takes the shape of the square pick box, where you move the cursor to the desired text and pick. The Edit Text dialog box appears, with the line of text you picked ready for editing (see fig. 21.17). The Attdef option refers to an attribute, which is covered in Chapter 17, "Filling Areas with Hatching."

▶ See "Working with Attributes," p. 713

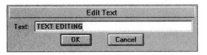

**Fig. 21.17**
The Edit Text dialog box displays the selected text, ready for editing.

**VI**

Advanced Editing

By default, the line of text to edit is highlighted in the edit box, with the cursor flashing at the end of the edit box. You can enter new text and the old text is automatically replaced. If you make a mistake at any time while editing text, you can click the Cancel button and reselect the desired text.

To edit text after the Edit Text dialog box is open, move the cursor anywhere inside the edit box and pick. This will remove the highlight around the text. After the highlight is removed from the text, any of the following procedures can be used to edit the text:

■ *Moving around inside the edit box.* The left and right arrow keys can be used to move the cursor back and forth in the edit box. You can also use the pointing device cursor (the arrow) to point anywhere on the line of text and click to place the typing cursor. You should use whatever method is the most comfortable.

■ *Insert mode.* After the cursor is at the desired location, type the text. This inserts the new text and shifts the existing text to the right.

■ *Backspace key.* Pressing the Backspace key removes the character or text to the left of the cursor, and moves the text to the right along with the cursor.

■ *Space bar.* Pressing the space bar inserts a space if you're in insert mode (press the insert key on the keyboard), and moves all the text to the right of the cursor.

■ *Highlighting text.* To highlight text in the edit box, move the pointing device cursor to the desired text and pick. Hold down the pick button while you drag the cursor across the text you want highlighted. When you're done highlighting all the proposed text, release the pick button.

■ *Removing highlighted text.* When text or a portion of the text is highlighted, press any key to remove the highlighted text or press the delete key.

■ *Control+X.* Control+X also deletes all of the highlighted text in the edit box.

# Renaming Object Traits (DDRENAME)

When working within AutoCAD you can assign names to several different components. Two of these components are layers and text styles. The DDRENAME command may be used to change the name of any of the following objects:

- Layer

- Linetype (Ltype)

- Text Style (Style)

- View

- Dimension Style (Dimstyle)

- Block

- User Coordinate System (UCS)

- Viewpoint Configurations (Vport)

To rename an object, you must have previously defined the object and given it a name. The Rename dialog box may be accessed by doing typing **ddrename** at the Command: prompt.

The DDRENAME command brings up the Rename dialog box shown in figure 21.18. The options within the dialog box enable you to select the type of object you want to rename. For example, selecting Layer from the Named Objects list displays all current layer names in the Items box. To change the name of a layer, select the name you want to change from the Items box. AutoCAD will display the name of the layer selected in the Old Name edit box. Type the new name in the Rename To edit box, and click the Rename To button. When you have completed renaming objects, click OK to return to the drawing editor.

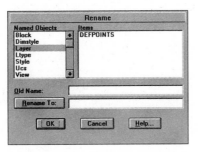

**Fig. 21.18**
The Rename dialog box is used to rename existing named objects, such as layers and linetypes.

**VI**

**Advanced Editing**

There also is a rename command available. If you use this command you can change the same items as DDRENAME but AutoCAD won't display a dialog box and the command is less interactive. Because dialog boxes are a large part of the AutoCAD user interface, the user should update all commands that use them to become more efficient.

# Removing Unwanted Objects (PURGE)

As you continue working on a drawing, it can become cluttered with extra layers, linetypes and text styles that you no longer need. Having extra objects in the drawing enlarges the size of the drawing file, increasing the time needed to load the drawing into AutoCAD. The PURGE command can be used to remove unwanted named objects from a drawing.

> **Note**
>
> You can purge the drawing at any time during the drawing session. This feature is new with AutoCAD Release 13. Before, you could only use purge at the beginning of your drawing session. This feature adds convenience to the command's functionality.

The PURGE command removes the following objects from a drawing:

- Blocks (Blocks)
- Dimension Styles (Dimstyles)
- Layers (LAyers)
- Linetypes (LTypes)
- Shapes (SHapes)
- Text Styles (STyles)
- APPID Table (For third-party applications)
- Multiple Lines Styles (Mline)
- All

▶ See "Using Symbols and XRefs," p. 677

To access the PURGE command, type **purge** at the Command: prompt. AutoCAD allows you to specify the type of objects you want to delete. Normally, you should select the ALL option to clear everything you don't need. PURGE only removes named objects that aren't used in the drawing. AutoCAD also prompts you for confirmation before deleting any objects.

## Tutorial: Modifying Object Characteristics

In this tutorial you'll use the commands introduced in this chapter to modify the Hot-tub symbol that was created in Chapter 4 and shown in figure 21.19.

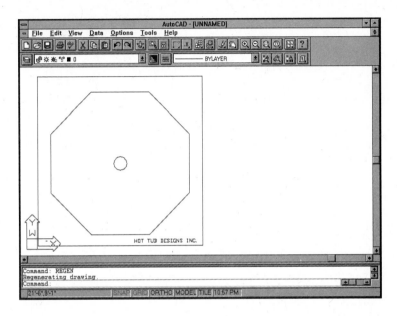

**Fig. 21.19**
Modifying object characteristics of the Hot tub Symbol.

1. Select Open in the Standard toolbar. In the File Name input box in the Open Drawing dialog box, type **C:\UAW13\21DWG01** and press Enter or click OK. This loads the Hot-tub symbol.

2. Create a new layer called HOTTUB.

3. Select DDLMODES from the Modify toolbar and press Enter. The Layer Control dialog box appears as shown in figure 21.20.

4. Type **hottub** in the edit box and click New. The HOTTUB layer will appear in the Layer Name column.

5. Click OK to close the dialog box.

**Fig. 21.20**
Using
DDLMODES to
create the
HOTTUB layer.

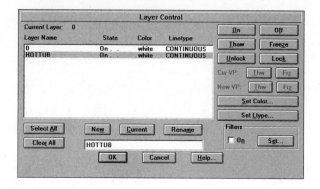

6. Now change the layer of the symbol. It's currently on layer 0.

   Change the symbol to the new layer HOTTUB that you just created.

7. At the Command: prompt, type **ddchprop** and press Enter.

   At the Select objects: prompt, type **all** and press Enter.

   At the Select objects: prompt, press Enter.

   The Change Properties dialog box appears as shown in figure 21.21.

8. Click the Layer button. The Select Layer dialog box appears as shown in figure 21.22.

9. Select the HOTTUB layer and click OK. The Select Layer dialog box will close.

10. Click OK in the Change Properties dialog box to accept the changes.

**Fig. 21.21**
Using the Change
Properties dialog
box to change the
properties of the
Hot tub symbol.

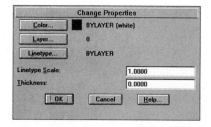

11. Now change the size of the drain in the Hot tub symbol.

    Select Properties from the Object Properties toolbar. At the Select objects: prompt, select the circle in the middle of the symbol that represents the drain.

The Modify Circle dialog box appears as shown in figure 21.23.

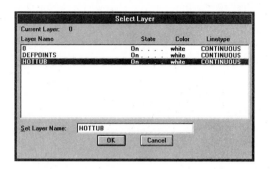

**Fig. 21.22**

Changing the layer
of the Hot tub
symbol geometry.

**12.** In the Radius edit Box, change the 5" to 6" and click OK. Notice that the size of the drain is now larger.

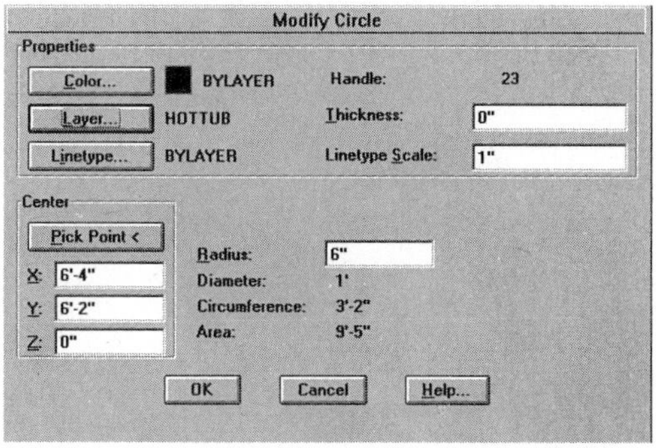

**Fig. 21.23**

Change the size of
the hot tub drain
using the Modify
Circle dialog box.

**13.** The text on the lower right of the symbol is too small to be read.

Use the DDMODIFY command to make it larger. Select Properties from the Object Properties toolbar.

At the Select object to modify: prompt, select the text. The Modify Text dialog box appears as shown in figure 21.24.

In the Height edit box, change 1" to 3" and click OK. The Modify Text dialog box is closed and the text is enlarged.

**14.** Finally, change the name of the Hot tub layer to HOT-TUB.

Select Rename from the Data menu. The Rename dialog box appears as shown in figure 21.25.

**VI**

**Advanced Editing**

**15.** Click Layer in the Named Objects column.

Then click HOTTUB in the Items column.

HOTTUB will appear in the Old Name input box as shown in figure 21.25.

**Fig. 21.24**

Change the size of the text in the Hot tub symbol.

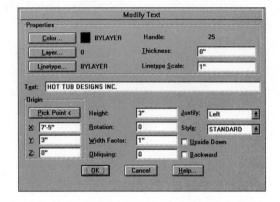

**16.** In the Rename To input box, type **hot-tub** and click the Rename To button.

Click OK to accept the renaming of the layer.

**Fig. 21.25**

Changing the Name of the HOTTUB Layer to HOT-TUB.

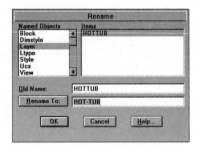

# From Here...

Besides geometry creation, AutoCAD offers several powerful commands to change an existing object. The DDCHPROP command allows you to easily move several objects to a different layer. For more in-depth changes, the DDMODIFY command not only lists the current database information for an existing object, but allows you to change the information.

Text can be edited with either the DDMODIFY or DDEDIT command. Rename existing objects with the DDRENAME command. Purging your drawing of unwanted objects is a good file management practice. Proper use of the PURGE command reduces file size, creating more space on your storage media for additional files.

For more information about what you can do with AutoCAD, see the following chapters:

- Chapter 5, "Creating Basic Geometry," shows you how to create basic geometry such as circles, arcs, and lines.

- Chapter 19, "Using Polylines," introduces you to the proper use and creation of polylines.

- Chapter 32, "Introduction to Solid Modeling Concepts," explains how to create and modify solid models.

**VI**

**Advanced Editing**

# Chapter 22

# Getting Information from Your Drawing

One advantage of using AutoCAD over manual drafting is the great deal of information AutoCAD stores about the drawing. This information is stored in a database. The information in the database may be accessed through a variety of commands. In this chapter, you'll learn how to extract information from AutoCAD's database. After completing this chapter you'll be able to:

- List the current status of AutoCAD (STATUS)

- List the information stored for drawing objects (LIST and DBLIST)

- Determine a distance and angle (DIST)

- Locate the coordinates of a point on-screen (ID)

- Calculate the area of a given shape (AREA)

- Keep track of the time spent on a drawing (TIME)

Calculating area or determining the distance and angle of a line can be very time-consuming and tedious work on a manually drawn object. The database AutoCAD creates is in a form that is easy to access and manipulate. By simply entering LIST and selecting a line, AutoCAD displays the line's distance and angle in the current units. Commands such as LIST, DBLIST, and STATUS display all the information stored for a specific object or for the entire drawing database.

AutoCAD also offers additional commands which are very useful when determining the area and perimeter of an object. By picking points on an object, AutoCAD calculates the object's area and perimeter. You also can easily add and subtract objects, such as an island, from the area.

Many individuals using AutoCAD on a daily basis are very concerned with the amount of time it takes to create and revise drawings. This information is often essential for billing purposes. AutoCAD automatically begins a timer whenever a drawing is started or revised. Issuing the TIME command displays this information on-screen.

# Listing the Status of AutoCAD (STATUS)

To obtain current information about your drawing, AutoCAD provides the STATUS command. The STATUS command may be accessed by:

- Choosing Status from the Data pull-down menu.

  or

- Entering **status** at the Command: prompt.

When the STATUS command is invoked, AutoCAD switches to a text window and generates a report based on the current drawing. The STATUS command reports information on the following:

- Name of the drawing

- Number of objects in the drawing

- The limits setting for current space (model space or paper space)

- The drawing's actual extents (model space or paper space)

- The limits of the current display

- The insertion base point

- Snap spacing

- Grid spacing

- Current space (model space or paper space)

- Object snap modes (endpoint, intersection, etc.)

- Current layer, color, linetype, thickness, and elevation

- The on/off Settings for fill, ortho, snap, grid, Qtext, and tablet

- Available disk space and swap file size, physical memory, swap file space

When reporting the Drawing Limits, AutoCAD compares the physical limits of the drawing to the actual limits you set. The space is either model space or paper space. If any objects are located outside the limits, AutoCAD responds with ***OVER in the model space uses section. All coordinates and distances displayed with the STATUS command are in the format specified in the most recent UNITS command. Entering **status** at the Dim: prompt reports the values and descriptions of all dimension variables.

AutoCAD also reports the amount of disk space available at the Free disk: line. As you continue creating geometry and the file size grows, you should maintain enough free space available at the Free disk: line equal to the size of the drawing. When working on a drawing, AutoCAD creates a variety of temporary files that are not saved with your drawing file. Because the temporary files are not saved as part of the drawing but are necessary when working on the drawing, you need extra disk space available when the drawing file is open.

---

### Troubleshooting

*Sometimes when I am working on a drawing, the computer seems really slow. What can I do to speed up AutoCAD?*

Several factors can cause your computer to slow down when running AutoCAD. The number of programs you currently have running in Windows is one factor. Hold the Control key down and press Escape (Ctrl+Esc). This brings up the Task List dialog box. Close everything but Program Manager and AutoCAD. This helps free up some system resources. If the computer consistently seems to access the hard drive when using AutoCAD, consider adding more memory to the computer. Adding more memory not only improves AutoCAD's performance, but other programs' performance as well.

---

## Tutorial: Listing the Status of a File

In this tutorial you load the hot-tub symbol from the workdisk and list the status of the file. This file should remain open for all subsequent tutorials in this chapter.

1. Choose the Open button from the Standard toolbar. If the AutoCAD dialog box appears, choose No unless you want to save the current drawing. If you want to save the current drawing, choose Yes and enter a path and drawing name.

**VI**

**Advanced Editing**

2. In the Select File dialog box, change to the appropriate drive and directory (C:/UAW13) and choose file 22DWG01. Your screen should resemble figure 22.1.

**Fig. 22.1**
Loading the completed hot-tub symbol from the workdisk.

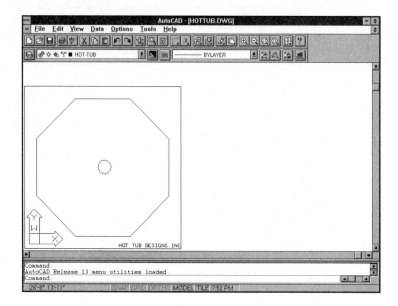

3. Choose Data, Status.

The AutoCAD text screen appears and the status information for the hot-tub symbol file appears as shown in figure 22.2. The information on your screen may vary from that of figure 22.2 because of the difference in your computer's configuration.

4. To return to the drawing area, press the F2 function key. The screen should now revert to figure 22.1. The next tutorial in this chapter continues from here.

**Fig. 22.2**
Listing the status of the hot-tub symbol file.

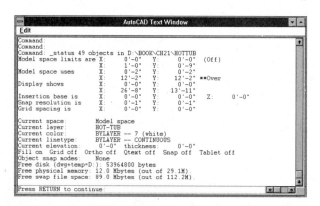

# Listing Object Information (LIST and DBLIST)

To obtain information about selected objects in your drawing, use the LIST command. The LIST command displays information about any selected objects within the drawing. The LIST command may be accessed by:

- Choosing the List button on the Object Properties toolbar.

- Entering **list** at the Command: prompt.

To use the LIST command, select the objects you want information about at the Select objects: prompt. When you have completed selecting objects, press Enter. AutoCAD displays the information on the selected objects on the screen.

The DBLIST command refers to Database List. This command displays *all* information about *every* object in the current drawing. The information provided with the DBLIST command is in the same format as the LIST command. As soon as you enter the DBLIST command, the data begins scrolling on-screen. The scrolling automatically stops when a complete page has been filled with information. To continue scrolling to the next page, press Enter.

---

**Caution**

Using the DBLIST command on a large drawing can take a long time to display all of the information. To display database information, it is usually more beneficial to select individual objects with the LIST command. To stop the DBLIST command, press Esc. This ends the scrolling and returns you to the drawing editor.

---

## Tutorial: Listing the Objects of a File

In this tutorial you list the object properties in the hot-tub symbol using both the LIST and DBLIST commands.

1. Continue from the previous tutorial. Begin this tutorial by first listing object properties singularly. Choose the List button from the Standard toolbar.

2. At the Select objects: prompt, select the outside edge of the hot-tub symbol as shown in figure 22.3 and press Enter.

**VI**

**Advanced Editing**

**Fig. 22.3**

Selecting the outside edge of the hot-tub symbol.

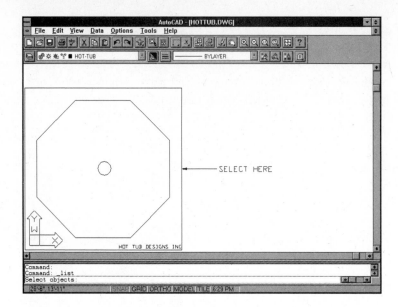

The AutoCAD text screen appears as shown in figure 22.4.

AutoCAD displays a Press RETURN to continue: prompt at the bottom of the screen. Press Enter to view the remaining information as shown in figure 22.5. Review the information in the AutoCAD text screen.

3. Press the F2 function key to return to the drawing area. Your screen now reverts back to figure 22.3.

4. Next list all of the objects found in the hot-tub drawing symbol file.

    Command: **dblist**

5. The AutoCAD text screen appears and you notice that AutoCAD begins a list of all objects found in the hot-tub drawing file. The list is similar to the list produced in step #1 of this tutorial. Review the list.

6. When the Press RETURN to continue:prompt appears, press Enter to continue the list. If you don't want to review the complete list, the DBLIST command can be canceled by pressing the Escape key.

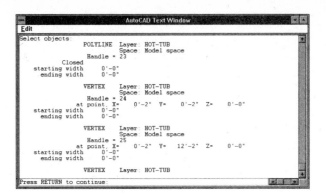

**Fig. 22.4**
Viewing the
AutoCAD text
screen list of the
information for
the outside edge
of the hot-tub
symbol.

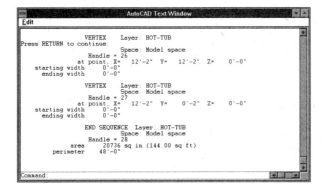

**Fig. 22.5**
Displaying the
complete list of
the outside edge
of the hot-tub
symbol.

# Reporting Distances and Angles (DIST)

To find the distance and angle between two points, use the DIST command. The DIST command is accessed by:

- Choosing the List button on the Object Properties toolbar brings up a fly-out menu, showing the Distance button.

- Entering **dist** at the Command: prompt.

To use the DIST command, select two points on the screen. The DIST command displays the distance and angle of the line. It also gives the delta $x$, $y$, and $z$ dimensions.

**VI**

**Advanced Editing**

## Tutorial: Using the DIST Command

In this tutorial you use the DIST command to determine the diagonal distance across the corners of the hot-tub symbol.

**Tip**

To ensure accuracy when using the DIST command, use OSNAP commands to pick locations. Alternatively, make sure the point locations lie on snap points and snap is turned on.

1. Continue from the previous tutorial. Choose the Distance button from the List fly-out menu.

2. First, select the upper-right corner of the hot-tub symbol as shown in figure 22.6. Use the INTersection osnap to ensure that your selection is exactly on the corner.

   > First point: *int*

3. Next, select the lower-left corner of the hot-tub symbol as shown in figure 22.7. Again, use the INTersection osnap.

   > Second point: *int*

4. Unlike the LIST command, the AutoCAD text screen does not appear. This information for the DIST command appears in the Command: prompt area as shown in figure 22.7. The distance should equal 17' as shown in figure 22.7.

**Fig. 22.6**
Selecting the upper-right corner of the hot-tub symbol.

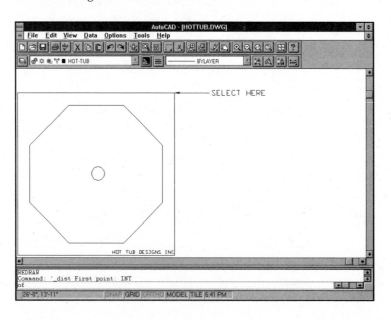

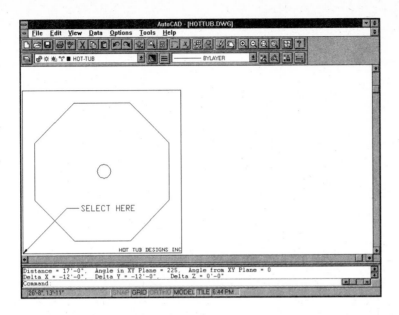

**Fig. 22.7**
Selecting the
lower-left corner
of the hot-tub
symbol. The DIST
information
appears in the
Command: prompt
area.

# Locating Points (ID)

As you are working on a new drawing or editing an existing drawing, it is often necessary to determine the coordinates for a specific location. The ID command is used to display information about a point location, giving its coordinates. The ID command is accessed by one of the following methods:

- Choosing the List button on the Object Properties toolbar to bring up a fly-out menu. The first button is Locate Point.

- Entering **id** at the Command: prompt.

To use the ID command, pick the point to be identified. Use the proper osnap mode to ensure accuracy.

The ID command also performs another important function. As you use ID to locate a point, the coordinates of the last point entered are stored in the LASTPOINT system variable. This is very useful when you want to begin drawing at a set distance from a specific point rather than a point you pick.

For example, to locate the center of a circle located .38 on the *x* and *y* axis from the corner of an object, select ID and pick the corner as shown in figure 22.8. Next, select CIRCLE and enter a relative coordinate. The command sequence is shown in the following example:

**VI**

**Advanced Editing**

```
Command: id
Point: int Use the OSNAP-INTersection of (select the corner)
Command: circle
3P/2P/TTR/<Center point>: @-.38,.38
```

This uses the LASTPOINT variable found with the ID command, locating the center of the circle with a Relative coordinate.

```
Diameter/<Radius>: d
Diameter: .38
Command:
```

Whenever you use the ID command, it automatically resets the LASTPOINT system variable to the value of the ID point. Using the @ sign tells AutoCAD to use the LASTPOINT value.

The From object snap also can be used to begin drawing at a set distance from a specific point. The From object snap makes a temporary reference point as the basis for locating subsequent points.

**Fig. 22.8**
Locating the center of a circle using the ID command to set the LASTPOINT system variable.

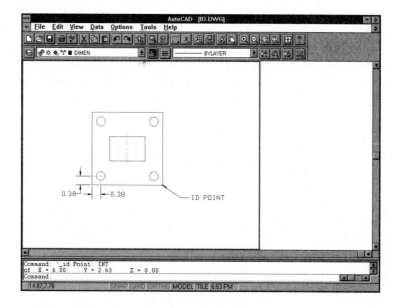

## Tutorial: Using the ID Command

In this tutorial, you use the ID command to determine the location of the upper-right corner of the hot-tub symbol.

1. Continue from the previous tutorial. Choose the Locate Point button from the List fly-out menu.

2. Select the upper-right corner of the hot-tub symbol as shown in figure 22.6. Use the INTersection osnap to ensure your selection is exactly on the corner.

> Point: *int*
>
> of *Select the upper-right corner as in figure 22.6.*

3. The point ID information appears in the Command: prompt area as shown in figure 22.9. This information gives us the *x*, *y*, and *z* coordinates of the upper-right corner of the hot-tub symbol.

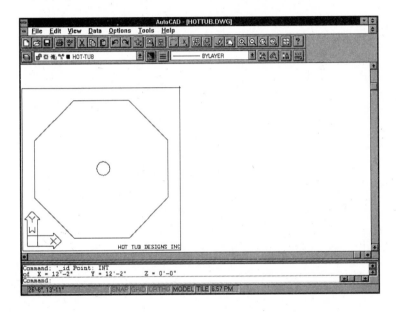

**Fig. 22.9**
Viewing the ID Information for the upper-right corner of the hot-tub symbol in the Command: prompt area.

# Calculating Area (AREA)

Calculating boundary area is required in many disciplines. A contractor may need to determine the square footage in a building or room to estimate building cost. A machinist may need to calculate the surface area of a part to determine the amount of protective coating needed.

One advantage of working with AutoCAD is the ease in which the drawing database may be used to make area calculations on a given drawing. The AREA command may be accessed by:

■ Choosing the List button on the Objects Properties toolbar brings up a fly-out menu, showing the Area button.

**VI**

**Advanced Editing**

- Entering **area** at the Command: prompt.

The basic function of the AREA command is to find the area of any pre-defined circle or polyline. The following command sequence calculates the area for a selected object:

```
Command: area<First point>/Object/Add/Subtract: o
Selectobjects: Select object.
Area=(x.xx), Circumference=(x.xx)
```

## Tutorial: Using the AREA Command

In this tutorial, you use the AREA command to determine the area of the drain in the hot-tub symbol.

**1.** Continue from the previous tutorial. Choose the Area button from the Inquiry fly-out menu.

**2.** Use the Object option and select the circle that represents the drain as in figure 22.10.

```
<First point>/Object/Add/Subtract: o
Select objects: Select the drain as shown in figure
        22.10.
```

**Fig. 22.10**

When you use the object option of area to calculate the area of the hot tub drain, the area information appears in the Command: prompt section.

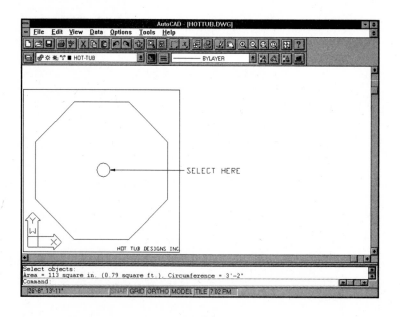

**3.** The area of the circle appears in the Command: prompt area as shown in figure 22.10.

## Finding Area (AREA First point)

With the AREA First point option, you pick points to define a boundary and AutoCAD calculates the area and perimeter of the boundary. When you pick two points, AutoCAD calculates the distance between them as the perimeter. If you pick three or more points, AutoCAD connects all of the points to create an imaginary polygon. AutoCAD reports the area and perimeter of the polygon. Pressing Enter at the Next point: prompt ends the pick point process. The following command sequence calculates the area for a selected object as shown in figure 22.11:

```
Select the Area button from the List fly-out menu.
<First point>/Object/Add/Subtract: Select the first point (1).
Next point: Select the second point (2).
Next point: Select the third point (3).
Next point: Select the fourth point (4).
Next point: Select the fifth point (5).
Next point:
```

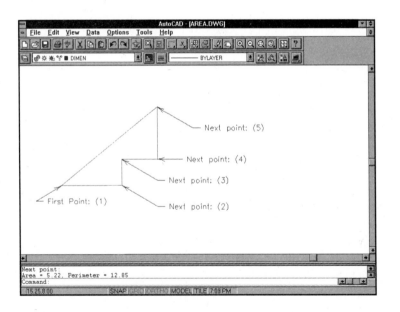

**Fig. 22.11**

Using the pick point option of area to calculate the area and perimeter of an object.

When calculating area with the First point option, shapes or lines do not have to be closed for AutoCAD to calculate their area. If the shape is not closed, AutoCAD calculates the area as if a line connected the first and last points. Specifically, AutoCAD automatically closes the area back to the starting point.

**VI**

**Advanced Editing**

First point is the default mode of the AREA command. To calculate the area of a shape, pick all vertices of the shape. To increase speed and accuracy, set a running OSNAP to INTersection or ENDpoint to help pick the vertices. Note the First point option only works with shapes created with straight lines.

> **Note**
>
> Using the AREA First point option to calculate area can be time-consuming since you must pick every vertex on the object. One option is to use the BPOLY command, discussed in the upcoming section "Developing a Boundary with BPOLY." If you know you are going to calculate areas on an object, consider creating the geometry with the PLINE command instead. Then you can use the Object option and select the entire object.

## Adding and Subtracting Features (AREA Add and Subtract)

The AREA command also allows you to add and subtract closed objects from the calculated area. You also can use the pick point method to define an area to add or subtract. AutoCAD keeps a running total of the area, based on the objects you select. You can switch back and forth between the add and subtract modes as needed. You can also mix point selection methods with object selection to define the boundary you want calculated.

## Tutorial: Using the AREA Command

In this tutorial, you use the AREA command to determine the area of the top face of the hot-tub symbol as shown by the hatched area in figure 22.12.

1. Continue from the previous tutorial. Choose the Area button from the List fly-out menu.

2. You first use the Add option. Once you are in the add mode, use the Object option and select the outside rectangle as shown in figure 22.13.

   ```
   <First point>/Object/Add/Subtract: a
   <First point>/Object/Subtract: o
   (ADD mode) Select objects: Select the outside
         rectangle as shown in figure 22.13.
   ```

3. The area of the rectangle is displayed in the Command: prompt area.

   ```
   Area = 20736 square in. (144.00 square ft.), Perimeter =
   48'-0", Total area = 20736 square in. (144.00 square ft.).
   ```

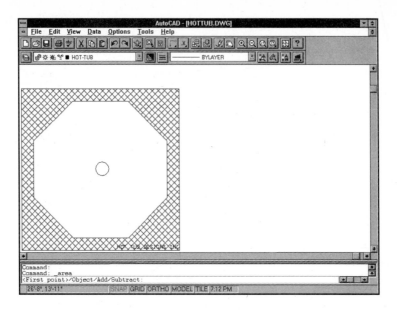

**Fig. 22.12**
Determining the
area of the top face
of the hot-tub
symbol.

4. To find the area required, you must subtract the area of the octagon.
   Change from the add mode to the subtract mode.

   ```
   (ADD mode) Select objects:
   <First point>/Object/Subtract: s
   ```

5. Use the object mode and select the octagon as shown in figure 22.13.
   After you enter the object mode, the prompt shows that you are in the
   subtract mode. When you select the octagon, its area is subtracted from
   the area of the rectangle.

   ```
   <First point>/Object/Add: o
   (SUBTRACT mode) Select objects: Select the octagon as
       shown in figure 22.13.
   ```

6. The area of the octagon is displayed in the Command: prompt area and is
   equal to 12,321 square inches (85.56 square feet).

   Notice that this time the total area is no longer equal to the area of the
   octagon, but is the area of the rectangle minus the area of the octagon.
   So the area of the surface is 8,415 square inches (58.44 square feet).

**VI**

**Advanced Editing**

**Fig. 22.13**
Using the Area–
Subtract option to
determine the area
of the top face of
the hot-tub
symbol.

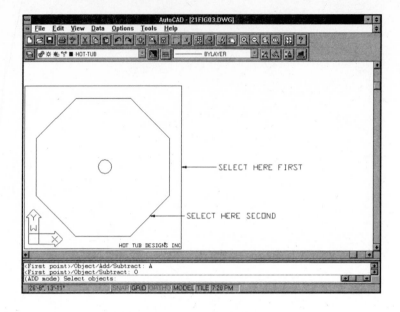

## Developing a Boundary with BOUNDARY

◀ See "Creating
Hatched Areas
Using Bound-
ary Hatch
(BHATCH),"
p. 488

Calculating an area with the First point selection can be a tedious process.
The BOUNDARY command automatically creates a polyline that bounds an
area. The area must be totally closed for the BOUNDARY command to work,
however.

In Chapter 17, "Filling Areas with Hatching," an option was used in the
BHATCH command that automatically generated a polyline boundary when
hatching an area. The BOUNDARY command performs the same function
without generating a hatch. Because the BOUNDARY command does not
automatically close a boundary, you must draw lines across any openings
before using BOUNDARY to correctly define the polyline boundary. The
BOUNDARY command may be accessed by one of the following methods:

■ Choosing the Rectangle button on the Draw toolbar brings up a fly-
out menu, showing the Boundary button.

■ Entering **boundary** at the Command: prompt.

◀ See "Using
Polylines,"
p. 573

When the BOUNDARY command is issued, the Boundary Creation dialog box
appears as shown in figure 22.14. Pick Points in the BOUNDARY command
works the same way as Pick Points in the BHATCH command. The BOUND-
ARY command creates a polyline that can be used with the AREA–Object
option.

**Fig. 22.14**
The BOUNDARY command is used to create a polyline that bounds an area.

> **Note**
>
> When the geometry is complex, the BOUNDARY command may have trouble defining the boundary. When this happens, use the Ray Casting Option of the Boundary Creation dialog box to get the desired result.

# Keeping Track of Time (TIME)

The clock within your computer automatically keeps track of the current date and time. AutoCAD uses this clock to maintain accurate time information about your drawing. The TIME command may be accessed by one of the following methods:

- Choose Time from the Data pull-down menu.

- At the Command: prompt, enter **time.**

When the TIME command is issued, AutoCAD displays the time information on-screen and responds with the following prompt:

    Display/ON/OFF/Reset:

The four options affect only the elapsed timer. This allows the timer to be used as a stopwatch. Time is not updated with the QUIT command because quit does not indicate that anything has been done in the drawing and that any time needs to be recorded. If you SAVE and then QUIT, the SAVE updates the timer.

The Reset option resets the elapsed timer to zero and turns the clock back on. To view the display again after resetting the clock, choose the Display option.

Off turns off the elapsed timer; On turns the timer back on. The time display contains the following information:

- *Current time.* Displays the current time and date according to the computer. Because AutoCAD uses the computer's clock, you must make sure the computer's date and time are set properly.

- *Created.* This is the date and time the current drawing was started.

- *Last updated.* The time the current drawing file was last updated. This time is updated whenever the SAVE or END command is issued.

- *Total editing time.* The total amount of time spent in all drawing sessions with the current drawing. If you end a drawing session with QUIT, the session's time is not recorded. This time includes all time the drawing file was open, whether you were working on the drawing or doing something else, like going to the gym. As long as the file is open, time is added to the Total editing time.

- *Elapsed timer (on).* This timer is affected by the Reset option. It can be turned On, Off, or Reset.

- *Next automatic save in.* Indicates the next time the drawing is automatically saved by AutoCAD. The system variable SAVETIME determines this time.

## Tutorial: Using the TIME Command

In this tutorial you use the TIME command to determine when the hot-tub symbol file was created. You also learn how to use the Elapsed Timer to record and measure the amount of elapsed time you are working on a drawing for.

1. Continue from the previous tutorial. Choose Time from the Data pull-down menu.

   The time summary is displayed in the AutoCAD text screen as shown in figure 22.15. Your screen is identical to figure 22.19. Notice the time and date that the hot-tub symbol was created.

2. Reset the timer, turn it on, and wait approximately 15 seconds.

   ```
   Display/ON/OFF/Reset: r
   Display/ON/OFF/Reset: on
   ```

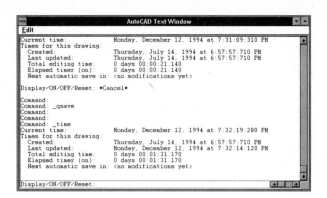

**Fig. 22.15**
Viewing the time
information for
the hot-tub
symbol file in the
AutoCAD text
screen.

**3.** After waiting approximately 15 seconds, turn the timer off.

> Display/ON/OFF/Reset: off

**4.** Display the time and note the elapsed time.

> Display/ON/OFF/Reset: **d**

The time summary is displayed once again in the AutoCAD text screen.
Look at the Elapsed timer section. Notice that the timer is off and the
elapsed time is approximately 15 seconds, as shown in figure 22.16.
Press the F2 function key to return to the drawing area.

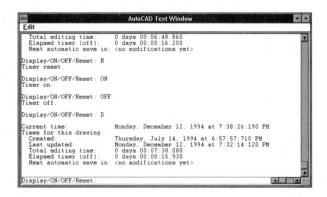

**Fig. 22.16**
Viewing the
elapsed timer
section of the time
information.

**VI**

**Advanced Editing**

# From Here...

The ability to easily access the drawing database is an important part of using AutoCAD. While the STATUS, LIST, and DBLIST commands give complete information on selected objects, this information cannot be changed.

The ID command can be very useful to locate points in a drawing and set the LASTPOINT system variable. Properly used, ID can greatly speed up drawing time. Setting the LASTPOINT variable can be used to begin drawing at a set distance from a given point rather than at a point you pick.

Calculating AREA is also easily accomplished using AutoCAD. Used in conjunction with the BOUNDARY command, area calculations on complex geometry is greatly simplified. Keeping track of time is another feature that can be very useful, especially in billing situations. Since AutoCAD automatically starts the clock each time you open a drawing file, you always have accurate information on when the drawing was started, edited, and how much time you spent working on it.

The amount of time spent working on a drawing is usually a major consideration when using AutoCAD. The ability to use the same geometry in several different drawings can lessen the time spent working on a drawing considerably. AutoCAD also allows you to attach information to a drawing. For example, you could attach the cost and manufacturer of a door to a door symbol. This information is saved with the drawing, and is available for export to other programs. These important topics are covered in the upcoming chapters:

- Chapter 23, "Using Symbols and XRefs," discusses the ability to use the same geometry in several different drawings.

- Chapter 24, "Working with Attributes," explains a method of attaching information to a drawing.

# On Your Own

Load the drawing 22DWG02 from your UAW13 subdirectory. Your drawing should look like figure 22.17. Calculate the amount of carpeting required to cover the kitchen and living room. Include the closet in the living room. Do not include the area by the fireplace (layer fireplace) or by the breakfast bar, appliances, and counter top (layer kitchen) in the kitchen. Keep an accurate record of your time.

**Fig. 22.17**
Calculate the square footage of carpeting required to cover the kitchen and living room in the apartment.

Hints:

■ After loading the drawing, set the timer. This enables you to keep an accurate record of your time.

■ Use the AREA command to calculate the total area in both the living room and kitchen. Use the AREA–Add option to include the closet. Use the AREA–Subtract option to remove the fireplace and kitchen counter areas.

■ Check your time, and then reset the timer. Calculate the area again, this time using the BOUNDARY command. Compare your answers and time.

**VI**

**Advanced Editing**

# Part VII

# Using Symbols and Attributes

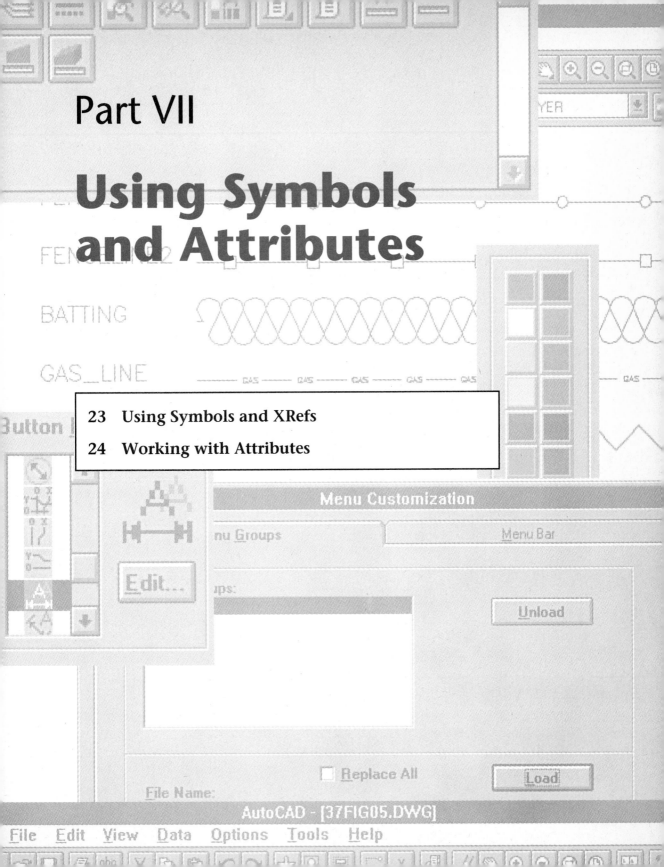

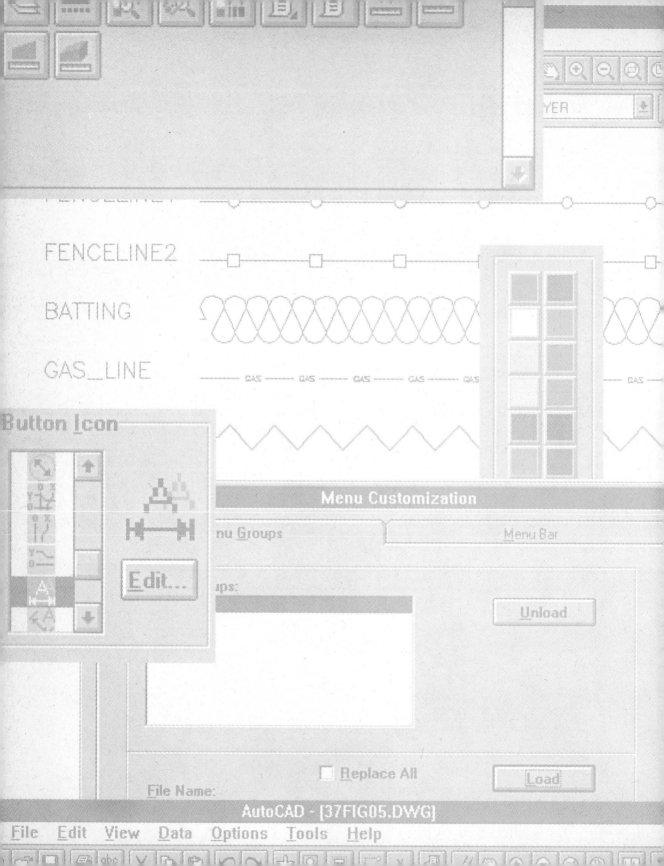

FENCELINE2

BATTING

GAS_LINE

**Button Icon**

Edit...

**Menu Customization**

nu Groups                                    Menu Bar

ups:

Unload

☐ Replace All                               Load

File Name:

AutoCAD - [37FIG05.DWG]

File   Edit   View   Data   Options   Tools   Help

# Chapter 23

# Using Symbols and XRefs

One advantage of using AutoCAD over manual drafting techniques is the ability to copy existing geometry to other locations in the drawing. AutoCAD also lets you copy existing geometry between drawings. For example, you could use the symbol for a water closet created in one drawing in several other drawings. This chapter discusses AutoCAD's ability to use geometry created in one drawing in one or several other drawings. In this chapter you learn to:

- Use the Object Grouping function to group objects

- Create a symbol library with the BLOCK command

- Write a section of a drawing to a file with the WBLOCK command

- Insert a symbol into a drawing (INSERT, DDINSERT)

- Insert multiple symbols into a drawing (MINSERT)

- Specify a new insertion point of a symbol with the BASE command

- Break a block apart into separate objects (EXPLODE)

- Insert shapes using the SHAPE command

- Reference another drawing (XREF)

Many drawings contain common geometric elements called *symbols*. In architecture, symbols are often used for door openings and kitchen appliances. Mechanical drawings may use a symbol for a nut or bolt. In manual drafting, these symbols may be placed in the drawing with a template.

AutoCAD can store these symbols for later use. AutoCAD has a command called BLOCK that allows you to define a group of objects as a single object. Once defined, these symbols, or *blocks,* can be inserted into a drawing full-size, scaled, or rotated.

The GROUP command allows you to create a series of named selection sets. One of the major differences between this command and the BLOCK command is the ability to select a series of objects based on their group association. As you explore the group command you will no doubt find it a much more convenient method of grouping objects within a drawing than using the BLOCK command.

◀ See "Under-
standing Selec-
tion Sets,"
p. 211

If you have the time and patience, you can create shapes. *Shapes* are similar to blocks but involve the use of codes instead of drawing tools. Although shapes are difficult to create, they are very easy to insert, and AutoCAD uses them to create complex linetypes.

AutoCAD also allows you to *reference* a drawing. When another drawing is referenced, it becomes part of the drawing on the screen, but its content isn't actually added to the current drawing file. These referenced drawings are referred to as *dependent symbols.* If you revise a dependent symbol, the drawing it references is automatically updated the next time it's opened in AutoCAD.

# Using Groups

Similar to blocks, *groups* allow you to group objects together in a named selection set. One of the key differences between GROUP and BLOCK is that an object can be assigned to more than one group. You will find this command useful if you have a large number of objects that you want to modify at one time. You access the GROUP command by doing either of the following:

- Select the Object Group button on the Standard toolbar.

- Type **group** at the Command: prompt.

When you access the GROUP command, the Object Grouping dialog box appears as shown in figure 23.1, and you are presented with the following options:

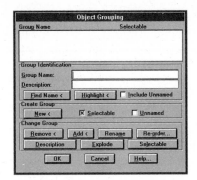

**Fig. 23.1**
The Object
Grouping dialog
box.

- *Group Name.* Enter a group name here. The group name convention is the same as the layer naming conventions and can be up to 31 characters long. AutoCAD converts the name to uppercase. Once a name has been given to the group, that name appears in the Group Name listing.

- *Description.* Enter a descriptive phrase for the group. The description can be up to 64 characters in length and is optional.

- *Find Name.* Allows you to select an object and then list the name of the group or groups with which the object is associated.

- *Highlight.* Shows all objects within a group. The group objects are shown in the drawing area.

- *Include Unnamed.* Allows you to view unnamed groups in the dialog box.

- *New.* Creates a new group from the objects you have selected.

- *Selectable.* Determines whether a group can be selected when a single object within the group is picked. If a group is unselectable, selecting any object within the group only selects that single object.

- *Unnamed.* Creates a group without a given name. AutoCAD assigns an anonymous name, *AN where *N* is a sequential number that indicates the new number of unnamed groups as they are created.

- *Remove.* Removes objects from a group. You can remove all objects within a group, but the group is still defined. Removing objects from a group doesn't remove them from the drawing.

- *Add.* Adds objects to a group.

■ *Rename*. Renames a selected group to the name found in the Group Name edit box. Select the group first, type the new group name in the Group Name edit box, and then click the Rename button.

■ *Re-order*. Selecting this button immediately displays the Order Group dialog box. In this dialog box you can change the order of the objects in a group. Objects are numbered as they are selected into the group. Re-ordering allows you to reverse the numbering scheme or change the scheme one by one.

■ *Description*. Changes the existing description of a group. Uses the same procedure as Rename.

■ *Explode*. Deletes a group. Select the group you want to delete from the list, then click the Explode button. The group definition is deleted but the objects remain in the drawing.

■ *Selectable*. Allows you to change whether an existing group is selectable.

# Using Blocks to Represent Symbols

Drawing an object once, with the ability to insert it into several other drawings, is one of the greatest timesaving features of AutoCAD. A block may be defined as a single object that is composed of many other objects. You can create objects as you normally would, using any of AutoCAD's drawing and editing tools. These objects can then be compiled into a block for use as a symbol in your drawing. Several advantages to using blocks are:

■ *Ability to share blocks*. A copy of a block can be stored on disk for use in other drawings. If you work with a standard set of symbols, for example, one person can draw the symbols and then share them with everyone else. This collection of standardized symbols can be called a *symbol library*.

■ *Reduction in file size*. When the COPY command is used, all of the objects are duplicated. For example, you have a symbol in a drawing that consists of 100 objects. When you COPY the objects, you duplicate the objects. If you COPY them 10 times, you have added 1000 new objects to the drawing file. If you make the objects a block and insert it 10 times, you only create 110 objects. 100 objects are for the original block, with 10 for each block. When you use blocks in your drawing, you can save a great amount of disk space.

- *Ease of modification.* If a block is updated or changed in a drawing, AutoCAD automatically updates all symbols based on that block. For example, if you decide to change the symbol for an electrical outlet, you first redefine the BLOCK definition of the outlet. AutoCAD automatically updates all electrical outlets based on the new BLOCK definition.

- *Ability to attach information.* When a block is created, you can attach information to it. This information can be extracted and used in other programs. These pieces of information are called *attributes*. For more information see Chapter 24, "Working with Attributes."

A block can be any symbol or entire drawing that you need to use more than once. Before you begin a drawing, create a rough sketch of the drawing. Look for assemblies, symbols, shapes, and notes that are used more than once. This information can be drawn once, then saved as a block.

## Creating Symbol Libraries (BLOCK)

To make a block, begin creating geometry using any AutoCAD commands. When you've finished creating the geometry, determine where the best place on the symbol to use as an insertion point. When the block is inserted into the drawing, the symbol is placed with its insertion point on the screen crosshairs.

Once the symbol is created and the insertion point determined, use the BLOCK command. Either of the following gives you access to the BLOCK command:

- Select the Block button on the Draw toolbar to bring up a fly-out menu, showing the different options for the BLOCK command.

- Type **block** at the Command: prompt.

Once you've invoked the BLOCK command, AutoCAD prompts for the name and insertion point. The block name may not exceed 31 characters. Additionally, use the appropriate OSNAP command or coordinate values when specifying the insertion point. You can use any selection set method such as Window, Fence, or Crossing to pick the objects that make up the block. The following command sequence is used when defining a block:

```
Select Block from the Draw toolbar.
Block name (or ?): Type in the block name.
Insertion base point: Pick the insertion point using OSNAP
    or by entering coordinates.
```

```
Select Objects: Select the objects comprising the symbol,
    using any selection set method.
Select Objects:
```

**Tip**
After creating the
block, the original
defining objects
are erased from the
screen. To restore
these objects,
type **oops** at the
Command: prompt
or select the Oops
button from the
Miscellaneous
toolbar.

When you have completed the BLOCK command sequence, the original
defining objects are erased from the screen. The defined block is now part of
the current drawing file. It may not be used in any other drawing—only the
one it was created in. Saving the block to be used in another file is discussed
in "Writing Blocks to a File" later in this chapter.

A block can be created from any objects that are already in your drawing. If
you create a symbol for a door, for example, you can use the BLOCK command to create a block from its objects. The block definition is now stored
with the drawing, and the original objects disappear from the screen. Once
the block is created, it may be inserted into the drawing as many times as
needed.

### Tutorial: Creating a Bathtub Symbol

In this tutorial you load the apartment floor plan, as shown in figure 23.2,
and create a bathtub symbol to be used in the apartment floor plan. The
apartment floor plan drawing is used in all subsequent tutorials in this
chapter.

**1.** Select Open from the Standard toolbar.

In the File Name input box in the Open Drawing dialog box, type
**C:\UAW13\23DWG03** and press Enter or click OK. This loads the
apartment floor plan as shown in figure 23.2.

**Fig. 23.2**
Loading the
apartment floor
plan.

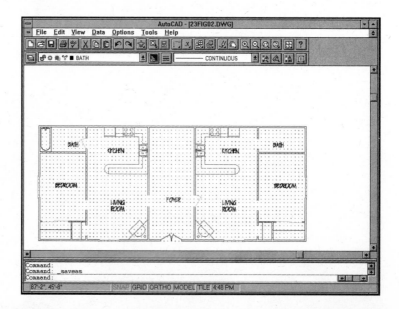

**2.** Change the view to display the left bathroom.

Select Named Views from the Standard toolbar.

The View Control dialog box appears as shown in figure 23.3. Select the Leftbath view as shown in figure 23.3, click the Restore button, and then click OK to select the new view. The screen zooms into the left bathroom as shown in figure 23.4.

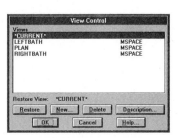

**Fig. 23.3**
Using the View Control dialog box to select the Leftbath pre-defined view.

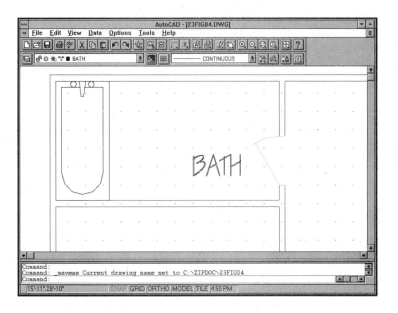

**Fig. 23.4**
Viewing the left bathroom to create a bathtub symbol block.

**3.** Now create the bathtub symbol block. Select Blocks from the Draw toolbar.

```
Insertion base point: 1'10",29'8"
Select objects: Window around the bathtub as shown in
     figure 23.5.

Select objects:
```

The bathtub disappears. Because the symbol is needed in this location, it may be helpful to bring it back by selecting the Oops button from the Miscellaneous toolbar.

**Fig. 23.5**
Use the window selection to select the objects to be included in the bathtub symbol block.

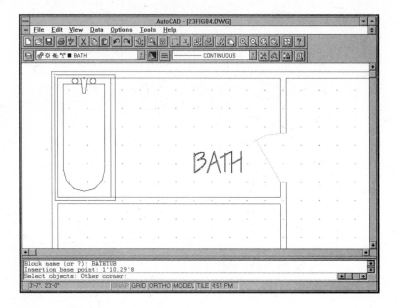

**4.** Return the bathtub drawing to its original position.

Select the Oops button from the Miscellaneous toolbar.

The bathtub drawing is redisplayed within the drawing area in its original position.

### Listing Blocks in the Current Drawing

To list the blocks defined in the current drawing, first enter the BLOCK command. At the Block name (or ?): prompt, enter a question mark as follows:

    Select Block from the Draw toolbar. Block name (or?):**?**
    Block(s) to list<*>:

This brings up a list of all blocks currently defined in the drawing. The following information is displayed in the text window:

```
Defined Blocks
(This area lists all blocks, alphabetically by name, defined in the drawing)
User            External        Dependent       Unnamed
Blocks          References      Blocks          Blocks
0               0               0               0
```

*User blocks* are blocks you created. *External references* are other drawings referenced with the XREF command. The XREF command is discussed later in "Using External References" later in this chapter. *Dependent blocks* are blocks that reside in an Xref drawing. *Unnamed blocks* are certain types of objects, such as associative dimensions or hatch patterns.

### Tutorial: Using BLOCK with the ? Option

**1.** Continue from the previous tutorial.

**2.** Select Block from the Draw toolbar.

```
Block name (or ?): ?
Block(s) to list<*>:
```

Notice that the bathtub is now listed as a block within the tutorial file.

### Creating Blocks on Layer 0

When objects are created on specific layers and blocked, they retain their original characteristics when inserted back into the drawing. To have a block adopt the characteristics of the current layer, create the original objects on layer 0.

When objects are created on layer 0 and blocked, the objects "float through" to the current layer and inherit the color and linetype of the current layer. The following list summarizes block creation, layers, and layer 0:

- *Maintain original object color and linetype.* To maintain the color and linetype with which the objects were originally created, draw the initial objects with the color, linetype, and layer you want. After creating the objects, block them. When the block is inserted back into the drawing, they retain their original color and linetype regardless of the current color, linetype, or layer.

- *Adopt characteristics of the current color and linetype.* To have objects adopt the current color and linetype, initially create the objects on layer 0. After creating the objects on layer 0, block them. When the block is inserted back into the original drawing, they adopt the current color and linetype.

- *Using Object Creation Modes dialog box.* Leave the Color and Linetype settings to the default Bylayer.

### Using Layers to Create Blocks

When blocks are created, the objects used to define the block may be drawn on various layers. Specify the color and linetype's bylayer when creating blocks. When you insert a block, the objects are placed in the drawing as well as the layers in which they were created. This is an easy way to assist in the standardization of layers. Create blocks such as doors on a layer called doors; when that block is inserted by anyone, the layer is automatically created. It's important to note that the block can be inserted on any layer and the new layers are still created unless there are duplicate layer names. If the layer that the block is inserted on is frozen or turned off, that block won't be displayed. Also, the layers that are newly created by inserting blocks can be manipulated individually, but the layer setting that the block was inserted on has precedence. If the block is exploded, the objects of the former block are no longer associated with the layer that the block was placed on. The block objects are now separate objects on their predefined layers.

### Using BYBLOCK with Blocks

◀ See "Modifying Object Characteristics," p. 625

The Object Creation Modes dialog box (DDEMODES), shown in figure 23.6, controls the current settings for Color and Linetype. Selecting the Color option in the Object Creation Modes (DDEMODES) dialog box brings up the Select Color dialog box. One option in the Select Color dialog box is to set the Logical Colors Byblock (see fig. 23.6).

**Fig. 23.6**
The default color and linetype can be set with the Object Creation Modes dialog box.

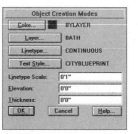

**Fig. 23.7**
The default object color can be set to Byblock in the Select Color dialog box.

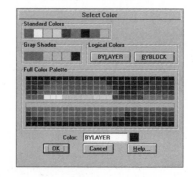

Byblock for color or linetype causes all the objects in the block to take on the settings of the insertion layer (assuming that the block was originally drawn on layer zero). Any change in the insertion layer affects the block as a whole. This is different than using Bylayer.

## Writing Blocks to a File (WBLOCK)

A block created from a group of objects can only be used in the current drawing. The WBLOCK command writes all or part of a drawing to a file. When you WBLOCK a group of objects, you essentially create a block and copy it to a new drawing file on the disk. This drawing file is no different than any other drawing file you create and save.

Once the WBLOCK definition is written to a file, it can be used outside of the current drawing. The WBLOCK command enables you to export symbols created in a drawing to use in other drawings. The WBLOCK command may be accessed by:

- Selecting the Block button on the Draw floating toolbar. The third button is the Wblock button.

- Typing **wblock** at the Command: prompt.

When you enter the WBLOCK command, the Create Drawing File dialog box appears. Select the drive, path, and name of the Wblock file to create. Don't include a file extension, since AutoCAD assumes you are creating a DWG file and automatically adds it.

> **Note**
>
> Proper file management techniques are very important when using blocks. One of the greatest benefits of AutoCAD is the capability to store common symbols for future use. The ability to easily locate a symbol after it has been stored on the disk is just as important as how it was created.

After entering the drive, path, and name, AutoCAD prompts you for a block name. Enter the name of the block you wish to write to the disk. The following list summarizes responses to the Block name: prompt:

- Block name: *Specify the name of the block to write to disk*. This option writes an *existing* block file to disk.

- Block name: = The = (equal) sign means that you want to create a Wblock of an existing block and that the existing block has the same name as the one you already entered for the wblock.

- `Block name:*` Typing the * (asterisk) writes the entire drawing to disk. Using the * option with the WBLOCK command doesn't write unreferenced symbols (layers, blocks, linetypes, text styles, and dimension styles) to the drawing file. Using this technique is similar to applying the PURGE command to your drawing. By dropping unused symbols from the drawing, the drawing file is reduced in size. Once the block is created, you must remember not to save any changes to the current file or the block will be over-written.

- `Block name:` *(Press spacebar or Enter)* Pressing the spacebar or Enter key causes AutoCAD to prompt for the `Insertion base point:`. After selecting the Insertion base point, you are prompted to `Select objects:`. Using this method allows you to write a group of objects to disk without first making them into a block with the BLOCK command.

> **Note**
>
> Using the WBLOCK command creates a standard AutoCAD DWG drawing file which can be edited. It's also important to note that the insertion point of the block drawing file is now the origin for the drawing file.

### Tutorial: Using WBLOCK to Create a Door Symbol

In this tutorial you create a Wblock of the 2'8" door symbol found in figure 23.2. Before you start, you need to restore your drawing area view as shown previously in figure 23.2.

1. Continue from the previous tutorial. Restore the view so that the complete apartment floor plan can be seen within the drawing area.

   Select Named Views from the View pull-down menu.

   The View Control dialog box appears as shown previously in figure 23.3. Select the Plan view, click Restore, and then click OK to select the new view. The screen displays the complete floor plan within the drawing area as shown earlier in figure 23.2.

2. Zoom in on the door drawing to convert it to a symbol.

   Select Zoom Window from the Standard toolbar.

   ```
   All/Center/Dynamic/Extents/Left/Previous/Vmax/Window/
       <Scale(X/XP)>:
   ```

Create a window similar to that shown in figure 23.8. The view should now resemble the one shown in figure 23.9.

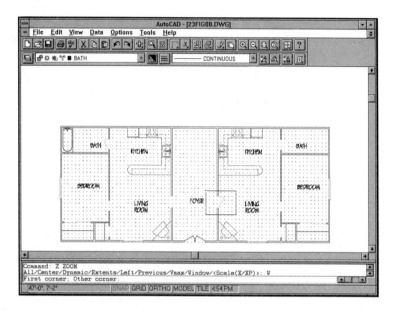

**Fig. 23.8**

Using Window to zoom in on the door.

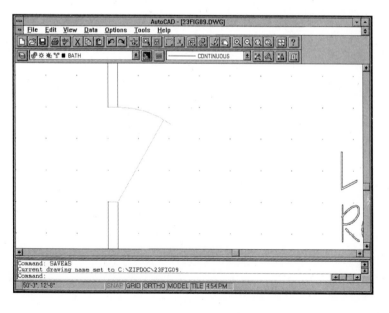

**Fig. 23.9**

Displaying the door separately in the drawing area.

**3.** Create a Wblock of the door symbol.

> Command: **wblock**

The Create Drawing File dialog box appears as shown in figure 23.10. In the File Name input box type **C:\UAW13\23DWG01** and click OK.

**Fig. 23.10**

Using the Create Drawing File dialog box to name the 23DWG01 Wblock.

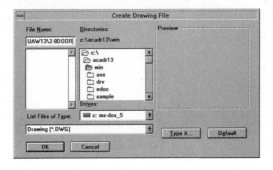

> Block name (or ?):
> Insertion base point: **42',12'**
> Select objects:

Create a window around the door as shown in figure 23.11.

**Fig. 23.11**

Using the Window Selection method to select the door in the apartment floor plan.

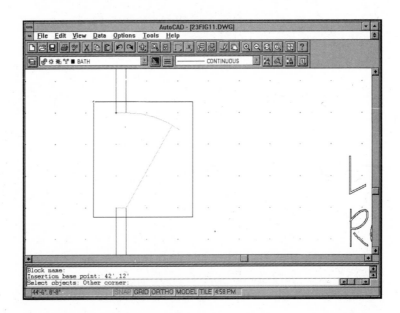

> Select objects:

The door drawing disappears and is saved to a Wblock file for later use in this or another drawing.

**4.** Now return the door drawing back to its original position.

> Command: **oops**

The door drawing is restored back to its original location on the apartment floor plan drawing.

## Points to Consider when Creating a Block

When creating a block or wblock, several factors affect your ability to use the block. The layer, color, linetype, insertion point, and size the block was drawn at all affect the block when you try to use it. Following are tips that help in the creation of blocks and avoid confusion when creating and later inserting blocks.

- *Layer, color, and linetype.* To have the block take on the characteristics of the layer on which it is inserted, all the block's objects must be on layer 0 (zero) when you create the block and the color and linetype variables must be set to bylayer.

  If the block was created from objects on any layer other than layer 0 (zero), the block retains the characteristics of that layer. If the block objects were created on several layers, the block's objects remains on the original layers when inserted. If the block was created on a layer that doesn't exist in the current drawing, AutoCAD recreates that layer when the block is inserted.

- *Drawing a block to scale.* When creating a block, draw all the objects that comprise the block to *unit size*. For example, suppose you draw an electrical outlet symbol 1 unit wide. When scaling the block in a different drawing, AutoCAD automatically scales the block for you. If you want the electrical outlet symbol to be 2 units across in the new drawing, from the INSERT command specify a scale factor of 2. If the block should be half a unit, use a scale factor of .5.

- *Defining the insertion base point.* The BLOCK command's Insertion base point: prompt asks you to define a reference point on the block. This reference point is used when inserting the block into the drawing. Select a reference point that is convenient for future reference. For example, the center or lower-left corner are commonly used as reference points.

**Tip**

Existing block names can be changed with the Rename dialog box (DDRENAME).

## Inserting Symbols into a Drawing (INSERT, DDINSERT)

After defining a block in a drawing, the block can be inserted into the drawing. Additionally, you can insert any drawing file (including files created with the WBLOCK command) into a drawing as a block. AutoCAD provides the INSERT, DDINSERT, and MINSERT commands for inserting a block into a drawing.

When inserting a block into a drawing, you must specify four things:

- The name of the block or file to insert.

- The point where you want the block inserted.

- The block scale in the *x*-, *y*-, and *z*-axis.

- The rotation of the block.

If you type **insert** at the Command: line, AutoCAD prompts you for this information. The DDINSERT command is similar to the INSERT command in the way it inserts blocks or files into a drawing. The DDINSERT command opens the Insert dialog box that can be used to locate the block or file name and specify the insertion parameters. In most cases the DDINSERT command is easier to use, and it's the one used in this chapter. The Insert dialog box can be accessed by:

- Selecting the Insert Block button on the Draw floating toolbar brings up a fly-out menu. The second button is the BLOCK button.

- Typing **ddinsert** at the Command: prompt.

The Insert dialog box is shown in figure 23.12. To select a block that is already defined in the drawing, select the Block button. This causes the Defined Blocks dialog box to appear as shown in figure 23.13.

**Fig. 23.12**
Use the Insert dialog box to insert blocks easily.

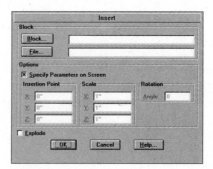

**Fig. 23.13**
The Defined Blocks dialog box lists all blocks currently defined in the drawing.

To insert a file into the drawing as a block, select the File button. This causes the Select Drawing File dialog box to appear as shown in figure 23.14. Change to the appropriate drive and directory and choose the desired file.

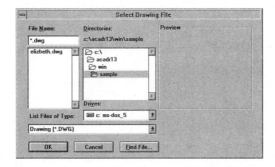

**Fig. 23.14**
The Select Drawing File dialog box allows you to select a file to insert into the current drawing as a block.

The insertion point, scale, and rotation of the block can be set in the edit boxes in the Insert dialog box. By default, the Specify Parameters on Screen box is checked. If this option is used, you are returned to the drawing editor after selecting the appropriate block or file and selecting OK. You are then prompted to specify the insertion point, scale, and rotation parameters at the Command: prompt. AutoCAD dynamically changes the appearance of the block as you specify the rotation and scale values.

> **Note**
>
> The insertion base point specified when the block was created is the point at which the block is now inserted. If you're inserting a drawing file where you didn't specify a base point, the origin (0,0,0) becomes the insertion base point by default.

To change the parameters in the Insert dialog box, remove the check in the Specify Parameters on Screen checkbox. Type the appropriate values in the text boxes. Setting the parameters in the Insert dialog box doesn't allow you to see the size and orientation of the block prior to insertion.

> **Note**
>
> When inserting entire drawings it's often easier to remove the check in the Specify Parameters on Screen box and set the values in the Insert dialog box. Since entire drawings have the insertion base point set to 0,0,0, this option can speed up block insertion. 0,0,0 refers to the origin of the drawing being inserted. Setting the values in the Insert dialog box speeds things up because AutoCAD doesn't have to try and represent the drawing as you alter the insertion point, scale, and rotation on screen.

### Tutorial: Inserting Symbols into a Drawing

In this tutorial you learn how to insert the bathtub and 2-8 door symbols that you created in the previous tutorials. Begin by first inserting the bathtub symbol.

1. Continue from the previous tutorial. Change the view to display the right bathroom.

   Select Named Views from the View pull-down menu.

   The View Control dialog box appears as shown previously in figure 23.4. Select the RIGHTBATH view, click the Restore button, and then click OK to select the new view. The screen zooms into the left bathroom as shown in figure 23.15.

**Fig. 23.15**
Using the View Control dialog box to select the Rightbath predefined view.

2. Select Insert Block from the Draw toolbar.

   The Insert dialog box appears as shown in figure 23.16. Click the Block button. The Defined Blocks dialog box appears as shown in figure 23.17. Select the bathtub symbol and click the OK button. Bathtub appears in the Block input box of the Insert dialog box. To select the symbol for insertion click OK in the Insert dialog box as well.

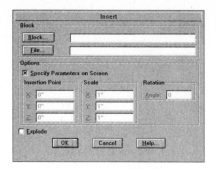

**Fig. 23.16**
Use the Insert
dialog box to insert
the bathtub
symbol.

**Fig. 23.17**
Use the Defined
Blocks dialog box
to select the bath-
tub symbol for
insertion into the
apartment floor
plan's right
bathroom.

```
Insertion point: 70'2",29'8"
X scale factor <1>/Corner/XYZ:
Y scale factor (default=X):
Rotation angle <0>:
```

The bathtub symbol is inserted into the bathroom as shown in figure
23.18. Notice that the vertical line on the left of the bathtub is blue.
Change this so that it's consistent with the symbol colors of the other
objects in the next tutorial.

3. You're now ready to add the 23DWG01 symbol to the bathroom drawing. Before inserting the 23DWG01 symbol, change to the Doors layer.
   Use the layer control function in the toolbar and change to the DOORS
   layer.

4. Now insert the 23DWG01 symbol.

   Select Insert Block from the Draw toolbar.

**Fig. 23.18**
The right bath-
room with the
bathtub symbol
inserted.

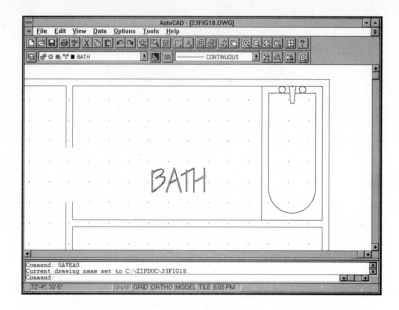

The Insert dialog box appears as shown in figure 23.16. Click the <u>B</u>lock
button. The Defined Blocks dialog box appears as shown in figure
23.17. Select the 23DWG01 symbol. Click OK and the 23DWG01
appears in the Block input box of the Insert dialog box. To select the
symbol for insertion click OK in the Insert dialog box as well.

```
Insertion point: endp of
```

Make the selection as shown in figure 23.19.

**Fig. 23.19**
Selecting the
insertion point of
the 23DWG01
symbol.

```
X scale factor <1>/Corner/XYZ:
Y scale factor (default=X):
Rotation angle <0>: 180
```

The block is inserted on the drawing and is placed on the DOORS layer as shown in figure 23.20.

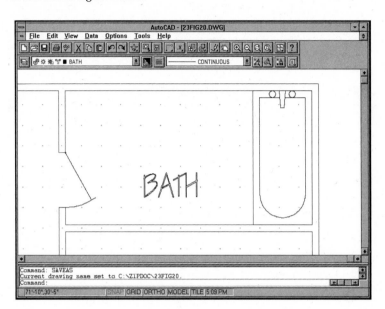

**Fig. 23.20**
The bathroom after the bathtub and 23DWG01 symbols have been inserted.

## Specifying a New Insertion Point (BASE)

The INSERT or DDINSERT command can be used to insert an entire drawing into the existing drawing. By default, the drawing being inserted has a base insertion point of 0,0,0. The BASE command can be used to change the insertion point for the new drawing. The BASE command can be accessed by typing **base** at the Command: prompt.

To determine the best location for the base point, examine the drawing view and the location of the inserted drawing. After you redefine the base point, all subsequent drawings are inserted at that point.

## Breaking Blocks Apart (EXPLODE)

When you create a block from a group of objects in AutoCAD, it's defined as a single object. The individual objects in the block definition can't be edited.

When a block is exploded, the block definition is removed and the block is broken down into its individual objects. Exploding a block creates a drawing database entry for each object in the block. Exploding a block can have a significant effect on the size of a drawing. The EXPLODE command is used to explode an existing block. The EXPLODE command can be accessed by:

- Selecting the EXPLODE button on the Modify floating toolbar.

- Typing **explode** at the Command: prompt.

After the block is exploded, the individual objects that were part of the block can now be edited. Exploding a block only affects the selected block and doesn't affect any other blocks with the same name.

> **Note**
>
> Release 13 allows you to explode a block that wasn't uniformly scaled.

**Tip**

You can use the Insert dialog box (DDINSERT) to explode a block before it's inserted. Simply place a check in the Explode checkbox.

### Tutorial: Exploding a Block and Changing the Layer of a Block Object

As mentioned in the previous tutorial, the left vertical line of the bathtub symbol isn't the same color as the other objects in the symbol. In this tutorial you'll explode the symbol and make the change to the object.

1. Continue from the previous tutorial.

   ```
   Command: ddchprop
   Select objects: Select the left vertical line of the
        bathtub symbol.
   ```

   Notice that the whole symbol is selected. It's necessary to explode the block before any objects can be modified. Press the Esc key to cancel the DDCHPROP command.

2. Use the EXPLODE command before modifying block objects.

   Select Explode from the Modify toolbar.

   ```
   Select objects: Select any portion of the bathtub
        symbol.
   ```

   The bathtub symbol is highlighted.

   ```
   Select objects:
   ```

   There is no apparent change in the block, but upon further inspection you'll notice that you may now modify the block objects.

3. Modify the block object layer properties.

   ```
   Command: ddchprop
   Select objects: Select the left vertical line of the
        bathtub symbol.
   Select objects:
   ```

Notice that the vertical line is on the walls layer. Use the Change Properties dialog box to change the line from the walls layer to the bath layer.

## Inserting More than One Block (MINSERT)

The MINSERT (Multiple INSERT) command combines the features of the INSERT and ARRAY commands for block insertion. All blocks in the array are recognized as a single object. Using the MINSERT command for inserting and arranging blocks not only saves time but disk space as well. The MINSERT command can be accessed by:

■ Selecting Insert Multiple Blocks from the Miscellaneous toolbar.

■ Typing **minsert** at the Command: prompt.

```
Block name (or ?): Enter name of block.
Insertion point: Type in or select coordinates to
    insert block.
X scale factor <1> / Corner / XYZ: Press Enter or
    change scale.
Y scale factor (default=X): Press Enter or change
    scale.
Rotation angle <0>: Enter angle.
Number of rows (---) <1>: Enter number of rows.
Number of columns (¦¦¦) <1>: Enter number of columns.
```

> **Note**
>
> All blocks included in the MINSERT array have the same scale and rotation. Additionally, blocks inserted with MINSERT can't be exploded.

◀ See "Producing Arrays of Objects (ARRAY)," p. 292

## Updating a Symbol

To edit a block, it first must be broken down into its original objects. This is especially important when an entire drawing is inserted. The EXPLODE command is used to break the block apart into its individual objects. To make sure the block was exploded properly, select any object that was formally part of the block. Only that object should be highlighted.

Occasionally situations arise when a block must be edited. AutoCAD allows you to redefine an existing block, even if it has been placed on the drawing many times. To update a symbol defined as a block, use the following procedure:

1. Insert the block you want redefined anywhere on the drawing.

2. Explode the block just inserted with the EXPLODE command.

3. Edit the block using any of AutoCAD's editing commands.

4. Redefine the block using the BLOCK command.

5. When prompted for the name, give the edited block the same name it had before. Answer Yes when AutoCAD prompts `Redefine it? <N>`.

6. Specify the same insertion point on the edited block as the original.

7. All blocks that were inserted are updated when the BLOCK command is completed.

If you try to redefine the block without using the EXPLODE command, the following error message is displayed and the command is aborted:

```
Block <name> references itself
*Invalid*
```

The error message alerts you that you're trying to re-create a block that already exists. Use the EXPLODE command on the block and redefine it.

## Editing Blocks with Grips

Because AutoCAD defines blocks as a single object, a block normally displays one grip. This single grip is located at the insertion point of the block. This grip can be used to perform all the Grip auto edit functions such as move and copy on the block.

The GRIPBLOCK system variable is used to control the display of grips within a block. The easiest way to control the GRIPBLOCK variable is with the Grips dialog box. The Grips dialog box can be accessed by:

■ Selecting Grips from the Settings pull-down menu.

■ Typing **ddgrips** at the `Command:` prompt.

To enable the GRIPBLOCK variable, check the box labeled Enable Grips Within Blocks in the Grips dialog box.

The default setting for the GRIPBLOCK variable is 0 or off. When GRIPBLOCK is off, the block displays a single grip. When GRIPBLOCK is set to 1 or on, all individual objects within the block display grips as if they were single objects. This can be useful if you need to edit the basepoint in the block.

Even though each individual object displays its grips when GRIPBLOCK is set to 1, you can't use the grips to edit the individual objects within the block—only the basepoint. The block must first be exploded to edit the individual objects.

### Nesting Blocks

Nested blocks are simply blocks that contain other blocks. You can create a block that contains another block by just selecting the block as the object to include in the new block. If you explode a block that contains a block, it converts the first block to all the individual objects and the second block is unaffected. To separate the second block, you must explode it as well. It is possible for a block to contain another block, which can contain another block, which could contain the first block.

# Using Shapes to Represent Symbols

Another method of representing or inserting symbols is to use shapes. The methods used to insert shapes and blocks are similar. The difference however, is in the creation of a shape. When creating a block, you can use the standard AutoCAD drawing commands to create the object. To create a shape, you must use a special coding system that was developed by Autodesk. To create this shape file you would use a text editor or word processor that is capable of saving an ASCII format file with an SHX extension. A sample file is shown below:

```
*230,6,DBOX
014,010,01C,018,012,0
```

As you can see, the coding is very cryptic and without some kind of reference or prior knowledge of these codes, it can be very difficult to create a shape. If you would like to learn more about creating shapes, refer to the AutoCAD Release 13 *Customization Guide*. Although shapes are more difficult to create, many third-party developers supply shape libraries such as architectural symbols that can speed up the creation of complex drawings.

It's important to note that before a shape can be used, it must be loaded using the LOAD command. The sequence for using a shape is as follows, starting with the LOAD command.

- Select Shape File from the Data pull-down menu.

- Type **load** at the Command: prompt.

In the the Select File dialog box select or type in the name of the shape file that you wish to load.

Once the shape file is loaded, type **shape** at the Command: prompt to place the shape.

```
Shape name (or ?)<current>: Enter the name of the shape
    file previously loaded.
Start point: Specify the start point or insertion point of
    the shape.
Height<1.0000>: Specify the height of the shape.
Rotation angle <0>: Specify the rotation of the shape.
```

# Using External References (XREF)

When working on a drawing, sometimes you need information stored in another drawing. One method is creating a Wblock of the information and inserting the block into the current drawing. Or you could simply insert the entire drawing. This procedure increases the size of the drawing by the size of the inserted block, however.

AutoCAD provides another means for inserting one drawing into another. *External references*, or *Xrefs*, appear in the drawing but aren't actually part of the drawing. Several examples of how Xrefs may be used are:

■ *Title Block.* An external reference drawing could serve as the title block used in a drawing. Since the title block is usually the same for every drawing, it doesn't need to be stored with the drawing. By attaching the title block as an external reference drawing, you can still see the title block with the drawing while saving disk space.

■ *Master Drawings.* Xrefs can allow you to assemble a master drawing from a set of component drawings, some of which are still subject to change. The Xref component drawings aren't stored with the current drawing, but reloaded when needed. Because Xrefs are reloaded, they always reflect the latest revisions.

■ *Workgroup Design.* Workgroup design refers to a group of people that work together as a team on a design project. For example, suppose a new intersection needs to be designed. The design has many aspects— site-grading plan, lighting and signal plan, and a landscaping plan. Complex jobs like this are often designed by a team of engineers rather than by a single individual. The team is called a *workgroup*.

In a project such as this, coordinating the design can be difficult. Each person in the workgroup must rely on the other members for information about the design. All the areas are related. For example, everyone needs to know what the site plan looks like so they can design their part of the intersection.

Each person could insert the site plan into their drawing as a block. If the site plan is inserted as a block, however, the landscaping designer has no way of knowing if the site plan changes because the site plan block won't update automatically.

Xrefs can keep all the different drawings up to date. If the site plan is attached to each engineer's drawing as an Xref, it isn't actually a part of their drawing. If the site plan is changed for some reason, the change occurs automatically each time the other engineers load their drawing, plot, or manually update the Xref in their drawing. Any changes to one drawing can be automatically updated in the other designs. If a change occurs, each engineer in the workgroup knows almost immediately and can modify their design accordingly.

Xrefs also can be attached temporarily to a drawing. For example, suppose you're designing a mechanical part that attaches to another part. The design for the other part has already been completed. You could attach the design for the other part to your drawing as an Xref to provide a reference to use. By using the completed design as an Xref, you can guarantee your part matches the other one. To access the XREF command:

- Display the External References toolbar (see fig. 23.21).

- Type **xref** at the Command: prompt. The following prompt is displayed:

      ?/Bind/Detach/Path/Reload/Overlay/<Attach>:

**Fig. 23.21**
The Xref toolbar has eight different tools.

The Xref function allows you to reference objects for object snaps, set referenced layers and linetypes, or use referenced dimension and text styles. You cannot change or otherwise modify any of the objects of the Xref file. You can change the layer color and linetype, but only for the current file. It doesn't change any of the settings for the externally referenced file.

## Listing Referenced Drawings (XREF ?)

The ? option lists all the drawings referenced by the current drawing. The following command sequence lists all currently referenced drawings:

```
Command: xref
?/Bind/Detach/Path/Reload/Overlay/<Attach>:?
Xref(s) to list <*>:
```

AutoCAD lists each externally referenced drawing name and path in which the drawing is located. The List option in the Xref toolbar also lists the externally referenced drawings.

## Referencing Another Drawing (XREF Attach)

The default Xref option at the Command: line, Attach, adds a referenced drawing to the current drawing. AutoCAD prompts with Xref to Attach:, where you supply the path and name of the file to attach.

When the Attach option is selected from the External References toolbar, the Select File to Attach dialog box appears. The dialog box appears with options to select the drive, directory, and file name of the drawing you want to use as the external reference. The drive and path to the selected file is used to reload the Xref each time the master drawing is opened, regenerated, or plotted.

> **Note**
>
> An Xref drawing may itself have external references to other drawings. Autodesk calls this *nesting* an Xref because one Xref is contained or nested within another. Using this technique, you can create chains of external references. For example, you can create and save a drawing called A. You can then create a new drawing called B and attach drawing A as an Xref. You can then create a new drawing C and attach drawing B as an Xref. Drawing C contains the Xref of drawing B and the Xref inside B of drawing A. Drawing A is a nested Xref.
>
> Chains or nested Xrefs may not loop back on themselves. To continue with the example, AutoCAD will not let you attach drawing C as an Xref to drawing A. Autodesk call this a *circular* reference. If you attempt a circular reference, AutoCAD displays a warning message and stops the attachment.

After selecting the file to Xref, AutoCAD prompts for the insertion point, scale, and rotation to attach the referenced drawing. This is the same information asked for when inserting a block. The XREF command doesn't offer a dialog box to preset insertion point, scale, and rotation.

After the Xref has been attached, it contains only one grip like a block. The grip is located at the Xref insertion point. You can use the grip to modify the Xref with any of the auto edit modes.

Although you can't change or modify the Xref, you can use OSNAP modes to snap to points on the Xref. This makes it possible to use the geometry in the Xref as if it actually is part of your drawing.

When the source drawing for the Xref changes, the changes appear in your drawing whenever you load the drawing, regenerate it, or plot it. You can also force the Xref to update itself with the Xref Reload option.

## Layers and Named Objects with XREFs

When a drawing is attached as an Xref, each Xref can have unique layers, layers similar to the master drawing. When an Xref is attached, the new layer names appear in the master drawing with a prefix containing the name of the Xref.

For example, you attach a drawing called FLPL that contains a layer called Wall. The Wall layer is renamed FLPL|WALL and appears with that new name in the Layer Control dialog box in the master drawing.

You can change the color, linetype characteristic, freeze, thaw, and turn on or off any Xref layer. You can't make the Xref layers current, however. This is because the layers are only *borrowed* from the Xref drawing.

Other named objects included in the externally referenced drawing are also brought into the current drawing. These include blocks, dimension styles, layers, linetypes, text styles, and named views. Like layers, these named objects are prefixed by the name of the Xref, such as Flpl|Newline.

### Tutorial: Attaching a File to a Drawing Using XREF

In this tutorial you use the 23DWG02 file to attach stairs to the apartment floor plan drawing. To do this, you use the Xref Attach function.

1. Continue from the previous tutorial. To begin, restore the view so that all the floor plan is displayed within the drawing area.

2. Select Named Views from the Standard toolbar.

   The View Control dialog box appears as shown previously in figure 23.15. Select the Plan view, click the Restore button, and then click OK to select the new view. The screen displays the entire apartment floor plan.

**3.** Insert the stair (23DWG02) drawing using the XREF command.

```
Select Attach from the External Reference toolbar.
Xref to Attach: C:\UAW13\23DWG02
23DWG02 loaded.
```

Verify that the file has been properly loaded. The next prompts are identical to those found when inserting a block.

```
Insertion point: 0,0
X scale factor <1>/Corner/XYZ:
Y scale factor (default=X):
Rotation angle <0>:
```

The stair (23DWG02) drawing is now included with the apartment floor plan as shown in figure 23.22.

**Fig. 23.22**

Using XREF to reference the stairs drawing.

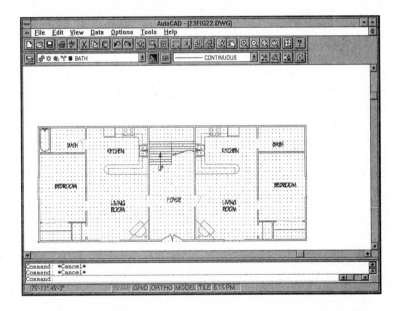

## Detaching a Referenced Drawing (XREF Detach)

An externally referenced drawing remains attached until you detach it. The Xref doesn't detach when you end or quit the drawing. If you no longer need the referenced drawings, you can remove it by selecting Detach from the Xref toolbar. When you select Detach, the following prompt appears:

```
Xref(s) to Detach:
```

Type the drawing name, or an asterisk (*) to detach all referenced drawings. You can't detach a nested Xref file if its master file isn't detached.

> **Caution**
>
> If an Xref drawing file is deleted from your hard drive, but the Xref isn't detached from the master drawing, AutoCAD continues to search for it when the drawing is loaded or plotted. AutoCAD displays an error message stating the Xref file is not found. To avoid this message, detach the Xref from your drawing.

### Tutorial: Detaching a File from a Drawing Using XREF

In this tutorial, detach the 23DWG02 file from the apartment floor plan drawing using the Xref detach function and then list the Reference drawing using the ? option. Begin by first detaching the 23DWG02 file.

**1.** Continue from the previous tutorial.

```
Select Detach from the External Reference toolbar.
Xref to Attach: 23dwg02
```

The Xref is removed from the drawing.

**2.** Undo the last step to continue on with the tutorial.

```
Command: u
```

**3.** Next, list the referenced drawing.

```
Select List from the External Reference toolbar.
Xref(s) to list <*>:
```

The AutoCAD text screen appears as shown in figure 23.23.

**Fig. 23.23**
Listing the referenced drawings in the apartment floor plan.

## Permanently Attaching a Referenced Drawing (XREF Bind, XBIND)

*Dependent symbols* refer to named items such as blocks, dimension styles, layers, linetypes, and text styles. When you reference a drawing, you can't directly use any of its dependent symbols. For example, a layer that exists only in the referenced drawing can't be made current in the master drawing.

If the referenced drawing has a block, dimension style, layer, linetype, or text style you want to use on the master drawing, you can permanently *bind* any of these dependent symbols to the master drawing. After creating a permanent bind, the dependent symbol can be used in the master drawing. The command sequence is as follows:

■ Select Bind from the External References toolbar.

■ Type **xref** at the Command: prompt.

> Block/Dimstyle/LAyer/LType/Style: *Select the dependent symbols you wish to bind.*

After selecting the dependent symbols to bind, AutoCAD prompts you for the dependent name. Enter the name of the Xref, followed by the pipe symbol(|), and then the name of the item to add. The following example shows the command sequence for binding two layers (TEXT and NOTES) from the Xref drawing border:

```
Command: xbind
Block/Dimstyle/LAyer/LType/Style: LA
Dependent Layer name(s):BORDER¦TEXT,BORDER¦NOTES
Scanning...
2 Layer(s) bound.
Command:
```

When the layer has been bound to the master drawing, it's renamed. The Border|Text layer becomes BORDER$0$TEXT. Binding an Xref to a drawing has certain advantages. If a drawing containing Xrefs needs to be sent to another individual, you must also send all of the Xref drawings associated with it. Not only must you send the files, but they must be in the same subdirectories they were in when they were attached to the drawing or they must be detached and then attached to change the location of the Xrefs. See "Updating a Referenced Drawing's Path (Xref Path)" later in this chapter.

Unless the person receiving the drawing creates the same directory structure and copies the Xref drawings to their original locations, the Xrefs will not load. *Binding* an Xref to the master drawing makes the Xref a permanent block in the drawing and eliminates the need for external files. Keep in mind, however, that dependent symbols bound to the master drawing become a permanent part of the drawing, increasing the master drawing file size.

## Updating the Referenced Drawing (RELOAD)

If another individual is working on a referenced drawing, you may want to see an updated version of that drawing. The Xref Reload option brings in the current version of a referenced drawing. When you select Reload from the Xref toolbar, the following prompt appears:

```
Xref(s) to reload:
```

You can type the name of an Xref to update, or enter an asterisk (*) to update all referenced drawings.

## Updating a Referenced Drawing's Path (Xref Path)

When you attach a drawing with XREF, AutoCAD stores the insertion base point, scale, and rotation of the Xref with the master drawing. It also stores the drive, path, and file name of the Xref source drawing.

If the drive or path change for the Xref drawing, you need to inform AutoCAD of the change. The PATH command is used as follows:

```
Select Path from the External Reference toolbar.
Edit path for which Xref(s): Type the name of the Xref you
        want to edit the path for.
Old path: AutoCAD displays the drive, subdirectory, and
        file name of the Xref drawing.
New path: Type in the new path and press Enter.
```

When AutoCAD finds the referenced drawing in its new path, it reloads the drawing file. This option appears as Change Path in the Xref cascading submenu.

## Overlaying a Referenced Drawing (Xref Overlay)

The Overlay function allows you to reference a drawing with an overlaid Xref within another drawing without that Xref appearing in the current drawing. This command doesn't allow for nested Xrefs unlike blocks and attached Xrefs. The command sequence is as follows:

- Select Overlay from the External Reference toolbar.

- Type **xref** at the Command: prompt.

- At the ?/Bind/Detach/Path/Reload/Overlay/<Attach>: command prompt, type **o** and press Enter.

## Understanding VISRETAIN

The VISRETAIN system variable allows you to control the layer visibility and settings from Xrefs. The VISRETAIN system variable is a switch and can only have two settings, on (1) or off (0). Turning the system variable on (1) maintains the layer settings from the Xref drawing. Any layer settings, On/Off,

Freeze/Thaw, Color, and Linetypes, are maintained within the current drawing. A setting of Off (0) allows you to change layer settings of the Xref drawing within the current drawing only. Changing the layer settings of the Xref won't change them in the Xref file, only the current file. You access the VISRETAIN system variable from the command prompt:

```
Command: visretain
New value for VISRETAIN <0>: Enter the disired value and
    press Enter.
```

## Clipping a Reference in a Viewport (XREFCLIP)

◀ See "Understanding Model Space and Paper Space," p. 369

If you Xref a drawing file and don't wish to see all of the Xref drawing file, you can use the XREFCLIP command to remove the unwanted geometry from the current file. One important thing to note before using this command is that you should already have a familiarity with the use of paper space and model space before using this command. AutoCAD creates a rectangular viewport of the size you specify to show the Xref.

Figure 23.22 shows a the apartment floor plan drawing with a staircase Xref.

**Fig. 23.24**
Showing an Xref in the apartment floor plan.

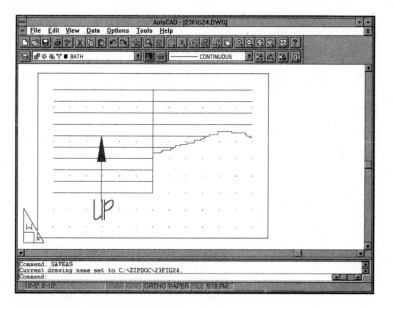

To access the XREFCLIP command:

■ Select Clip from the External Reference toolbar.

■ Type **xrefclip** at the Command: prompt.

Paper space/Model space is disabled. This routine won't run unless it's enabled.

- `Enable Paper/Model space? <Y>:` Press Enter to continue the command. If you enter an **N**, the command is terminated.

- `Xref Name:` Enter the name of the attached Xref you wish to clip.

- `Clip onto what layer?` Type a layer name that doesn't already exist.

- `First corner of clip box:` Select the first point of the rectangular area you wish to clip.

- `Other corner:` Select the other corner of the rectangular area you wish to clip.

- `Number of paperspace units.<1.0>:` Enter a positive value greater than one.

- `Number of model space units. <1.0>:` Enter a positive value greater than one.

- `Insertion point for clip:` Select the point to create the lower-left corner of the model space viewport.

AutoCAD creates a rectangular viewport from the sizes that you specified. It also only shows the section of the drawing that was selected to be displayed in the viewport. Remember, to remove this view, you must delete the viewport in paper space.

# From Here...

The ability to use information from other drawings is one of the greatest benefits of using AutoCAD. The methods of using existing geometry were the BLOCK, WBLOCK, GROUP, SHAPE and XREF commands.

For more information about paper/model space and working with attributes see the following chapters.

- Chapter 13, "Understanding Model Space and Paper Space," shows you how use model/paper space to create views of objects and then scale them for plotting.

- Chapter 24, "Working with Attributes," explains how to attach and use attributes to assign certain values to objects.

# On Your Own

Continue from the previous tutorial. Use the symbols created in previous chapter tutorials and those from the tutorials in this chapter, to finish the apartment floor plan.

Hints:

1.  Locate the insertion point of all symbols before starting.

2.  Examine the drawing and determine if a rotation of the symbol is required. Also, consider the scale of the symbol.

3.  If you have not completed all of the tutorials up to this point, create the necessary symbols from scratch.

# Chapter 24

# Working with Attributes

In the previous chapter, you learned about blocks. Blocks allow you to reuse parts of your drawing in the current drawing, another drawing, or whole drawings as parts of other drawings. Blocks make it possible for you to create symbol libraries and standard details that you can use over and over without having to redraw them on each new project. Blocks can be improved by adding another object to them: *attributes*. Attributes allow you to attach text information to your blocks, which can later be extracted for analysis in database and spreadsheet programs.

Attributes also are handy for entering text that changes with each insertion of a particular block. For example, you can define attributes in your standard title block that prompt for the drafter's name, current date, and project ID number each time someone inserts the title block into a drawing.

In this chapter, you learn to use:

- ■ ATTDEF to define your attributes from the command line

- ■ DDATTDEF to define your attributes with a dialog box

- ■ DDEDIT to the three parts—attribute tag, attribute prompt, and default attribute value—of your attribute definitions in one dialog box

- ■ ATTEDIT to edit your attribute definitions from the command line

- ■ DDATTE to edit attributes in a dialog box

- ■ ATTEXT to extract information from attributes at the command line

- ■ DDATTEXT to extract attribute information using a dialog box

- ■ ATTREDEF to redefine a block and update the block's attributes

- ATTDISP to display all attributes

- ATTMODE to control the attribute display mode

- ATTDIA to determine the use of dialog boxes when editing attributes

- ATTREQ to determine either to accept the defaults or to prompt for values

# Adding Information to Blocks with Attributes

Attributes work only if you insert them into a drawing as a block. To create an attribute, you follow a three-step process. First, you define the attribute. Then, you include the attribute definition as part of a block. Finally, you insert the block and enter data at the attribute prompts. At this point, the attribute and block become part of your drawing.

## Defining an Attribute (ATTDEF, DDATTDEF)

Most commands that create and modify attributes are available in both the AutoCAD Command: line and dialog box versions. To create an attribute, you can:

- Type **attdef** (Attribute Define) at the Command: prompt.

- Type **ddattdef** at the Command: prompt or click the Define Attribute icon from the Attribute toolbar to use the DDATTDEF dialog box.

> **Note**
>
> The toolbar for attributes must be activated before you can access it. It's not a default toolbar, but once it's activated, it will remain on-screen until you close it. To activate the toolbar icons for attributes, choose Tools, Toolbars, Attributes. You can move the toolbar shown in figure 24.1 to the toolbar icons area across the top and leave it open for future use.

If you use DDATTDEF to define your attributes, AutoCAD provides a dialog box in which you can enter an attribute definition's settings. It's more convenient to use the dialog box because it's like a one-stop shopping center; you can make all your selections at one time.

**Fig. 24.1**
The Attribute
toolbar icons are
first activated.

## Attribute Settings

When you define an attribute, you assign various settings that govern two categories: how the attribute is displayed and the information the attribute conveys. The display settings are the same as those you used when you created text:

- Insertion point
- Justification
- Text style
- Height
- Rotation

In figure 24.2, in the lower half of the dialog box are the Insertion Point and Text Options areas in which you adjust these settings. In the top half of the dialog box are the Mode and Attribute areas in which you define the attribute.

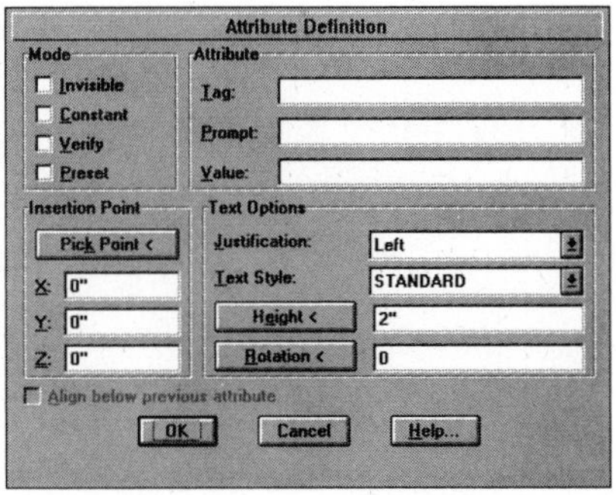

**Fig. 24.2**
The Attribute
Definition dialog
box appears like
this when loaded.

## Attribute Tag, Prompt, and Value

The most basic attribute is composed of a *tag*, a *prompt*, and a *value*. The tag categorizes the attribute, such as COST, MANUFACTURER, NAME, or TELEPHONE_NUMBER. The tag is actually the name of the attribute and is used to sort attributes when performing an attribute extraction.

AutoCAD uses the prompt to ask you what value the attribute will have when you insert it into a drawing. For example, a prompt could be "Enter the item's cost:". The value is what a particular instance of the attribute will say when it is inserted into the drawing, such as $12.50. If attreq is turned on, this is the prompt that you will see for the attribute (see Appendix C, "System Variables Reference," for more information).

When you define an attribute, you can supply a default value that AutoCAD uses if you do not supply a value when you insert the attribute. The default value is often set to the most common value used. For example, on a relay coil in a schematic you have a common value like "L2" on one side of all AC relays. In this case, it would make sense to assign a default value of "L2" to the attribute rather than entering "L2" each time the block is inserted.

---

**Troubleshooting**

*I created my attributes and misspelled some of the values. Do I have to re-create the attribute from scratch?*

Don't worry if you make a mistake when defining an attribute. You can use DDEDIT to edit the Tag, Prompt, and Value fields on an attribute definition before you make it into a block. This is explained in the section, "Editing Attribute Definitions (DDEDIT)," later in this chapter.

---

## Attribute Mode Settings

You can define attributes that exhibit any combination of four modes: Invisible, Constant, Verify, and Preset, with the exception that Constant attributes cannot also be Verify or Preset attributes. Each mode has a specific effect on the attribute when you insert it into a drawing:

**Tip**
Invisible attributes are handy in blocks with many attributes used primarily for extraction since they won't clutter your drawing. Because you're extracting and viewing them elsewhere, you don't need to see them on-screen.

- *Invisible.* This attribute, when inserted, will be invisible. If you need to edit invisible attributes after you have inserted them, you can use the ATTEDIT or DDATTE commands, discussed later. You can make AutoCAD display invisible attributes on-screen with the ATTDISP command, which is discussed later.

- *Constant.* Constant attributes always take the same value when you insert them. You assign the value when you define the attribute. Constant attributes don't have a prompt and can't be edited.

- *Verify.* When you insert a Verify attribute, AutoCAD prompts you twice for the value so that you can change your answer before AutoCAD inserts it into the drawing. Verify mode is handy if you're creating attributes that can be easily misspelled or otherwise mistakenly typed.

- *Preset.* Like Constant attributes, Preset attributes always have the same value when you insert them. Unlike Constant attributes, however, you can edit their values later.

As you can see from figure 24.2, to set an attribute mode with the DDATTDEF command, simply select the appropriate check box. If you use the ATTDEF command instead, AutoCAD displays this prompt:

```
Attribute modes - Invisible:N Constant:N Verify:N Preset:N
Enter (ICVP) to change, RETURN when done:
```

To toggle a mode, type the first letter, in upper- or lowercase, of the mode you want to set (**i**, **c**, **v**, or **p**), and then press Enter. AutoCAD redisplays the mode prompt with the mode you specified (in this case, Invisible) set to Y:

```
Attribute modes - Invisible:Y Constant:N Verify:N Preset:N
Enter (ICVP) to change, RETURN when done:
```

You can continue to set as many modes as you want; unlike the DDATTDEF command, ATTDEF allows you to set Constant, Verify, and Preset to Y, although the Constant setting overrides the others. After you've set the modes as you want, press Enter to move on to the rest of the attribute definition settings. Mode settings remain in effect until you change them.

## Attribute Insertion Point Settings

The Insertion Point area of the Attribute Definition dialog box lets you specify where the attribute definition will appear on your drawing. If you choose the Pic<u>k</u> Point < button, the dialog box temporarily disappears so that you can pick a point on your drawing. If you already know the specific point where you want the attribute to appear, you can, instead, enter the <u>X</u>, <u>Y</u>, and <u>Z</u> coordinates in the appropriate edit boxes. You can move the attribute to a different point at any time.

The ATTDEF command leads you through the prompts for attribute mode, tag, prompt, and default value before asking:

```
Justify/Style/<Start point>:
```

You may remember a similar prompt from the TEXT and DTEXT commands. It works the same way here. You can type, in either upper-or lowercase, **J** to select one of AutoCAD's text justification options, **S** to select a different text style, or you can pick an insertion point on the drawing. Of course, you also can type in specific coordinates rather than picking a point.

**Tip**

When using the ATTDEF command, you can enter the justification you want at the `Justify/Style/ <Start point>:` prompt without first selecting Justify.

◄ See "Defining
a Text Style,"
p. 462

◄ See "Justifying
Text," p. 470

◄ See "Editing
Text (CHANGE,
DDEDIT, and
DDMODIFY),"
p. 476

## Attribute Text Option Settings

In the Text Options area of the Attribute Definition dialog box, you can specify the attribute text's justification, style, height, and rotation. You can select justification and style from the pop-up lists, or type in your choices. You can type height and rotation in the edit boxes, or click the adjoining buttons to specify height and rotation by picking points on the screen.

As discussed in the previous section, when you use the ATTDEF command, you pick justification and style options at the `Justify/Style/<Start point>:` prompt. After you get past that point, AutoCAD prompts separately for height and rotation angle. You can type values, or pick points on-screen to show height and rotation values.

## Editing Attribute Definitions (DDEDIT)

You may sometimes find that you need to change an attribute's tag, prompt, or value before you make it into a block. The DDEDIT command provides an easy way to edit attribute definitions. To use DDEDIT, type **ddedit** at the `Command:` prompt.

**Tip**

After the attribute definition is made into a block, it becomes an attribute. DDEDIT can only edit an attribute definition. Therefore, the block must be exploded so that the attribute reverts to an attribute definition.

AutoCAD prompts you to:

        `<Select a TEXT or ATTDEF object>/Undo:`

Select the attribute definition that you want to edit. A dialog box appears in which you can edit the attribute's tag, prompt, or value (see fig. 24.3). You can use standard Windows text editing options in these fields. Interestingly, if you're editing a Constant or Preset attribute definition, DDEDIT lets you enter an attribute prompt, which is discarded when you put the attribute into a block.

**Fig. 24.3**
The DDEDIT command lets you edit attribute definitions that are not yet part of a block.

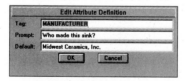

While you can only edit attribute definitions one at a time with the DDEDIT command, the command stays active until you press Enter at the `<Select a TEXT or ATTDEF object>/Undo:` prompt. That way, you can sequentially edit attribute definitions without having to restart the command between edits.

## Making a Block of Your Attributes

You can create a block with nothing in it but attributes. This is useful for adding Bill of Material, Change, or other required text information to a drawing. To create a block of attributes, you will follow the same procedures as you did for creating a block in Chapter 23.

> **Note**
>
> Unlike creating a block, the order of attribute selection is important. The order in which AutoCAD inserts a block is last to first. This means that the last object created in the block will be the first object inserted, including attributes. If you want your attributes to prompt you in a particular order, you must select them in that order when making a block that includes those attributes. Doing so overrides the standard way in which AutoCAD inserts a block with respect to the attributes only. The first attribute that you selected when prompted for objects at the time of block creation will be the first attribute that you receive a prompt for. Conversely, the last attribute selected will be the last one you are prompted for.

## Tutorial: Defining and Inserting an Attribute

Now that you've seen how to define an attribute, try one of your own. In the directory UAW13, you should find the drawing 24DWG01, an apartment floor plan. Open the drawing, making sure that the system variable ATTDIA is set to 1 and that the Draw toolbar is active on your screen. Follow these steps and review the figures as you go.

> **Note**
>
> You can save yourself a lot of time if you set up your prototype drawing with some of these settings, such as ATTDIA set to your preferences. See Chapter 3, "Understanding Prototypes," for more information on setting up your prototype drawing.

1. Start AutoCAD and open the drawing 24DWG01.

2. Select the <u>Z</u>oom <u>W</u>indow button, and draw a window around the bathroom in the upper-right corner.

   Let's make some attributes for the sink, and then make the sink and its attributes into a block.

3. Select the Define Attribute icon in the Attribute toolbar.

   AutoCAD displays the Attribute Definition dialog box.

4. In the Attribute Tag field, type **MANUFACTURER**. In the Prompt field, type **Who made this sink?**. In the Value field, type **Midwest Ceramics, Inc.**

5. Click the Text Style pop-up list in the Text Options area. Choose the STANDARD style.

6. Click the Height < edit box, and enter a new height of **3"**.

7. Click the Pick Point < button in the Insertion Point area.

   The dialog box closes.

8. Double-click the SNAP button on the status bar at the bottom of the screen to turn on snap mode. Pick the point 17'–3", 29'–5".

   The dialog box reappears (see fig. 24.4). You see the coordinates of the point you picked automatically entered in the X and Y edit boxes in the Insertion Point area.

**Fig. 24.4**
The completed
Attribute Defini-
tion dialog box.

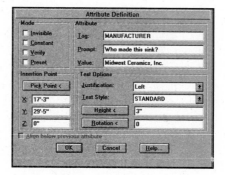

9. Choose OK.

   You should see the word MANUFACTURER written across the sink's upper-left corner (see fig. 24.5).

10. Press Enter to repeat the DDATTDEF command, and follow steps 4 through 9 to create another attribute. For the Tag, enter **PRICE**. For the Prompt, enter **How much does it cost?** For the Value, enter: **$175.00**. Instead of picking a point, select the Align Below Previous Attribute check box at the bottom of the dialog box (see fig. 24.6). Then choose OK.

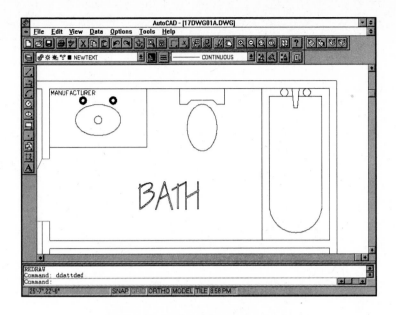

**Fig. 24.5**
The sink with the attribute definition in place.

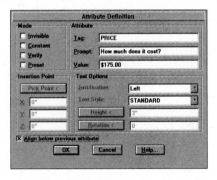

**Fig. 24.6**
The completed Attribute Definition dialog box has the Align Below Previous Attribute check box selected.

11. Select the <u>B</u>lock icon from the Draw toolbar. Create a block called SINK that includes the two lines that form the cabinet, the ellipse that represents the sink, the drain circle, the donut taps, and the two attributes. Make the insertion base point the intersection of the two cabinet lines.

**Tip**
Select your attributes first when creating a block. This ensures that you are prompted for attribute values in order.

12. Insert SINK at coordinates 21'-6",27'-2" with an XY scale factor of 1 and a 0 rotation. The command prompts should look like the following:

```
Command: insert
Block name (or ?): sink
Insertion point: 21'6",27'2"
X scale factor <1> / Corner / XYZ: 1
Y scale factor (default=X):
Rotation angle <0>: 0
```

The Enter Attributes dialog box shown in figure 24.7 appears. Note that the order for the attributes is consistent with the order in which you selected them when creating the block. Change How much does it cost? to **$185.00**, and then choose OK.

**Fig. 24.7**
The Enter
Attributes dialog
box appears when
you insert a block
with attributes.

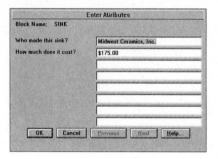

Now that you have successfully created a block with attributes, save it as 24DWG01A for future use. You will be doing more to this drawing later in this chapter.

# Editing Attributes in a Block (ATTEDIT, DDATTE, ATTREDEF)

Even after you have created your attribute definitions, perhaps edited them with DDEDIT, placed them into blocks, and inserted the blocks into your drawings, you may still need to edit the attribute values. AutoCAD provides the ATTEDIT and DDATTE commands to edit attributes in a block, and ATTREDEF is used to add or modify attributes in an existing block definition.

> **Note**
>
> After a block with an attribute is inserted, the attribute becomes an *attrib* type object. While you are defining an attribute, it is an *attdef* type object and can be modified with the CHANGE command as well as DDEDIT, MODIFY and DDMODIFY. CHANGE cannot change attributes once they become an attrib type object. Refer to the table on DXF object types for more information on object types.

## Using ATTEDIT to Edit Attributes in a Block

Although it's easy to use because it's a dialog box, the DDATTE command is limited in its functionality. DDATTE allows you to edit only attribute values and only on one block's attributes at a time. To access DDATTE:

1. Select the DDATTE icon from the Attribute toolbar.

2. AutoCAD prompts you to `Select block:`. Choose the block whose attributes you want to edit.

   AutoCAD displays the Edit Attributes dialog box with all the block's variable attributes displayed (see fig. 24.8). Each line in the box contains an attribute prompt and an edit box that contains the attribute's current value. You can use standard Windows text editing methods to change the text in the edit boxes. Pressing Enter or Tab cycles among the edit fields; Tab also cycles through the dialog box buttons at the bottom of the dialog box.

3. After you have completed editing, you choose the OK button to exit the command, update the attributes, and close the dialog box.

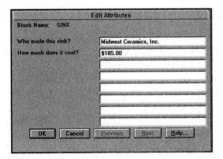

**Fig. 24.8**
The Edit Attributes dialog box lets you edit the attribute values of a single block's variable attributes.

## Editing Attributes with ATTEDIT

If you need to edit more than an attribute's value or you want to edit attributes globally, use the ATTEDIT command. To access ATTEDIT:

1. Type **attedit** at the `Command:` prompt.

2. Select the Edit Attribute Globally icon from the Attribute toolbar.

AutoCAD prompts with:

    Edit attributes one at a time? <Y>

If you reply N to this question, you can edit attributes globally. At this point, the command's prompts diverge. Let's discuss individual editing first.

## Editing Individual Attributes

If you accept the default of Y at the `Edit attributes one at a time?` prompt, AutoCAD proceeds with individual attribute editing. You can first narrow the selection set of attributes to edit. AutoCAD displays three prompts sequentially:

```
Block name specification <*>:
Attribute tag specification <*>:
Attribute value specification <*>:
```

You can enter specific block names, tags, and values at these prompts, or combinations of text and wildcard characters (?,*) to restrict which attributes the command selects for editing. After you've narrowed the search, AutoCAD prompts `Select attributes:`. You can use any of AutoCAD's object selection methods—windows, crossing boxes, or fences—to select attributes that you want to edit.

---

**Caution**

The `Select attributes:` prompt works a bit differently from AutoCAD's standard `Select objects:` prompt. When you select an object (or objects with, say, a window) and press Enter, AutoCAD displays a new `Select objects:` prompt. AutoCAD only issues one `Select attributes:` prompt, though. You select all the attributes that you want to edit at that one prompt; only after you press Enter does AutoCAD continue with the command.

---

**Note**

You can now see the power that AutoCAD provides by combining the capability to narrow the set of attributes with its object selection methods. You may be looking at a drawing of an office floor plan. Your task is to edit a few attributes out of perhaps hundreds. Start the ATTEDIT command, specify a particular block name whose attributes you want to edit, and then window the entire drawing. AutoCAD searches the drawing database for you, and selects only those attributes associated with the particular block that you had named. AutoCAD saves you the trouble of having to zoom and pan around the drawing to individually pick only those attributes that you want to edit.

---

After you narrow your selection set and select the attributes that you want to edit, press Enter. AutoCAD confirms the number of attributes selected and prompts:

```
Value/Position/Height/Angle/Style/Layer/Color/Next <N>:
```

You will also notice that AutoCAD places a small x at the head of the first attribute you selected. If this behavior looks familiar, it should be; it echoes the PEDIT command's Edit vertex options. As when you edit polyline vertices, if you press Enter at this point to accept the Next default, AutoCAD moves the X to the next attribute in the selection set. This option provides you with one last chance to select only those attributes that you really need to edit. Unlike the Edit vertex prompt, though, the ATTEDIT command does not offer a Previous option. And, if you go forward with the Next command through all the selected attributes, AutoCAD ends the command. So be careful with the Next option, lest you accidentally go past an attribute that you really intended to edit and have to choose your selection set all over again.

With the X designator positioned on an attribute that you want to edit, you can finally actually change something. Type the first letter of one of the editing options (V, P, H, A, S, L, or C), or type the full word if you want. AutoCAD prompts for the change that you want to initiate.

In most cases, AutoCAD simply asks for a new designation. In the case of Value, though, AutoCAD first asks, Change or Replace? <R>:. You can choose Change to change only part of the attribute's current text; AutoCAD prompts for String to change:. Type the part of the text you want to change. Then AutoCAD asks for a New string:; enter the new text. When you choose Replace, AutoCAD asks for a New Attribute value:, at which point you enter the new text with which AutoCAD will replace all the current text. The following is what the command lines would look like to change values:

```
Command: attedit
Edit attributes one at a time? <Y>
Block name specification <*>:
Attribute tag specification <*>:
Attribute value specification <*>:
Select Attributes:
1 attributes selected.
Value/Position/Height/Angle/Style/Layer/Color/Next <N>: v
Change or Replace? <R>: c
String to change: Midwest
New string: MidWest
```

The following lines replace the value entirely:

```
Command: attedit
Edit attributes one at a time? <Y>
Block name specification <*>:
Attribute tag specification <*>:
Attribute value specification <*>:
Select Attributes:
1 attributes selected.
Value/Position/Height/Angle/Style/Layer/Color/Next <N>: v
Change or Replace? <R>:
New attribute value: Midwest Ceramics, Inc.
Value/Position/Height/Angle/Style/Layer/Color/Next <N>:
```

## Editing Global Attributes

If you start the ATTEDIT command and answer No to the `Edit attributes one at a time?` prompt, AutoCAD enters global attribute edit mode. In global editing, you can only edit attributes' values; you cannot change other characteristics, like height or color. Global editing does, however, save you the trouble of having to type the same old and new strings over and over as you would need to do if you were individually editing attributes.

After you select global edit mode, AutoCAD asks, `Edit only attributes visible on screen? <Y>`. You may be zoomed into a small corner of your drawing, but want to edit all the instances of a particular attribute that are in the drawing, regardless of whether you can see them. In this case, answer **N** to this prompt, and AutoCAD will find all the chosen attributes in the drawing without you having to do a perhaps time-consuming Zoom All or Zoom Extents command. When you choose this option, AutoCAD pops up the text screen window, and goes through the search-narrowing options that you saw when you edited attributes one at a time:

```
Block name specification <*>:
Attribute tag specification <*>:
Attribute value specification <*>:
```

Enter information at these prompts if you want. Should you want to edit only values in a specific block (such as the title block), you can narrow the global editing by entering the name of the title block at the `Block name specification <*>:` prompt. The same would apply if you wanted to globally edit a specific tag by entering the tag name in the `Attribute tag specification <*>:` prompt. Entering a value in the `Attribute value specification <*>:` would check every block and attribute visible for the entered value. See the section, "Editing Individual Attributes," in this chapter.

### Note

When you edit attributes globally and choose to edit attributes not visible on the screen, you probably will want to narrow your selection set. In this mode, AutoCAD does not give you the opportunity to select attributes individually, as it does when you edit only visible attributes. If you accept the "*" defaults, AutoCAD will evaluate every attribute in your drawing to see if it contains the text string you want to change. If you have a lot of attributes in your drawing, this evaluation could take a long time. You also run the risk of inadvertently changing values that you don't want to be changed, as AutoCAD will replace any occurrence in any attribute of the old text string with the new one.

If you accept the Y default at the `Edit only attributes visible on screen?` prompt, AutoCAD asks for block name, attribute tag, and attribute value specifications, so you can narrow your selection set. Then AutoCAD asks you to `Select attributes:`. Just as when you edited attributes individually, you can use any of AutoCAD's object selection methods to pick the attributes that you want to edit. After you've chosen them all, press Enter. If you choose Constant attributes, AutoCAD casts them out of the selection set.

From this point on, the command proceeds the same whether you're editing all attributes, or only those visible on the screen. AutoCAD prompts for a `String to change:`. You enter the text string. AutoCAD prompts for a `New string:`. You enter the new value. AutoCAD replaces the old with the new. If you're editing only visible attributes, AutoCAD dynamically replaces the text; you can watch it happen. If you're editing all attributes, AutoCAD replaces the text internally, and then regenerates the drawing when it's done to update the attribute values.

## Tutorial: Editing Attributes

Here you're going to make a few changes to the attributes in your drawing using the ATTEDIT command. The attribute text in the block is too big for the block and looks terrible. Because these changes are carried out at the `Command:` prompt, the actual AutoCAD commands are listed for you to follow. Press Enter after each command.

```
Select the Edit Attribute Globally icon in the Attribute
toolbar or enter at the Command:prompt attedit
Edit attributes one at a time? <Y>
Block name specification <*>:
Attribute tag specification <*>:
Attribute value specification <*>:
Select Attributes: c
First corner: 18'-1",29'-7"
Other corner: 17'-6",28'-11"
2 attributes selected.
Value/Position/Height/Angle/Style/Layer/Color/Next <N>: h
New height <0'-3">: 2"
Value/Position/Height/Angle/Style/Layer/Color/Next <N>: n
Value/Position/Height/Angle/Style/Layer/Color/Next <N>: h
New height <0'-3">: 2"
Value/Position/Height/Angle/Style/Layer/Color/Next <N>: v
Change or Replace? <R>: c
String to change: 8
New string: 7
Value/Position/Height/Angle/Style/Layer/Color/Next <N>:
Select the Redraw button to complete this tutorial.
```

Your drawing should look like figure 24.9 when you have completed the changes.

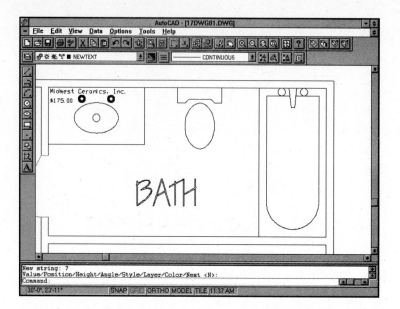

**Fig. 24.9**
The Sink block displays the changes.

# Changing the Default Display Setting (ATTDISP)

The ATTDISP (ATTribute DISPlay) command lets you override the normal attribute display modes, so that, for instance, you can make invisible attributes visible.

ATTDISP has the following three options:

```
Normal/ON/OFF <Normal>:
```

■ Normal is exactly what it seems; it leaves the display modes as they would normally be.

■ ON makes all attributes visible; you will use it primarily to make invisible attributes visible so that you can select and edit them with the DDATTE and ATTEDIT commands.

■ OFF makes all attributes invisible. If your drawing is cluttered, or you need to plot a drawing, but don't need to plot the attributes, you can make them temporarily invisible.

## Tutorial: Changing the Attribute's Display Setting

In this exercise, you will add two attributes that will be invisible to the SINK block. The first attribute will be the manufacturer's part number; the second will be the sink color.

1. Choose the Zoom Window button on the Standard toolbar. Draw a window around the bathroom in the upper-right corner.

2. Explode the SINK block created in the previous tutorial in this chapter.

   The attributes in the block revert to attribute definitions, and the objects are separate objects again.

3. Select the Define Attribute tool from the Attribute toolbar. Select the Invisible check box in the Mode area in the upper-left corner of the Attribute Definition dialog box.

4. In the Tag field, type: **PART_NO**. In the Prompt field, type: **What is the manufacturer's part number?**. In the Value field, type: **MS1228WT**.

5. Click the Text Style list box in the Text Options area. Choose the STANDARD style.

6. Click in the Height edit box, and enter a new height of **2"**.

7. Enter the *x*-coordinate **17'-3"** in the X insertion point.

8. Enter the *y*-coordinate **27'-3"** in the Y insertion point. Compare your screen to figure 24.10.

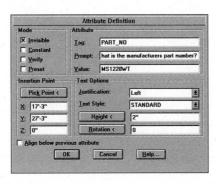

**Fig. 24.10**
The Attribute Definition dialog box is complete.

9. Click the OK button.

   You should see the word PART_NO written across the sink's lower-left corner, as shown in figure 24.11.

**Fig. 24.11**
The sink shows the attribute definition in place.

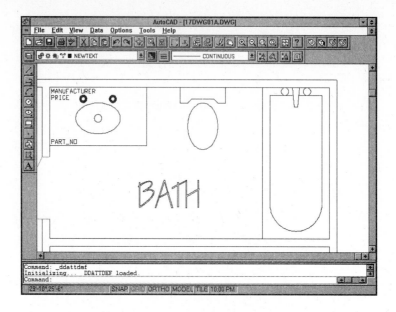

10. Press Enter to repeat the DDATTDEF command, and follow steps 4 through 8 to create another attribute. For the Tag, enter: **COLOR**. For the Prompt, enter: **What is the color of the sink?**. For the Value, enter: **WHITE**. Enter the *x*-coordinate of **21'-5"** and the *y*-coordinate of **27'-3"** for the insertion point (see fig. 24.12). Select Right from the Justification pop-up list, and click OK.

**Fig. 24.12**
The completed Attribute Definition dialog box uses the Text Options, Justification, Right.

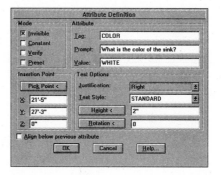

 11. Select the Block icon from the Draw toolbar. Enter the name **sink** and answer the prompt:

```
Block SINK already exists.
Redefine it? <N> y
```

Select the following objects: the two lines that form the cabinet, the ellipse that represents the sink, the drain circle, the donut taps, and the four attributes. Make the insertion base point the intersection of the two cabinet lines.

12. Insert SINK at coordinates 21'-6",27'-2" with a scale factor of 1 and rotation of 0. The Enter Attributes dialog box, shown in figure 24.13, will appear.

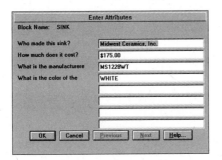

**Fig. 24.13**
The Enter Attributes dialog box is complete.

13. At the Command: prompt, enter the following commands:

```
Command: attdisp
Normal/ON/OFF <Normal>: on
Regenerating drawing.
```

Look at the SINK block and count the number of visible attributes. You should have four attributes (see fig. 24.14).

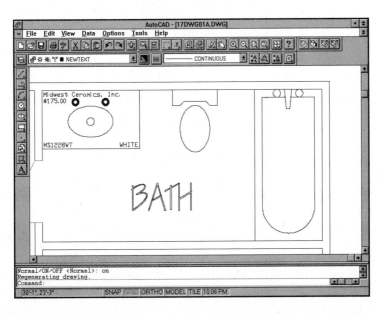

**Fig. 24.14**
The visible and the invisible attributes are in the SINK block.

Command:
ATTDISP Normal/ON/OFF <On>: **off**

Now count the number of visible attributes (see fig. 24.15). If you get more than zero, go back to step 2 and try again. This time, make sure that you selected the Invisible check box.

**Fig. 24.15**

Neither the visible nor the invisible attributes in the SINK block are displayed.

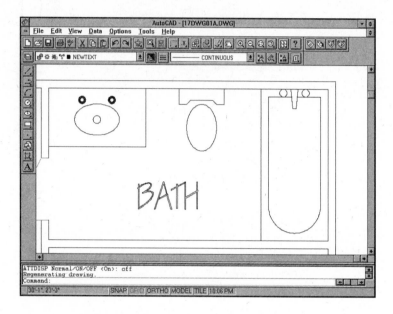

Command:
ATTDISP Normal/ON/OFF <Off>: normal

The block is now displayed normally, with two visible attributes only (see fig. 24.16).

## Using the ATTREDEF Command to Edit Attributes

A common problem is finding you need to edit, remove, or add an attribute in an inserted block. Fortunately there is a command to take care of this problem. ATTREDEF works on one block definition at a time, but not on one block at a time. The difference is that only one definition for each block is changed, but every insertion of that block will reflect those changes.

**Fig. 24.16**
The block
attributes are
displayed
normally.

The ATTREDEF command keeps existing attribute values if the attributes are
included in the redefined block. If an attribute was deleted, the values for
that attribute are deleted. New attributes will be given their default values
and will require editing with DDATTE or ATTEDIT. See the section, "Editing
Individual Attributes," in this chapter.

Using ATTREDEF is a three-step process. The first step requires you to copy or
reinsert and then explode the block with attributes that need to be redefined.
The second step is creating, editing, or deleting attribute definitions as
needed. Finally, you execute the ATTREDEF command and redefine the block
with the required changes. At this point, your drawing regenerates and your
changes are complete.

**Note**

ATTREDEF works on a block definition. When you explode a block, it removes the
definition and ATTREDEF cannot be used. Therefore, you must have more than one
instance of the block you want to redefine already existing in the drawing.

## Tutorial: Redefining Attributes in a Block with ATTREDEF

In this tutorial, you use the ATTREDEF command to clean up the clutter resulting from copying and rotating existing blocks. You will find the drawing 24DWG01B (see fig. 24.17) in the directory UAW13 that will be used in this tutorial. Open the drawing 24DWG01B and follow these steps:

1. Select the Zoom Window button from the Standard toolbar. Answer the prompts as follows:

        First corner: **2',35'**
        Other corner: **16',44'**

    Press Enter.

**Fig. 24.17**
The drawing of the apartment complex is expanded into a four-unit floor plan.

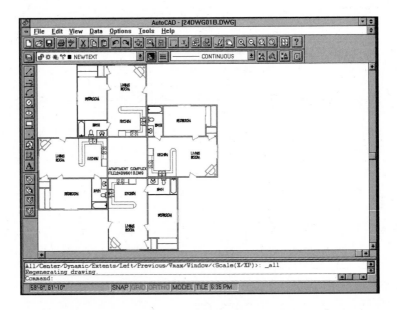

2. Choose the Insert Block button from the Draw Toolbar. Enter the following:

        Block name (or ?): **sink**
        Insertion point: **10',38'**
        X scale factor <1> / Corner / XYZ:
        Y scale factor (default=X):
        Rotation angle <0>:

    Pick OK to accept the default values for the attributes.

3. Select the Explode button from the Modify Toolbar. Select the block you just inserted and press Enter twice. The block explodes and looks like figure 24.18.

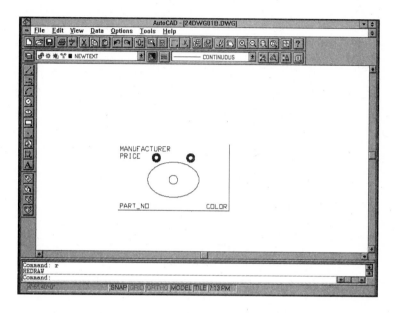

**Fig. 24.18**
The SINK block exploded with all the attribute definitions exploded.

```
Select objects: 1 found
Select objects:
```

4. Select the Properties button from the Object Properties toolbar and select the text MANUFACTURER. The Modify Attribute Definition dialog box in figure 24.19 will appear. Select the Invisible check box, and then choose OK.

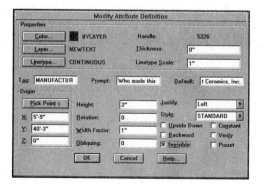

**Fig. 24.19**
The Modify Attribute Definition dialog box.

**5.** Press Enter, select the word PRICE, and repeat step 4.

**6.** Pick the Redraw View button from the Standard toolbar to clean up the drawing.

**7.** Select the Redefine Attribute button from the Attribute Toolbar, and enter the following:

```
Name of Block you wish to redefine: sink
Select objects for new Block...
Select objects: Select the objects for the sink block.
Select objects: 10 found
Select objects:
Insertion base point of new Block: int
of
```

Pick the two lines that intersect to make the lower-right corner of the sink, and press Enter.

At this point, the drawing regenerates and the inserted block that you just redefined disappears from your screen.

**8.** Select Zoom All from the Standard toolbar.

**9.** Select Zoom Window and zoom in on any one of the four bathrooms.

The attributes are not visible anymore and should look like figure 24.20. If they were still visible some would be upside down or sideways as shown in figure 24.21.

**Fig. 24.20**

The SINK block after it has been redefined.

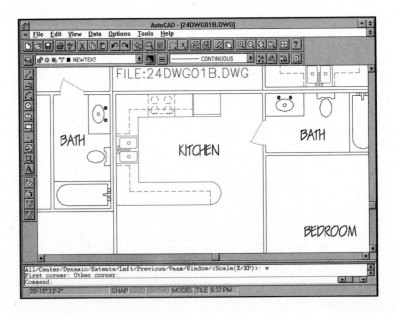

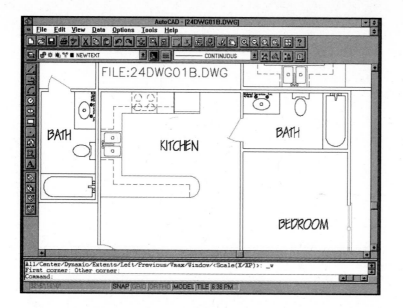

**Fig. 24.21**
This is what the
block looks like if it
is not redefined.

**VII**

Symbols & Attributes

# Extracting Information with Attributes

As stated at the beginning of this chapter, attributes have two primary purposes. You can use them to automatically prompt you for text that varies from drawing to drawing or insertion to insertion, but that is always associated with a particular block or symbol, such as a title block. Also, you can extract attribute information from a drawing into a format suitable for import into a database or spreadsheet program. You can use the extracted attribute data in programs like these to perform tasks for which they are more suited than AutoCAD, such as assembling bills of material, parts lists, cost estimates, and inventories. To extract the attribute data in a format suitable for use by another program, you first create a template file, and then you extract the data.

## Creating a Template File

The template file tells AutoCAD what format the extracted data will assume and which attributes' data will be included in the extract file. It must be an ASCII text file, and it must have a file extension of TXT. If you create the template file with a word processor, be sure to save it in ASCII format, not your word processor's native format. Otherwise, you can use any ASCII text editor, like Windows Notepad or DOS EDIT to create the template file. A simple template file might look like this:

| | |
|---|---|
| PART# | N010000 |
| COLOR | C007000 |
| MATERIAL | C025000 |
| COST | N007002 |

In this sample template file, the first column contains several attribute tags. The second column contains a code that tells AutoCAD the attribute data's type, whether numeric or character, the database or spreadsheet field's width, and the number of decimal places (applicable only to numeric data). Let's break down each of these fields into parts.

| Tag Name Places | | | Code Letter | Maximum Characters Allowed | Decimal (Numeric Values Only) |
|---|---|---|---|---|---|
| PART# | N010000 | = | Number | 10 | 0 |
| COLOR | C007000 | = | Character | 7 | |
| MATERIAL | C025000 | = | Character | 25 | |
| COST | N007002 | = | Number | 7 | 2 |

> **Note**
>
> Note that there are no decimal place entries for character fields and that no characters can be entered in a numeric field. Further care must be taken that you do not use the Tab key, add any extra spaces, or insert an additional line or carriage return at the beginning or end of the template file. If you have any problems with your attribute extraction, it's usually here that you find the culprit.

In addition to attribute tags, AutoCAD also recognizes certain predefined fields called Block Characteristics and Predefined Field Names. They contain information about the blocks from which you can extract the additional data.

| | |
|---|---|
| BL:NAME | C009000 |
| BL:X | N010004 |
| BL:Y | N010004 |

These fields are a sampling of the available fields that you can use to extract non-attribute block information. The BL: defines the fields as special, and, in the cases shown here, NAME is the block name; X is the block's X insertion point; and Y is the Y insertion point. These and all the other fields are explained fully in the *AutoCAD Command Reference*.

After you have constructed a template file, you can extract attribute data very easily. As with other attribute commands, you can use either an AutoCAD `Command:` line version (ATTEXT) or a dialog box version (DDATTEXT).

## Extracting Information (ATTEXT)

ATTEXT works on the AutoCAD `Command:` line. Type **attext** at the `Command:` prompt and press Enter. AutoCAD prompts:

```
CDF, SDF or DXF Attribute extract (or Objects)? <C>:
```

*CDF* stands for *Comma Delimited Format*, where the extract file's fields are separated by commas. *SDF* stands for *Space Delimited Format*; fields are fixed lengths that are padded with spaces and separated by spaces so that the columns align evenly. Database and spreadsheet programs usually can read one or the other. You need to determine ahead of time which type your program uses, so that you can extract the attribute data in the appropriate format. Also, you can extract data in AutoCAD's DXF format, although you would probably only use DXF if you wanted to import attributes into another CAD program. Finally, you can type **o** at the prompt, and AutoCAD lets you choose specific blocks whose attributes you want to extract. After you choose the blocks, AutoCAD displays the prompt:

```
CDF, SDF or DXF Attribute extract? <C>:
```

You choose the appropriate output format, and AutoCAD will extract attribute data only from the blocks you chose previously.

After you have chosen an extract format, AutoCAD prompts for the name of the template file to use, and then asks for the name of the extract file name.

```
Command: attext
CDF, SDF or DXF Attribute extract (or Objects)? <C>: s
Template file <C:\UAW13\SINK.TXT>: sink.txt
Extract file name < C:\UAW13\24DWG01A>:24dwg01s
1 records in extract file.
```

AutoCAD extracts the information from the drawing and deposits it into the extract file. The following line is a sample line from the extract file 24DWG01S.TXT created using the previous prompts.

```
SINK       1.0000  1.0000Midwest Ceramics, Inc.$175.00
MS1228WT         WHITE
```

## Extracting Information with a Dialog Box (DDATTEXT)

The DDATTEXT command accomplishes the same task as the ATTEXT command, only through a dialog box rather than from the Command: prompt. The File Format area, at the top of the dialog box, contains three radio buttons with which to choose your output format: CDF, SDF, or DXF. Below that, the Select Objects < button causes the dialog box to disappear so that you can choose specific blocks from which to extract attribute data. In the two edit boxes at the bottom, you enter the names of the template file and extract file. After you've entered this information, click OK, and AutoCAD will extract the data for you.

## Tutorial: Extracting Attribute Data

The first step in extracting attributes is to create a template file. You will do that first, and then you will use the DDATTEXT command to extract the attributes from your SINK block to a CDF text file.

1. Start Notepad and type the following exactly as it appears here. Remember, do not use the Tab key, do not add any line returns before or after the text, and save the file with the TXT extension.

    **BL:NAME**          **C008000**

    **BL:XSCALE**        **N008004**

    **BL:YSCALE**        **N008004**

    **MANUFACTURER**     **C035000**

    **PRICE**            **C010000**

    **PART_NO**          **C015000**

    **COLOR**            **C010000**

2. Save the file as SINK.TXT in the UAW13 directory. If you have trouble, use the template file CHPTR24.TXT in the UAW13 directory.

3. If you aren't in AutoCAD, start AutoCAD and open the drawing 24DWG01A that you used earlier in this chapter.

4. At the Command: prompt enter **ddattext**. The Attribute Extraction dialog box appears (see fig. 24.22).

5. Select the <u>C</u>omma Delimited File radio button.

**Fig. 24.22**
The Attribute
Extraction dialog
box shows all
information filled
out.

6. Choose the Select Objects < button. The dialog box disappears; you can select anywhere on the SINK block and press Enter. The dialog box reappears with 1 selected next to the Select Objects < button.

7. Pick the Template File button, and the Template File dialog box appears (see fig. 24.23). Select the template file you created in step 2, SINK.TXT, and choose OK.

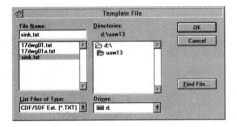

**Fig. 24.23**
The Template File
dialog box appears.

8. Accept the default file name, D:\UAW13\24DWG01A.TXT, in the Output File box by choosing OK.

9. Open Notepad and open the text file that you just created. It should look like the following line. Note the commas separating the fields.

```
'SINK', 1.0000, 1.0000,'Midwest Ceramics,
Inc.','$175.00','MS1228WT','WHITE'
```

Contrast this comma delimited line of text with the space delimited line of text shown earlier. The comma delimited file has uneven columns, while the space delimited file is arranged with even columns. The comma delimited file is particularly useful for importing into spreadsheets and databases. The space delimited files can be used for a quick, unformatted text printout.

10. Close Notepad without saving.

11. Close AutoCAD without saving.

# The AutoCAD SQL Extension

The AutoCAD SQL Extension was introduced in AutoCAD Release 12 and is commonly referred to as ASE. A drawing is in actuality a complex database of objects or records with properties or fields. A demand exists to be able to use data within a drawing for external or non-graphical purposes, such as reports and costing. It is also desirable to link data within a drawing to data that resides outside the drawing. Hence, Autodesk introduced ASE, the AutoCAD Structured Query Language Extension.

With ASE, you can manipulate information in a standard or relational database-management system (DBMS or RDBMS). To take advantage of ASE, you must have a database that supports SQL and is itself supported by data-base drivers supplied with AutoCAD. Why use ASE when you can use the familiar attributes? With ASE, you can perform far more sophisticated information extraction and manipulation. Indeed, the link can be both ways so that any changes in the database can be imported back into the drawing.

All drawing objects can be linked to an external database with ASE. Objects that are ASE-specific are called *displayable attributes*. These objects or attributes automatically update the database or the drawing if changed. Objects that are linked to an external database can provide information such as layer, object type, and color. Any information linked to the external database can be manipulated externally to change the drawing itself. For more information on ASE, read Chapter 13, "Accessing External Databases," in the *AutoCAD User's Guide* from Autodesk.

# From Here...

From this discussion of attributes, you might want to look at the following chapters:

- Chapter 16, "Working with Text," discusses using AutoCAD text.

- Chapter 23, "Using Symbols and XRefs," explains blocks.

- Chapter 36, "Exchanging Data with Windows Applications," explores different methods of extracting information from your drawings and analyzing it in other programs.

# On Your Own

Now that you've learned all about attributes, you should try defining, editing, and extracting them. On the disk included with this book, you will find the drawing 24DWG02, a hypothetical computer lab layout. Try using the following hints to create and manipulate your own attributes. Then you can look at the drawing 24DWG03, Computer Lab Layout—Complete, to see how you've done.

Hints:

1. Load the existing drawing 24DWG02. This is a drawing of a computer lab layout.

2. For the desk, computer, and plotter symbols, define the following attributes. Use a text height of 3".

3. For the desk symbol, define the following attributes, then create a block to include the attributes:

| Tag | Value | Prompt |
| --- | --- | --- |
| Description (Visible, Constant) | Table | Description |
| Vendor (Inv, Constant) | Steelcase | Vendor |
| Cost (Inv) | | Cost |

4. For the computer symbol, define the following attributes, then create a block to include the attributes:

| Tag | Value | Prompt |
| --- | --- | --- |
| Description (Constant) | Computer | Description |
| Type (Preset) | 486-66 | Type |
| Make | | Make |
| Cost (Inv) | | Cost |

5. For the plotter symbol, define the following attributes, then create a block to include these attributes:

| Tag | Value | Prompt |
|---|---|---|
| Description (Constant) | Plotter | |
| Model (Preset) | HP7475A | Model |
| Cost (Inv, Preset) | $1,042.00 | Cost |

6. Insert the attribute, labeling the computer lab equipment. Change the attribute display variable to check your values. Load 24DWG03 to compare results.

# Part VIII

# Isometrics and 3D Drafting

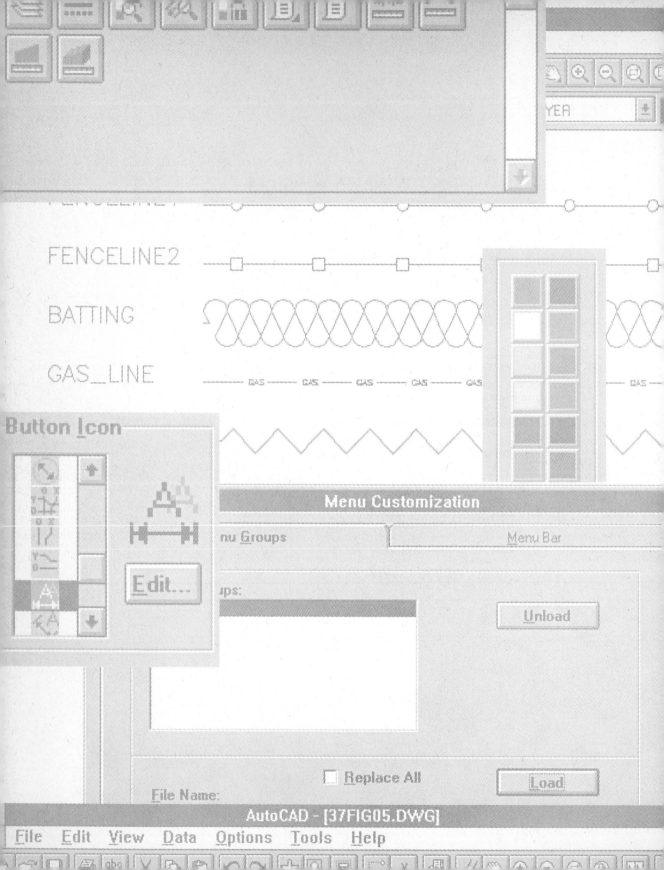

FENCELINE2

BATTING

GAS_LINE — GAS — GAS — GAS — GAS — GAS — GAS

**Button Icon**

Edit...

**Menu Customization**

nu Groups | Menu Bar

ups:

Unload

☐ Replace All   Load

File Name:

AutoCAD - [37FIG05.DWG]

File   Edit   View   Data   Options   Tools   Help

# Chapter 25

# Creating Isometric Drawings

Before AutoCAD was equipped with true 3D capabilities (and sometimes even now), designers created isometric drawings to communicate a three-dimensional design. Although isometric drawings only simulate the view of a 3D model, they still effectively communicate a 3D design. A good example might be an isometric piping plan (see fig. 25.1).

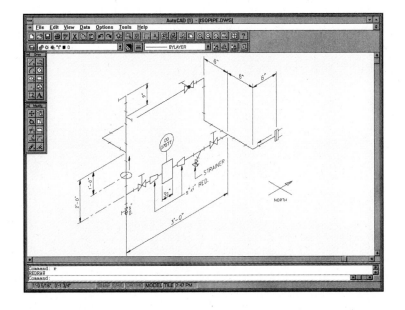

**Fig. 25.1**
An isometric piping plan can effectively communicate a 3D design.

This chapter examines the commands and methods needed to set up and draw in isometric. In this chapter you learn to:

- Set up a snap resolution in isometric planes (SNAP)

- Establish an isometric grid on the isometric plane (GRID)

- Switch isometric planes (ISOPLANE)

- Use the Drawing Aids dialog box to set up isometrics (DDRMODES)

- Draw isometric objects

- Draw nonisometric lines in an isometric drawing

## Setting Up an Isometric Drawing

Objects in an isometric drawing are drawn on one of three isometric planes. Each plane has a pair of axes. You can think of these axis pairs as your *X* and *Y* axes—although, technically they are not—when drawing objects on a particular isometric plane. For the top plane, the axis pairs are 30 degrees and 150 degrees; for the right plane, 30 degrees and 90 degrees; and for the left plane, 150 degrees and 90 degrees. The isometric planes are illustrated on the "cube" drawings in figure 25.2.

**Fig. 25.2**
Isometric drawing of cubes showing right, top, and left isometric planes.

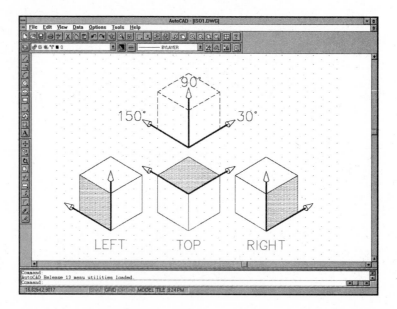

Before you can work in one of the isometric planes, you must first set the snap style to isometric. This allows you to "rotate" the crosshairs to match the current isoplane as well as snap to a specific resolution along that plane. In addition to snap, having a grid that corresponds to the snap resolution is helpful. The next two sections discuss in more detail setting up SNAP and GRID for use in an isometric drawing.

## Setting SNAP for Isometric Drawing

You learned about the basics of using the SNAP command in Chapter 2, "Creating Your First Drawing." The SNAP command is a drawing aid that simply assists the designer in producing the desired results. It is also an integral part of producing isometric drawings. You are allowed to set or toggle the current isoplane using the ISOPLANE command (discussed later in this chapter); but without having your snap style set to Isometric, you are not able to draw objects in an isometric plane. To set up an isometric snap style, follow these steps:

1. Choose <u>O</u>ptions, <u>D</u>rawings Aids, or enter **ddrmodes** at the Command: prompt. The Drawing Aids dialog box appears (see fig. 25.3).

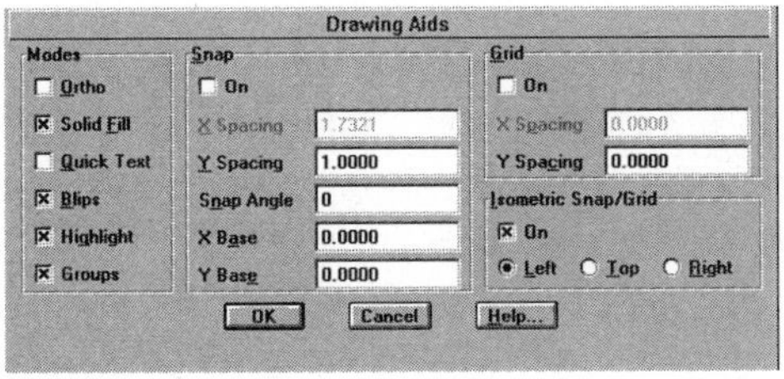

**Fig. 25.3**

The Drawing Aids dialog box can be used to quickly set up tools such as Snap and Grid.

2. In the <u>I</u>sometric Snap/Grid section of the dialog box, select the On check box if it is not checked.

3. Choose OK to accept these settings.

> **Note**
>
> You do not have to have SNAP turned on (refer to fig. 25.2) to have an active snap style of isometric. If, in addition to an isometric snap style, you want to restrict your coordinates to a specific snap resolution, simply turn SNAP on while in the Drawing Aids dialog box.

## Setting GRID for Isometric Drawing

Grid is another drawing aid that works hand-in-hand with snap. When the snap style is set to Isometric and GRID is turned on, you will see a grid of dots which acts as a visual aid for drawing isometric objects. You will notice that the grid corresponds to the isometric axes—30 degrees, 90 degrees, and 150 degrees.

**Fig. 25.4**

A sample isometric snap grid used to aid point selection in an isometric plane.

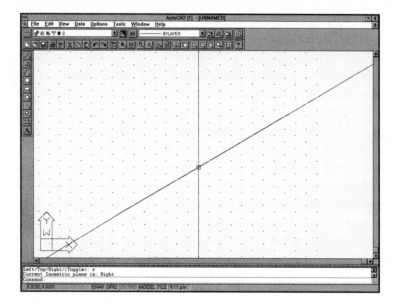

To turn your Grid on, follow these steps:

1. Choose Options, Drawing Aids, or enter **ddrmodes** at the Command: prompt. The Drawing Aids dialog box appears.

2. In the Grid section of the dialog box, select the On check box if it is not checked.

3. Choose OK to accept these settings.

Notice that when the Isometric snap/grid value in the Drawing Aids dialog box is on, you are not allowed to specify different values for the X Spacing and Y Spacing for both Snap and Grid. You can only change the Y Spacing.

**Tip**

You may also find it easier to use the function key F7 or Ctrl+G to toggle the Grid on and off. You can also double-click the Grid button on the status bar.

> **Note**
>
> The grid does not get plotted. Like "blips" when BLIPMODE is on, it is simply a visual aid which can be easily turned on and off as needed.

## Setting the Isometric Plane

The ISOPLANE command is used to switch from one isometric plane to the other. You can select from Top, Left, or Right. Toggle, the default option, allows you to simply rotate to the next isoplane. For example, if your current isoplane is Top, choosing Toggle changes your current isoplane to Right. The toggle rotation order is from Top to Right to Left and so on. Refer to figure 25.2 for an example of each of the isometric planes. The following is an example of accessing the ISOPLANE command at the Command: prompt.

```
Command: isoplane
Left/Top/Right/<Toggle>:
```

> **Note**
>
> Instead of typing ISOPLANE at the Command: prompt, you may find it easier to use the Drawing Aids dialog box available from the Options pull-down menu. Also, you may use Ctrl+E to toggle the isoplane.

## Drawing Isometric Circles and Arcs

When representing circles and arcs on an isometric plane, you use the Isometric option of the ELLIPSE command. The ellipse is used to simulate a circle or arc on the current isometric plane as if viewed from an oblique angle.

When drawing isometric circles, first make sure the Snap style is set to isometric and then pick the Ellipse Axis, End tool or enter **ellipse** at the Command: prompt.

```
Command: ellipse
Arc/Center/Isocircle/<Axis endpoint 1>: i
Center of circle: Pick the centerpoint.
<Circle radius>/Diameter: Specify a radius.
```

When drawing isometric arcs, pick Ellipse Axis, End or enter **ellipse** at the Command: prompt. Then choose I at the <Axis endpoint 1>/Center/Isocircle: prompt. See figure 25.5 for an example of isometric arcs and circles.

```
Command: _ellipse
Arc/Center/Isocircle/<Axis endpoint 1>: a
<Axis endpoint 1>/Center/Isocircle: i
Center of circle: Pick the center point.
<Circle radius>/Diameter: Specify a radius.
Parameter/<start angle>: Enter start angle.
Parameter/Included/<end angle>: Enter end angle.
```

**Fig. 25.5**
An example of
isometric arcs and
circles.

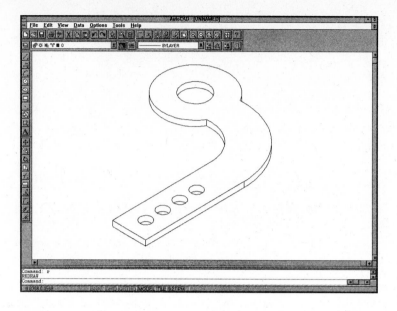

## Drawing Nonisometric Objects

The ISOPLANE and SNAP commands make it easy to translate any orthogonal object into an isometric one. However, any line that does not fall directly on the isoplanes or is on the planes, but not at exactly 90, 30, or 150 degrees, is considered a *nonisometric*, or foreshortened, object. Figure 25.6 shows an example of nonisometric objects.

**Fig. 25.6**
An example of
nonisometric
objects.

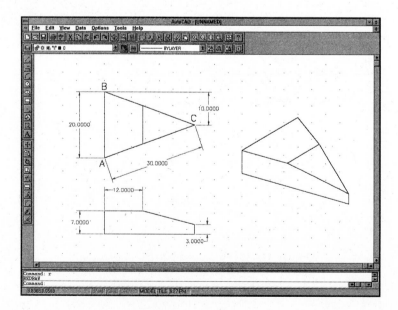

Lines A-C and B-C do not fall directly on one of the isoplanes, and are therefore nonisometric in nature. Although figure 25.6 shows that lines A-C and B-C have a length of 30 units, they cannot be drawn using this length in the isometric view. Only those lines drawn directly on one of the isoplanes can be drawn using the line's actual length. Using the box method with Auto-CAD's new construction lines, you can offset to find the intersections for the nonisometric lines (see fig. 25.7). Another method is to use the geometric calculator (CAL). CAL is used in the tutorial later in this chapter.

◀ See "Drawing Infinite Lines (XLINE)," p. 449

◀ See "Drawing Rays (RAY)," p. 454

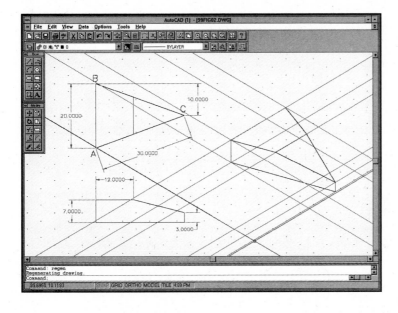

**Fig. 25.7**
Using construction lines; the box method.

VIII

Isometrics & 3D Drafting

## Tutorial: Isometric Drafting

In this tutorial, you practice what you have learned in this chapter. You set up and draw an isometric view using the dimensions shown in the top and side views in the drawing 25DWG01 (see fig. 25.8) found in your UAW13 work directory. Follow these steps:

1. Open the drawing 25DWG01 in your UAW13 work directory.

2. Choose Options, Drawings Aids. The Drawing Aids dialog box appears. Set values in the Drawing Aids dialog box to match those shown in figure 25.9.

**Fig. 25.8**
The finished
isometric tutorial
drawing
25DWG01.

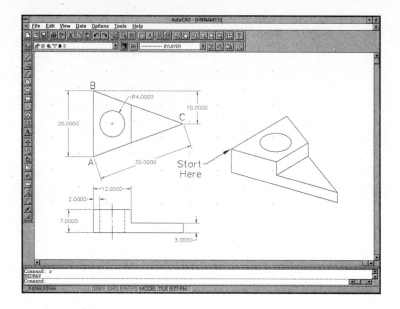

3. Verify that the current isoplane is top (look at the crosshairs).

4. Draw a line from the point shown as "Start Here" in figure 24.8 to a
   point @20<30.

**Fig. 25.9**
Correct settings
for 25DWG01
tutorial.

Choose the Line button, from the Draw toolbar.

> From point: *Pick approximate "start here" point.*
>
> To point: **@20<30**

Stay in the LINE command.

Because the line B-C in the isometric view does not fall on one of the
isometric planes, it is considered to be a nonisometric line. The distance
between B-C (30.0) cannot, therefore, be directly translated to the isometric view. You can calculate point C in the isometric view using the
CAL command in the next step.

5. Continue drawing the line. Enter **'cal** at the To point: prompt.

   ```
   To point: 'cal
   ```

6. Enter the expression **mid+[dist(mid,end)<330]**.

   ```
   >>Expression: mid+[dist(mid,end)<330]
   ```

7. For the first MID point selection, choose the isometric line which represents line A-B.

8. For the second MID point selection, choose the line on the top view between A-B.

9. For the END point selection, choose near point C on the top view.

10. Close the line.

    ```
    To point: c
    ```

11. Choose the Copy command from the toolbar, and select the first isometric line drawn. Displace a copy of the line 12<330.

    ```
    <Base point or displacement>/Multiple: 12<330
    Second point of displacement:
    ```

12. Continue using copy and trim to achieve the view shown in figure 25.10 and figure 25.11.

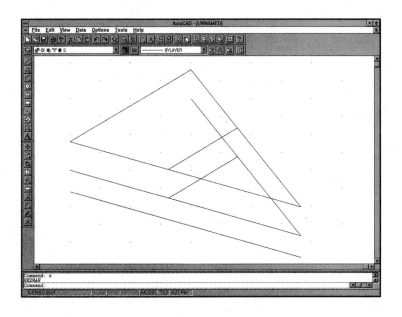

**Fig. 25.10**
25DWG01 after copy operations.

**Fig. 25.11**
25DWG01 after trim operations.

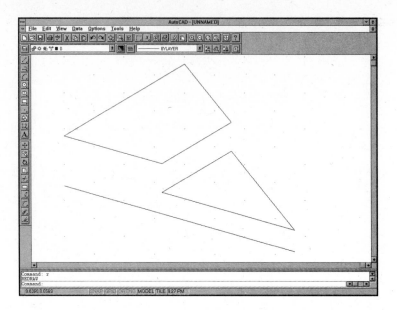

 **13.** Choose the Ellipse command from the Draw toolbar.

**14.** At the `Arc/Center/Isocircle/<Axis endpoint 1>:` prompt, enter **I**.

**15.** For the `Center of circle:` prompt, use the CAL command with the following expression (see fig. 25.12):

```
Center of circle: 'cal
>>Expression: mid+[6<330]
>>Select object for MID snap: Select the isometric
line which represents line A-B in the isometric view.
```

**16.** Enter a radius of 4.0.

Your drawing should now look like the one in figure 25.12. Finish the drawing by drawing lines between the endpoints.

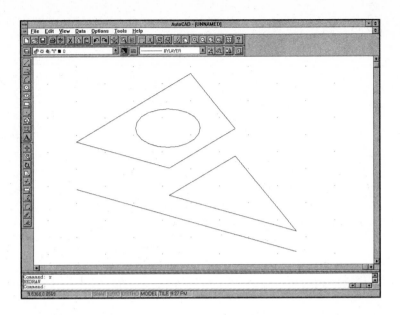

**Fig. 25.12**
25DWG01 near
completion.

**VIII**

# From Here...

When drawing isometric drawings, keep in mind that you are not actually drawing in 3D, but simply simulating a three-dimensional drawing. Some dimensions from Plan and Side views cannot be directly translated into the isometric view; these are nonisometric lines. Remember to use the geometric calculator (CAL) to aid you in these cases. For more information on two-dimensional object creation commands, editing, and other techniques, see the following chapters:

- Chapter 1, "Introducing AutoCAD," gives you a refresher on setting SNAP.

- Chapter 5, "Creating Basic Geometry," provides you with a discussion on general object creation.

- Chapter 11, "Editing with Grips," gives you information on an extremely productive editing tool, grips.

# On Your Own

Load the drawing 25DWG02 from your UAW13 work directory and draw the isometric view using the top view, side view, and figure 25.13 as your guide.

**Fig. 25.13**

25DWG02 completed isometric drawing.

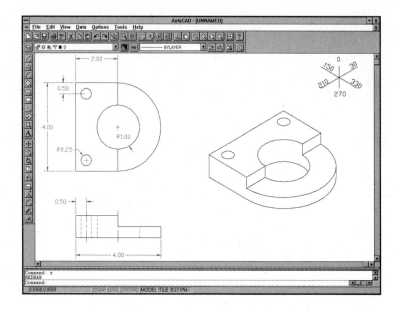

Hints:

1. Examine the top and side views to see which dimensions can be directly translated to the isometric view.

2. Use the ELLIPSE command with the arc and isocircle options.

3. Use copy and trim as needed.

# Chapter 26

# Introduction to 3D Modeling

When you stop and think about it, CAD is nothing more than a communications tool. You're trying to communicate an idea or design to someone. You may be designing a house or something as complex as a car, but one thing is still true—you need to clearly relay your ideas to the client and builder. Drawings produced by hand using pencil and paper on a drafting table and flat, two-dimensional drawings produced using CAD can be limited in the amount of information they relay. It is sometimes hard for the client and builder to "visualize" what is intended by the designer with such a limited view. This failure to communicate can cost the designer and the client money. 3D Modeling offers many features (one of which is better communication) which flat, two-dimensional drawings just cannot provide.

For example, what do architects and car companies do to help their clients visualize their proposed design? They build a three-dimensional model. Sometimes this model is made from wood or clay, but many times it's not made at all. They simply create a "virtual" three-dimensional model on CAD, using the tools and techniques you'll be learning to use in the next six chapters. By *virtual*, we mean the object doesn't actually exist in the real world (yet).

In this chapter, you get a glimpse of some of the drawing aids and tools AutoCAD uses to communicate ideas three dimensionally. You also learn how to do the following:

- Use CHPROP or DDCHPROP to change an object's properties (layer, color, linetype, linetype scale, elevation, and thickness)

- Use the ELEV command to set the current elevation

- Alter your viewpoint of the model with the VPOINT command

- Use a friendlier, dialog box-based version of VPOINT, the DDVPOINT command

- Add surfaces to the model with the 3DFACE command

- Remove hidden lines from view with HIDE

- Generate shaded images of your models with the SHADE command

- Control the way your shaded image is displayed with SHADEDGE

**Fig. 26.1**
An example of a virtual three-dimensional model.

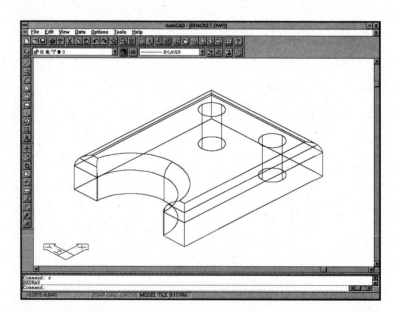

# Types of Three-Dimensional Models

In this section, you take a look at the three different types of three-dimensional models you can produce in AutoCAD:

- Wireframe Models

- Surface Models

- Solid Models

Each of these models has its own place in the design process. For example, you may find that you only need to produce wireframe models. You may want to start with a wireframe and later add "skin" to it, making it a surface model. You may then want to render the surface model for some presentation. If you need to do some type of analysis on the model, you'll want to create a solid model.

## Advantages of Drawing in Three Dimensions

Producing three-dimensional drawings, whether they are wireframe, surface, or solid models, provides many benefits over two-dimensional drawings. Keep in mind that even though isometric drawings appear as if they are three-dimensional, they are not. Isometric drawings are simply two-dimensional drawings that simulate 3D. Therefore, most of the advantages of drawing in 3D that are discussed in this section do not apply to isometric drawings.

◀ See "Creating Isometric Drawings," p. 747

As discussed in the introduction of this chapter, CAD drawings are meant to be a communications tool. Because communication is so important, when the design cannot easily and accurately be conveyed with a flat, two-dimensional drawing, it's time to do that design in 3D. Therefore, one of the primary benefits is better communication.

Part of communicating the design to the client and builder means having the ability to provide drawings of any view of the model. In the two-dimensional world, this means redrawing that particular view, if you can. In the three-dimensional world, it's a simple matter of changing your view of the model and replotting. Because the model was drawn in 3D, it's a virtual representation of what the part, building, roadway, and so on will look like. It's like walking around your house taking pictures at different angles.

Another advantage is that you can design the model once and quickly produce a multiview drawing (top, side, perspective, and so on) utilizing Paper Space. This means that features on a CAD model can quickly be altered and redisplayed to the client. Changing a feature in one view automatically affects that feature in other views. However, if the designer built a physical model of the design from wood or clay, for example, it may need to be completely remodeled. For more information on Paper Space, see Chapter 13.

The following is a list of some of the advantages of drawing in 3D:

- One model, many views

- Easier to visualize intended design

- Easier to catch mistakes

- No need to create physical prototype models (wood, clay)

**VIII**

**Isometrics & 3D Drafting**

- Surface models can be rendered into photorealistic images

- Solid models can be translated into CNC code (Computerized Numerical Code) to create real models

## Wireframe Models

Wireframe models are created using objects such as lines, arcs, and circles. They are the easiest of the three models to produce. A good way to visualize a three-dimensional wireframe model is to picture a cube made out of toothpicks. Imagine that the toothpicks are glued together at each corner of the cube. The toothpicks represent AutoCAD lines at each edge. Looking straight down on the cube, you'll see the lines of the cube created in the XY plane. From the front or back of the cube, you'll see the XZ plane; and from either side, you'll be looking at the YZ plane. Don't get too confused about all this talk of X, Y, and Z planes; they are discussed in more detail later. In the section "Creating a Simple Wireframe Model," you'll have a chance to practice building a three-dimensional wireframe model (see fig. 26.2).

**Fig. 26.2**
Some examples of simple wireframe models.

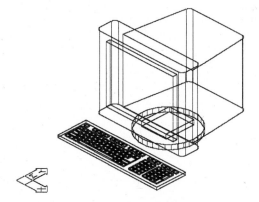

## Surface Models

In the previous section, you took a look at what a wireframe model is. You imagined a cube built out of toothpicks, joined at the corners with some glue. Now let's say you're going to use this cube of toothpicks as the base for a small model house. You add some more toothpicks to form the roof. You still have a wireframe model though. The problem is that you can see right through this model house; what you need to do is put some walls and a ceiling on it. You can cut out some thin cardboard that matches the sides of the cube and ceiling and glue them to the edges of the toothpicks. You now have a surface model, with the cardboard acting as your surface! The toothpicks represent lines in AutoCAD, and the cardboard represents 3D surface objects like 3D faces.

Although you do not have to start a surface model by first producing a wireframe model, it usually helps to do so. If you know ahead of time that you won't need the objects that were used to produce the wireframe, simply put those objects on a different layer. You might want to call the layer "Wireframe." After you've added your 3D surfaces, you can freeze or delete the objects on the "Wireframe" layer and then purge that layer.

Surface models go one step further in communicating the design. Where wireframe models give you a skeletal view of an object, surface models add the skin. They can be shaded using the SHADE or RENDER commands, or rendered to produce photorealistic images using programs such as AutoVision and 3D Studio. Figure 26.3 shows some examples of 3D surface models.

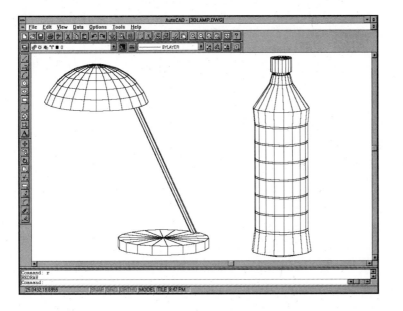

**Fig. 26.3**
Some examples of
3D surface models.

## Solid Models

You first produced a wireframe model by gluing toothpicks together. Then you glued some thin cardboard to the sides of the cube, making a surface model. Solid models, however, are much different than either surface models or wireframe models. Using these models as examples, you might say that a solid model is a cube cut out of wood or some other material. It is a "virtual" solid object.

AutoCAD was first able to produce solid models with the introduction of the Advanced Modeling Extension, or AME. AME was an add-on product for AutoCAD Release 12 that used Extended Object Data to attach information to primitives. Other operations allowed the designer to perform Boolean operations on primitives to produce a final model. A solid modeler, with much more sophistication than it's predecessor (AME), is now included with AutoCAD. With this solid modeler, it is much easier to create basic primitive shapes (box, cone, sphere, wedge, and so on) and then use Boolean commands to combine them into a complex solid model.

Solid models aren't only used to communicate a visual idea or design, but are often used as virtual prototype models on which analysis is performed. The analysis may include stress handling, weight, stability, FEM (finite element method), and so on. This is where the information being communicated needs to be very accurate.

### Note

You can produce wireframe, surface, and solid models in AutoCAD as it comes "out of the box." In Release 13, you no longer need to purchase an add-on product, such as AME, for solid modeling.

For more specific information on the solid modeler, and solid modeling techniques, see Chapter 32, "Introduction to Solid Modeling Concepts."

# Introduction to Three-Dimensional Drawing

You've looked at the different types of 3D models you can produce using AutoCAD, but you must first have a good understanding of 3D coordinates. If this is your first time drawing in 3D, up to now you've only worked with two of the three available coordinates—*X* and *Y*. The *Z* coordinate has always been there, it's just been defaulting to zero. So in fact, you have been drawing in 3D. It's just that everything you have been drawing is flat!

In this section, you'll take another look at the AutoCAD coordinate system. This time, you take advantage of the *Z* axis. Afterwards, you'll learn about some of the rules and tools that will help you understand and effectively work in 3D space.

## Coordinate Systems

A good understanding of the AutoCAD coordinate system (Cartesian coordinates) is paramount to being a productive user. What drawing or editing command does not in some way require coordinate (point) information? When you draw a line, it's from a "starting point" to an "ending point." When you copy an object, it's from one point to another. The more you understand about the methods of providing point information to AutoCAD, the more productive you'll be.

A good place to start is to look at the lower-left corner of your AutoCAD screen. If the system variable UCSICON is turned on, you'll see an icon like the one in figure 25.4. This illustration shows the UCS in plan view; therefore positive *X* coordinates go from the left of your screen to the right, and positive *Y* coordinates go from the bottom of your screen to the top. Chapter 27, "Understanding 3D Coordinate Systems," gives you a closer look at the UCS and UCSICON.

**Fig. 26.4**
The User Coordinate System Icon (UCSICON).

## Z Axis

Now that you've had a review of the AutoCAD coordinate system, you need to know about the next coordinate in the family—the *Z* axis. In a minute, you'll learn about a rule called the Right Hand Rule. This rule is good for helping you visualize and remember in which direction *Z* is heading. For now, let's concentrate on something you'll spend a lot of time looking at— your monitor. In figure 26.5, you can clearly see that the positive *Z* axis is extending out from the monitor. That would naturally mean that negative *Z* coordinates go back into the monitor (not really, but you can think of it that way!).

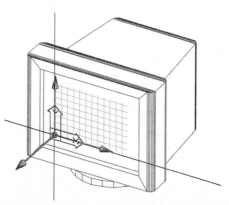

**Fig. 26.5**
A visual example of the X,Y,Z coordinate system.

Because the USCICON indicates both positive *X* and positive *Y* axes, positive *Z* will be extending straight up (towards you, that is) when in plan view (as was illustrated in figure 26.5). There's another easy way to visualize this rule; it's called the Right Hand Rule.

## Right Hand Rule

The Right Hand Rule, like using your screen, is an easy way to visualize and remember what's going on with *X*, *Y*, and *Z* coordinates. When you first start drawing in 3D, keeping each of these axes straight can be a mental chore. Using these tips eases the frustration and helps get you on your way to designing in 3D.

To use the Right Hand Rule, follow these steps:

1. Hold out your right hand with your fingers closed.

2. Rotate your wrist so that your palm is facing up (towards you).

3. Extend your index (pointing) finger straight out.

4. Extend your middle finger towards you, at a 90-degree angle from your index finger.

5. Last of all, stretch your thumb out to your right.

Your hand should look something like figure 26.6.

**Fig. 26.6**
The Right Hand Rule.

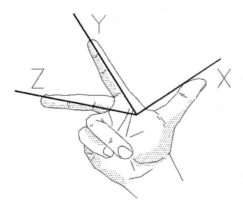

As you can see in figure 26.6, your thumb represents the positive *x*-axis; your index finger represents the positive *y*-axis; and your middle finger represents the positive *z*-axis. As you move your hand around (keeping your fingers in place), notice the relationship each axis has to the other. You'll start to visualize how easy it is to rotate the X,Y,Z coordinate system around to suit your needs. This is referred to later as a UCS, or a User Coordinate System.

---

**Troubleshooting**

*I can't or am unable to perform the Right Hand Rule.*

If you are unable to perform the Right Hand Rule, you alternatively can use the left hand. In this case, the index finger represents positive *Y*, the middle finger positive *X*, and the thumb positive *Z* axes.

---

# Creating a Simple Three-Dimensional Wireframe Model

**VIII**

**Isometrics & 3D Drafting**

In this section, you will start to use some of the things you have learned previously about 3D. You begin by changing the way you look at the drawing using the VPOINT command. Then, you'll learn about drawing objects in 3D space using 3D coordinates—absolute, relative, and polar (spherical).

## Changing the Viewpoint (VPOINT)

Before you start creating the 3D wireframe model of a sofa, you should view it three dimensionally, rather than just in plan view. One way you can accomplish this is by using the VPOINT command. The VPOINT command does just what its name indicates—it allows you to change your point of view of the object. Don't get confused into thinking that you're somehow rotating the object itself. You're not rotating or moving the object to fit your point of view; rather, you're the one moving (not physically, of course). Just imagine that the sofa is actually in front of you. You are looking at it from the front, but you want to look at it from the side. Do you move the sofa? No, you move around the room to obtain the desired point of view. It's true with all of AutoCAD's display commands of which VPOINT is one. You can access the VPOINT command by selecting 3D Viewpoint from the <u>V</u>iew pull-down menu, or by entering **vpoint** at the Command: prompt.

```
Command: vpoint
Rotate/<View point>:
```

**Tip**
You cannot use the VPOINT command while in Paper Space.

Later in this chapter, you will examine two ways to change the viewpoint using either preset values or a dialog box interface (DDVPOINT).

One of the easiest ways to use the VPOINT command is to simply press Enter at the `Rotate/<View point>:` prompt. This brings up an axis and target screen like the one shown in figure 26.7. You may find that using this method is a little easier to visualize than the Rotate option. With this option, practice makes perfect.

```
Command: vpoint
Rotate/<View point>:
```

**Fig. 26.7**

The VPOINT commands Axis and Target options.

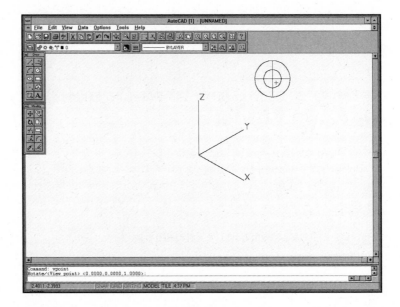

To effectively use this option of VPOINT, you need to pay close attention to the target. As you move your pointing device around, you'll obviously notice the axis rotating and changing. Also notice that there is a small plus sign (+) in the target. You use this target crosshair as a navigational aid. The target is divided into four quadrants. Each of those quadrants is again divided. If the crosshair is in the inner circle, it's as if you are above the model looking down on it. If the crosshair is in the outer circle, it's as if you are below the model looking up at it. If the crosshair is right on the middle circle, it's as if you are looking perpendicular to the model. The quadrants represent where you would be standing looking back at the model, which is always in the middle of the quadrants.

The last option you'll examine for VPOINT is using $x$, $y$, and $z$ coordinates to define the viewpoint. Using this method, you simply tell the VPOINT command where you want to be in 3D space. You are always looking back at the drawing's origin point (0,0,0), so that is your target point. When you first start AutoCAD, you're in what's called "plan view." Your VPOINT setting is 0,0,1. In other words, you're looking down on the model from the absolute point 0,0,1 to the origin point 0,0,0. Try keying in some coordinates like 4,5,6 or 10,20,30 and see what results you get. Fig. 26.8 illustrates this option.

```
Command: vpoint
Rotate/<View point>: 4,5,6
```

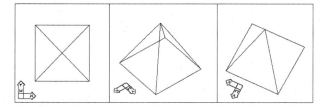

**Fig. 26.8**
Using the VPOINT command's default Viewpoint option.

**VIII**

Isometrics & 3D Drafting

Now that you know how to alter your view so that you can see the model from a three-dimensional point of view, get ready to draw a wireframe model of a sofa.

## Tutorial: Setting Up Your 3D View

In this tutorial, you set up a three-dimensional view. This is done in preparation for future tutorials in which you will be drawing a 3D wireframe model of a sofa.

To set up the three-dimensional view for the sofa exercise using the VPOINT command, follow these steps:

1. From the Standard toolbar, click the New button, or choose File, New. Name the drawing 3DSOFA and press OK.

2. Choose View, 3D Viewpoint, Vector.

3. Choose the Rotate option by entering **r** at the prompt.

4. For the angle in XY plane from X axis, enter **45**.

5. For the angle from XY plane, enter **30** (see fig. 26.9).

6. Save your work! Click the Save button on the toolbar. The QSAVE command is executed.

Stay in this drawing; you will continue this tutorial later.

**Fig. 26.9**

Specifying angles
for the VPOINT
Rotate option.

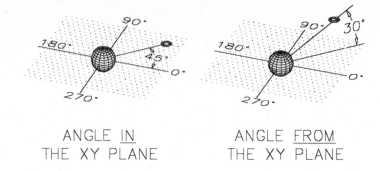

## Using 3D Coordinates

With the viewpoint adjusted to a rotation of 45 and 30 degrees (from the
previous section), you'll be able to see what you're doing from a three-
dimensional point of view. Later, we'll examine a command that will allow
you to view the model from several points of view (plan, side, 3D, and so on)
on the same screen. For now, use this view (see fig. 26.10).

**Fig. 26.10**

A wireframe model
of a sofa.

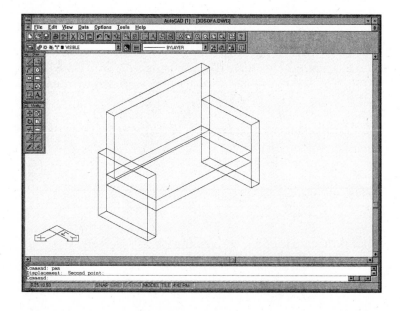

You are set up to start drawing objects using 3D coordinates. You start this
wireframe sofa by generating the side arms using lines. Entering 3D coordinates is every bit as easy as entering them in 2D; you just have to keep in
mind that you now have to enter some value for the z coordinate. For example, if you wanted to draw a line from 0,0,0 to a point in 3D space using

absolute coordinates, you might enter a value like 10,20,5. Just like with 2D coordinates, each coordinate is separated by a comma in the order *x,y,z*. When entering relative coordinates, preface the point with an @ symbol. This keys AutoCAD that this is something other than an absolute coordinate. An example is @2,3,4. From your last point, 2 over in the *x* axis, 3 up in the *y* axis, and 4 up in the *z* axis.

## Tutorial: Drawing the Sofa's Arms

This is a continuation of the previous tutorial. Make sure you have completed the previous tutorial before proceeding with this one.

To start building the side arms of the sofa, follow these steps:

1. From the Draw toolbar, click the Line button or enter **line** at the `Command:` prompt.

2. At the `From point:` prompt, enter **1.5,1.75,0**.

3. Continue drawing the line using the following relative coordinates (entry of the *z* coordinate is optional here, 0 is the default):

```
To point: @0,3,0
To point: @0.5,0,0
To point: @0,-3,0
To point: C
```

Now, you could draw the top of the arm in a similar manner, but why do that when it's the same as the bottom? Instead, you just copy these lines up 3.0 units to form the top of the arm. Follow these steps:

1. From the Modify toolbar, click the Modify Object button.

2. Select the last four lines you drew, which represent the bottom of the sofa arm.

3. At the `<Base point or displacement>:` prompt, enter **0,0,3**.

4. When prompted for the second point, just press Enter.

> **Note**
>
> By not supplying a second point, you're telling AutoCAD to simply displace the object a specific distance, the first value you enter at the `<Base Point...>:` prompt.

5. Click the Running Snap Object button on the Object Snap toolbar and set a running object snap of Endpoint. Connect the corners using the LINE command.

Because the arm on the other side of the sofa is the same, there is no reason to draw it again. Simply copy the arm you just drew 6.25 units over to the other side of the sofa by following these steps:

1. Click the Copy Object button on the Modify toolbar.

2. At the `Select objects:` prompt, select the twelve lines you just drew for the sofa arm.

3. At the `<Base point or displacement>/Multiple:` prompt, enter **6.25,0,0**.

4. When prompted for the second point, press Enter.

Now draw the cushion of the sofa by following these steps:

1. Click the Line button on the Draw toolbar.

2. Turn the running object snap of Endpoint off and then draw the cushion using the following coordinates:

```
From point: 2.0,1.75,1.25
To point: 2.0,4.75,1.25
To point: @5.75,0
To point: @3<270
To point: C
```

> **Note**
>
> You can mix and match coordinate input methods. You can use Absolute, Relative, Polar, and so on, any time you're asked to enter point information (for example, To `point:`)

3. Copy the cushion bottom up 0.5 units in the Z axis to form the top (see fig. 26.11).

4. Click Erase on the Modify toolbar, and erase the sofa cushion you just drew. In a later tutorial you will draw it again using another method.

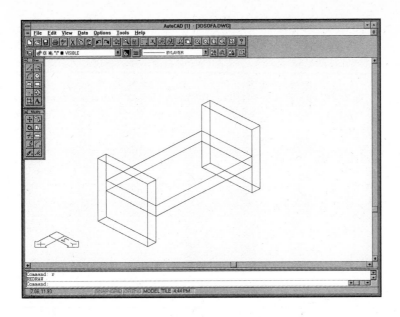

**Fig. 26.11**
Wireframe model
of the sofa's arms
and cushion.

## Using Polar 3D Points

AutoCAD provides two methods of supplying polar 3D point information—
spherical and cylindrical.

Spherical coordinate entry is similar to 2D polar coordinate entry, but with
an additional angle. When supplying a polar coordinate to an AutoCAD command in 2D, you use the syntax *dist<angle*, because you're not worried about
any other plane than the XY plane. With spherical coordinates, you enter the
coordinate using the syntax *dist<angle1<angle2* where *angle1* is the angle in
the XY plane, and *angle2* is the angle from the XY plane. You could use this if
you wanted to draw a line from 0,0,0 to a point 30 degrees in the XY plane
and 45 degrees from the XY plane. See figure 26.12 for an example.

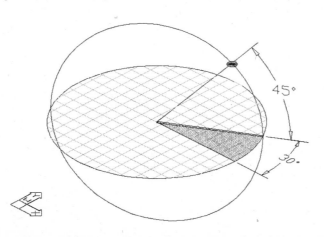

**Fig. 26.12**
Using spherical
coordinates to
locate points.

Cylindrical coordinate entry is like combining 2D polar coordinates and absolute or relative *Z* coordinate point information. You enter cylindrical coordinates using the syntax *dist<angle,Z*, where *dist* is the distance you want to travel, *angle* is the angle in the XY plane you want to rotate, and *Z* is the absolute Z coordinate of the new point. If the cylindrical coordinate entry is prefaced with an @ (which indicates a relative coordinate), then the *distance, angle* and *Z* values are not from the current UCS's origin (0,0,0), but rather the last entered point. See figure 26.13 for an example.

**Fig. 26.13**
Using cylindrical coordinates to locate points in 3D space.

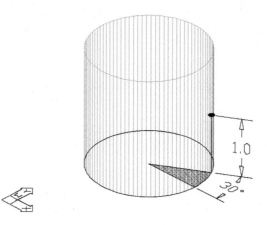

Look at the finished wireframe sofa model in figure 26.14 and finish drawing the back using any of the coordinate input methods discussed so far. Remember, you should only have to draw one side and then copy it using the COPY command's displacement technique.

**Fig. 26.14**
Finished wireframe model of the sofa.

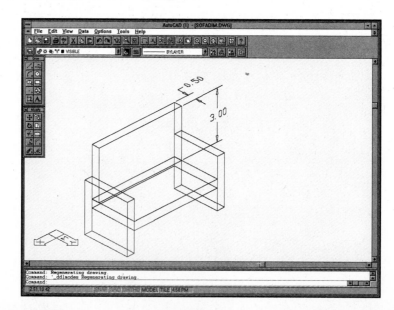

# Creating a Simple Three-Dimensional Surface Model

Wireframe models are fine for some 3D modeling tasks; but for those models you plan on presenting to a client, you may want to go ahead and create a surface model. Wireframes are a good place to start, and should be understood before attempting to move on to surface models. You can use them as a framework to which surfaces can later be added. So if you start out with a wireframe and later decide you need a surface model, you don't have to start from scratch. In this section, you'll be starting from scratch, but only so you can see some other techniques. You'll learn how to set an elevation using the ELEV command. Part of the ELEV command is setting the extrusion thickness (the positive direction of the *z* axis of any UCS) for newly created objects.

## Adding Elevation (ELEV)

When drawing objects and specifying points without supplying a *z* coordinate, AutoCAD automatically supplies that information for you. AutoCAD gets this information (the default Z coordinate) from a system variable called ELEVATION. You can supply the elevation information by either directly accessing the system variable ELEVATION from the Command: prompt or through the ELEV command, which, in addition to setting the current elevation, allows you to specify the extrusion thickness. *Extrusion* simply means the positive direction of the *z* axis of any UCS.

```
Command: elev
New current elevation <0.00>: Enter a value.
New current thickness <0.00>: Enter a value.
```

The base of your sofa is 1.25 units off the floor (which has an elevation of 0.0). So that you don't have to enter the same *Z* coordinate for each of the four lines around the base, set an elevation of 1.25. In the following tutorial, you use this elevation setting to draw the base of the sofa.

## Tutorial: Drawing the Base of the Sofa

This is a continuation of the previous tutorial. Make sure you have completed the previous tutorial before proceeding with this one. You should have erased the sofa cushion in the last tutorial. If you haven't, do so before proceeding.

1. Click the Object Creation button in the Object properties toolbar or choose <u>D</u>ata, <u>O</u>bject Creation. The Object Creation Modes dialog box appears (see fig. 26.15).

**VIII**

**Isometrics & 3D Drafting**

**Tip**

You can use the Object Creation Modes dialog box to set elevation and thickness as well as other object properties like the current color.

**Fig. 26.15**
Use the Object
Creation Modes
dialog box to set
elevation and
thickness.

2. Set the Elevation to 1.25. Click OK to accept changes.

3. Click the Line button on the Draw toolbar.

4. Draw a rectangle (see fig. 26.16) using the following command
sequence:

```
From point: 2,1.75
To point: @0,3
To point: @5.75,0
To point: @0,-3
To point: C
```

**Fig. 26.16**
Set the elevation
and then draw the
base of the sofa.

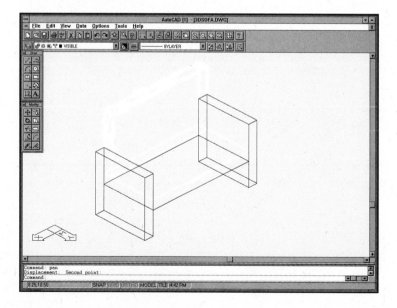

## Giving Objects Thickness

The cushion on the sofa is 0.5 units thick. Instead of copying the base of the
cushion up and connecting the edges like you did with the wireframe sofa
model, you can simply modify the extrusion thickness. In other words, you'll

extrude the object 0.5 units upward. This method doesn't actually produce a surface model, but it's a quick-and-dirty way to build a frame to which surfaces can be added.

Like elevation, the extrusion (positive Z direction) thickness value is stored in a system variable called THICKNESS. When THICKNESS is set to a value other than zero, the object drawn automatically is extruded by that value. Thickness can be set to either a positive or negative value. If positive, the object is extruded upward. If negative, it's extruded downward (see fig. 26.17).

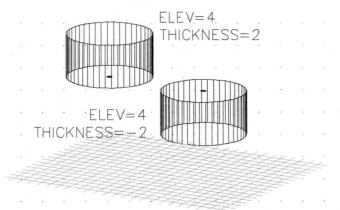

**Fig. 26.17**

Elevation of 4.0 with extrusion thickness of 2.0 and –2.0.

Because the cushion was already drawn with a thickness setting of 0.0, you'll use DDCHPROP to change the THICKNESS property of those objects. You can go ahead and change the extrusion thickness value for the sofa cushion.

## Tutorial: Drawing the Cushion of the Sofa

This is a continuation of the previous tutorials. Make sure you have completed the previous tutorials before proceeding with this one.

1. At the Command: prompt, enter **ddchprop**.

2. Select the lines that make up the sofa cushion (four total).

3. Enter **0.5** for the thickness.

4. Click OK to accept changes.

Your drawing should now look like figure 26.18.

VIII

Isometrics & 3D Drafting

**Fig. 26.18**

The sofa cushion after changing thickness.

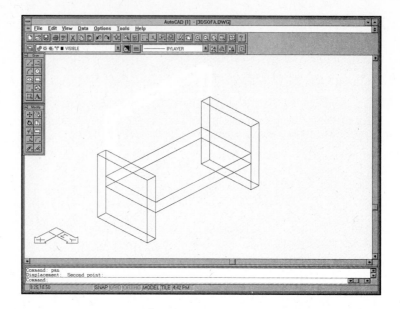

Now, in preparation for drawing the back of the sofa, set another elevation and thickness using the Object Creation Modes dialog box.

1. Click the Object Creation button on the Object properties toolbar or choose <u>D</u>ata, <u>O</u>bject Creation. The Object Creation Modes dialog box appears.

2. Set the new current <u>E</u>levation to **1.75**.

3. Set the new current <u>T</u>hickness to **3.0**.

Draw the back of the sofa following this command sequence:

1. Click the Line button on the Draw toolbar.

2. Draw four lines using the following coordinate input:

```
From point: 2.0,1.75
To point: @0,0.5
To point: @5.75,0
To point: @0,-0.5
To point: C
```

As with the wireframe you drew earlier, the arms on the sofa are 0.5 units wide by 3 units tall by 3 units high. Erase the arms you drew earlier and re-draw them with the new Elevation and thickness settings. Set the ELEVA-TIONto 0 and THICKNESS to 3. Draw one arm and copy it over to the other side of the sofa.

## Adding 3D Surfaces (3DFACE)

At this point in the project, it looks like you have another wireframe of the sofa, and basically you do. Use the extruded lines endpoints as a framework for the placement of 3D Faces (see fig. 26.19).

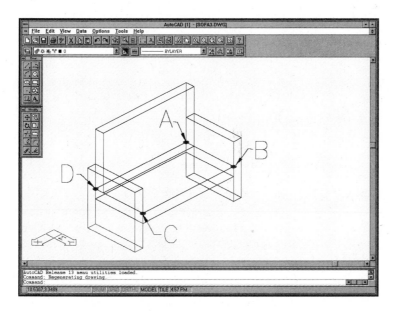

**Fig. 26.19**
Use the wireframe model of the sofa as a framework for adding 3D Faces.

## Tutorial: Adding Surfaces to the Sofa

This is a continuation of the previous tutorial. Make sure you have completed the previous tutorial before proceeding with this one.

> **Note**
>
> For purposes of shading later on, you may want to use different colors for the back, cushion, and arms of the sofa. This will make it easier for you to see what is going on with your design.

Place 3D Faces on the model using the following commands:

1. Choose <u>O</u>ptions, Running <u>O</u>bject Snap and set a running object snap of Endpoint. You may already have it set to endpoint; if so, pick OK.

2. Click the 3D face button on the Surfaces toolbar.

3. Select points as prompted:

```
First point: select point A
Second point: select point B
Third point: select point C
Fourth point: select point D
Third point: Enter
```

**Tip**
Pressing Enter at
the second Third
point: prompt,
and then again at
the Command:
prompt places you
back into the
3DFACE com-
mand. Here you
can start fresh
with a First
point: pick.

4. Using Step 3 as an example, continue placing 3D Faces on the remaining edges until done.

> **Note**
>
> Chapter 28, "3D Modeling Essentials," discusses the 3DFACE command in more detail.

## Changing the Viewpoint (DDVPOINT)

Earlier you looked at the VPOINT command. The VPOINT command was used to allow you to alter the way in which you viewed the model. One of the options of VPOINT was Rotate. The DDVPOINT command gives you a dialog box with preset rotation values (see fig. 26.20). You'll find this dialog box much easier to use when you want to specify a rotation like you used earlier (45 degrees by 30 degrees).

**Fig. 26.20**
Using the
DDVPOINT
command displays
the Viewpoint
Presets dialog box.

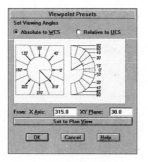

To set your Viewpoint rotation to 315 degrees by 30 degrees, simply pick 315 on the left and +30 on the right. You could also enter those same values manually in the From X Axis and XY Plane edit boxes.

Besides the Viewpoint Presets dialog box, Release 13 has provided a 3D Viewpoint Presets pull-down menu under View. Here you are able to select preset view configurations from the pull-down menu. Refer to figure 26.21 for a list of view options available. Notice that the pull-down menu gives you four isometric preset view configurations, as well as some standard views such as plan, top, bottom, right, left, and so on.

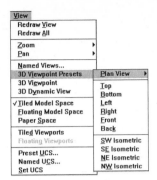

**Fig. 26.21**
Use the 3D
Viewpoint Presets
option of the View
pull-down menu.

## Making the 3D View More Realistic

One of the reasons for creating a surface model in the first place is to clearly and realistically communicate a design to someone. In this section, you'll look at two commands that allow you to view your surface models in a manner more in-line with what the model will look like in the real world. The first command, HIDE, simply removes from view those lines that you would not normally see from your current viewing position. It's the type of view you manually produce with an isometric drawing. Next, you can add a little life to the surface model and obtain a somewhat realistic view using the SHADE command. SHADE doesn't allow you to define materials or lights like AutoVision does, but it's still a quick and easy way to present your model.

### Removing Hidden Lines (HIDE)

One of the benefits of producing a surface model over a wireframe is that hidden line removal can be done on the model. To remove those lines on the model that you would not normally see from your current point of view, use the HIDE command.

You may access the HIDE command by either clicking the Hide button on the Render toolbar, or by entering **hide** at the Command: prompt. AutoCAD indicates that the drawing is regenerating, and begins a percentage countdown of hidden lines removed. After the HIDE command's percentage complete reaches 100 percent, the image with hidden lines removed is displayed (see fig. 26.22).

> **Note**
>
> You will only want to use the HIDE command in Model Space. Paper Space and Hidden Line Viewports are discussed later in this chapter.

VIII

Isometrics & 3D Drafting

**Fig. 26.22**
Sofa after removing hidden lines with HIDE.

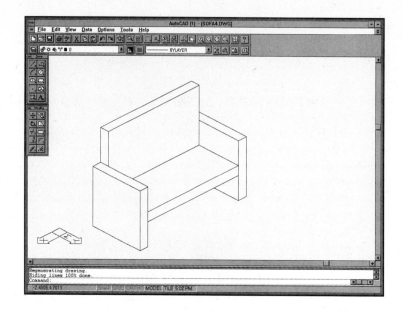

### Shading the Object (SHADE)

▶ See "Understanding Rendering Concepts," p. 949

Using the SHADE command goes one step further than HIDE alone. With the SHADE command, AutoCAD does both a hidden line removal and "paints" the surface of the model. The color that a particular surface on the model appears as depends on the color of the object, the type of video card and/or monitor you have, and the current setting of the system variable SHADEDGE.

Unlike using AutoCAD's RENDER command, AutoVision, or 3D Studio, SHADE can only use one light source. This light is directly behind your viewpoint. You could also say that it is inside of or behind your eye. When you have the SHADEDGE system variable set to either 0 or 1 (which requires 256 colors), AutoCAD shades the faces of the object with consideration to the angle the face is to your viewpoint. Those faces that are closer to being perpendicular to the view reflect more light than those at a greater angle to the view. The amount of light that is diffuse reflection and ambient is controlled by the system variable SHADEDIF.

SHADEDIF default setting is 70, which means that 70 percent of the light available to the scene is diffuse and the remaining 30 percent is ambient. Although you are allowed to set the SHADEDIF system variable to a value between 0 and 100, it's recommended that you leave it set at or around 70. This produces more realistic shadings in the scene. You also would not want to have any diffuse reflection (SHADEDIF set to 0), because this causes the shaded object to appear unrealistically bright. Not enough diffuse reflection causes the object to have unnaturally dark shaded edges.

### Controlling the Shaded Rendering (SHADEDGE)

Use Table 26.1 to determine which value SHADEDGE should be set to for your application. See figure 26.23 below for an example of a shaded model.

| Table 26.1 | Possible SHADEDGE Settings |
|---|---|
| **SHADEDGE Value** | **Type of SHADE Produced** |
| 0 | Shaded faces, edges of objects not highlighted |
| 1 | Shaded faces, with edges of the object highlighted using current background color |
| 2 | Faces shaded using the current background color, with edge color determined by the objects color, gives same results as using the HIDE command |
| 3 | Faces are not shaded, but are drawn in the color of the object with edges of the object highlighted using current background color, default value |

### Note

SHADEDGE settings of 0 and 1 require a 256-color display adapter and standard AutoCAD 256-color map.

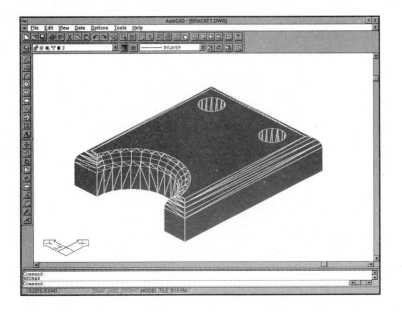

**Fig. 26.23**
Using the SHADE command adds life to the model.

VIII

Isometrics & 3D Drafting

> **Note**
>
> The system variables DISPSILH (Display Silhouette) and FACETRES (Facet Resolution) can be used to improve the quality of the image generated with the HIDE or SHADE commands. Setting DISPSILH to 1 removes the "tesselation" lines on curved surfaces such as those shown in figure 26.23. FACETRES controls the number of facets used to generate a surface.

# From Here...

Drawing in 3D is really no harder than drawing in 2D. In many cases, you use the exact same commands. You simply are adjusting your point of view or UCS (User Coordinate System) and then using regular 2D commands (like LINE). For more information on 2D object creation commands, editing, and other techniques, see the following chapters:

- Chapter 5, "Creating Basic Geometry," discusses general object creation.

- Chapter 6, "Using Object Snaps," discusses the benefits of using object snaps when modeling in 3D.

- Chapter 10, "Editing Techniques," gives you a refresher on editing commands and techniques.

- Chapter 11, "Editing with Grips," provides information on a useful editing tool, grips.

- Chapter 19, "Using Polylines," provides you with a review of how you can alter your UCS and still draw 2D polylines although there is a 3D POLY command.

# On Your Own

Load the drawing 26DWG01 and experiment changing your viewpoint, removing hidden lines, shading, and so on.

Hints:

1. Use either the VPOINT or DDVPOINT commands to change your view point. Try accessing these commands from the pull-down menu and from the Command: prompt.

2. Create a more realistic view of the model using the HIDE and SHADE commands. Experiment with various values for the SHADEDGE system variable.

3. Try using CHPROP or DDCHPROP to alter some of the objects and reshade or hide the model.

# Chapter 27

# Understanding 3D Coordinate Systems

In this chapter, you examine two aspects of understanding and working effectively with 3D coordinate systems. The first examines building new 2D and 3D points by filtering out the point component information you want. The second discusses escaping the bounds of the World Coordinate System (WCS) by creating your own coordinate system, a User Coordinate System (UCS).

In this chapter, you learn to:

■ Create a new UCS (User Coordinate System)

■ Control the display and origin of the UCSICON

■ Restore saved UCS configurations with DDUCS

■ View the current UCS plan view with PLAN

■ Control the initial view of a newly created UCS with UCSFOLLOW

## Using Point Filters

To be a productive user, you need a good understanding of the AutoCAD coordinate system and the tools used to supply point information to AutoCAD commands. One of the nicer point-related tools is *point filters*. Point filtering can be used to build both 2D and 3D points. The term "build" is used because, in essence, that's what this tool does. It filters out requested portions of one point (which again is the form *x,y,z*) and combines that information with the remaining components of another point.

A good example of when to use point filters would be when you have a plan and side view of a part. As in figure 27.1, the object in plan view has a hole in the middle of the part. This feature needs to be shown accurately on the side view. One method would be to draw construction lines from the top and bottom quadrants of the circle, with ORTHO on, and later trim the line. This method works, but there is no need to draw the construction lines in the first place.

**Fig. 27.1**
There is no need to draw construction lines. Use point filters.

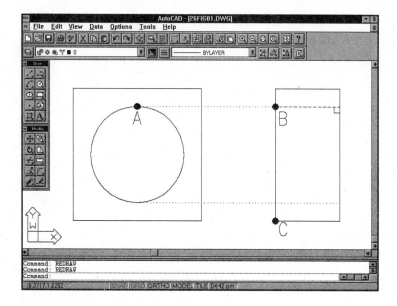

Looking at figure 27.1, it's clear that points A and B should have the same value for the *y*-axis. The X and Z values for point B will be the same as point C. Using point filters, you can combine the Y value from point A to the X and Z values from point C to form a new point, point B (see Table 27.1).

| Table 27.1 | Using a .Y Point Filter | | |
|---|---|---|---|
| | **X** | **Y** | **Z** |
| Point A | 2.5 | 3.625 | 0.0 |
| Point B (new) | 5.25 | 3.625 | 0.0 |
| Point C | 5.25 | 1.0 | 0.0 |

To perform a point filter, at any `Point:` prompt (`From point:`, `To point:`, `Base point:`, and so on) enter a period (.) followed by the component(s) you want to "hold" or filter on. Additionally, you can select a point filter option from the Point Filter toolbar or from the Point Filter fly out on the Standard toolbar. For example:

```
Command: line
From point: .y
of qua
of select circle at point A.
(need XZ) end
of select line at point C.
To point: per
to select line opposite point B.
```

The prompt (`need XZ`) means that this is the information AutoCAD needs to complete the point. A point must have $x$, $y$, and $z$ for it to be a valid point.

You are allowed to mix and match point filtering components as needed. The following examples show the methods available:

- .X, then (need YZ)

- .Y, then (need XZ)

- .XZ, then (need Y)

- .YZ,then (need X)

- .XY, then (need Z)

- .Z, then (need XY)

**VIII**

Isometrics & 3D Drafting

## Tutorial: Using Point Filters

In this tutorial you will practice using the point filtering technique. Use figure 27.1, shown earlier, as a guide and follow these steps:

1. Choose the Open button and select 27DWG01 from the C:\UAW13 subdirectory.

2. Choose the Line button.

3. At the `From point:` prompt, select the .Y button from the Point Filter fly out on the Standard toolbar.

   ```
   Command: _line From point: .y
   ```

4.  Filter on the upper quadrant of the circle (point A in fig. 27.1).

    ```
    of qua
    ```

5.  Satisfy the (need XZ) prompt by selecting the endpoint of the upper-left corner of the side view (above point B in fig. 27.1).

    ```
    of (need XZ): end
    of
    ```

6.  Finish by drawing the line to a point perpendicular to the other side.

    ```
    To point: per
    to
    ```

7.  Repeat these steps for the lower quadrant of the circle.

# Understanding the User Coordinate System (UCS)

So far, you've done everything in a fixed coordinate system called the World Coordinate System (WCS). For 2D drawings and simple 3D models (like the sofa in Chapter 18, "Dimensioning a Drawing"), working in the WCS alone is fine. When it comes to more complicated models, however, you need a little more flexibility. For example, consider the wireframe model of a small house in figure 27.2. Say that you want to draw a skylight on the roof. You could do this within the WCS, but it would be much more difficult. Some objects, such as circles and text, are constrained to a plane that is parallel to the XY plane of the current UCS. For example, if the skylight in figure 27.2 was circular, the XY plane of the UCS would need to be parallel to the roof in order to correctly draw the circle.

By using the UCS command to change the coordinate system to match the plane of the roof, it becomes much easier to draw the skylight (see fig. 27.3).

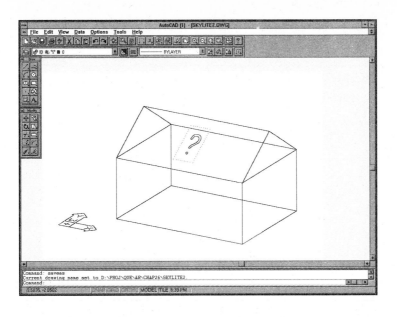

**Fig. 27.2**
Drawing a skylight
on a wireframe
house model in
the WCS.

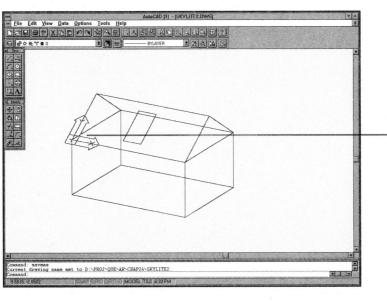

**Fig. 27.3**
Drawing a skylight
on a wireframe
house model in a
new UCS.

UCS icon

**VIII**

**Isometrics & 3D Drafting**

## Understanding the Coordinate System Icon (UCSICON)

As shown in figure 27.3, the User Coordinate System icon (UCSICON) is used to orient yourself to the newly generated XYZ plane. Without this icon, it would be easy to get confused as to the direction of the positive $x$-, $y$-, and $z$-axes.

The UCS icon not only indicates the direction for $x$, $y$, and $z$, it also indicates the following:

■ When the W appears, as in fig. 27.4, this indicates you are in the WCS; otherwise, you're in a UCS (see fig. 27.5).

**Fig. 27.4**

Icon indicating WCS.

**Fig. 27.5**

Icon indicating a UCS.

■ Figure 27.6 shows the UCS icon when displayed at the current UCS origin (0,0,0) point. The (+) on the UCS icon indicates that the UCS icon is at the origin.

**Fig. 27.6**

UCS icon at the origin point (0,0,0).

■ Figure 27.7 shows whether your viewpoint is above or below the model. Notice the missing lines in figure 27.8 (below view).

**Fig. 27.7**

UCS icon showing above view.

**Fig. 27.8**

UCS icon showing below view.

■ Figure 27.9 shows how the UCS icon appears when your viewpoint is perpendicular (or within one degree of being perpendicular) to the UCS. When you see this icon, it is recommended that you do not attempt to specify coordinates in the viewport using your pointing device.

**Fig. 27.9**
UCS icon showing view is almost perpendicular to UCS.

## Managing the UCS Icon

As you saw in the preceding section, the UCS icon is very useful for keeping tabs on where you are in 3D space. There are times when you want the UCS icon to be displayed at the origin point, or perhaps not displayed at all. The UCSICON command is used to control the visual aspects of the UCS icon. When you access UCSICON from the Command: prompt, you are presented with a list of options from which to choose.

    Command: **ucsicon**

Choose Options, UCS, Icon.

Choose Options, UCS, Icon Origin.

The UCSICON command displays the following prompt:

    ON/OFF/All/Noorigin/ORigin <ON>

Here is an explanation of each of these options:

| Option | Does This |
| --- | --- |
| ON | Displays the UCS icon. |
| OFF | Hides the UCS icon. |
| All | Controls visibility changes in all active viewports. |
| Noorigin | Places the UCS icon in the lower-left corner of screen, regardless of origin. |
| ORigin | Places the UCS icon at the UCS's origin point (if able). If the origin point is off-screen, the icon defaults to being displayed in the lower-left corner. |

> **Note**
>
> UCSICON is also a system variable. A value of 1 indicates the UCS icon is on (displayed). A value of 0 indicates it is off (not displayed). A value of 2 indicates the icon is displayed at the origin point of the current UCS.

VIII

Isometrics & 3D Drafting

---

**Troubleshooting**

---

*I don't want to turn the UCS icon off, but it's in my way. Is there any way to move it to a different part of the screen temporarily?*

No. The UCS icon only can be in one of three states; On, Off, and displayed at the Origin (0,0,0) point. If it is blocking your view, either pan the display, or temporarily turn off the UCS icon. Turn it back on when you are done with your operation.

---

## Tutorial: Turning the UCS Icon On

For future exercises, make sure that the UCS icon is displayed by doing one of the following:

- Choose Options, UCS, Icon. If On has a check mark by it, the UCS icon is already on. If not, select On.

- At the Command: prompt, enter **ucsicon**. Then at the ON/OFF/All Noorigin/ORigin: prompt, enter **on.**

## Tutorial: Changing the Appearance of the UCS Icon

In this tutorial, you use the ZOOM, PAN, and DDVPOINT commands to alter the display. Each time you alter the display, notice the appearance of the UCS icon.

1. Choose the Open button and select 27DWG02 from the C:\UAW13 subdirectory.

   Notice the location and appearance of the UCS icon.

2. Set the UCS icon to origin. Open the Options menu and choose UCS, Icon Origin.

   Notice that the position and appearance changes to the UCS icon. Specifically, notice the plus sign (+) at the actual origin location.

3. Open the View menu and choose 3D Viewpoint Presets, or enter **ddvpoint** at the Command: prompt.

4. Select 315 for the angle from x-axis and 30 for the angle in XY plane. Press OK to accept the settings.

   Notice the appearance of the UCS icon in this 3D-rotated view.

5. Press Enter to reenter the DDVPOINT command.

6. Now use the settings 315 and –30.

   What does the UCS icon look like when viewing the model from below?

7. Select Zoom Previous.

8. Select Pan, and enter a displacement of **–5,–5**.

Notice that when the model moves off the screen, and the UCS icon is set to *origin*, the icon automatically resets to the lower-left corner when it is unable to be displayed at the actual origin location.

## Relocating the UCS in 3D

The UCS command is very flexible when it comes to setting up a new coordinate system. The new coordinate system you create controls the orientation for 2D objects (like circles and text), the extrusion direction for THICKNESS, and the rotation axis for the ROTATE command. To set up a new UCS, enter **ucs** at the Command: prompt. You are presented with the following command options list:

```
Command: ucs
Origin/ZAxis/3point/OBject/View/X/Y/Z/Prev/Restore/
Save/Del/?/<World>:
```

This is a rather long list of options, but don't let that intimidate you. Each option is examined in this section. After you feel comfortable with each option of the UCS command, you may find it easier to use the UCS toolbar and fly out on the Standard toolbar. In the following section, each icon is shown with the appropriate option.

## Opening the 3DCOORDS Tutorial Drawing

Throughout this section, the sample drawing 27DWG03 will be used. Open that drawing now by following these steps:

1. Choose the Open button and select 27DWG03 from the C:\UAW13 subdirectory.

2. Choose OK to accept.

### Changing the UCS Origin

The first option, Origin, allows the repositioning of the origin point, or 0,0,0. The WCS's origin point will always be fixed. You need a fixed, absolute point (like the North Pole) to refer to. But, via the UCS command, you are able to indicate a new point in 3D space that you'd like to act as 0,0,0.

**VIII**

**Isometrics & 3D Drafting**

Using drawing 3DCOORDS as an example, set the origin point to the corner of the model at point A (see fig. 27.10).

**Fig. 27.10**
Using UCS's Origin option, set the origin point at point A.

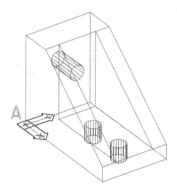

Notice the appearance of the UCS icon as you go through each of these options. If you need to, refer to figures 27.4 through 27.9 for an explanation.

### Rotating the UCS

Four UCS command options are specific to rotating the coordinate system: ZAxis, X, Y, and Z (yes, there is a difference between the option ZAxis and the option Z).

### ZAxis

Using the ZAxis option allows you to reposition the z-axis itself, as illustrated in figure 27.11. You are first asked to supply the new origin point (press Enter if you want it to remain at its current location) and then to supply a point somewhere along the new positive z-axis. Here is an example of this option in use:

```
Command: ucs
Origin/ZAxis/3point/OBject/View/X/Y/Z/Prev/Restore/
Save/Del/?/<World>: za
Origin point <0,0,0>: Pick a point.
Point on positive portion of Z-axis <10.25,6.5,1.0>:
@1,1.5,2
```

### XAxis

The XAxis option allows you to rotate the current coordinate system around the x-axis forming a new coordinate system. This is illustrated in figure 27.12.

Pay special attention to the direction of positive rotation. This command option has the form:

```
Command: ucs
Origin/ZAxis/3point/OBject/View/X/Y/Z/Prev/Restore/
Save/Del/?/<World>: x
Rotation Angle about X axis <0>: 90
```

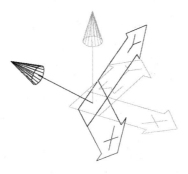

**Fig. 27.11**
Creating a new UCS by repositioning the z-axis.

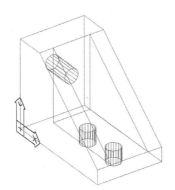

**Fig. 27.12**
Creating a new UCS by rotating about the x-axis.

### YAxis

As with the XAxis option, the YAxis option allows the creation of a new coordinate system (a UCS) as a result of rotating the current coordinate system about the y-axis. Again, notice the direction in which positive angles rotate (see fig. 23.13).

```
Command: ucs
Origin/ZAxis/3point/OBject/View/X/Y/Z/Prev/Restore/
     Save/Del/?/<World>: x
Rotation Angle about X axis <0>: 90
```

**Fig. 27.13**
Creating a new
UCS by rotating
about the *y*-axis.

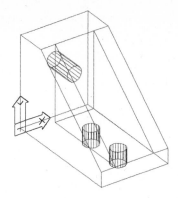

### ZAxis

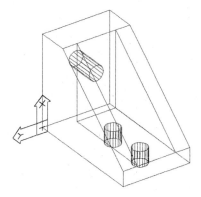

Creating a new coordinates system by rotating about the *z*-axis is the same as
for *x* and *y* (see fig. 27.14).

**Fig. 27.14**
Creating a new
UCS by rotating
about the *z*-axis.

### 3point

The 3point option of the UCS command is probably the most versatile option
available. You are prompted to supply three pieces of information:

- A new origin point

- A point that defines the new coordinate system's positive *x*-axis

- A point that defines the new UCS's positive *y*-axis

◀ See "Right
Hand Rule,"
p. 766

By picking points (or entering in WCS absolute, relative, or polar coordinates)
for the positive *x*- and *y*-axes, you are automatically defining the positive
*z*- axis. No need to worry about that. If you have trouble visualizing what
direction positive *z* is heading off in, try using the Right Hand rule.

### Tutorial: Creating a UCS Using 3 Points

If you don't have the sample drawing 27DWG03 still open, open it again now. Create a UCS along the sloped front of the part at points A, B, and C (point A being the origin; point B, the *x*-axis; and point C, the *y*-axis) by following these steps:

1.  Select the UCS 3point button, or at the Command: prompt, enter **ucs** and select the 3point option.

2.  For the origin point, choose point A.

3.  For the point on the positive portion of the *x*-axis, choose point B.

4.  For the point on the positive portion of the *y*-axis, choose point C.

If the UCS icon is still set to Origin, your screen should appear like the one shown in figure 27.15. It's not necessary that the UCS icon be set to Origin. However, at first, you may find it useful in order to keep a mental note of where your origin point (0,0,0) is.

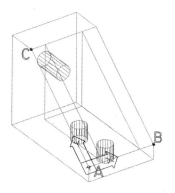

**Fig. 27.15**
Creating a UCS with the 3point option.

### Aligning the UCS with an OBject

A quick way to switch to a new UCS is to use the OBject option of the UCS command. With this option, AutoCAD examines the object you select and determines what UCS settings it was produced under. The information AutoCAD uses to set up the new UCS is dependent upon the object selected. Table 27.2 indicates the way in which AutoCAD creates a new UCS for each object type you select.

```
Command: ucs
Origin/ZAxis/3point/OBject/View/X/Y/Z/Prev/Restore/
Save/Del/?/<World>: ob
```

**Note**

You cannot use 3D Polylines, Viewports, and Polygon Meshes as object selections to define a UCS.

**Table 27.2 Using the UCS OBject Option**

| Object Type | Creation of UCS |
|---|---|
| Arc | The UCS origin is at the Arc's center point. The positive x-axis is from the center to the endpoint of the arc. |
| Circle | The UCS origin is at the Circle's center point. The positive x-axis is from the center to the point of selection. |
| Line | The endpoint closest to where you select becomes the UCS origin. The positive x-axis is from the new origin to the opposite endpoint. |
| Polyline (2D) | The UCS origin is at the start point. The positive x-axis is from the start point to the first vertex point. |
| Solid | The first point on the Solid is used as the new origin. The positive x-axis is from the new origin to the second point. |
| 3DFace | The first point of the 3DFace is used as the new origin. The positive x-axis is from the new origin to the second point, and the positive y-axis is from the new origin to the fourth point on the 3DFace. |
| Point | The UCS origin is at the point. The x-axis is determined by an arbitrary algorithm. |
| Text, Insert, Attribute, Shape | The UCS origin is placed at Attdef, the object's insertion point. The positive x-axis is from the new origin to a point along the same angle as the object's rotation. |
| Dimension | The UCS origin is at the midpoint of the dimension text. The positive x-axis is parallel to the UCS that the dimension was created under. |
| Trace | The first point of the object is used as the new origin. The positive x-axis is from the new origin along the Trace's center line. |

> **Note**
>
> As Table 27.2 shows, AutoCAD uses an arbitrary algorithm to locate the axes of the UCS when you attempt to align the UCS on a point object. You may find that AutoCAD's choice of axes alignment does not match the UCS you had when the point was drawn. That may be a problem if you need to reset the UCS to an exact previous setting based on a point. To avoid the problem, use the UCS Save and Restore options discussed later.

---

**Troubleshooting**

*Using the OBject option produces an unexpected UCS configuration.*

Because the OBject option is using an arbitrary algorithm to locate the axes of the UCS, the *x*- and *y*-axes may not be oriented the way you would expect. Try locating 3 points on the object and use the 3point option.

---

### Aligning the UCS with a View

To create a new coordinate system that is perpendicular to your current view-point, use the View option of the UCS command (see fig. 27.16).

```
Command: ucs
Origin/ZAxis/3point/OBject/View/X/Y/Z/Prev/Restore/
Save/Del/?/<World>: v
```

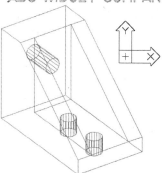

**Fig. 27.16**
Setting up a UCS that is perpendicular to your current viewpoint.

Using the View option is the easiest way to set up a UCS that allows you to place notes or other annotations on a 3D view.

### Saving a UCS (DDUCS)

After you set up one or several different UCSs (using one of the options discussed earlier), it would be nice if AutoCAD provided you with a way to save those settings. It does! In the same way you can save a view using the VIEW command and easily recall it later, you can save a UCS. This makes it much easier to return to that UCS for additional modeling later without having to go through rotations and other manipulations to set up the UCS. Doing it once is enough.

For example, if you are designing an apartment building, somewhere in the modeling process there will come a time to work on the roof. For the roof you'll have at least two UCSs, one for each slope. You may find the need to switch back and forth from one side of the roof to the other while modeling. Having a saved UCS makes this much easier to do.

To save the UCS configuration, do one of the following:

- Choose the Save UCS button from the UCS toolbar.

- From the <u>V</u>iew pull-down menu, choose <u>S</u>et UCS, then <u>S</u>ave.

At the `?/Desired UCS name:` prompt, enter the name you want to save this UCS under.

- At the `Command:` prompt, enter **ucs**, and then choose Save.

To restore a previously saved UCS, do one of the following:

- Choose the Restore UCS button from the UCS toolbar.

- From the <u>V</u>iew pull-down menu choose <u>S</u>et UCS, then <u>R</u>estore.

  At the `?/Name of UCS to restore:` prompt, enter the name of the UCS you wish restored.

- At the `Command:` prompt, enter **ucs**, and then choose Restore.

Another method is to use the UCS Control dialog box (see fig. 27.17). This dialog box can be used to save, list, restore, rename, and delete UCS configurations. To access the dialog box from the Standard or UCS toolbars, choose the Preset UCS button, or enter **dducs** at the `Command:` prompt.

**Fig. 27.17**
The DDUCS
command brings
up the UCS
Control dialog
box.

**VIII**

Isometrics & 3D Drafting

After you see the UCS Control dialog box, you may choose to perform one of
the following options:

### Save

To save your current UCS settings, in the UCS Control dialog select from the
UCS Names list *No Name*. Highlight *No Name* in the edit box next to the
Rename To: command button, give it a new name, and select Rename To:.
Select OK to accept changes.

You also can save the current UCS settings by clicking Save UCS button on
the UCS toolbar, or by entering **ucs** at the Command: prompt; then enter **s** for
Save. At the ?/Desired UCS name: prompt, enter a name for the UCS.

```
Command: ucs
Origin/ZAxis/3point/OBject/View/X/Y/Z/Prev/Restore/
    Save/Del/?/<World>: s
?/Desired UCS name: Enter ? or a name.
```

### Restore

To restore a saved UCS using the DDUCS command, simply select the UCS
you want to restore from the UCS Names list, and then choose Current, OK.

If using the toolbar, choose the Restore UCS button, or enter **ucs** at the Command: prompt, **r** for restore, and the name of the saved UCS. If you forget the
name of the saved UCS, use the **?** option to bring up a list of saved UCSs.

```
Command: ucs
Origin/ZAxis/3point/OBject/View/X/Y/Z/Prev/Restore/
    Save/Del/?/<World>: r
?/Name of UCS to restore: Enter ? or a name.
```

### Previous

To restore the UCS that was in use prior to the current UCS, select *Previous*
from the UCS Control dialog (DDUCS), and then choose Current, OK.

If using the UCS toolbar, choose the Previous UCS button or at the `Command:` prompt, enter **ucs**, and then **p** for previous.

```
Command: ucs
Origin/ZAxis/3point/OBject/View/X/Y/Z/Prev/Restore/
    Save/Del/?/<World>: p
```

### ?

A listing of saved UCSs is automatically available by using the DDUCS command. For a listing of saved UCSs from the `Command:` prompt, enter **ucs**, and then press **?**. You may supply wildcards if you want.

```
Command: ucs
Origin/ZAxis/3point/OBject/View/X/Y/Z/Prev/Restore/
    Save/Del/?/<World>: ?
```

### Del

After you use the Save option of the UCS command to save a UCS configuration, you may find the need to remove it from the list of saved coordinate systems. To do this from the UCS Control dialog box, select the saved UCS name from the list and choose the Delete button. From the `Command:` prompt, you can use the UCS command's del option.

```
Command: ucs
Origin/ZAxis/3point/OBject/View/X/Y/Z/Prev/Restore/
    Save/Del/?/<World>: d
UCS name(s) to delete <none>: Enter a name.
```

### Setting the UCS to the World Coordinate System

AutoCAD provides you with a method of returning home, so to speak. Any time you want to return to the default World Coordinate System (WCS), you can use the default option, World. With this option, you're not actually creating a new UCS; you're restoring one that's already there—the WCS.

To return to the World Coordinate System (WCS), do one of the following:

- Choose the World UCS button from the UCS fly out on the Standard toolbar.

- Choose the World UCS button from the UCS toolbar.

- At the `Command:` prompt, enter **ucs** followed by **w** for World.

1. Choose <u>V</u>iew, <u>P</u>reset UCS. The UCS Orientation dialog box appears (see fig. 27.18).

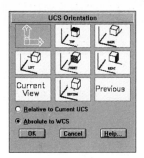

**Fig. 27.18**
Using the UCS
Presets dialog box.

2. Choose the UCS icon that represents the WCS in the upper-left corner of the dialog box.

3. Choose OK to accept.

---

**Note**

You also can use the UCS Presets dialog box (DDUCSP command) to set up a new UCS for the top, back, left, front, right, and bottom sides. In addition, it can be used to set the UCS to the current view and restore the previous UCS.

---

**VIII**

**Isometrics & 3D Drafting**

---

**Troubleshooting**

*I have no idea what UCS I'm in or how it's configured. What should I do?*

Your best bet would be to return to the WCS using one of the methods you just read about. In the WCS, you know where you are and can work your way forward again.

---

## Using the PLAN Command with the UCS (PLAN)

After you set up a new User Coordinate System (UCS), you may want to view it in plan view. To understand what *plan view* means, imagine that you are in a hot air balloon looking straight down on your 3D model. This is also identical to having a VPOINT setting of 0,0,1 relative to the current UCS.

Access the PLAN command by doing one of the following:

■ Open the View pull-down menu and choose 3D Viewport Presets, then Plan View.

■ At the Command: prompt, enter **plan**.

The PLAN command displays the following prompt:

&lt;Current UCS&gt;/Ucs/World: *Enter an option or press enter.*

The PLAN command provides three options to set the current plan view:

- *Current UCS.* Displays a plan view of the current UCS.

- *World Coordinate System (WCS).* Restores the plan view of the WCS.

- *Saved UCS.* Displays a plan view of a previously saved UCS.

### Using PLAN Command with a Previously Saved UCS

To change to the plan view of a previously saved UCS, do one of the following:

- From the View pull-down menu, choose 3D Viewpoint Presets, then Plan View.

- From the Command: prompt, enter **plan**. Then enter **u** at the &lt;Current UCS&gt;/Ucs/World: prompt.

AutoCAD asks for the name of the UCS for which to regenerate the plan view. Enter the name of a previously saved UCS or ? to obtain a listing.

### Creating a Plan View when Changing UCS (UCSFOLLOW)

When the system variable UCSFOLLOW is turned on (value of 1), you are automatically placed in plan view every time you change the UCS.

> **Note**
>
> UCSFOLLOW has no effect in Paper Space.

# From Here...

A good understanding of the 2D coordinate system is necessary for effective manipulation of UCSs. Review some of the following chapters if you need a refresher:

- Chapter 4, "Understanding Coordinates and Units," provides a discussion on AutoCAD's coordinate system.

- Chapter 12, "Viewing a Drawing," discusses commands used to control and change the way you view your work.

# On Your Own

Create a new 3D wireframe model of a chair. Name your drawing 3DCHAIR. Use figure 27.19 and the dimensions shown as a guide.

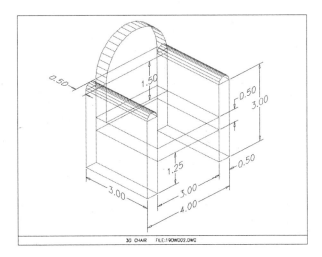

**Fig. 27.19**
A 3D wireframe
model of a chair.

Hints:

1. Use the UCS command to alter the UCS as needed.

2. Use the ELEV command as needed to control thickness and elevation.

3. Try using CHPROP or DDCHPROP to alter some of the object's thicknesses.

# Chapter 28

# 3D Modeling Essentials

At times you may need to create more complex models than those introduced in the previous two chapters. This chapter introduces you to the commands essential to producing complex 3D surface models. In this chapter you learn to:

- Create a polyline in 3D space using the 3DPOLY command

- Generate solid-filled polygons with the SOLID command

- Place a three- or four-sided 3D surface using 3DFACE

- Use 3DMESH to generate a free-form polygon mesh

- Create a polyface mesh with the PFACE command

- Control M direction mesh density with the SURFTAB1 system variable

- Control N direction mesh density with the SURFTAB2 system variable

- Construct a tabulated surface with the TABSURF command

- Construct a ruled surface using the RULESURF command

- Construct a surface of revolution with the REVSURF command

- Define a surface between edges using the EDGESURF command

This chapter examines the creation of a 3D polyline; how to create a solid area (not solid modeling) using the SOLID command; and how to extrude a solid by adding thickness, giving it the appearance of a complete surface model. Then, this chapter revisits 3D faces, the common foundation and building blocks for all surface models. For example, if you took a surface model produced by a command such as REVSURF and then broke it down (exploded it) into its individual elements, you would find that those individual objects are 3D faces. Another type of complex surface is called a polygon mesh. You can think of a polygon mesh as a "block" of any number of rows and columns of 3D faces. Just like blocks, polygon meshes are treated by AutoCAD as one object, in this case, a special type of polyline. When a polygon mesh is exploded, it too breaks down into individual 3D face objects.

AutoCAD provides a rich set of commands which allow the creation of polygon meshes in a variety of different situations. For example, you may want to place a surface between two edges by using the RULESURF command. In another situation you may want to revolve a profile to create a complex surface using REVSURF. Whatever the situation, in most cases you will have the command you need to generate the surface.

A good example would be the 3D lamp (see fig. 28.1)—a simple wireframe on the left, and the finished surface model on the right. The wireframe only contains those objects needed to aid in the creation of the surface model. The base of the lamp was created using RULESURF, the arm of the lamp with TABSURF, and the lamp dish with REVSURF.

**Fig. 28.1**

A 3D surface model of a lamp created from a simple wireframe model using RULESURF, TABSURF, and REVSURF.

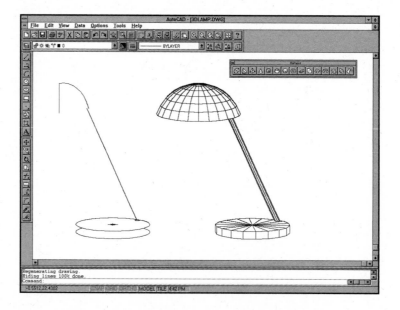

# Creating 3D Polylines (3DPOLY)

3D polylines free you from the limitation that 2D polylines have of not being allowed to enter vertex information using 3D coordinates, but they are limited in other areas. For example, with the 3DPOLY command, you cannot generate polylines with arc segments or add width as you can in 2D.

3D polylines can only be comprised of straight line segments between each vertex point. But then, of course, with the PLINE command you can't draw a polyline in 3D space, so there are some trade-offs.

When drawing a 3D polyline , you are prompted for the first vertex point with the familiar From point: prompt (see fig. 28.2). After supplying the first point, the only options the 3DPOLY command has are for the <Endpoint of line>, Close, and Undo.

To access the 3DPOLY command use one of the following methods:

- Select the 3D Polyline button from the polyline fly out on the Draw toolbar.

- Enter **3dpoly** at the Command: prompt.

AutoCAD prompts you with:

```
Command: 3DPOLY

From point: Select a point.

Close/Undo/<Endpoint of line>:
```

◀ See "Drawing Polylines (PLINE)," p. 573

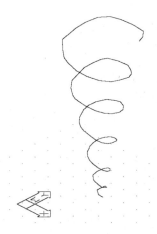

**Fig. 28.2**
An example of a 3D polyline.

# Tutorial: Working with 3D Polylines

This tutorial gives you a chance to try the 3DPOLY command. Start a new drawing, and follow the instructions below:

**1.** Select the New button, and name your drawing 3dptest.

VIII

Isometrics & 3D Drafting

2. Enter **ddvpoint** at the Command: prompt, and rotate the view 315 degrees from the X axis and 30 degrees in the XY plane.

3. Select the 3D Polyline button from the Polyline fly out on the Draw toolbar, or enter **3dpoly** at the Command: prompt.

   Command: **3dpoly**

4. At the From point: prompt, select a point on the screen.

   From point: *Specify a point.*

5. Following the prompts, finish drawing the 3D polyline.

   ```
   Close / Undo / <Endpoint of line>: @0,0,1
   Close / Undo / <Endpoint of line>: @1,0,0
   Close / Undo / <Endpoint of line>: @0,0,-1
   Close / Undo / <Endpoint of line>: @0,1,0
   Close / Undo / <Endpoint of line>: @0,0,1
   Close / Undo / <Endpoint of line>: @-1,0,0
   Close / Undo / <Endpoint of line>: @0,0,-1
   Close / Undo / <Endpoint of line>: c
   ```

# Creating Faces

Chapter 26, "Introduction to 3D Modeling," compared a wireframe to toothpicks joined together at each corner by glue. Imagine again a 1 x 1 x 1 cube made out of toothpicks. No matter from what angle you view the model, you can still see through to the opposite side. Now, imagine that you have glued some very thin paper to each side of the cube. Your view is restricted to the face closest to you. You cannot see through to the opposite side.

A face can be thought of as an infinitely thin opaque layer of paint on an object. Remember, surface models are not solid. The face of the surface doesn't actually have any depth to it. It is simply used by AutoCAD to simulate opacity.

## Creating Solid Areas (SOLID)

> **Note**
>
> Don't get confused by the name of this command. It is not used to create solid models, but rather opaque, filled (solid) regions.

Although the SOLID command does not actually produce a "face," the result of the command is similar in that it allows the production of a triangular or rectangular opaque region. To understand opacity, imagine you are holding a sheet of glass in front of you. You can see through it—it's transparent. If paint were to be sprayed onto the glass, it would become opaque, not allowing you to see objects behind the glass. Likewise, any object behind a solid is removed from view if FILLMODE is on or, in a 3D view, if hidden line removal or shading is performed. Therefore, it is like having a face there. The system variable FILLMODE controls whether the solid is displayed as a filled, opaque region.

> **Note**
>
> When viewing a solid in a view other than plan, the solid will not display filled even if FILLMODE is turned on.

The SOLID command can be accessed by either of these methods:

- Select the 2D Solid button from the Polygon fly out on the Draw toolbar.

- Enter **solid** at the Command: prompt.

After issuing the SOLID command, you are prompted for a series of points. A minimum of three points must be supplied, and no more than four points per solid are allowed. If a fourth point is supplied, the SOLID command will cycle back to a request for another third and fourth point, using the previous solid's third and forth points as its own first and second.

```
Command: solid
First point: Pick a point.
Second point: Pick a point.
Third point: Pick a point.
Fourth point: Pick a point.
Third point: <ENTER>
```

> **Note**
>
> With the SOLID command, you can only enter 2D points at each of the point prompts. To generate a true surface in 3D, use the 3DFACE command.

The SOLID command behaves a little differently than the 3DFACE command (discussed in "Creating 3D Faces" later in this chapter). As you can see in figure 28.3, you have to pay special attention to the order in which points are picked when creating a solid. Picking points in the same order you do when creating 3D faces would result in a "bow tie" effect.

**Fig. 28.3**
The order in which points are selected for a solid is important.

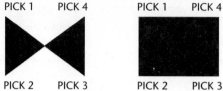

Just as you can extrude lines, arcs, circles, and so on, you can extrude a solid by adjusting its thickness property. Unlike extruding a set of closed lines, or polylines, extruding a solid gives it the appearance of having surfaces on every edge. In figure 28.4, you see a closed polyline extruded on the left and a solid that was extruded on the right. Notice that the solid, when hidden lines are removed, appears to have faces on all sides.

**Fig. 28.4**
Examining the difference between a Polyline and Solid extrusion.

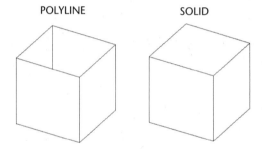

## Creating 3D Faces (3DFACE)

3D faces are the simplest of the 3D surface objects to generate. Like solids produced with the SOLID command, 3D faces can be triangular or rectangular. As with solids, a 3D face must have at least three corners and no more than four. The difference is that with the 3DFACE command you are allowed to pick the points in either clockwise or counterclockwise order, rather than in a "Z" or "N" fashion. Unlike a SOLID, with a 3D face, each corner of the face can have a different Z coordinate.

You can access the 3DFACE command by using either of the following methods:

■ Select the 3D Face button from the Surfaces toolbar.

■ Enter **3dface** at the Command: prompt.

You are prompted to specify each corner as shown below.

```
Command: 3dface
First point: 1,1
Second point: 2,1
Third point: 2,2,1.5
Fourth point: 1,2,1.5
Third point:
```

Both solids and 3D faces are opaque, but only solids are filled with the object color prior to performing a SHADE. A 3D face appears as if it were a wireframe until you perform a hidden line removal, shade, or render the scene (see fig. 28.5). With hidden line removal, the 3D face object is not filled (painted) with any color, but does "hide" from view those objects that would be behind it according to the current viewpoint. The edge of the 3D face takes on the original color of the 3DFACE object, and the actual face is displayed in the default background color. When using the SHADE command, a 3D face is displayed according to the settings of the system variables SHADEDGE.

◀ See "Making the 3D View More Realistic," p. 781

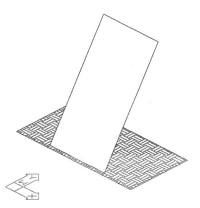

**Fig. 28.5**
The result of performing hidden line removal on a 3DFACE.

With a little forethought, you can quickly add faces to wireframe models such as the one in figure 28.6. Because the 3DFACE command uses third and fourth points selected on the last 3DFACE (like the SOLID command does), you can use this to your advantage. Instead of terminating the 3DFACE command by not picking a new third point, you can continue selecting points to produce additional, adjoining faces in one operation. Figure 28.6

**VIII**

Isometrics & 3D Drafting

also illustrates a potential picking order. When you reach point 4, you are prompted again for a new third point, which in this example is pick point number 5. The 3DFACE command continues asking for third and fourth points, using the previous face's third and fourth points as its first and second points. To stop, simply press Enter at any Third point: prompt.

**Fig. 28.6**
You can add several 3D faces to a wireframe model at once.

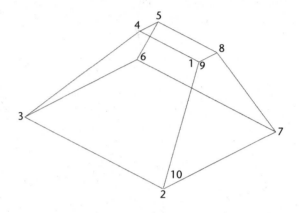

> **Note**
>
> If you do not supply the 3DFACE command a point at the Fourth point: prompt, a triangular 3D face is the result.

```
Command: 3dface
First point: point 1
Second point: point 2
Third point: point 3
Fourth point: point 4
Third point: point 5
Fourth point: point 6
Third point: point 7
Fourth point: point 8
Third point: point 9
Fourth point: point 10
Third point:
```

**Tip**
Using a running object snap of Endpoint makes the selection of 3DFACE points much faster when using a wireframe as a reference.

Any time you do not want an edge of the 3D face to be visible, preface the point selection with the letter "I" or the word "invisible." The edge from that point selection to the next is not displayed. In figure 28.7 on the left is the model with 3D faces having all edges visible. The example on the right shows why you might want to set the edge between selection points 3 and 4 to invisible.

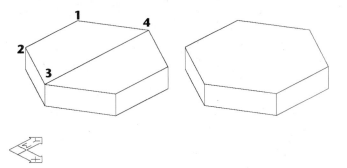

**Fig. 28.7**
Example of
setting a 3D faces
edge to invisible.

> **Note**
>
> To view the invisible edges of a 3DFACE for editing purposes, set the system variable
> SPLFRAME to a value other than zero (0), then perform a REGEN. To "hide" the
> invisible edges again, set SPLFRAME back to 0 and regen.

**Tip**
Use the EDGE
command from
the Surfaces
toolbar to make
surface edges (like
those on 3D Faces)
invisible.

**VIII**

**Isometrics & 3D Drafting**

# Creating 3D Surfaces

The 3D surface models that have been created thus far are very simple
models, usually using a wireframe as a skeletal structure to which to attach
the faces. When any surface model is broken down to its simplest form, in
other words exploded, the individual surfaces are nothing but 3D faces. Even
though this is true, it would be very difficult to produce a model like the one
shown in figure 28.8 only using 3D Faces. AutoCAD has a set of commands
that makes the creation of complex surface models easier. Four 3D surface
commands (TABSURF, RULESURF, REVSURF, and EDGESURF) and two system
variables (SURFTAB1 and SURFTAB2) are discussed in the next section.

## Specifying the Mesh Density (SURFTAB1 and SURFTAB2)

Before talking about controlling the mesh density, you should know what a
mesh is. Figure 28.9 shows an example of a polygon mesh. To visualize what
a polygon mesh is, think of a net at the circus. Picture in your mind the rows
and columns of rope tied together. Think of the rectangular area between
each knot in the net as the surface, or face, of the object. The knots themselves can be thought of as the corners or vertex points for the surface. You
can think of a Polyface Mesh as a 3D face with multiple vertex points, not
just three or four created using the 3DFACE command.

**Fig. 28.8**
An example of a
more complex
surface model.

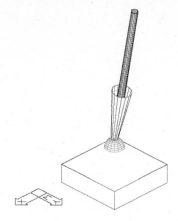

**Fig. 28.9**
An example of a
polygon mesh.

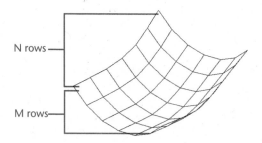

Two system variables are used to control the density of the mesh, SURFTAB1
and SURFTAB2. SURFTAB1 controls the number of columns in the M direction, and SURFTAB2 controls the number of rows in the N direction. As you
will see later, not all the 3D surface commands use both system variable settings. Some take into account only the setting of SURFTAB1, or in other
words, the number of (M) columns.

The spheres in figure 28.10 show the effects of having different SURFTAB1
and SURFTAB2 settings. Figure 28.10 also illustrates the direction for M and
N. The (M) columns travel around the sphere and the (N) rows travel up and
down the sphere.

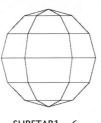  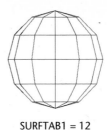

**Fig. 28.10**
Spheres modeled
with various
SURFTAB1 and
SURFTAB2
settings.

| SURFTAB1 = 6 | SURFTAB1 = 6 | SURFTAB1 = 12 |
|---|---|---|
| SURFTAB2 = 6 | SURFTAB2 = 12 | SURFTAB2 = 6 |

## Creating a Polygon Mesh (3DMESH)

One of the more common uses of the 3DMESH command is to produce a 3D topologically rectangular mesh. You may have also heard this type of mesh referred to as a *terrain model*. A 3DMESH is defined by specifying the number of vertices in the columns and rows, or in other words the M direction and N direction. For each vertex location, you are asked to supply a 3D point location. Figure 28.11 is an example of a $4 \times 3$ polygon mesh.

To access the 3DMESH command use one of the following methods:

- Select the 3D Mesh button from the Surfaces toolbar.

- Enter **3dmesh** at the Command: prompt.

The following example illustrates the promptings for a $4 \times 3$ polygon mesh.

```
Command: 3dmesh
Mesh M size: 4
Mesh N size: 3
Vertex (0, 0): 1,1,0
Vertex (0, 1): 1,2,-.25
Vertex (0, 2): 1,3,0.25
Vertex (1, 0): 2,1,-.5
Vertex (1, 1): 2,2,0
Vertex (1, 2): 2,3,.5
Vertex (2, 0): 3,1,.25
Vertex (2, 1): 3,2,0
Vertex (2, 2): 3,3,.25
Vertex (3, 0): 4,1,0
Vertex (3, 1): 4,2,-.25
Vertex (3, 2): 4,3,.5
```

**VIII**

**Isometrics & 3D Drafting**

**Fig. 28.11**
An example of a
4 x 3 polygon
mesh created with
the 3DMESH
command.

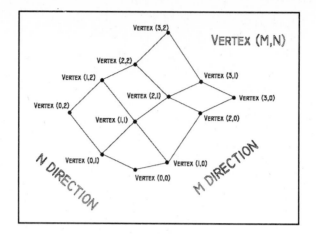

When specifying the number for M and N, you must enter a number between 2 and 256. The number of vertices you must supply points for is determined by multiplying these two values together (M × N). For the example in figure 28.11, 4 × 3 is 12, so a total of 12 vertex points were entered. Also, notice in this example that the vertices for the columns (M direction) were entered first, then after each column entered, the points for the rows (N direction).

> **Note**
>
> Unless you are using the 3DMESH command in a script or AutoLISP routine, you will most likely find creating any 3DMESH very time-consuming. You may find it easier to use a command like EDGESURF to create complex surface meshes.

## Tutorial: Generating a 3D Mesh

This tutorial is meant to reinforce the information you just read about the 3DMESH command, and give you a chance to try it. Start a new drawing, and follow the instructions below:

1. Select the New button, and name your drawing **3dmtest**.

2. Choose the 3D Mesh button from the Surfaces toolbar, or enter **3dmesh** at the Command: prompt.

3. Create a 4 x 3 mesh as shown in the prompts.

```
Command: 3dmesh
Mesh M size: 4
Mesh N size: 3
```

4. Continue by suppling vertex information as follows.

```
Vertex (0, 0): 1,1,0
Vertex (0, 1): 1,2,-.25
Vertex (0, 2): 1,3,0.25
Vertex (1, 0): 2,1,-.5
Vertex (1, 1): 2,2,0
Vertex (1, 2): 2,3,.5
Vertex (2, 0): 3,1,.25
Vertex (2, 1): 3,2,0
Vertex (2, 2): 3,3,.25
Vertex (3, 0): 4,1,0
Vertex (3, 1): 4,2,-.25
Vertex (3, 2): 4,3,.5
```

5. Use DDVPOINT to adjust the view of your 3Dmesh as needed.

## Creating a Polyface Mesh (PFACE)

With a 3DMESH, each face of the polygon mesh is defined by four vertex points. A polyface mesh is generated using the PFACE command, where each face can contain any number of vertices. It is like being able to place an irregular shaped 3DFACE, not being restricted to the three or four points normally used to define it.

Because you enter all the vertex points first, and then specify which vertex is on which face, it is a good idea to use a wireframe model as a guide. Pick the points on the wireframe model in a logical order, then specify which vertex belongs to which face.

You can access the PFACE command by entering **pface** at the Command: prompt.

```
Command: pface
Vertex 1: 3,2,0
Vertex 2: 3,1,0
Vertex 3: 2,1.5,0
Vertex 4: 1,1,0
Vertex 5: 1,2,0
Vertex 6: 1,2,1
Vertex 7: 2,2,1.5
Vertex 8: 3,2,1
Vertex 9:
Face 1, vertex 1: 1
Face 1, vertex 2: 2
Face 1, vertex 3: 3
Face 1, vertex 4: 4
Face 1, vertex 5: 5
Face 1, vertex 6:
```

```
Face 2, vertex 1: 1
Face 2, vertex 2: 5
Face 2, vertex 3: 6
Face 2, vertex 4: 7
Face 2, vertex 5: 8
Face 2, vertex 6:
Face 3, vertex 1:
```

In the previous example, vertex points 1 through 5 lie on face 1. Vertex points 1,5, and 6 through 7 lie on face 2 (see fig. 28.12).

**Fig. 28.12**

An example of a polyface mesh created with PFACE command.

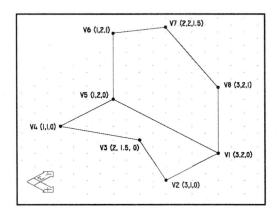

## Tutorial: Generating a Polyface Mesh

In this tutorial, you create a polyface mesh which consists of two faces with a total of nine vertices (see fig. 28.12). Start with a clean drawing, and follow these steps:

**1.** Select the New button, and name your drawing pftest.

**2.** Enter **pface** at the Command: prompt.

**3.** Enter the coordinates for each vertex as shown.

```
Command: pface
Vertex 1: 3,2,0
Vertex 2: 3,1,0
Vertex 3: 2,1.5,0
Vertex 4: 1,1,0
Vertex 5: 1,2,0
Vertex 6: 1,2,1
Vertex 7: 2,2,1.5
Vertex 8: 3,2,1
Vertex 9: Press Enter.
```

4. Indicate which vertices belong to face number 1 on the polyface mesh. Follow the prompts below.

```
Face 1, vertex 1: 1
Face 1, vertex 2: 2
Face 1, vertex 3: 3
Face 1, vertex 4: 4
Face 1, vertex 5: 5
Face 1, vertex 6:
```

5. Indicate which vertices belong to face number 2.

```
Face 2, vertex 1: 1
Face 2, vertex 2: 5
Face 2, vertex 3: 6
Face 2, vertex 4: 7
Face 2, vertex 5: 8
Face 2, vertex 6:
```

6. Because this is a polyface mesh consisting of only two faces, press Enter at the `Face 3, vertex 1:` prompt to terminate the process.

```
Face 3, vertex 1: Enter
```

## Tabulated Surfaces (TABSURF)

In Chapter 26, "Introduction to 3D Modeling," the THICKNESS system variable was used to control an object's extrusion thickness. You can create similar results using the TABSURF command. Creating tabulated surfaces with the TABSURF command is much like extruding an object by setting its thickness, but with a lot more flexibility. Besides being more flexible, with TABSURF you are actually generating 3D surfaces, rather than just an extrusion.

With THICKNESS, you could only extrude an object in its positive or negative Z axis. TABSURF allows you to generate a tabulated surface in any direction using a direction vector. The direction vector, which can be a line or polyline, is used to determine the direction and distance to tabulate the selected object. Figure 28.13 shows the results of tabulating a circle (the path curve) using a line as the direction vector.

To access the TABSURF command use one of the following methods:

- Select the Extruded Surface button from the Surfaces toolbar.

- Enter **tabsurf** at the `Command:` prompt.

**Fig. 28.13**
Use TABSURF to
tabulate a circle
along a direction
vector.

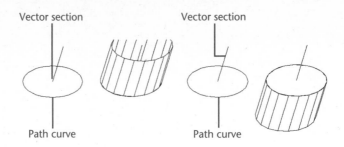

## Tutorial: Using Tabsurf

In this tutorial, you begin to build the surface model of the 3D lamp in
figure 28.1. Start by opening up the drawing DESKLAMP.DWG, which is a
wireframe model you will use as a guide. Build the neck of the lamp by following these steps:

1.  Select the Open button and change to your work directory, C:\UAW13.

2.  Select the file 28DWG01 from the list and press OK.

3.  At the Command: prompt, enter **surftab1** and set it to **8.**

4.  Select the Extruded Surface button from the Surfaces toolbar, or enter
    **tabsurf** at the Command: prompt.

5.  Select the small circle for the path curve (see fig. 28.14).

6.  Select the line as shown for the direction vector (see fig. 28.14).

This same drawing is used in the remainder of the tutorials in this chapter.

> **Note**
>
> It does matter where you select the direction vector. Choosing at one end of the line
> will cause the direction to be from that point towards the opposite endpoint and vice
> versa.

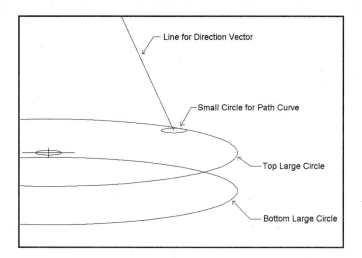

Line for Direction Vector

Small Circle for Path Curve

Top Large Circle

Bottom Large Circle

**Fig. 28.14**
Use TABSURF to generate the neck of the 3D lamp.

**VIII**

**Isometrics & 3D Drafting**

> **Note**
>
> Because only columns in the M direction are being generated, TABSURF uses the SURFTAB1 setting. There is no need to set the SURFTAB2 system variable for this command.

## Ruled Surfaces (RULESURF)

When you have to generate a ruled surface between two edges, use the RULESURF command. Examples of ruled surfaces include cones and cylinders where the surface is defined by the motion of a straight line. Figure 28.15 illustrates some common ruled surfaces.

To access the RULESURF command use one of the following methods:

- Select the Ruled Surface button from the Surfaces toolbar.

- Enter **rulesurf** at the Command: prompt.

AutoCAD prompts you with:

```
Command: rulesurf
Select first defining curve:
Select second defining curve:
```

**Fig. 28.15**
Common
examples of ruled
surfaces.

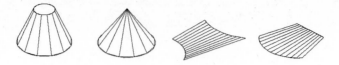

When using the RULESURF command, you are prompted for the first and second defining curves. You can think of these curves as the opposing edges of the ruled surface. The two edges used to define the ruled surface can be either closed or open objects. Closed objects can include Circles, Points, and closed 2D or 3D Polylines. Open objects can include Arcs, Lines, open 2D or 3D Polylines, and Points. If the first object selected is a closed object, the second object must be a closed object as well. Points are the one object that can be used as a "defining curve" for both open and closed objects.

## Tutorial: Using RULESURF

This tutorial continues with the 3D lamp and creates the lamp's base by following these steps:

1. Set SURFTAB1 to **18** at the Command: prompt.

2. Select the Ruled Surface button from the Surfaces toolbar, or enter **rulesurf** at the Command: prompt.

3. When prompted for the first defining curve, select the large circle on the bottom (see fig. 28.14).

4. Select the other large circle just above your first selection for the second defining curve (see fig. 28.14).

When generating a ruled surface between two circles, you can select each circle at any point. This is because circles are closed objects and, therefore, the resulting ruled surface is not affected by where you selected them. However, when creating ruled surfaces between open objects, such as lines and arcs, you have to pay special attention to where you select each defining curve. When selecting the defining curves, select them on the same side of each of the objects. Figure 28.16 shows what happens when you select the objects incorrectly.

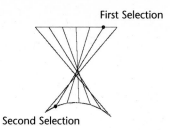

First Selection

Second Selection

**Fig. 28.16**
The result of
incorrectly
selecting the
defining curves of
a ruled surface.

Now that you have the sides of the lamp base, you can put a top on the base. In figure 28.17, notice the point object in the middle of the top circle. As mentioned earlier, you may use points for either open or closed objects. Use the point as the second defining curve for the next ruled surface created. Continuing with the tutorial, follow these steps to create the top of the lamp base.

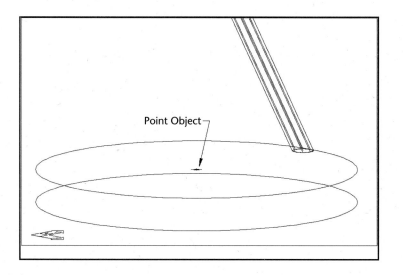

Point Object

**VIII**

Isometrics & 3D Drafting

**Fig. 28.17**
Select a point as a
defining curve.

5. Select the Move button from the Modify toolbar and enter L for last at the Select objects: prompt to select the ruled surface last created.

6. Enter **6,6** for the base point.

7. Press Enter. Don't supply a second point of displacement.

> **Note**
>
> The ruled surface was moved out of the way temporarily because it can't be used as a defining curve for the RULESURF command. Use this technique anytime you find a surface is in the way; but be sure to move it back when you are done.

8. Select the Ruled Surface button from the Surfaces toolbar, or enter **rulesurf** at the Command: prompt.

9. Select the large circle on top when prompted for the first defining curve.

10. Select the point in the middle of the circle you just selected when prompted for the second defining curve.

11. Select the Move button from the Modify toolbar and select the ruled surface you moved earlier.

12. Enter **6, 6** as the base point. This moves it back to where it was in the first place.

Your model should appear like the one in figure 28.18.

**Fig. 28.18**
Your 3D lamp should now look like this.

## Surfaces of Revolution (REVSURF)

Any time you need to generate a complex circular surface model of an object such as a wine glass, soda can, bottle, bowl, flashlight, and so on, use the REVSURF command (see fig. 28.19). Simply provide the REVSURF command with a profile, a rotation axis, and starting and ending angles. As a result, a polygon mesh of M columns by N rows is produced. The M columns value is determined by the SURFTAB1 setting and the N rows value is determined by the SURFTAB2 setting.

To access the REVSURF command, use one of the following methods:

- Select the Revolved Surface button from the Surfaces toolbar.

- Enter **revsurf** at the Command: prompt.

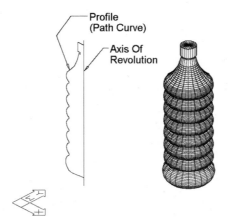

**Fig. 28.19**
A 3D Surface model of a water bottle produced using REVSURF.

## Tutorial: Using REVSURF

This tutorial continues building surfaces onto the 3D lamp. The only feature the lamp is missing is the lamp dish. Create the lamp dish by following these steps:

1. Select the Revolved Surface button from the Surfaces toolbar, or enter **revsurf** at the Command: prompt.

2. Select the arc at the top of the lamp for the path curve (see fig. 28.18).

3. Select the line at the end of the arc for the axis of revolution.

4. Press Enter to except the default starting angle of 0.

5. Press Enter to except the default of <Full Circle> for the include angle.

   The 3D lamp surface model is now complete! Adjust your view and try removing the hidden lines with the HIDE command.

◀ See "Removing
Hidden Lines
(HIDE)," p. 781

**6.** Select the Hide button from the Render toolbar, or enter **hide** at the
Command: prompt.

Your view should be similar to the one in figure 28.20. Be sure to save
this file. It is used in other exercises in this chapter.

**7.** Select Save from the Standard toolbar.

**Fig. 28.20**
A completed 3D
lamp surface
model.

## Tutorial: Creating a 3D Bowling Pin

In the 3D lamp completed above, you used a simple object (in this case an
arc) as the object to revolve. Generating a profile from a polyline allows the
creation of much more interesting surfaces of revolution. Open the drawing
BOWLPIN.DWG and follow these steps to produce a 3D surface model of a
bowling pin:

**1.** Select the Open button form the toolbar, and change to your work
directory, C:\UAW13.

**2.** Select the file 28DWG02 from the list and press OK.

**3.** At the Command: prompt, set SURFTAB1 and SURFTAB2 to **12**.

**4.** Select the Revolved Surface button from the Surfaces toolbar, or enter
**revsurf** at the Command: prompt.

**5.** Select the polyline representing the profile of the bowling pin as the
path curve.

**6.** Select the vertical line as the axis of revolution.

7. Choose a starting angle of 0 and revolve full circle (default options).

8. Use DDVPOINT to adjust your view as needed (see fig. 28.21).

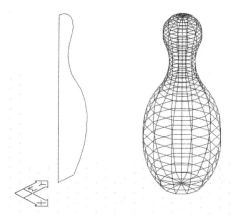

**Fig. 28.21**
A completed 3D
surface model of
bowling pin.

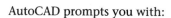

## Edge-Defined Surface Patches (EDGESURF)

The EDGESURF command generates a polygon mesh like the 3DMESH command would do, but without the requirement to specify each vertex location. By selecting four edges, AutoCAD calculates the location of each vertex along the mesh for you. The resulting mesh is considered to be a Coons surface patch. A Coons patch is a set of 3D surfaces interpolated between the two sets of edges.

To access the REVSURF command use one of the following methods:

- Select the Revolved Surface button from the Surfaces toolbar.

- Enter **revsurf** at the Command: prompt.

AutoCAD prompts you with:

```
Command: edgesurf
Select edge 1: Select an object.
Select edge 2: Select an object.
Select edge 3: Select an object.
Select edge 4: Select an object.
```

The objects used to define each of the four edges, as shown in the prompts above can be either arcs, circles, lines, or open polylines (2D or 3D). The one rule you must follow when generating these objects for use as edges with the EDGESURF command is that the starting or ending point of the object be the same as the starting or ending point of the adjoining edge (see fig. 28.22).

**Fig. 28.22**
An example of a
Coons patch
created with the
EDGESURF
command.

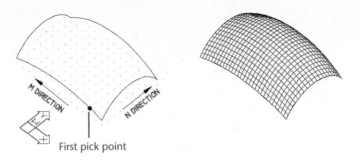

When creating a mesh with the EDGESURF command, the first edge you select and where you select it determines the M direction (rows). Worry about this only if you have different values assigned to SURFTAB1 and SURFTAB2. SURFTAB1 is used to control how many faces are divided along the M direction. SURFTAB2 is used to control how many faces are divided along the N direction.

## Tutorial: Using EDGESURF

This tutorial uses the EDGESURF command. Use drawing EDGELAB.DWG from the disk included with this book.

1. Select the Open button and change to your work directory, C:\UAW13.

2. Select the file 28DWG03 from the list and press OK.

3. Set SURFTAB1 and SURFTAB2 to **12** at the Command: prompt.

4. Select the Edge Surface button from the Surfaces toolbar, or enter **edgesurf** at the Command: prompt.

5. Select the edges as shown in figure 28.23. Keep in mind that the first edge selected controls the M direction.

```
Select edge 1: Select edge 1.
Select edge 2: Select edge 2.
Select edge 3: Select edge 3.
Select edge 4: Select edge 4.
```

The resulting mesh should look like the mesh in figure 28.22.

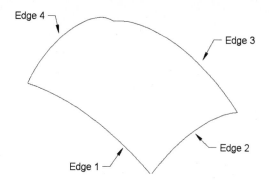

**Fig. 28.23**
Select the edges for
edgesurf tutorial.

**VIII**

**6.** Erase the mesh and alter the values for SURFTAB1 and SURFTAB2. Try using a larger value for one of the variables. Select the edges in a different order to show the effects the SURFTAB variable has on both the M and N directions of the mesh.

# Using 3D Objects

Commands and methods for creating surface geometry were discussed in previous sections. AutoCAD also provides you with another method of producing some common surface models. Some of these common shapes include cones, cubes, spheres, torus and more (see figs. 28.24–28.32). The following list of shapes is available from the Surfaces toolbar (the alternate Command: line entry is shown as well):

**Fig. 28.24**
The Surfaces toolbar.

■ *Box.* Creates a 3D box surface model.

```
Command: ai_box
Corner of box: Specify a point.
Length: 1
Cube/<Width>: 2
Height: 1.5
Rotation angle about Z axis: 0
```

**Fig. 28.25**
An example of a
box surface model.

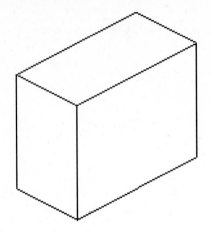

 ■ *Wedge.* Creates a 3D surface model with a sloped face tapering along the
X-axis.

```
Command: ai_wedge
Corner of wedge: Specify a point.
Length: 2
Width: 1
Height: .75
Rotation angle about Z axis: 0
```

**Fig. 28.26**
An example of a
wedge surface
model.

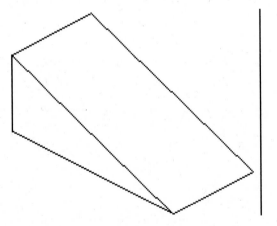

 ■ *Pyramid.* Creates a surface model of a pyramid (4-sided) or tetrahedron
(3-sided).

```
Command: ai_pyramid
First base point: Specify a point.
Second base point: Specify a point.
Third base point: Specify a point.
Tetrahedron/<Fourth base point>: Specify a point.
Ridge/Top/<Apex point>: Specify a point.
```

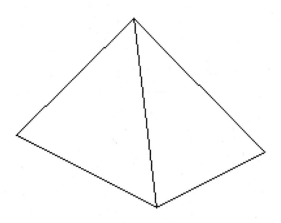

**Fig. 28.27**
An example of a pyramid surface model.

■ *Cone.* Creates a 3D surface model of a cone.

```
Command: ai_cone
Base center point: Specify a point.
Diameter/<radius> of base: 2
Diameter/<radius> of top <0>:
Height: 1
Number of segments <16>:
```

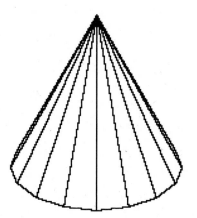

**Fig. 28.28**
An example of a cone surface model.

**VIII**

**Isometrics & 3D Drafting**

■ *Sphere.* Creates a 3D surface model of a sphere.

```
Command: ai_sphere
Center of sphere: Specify a point.
Diameter/<radius>: .25
Number of longitudinal segments <16>:
Number of latitudinal segments <16>:
```

**Fig. 28.29**
An example of a
sphere surface
model.

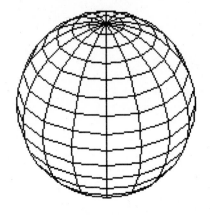

■ *Dome.* Creates a surface model of an open dome.

```
Command: ai_dome
Center of dome: Specify a point.
Diameter/<radius>: 1.25
Number of longitudinal segments <16>:
Number of latitudinal segments <8>:
```

**Fig. 28.30**
An example of a
dome surface
model.

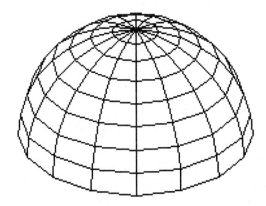

■ *Dish*. Creates a surface model of an open dish.

```
Command: ai_dish
Center of dish: Specify a point.
Diameter/<radius>: .625
Number of longitudinal segments <16>:
Number of latitudinal segments <8>:
```

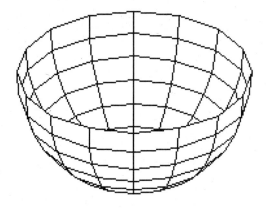

**Fig. 28.31**
An example of a
dish surface
model.

■ *Torus*. Creates a closed torus surface model.

```
Command: ai_torus
Center of torus: Specify a point.
Diameter/<radius> of torus: .5
Diameter/<radius> of tube: .25
Segments around tube circumference <16>:
Segments around torus circumference <16>:
```

**Fig. 28.32**
An example of a
closed torus
surface model.

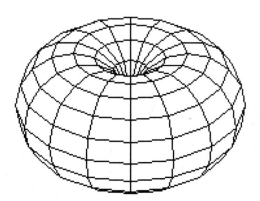

### Tutorial: Placing Predefined 3D Objects

Open a new drawing and spend some time experimenting with each of these shapes. If you want, use the values for each shape as shown in command line examples above (they were given as an example of what to do). Use these values as a starting point, but see what happens when you use your own values.

> **Note**
>
> Because these commands are menu driven, a lot of times you do not have to worry about setting SURFTAB1 and SURFTAB2. The system variables are set for you according to the values you enter at the prompts for the various 3D objects.

Use these predefined 3D object commands anytime you need a cube, cone, sphere, or another 3D surface model that can be created here. This saves you a lot of time and effort.

# From Here...

This chapter discussed the essentials of producing 3D surface models. You have to clearly visualize what is going on in 3D space to effectively use these tools. These chapters address setting up User Coordinate Systems, and various tools for viewing your model:

- Chapter 27, "Understanding 3D Coordinate Systems," discusses setting up and using UCSs.

- Chapter 30, "Viewing a 3D Model," covers the commands and tools used to control the display of your model in 3D space.

# On Your Own

Reinforce your knowledge of this chapter by completing these exercises.

1. Open a new drawing called ANGBLOCK.DWG. Create the surface model of the Angle Block using the dimensions shown in figure 28.33.

2. Open a drawing and name it LPLATE.DWG to produce the surface model you see in figure 28.34 (use the dimensions shown in fig. 28.35 as a guide).

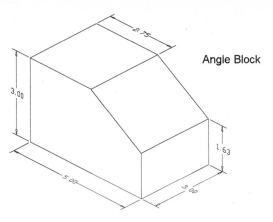

Angle Block

**Fig. 28.33**
Guide for the
Angle Block
exercise.

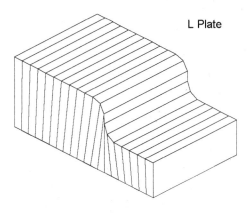

L Plate

**Fig. 28.34**
A finished L-Plate
surface model.

**VIII**

**Isometrics & 3D Drafting**

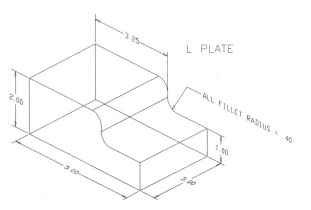

L PLATE

ALL FILLET RADIUS = .40

**Fig. 28.35**
Guide for the
L-Plate exercise
dimensions.

Hints:

- Draw the Angle Block using the 3DFACE and PFACE commands.

- Draw the wireframe model of the L-Plate (as shown in fig. 28.35), then use RULESURF.

# Chapter 29

# 3D Editing Essentials

Having the ability to modify an object after it is created is one of the reasons AutoCAD is so beneficial. It's thought by some that a typical, productive user will spend around 20 percent of his time creating new geometry (lines, arcs, circles, and so on) and the rest of the time using editing techniques. A quick glance at the commands available to AutoCAD tells you where a lot of the focus is. It's on commands that modify existing geometry and construct new geometry from existing geometry.

This chapter examines some of the commands that are used when modifying 3D objects. Other commands that will be looked at in this chapter allow you to get information from the object. In this chapter, you learn how to:

- Change object properties using CHPROP and DDCHPROP

- Edit polylines with PEDIT

- Use EXPLODE to separate complex objects

- Get data from the object with LIST

- Find the distance between two points using DIST

- Find the area of an object with the AREA command

- Rotate objects in 3D space with ROTATE3D

- Mirror objects in 3D space using MIRROR3D

- Edit polylines with PEDIT

- Create an array in 3D space using 3DARRAY

Besides the commands listed above, this chapter also examines 3D object modification techniques using grips. Grips were introduced in Release 12 of

◀ See "Editing
with Grips,"
p. 301

AutoCAD, but continue to make editing of complex surfaces and meshes, as well as other objects, much easier in Release 13.

# Editing Commands and the Current UCS

In AutoCAD Release 13, when using commands such as BREAK, CHAMFER, FILLET, EXTEND, and TRIM, the extrusion direction of the objects selected does not need to be parallel to the z axis of the current UCS. It is possible to edit objects using these commands without first making the UCS parallel to all selected objects.

◀ See "Under-
standing 3D
Coordinate
Systems,"
p. 785

Take, for example, the wireframe model in figure 29.1. In Release 12, if you want to fillet the front edge, you first need to change the UCS to match the side of the wireframe (see fig. 29.2). This is due to the fact that the FILLET command (among others) is not designed to work with 3D objects; you have to trick it into thinking it's working with 2D objects. Release 13, however, allows you to fillet and chamfer objects that do not lie on the same plane (that is, the objects have differing Z coordinates). This addition allows you to concentrate on the editing at hand, rather than worrying about constantly changing the UCS.

There are certain instances, however, when having the UCS parallel to the objects being modified is still important. Using the OFFSET command is an example of this. In this case, the offset would still be performed, but the results of the offset may not be what you expected. Rotating the UCS to be parallel to the object(s) selected gives you the desired offset results.

**Fig. 29.1**
A 3D wireframe model created in the UCS.

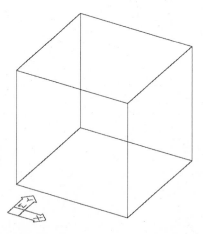

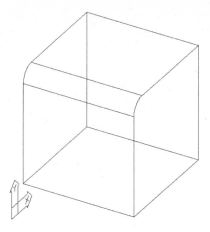

**Fig. 29.2**
The 3D wireframe
after being filleted
with the 2D
FILLET command.

# Editing Commands for 3D Objects

Previously, you learned about working with some of the 2D editing commands in 3D space. AutoCAD does provide editing commands that are specifically designed to work in 3D space. This section examines those commands.

## Rotating in 3D (ROTATE3D)

The ROTATE3D command is used to rotate objects around a three-dimensional axis. Unlike the ROTATE command which rotates objects around a 2D axis determined by the current UCS, the axis used with ROTATE3D can be anywhere in 3D space. The axis can be specified by using two points, by selecting an object, specifying the $x$, $y$, or $z$ axis of the current UCS, or selecting View (which is Z direction of the current view).

You can access the ROTATE3D command by using one of the following methods:

- Select 3D Rotate from the Rotate flyout on the Modify toolbar.

- At the Command: prompt, enter **rotate3d**.

The following options list appears:

```
Command: rotate3d
Select objects: Select object(s).
Axis by Object/Last/View/Xaxis/Yaxis/Zaxis/<2points>:
```

After you have decided which option to use to define the axis, you are presented with the following options:

```
<Rotation angle>/Reference:
```

**VIII**

Isometrics & 3D Drafting

◀ See "Rotating
Objects
(ROTATE),"
p. 255

This option functions the same as the ROTATE command. You can enter the desired angle of rotation (around your newly defined axis), or enter **r** to specify a reference angle.

◀ See "Right
Hand Rule,"
p. 766

The default option, 2points, is illustrated in figure 29.3. In this example, point 1 to point 2 defines the positive direction of the rotation axis. The rotation angle you specify follows the right hand rule.

**Fig. 29.3**

Using the 2points option under ROTATE3D.

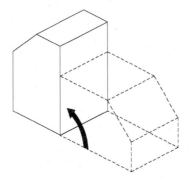

## Mirroring in 3D (MIRROR3D)

 Unlike its 2D counterpart (MIRROR), which uses a vector to define a mirror line, the MIRROR3D command creates a mirror image of objects around a plane. This plane can be specified using any of the options shown in the command listing below. The default option, 3point, is illustrated in figure 29.4.

You can access the MIRROR3D command by:

■ Selecting 3D Mirror from the Copy flyout on the Modify toolbar.

■ Entering **mirror3D** at the Command: prompt.

AutoCAD displays the following prompts:

```
Command: mirror3d
Select objects: Select object(s).
Plane by Object/Last/Zaxis/View/XY/YZ/ZX/<3points>:
```

When using the Object option, you are prompted to select a circle, arc, or 2D-polyline segment. The plane that the selected object lies on is used as the mirroring plane.

```
Pick a circle, arc, or 2D-polyline segment:
```

The Zaxis option allows you to select a point on the plane and then specify a point which is normal to the first point selected. As defined by Autodesk in the Glossary of the User Guide, a normal is "a vector perpendicular to a face or surface at the point where it is drawn."

The XY, YZ, and XZ options are used to specify a plane that is parallel to the XY plane, the YZ plane, or the XZ plane of the current UCS.

A plane through a selected point which is parallel to the current viewport's viewing plane can be achieved by using the View option.

After you have defined the mirroring plane, you will be asked the customary question, `Delete old objects? <N>`. This is the same prompt you saw with the 2D MIRROR command.

◀ See "Creating Mirror Images (MIRROR)," p. 258

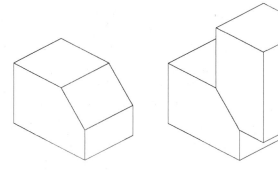

**Fig. 29.4**
Using the 3point option under mirror3D.

**VIII**

**Isometrics & 3D Drafting**

## Arraying in 3D (3DARRAY)

Just as with the ARRAY command, 3DARRAY can be used to create either rectangular or polar arrays. The main difference is that arrays created under 3DARRAY are three-dimensional arrays. When creating a rectangular 3D array, you are prompted for rows, columns, and levels (see fig. 29.5). With a 3D polar array, the main difference is evident when specifying the center point of the array. Because you are working in 3D space, you must specify a second point to define the axis of rotation (see fig. 29.6).

The 3DARRAY command can be accessed by:

- Selecting 3D Rectangular Array from the Copy flyout on the Modify toolbar.

- Selecting 3D Polar Array from the Copy flyout on the Modify toolbar.

- Entering **3darray** at the `Command:` prompt.

Here's an example of what AutoCAD displays when using either the 3D Rectangular Array icon or entering **3darray** followed by **r** at the `Command:` prompt.

```
Command: 3darray
Select objects: Select object(s).
Rectangular or Polar array (R/P): Enter an option.
```

If you select **r** for rectangular, the following prompts are presented:

```
Number of rows (--)<1>: Enter a positive number.
Number of columns (¦¦¦)<1>: Enter a positive number.
Number of levels (...)<1>: Enter a positive number.
```

After this information is supplied, you will need to tell AutoCAD the distance between each row, column, and level (if more than one level was selected).

```
Distance between rows (--): Enter a value.
```

**Fig. 29.5**

Creating a rectangular 3D Array.

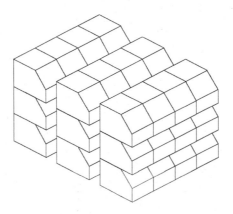

```
Distance between columns (¦¦¦): Enter a value.
Distance between levels (...): Enter a value.
```

If you selected **p** for polar or picked the 3D Polar Array icon, the following prompts are presented (see fig. 29.6):

```
Number of items: Enter a positive number.
Angle to fill <360>: Enter a value.
Rotate objects as they are copied? <Y>: Enter Y or N.
Center point of array: Specify a point (point 1).
Second point on axis of rotation: Specify a point (point 2).
```

### Tutorial: Editing in 3D (ROTATE3D, MIRROR3D, and 3DARRAY)

In this tutorial, you practice using the previously discussed 3D editing commands ROTATE3D, MIRROR3D, and 3DARRAY. A practice drawing has been provided for you. Open the practice drawing, as instructed below, and perform each task as directed.

**1.** Select Open and change to your working directory, C:\UAW13.

2. Select the file 29DWG01.DWG from the list and choose OK.

3. Select 3D Rotate from the Rotate flyout on the Modify toolbar, or enter  **rotate3d** at the Command: prompt.

    Command: **rotate3d**
    Select objects:

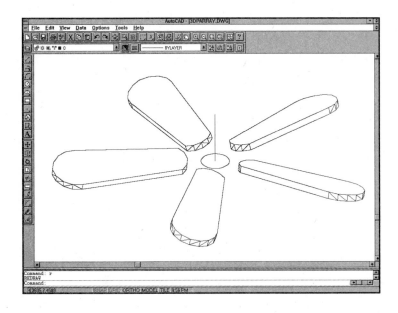

**Fig. 29.6**
Creating a polar
3D Array.

4. At the Select objects: prompt, select Arm 2 and Grip, as illustrated in figure 29.7.

5. At the Axis by Object/Last/View/Yaxis/Zaxis/<2points>: prompt, enter **e** for Axis by Object.

    Axis by Object/Last/View/Yaxis/Zaxis/<2points>: **e**

6. At the Pick a line, circle, arc, or 2D-polyline segment: prompt, select the magenta line labeled Rotation Axis (see fig. 29.7).

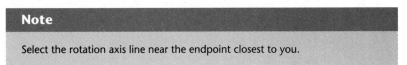

**Note**

Select the rotation axis line near the endpoint closest to you.

7. At the <Rotation angle>/Reference: prompt, enter an angle of **10**.

> **Note**
>
> Positive rotation is clockwise along the extrusion direction of the rotation axis—in this case, the line.

Your drawing should look like figure 29.8.

**Fig. 29.7**
Practice drawing
29DWG01.DWG.

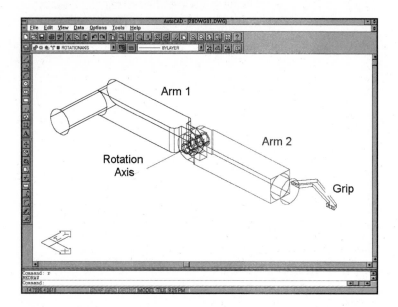

**Fig. 29.8**
Arm3d drawing
after 3D rotation.

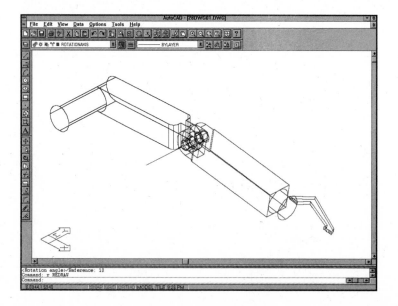

8. Zoom in on the arms grip, as illustrated in figure 29.9.

9. Select 3D Mirror from the Copy flyout on the Modify toolbar, or enter
   **mirror3d** at the Command: prompt.

   ```
   Command: mirror3d
   Select objects:
   ```

10. At the Select objects: prompt, select the grip (see fig. 29.9).

11. At the Plane by Object/Last/Zaxis/View/XY/YZ/ZX/<3points>: prompt,
    use the default option of **3points** and select points 1, 2, and 3 (see
    fig. 29.9).

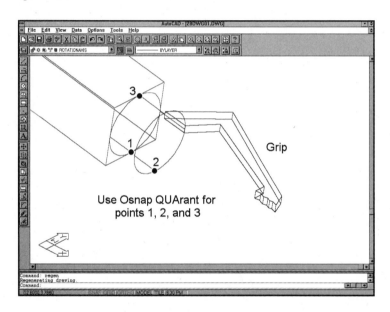

**Fig. 29.9**
Zoom in on the grip.

12. When prompted to Delete old objects? <N>, accept the default of No.

    You may want to use the HIDE command at this point to better visual-
    ize the results. Otherwise, continue with the exercise. You erase the last
    object drawing (the mirrored grip) to set up the exercise for the next
    command, 3DARRAY.

13. Select Erase from the Modify toolbar, or at the Command: prompt, enter
    **erase**. Select the last object.

    ```
    Command: erase
    Select objects: last
    1 found
    Select objects:
    ```

14. Select 3D Polar Array from the Copy fly out on the Modify toolbar, or enter **3darray** at the Command: prompt.

>     Command: **3darray**
>     Select objects:

15. At the Select objects: prompt, select Grip (refer to fig. 29.9).

16. At the Number of items: prompt, enter **4.**

>     Number of items: **4**

17. For the Angle to fill <360>:, press Enter to accept the default of 360.

>     Angle to fill <360>:

18. Answer Yes to the Rotate objects as they are copied? <Y>: prompt.

>     Rotate objects as they are copied? <Y>:

19. For the Center point of array:, use the object snap center and select near point 1 (refer to fig. 29.9).

20. For the Second point on axis of rotation:, use the object snap center and select near point 2 (refer to fig. 29.9).

21. Select Hide from the Render toolbar, or at the Command: prompt, enter **hide**.

>     Command: **hide**

Your drawing should look like the one in figure 29.10.

**Fig. 29.10**
Grip after
3DARRAY and
HIDE.

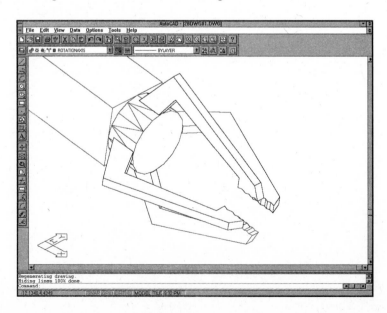

## Changing the Properties of Objects (CHPROP and DDCHPROP)

You may use either the CHPROP or DDCHPROP commands to change properties of objects. Some properties, such as the layer, color, and linetype, are not specific to 3D. These properties can be adjusted regardless of whether the object is 2D or 3D. Other properties, such as elevation and thickness, also can be adjusted on 2D objects, but fall closer in line with the 3D discussion.

◀ See "Modifying Object Characteristics," p. 625

3D objects, such as 3D polylines, 3D faces, polygons, and polyface meshes, cannot actually receive thickness. When you use either of the property commands, CHPROP or DDCHPROP, you are given the option to change the thickness of these objects, but nothing actually happens. A 3D face object, for example, is already a 3D object. For 3D objects, simply use the CHPROP or DDCHPROP commands to alter properties like layer, linetype, and color.

◀ See "3D Modeling Essentials," p. 807

## Editing 3D Polylines (PEDIT, GRIPS)

One of the commands you can use to alter 3D polyline objects is the PEDIT command. You also will learn how this is done using grips later in this chapter.

You can access the PEDIT command by:

- Selecting Edit Polyline from the Special Edit flyout on the Modify toolbar.

- Entering **pedit** at the Command: prompt.

```
Command: pedit
Select polyline:
Close/Join/Width/Edit vertex/Fit/Spline/Decurve/
    Ltype gen/Undo/eXit <X>:
```

When you originally created a 3D polyline using the 3DPOLY command, you noticed some limitations there. Likewise, you are limited in how and what you can edit on the object. Due to the fact that 3D polylines cannot have arc segments, notice that one of the PEDIT options that is missing is Fit curve.

◀ See "Using Polylines," p. 573

```
Command: pedit
Select polyline:
Close/Edit vertex/Spline curve/Decurve/Undo/eXit <X>:
```

A much easier way to edit 3D polylines is by utilizing grips. Figure 29.11 shows grips at each vertex point along the 3D polyline. Selecting a grip turns it into a "hot" grip that activates pre-set AutoCAD commands, such as STRETCH. STRETCH, for example, can be used to move a vertex to a new location.

◀ See "Editing with Grips," p. 301

**VIII**

Isometrics & 3D Drafting

**Fig. 29.11**

Editing a 3D
polyline using
grips.

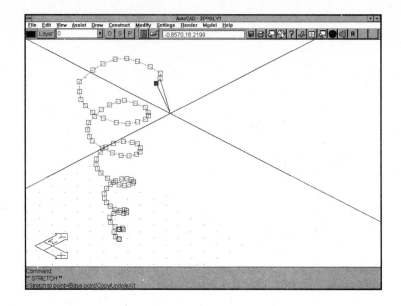

**Tip**

Use the PEDIT
command to add
a spline curve,
close, or open a
3D polyline.
Use grips for other
editing operations.

## Editing 3D Polygon Meshes (PEDIT, GRIPS)

The PEDIT command also plays an important role in the editing of polygon
meshes. Later in this section, you will use the LIST command to view a report
from a 3D polygon mesh object. What you will see, at that time, is that a
polygon mesh is actually a special type of polyline. Because the PEDIT command is used to edit all types of polylines (2D, 3D, and mesh), you can use it
to edit a 3D polygon mesh as well.

Notice the differences between the options available to a 3D polyline and a
polygon mesh when using the PEDIT command. Two of the additional options are Mopen/Mclose and Nclose/Nopen. Like a 2D or 3D polyline, a polygon mesh (which is a special type of polyline) also can be closed. Due to the
fact that a mesh is defined by a number of vertices in the M direction and N
direction, it has the ability to be open or closed in both of those directions.
The PEDIT command will provide the appropriate prompting depending
on the open or closed state of either of the directions of the mesh (see
fig. 29.12).

The PEDIT command can be accessed by using one of the methods below:

- Select Edit Polyline from the Special Edit flyout on the Modify toolbar.

- Enter **pedit** at the Command: prompt.

```
Command: pedit
Select polyline:
Edit vertex/Smooth surface/Desmooth/Mopen/Nopen/Undo/
    eXit <X>: m
```

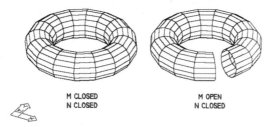

M CLOSED
N CLOSED

M OPEN
N CLOSED

**Fig. 29.12**
3D polygon mesh
before and after
opening the M
direction using
PEDIT.

Another one of the options that differs is the Smooth surface option. This
option allows you to fit one of three different types of smoothed surfaces to
the mesh (see fig. 29.13). The type of surface fit is determined by the system
variable SURFTYPE. See Table 29.1 for a list of possible settings for SURFTYPE.

| Table 29.1   SURFTYPE System Variable Settings | |
|---|---|
| **SURFTYPE Setting** | **Surface Type Fit to Mesh** |
| 5 | Quadratic B-Spline |
| 6 | Cubic B-Spline |
| 8 | Bezier Surface |

```
Command: pedit
Select polyline:
Edit vertex/Smooth surface/Desmooth/Mclose/Nclose/Undo/
    eXit <X>: s
```

As with the 3D polylines, using grips is a much easier method of editing 3D
polygon meshes, especially when moving vertex locations. Figure 29.14
shows grips being used to relocate a vertex on the mesh.

## Separating 3D Polylines and Meshes (EXPLODE)

As you saw in Chapter 23, "Using Symbols and XRefs," the EXPLODE command is used to break down a complex object, such as a polyline or block,
into individual elements. When the EXPLODE command is used to separate a
3D polyline, the result is individual line segments with starting and ending
points in 3D space at the original 3D polyline's vertex locations.

**VIII**

**Isometrics & 3D Drafting**

When a 3D polygon or polyface mesh is exploded, it is divided into individual 3D face objects, with the 3D faces' edge points being equivalent to the original 3D polygon's vertex locations. Figure 29.15 serves as an example, with a polygon mesh on the left and a polygon mesh that has been exploded with the EXPLODE command on the right. Each is being edited using grips.

**Fig. 29.13**
Using PEDIT to fit a Smooth surface to a mesh with different SURFTYPE system variable settings.

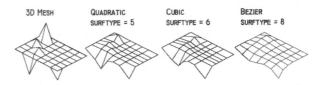

**Fig. 29.14**
Editing a 3D polygon mesh using grips.

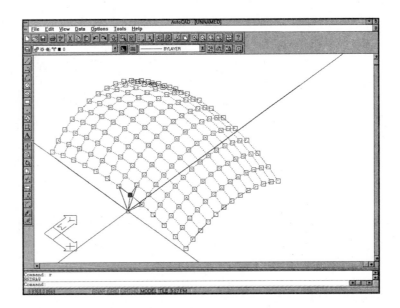

### Tutorial: Working with 3D Polylines, Meshes, and Polyfaces

This tutorial reinforces the information in the previous sections by allowing you to work hands-on with some of the commands and processes you just read about. You will start by opening an existing drawing, which you will use to practice the PEDIT command, grips, and the EXPLODE command. Follow these steps:

1. Select Open and change to your work directory, C:\UAW13.

2. Select the file 29DWG02.DWG from the list and choose OK (see fig. 29.16).

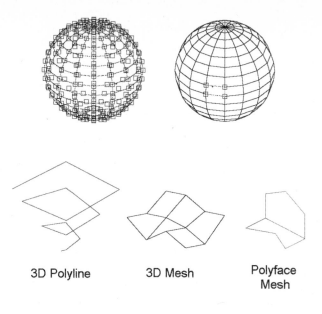

**Fig. 29.15**
Editing a polygon
mesh and a 3D
face from an
exploded polygon
mesh using grips.

3D Polyline          3D Mesh          Polyface
                                       Mesh

**Fig. 29.16**
The practice
drawing,
28DWG02.DWG.

4. Select Edit Polyline from the Special Edit flyout on the Modify toolbar, or enter **pedit** at the Command: prompt.

   ```
   Command: pedit
   Select polyline:
   ```

5. At the Select polyline: prompt, select the 3D Polyline as illustrated in figure 29.16.

6. At the Close/Edit vertex/Spline curve/ Decurve/Undo/eXit <X>: prompt, enter **s** for Spline curve.

   ```
   Close/Edit vertex/Spline curve/Decurve/Undo/eXit <X>: s
   Close/Edit vertex/Spline curve/Decurve/Undo/eXit <X>:
   ```

   The 3D Polyline in your tutorial drawing should look like the one in figure 29.17.

   Next, you will use grips to edit one of the vertices on the 3D Mesh. First, check to make sure that grips are enabled and ready to use.

7. From the Options menu, choose Grips or at the Command: prompt, enter **ddgrips.**

   ```
   Command: ddgrips
   ```

8. Verify that grips are enabled and choose OK.

9. Place the crosshairs on top of some portion of the 3D mesh and select it with the Pick button.

VIII

Isometrics & 3D Drafting

**Fig. 29.17**
3D polyline after
being splined
using PEDIT.

10. Pick the hot grip, as shown in figure 29.18.

11. At the `<Stretch to point>/Base point/Copy/Undo/eXit:` prompt, enter
    an offset value of **@0,0,.5**

    ```
    ** STRETCH **
    <Stretch to point>/Base point/Copy/Undo/eXit: @0,0,.5
    ```

The 3D mesh in your tutorial drawing should look like the one in figure
29.19.

**Fig. 29.18**
3D mesh with
grips enabled and
hot grip selected.

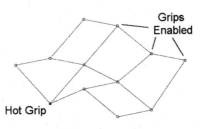

**Fig. 29.19**
3D mesh after
vertex edit using
grips.

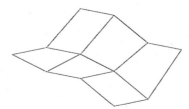

# Getting Information from 3D Objects

It may be necessary to retrieve information from a 3D object for verification or for other calculations. This section looks at three commands that do just that. You learn how to:

◀ See "Getting Information from Your Drawing," p. 653

- Use LIST to get information from the 3D object

- Use DIST to find the distance between two points

- Use AREA to find the area of an object

## Listing 3D Object Information (LIST)

The LIST command is used to retrieve data for a specific object or group of objects found in the drawing database. The amount and type of information returned by the LIST command is relative to the object that's selected. Two examples below show the data that's returned after selecting a 3D face and a 3D polygon mesh.

Partial listing for a 3D face object:

```
              3D FACE   Layer: 0
                    Space: Model space
   first point, X=   1.6198  Y=   3.6870  Z=   0.0000
   second point, X=  2.7616  Y=   3.6870  Z=   0.0000
   third point, X=   2.7616  Y=   5.0990  Z=   0.0000
   fourth point, X=  1.6341  Y=   5.0990  Z=   0.0000
   Listing for a polygon mesh:
       POLYLINE  Layer: MODEL
                    Space: Model space
        2x7 mesh

       VERTEX    Layer: MODEL
                    Space: Model space
Mesh
   at point, X=   4.2458  Y=   3.0880  Z=   2.0143

       VERTEX    Layer: MODEL
                    Space: Model space
Mesh
   at point, X=   4.4661  Y=   3.1810  Z=   2.2650

       VERTEX    Layer: MODEL
                    Space: Model space
-- Press RETURN for more --
```

As shown, when listing data on a 3D polygon mesh, the actual object type is a polyline. In addition, the number of faces in the M × N direction is listed.

**VIII**

**Isometrics & 3D Drafting**

### Reporting 3D Distances and Angles (DIST)

Use the DIST command (see fig. 29.20) to obtain information such as the distance between two points in 3D space. Other information includes the angle between the two points in and from the XY plane of the current UCS.

If, when using the DIST command, you omit the z coordinate, the value of the current ELEVATION system variable setting is used.

**Fig. 29.20**
Information retrieved from the DIST command.

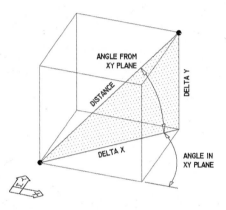

◄ See "Adding Elevation (ELEV)," p. 775

> **Note**
>
> Adjust your view as needed and use the appropriate object snaps to ensure selection of the correct point on the object. Sometimes, your view may restrict correct selection and the information returned will not be representative of your intended selection.

> **Note**
>
> The distance value calculated between the two point selections is stored in the DISTANCE system variable, where it can be retrieved for later use.

### Calculating 3D Area (AREA)

► See "System Variables Reference," p. 1147

When calculating the area of objects in 3D space, you will experience some of the same types of problems you did earlier using the FILLET command. Although the AREA command allows you to enter 2D or 3D points, or select an object with 2D or 3D points, each point much be parallel to the current UCS. To visualize this invisible plane, imagine that a thin sheet of glass is projected through and touching each object's endpoint. If one of the objects or points selected doesn't touch the glass, it's not parallel to that plane (or, in other words, the current UCS).

Figure 29.21 serves as an example. Here, you need to figure the area of the beveled front edge of the cube. You will not be able to use the AREA command here successfully without first altering the UCS. One of the easiest options of the UCS command, in this scenario, would be the 3point option. After you have set up the UCS to match the beveled edge, you are ready to gather the AREA data.

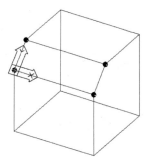

**Fig. 29.21**
Finding the area in
3D space with the
help of a UCS.

**VIII**

**Isometrics & 3D Drafting**

If you had attempted to find this area without first setting up the UCS, you would have received the following error message upon selecting the same points:

```
Points had differing Z coordinates.
```

If selecting an object, rather than selecting points as you did in the previous example, the rules are the same. Each point in the object must be parallel to the current UCS, otherwise you will receive the error message:

```
Object not parallel with UCS.
```

Or, if the object is a 3D polyline:

```
3D Polyline vertices had differing Z coordinates.
```

## Using the Geometric Calculator (CAL)

The CAL command is like having a built-in geometric calculator within AutoCAD. Although CAL can be used for simple real and integer expressions, such as 1+1, its real power shows when calculating point (vector) expressions. The expression that is to be evaluated by CAL can include point information obtained by using built-in functions equivalent to AutoCAD's normal object snap modes. For example, to find the midpoint between two endpoints, you could enter the expression **(end+end)/2**. CAL performs vector math on the expression, adding the two endpoints selected together, and then dividing the resulting value by 2. Figure 29.22 illustrates this expression.

**Fig. 29.22**
Finding the midpoint between two endpoints.

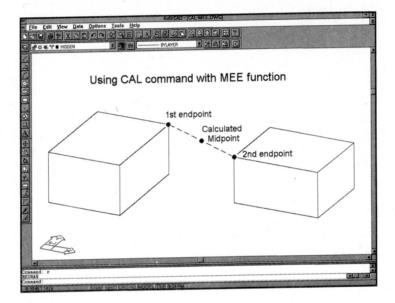

CAL offers many built-in functions for performing a large variety of tasks. Some of the built-in functions are known as *shortcut functions*. These shortcut functions are quicker ways to perform the same expression, but with much less typing. Take, for example, the expression *(end+end)/2* used earlier; the shortcut function is *mee*, which stands for midpoint between two endpoints. In the command line example that follows, you may want to draw a line whose starting point is at the midpoint between two endpoints. The two methods are shown:

```
Command: line
From point: 'cal
>> Expression: (end+end)/2
>> Select object for END snap: Select an object.
>> Select object for END snap: Select an object.
To point: Pick a point.
To point:
```

The second method follows:

```
Command: line
From point: 'cal
>> Expression: mee
>> Select one endpoint for MEE: Select an object.
```

```
>> Select another endpoint for MEE: Select an object.
To point: Pick a point.
To point:
```

Both expressions produce the same results, but using *mee* is the obvious choice.

Other variations of object snap modes can be used as well. When using object snaps in the expression, it's only necessary to enter the first three letters of the object snap. For example, if you wanted to find a point that was 5 units in the $x$ axis, 6 units in the $y$ axis, and 2 units in the $z$ axis away from the center of a circle, you could use the following expression:

```
Command: 'cal
>> Expression: cen+[5,6,2]
>> Select object for CEN snap: Select an object.
```

Here you are combining the results returned from the center object snap to a point 5,6,2. Notice the brackets ([]) around the manual point you enter.

There are many more functions that you can perform using CAL, such as calculating a normal vector, converting points between UCS and WCS, calculating a distance, obtaining an angle or radius, and much more. For a full list of syntax and functions, refer to the CAL command in the AutoCAD Release 13 Command Reference.

## Tutorial: Getting Information and Calculating Points in 3D

This tutorial continues where you left off in the previous section. If you do not still have the tutorial drawing 29DWG02.DWG open, open it back up by following these steps:

1. Select Open and change to your work directory, C:\UAW13.

2. Select the file 29DWG02.DWG from the list and choose OK (see fig. 29.23).

   To begin with, you will use the LIST command to verify that the object on the far right of the drawing is a pface mesh. Then, after exploding the pface using the EXPLODE command, you will use the LIST command again to see into what type of object the pface was broken down. Continue the tutorial with these steps:

3. Select List from the Object Properties toolbar, or enter **list** at the `Command:` prompt.

```
Command: list
Select objects:
```

**Fig. 29.23**
The practice
drawing,
29DWG02.DWG.

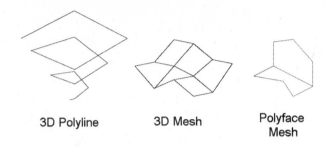

3D Polyline        3D Mesh        Polyface
                                  Mesh

4. At the Select objects: prompt, select the pface mesh.

   Here is a partial listing of what the LIST command returns. Notice that the object type is a special type of polyline called a polyface mesh.

```
Select objects:
                    POLYLINE   Layer: PFACE_MESH
                               Space: Model space
                   Handle = 41
        Polyface mesh

                    VERTEX     Layer: PFACE_MESH
                               Space: Model space
                   Handle = 42
        Polyface vertex
            at point, X=  14.2086  Y=   9.2423  Z=   0.0000

                    VERTEX     Layer: PFACE_MESH
                               Space: Model space
                   Handle = 43
        Polyface vertex
            at point, X=  14.2086  Y=   8.2423  Z=   0.0000

                    VERTEX     Layer: PFACE_MESH
                               Space: Model space
                   Handle = 44
        Polyface vertex
            at point, X=  13.2086  Y=   8.7423  Z=   0.0000
Press RETURN to continue:
```

5. Return to the Graphics screen and select Explode from the Modify toolbar, or enter **explode** at the Command: prompt. Select the pface mesh.

```
Command: _explode
Select objects:
```

**6.** Repeat step 5 above, using the LIST command to list the exploded pface mesh. What type of object is the polyface mesh comprised of?

Now practice using the DIST, CAL, and AREA commands. You will use the pface object that was just exploded for the remainder of this tutorial. You may want to zoom on the old pface object for a clearer view. Continue the tutorial by following these steps:

**7.** Select Distance from the List flyout on the Object Properties toolbar, or at the Command: prompt enter **dist**.

> Command: **dist**

**8.** At the First point: prompt, select Calculator from the Snap From flyout on the Standard toolbar, or at the Command: prompt enter **'cal**.

> First point: **'cal**

**9.** When prompted for the >> Expression:, enter **mee**.

> >> Expression: **mee**

**10.** For the >> Select one endpoint for MEE:, select at point A (as shown in fig. 29.24).

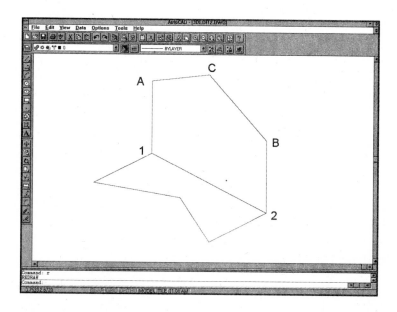

**Fig. 29.24**
Working with DIST, CAL, and AREA.

**11.** For the >> Select another endpoint for MEE:, select at point B (as shown in fig. 29.24).

**VIII**

**Isometrics & 3D Drafting**

12. At the Second point: prompt, use the object snap Endpoint, and select at point C (as shown in fig. 29.24).

    The DIST command (with the help of the CAL command) displays the distance from the midpoint between A and B to point C. Now find the area using these same points as a guide.

13. Set up a running object snap. Select Running Object Snap from the Snap From flyout on the Standard toolbar, or at the Command: prompt enter **ddosnap**.

    > Command: **ddosnap**

    Because points cannot have differing Z coordinates when using the AREA command, let's set up a UCS that matches the plane these lines are on using the 3point option. Follow these steps:

14. Select 3Point UCS from the Preset UCS flyout on the Standard toolbar, or from the View menu, choose Set UCS, then 3 Point.

15. For the Origin point <0,0,0>:, select at point 1 (see fig. 29.24).

16. For the Point on positive portion of the X-axis:, select at point 2 (see fig. 29.24).

17. For the Point on positive-Y portion of the UCS XY plane:, select at point A. (see fig. 29.24).

 18. Access the AREA command by selecting Area from the list flyout on the Object Properties toolbar, or at the Command: prompt, enter **area**.

19. At the <First point>/Object/Add/Subtract: prompt, pick point A. Then at the Next point: prompts, select points B and C. After selecting point C, press Enter at the Next point: to terminate the AREA command. Use the ENDpoint object snap to select the points.

    > The AREA command displays the following results:
    > Area = 0.5000, Perimeter = 4.2361

## From Here...

This chapter discussed the essentials of editing 3D surface models. Editing encompasses a large portion of the time you will spend in front of the AutoCAD screen. Refer to the following chapters for information on editing commands, as well as the coordinate systems:

■ Chapter 9, "Understanding Selection Sets." Selection sets are something that are important, no matter what editing command you use.

■ Chapter 10, "Editing Techniques." Here you can get a refresher on some of the basic editing techniques and commands.

■ Chapter 11, "Editing with Grips." If you skipped over this chapter, you'll want to go back and read it. Grips are a great way to edit in either 2D or 3D.

■ Chapter 22, "Getting Information from your Drawing," provides a good review of the LIST command.

■ Chapter 27, "Understanding 3D Coordinate Systems," discusses setting up and using UCSs.

**VIII**

Isometrics & 3D Drafting

# Chapter 30

# Viewing a 3D Model

Chapter 19, "Using Polylines," looked at two commands that are used to control the display of 3D Models: VPOINT and DDVPOINT. In this chapter, other display control commands commonly used in 3D modeling are discussed. This chapter covers the following:

- Using DVIEW to setup a perspective view or parallel projection

- Dividing the screen using the VPORTS command

- Using REDRAWALL to refresh all viewports

- Using REGENALL to recalculate the display of all viewports

These commands, specifically DVIEW and VPORTS, continue to reinforce the discussion that 3D models are communication tools. What's more, these commands also allow AutoCAD to better communicate information about the model back to you, the designer. If the methods available for viewing the model were restrictive, you may not be able to accurately design the model.

## Dynamically Changing the Viewpoint (DVIEW)

The DVIEW command (short for Dynamic VIEW) takes a different approach to display control than the VPOINT command. With DVIEW, terms such as Camera and Target are used to illustrate where you are standing and where your focus is on the model. Take, for instance, a professional photography studio. Many studios mount a low-power laser under the camera to precisely indicate the *target* or center of view. A red dot represents the target point. The DVIEW command does this for you, too (without using a real laser of course). The laser beam is representative of an invisible line between the Camera and Target locations (see fig. 30.1).

**Fig. 30.1**
You can use DVIEW to set up a three-dimensional view.

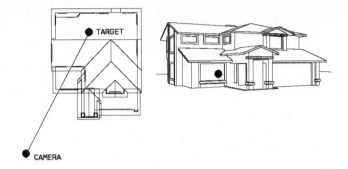

Besides being able to move around the model and to change the view by repositioning the target and/or camera, the DVIEW command has several other options. For example, you can turn on DVIEW's perspective mode by specifying the distance the camera is from the target. Figure 30.2 shows a model of a car in original parallel projection and the result of using the DVIEW command with perspective viewing turned on.

**Fig. 30.2**
You can show parallel (left) and perspective (right) for viewing.

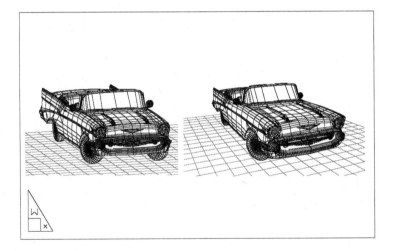

You also can use the DVIEW command to create a *cut-away*, or section view of your model. This is done by setting up and positioning a front and back *clipping plane* (a boundary that defines or clips the field of view). One of the biggest limitations to this command is that the clipping plane can only be setup perpendicular to the current view. Cut-away views are good for those times when geometry is blocking the view. For example, with the model shown in figure 30.3, after a hidden line removal is performed, all you can see is a wall. By setting up a clipping plane, however, you can cut into the wall to see the model behind it.

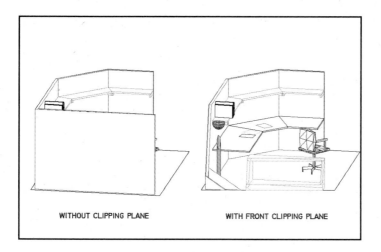

**Fig. 30.3**
You can use a clipping plane with DVIEW.

Other options of the DVIEW command allow you to change the Camera and Target by specifying the angle each has to the other. The options include Camera to Target, Target to Camera, Pan the display, Zoom the display, Twist the display, and perform hidden line removal on the selected DVIEW objects.

After a perspective view has been set using the Distance option, you can switch back to parallel projection by using the Off option. The Undo option is used to reverse any of the operations performed with the DVIEW command options.

To access the DVIEW command, use one of the following methods:

■ Select 3D Dynamic View from the View pull-down menu.

■ At the Command: prompt type **dview**.

```
Command: dview
Select objects:
CAmera/TArget/Distance/POints/PAn/Zoom/TWist/CLip/Hide/Off/Undo/<eXit>
```

Each of these options is discussed in later sections.

## Selecting Objects to View

Before any of the DVIEW options mentioned in the previous section are available to you, it's necessary to first build a selection set. The first prompt after entering the DVIEW command is Select objects:. You may use any of the methods available to build this selection set (Window, Crossing, Fence, and so on). The objects you select (if any) are used as a display reference while adjusting the view. If you do not select any objects, AutoCAD searches the Block Tables section of the drawings database for a block record called DVIEWBLOCK. If found, the DVIEWBLOCK is used as the reference object in DVIEW; otherwise, AutoCAD creates this block for you automatically (see fig. 30.4).

**Fig. 30.4**
Using DVIEW with no selection set brings up the DVIEWBLOCK.

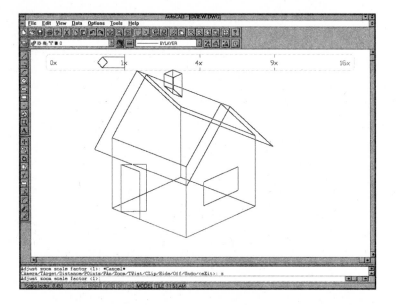

When selecting objects, don't think you have to select everything. This slows down the dynamic nature of the command. The more information DVIEW has to deal with, the choppier the dynamic redraws are. Select only enough objects to give you a good idea of the position and size of the overall model.

## Changing the View with DVIEW Options

After selecting the reference objects, the DVIEW command presents you with a list of options shown in the following Command: line example. Each has its own purpose and is discussed in detail in the following sections.

```
Command: dview
Select objects:
CAmera/TArget/Distance/POints/PAn/Zoom/TWist/CLip/Hide/Off/Undo/<eXit>
```

### CAmera, TArget, and POints

The CAmera, TArget, and POints options of the DVIEW command are responsible for controlling the placement and position of the CAmera and TArget. Keep in mind, the camera is from your point of view and the target is your focal point.

The CAmera and TArget options are very similar in operation. The CAmera option is used to adjust the location of the camera by adjusting the angle relative to the target. TArget is used to adjust the position of the target by specifying the angle relative to the camera. Figure 30.5 illustrates the relationship the Camera and Target have to each other.

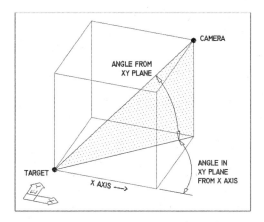

**Fig. 30.5**

Use the CAmera and TArget options of the DVIEW command.

When you first enter the CAmera or TArget options, you are presented with the following prompt:

```
CAmera/TArget/Distance/POints/PAn/Zoom/TWist/CLip/Hide/Off/Undo/<eXit>: ca
Toggle angle in/Enter angle from XY plane <10.00>:
```

At this point, notice that the angle listed in the status line changes as you move the cursor (mouse) up and down. This serves as a dynamic indication of the angle from the XY plane. If you want to view the angle in the XY plane from the X axis, enter **t** to toggle to that mode.

```
Toggle angle in/Enter angle from XY plane <10.00>: t
Toggle angle from/Enter angle in XY plane from X axis <-45.00>:
```

The POints option is used to setup the locations of both the camera and the target. When using this option, you are first asked to specify the location of the target and camera. You may use any of the point entry methods available to AutoCAD. For example, you can enter in values (such as 0,0,10) or pick a point using an object snap (such as endpoint).

### Tutorial: Using the POints Option

Practice using the POints option by opening the drawing 30DWG01 on the work disk and following these steps:

1. Choose <u>V</u>iew, 3D <u>D</u>ynamic View.

2. At the `Select objects:` prompt, select the office door, the desk, the phone, and the chair. You also might want to select some of the walls (in green).

3. Enter **po** to select the POints option.

4. Using the object snap of `Endpoint`, select the upper corner of the phone (on the desk) as the target point.

5. When prompted to select the camera point, enter **17'6",3'6",6'** (this is the point directly inside the door, as if a 6' tall person were standing there); refer to figure 30.6.

6. Stay in the DVIEW command. You use it in a later tutorial.

**Fig. 30.6**

Set up the view with the POint option of DVIEW.

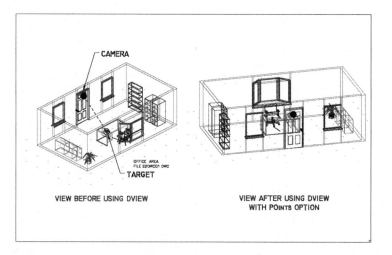

VIEW BEFORE USING DVIEW        VIEW AFTER USING DVIEW WITH POINTS OPTION

### Distance, Off, Zoom, Pan, Twist

After the camera and target are set up, the Distance, Off, Zoom, Pan, and Twist DVIEW command options are used to further alter the display.

Selecting the Distance option turns on perspective viewing. Use the Off option to turn off perspective viewing (parallel projection). Perspective viewing offers a more realistic view of the model than parallel projection. Objects in the scene that are far away appear as if they are smaller; objects closer seem larger. To set the distance the camera is from the target, enter a number at the New camera/target distance: prompt, or use the slider to specify the value. When using the slider bar (see fig. 30.7), moving to the right increases the distance the camera is from the target, and to the left decreases the distance.

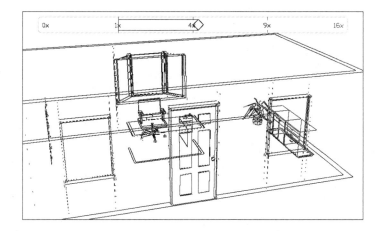

**Fig. 30.7**
Use the slider to specify distance.

**VIII**

**Isometrics & 3D Drafting**

What takes place when using the Zoom option depends on whether perspective mode is on. As you just saw, when you use the Distance option, and specify the distance the camera is from the target, the perspective mode is turned on. In perspective mode, the Zoom option is used like a dynamic lens changer. It's like having a bag full of every lens ever made for your 35mm camera! As with the Distance option, you may choose to type in the lens value, or use the slider to choose the lens value.

The Pan option works just like the PAN command does outside the DVIEW command. You use this option to fine-tune your view. When specifying points for the panning action, enter coordinates only when you're not in perspective mode. In this mode, only on-screen point selection is available (which, in almost every case, is all you need).

The Twist option allows you to rotate the view around the current line of sight (which is defined by the camera and target). As with other AutoCAD commands that use angles, the angles are measured counterclockwise, with angle zero starting at the right of your screen.

◀ See "Panning the Display (PAN)," p. 352

**Tutorial: Using the Distance, Zoom, Pan, and Off Options**

You should still be in the DVIEW command from the previous tutorial. Continue setting up the scene from the previous tutorial by following these steps:

1. Select the Distance option.

```
CAmera/TArget/Distance/POints/PAn/Zoom/TWist/CLip/Hide/
    Off/Undo/<eXit>: d
```

2. Enter the number directly, or use the slider to set the distance to 8'. This gives you a view as if you were looking through a 50mm lens attached to a 35mm camera.

3. Now change the size of camera lens using the Zoom option. Select the Zoom option.

```
CAmera/TArget/Distance/POints/PAn/Zoom/TWist/CLip/Hide/
    Off/Undo/<eXit>: z
```

4. Enter a lens value of 35 (for 35mm lens).

```
Adjust lenslength <50.000mm>: 35
```

Notice the change in the view. It's like you just changed the lens on your camera!

5. Now pan the display slightly using the Pan option. Select the Pan option.

```
CAmera/TArget/Distance/POints/PAn/Zoom/TWist/CLip/Hide/
    Off/Undo/<eXit>: pa
Displacement base point:
Second point:
```

6. For the displacement point, select a point near the middle of the phone.

7. For the second point, pan to the right until the chair is in the middle of your crosshairs and pick again.

Notice that the target point was what was actually being panned.

8. Select the TWist option.

```
CAmera/TArget/Distance/POints/PAn/Zoom/TWist/CLip/Hide/
    Off/Undo/<eXit>: tw
```

9. Twist the view 45 degrees.

```
New view twist <0.00>: 45
```

This causes the camera to roll about the camera/target axis.

**10.** Set the twist angle back to 0.

```
CAmera/TArget/Distance/POints/PAn/Zoom/TWist/CLip/Hide/
    Off/Undo/<eXit>: tw
New view twist <0.00>: 0
```

A distance value is in place; therefore, the views you see are perspective views (notice the UCSICON in the lower-left corner of the screen). Turn perspective viewing off.

**11.** Select the Off option.

```
CAmera/TArget/Distance/POints/PAn/Zoom/TWist/CLip/Hide/
    Off/Undo/<eXit>: off
```

The view returns to parallel projection and the original camera/target distance.

### Hide and Clip

The Hide and Clip options of the DVIEW command are used to remove portions of the model from view. The Hide option works identical to the HIDE command except that only the reference objects are hidden in DVIEW (that is, the objects you selected at the Select objects: prompt of the DVIEW command). Go ahead and use the Hide option now (from the previous exercise). Your view should look like figure 30.8.

◄ See "Removing Hidden Lines (HIDE)," p. 781

**Fig. 30.8**
Use the Hide option of the DVIEW command.

The Clip option is used to set up a clipping plane as discussed earlier. A *clipping plane* can be thought of as an invisible knife that cuts off a part of your model (either from the front or back of the model according to your current viewpoint). In the case of a front clipping plane, the portion of the objects that touch the plane forward (perpendicular to your current viewpoint) are removed from view. These objects are not erased from the drawing, but rather temporarily not displayed; just like hidden lines are only temporarily not shown. A back clipping plane removes from view those objects which intersect the clipping plane on back (away from view). Figure 30.9 illustrates both front and back clipping planes.

**Fig. 30.9**
An example of front and back clipping planes.

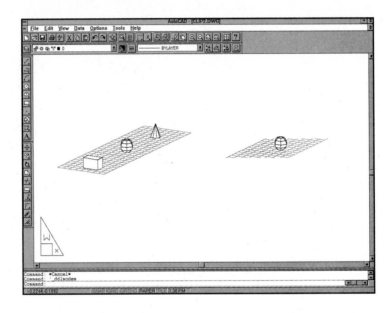

**Tip**
To reverse an operation you have performed using one of the DVIEW command options, use the Undo option.

When setting up front and back clipping planes, you are asked to specify a distance from the target. You may enter a specific value, or use the slider until you achieve the results wanted.

## Tutorial: Using DVIEW's Hide and Clip Options

1. Select the Open button and change to your working directory, C:\UAW13.

2. Select 30DWG02 from the file list, and select OK (see fig. 30.10).

3. Select 3D Dynamic View from the View menu, or at the `Command:` prompt, type **dview**.

    ```
    Command: dview
    ```

4. At the `Select objects:` prompt, type **all**.

    ```
    Select objects: all
    454 found
    Select objects:
    ```

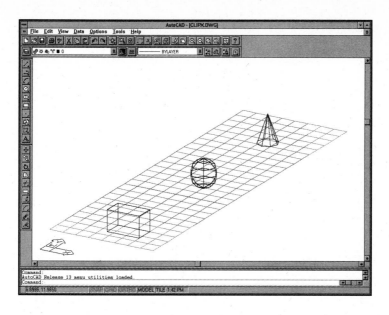

**Fig. 30.10**
Open the tutorial
drawing,
30DWG02.

**VIII**

**Isometrics & 3D Drafting**

**5.** Type **cl** to select the Clip option.

```
CAmera/TArget/Distance/POints/PAn/Zoom/TWist/CLip/Hide/
    Off/Undo/<eXit>: cl
```

**6.** Start with the back clipping plane. Type **b** at the Back/Front/<Off>:
prompt.

```
Back/Front/<Off>: b
```

**7.** Enter a value of **–5** for the distance from the target point.

```
ON/OFF/<Distance from target> <16.4959>: -5
```

**8.** Now setup the front clipping plane. Type **cl** at the prompt to reenter
the Clip option, then type **f** (for front).

```
CAmera/TArget/Distance/POints/PAn/Zoom/TWist/CLip/Hide/
    Off/Undo/<eXit>: cl
Back/Front/<Off>: f
```

**9.** Enter a value of **5** for the distance from the target point.

```
Eye/ON/OFF/<Distance from target> <1.0000>: 5
```

**10.** Hide the view using the Hide option.

```
CAmera/TArget/Distance/POints/PAn/Zoom/TWist/CLip/Hide/
    Off/Undo/<eXit>: h
Hiding lines 100% done.
```

```
CAmera/TArget/Distance/POints/PAn/Zoom/TWist/CLip/Hide/
    Off/Undo/<eXit>:
Regenerating drawing.
```

Your tutorial drawing should look like figure 30.11.

**Fig. 30.11**
The 30DWG02 tutorial drawing is finished.

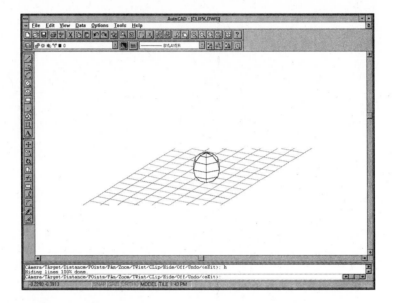

# Displaying More Than One View (VIEWPORTS or VPORTS)

When working in 3D, it's sometimes very easy to get frustrated. Errors when editing objects in 3D space is one of these frustrations. In this case, it would be nice to be able to view the model from many different angles at the same time. With the VPORTS command, you can split your model space screen into several different view "ports." In one view, you have clear access to the top of your model. In another, you can see the back. And maybe in a third, you can view the model isometrically. You can make accurate selections editing when you're able to view the model with VPORTS.

Because the VPORTS command is only used to create tiled viewports, it can only be used in model space with TILEMODE set to 1. For information on setting up floating viewports, refer to Chapter 13, "Understanding Model Space and Paper Space," and Chapter 31, "Plotting a 3D Model."

To access the VPORTS command use one of the following methods:

■ Open the <u>V</u>iew menu and choose Tile<u>d</u> Viewports.

■ At the Command: prompt, type **vports**.

The viewports in figure 30.12 were set up using the VPORTS command with the following options:

```
Command: vports
Save/Restore/Delete/Join/SIngle/?/2/<3>/4:
Horizontal/Vertical/Above/Below/Left/<Right>:
```

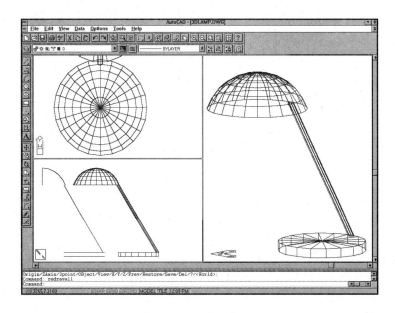

**Fig. 30.12**
You can split up the viewing windows with VPORTS.

As you can see in the previous command line, AutoCAD provides several methods of setting up viewports. After the viewports are setup the way you want, you might want to save that setting for later retrieval. To save the settings, use the Save option; to retrieve a viewport configuration, use the Restore option. The Delete option can be used to purge unwanted saved viewport configurations.

Other options of the VPORTS command allow you to join two viewports to form a single viewport. When joining viewports, the view and display properties of the first view selected are used by the newly joined view. Any time you want to revert to one view (the default view configuration when starting AutoCAD), use the SIngle option.

AutoCAD also provides a more user friendly method of choosing viewport layouts than the manual command line entry method. Figure 30.13 shows the Tiled Viewport Layout dialog box. To activate the dialog box, choose View, Tiled Viewports, then choose Layout. With this dialog box, you can choose from several tiled viewport layouts. Besides the graphical representation of a particular layout on the right side of the dialog box, there is a text listing of the layouts on the left side. Select the icon or the text description on the left.

**Fig. 30.13**
Using the Tiled
Viewport Layout
dialog box.

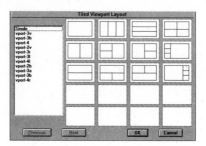

## Tutorial: Creating Viewports with the VPORTS Command

In this tutorial, you learn to setup a tiled viewport configuration (see fig. 30.14). The tutorial uses the Tiled Viewport Layout dialog box first, and then examines the methods needed to produce the same viewport configuration manually with the VPORTS command. Start with the dialog box and follow these steps:

1. Start a new drawing by selecting the New button. Name your drawing **vplayout** and choose OK.

2. Make sure the system variable tilemode is on (1). Choose View, Tiled Model Space or type **tilemode** and **1** at the Command: prompt.

3. Choose View, Tiled Viewports.

   You are presented with the Tiled Viewport Layout dialog box (refer to fig. 30.13).

4. Select the lower-right button, which represents a list of four vports (one large viewport on the left, and three small viewports on the right).

   Your screen is divided into the viewport layout selected. Use the Single option of the VPORTS command to set the screen back to a single viewport. Continue the tutorial, this time doing the same operation manually.

5. Type **vports** at the Command: prompt.

   Command: **vports**

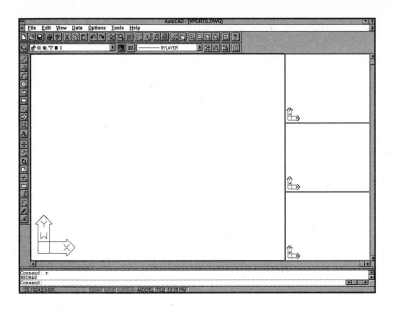

**Fig. 30.14**
You can select a viewport from one large viewport or three smaller ones.

6. At the `Save/Restore/Delete/Join/SIngle/?/2/<3>/4:` prompt, type **2**

   `Save/Restore/Delete/Join/SIngle/?/2/<3>/4:` **2**

7. Select the default of Vertical.

   `Horizontal/<Vertical>:`

8. Press Enter to re-issue the VPORTS command. Divide the viewport on the right in half, vertically. At the `Save/Restore/Delete/Join/SIngle/?/2/<3>/4:` prompt, enter **2**.

   `Save/Restore/Delete/Join/SIngle/?/2/<3>/4:` **2**
   `Horizontal/<Vertical>:`

9. Press Enter to re-issue the VPORTS command. Divide the far right viewport into three viewports using the Horizontal option.

   `Save/Restore/Delete/Join/SIngle/?/2/<3>/4:` **3**
   `Horizontal/<Vertical>:` **h**

You should have one larger viewport on the left, a small vertical viewport to the right of that, then three small viewports on the right of the screen. The last step is to join the large viewport on the left to the smaller vertical viewport to its immediate right. If you have exited the VPORTS command, reenter it now. Continue the tutorial by following these steps:

10. At the `Save/Restore/Delete/Join/SIngle/?/2/<3>/4:` prompt, type **j**.

    `Save/Restore/Delete/Join/SIngle/?/2/<3>/4:` **j**

11. For the dominant viewport, select the large viewport on the far left.

> Select dominant viewport <current>: *Select large viewport*
> *on left.*

12. For the viewport to join, select the viewport to its right.

> Select viewport to join: *Select smaller, vertical*
> *viewport.*

As you can see, unless you have the need for a tiled viewport layout that is not available on the Tiled Viewport Layout dialog, it's much easier to use the dialog box.

## Redrawing All Viewports (REDRAWALL, REGENALL)

◄ See "Viewing a Drawing," p. 331

When working with and editing objects in multiple views, it's often necessary to clean up the display. There can be ghost images left behind from a former editing operation or other command. You can refresh or completely regenerate the view in all active viewports at the same time. The REDRAWALL command refreshes the view, taking the information that's already in video memory and repainting the screen. The REGENALL command completely recalculates the way the image is displayed by going to the drawing database and scanning each and every object. Each active viewport is regenerated.

To access the REDRAWALL command do one of the following:

■ Select the Redraw All button from the Redraw flyout on the Standard toolbar.

■ At the Command: prompt, type **redrawall**.

To access the REGENALL command do the following:

■ At the Command: prompt, type **regenall**.

## From Here...

This chapter addressed model space. When creating the model, you may find it easier to work in just model space, utilizing various viewport layouts. When it comes time to put the design on paper, the best choice for the page layout is paper space. When working with a floating paper space viewport, a lot of what you learned in this chapter will apply. Refer to the following chapters for more information on modeling:

- Chapter 13, "Understanding Model Space and Paper Space," reviews the paper space environment.

- Chapter 31, "Plotting a 3D Model," looks at some of the tools used to set up and plot a 3D model.

# On Your Own

Load the drawing of a counter bore (30DWG03) and experiment changing your viewpoint with the DVIEW command, setting up the target and camera, and setting up perspective mode (see fig. 30.15).

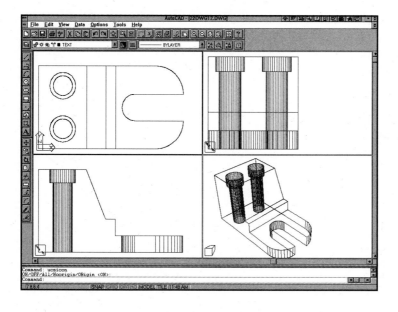

**Fig. 30.15**
A counter bore model is used to practice using the DVIEW command.

**VIII**

**Isometrics & 3D Drafting**

Here are some hints:

1. Use the DVIEW command to create a perspective view of the model.

2. Create a four viewport configuration with a front, top, right side, and isometric view.

# Chapter 31

# Plotting a 3D Model

Previous chapters have dealt with topics such as creating, viewing, and managing 3D models. The final result of these drawings is to plot them out using a hard copy device such as a plotter or printer. This is usually the final method of communicating our ideas. In this chapter you'll examine the setup and plotting of 3D models, by learning how to:

- Use MVSETUP to setup the specifications of a drawing

- Create and control floating viewports with MVIEW

- Set up a perspective view using DVIEW

- Control object visibility in each viewport with DDLMODES

VIII

Isometrics & 3D Drafting

## Using MVSETUP

MVSETUP, short for Model View Setup, is an AutoLISP routine used to help you set up and prepare your drawing for plotting. Depending on the current setting of the TILEMODE system variable, MVSETUP will go one of two directions. If TILEMODE is on (a value of 1), you're restricted to working in just model space, and can use MVSETUP only to set up the Units type, global scale factor, and paper size. If TILEMODE is off (a value of 0), you can use MVSETUP to insert any number of predefined title blocks, as well as create and manage floating viewports in paper space.

◀ See "Understanding Model Space and Paper Space," p. 369

One of the main benefits of designing in 3D is that the resulting model can be viewed from any angle in a number of different floating viewports in paper space. One model can be utilized to produce several paper space plots. Although MVSETUP can also be used under model space to automate drawing preparation, this section will deal only with the options available to MVSETUP under paper space (TILEMODE off).

The MVSETUP command can be accessed by choosing View, Floating Viewports and then MV Setup from the fly-out menu. If the Floating Viewports option is disabled (grayed out), this simply means that TILEMODE is turned on (1). In order to enable this option, you can either turn TILEMODE off first, by choosing View, Paper Space as shown in figure 31.1, or by entering **mvsetup** at the Command: prompt and answering Yes to the Enable paper space? (No/<Yes>): prompt that follows. After you're in the MVSETUP command, you'll notice a list of options as shown below.

```
Command: mvsetup
Align/Create/Scale viewports/Options/Title block/Undo:
```

**Fig. 31.1**
The Floating Viewports option under the View menu.

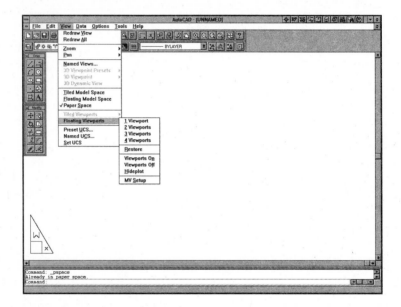

## Setting Options

One option under MVSETUP is Options. This is where you specify the layer the title block will be inserted onto, whether or not you want the limits reset to match the extents of the drawing after title block insertion, whether the size and point locations are to be translated to inch or millimeter paper units, and whether the title block should be inserted as a block or as an external reference.

When you choose the Options option, you'll be presented with the following:

```
Command: mvsetup
Align/Create/Scale viewports/Options/Title block/Undo: o
Set Layer/LImits/Units/Xref:
```

- *Set Layer.* This option allows you to specify the layer on which the predefined title block (discussed in the next section) is to be inserted. You are asked to enter a layer name or . (period) for current layer. Entering a period (.) will cause the title block to be inserted on the current layer. If you enter the name of a layer that doesn't exist, it will be created for you.

- *Limits.* Use this option to indicate that you want the limits of the drawing to match the extent of the drawing after a predefined title block has been inserted.

- *Units.* With this option you can specify whether the paper space units for sizes and point locations are translated into feet, inches, meters, or millimeters. At the `Feet/Inches/Meters/Millimeters? <in>:` prompt, select the appropriate value.

- *Xref.* Controls whether the predefined title block is inserted as a block or externally referenced as a cross-reference. At the `Xref Attach or Insert title block? <Insert>:` prompt, type **x** to attach the title block as a cross-reference, or simply accept the default of Insert by pressing Enter.

## Inserting a Predefined Title Block

Once the MVSETUP preferences have been set using the Options option (as discussed above, and if necessary), the Title block option can be used to insert a predefined title block. When you enter this option you'll be presented with the following list of sub options:

```
Delete objects/Origin/Undo/<Insert title block>:
```

The Delete Objects option allows you to select objects in paper space for deletion. The next option, Origin, is used to specify the origin (0,0,0) point for the title block you have or are getting ready to insert. The Undo option, much like the UNDO command, is used to reverse an operation you have performed during this session of MVSETUP. The default, Insert Title Block, presents a list of predefined title blocks you can choose to insert as well as other options for adding items to and deleting items from the list. This list is derived from information stored in a default file named mvsetup.dfs, which is automatically created the first time you use MVSETUP. Below is the list of title block options available initially.

```
0:      None
1:      ISO A4 Size(mm)
2:      ISO A3 Size(mm)
3:      ISO A2 Size(mm)
```

```
4:       ISO A1 Size(mm)
5:       ISO A0 Size(mm)
6:       ANSI-V Size(in)
7:       ANSI-A Size(in)
8:       ANSI-B Size(in)
9:       ANSI-C Size(in)
10:      ANSI-D Size(in)
11:      ANSI-E Size(in)
12:      Arch/Engineering (24 x 36in)
13:      Generic D size Sheet (24 x 36in)
Add/Delete/Redisplay/<Number of entry to load>:
```

Select the number that corresponds to the title block definition you want to use. For additional information on adding and deleting items on this list, please refer to the online documentation that comes with AutoCAD.

Figure 31.2 shows the title block that is inserted after using MVSETUP with option number 7 (ANSI-A) as shown in list above.

**Fig. 31.2**
ANSI-A Size title block created by MVSETUP.

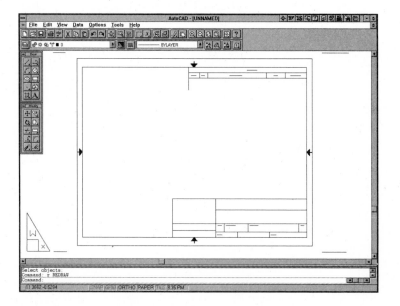

## Creating Floating Viewports

In model space, you could only split the screen up by using the VPORTS command to create *tiled* viewports. Paper space frees you from the limitation of model space's viewports, and allows you to create floating (non-tiled) viewports. This section examines two methods of creating floating viewports; one using an option in the MVSETUP routine itself, and the other using the MVIEW command.

## Using the Create Option

When using the Create option under the MVSETUP routine to create new floating viewports, you must first choose from this list of available viewport layouts:

◄ See "Under-standing Model Space and Paper Space," p. 369

```
Command: mvsetup
Align/Create/Scale viewports/Options/Title block/Undo: c
Delete objects/Undo/<Create viewports>:
Available Mview viewport layout options:
      0:  None
      1:  Single
      2:  Std. Engineering
      3:  Array of Viewports
Redisplay/<Number of entry to load>:
```

For the purpose of this chapter, you need to examine option number 2, Standard Engineering. This option automates the process of setting up four viewports, and then adjusting each view to match a commonly used viewing configuration (see fig. 31.3).

```
Redisplay/<Number of entry to load>: 2
Bounding area for viewports. Default/<First point>:
    Select the lower corner of bounding area.
Other point: Select the upper corner of bounding area.
Distance between viewports in X. <0.0>:
Distance between viewports in Y. <0.0>:
```

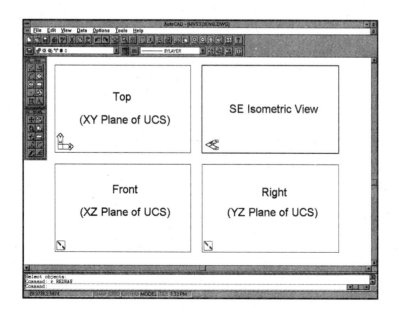

**Fig. 31.3**
The Standard Engineering Layout option.

**VIII**

**Isometrics & 3D Drafting**

The bounding area for viewports can be defined in one of two ways. The option Default uses information derived from the default file mvsetup.dfs mentioned earlier. Each predefined title block has been defined with a default bounding area built in. If you want to supply your own bounding area, simply pick two points, much like you would when using ZOOM Window.

### Using the MVIEW Command

Although the MVSETUP routine automates a lot of the steps involved in setting up floating paper space viewports (as previously shown), you may still want to add viewports manually, or add to what MVSETUP is able to do. The MVIEW command, which is actually being used by the MVSETUP routine, is always available for this task. To access MVIEW, follow these steps:

1. Choose <u>V</u>iew, Floating Viewports.

2. Enter **mview** at the Command: prompt.

The MVIEW command displays the following prompt:

```
Command: mview
ON/OFF/Hideplot/Fit/2/3/4/Restore/<First Point>:
```

## Setting the Viewports Scale

In Chapter 13, "Understanding Model Space and Paper Space," you used the ZOOM command with the XP option to specify the viewports scale factor in relationship to paper space. Actually, the same command is being used here with the Scale option of the MVSETUP routine. The only difference is that you aren't directly aware of it. When using the Scale option of MVSETUP, you must first select the floating viewports to scale. Keep in mind, you're not actually scaling the viewport as you might with Grips or the SCALE command, but rather setting up a ratio between paper space and model space.

◄ See "Scaling Paper Space Viewports," p. 385

If you select more than one viewport for scaling, a prompt appears asking you whether this scaling operation is to be interactively or uniformly performed. If only one viewport was selected, this prompt is skipped, and you move on to supplying the units value.

```
Set zoom scale factors for viewports. Interactively/<Uniform>:
```

Selecting the default option of Uniform will scale all selected viewports to the same paper space to model space ratio. This ratio (or scale) is calculated by supplying information to the following prompts:

```
Number of paper space units. <1.0>:
Number of model space units. <1.0>:
```

If you choose Interactively, you're prompted for the paper space and model space units for each viewport (using the same prompts as shown above).

Just as when you're using ZOOM XP, the paper space units are divided by the model space units to achieve the proper ratio. For example, if the paper space border was full size at 36" × 24" and each viewport was to have the scale 1/4"=1', then the ratio would be 1:48. (1 paper space unit to every 48 model space units. When it's time to plot, be sure to plot from paper space using a scale of 1=1.) Since the viewports have been scaled, they will plot out to the correct scale.

# Controlling the Display of the Viewport

Using MVSETUP or MVIEW to create and set up floating viewports is one thing, getting the final plot to look just the way you want it to may be another story. AutoCAD has some nice tools to help you align the viewports, remove hidden lines, set up perspective views, and much more. This section will examine some of the tools and methods you can use to set up and plot great looking, multiple view documents.

## Aligning Viewports (MVSETUP)

The Align option under MVSETUP provides a fast and easy way to line up multiview drawings. Earlier you saw how to use the MVSETUP routine to set up a standard engineering viewport layout. Sometimes, the objects in the top, front, and right views don't line up with each other. Using the PAN command will get you close (eyeball it in), but using options like Horizontal and Vertical Alignment is much easier and more accurate.

When you access the Align option, you'll be given another list of options. These are the methods of alignment from which you can choose.

```
Command: mvsetup
Align/Create/Scale viewports/Options/Title block/Undo: a
Angled/Horizontal/Vertical alignment/Rotate view/Undo:
```

Figure 31.4 shows a standard engineering layout, but the views of the model don't line up with each other. Figure 31.5 shows the results of using MVSETUP Alignment options Horizontal and Vertical.

**Fig. 31.4**
Multiview drawing
before viewport
alignment.

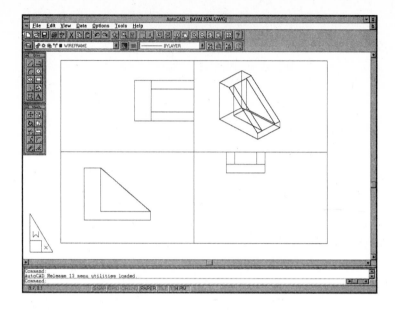

**Fig. 31.5**
Multiview drawing
after horizontal
and vertical
viewport
alignment.

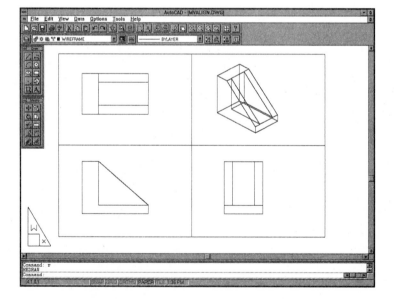

### Angled

Use the Angled option to pan the display in a viewport in a direction specified by a distance and an angle specified from a basepoint. First select the
Basepoint, which is the point in the view from which you are panning. Next,
select a point in the view you are panning. This point will be panned
(moved) to a point determined by your next two responses; the distance and
angle from the basepoint. The prompts are as follows:

```
Command: mvsetup
Align/Create/Scale viewports/Options/Title block/Undo: a
Angled/Horizontal/Vertical alignment/Rotate view/Undo: a
Basepoint: _Select a point.
Other point: _Select a point in the viewport to be panned.
Specify the distance and angle to the new alignment point
in the current viewport where you specified the basepoint.
Distance from basepoint: Enter the distance.
Angle from basepoint: Enter the angle.
Angled/Horizontal/Vertical alignment/Rotate view/Undo:
Align/Create/Scale viewports/Options/Title block/Undo:
```

### Horizontal

Use the Horizontal option to line up viewports that are positioned horizontal to each other (see fig. 31.6). Here again you select a basepoint and a second point. The second point is in the viewport you are aligning to the basepoint viewport. The basepoint can be the endpoint of a line, center of a circle, or other object that is visible in both views. The second point selected will be panned to align itself with this point.

```
Command: mvsetup
Align/Create/Scale viewports/Options/Title block/Undo: a
Angled/Horizontal/Vertical alignment/Rotate view/Undo: h
Basepoint: _Select a point.
Other point: _Select a point in the viewport to be panned.
```

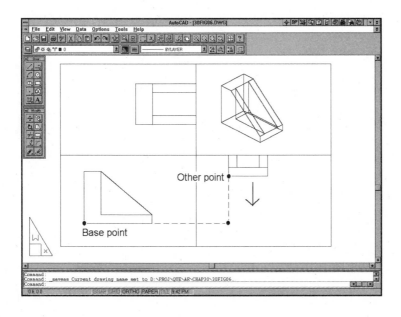

**Fig. 31.6**
Performing
Horizontal viewport
alignment.

### Vertical Alignment

The Vertical Alignment option lines up viewports that are positioned vertical to each other (see fig. 31.7). As with Horizontal Alignment, you select a basepoint and a second point. Again, the second point selection is in the viewport you are aligning to the basepoint viewport. The basepoint can be the endpoint of a line, center of a circle, or other object that is visible in both views. The second point selected will be panned to align itself with this point.

```
Command: mvsetup
Align/Create/Scale viewports/Options/Title block/Undo: a
Angled/Horizontal/Vertical alignment/Rotate view/Undo: v
Basepoint: _endp of
Other point: _endp of
```

**Fig. 31.7**
Performing vertical viewport alignment.

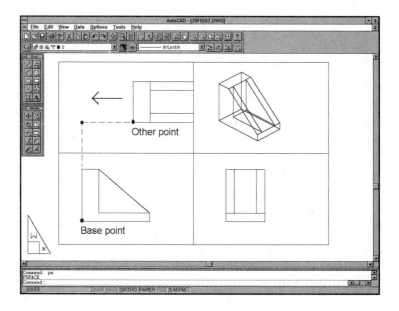

### Rotate View

◀ See "Dynamically Changing the Viewpoint (DVIEW)," p. 865

You can rotate the view in a viewport around a selected basepoint with the Rotate View option. It automates the process of using the DVIEW command to change the view twist. This option is used primarily when the UCS is parallel to the screen and in conjunction with the Angled option to align angled views.

**Undo**

Use the Undo option to reverse an alignment operation performed in MVSETUP with the Align option. It's good for the current MVSETUP session only. Use the UNDO command (not the MVSETUP commands Undo option) to reverse previous uses of MVSETUP in this drawing session.

## Tutorial: Aligning Viewports

In this tutorial, you'll work with an existing multiview drawing that has been set up using MVSETUP. The viewport layout in this tutorial is the Standard Engineering layout. Align the Top and Right side views to the Front view. Your final result should match the drawing shown in figure 31.8. To begin, follow these steps:

1. Choose Open from the Standard toolbar and change to your work directory, C:\UAW13.

2. Select 31DWG01 from the file list and click OK.

3. Choose <u>V</u>iew, MV <u>S</u>etup, or enter **mvsetup** at the Command: prompt.

    ```
    Command: mvsetup
    ```

4. At the Align/Create/Scale viewports/Options/Title block/Undo: prompt, enter **a** for Align. Then enter **h** for Horizontal Alignment.

    ```
    Align/Create/Scale viewports/Options/Title block/Undo: a
    Angled/Horizontal/Vertical alignment/Rotate view/Undo: h
    ```

5. For the base point, select point B in the Front view.

    Hint: Use an object snap of endpoint.

6. For the Other point, select point A in the Right view.

7. Perform a vertical alignment using point B as the base and point C as the point to align vertically to B.

**Fig. 31.8**

Results of aligning
viewports in the
31DWG01
tutorial.

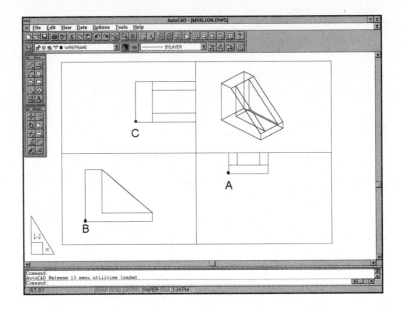

## Hidden Line Viewports (MVIEW)

When plotting, one of the options available in the plot dialog box is Hidden
Line Removal. Hidden Line Removal affects all viewports, even if you only
want to have hidden lines removed in one or two of them. The MVIEW command allows you to specify a particular floating viewport that needs to have
hidden lines removed. Remember, this refers to lines which are obscured by
geometry, not lines drawn in the hidden linetype.

Choose View, Floating Viewports, or enter **mview** at the Command: prompt.
At the prompt that follows, select Hideplot.

```
Command: mview
ON/OFF/Hideplot/Fit/2/3/4/Restore/<First Point>: h
```

Select only the viewport(s) you want to have hidden lines removed from at
plot time.

◄ See "Removing
Hidden Lines
(HIDE)," p. 781

> **Note**
>
> Because floating viewports are paper space objects, make sure you are in paper space
> before attempting to select them under the Hideplot option of MVIEW. Attempting
> to select the viewport in model space will only result in frustration! You also need to
> make sure the layer that the viewports reside on is thawed—otherwise you won't be
> able to select them.

## Perspective View (DVIEW)

Setting up a perspective view of your model gives you a more realistic representation of your 3D model than parallel projection can provide. A perspective view can easily be set up by indicating the distance the target point is from the camera point under DVIEW's Distance option. Other options under DVIEW can be used in conjunction with Distance to pan, zoom, and twist the view to achieve the desired effect. The DVIEW command is covered in more detail in Chapter 30, "Viewing a 3D Model."

## Layer Control (DDLMODES)

When you set up your final plot in paper space, each floating viewport can be set up to display only the information you want shown. You have the freedom to freeze and thaw layers on a viewport by viewport basis. To do this, access the DDLMODES command, by clicking the button on the Standard toolbar.

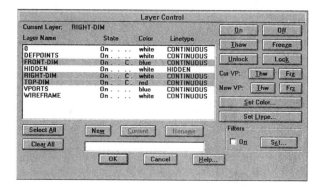

**Fig. 31.9**
Controlling viewport layer visibility with DDLMODES.

AutoCAD provides two methods of controlling the layer visibility in floating viewports. In an existing viewport, make it the current viewport and select either the Thw (thaw) or Frz (freeze) button next to the words Cur VP: in the Layer Control dialog box (DDLMODES)(see fig. 31.9). Layer visibility of viewports that are created later using MVIEW are controlled by selecting Thw or Frz next to the words New VP:. Freezing a layer in the current viewport places a C in the State column of the Layer Control Dialog box. You can see that a particular layer won't be displayed in new viewports if an N is present in the State column.

◄ See "Understanding Layers," p. 175

## Tutorial: Multiview Dimensioning Control

In this tutorial, you'll work with an existing multiview drawing that has already been dimensioned. Dimensions that correspond to each view have been placed on separate layers. For example, those dimensions which show up in the Top view are on the Dim-Top layer. In each viewport, freeze those layers that should not be displayed until your drawing looks like the one in figure 31.10. Follow these steps:

1. Choose Open and change to work directory, C:\UAW13.

2. Select 31DWG02 from the file list and click OK.

3. Make sure you're in model space within a paper space viewport by either double-clicking Paper in the status bar (which switches you to model space), selecting Model Space from the View menu, or entering **ms** at the Command: prompt.

4. In model space, select the upper-left viewport, making it the current viewport.

5. Select the layers button from the Standard toolbar, or enter **ddlmodes** at the Command: prompt.

6. In the Layer Control dialog box, find and select the layers Front-Dim and Right-Dim.

7. Next to the words Cur VP: click Frz.

8. Repeat steps 5 through 8 for the Front and Right viewports freezing layers, Top-Dim and Right-Dim in the Front viewport, and Top-Dim and Front-Dim in the Right viewport. Figure 31.10 shows the final results.

**Fig. 31.10**
Multiview
Dimension
drawing after layer
visibility changes.

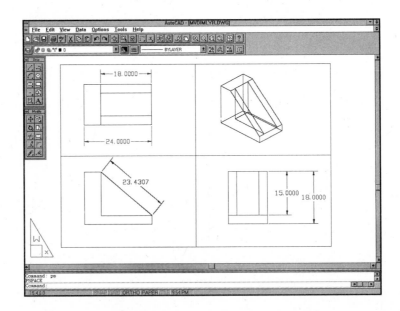

# From Here...

This chapter discussed some of the commands, methods, and tools used to set up a 3D model for plotting. A good comfort level with paper space is needed to achieve effective results with these commands. If you're still unsure of your knowledge of paper space, take a minute to review chapter 13, "Understanding Model Space and Paper Space"—it will be well worth your time. Paper space is a wonderful tool in the hands of a knowledgeable user. Commands like MVSETUP, MVIEW, DVIEW, and so on make using paper space much easier and effective.

- Chapter 7, "Understanding Layers," gives valuable information about something that is a must to know when working on multiview drawings.

- Chapter 12, "Viewing a Drawing," provides a refresher on some of the basic view control commands.

- Chapter 13, "Understanding Model Space and Paper Space," discusses paper space and model space as they are used with multiview and 3D models.

- Chapter 14, "Plotting a Drawing," reviews plotting a drawing from the Plot dialog box.

# On Your Own

Reinforce the commands and techniques discussed in this chapter by setting up some paper space drawings. Select from any of the models drawn in previous chapters.

Hints:

1. Use MVSETUP to automate the insertion of a title block and floating viewports.

2. In multiview configurations (like Std. Engineering), try using MVSETUPs Align options.

3. Set up various dimensioning layers for various scales and views, controlling the visibility of each as needed in each viewport.

# Part IX

# Solid Modeling and Rendering

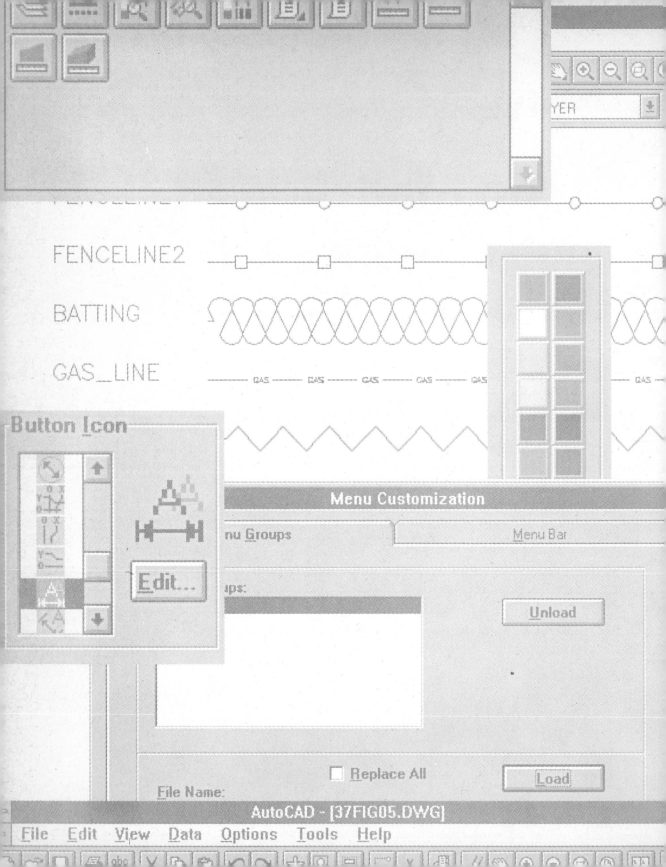

FENCELINE2 ──□──□──□──□──

BATTING ◠◠◠◠◠◠◠◠◠◠◠◠

GAS_LINE ── GAS ── GAS ── GAS ── GAS ── GAS ── GAS ──

## Button Icon

Edit...

## Menu Customization

nu Groups          Menu Bar

ps:

Unload

□ Replace All          Load

File Name:

AutoCAD - [37FIG05.DWG]

File   Edit   View   Data   Options   Tools   Help

# Chapter 32

# Introduction to Solid Modeling Concepts

A solid model presents a clear and informationally complete representation of a physical object. The concept, as well as construction procedures, differ from both three-dimensional wireframe and surface models. This chapter introduces you to creating solid models. At the completion of this chapter, you will be able to do the following:

- Create a solid model from a two-dimensional shape

- Create solid models from solid primitives

- Construct composite solid models by adding and subtracting solid objects

- Edit solid models

While AutoCAD solid modeling automates most of the three-dimensional model creation, you still need a good understanding of AutoCAD's coordinate system and use of views before attempting to create a solid model. Take some time to review the previous 3D coordinate system chapters before beginning this chapter.

◄ See "Introduction to 3D Modeling," p. 759

◄ See "Understanding 3D Coordinate Systems," p. 785

The majority of man-made objects around you were manufactured using a centuries-old process. The process starts with an idea. The idea is perfected by constant design changes involving testing, modification, and re-testing. The object is finally built to the designers' specifications.

Until several years ago, this process was done manually on paper. Different types of engineering drawings and pictorial representations of the object were created. Drawings of three-dimensional objects were represented on flat two-dimensional paper. A standard method of representing three-dimensional objects on two-dimensional paper, called *orthographic projection*, was developed. Two-dimensional drawings are limited because they are two-dimensional descriptions of three-dimensional objects which must be interpreted. This is where the fundamental difference between two-dimensional drawings and three-dimensional objects lies.

A 3D model created on the computer can be analyzed as though it really exists. This allows much more accurate and effective interaction between the designer and his idea. Generally, there are three different categories of 3D modeling in AutoCAD: wireframe modeling, surface modeling, and solid modeling. Each method has particular advantages and disadvantages and can produce an appropriate result for a particular design or application.

# Wireframe Models

◀ See "Creating a Simple Three-Dimensional Wireframe Model," p. 767

A *wireframe model* is basically a skeletal description of a three-dimensional object. It is the simplest of the 3D modeling methods.

## Advantages of Wireframe Models

Creating three-dimensional models with a wireframe has several advantages over other methods of three-dimensional model creation. These are:

- Wireframe models are the simplest of 3D modeling methods—they are easy to generate.

- The majority of 2D commands can be used to create a 3D model. All you need to do is add a Z coordinate.

- The wireframe model can be quickly plotted or printed.

## Disadvantages of Wireframe Models

There are also several disadvantages to creating three-dimensional models with the wireframe technique. These are:

- Wireframe models contain a minimum amount of information. For example, no data exists describing the space between the edges of a object.

- It is difficult to determine the intersections of surfaces.

■ Hidden line removal and shaded renderings cannot be produced automatically.

# Surface Models

A *surface model* is a three-dimensional model containing information about the profile edges of the object and the relationship between those edges. A surface model can be thought of as an infinitely thin shell covering the shape of the model. Surface models are created by placing three-dimensional closed flat and curved surface elements together to define the volume of the object.

◄ See "Creating a Simple Three-Dimensional Surface Model," p. 775

## Advantages of Surface Models

The advantages to creating a three-dimensional model using the surface technique are numerous. These advantages are:

■ Information is provided about the profile edges of the model—hidden-line removal is possible.

■ Faceted models can be created for shaded renderings.

■ A database can be provided for numerical code generation.

■ You can easily visualize curved surfaces.

■ You can find the intersection of surfaces in space.

## Disadvantages of Surface Models

The disadvantages to creating a three-dimensional model using the surface model technique are:

■ Surface models are made up of surfaces that may have no link to the wireframe geometry from which they were created. This makes it possible to create a model that is not topologically closed—it doesn't have a top or bottom (see fig. 32.1).

■ It is possible to create a model having surfaces that intersect themselves. This makes it possible to create a model that would be difficult, if not impossible, to build (see fig. 32.2).

**Fig. 32.1**
A disadvantage to creating a three-dimensional surface model is that it's possible to create an invalid model containing no top or bottom.

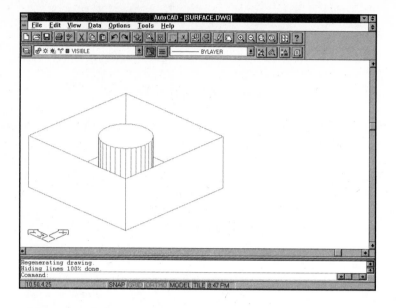

**Fig. 32.2**
It's possible to create an invalid surface model that contains surfaces that intersect each other.

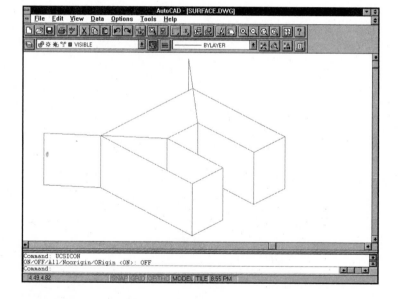

# Solid Models

A *solid model* contains a complete representation of the shape of a physical object. Solid modeling is different from wireframe or surface modeling in two ways. First, the solid model is more informationally complete than wireframe or surface models. Second, constructing a solid model is more straightforward than constructing wireframe or surface models. Surface modeling is different because it uses a "building blocks" approach in the creation of the physical object. The object is created primarily by adding and subtracting smaller primitive objects, until the final object is complete.

## Advantages of Solid Models

Solid modeling has several advantages over wireframe and surface modeling in the creation of three-dimensional physical objects. These advantages are:

- Solid models are the most informationally complete 3D models.

- Due to the amount of information contained in solid models, they support a wide variety of external applications, such as finite element analysis.

- Many solid modeling packages have internal tests to check the validity of the model. This prevents the creation of nonsense objects.

## Disadvantages of Solid Models

Like all modeling techniques, there are several disadvantages to creating a physical object with the solid modeling technique. These are:

- Until recently, solid modeling was expensive and not included in many CAD packages.

- Due to the high amount of information contained in a solid model, solid modeling software requires expensive, state-of-the-art hardware.

- Depending on the hardware, solid modeling can be slow and difficult to use.

- When creating parts that have arbitrary surfaces, solid models may not be as precise as surface or wireframe models because they use primitives to construct the object.

Solid models are far more useful than wireframe or surface models. Applications requiring deep analytical evaluation, such as volumetric, mass, and moment of inertia computations, require more information than wireframe or surface models can provide. The main limitations to solid modeling were the steep computing requirements and high cost of the software.

With the price-performance ratio of personal computers continuing to drop, solid modeling on the desktop is becoming a reality. Graphical user interfaces, such as Windows, are making application software like solid modeling easier to use. As the price of hardware continues to drop and software becomes easier to use, solid modeling is likely to gain a wider range of acceptance.

AutoCAD Release 13 includes the use of ACIS technology for the first time in AutoCAD. ACIS technology allows for more complete and exact representations of objects. For example, AutoCAD Release 13 uses ACIS technology to create the ellipse object and accurate spline curves with tangent points. ACIS technology also allows AutoCAD to create accurate 3D solid models without a great deal of the overhead or limitations inherent in the Advanced Modeling Extension (AME) used with Release 12. ACIS technology also makes editing a 3D solid easier, more accurate, and faster. If you are familiar with AME, you should pay close attention to the drafting and editing methods described in the solid modeling chapters. You may find that you can now draft in ways that were previously impossible or took a great deal of planning and forethought that could have been better spent on design rather than drafting.

# Introduction to Solid Modeling Definitions and Concepts

Solid modeling is similar to wireframe and surface modeling. In fact, a solid model may look identical to a similarly created wireframe or surface model. The difference is that AutoCAD recognizes the solid model as a single object with physical characteristics.

With a solid model you can calculate and analyze its weight, density, thermal conductivity, and other properties. Solid modeling is fully integrated into AutoCAD. You can combine solid and non-solid geometry in the same file using familiar AutoCAD commands to manipulate them.

As previously mentioned, AutoCAD Release 13 now uses the ACIS engine to create a Boundary Representation (B-REP) of the solid. Release 12 created a CSG tree (*Constructive Solid Geometry*) of the composite solid. Because there is no CSG tree used in the ACIS engine, the SOLSEP or SOLCHP commands you used with Release 12 can't be used with Release 13 solid models. When creating solids with the Release 13 ACIS engine you still create primitives and use Boolean operations to create a composite solid. Blocks, cones, and spheres are several examples of solid primitives that can be used. These primitives are combined by Boolean (addition, subtraction) operations to form complex solids. This change from the CSG approach to the ACIS modeling engine accounts for most of the speed increase in Release 13 solid modeling, and also some loss of functionality over the Release 12 AME.

As the model is created, its boundary representation and a record of what primitive shapes were used to create it are maintained. Using the ACIS B-REP modeling technique found in Release 13, a solid is defined by first creating its boundaries (surfaces and curves) and then creating a volumetric solid from those elements. The solid contains links back to those elements. If the bounding curves are changed the solid should change with them. This allows more flexible entity creation, but it carries the complexity for the user of surface creation. Using this data, you can directly analyze the solid model to obtain accurate information about its weight, mass, volume, surface area, and much more.

# Creating Solid Models from Two-Dimensional Shapes

A solid primitive's profile can be defined by using existing geometry. You can create tapered extrusions or solidify extruded polylines. These commands are useful when you have existing 2D geometry you want to turn into a 3D solid model.

> **Note**
>
> Your 2D geometry must be a polyline, closed object (a circle, ellipse, or region) to extrude or solidify. If your geometry is not a polyline, you can use the PEDIT command to turn it into one.

The majority of solid modeling commands are available in the Solids floating toolbar, shown in figure 32.3. You can access the Solids toolbar by choosing Tools, Toolbars, Solids.

◀ See "Editing Polylines (PEDIT)," p. 586

### Extruding 2D Geometry

One method for creating solid primitive objects is to extrude existing 2D objects. Extrusion allows you to create complex tapered extrusions as shown in figure 32.4. You can extrude polylines, polygons, 3D polylines, circles and ellipses. The EXTRUDE command can be accessed using these steps:

- Select the Extrude button on the Solids floating toolbar.

- Enter **extrude** at the Command: prompt.

When extruding polylines, the polyline must contain at least three but no more than 500 vertices. Because the polyline is limited to 500 vertices, it is recommended you do not attempt to extrude polylines that have been curved or spline fit with the PEDIT command. Additionally, you cannot extrude polylines that contain crossing or overlapping segments.

**Fig. 32.3**

The Solids floating toolbar contains most of the solids modeling commands.

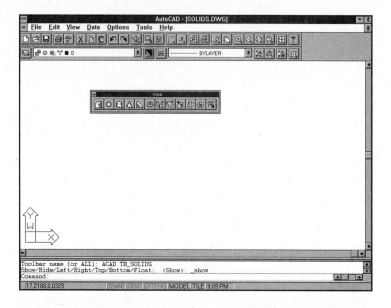

**Fig. 32.4**

Existing 2D geometry can be extruded in complex tapered shapes.

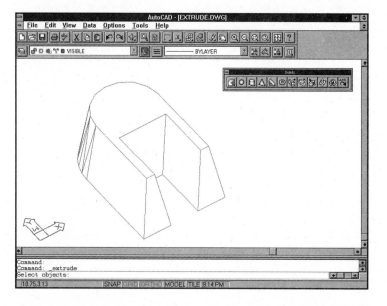

The extrusion angle must be 0 or greater, and less than 90. If you use a negative value for the extrusion height, the solid will be extruded in the negative Z direction.

You can use the REGION command to create 2D regions that can be extruded into 3D solids. A *region* is a closed loop object, essentially a 2D solid. To create a region, you simply draw the objects (closed lines, circles, closed polylines, and so on) necessary to create the desired *closed* shapes and then use the REGION command to change the objects (closed lines, circles, closed polylines, and so on) into regions. To edit the regions into a complex single region, use the solid modeling, Boolean commands discussed later in the "Constructing Composite Solid Models" section. You can edit separate regions into a single, complex 2D region, then extrude that region into a 3D solid. This is an effective way of creating complicated 3D solids. You can access the REGION command in either of the following ways:

- From the Draw toolbar, choose Rectangle, Region.

- At the Command: prompt, enter **region**.

### Tutorial: Extruding 2D

For this tutorial, you will create basic 2D geometry and extrude it into a 3D solid model. Before doing so, you will first change the viewpoint orientation so that you can view the model, as it is being created, in three dimensions.

1. Choose the New button from the Standard toolbar. If the AutoCAD dialog box appears, choose No unless you want to save the current drawing. If you want to save the current drawing, choose Yes and enter a path and drawing name. At the New Drawing dialog box click the OK button or press Enter.

2. For this tutorial, you will use the Draw toolbar and the Solids toolbar. Anchor the Draw toolbar to the right of the screen, and the Solids toolbar to the left of the screen. Close any other floating toolbars. This arrangement is not necessary for using the toolbars but it does give you access to all of the commands with a minimum of clutter. See figure 32.5 for an example of what the toolbars look like when docked in this manner.

3. To obtain an accurate view of the model, use the VPOINT command and type in the viewpoint.

   ```
   Command: vpoint
   Rotate/<View point> <0.0000,0.0000,1.0000>: .5,-.5,.7071
   ```

   Your screen should now look similar to the one shown in figure 32.5, with the toolbars anchored to the left and right side of the screen.

**Fig. 32.5**
Changing the
viewpoint
orientation to
better visualize the
hose connector as
it is created.

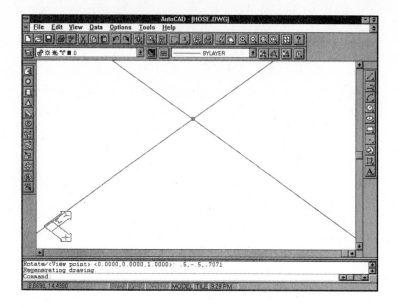

4. Next you will create a rectangle to serve as the base for the hose connector. Select the Rectangle button from the Draw toolbar.

```
First corner: 0,0
Other corner: 5,5
```

5. After creating the rectangle, you may not be able to see the entire rectangle on-screen. A ZOOM command will remedy the problem. First, select the Zoom Extents button. Then, select the Zoom Scale button, and use a scale factor of .8.

```
All/Center/Dynamic/Extents/Left/Previous/Vmax/Window/
    Scale(X/XP)>: .8
```

You should now be able to see the complete rectangle as shown in figure 32.6.

6. Next, fillet the corners of the rectangle. Select the Fillet button from the Chamfer fly-out button. The Chamfer button is located on the Modify floating toolbar. First, set the fillet radius as follows:

```
Polyline/Radius/Trim/<Select first object>: r
Enter fillet radius<0.0000>: 1
```

7. To fillet the polygon, press Enter at the Command: prompt to reenter the FILLET command, then select the polygon. Your screen should now look like figure 32.7.

```
Command:
Polyline/Radius/Trim/<Select first object>: P
Select 2D polyline: Select the rectangle.
4 lines were filleted
```

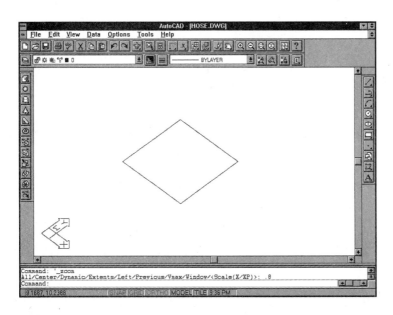

**Fig. 32.6**
Using the ZOOM command to display the rectangle.

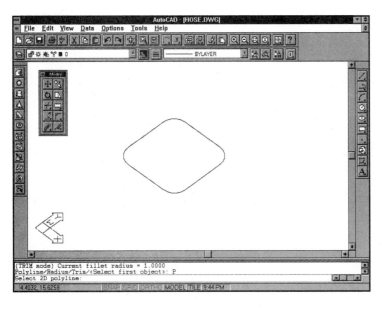

**Fig. 32.7**
The FILLET Command can be used to fillet a rectangle with the polyline option.

**IX**

Solid Modeling & Rendering

**8.** Now extrude the 2D shape into a 3D solid model. Select the Extrude button from the Solids toolbar.

```
Select objects: Select the 2D shape.
Select objects:
Path/<Height of extrusion>: 1
Extrusion taper angle <0>:
```

The 2D shape is extruded into a 3D solid model as shown in figure 32.8. Save your work as hose in the UAW13 subdirectory. The next tutorial continues from here.

**Fig. 32.8**
Use the EXTRUDE command to convert a 2D shape into a 3D solid model.

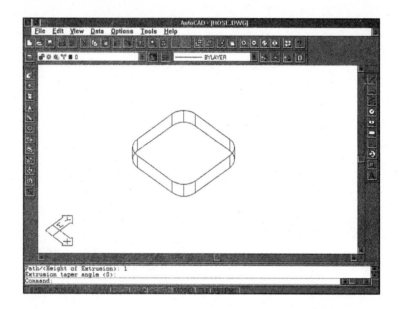

# Creating Solid Models with Solid Primitives

Solid primitives are the basic building blocks of every solid model. One method for creating primitive models is extruding or solidifying existing geometry.

AutoCAD offers several predefined solid primitives, such as a box, sphere, and wedge. They can be combined, subtracted, or intersected to create complex shapes. The subsequent models are highly accurate, with no interfering surfaces. Primitives are used to define the basic masses of the model. The model can be refined later with Boolean operations to create an accurate representation of your design.

## Solid Box

Two options are available to create a rectangular solid (or box). The base of the box is created parallel to the current User Coordinate System. You can access the Solid Box options by doing one of the following:

- Select Box on the Solids toolbar. This brings up a fly-out menu, containing the Center and Corner options.

- Enter **box** at the Command: prompt. AutoCAD responds with the following:

      Center/<Corner of Box><0,0,0>: *Select a corner of the*
            *box, or enter* c *to select the center point of the*
            *box.*

- The default option is to specify the box by the Corner. To change to the Center option, respond to the prompt with Center.

The two options for creating a solid box are corner and center. Both of these options are available as flyouts when selecting the Box button on the solids toolbar.

- *Box Corner Option.* By selecting the Box Corner option with either the toolbar or at the Command: prompt, you can create a box by selecting the opposite corners in the *x-y* plane and specifying a height. You can also enter negative values for the opposite corner and height as shown in figure 32.9.

- *Box Center Option.* You can also create a solid box by specifying the center point, one corner, and the height. Negative values for the opposite corner and height can also be used.

## Solid Cylinder

A solid cylinder can be created with either a circular or elliptical base. When defining the solid cylinder, the ends of the cylinder are parallel to the current UCS *x-y* plane as shown in figure 32.10.

You can create a solid cylinder by doing one of the following:

- Select the Cylinder button from the Solids toolbar. This invokes a fly-out menu, showing the Elliptical and Center buttons.

- Enter **cylinder** at the Command: prompt. AutoCAD responds with the following prompt:

      Elliptical/<center point> <0,0,0>: *Select a center*
            *point, or enter* e *to create an elliptical cylinder.*

**Tip**

To create a cylinder with one end larger than the other, use the EXTRUDE command described earlier in this chapter.

IX

Solid Modeling & Rendering

**Fig. 32.9**

A solid box can be created with the Corner option using positive or negative values.

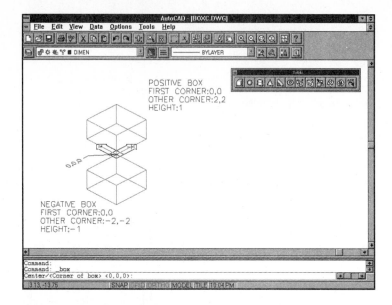

**Fig. 32.10**

Solid cylinders can contain circular or elliptical bases.

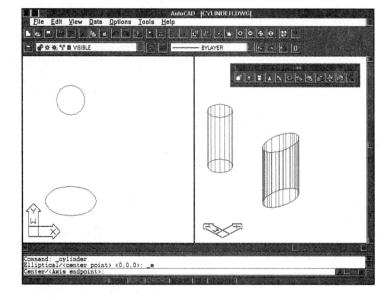

Now use one of the following options:

■ *Specify the Center Point.* This creates a solid cylinder by specifying the center point, radius or diameter, and height.

■ *Specify an Elliptical Cylinder.* This creates a solid ellipse. The top and bottom of the elliptical cylinder are always equal.

### Tutorial: Creating Holes and Cylinders

This tutorial will show you how to create cylinders that will later represent holes and cylindrical shapes on the hose connector solid model. This tutorial continues from the previous one in this chapter.

1. Create a cylinder to represent a hole and then make three copies. Select the Cylinder Center button from the Cylinder fly-out menu.

   ```
   Elliptical/<Center point> <0,0,0>: 1,4
   Diameter/<Radius>: .25
   Center of other end/<Height>: 1
   ```

   A cylinder is created (see fig. 32.11).

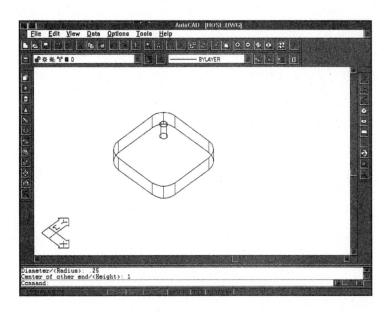

**Tip**

Solid cylinders can be used to bore holes in other solid objects with the SUBTRACT command.

**Fig. 32.11**
Use the CYLINDER command to create cylinders for later subtraction from the base.

2. Three more copies of the cylinder are needed to complete the base of the hose connector. Use the ARRAY command to make these copies. Select the Rectangular Array button from the Copy fly-out menu. The Copy button is located on the Modify floating toolbar.

   ```
   Select objects: Select the cylinder.
   Select objects:
   Rectangular or Polar array(R/P)<R>: _r
   Number of rows(---)<1>: 2
   Number of columns(┆┆┆)<1>: 2
   Unit cell or distance between rows(---): -3
   Distance between columns (┆┆┆): 3
   ```

   Three more cylinders are created (see fig. 32.12).

IX

Solid Modeling & Rendering

**Fig. 32.12**
Use the ARRAY command to create three additional cylinders for later subtraction from the base.

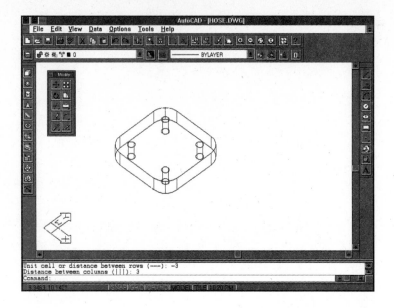

3. Create the hose fittings next. Select the Cylinder Center button. Enter the center location for the cylinder first, followed by the diameter and height.

```
Elliptical/<center point> <0,0,0>: 2.5,2.5,-3
Diameter/<Radius>: 1
Center of other end/<Height>: 7
```

A cylinder representing the hose fittings is created as shown in figure 32.13.

4. To complete the basic geometry for the hose connector, create a cylinder that will later be subtracted from the hose fittings to allow for material passage through the hose connector. Select the Cylinder Center button.

```
Command:
Elliptical/<Center point> <0,0,0>: 2.5,2.5,-3
Diameter/<Radius>: .75
Center of other end/<Height>: 7
```

A cylinder representing a hole through the hose connector is created as shown in figure 32.14. The next tutorial continues from here.

## Solid Wedge

A solid wedge is constructed with the bottom parallel to the current UCS with the slanted face sloping downward in the *x* direction. A variety of wedges is shown in figure 32.15. Wedges are useful for creating objects containing sloping surfaces. They can be combined using Boolean operators to create complex surfaces.

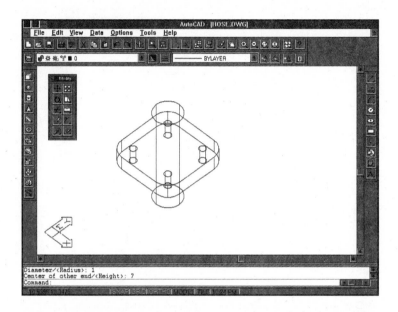

**Fig. 32.13**
Create a cylinder to represent the outside of the hose connector.

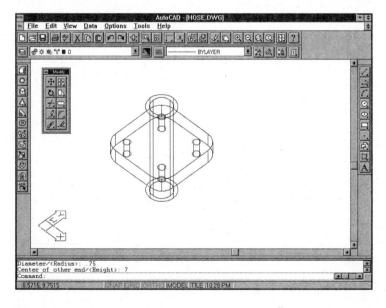

**Fig. 32.14**
Create a cylinder to represent the hole through the hose connector.

**IX**

Solid Modeling & Rendering

**Fig. 32.15**
You can create a
variety of solid
wedges which can
be combined to
create complex
surfaces.

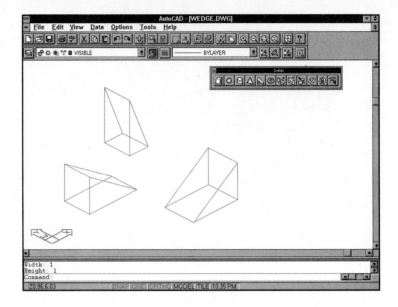

The WEDGE command can be accessed by performing one of the following:

 ■ Select the Wedge button on the Solids toolbar. This brings up a fly-out menu, showing the two wedge options—Center and Corner.

■ Enter **wedge** at the Command: prompt. AutoCAD responds with:

```
Center/<Corner of wedge><0,0,0>:Select a location for
    the corner of the wedge, or enter Center to
    select the center location for the wedge.
```

After entering the WEDGE command, either through the toolbar or the Command: prompt, you are given two options for creating a wedge. These options are to create a wedge by specifying the center point, or to specify a corner point.

 ■ *Specify the Center Point.* First, locate the center point of the wedge bottom. Next, locate the corner of the wedge and specify the height. The height will be parallel to the *z* axis, and can be positive or negative.

 ■ *Specify a Corner Point.* You are prompted for length, width, and height when creating the wedge. The length and width can be specified by entering coordinates or picking opposite corners of the base, similar to the method for specifying a solid box.

## Solid Cone

The cone primitive allows you to create circular or elliptical cones (see fig. 32.16). A solid cone is symmetrical and comes to a point along the z axis. The base of the cone is always parallel to the current UCS.

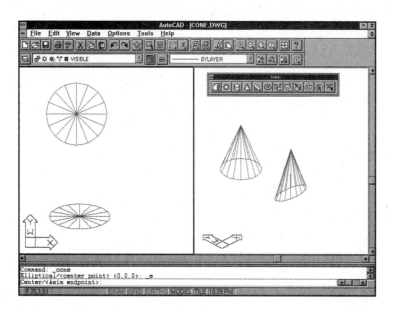

**Fig. 32.16**
Circular and elliptical cones can be created with AutoCAD.

Do one of the following to create a solid cone:

■ Select the Cone button from the Solids toolbar. This brings up a fly-out menu, showing the two option buttons for creating a cone—Elliptical and Center.

■ Enter **cone** at the Command: prompt. AutoCAD issues the following prompt:

```
Elliptical/<Center point><0,0,0>:Specify the center
    point of the cone, or enter E to create an
    elliptical cone.
```

After entering the CONE command through the toolbar or Command: prompt, you are given two options. You can specify the center point of the cone, or create an elliptical cone.

◄ See "Drawing Ellipses (EL-LIPSE)," p. 443

■ *Specify the Center Point.* The center point option prompts for the center of the cone, followed by the radius or diameter and height.

■ *Specify an Elliptical Cone.* The prompts for defining the base of an elliptical cone are the same as AutoCAD's ellipse command prompts.

**IX**

**Solid Modeling & Rendering**

## Solid Sphere

Spherical solid objects are round, as shown in figure 32.17. They are used for all round or partially round objects. Objects such as dishes, globes, balls, and domes all begin as spheres. To define a partial sphere such as a dome or dish, first define the sphere, then use other solids and Boolean operators to create the desired object.

**Fig. 32.17**
Solid spheres form the basis for other solid objects such as dishes, globes, or domes.

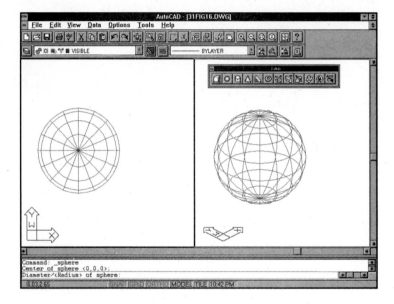

You can access the SPHERE command by:

■ Selecting the Sphere button on the Solids toolbar.

■ Entering **sphere** at the Command: prompt.

After entering the SPHERE command through the toolbar or Command: prompt, you are prompted for two pieces of information. To create a solid sphere, you must supply the sphere's center point and either a radius or diameter.

## Solid Torus

A torus is a cylindrical tube that joins back on itself. Classic examples of tori are a bicycle inner tube or a doughnut. The diameter or radius of a torus defines an imaginary circle running through the center of the torus' tube as shown in figure 32.18. The tube itself is defined by a radius or diameter.

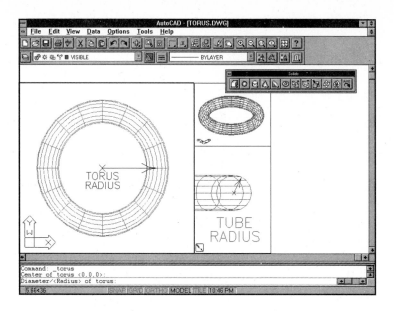

**Fig. 32.18**
To create a solid torus, you must define the torus radius and tube radius.

Access the TORUS command by:

- Selecting the Torus button on the Solids toolbar.

- Entering **torus** at the Command: prompt.

After entering the TORUS command through the toolbar or Command: prompt, you first have to specify a center point for the torus. Next specify the torus radius or diameter and the tube radius or diameter.

AutoCAD enables you to specify a torus with a tube radius greater than the torus radius. This allows you to create a torus with no hole in the middle. A wireframe/surface model torus drawn with the 3D command cannot have a tube radius greater than the torus radius

# Constructing Composite Solid Models

The first step in constructing a composite solid model is the creation of one or more primitives. The next step is to use the Boolean operators of union, subtract, or intersect to create a composite solid. The use of the Boolean operators is where the true power of the AutoCAD solid modeling lies.

By generating composites of solid primitives, you can create complex solid objects. These complex solids can be further composited with more

primitives or even other complex solids. Although Boolean operators are normally performed on two solids at a time, you can apply Boolean operators to multiple solids.

## Adding Solid Objects

The UNION command combines two or more intersecting solid objects to create one single complex solid (see fig. 32.19). The objects added together must be either primitive or composite solids. Although the solids do not have to intersect to be joined into one complex solid, you do not see any change in the objects if they are not actually touching. You can access the UNION command by:

**Fig. 32.19**
The union of a solid box and sphere, creating a complex solid.

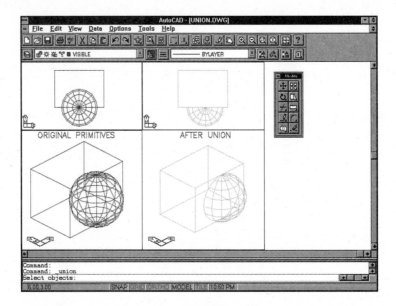

After entering the UNION command through the toolbar or Command: prompt, you are prompted to select objects. Select the solid objects to union. Any intersecting volume is eliminated. The resulting composite solid includes the volume enclosed by all of the selected solids. The union of two or more solids is frequently used to build complex shapes needed in most design work.

■ Selecting the Union button. The Union button is located on the fly-out menu that appears when you select the Explode button. The Explode button, located on the Modify toolbar, activates the flyout button containing Union. This is shown in figure 32.20.

■ Entering **union** at the Command: prompt.

**Fig. 32.20**
The Union button
is located on the
Explode fly-out
menu.

### Tutorial: Using the UNION Command to Add Solids

In this tutorial, you will use the UNION command to make the base plate
and the hose fitting one object. Presently, they are two separate objects, an
extruded polygon and a cylinder. This tutorial is continued from the previous
one in this chapter.

1. Select the Union button from the Explode fly-out menu. The Explode
   button is located on the Modify toolbar.

   > Select objects: *Select the extruded polygon and the
   > cylinder as shown in figure 32.21. The order of
   > selection is not important.*

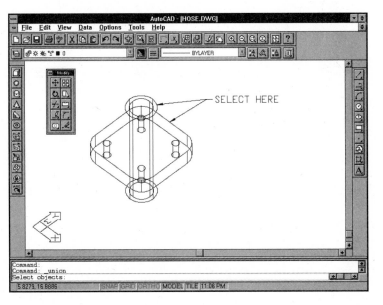

**Fig. 32.21**
Selecting the
extruded polygon
and the cylinder
to be unioned.

   > Select objects:

2. After selecting the objects and pressing Enter, AutoCAD computes the
   new complex solid. The database is updated and the object in figure
   32.22 is created.

**IX**

Solid Modeling & Rendering

3. To get a better idea of what your object looks like, perform a Shade or Hide on the object. These commands are available on the Render toolbar. After issuing the SHADE or HIDE commands, remember to REGEN the screen. The next tutorial will continue from here.

**Fig. 32.22**
Viewing the hose connector after the base plate and the hose fittings have been unioned.

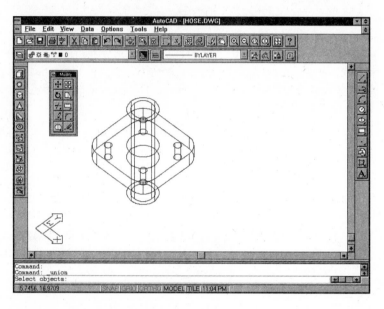

## Subtracting Solid Objects

◄ See "Making the 3D View More Realistic," p. 781

Subtracting two solid objects involves two selections. The first selection is used to define the primary or *source* object. The second selection defines the object that is subtracted from the first. The intersecting volume between the solids is replaced with a void (see fig. 32.23). Subtracting does not create one complex solid out of the selected solids the way UNION does. Like the UNION command, the selected solids do not have to intersect. But unlike UNION, if there is no intersection, nothing happens when you run SUBTRACT. You can access the SUBTRACT command by:

■ Selecting the Explode button, which brings up a fly-out menu containing Subtract. The Explode button is located on the Modify toolbar.

■ Entering **subtract** at the Command: prompt.

Two intersecting solid objects are selected, with the intersecting volume removed from the first selected object. Subtracting two solid objects can be used to bore holes, create grooves, or any other creative uses in which the volume of one solid is subtracted from another.

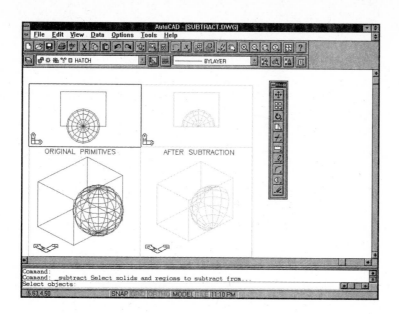

**Fig. 32.23**
Subtracting solid
objects results in a
void where the
two objects
intersected.

## Tutorial: Subtracting Cylinders to Create Holes

In this tutorial you will use the SUBTRACT command to subtract all the cylinders that represent holes in the Hose Connector drawing. Although the cylinders appear as holes, they are still solid material and must be subtracted before they will appear and be calculated as holes.

1. Continue from the previous tutorial. To select the cylinders for subtraction without interference from the other objects that comprise the hose connector, it will be necessary to change the viewpoint orientation.

   ```
   Command: vpoint
   Rotate/<View point> <0.0000,0.0000,1.0000>: .6964,
       -.1228,.7071
   ```

   The vpoint orientation changes are shown in figure 32.24.

2. Next, enter the SUBTRACT command and select the base plate. Select Subtract from the Explode fly-out menu.

   ```
   Select solids and regions to subtract from...
   Select objects: Select the base plate as shown in
       figure 32.25. Be careful not to select any cylin-
       drical object. Order of selection is important
       for this step. After selecting the base plate,
       the base plate and the exterior of the hose
       fitting is selected and highlighted. AutoCAD will
       respond 1 found.
   Select objects: Press Enter to terminate the selection
       of solids to extract from.
   ```

**3.** At this point you are still in the SUBTRACT command. You selected one solid from which to subtract, which contained the base plate and exterior of the hose fitting. Next, select the objects to subtract from them.

**Fig. 32.24**

Change the viewpoint orientation to allow for easier selection of cylindrical objects.

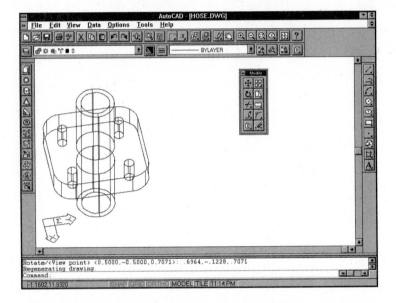

**Fig. 32.25**

Selecting the base plate as the source object for subtraction.

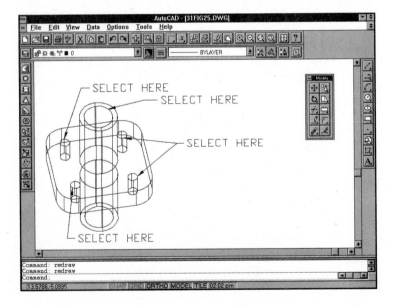

```
Select solids and regions to subtract...
Select objects: Select the cylinders as shown in
      figure 32.26.
Select objects:
```

AutoCAD computes the new solid. The database is updated and the object shows no apparent change. The only visual verification is the return of the Command: prompt.

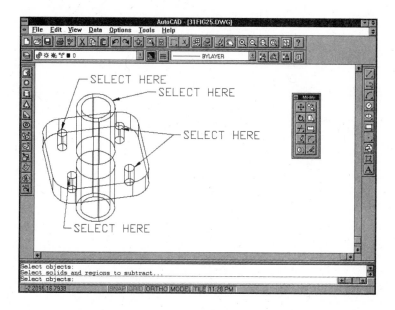

**Fig. 32.26**
Select the cylinders (that represent holes) to be subtracted from the base plate.

4. To check the model, perform a Shade or Hide. Make sure you regenerate the screen after performing the shade or hide commands. The next tutorial continues from here.

**IX**

**Solid Modeling & Rendering**

### Note

To make object selection easier and to create an object that can visibly change when you subtract, you can draw the solid primitives longer or larger than necessary. For example, in the preceding tutorial, you can draw the four cylinders with a height longer than the base plate is thick. That makes the cylinders stick out from the top or bottom of the base plate. When you perform the subtraction, you can easily use the bits of the cylinders that stuck out as selection points and you know when the subtraction is complete because the extra bits disappear. You should note, however, that AutoCAD knows that the full primitive existed before subtraction and stores that information in the drawing database.

## Intersecting Solid Objects

The Intersection option creates a new solid out of the intersecting volume of two or more selected solids. All of the selected solids must have a common intersecting area (see fig. 32.27). A new solid is created, using only the intersecting volume of the selected solids. You can access the INTERSECTION command by:

- Selecting the Intersection button on the Explode fly-out menu. The Explode button is located on the Modify toolbar.

- Entering **intersect** at the Command: prompt.

**Fig. 32.27**

Only the intersecting volume of the selected solids remain when using the intersection option.

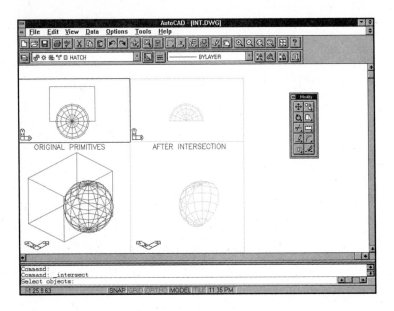

After accessing the INTERSECTION command through the toolbar or Command: prompt, select the two intersecting solids. Only the intersecting or common volume of the selected solids remain.

You can intersect solids that do not actually have an intersecting area. The result is a null space which AutoCAD notes in the command line and deletes. The net effect of intersecting solids that do not share a common area is that the solids and the resulting null area are all erased.

# Editing Solid Models

The ease of editing solid models makes working with solids an attractive alternative to surface modeling. Even if you do not need the analysis capabilities of solids, basic editing such as filleting or chamfering edges is easily accomplished on the solid model.

AutoCAD Release 13 allows for accurate and simple filleting and chamfering of 3D solids.

**RELEASE**

## Filleting Solids

To fillet the edge of a solid, pick the target edges and supply the fillet dimension. Figure 32.28 shows a solid box which has fillets across the edges. You can access the FILLET command by:

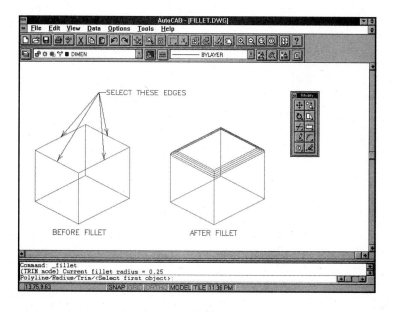

**Fig. 32.28**
The FILLET command allows you to fillet multiple edges in one command.

- Selecting the Fillet button on the Features fly-out menu. The Feature button is located on the Modify toolbar.

- Entering **fillet** at the Command: prompt.

Using the FILLET command on a solid model uses the same commands and prompts as if you are creating a 2D fillet.

◀ See "Filleting
Objects
(FILLET),"
p. 278

### Tutorial: Using the FILLET Command on a Solid Model

In this tutorial, you will use the FILLET command to create a solid fillet between the base plate and the hose fittings.

1. Continue from the previous tutorial. If you shaded or removed the hidden lines in the previous tutorial, make sure you regenerate your drawing before proceeding.

2. Select the Fillet button on the Features fly-out menu and select the first object.

   ```
   (TRIM mode) Current fillet radius = 1.000
   Polyline/Radius/Trim/<Select first object>: Select the
         top edge of the hose fitting as shown in figure
         32.28.
   Chain/Radius/<Select edge>:
   Enter radius <1.000>: .25
   Chain/Radius/<Select edge>: Select the bottom edge of
         the hose fitting as shown in figure 32.29.
   Chain/Radius/<Select edge>:
   ```

3. After selecting the edges and pressing Enter, AutoCAD computes the new solid. This process takes a few seconds and isn't instantaneous. The database is updated and a fillet is created (see fig. 32.30).

**Fig. 32.29**

You can use the FILLET command to create a solid fillet between the base and outside cylinder of the hose clamp.

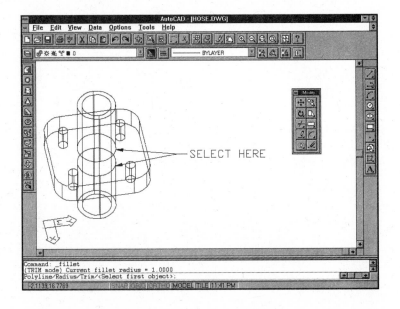

4. To check the model, perform a Shade or Hide. Make sure you regenerate the screen after performing the shade or hide commands. The next tutorial continues from here.

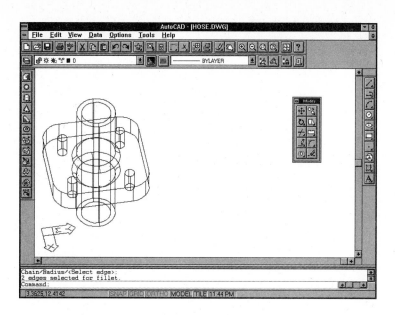

**Fig. 32.30**
Creating a fillet
between the base
plate and the hose
fittings.

## Chamfering Solids

The CHAMFER command allows you to chamfer selected edges of an existing solid. You can supply different dimensions along each direction of the chamfer (see fig. 32.31). You can access the CHAMFER command by:

- Selecting the Chamfer button on the Features fly-out menu. The Feature button is located on the Modify toolbar.

- Entering **chamfer** at the Command: prompt.

As with the FILLET command, using the CHAMFER command on a solid model uses the same commands and prompts as if you are creating a 2D chamfer.

### Tutorial: Using the CHAMFER Command on a Solid Model

You will finish the geometry creation of the hose connector by creating a chamfer on the end of the top and bottom hose fittings. This chamfer allows a hose to be easily connected to the top and bottom of the hose connector.

◄ See "Chamfering Objects (CHAMFER)," p. 282

1. Continue from the previous tutorial. Make sure you regenerated your drawing before proceeding if you shaded or removed the hidden lines in the previous tutorial.

2. Select the Chamfer button on the Features fly-out menu and select the top surface on the hose clamp.

**Fig. 32.31**

The CHAMFER command can be used to apply chamfers to a solid model.

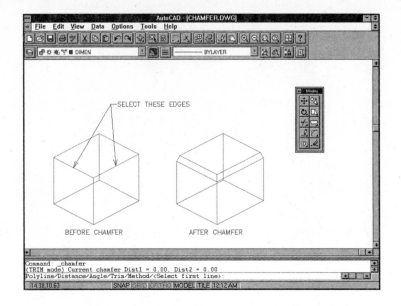

```
(TRIM mode) Current chamfer Dist1 = 0.0000, Dist2 =
    0.0000
Polyline/Distance/Angle/Trim/Method/<Select first
    line>: Select the surface as shown in figure
    32.31.
Select base surface:
Next/<OK>:
Enter base surface distance: .2
Enter other surface distance: .2
Loop/<Select edge>: Select the same location as shown
    in figure 32.32.
Loop/<Select edge>:
```

3. After completing the chamfer, AutoCAD calculates the new solid. This process takes a few seconds. The database is updated and a chamfer is created along the top of the hose fittings. Next, re-enter the CHAMFER command and chamfer the bottom surface on the hose clamp.

```
Command:
(TRIM mode) Current chamfer Dist1 = 0.2000, Dist2 =
    0.2000
Polyline/Distance/Angle/Trim/Method/<Select first
    line>: Select the surface as shown in figure
    32.32.
Select base surface:
Next/<OK>:
Enter base surface distance <0.2000>:
Enter other surface distance <0.2000>:
Loop/<Select edge>: Select the same location as shown
    in figure 32.33.
Loop/<Select edge>:
```

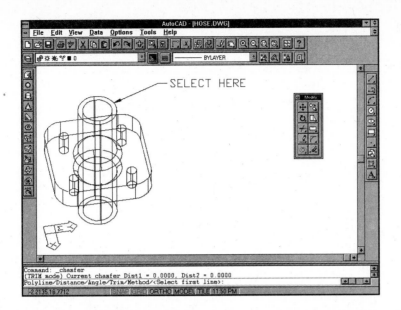

**Fig. 32.32**
Select the top
surface and edge
for the CHAMFER
command.

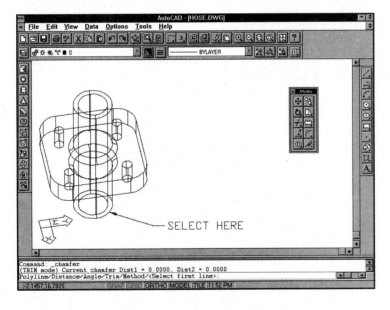

**Fig. 32.33**
Select the bottom
surface and edge
for the CHAMFER
command.

**IX**

Solid Modeling & Rendering

4. After completing the final chamfer, AutoCAD calculates the new solid. This process is not instantaneous, it takes a few seconds. After the database is updated, a chamfer is created along the bottom of the hose fittings. The geometry is now complete as shown in figure 32.34.

**Fig. 32.34**
The completed
geometry of the
hose connector.

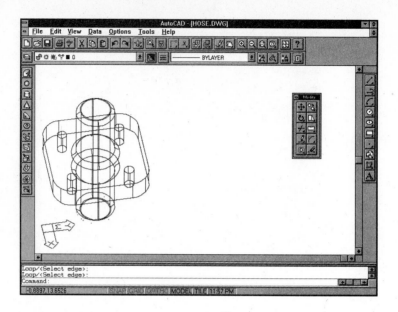

## Viewing Solid Models

◀ See "Removing
Hidden Lines
(HIDE)," p. 781

Solid models can be viewed with the HIDE or SHADE command without any
modification. For more information on the HIDE and SHADE commands, see
Chapter 30, "Viewing a 3D Model."

◀ See "Shading
the Object
(SHADE),"
p. 782

**Tutorial: Using the SHADE and HIDE Commands to View a Solid Model**
This final tutorial shows you how to use the SHADE and HIDE commands to
view the solid model of the hose connector. This tutorial continues from the
previous one in this chapter.

1. First, use the HIDE command to remove the hidden lines from the hose
   connector. Do this by selecting the Hide button from the Render
   toolbar.

   The hose connector hides the hidden lines (see fig. 32.35). Notice that
   it is easier to visualize the object when viewed this way.

2. Next, use the SHADE command on the solid model. Select the Shade
   button from the Render toolbar.

   The hose connector is shaded as shown in figure 32.36.

You have now completed the solid model of the hose connector.

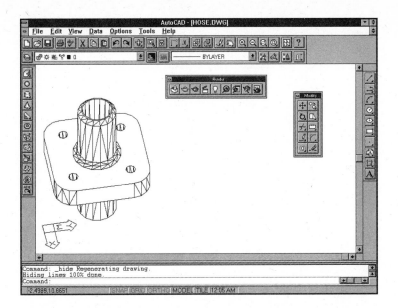

**Fig. 32.35**
Use the HIDE
command to
remove hidden
lines on the solid
model of the hose
connector.

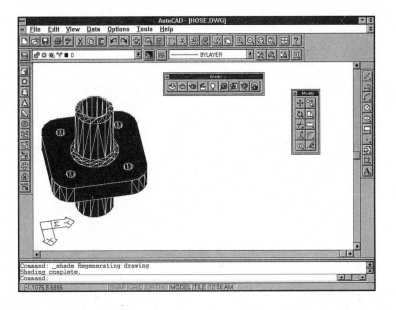

**Fig. 32.36**
Use the SHADE
command to
shade the solid
model of the hose
connector.

**IX**

**Solid Modeling & Rendering**

# From Here...

Solid modeling has long been one of the best methods for creating three-
dimensional objects. Initial problems with solid modeling were inadequate
hardware and expensive software. Solid modeling requires the computer
to perform many mathematical calculations when creating the model.

Until recently, personal computers did not have the necessary power to efficiently perform solid modeling. With solid modeling now an integral part of AutoCAD, it is possible to efficiently and effectively create three-dimensional solid models on the desktop.

Solid modeling in AutoCAD is an excellent method for creating three-dimensional objects. Both wireframe and surface models can create nonsense objects that would be impossible to manufacture. With solid models, it is much easier to pinpoint design flaws due to the ability to create interference-free models. Solid models are well-suited to mechanical design when analysis and interference checking are important.

Creating and editing a solid model is generally easier than creating a wireframe or surface model. A solid can be constructed from existing 2D geometry, or assembled from primitives. Solid models are an excellent way to create complex three-dimensional geometry.

For more information about making your solid model appear more realistic, creating 2D views from a solid, and generating various reports on a solid model, see the following chapters:

- Chapter 33, "Working with Solid Models," explains the method for constructing 2D views and generating mass reports from a solid model.

- Chapter 34, "Understanding Rendering Concepts," shows you how to apply lights and textures to your completed solid model to make it appear more realistic.

# On Your Own

Using the solid modeling tools introduced in this chapter, create a solid model of the object found in figure 32.37.

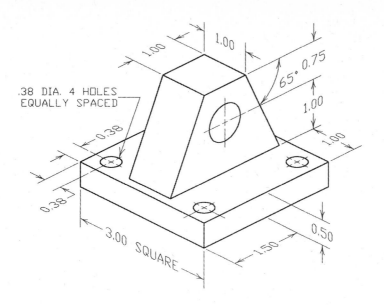

**Fig. 32.37**
Using the different solid modeling commands introduced in this chapter, create the object.

Hints:

**1.** Use both primitives and extruded 2D polygons.

**2.** Try using layers and different colors for the polygons and primitives.

**3.** When you complete the model, be sure to use both the HIDE and SHADE commands to view your model.

# Chapter 33
# Working with Solid Models

When a solid model is created, you have a complete representation of a physical object. AutoCAD Release 13 uses boundary representation of a solid using the new ACIS modeling technology. Release 12 users will note that AutoCAD Release 13 has taken away many of the inherent analysis commands, such as the materials definition. Not to worry, with the addition of the AutoSURF and Designer add-on modules, you can generate 2D orthographic and auxiliary projections from the 3D model, as well as analyze solids more efficiently than ever before. Alone, AutoCAD allows you to create temporary profile views using the HIDE or SHADE commands.

In this chapter, you learn how to:

- Calculate mass properties of a solid model

- Construct a 2D view from a solid model

- Construct a sectioned profile from a solid model

◀ See "Removing Hidden Lines (HIDE)," p. 781

◀ See "Shading the Object (SHADE)," p. 782

◀ See "Viewing a 3D Model," p. 865

Normally, there are several phases in the development cycle of a product. Typically, a part starts with an idea. The part is first designed and modeled conceptually. An engineering analysis is performed on the part to check for failure under load conditions. Based on the analysis, recommendations are made for modification. This information is sent to the drafting department where the drawing is created. The completed drawings are then sent to manufacturing.

In the past, design, analysis, drafting, and manufacturing were all separate departments. The designer, drafter, and manufacturer did not work off of a common database. Each department re-created the geometry for its own specific application.

IX

Solid Modeling & Rendering

Today, this is beginning to change. The manufacturing industry is moving toward integration, with the different departments working off a common database. This avoids duplication of work and promotes more departmental interaction during the product development cycle.

Solid modeling is a quick and efficient way of building a 3D model that can be used for engineering analysis, manufacturing, and drafting. The ability to use solid models for different applications is why solid models are the most efficient and popular computer models.

AutoCAD uses solid models very effectively in Release 13. In Releases 11 and 12, solid modeling was provided by AME (Advanced Modeling Extension). AME was an add-on package that had to be purchased separately from Autodesk. Solid modeling is now included and part of the core code in Release 13. Not only is it in the core code, it also uses the ACIS solid modeling engine. The inclusion of the ACIS engine allows AutoCAD to create more accurate and usable solid models than in previous releases of AutoCAD. AutoCAD can now import and export ACIS solid models, which is a major asset to mechanical engineering firms using other CAD/CAM systems that also use ACIS technology. By connecting the ACIS engine and Designer, an Autodesk parametric dimensioning package, mechanical engineers and draftsmen now have a very powerful design and engineering tool.

# Generating Mass Property Reports

After a model is created, you can obtain information about its physical properties using the MASSPROP command.

## Generating Mass Properties (MASSPROP)

The mass properties can be displayed or calculated on a selected solid using the MASSPROP command. The following commands can be used to calculate the mass properties of a solid:

- Select Mass Properties from the List fly-out toolbar menu.

- Enter **massprop** at the Command: prompt. This brings up a text screen that shows the mass properties of the solid.

AutoCAD calculates the mass properties of a solid using algorithms from the ACIS modeling engine. The mass properties for a solid cube are shown in figure 33.1.

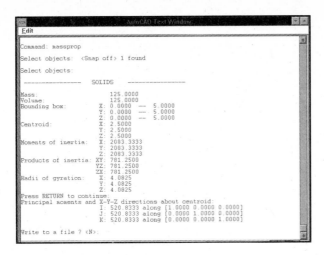

**Fig. 33.1**
Mass properties
displayed for a
solid cube.

The information provided by the mass calculations can be used by third-party applications to analyze the structural, thermal, and kinetic characteristics of the solid model. After calculating the mass properties, you can save the information to a file by answering Y at the `Write to a file?<N>:` prompt at the end of the mass properties calculations.

The following information is provided when you calculate the mass properties of a solid:

- Mass

- Volume

- Bounding box

- Centroid

- Moments of inertia

- Products of inertia

- Radii of gyration

- Principal moments and X, Y, Z directions about a centroid

**Tip**
MASSPROP also
can be used to find
the properties of
regions.

### Tutorial: Calculating the Mass Properties of the Hose Connector Model

In this tutorial, you'll calculate the mass properties of the hose connector model.

**IX**

**Solid Modeling & Rendering**

**Fig. 33.2**
The finished hose
connector model.

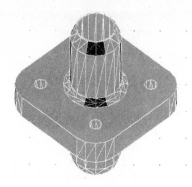

 **1.** Select Open from the Standard toolbar.

The Select File dialog box appears. In the File Name text box, type
**C:\UAW13\33DWG01** and press Enter or click the OK button.
When the file is loaded, your screen should resemble figure 33.2.

**2.** Select Mass Properties from the List fly-out toolbar menu.

```
Select objects: Select the hose connector model.
Select objects: Press Enter.
```

The text screen appears showing the mass properties (see fig. 33.3). Use the
scroll bar to move through the calculations. When you're through looking at
the mass properties for the hose connector, choose No when prompted to
**save** as a file and click the OK button.

**Fig. 33.3**
Viewing the mass
properties of the
hose connector
model.

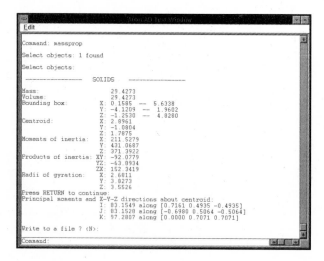

# Creating 2D Views, Profiles, and Sections from a Solid

One of the main advantages of creating 3D models to a drafter, engineer, or architect is obtaining complex 2D views, profiles, and sections. Creating these views often means the user has to have a firm foundation in orthographic projection and 3D projection theory. Using a 3D solid model, the user needs to choose the view he wants and then create the view using the VPOINT command.

◀ See "Changing the Viewpoint (DDVPOINT)," p. 780

## Tutorial: Constructing a 2D View and Profile of a Solid

As you found in Chapter 30, "Viewing a 3D Model," it's very easy to obtain a needed view of a model. This view can then be used to determine the usability of the solid model and the fit between two or more parts. To construct a 2D view of a solid, use the commands in Chapter 30, as well as the HIDE command. For example, to construct the front view of the hose connector that was created in Chapter 32, "Introduction to Solid Modeling Concepts," follow these steps:

1. Choose 3D Viewpoint, Rotate from the View menu.

2. Make changes to the Viewpoint Presets dialog box, as shown in figure 33.4.

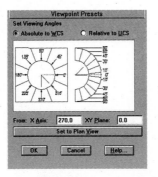

**Fig. 33.4**
Set the Viewpoint Presets dialog box to obtain the front view of the hose connector.

**IX**

**Solid Modeling & Rendering**

3. Select Hide from the Render toolbar.

   After these commands are executed, you should have a view similar to figure 33.5.

4. Be sure not to close this file. It will be used in the next tutorial.

**Fig. 33.5**
View the hose
connector after
executing the
HIDE command.

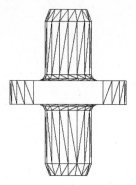

◀ See "Under-
standing Model
Space and
Paper Space,"
p. 369

When these steps are used in conjunction with model/paper space, you can obtain hardcopy views of the solid (see fig. 33.6).

**Fig. 33.6**
Obtain multiple
views of the hose
connector model
using paper space/
model space.

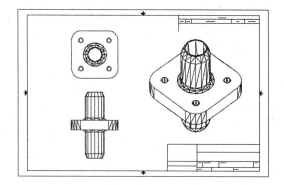

If you desire a more detailed view or representation of a solid model, consider adding Designer to your software library. With Designer, you can obtain any view and then have it dimensioned to your specifications. Designer is a parametric dimensioning package that allows you to change the size of a feature by changing the value in the dimension. If you need these functions and want to exploit the full use of solid models, consider an investment in Designer.

**Note**

The HIDE command is not the only command that allows you to view the profile of a solid model. You also can use the SHADE command. The SHADE command gives a more realistic view of the object (see fig. 33.7).

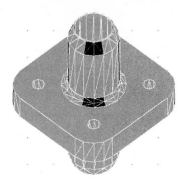

**Fig. 33.7**
Use SHADE to obtain a profile view of the hose connector model.

## Constructing a Sectioned Profile of a Solid (SECTION)

Because the solid model creates a complete description of the object, you can cut through any portion of it to create a section view. Section views are very handy in determining the inside features of an object that do not appear from the outside of the model. The SECTION command cuts through the object at a defined plane. That plane is the plane that best shows the description of the interior features you wish to show. You can access the SECTION command using one of the following methods:

- Select Section from the Solids toolbar.

- Type **section** at the Command: prompt. This displays the prompt options.

The following command sequence is used to create a sectional view of a solid:

Select Section from the Solids toolbar.

```
Select objects: Pick the model you want to section.
Select objects:
Section plane by Object/Zaxis/View/XY/YZ/ZX/<3points>: xy
Point on XY plane <0,0,0>:
```

A region is created on the current layer that is an outline of the section from the chosen plane. The region that's created is placed at the location of the defined plane. You can use the MOVE command to move the section off the model for later use. After you move the sectioned region, use the BHATCH command to place a hatch within the section boundary.

◀ See "Filling Areas with Hatching," p. 487

The section command doesn't have to be used to create sections only. You also can use this command to create a profile from a solid that can be used to assist in the creation of orthographic views of a model for later dimensioning. To do this, be sure the section plane is placed on the profile of the model.

IX

Solid Modeling & Rendering

◀ See "Hide and Clip," p. 873

You also can create a section by using the Hide and Clip options of the DVIEW command. Although these options also provide a section, remember these are only views; as such, they can't be hatched or used to create working drawings.

### Tutorial: Using the SECTION Command to Create a Section View of the Hose Connector Model

In this tutorial, you'll use the SECTION command to create a section view of the hose connector model.

1. Continue from the previous exercise.

2. Create a new layer called Section and make it the current layer.

3. Create a section view of the hose connector model.

4. Select Section from the Solids toolbar.

```
Select objects: Select the hose connector model.
Select objects:
Sectioning plane by Entity/Last/Zaxis/View/XY/YZ/ZX/
     <3points>:
```

5. Use the MID object snap to pick the three points shown in figure 33.8. AutoCAD creates the section view and places it within the model.

**Fig. 33.8**
Pick three points to define the sectioning plane.

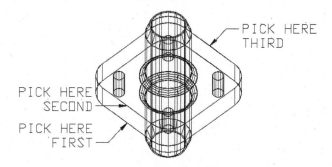

PICK HERE THIRD

PICK HERE SECOND

PICK HERE FIRST

6. Use the MOVE command to place the section view away from the model (see fig. 33.9). Select Zoom All if necessary.

7. When moved, the section view is incomplete. Complete the view and add hatching, as shown in figure 33.10.

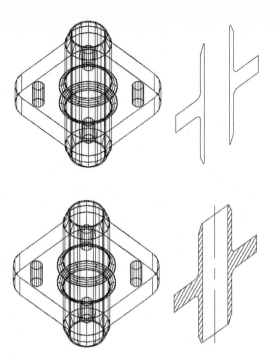

**Fig. 33.9**
Move the section
view away from
the hose connec-
tor model.

**Fig. 33.10**
Completed
section of the
hose connec-
tor model.

# From Here...

The power of solid modeling lies not only in the creation of the geometry, but in what can be done with the completed model. A variety of materials can be assigned to the model and then analyzed. AutoCAD has several materials built in, and you can add more from outside sources or define your own. AutoCAD then calculates mass properties of the solid, directly related to its material.

Two-dimensional views also can be constructed from the solid model. You can create a sectioned or an image profile of the solid. Used with the model and paper space capabilities of AutoCAD, a complete 2D orthographic drawing can be created from the solid.

For more information about exchanging information with other applications and ACIS technology, see the following chapters:

■ Chapter 36, "Exchanging Data with Windows Applications," shows you how to import mass properties data into other Windows Applications, such as spreadsheets and word processors.

**IX**

**Solid Modeling & Rendering**

■ Appendix A, "New Features in AutoCAD Release 13 for Windows," explains new features and gives details about ACIS technology.

# On Your Own

Using the hose connector model, re-create figure 33.6 and plot to your hardcopy device.

Hints:

**1.** Use model space and paper space.

**2.** Use MVSETUP to create a B size border.

**3.** Use a scale factor of .6217 for the front and top views.

**4.** Use a scale factor of 1 for the isometric view.

**5.** Add an additional view showing the section of the hose connector.

# Chapter 34

# Understanding Rendering Concepts

Often you may want to see a realistic picture of what your design will actually look like when it is complete. A wireframe, surface, or solid model created in AutoCAD does not show any depth, shadows, shading, or reflection; however, creating a rendered image gives you a chance to preview alternate designs without having to build a prototype. In this chapter, you will load a sample 3D model and accomplish the following objectives:

- Understand rendering concepts

- Create different views of a 3D model

- Create a one-point and two-point perspective view of the 3D model

- Use lights in the 3D model

- Create a scene with the 3D model

- Apply a material to the 3D model

- Save and display a rendered image

## Understanding Rendering Techniques

The AutoCAD SHADE command produced a shaded picture of the 3D model in the current viewport. Although the shaded image could be used to check the accuracy of 3D models, it did have several limitations. The shaded image was pixel-based and could not be plotted. The shaded model had one light source located directly behind the viewer's position and could not be altered.

◀ See "Introduction to 3D Modeling," p. 759

Creating more realistic renderings of a 3D model than SHADE can produce is very easy with AutoCAD. By selecting Render from the Render toolbar and using the default settings in the Render dialog box, you can obtain a much more realistic picture of a 3D model than with the SHADE command.

> **Note**
>
> Before you can render, you must first have your rendering device configured. For more information on configuring your rendering device, see the AutoCAD installation guide.

The LIGHT command gives you complete control over lighting your 3D model. You can place point, distant, or direct lights on your model. The different light sources also can be adjusted for intensity.

You also can create scenes with a named view with any number of lights. The final rendered scene image can be saved in a variety of file formats. RENDER also allows you to devise and assign different materials to your model.

# Rendering Terms and Definitions

With the rendering capabilities of AutoCAD, you can work with surface textures, lights, and shading. When creating a photo-realistic rendering, AutoCAD assumes different roles. You must understand what lights, materials, and scenes are, and why they are important. This section discusses the type, color, and intensity of lighting and its effect on 3D model surfaces. Additionally, the creation and use of textures and scene creation are covered.

The majority of render commands are available in the Render toolbar as shown in figure 34.1.

**Fig. 34.1**
The Render toolbar contains the majority of the render commands.

## Views

Before creating a rendering, you must define the correct view of the 3D model. Selecting the proper 3D view is important when creating the 3D model and essential in rendering. The view is combined with lights to make a scene. The scene is then rendered to create the final image.

Several of AutoCAD's commands can be used to create an appropriate view. The two most common commands are DVIEW and VPOINT. The VPOINT command allows you to select the proper viewpoint and view angle of the 3D model. This can be done by entering data from the keyboard or selecting a point on the compass and axes tripod. Alternatively, you can use the DDVPOINT command to access the Viewpoint Presets dialog box and set the view.

◄ See "Changing the Viewpoint (VPOINT)," p. 767

Although both the VPOINT and DDVPOINT commands allow you to create a view of the entire drawing, you cannot create a perspective view using either command.

The DVIEW command allows you to create 3D parallel projection or perspective views dynamically. After selecting objects in the drawing, you can enter camera and target points and preview the image of the selected objects on the screen.

◄ See "Dynamically Changing the Viewpoint (DVIEW)," p. 865

Perspective views are created by selecting the Distance option when using the DVIEW command.

## Lights

Placing lights into a scene affects the object's colors and can cast shadows. You can combine any number of lights within a view to create a scene to render. Additionally, you can increase or decrease the intensities of the lights, and turn the lights on or off.

AutoCAD uses four different types of lights: ambient light, point lights, distant lights, and spotlights. To access the Lights dialog box, follow these steps:

**Tip**

After you have created a good view of the object, save it with the DDVIEW command. Later you can restore, rename, or delete the view in any viewport.

1. Select the Lights button on the Render toolbar.

2. Type **light** at the Command: prompt.

The Lights dialog box, as shown in figure 34.2, allows you to perform several modifications to a light.

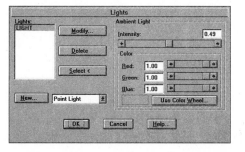

**Fig. 34.2**
In the Lights dialog box, you can perform several modifications to new and existing lights.

### Ambient Light

*Ambient light* is like natural light. It has the same intensity everywhere, with all faces receiving the same amount of light. Ambient light cannot create highlights on objects. The intensity can be changed with the slider bar shown in figure 34.2. The intensity can range from 1 (full intensity) to 0 (off). You cannot concentrate an ambient light in one area.

Ambient light can be compared to light found at twilight, or just before the sun rises. If you only have ambient light present in your scene, rendered objects can appear as solid, flat silhouettes.

In summary, ambient light is the overall lighting of AutoCAD surfaces. Because each surface is illuminated with the same amount of light, you could not determine two adjoining faces of a box if this was the only light on your model. And because the ambient light has no source, it is the most unrealistic type of light. You do not need to insert an ambient light into the model because it is always present, unless you turned it off by setting its intensity to 0.

### Distant Light

A *distant light* is a directional light source with parallel rays. The intensity of distant light can be changed, with the intensity remaining the same on all objects. Depending upon its location, it strikes all objects in the scene on the same side. A distant light is useful to light a backdrop uniformly in a scene.

A distant light can be compared to the sun. To create a distant light, select Lights from the Render toolbar. The Lights dialog box appears (see fig. 34.3). Select Distant Light from the pop-up menu and then select New. This brings up the New Distant Light dialog box.

**Fig. 34.3**
The Lights dialog box allows you to select three different types of lights.

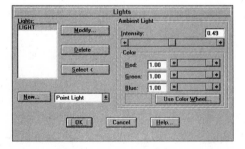

In the Light <u>N</u>ame text box, you must give the new distant light a name. The name must be unique, with eight characters or less. You can change the intensity of the light by adjusting the Intensity slider bar.

The Position area of the New Distant Light dialog box allows you to change the location of the distant light using Azimuth and Altitude settings or by specifying the Light Source Vector. If the Light Source Vector option is used, the Azimuth and Altitude are automatically updated.

---

**Note**

The location of a distant light is not critical in terms of its distance from the object in the scene. To avoid confusion in your scene, position your distant lights near the edge of the drawing extents. The direction the light points is critical; make sure that it is pointing at the model.

---

The color of any light can be changed directly in the Lights dialog box or you can use the Color dialog box by selecting the Use Color <u>W</u>heel button. Here you can modify the color of the light. The colors displayed in this dialog box depend upon your video card and screen resolution. The Color dialog box is displayed in figure 34.4.

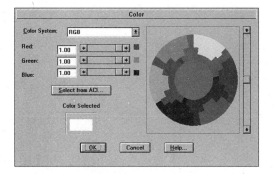

**Fig. 34.4**
The Color dialog box allows you to change the color of a light.

In summary, distant light is inserted with a target point and light location. These points determine the direction of the parallel beams of light, which extend to eternity. Its light intensity does not change over distance.

### Point Light

A *point light* is similar to a light bulb. Its intensity falls off over distance, and it shines out in all directions. Because the intensity of a point light weakens over distances, surfaces further from the light source appear darker than surfaces closer to the light source. You can use point lights to create a variety of lighting effects.

To create a point light, select Lights from the Render toolbar. The Lights dialog box appears as shown in figure 34.2. Select Point Light from the pop-up menu and then select New. This brings up the New Point Light dialog box (see fig. 34.5).

**Fig. 34.5**
With the New Point Light dialog box, you can define a point light.

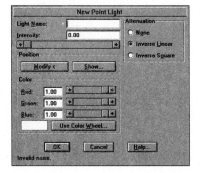

Defining a new point light is very similar to defining a new distant light. You must name the light; you can adjust its location and color. When prompted for location, however, you are only prompted to enter the light location. Because the point light shines in all directions like a light bulb, you do not need to specify a target. The attenuation of the light also can be adjusted. Changing the attenuation controls how the light diminishes over a certain distance.

In summary, a point light is inserted at a location you specify. You do not need a direction vector because this light shines in all directions. Surfaces close to the light appear brighter than surfaces at a distance.

### Spotlight

A *spotlight* has a directional cone of light. When specifying a spotlight, you can set the target and distance in addition to the dimensions of the cone, as shown in figure 34.6.

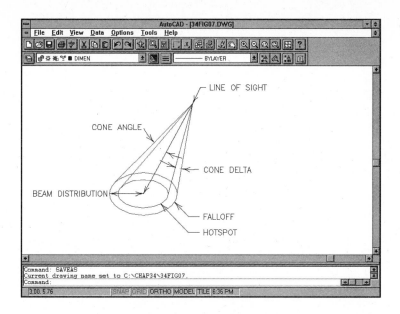

**Fig. 34.6**
The parts of a
spotlight cone.

To create a spotlight, select Lights from the Render toolbar. The Lights dialog
box appears (refer to fig. 34.2). Select Spotlight from the pop-up menu and
then select <u>N</u>ew. This brings up the New Spotlight dialog box shown in
figure 34.7.

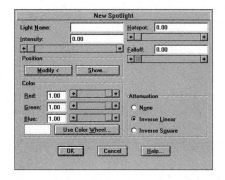

**Fig. 34.7**
The New Spotlight
dialog box is used
to define a new
spotlight.

Defining a new spotlight is similar to defining a new distant light. You must
name the light; you can adjust its location and color.

A spotlight consists of an inner cone and outer cone, as shown in figure 34.6.
The inner cone, referred to as the *hotspot,* is the brightest or most intense part
of the light. The outer cone, or *fall-off,* is the fade-out or fringe area of the
beam created as you move away from the hotspot. When the hotspot and
fall-off are equal, the light beam has a sharp edge. As the fall-off becomes
larger than the hotspot, the edge of the beam becomes fuzzier and softer.

**IX**

**Solid Modeling & Rendering**

In summary, a spotlight is defined with an insertion point, a direction vector, and a specified angle describing the cone of light. Surfaces close to the spotlight appear brighter than surfaces at a distance.

### Light Effects on Surfaces

With point lights or spotlights, the brightness of the surface is dependent on the following three factors:

■ *Angles.* When AutoCAD renders the faces of a model, the brightness of the face is determined by the angle at which the light rays strike the faces. Faces perpendicular to the light rays receive the most light and appear the brightest. When the angle between the light rays and the face increases, the amount of light striking the face decreases, and the surface appears darker. This is shown in figure 34.8.

**Fig. 34.8**

The brightness of a face is determined by the angle at which the light rays strike the faces.

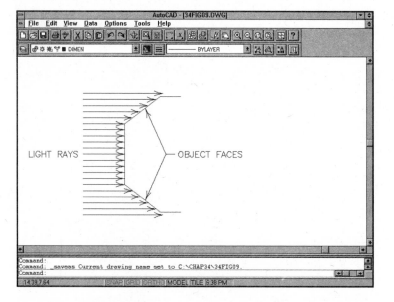

In summary, a surface that shines the brightest is one in which the light is shining perpendicular to the surface. The further a surface is from a 90-degree angle to the light source, the darker it appears.

■ *Reflectivity.* The brightness of a face also is determined by the number of light rays reflected off it. Light rays are reflected off a surface (angle of reflection) at the same angle at which they strike it (angle of incidence). The following two factors influence the amount of light reflected off of a surface:

*Angle at which the object is viewed in relation to the angle at which the light strikes it.* The brightness of reflected light is primarily dependent upon the number of light rays that reach your eyes. The amount of light you see reflected depends upon the angle at which you view the object, as shown in figure 34.9.

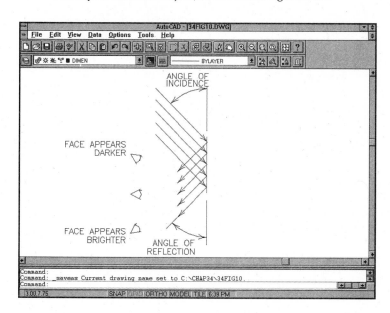

**Fig. 34.9**
The angle at which you view the object determines how much reflected light you see.

*Type of Surface.* The type of surface on the face of an object also affects the amount of light reflected. A smooth and polished surface reflects more light than a rough surface. Surfaces that are not smooth are called *matte* surfaces. When light rays hit a matte surface, light is reflected in many directions. Figure 34.10 shows the difference between smooth and matte surfaces.

■ *Distance.* The further an object is from the light source, the less light reaches it. A point light is like a light bulb, with the intensity decreasing the further an object is from the light. AutoCAD allows you to adjust this fall-off in three different ways. These three options are available in the Lights dialog box, shown in figure 34.5.

*No̲ne.* This applies the same light intensity regardless of the distance between the light and object. No fall-off is calculated.

**IX**

**Solid Modeling & Rendering**

*Inverse Linear.* The illumination decreases in inverse proportion to the distance between the light and object. For example, if an object is four units away from the light source, it receives one-quarter the amount of light. If it is two units away, it receives one-half the amount of light.

*Inverse Square.* The illumination decreases in inverse proportion to the *square* of the distance between the light and object. For example, if an object is two units away from the light source, it receives one-quarter the amount of light.

**Fig. 34.10**
Shiny surfaces reflect light more evenly than matte surfaces.

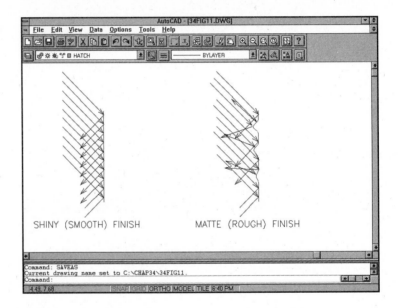

By selecting the appropriate radio button in the point light fall-off area, you can change the amount of illumination an object receives. The light fall-off is fastest with the Inverse Square option.

## Materials

Assigning materials allows the object to appear more realistic. In AutoCAD you can simulate materials by adjusting their color, transparency, and reflectivity. Materials can be created or exported from a material library. They are then assigned to an object color, a specific AutoCAD Color Index (ACI) number, a layer, or a block. To create a new material:

- Select the Materials button on the Render toolbar.

- Type **rmat** at the Command: prompt.

The Materials dialog box, as shown in figure 34.11, allows you to perform several different functions on a surface.

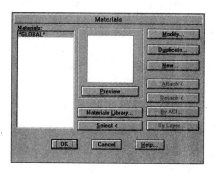

**Fig. 34.11**
You can create or modify a surface material in the Materials dialog box.

To create a material, select the New button in the Materials dialog box. This displays the New Standard Material dialog box as shown in figure 34.12.

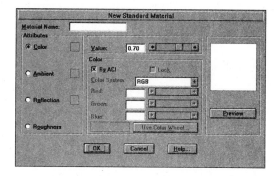

**Fig. 34.12**
The New Standard Material dialog box is used to specify the values for a new material.

The New Standard Material dialog box is used to name the material and to set the Color, Ambient, Reflection, and Roughness of the material. Select the color for these settings by selecting the Set Color button. This brings up the Color dialog box as shown in figure 34.4. You can modify the following settings:

- *Color.* Adjusts the color of the material. The color can be adjusted using the AutoCAD Color Index (ACI) setting or by manually changing them using the Red, Green, and Blue (RGB) sliders.

- *Ambient.* Ambient color is the background color. The value (the default value is .3, or 30 percent) determines how much color is reflected from the surface. The effect of this color is not dependent upon the viewpoint. In most cases, you should leave this to the default value.

■ *Reflection.* Changes the material's reflective color. This color is slight in most applications and appears near the specular point of the object. Once again the value is a percentage.

■ *Roughness.* Determines the size of the specular reflection or highlight. The smaller the roughness number, the shinier the surface appears.

After you have given the material a name and set the appropriate parameters, preview the material by selecting the Preview button. After selecting OK, you are taken back to the Materials dialog box. To assign the material to an object, select the Attach< button. You are then prompted to select the object to attach the material. The material name appears on the object as a reminder.

### Attaching a Material to an Object

You can attach a material to objects three different ways: by objects, ACI number, or layer. All these options appear in the Materials dialog box.

To assign a material to an object, use the Attach< command as described earlier. It also is important to note that the Detach< selection unassigns a material from an object. Selecting the ACI option allows you to attach the material to an AutoCAD color index number. For example, if you attached a material to ACI number 1, all objects with that color are assigned the material. To assign to an ACI, select By ACI. The Attach by AutoCAD Color Index dialog box appears, and you can attach using the ACI list provided.

### Editing a Material

To delete a material, select the Materials Library button. The Materials Library dialog box appears.

This dialog box allows you to create and save the materials you have created, as well as delete them. You also can load material libraries that have been created by someone else.

To modify a material, choose the material in the Materials dialog box, and then choose Modify. This displays the Modify Standard Material dialog box, which is identical to the New Standard Material dialog box (refer to fig. 34.12).

## Scenes

A *scene* consists of a view and lighting data. The first step in creating a scene is to define one or several views of the model. Use the VIEW, VPOINT, or DVIEW commands to set the viewpoint; then save it with the VIEW command. After you have created and saved one or several views, the second step is to place the necessary lights if they are needed.

Once you have created one or several views and inserted the lights, you are ready to create a scene. To access the Scenes dialog box, follow these steps:

**1.** Select the Scenes button on the Render toolbar.

**2.** Type **scene** at the Command: prompt.

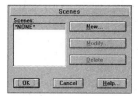

The Scenes dialog box allows you to create a <u>N</u>ew scene, <u>M</u>odify an existing scene, or <u>D</u>elete a scene (see fig. 34.13).

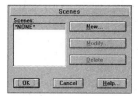

**Fig. 34.13**
The Scenes dialog box can be used to create a new scene, modify an existing scene, or delete a scene.

Selecting <u>N</u>ew brings up the New Scene dialog box, shown in figure 34.14. After giving the new scene a name, select one of the previously defined views you created in the <u>V</u>iews box. Next, select one or more previously defined lights in the <u>L</u>ights box. When you select Render, AutoCAD finds the current scene selected and renders that view with the applicable lights.

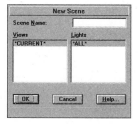

**Fig. 34.14**
The New Scene dialog box lists available views and lights.

By making different scenes, you can use a combination of views and lights to create many different effects.

## Setting Render Preferences

The Rendering Preferences dialog box provides several options and settings for rendering. By default, AutoCAD is configured so that you can create a rendering of your model without changing any of the following settings. Depending upon the type of video card you are using, not all the options may be available. To access the Rendering Preferences dialog box, perform these steps:

**IX**

**Solid Modeling & Rendering**

1. Select the Render Preferences button on the Render toolbar.

2. Type **rpref** at the Command: prompt.

The Rendering Preferences dialog box, shown in figure 34.15, allows you to set many of the rendering options. The following list describes the rendering options.

**Fig. 34.15**

The Rendering Preferences dialog box is used to set many of the rendering parameters.

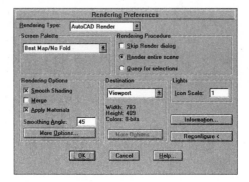

■ *Rendering Type.*

> *AutoCAD Render.* This is the default rendering type. Other types can be added. One example is AutoVision, which is another rendering add-on developed by Autodesk that allows for more detailed lights and material assignments.

■ *Rendering Options.*

> *Smooth Shading.* Produces the highest quality rendering by smoothing out the faces and blending the colors across the faces. Slows down rendering.

> *Merge.* Allows you to overlay images only if you use a 24-bit full-color display device. This option allows you to render one scene, store it in the frame buffer, and then render another scene and merge the two together in the frame buffer. If this option is off, AutoCAD begins each new rendering with a black screen.

> *Apply Materials.* Any materials you created and assigned to the models are used when rendering. Although this creates a high-quality rendering, it also increases rendering time.

*Smoothing Angle.* Allows you to specify what angles are defined as edges. The default is 45, which means that any angle greater than 45 degrees is rendered as an edge.

Selecting the More Options button provides the following rendering options:

*Gouraud.* Renders the scene with the Gouraud shading process. Gouraud is the mathematical method used to determine the light intensity on the object.

*Phong.* Uses a more sophisticated process of shading than Gouraud. Phong shading analyzes each pixel and determines the light intensity. Phong shading requires more time to render than Gouraud.

*Discard Back Faces.* Disregards all hidden faces when rendering. This option does not delete the faces. Choosing this option decreases rendering time because these faces are not factored into the calculations.

*Back Face Normal is Negative.* Allows you to choose which faces are back faces.

■ *Screen Palette.* This area will be grayed out and not available for selection if your graphics card does not support rendering to a viewport. Consult the AutoCAD Render manual for more information.

■ *Rendering Procedure.*

*Skip Render Dialog.* Allows you to render without displaying the Render dialog box.

*Render Entire Scene.* Renders all objects within a scene.

*Query For Selections.* Allows you to select the objects to render within a scene by prompting you to select those objects.

■ *Destination.*

*Viewport.* Renders to the AutoCAD viewport.

*Render Window.* Renders to a separate window.

*Hard Copy.* This option is only displayed if you have configured a rendering output device. This allows you to render directly to a printer. See the AutoCAD installation manual for more information.

**IX**

**Solid Modeling & Rendering**

*File.* Renders to a file.

*More Options.* If you choose file for your destination, use the More Options selection to specify the file type and destination of the file. A discussion of the file types and their uses is beyond the scope of this book. Generally, use this option if you want to incorporate your rendering inside a word-processing document or an electronic slideshow. Many times it is necessary to save the rendering to a file so it can be printed using a third-party program.

### Displaying Rendering Statistics

Follow these steps to display statistics on your renderings:

1. Select the Statistics button on the Render toolbar.

2. Type **stats** at the Command: prompt.

The Statistics dialog box, displayed in figure 34.16, displays information on the rendering that cannot be altered. The information can, however, be saved to a file.

**Fig. 34.16**
The Statistics dialog box displays current information about the rendering.

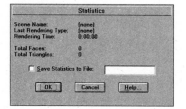

# Creating a Simple Rendering with AutoCAD

In this tutorial, you create 3D views of the bowling model. To begin, load the bowling model. This file is used for all tutorials in this chapter.

1. Select <u>O</u>pen from the Standard toolbar.

2. In the File Name edit box, type **C:\UAW13\34DWG01**; press Enter or click the OK button. After the file is loaded, your screen should resemble figure 34.17.

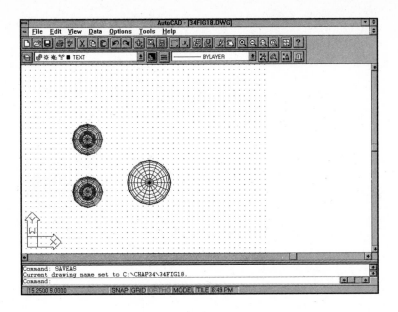

**Fig. 34.17**
Loading the
bowling model.

## Tutorial: Creating Views of the 3D Model

1. Select 3D Dynamic View from the View menu.

```
Select objects: all
Select objects:
CAmera/TArget/Distance/POints/PAn/Zoom/TWist/CLip/Hide/Off/Undo/
    <eXit>: ca
Toggle angle in/Enter angle from XY plane <90.00>: 30
Toggle angle in/Enter angle from XY plane from X axis<90.00>: -30
CAmera/TArget/Distance/POints/PAn/Zoom/TWist/CLip/Hide/Off/Undo/
    <eXit>:
```

The view changes, as shown in figure 34.18.

2. Select Named Views from the View toolbar and save this view setting as
VIEW1.

**IX**

**Solid Modeling & Rendering**

**Fig. 34.18**
Changing the
Camera View of
the bowling
model.

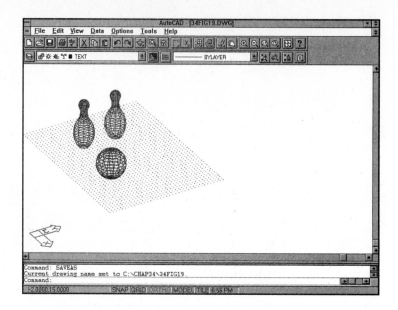

## Tutorial: Creating a Perspective View of the 3D Model

In this tutorial, use the DVIEW command to create a two-point perspective view of the bowling model.

1. Continue from the previous tutorial.

   ```
   Select 3D Dynamic View from the View toolbar.
   Select objects: all
   Select objects:
   CAmera/TArget/Distance/POints/PAn/Zoom/TWist/CLip/Hide/Off/
       Undo/<eXit>: po
   Enter target point <default>: 0,0,0
   Enter cameral point <default>: 21,21,3
   CAmera/TArget/Distance/POints/PAn/Zoom/TWist/CLip/Hide/Off/
       Undo/<eXit>: d
   New camera/target distance: 30
   CAmera/TArget/Distance/POints/PAn/Zoom/TWist/CLip/Hide/Off/
       Undo/<eXit>:
   ```

   The view changes, as shown in figure 34.19.

2. Select Named Views from the View toolbar and save this view setting as VIEW2.

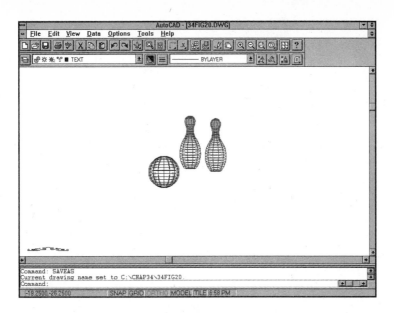

**Fig. 34.19**
Changing the
camera view of the
bowling model.

## Tutorial: Using Lights in the 3D Model

In this tutorial, you add a point light to the bowling model scene.

1. Continue from the previous tutorial. Select Lights from the Render toolbar. The Lights dialog box appears, as shown in figure 34.20.

2. Choose the Point Light option and click the New button. The New Point Light dialog box appears (see fig. 34.21). In the Light Name edit box enter **POINT1**. Change the Intensity to 1.00 and click the OK button. Use the default location for this tutorial. The Lights dialog box will reappear. The POINT1 light is now listed under the lights column. Click OK to accept the light.

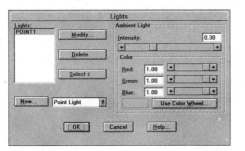

**Fig. 34.20**
The Lights dialog box.

**IX**

**Solid Modeling & Rendering**

**Fig. 34.21**
Using the New
Point Light dialog
box to create a
new light for the
bowling model.

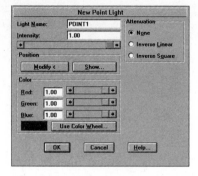

3. Select Render from the Render toolbar. Then choose the Render option
   in the Render dialog box. The objects are rendered, as shown in
   figure 34.22.

**Fig. 34.22**
The rendered
bowling model
after a point light
has been modified
and added.

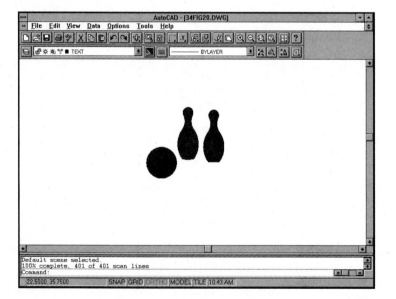

## Tutorial: Using Scenes in the 3D Model

In this tutorial, use the SCENE command to create a scene for the bowling
model.

1. Continue from the previous tutorial. Select Scene from the Render
   toolbar. The Scenes dialog box appears, as shown in figure 34.23.

2. Click the <u>N</u>ew button. The New Scene dialog box appears (see fig. 34.24).

3. In the Scene <u>N</u>ames edit box type **standard**.

4. Select VIEW1 and the POINT1 light.

5. Click the OK button to create the new scene. The Scenes dialog box reappears. Notice that the Standard Scene is now shown in the Scenes Column.

6. Click the OK button to accept the new scene changes.

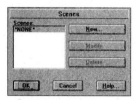

**Fig. 34.23**
Using the Scenes dialog box to create a scene in the bowling model.

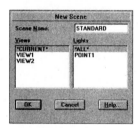

**Fig. 34.24**
Using the New Scene dialog box to create and change the settings of a scene for the bowling model.

7. Select Render from the Render toolbar. Select Render Scene in the Render dialog box.

   The objects are rendered as shown in figure 34.25. Notice that the scene is now rendered from the VIEW1 orientation created earlier in the chapter.

**Fig. 34.25**

The rendered bowling model after a scene has been created.

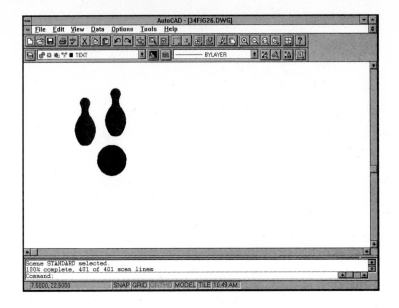

## Tutorial: Using Materials in the 3D Model

In this tutorial, use the MATERIAL command to create and assign a material to the bowling model.

**1.** Continue from the previous tutorial.

    Command: **regen**

Reverts the screen to a wireframe representation.

**2.** Select Materials from the Render toolbar. The Materials dialog box appears (see fig. 34.26).

**3.** Click the New button to create a new material. The New Standard Material dialog box appears (see fig. 34.27).

**4.** In the Material Name edit box, type **finish1** to name the new material being created.

**5.** Turn off the Color By ACI option.

**6.** Change the blue setting to 100 percent or 1.00 and the roughness setting to 1.00.

**7.** Click the Preview button. The dialog box changes, as shown in figure 34.28.

**8.** Click the <u>A</u>ttach< button.

```
Gathering objects...0 found*Cancel*
Select object"": Select the bowling ball.
Select objects:
```

**9.** The Materials dialog box returns. Click OK to accept the material attachment to the bowling ball.

**10.** Select Render from the Render toolbar.

**11.** Select Render Scene in the Render dialog box.

**12.** View the rendering and notice the changes in the material.

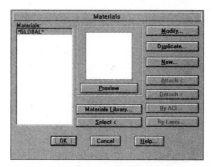

**Fig. 34.26**
The Materials dialog box.

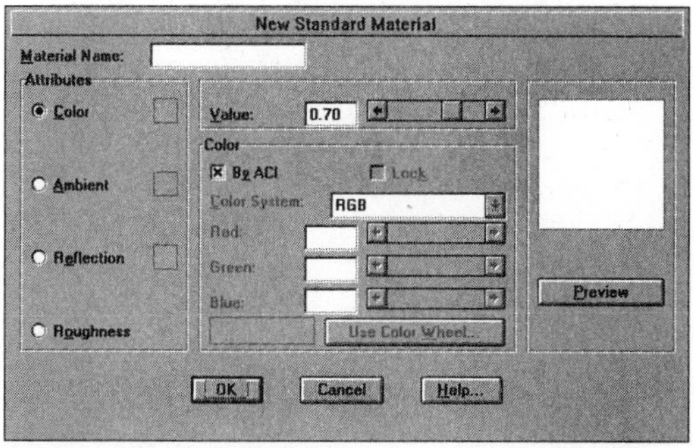

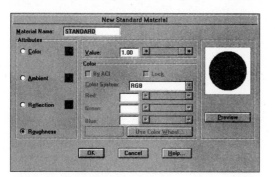

**Fig. 34.27**
Using the New Standard Material dialog box to create a new material for the bowling model.

**Fig. 34.28**
Previewing the new standard material created for the bowling model.

## Tutorial: Saving and Displaying Rendered Images

Up to this point, you have learned how to create a rendering of a scene or object. There are very few times when you want someone to wait for AutoCAD to render your scene so they can see your handy work. In the following text, you will learn how to save the scenes that you render, as well as replay them in AutoCAD to display them.

In this tutorial, use the SAVEIMG and REPLAY commands to save the rendered bowling model image created in the last chapter; then redisplay it.

1. Continue from the previous tutorial. From the Tools menu select Image Save. The Save Image dialog box appears (see fig. 34.29).

2. Using the default settings, click the OK button. The Image File dialog box appears.

3. Save the image as **C:\UAW13\BOWLING**.

**Fig. 34.29**

Using the Save Image dialog box to save the rendered image of the bowling model.

4. From the Tools menu, select Image, View. The Replay dialog box appears.

5. In the Filename edit box type **C:\UAW13\BOWLING**.

6. Click the OK button to replay the render file. The Image Specifications dialog box appears (see fig. 34.30).

7. Click the OK button to accept the default settings. The rendering of the bowling model is displayed in the drawing area.

8. At the Command: prompt enter **regen.**

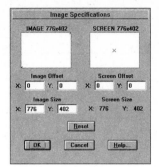

**Fig. 34.30**
Setting the image
specifications to
replay the bowling
model rendering.

# From Here...

For more information about creating solid models, refer to the following chapters:

- Chapter 32, "Introduction to Solid Modeling Concepts," explains how to create and modify solid models.

- Chapter 33, "Working with Solid Models," explains how to create a custom view from a solid model.

# On Your Own

Make a rendering of the Eye Bracket. Create different views, including a perspective. Set up lights, scenes, and apply materials. Save several rendered images.

Hints:

1. Begin by opening the Eye Bracket surface model, 34DWG02. This is a 3D surface model.

2. Using the DVIEW command, create and save several different views, including a perspective view.

3. Set up several different lights, including a spotlight.

4. Create several different scenes using different views and light combinations.

5. Apply a material to the model.

6. Render the different scenes and save them to disk.

**IX**

**Solid Modeling & Rendering**

# Part X

# Using and Managing Drawing Data

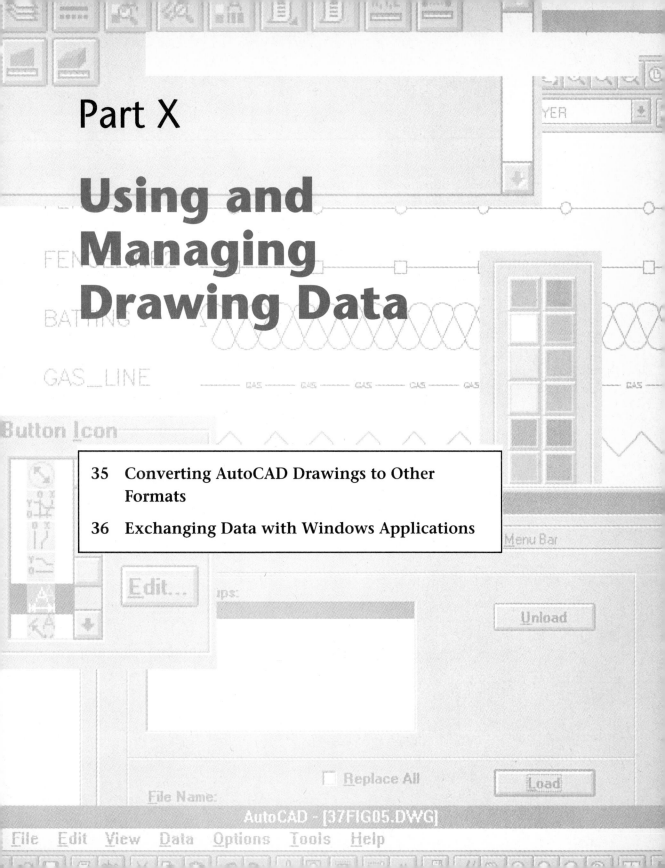

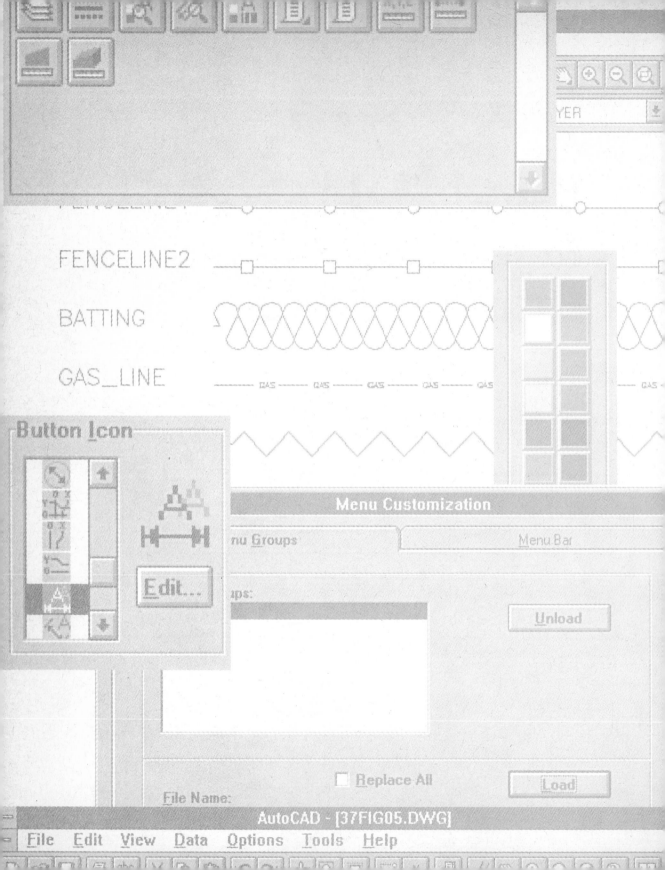

FENCELINE2

BATTING

GAS_LINE          GAS      GAS      GAS      GAS      GAS      GAS

## Button Icon

Edit...

## Menu Customization

nu Groups                    Menu Bar

ps:                          Unload

☐ Replace All                Load

File Name:

AutoCAD - [37FIG05.DWG]

File   Edit   View   Data   Options   Tools   Help

# Chapter 35

# Converting AutoCAD Drawings to Other Formats

Eventually, you'll want to exchange information between your AutoCAD drawings and other programs. AutoCAD provides a variety of methods for importing and exporting data. The ability to exchange information with other programs is a powerful feature of AutoCAD. At the conclusion of this chapter you'll be able to do the following:

- Export information contained in an AutoCAD drawing in the DXF format with the DXFOUT command

- Import information in the DXF format from other programs into AutoCAD with the DXFIN command

- Import specially coded DXB binary files into AutoCAD with the DXBIN command

- Import raster files in the PCX, GIF, and TIF formats into AutoCAD with the PCXIN, GIFIN, and TIFFIN commands

- Import and export PostScript files with the PSIN and PSOUT commands

- Import standard Windows bitmap images (BMP files) into AutoCAD

- Import and export Windows metafiles into AutoCAD with the WMFOUT, WMFOPTS, and WMFIN commands

> **Note**
>
> Autodesk is going to great lengths to standardize the DWG file format across all of its applications. As new versions of Autodesk applications become available, you should be able to transfer drawing files between them without having to import and export files as DXF files.

# Converting AutoCAD Drawings to DXF Format

While standardization is elusive in the CAD industry, significant efforts have been made to allow CAD users to translate files among different programs. The DXF (Drawing Exchange File) format developed by Autodesk has become the accepted standard for translating files among different CAD programs.

Files created with the DXF format can be written in standard ASCII code. ASCII stands for American Standard Code for Information Interchange. If the information contained in a DXF file is in ASCII code, the file can be read by any computer.

Unfortunately when attempting to translate a CAD drawing, information is often lost in the translation. Often the translation isn't exactly like the original drawing. The problem isn't the DXF translation or ASCII code, but rather the way in which different CAD programs create objects, layers, and other drawing elements.

AutoCAD allows you to use layer names; other programs may use only numbers. Even if you use a numbering system to define your layers, they may not translate into exactly the same layers in a different program. While drawing translation may seem like a major problem, it often creates only minor problems. This, of course, depends upon the drawings translated and the CAD systems involved.

## Writing a DXF file (DXFOUT)

The DXFOUT command creates a file with the DXF extension. The default is an ASCII file created from the AutoCAD drawing. To create a DXF file from your current drawing, do either of the following:

- Enter **dxfout** at the Command: prompt. This opens the Create DXF File dialog box, as shown in figure 35.1

■ Select <u>F</u>ile, <u>E</u>xport to open the Export Data dialog box (see fig. 35.2). Select the arrow under <u>L</u>ist Files of Type to show the different options available for exporting your drawing, including DXF.

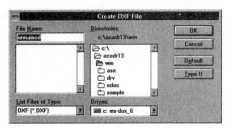

**Fig. 35.1**
The Create DXF File dialog box can be used to create a DXF file from your current drawing.

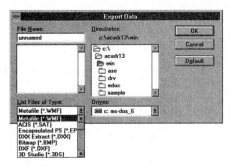

**Fig. 35.2**
The Export Data dialog box can be used to export your drawing in a variety of file formats, including DXF.

After you've accessed either the Create DXF File or the Export Data dialog box, enter the File <u>N</u>ame and click OK. You don't need to enter a DXF extension—AutoCAD automatically appends this to the file you specify. If you have previously named the drawing, the file name appears by default in the edit box. Click OK in either dialog box, and AutoCAD prompts:

```
Enter decimal places of accuracy (0 to 16)/Objects/Binary <6>:
```

The Objects option allows you to select specific objects in your drawing to include in the DXF file. If you choose this option, only objects you select are placed in the file. After choosing the Objects option and selecting the objects, AutoCAD prompts for the desired accuracy as before.

When AutoCAD prompts for decimal places of accuracy, you can specify a precision of up to 16 places for floating-point numbers. While it would seem logical to always use the highest setting (16) for decimal places of accuracy, this increases file size, and consequently the time needed to create and read the DXF file. Also, depending on what you are going to do with the DXF file, other programs do not need or cannot use floating-point numbers with a precision of 16 decimal places. To help determine what decimal places of accuracy to use, check the application you are going to use the DXF file with and what kind of precision the application needs and can use.

### Writing a Binary DXF File (DXFOUT)

The standard DXF file is in ASCII format. You also have the option of creating a binary form of the DXF file. To create a binary DXF file, enter **b** at the DXFOUT prompt as shown:

```
Enter decimal places of accuracy (0 to 16)/Objects/Binary
     <6>: b
```

This creates a binary form of the DXF file. *Binary code* is composed of data in the form of bits having a value of 1 or 0. The advantage of creating a binary file is that it can be up to 25 percent smaller, and is just as accurate. AutoCAD can read a binary file quicker than an ASCII file. A standard ASCII file can be read or edited with most word processors, including the Microsoft Write program contained in Windows. The disadvantage of a binary DXF file is that it can't be easily read or edited with a word processor program like an ASCII file can.

### Contents of an ASCII DXF File

Understanding the contents of an ASCII DXF file is important when customizing or programming AutoCAD. The contents of an ASCII DXF file are arranged into the following four sections:

- *Header*. Lists every drawing variable and its value.

- *Tables*. Contains named items such as layers, linetypes, styles, and views.

- *Blocks*. All objects and their values that make up blocks in the drawing are listed in this section.

- *Objects*. Objects used in the drawing are located here.

You can display the contents of a DXF file with any ASCII file editor or viewer such as Windows Write. Most DXF files will probably be too large for Windows Notepad.

```
Command: type
File to list: Enter path and file name of DXF file to list.
```

After pressing Enter, you can press Ctrl+S to stop the screen from scrolling.

**Note**

As a last attempt, a DXF file can be used to recover a corrupted AutoCAD drawing file. To create a DXF file from a corrupted drawing, begin to load the drawing into AutoCAD. Once the drawing has started loading, press Escape to stop AutoCAD from loading the entire drawing. This should be done before it reaches the corrupted part of the drawing when the system locks up. When the Command: prompt appears, use DXFOUT to write a DXF file. You can load the DXF file into any standard text editor. After loading the file, search through it and look for any unusual data. If you find data that doesn't appear correct, delete it. After saving the file in ASCII format, use DXFIN to bring the drawing back into AutoCAD. You'll lose all objects whose data you deleted from the file, and any objects that have not yet loaded after pressing Escape. While you most likely will lose objects using this process, it may be preferable to redrawing the entire drawing.

Note that this method should only be considered as a last attempt at recovering a corrupted drawing file. You should use it only after trying your backups, AutoCAD's drawing recovery procedures, and third-party drawing recovery programs.

## Reading a DXF file (DXFIN)

The DXFIN command allows you to create an AutoCAD drawing file (DWG) from a DXF file. If you want to import all objects, layers, text styles, and attributes of the DXF file, it's important to begin a new drawing using the No Prototype option. To begin a new drawing using the No Prototype option, select the New button on the standard toolbar. In the Create New Drawing dialog box, select the No Prototype option.

If you import a DXF file into an existing drawing or do not select the No Prototype option, only the objects of the DXF file are inserted. All layers, text styles and attributes of the existing drawing override those of the DXF file. To import a DXF file, do one of the following:

- Enter **dxfin** at the Command: prompt. This brings up the Select DXF File dialog box, as shown in figure 35.3

- Choose File, Import to open the Import File dialog box (see fig. 35.4). Select the arrow under List Files of Type to show the different options available for importing data into your drawing, including DXF.

**Fig. 35.3**
The Select DXF
File dialog box can
be used to import
a DXF file into
your current
drawing.

**Fig. 35.4**
The Import File
dialog box can be
used to import
a variety of
information into
your drawing in
different file
formats, including
DXF.

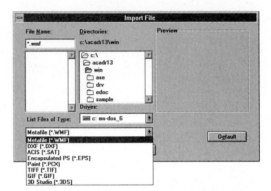

After you select the file and click OK, AutoCAD imports the file into your
current drawing. If you import the DXF file into an existing drawing or begin
a new drawing without using the No Prototype option, AutoCAD prompts:

```
Not a new drawing--only OBJECTS section will be input.
```

# Drawing Exchange Binary (DXBIN) Files

As mentioned in the previous section, DXF files are a complete ASCII representation of the AutoCAD drawing. These files can be written and read by
AutoCAD and many other programs. Other programs need to provide simple
geometric input into AutoCAD. The DXB (drawing exchange binary) format
was designed for this purpose. The DXB format is even more compact than
the DXF binary format, and hence is limited in the objects it can represent.
To input a DXB file:

1. Enter **dxbin** at the Command: prompt. This opens the Select DXB File
   dialog box as shown in figure 35.5.

2. In the Select DXB File dialog box, enter the name of the file. You don't
   need to include the DXB extension; it's assumed.

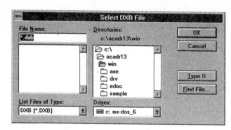

**Fig. 35.5**
The Select DXB
File dialog box is
used to import
DXB files.

# Importing Raster Files into AutoCAD

When you create an AutoCAD drawing file, it's composed of vectors. A *vector* is defined as an object that is completely specified by magnitude and direction. In AutoCAD, a vector is defined by XYZ coordinates, and has no relationship to the physical pixels you see on your monitor. The pixels on your monitor are used simply to display the drawing on the screen.

As opposed to vectors, many drawing, painting, and presentation programs are saved as raster files. *Raster files* define the objects by location and color of the actual screen pixels. Raster files are also known as *bitmap* images.

AutoCAD's ability to import raster files opens up a wide range of possibilities. You can use two basic file types in your drawing: vector and raster. You can import a raster file, edit it, and save it as a drawing file. The manner in which you edit the raster image—rotate, mirror, and so on—is up to you.

One use of raster images is sketching or tracing the image. For example, you may require a line drawing of an image that is currently available as a PCX file. After importing the raster image you could use the appropriate commands to sketch or trace the image. After sketching or tracing the object, you could delete or freeze the original raster image. The remaining object could be further enhanced with AutoCAD to create the type of drawing needed.

There are several different formats of raster files that are widely used for presentation graphics and desktop publishing. AutoCAD allows you to work with the following three common types of raster files:

- *PCX (Personal Computer Exchange)*. Raster file format developed by the Z-Soft Corporation, and commonly used by programs such as PC Paintbrush.

- *GIF (Graphics Interchange Format)*. Image format developed by the CompuServe network. CompuServe is a computer information network that can be accessed by modem. It provides a variety of information, including pictures GIF format.

■ *TIF(F) (Tagged Image File Format).* Raster format developed by Aldus and Microsoft.

If you have a raster image you'd like to import into AutoCAD and the image isn't one of the three listed above, the image can be converted from one format to another with third-party and screen capture software. One highly rated program for image converting and capturing is the HiJaak Graphics Suite for Windows by Inset.

## Importing PCX files (PCXIN)

The PCXIN command allows you to import a PCX raster file into AutoCAD. To import a PCX file into AutoCAD, do one of the following:

■ Enter **pcxin** at the Command: prompt. AutoCAD then prompts:

    Initializing. . .PCX file name:

■ Choose File, Import to open the Import File dialog box (refer to fig. 35.4). Select the down arrow under List Files of Type to show the different options available for importing your drawing, including PCX.

After selecting the file with either method, AutoCAD prompts:

    Insertion point<0,0,0>: Select a point.
    Scale factor: Enter a scale factor and press Enter.

◀ See "Inserting Symbols into a Drawing (INSERT, DDINSERT)," p. 692

When inserting the image, it's moved and displayed quickly because the image is shown as a box with the name of the file inside. Because the image is inserted as a block, you must select the insertion point and scale factor. The image is displayed on the screen.

## Importing GIF Files (GIFIN)

The GIFIN command is similar to the PCXIN command. To import a GIF file into AutoCAD, do one of the following:

■ Enter **gifin** at the Command: prompt. AutoCAD prompts:

    Initializing. . .GIF file name:

■ Choose File, Import to open the Import File dialog box (refer to fig. 35.4). The GIF option appears under the List Files of Type box.

After selecting the file with either method, AutoCAD gives you the same prompts as with the PCXIN command.

## Importing TIF Files (TIFFIN)

With the TIFFIN command you can import TIF files into your AutoCAD drawing. The use of the TIFFIN command is similar to the GIFIN and PCXIN commands. To import a TIF file into AutoCAD, do either of the following:

- Enter **tiffin** at the Command: prompt. AutoCAD prompts:

    Initializing. . .TIF file name:

- Open the Import File dialog box (File, Import), and select the TIF option under the List Files of Type box.

After selecting the file with either method, AutoCAD gives you the same prompts as with the PCXIN and GIFIN commands.

### Tutorial: Importing a Raster File into AutoCAD

In this tutorial you import a PCX raster file into AutoCAD. Begin by opening a new drawing.

1. Select the New button from the Standard toolbar. Enter a path and name for the drawing if you desire.

2. Choose File, Import to access the Import File dialog box.

3. Click the down arrow under List Files of Type to display files available for import. Select the Paint (*.PCX) option.

4. Change to the UAW13 subdirectory and select the WHEELCHR.PCX file.

5. After the file finishes loading, AutoCAD asks for the insertion base point.

    Insertion point <0,0,0>: **2,2**

6. Use 4 for the scale factor, then press Enter. Your screen should now look like figure 35.6

    Scale factor: **4**

**Fig. 35.6**
The inserted wheelchair raster symbol.

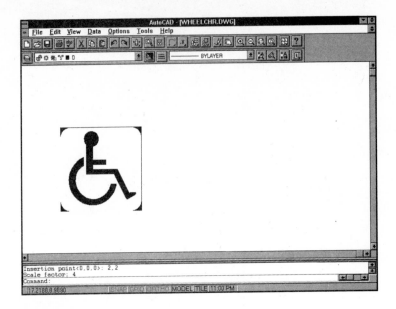

# Working with Bit-Mapped Files (BMPOUT)

You can use the BMPOUT command to create a bitmap image of the objects in your drawing. To create a bitmap image of your drawing, do either of the following:

- Enter **bmpout** at the Command: prompt. The Create BMP File dialog box appears as shown in figure 35.7.

- Open the Export Data dialog box by choosing File, Export (refer to fig. 35.2). Select the down arrow under List Files of Type. The Bitmap (*.BMP) option is listed along with several others.

**Fig. 35.7**
You can create a bitmap image of the objects in your drawing by using the Create BMP File dialog box.

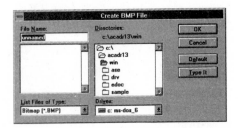

After entering the file name for the bitmap image using either method, AutoCAD prompts:

> Select objects: *Create a selection set of all objects you want included in the bitmap image.*

# Working with Windows Metafiles

A windows metafile, unlike bitmaps, is a vector image that can be scaled and printed with no loss of resolution when imported back into AutoCAD or some other Windows-based application. Objects in the metafile format have the file extension WMF (Windows Metafile Format). You can import metafiles into AutoCAD and export AutoCAD objects as metafiles.

## Exporting Windows Metafiles (WMFOUT)

The WMFOUT command gives you the option of saving all or part of a drawing in the WMF. This is similar to the COPYCLIP command, except the objects you select are written to disk as a WMF file. To export objects into a metafile, do one of the following:

▶ See "Exchanging Data with Windows Applications," p. 993

- Enter **wmfout** at the Command: prompt. This brings up the Create WMF File dialog box, as shown in figure 35.8.

- Choose File, Export to access the Export Data dialog box (refer to fig. 35.2). Select the arrow under List Files of Type to show the different options available for exporting your drawing. The default option is Metafile (*.WMF).

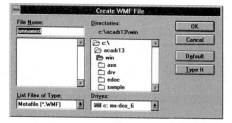

**Fig. 35.8**
You can export AutoCAD objects in the Windows Metafile format by accessing the Create WMF File dialog box.

By default, the metafile is saved with the same file name as the current drawing. You have the option of specifying a different drive or directory and entering a new file name in the File Name edit box. When you have completed your changes, click OK. The graphics window re-appears and you may use any of the AutoCAD selection set options at the Select objects: prompt.

## Importing Windows Metafiles (WMFOPTS, WMFIN)

The WMFIN command can be used to import metafiles into AutoCAD. To access the WMFIN command, do one of the following:

■ Enter **wmfin** at the Command: prompt. This brings up the Import WMF dialog box, as shown in figure 35.9. The file you select is displayed in the Preview box.

■ Select File, Import to access the Import File dialog box (refer to fig. 35.4). The default option is Metafile (*.WMF). The file selected appears in the Preview box.

**Fig. 35.9**
The Preview box allows you to preview the metafile before importing it into your drawing.

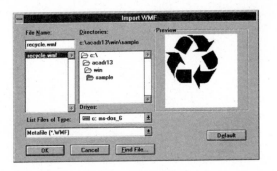

◀ See "Inserting Symbols into a Drawing (INSERT, DDINSERT," p. 692

After selecting the proper file, the WMFIN command is similar to the INSERT command at this point. AutoCAD displays the following prompts:

```
Insertion point: Select an insertion point.
Scale factor <1>/Corner/XYZ: Select a point, enter a value
     and press Enter, or press Enter to accept the default
     scale factor.
Y scale factor (default=X): Enter a new scale factor and
     press Enter, or press Enter to accept the default
     scale factor.
Rotation angle <0>: Select a point, enter a value and press
     Enter, or press Enter to accept the default rotation
     angle.
```

The metafile is inserted as a block object on the current UCS with its insertion point at the upper-left corner of the block. The imported metafile retains the layer, color, and linetype properties that it was originally created with. Unlike normal block insertions, however, it doesn't inherit the color and linetype properties of the receiving layer if it was created on Layer 0.

You can determine the properties of an imported metafile by accessing the WMF Import Options dialog box as shown in figure 35.10. To access the WMF Import Options dialog box:

- Enter **wmfopts** at the Command: prompt.

- Select File, Options, WMF Options.

**Fig. 35.10**
The WMF Import Options dialog box allows you to modify the properties of an imported metafile.

The two check boxes in the WMF Import Options dialog box perform the following functions on imported metafiles:

- *Wire Frame (No Fills).* This controls the fill of objects such as donuts, solids, traces, or wide polylines. When the box is checked, objects are imported as wireframes. When the box isn't checked, objects are imported filled.

- *Wide Lines.* When this box is checked, the lines and borders of the objects maintain their original width. If the box isn't checked, the object lines are imported with zero width.

Figure 35.11 shows the effect of these two options on an imported metafile.

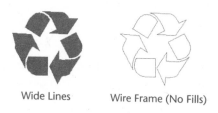

Wide Lines          Wire Frame (No Fills)

**Fig. 35.11**
An example of a metafile showing wide lines and wire frame (no fills).

# Working with PostScript Files

PostScript is a copyrighted page description language developed by Adobe Systems. It's used extensively in the desktop publishing industry. With the PSIN and PSOUT commands, AutoCAD gives you the ability to work with PostScript fonts and files. Combining this with the ability to work with raster files such as PCX, GIF, and TIF, you can create presentation graphics with AutoCAD.

## Importing PostScript Files (PSIN)

The PSIN command allows you to import a PostScript file into AutoCAD. A PostScript file has the EPS extension. The PSIN command is similar to the

INSERT or GIFIN commands because all it asks for is an insertion point and scale factor. To insert a PostScript file into AutoCAD:

- Enter **psin** at the Command: prompt.

- When the Select PostScript File dialog box appears, select the file and click OK. AutoCAD prompts:

      Insertion point<0,0,0>: *Enter the insertion point.*
      Scale factor: *Enter the scale factor.*

Once you've placed your PostScript object on the drawing, you can save it as a drawing file or output it again as a PostScript file with the PSOUT command.

## Exporting PostScript Files (PSOUT)

Any drawing created in AutoCAD can be converted to a PostScript file with the PSOUT command. This command is normally used if PostScript fonts or images were added to the drawing. To output an AutoCAD drawing as a PostScript file:

- Enter **psout** at the Command: prompt.

- In the Create PostScript File dialog box, enter the name and the path where you want to save the file, and click OK. AutoCAD prompts:

      What to plot--Display, Extents, Limits, View, or
          Window <D>:*Select what you want to plot.*

      Include a screen preview image in the file? (none/EPSI/TIFF)
          <None>: *If you want to include a preview image,
          select EPSI or TIFF, or press Enter if you don't
          want to include a preview image.*

> **Note**
>
> The screen preview image can be used with other desktop publishing programs to view the PostScript file. If you select the EPSI or TIFF options, you're prompted for the image size. The default size is 128×128 pixels. This is a good choice since it doesn't slow down the software you're importing the image into.

      Size Units (Inches or Millimeters) <Inches>: *Select
          the appropriate units.*
      Specify scale by entering:
      Output Inches=Drawing Units or Fit or ? <Fit>: *Press
          Enter to select fit as the default, or enter a
          scale.*

The text window now displays a list of "Standard values for output size."

```
Enter the Size or Width, Height (in Inches) <USER>: Choose
    from the list and type the letter, or enter a new
    size.
```

AutoCAD creates a PostScript file which can be printed by any PostScript output device.

> **Note**
>
> An EPS file created with the PSOUT command can only be printed by a PostScript printer.

## Working with AutoCAD Drawings and Other Formats

In addition to the formats mentioned previously, AutoCAD also has the ability to export and import other formats. The following list summarizes other import/export options.

### 3D Studio

With the 3DSIN and 3DSOUT commands, you can import and export AutoCAD drawings directly with 3D Studio. With the 3DSIN command, you can import 3D Studio geometry and rendering data into AutoCAD. This includes meshes, maps, materials, lights, and cameras.

You can export your AutoCAD geometry and accompanying rendering data to 3D Studio with the 3DSOUT command. Using 3DSOUT converts any named views to 3D Studio cameras, and any AutoVision lights you created are converted to the nearest 3D Studio equivalent. Files created with 3DSOUT contain the 3DS file extension.

### ACIS Solid Models

ACIS solid modeling provides a format that can be used to import and export ACIS solid models. This information is stored in an SAT ASCII file. The ACISIN and ACISOUT commands allow you to import and export ACIS solid models with AutoCAD.

The AMECONVERT command can be used to convert AME Release 2 or 2.1 region or solid models into AutoCAD.

### Stereo Lithography

The SLTOUT command allows you to create a file that is compatible with Stereo Lithography devices. These files have an STL extension.

Stereo lithography is a process based on the principle of hardening a material that reacts with a laser light into a specific shape. Many industries are using stereo lithography as a rapid and inexpensive method of producing prototypes. One major application is in the area of making molds and dies for casting and injection molding. With the SLTOUT command, AutoCAD has the capability to transfer geometrical data to the stereo lithography apparatus.

### IGES

Unlike AutoCAD Release 12, AutoCAD Release 13 doesn't provide IGES import and export commands. While Release 12 had these commands, they didn't work very well and a separate application was developed to handle importing and exporting IGES formats. If you need to work with IGES files, contact your AutoCAD dealer or Autodesk for information on applications that support IGES in AutoCAD.

# From Here...

Because little standardization exists in the CAD industry, the ability to import and export AutoCAD drawings in a variety of formats is very important. The DXF format, developed by Autodesk, is quickly becoming the preferred method for exchanging drawings with other CAD systems.

The ability to import raster files into AutoCAD greatly increases its capability. If you have a company logo, for example, you can scan it and import it into AutoCAD with the GIFIN, PCXIN, or TIFIN options. With the ability to import raster files and PostScript files into AutoCAD, you can create presentation graphics using a variety of file formats.

For more information on exchanging data with other windows applications and customizing AutoCAD see the following chapters:

■ Chapter 36, "Exchanging Data with Windows Applications," explains how to use your AutoCAD drawing in conjunction with other Windows programs.

■ Chapter 37, "Customizing AutoCAD," shows you how to take advantage of AutoCAD's ability to customize its interface and menus.

# On Your Own

Importing files can be very useful if you need a symbol that isn't available in AutoCAD. Import the metafile COMPASS.WMF into a new drawing.

# Chapter 36

# Exchanging Data with Windows Applications

Users of general business productivity applications, such as word processing, desktop publishing, and business charting, were among the first to adopt Microsoft Windows as their graphical environment of choice. Autodesk saw in the phenomenal acceptance of Windows an opportunity to move its users to the ease of use, consistency, and inter-application communication capabilities they already were familiar with from their other applications.

AutoCAD's Windows Extension for Release 11 was the first time users could run AutoCAD as a native Windows application, but its implementation was not full-featured because it lacked support for add-ons, such as the AutoCAD Modeling Extension. Nevertheless, it provided a taste of what to expect in future versions by way of its interaction with other Windows applications.

Release 12 for Windows was the first complete implementation of AutoCAD that included all of the features found on other platforms and introduced a sample tool palette as an alternative means of invoking its commands. Now, with Release 13, Autodesk has gone a step further by making Windows its primary development platform so that users see features, such as resizable and overlapping view windows, multiple floating toolbars, and others, first on Windows. Neither of these interface features are implemented under the DOS version.

In contrast to all the previous chapters in this book, this chapter does not discuss AutoCAD's drawing and editing features. In this chapter, you're exposed to AutoCAD's implementation of data exchange capabilities, both for receiving and sending information. This chapter covers the following concepts:

- Exchanging data using the Windows Clipboard

- Embedding and linking OLE objects

- Using AutoCAD as a DDE client and a DDE server

Whether you want to simply understand AutoCAD's inter-application communication capabilities, gain a sense of tasks it can help tame, or follow along on your computer to try out the DDE exercises, you should read this chapter.

# Using the Clipboard

Interface consistency, one-stop configuration, and multitasking are important Windows benefits, and perhaps the reason for its immense popularity. But the most important benefit of all is its support for inter-application communication. It used to be that if you wanted to share data between applications, you'd write a file from one in a format supported by another, and then read the external file using the second application's import filters. Though this process works, its drawbacks are the tedious nature of the file export and import process and the static nature of the data transfer. That is, changes in the source application mean that data in the target application is no longer current and the export/import process must be reinitiated to keep the data in synchronization.

In the context of this chapter, *inter-application communication* refers to the exchange of data, both static and dynamic, between diverse applications. This embraces the Windows Clipboard, the Windows Object Linking and Embedding (OLE) protocol, and the Windows Dynamic Data Exchange (DDE) protocol.

As noted above, the traditional method of data transfer between applications involving external file export and import procedures is tedious and also static. Windows provides an integrated facility, the Clipboard, to simplify transferring both graphics and text data between applications. Though the data transferred using the Clipboard is static—that is, edits in the source application are not automatically reflected in the target application—the process is much simpler.

The *Clipboard* is an integrated facility within Windows that enables the copying and pasting of data between applications. The application from which you copy data is termed the *source*, and the application into which you paste the data is termed the *target*.

To use the Clipboard, simply select an object of interest (text or graphic) in the source application, and choose Edit, Copy to transfer a copy of the object to the Clipboard. Follow this by switching to the target application and choosing Edit, Paste.

> **Note**
>
> By using the Clipboard you end up with a good replica of the AutoCAD drawing in your document, However, any associated accuracy or intelligence is lost. Windows performs a translation when transferring data using the Clipboard.

> **Note**
>
> Users of AutoCAD for DOS should take special note: Contrary to canceling an active command, as it does in the DOS version, the Ctrl+C keystroke combination invokes the copy to Clipboard command in AutoCAD for Windows. Use the Esc key to cancel a command.

**Tip**

You can use the Windows standard keystroke combination shortcuts, Ctrl+C, Ctrl+X, and Ctrl+V for the Copy, Cut, and Paste commands respectively.

**X**

**Using Drawing Data**

The following tutorial demonstrates how to use the Windows Clipboard with an example that shows you how to paste text from Windows Write into AutoCAD.

## Tutorial: Pasting Text from Windows Write into AutoCAD

Placing text is an important part of creating a finished drawing. Most of you probably already have a standard set of notes stored on disk for use on a variety of projects. In the following exercise, enter text in the Windows accessory application Write and transfer it to AutoCAD using the Clipboard.

1. If AutoCAD is not already running, start it by double-clicking its icon in Program Manager's AutoCAD R13 group window.

2. Start Windows Write by switching to Program Manager (press Ctrl+Esc to display the Windows Task List, select Program Manager, and click the Switch To button) and double-clicking its icon in the Accessories group window.

3. With Windows Write active, type in **AutoCAD Release 13 for Windows.**

4. Highlight the text and choose Edit, Copy to place a copy of the selected text in the Windows Clipboard (see fig. 36.1).

**Fig. 36.1**

With Write active, type in some text, highlight it, and choose Edit, Copy.

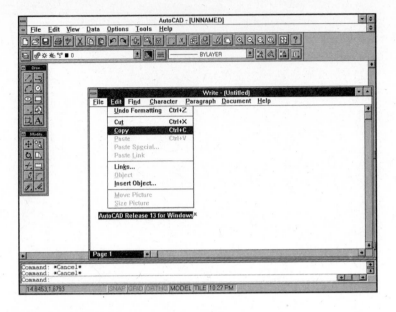

**5.** Switch to AutoCAD, and click the Text icon (the bottom-right icon in the Draw floating toolbar). Alternatively, at the Command: prompt, type **mtext** and press Enter.

**Tip**

Windows users of old will find the earlier shortcut keys for Cut (Shift+Delete), Copy (Ctrl+Insert), and Paste (Shift+Insert), still work.

**6.** Pick two points for the location of the text block.

```
Attach/Rotation/Style/Height/Direction/<Insertion point>:
Pick a point near the upper-left corner in your drawing
    area.
Attach/Rotation/Style/Height/Direction/Width/2Points/
<Other corner>: Pick another point near the lower-right
    corner in your drawing area.
```

**7.** The Edit MText dialog box appears. With the cursor in the edit field, press Ctrl+V to paste the text from the Clipboard to the dialog box. Your AutoCAD screen should look similar to the one shown in figure 36.2.

**8.** Click the OK button in the Edit MText dialog box to place the text in your drawing.

The process of pasting a graphic from AutoCAD to another application, such as a word processor, is also similar. Click the Copy icon in the Standard toolbar (or press Ctrl+C, or choose Edit, Copy) and select objects to copy to the Clipboard. After the graphic is on the Clipboard, you can choose Edit, Paste from within the other application to complete the process.

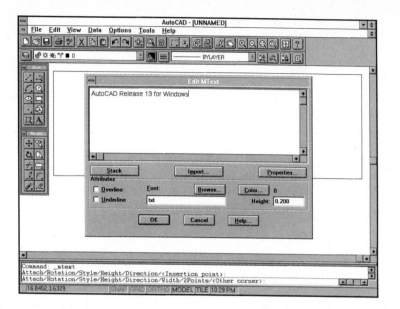

**Fig. 36.2**
With the cursor in the Edit field, press Ctrl+V to place the text from the Clipboard to the Edit MText dialog box.

> **Note**
>
> The Edit menu in AutoCAD offers a Copy command and a Copy View command. The Copy command prompts you for objects to copy to the Clipboard, and the Copy View command copies the contents of the current view to the Clipboard in a single step.

> **Note**
>
> To paste a graphic from AutoCAD to either a DOS application or to an application that does not support the Windows Clipboard, export it in a supported format, preferably a vector format such as an HPGL plot file, and then import the file in the other application.

# Using Object Linking and Embedding (OLE)

The transfer of data using the Clipboard, as shown in the previous section, is the simplest from among the several data exchange mechanisms available in Windows. A more sophisticated data exchange facility is *OLE*, which stands for *object linking and embedding*.

Although the process of linking or embedding an object from one application to another is similar to that of using the Clipboard, there is one important difference. The OLE object knows the application in which it was created. Thus, if you embed or link a graphic from AutoCAD as an OLE object in Windows Write, double-clicking the graphic in Write loads it—ready for editing—in AutoCAD. And if AutoCAD were not active, double-clicking the graphic also starts AutoCAD.

In an OLE transaction, the source application in which the object is created is called the OLE *server*, and the target application that accepts the object is called the OLE *client*. AutoCAD is both an OLE server and a client. Its drawings can be included in any OLE client application, and objects, such as a sound annotation, also can be included in AutoCAD drawings.

As you may have guessed, linking and embedding are similar in many ways, yet they differ in how the target document that contains the graphic stores information.

*Embedding* an AutoCAD drawing in another application means that a copy of the drawing has been made and stored in the document. There is no association between the drawing file and the graphic embedded in the document. In other words, if you edit the original drawing that formed the basis of the embedded object, the object remains unchanged because it is an independent copy. By the same token, when you double-click the embedded graphic in a document, the copy embedded in the document, and not the original drawing, is loaded in AutoCAD.

*Linking* a drawing, on the other hand, means that a link to the drawing and its view has been created in the document. Whereas embedding creates a copy of the selected objects from the original drawing, linking maintains information about where to find the original drawing and the name of the saved view to be linked. If you modify the original drawing, an update link command in the target document seeks out the original drawing and updates your document so the included graphic reflects the same information as that in the edited original drawing.

Another difference between embedding and linking an AutoCAD drawing, is that linking associates the current view of a drawing to a document and embedding copies selected objects from a drawing to a document.

## AutoCAD as an OLE Server

When you embed or link an AutoCAD drawing in another application, you use AutoCAD as an OLE server. When AutoCAD for DOS users want to insert a copy of a drawing in their word processor, they typically create a file on disk in a format the word processor understands, and then import the file in the document at the proper location.

But as an AutoCAD for Windows user, you have the ability to use OLE, in addition to the traditional DOS method of file export and import. One benefit of using OLE is that you need not worry about what graphic formats the target application accepts. As long as your application is an OLE client, it accepts data you send from AutoCAD.

Another benefit of using OLE is the nature of the additional information kept along with the drawing in the target document. Suppose you are in a network environment, and the marketing department creates an OLE link to one of your drawings. Also, suppose that you change the contents of your drawing after the marketing department had established the link. Now, when the marketing department opens its document at a later date, the copy of the graphic in their document is automatically updated.

For a hands-on tutorial on using AutoCAD as an OLE server, take a look at the exercise in the following section.

## Tutorial: Embedding a Graphic from AutoCAD in Windows Write

There are many times you may want to copy drawings you create in AutoCAD to other applications. In this exercise, you learn how to embed an AutoCAD drawing in Windows Write. This exercise works with any application—such as Lotus AmiPro or Microsoft Word—that is designed to be an OLE client. But Write was chosen in this instance because it is included in every copy of Windows.

Perform the following steps to embed an AutoCAD graphic as an OLE object in a Windows Write document:

1.  If AutoCAD is not already running, start it by double-clicking its icon in Program Manager's AutoCAD R13 group window.

2. Start Windows Write by switching to Program Manager (press Ctrl+Esc to display the Windows Task List, select Program Manager, and click the Switch To button) and double-clicking its icon in the Accessories group window.

3. Switch to AutoCAD and create, or open, the drawing you want to embed in Write.

4. Choose Edit, Copy from AutoCAD's menu bar if you want to embed selected objects from your drawing. You are prompted to select objects which are then sent to the Clipboard.

Or

Choose Edit, Copy View if you want to embed your current view. If you have not saved your current view, AutoCAD automatically creates one with a name, such as OLE1, prior to linking it.

5. Switch to Windows Write.

6. Choose Edit, Paste Special. Select the AutoCAD R13 Drawing Object format in the Paste Special dialog box and click the Paste Link button to embed the drawing in Write (see fig. 36.3).

**Fig. 36.3**
Select the AutoCAD R13 Drawing Object format in the Paste Special dialog box and click the Paste button to embed the drawing in Windows Write.

## AutoCAD as an OLE Client

AutoCAD has been an OLE server since Release 12. But its ability to accept OLE objects in a drawing is new to Release 13. What kind of objects could you possibly want to embed in your drawing? Consider sound!

If you have a sound board and a microphone attached to your computer, you can record your comments about a drawing as a sound file and embed it next to appropriate elements in the AutoCAD drawing. The embedded sound object appears as a Microphone icon in your drawing (see fig. 36.4).

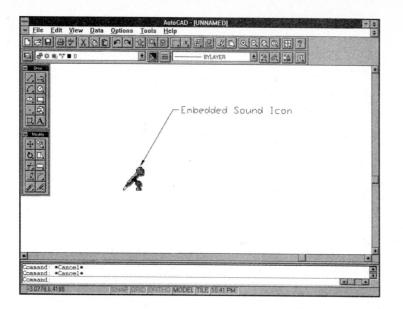

**Fig. 36.4**
Embedded sound
objects appear as a
Microphone icon
in a drawing.

## Tutorial: Embedding a Sound Object in an AutoCAD Drawing

As noted earlier, because AutoCAD is an OLE client, you can paste objects
from a variety of OLE server applications into your drawings. In the following
exercise, you embed a sound object in an AutoCAD drawing:

1. If AutoCAD is not already running, start it by double-clicking its icon in
   Program Manager's AutoCAD R13 group window.

2. Start the Sound Recorder by switching to Program Manager (press
   Ctrl+Esc to display the Windows Task List, select Program Manager, and
   click the Switch To button) and double-clicking its icon in the Accessories group window.

3. Open a sound file in the Sound Recorder. Choose File, Open and select
   one of the sample sound files from the Open dialog box. Alternatively,
   if you have the appropriate hardware, such as a microphone attached to
   your personal computer, you can record your own sound file.

4. Choose Edit, Copy from the Sound Recorder's menu bar to copy the
   sound object to the Clipboard.

5. Switch to AutoCAD, and choose Edit, Paste.

6. A microphone icon appears at the upper-left corner of your view window, indicating that the sound is now embedded.

To listen to your comments embedded in a drawing, all you do is double-click the microphone icon to load the sound in the Windows Sound Recorder. Click the Play button to play back your comments. Of course, if you send a sound annotated drawing to others, their computer must be equipped with a sound board and speakers to listen to your comments.

# Using Dynamic Data Exchange (DDE)

▶ See "What Are AutoLISP, ADS, and ARX?" p. 1049

Among the various data exchange mechanisms implemented in Windows, the most sophisticated is DDE. Earlier in this chapter, you learned how to transfer text from another application to AutoCAD via the Clipboard. You also learned how to embed and link AutoCAD drawings in other applications, and how to embed sound objects in your drawings. All of these tasks were accomplished by simply selecting choices from the Edit menu. DDE, on the other hand, is implemented as a set of macro functions in an application. Just like Lotus 1-2-3 for Windows and Microsoft Excel incorporate DDE functions in their macro language, AutoCAD extends AutoLISP to incorporate DDE specific functions. AutoCAD's DDE functions also can be invoked from within ADS and ARX applications.

Although you get good data exchange functionality from the Clipboard and OLE data exchange protocols, only DDE lets you create such useful and flexible applications as parametric part generation and automated Bill of Materials creation.

With DDE, you can set up AutoCAD and another application, such as a spreadsheet, to transfer not only data but also commands. Thus you can have a design calculation performed in Lotus 1-2-3 update a drawing in AutoCAD. And you can extract information from a drawing, such as a count of blocks in the drawing, and generate a chart from it in Microsoft Excel.

Let's start by first understanding the basics of DDE, and then move on to write simple DDE code that shows how to set up DDE conversations between AutoCAD and another application.

## Basic DDE Concepts

DDE is a mechanism for establishing a conversation between Windows applications. As in any interaction, one application initiates the conversation and the other responds. The application initiating a link is called the *DDE client*. The application responding to data and commands it receives is called the *DDE server*.

AutoCAD for Windows is designed to both initiate a DDE conversation and to respond to one. So, it is both a DDE client and a server. When you create a drawing in AutoCAD by remotely passing it commands from another application, you use AutoCAD as a DDE server. When you pass data from AutoCAD for further manipulation in another application, you use AutoCAD as a DDE client.

To initiate a conversation, a DDE client broadcasts a message to Windows with two pieces of information: an *application* name, and a *topic*. The application name refers to the DDE server, and the topic refers to an element of the DDE server, such as the command line, menu bar, document, or view, with which the DDE client wants to interact.

Windows does not limit applications to only a single DDE link. In other words, at a given time you can have multiple DDE conversations. Because there can be several concurrent DDE links, Windows needs to uniquely identify each. Thus any time a DDE client initiates a conversation, Windows assigns a unique integer number, called a *channel*, to that thread of conversation.

You must structure any DDE application you write to follow the sequence shown below:

- *Initiate the link.* The first step to writing a DDE application is to have the DDE client initiate a link through a function call from its macro language. The exact syntax of the function that initiates a link varies from application to application.

  In Lotus 1-2-3 for Windows, to initiate a link, use the function {DDE-OPEN "APPLICATION", "TOPIC"}.

  In Microsoft Excel, use the function =INITIATE("APPLICATION", "TOPIC").

  In AutoCAD, use the function (APPINIT "APPLICATION" "TOPIC" "EXECUTABLE").

When initiating a link from another application, the application name to use for AutoCAD is "AUTOCAD.R13.DDE," and the topic name for its command line is "SYSTEM." When the macro function to initiate a link is executed, Windows returns a channel number to identify the link.

■ *Exchange data.* After a link has been established, you can start to send and receive data from the client application. The channel number returned by Windows when the link was established must accompany the data you send via the client application's data transfer macro functions.

To pass the LINE command to AutoCAD from Lotus 1-2-3, use the statement {DDE-EXECUTE "LINE"}.

To pass the same command from Microsoft Excel, use the statement =EXECUTE(CHANNEL, "LINE").

If you use AutoCAD as a DDE client, use the function (POKE "CHANNEL" "ITEM" "DATA") to send data and the function (EXECUTE "CHANNEL" "COMMAND") to send a command to the DDE server application.

■ *Terminate the link.* The final step, after you have completed all the data exchange, is to terminate the DDE link to free up the system resources consumed by it. Again, this is done by a function call from the client application.

To terminate the link from Lotus 1-2-3, use the function {DDE-CLOSE}.

In Microsoft Excel, use the function =TERMINATE("CHANNEL").

In AutoCAD, use the function (TERMINATE "CHANNEL") to close a single channel, or the (DDEDONE) function to terminate all channels.

With the basic information presented here, you should be able to write your own DDE applications. The next section discusses the kinds of applications you can develop using DDE.

> **Note**
>
> If you do not yet feel comfortable with DDE concepts, don't worry. Later in this chapter, there is some actual code of working examples that exploit AutoCAD's DDE functionality.

# What Can DDE Do?

Just as AutoCAD places no restrictions on what you can draw with it, the variety of problems you can tackle through the use of DDE has no bounds. Spreadsheet software is probably the most important type of application you use to create DDE links. Of course, links can be created with any Windows application, such as a database, that incorporates DDE functionality.

Let's look at the two classes of applications you are most likely to develop using DDE: parametrics and Bill of Materials.

### Parametrics

The concept of parametrics is neither new nor specific to Windows. It has been around for years; many parametric utilities have been written in AutoLISP. Essentially, for our purposes, *parametrics* refers to the creation of shapes that are driven by numerical values. Thus, if you wrote a macro that prompted the user to key-in a length and a width for a rectangle and then proceeded to draw the shape with the values supplied, you would have written a parametric program.

For example, a parametric that is useful to a structural steel designer, who designs building or other structures out of standard steel shapes, is a parametric steel shapes library. The American Institute of Steel Construction (AISC) publishes the Steel Construction Manual that lists over a thousand standard steel shapes, such as wide flange beams, channels, tubes, and so on. You can maintain the dimensions of these shapes in a spreadsheet and write a DDE program to draw them in AutoCAD.

Another example is the parametric creation of all types of mechanical fasteners. Again, the fastener sizes and shapes have been standardized by the industry, and maintaining their dimensions in a spreadsheet allows you to create a DDE program to draw them in AutoCAD.

The benefit of using parametrics is that after you have all the dimensions that define a part, you can generate any desired view: section, plan, or elevation. Such flexibility is not possible if you use predrawn AutoCAD blocks for each shape.

Certainly, the two examples noted previously can be very well implemented in AutoLISP. So, why consider DDE? Because of its simplicity. Writing a parametric steel shapes program in AutoLISP requires a fairly sophisticated knowledge of the language, and the code you write is long and time-consuming.

By using a spreadsheet's built-in data query functions to locate the dimensions corresponding to a specific part name, you can do in one line of code what would require significantly more effort to write in AutoLISP. Thus if you know the basics of your spreadsheet macro language, you can leverage that knowledge to create utilities for AutoCAD, even though you may not know AutoLISP.

Spreadsheets are a great tool for evaluating various design alternatives easily and quickly. When you combine their number-crunching power with DDE links to AutoCAD, you can have designs that you calculate drive the drawings that you want to create. This can be a very powerful combination.

All of the examples listed here use AutoCAD as a DDE server. Let's now explore yet another type of application that uses AutoCAD as a DDE client.

### Bill of Materials

You probably have heard the words "intelligent drawing" bandied around. In simple terms, it refers to non-graphic information that you attach to graphic elements in your drawing. For example, data attributes that you embed in a block, or external database links that you establish to any drawing object, are forms of intelligence that you impart to a drawing. Such non-graphic data can be extracted and sent to other applications for further processing.

An example that exploits this capability is the creation of a bill of materials. A facilities manager, who maintains information such as price and model number of furniture items in a building in the form of attributes in a block, can extract a count of symbols and send them to a spreadsheet using DDE commands. The table of information sent can then be formatted and printed as a bill of materials, or a count of inventory from the spreadsheet.

Similarly, a highway sound barrier panel manufacturer, who designs wall panels that line the sides of highways to reduce the level of noise from vehicular traffic, can generate a cost estimate from the plan drawing of the panel layout, if the appropriate non-graphic fields are embedded in the blocks he uses to draw them.

▶ See "Intro-
duction to
AutoLISP, ADS,
and ARX,"
p. 1049

Implementing examples such as the ones noted here requires you to extract non-graphic data from a drawing and send it to a spreadsheet. Because you can use AutoCAD as a DDE client in this scenario, a knowledge of AutoLISP is required.

With this said, let's get practical! The next two sections present very simple, yet illustrative examples that show how you can go about writing your own DDE application.

## AutoCAD as a DDE Client

Whenever you extract data from a drawing and want to pass it to another application, you use AutoCAD as a DDE client. AutoCAD implements a large set of DDE functions to perform a variety of tasks. This section presents an AutoLISP program that initiates a conversation with Microsoft Excel and draws a chart in it by sending data and commands via DDE function calls.

By reading through Listing 36.1, you learn how to initiate a DDE link from AutoCAD, send data and commands to Excel, and finally, how to terminate the link. In other words, you walk through all the steps needed to create a DDE application.

---

**Listing 36.1   Using AutoCAD to Create a Chart in Excel**

```
; AC13TOXL.LSP
; ============
; An AutoLISP program to demonstrates a DDE conversation between
; AutoCAD Release 13 for Windows and Microsoft Excel. Because
; AutoCAD initiates the link, and sends data and commands to Excel,
; it is the DDE client in this interaction.
;
; by Ranjit S. Sahai
;
(defun AC13TOXL()
  (xload "c:\\acadr13\\win\\sample\\ddelisp")
;
; INITIATE LINK
;
  (setq chnl (appinit "excel" "sheet1" "c:\\excel\\excel"))
;
; the appinit function starts Excel if it is not already running
; if you installed Excel in a drive and directory other than the
; default c:\excel, then substitute that path in the above state-
  ment
; something like d:\\mypath\\excel
;
; SEND TEXT AND NUMBERS TO SPECIFIC CELLS IN EXCEL
;
  ; The POKE command sends data to specified cell
  ;
  (poke chnl "r1c3" "Using AutoCAD Release 13 for Windows")
  (poke chnl "r2c3" "(AutoCAD is the DDE Client Here)")
  (poke chnl "r4c2" "Year")
  (poke chnl "r4c3" "Installed AutoCAD Seats")
  (poke chnl "r5c2" "'82")
```

*(continues)*

**Listing 36.1   Continued**

```
      (poke chnl "r6c2" "'84")
      (poke chnl "r7c2" "'86")
      (poke chnl "r8c2" "'88")
      (poke chnl "r9c2" "'90")
      (poke chnl "r10c2" "'92")
      (poke chnl "r11c2" "'94")
      (poke chnl "r5c3" "0")
      (poke chnl "r6c3" "10000")
      (poke chnl "r7c3" "50000")
      (poke chnl "r8c3" "150000")
      (poke chnl "r9c3" "400000")
      (poke chnl "r10c3" "650000")
      (poke chnl "r11c3" "1000000")
      (prompt "All data sent. ")
      (setq keypress (getstring "Press ENTER to create chart."))
      ;
      ; The EXECUTE command sends commands to Excel
      ;
      (execute chnl "[SELECT(\"r4c2:r11c3\")]")
      (execute chnl "[NEW(2)]")
      (prompt "Chart drawn. ")
      (setq keypress (getstring "Press ENTER to close Excel."))
      ;
      ;SELECT highlights data range, NEW(2) creates chart
      ;
   ; CLOSE EXCEL AND TERMINATE LINK
   ;
      (ddedone)                              ;Terminate link
      (setq chnl (initiate "excel" "system"))
         ;Start link again
      (execute chnl "[CLOSE(FALSE)]")
         ;but now to "system"
      (execute chnl "[CLOSE(FALSE)]")
         ;to be able to issue
      (execute chnl "[QUIT()]")
         ;File Close and Exit commands
      (ddedone)                              ;Terminate link
   ;
   ; OPTIONALLY UNLOAD AUTOCADS DDE MODULE
   ;
      (xunload "ddelisp")
   )
```

Listing 36.1 is a straightforward example that passes text and numbers to Excel, and then invokes its commands to select the data and create a chart. To re-create this example on your computer, open a text editor, such as the Windows Notepad, and type the entire text of this listing (see fig. 36.5).

> **Note**
>
> Although you may want to type the code for Listing 36.1 to get a better feel for its syntax, you don't have to. The code is included on the disk accompanying this book in the text file AC13TOXL.LSP.

```
                    Notepad - AC13TOXL.LSP
 File  Edit  Search  Help
; AC13TOXL.LSP
; =============
; An AutoLISP program to demonstrates a DDE conversation between
; AutoCAD Release 13 for Windows and Microsoft Excel. Because
; AutoCAD initiates the link, and sends data and commands to Excel,
; it is the DDE client in this interaction.
;
; by Ranjit S. Sahai

(defun AC13TOXL()
   (xload "c:\\acadr13\\win\\sample\\ddelisp")
;
; INITIATE LINK

   (setq chnl (appinit "excel" "sheet1" "c:\\excel\\excel"))
;
; the appinit function starts Excel if it is not already running
; if you installed Excel in a drive and directory other than the
; default c:\excel, then substitute that path in the above statement
; something like d:\\mypath\\excel
;
; SEND TEXT AND NUMBERS TO SPECIFIC CELLS IN EXCEL

   ; The POKE command sends data to specified cell
   ;
   (poke chnl "r1c3" "Using AutoCAD Release 13 for Windows")
   (poke chnl "r2c3" "(AutoCAD is the DDE Client Here)")
   (poke chnl "r4c2" "Year")
   (poke chnl "r4c3" "Installed AutoCAD Seats")
   (poke chnl "r5c2" "'82")
   (poke chnl "r6c2" "'84")
   (poke chnl "r7c2" "'86")
   (poke chnl "r8c2" "'88")
   (poke chnl "r9c2" "'90")
   (poke chnl "r10c2" "'92")
   (poke chnl "r11c2" "'94")
```

**Fig. 36.5**
You start by typing your code in a text editor such as Windows Notepad.

The next step is to save your code (or copy the file from the disk included with this book) in AutoCAD's support directory (c:\acadr13\win\support for a default installation) and give the file a name such as AC13TOXL.LSP. This makes the file available for loading in AutoCAD as an AutoLISP application. Load the application in AutoCAD by typing **(load "ac13toxl")** at the Command: prompt (see fig. 36.6).

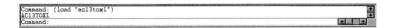

```
Command: (load "ac13toxl")
AC13TOXL
Command:
```

**Fig. 36.6**
Load your application in AutoCAD by using the AutoLISP LOAD function.

After the application is loaded, you can start it by typing **(ac13toxl)** at the Command: prompt. The first line of code defines the function name and is followed by the XLOAD function that loads DDELISP.EXE, an ADS application that extends the AutoLISP language with new DDE functions. This application must be loaded if you are to use DDE in AutoCAD.

Of the several ways AutoLISP provides to initiate a link, this example uses APPINIT as it is the most flexible. If Excel is already loaded, this function merely initiates the DDE link, but if Excel is not running, the function first starts the spreadsheet and then initiates the link.

---

**Note**

You may want to start Excel and tile it with AutoCAD on your Windows desktop. Doing so allows you to switch between both applications and watch how the AutoLISP controls Excel.

---

With the link established and the ID of the communication channel defined in the "chnl" variable, use the AutoLISP function POKE to transmit data from AutoCAD to Excel.

Although you have actually embedded numbers in the POKE function that you want to transmit from AutoCAD to Excel, normally you extract numbers from the drawing object database before incorporating them in the POKE function. It should be pointed out that AutoLISP numeric variables should first be converted to text strings prior to including them as parameters in the POKE function.

The application listing presented above first "poked" a few explanatory labels and column titles to cells in Excel. Then it sent the year and the data for the number of AutoCAD seats installed for that year (see fig. 36.7).

**Fig. 36.7**
Use the AutoLISP POKE function to transfer data from AutoCAD to Excel.

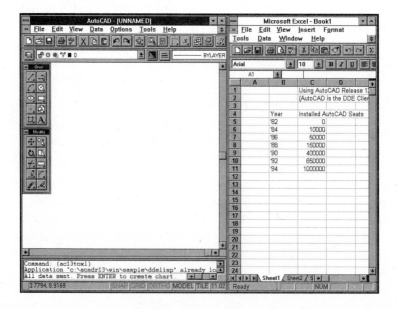

Next, to have Excel draw a chart from the data transmitted, use the AutoLISP EXECUTE function. The Excel macro command "[SELECT("R4C2:R11C3")]" selects the range of cells that you wish to include in a chart. The "[NEW(2)]" command creates a chart from the selected data (see fig. 36.8).

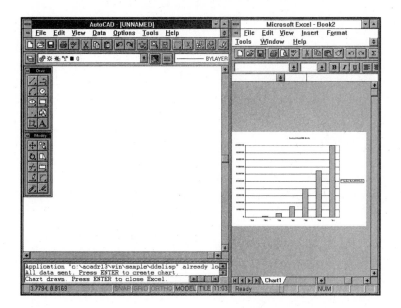

**Fig. 36.8**

The AutoLISP EXECUTE function uses DDE to send Excel its command to draw a chart.

Finally, the last few statements are used to close Excel. Notice that a new channel was established to the item "system" to be able to issue the File, Close and File, Exit commands in Excel. For the sake of recovering system resources used by DDE links, it is always wise to terminate open links.

## AutoCAD as a DDE Server

When another application sends data and commands to AutoCAD for it to execute, AutoCAD assumes the role of a DDE server. Because the other application is in control of the DDE interaction between the two, you must know that application's macro language. This example uses Lotus 1-2-3 for Windows to send data and commands to AutoCAD.

See figure 36.9 for an overview of the worksheet created in this section. The purpose of the worksheet is to generate a stair section. You supply the number of risers that you want to draw, along with the height of a riser, and the width of a tread. When you invoke the macro in 1-2-3, it initiates a conversation with AutoCAD and draws the stair section.

**Fig. 36.9**
This is an overview of the worksheet layout created.

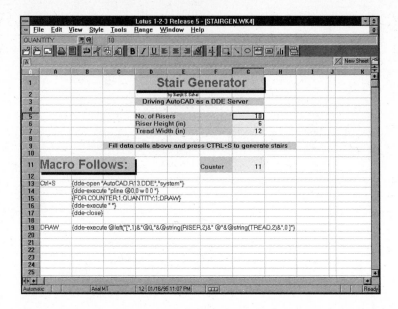

> **Note**
>
> Although you may want to re-create the spreadsheet based on the following tables to get a better feel for its syntax, you don't have to. The spreadsheet is included on the disk accompanying this book and is named STAIRGEN.WK4.

Before you start re-creating the worksheet shown in figure 36.10, take a moment to review the range names used. Define the names for cell ranges as shown in Table 36.1.

**Table 36.1 Range Names Used in Stair Generator Worksheet**

| Range Name | Cell Range | Description |
| --- | --- | --- |
| COUNTER | G11 | Counter variable used by FOR loop |
| DRAW | B19 | Subroutine name used by FOR loop |
| QUANTITY | G5 | Number of risers in stairs |
| RISER | G6 | Height of riser in inches |
| TREAD | G7 | Width of tread in inches |
| \S | F11 | Macro to draw stair section in AutoCAD |

> **Note**
>
> In Table 36.1, the range name \S assigns the keystroke Ctrl+S to the macro that starts at cell F11.

Table 36.1 defines the range names for all variables used in the spreadsheet. The advantage of using range names is twofold; first, it provides better code readability, and second, it offers flexibility while moving cell contents because references to variables in code are independent of cell addresses.

With Range Names as defined in Table 36.1 above, you can proceed to type in contents of cells, as shown in Table 36.2.

| Table 36.2   Contents of Stair Generator Worksheet for Lotus 1-2-3 | |
|---|---|
| **Cell** | **Contents** |
| D1 | Stair Generator |
| E2 | by Ranjit S. Sahai |
| D3 | Driving AutoCAD as a DDE Server |
| D5 | No. of Risers |
| D6 | Riser Height (in) |
| D7 | Tread Width (in) |
| C9 | Fill data cells above and press Ctrl+S to generate stairs |
| A11 | Macro Follows |
| F11 | Counter |
| A13 | Ctrl+S |
| A19 | DRAW |
| B13 | {dde-open "AutoCAD.R13.DDE","system"} |
| B14 | {dde-execute "pline @0,0 w 0 0 "} |
| B15 | {FOR COUNTER;1;QUANTITY;1;DRAW} |
| B16 | {dde-execute " "} |
| B17 | {dde-close} |
| B19 | {dde-execute @left("[",1)&"@0,"&@string(RISER,2)&" @"&@string(TREAD,2)&",0 ]"} |

> **Note**
>
> Cells G5, G6, and G7 are data cells in which you key in the number of risers, height of riser, and width of tread. These values are used by the macro that starts at cell B13 and its subroutine at cell B19.

After you have keyed in all the cell contents, as shown in Table 36.2, you are ready to use your Stair Generator. Start both AutoCAD and Lotus 1-2-3. Load the worksheet you just created in Lotus 1-2-3, if it is not already loaded, and tile both applications (see fig. 36.10).

**Fig. 36.10**
Tile AutoCAD and the Stair Generator worksheet in Lotus 1-2-3 as shown, and type in data values.

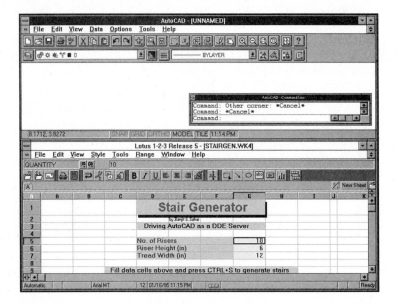

The code in the spreadsheet generates a stair in elevation starting from the last active point in AutoCAD. So before you generate a stair, pick a point near the lower-left corner of your drawing area in AutoCAD to make that point the last active point. AutoCAD prompts you to pick the other corner for a selection window. Press Esc to cancel this prompt and return to the Command: prompt.

Switch to Lotus 1-2-3. In the data cells G5, G6, and G7, type in the values **10**, **6**, and **12** respectively. With 1-2-3 active, press the keystroke Ctrl+S to create the stair section in AutoCAD (see fig. 36.11).

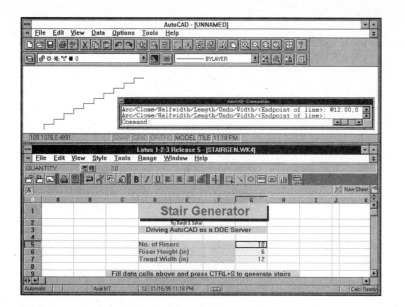

**Fig. 36.11**
Press Ctrl+S to create the stair section in AutoCAD.

### Note

This spreadsheet works fine with Release 13, but not with AutoCAD Release 12, or with AutoCAD Windows Extension (AWE) for Release 11. To make it work with Release 12, use the application name "AutoCAD.DDE", and to make it work with AWE Release 11, use the application name "AutoCAD" in cell B13.

Let's take a moment to examine the spreadsheet macro and understand the logic behind its workings. The macro code starts at cell B13, where it initiates a link with AutoCAD's command line. The application name for AutoCAD is *AutoCAD.R13.DDE* and the topic name for its command line is *system*.

The next line of code in cell B14 sends the PLINE command to AutoCAD along with the start point location of @0,0 (that is, relative coordinate of 0,0 with respect to the last point picked) and a start and end width of 0.

Cell B15 then invokes a loop that repeats the DRAW subroutine (located in cell B19) once each for the number of risers specified in cell G5. The DRAW subroutine essentially draws one riser and one tread using relative coordinate input with riser height and tread width, as specified in cells G6 and G7 respectively.

The line in cell B16 exits out of the PLINE command after all risers and treads have been drawn, and the line in cell B17 terminates the link with AutoCAD.

As should be clear by this example, you do not need to learn AutoLISP to program utilities for AutoCAD. If you know your spreadsheet macro language well, you can create useful utilities that can send commands to AutoCAD to do your bidding.

# From Here...

For more information about customizing various aspects of AutoCAD and programming in AutoLISP, see the following chapters:

- Chapter 37, "Customizing AutoCAD," shows you how to customize toolbars and menus, linetypes, shapes, and fonts.

- Chapter 38, "Introduction to AutoLISP, ADS, and ARX," introduces you to AutoCAD's programming languages, its benefits, and how to invoke sample programs you may come across.

# Part XI

# Customizing and Expanding AutoCAD Resources

FENCELINE2 ——□———□———□——

BATTING

GAS_LINE —— GAS —— GAS —— GAS —— GAS —— GAS —— GAS

## Button Icon

Edit...

## Menu Customization

nu Groups                    Menu Bar

ups:                                    Unload

☐ Replace All              Load

File Name:

AutoCAD - [37FIG05.DWG]

File   Edit   View   Data   Options   Tools   Help

# Chapter 37

# Customizing AutoCAD

Both this chapter and Chapter 38, "Introduction to AutoLISP, ADS, and ARX," discuss how to modify AutoCAD to your specific needs and tastes. If you are looking for instructions on how to install AutoCAD, you should refer to Appendix B: "Installing and Configuring." There you will find information about system requirements, the AutoCAD Configuration Menu, configuring AutoCAD for your hardware, and more.

Chapter 37 and 38 combine to give you an introductory overview toward altering AutoCAD's interface for your specific needs. The capability to customize the drafting program has been inherent since the earliest versions, and allows for the program to be adapted to a wide variety of users. It is this capability (and support by third-party developers) that has led to the success of the program.

An entire book could be dedicated to the details for developing custom applications for AutoCAD. Indeed, Autodesk has included with your software a separate manual just for this subject. This manual, the *AutoCAD Release 13 Customization Guide*, is referred to throughout this chapter. In this chapter, you get an abridged version of the features within AutoCAD that enable you to customize the program for your use. In addition, you learn where you can obtain further information should you wish to pursue the topics in greater detail.

In this chapter, you learn about the following:

- Customizing toolbars and menus

- Customizing linetypes, including an example of Release 13's new complex linetypes

- Customizing more complex graphical information

- Using third-party applications with AutoCAD

■ Using AutoCAD's programming languages

The discussion of customizing AutoCAD begins with an overview of the AutoCAD menu.

# Customizing Toolbars and Menus

The menu has long been one of the two sources of issuing commands to AutoCAD. Menus and the keyboard were once the sole means of interacting with the program. Now, there are also toolbars (in the Windows version of AutoCAD only), voice recognition, and we are on the verge of having 3D and Virtual Reality input devices.

In the Windows version of AutoCAD, there are five menu types and four menu features. All nine aspects of the menu reside in one text-based file that can be edited or created as you wish. The standard text file menu that comes with AutoCAD for Windows is ACAD.MNU, but you can load menus with other names such as menus created by third-party developers. (Third-party software is discussed at the end of this chapter.) The five menus and four features supported by AutoCAD for Windows are as follows:

Menus:

■ Pull-down and cursor menus

■ Screen menus

■ Image tile menus

■ Pointing device menus

■ Digitizing-tablet menus

Features:

■ Toolbars

■ Keyboard accelerators

■ Help string and tool tips

■ Menu groups

You were introduced to these AutoCAD menus and features in Chapter 1, through the discussions on "Understanding the Display," and the examples seen in "Using the Toolbars and Menus." Note, though, that although the toolbar definitions exist within the menu file, toolbars are not available in

AutoCAD for DOS. Therefore, menu files are not interchangeable between AutoCAD for DOS and AutoCAD for Windows. Menus written for the DOS version can, however, be loaded into AutoCAD for Windows, and as you will see, you are able to take part of menu files—whether created for DOS or Windows—and create a custom menu.

> **Note**
>
> AutoCAD for Windows can use menus created for the DOS version. Of course, there will be limitations by not having any toolbars or keyboard accelerators predefined. Unfortunately, the DOS version is not able to interpret the syntax of a menu for AutoCAD for Windows. Even though the source file for AutoCAD for DOS and AutoCAD for Windows uses the name ACAD.MNU, these files are not the same in syntax or content.

A new feature to Release 13 is the capability to load just part of a menu. This partial menu loading gives the users and third-party developers the ability to cross-reference menus and permit faster execution of AutoCAD commands. Unfortunately, this feature is only available in the Windows and Windows NT versions of AutoCAD, and will not be available in the DOS version.

> **Note**
>
> You will notice that AutoCAD comes with separate ACAD.MNU files for the DOS and Windows versions. The name of the menu you are currently using is saved inside each individual drawing file. Since the menu you are using is saved in the drawing, having two separate but similarly named files permits you to work on a drawing in the DOS version of AutoCAD and, at any time, open the drawing In AutoCAD for Windows without having to redefine a separate menu. By having the menus set up in this way, AutoCAD loads the correct menu for the proper platform of AutoCAD.

There are aspects to the AutoCAD for Windows menu that are not available in the DOS menu command structure. These offer more flexibility and convenience to the end user. For example, in the list shown previously you see a feature called *menu groups*. This feature allows you to load partial menus instead of an entirely new menu. Since AutoCAD can only have one menu loaded at a time, you must choose between add-in software or flip between packages as you need them if you are using the DOS version. If the menu is written using the features available in Windows, you have the ability to load part of a menu, or easily create a custom menu by assembling various parts of many menus. This feature is available by using the MENULOAD command, which is discussed later in this chapter.

It may be helpful to briefly cover the MENU command. This command allows you to load one menu in the drawing. Using this command, you may load any menu created for AutoCAD. This may be a menu that was provided with AutoCAD, purchased from a third-party developer, or one that you have created from scratch.

There are two files relating to an AutoCAD Menu in the DOS version of AutoCAD. There are four files that relate to the Windows versions. The text file that can be altered with any editor has the filename *.MNU, regardless of the AutoCAD platform. AutoCAD compiles this text file automatically the first time it's used or if it changed, and creates a version used by the system with the filename *.MNX for the DOS version, and *.MNC for the Windows versions. The other files for the Windows version include *.MNR, which is the resource file and holds the Bitmap images used by the menu, and *.MNS, the source menu file that is a text-based file created by AutoCAD.

In figure 37.1 you see the actual menu pull-down as seen in the standard ACAD.MNU. After, you see the syntax used.

**Fig. 37.1**

Just one of the pull-downs from the menu bar.

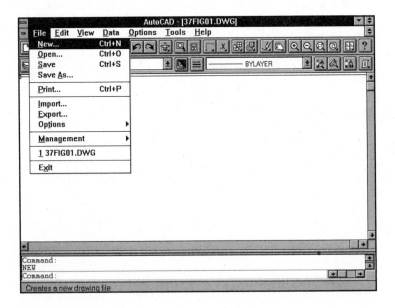

The syntax that follows corresponds to the pull-down seen in figure 37.1. This is just 26 lines of the 6,889 lines of code in the ACAD.MNU menu for the Windows platform.

```
***POP1
ID_File     [&File]
ID_New      [&New...\tCtrl+N]^C^C_new
```

```
ID_Open      [&Open...\tCtrl+O]^C^C_open
ID_Save      [&Save\tCtrl+S]^C^C_qsave
ID_Saveas    [Save &As...]^C^C_saveas
             [--]
ID_Print     [&Print...\tCtrl+P]^C^C_plot
             [--]
ID_Import    [&Import...]^C^C_import
ID_Export    [&Export...]^C^C_export
ID_Ioopts    [->Op&tions]
ID_Wmfopt      [WMF Op&tions...]^C^C_wmfopts
ID_Psqual      [PostScript &Quality]'_psquality
ID_Psdisp      [PostScript &Display]'_psdrag
               [--]
ID_Psprol      [<-&PostScript Prolog]'_psprolog
             [--]
ID_Mngt        [->&Management]
ID_Unlock      [&Unlock File...]^C^C_files
ID_Audit       [&Audit]^C^C_audit
ID_Recov       [<-&Recover...]^C^C_recover
             [--]
ID_MRU       [Drawing History]
             [--]
ID_Exit      [E&xit]^C^C_quit
```

## Customizing Menus with MENULOAD and MENUUNLOAD

Previously, you read about a feature within AutoCAD for Windows that enables you to load (and unload) part of a menu. There are two aspects to customizing your AutoCAD for Windows environment: customizing the menu and customizing the toolbars. First, you'll learn how to modify the menu by assembling parts of different menus into one. Following, you see an example of the MENULOAD and MENUUNLOAD commands that make this possible.

If you compare figure 37.2 with figure 37.1, you see the addition of two pull-down menus, Osnap and Shaft. Notice also, the missing pull-down, Tools.

The menu is customized with the MENULOAD command. With this command, you can attach parts of other menus called *partial menus* to the existing "base" menu. For purposes of this command and the syntax used within the menu itself, Autodesk refers to a complete menu as a menu *group*. From this group, you can select one or more parts to load into the base. Once MENULOAD is executed, the Menu Customization dialog box is displayed. As with all dialog boxes in AutoCAD, the system variable FILEDIA must be set to 1 or you will receive text prompts only. Figure 37.3 shows the Menu Groups dialog options to the command.

**XI**

Customizing AutoCAD

**RELEASE**

**Fig. 37.2**
A modified version
of AutoCAD's
standard menu.

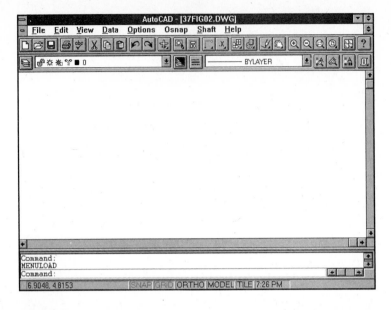

**Tip**
The MENULOAD
command does
not have an icon
"button." You can
access the com-
mand through the
keyboard or by the
pull-down menu
sequence: Tools,
Customize Menus.

**Note**

If you have the system variable FILEDIA set to 1, the MENULOAD and MENUUNLOAD
commands are identical. Using the command MENULOAD and setting the variable to
0 returns the prompt:

    Menu file name or . for none <acad>:

Using the MENUUNLOAD command returns:

    Enter the name of the MENUGROUP to unload:

**Fig. 37.3**
The Menu Groups
area allows you to
load other menu
groups.

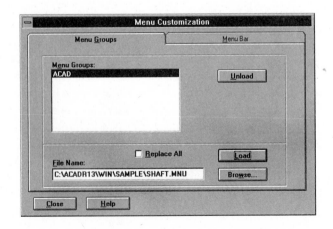

You can have many menus loaded under the Menu Groups area. As you can see in the figure, a sample menu provided with AutoCAD called "SHAFT" was loaded. The options that are available in the Menu Groups and seen in figure 37.3 are as follows:

- *Menu Groups:* This box lists the menu groups currently loaded.

- *File Name:* Under this prompt, type the name of the menu to load, or use the Browse option to find the menu.

- *Replace All:* Unloads all the menu groups listed and loads the single menu entered in the File Name: box.

- *Unload:* Selecting individual menu groups and picking Unload removes that single menu from the group's listing.

- *Load:* With a menu typed in the File Name box, the Load option loads the menu into the Groups listing. If the menu has not been previously compiled into the *.MNC file, AutoCAD automatically compiles the menu.

- *Browse:* This option displays the file dialog box with which you can find a menu file located on your storage device.

Once you have selected a menu to add to the Menu Groups, you can customize the current menu by going to the Menu Bar screen in the Menu Customization dialog box. The options for the Menu Bar are displayed in figure 37.4.

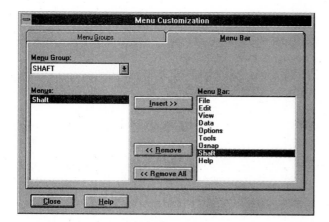

**Fig. 37.4**

The Menu Bar allows you to patch parts of a menu together in the current "base" menu.

As you can see in our example, the Shaft menu has been inserted from the left side of the screen into the menu Bar above the Help menu on the right side of the screen. Using the options seen in figure 37.4, the "Tools" menu has been removed and the "Osnap" menu from the ACAD.MNU menu group has been added. The options for the Menu Bar are as follows:

- *Menu Group:* This pop-up listing shows the loaded menu groups. These groups are loaded as seen previously in figure 37.3.

- *Menus:* The menus associated with the menu group seen under the Menu Group option are listed under this heading.

- *Menu Bar:* The Menu Bar lists the pull-down menus seen in the current or "base" menu. The first item in the list represents the left-most item in the menu.

- *Insert:* The Insert option places the highlighted menu in the window on the left within the menu bar shown on the right. It is inserted above the selected (highlighted) pull-down seen on the right.

- *Remove:* The Remove option deletes the selected pull-down from the menu bar.

- *Remove All:* This option removes all the pull-down menus from the Menu Bar, thus allowing you to create a menu from scratch.

- *Close:* By closing the dialog box, you accept the changes to the menu.

After selecting Close from this screen, AutoCAD displays the menu seen in figure 37.2.

Another aspect of customizing menus includes customizing the AutoCAD toolbars. Let's continue the discussion on customizing your environment by demonstrating how to change the AutoCAD toolbars.

## Customizing Toolbars with TBCONFIG

Another feature useful in customizing AutoCAD's environment is the ability to alter the toolbars. Toolbars are covered in Chapter 1, under "Understanding the Display," and the examples seen in "Using the Toolbars and Menus." In this section, you discover the method by which you can alter the toolbars to improve your drawing efficiency.

The toolbars are altered through a series of dialog boxes. Within these dialog boxes, you can change the existing toolbars, create a new toolbar from

**Tip**
The capability to load partial menus is only available in the Windows version of AutoCAD. AutoCAD for Windows can read menus that were written for previous versions and for the DOS version of Release 13.

scratch, define a series of keystrokes called macros to a button, and even create a button's picture with a Button Editor. The main dialog box is seen in figure 37.5. To access the Toolbars dialog box, perform the following steps:

- Enter the command **tbconfig** from the keyboard.

- Click the Return button while pointing at a tool icon.

- Select the Tools pull-down menu and the Customize Toolbars option.

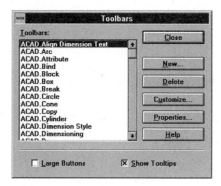

The options on the Toolbars dialog box are as follows:

- *Toolbars:* Here you see the toolbars available. Preceding each toolbar is the menu name to which they are associated. In the figure, for example, the toolbar for Align Dimension Text can be found within the AutoCAD menu group.

- *Close:* Closes the dialog box and saves the changes to the toolbars.

- *New:* Displays the New Toolbar dialog box. This option is discussed in more detail later in this chapter.

- *Delete:* Removes the highlighted toolbar.

- *Customize:* This option displays the Customize Toolbars dialog box and is used to organize the toolbars into categories. This option is discussed further later in this section.

- *Properties:* With the Properties option, the Toolbar Properties dialog box is displayed. Here you can modify the settings that affect the display and name of individual toolbars. This option is discussed in more detail shortly.

■ *Large Buttons:* Selecting this option changes the toolbar icons from 16 × 16 pixels to 32 × 32 pixels.

■ *Show Tooltips:* When the Show Tooltips box is filled in, AutoCAD displays the tool's name when the pointing device pauses on the toolbar.

### Creating New Toolbars

One of the options on the main dialog box allows you to create a new toolbar. When selected, the New option seen in figure 37.5 displays the dialog box in figure 37.6.

**Fig. 37.6**

With the New Toolbar dialog box, you can create blank toolbars.

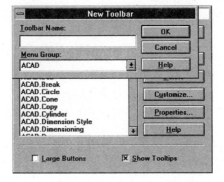

With the New Toolbar dialog box, you can create blank toolbars and assign them to a menu file. After you create a new toolbar, use the Customize Toolbars option to place icons within the new toolbar. The options for New Toolbars seen in figure 37.6 are as follows:

■ *Toolbar Name:* Enter the name of the new toolbar in this box.

■ *Menu Group:* The menu group listed here holds the new toolbar after it is created. You cannot enter a menu name here unless it has been loaded. See the MENULOAD command, discussed earlier in this chapter.

### Adding Tools to an Existing Toolbar

Another option in the main Toolbars dialog box (seen in figure 37.5) is Customize. Once this option is selected, you see the dialog box in figure 37.7.

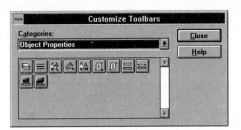

**Fig. 37.7**
Using the
Customize
Toolbars dialog
box, you can add
or delete tools
from the toolbars
on the display.

With Customize Toolbars, you can drag and drop tools from the categories right into existing toolbars. When dropped, the new tools are placed where the cursor was located in the toolbar. You can also remove tools from toolbars on the display by dragging from the toolbars and dropping on the Customize Toolbars dialog box.

The option seen in the Customize Toolbars dialog box is as follows:

- *Categories:* These are predefined groupings of icons that make it easier to find the tools you are looking for. It includes a miscellaneous and a custom category for creating your own custom tools.

### Modifying Toolbar Properties

You can also customize the properties of existing toolbars. This includes changing the name, the description (which is displayed in the status bar as the pointing device moves over the toolbar), and if the toolbar is displayed or not. This is done with the <u>P</u>roperties option of the Toolbars dialog box seen in figure 37.5. This option displays the Toolbar Properties dialog box seen in figure 37.8.

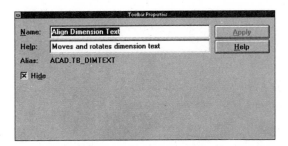

**Tip**
Within the Customize Toolbars dialog box, you can copy a tool from one toolbar to another by pressing the Ctrl key while dragging and dropping.

**XI**

**Customizing AutoCAD**

**Fig. 37.8**
The Toolbar
Properties dialog
box affects the
name and display
of the toolbar.

- *Name:* The name is displayed in the top bar of each toolbar.

- *Help:* The text in this box is displayed in the status bar when the pointing device moves over the toolbar.

- *Alias:* This value, which cannot be changed, shows the name AutoCAD uses internally. The name begins with the menu group and is followed by the toolbar name as it appears in the ACAD.MNU file. This text string corresponds to the toolbar alias in the Toolbar dialog box.

- *Hide:* Selecting this toggle and then selecting Apply either displays or hides the toolbar you are customizing.

### Assigning Macros to Buttons

With the Button Properties dialog box, you can control the command, name, and icon associated with a tool. You can even edit the button's graphic icon. The dialog box used for these options is seen in figure 37.9. To open this dialog box, click the Return button on the pointing device while pointing at a tool icon when the Toolbars menu is displayed.

**Fig. 37.9**
The Button Properties dialog box allows you to modify the task a tool performs.

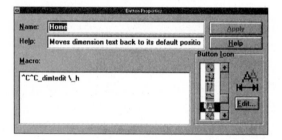

- *Name:* Sets the tool's name. This name is displayed when the pointing device passes over the icon if the Show Tooltips option is checked in the Toolbars dialog box.

- *Help:* The text in the Help box is displayed in the status bar when the pointing device passes over the tool.

- *Macro:* Here, you can place a command or series of keystrokes. When the button is pressed, the commands are entered as if typed at the keyboard. For more information on the syntax needed when creating macros, see Chapter 4 of the *AutoCAD Customization Guide*, "Custom Menus."

- *Button Icon:* In this scrolling list you can select from many predefined button icons. Pressing the Edit button opens the Button Editor, discussed next.

### Drawing Your Own Buttons

AutoCAD enables you to modify the button icons used in the toolbars. You begin by opening the Button Properties dialog box discussed previously. Afterward, you select a button icon from the scrolling list and press the Edit button. The Button Editor is displayed as seen in figure 37.10.

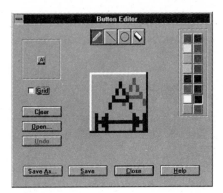

**Fig. 37.10**

With the Button Editor, you can change the icon of any tool.

The button editor functions much the same as many popular painting programs. The options seen in this dialog box includes the following:

- *Image:* The icon's image is displayed in both large form called the Editing Area, and at a reduced scale. The smaller version, seen in the upper-left corner, helps you understand how your changes appear when done. The large picture in the center is where you edit the image.

- *Editing Tools:* The editing tools located on the top of the dialog box are used to modify the image. They are:

| | |
|---|---|
| Pencil | Change one pixel at a time in the color selected. Dragging the pointing device changes all the pixels it touches. |
| Line | This draws a straight line in the color selected. Pick a point and drag it to the end of the line. A temporary line is displayed until you release the button. |
| Circle | Circle creates an approximated circle in the image editing area. The circle is created much the same as the line in that you pick a point that represents the center and drag it to represent the radius. When the pointing device button is released, the circle is created. |

Erase        This tool erases one pixel at a time. Just like the Pencil, you can affect more than one pixel by holding the pointing device button down and dragging it across the editing area.

- *Editing Area:* The editing area is located in the center of the dialog box and is where you can alter the image.

- *Color Palette:* On the right, you see the color palette. This sets the current color used by the editing tools.

- *Grid:* This toggle turns a grid on and off that shows the pixels of the icon.

- *Clear:* This option erases the entire image.

- *Open:* This option allows you to open any Bitmap image for editing. These files are stored with the filename *.BMP.

- *Undo:* The Undo option removes the effects of the last action.

- *Save As... / Save:* These options save the customized icon as a Bitmap file.

- *Close:* Closes the dialog box. If you haven't saved the changes, you are prompted to do so.

### Changing Fly-out Toolbars

The last aspect to customizing the toolbars is changing the Fly-out toolbars. You can use the dialog box seen in figure 37.11 by clicking the Return button of the pointing device on a tool with a fly-out while Toolbars is displayed.

**Fig. 37.11**
The Fly-out Properties dialog box allows you to change the properties of fly-out tools.

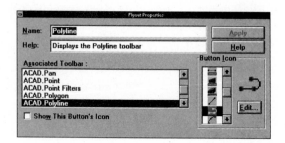

This dialog box functions much the same as the Button properties dialog box discussed earlier. The options seen in figure 37.11 are as follows:

- *Name:* The name of the tool.

- *Help:* This text is displayed in the status bar when the pointing device passes over the tool.

- *Associated Toolbar:* This specifies the toolbar that is associated with the fly-out icon.

- *Show This Button's Icon:* Selecting this option forces the icon to remain with the current tool. Turning the option off replaces the tool with the previous tool selected from the fly-out.

- *Button Icon:* The scrolling list allows you to select from many predefined button icons. Pressing the Edit button opens the Button Editor, discussed earlier.

This concludes our discussion on customizing AutoCAD menus and toolbars. For more information, see the *AutoCAD Release 13 Customization Guide* and *Customizing AutoCAD 13* by New Riders Publishing.

Although it's relatively painless to modify an AutoCAD menu once comfortable with the required syntax, most beginning users leave the menu customizing to third-party developers and focus on other areas of the program. These other areas usually include changing the prototype drawing's layers and colors, creating a library of commonly used details, or even creating special linetypes to give the drawings the appearance needed. In the next section, you learn how to create customized linetypes, including Release 13's complex linetypes.

**XI**

Customizing AutoCAD

---

**Note**

Using an editor or word processor to create or modify AutoCAD menus has been discussed earlier. The same method can be used to alter linetypes, styles, shapes, and program code. Note that if you elect to customize these, your word processor must be able to handle large file sizes and be able to save the finished file in an ASCII text file.

# Customizing Linetypes

As you have already seen, AutoCAD provides a variety of linetypes from which to choose. You may want to visit Chapter 8, "Understanding Linetypes," for an overview of these objects. As with most of the aspects of AutoCAD, you have the ability to customize the linetypes provided and create new ones as well. Generally, there are two type of linetypes for AutoCAD:

- Simple linetypes

- Complex linetypes

Both of these linetypes are defined in a text file that can be created or edited with any word processor. They are defined in a file with a filename *.LIN. AutoCAD Release 13 comes with two linetype files: ACAD.LIN and LTYPESHX.LIN. The discussion of linetypes begins with Simple Linetypes.

## Simple Linetypes

Until Release 13, all linetypes were limited to dashes, dots, and spaces. Linetypes with these characteristics are now referred to as "simple." You will learn how to create your own simple linetypes, but look first at some linetypes and the syntax supplied with AutoCAD in the file ACAD.LIN.

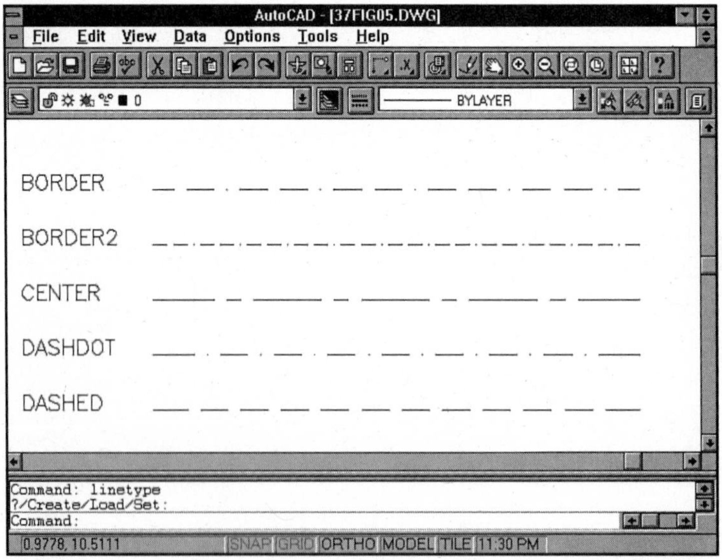

**Fig. 37.12**

A sample of some simple linetypes supplied in ACAD.LIN.

The following is syntax for just some of the linetypes supplied in the
ACAD.LIN file. These correspond to the lines displayed in figure 37.12.

```
*BORDER,__ __ . __ __ . __ __ . __ __ . __ __ . __ __ . __ __ .
A,.5,-.25,.5,-.25,0,-.25

*BORDER2,__.__.__.__.__.__.__.__.__.__.__.__.__
A,.25,-.125,.25,-.125,0,-.125

*CENTER,____ _ ____ _ ____ _ ____ _ ____ _ ____ _ ____ _ ____ _
A,1.25,-.25,.25,-.25

*DASHDOT,__ . __ . __ . __ . __ . __ . __ . __ . __ .
A,.5,-.25,0,-.25

*DASHED,__ __ __ __ __ __ __ __ __ __ __ __ __ __
A,.5,-.25
```

As you can see, the source code contains two lines for each linetype.
The specific syntax is as follows:

```
*linetype-name [, description]
alignment,patdesc-1,patdesc-2, ...
```

Each linetype code begins with an asterisk and name, which has no spaces.
The description is optional and may be graphical (using dashes and periods)
or text (such as "USE THIS LINETYPE FOR COLUMN CENTERLINES"). You
see this description if you list the linetypes, such as using the LINETYPE List ?
command sequence.

The second line of code contains the alignment and the pattern descriptions.
You will notice all the linetypes in the example shown begin with A, this is
the only alignment currently supported by AutoCAD. This alignment instructs AutoCAD to start and stop each line with a dash, and spaces the
dashes and dots equally between the beginning and ending points.

The Pattern Descriptions, *patdesc-n,* which follow, define the pen strokes as
the line is drawn. The descriptions include the distance and whether the
pen is up or down. Numbers represent the distance the pens travel, and a
positive value indicates the pen is down. Conversely, a negative number tells
AutoCAD the distance to travel with the pen up. A 0 used in the linetype
definition produces a dot. Linetypes with an alignment of "A" must begin
with the pen down, and therefore must have a starting value of 0 or greater.

Here, you see a brief example that shows how to create a simple linetype. AutoCAD provides a method of defining linetype by using the LINETYPE Create command sequence. Although this method is available, it's recommended that you use a simple text editor. Using a text editor is far more forgiving should you mistype the code, and you cannot use LINETYPE Create to define complex linetypes (discussed shortly). For more information on the LINETYPE command, see Chapter 8 of this book, "Understanding Linetypes."

**Tutorial: Creating a Simple Linetype**

Using a text editing program such as the Notepad program in Windows, create a file called SAMPLE.LIN. You can place comments anywhere in this file by placing a semicolon (;) at the beginning of the line, as demonstrated in the following lines. Type the following code to create the linetype called Sample_line:

```
;  This linetype file defines a sample line
;
*Sample_line, _____  _  .  _  _____  _  .  _  _____
  _  .  _  _____  _  .  _
A,1.25,-.25,.25,-.25,0,-.25,.25,-.25
```

After typing the text, save the line file. Using AutoCAD's LINETYPE command, load the Sample_line file, and set the current linetype to be Sample_line. Now, using AutoCAD's LINE or PLINE command, you can create figure 37.13.

See the line displayed by AutoCAD in Figure 37.13. Note that the spacing of the line's dashes and dots relies on the system variable LTSCALE. See Chapter 8, "Understanding Linetypes," and Appendix C, "System Variables Reference," for discussions on the linetype scale and LTSCALE.

---

**Caution**

It's always best to create a separate file for your own linetypes instead of appending to AutoCAD's default file: ACAD.LIN. If you save the linetypes to a separate file, you are able to copy it to other systems within your office more easily, as well as ensure that linetypes are not lost as you upgrade software in the future. This procedure should apply to any custom files you create, such as menus, hatches, shapes, or fonts.

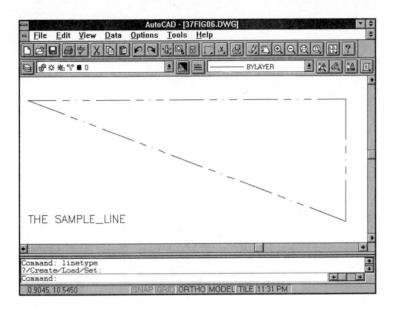

**Fig. 37.13**
The sample
linetype created
with the lines of
code in the text.

Now that you have an understanding of how to create simple linetypes, you can move on to Complex Linetypes. You will find that these are created in the same manner and use syntax similar to the simple linetypes.

## Complex Linetypes

Release 13 now gives us the ability to create linetypes that are far more complex and that can be used by most every type of user. Complex Linetypes go beyond those discussed earlier by allowing you to embed text and even graphics within the line. This has been long awaited by many users, and when you see how easy it is, you may be tempted to create a great deal of complex linetypes.

To begin with, here's a brief sample of some of the complex linetypes supplied with AutoCAD. These are located in the file LTYPESHP.LIN.

> **Note**
>
> Although Autodesk has separated simple and complex linetypes into two separate files, both types could have been placed in one file. As shown in the text, there is only a slight change in the syntax.

XI

Customizing AutoCAD

Complex linetypes can include the following in addition to dashes, dots, and spaces:

■ Embedded text

■ Embedded shapes

The example to follow shows a sample of some of the complex linetypes furnished with AutoCAD Release 13. Let's begin with the AutoCAD screen showing the lines as they would appear in the drawing. Then, you'll see the source code for these lines. This information is located in the file: LTYPESHX.LIN and can be customized with any word processor. Finally, as you can see in the source code, the shape files are located in the shape file: LTYPESHP.SHX. The source code for this file is listed at the end. (You can find this source code in the text file LTYPESHP.SHP.)

The syntax for these lines can be found in LTYPESHX.LIN and corresponds to the lines displayed in figure 37.14.

**Fig. 37.14**
A sample of complex linetypes provided in LTYPESHX.LIN. Note that the linetype's scale factor plays a role in the visibility of these symbols.

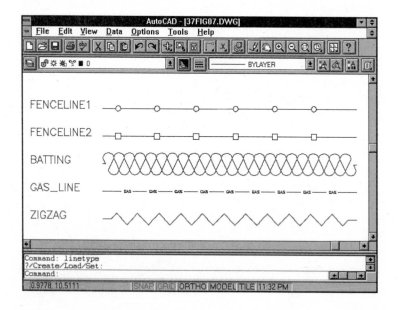

The source code in the file LTYPESHP.LIN is listed as follows. Note the similarities to simple linetypes.

```
*FENCELINE1,----0-----0----
A,.25,[CIRC1,ltypeshp.shx,s=.1],-.2,1
```

```
*FENCELINE2,----[]-----[]----
A,.25,[BOX,ltypeshp.shx,s=.1],-.2,1

*BATTING,
A,.0001,[BAT,ltypeshp.shx,s=.1],-.4

*GAS_LINE,----GAS----GAS----GAS----GAS
A,.5,-.2,["GAS",STANDARD,S=.1,R=0.0,X=-0.1,Y=-.05],-.25

*ZIGZAG,/\/\/\/\/\/\/\/\/\/\/\/\
A,.0001,[ZIG,ltypeshp.shx,s=.2],-.8
```

You will notice that the change in syntax from the simplex linetype includes information in brackets. This information lists the shape name, the files where it can be located, the scale factor, relative rotation, absolute rotation, and offsets in the X or Y directions.

For example, in the description for "GAS_LINE," you see a scale factor "S" of .1 or 10% of the shape's scale as defined in the source file. Next, you see "R," which stands for the relative rotation that identifies the shape's rotation as 0 with respect to the line's direction. The variable "A" could have been used to identify an absolute rotation that would be used to rotate the symbol relative to the origin. Next, you see an "X" and a "Y" value that identifies the offset in the X and Y directions from the endpoint of the linetype definition vertex. These values shift the symbol in relation to the line and are not scaled by the "S" variable seen previously. For additional information regarding the variables used for Complex Linetypes, see the *AutoCAD Release 13 Customization Guide*.

The actual source code for the LTYPESHP.SHX file is shown here. This file is used to define the shape files in the linetypes shown previously.

The following source code defines the shapes seen in the complex linetypes shown previously. You can find this code in the file LTYPESHP.SHP.

```
*133,4,CIRC1
10,1,-040,0

*132,6,BOX
014,020,02C,028,014,0

*134,10,BAT
025,10,2,-044,04B,10,2,044,025,0

*131,4,ZIG
012,02E,012,0
```

This completes our discussion on linetypes, both simple and complex. A brief explanation of what is entailed in customizing AutoCAD's linetype has been offered. If you are interested in modifying the linetypes provided by Autodesk, or if you would like to create your own, it's recommend you review Chapter 2, "Linetype and Hatch Patterns," of *AutoCAD Release 13 Customization Guide* by New Riders Publishing.

# Customizing More Complex Graphical Information

Along with customizing linetypes, Autodesk allows users to customize the more advanced graphical aspects of AutoCAD. This includes the following:

- Hatch patterns

- Postscript Fill Patterns

- Shapes and Fonts

These three have been separated from the discussion on customizing linetypes because of the higher level of programming needed for these objects. You may find that although your needs dictate alternating the default AutoCAD setup for these objects, it's not feasible for beginning users to mount the learning curve for customizing all the graphical aspects of AutoCAD.

As many users find out, it often seems to be more practical to purchase a third-party add-in package for this need. (These add-in packages are discussed near the end of this chapter.) For the next three sections, you learn about these three types of objects, and in general terms, how they may be customized. Let's begin the discussion on customizing the complex graphical objects by covering hatch patterns.

## Customizing Hatch Patterns

Most people are surprised to find that creating custom hatch patterns can be quite simple. On the other hand, it can also be overwhelming. Which of the two is true for you depends on the type and complexity of the hatch desired. Since most of the simpler hatches are provided with AutoCAD, users often look to add-in packages to fill their AutoCAD "toolbox" of hatches.

Hatch patterns are discussed in Chapter 17, "Filling Areas with Hatching." For an overview of this feature and the new Release 13 features for creating hatched objects, you should review that chapter.

The syntax for hatch patterns is the same as that for simple linetypes. You can think of the definitions for simple linetypes as one-dimensional, that is, one line of code that tells the computer how to draw the linetype by raising and lowering the pen as it proceeds along the length of the line.

Hatch pattern definitions take the same approach but allow you to have multiple lines of code. Each line of code can draw it's own line of dashes, dots, and spaces. The patterns are defined by giving each "line" a relative start point and a rotation, along with the instructions for dashes, dots, and spaces. The hatch pattern gets its appearance by drawing each of the individual "lines" until the area is full.

Figure 37.15 shows two hatch patterns—one that is rather simple and one that is more complex. The corresponding syntax for these patterns is also listed. Syntax for AutoCAD hatch patterns is placed in a text file with the filename *.PAT. AutoCAD comes with one pattern file—ACAD.PAT—from which this example was taken.

XI

Customizing AutoCAD

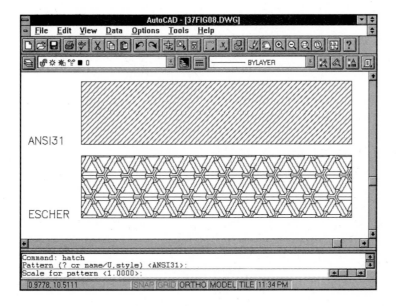

**Fig. 37.15**

Two of the hatch patterns supplied with AutoCAD.

This is the syntax from the ACAD.PAT file for the two hatch patterns seen in figure 37.15. Notice the complexity of each.

```
*ANSI31, ANSI Iron, Brick, Stone masonry
45, 0,0, 0,.125

*ESCHER, Escher pattern
60, 0,0, -.6,1.039230484, 1.1,-.1
180, 0,0, -.6,1.039230484, 1.1,-.1
300, 0,0, .6,1.039230484, 1.1,-.1
60, .1,0, -.6,1.039230484, .2,-1
300, .1,0, .6,1.039230484, .2,-1
60, -.05,.08660254, -.6,1.039230484, .2,-1
180, -.05,.08660254, -.6,1.039230484, .2,-1
300, -.05,-.08660254, .6,1.039230484, .2,-1
180, -.05,-.08660254, -.6,1.039230484, .2,-1
60, -.4,0, -.6,1.039230484, .2,-1
300, -.4,0, .6,1.039230484, .2,-1
60, .2,-.346410161, -.6,1.039230484, .2,-1
180, .2,-.346410161, -.6,1.039230484, .2,-1
300, .2,.346410161, .6,1.039230484, .2,-1
180, .2,.346410161, -.6,1.039230484, .2,-1
0, .2,.173205081, -.6,1.039230484, .7,-.5
0, .2,-.173205081, -.6,1.039230484, .7,-.5
120, .05,.259807621, .6,1.039230484, .7,-.5
120, -.25,.08660254, .6,1.039230484, .7,-.5
240, -.25,-.08660254, .6,1.039230484, .7,-.5
240, .05,-.259807621, .6,1.039230484, .7,-.5
```

You can find more information on the syntax needed for altering the hatches provided or creating your own patterns in the *AutoCAD Release 13 Customization Guide,* or in *Customizing AutoCAD 13,* both by New Riders Publishing.

## Customizing PostScript Fill Patterns

Although hatch patterns are commonly used to fill areas of your drawing, you may also use Postscript fill patterns. The feature was first introduced in Release 12 of AutoCAD. AutoCAD allows you to apply Postscript fill patterns using the PSFILL command.

Postscript fill patterns are similar in usage to hatch patterns. AutoCAD also supports PostScript fonts, the exporting of AutoCAD drawing files in Encapsulated PostScript (EPS) files, and the importing of EPS files into the AutoCAD drawing.

To customize PostScript fill patterns, you edit the ACAD.PSF file. The PostScript parameters are located in this ASCII file and include pattern names and values that define the fill pattern. Should the drawing file be exported (using AutoCAD's PSOUT command) in the Encapsulated PostScript file format, this information is encoded in the EPS file. For more information on the parameters used to define PostScript Fill Patterns, see Chapter 3, "Shapes, Fonts, and PostScript Support," of *AutoCAD Release 13 Customization Guide* by New Riders Publishing.

## Customizing Shapes and Fonts

Shapes and fonts are other types of advanced graphical objects that can be customized. Shapes and fonts in AutoCAD use the same type of source code. Beginning users, however, don't often concern themselves with customizing shape files. There are two reasons for this: first, the time involved to define a shape or font is significant compared to linetypes, or even hatch patterns; and second, a tremendous amount of affordable third-party programs exist that make the process of creating a shape file from scratch quite a burden.

AutoCAD shapes are covered in Chapter 23, "Using Symbols and XRefs." These objects can be simple or quite complex. As you've seen earlier in this chapter, they can now be placed within complex linetypes. These objects are similar to fonts, hatch patterns, and linetypes in that they are defined by an ASCII text file. Within this file are the parameters that identify whether the pen is up or down when drawing the image, and the direction and the length of the vector.

Take fonts for example. AutoCAD supports PostScript font files. Many programs, including AutoCAD, come with a substantial amount of PostScript fonts. You can also obtain CD-ROMs that contain hundreds of fonts for pennies each. You may have also heard of application programs that allow you to draw a symbol in AutoCAD and have it define the source code for the font file or shape file. These are strong reasons for considering how much effort should be given to creating shape files.

For the sake of the discussion, however, the files and approach to creating a shape file are explained. Although AutoCAD can read PostScript fonts, the source file for these are different than AutoCAD fonts. AutoCAD fonts and shapes use the extension: *.SHP. This *.SHP is the text file, which is compiled by the user with the COMPILE command. As a result, a file is created with the name: *.SHX.

**XI**

Customizing AutoCAD

**Tip**
You can compile more frequently used PostScript fonts into *.SHX files that load faster at the expense of hard drive space.

The syntax for a shape file is similar to the instructions seen in linetype definitions. Namely, you define vectors with length and direction, and include instructions for moving the pen up and down. For more information on how to create or modify shape files, see Chapter 3 of the *AutoCAD Release 13 Customization Guide*, "Shapes, Fonts, and PostScript Support."

# Using Third-Party Applications with AutoCAD

As discussed earlier, many users of all levels rely on third-party developers to help with customization of AutoCAD. The simpler packages can be *freeware* or *shareware* programs that perform some function not seen in AutoCAD. These packages can be acquired and used with a nominal charge, or even no cost at all. Packages can also be complete add-ins that work with AutoCAD but completely control how you interact with the program. It's not uncommon for these larger packages to be every bit as complex as AutoCAD itself and in some cases, cost more than AutoCAD itself!

Let's begin by defining what add-in packages are, who creates and supports them, why they are so common, and where you can obtain these applications. First, add-in packages are not stand-alone. That is, they require you to purchase AutoCAD in order to be of any use. In the past, these applications were commonly referred to as menus because they replaced the AutoCAD menu with a menu that matched your drawing needs.

Even now, some users refer to the larger programs as menus, but they are often quite a bit more. Add-in applications can range from rendering applications, industry standard details, structural calculation programs (which use AutoCAD to show stresses and deflections), three-dimensional object creation (such as used for HVAC piping design), even add-ins that run benchmarks within AutoCAD to help you tweak the performance of your CAD station.

As discussed earlier in this chapter, the menu is one of the major ways for interaction with AutoCAD. Most complex third-party applications completely replace the AutoCAD menu with their own. In addition, they provide details, symbols, fonts, and hatch patterns that you can use. The simpler add-in applications might be a few lines of programming code. Often you will find these programs published in magazines that support the AutoCAD community, or available for download from local user groups or the AutoCAD Forum on the CompuServe Information Service.

Who creates these add-in applications? Well, applications usually start with individuals such as you, who want AutoCAD to work in a particular manner, or produce a specific type of drawing. Even a complex program like AutoCAD cannot be everything to every drafter in every office. As such, programmers—referred to as Developers—sometimes create a solution for their own needs. If they think others would be interested in it, they may circulate it for free (freeware) or for a nominal charge (shareware). In the case of large, expensive applications, these are often created by software companies which are similar to Autodesk, but separate. They have a symbolic relationship with Autodesk because the success of their products relies on the seamless and transparent interaction of AutoCAD.

As has been the case, developing programs and add-on applications for AutoCAD has become an industry in itself. With any product in today's marketplace, support can make all the difference in sales. In cases of simple freeware programs, they are commonly used by a significant number of users before they gain a reputation for being a tool every user should have in his AutoCAD toolbox.

Software companies that develop add-in applications usually test, debug, and ship their programs in a manner similar to Autodesk. You will find that add-in applications are always issued after Autodesk ships its releases. Developers usually create their applications while the latest AutoCAD release is being developed, but—in order to ensure compatibility with AutoCAD—they usually test their programs with the actual release before shipping their products. This testing offers you better support and a better product.

Part of the strength of Autodesk is its support of, *and for*, the third-party market. It truly is a win-win-win situation for developers, Autodesk, and you the user. Developers win because of Autodesk's commitment to an open architecture and easily customizable program, as you have seen demonstrated in this book and specifically in this chapter. Autodesk benefits because the support of the third-party market has helped concentrate on the features needed by the majority of users. The third-party market has also helped make AutoCAD the industry standard and dominant factor in the Computer Aided Drafting market. Obviously, you, and other users, benefit from the assortment of tools that can make your day-to-day drafting more efficient and accurate.

The capability for third-party developers to create reliable products that work in conjunction with AutoCAD has become more and more important with each new release. This capability to interact with other external programs and applications is known as *interoperability*. Adhering to industry standards has always been important in the DOS platform, but is paramount to Windows programs interacting properly. With Release 13, Autodesk has adopted a number of industry standards to ensure the best interaction possible of AutoCAD with add-in packages.

AutoCAD interoperability standardized for Release 13 includes the following:

- Adherence to Windows Object Linking and Embedding (OLE)

- AutoCAD SQL Environment for database management (ASE)

- The capability to read drawings created with previous versions of AutoCAD

- AutoCAD Runtime Extension (ARX) for faster and more efficient add-in programs

- Application Integration Guidelines (AIG) guarantee that applications built on top of AutoCAD integrate correctly

- Peripheral Support provided by both Autodesk and the manufacturers, including compatibility, graphics, and output

How do you get a list of these developers and add-in applications? You may have already seen the AutoCAD *Resource Guide* that ships with each copy of AutoCAD. This guide came with AutoCAD Release 12, and has been updated and reissued with Release 13. This guide contains over 4,000 application-specific programs, add-in programs, device drivers, and developer contact information to aid you in your search. In addition, you can find detailed discussions on specific applications in *Killer AutoCAD Utilities, 2nd Edition* published by New Riders Publishing.

Other means of finding add-in packages include magazines designed strictly for the AutoCAD community. You should find subscription forms for indus-try magazines in your AutoCAD package. Not only do developers advertise in these journals, but the magazines often feature small programs that you can enter or modify for your own use. Finally, resources such as local users groups, bulletin boards, the Autodesk forum on CompuServe, as well as your Autodesk dealer, are there to help. These resources can often help users find the add-in to suit their needs.

This concludes the discussion on add-in applications for AutoCAD. To conclude the discussion of customizing AutoCAD, a brief discussion on AutoCAD's programming languages follows.

In the preceding section, it was mentioned that third-party applications often include programs to make your drafting in AutoCAD easier. In the next chapter, "Introduction to AutoLISP, ADS, and RX," our discussion of customizing AutoCAD continues by covering the programming languages that can be utilized to make AutoCAD more productive for your needs. With a basic understanding of these programs, you are in a better position to determine the task and skills needed as you pursue customizing AutoCAD.

# From Here...

This concludes the chapter on customizing AutoCAD. In this chapter you have seen the method and examples for how to change the default AutoCAD configuration. The customization of the following has been discussed and demonstrated: toolbars and menus; linetypes, including Release 13's new complex linetypes; complex graphical information such as hatches, PostScript fills, shapes and fonts; and third-party applications.

For more information about customizing AutoCAD, see the following chapters of this book:

- Chapter 1, "Introducing AutoCAD," shows examples of the AutoCAD toolbars and menus in the section "Using the Toolbars and Menus."

- Chapter 8, "Understanding Linetypes," and Appendix C, "System Variables Reference," provide discussions on the linetype scale and the LTSCALE variable.

- Chapter 17, "Filling Areas with Hatching," includes an overview of hatching and the new Release 13 features for creating hatched objects.

- Chapter 23, "Using Symbols and XRefs," discusses AutoCAD shapes.

- Chapter 38, "Introduction to AutoLISP, ADS, and ARX," complements this chapter with a discussion on the programming languages used to customize AutoCAD.

- Appendix B, "Installing and Configuring AutoCAD," provides instructions on the installation of AutoCAD, including information about system requirements, information on the AutoCAD Configuration Menu, configuring AutoCAD for your hardware, and more.

**XI**

**Customizing AutoCAD**

For more information about customizing AutoCAD use these resources:

- *The AutoCAD Release 13 Customization Guide's* Chapter 2, "Linetypes and Hatch Patterns," for information relating to modifying linetypes and hatch patterns.

- *The AutoCAD Release 13 Customization Guide's* Chapter 3, "Shapes, Fonts, and PostScript Support," for an explanation on the parameters used to define PostScript Fill Patterns.

- *AutoCAD Resource Guide* that contains over 4,000 application specific programs, add-in programs, device drivers, and developer contact information.

And finally, the following books for further information on the advanced aspects of customizing AutoCAD are recommended:

- *Customizing AutoCAD 13,* by New Riders Publishing.

- *Killer AutoCAD Utilities, 2nd Edition* published by New Riders Publishing.

# Chapter 38

# Introduction to AutoLISP, ADS, and ARX

Adaptability. This one word easily describes the reason for AutoCAD's success. The programmers at Autodesk decided during the early days in the development of the program that they would make AutoCAD easily customizable by the end users. They knew that users of their software would find new commands they wanted to add or existing commands they wanted to change.

AutoLISP, ADS, and ARX are the names of the programming languages that provide hooks into the AutoCAD program. With these tools, end users can turn AutoCAD into the exact software needed to accomplish their drafting and design tasks.

This chapter answers the following questions you might have concerning AutoLISP, ADS, and ARX:

- What exactly are AutoLISP, ADS, and ARX, and what can they do for me?

- How do I load a program and run it?

- If I find a program I really like, how do I make it available for everyday use?

## What Are AutoLISP, ADS, and ARX?

AutoLISP, ADS, and ARX are acronyms for three of the programming languages that come with AutoCAD. Programs written in these languages communicate with AutoCAD to manipulate drawings through information supplied by the CAD operator. These powerful yet easy-to-learn languages have given many individuals the ability to create new commands that do the things they need to do on the job.

## What Is AutoLISP?

AutoLISP was the first programming language built into the AutoCAD program. It has been available since AutoCAD version 2.18, which was released in January 1986.

The name comes from a combination of AutoCAD and LISP. The term *LISP* stands for *LISt Processing*. It has its origins in Common LISP, a programming language that is easy to learn and has been used for artificial intelligence research.

Autodesk took Common LISP, deleted some of the features that didn't apply to graphics work, kept some others, added new features unique to CAD work, and called this new programming language AutoLISP. Autodesk then added an AutoLISP interpreter/evaluator to the AutoCAD program itself. The evaluator reads this AutoLISP code and hands it to AutoCAD to perform various operations.

Therefore, AutoLISP essentially can be thought of as an extended set of commands that are available in AutoCAD, just like the LINE or MOVE commands. There are about 200 of these AutoLISP commands, and each performs a certain function. These functions can:

- Do mathematical calculations
- Prompt for information
- Store values for later use
- Execute standard AutoCAD commands
- Read and write files
- Select objects on the screen
- Print information to the screen
- Test for certain conditions and act on them accordingly
- Modify drawing objects

As each function is run, it returns a value. A function that prompts for information shows a prompt on-screen, waits for the user to respond, and then returns the user's response. For example, the function (getreal "Enter a real number :"), will prompt the user and wait until they supply a real number value. This response can then be stored in memory by another function. A mathematical function can retrieve this value stored in memory to perform some desired calculation and return the value it comes up with back to the user.

By chaining or combining all these functions into a group, you can create specialized programs that can be used in your particular line of work. This is where AutoCAD has the edge over other CAD programs. Users that draw doohickeys all day long can write an AutoLISP program that turns regular AutoCAD into an automated doohickey drawing program. By allowing the users to customize the program to their work requirements, AutoCAD can be turned from a generic design and drafting program into an application-specific program that creates exactly the items your company manufactures.

## What Is ADS?

In October 1990, Autodesk added ADS (AutoCAD Development System), a C programming language interface, to AutoCAD Release 11. An ADS application is a compiled C program that communicates with the user and AutoCAD via AutoLISP. Because ADS applications are compiled, they run faster than AutoLISP. ADS also has a larger command base and can access the operating system. You can do many things in ADS that you cannot do in AutoLISP, and you can do them faster.

## What Is ARX?

ARX (AutoCAD Runtime Extension) is new in Release 13. It is designed as a replacement for ADS for serious developers. Just like an ADS program, ARX is written in C code and compiled. Unlike ADS, which must communicate through the AutoLISP interpreter, ARX communicates directly with the core AutoCAD code. This makes it faster, more stable, and less complicated than ADS.

# The Benefits of Using AutoLISP, ADS, and ARX

Everyone looks for ways to make their work easier. That is why people purchase AutoCAD in the first place. They get tired of working with manual drawings that are hard to change, get torn and dirty, and occasionally get lost. After they start using AutoCAD, they see how quickly their drawings come together and how much easier the drawings are to modify after they are created.

As users continue using AutoCAD, they pick up on the more advanced commands that AutoCAD offers. They start with LINE, COPY, ERASE and other commands and soon graduate to more advanced commands like PEDIT and 3DMESH. They see the benefits that these additional commands offer.

**XI**

**Customizing AutoCAD**

AutoLISP, ADS, and ARX functions enable you to go even further than the standard AutoCAD commands. By intermixing the functionality of the standard command set with the added power provided by the AutoLISP, ADS, and ARX functions, you can create a program that does the following:

- Prompts the user for design parameters, and creates an object in the drawing based on those parameters

- Enables the user to select objects on the drawing and make modifications to them that standard AutoCAD commands can't do

- Scans through all the objects on the drawing, locates certain ones, and makes changes to those found based on what the user wants

Even if you decide to never use or write an AutoLISP, ADS, or ARX program, you can still produce your drawings in a timely manner. However, just think about all the additional, helpful commands you'll be missing.

> **Note**
>
> Due to changes in the programming languages and AutoCAD, AutoLISP programs may have to be rewritten for each new release of AutoCAD. ADS and ARX applications may have to be rewritten, and will definitely have to be recompiled.

## Using AutoLISP, ADS, and ARX in Your Daily Work

**Tip**
The Autodesk forum on CompuServe has AutoLISP files available for downloading and also has message areas that allow you to communicate with AutoCAD programmers.

AutoCAD ships with several sample AutoLISP, ADS, and ARX programs. These programs can be found in the SAMPLE directory under the AutoCAD directory you created during the installation procedure. They provide features not found in the standard AutoCAD commands. These programs were written by programmers at Autodesk and serve as good examples of how AutoLISP, ADS, and ARX programs should be written.

AutoLISP programs also can be found on computer bulletin board systems (or BBSs) around the country. CompuServe has a section reserved for the uploading and downloading of these files. Many were written by users who wanted a better way to tackle a particular AutoCAD problem.

To use any AutoLISP program you write, download, or purchase, you have to load the file from disk into memory and type in the program name.

## Loading and Running Programs

The disk included with this book contains a sample AutoLISP program called TMODIFY.LSP. This program was written to streamline the modification of text objects on a drawing.

By now you have learned that the AutoCAD CHANGE command can be used to modify the existing height, rotation, and string value of a piece of text. There is only one problem. To change only one trait you must cycle through a series of prompts to get to the trait you want to change. This situation is aggravated when you want to change a certain trait to the same value on several selected text objects. Now, you have to cycle through the entire series of prompts for each text object. This is very time-consuming.

TMODIFY automates the prompt-cycling process. It saves you precious time that could be spent doing other tasks.

> **Note**
>
> When you load a program, it is placed in memory. If you load another program with the same name, the new program will replace the old one in memory. This is called *redefining a program*. Be careful not to redefine any programs, especially the ones loaded by AutoCAD. Check the AutoCAD documentation for details on naming functions.

### Loading a Program

To run any AutoLISP, ADS, or ARX program, you must tell AutoCAD to read the program from the disk and load it into memory. There are three functions that accomplish this task:

- `(load "filename")` is used to load an AutoLISP program. AutoLISP programs have a file name extension of LSP. The (LOAD) function requires only the file name without the extension.

- `(xload "filename")` is used to load an ADS program. ADS programs have a file name extension of EXE. The (XLOAD) function requires only the file name without the extension.

- `(arxload "filename")` is used to load an ARX program. ARX programs have a file name extension of ARX. The (ARXLOAD) function requires only the file name without the extension.

To run the program that is contained in the TMODIFY.LSP file on the disk, you must tell AutoCAD to read the contents of the file. This is done through the AutoLISP (LOAD) function.

---

**Caution**

Do not confuse the AutoCAD LOAD command with the AutoLISP (LOAD) function. The LOAD command looks for a shape file to load. The (LOAD) function looks for a DOS file that contains an AutoLISP program.

The LOAD command displays a dialog box, and you will get an error message if you attempt to use the dialog box to load an AutoLISP routine. (LOAD) simply loads an application; it does not display a dialog box.

---

### Tutorial: Loading an AutoLISP Program

In this tutorial, you load the TMODIFY.LSP file. Type the following after the Command: prompt to get the contents of the file (the command can be typed in uppercase and/or lowercase, but the parentheses and quotes are required):

```
Command: (load "C:/UAW13/TMODIFY")
```

---

**Note**

The C in this command line represents the drive that contains the program files you installed from the disk in this book. If the drive that has the TMODIFY.LSP file on it is something other than the C drive, substitute that drive letter for C in the command line.

---

**Caution**

You cannot use a single backslash (\) in the path specified by the LOAD function. You must use either two backslashes (\\) or a single forward slash (/).

---

If you typed in the command line properly, you will get the phrase C:TMODIFY echoed back to the command line. This means that AutoCAD has read the contents of the TMODIFY.LSP file and found a program called TMODIFY in it that has been defined as a new AutoCAD command.

If you didn't get the phrase C:TMODIFY echoed back to you, check for the following common mistakes:

- Forgetting to put the parentheses at the start and end of the command line you typed in

- Not enclosing the name of the file to load in quotation marks

- Using a single backslash (\) character instead of two backslashes (\\) or a single forward slash (/) character

- Designating the wrong drive specification in front of the file name

- Misspelling the name of the file

### Note

If you get a response on-screen like 1>, this means that either one or the other of the parentheses or quotation marks are missing. Don't panic.

All you have to do is press Esc to get back to the Command: prompt. Then retype the line to load the program.

After you've gotten the proper response, you can try the program.

Because this program was designed to modify existing text objects on the drawing, make sure that the drawing you're trying this out on has a few text objects on which to experiment. If it doesn't, then take the time right now to place a few on the drawing. Use figure 37.1 as an example.

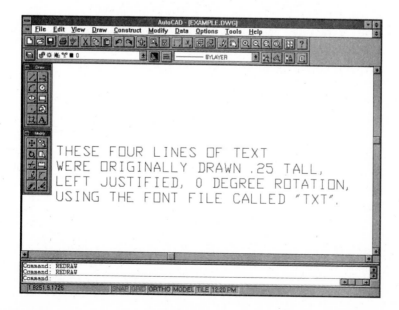

**Fig. 37.1**
Some sample text objects to be modified with the TMODIFY program.

### Tutorial: Running a Program

Now that you have the program loaded and some guinea pig text objects to work with, use these steps to run the program:

1. At the Command: prompt type **tmodify**.

   You get the following message on-screen:

   ```
   TMODIFY-Text Modifier Program
   Select objects:<pick text objects to change>
   ```

   At this point, the program is waiting for you to pick the text objects that need changing. Pick the four text objects on your example screen. You may do this on an individual basis, or window around them all. After you have the text objects selected, press Enter to get to the next part of the TMODIFY program.

2. You are first asked for a new text height.

   ```
   New text HEIGHT ? .125
   ```

3. You are now prompted for a new angle. You don't want to supply a new one so press Enter to go to the next prompt.

   ```
   New text ANGLE ?
   ```

4. The program prompts you to change the text wording, but for now leave the wording as is.

   ```
   New text STRING ?
   ```

   The program runs against the text objects you previously selected. It sets a height value of .125 for each text object. The text strings on the screen flash and reappear with their new height settings.

Type **tmodify** to run the program again. This time change the height, rotation, and string value of each piece of text.

1. Select the first and second lines of text on the drawing.

2. Supply new values for all three prompts.

   ```
   New text HEIGHT ? .1875
   New text ANGLE ? 15
   New text STRING ? CHANGING TEXT OBJECTS IS A BREEZE
   ```

   The text objects flash, and you end up with text that looks like the screen in figure 37.2.

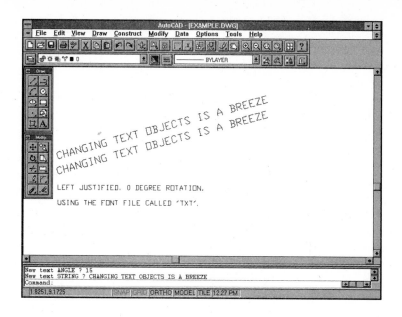

**Fig. 37.2**

Here's how the sample text objects look after modification by the TMODIFY program.

The TMODIFY program is nothing fancy, but it gets the job done. It doesn't have any *error checking*. This means that if the program encounters unexpected input, it will probably "bomb out." This is nothing to be alarmed about, because you can always use the AutoCAD UNDO command to back your way out of any unexpected results. Don't be afraid to try running any AutoLISP programs you receive. There is virtually nothing that an AutoLISP program can do to permanently harm your drawing that can't be corrected with the UNDO command. If you want to be absolutely sure you do no harm to a drawing, then run the program on a drawing that is expendable. You can also make a copy of one of your drawings and test your programs on the copy.

> **Note**
>
> The AutoLISP programs you load into memory are available only while you remain on a particular drawing. They are cleared out of memory and have to be reloaded when you exit the drawing and call up a different drawing. The file remains on the disk, however, and is not affected in any way.
>
> ADS and ARX programs loaded into memory are not cleared out of memory until you exit AutoCAD completely. Therefore, they are available from drawing to drawing without having to reload.

### The Autodesk Interoperability Guidelines

AutoLISP, ADS, and ARX applications are written by programmers all over the world. Each application defines functions that may redefine AutoCAD's functions or another developer's functions. Each of these applications might come with new support files or replacement files for existing AutoCAD files. Any replacement support file may overwrite a custom support file provided by a different application. Because of these and other potential problems, Autodesk developed interoperability guidelines.

The Autodesk interoperability guidelines are a set of rules governing how your applications and their functions may be named; what files you may edit, replace, or add; how the application must work with AutoCAD; and so on. All of these guidelines ensure that each developer's application will work with AutoCAD and with other developer's applications. If you are shopping for applications, check to see if they meet the guidelines. For more information on the guidelines, consult your AutoCAD documentation or contact Autodesk.

## Adding Programs to the Pull-Down Menu

As you can see, TMODIFY is a program you might want to access regularly. You might feel that it ranks right up there with your repertoire of AutoCAD commands. There is one hitch. You don't want to have to retype the (load "filename") command line every time you switch from one drawing to another.

There are three ways to make your program accessible at the touch of a button:

- Edit your menu file, ACADFULL.MNU, and put some code behind a menu selection.

- Edit a file called ACAD.LSP, which AutoCAD automatically loads every time you call up a drawing, and put the AutoLISP code in it or call the other AutoLISP file from it.

- Add the load line to the MNL file for your current menu. When the menu loads, the associated MNL file loads also.

To perform any of these tasks, you must first be familiar with a text editor or word processor that is capable of saving files in ordinary ASCII format. *ASCII* is an acronym for American Standard Code for Information Interchange.

Most editors and word processors allow you to format the text on-screen in various ways, such as making text bold, italic, a different color, and so on.

For the program to know these settings when you call up the document the next time, it writes the text information out to the file along with the control codes that describe these formatting options. This is great for the word processing program, but not so good for AutoCAD. AutoCAD has no idea what these control codes are or what to do with them.

It is important that whatever program you use to edit the ACADFULL.MNU or ACAD.LSP file has an option to save in ASCII format. This option can be called non-document mode, text-only mode, DOS text mode, or ASCII mode.

You can use Windows Notepad or Windows Write. Be warned, however, that Notepad cannot hold large files. You also can use the DOS EDIT text editor on smaller menu files. Windows Write can hold bigger files than EDIT.

---

### Caution

Saving the ACADFULL.MNU or ACAD.LSP file in non-ASCII format usually makes it unreadable by AutoCAD. Make sure that when you edit and save either file, you are saving in ASCII format.

It is strongly suggested that you also make a back-up copy of the file you are going to modify. This allows you to go back to the original file in case you made unwanted changes.

---

You can add code to the ACADFULL.MNU file. This allows you to pick your favorite programs from the menu. Any application—AutoLISP, ADS, or RX—can be added to the menu file. The process is essentially the same, regardless of the programming language. You have to add the code to the menu and make sure the code is loaded before you call it.

### Tutorial: Adding TMODIFY.LSP to Your Pull-Down Menu

The ACADFULL.MNU file contains the source code for all your pull-down, side-screen, toolbar, and tablet selections. This tutorial puts the code used to load and run the TMODIFY program in a new pull-down menu at the top of the screen. This pull-down menu is named AutoLISP.

1. Using your text editor or word processor, open the ACADFULL.MNU file located in the SUPPORT directory under your main AutoCAD directory. Locate the pull-down section of the file that looks like the following:

```
***POP10
ID_Help    [&Help]
ID_Helpcts [&Contents...]'_help
```

```
ID_Helpsrc [&Search for Help on...]^P(help "" ""
"help_partialkey") ^P
ID_Helphow [&How to Use Help...]^P(help "" ""
"help_helponhelp") ^P
            [--]
ID_Whatnew [&What's New in Release 13...]^P(playtbk
"whatsnew") ^P
ID_Qtour    [&Quick Tour...]^P(playtbk "quiktour") ^P
ID_Lrnacad [&Learning AutoCAD...]^P(help "tutorial.hlp") ^P
            [--]
ID_About    [&About AutoCAD...]^C^C_about
//
//   Begin AutoCAD ToolBars
//
***TOOLBARS
```

This ***POP10 section of the menu is the last pull-down menu at the top
of the screen on the far right. The definition for the toolbars follows the
pull-down section.

2. Place the new AutoLISP pull-down section after the POP10 section in the
   menu. This will make it POP11. Using your text editor, make the following changes (shown here in bold) to the menu file:

```
***POP10
ID_Help     [&Help]
ID_Helpcts [&Contents...]'_help
ID_Helpsrc [&Search for Help on...]^P(help "" ""
"help_partialkey") ^P
ID_Helphow [&How to Use Help...]^P(help "" ""
"help_helponhelp") ^P
            [--]
ID_Whatnew [&What's New in Release 13...]^P(playtbk
"whatsnew") ^P
ID_Qtour    [&Quick Tour...]^P(playtbk "quiktour") ^P
ID_Lrnacad [&Learning AutoCAD...]^P(help "tutorial.hlp") ^P
            [--]
ID_About    [&About AutoCAD...]^C^C_about
***POP11
[AutoLISP]
[TMODIFY]^C^C^C^P(load "C:/UAW13/TMODIFY");TMODIFY;^P
//
//   Begin AutoCAD ToolBars
//
***TOOLBARS
```

You have made the TMODIFY program accessible by just a pick off the
screen. There is just one thing to note. The TMODIFY.LSP file in this
case was copied into the UAW13 directory on the hard drive so that you

don't have to lug a floppy disk around. It can be put into whatever directory you choose; just put the correct path name in place of `C:/UAW13/`.

The `^C`s in the menu line perform the normal "cancels" to make sure any command that might be currently active when this menu item is picked is aborted.

The `^P`s toggle the commands that are run on this line on and off.

Semicolons (;) act as carriage returns.

3. If you find other programs you would like to add, just list them after the TMODIFY line, as in the following:

```
***POP11
[AutoLISP]
[TMODIFY]^C^C^C^P(load "C:/UAW13/TMODIFY");TMODIFY;^P
[GIZMO  ]^C^C^C^P(load "C:/LSPFILES/GIZMO");GIZMO;^P
[LINEFIX]^C^C^C^P(load "C:/LSPFILES/LINEFIX");LINEFIX;^P
```

4. After making your changes to the menu file, save it as regular ASCII. Now call up AutoCAD and reload your menu file. Notice that in the pull-down menu at the top of the screen, there is a new menu selection available on the far right with the heading of AutoLISP. Click it, and you will see TMODIFY (see fig. 37.3). Select TMODIFY and your AutoLISP program will be loaded and run.

**Fig. 37.3**
The AutoLISP program TMODIFY is added to the screen pull-down menu.

XI

Customizing AutoCAD

The second method mentioned earlier in this chapter to automatically load your favorite AutoLISP routines can be done via the use of the ACAD.LSP file. The ACAD.LSP file usually resides in the SUPPORT directory under your AutoCAD directory.

When you call up a drawing, AutoCAD looks to see if a ACAD.LSP file exists. If AutoCAD finds ACAD.LSP, it loads whatever AutoLISP programs are contained inside it. What this means is that you can put the contents of the TMODIFY.LSP file at the bottom of the ACAD.LSP file, and have AutoCAD load it into memory for you every time you call up another drawing. Then, all you have to do is type **tmodify** at the Command: prompt whenever you want to run the program.

You can add the TMODIFY.LSP file to the ACAD.LSP file in two ways:

- Use your editor and merge the contents of TMODIFY.LSP to the bottom of the ACAD.LSP file.

- Edit the ACAD.LSP file and put a line at the bottom of the file that executes the AutoLISP (LOAD) function. For example:

    ```
    (load "C:/UAW13/TMODIFY")
    ```

The last method to automatically load your AutoLISP programs is by putting the AutoLISP code in an MNL file with the same name as the regular menu file you use on a daily basis. So, if you regularly use the ACADFULL.MNU file on your drawings, create an ACADFULL.MNL file with your favorite AutoLISP code included as its contents. Whenever the MNU file is loaded, the associated MNL file is also loaded.

## From Here...

What you've seen in this chapter may be as far as you want to go in your understanding of AutoLISP, ADS, and ARX. You now know what AutoLISP, ADS, and ARX programs are, how to load and run them, and how to make them accessible in your daily work. If you're feeling a little more adventurous, and want to write your own programs, please refer to the *AutoCAD Customization Guide* for more details on AutoLISP, ADS, and RX programming. This book is available in the documentation package that came with your AutoCAD software.

To enhance your knowledge as it relates to programming, please review the following chapters in this book:

- Chapter 21, "Modifying Object Characteristics," explains the options available in the CHANGE and DDMODIFY commands that can be used to modify text objects.

- Chapter 37, "Customizing AutoCAD," has a section on customizing toolbars and menus.

Here are also a few other things you might want to do now that you know what AutoLISP, ADS, and ARX programs can do for you:

- Subscribe to one or two of the AutoCAD-oriented magazines. There are usually example AutoLISP programs in these magazines that can be typed in and run. The magazines also contain advertisements for programs that can be purchased and added to your AutoCAD command arsenal.

- Enroll in an AutoLISP or ADS class at the AutoCAD training center in your area. Many AutoCAD dealers also hold classes in customizing AutoCAD through AutoLISP and ADS programming.

- Join an AutoCAD users' group. Members are usually ready and willing to trade programs and help troubleshoot programming problems. Some members also write custom programs.

# On Your Own

Instead of adding the TMODIFY program to the AutoLISP pull-down menu at the top of the screen, put TMODIFY in the right side-screen menu as a selection.

Hints:

1. The same menu file, ACADFULL.MNU, also contains the right side-screen menu coding.

2. The screen menu coding begins in the file at the "***SCREEN" section heading.

3. The code that goes on the line in the file is the same as the code for the pull-down menu, except for the section of the menu file in which the code should be placed.

4. Remember to reload the menu file to recompile it after you have made your changes.

XI

Customizing AutoCAD

# Appendixes

FENCELINE2 ——□——□——□——□——□——

BATTING

GAS_LINE —— GAS —— GAS —— GAS —— GAS —— GAS —— GAS ——

## Button Icon

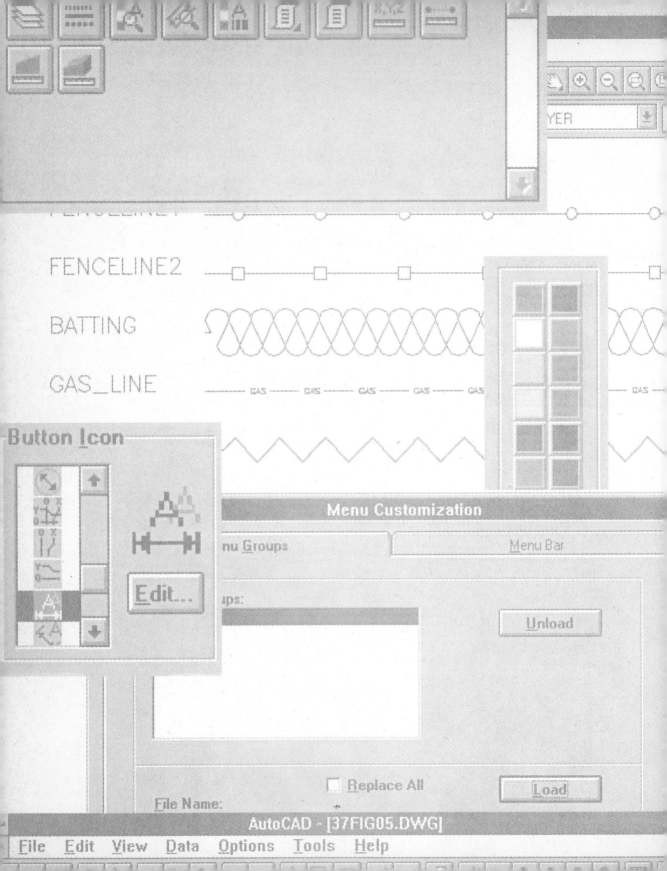

Edit...

### Menu Customization

nu Groups | Menu Bar

ups:

Unload

☐ Replace All

Load

File Name:

AutoCAD - [37FIG05.DWG]

File  Edit  View  Data  Options  Tools  Help

# New Features in AutoCAD Release 13 for Windows

As an early adopter of AutoCAD, I've lived through many updates, changes, and new versions. It's always a chore to learn about what's new and to change old habits to take advantage of advanced tools. Yet, once I got used to the new tools, it's hard to imagine how I survived without them.

Glancing through an old AutoCAD manual highlights this fact. Think of what it was like before the "new" version 1.4 features such as polar arrays, WBLOCK command, LINE Close option, ZOOM Previous, and using the space bar as a return key. The "Advanced Drafting Extensions" package option included such *extras* as hatching, display of units in feet and inches, BREAK and FILLET commands. These and other ACAD v1.4 features were explained in a 180-page, three-ring binder manual. The software came on three double-density disks, and AutoCAD required a minimum of dual floppy drives and 256K RAM to run. My, how things change!

So what has changed with the latest release of AutoCAD? In this appendix, you'll see selected new and improved features that you may someday wonder how you managed without, including the following:

- New construction objects

- New and enhanced drawing objects

- Improved hatching features

- New and enhanced dimensioning capabilities

**Appendixes**

- Advanced text features

- Changes and additions to available drawing aids

- New and improved editing functions

# Construction Objects

There are two new construction objects in this release of AutoCAD: infinite construction lines (XLINE) and rays (RAY). Both are similar in function, and are defined by two points. Whereas a ray uses the first point specified as a beginning point and continues indefinitely in the direction specified by the second point, an XLINE passes through both points and is infinite in both directions.

## Infinite Construction Lines (XLINE)

◄ See "Drawing Infinite Lines (XLINE)," p. 449

The XLINE command is used to place one or more lines of infinite length that can be used to aid in constructing the drawing. After placement, object snap modes can be used to lock onto the infinite line for locating other geometry.

Although an infinite line has no termination, it doesn't affect the extents of the drawing area. This will be appreciated by users who have had plots or zooms influenced by an erased reference line that previously passed outside the extents of the drawing area.

For convenience, these construction lines can be located on a separate layer and frozen or turned off to keep them from plotting. Although an infinite line can't display as any linetype other than continuous, you can assign it a faint color to keep it from interfering with the main drawing view.

## Rays (RAY)

Like infinite lines, rays are used for construction purposes. Unlike an infinite line, a ray has a termination point at one end that may help keep your drawing from becoming too cluttered with reference objects.

A ray can also be assigned to a specific layer and have an associated color. Again, the drawing extents don't take into account any ray objects when calculating plot or zoom areas.

◀ See "Drawing
Rays (RAY),"
p. 454

> **Note**
>
> In addition to using XLINE and RAY to create construction lines, you can also use them to help orient yourself in 3D space. By drawing a ray or infinite line along a UCS axis, you can tell at a glance how you are oriented in relation to the UCS.

# Drawing Objects

You will see three drawing objects that are new or enhanced in this version of AutoCAD. First, there are multilines—powerful "multiple line" objects that can be configured to display in a variety of ways. Second, the linetype selection has been greatly enhanced by the addition of complex linetypes that include text or symbols. And third, ellipses are constructed as a true ellipse rather than polyline segments, making them easier to work with.

## Multilines (MLINE)

If you've ever offset a line or lines and had to work with the resultant group of lines as one, you'll love the new MLINE command. Multiple line segments, called *elements*, are drawn as one object just as you would draw a single line. The resultant multiline can then be manipulated as one item in the drawing, much like a polyline.

Multilines consist of up to 16 elements, each with its own color and linetype. Once a multiline is defined, it can be saved for future use by naming it in the Multiline Styles dialog box (see fig. A.1).

**Fig. A.1**
The Multiline Styles dialog box allows you to enter, save, and load multiline configurations.

Each element of the multiline style is defined using the Element Properties dialog box (see fig. A.2). The element's offset from centerline is indicated, along with its individual color and linetype. By combining the various options, you can create multilines to represent things such as streets with sidewalks, building walls, wiring diagram multipole connections, and so on.

**Fig. A.2**

Multilines can have as many as 16 elements defined, with an associated color and linetype for each.

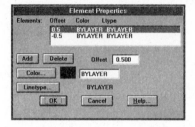

The multiline style can be further refined using the Multiline Properties dialog box (see fig. A.3). Here, you can indicate whether you want joints to be shown at each bend of the multiline, what type of end cap you want at the start and end of the elements, and whether you want the multiline filled with color.

**Fig. A.3**

Properties for multilines can include whether to display joints, what type of end caps appear, and whether the multiline is filled.

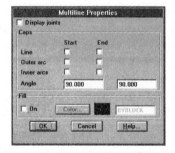

End caps can be either straight lines or arcs. In addition, an angle can be specified for the end cap line to provide a bevel at the beginning or stopping point.

When drawing a multiline, you can specify how it's justified. In addition to drawing the multiline centered along the points defining the line, it can also be justified above or below. If desired, you can also specify a scale for the multiline. The offset of all elements are adjusted by the scale factor indicated.

Multilines are limited to straight segments because, unlike polylines, there is no option for arc segments. However, object snap works with individual multiline elements, so you can manually join straight segments with arcs or polylines.

A separate facility is provided for editing multilines. Multiline cross and tee intersections can be automatically cleaned up, vertices can be added or removed, and the entire multiline or individual elements can be broken. The Multiline Edit Tools dialog box provides visual selection of editing options (see fig. A.4).

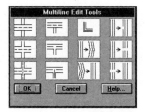

**Fig. A.4**
The Multiline Edit Tools dialog box allows you to clean up multiline intersections, add or remove vertices, and break elements.

> **Note**
>
> The MLINE command replaces the old DLINE command and offers more features that are easier to use.

◄ See "Using Multilines," p. 597

## Complex Linetypes

In addition to linetypes consisting of segments of lines and dots, you can now select from a collection of more complex linetypes that include shapes or text. This new feature provides a simple way to draw connecting items, such as railroad tracks, fence posts, insulation batting, utility lines, or topographical map elevation lines (see fig. A.5).

AutoCAD ships with a library of complex linetypes already defined, and users and third-party vendors can create their own. The AutoCAD Customization Guide provides details on the format for defining your own complex linetypes.

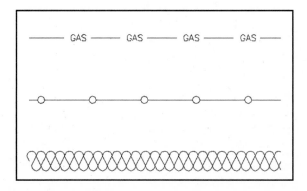

**Fig. A.5**
Complex linetypes can be defined that include text or symbols as an integral part of the object.

The size of text and shapes within a complex linetype are affected by the LTSCALE and CELTSCALE settings. Therefore, a single linetype may be used for a variety of functions by setting the object or global linetype scale as required (see fig. A.6).

**Fig. A.6**
Complex shape linetypes can change appearance with varying linetype scale settings.

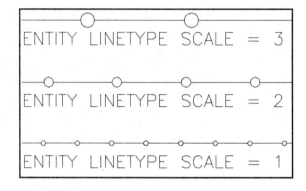

## True Ellipses

◄ See "Customizing AutoCAD" p. 1019

With this release of AutoCAD, the ellipse object has been redesigned to be a mathematically generated true ellipse. Previously, an ellipse was generated in AutoCAD by drawing polyline segments through points specified as the ellipse axis endpoints.

Breaking or trimming an ellipse, and working with ellipse linetypes has long been an ordeal for AutoCAD users. Although this new feature doesn't provide a dramatic visual difference in drawings, it's a welcome change for anyone who has tried to edit ellipses in the past. Also, the new style ellipse is more accurate—both as a full ellipse, and as elliptical arc segments.

# Hatching

◄ See "Drawing Ellipses (ELLIPSE)," p. 443

Hatching functions have received a facelift in the new version of AutoCAD. Users who have become dependent on associative dimensions will appreciate having the associative feature extended to hatching. Simplified boundary definition—provided in the previous release of AutoCAD—has been enhanced further. Plus, hatches can now be edited when required, rather than having to erase and redraw them.

## Associative Hatching

Anyone who has worked with hatching in AutoCAD will cheer the fact that hatching is now associative. Previously, any change to hatched geometry required that the existing hatch be erased and redefined to match the new geometry. Now, when you move, stretch, or erase objects within a hatched area, the hatching updates automatically.

The following figures show an example of associative hatching. In the first, an area to be stretched is selected. After the geometry is modified, the hatch area updates to match the new boundary (see figs. A.7 and A.8).

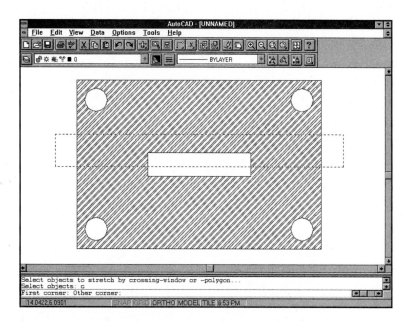

**Fig. A.7**
Editing hatched geometry now updates the associated hatching automatically.

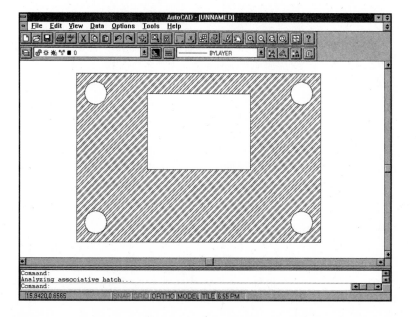

**Fig. A.8**
The hatched drawing after stretching the inner cutout area.

### Enhanced Boundary Selection

A new facility was added in the previous version of AutoCAD to allow hatch boundary specification by pointing to an enclosed area of the drawing. If there were any objects within that area that should not be hatched over, you had to indicate that they were to be excluded.

With this release, the boundary selection has been simplified further by having AutoCAD automatically hatch around anything inside the enclosed hatching area. The boundary definition can be further refined using the Select Objects, Remove Islands, and Advanced options from the Hatching dialog box. After selections are made, you can click the Preview Hatch button to see what the hatching will look like before it is actually drawn.

### Editing, Updating, and Redefining Existing Hatches

In addition to updating the hatch areas when associated geometry is changed, the hatch itself can be modified dynamically now. Using the Hatchedit dialog box, an existing hatch area can be redefined to change any parameter, including pattern, scale, or angle of the hatch (see fig. A.9).

**Fig. A.9**
Use the Hatchedit dialog box to modify properties of an existing hatch, instead of erasing and drawing it again.

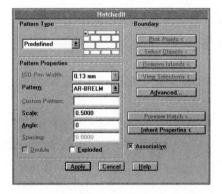

In previous versions of AutoCAD, each change to a hatch required that the existing object be erased and replaced with a new hatch pattern. This could cause problems when you couldn't remember—or didn't know—the original hatch pattern name, scale, or angle. The new hatch edit capability will be greatly appreciated by anyone who has been caught in that trap.

# Dimensioning

There are several changes to dimensioning capabilities in this version of AutoCAD, including enhanced leaders, geometric tolerancing, and improvements in definition of dimension styles.

## Mainstream Dimension Commands

All dimension commands have been moved from the dimension subcommand prompt to the main command prompt. The older DIM and DIM1 commands are still available for consistency with existing menus and scripts, however.

## Improved Leaders

With this release of AutoCAD, dimension leaders finally join other dimension objects in being associative. The arrowhead and leader line are now a single item. Gone are the days of orphaned leader arrows floating around the drawing.

Leaders now have a format option that controls the appearance of the leader line and arrowhead. The line can be straight, or a SPLINE curve, with or without an arrow (see fig. A.10).

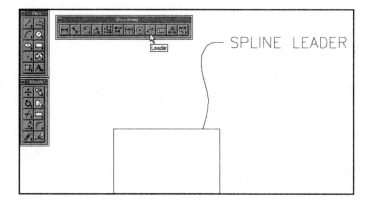

**Fig. A.10**
Leaders can now be formatted as SPLINE curves, and arrowheads are optional.

Leader text has gained flexibility as well. In addition to single-line annotation entered at the command line, the text can be copied from an existing piece of text, or entered as paragraph text. Multiline paragraph text can contain special codes for fonts and other features (see the section on text, later in this appendix).

In addition to text, the leader annotation can also be a user-specified block, or a geometric tolerance object.

## Geometric Tolerancing

The new geometric tolerancing capability provides a simplified method of creating standard ANSI tolerance notation. The resultant *feature control frame* contains all symbols and notation in proper format.

The tolerance is created using two dialog boxes. The first allows selection of an appropriate geometric characteristic symbol (see fig. A.11), which is then entered into the second dialog box for additional input (see fig. A.12).

**Fig. A.11**

The Symbol dialog box is the first step in creating a geometric tolerance.

**Fig. A.12**

After specifying the geometric characteristic symbol, a Geometric Tolerance dialog box receives input for the remainder of the required information.

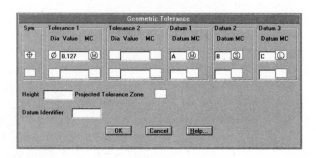

## Improved Styles

◀ See "Additional Dimensioning Features," p. 560

The function of dimension styles has been enhanced with this release to include style families, as well as style overrides. Also, each dimension object now has a style assigned to it in order to take advantage of the new features.

Styles are defined using the Dimension Styles dialog box (see fig. A.13). A style *family* can have variations to the basic *parent* style defined for each type of dimension object. In this way, entirely new styles are not required in order to have different settings on linear and radial dimensions, for example. When a particular style is in effect, newly created dimensions take on the characteristics defined for their own type of dimension within the family.

**Fig. A.13**

The Dimension Styles dialog box allows the user to define, save, and recall dimension styles.

After the style is defined, it can be named and saved for future use. The dialog box allows selection of available styles to be used as the current style for drawing dimensions.

In some instances, it may be desirable to change a dimension setting for one or more dimensions without setting up a new style. In this case, you can override a dimension style by setting it current, and then making changes to the individual style settings. When this is done, the current style name will have a plus sign preceding it, indicating that style *overrides* are in effect. New dimensions drawn are created using the current style and override settings. This is convenient for temporarily suppressing extension lines, for example, without having to create a separate style. Reselecting the original style from the dialog box resets it as current.

In all cases, dimension objects carry information about the style used to create them, including any overrides that were in effect. The relevant dimension settings remain a part of that object until it is modified to change the associated style or override settings.

## Enhanced Dialog Boxes

The Dimension Styles dialog box (refer to fig. A.13) includes buttons that call additional dialog boxes for setting the individual dimension properties. With this release of AutoCAD, the dimension Geometry, Format, and Annotation dialog boxes have been made easier to use.

◀ See "Creating Dimension Styles," p. 508

The Geometry dialog box has graphical indications of what arrowhead and center mark settings will look like. Changes in the settings modify the display to assist the user in understanding what the dimension will look like. As a shortcut, the graphic itself can be clicked repeatedly to toggle between available settings. Colors for dimension and extension lines can be selected using the appropriate Color button, or by clicking on the color box (see fig. A.14).

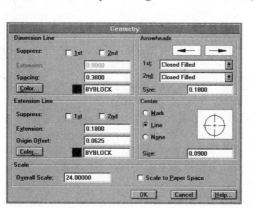

**Fig. A.14**
The Geometry dialog box simplifies specification of dimension characteristics.

Appendixes

Similar to specifying geometry, the Format dialog box provides a graphical representation of what dimension formats will look like, depending upon the settings selected. Settings can be selected from a list, or the graphic can be clicked to toggle through the available options. If changes to one setting affect another, the display shows the changes visually by updating the other related graphic (see fig. A.15).

**Fig. A.15**

The Format dialog box provides visual clues about changes to dimension settings that can be toggled by clicking the associated diagram.

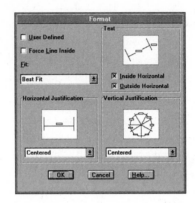

Lastly, the Annotation dialog box provides an easy way to see what changes in the dimension text settings will look like. Examples of limits, tolerances, and so on are reflected in the display of primary and alternate units. As with the Geometry Dialog Box, color of dimension text can be selected using either the button or color graphic (see fig. A.16).

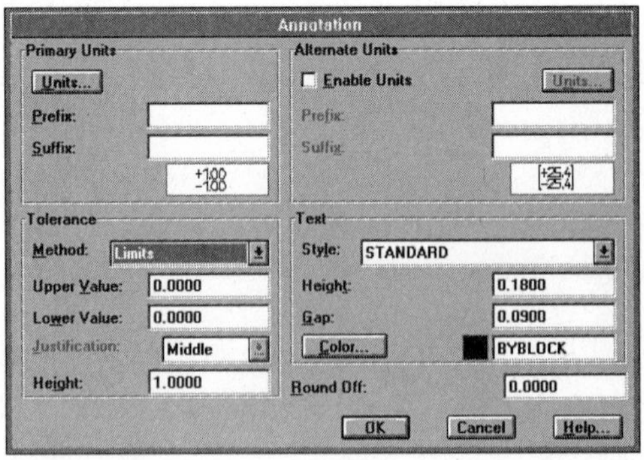

**Fig. A.16**

The Annotation dialog box allows entry of values to control dimension text formatting.

## Linear Dimensioning Creation and Editing

You can now create linear dimensions more intuitively by specifying the origin points and then dynamically dragging the horizontal and vertical dimensions. The final dimension type and location are determined by selecting the desired position of the dimension line and text. Because of this capability to specify dimension types on the fly, all horizontal, vertical, and rotated dimensions are now handled by a single DIMLINEAR command.

Additional linear dimension options allow entry of alternate text, specification of the text angle, and whether the dimension line is to be rotated. The text angle can be indicated for a given dimension and will take precedence over current dimension style settings.

After creation, linear dimensions can easily be edited using the DIMEDIT command to change text characteristics. Text can also be moved by dragging its grip, which automatically repositions the dimension and extension lines to maintain their location relative to the text.

# Text

There are several enhancements and additions to AutoCAD's text capabilities with this release. Paragraph text objects are now supported that can include a variety of formatting codes. A built-in spelling checker looks for misspelled words in both text and dimensions. Plus, Unicode character sets are now supported, as are PostScript Type 1 and TrueType fonts.

◄ See "Linear Dimensioning," p. 537

## Multiline Paragraph Text (MTEXT)

You can now create paragraphs of text and have them inserted as an individual object within your drawing. The MTEXT command allows you to work with text and formatting in an editor, and then returns the text to your drawing when finished. Multiline text can include a variety of formatting within the paragraph (see fig. A.17).

Some of the formatting features that can be used with paragraph text include the following:

- Under and overscore

- Specification of text color

- Indication of font to be used

- Change of text height

Appendixes

- Modification of tracking, or spacing between characters

- Oblique angle of the text

- Width factor of the text

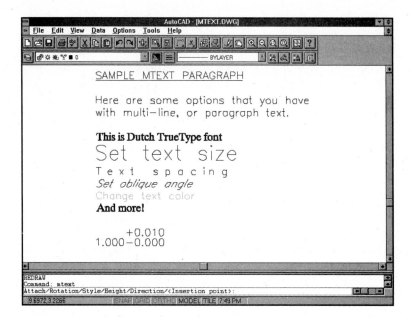

**Fig. A.17**
Multiline text can include codes for a variety of formatting effects.

Also, you can create stacked text for use in making tolerances or fractions. The Edit MText dialog box provides an input area for typing and formatting text (see fig. A.18). If desired, you can also specify an external editor of your choice, and use special codes to indicate formatting options.

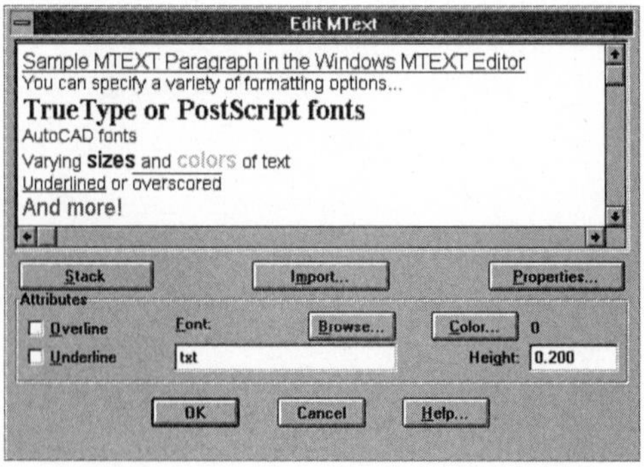

**Fig. A.18**
The Edit MText dialog box is used to type and format paragraph text.

All the available formatting can be mixed and matched within the text to operate on specific characters, lines, or entire sections. Remember that when the paragraph is drawn in AutoCAD, it is a single object, so changes to text appearance must be handled within the dialog box or external editor.

Note that when using an external editor, carriage returns are ignored when the text is returned to the drawing editor. Therefore, if you use an editor with word wrap, your spacing may not be as expected. Problems can also occur if your editor removes blank spaces from the end of lines, since this may cause words to run together. AutoCAD, however, provides a code to force a new line if required.

The MTEXT command prompts you for paragraph width, wrapping text as necessary to stay within the specified boundaries. Text is wrapped, if required, to stay within the boundary you specify. When you specify the width for a paragraph by defining a boundary box, the text is not restricted to the height of that area. If necessary, the text "spills" out of the box top or bottom if it's too long to fit within the area you indicate. One of the MTEXT options is Attachment, which indicates both the justification of the paragraph and the direction of spill for excess text. There are nine settings, including top, middle, and bottom for left, center, or right justification.

You also have the opportunity to specify a default text style and height when issuing an MTEXT command. This determines a base setting for text within the paragraph, although changes can still be made by using the special formatting codes mentioned earlier. There is also an option to indicate flow direction for those languages where text does not run left to right. Additionally, the entire paragraph can be rotated around the attachment point at an angle that you specify.

Once the paragraph text is created, you can edit either the content or the characteristics of the paragraph itself. If you need to change the text or internal formatting, you are taken to the editor to make changes. Changing the paragraph itself is done using the Mtext Properties dialog box, where you can modify text style or height, direction, attachment, width, or rotation (see fig. A.19).

**Fig. A.19**
The Mtext
Properties dialog
box can be used
to change the
definition of
paragraph text.

## Built-In Spelling Check

◄ See "Entering
Text with
MTEXT,"
p. 475

If you use a computer for word processing, you're probably already familiar
with the convenience of having a spelling checker to look for incorrectly
spelled words. You've probably also wished more than once that AutoCAD
had a similar feature to look through your drawing text for you. Finally, it's
here!

The internal spelling checker in AutoCAD combs your entire drawing—or
specific items that you select—and reports any unrecognized words that
it finds. Both line and paragraph text can be checked using the SPELL
command.

When an incorrect or unrecognized word is located, it's displayed in the
Check Spelling dialog box, where you can do any of the following: make
corrections, look up alternate words, add correctly spelled words to the
dictionary, ignore text that is flagged as bad, and change to a different
dictionary. The word in question is shown in context for your reference
(see fig. A.20).

**Fig. A.20**
The built-in
spelling checker
can help flag
misspellings in
text.

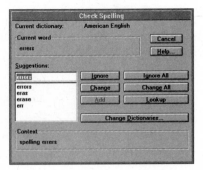

AutoCAD comes with a collection of spelling dictionaries for various dialects of English. When checking for words, AutoCAD looks in both the main dictionary and the current custom dictionary. Any words that you select for addition are put into the custom dictionary, which can be edited with a standard ASCII editor.

## Unicode Support

This release of AutoCAD brings a change in the font coding used in the past. In order to handle text for languages with large numbers of characters, accents, or glyphs, the supplied fonts now use a Unicode character encoding scheme.

◀ See "Spell Checking a Drawing (SPELL)," p. 481

Unicode fonts can support over 65,000 characters and require a different coding sequence than has been used in previous versions of AutoCAD. To allow time for transition from old fonts that you might have acquired over the years, the previous font SHX files are still supported in this version of AutoCAD. They will, however, be dropped in a future release.

## TrueType and PostScript Type 1 Font Support

The change in format for AutoCAD fonts will eventually make some existing third-party fonts unusable. With this version of AutoCAD, however, you can use TrueType and Postscript Type 1 fonts, several of which are supplied with AutoCAD. This new feature opens up a world of new options in formatting text appearance.

Any font type can now be used as the basis for a text style. To use a TrueType or PostScript font, simply supply the filename when prompted for a font name. Multiline paragraph text can include formatting to specify one of these fonts for use (see fig. A.21).

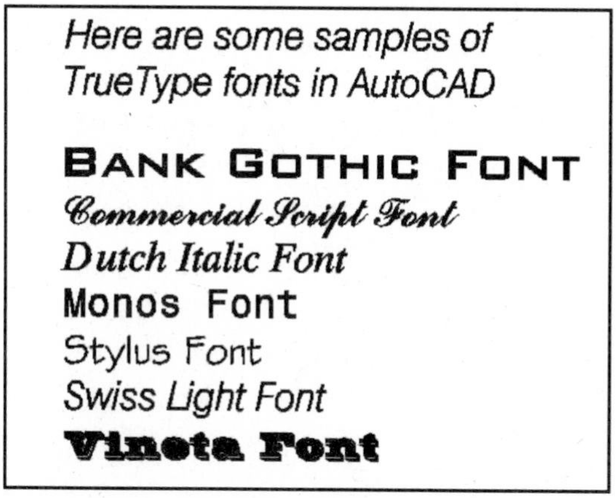

**Fig. A.21**
Text styles can now use TrueType and Adobe fonts besides standard AutoCAD fonts.

Appendixes

Because heavy filled fonts can slow drawing operations, a system variable is provided to control whether fonts are filled in, or simply drawn as outlines. Unfilled fonts also plot as outlines until the fill is turned back on.

> **Note**
>
> Filled TrueType fonts can now be displayed as 3D objects. You can place text using a filled TrueType font at any location and orientation in 3D space and AutoCAD will display the text as a filled TrueType font.

# Drawing Aids

This version of AutoCAD brings new features and commands to make working with drawings easier. There are object groups that allow collections of objects to be named and handled as one without having to create a block, and new object snap modes fill in some gaps. Linetype scale can now be set by individual object, providing greater flexibility in controlling the drawing appearance. Additionally, selecting objects by pick is simplified through use of object selection cycling.

## Object Groups

The new object group feature allows you to specify a collection of objects that can be manipulated as one object. Unlike a normal selection set, the items within a group can be named and saved with the drawing. Groups have some features in common with blocks, although they are more flexible in that individual objects within the group can be manipulated.

A group is created by selecting objects to be included and giving them a name and description. If the group is defined as selectable, selecting one object in the group selects the entire group. The group objects are only selected, however, if they would be individually selectable under current drawing conditions. For example, if a group contains objects on a layer that is frozen, those items are not selected when the group is picked. The Object Grouping dialog box allows you to fully manipulate grouped items (see fig. A.22).

An object group can be used any time AutoCAD prompts you to select items. Group names can be used to select objects for editing commands such as COPY, ERASE, MIRROR, and ARRAY. You simply indicate that the objects you want to select are a group, and provide the group name (see fig. A.23).

**Fig. A.22**
The Object
Grouping dialog
box allows
manipulation of
grouped objects.

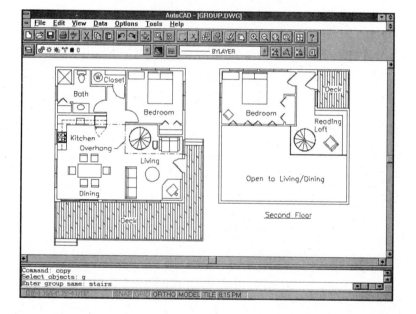

**Fig. A.23**
Once objects have
been grouped, the
group name can be
entered at any
prompt that
requests that you
select objects.

Adding and deleting items from a group is much simpler than with blocks. Use the dialog box Add or Remove buttons to select items for addition or deletion. You can change the group name or description, and toggle whether it is selectable.

Objects can be part of multiple groups. Therefore, AutoCAD has provided the Find Name and Highlight buttons to assist with managing groups and their objects. If you want to see what groups an object belongs to, use the Find Name feature to bring up a list. This lets you know what other groups might be affected by deleting that object, for example. To find a group of objects on-screen, use Highlight to indicate where they are.

When a group is copied or arrayed, the resultant duplications don't have the same name as the original object-like blocks. Each additional copy of the group receives an *anonymous* name *A*n, where *n* increments for each new group. These anonymous groups can be listed and manipulated in the Object Grouping dialog box by selecting the Include Unnamed box (refer to fig. A.22).

If desired, you can change the order of objects within a group. This would be useful in certain cases for processing the group components in programming code. From a user standpoint, you might want to put one item at a different location in the group order if it's near or on top of another item. This would make one item visible over the other.

Once a group is no longer needed, you can explode it to remove the definition from the drawing. This does not alter the objects within the group, if any, but just deletes the group from the drawing.

## New Object Snaps

◀ See "Using Groups," p. 678

There are two new object snaps in this release of AutoCAD, and a change in the way that others work with the new ellipse object. Since ellipses are now mathematically generated and not made up of polyline segments, the CENter, QUAdrant, and TANgent OSNAP modes work with an ellipse object as you expect them to.

The first new object snap mode is From. By itself, From doesn't snap to any particular object type. Instead, it's used to establish a reference point from which you can specify a relative location. From can be used with other object snap modes to locate a point, for example, a certain distance *from* the ENDpoint of a line. It should be considered an object snap modifier rather than an actual Osnap mode.

The APParent Intersection mode, however, is used like any other object snap. It prompts for two objects and finds their actual or implied intersection point. In complex drawings, APP can be used instead of INTersection in places where it might be difficult to lock onto one of several intersections in close quarters. In 2D drawings, APP can be used to lock onto a point where two objects *would* intersect if they continued far enough (see fig. A.24). For 3D users, APP locates a point where two objects appear to meet in the current view, even though they don't actually meet in 3D space.

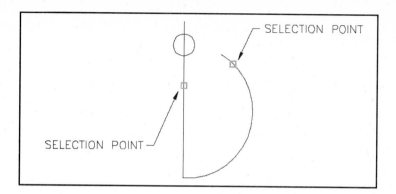

**Fig. A.24**
Using the Apparent Intersection Osnap mode, a circle is drawn where the arc and line would meet, if the arc were extended.

## Linetype Scale by Object

Objects that can have a linetype assigned now can also have an associated linetype scale. This should prevent a great deal of aggravation for those hidden or center lines that are just too short to warrant a break. You can now change the linetype scale and force a break to appear without having to manually split the line into multiple pieces.

◄ See "Understanding Object Points and Object Snap," p. 150

The object linetype scale is also useful with the new complex linetypes that can include shapes or text as part of the line. By changing the scale individually, each linetype can assume a variety of appearances (refer to fig. A.6). When modifying objects now, the scale may be changed along with other properties (see fig. A.25).

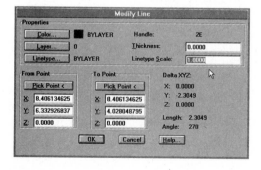

**Fig. A.25**
Use the Modify Line dialog box to change the LTSCALE of individual objects.

## Object Selection Cycling

When working on a complex drawing, it's often difficult to select the correct object by picking. With several objects falling inside the pickbox, AutoCAD is likely to grab the wrong one at any given time. You can always make the pickbox smaller to make it less likely that multiple items are captured, but that also makes it less likely that you'll be able to easily select what you're

◄ See "Adjusting the Linetype Scale," p. 628

trying to get. Another option is to zoom in for a closer look, but that takes time and is distracting.

AutoCAD's solution to the problem is object selection cycling. Go ahead and enlarge that pickbox to keep from squinting. Then, hold down the Ctrl key when you press the pick button to select an object. If AutoCAD highlights one that you don't want, press the pick button again to move to the next item within the pickbox range. Repeat until you get the item you want.

# Editing

◀ See "Object Selection Cycling," p. 232

Some editing commands have received updates and enhancements with this release of AutoCAD, including TRIM, EXTEND, PURGE, and EXPLODE. Also, we'll look at the new LENGTHEN command, which is deceptively named since it can also shorten objects.

## LENGTHEN Command

The LENGTHEN command combines features of several commands, including CHANGE, BREAK, TRIM and EXTEND, but provides greater control over the object being edited. LENGTHEN operates on one item at a time, however.

LENGTHEN works on nonclosed objects, such as lines, polylines, splines, and arcs. You are given the option of changing the length or angle of objects in a variety of ways. The delta length or angle can be indicated either as a positive or negative value. Positive adds to the item, whereas negative removes a portion. In either case, the end closest to the pick point is operated on by the command.

You can also specify the change as a percent of current length or angle, or as an ending total length or angle. Additionally, there is a Dynamic option that allows you to drag the end to a desired location.

Unlike using the STRETCH command on an arc, dynamically dragging using the LENGTHEN command does not change the arc center point or radius. It provides a more natural feel for making visual changes. When used on a polyline or spline, the total length is used for calculating length changes, not just the end segment.

To assist you in deciding what changes need to be made, the LENGTHEN command reports on a selected object's current length and, if appropriate, included angle. This provides a quick and convenient method for determining the distance around an arc segment, or along a spline or polyline, without having to use the LIST command.

## Improved TRIM and EXTEND Commands

While the AutoCAD programmers were working to add an apparent intersection object snap, they decided to include the concept as an enhancement to the TRIM and EXTEND commands. Both of these now work with a selected boundary that doesn't actually cross the area being trimmed or extended to.

◀ See "Changing Object Lengths (LENGTHEN)," p. 274

As shown in the following figures, the selected boundary edge doesn't actually extend to where the lines are trimmed or the arc extended. AutoCAD uses this *implied* boundary to calculate the correct points for editing the objects (see figs. A.26 and A.27).

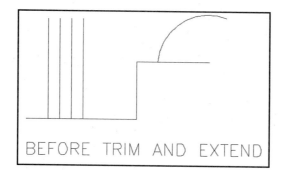

BEFORE TRIM AND EXTEND

**Fig. A.26**
Before editing to TRIM the vertical lines and EXTEND the arc.

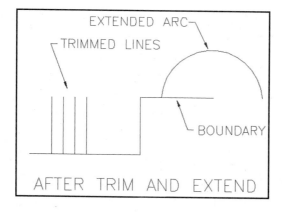

EXTENDED ARC
TRIMMED LINES
BOUNDARY
AFTER TRIM AND EXTEND

**Fig. A.27**
After editing, the lines are trimmed and the arc extended to the selected boundary line, even though it doesn't cross the necessary points.

## PURGE At Any Time

Ever since the PURGE command was introduced, users have wished that it could be used during the drawing session rather than just after entering a drawing. Finally, this capability was added to the new release, providing a way to keep drawing size down during long drawing and editing sessions. Purging a drawing to remove unused blocks, layers, linetypes, and such, helps to reduce REGEN time, and makes listings of these objects more manageable. Use it often.

◀ See "Using the Editing Commands," p. 240

**Appendixes**

### Improved EXPLODE Command

◀ See "Removing Unwanted Objects (PURGE)," p. 289

The EXPLODE command has been improved to allow editing blocks that were inserted with a differing *X* and *Y* scale factor. It now also works on blocks inserted at negative scale factors. Previously, these blocks were rejected by EXPLODE.

# 3D Modeling

◀ See "Breaking Blocks Apart (EXPLODE)," p. 697

AutoCAD has come a long way from its 2D drafting roots. Although 2D drafting continues to be the application most users use AutoCAD for, there has been significant interest in 3D modeling in recent years.

In Release 13, Solid Modeling has been integrated into the basic command set by incorporating the ACIS geometry kernel into the core AutoCAD database. The ACIS (American Committee for Interoperable Standards) geometry kernel has also provided other significant enhancements that include creation of true ellipses and splines defined as NURBS (Nonuniform Rational B-Spline) curves. In Release 12, Solid Modeling commands were available with the add-on AME (Advanced Modeling Extension) package. AME is discontinued in Release 13, as most of the functionality is available to users free of cost within the base Release 13 package.

Solid Modeling functionality in Release 12 suffered from lack of performance and large file sizes. Both of these concerns were corrected with the integrated solid modeling capability of Release 13. Also, basic editing functions such as union, subtract, intersection, fillet, and chamfer are available from the command prompt or from menus. With the AME package, users could edit the CSG (Constructive Solid Geometry) tree using the SOLCHP command. This is not available in Release 13 as the solids do not maintain the CSG tree. SOLPROF (used to create 2D profiles) and SOLSEP (used to separate Boolean operations) have also been discontinued. For more details refer to Chapters 32 and 33, which cover the Solid Modeling commands.

To help users of the AME package migrate to Release 13's Solid Modeling capabilities, a command called AMECONVERT has been added. This converts AME models into Release 13 Solids. Users needing more advanced Solid Modeling capabilities should consider Designer or AutoSurf for complex surfaces. Both of these packages will be available for Release 13.

In Release 13, editing commands are less UCS dependent. Extrusion direction of selected objects no longer needs to be parallel to the Z-axis of the current UCS. This affects editing commands such as EXTEND, TRIM, OFFSET, BREAK and FILLET.

## Rendering

An integral part of 3D modeling is the capability of rendering, which allows for creation of realistic 3D images. These images can be used to aid in better visualization or may be used in marketing documents and presentations. With Release 12, Rendering became part of the basic AutoCAD command set. In Release 13, this functionality has been further enhanced.

This enhancement includes the addition of spotlights as another light source, along with point and distant lights. Also, lights can now be assigned colors. This helps simulate better images. A Materials Library is now included that allows users to assign realistic texture maps to objects based on the type of material used. Material properties can be modified and previewed before being used.

Rendered images can now be saved in several widely used formats including TGA, TIFF, GIF, Postscript, PCX , X11, PBM, PGM, PPM, BMP, SUN, FITS, and IFF. For more details refer to Chapter 34, "Understanding Rendering Concepts."

If you require additional rendering capabilities, you could use AutoVision R2. This add-on package provides the capability to create shadows, along with the provision to add texture and bump maps to objects. It can also simulate transparency and refraction.

Rendering created in AutoCAD can be exported to 3D Studio using the new 3DSOUT command. They can then be used for advanced rendering and animation capabilities available in that product. 3D Studio-created images can also be incorporated into an AutoCAD rendering using the new 3DSIN command.

# Miscellaneous

There are some other changes that can't really be grouped elsewhere, so they are grouped here at the end.

AutoCAD now includes the capability to import and export ACIS .*sat* files for use with new solid modeling features. The dialog boxes for opening files and inserting blocks have been enhanced to add a thumbnail view of drawings as you scroll through the directory list. And a new type of Xref has been added to simplify the use of shared drawings.

## ACIS Technology

With the addition of solid modeling capabilities in this release of AutoCAD, Autodesk has also included a function to import and export ACIS files in ASCII (.sat) format. This allows transfer of relevant 3D information from other programs that use this format.

Using the ACISIN and ACISOUT commands, you can provide the name of an ACIS *.sat* file to transfer data to or from AutoCAD. With widespread usage of the ACIS geometry kernel, ACIS could become a standard for transferring solid geometry between different CAD packages.

## Drawing Preview at File Open or Block Insert

The Open Drawing dialog box now includes a thumbnail view of drawing files as they are highlighted in the directory list. The same feature has been included for selecting a file for block insertion. Both provide a visual clue about drawing content to serve as a reminder of what that eight-character name really means.

The Open Drawing dialog box allows you to specify that a file be opened in read-only mode. Also, you can select which view of the drawing to display when it is opened (see fig. A.28). The thumbnail view won't be displayed if the file isn't in Release 13 format, although you can use MAKEPREVIEW to create thumbnails of pre-Release 13 drawings.

**Fig. A.28**
The Select File
dialog box
includes a
thumbnail view of
the highlighted
drawing file.

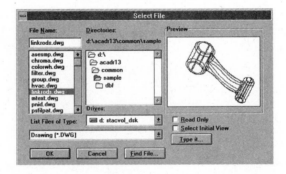

When inserting a block using DDINSERT, you have an option within the dialog box to select a file from disk (see fig. A.29). A file name can be entered directly, or you can use the File button to bring up the Select Drawing File dialog box.

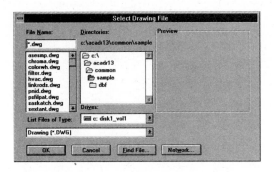

**Fig. A.29**
Using the File button takes you to the Select Drawing File dialog box.

The Select Drawing File dialog box includes a Find File button which will take you to the visual drawing browse mode. Once in the Browse/Search dialog box, you can toggle between functions using the Browse and Search tabs. Browse mode provides a view of all drawing files within the selected directory. The Size selection allows you to specify viewing of small, thumbnail pictures for each drawing, or two slightly larger sizes (see fig. A.30).

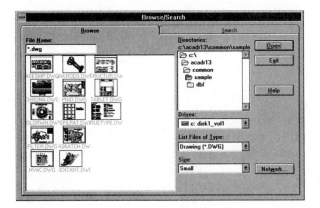

**Fig. A.30**
The Browse/Search dialog box Browse mode provides small, medium, or large graphics of drawing files within the selected directory.

To help you find drawings when you don't know where they're stored, use the Search tab. This section of the dialog box allows you to specify a file name pattern, date or time specification, and drive or directory location for the search. All files that match your criteria are shown in the graphic area, along with their full path and file name (see fig. A.31).

**Appendixes**

**Fig. A.31**
The Browse/
Search dialog box
provides a search
function to assist
with locating
drawings that
match criteria you
specify.

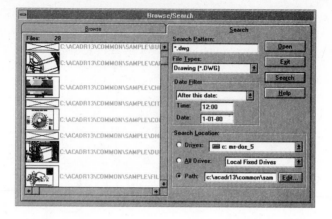

## Overlay Xrefs

Previously, when a drawing included an Xref to another file, the included reference drawing was passed along if the container drawing was used as an Xref itself in some other file. This could become confusing, and even create problems if a drawing tried to reference some other file that referenced back to it.

◄ See "Overlaying a Referenced Drawing (Xref Overlay)," p. 709

With this version of AutoCAD, overlay Xrefs have been introduced as an alternative to the original style Xref. The new overlay files behave in a similar manner to previous Xrefs, but when a drawing containing an overlay Xref is itself used as an Xref, the overlay information does not pass through. Overlay Xrefs go only one "layer" deep. The original style of Xref is now referred to as an *attached* Xref.

# From Here...

This is only a partial list of the new features in AutoCAD Release 13. Throughout the book, you will find icons similar to this one, which indicate new and enhanced features. For more information, look at the sections indicated for each item shown previously, or thumb through to find the New Feature icons.

# On Your Own

For another look at some of the new features and improvements to existing commands, use the AutoCAD Help pull-down menu to view examples and descriptions online.

# Appendix B

# Installing and Configuring AutoCAD

This appendix describes AutoCAD's installation and configuration procedures. Although this appendix discusses many configuration settings and setup techniques you can use to control AutoCAD and improve its performance, AutoCAD supports too many devices to cover all configuration details. If you find your interest piqued and you want more details, please see the *AutoCAD Installation Guide for Windows*. Use it to determine what configuration settings provide optimal performance for your system and drawings when you experiment on your own. This appendix covers the following:

■ Minimum system requirements for installing and running AutoCAD Release 13

■ Preparing your system for AutoCAD Release 13 installation

■ Installing AutoCAD Release 13 on a typical system

■ Installing AutoCAD Release 13 on a network

■ Running AutoCAD efficiently in the Windows environment

■ Troubleshooting your installation

In the past, many dealers have provided installation of AutoCAD as part of the value-added services offered to their customers. Some dealers offered discounts on the software in exchange for customers installing the software on their own systems. This can be an equitable arrangement for the knowledgeable user. However, for the first-time buyer or novice user, dealer installation of AutoCAD is highly recommended. In fact, in the future AutoCAD dealers may have no choice in this matter. Autodesk is in the process of restructuring its distribution system for its products. Autodesk is attempting to create a closer dealer-customer relationship in which the dealer is more knowledgeable of the Autodesk products offered. Autodesk is taking this action with the thought that dealers will be able to offer more and better services for its customers. It has yet to be seen how this affects product pricing and standard versus optional services that dealers offer.

# Requirements and Recommendations for Installation

As with any program, how you use AutoCAD determines the type of hardware best suited to your application. If you use AutoCAD in an educational environment, you may not require hardware as powerful as that used in a production environment. AutoCAD for Windows requires the following hardware and software for a minimum configuration:

- PC or MS-DOS Version 5.0 or later.

- Microsoft Windows 3.1 or Windows for Workgroups 3.11. Your computer must run Windows in enhanced mode. AutoCAD will not run in standard mode or in real mode.

- A copy of Win32s 1.20 or later installed on your system prior to installing AutoCAD. Autodesk supplies this program. The installation routine automatically searches for Win32s and prompts the user to install the program if needed.

- An 80386DX-, 80486DX-, or Pentium-based computer. In an educational environment, an 80386DX-based system may work. Production drafters should have at least an 80486/33 system.

- A math coprocessor for 80386-based systems. 80486DX and Pentium chips contain an integrated coprocessor.

- A disk drive with 1.2M or 1.44M capacity.

- A hard disk with at least 23M of free disk space for the minimum installation of AutoCAD for Windows.

**Note**

The hard drive space required soars to 88M if you want to do a Custom installation and copy all the files Autodesk includes. These requirements do not include space for your drawing files.

■ A permanent swap file of 40M.

■ A minimum of 16M RAM. If you create large drawings, AutoCAD operates faster if you add more than the 16M minimum.

■ A graphics card and monitor capable of displaying a VGA or better resolution and compatible with Microsoft Windows.

■ A Windows-supported pointing device, such as a mouse. If you would rather use a digitizing tablet in place of the required mouse, you need an extra serial port and tablet. For more information on digitizers, see Appendix D, "Working with Digitizers."

■ If you have an international or network version of AutoCAD Release 13, you need an IBM-compatible parallel port for the hardware lock that comes with these versions of AutoCAD.

■ If you want to plot your drawings, you need a printer or plotter that is either supported by AutoCAD or comes with its own drivers for AutoCAD. You can also print to the Windows system printer, if the printer has been configured through the Windows control panel.

■ If you plan to install AutoCAD using the CD-ROM data you will need a CD-ROM drive.

■ If you intend to install both Windows and DOS platforms you will need additional hard disk space to accommodate both versions.

**Tip**

Update your DOS operating system to version 6.2. DOS version 6.2 offers valuable features for a customized environment and for optimizing Windows performance.

**Caution**

Before beginning any software installation, always make a backup copy of your distribution disk(s). Always install the software from the backup set of disks, not the originals. You should also keep a backup copy of your DOS distribution disks. If you are installing from a CD, you should make a backup of the floppy disk that comes with the CD and start your installation from the backup. Your CD should be safe from most common forms of damage and does not need to be backed up. The only way to back up the CD is with special CD writing equipment or with tape.

**Appendixes**

# Making Backups

The following sections cover steps that you should always take before installing any new software on your system. These steps protect the investment you have made in your system to date, while saving you time in the event an error occurs while installing or updating your software. It is never a question of whether a system error will affect you, it is a question of when an error will arise. Taking these steps will help you recover quickly from almost any catastrophe and get your system back on-line with minimal effort.

## Backing Up Your Original Disks

Before making backup copies of your distribution disk(s), push the write-protect tab to the open position on each original disk to prevent accidental erasure or damage to the disk. You need the same number and type of backup disks as your distribution set. As previously mentioned, if you are installing from a CD, you should back up the one disk that comes with the CD. You do not need to back up the CD.

Use COPY DISK to back up your disks. COPY DISK is a Windows command that allows you to copy the entire contents of one disk to another quickly. If you have a single floppy drive, insert the first original (source) disk in drive A: and follow these steps:

1. Open File Manager in the Main program group from the Windows Program Manager.

2. Select Disk from the menu bar.

3. Select Copy Disk from the pull-down menu.

4. In the Copy Disk dialog box select the OK button to verify that the source disk is in drive A:, which also is the Destination drive.

5. In the Confirm Copy Disk dialog box, select Yes to verify that you want to continue. As the dialog warns, be certain that the destination disk is empty or does not contain information you need.

6. If you have not already, insert the source disk and select OK.

7. Windows begins copying the data. Insert the destination disk when prompted and select OK.

If you have two disk drives that are the same size and density (both 5 1/4" or both 3 1/2"), place the first distribution disk in drive A: and a backup (target) disk in drive B: and repeat the steps above, replacing step 4 with the following:

> In the Copy Disk dialog box select B: as the Destination In:, then select the OK button to verify the settings. This command copies everything on the disk in the A: drive to the disk in the B: drive.

The *source disk* is the disk you are copying (your original distribution disk), and the *target disk* is your duplicate (backup) disk. Your target disk does not have to be formatted. COPY DISK formats it for you.

If you see `Error reading drive A` messages while attempting to copy a disk, please contact your AutoCAD dealer before continuing. Your AutoCAD disk(s) may be defective; if they are, your dealer can return them to Autodesk for a new copy.

### Backing Up Your Existing Files

Installation of Windows applications has a far-reaching effect on many system files. Most of these system files were not even in a DOS system, so many users are not yet familiar with them. For this reason, if no other, you should do a complete system backup before installing any new software. If something goes wrong while installing your new program, you could easily spend a day trying to get your system back to its original state. If time and backup equipment are issues, you should at the very least back up your DOS and Windows system files, AUTOEXEC.BAT, CONFIG.SYS, SYSTEM.INI, and WIN.INI.

Perhaps the single most important step you can take to ensure that the time and money you have invested in your AutoCAD system is not wasted is to start a daily tape backup system. If you do not already have a tape drive for system backups, you should seriously consider investing in one. With a tape drive unit, you can automate the backup system, allowing an unattended backup of your system. If you do not have a tape drive, you can back up your system using floppy disks and the DOS BACKUP (5.0) or MSBACKUP (6.0 and higher) command. This command is different for each DOS version. Refer to your DOS manual for the correct name and syntax.

# Optimizing Your Hard Disk's Performance

The speed at which files are accessed on your hard disk significantly affects AutoCAD's performance because it must swap program and drawing data

**Tip**
Keep each program you use (like AutoCAD) in its own subdirectory. File access is faster and and it is easier to install future program upgrades.

in and out to disk when the drawing becomes too big to fit entirely into available RAM. Disk access time is also important when it comes to loading and storing drawing files, inserting blocks, and loading other files. If you are installing AutoCAD onto a computer that you have been using for awhile, you should defragment the disk before installation. A defragmented hard disk runs faster and more efficiently.

## Disk Fragmentation

When you erase a file from your hard disk, DOS makes the sectors of the hard disk that were occupied by that file available for new files. A new file may require more space than is available in that group of sectors. When you place the new file on the hard disk, DOS puts as much of the file as it can into the newly available space and then looks for another section somewhere else on the drive for the rest of the file. Thus, the file's contents are scattered around the hard disk, or *fragmented*, rather than placed into a single block of space on the disk. It takes longer for programs to find all the parts of a file if the files are fragmented than if they are placed into a single block of space on the hard disk. The more you use the disk and the more files you erase and store on it, the more fragmented the disk becomes and the longer it takes your programs to find files.

Because AutoCAD creates a large number of temporary files, it is quite likely that your hard drive will become highly fragmented. This situation will seriously degrade AutoCAD's performance. Because of this, AutoCAD requires that you have a large section of your drive reserved as a permanent swap file, used for the temporary files it creates. This is done by the Windows permanent *swap file* discussed later in this appendix.

The swap file must be a minimum of 40M. This space must be a contiguous blank area on your hard disk. Although your system might report you have 40M available, it is highly unlikely that it is a contiguous area. This is why you will want to run the disk defragmenting program before creating the swap file. It is also a good idea to run the defragmentation program periodically to clean-up the data files on your hard drive.

## Defragmenting and Reformatting

If your drive has been in use for a long time, you may want to defragment the disk. Defragmenting reorders the files, moving the data around so that your files are once again stored in contiguous sectors. Additionally, your defragmentation utility may allow you to take any small groups of unused sectors that were previously in between files and reallocate them into a large group. The DEFRAG command that comes with DOS 6.0 and higher

**Tip**
Use a disk optimizer or defragmentation program frequently to speed up file access on your hard disk.

defragments your files and optionally places the files together in a contiguous block and creates a large contiguous blank area for future files, minimizing the distance between existing files. DEFRAG uses the term *compress* when referring to defragmenting the files and placing the files together, leaving a large blank area. Do not confuse this with compressing the files on the drive using DRVSPACE or Stacker. DEFRAG optimizes your drive's performance; it does not actually reduce the size of the files.

> **Note**
>
> If your system is currently set up to use a permanent swap file in Windows, remove the swap file before defragmenting and compressing your disk. Add the swap file back after you have finished. For additional information, refer to "Configuring a Permanent Windows Swap File," later in this appendix.

You can buy commercial disk management programs that allow you to defragment the disk, and to check and adjust other operating parameters of your hard disk, such as the disk's interleave factor (the ordering of the sectors on the disk). The later versions of DOS 6.*x* also provide many of these commands to help you maintain your disk. Refer to your DOS user's manual for details on CHKDSK, DEFRAG, SCANDISK, MSAV, and more.

Also, you should be aware of programs that tout the capability to double your hard disk's capacity. They do so at the expense of sacrificing your drive's file access speed. As discussed previously, this is critical considering the fact that AutoCAD makes heavy use of accessing drawing and swap files.

As an alternative to defragmenting the drive, you can choose to reformat. If you have a tape drive, as mentioned in the "Backing Up Your Existing Files" section earlier in this appendix, this method can save time over defragmenting a very large and very fragmented hard disk. Because the entire disk is freed by reformatting, you achieve the same effect as defragmenting and removing small blank spaces when you copy your files back onto the disk; they are copied into contiguous sectors because there is plenty of free space on the disk.

You can defragment your disk without losing data, but reformatting destroys any existing data on your hard disk. Before you consider reformatting the hard disk, make sure that you have completed the earlier outlined backup of all files on the drive, and that you know how to restore them after you reformat it. Make sure that you can install the software necessary for restoring your backup, and make sure that you have more than one up-to-date backup.

**Appendixes**

# Before Installation

Along with the issues covered in this section, as a precautionary measure, you may want to review "Troubleshooting the Installation" later in this appendix. This section can help you avoid any of the common errors that might occur while you install and configure AutoCAD. If you're upgrading from an earlier version of AutoCAD, follow these guidelines:

- Leave the earlier version installed on your computer until you are confident that Release 13 has been installed and runs correctly. Install Release 13 in a different directory or on a different drive from the older release until Release 13 is up and running.

- Make backup copies on floppy disks of any customized files you have created or installed. These include AutoLISP programs (LSP), prototype drawings (DWG), shape and text font files (SHP and SHX), customized help files (HLP and HDX), menu files (MNU and MNX), and custom linetype (LIN) and hatch pattern (PAT) files.

> **Note**
>
> AutoCAD Release 13 for Windows creates additional menu files and compiles the menu to an MNC file.

- You may have to make modifications to your AUTOEXEC.BAT and CONFIG.SYS files. Make sure that you have backups of these files.

## Freeing Conventional Memory Using MemMaker

MemMaker is a utility program provided in DOS 6.0 and later. Using MemMaker, you are able to free conventional memory by loading device drivers, TSRs, and other programs into the upper memory area. If you find that you do not have enough conventional memory to run AutoCAD or the AutoCAD installation program, you may want to try using MemMaker to free some memory.

You can check the amount of free memory your system has by entering the DOS command MEM at the DOS prompt. MEM reports back the Total, Used, and Free amounts of memory for Conventional, Upper, Reserved, and Extended (XMS) memory types. It also reports the largest executable program size, which is the number you are most interested in knowing.

Before you use MemMaker, you should be aware that it is not without its own set of limitations. If you have busy CONFIG.SYS and AUTOEXEC.BAT files, you may find it difficult to use MemMaker. Make sure that you have backups of your CONFIG.SYS and AUTOEXEC.BAT files before you start MemMaker. Refer to your DOS manual for details on using MemMaker. If you are familiar with the settings in your CONFIG.SYS and AUTOEXEC.BAT files, use MemMaker to do the majority of the configuration. Then you can go in and optimize any settings that might need adjustment.

# Installing Your Software

Now that you have prepared an environment suitable for AutoCAD, you are ready to begin the actual installation. This section covers the installation of AutoCAD in a stand-alone PC environment. First complete the next section, "Installing Win32s 1.20 or Later," before starting the AutoCAD setup. Win32s is a utility program provided by Autodesk and is required to run AutoCAD.

**Tip**

If you should encounter problems when you install Win32s or AutoCAD, you can refer to the section "Troubleshooting the Installation," at the end of this appendix.

## Installing Win32s 1.20 or Later

The Win32s application is a bridge utility that allows you to run applications that address 32 bit CPUs. It is required until the next version of the Windows operating system is released. The AutoCAD installation program automatically detects if Win32s is installed on your system. If it is not already on your system, you will see the information dialog box (see fig. B.1). You are then required to exit and install the program before you are allowed to continue.

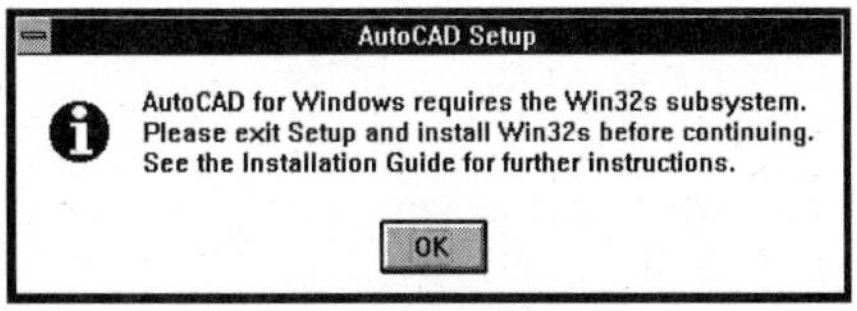

**Fig. B.1**
The WIN32s information dialog box.

Install the Win32s program using a standard Windows SETUP program. The installation program automatically creates the necessary directories, Windows Program Group, and Program Items. It copies files, edits your SYSTEM.INI file, and attaches icons for you. It also gives you the option to install FREECELL, a program that allows you to test the Win32s program to be sure it is operating.

To install Win32s, follow these steps:

1. Have disks 23 and 24 available if you are using disks to install AutoCAD.

2. Insert disk 23 in drive A: or B:, or if you are using a CD, make sure that it is in your CD drive.

3. From Windows Program Manager, choose File, Run.

4. Type **X:setup** (*X:* is the drive letter of the floppy or CD drive for the media you are using).

## Using the AutoCAD Installation Program

You install AutoCAD for Windows with a standard Windows SETUP program that automatically creates the necessary directories and Windows Program Groups and Items, copies files, attaches icons, and personalizes AutoCAD for you. It also lets you install only those groups of files that you want, which can save you significant disk space if you do not want source, bonus, and sample files installed on your hard disk.

You need at least 23M of free space on your disk for executable and support files to install a minimum AutoCAD configuration. A full installation requires 88M and includes executable and support files, learning tools, application development tools, external database access, examples and samples, and TrueType and PostScript fonts along with source SHX files, speller dictionaries for three dialects of English, and an electronic documentation viewer. The typical installation requires 46M, which includes executable and support files, U.S. dictionary, fonts, sample drawings and LISP routines, ASE files, peripheral drivers, learning tools, and on-line documentation (CD only). If you do not have enough space to install the files you have selected, INSTALL alerts you to that fact.

To install AutoCAD, follow these steps:

1. Insert disk 1 into drive A or B (even if you are using the CD installation, you still have disk one in addition to the CD).

2. From Windows Program Manager, choose File, Run.

3. Type **A:setup** or **B:setup**.

4. Enter your name, company, and AutoCAD dealer information (this information is displayed when you start AutoCAD) in the Personal Data dialog box (see fig. B.2).

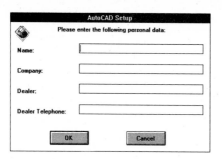

**Fig. B.2**
The Personal Data
dialog box.

5. Next, select which platform you want to install. Choose Windows Only
   for only the Windows version; choose Windows and DOS if you want
   both (see fig. B.3). The hard disk space requirements discussed previously assume a Windows Only installation.

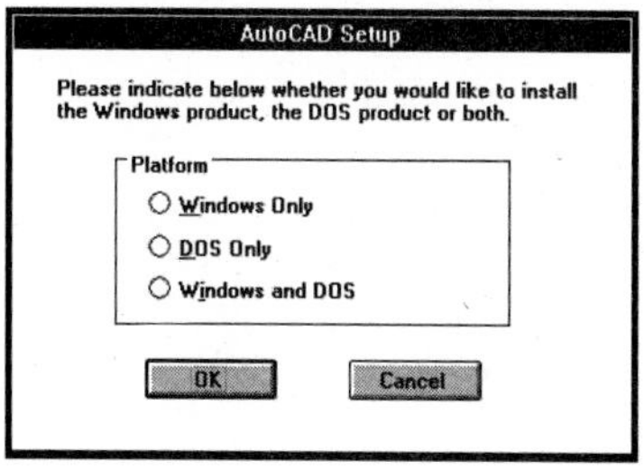

**Fig. B.3**
The AutoCAD
Setup screen,
Platform dialog
box.

6. Choose what type of installation you want. Review the three options
   and follow the instructions for the installation of your choice (see
   fig. B.4).

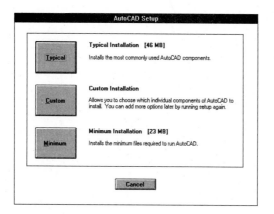

**Fig. B.4**
The AutoCAD
Setup screen,
Installation dialog
box.

**Appendixes**

- Selecting Typical Installation automatically chooses the AutoCAD Executable and Support files along with a combination of Shared Files.

- Selecting Custom Installation brings up an Installation Options dialog box. Select the options that meet your needs. You also can select the Fonts and Dictionaries buttons to select subsets of those options. As you select options, you also have the opportunity to deselect options by picking the highlighted selection box again.

After you have completed your selections, choose the Continue button to move to the next dialog box. If you want, you can choose the Select All button to do a complete installation. As you make your selections, the Total Disk Space Required reference changes so that you can monitor the hard disk space requirements. If you do not like your selections, you can choose the Clear All button to start over. To see the dialog boxes that appear during a custom installation refer to figures B.5, B.6, B.7, and B.8.

**Fig. B.5**
The AutoCAD Setup screen, Installation Options dialog box.

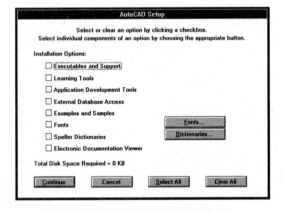

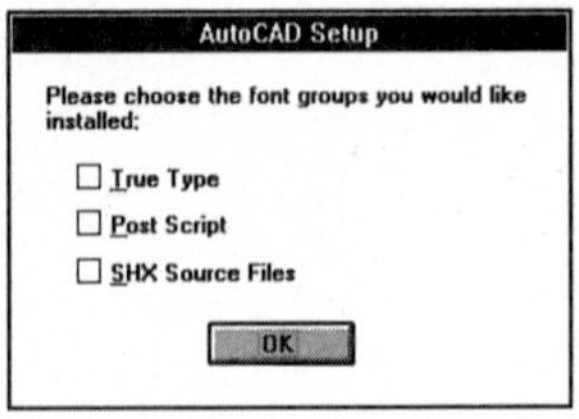

**Fig. B.6**
The AutoCAD Setup screen, Font dialog box.

**Fig. B.7**
The AutoCAD
Setup screen,
Dictionary dialog
box.

**Fig. B.8**
The AutoCAD
Setup screen after
custom installation
is completed.

■ Selecting <u>M</u>inimum Installation automatically selects the
AutoCAD executable files along with a minimal number of shared
files.

**7.** After you select the type of installation you want and choose <u>C</u>ontinue,
the Directory Confirmation dialog box opens. This dialog box allows
you to confirm your directory settings in edit boxes. It also shows you
the amount of space your files occupy. If you feel your option settings
are not correct, select the <u>I</u>nstall Options to return to the previous dialog box. When everything is correct, select the <u>C</u>ontinue button. The
screen should look like figure B.9; the only difference is the amount of
space required for the files you selected or your directory structure. The
amount of space required depends on which type of installation you
chose.

Appendixes

**Fig. B.9**
The AutoCAD
Setup screen,
directory confir-
mation dialog box.

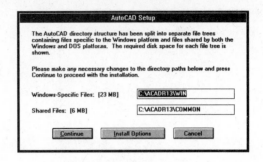

8. You get one of two inquiry dialog boxes. If you are installing Release 13 for the first time, you are prompted with The "C:\ACADR13\WIN" directory does not exist do you want to create it? If you are reinstalling Release 13, you are prompted with The C:\ACADR13\WIN directory already exists. Install anyway?. Select the Yes button, for whichever prompt you receive. See figure B.10 and B.11 for examples of the warning dialog boxes.

**Fig. B.10**
The AutoCAD
Setup screen,
directory does not
exist dialog box.

**Fig. B.11**
The AutoCAD
Setup screen,
directory already
exists dialog box.

9. If you are installing AutoCAD from a CD, enter the drive of your CD player in the CD Drive Letter dialog box. Select OK to continue. If you are using a floppy drive, change disks as you are prompted. Figure B.12 shows you the CD-ROM drive edit box and screen.

**Fig. B.12**
The AutoCAD
Setup screen, CD
drive letter dialog
box.

10. After AutoCAD is finished copying files from your data source, an information dialog box tells you the installation is complete (see fig. B.13).

**Fig. B.13**
The AutoCAD
Setup screen,
installation is
complete dialog
box.

The AutoCAD setup is complete. You may now configure AutoCAD. If any of your hardware requires an ADI driver that is not supplied with AutoCAD, install it according to the manufacturer's instructions before configuration.

## Adding Directories to AutoCAD's Support Path, Changing Icons, and Editing ACAD.INI

The SETUP program automatically constructs a path to the standard AutoCAD support directories, but if you have placed other support files, such as third-party fonts or applications in other directories, you must add them to that path. There are several ways you can change this information. This section covers two of the methods: through the program group and by the ACAD.INI file. Other options you can change while you are accessing the files are also discussed.

### Adding Directories to AutoCAD's Support Path and Changing Icons in the Program Group

After you have finished installing AutoCAD, you are returned to the Windows Program Manager. You should have a new Program Group open for your AutoCAD files (see fig. B.14). To change or add AutoCAD support directories from the Program Item Properties dialog box, follow these steps:

1. From the Program Manager, double-click the AutoCAD Program Group (if it is not already open). When the Program Group opens, click the AutoCAD icon and choose File, Properties. Windows opens the Program Item Properties dialog box.

2. Click the Command Line edit box.

   You should see something similar to the following (depending on where you installed AutoCAD):

   ```
   c:\acadr13\win\acad.exe /s c:\acadr13\win;
   c:\acadr13\win\support; c:\acadr13\common\support;
   c:\acadr13\common\fonts;
   ```

Appendixes

The /s tells AutoCAD that the path that follows indicates support directories.

3. Add your own support directory names to the end of this line, separating directory names with semicolons.

You may click the Change Icon box to select from among several AutoCAD icons to display on the Windows desktop.

**Fig. B.14**
The AutoCAD Release 13 Program Group.

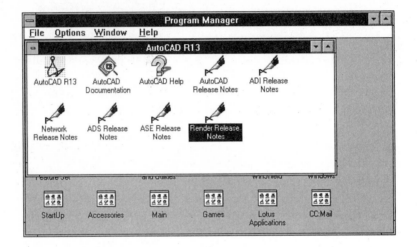

**Editing ACAD.INI to Add Directories to AutoCAD's Support Path and Other AutoCAD Settings**

**Tip**

INI files typically are associated with the NOTEPAD.EXE program. This allows you to double-click the ACAD.INI file in File Manager to launch the program.

Each Windows application has an INI file that contains program settings referenced by Windows when it starts the application. The ACAD.INI file contains environment settings, support paths, preferences, and screen settings. If AutoCAD cannot locate files it needs to run, it may become necessary to edit the support path or environment settings in the INI file.

You can edit this file from within Windows using a text editor like Notepad. The ACAD.INI file is located in the C:\ACADR13\WIN directory. The directory may vary, depending on the path you entered at installation.

**Note**

Most of the ACAD.INI settings are accessible through the Preferences dialog boxes in the AutoCAD program. Choose Options, then Preferences from the pull-down menu. See "Setting Your Preferences in AutoCAD," later in this appendix.

The ACAD.INI file is divided into several sections that each have a section title within [ ]s. Lines enclosed in [ ]s or beginning with a semicolon are not read by Windows when it references the file.

For this section, the information we are interested in is located under the title [General]. Look for the ACAD= line. This is the line that specifies the support path AutoCAD searches for files it references. Notice two lines down ACADDRV=. This line sets the path where AutoCAD looks for driver files. If you have a problem getting AutoCAD to load a device driver, check this path. After this heading, the majority of the information deals with screen settings for the program window, menus, toolbars, and so on. Refer to figure B.15 to see a listing of the first part of the ACAD.INI file.

**Tip**
Print out a copy of the ACAD.INI file and keep it with your AutoCAD manuals for future reference and troubleshooting.

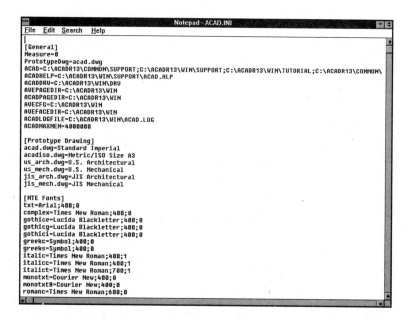

**Fig. B.15**
The ACAD.INI file in Notepad.

# Starting and Configuring AutoCAD for Windows

You have now finished the automated installation and verified that your support directories are correct. You are almost ready to start AutoCAD. This section covers the steps necessary to configure AutoCAD for your hardware and operating preferences. You need to complete one more step before starting the actual AutoCAD configuration. That is to make sure that you have installed ADI drivers for the hardware accessories you use with AutoCAD.

Appendixes

The following section discusses ADI drivers. From there, you begin the configuration process, setting up your hardware and the way you want AutoCAD to appear and function.

## ADI Drivers

ADI (Autodesk Device Interface) drivers are device driver programs for peripherals such as plotters, video cards, and digitizers. All AutoCAD for Windows drivers other than null drivers are of the ADI type. AutoCAD for Windows ADI drivers only work with AutoCAD for Windows; real-mode and protected mode ADI drivers used with DOS AutoCAD 386 do not work with AutoCAD for Windows. If you do not already have the most recent ADI drivers for your equipment, you need to contact the manufacturer of your digiziter and plotter to request an up-to-date copy. You also need to refer to the documentation provided with the driver to help with its installation.

## Configuring AutoCAD for Your Hardware

You are now ready to start AutoCAD and begin the configuration process.

1. If the AutoCAD Program Group window is not displayed, double-click the AutoCAD Release 13 Program Group icon in the Program Manager. The AutoCAD Program Group window is displayed.

2. From within the AutoCAD Release 13 Program Group, double-click the AutoCAD Program icon to launch AutoCAD.

After AutoCAD has loaded, the AutoCAD Text Window appears on-screen. The screen prompts you for information regarding your video display, digitizer, and plotter. Figure B.16 shows the digitizer and plotter screens. The configuration steps are as follows:

1. From the `Available video Display` list, select the appropriate display for your system. For most users that will be option 1, the Accelerated Display Driver. Selecting the Windows Display Driver will disable many of the speed enhancements that are associated with the Accelerated Display. As mentioned at the start of this appendix, every user's system is different; if you are not certain which to choose, try both options to see the results.

   ■ Accelerated Disp. Drvr., by Rasterex (Int'l) a.s. for Autodesk, Inc.

   ■ Windows Display Driver, by Autodesk, Inc.

The AutoCAD Text
Window displaying
configuration
prompts.

2. If you select the first video display, you are prompted Do you want to
   configure the driver? <N>:. If you enter Y, a DSAI Configuration dialog box appears that allows you to configure the Accelerated Display
   Driver. There are two options in this dialog box:

   ■ To bypass the Graphics Display Interface (GDI) that Windows uses
     to control the display of windows and other objects displayed on
     the graphics screen, select the GDI Bypass box. Selecting GDI
     bypass increases the display speed when doing a redraw. Selecting
     this option may cause incompatibility with some display drivers.
     If problems occur with your display, disable this option.

   ■ The second option is to use a Display List. Using a display list
     allows you to operate with a faster and more efficent graphics
     window. It also is required if you want to use the Aerial View
     feature in AutoCAD. However, if your system is low on memory,
     you may have to disable this feature.

3. No matter which display you choose, you can adjust the aspect ratio of your graphics screen. You need to adjust this ratio if circles appear elliptical or squares appear rectangular.

For now, at the `If you have previously measured the height and width of a square on your graphics screen, you may use these measurements to correct the aspect ratio. Would you like to do so? <N>:` prompt, accept the default by pressing Enter.

4. Next, you are asked to select the type of digitizer your system uses. The nine options listed after the `Available digitizer:` prompt are as follows:

```
1. Current System Pointing Device
2. Calcomp 2500 (obsolete) and 3300 Series ADI 4.2 - by
   Autodesk, Inc
3. Hitachi HICOMSCAN HDG Series ADI 4.2 - by Autodesk, Inc
4. Kurta IS/ONE (obsolete) ADI 4.2 - by Autodesk, Inc
5. Kurta XLC, IS/THREE (obsolete) ADI 4.2 - by Autodesk,Inc
6. Kurta XLP, ADI 4.2 - by Autodesk, Inc
7. Summagraphics MicroGrid v1.1 (Series II or later) ADI4.2
   - by Autodesk, Inc
8. Summagraphics MM Series v2.0, ADI 4.2 - by Autodesk, Inc
9. Wintab Compatible Digitizer ADI 4.2 - by Autodesk, Inc
```

Select the appropriate digitizer for your system. For specific information on configuring your digitizer see Appendix D, "Working with Digitizers."

▶ See "Digitizers Supported by AutoCAD," p. 1211

5. Next, you are asked to select the type of plotter to which your system has access. Fifteen options are listed at the `Available plotter:` prompt, as follows:

```
 1. None
 2. AutoCAD file output formats (pre 4.1) - by Autodesk, Inc
 3. CalComp ColorMaster Plotters ADI 4.2 v2.8 - by Autodesk
 4. CalComp DrawingMaster Plotters ADI 4.2 v2.8 - by Autodesk
 5. CalComp Electrostatic Plotters ADI 4.2 v2.8 - by Autodesk
 6. CalComp Pen Plotters Plotters ADI 4.2 v2.8 - by Autodesk
 7. Canon Laser Printer ADI 4.2 - by Autodesk
 8. Hewlett-Packard (HP-GL) ADI 4.2 - by Autodesk, Inc
 9. Hewlett-Packard (PLC) LaserJet ADI 4.2 - by Autodesk, Inc
10. Hewlett-Packard (PLC) PaintJet/DeskJet ADI 4.2 - by
    Autodesk, Inc
```

11. Hewlett-Packard HP-GL/2 devices, ADI 4.2 - for Autodesk
    by HP
12. Houston Instrument ADI 4.2 - by Autodesk, Inc
13. PostScript device ADI 4.2 - by Autodesk, Inc
14. Raster file export ADI 4.2 - by Autodesk, Inc
15. System Printer ADI 4.2 - by Autodesk, Inc

The prompts that follow depend on your plotter selection. If you find
yourself needing more specific information, refer to your plotter
manual.

6. The next option is for the default login name. This default is taken from
   when you personalized AutoCAD during installation. The login name is
   used to identify the owner of a locked file. If your system is in a network environment and accesses files from a server, you want to utilize
   this option. The login name must be one to thirty characters in length
   and begin with a nonblank character. Spaces are permitted between
   characters. At the Enter default login name or . for none <my name,
   my company>: prompt, type the correct response for your situation and
   press Enter.

7. You are now prompted to tell AutoCAD if you want to enable file locking. If you are working in a networking environment, file locking is
   automatically enabled. Even if you are configuring for a single-user
   workstation in a networking environment, it is best to enable this
   feature. This allows you to access files kept on a server or in shared
   directories over the network. If you are not working in a networking
   environment you can safely disable file-locking. At the Do you wish to
   enable file-locking? <Y>: prompt, respond accordingly.

> **Caution**
>
> If file locking is enabled and AutoCAD or your system were to crash, you
> would be locked out of the drawing file, possibly AutoCAD as well. Delete
> the lock files, from either DOS or Windows, to reenable the drawing and/or
> AutoCAD. A lock file usually has the same names as the locked file but with a K
> as the last character of the extension. If the drawing file DRAWING.DWG were
> locked, the accompanying lock file would be DRAWING.DWK.

Appendixes

8. If you chose the English dictionary option when you installed AutoCAD, you are given the option to select a version of the English dialect to use. The three choices at the Available spelling dialects: list are as follows:

```
1. American English
2. British English (ise)
3. British English (ize)
```

Enter your selection at the Select dialect number or ? to repeat list <1>: prompt.

9. After you have completed these steps, AutoCAD reports your choices to the screen. Press Enter to continue. The Configuration menu appears (see fig. B.17).

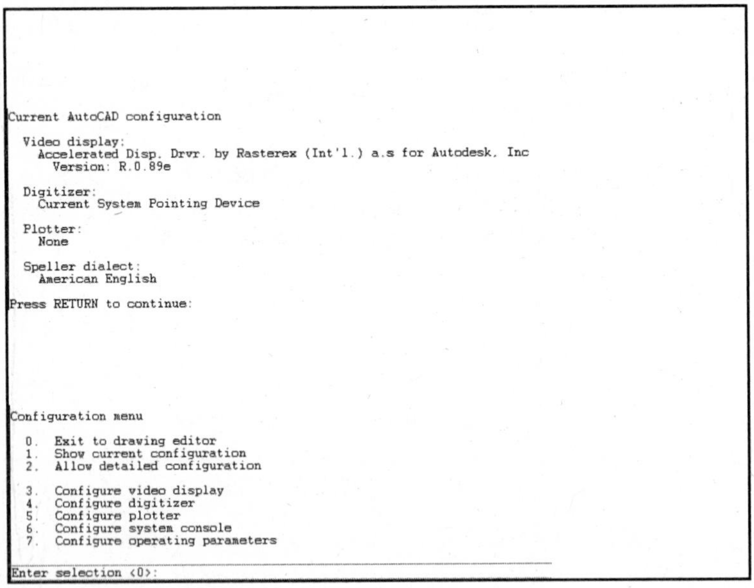

**Fig. B.17**
The Configuration menu.

```
Current AutoCAD configuration

  Video display:
    Accelerated Disp. Drvr. by Rasterex (Int'l.) a.s for Autodesk, Inc
        Version: R.0.89e

  Digitizer:
    Current System Pointing Device

  Plotter:
    None

  Speller dialect:
    American English

Press RETURN to continue:




Configuration menu

  0.  Exit to drawing editor
  1.  Show current configuration
  2.  Allow detailed configuration

  3.  Configure video display
  4.  Configure digitizer
  5.  Configure plotter
  6.  Configure system console
  7.  Configure operating parameters

Enter selection <0>:
```

## AutoCAD Configuration Menu

In the preceding section, you completed the hardware configuration for AutoCAD. Accepting the 0 default displays a message telling you that typing N discards all configuration changes and asks if you want to keep them. Accepting the Yes default causes AutoCAD to exit from the Configuration menu, bringing you into AutoCAD's drawing editor. Before going into the editor, examine the options in the Configuration menu:

■ At the 1. Show current configuration prompt, Enter **1**. AutoCAD displays your current configuration. At the Press Enter to continue: prompt, press Enter to end the option. This is a standard prompt displayed at the end of each option outlined in this section. This step is not mentioned in the remaining menu options. It is assumed that you will do so to end the following options.

■ At the 2. Allow detailed configuration prompt, Enter **2**. At the Do you want to do detailed device configuration? <N> prompt, enter **Y**. AutoCAD displays the prompt Additional questions will be asked during configuration. This allows you access to additional configuration options for items 3 through 5. The questions vary with each device.

■ Selecting options 3 through 5 repeats the setup screens you saw at installation.

■ At the 6. Configure system console prompt, enter **6**. Configure the console by selecting "Preferences" from the AutoCAD "File" menu appears in the Message box. Select OK or press Enter to remove the box.

■ At the 7. Configure operating parameters prompt, enter **7**. The last option displays the Configure operating parameters menu (see fig. B.18 for a list of menu options). This menu has 11 options that can be accessed by the Preferences dialog box in the AutoCAD editor. These options are covered in detail in "Setting Your Preferences in AutoCAD" later in this appendix. Press Enter to select 0 and exit back to the Configuration menu.

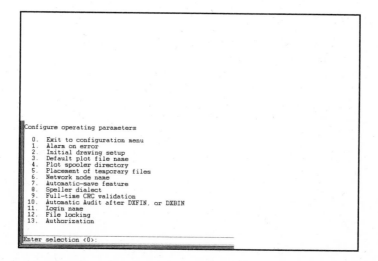

**Fig. B.18**
The Configure operating parameters menu.

```
Configure operating parameters

 0.  Exit to configuration menu
 1.  Alarm on error
 2.  Initial drawing setup
 3.  Default plot file name
 4.  Plot spooler directory
 5.  Placement of temporary files
 6.  Network node name
 7.  Automatic-save feature
 8.  Speller dialect
 9.  Full-time CRC validation
10.  Automatic Audit after DXFIN. or DXBIN
11.  Login name
12.  File locking
13.  Authorization

Enter selection <0>:
```

Appendixes

With AutoCAD installed and your review of the Configuration menu completed, you are ready to enter the AutoCAD editor. Press Enter to exit to the drawing editor. AutoCAD displays the following message: If you answer N to the following question, all configuration changes you have just made will be discarded. Keep configuration changes? <Y>. Press Enter to accept the configuration.

### Obtaining and Entering Your Personal Authorization Code

A new feature of AutoCAD Release 13 that will take some veteran users by surprise is the need to obtain an authorization code for your software. This is part of Autodesk's new strategy for registering users of its software.

You can obtain the code before you install the software by contacting Autodesk at 800-551-1490, or you can install the software before obtaining the code. However, if you do not contact Autodesk for the code within 30 days from installation, AutoCAD will lock you out of the drawing editor. Until you have entered the authorization code, each time you enter the drawing editor AutoCAD reminds you that you must still enter the code. To obtain your code and register your software you have to provide Autodesk with the following information:

- Your name, company, address, city, state, ZIP code and phone number

- The dealer from whom you purchased your software

- The date of purchase

- The AutoCAD serial number from a previous version, if you are upgrading

- The AutoCAD serial number from your new version

To enter your authorization code follow the steps outlined as follows:

1. At the Configuration menu (refer to fig. B.17), type **7** to open the Configure operating parameters menu.

2. At the Configure operating parameters menu (refer to fig. B.18), type **13** to select the Authorization option.

3. At the Enter authorization code for this serial number: prompt, enter the authorization code Autodesk supplied to you and press Enter.

4. Exit the Configure operating parameters menu by typing **0** and pressing Enter.

**5.** At the Configuration menu type **0** and press Enter to exit that menu.

**6.** At the `Keep configuration changes? <Y>` prompt, press Enter to accept the changes.

Your software is now registered. If you had previously installed AutoCAD without entering the authorization code, the reminder prompt that had appeared in the drawing editor should no longer be displayed.

## Reconfiguring AutoCAD

Now that you are in the drawing editor with AutoCAD installed, you can always reconfigure your setup by choosing Options, and either Preferences or Configure from the pull-down menu. AutoCAD displays your current configuration.

### Using Configure to Set Up AutoCAD

To configure or change a device driver, select the item you want to change from the configuration menu. AutoCAD prompts you for values for each device. When you choose to configure a particular device in AutoCAD's configuration menu, AutoCAD looks on your hard disk for the appropriate driver files. If it does not find the driver files, it prompts you to enter the drive and directory where they are located. Insert your backup disk that contains the drivers and press Enter. AutoCAD reads the contents of the disk and displays the drivers for you. Refer to the previous section "AutoCAD Configuration Menu," if you need further assistance to change the device(s).

### Setting Your Preferences in AutoCAD

The Preferences dialog box allows you to set variables in five different panes: System, Environment, Render, International, and Misc. These settings allow you to configure AutoCAD to work the way you do. Figure B.19 shows the Preferences dialog box. To access the Preferences dialog box, follow these steps:

**1.** Select Options, Preferences from the pull-down menu.

**2.** At the `Command:` prompt, type **preferences** and press Enter.

The following settings are available in the System pane of the Preferences dialog box (see fig. B.19).

**Fig. B.19**
The Preferences
dialog box.

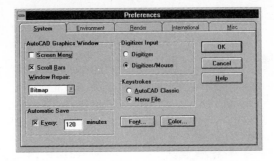

The AutoCAD Graphics Window area offers you variables to control the display of the screen:

- *Screen Menu*. Click this box if you want to use the screen menu.

- *Scroll Bars*. Click this box if you want to use the vertical and horizontal scroll bars on the drawing window.

- *Window Repair*. Select the mode you want to use for reconstructing the graphics window image when an overlying window is removed. Unless you use a third-party display driver, the default is BITMAP. If other options are available, they are listed in the pop-up list.

The Automatic Save area allows you to enable AutoCAD's automatic save command and set the save interval:

- *Every*. Check this box to enable the automatic save feature.

- *Minutes*. Enter the automatic save interval in this edit box.

The Digitizer Input area allows you to configure AutoCAD to accept input from a digitizer or a digitizer/mouse.

► See "Configuring the Digitizer," p. 1213

- *Digitizer*. Accepts input from your configured digitizer only.

- *Digitizer/Mouse*. Accepts input from the pointing device last moved or last sent a coordinate. This is the default option (usually the desired option).

The Keystrokes area offers two check boxes to control how AutoCAD interprets keystrokes:

◄ See "Using the AutoCAD Drafting Tools," p. 55

- *AutoCAD Classic*. Mode toggles to function regardless of the definitions of the accelerator.

- *Menu File*. Accelerators take precedence over the mode toggles.

The remaining buttons on the System pane are as follows:

■ *Fo*n*t button.* Displays the Font dialog box. Use this dialog box to select the font and size that AutoCAD uses for displaying text in the graphics and text windows.

■ *Color button.* Allows you to choose colors for the following screen areas: Graphics window background, Graphics text background, Graphics text color, Text window background, and Text window text color. You can use any of the standard system colors, or make your own custom colors using the R, G, and B slides. Changes are displayed on the left side of the dialog box.

The Environment pane of the Preferences dialog box is used primarily for setting directory paths. All the path boxes work with the Browse button. This allows you to scan your system's directory tree and select a new path or file name to insert in the edit box (see fig. B.20).

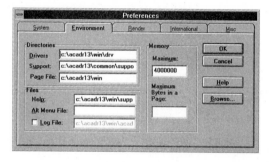

**Fig. B.20**
The Preferences dialog box, Environment pane.

The Directories area offers these edit boxes for entering directory references:

■ *Drivers.* Enter the path and directory in which AutoCAD is to search for ADI drivers. This information may be stored in the ACADDRV environment variable.

■ *Support.* Enter the path and directory in which AutoCAD is to search for files. This includes text fonts, menus, LISP files, linetypes, hatch patterns, and drawing files. This information may be stored in the ACAD environment variable.

■ *Page File.* Enter the path and directory in which AutoCAD is to place the first page file. This information may be stored in the ACADPAGEDIR environment variable.

The Files area offers the following edit boxes for entering references for support files that AutoCAD accesses:

- *Help*. Enter the file name and path for the Windows AutoCAD or platform-independent help files. The file name and path also may be stored in the ACADHELP environment variable.

- *Alt Menu File*. Enter the name of an alternate menu file to swap with the standard AutoCAD tablet menu. This file name also may be stored in the ACADALTMENU environment variable.

- *Log File*. Select the option box and enter the directory path where you want the ACAD.LOG file stored. This file holds the entire contents of the text window for your editing sessions. The file also may be stored in the environment variable ACADLOGFILE.

The Memory area offers two edit boxes for entering values to control the AutoCAD page file:

- *Maximum*. This value sets the amount of memory, in bytes, that the pager can receive from Windows. The environment variable ACADMAXMEM also may hold this value.

- *Maximum Bytes in a Page*. Set the maximum number of bytes for the first page file. The value also may be stored in the ACADMAXPAGE environment variable.

> **Note**
>
> Settings saved in the ACAD.INI file take precedence over environment settings. If you do not save changes made in the environment pane to the ACAD.INI file, the changes are used in the current AutoCAD session.

The Render pane of the Preferences dialog box is used primarily for setting directory paths for the rendering environment. Like the Environment pane, all the path boxes work with the Browse button (see fig. B.21).

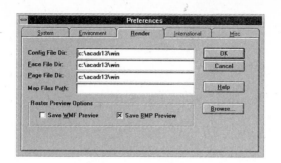

- ■ *Config File Dir.* Specify the rendering configuration file location. String also may be stored in the AVECFG environment variable.

- ■ *Face File Dir.* Specify a directory for the temporary storage of faces and meshes. The string also may be stored in the AVEFACEDIR environment variable.

- ■ *Page File Dir.* Specify a directory for the first page file. The string also may be stored in the AVEPAGEDIR environment variable.

- ■ *Map Files Path.* Enter a directory for the map files in this edit box. The string also may be stored in the AVERDFILE environment variable.

The Raster Preview Options area has two check boxes. They control if a preview drawing is displayed when using the File, Open command, and what type of format is used.

- ■ *Save WMF Preview.* Check this box to save and display preview files in Windows Metafile Format.

- ■ *Save BMP Preview.* Check this box if you want to save and display preview files in Bit Map format.

The International pane of the Preferences dialog box is used for setting international variables. The pane has three options (see fig. B.22).

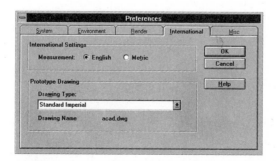

The International Settings area has one setting:

■ *Measurement.* Offers two choices: English or Metric. Select the units of measure you want to use for international measurement.

The Prototype Drawing area reports two settings:

■ *Drawing Type.* Select the type of drawing you want for your prototype drawing. The six choices are Standard Imperial, Metric/ISO Size A3, U.S. Architectural, U.S. Mechanical, JIS Architectural, or JIS Mechanical.

■ *Drawing Name.* Displays the name of your default prototype drawing. This setting changes depending on which drawing type you select from the Drawing Type pop-up list.

The Misc pane of the Preferences dialog box is used to set a variety of options (see fig. B.23).

**Fig. B.23**

The Preferences dialog box, Misc pane.

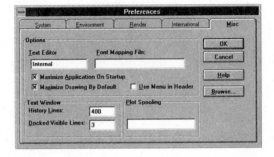

The Options area has the following commands:

■ *Text Editor.* Enter the name of the text editor that the MTEXT command is to use. The program directory must reside in Support edit box of the Directories area on the Environment pane.

■ *Font Mapping File.* Enter the font mapping file to be used by the MTEXT command.

■ *Maximize Application On Startup.* Maximizes the AutoCAD window at startup.

■ *Maximize Drawing By Default.* Maximizes the AutoCAD drawing window at startup.

■ *Use Menu in Header.* Loads the last menu used to edit the current drawing, rather than using the menu currently loaded in the drawing editor.

The Text Window area offers these commands:

- *History Lines*. Enter the number of lines you want showing in the command window above the command line in this edit box. These are the number of lines that you can scroll back through.

- *Docked Visible Lines*. Specifies the number of lines showing in the command window when it is docked.

- *Plot Spooling*. Allows you to enter the conditions for using a plot spooling application. The option sets the ACADPLCMD environment variable.

# Installing AutoCAD on a Network

Portions of the following information have been reprinted from the *AutoCAD Installation Guide*, with permission from Autodesk, Inc. You can install AutoCAD on either the server of a local area network or on the local hard disks of individual workstations. In both cases, users can share data on the server hard disk and store drawings they don't want to share on a local hard disk. Each method offers certain benefits:

◄ See "What Is Autospool?" p. 420

- Installing AutoCAD on the local hard disk of each workstation offers more protection if a server crashes. Users can access data in a shared network directory.

- Installing AutoCAD on the server hard disk enables users to share a single copy of the executable files, takes up less disk space, and simplifies the task of installing or upgrading software.

To install AutoCAD on your network, follow the steps outlined in the next section. Some of the steps were covered earlier in the appendix. When appropriate, you are referred to these sections.

> **Note**
>
> Before installing AutoCAD on a network, attach the hardware lock. For detailed instructions, see the next section "Installing the AutoCAD Hardware Lock."

**Appendixes**

## Installing the AutoCAD Hardware Lock for International and Network Versions

When you install the network version of AutoCAD or a single-user international version, you must attach a hardware lock to your system's parallel port. The lock only affects AutoCAD. You can still connect other peripheral devices to the same parallel port; other programs run with the hardware lock in place.

> **Note**
>
> If the hardware lock you have is faulty or damaged, you must contact your dealer to receive a replacement.

> **Caution**
>
> Do not remove the lock while running AutoCAD. Removing the lock can freeze your display, resulting in lost data or causing AutoCAD to fail. If the lock is removed while you are running AutoCAD, save your drawing, quit AutoCAD, exit Windows, and turn off your computer. Reinstall the hardware lock.

### Installing an International Version Hardware Lock

If you are installing an international version of AutoCAD as a single-user, follow these steps:

1. Turn off your computer and all peripheral devices.

2. Attach the male connector of the hardware lock to a parallel port of your computer. If all parallel ports are in use, disconnect one of the peripheral devices and connect the hardware lock to the open parallel port. Reconnect the peripheral device to the female end to the lock.

Continue on to the sections "Installing the AutoCAD Network Software" and "Verifying Environment Variables."

> **Note**
>
> If you are cascading the Rainbow SuperPro lock with other manufacturer's locks, position the Rainbow SuperPro last in the chain. Doing this should prevent any conflicts.

**Installing a Network Hardware Lock**

If you are installing AutoCAD on a network, you are required to install a hardware lock. The network hardware lock holds your licensing information. It comes configured for two AutoCAD licenses. If all you need are two licenses, you are ready to install the lock. However, if you need more than two licenses with a single lock, you need to upgrade the network lock. Refer to the section "Upgrading the Network Lock with Additional Licenses," for details on adding more licenses.

A network server lock (NSL) grants licenses with a security server software module (SSSM). The SSSM establishes a license server and broadcasts its presence with the server advertising protocol (SAP). The NSL must be attached to a parallel port on the license server computer before an SSSM is loaded.

The lock supports two networks: IPX and NetBIOS. Novell uses IPX. Windows for Workgroups can use either IPX or NetBIOS.

The following SSSMs are provided:

- *NSRVNI.NLM.* A Novell Netware loadable module (NLM) for establishing a license server on a Netware 3.x or 4.x file server.

- *NSRVDI.EXE.* A DOS TSR (terminate-and-stay-resident) program for establishing a license server on a client computer with the IPX network protocol driver loaded.

- *NSRVDN.EXE.* A DOS TSR program for establishing a license server on a client computer with the NetBIOS network protocol driver loaded.

> **Note**
>
> You can have multiple network locks on a license server. If you have multiple network locks, it is recommended that you create separate license servers for each lock and distribute the AutoCAD software among them. This permits AutoCAD users to continue working even if one license server fails.

**Installing the Hardware Lock in a Novell Network.** If you have another application that uses a NetSentinel™ hardware lock, it may use a different version of the security server module. Use the latest version of the security server software. AutoCAD ships with NSRVNI.NLM version 4.0.

**Appendixes**

> **Note**
>
> On client machines that receive a license from the Novell server, run the network version of AutoCAD and verify that the NWIPXSPX.DLL file exists in the Windows directory before you attach the network lock.

> **Note**
>
> Using the SAP, the SSSM communicates with the hardware lock and notifies client workstations that it has a hardware lock.

To attach the network lock to the server's parallel port and install the SSSM on the server as the network license manager, follow these steps:

1. Turn off the server and peripheral devices.

2. Connect the network lock to the server's parallel port.

> **Caution**
>
> Do not attach more than one NetSentinel™ lock to your parallel port at a time. AutoCAD does not function with more than one lock attached to the same port. During startup, the module gets the number of authorized network licenses from the network lock.

3. Unload any existing version of the SSSM, from memory. To do so, enter one of the following according to your system platform:

   - *Novell running IPX*. At the DOS prompt, enter **nsrvni /r** (reserved unload) or **nsrvni /u** (unconditional unload).

   - *DOS running IPX*. At the DOS prompt, enter **nsrvdi /r** (reserved unload) or **nsrvdi /u** (unconditional unload).

> **Note**
>
> In nsrvni, *n* indicates Novell, and *i* indicates IPX. In nsrvdn, *d* indicates DOS, and i indicates IPX.

4. To update the server's startup file with the current SSSM, enter the following according to your system network environment:

- *Novell running IPX.* Enter **nsrvni** into the AUTOEXEC.NCF file, as in the following example:

   **load nsrvni**

- *DOS running IPX.* Enter **nsrvni** into the AUTOEXEC.BAT file. Use the following example, and provide the directory and server name according to your system:

   **r:\directory\server\dos\nsrvdi**

- License servers also can have a department name attached to them, which allows clients to request licenses from specific departments. To assign a department name to a license server, add a command line option during license server startup. Use one of the following examples depending on whether your system is DOS (DN) or Novell (NI):

   **NSRVDN /DN:sales**

   **load NSRVNI /DN:sales**

- The department name can have a maximum of seven characters. Up to ten license servers can coexist per each department name. You can use any alphanumeric or (underscore character) for department name.

5. Update the startup file to point to the license SSSM; either NSRVNI.EXE or NSRVDN.EXE, whichever is appropriate for your environment.

6. For the changes to the startup file to take effect, you must reboot and restart the server to access the server module.

**Installing the Hardware Lock in a Windows for Workgroups Network.**
You allow Windows for Workgroups to access NetBIOS by entering **net start netbeui** at the DOS prompt.

This starts the Windows for Workgroups access layer to DOS NetBIOS. *NetBEUI* stands for *NetBIOS Extended User Interface Service.*

**Tip**
To verify the services that have been started, enter **net start /list** at the DOS prompt.

**Appendixes**

> **Note**
>
> To issue licenses, the license manager workstation does not need to be running Windows for Workgroups, but must have it installed and the network connection enabled.

After verifying that NetBIOS has started, follow these steps to attach the network lock and install the software on the server:

1. Turn off the server and peripheral devices.

2. Connect the network lock to the server's parallel port.

> **Caution**
>
> Do not attach more than one NetSentinel™ lock to your parallel port at a time. AutoCAD does not function with more than one lock attached to the same port. During startup, the module gets the number of authorized network licenses from the network lock.

3. Unload any existing version of the SSSM. To do so, enter one of the following according to your system platform:

   - *DOS running IPX.* At the DOS prompt, enter **nsrvdi /r** (reserved unload) or **nsrvdi /u** (unconditional unload).

   - *DOS running NetBIOS.* Enter **nsrvdn /r** (reserved unload) or **nsrvdn /u** (unconditional unload) at the DOS prompt.

> **Note**
>
> In nsrvdi, *d* indicates DOS, and *i* indicates IPX. In nsrvdn, *d* indicates DOS, and *n* indicates NetBIOS.

4. To update the server's startup file with the current SSSM, enter the following according to your system network environment:

   - *DOS running IPX.* Enter **nsrvd** in the AUTOEXEC.BAT file. Use the following example; provide the directory and server name according to your system:

     **r:\directory\server\dos\nsrvdi**

- *DOS running NetBIOS.* Enter **nsrvdn** in the AUTOEXEC.BAT file. Use the following example; provide the directory and server name according to your system:

    **r:\directory\server\dos\nsrvdn**

- *Novell running IPX.* Enter **nsrvni** in the AUTOEXEC.NCF file as shown in the following example:

    **load nsrvni st**

- License servers also can have a department name attached to them, which allows clients to request licenses from specific departments. To assign a department name to a license server, add a command line option during license server startup. Use one of the following examples depending upon whether your system is DOS (DN) or Novell (NI):

    **NSRVDN /DN:sales**

    **load NSRVNI /DN:sales**

- The department name can have a maximum of seven characters, and up to ten license servers can coexist per each department name. You can use any alphanumeric or (underscore character) in the department name.

5. For the changes to the startup file to take effect, you must reboot and restart the server to access the server module.

### Specifying the License Server

The network licensing routines in AutoCAD search the network for the first responding licensed server to use. The client system can specify multiple department names to search for a license.

To search for a license, set the ACADSERVER environment variable with the department names you want to search. If you have multiple network license managers, you can specify from which license manager to get your license by indicating each department name separated by semicolons (see the following example):

    **set ACADSERVER=dept1;dept2;dept3**

The search request begins with dept1. If no license is found, dept2 is requested, and so on until a license is found. If the environment variable ACADSERVER is not defined; the default department name NETINEL is used. If ACADSERVER is found, the default department names that have been defined are used.

### Upgrading the Network Lock with Additional Licenses

To upgrade a network lock for more than two AutoCAD licenses, complete the following:

1. Obtain an authorization code.

2. Update the network lock with the code and the number of network licenses. Also, update the SSSM with the number of licenses available.

> **Note**
>
> When you update the network lock, use the network copy of AutoCAD. AutoCAD associates its serial number with the lock serial number. An updated network lock grants licenses only to the AutoCAD serial number for which it is updated.

> **Caution**
>
> Before you upgrade an installed network lock, make sure that no AutoCAD sessions are using the lock.

**Obtaining an Authorization Code.** You must obtain an authorization code from your dealer by purchasing additional licenses for your network lock. To purchase additional licenses, provide your dealer the following information:

- The AutoCAD serial number

- The network lock serial number

- The number of AutoCAD licenses purchased for the lock and the authorization code from any previous upgrade

To obtain this information, run the AutoCAD configuration with the network lock used as a local hardware lock. To use the network lock as the local lock, attach the network lock to the parallel port of the workstations that are running the current version of AutoCAD.

When you start the AutoCAD configuration with the network lock as the local lock, an additional menu item appears in the AutoCAD Configuration Operating Parameters menu:

```
xx. Network Lock Authorization
```

Select this item to display the AutoCAD serial number, the lock's serial number, and the current number of licenses the lock authorizes. If the authorization is not the initial authorization, AutoCAD also displays previous authorization codes.

> **Note**
>
> You can update the network lock information only once per AutoCAD session. You must quit and restart AutoCAD each time you update the network lock.

**Updating Your Network Lock.** To change the number of authorized licenses, you must start AutoCAD with the network lock as the local lock. When you update the network lock, you must also update the SSSM by unloading and reloading it.

1. Unload the SSSM, from memory. To do so, enter one of the following according to your system platform:

   - *DOS running IPX.* At the DOS prompt, enter **nsrvdi /r** (reserved unload) or **nsrvdi /u** (unconditional unload).

   - *DOS running NetBIOS.* At the DOS prompt, enter **nsrvdn /r** (reserved unload) or **nsrvdn /u** unconditional unload).

2. Start the network copy of AutoCAD with the network lock as a local lock.

3. Start the AutoCAD configuration. From the Configuration menu, choose Configure Operating Parameters, item 7. From the Operating Parameters menu, choose xx. Network Lock Authorization.

   AutoCAD displays the current network lock information. In the following example, the lock has been updated twice:

```
Your AutoCAD serial number is: 123-12345678
Information for this lock:
      Network lock serial number: 1A2B
      Current number of network licenses: 11
Current network authorization code: 00000AAAA for 11
      licenses
Previous authorization code: 9999FFFF for 7 licenses
```

Appendixes

To obtain more network licenses for this lock, you need to provide the AutoCAD and network lock serial numbers, along with the most recent valid network license count and authorization code.

4. Respond to the following prompts:

   `Do you have an authorization code for at least nn licenses?`

   - If you enter N, AutoCAD returns to the Operating Parameters menu.

   - If you enter Y, AutoCAD displays prompts to change the number of network lock licenses:

     `Enter the new number of licenses: Enter the`
     `    number of licenses.`

     `Enter the new authorization code: Enter the`
     `    authorization code.`

   ---

   **Caution**

   If the number of licenses and the corresponding authorization code are not correct, the network lock is unusable on the network. It will still function as a local lock.

   ---

   **Note**

   The network lock code can be changed 100 times. If this is change 100, AutoCAD displays the following prompt before you enter the number of licenses and the code:

   `Warning: This is the last time you can update this lock.`
   `Do you wish to continue? <N>`

5. Respond to the following confirmation prompt:

   `Is the information correct: <N>`

   - If you enter N, AutoCAD returns to the Operating Parameters menu without updating the lock.

   - If you enter Y, AutoCAD updates the network lock and displays the following information:

     `The network lock has been updated.`

6. Because you can run network authorization only once for each session, you must quit and restart AutoCAD after you update the network lock. Use the network lock authorization configuration to check the network lock authorization. AutoCAD displays the new lock information as the current settings.

7. If necessary, move the network lock back to the server and restart the computer as a server. Load the SSSM on the server to update it with the new number of authorized licenses.

### Restoring an Authorization Code

If you update the hardware lock with an incorrect number of licenses or authorization code, follow these steps to restore the last correct settings:

1. Exit and restart AutoCAD with the network lock as the local lock.

2. Start the AutoCAD configuration. From the Configuration menu, choose Configure Operating Parameters, item 7. From the Operating Parameters menu, choose xx. Network Lock Authorization.

3. AutoCAD displays the current network lock information. In the example that follows, the last entered authorization code or number of licenses is incorrect:

```
Your AutoCAD serial number is: 123-12345678
Information for this lock:
Network lock serial number: 1A2B
Current number of network licenses: 0
Current network authorization code: 00000AAAA for 12
    licenses is INVALID
Previous authorization code: 9999FFFF for 7 licenses
```

To obtain more network licenses for this lock, you need to supply the AutoCAD and network lock serial numbers along with the most recent valid network license count and authorization code.

If the most recent authorization code is invalid, you can reuse a previous valid authorization code. For example, AutoCAD displays the following prompt:

```
Do you want to reset the lock to 7 licenses and
authorization code 9999FFFF?
```

■ Enter Y to use the most recent valid authorization code; return to the Operating Parameters menu.

■ Enter N to display the prompts to update network lock authorization.

### Security Server Command Line Options

When you load the security server software module (SSSM), you can use the /? option to list the command line options available to your security server. The following options list is an example of what may be displayed:

■ */DN:<name>*. Changes the server's department name from NETINEL to *<name>*.

■ */H:<nnn>*. Sets maximum number of licenses that can be used at any time on server *<name>*.

■ */MS:<nnn>*. Sets maximum number of servers running in the server's department and using the server's protocol *<nnn>*. Value ranges from 1 to 10, and is used to determine the range of server names.

■ */N:<nnn>*. Sets the name displayed by the monitor for the server to *<name>*.

■ */P*. Overrides the server's use of BIOS parallel port table addresses and uses the standard values 0x278, 0x378, and 0x3BC.

■ */P:<port>*. Overrides the server's use of the BIOS parallel port table addresses and uses the hexadecimal address *<port>*. Up to three addresses may be specified.

■ */Q*. Suppresses sign-on messages.

■ */R*. Conditionally unloads a previous instance of the server from memory if there are no open security sessions.

■ */S:<nnn>*. Sets the maximum number of clients that can actively communicate with the server at one time to *<nnn>*.

■ */ST*. Enables strict license time-out enforcement. Active licenses are immediately revoked and made available for reuse if no query is performed within the key's configured time-out interval.

## Installing the AutoCAD Network Software

Now that you have set up your system and the network environment for AutCAD, you are ready to begin the actual installation. While the installation of the networking version of AutoCAD is basically the same as the single-user installation, this section does cover several steps that are unique. When the installation steps are identical, you are referred back to the appropriate sections of the single-user installation material in this appendix.

1.  Start the install program as you would for a single-user. For detailed instructions on how to install AutoCAD, see "Installing Your Software," earier in this appendix.

2.  Create the following AutoCAD directories on your file server's hard disk:

    ■ For temporary and swap files: \acad_tmp

    ■ For the configuration file: \acad_cfg

3.  Follow your network's instructions for setting up user access to the directories created in step 1.

## Verifying Environment Variables

Verify that your environment variables are set to match the workstation you are configuring. For details on how to do this, see "Adding Directories to AutoCAD's Support Path, Changing Icons, and Editing ACAD.INI," earlier in this appendix.

## Configuring AutoCAD to Operate in a Network

You have now finished the automated installation and verified that your support directories are correct. You are almost ready to start AutoCAD. The steps required to configure the network version of AutoCAD are identical to the single-user version. The sequence and sections are outlined for you below.

1.  Configure the server for network users by starting AutoCAD and making the appropriate selections from the Configuration menu. For detailed instructions on options available from the Configuration menu, see "Starting and Configuring AutoCAD for Windows," earlier in this appendix.

2.  Use the Preferences dialog box within AutoCAD to set your environment variables. Refer to "Setting Your Preferences in AutoCAD," earlier in this appendix for information on using the Preferences dialog box.

## Handling Shared Files

If you are aware of the possible pitfalls and your system is properly configured, working with shared files in a networking environment can offer advantages over stand-alone workstations. This section addresses three areas:

file locking, file permissions, and permissions for AutoCAD executables and login files. Following the suggestions covered in this section should help you avoid any file handling problems that might arise later.

### File Locking

AutoCAD prevents users from changing the same file at the same time through an internal file-locking mechanism. When a user opens a file, AutoCAD creates a lock file with the same prefix as the open file and the extension DWK. The login name identifies the owner of a lock file.

File locking is automatically enabled when you install a network configuration on a server hard disk. It is recommended that you enable file locking when configuring for single-user workstation installations of AutoCAD. This allows users to access data in a shared network directory.

### File Permissions

File permissions must be established for individual files and directories. Under DOS, you can control permissions for files with the ATTRIB command. In Windows, use File Manager to control permissions for files. Incorrect file permissions can prevent AutoCAD from creating and deleting lock files, or simultaneously accessing files from multiple network nodes.

### Permissions for AutoCAD Executable and Login Files

If the ACAD.EXE file is installed on a network server, its file permission must allow it to be opened and executed by two or more users. On some networks, the ACAD.EXE file must be a read-only file or be located in a read-only directory.

> **Note**
>
> You should give the same permissions for directories and files to all AutoCAD users on a network.

## Verifying Your Network Installation

Now that you have completed the installation and configuration of AutoCAD, configure the workstations on your network and verify they are operating properly. To configure each workstation follow these steps:

1. Each workstation must have its own local configuration files, ACAD.CFG and ACAD.INI. When you create an AutoCAD icon, use the ACADCFGW variable to point to the directory on each node that contains this file.

2. Each workstation should have its own MNU and MNL menu files. Place these files in a directory listed by the node's /s switch or environment setting.

3. Each workstation should have a local copy of the main prototype drawing file, such as ACAD.DWG. This prevents minor delays caused by users simultaneously accessing a central prototype.

4. Use the Operating Parameters menu to set the location of temporary files, specify the workstation name, and specify the login name. These options become part of the ACAD.CFG file and must be locally defined for each workstation.

To avoid potential problems on your network, verify that AutoCAD loads and operates correctly on each workstation. Follow these steps at every AutoCAD workstation to verify operation:

1. Log in as the primary workstation user.

2. Verify that the hardware lock has been installed properly.

3. Start AutoCAD by double-clicking the AutoCAD icon.

4. From the File menu, choose Open to edit an existing drawing.

5. From the Windows File Manager, verify that the appropriate drawing and lock files exist in the drawing directory. Then return to AutoCAD.

6. Plot or print a drawing on each plotter or printer accessible to the user.

7. Exit AutoCAD.

# Configuring Your Windows and DOS System Files

This section covers how to set up your Windows and DOS environments to operate efficiently. Adding or changing a few lines in these files can have a major effect on the performance of your system and AutoCAD. In this section, you will review your swap file settings in Windows and take a closer look at your CONFIG.SYS and AUTOEXEC.BAT files in DOS. You will also learn some tips and tricks that will help you get the most out of your system.

Appendixes

## Configuring a Permanent Windows Swap File

To use AutoCAD Release 13 effectively, a permanent swap file is essential. Autodesk recommends a minimum swap file size of 40M. Windows, however, only allows you to use the largest contiguous section of your free hard disk space for a permanent swap file. This is another reason why it is important to optimize your disk prior to installing AutoCAD.

The advantage of using a permanent versus a temporary swap file is faster access to your data. Because the permanent file uses a contiguous section of your hard disk, all the data is located in one area. This reduces the amount of time it takes the pager to find information that was written out to the swap file. A permanent swap file also guarantees a minimum available amount of swap space.

To set up the swap file, access the Virtual Memory dialog box, which is part of the Control Panel Program Group in Windows. Follow these steps to access and set up the swap file:

1. Make sure that all your applications are closed. Adjusting the virtual swap space requires you to close Windows and then restart Windows.

2. From the Main Program Group in the Program Manager, double-click the Control Panel Program Group. This displays the Group window.

3. From the Control Panel Program Group window, double-click the Enhanced Icon to launch the program.

4. Select the Virtual Memory button.

5. Review and note your current Swapfile Settings in the event you need to change them back to their original values. Select the Change button.

6. You should be in the Virtual Memory dialog box. From the New Swapfile Settings area, select Permanent from the Type: pop-up list.

7. Enter a minimum of 40,000K in the New Size edit box. If this value is more than the Maximum Size: shown in the New Swapfile Settings area, use the value shown by Maximum Size: edit box.

8. Now select the OK button in the Virtual Memory dialog box.

9. Select the Yes button at the next Virtual Memory caution dialog box.

10. When prompted to Restart Windows Now?, in the next Virtual Memory dialog box, select the Continue button rather than pressing the Restart Windows button. Windows does not always respond properly to being restarted by CTRL+ALT+DEL or by using the Restart Windows option.

The most reliable method is to use Continue and exit Windows as you normally would.

You should now have a 40M permanent swap file set up on your hard disk. After restarting Windows, go back through these steps to confirm your settings.

## Configuring Your DOS Boot Files

When your system boots, the CPU runs through a self-test, and then reads two hidden files from the root directory of your boot drive. Under MS-DOS, these files are called IO.SYS and MSDOS.SYS. The system looks for two startup files, CONFIG.SYS and AUTOEXEC.BAT, in your root directory.

CONFIG.SYS contains entries that load system-level device drivers such as memory managers, RAM drives, and disk caches. You also can load device drivers for peripherals such as a mouse in CONFIG.SYS. In addition, CONFIG.SYS should contain entries that set the number of files that a program can have open at one time, and that specify the number of disk buffers to be created by the system. Generally, the files loaded in the CONFIG.SYS file have an SYS extension although EXE and COM are also possibilities.

AUTOEXEC.BAT contains entries that set your system prompt, set your path, load drivers for networking, run a mouse or disk cache program and other system variables, and run batch files or other programs to execute automatically during startup. The files loaded from AUTOEXEC.BAT are usually BAT, EXE, or COM files.

## Tailoring Your CONFIG.SYS File

CONFIG.SYS is read automatically by the system at boot, and must be located in the root directory of the boot disk. To examine your CONFIG.SYS file, open it in Notepad by performing these steps:

1. Double-click the Accessories icon in the Windows Program Manager.

2. Double-click the Notepad icon.

3. Choose File, Open.

4. Double-click the [..] symbol at the top of the Directories box.

5. Type **config.sys** in the Filename box.

A typical CONFIG.SYS file contains the following lines:

```
BUFFERS=20
FILES=50
```

**Tip**

Keep your AUTOEXEC.BAT and CONFIG.SYS files as uncluttered as possible.

**Tip**

Only install device drivers that are necessary in CONFIG.SYS. You can load a COM device driver from the DOS command line or a batch file, rather than a SYS device driver in CONFIG.SYS.

**Appendixes**

```
BREAK=ON
SHELL=C:\COMMAND.COM /P /E:1024
STACKS=9,254
```

**Tip**

Type SYSEDIT at
the File, Run, pull-
down menu in
Windows to open
all your system
files in a
Notepad editing
environment.

You can edit or create a CONFIG.SYS file in your root directory using
Notepad. Use the following discussion to help you in any modifications. Note
that the SETUP program may have modified your CONFIG.SYS for you.

The BUFFERS line allocates RAM to hold your recently used data. If a program
frequently accesses recently used data, buffers reduce disk accesses and increase speed. Each two-buffer increment uses 1K of base (conventional) DOS
memory. You may have to use a smaller number if AutoCAD runs short of
memory. AutoCAD recommends 20 buffers (ten if you are using a caching
program, such as SMARTDrive). Windows also recommends 20 buffers. Depending on what other software you run, setting more than 20 buffers does
not offer any benefit and may hinder performance.

The FILES line tells DOS the maximum number of files your applications
expect to have open at one time. FILES uses very little memory; a large value
helps with AutoCAD and AutoLISP. AutoCAD recommends 50 files; Windows
recommends 30. Because AutoCAD requires more, use the AutoCAD
recommendation.

The SHELL line defines the command processor to be used by DOS. By default, the system command interpreter is COMMAND.COM. Setting SHELL in
CONFIG.SYS allows you to specify the amount of RAM to store environment
variable settings and other information. AutoCAD and AutoLISP use several
of these. If you receive the error message, Out of environment space, you may
need to try a higher number. Increase the number, reboot, and try the operation that caused the error again. Repeat the process if needed until the error
message disappears. AutoCAD recommends a minimum environment space
of 750, while Windows recommends a minimum of 1,024. Use the larger size.

The STACKS line is included for older Windows applications and is not
relevant to AutoCAD for Windows.

With the later versions of DOS 6.x you can create multiple configurations in
your CONFIG.SYS file. When you boot the machine, you are presented with a
menu that allows you to select a particular configuration. You also can build
multiple configurations into your AUTOEXEC.BAT file by setting environment variables in your CONFIG.SYS file and using the variable settings with
IF and GOTO lines in your AUTOEXEC.BAT file to run only selected parts of
the AUTOEXEC.BAT file. This can be a solution for users who need to create
multiple operating environments. Refer to your DOS manual for details on
setting up multiple CONFIG.SYS files.

### Tailoring Your AUTOEXEC.BAT File

AUTOEXEC.BAT is a batch file like any other, with one important exception: DOS automatically executes AUTOEXEC.BAT every time the system is booted. Like CONFIG.SYS, AUTOEXEC.BAT must be in the root directory.

The AUTOEXEC.BAT file is the place to install your TSR programs. It also is the place to install the other setup programs and DOS environment settings that you need to complete an application environment. Examine your AUTOEXEC.BAT file in Notepad, using the procedure described earlier for the CONFIG.SYS file. Your AUTOEXEC.BAT file should include the following lines:

```
PROMPT=$P$G
PATH C:\:C:\DOS
```

Other information may follow. Your path may include other directories. It is not necessary to place your AutoCAD directory in the path because you specified the location of the AutoCAD executable file when you installed the program.

Edit or create your AUTOEXEC.BAT in your root directory using Notepad. Use the following discussion to help you with any modifications. Your AUTOCAD.BAT file also may contain settings shown in the startup batch file later in this appendix.

PROMPT $P$G is extremely valuable. It causes the DOS prompt to display your current directory path so that you do not get lost.

PATH is essential for automatic directory access to programs and DOS commands. The C:\ root and C:\DOS paths are essential to our recommended setup. If your DOS files are in a different directory, substitute the directory.

Use whatever is relevant to your setup. It is more than likely that your path contains additional directories. In fact, when you install Windows, your Windows directory is automatically added to your path by the Windows installation program if you choose to let it. The CONFIG.SYS and AUTOEXEC.BAT changes do not take effect until you reboot your computer. To perform a warm reboot of your system, press Ctrl+Alt+Del.

# Starting AutoCAD with Specific Drawing Files

If you want to start AutoCAD and have it automatically enter the drawing editor and load a particular drawing, Windows offers two methods by which you can automate loading individual drawing files. The first option uses File, Run and the second option involves setting file-program associations.

### Using Windows Run Option

Choose File, Run in Program Manager. In the Run dialog box, type **acad.exe** (the path name for AutoCAD's directory) and the path name and file name for the drawing you want to load. For example, if AutoCAD is located on your C drive in the ACADR13\WIN directory; your drawings are in a directory called DWGS; and you wanted to load a drawing called PART, you would type the following in the dialog box:

> **c:\acadr13\win\acad.exe c:\dwgs\part.dwg**

### Associating Drawing Files with AutoCAD in Windows File Manager

Windows allows you to associate data files that have the same file name extension with their parent applications. After you create the association, run the application and load an associated data file by double-clicking on the file's icon or the file name in Windows File Manager. To create an association between AutoCAD and its drawing files, run File Manager and highlight a drawing file. Then, choose Associate from the File menu. In the Associate dialog box, type the path name and the name of the AutoCAD executable file:

> **c:\acadr13\win\acad.exe**

Choose OK, and all files with the DWG extension are associated with AutoCAD.

### Troubleshooting the Installation

You may encounter problems as you install or start to configure AutoCAD. This section outlines potential pitfalls. By reviewing this section before you start installing AutoCAD, you will hopefully be able to avoid trouble during installation. If you still run into difficulty, this section should help you identify the problem, allowing you to recover and get your system back to where you started. The following is a list of common problems to avoid, and some tips that can help save time:

- Make sure that you have covered all steps outlined in this appendix prior to installing AutoCAD.

- Make sure you have original backup copies of your CONFIG.SYS, AUTOEXEC.BAT, SYSTEM.INI, WIN.INI, and ACAD.INI files on a floppy disk.

- If your system locks up, stops responding to your entries, you will have to reboot the computer. You can try to warm boot your system by pressing Ctrl+Alt+Del, but it is quite possible you will have to do a cold boot.

- After your system is back on-line, from a system lock up, you will need to clean-up the Windows and AutoCAD files that were left open. Windows will create temporary files with the extension *.tmp, while AutoCAD's temporary files have the extension *.ac$. Remove these files while you are in DOS, since new temporary files will be created once you restart Windows (at least Windows files). You will also want to perform a chkdsk /f on the drive that contains these files, just to be certain everything is cleaned off the hard drive.

- To make the previous task easier, locate all your temporary files in a single directory such as c:\temp. This way you have only one place to look for files that should be deleted, making the job of cleaning up much easier. To set the temporary file directory in AutoCAD use option 5 of the Configure operating parameters menu. For Windows you will want to add the following line to your AUTOEXEC.BAT file SET TEMP=E:\SWAP.

- If you must reboot your system in the middle of installing Win32s or AutoCAD, some clean-up is necessary. Remove all the partial files and directories that had been created prior to the failure of the installation. Take note of directories created and files that are altered as these programs are installed. Check your system files. If they were modified, replace them with your original backup copies.

> **Note**
>
> Check the date and time stamps to see if files have been modified. If you are in DOS, do a directory listing by using the DIR command. If you are in Windows, open the File Manager and select the correct directory. Be certain that All File Details is checked in the View pull-down, so you can see the date, time, and file size.

- If your Win32s installation fails you, remove all the files, directories, and any reference to Win32s in the SYSTEM.INI file; this allows the installation program to properly install Win32s.

- If you start to install AutoCAD and the install program finds you do not have enough hard disk space, AutoCAD displays the warning dialog box shown in figure B.24. AutoCAD may temporarily require as much as 4M

**Appendixes**

of additional disk space to install properly. If you want to load the files you selected, you will have to exit the install program and free additional disk space.

**Fig. B.24**
The not enough disk space warning dialog box.

- If you had a previous version of AutoCAD installed on your system, be sure that you install AutoCAD Release 13 in a different directory.

- If you are having difficulty starting AutoCAD after it has been installed, remove any set commands and path references in the AUTOEXEC.BAT that refer to your original AutoCAD installation. Make sure that your new ACAD.INI file does not reference any of your original AutoCAD information. Review the SYSTEM.INI and WIN.INI files for any old references to AutoCAD. You can leave these lines in the file, if you tell Windows how to ignore them. Use a semicolon at the start of the line. This tells Windows to treat the line as if it were a comment, not a command.

## From Here...

For more information about getting started with AutoCAD Release 13, see the following appendixes and chapter:

- Chapter 1, "Introducing AutoCAD," starts to explore AutoCAD, providing hands-on use and tutorials that help you learn how to put AutoCAD to work for you.

- Appendix A, "New Features in AutoCAD Release 13 for Windows," provides an outline of new commands and features included in AutoCAD Release 13.

- Appendix D, "Working with Digitizers," covers setup and user tips related to working with a digitizer tablet.

# Appendix C

# System Variables Reference

AutoCAD *system variables* catalog every aspect of the drawing editor's environment, including such details as the current snap increment or whether dialog boxes are activated. Because, by definition, a variable can assume diverse values, you can change the values of AutoCAD's system variables to modify the drawing environment. (Dimensioning and Solid Modeling variables are discussed in their respective chapters.)

## Accessing System Variables

Accessing system variables can be done in a general manner by using the SETVAR command or by choosing Options, System Variables, and then Set from the pull-down menu. You can access a specific system variable by using the command that sets the system variable. You also can type the system variable name itself at the Command: prompt. You can set a snap increment, for example, by entering SETVAR at the AutoCAD Command: prompt and then entering SNAPUNIT, which is the system variable that holds the value of the snap increment. You also can issue the SNAP command or type SNAPUNIT at the Command: prompt. AutoLISP programmers also can access system variables with the GETVAR and SETVAR AutoLISP functions. ADS programmers can use ADS_GETVAR and ADS_SETVAR. On the rare occasion that a system variable and a command share the same name, you must use SETVAR to directly access the system variable.

AutoCAD defines some system variables as *read-only*, meaning that you can't directly change their value with SETVAR. Some read-only variables can be set with other AutoCAD commands; others are untouchable. ACADVER, the current AutoCAD version number, is an untouchable variable.

When you use the SETVAR command, AutoCAD first prompts for a variable name. You can enter a name or a question mark (**?**) to see a list of variables and their current values. If you enter **?**, AutoCAD asks which variables to list. You can type an asterisk (**\***) to list almost all the variables, a variable name to list a single variable, several names (which must be separated by commas), or a wildcard pattern. If you enter a variable name, AutoCAD either prompts for a new value or, in the case of a read-only variable, shows the variable's current value and informs you of its read-only status.

Although SETVAR enables you to access system variables, some system variables are not listed with the question mark (?) then asterisk (*) option of SETVAR. These variables are ERRNO, RIASPECT, RIBACKG, RIEDGE, RIGAMUT, RIGREY, RITHRESH, MACROTRACE, RE-INIT, USERI1-5, USERR1-5, and USERS1-5. To access these system variables, you must either enter the variable name at the Command: or SETVAR prompt, or enter the command that sets the system variable, if such a command exists.

Table C.1 is set up in five columns. The first column contains each system variable's name. The second column indicates the variable's type. General system variables are categorized into the following types:

| Type | Meaning |
| --- | --- |
| String | The variable is a text string. |
| Integer | The variable is a whole number. |
| Real | The variable is a decimal number. |
| 2D Point | The variable is a point specified by X and Y values. |
| 3D Point | The variable is a point specified by X, Y, and Z values. |

The third column tells the AutoCAD command that sets the system variable when such a command exists. The fourth column shows the variable's default value. The fifth column indicates where the system variable is saved.

Most system variables are saved in the ACAD.CFG configuration file. Some variables, however, are saved in the drawing and some are not saved. System variables saved in ACAD.CFG are marked *CFG;* those saved in the drawing are marked *DWG;* and variables that are not saved are marked *NS*. All read-only variables also are marked with an *RO*. System variables new for Release 13 are shown in bold.

| Table C.1 | System Variables | | | |
|---|---|---|---|---|
| **Variable Name** | **Type** | **Command Name** | **Default Setting** | **Saved In** |
| ACADPREFIX | String | | Varies | NS, RO |
| ACADVER | String | | "13","13a", "13_c1", etc. | NS, RO |
| AFLAGS | Integer | DDATTDEF ATTDEF | 0 | NS |
| ANGBASE | Real | DDUNITS UNITS | 0.0000 | DWG |
| ANGDIR | Integer | DDUNITS UNITS | 0 | DWG |
| APERTURE | Integer | DDOSNAP APERTURE | 10 | CFG |
| AREA | Real | AREA LIST | 0.0000 | NS, RO |
| ATTDIA | Integer | | 0 | DWG |
| ATTMODE | Integer | ATTDIST | 1 | DWG |
| ATTREQ | Integer | | 1 | DWG |
| AUDITCTL | Integer | | 0 | CFG |
| AUNITS | Integer | DDUNITS UNITS | 0 | DWG |
| AUPREC | Integer | DDUNITS UNITS | 0 | DWG |
| BACKZ | Real | DVIEW | 0.0000 | DWG, RO |
| BLIPMODE | Integer | BLIPMODE | 1 | DWG |
| CDATE | Real | TIME | Varies | NS, RO |
| CECOLOR | String | DDEMODES COLOR | "BYLAYER" | DWG |
| **CELTSCALE** | Real | DDEMODES LINETYPE | 1.000 | DWG |
| CELTYPE | String | DDEMODES LINETYPE | "BYLAYER" | DWG |
| CHAMFERA | Real | CHAMFER | 0.0000 | DWG |

(continues)

| Table C.1 Continued | | | | |
|---|---|---|---|---|
| **Variable Name** | **Type** | **Command Name** | **Default Setting** | **Saved In** |
| CHAMFERB | Real | CHAMFER | 0.0000 | DWG |
| **CHAMFERC** | Real | CHAMFER | 0.0000 | DWG |
| **CHAMFERD** | Real | CHAMFER | 0.0000 | DWG |
| **CHAMMODE** | Integer | CHAMFER | 0 | NS |
| CIRCLERAD | Real | DDLMODES | 0.0000 | NS |
| CLAYER | String | DDEMODES LAYER | "0" | DWG |
| CMDACTIVE | Integer | CMDACTIVE | 0 | NS, RO |
| CMDDIA | Integer | | 1 | CFG |
| CMDECHO | Integer | | 1 | NS |
| CMDNAMES | String | | "Standard" | NS |
| **CMLJUST** | Integer | | 0 | CFG |
| **CMLSCALE** | Real | | 1.0000 | CFG |
| **CMLSTYLE** | String | | " " | CFG |
| COORDS | Integer | ^D F6 | 1 | DWG |
| CVPORT | Integer | VPORTS | 2 | DWG |
| DATE | Real | TIME | Varies | NS, RO |
| DBMOD | Integer | | 0 | NS, RO |
| **DCTCUST** | String | | " " | CFG |
| **DCTMAIN** | String | | "enu" | CFG |
| **DELOBJ** | Integer | | 1 | DWG |
| DIASTAT | Integer | | 1 | NS, RO |
| **DISPSILH** | Integer | | 0 | DWG |
| DISTANCE | Real | DIST | 0.0000 | NS |
| DONUTID | Real | | 0.5000 | NS |
| DONUTOD | Real | | 1.0000 | NS |

| Variable Name | Type | Command Name | Default Setting | Saved In |
|---|---|---|---|---|
| DRAGMODE | Integer | DRAGMODE | 2 | DWG |
| DRAGP1 | Integer | | 10 | CFG |
| DRAGP2 | Integer | | 25 | CFG |
| DWGCODEPAGE | String | | Varies | DWG |
| DWGNAME | String | | "UNNAMED" | NS, RO |
| DWGPREFIX | String | | "C:\ACADR13\ WIN\" | NS, RO |
| DWGTITLED | Integer | NEW | 0 | NS, RO |
| DWGWRITE | Integer | OPEN | 1 | NS |
| **EDGEMODE** | Integer | TRIM EXTEND | 0 | NS |
| ELEVATION | Real | ELEV DDEMODES | 0.0000 | DWG |
| ERRNO | Integer | | 0 | NS |
| EXPERT | Integer | | 0 | NS |
| **EXPLMODE** | Integer | EXPLODE | 1 | DWG |
| EXTMAX | 3D point | | −1.000E+20, −1.000E+20 | DWG, RO |
| EXTMIN | 3D point | | 1.0000E+20, 1.0000E+20 | DWG, RO |
| **FACETRES** | Real | | 0.5000 | DWG |
| **FFLIMIT** | Integer | | 0 | CFG |
| FILEDIA | Integer | | 1 | CFG |
| FILLETRAD | Real | FILLET | 0.0000 | DWG |
| FILLMODE | Integer | FILL | 1 | DWG |
| **FONTALT** | String | Text | "txt" | CFG |
| **FONTMAP** | String | Text | "" | CFG |
| FRONTZ | Real | DVIEW | 0.0000 | DWG, RO |
| GRIDMODE | Integer | DDRMODES GRID F7 | 0 | DWG |

(continues)

**Table C.1   Continued**

| Variable Name | Type | Command Name | Default Setting | Saved In |
|---|---|---|---|---|
| GRIDUNIT | 2D point | DDRMODES GRID | 0.0000,0.0000 | DWG |
| GRIPBLOCK | Integer | DDGRIPS | 0 | CFG |
| GRIPCOLOR | Integer | DDGRIPS | 5 | CFG |
| GRIPHOT | Integer | DDGRIPS | 1 | CFG |
| GRIPS | Integer | DDSELECT | 1 | CFG |
| GRIPSIZE | Integer | DDGRIPS | 3 | CFG |
| HANDLES | Integer | HANDLES | 1 | DWG, RO |
| HIGHLIGHT | Integer | | 1 | NS |
| HPANG | Real | BHATCH HATCH | 0 | NS |
| **HPBOUND** | Real | BHATCH HATCH | 1 | DWG |
| HPDOUBLE | Real | BHATCH HATCH | 0 | NS |
| HPNAME | String | BHATCH HATCH | " " | NS |
| HPSCALE | Real | BHATCH HATCH | 1.0000 | NS |
| HPSPACE | Real | BHATCH HATCH | 1.0000 | NS |
| INSBASE | 3D Point | BASE | 0.0000,0.0000, 0.0000 | DWG |
| INSNAME | String | DDINSERT INSERT | " " | NS |
| **ISOLINES** | Integer | SURFACE | 4 | DWG |
| LASTANGLE | Real | ARC | 0 | NS, RO |
| LASTPOINT | 3D Point | | 0.0000,0.0000, 0.0000 | NS |
| LENSLENGTH | Real | DVIEW | 50.0000 | DWG |

| Variable Name | Type | Command Name | Default Setting | Saved In |
|---|---|---|---|---|
| LIMCHECK | Integer | LIMITS | 0 | DWG, RO |
| LIMMAX | 2D Point | | 12.0000,9.0000 | DWG |
| LIMMIN | 2D Point | | 0.0000,0.0000 | DWG |
| **LOCALE** | String | | "en" | NS, RO |
| LOGINNAME | String | CONFIG | Varies | NS, RO |
| LTSCALE | Real | LTSCALE | 1.0000 | DWG |
| LUNITS | Integer | DDUNITS UNITS | 2 | DWG |
| LUPREC | Integer | DDUNITS UNITS | 4 | DWG |
| MACROTRACE | Integer | | 0 | NS |
| MAXACTVP | Integer | | 16 | NS |
| MAXSORT | Integer | | 200 | CFG |
| MENUCTL | Integer | | 1 | CFG |
| MENUECHO | Integer | | 0 | NS |
| MENUNAME | String | MENU | "C:\ACADR13\ WIN\SUPPORT\ ADAC.mnc | DWG, RO |
| MIRRTEXT | Integer | | 1 | DWG |
| MODEMACRO | String | | " " | NS |
| **MTEXTED** | String | MTEXT | "Internal" | CFG |
| OFFSETDIST | Real | OFFSET | –1.0000 | NS |
| ORTHOMODE | Integer | ^O F8 | 0 | DWG |
| OSMODE | Integer | DDOSNAP | 0 | DWG |
| PDMODE | Integer | | 0 | DWG |
| PDSIZE | Real | | 0.0000 | DWG |
| **PELLIPSE** | Integer | ELLIPSE | 0 | DWG |
| PERIMETER | Real | AREA, DBLIST, LIST | 0.0000 | NS, RO |

(continues)

**Table C.1 Continued**

| Variable Name | Type | Command Name | Default Setting | Saved In |
|---|---|---|---|---|
| PFACEVMAX | Integer | | 4 | NS, RO |
| PICKADD | Integer | DDSELECT | 1 | CFG |
| PICKAUTO | Integer | DDSELECT | 1 | CFG |
| PICKBOX | Integer | | 3 | CFG |
| PICKDRAG | Integer | DDSELECT | 0 | CFG |
| PICKFIRST | Integer | DDSELECT | 1 | CFG |
| **PICKSTYLE** | Integer | DDSELECT | 3 | DWG |
| PLATFORM | String | | Platform Dependent | NS, RO |
| PLINEGEN | Integer | | 0 | DWG |
| PLINEWID | Real | PLINE | 0.0000 | DWG |
| PLOTID | String | PLOT | " " | CFG |
| **PLOTROTMODE** | Integer | PLOT | 1 | DWG |
| PLOTTER | Integer | PLOT | 0 | CFG |
| POLYSIDES | Integer | POLYGON | 4 | NS |
| POPUPS | Integer | | 1 | NS, RO |
| **PROJMODE** | Integer | TRIM EXTEND | 2 | CFG |
| PSLTSCALE | Integer | | 1 | DWG |
| PSPROLOG | String | | " " | CFG |
| PSQUALITY | Integer | | 75 | CFG |
| QTEXTMODE | Integer | QTEXT | 0 | DWG |
| **RASTERPREVIEW** | Integer | | 0 | DWG |
| REGENMODE | Integer | REGENAUTO | 1 | DWG |
| RE-INIT | Integer | REINIT | 0 | NS |
| **RIASPECT** | Real | GIFIN TIFFIN | 0.0000 | NS |
| **RIBACKG** | Integer | | 0 | NS |

| Variable Name | Type | Command Name | Default Setting | Saved In |
|---|---|---|---|---|
| **RIEDGE** | Integer | GIFIN, TIFFIN PCXIN | 0 | NS |
| **RIGAMUT** | Integer | GIFIN, TIFFIN PCXIN | 256 | NS |
| **RIGREY** | Integer | | 0 | NS |
| **RITHRESH** | Integer | | 0 | NS |
| SAVEFILE | String | CONFIG | "AUTO.SV$" | CFG, RO |
| SAVEIMAGES | Integer | | 0 | DWG |
| SAVENAME | String | SAVEAS | " " | NS, RO |
| SAVETIME | Integer | CONFIG | 120 | CFG |
| SCREENBOXES | Integer | CONFIG | 26 | CFG, RO |
| SCREENMODE | Integer | F1 F2 (WINDOWS) | 0 | CFG, RO |
| SCREENSIZE | 2D Point | Varies | | RO, NS |
| SHADEDGE | Integer | | 3 | DWG |
| SHADEDIF | Integer | | 70 | DWG |
| SHPNAME | String | SHAPE | " " | NS |
| SKETCHINC | Real | SKETCH | 0.1000 | DWG |
| SKPOLY | Integer | | 0 | DWG |
| SNAPANG | Real | DDRMODES SNAP | 0 | DWG |
| SNAPBASE | 2D Point | DDRMODES SNAP | 0.0000,0.0000 | DWG |
| SNAPISOPAIR | Integer | DDRMODES SNAP | 0 | DWG |
| SNAPMODE | Integer | DDRMODES SNAP | 0 | DWG |
| SNAPSTYL | Integer | DDRMODES SNAP | 0 | DWG |
| SNAPUNIT | 2D Point | DDRMODES SNAP | 1.0000,1.0000 | DWG |

Appendixes

(continues)

| Table C.1 | Continued | | | |
|---|---|---|---|---|
| **Variable Name** | **Type** | **Command Name** | **Default Setting** | **Saved In** |
| SORTENTS | Integer | DDSELECT | 96 | CFG |
| SPLFRAME | Integer | | 0 | DWG |
| SPLINESEGS | Integer | | 8 | DWG |
| SPLINETYPE | Integer | | 6 | DWG |
| SURFTAB1 | Integer | | 6 | DWG |
| SURFTAB2 | Integer | | 6 | DWG |
| SURFTYPE | Integer | | 6 | DWG |
| SURFU | Integer | | 6 | DWG |
| SURFV | Integer | | 6 | DWG |
| SYSCODEPAGE | String | | Varies | NS, RO |
| TABMODE | Integer | TABLET F10 | 0 | NS |
| TARGET | 3D Point | DVIEW | 0.0000,0.0000, 0.0000 | DWG, RO |
| TDCREATE | Real | TIME | Varies | DWG, RO |
| TDINDWG | Real | TIME | Varies | DWG, RO |
| TDUPDATE | Real | TIME | Varies | DWG, RO |
| TDUSRTIMER | Real | TIME | Varies | DWG, RO |
| TEMPPREFIX | String | | " " | NS, RO |
| TEXTEVAL | Integer | | 0 | NS |
| **TEXTFILL** | Integer | TEXT | 1 | DWG |
| **TEXTQLTY** | Real | TEXT | 50 | DWG |
| TEXTSIZE | Real | TEXT | 0.2000 | DWG |
| TEXTSTYLE | String | TEXT STYLE | "STANDARD" | DWG |
| THICKNESS | Real | ELEV DDEMODES | 0.0000 | DWG |

| Variable Name | Type | Command Name | Default Setting | Saved In |
|---|---|---|---|---|
| TILEMODE | Integer | TILEMODE | 1 | DWG |
| **TOOLTIPS** | Integer | | 1 | CFG, WO |
| TRACEWID | Real | TRACE | 0.0500 | DWG |
| TREEDEPTH | Integer | TREESTAT | 3020 | DWG |
| TREEMAX | Integer | | 10000000 | CFG |
| **TRIMMODE** | Integer | TRIM | 1 | NS |
| UCSFOLLOW | Integer | | 0 | DWG |
| UCSICON | Integer | UCSICON | 1 | DWG |
| UCSNAME | String | DDUCS UCS | " " | DWG, RO |
| UCSORG | 3D Point | DDUCS UCS | 0.0000,0.0000, 0.0000 | DWG, RO |
| UCSXDIR | 3D Point | DDUCS UCS | 1.0000,0.0000, 0.0000 | DWG, RO |
| UCSYDIR | 3D Point | DDUCS UCS | 0.0000,1.0000, 0.0000 | DWG, RO |
| UNDOCTL | Integer | UNSO | 5 | NS, RO |
| UNDOMARKS | Integer | UNDI | 0 | RO, NS |
| UNITMODE | Integer | | 0 | DWG |
| USERI1-5 | Integer | | 0 | DWG |
| USERR1-5 | Real | | 0.0000 | DWG |
| USERS1-5 | String | | "" | NS |
| VIEWCTR | 3D Point | PAN ZOOM | Varies | DWG, RO |
| VIEWDIR | 3D Point | DVIEW | 0.0000,0.0000, 1.0000 | DWG, RO |
| VIEWMODE | Integer | DVIEW UCS | 0 | DWG, RO |

(continues)

Appendixes

| Table C.1 | Continued | | | |
|---|---|---|---|---|
| **Variable Name** | **Type** | **Command Name** | **Default Setting** | **Saved In** |
| VIEWSIZE | Real | VIEW ZOOM | Varies | DWG, RO |
| VIEWTWIST | Real | DVIEW | 0 | DWG, RO |
| VISRETAIN | Integer | | 0 | DWG |
| VSMAX | 3D Point | PAN VIEW ZOOM | Varies | NS, RO |
| VSMIN | 3D Point | PAN | Varies | NS, RO |
| WORLDUCS | Integer | UCS | 1 | NS, RO |
| WORLDVIEW | Integer | DVIEW UCS | 1 | DWG |
| XREFCTL | Integer | | 0 | CFG |

# Categorizing System Variables

The remainder of the System Variables Reference groups and describes the system variables according to their use, rather than alphabetically. This method of organization enables you to find a variable by the task that you want to perform, without having to know the variable's name. If you know the system variable name, you can look it up in Table C.2 and get the group number. When appropriate, the possible values of the system variable are listed after the variable description.

| Table C.2 | System Variable Index | | | | |
|---|---|---|---|---|---|
| **Variable** | **#** | **Variable** | **#** | **Variable** | **#** |
| ACADPREFIX | 1 | ACADVER | 1 | AFLAGS | 23 |
| ANGBASE | 6 | ANGDIR | 6 | APERTURE | 2 |
| AREA | 18 | ATTDIA | 23 | ATTMODE | 23 |
| ATTREQ | 23 | AUDITCTL | 2 | AUNITS | 6 |

| Variable | # | Variable | # | Variable | # |
|----------|---|----------|---|----------|---|
| AUPREC | 6 | BACKZ | 26 | BLIPMODE | 2 |
| CDATE | 33 | CECOLOR | 3 | CELTSCALE | 5 |
| CHAMFERA | 12 | CHAMFERB | 12 | CHAMFERC | 12 |
| CHAMFERD | 12 | CHAMMODE | 12 | CIRCLERAD | 12 |
| CLAYER | 3 | CMDACTIVE | 2 | CMDDIA | 13 |
| CMDECHO | 2 | CMDNAMES | 2 | CMLJUST | 12 |
| CMLSCALE | 12 | CMLSTYLE | 12 | COORDS | 2 |
| CVPORT | 25 | DATE | 34 | DBMOD | 31 |
| DCTCUST | 7 | DCTMAIN | 7 | DELOBJ | 3 |
| DIASTAT | 13 | DISPSILH | 19 | DISTANCE | 18 |
| DONUTID | 12 | DONUTOD | 12 | DRAGMODE | 8 |
| DRAGP1 | 8 | DRAGP2 | 8 | DWGCODEPAGE | 2 |
| DWGNAME | 30 | DWGPREFIX | 30 | DWGTITLED | 30 |
| DWGWRITE | 30 | EDGEMODE | 12 | ELEVATION | 3 |
| ERRNO | 35 | EXPERT | 2 | EXPLMODE | 22 |
| EXTMAX | 4 | EXTMIN | 4 | FACETRES | 27 |
| FFLIMIT | 29 | FILEDIA | 13 | FILLETRAD | 12 |
| FILLMODE | 2 | FONTALT | 29 | FONTMAP | 29 |
| FRONTZ | 26 | GRIDMODE | 9 | GRIDUNIT | 9 |
| GRIPBLOCK | 11 | GRIPCOLOR | 11 | GRIPHOT | 11 |
| GRIPS | 11 | GRIPSIZE | 11 | HANDLES | 2 |
| HIGHLIGHT | 2 | HPANG | 20 | HPBOUND | 20 |
| HPDOUBLE | 20 | HPNAME | 20 | HPSCALE | 20 |
| HPSPACE | 20 | INSBASE | 21 | INSNAME | 21 |
| ISOLINES | 19 | LASTANGLE | 18 | LASTPOINT | 18 |
| LENSLENGTH | 26 | LIMCHECK | 4 | LIMMAX | 4 |

(continues)

**Table C.2  Continued**

| Variable | # | Variable | # | Variable | # |
|----------|----|----------|----|----------|----|
| LIMMIN | 4 | LOCALE | 1 | LOGINNAME | 1 |
| LTSCALE | 5 | LUNITS | 6 | LUPREC | 6 |
| MACROTRACE | 33 | MAXACTVP | 25 | MAXSORT | 13 |
| MENUCTL | 13 | MENUECHO | 13 | MENUNAME | 13 |
| MIRRTEXT | 7 | MODEMACRO | 33 | MTEXTED | 7 |
| OFFSETDIST | 12 | ORTHOMODE | 2 | OSMODE | 2 |
| PDMODE | 15 | PDSIZE | 15 | PELLIPSE | 12 |
| PERIMETER | 18 | PFACEVMAX | 19 | PICKADD | 11 |
| PICKAUTO | 11 | PICKBOX | 11 | PICKFIRST | 11 |
| PICKSTYLE | 11 | PLATFORM | 1 | PLINEGEN | 19 |
| PLINEWID | 19 | PLOTID | 28 | PLOTROTMODE | 28 |
| PLOTTER | 28 | POLYSIDE | 12 | POPUPS | 13 |
| PSLTSCALE | 5 | PSPROLOG | 29 | PSQUALITY | 29 |
| QTEXTMODE | 7 | RASTERPREVIEW | 29 | REGENMODE | 2 |
| RE-INIT | 35 | RIABACKG | 29 | RIGAMUT | 29 |
| RIASPECT | 29 | RIEDGE | 29 | RIGREY | 29 |
| RITHRESH | 29 | SAVEFILE | 30 | SAVENAME | 30 |
| SAVEIMAGES | 3 | SAVETIME | 30 | SCREENBOXES | 13 |
| SCREENMODE | 14 | SCREENSIZE | 14 | SHADEDGE | 28 |
| SHADEDIF | 27 | SHPNAME | 21 | SKETCHINC | 24 |
| SKPOLY | 24 | SNAPANG | 10 | SNAPBASE | 10 |
| SNAPISOPAIR | 10 | SNAPMODE | 10 | SNAPSTYL | 10 |
| SNAPUNIT | 10 | SORTENTS | 11 | SPLFRAME | 19 |
| SPLINESEGS | 19 | SPLINETYPE | 19 | SURFTAB1 | 19 |
| SURFTAB2 | 19 | SURFTYPE | 19 | SURFU | 19 |

| Variable | # | Variable | # | Variable | # |
|----------|---|----------|---|----------|---|
| SURFV | 19 | SYSCODEPAGE | 1 | TABMODE | 13 |
| TARGET | 26 | TDCREATE | 24 | TDINDWG | 24 |
| TDUPDATE | 24 | TDUSRTIMER | 24 | TEMPPREFIX | 1 |
| TEXTEVAL | 7 | TEXTFILL | 7 | TEXTSTYLE | 7 |
| TEXTQLTY | 7 | THICKNESS | 3 | TILEMODE | 2 |
| TRACEWID | 12 | TOOLTIPS | 1 | TREEDEPTH | 31 |
| TREEMAX | 16 | TRIMMODE | 12 | UCSFOLLOW | 16 |
| UCSICON | 13 | UCSNAME | 16 | UCSORG | 16 |
| UCSXDIR | 16 | UCSYDIR | 16 | UNDOCTL | 17 |
| UNDOMARKS | 17 | UNITMODE | 6 | USERI1-5 | 32 |
| USERR1-5 | 32 | USERS1-5 | 32 | VIEWCTR | 25 |
| VIEWDIR | 26 | VIEWMODE | 26 | VIEWSIZE | 25 |
| VIEWTWIST | 26 | VISRETAIN | 22 | VSMAX | 25 |
| VSMIN | 25 | WORLDUCS | 16 | WORLDVIEW | 26 |
| XREFCTL | 22 | | | | |

## Caution

If any of the system variables are reset by an application, they may remain set after the application is completed. To prevent this, the application should specifically reset the variables to their original values. The application also should have a function that runs in the event of an application error that resets the system variables.

# 1 System-Setting Variables

The *system-setting variables* hold general system information and settings. These variables are used to gather environment information rather than reset the environment. They are all read-only and cannot be changed by any AutoCAD command.

### ACADPREFIX

ACADPREFIX stores the directory path set by the ACAD DOS environment variable. The install process for AutoCAD can create a start-up batch file called ACADR13.BAT. The ACAD environment variable is included in the batch file with the paths of the separate AutoCAD modules added as warranted by the installation. You can add directories to the path to increase the area searched for files. Use the DOS SET command to set the ACAD DOS environment variable.

### ACADVER

ACADVER stores the release number. This number varies with each release and update, and may contain values such as 13 or 13a.

### LOCALE

LOCALE displays the ISO language code of the current AutoCAD version you're running.

### LOGINNAME

LOGINNAME stores the user's login name. The login name may be stored in the configuration file or, if AutoCAD is so configured, entered with each startup. Access to the login name is provided for any on-line programs that need to know the name of the current draftsperson.

### PLATFORM

PLATFORM stores the name of the hardware AutoCAD is running on. This is used by third-party developers to identify the platform in use and work within its idiosyncrasies. The following are valid responses:

```
Microsoft Windows NT Version 3.5 (x86)
Microsoft Windows (Intel) Version 3.10
386 DOS Extender
```

### SYSCODEPAGE

SYSCODEPAGE stores the code page, as determined from the operating system. The *code page* identifies the keyboard character set or language being used.

### TEMPPREFIX

TEMPPREFIX stores the directory configured for placement of AutoCAD's temporary files. The directory defaults to the current drawing directory. In the event of a system crash, you should look for any system files stored on the disk as files or file fragments.

### TOOLTIPS

TOOLTIPS allows you to turn off the display of the tooltips when you place the pointing device over one of the tools:

> 0=Turns the tooltips display off
>
> 1=Turns the tooltips display on

## 2 Drawing-Mode Variables

The *drawing-mode variables* enable you to set the drawing environment's basic modes of operation and activate or deactivate some of AutoCAD's command responses.

### APERTURE

APERTURE controls the height, in pixels, of the snap target. The default value is 10. The target usually is made smaller to aid selection in dense drawings and larger to reduce the need for precise target placement in less dense drawings.

### AUDITCTL

AUDITCTL controls the creation of an audit report file (*.ADT). An audit report file contains the results of the AUDIT commands, which check the drawing database's integrity.

> 0=Disables the audit report file (the default)
>
> 1=Enables the audit report file

### BLIPMODE

BLIPMODE controls the placement of pick marks made during cursor selection.

> 0=No pick marks
>
> 1=Pick marks on (the default)

## CMDACTIVE

CMDACTIVE lists the type of command, if any, that is currently active. This information is useful when writing AutoLISP, ADS, or ARX applications, when you need to know what command is active at any given moment.

## CMDECHO

CMDECHO controls the echoing of prompts and input to the command line during AutoLISP routines. Developers frequently turn the echo off to speed up, and clean up, the appearance of their applications.

0=Turns command-line echo off

1=Turns command-line echo on (the default)

## CMDNAMES

CMDNAMES displays, in English, the name of the command, if any, that is currently active. Any transparent commands also are displayed. For example: CIRCLE'PAN indicates that the CIRCLE command has been issued, and that the PAN command is now being used transparently during the CIRCLE command. A response of " " (the default) indicates that no command is currently active.

## COORDS

COORDS controls the coordinate display in the status area of the graphics screen. By default, the coordinate display is on and updates as the cursor is moved. If the coordinate display is turned off by using F6, ^D, or double-clicking the coordinate display at the bottom of the screen, the coordinate display is updated only if a point is picked by using the cursor. If the coordinate display is turned back on by using F6, ^D, or double-clicking the coordinate display at the bottom of the screen, then the coordinate display is updated as the cursor is moved; and after a point is picked, the angle and distance of the cursor from the previous pick point will be shown during second point prompts. A final selection of F6 or ^D, or double-clicking on the coordinate display at the bottom of the screen, returns the coordinate display to its original status.

0=Coordinate display is updated at pick points only.

1=Coordinate display is continuously updated with absolute coordinates as the cursor is moved.

2=Coordinate display is continuously updated with absolute coordinates as the cursor is moved. The coordinate display changes to angle and distance during second point prompts.

## DELOBJ

DELOBJ controls whether objects used to create other objects are retained or deleted from the drawing database. For example, if you are extruding a polyline into a solid, the polyline will be either retained or deleted after extruding the solid depending upon the setting of the DELOBJ variable.

0=Objects are deleted.

1=Objects are retained.

## DWGCODEPAGE

DWGCODEPAGE stores the drawing-code page. DWGCODEPAGE is set to the value of SYSCODEPAGE when a drawing is started, but otherwise is not maintained. The code page identifies the keyboard character set or language being used.

## EXPERT

EXPERT suppresses or enables successive levels of prompts that AutoCAD uses to warn the user in the event of potentially dangerous editing. With each level of EXPERT, a new level of warning, plus all those previous to the level, are suppressed. Because of the far-reaching effects of some editing changes, EXPERT should be used with care.

0=All prompts are issued as normal (the default).

1=Suppresses the regeneration and current layer off warnings.

2=Suppresses the BLOCK and WBLOCK redefinition and overwrite prompts.

3=Suppresses the linetype redefinition or reloading prompts.

4=Suppresses the redefinition of UCS and viewport prompts.

5=Suppresses the redefinition and override of dimension style prompts.

### FILLMODE

FILLMODE controls the appearance of solids, traces, and polylines. With fill on, these objects are shown as solid where applicable. With fill off, the objects are shown as outlines.

0=Fill is off.

1=Fill is on (the default).

### HANDLES

HANDLES stores the results of the HANDLES command. For Release 13, handles are always on, so the value is always 1 (On). The HANDLES command merely reports that the handles are on. A *drawing handle* is a hexidecimal number that is permanently assigned to an object and remains with that object even after the drawing is closed. Object names also are hexidecimal codes that identify drawing objects, but they are not permanently stored with the drawing.

1=Handles are enabled.

### HIGHLIGHT

HIGHLIGHT controls the highlighting of selected objects.

0=OFF. Highlighting is turned off.

1=ON. Highlighting is turned on (the default).

> **Note**
>
> Grip-mode editing is not affected by HIGHLIGHT's setting.

> **Caution**
>
> Some display list drivers affect the appearance of highlighted objects. If HIGHLIGHT does not work consistently, you may be using a Display List Driver that disrupts HIGHLIGHT.

### ORTHOMODE

ORTHOMODE controls the orthogonal drafting mode. With ORTHOMODE on, coordinate entry is read from the cursor along the 0, 90, 180, and 270 degree points only. After a point is picked, the rubberband cursor extends horizontally or vertically from the pick point to a crosshair line. The rubberband cursor extends to the farther crosshair.

0=Orthagonal mode is turned off (the default).

1=Orthagonal mode is turned on.

### OSMODE

OSMODE sets the object snap mode. The value can be any of the modes shown or a sum of any of the modes to make multiple selections.

| | |
|---|---|
| 0= NONe (the default) | 64=INSertion |
| 1= ENDpoint | 128=PERpendicular |
| 2= MIDpoint | 256=TANgent |
| 4= CENter | 512=NEArest |
| 8= NODe | 1024=QUIck |
| 16= QUAdrant | 2048=APPint |
| 32=INTersection | |

### REGENMODE

REGENMODE controls automatic regeneration. If REGENMODE is set to 1 (the default), AutoCAD performs a regeneration whenever the need arises. If REGENMODE is set to 0, you are prompted before AutoCAD performs a re-generation.

0=OFF. Drawing regeneration will be prompted.

1=ON. Drawing regeneration is automatic.

### TILEMODE

TILEMODE controls the availability of paper space to maintain Release 10 compatibility. If TILEMODE is set to 1 (the default), you must work in model space. If you want tiled viewports, use the VPORTS command. If TILEMODE is set to 0, you can go into paper space and use MVIEW to set up floating viewports.

1=ON. No paper space, use VPORTS.

2=OFF. Paper space available, use MVIEW.

## 3 Object-Mode Variables

The *object-mode variables* control the attributes of objects drawn after the variables are set. You can reset the variables to apply different attributes, such as color or linetype, to different objects. Each of these variables can be set by using the DDEMODES command.

### CECOLOR

CECOLOR sets the color for any objects drawn after CECOLOR is set. The color can be BYLAYER (the default), BYBLOCK, a color name, or a string representing a color number between 1 and 255. BYLAYER color means that the object has the same color as the layer. BYBLOCK means that the object appears white until it is inserted into a drawing; then the object takes on the current color, either explicitly set or the current layer color.

### CELTYPE

CELTYPE sets the linetype for any objects drawn after CELTYPE is set. The linetype can be provided by AutoCAD, user-defined, BYLAYER (the default), or BYBLOCK. The 38 linetypes provided by AutoCAD are stored in ACAD.LIN and, with the exception of continuous and hidden, must be loaded with the LINETYPE command before they can be used by the Layer Control dialog box.

### CLAYER

CLAYER sets the layer for any objects drawn after CLAYER is set. All drawings begin with a single layer 0 (the default). Any layers you want to use after that must be created with the LAYER or DDLMODES commands. You can use CLAYER as a quick method to change layers once they have been defined.

### ELEVATION

ELEVATION sets the height, along the *z*-axis of the current UCS, of any objects drawn after ELEVATION is set. The default is 0. No limits are set on the *z*-axis, so the elevation has no practical limit. ELEVATION can be set with the ELEV command or DDEMODES.

### THICKNESS

THICKNESS sets the extrusion height, along the *z*-axis, of any objects drawn after THICKNESS is set. The default is 0. No limits are set on the *z*-axis, so the thickness has no practical limit. THICKNESS can be set with the ELEV command, after ELEVATION, or with DDEMODES.

## 4 Limits and Extents

The *limits and extents variables* control the boundary of your drawing and AutoCAD's behavior in accordance with the boundary.

### EXTMAX

EXTMAX is a World Coordinate System point that marks the uppermost right-hand corner of the drawing on the WCS X-Y plane for the current space. As the drawing expands along the positive $y$-axis or along the positive $x$-axis, EXTMAX is recalculated. If objects are removed, EXTMAX is recalculated to a point closer to the origin when ZOOM All or ZOOM Extents is issued.

### EXTMIN

EXTMIN is a World Coordinate System point that marks the lowermost left-hand corner of the drawing on the WCS X-Y plane for the current space. As the drawing expands along the negative $y$-axis or along the negative $x$-axis, EXTMIN is recalculated. If objects are removed, EXTMIN is recalculated to a point closer to the origin when ZOOM All or ZOOM Extents is issued.

### LIMCHECK

LIMCHECK sets the limits checking for the current space—either model or paper. If LIMCHECK is on, AutoCAD will not accept points outside the current limits.

> 0=Limits checking is turned off (the default).

> 1=Limits checking is turned on.

### LIMMAX

LIMMAX is a World Coordinate System point that marks the uppermost right-hand point of the drawing limits on the WCS X-Y plane for the current space.

### LIMMIN

LIMMIN is a World Coordinate System point that marks the lowermost left-hand point of the drawing limits on the WCS X-Y plane for the current space.

### SAVEIMAGES

This system variable controls whether images of objects created by other AutoCAD applications are written as graphic metafiles. Depending on the value, the application that was used to create the objects may have to be loaded to display the objects. The possible value areas follow:

> 0=The application's definition of the objects controls whether to save their graphical description of objects. Solid, body, and region objects are not saved.

> 1=Always saves images.

> 2=Never saves images.

## 5 Line-Scale Variables

The *line-scale variables* control the model space and paper space linetype scaling.

### CELTSCALE

The CELTSCALE variable allows you to set the current global linetype scale *per object*. Prior to Release 13, you could only change the linetype scale for all objects globally with the LTSCALE command, instead of individually.

### LTSCALE

LTSCALE sets the global linetype scale for model space. The linetype scale determines how big the dashes and gaps are in a line, relative to the current drawing. LTSCALE may need to be set differently, depending on whether you want to view the drawing or plot it.

**Tip**

If you want to view the drawing, try an LTSCALE similar to your drawing scale. If you are going to plot the drawing, try an LTSCALE that is 0.3 to 0.5 times your drawing scale.

### PSLTSCALE

PSLTSCALE controls the paper-space scaling of model-space linetypes. Because paper space is usually set up with a scale factor of 1:1 and you can have multiple viewports with different scales, linetype scaling is very important in paper space. If you want the linetypes in the MVIEW viewports to appear the same regardless of the scale of the viewport, leave PSLTSCALE at the default setting of 1. If you do not want the linetype scaling to be controlled by the MVIEW viewport scaling, set PSLTSCALE to 0.

   0=Linetypes are not scaled, in relation to Paper Space.

   1=Linetypes are scaled, in relation to Paper Space (the default).

## 6 Units Variables

The *units variables* control the units and degree of precision that AutoCAD uses. AutoCAD always maintains the same level of internal accuracy for calculations, but you can control the external appearance of the drawings units and precision. With the exception of UNITMODE, all the variables can be set with the DDUNITS or UNITS commands.

### ANGBASE

ANGBASE sets the direction of angle 0 in the current UCS. The value can be anywhere from 0 (the default) to 360.

### ANGDIR

ANGDIR sets the direction of angle measured in the current UCS.

> 0=Counterclockwise (the default)
>
> 1=Clockwise

### AUNITS

AUNITS sets the unit of measure for angular drawing.

> 0=Decimal degrees (the default)
>
> 1=Degrees/Minutes/Seconds
>
> 2=Grad
>
> 3=Radians
>
> 4=Surveyor's units

### AUPREC

AUPREC sets the precision, in decimal places, of angular measure. AutoCAD maintains the same level of internal accuracy. AUPREC affects the external appearance of angular measures. Valid entries are from 0 (the default) to 8.

### LUNITS

LUNITS sets the unit of measure for linear drawing.

> 1=Scientific
>
> 2=Decimal
>
> 3=Engineering
>
> 4=Architectural
>
> 5=Fractional

### LUPREC

LUPREC sets the precision, in decimal places or denominator, of linear measure. AutoCAD maintains the same level of internal accuracy. LUPREC affects the external appearance of linear measures. Valid entries for decimal units are from 0 to 8; 4 is the default.

## UNITMODE

**Tip**

To make AutoCAD
accept your frac-
tional feet and
inches input or
surveyor's units
as entered, set
UNITMODE to 1.

UNITMODE controls the way AutoCAD displays fractional feet and inches and surveyor's angles. Because you cannot enter a space when entering coordinates, fractional feet and inches and surveyor's units use a hyphen or are run together. To make the output easier to read, AutoCAD can alter the input by adding spaces in the appropriate places. UNITMODE determines whether AutoCAD alters the input.

0=AutoCAD alters the input (the default).

1=AutoCAD accepts the input and does not add spaces.

## 7 Text Variables

The *text variables* control AutoCAD's text functions and the way other functions deal with text. New to Release 13 is the spell-checking function. Dictionary variables control the location and choice of dictionaries to be used.

## DCTCUST

DCTCUST displays the current custom spelling dictionary path and file name. A custom spelling dictionary can be used to add words you have identified that are not in the standard dictionary. To change to a custom dictionary during a spell check, select Change Dictionaries in the Check Spelling dialog box. Enter a name in the Custom Dictionary text box. You can also select from a list of dictionaries with the Browse function. A custom dictionary has a CUS file extension.

## DCTMAIN

DCTMAIN displays the current main spelling dictionary file name. The full path is not shown because this file is expected to reside in the \support directory. You can specify a default main spelling dictionary using the SETVAR command. To change the main dictionary during a spell check, select Change Dictionaries in the Check Spelling dialog box. Select the Main Dictionary arrow and select a dictionary from the list.

## MIRRTEXT

MIRRTEXT controls the results of the MIRROR command on text. By default, text is mirrored along with other objects. Because this can make the text difficult to read, MIRRTEXT enables you to prevent text from being reversed when it is copied with the MIRROR command.

0=Text is not reflected when copied by the MIRROR command.

1=Text is reflected when copied by the MIRROR command.

> **Note**
>
> Dimension text is not affected by MIRRTEXT. Dimension text is never reflected when copied by the MIRROR command.

### MTEXTED

MTEXTED allows you to change to a third-party ASCII text editor to use for creating paragraph text. This can also be done in the Preferences dialog box.

### QTEXTMODE

QTEXTMODE controls the appearance of text. If QTEXTMODE is off (the default), text appears normally. If QTEXTMODE is on, text is replaced by a rectangle that redraws and regenerates faster than text.

> 0=OFF. Text is shown normally (the default).
>
> 1=ON. Text is replaced with a rectangle.

### TEXTEVAL

TEXTEVAL controls the way text prompts interpret your entries. If TEXTEVAL is on (the default), all text beginning with "(" or "!" is interpreted as an AutoLISP expression. If TEXTEVAL is off, all text is taken literally.

> 0=OFF. Text is not evaluated for AutoLISP expressions.
>
> 1=ON. Text is evaluated for AutoLISP expressions (the default).

> **Note**
>
> DTEXT takes all text input as literal, regardless of TEXTEVAL's setting.

### TEXTFILL

TEXTFILL controls the display of Bitstream, TrueType, and Adobe Type 1 fonts. By displaying text as outlines, you can improve drawing speed. You can also improve drawing speed by setting the QTEXT variable to display text as frames only. To plot filled-in text, change TEXTFILL to 1.

> 0=Displays text as outlines
>
> 1=Displays text as filled images

**Tip**

If you have a large amount of text in a drawing and you need to see where it is but not what it says, you can use QTEXTMODE to display the text as rectangles. This speeds up redraws and regenerations of the drawing.

**Appendixes**

### TEXTQLTY

TEXTQLTY sets the resolution of text created with Bitstream, TrueType, and Adobe Type 1 fonts. Increasing the value of TEXTQLTY can make text easier to read on the display. Increasing the value, however, increases the display and plotting speed. Lowering the values increases the display and plotting speed, but makes text more difficult to read on the screen. Valid values are 0 to 100.0. The default value is 50, which sets the text resolution to 300 dpi. Setting the value to 100 sets the resolution to 600 dpi.

### TEXTSIZE

TEXTSIZE sets the height of text drawn after TEXTSIZE is set. TEXTSIZE does not affect the current text style's settings. The default value is 0.2000.

> **Note**
>
> If the current text style has a fixed height, TEXTSIZE is ignored.

### TEXTSTYLE

TEXTSTYLE sets the current text style's name. The default is STANDARD. You can enter any defined style. Use the STYLE command to set or create text styles.

## 8 Drag-Mode Variables

The *drag-mode variables* control where and when AutoCAD redraws a selected image as the image is being dragged across the screen.

### DRAGMODE

**Tip**

If you are dragging a complex object, you can set DRAGMODE to 0 or 1 to stop automatic dragging and to speed up placement of the complex object.

DRAGMODE controls whether objects are shown as they are dragged into position. An example of this is the CIRCLE command. When you draw a circle, you are prompted for a center point, and then you can drag the circle in and out to set the radius. DRAGMODE can be set to one of three levels. If DRAGMODE is set to 0, all dragging is suppressed. If DRAGMODE is set to 1, dragging is enabled if you enter **drag** at the Command: prompt. If DRAGMODE is set to 2 (the default), the dragging is automatic and performed whenever possible.

0=OFF. All dragging is suppressed.

1=ON. Dragging is enabled when requested with DRAG.

2=Automatic. Dragging is done whenever possible (the default).

### DRAGP1

DRAGP1 determines when an object being dragged should be regenerated, based on a distance moved. The default is 10.

### DRAGP2

DRAGP2 determines when an object being dragged should be regenerated, based on a fast drag-sampling rate. The default is 25.

## 9 Grid-Mode Variables

The *grid-mode variables* control the existence and size of the background grid.

### GRIDMODE

GRIDMODE controls the display of the grid. The grid also can be set by pressing F7, or by using the GRID and DDRMODES commands. The grid is altered only in the current viewport and is aligned with the current UCS.

> 0=OFF. The grid is off (the default).
>
> 1=ON. The grid is on.

### GRIDUNIT

GRIDUNIT sets the X and Y spacing for the grid in the current viewport.

## 10 Snap-Mode Variables

The *snap-mode variables* control the existence, origin, size, angle, and mode of the snap feature. These variables enable you to have a rotated grid plane or three isometric grid planes.

### SNAPANG

SNAPANG sets the degree of rotation of the snap/grid, relative to the current UCS in the current viewport. Valid entries are from 0 to 360.

### SNAPBASE

SNAPBASE sets the point of origin for the snap/grid in the current viewport with current UCS coordinates.

### SNAPISOPAIR

SNAPISOPAIR sets the current isometric plane for the current viewport. The isometric snap style is set with SNAPSTYL, the Style option of the GRID command, or DDRMODES.

**Tip**

If your digitizer has a tendency to twitch, you can set DRAGP1 to a high number to prevent regenerations.

**Tip**

If your digitizer has a high, fast motion setting, you can set DRAGP2 high to maintain speed in fast motion jumps.

**Appendixes**

0=Left plane (the default)

1=Top plane

2=Right plane

### SNAPMODE

SNAPMODE turns the snap feature on and off for the current viewport.

0=OFF. Sets the snap off (the default).

1=ON. Sets the snap on.

### SNAPSTYL

SNAPSTYL sets the snap to the default standard orthagonal mode or isometric mode.

0=Standard mode

1=Isometric mode

### SNAPUNIT

SNAPUNIT sets the X and Y spacing for the current viewport.

## 11 Grip and Selection Variables

The *grip variables* and *selection variables* control the appearance and behavior of grips, selected objects, and selection modes.

### GRIPBLOCK

GRIPBLOCK controls the appearance of grips in blocks. If you set GRIPBLOCK to 1, all the objects in the block will display grips when selected.

0=OFF. Displays a grip at the block insertion point only (the default).

1=ON. Displays a grip for each element in the block.

### GRIPCOLOR

GRIPCOLOR sets the color of unselected grips. Unselected grips are drawn as a box outline. The default color is 5. A valid entry is an integer from 1 to 255.

## GRIPHOT

GRIPHOT sets the color for selected grips. A selected grip is drawn as a solid box. The default color is 1. A valid entry is an integer from 1 to 255.

## GRIPS

GRIPS enables or disables grip mode editing. Grip mode editing enables you to use grips to create a selection set and enter STRETCH, MOVE, ROTATE, SCALE, and MIRROR edit modes.

> 0=OFF. Disables grip-mode editing.
>
> 1=ON. Enables grip-mode editing (the default).

## GRIPSIZE

GRIPSIZE controls the size of the grips in pixels. The default value is 3. A valid entry is an integer from 1 to 255.

## PICKADD

PICKADD controls the selection of objects using noun/verb selection. If PICKADD is set to 0, each selection replaces the last selection set rather than being added to it. Objects can be added to a selection set if you press and hold down the Shift key while making selections. If PICKADD is set to 1 (the default), each selected object is added to the selection set. You can also remove selected objects from the selection set if you press and hold down the Shift key and pick objects that are already included in the selection set.

## PICKAUTO

PICKAUTO controls automatic windowing when selecting objects. If PICKAUTO is off, you must click directly on an object at the `Select objects:` prompt to select it. After you click once, automatic windowing is returned as a selection method. If PICKAUTO is on, you can window objects at the `Select objects:` prompt without issuing a Window or Crossing option.

> 0=OFF. Disables automatic windowing at the `Select objects:` prompt for the first selection.
>
> 1=ON. Enables automatic windowing at the `Select objects:` prompt (the default).

## PICKBOX

PICKBOX controls the height of the object-selection target box in pixels.

### PICKDRAG

PICKDRAG controls the method used to draw an automatic selection window. If PICKDRAG is 0 (the default), you draw a window by clicking at one corner, dragging the pointing device, and clicking at the opposite corner. If PICKDRAG is 1, you draw a window by clicking and holding the digitizer button at one corner, dragging the pointing device, and releasing the button at the opposite corner.

> 0=OFF. Automatic windows are drawn with two separate clicks (the default).

> 1=ON. Automatic windows are drawn with a click and hold, then drag, then release.

### PICKFIRST

PICKFIRST controls the noun/verb selection of objects before editing. If PICKFIRST is 0, you must enter an editing command before you begin selecting objects. If PICKFIRST is 1, you can select objects (the noun) and then enter an editing command (the verb). The previously selected objects are automatically selected by the editing command.

> 0=OFF. Disables noun/verb selection.

> 1=ON. Enables noun/verb selection (the default).

### PICKSTYLE

PICKSTYLE controls how groups and associative hatches are selected. Release 13 allows you to define a group as a named selection set of objects.

> 0=No group selection or associative hatch selection

> 1=Group selection

> 2=Associative hatch selection

> 3=Group selection and associative hatch selection

### SORTENTS

SORTENTS controls the order in which the drawing database is sorted. AutoCAD uses an *octal tree* to store the objects on the virtual screen. The virtual screen is divided into rectangular regions and subregions. The objects are stored in an eight-level tree based on their region and subregion location. Because objects are stored based on their location, object selection, zooming, regeneration, and redrawing are much faster. If, however, you need the objects to be sorted by their order of creation rather than by their location, you can reset SORTENTS. You can enter one of the following options or the sum of the options you would like to use:

0=Disables SORTENTS, the octal tree sorting is used for every AutoCAD function.

1=Sort for object selection. This turns octal-tree sorting off when selecting objects, so that the most recently drawn item is selected when two or more objects overlap at the selection point.

2=Sort for object snap. This turns octal-tree sorting off when object snaps are in use. This enables the QUIck object snap to find the most recently drawn object.

4=SOrt for redraws. This turns the octal tree off when the drawing is redrawn. This is done only if it is important that the objects be re-drawn in their order of creation.

8=Sort for MSLIDE slide creation. This turns octal-tree sorting off when a slide is displayed with MSLIDE. This is done when you need the slide to be drawn in the order in which component parts were drawn.

16=Sort for regeneration. This turns octal-tree sorting off when the draw-ing regenerates. This is done when it is important that the objects be regenerated in the order of their creation.

32=Sort for plotting. This turns octal-tree sorting off when plotting. This usually is not a concern because both AutoCAD and most plotters have their own object-sort routines. This is important if you are plot-ting to an image file and you need the objects to be drawn in the order of their creation. The default is on.

64=Sort for PostScript output. This turns octal-tree sorting off when us-ing PostScript output commands. This is done so that the objects are drawn in the order of their creation.

## 12 Drawing-Function Variables

The *drawing-function variables* store the default values of the drawing and editing functions, such as radii, diameters, width, and distances. These vari-ables enable AutoCAD to remember your last entry in a drawing command and use it as the default the next time you use the command. Release 13 now allows you to trim and extend objects to apparent intersections of objects in 3D space even if they do not intersect in the same plane.

**Tip**

The Object Sort Method button in the Object Selec-tion Settings dialog box enables you to set SORTENTS with a dialog box.

**Appendixes**

### CHAMFERA

CHAMFERA sets the default distance to trim the first line selected when using the CHAMFER command. Each use of CHAMFER resets the value.

### CHAMFERB

CHAMFERB sets the default distance to trim the second line selected when using the CHAMFER command. Each use of CHAMFER resets the value.

### CHAMFERC

A new function in Release 13 allows you to chamfer two objects by specifying a location on the first object selected (the chamfer length) where the chamfer line will start, and then specifying an angle the chamfer line will form with this object. CHAMFERC stores the chamfer length.

### CHAMFERD

CHAMFERD sets the chamfer angle when using the angle method to define a chamfer. This is used in conjuction with CHAMFERC, which stores the value for the chamfer length.

### CHAMMODE

CHAMMODE sets the input method by which AutoCAD creates chamfers. You have two options that can be used to specify chamfers. You can specify the two chamfer distances or specify the chamfer length and angle the chamfer line will form with this object.

> 0=Requires two chamfer distances.

> 1=Requires one chamfer length and an angle.

### CIRCLERAD

CIRCLERAD holds the default circle radius. Each use of CIRCLE resets the value. To specify no default, enter **0**.

### CMLJUST

The CMLJUST variable determines how a multiline is drawn between the specified points. It specifies multiline justification.

> 0=Top. The multiline is drawn below the cursor.

> 1=Middle. The origin of the multiline is centered at the cursor.

> 2=Bottom. The multiline is drawn above the cursor.

### CMLSCALE

The CMLSCALE variable stores the scale value for the current multiline. This scale does not affect the linetype scale. This scale factor is based upon the initial width of the multiline, fixed when the multiline style was defined. It controls the overall width of a multiline. For example, a scale factor of 2.0 produces a multiline twice as wide as the original style definition. A zero scale factor collapses the multiline into a single line. Using a negative scale factor flips the order of the offset lines (the smallest or most negative line is placed on top when the multiline is drawn from left to right).

### CMLSTYLE

CMLSTYLE is used to set the style for the multiline to use. AutoCAD has several predefined styles located in the Multiline Style library (ACAD.MLN). See MSTYLE in Chapter 20, "Using Multilines," for more information on loading multiline styles.

### DONUTID

DONUTID sets the default interior diameter of a DONUT. The value can be 0 to create a solid fill circle.

### DONUTOD

DONUTOD sets the default outside diameter of a DONUT. The value must be greater than 0. If the value of DONUTID is greater than DONUTOD, the values are switched and used as defaults for the next DONUT command.

### EDGEMODE

With the TRIM and EXTEND commands, you can trim or extend an object to another object's implied edge, or to an object that intersects it in 3D space. EDGEMODE controls how TRIM and EXTEND determine cutting and boundary edges.

0=Uses the selected edge without an extension.

1=Extends or trims the object to an imaginary extension of the cutting or boundary object. This could be another object's implied edge, or another object that intersects it in 3D space.

### FILLETRAD

FILLETRAD sets the default radius of the FILLET command. To specify no radius, enter **0**.

### OFFSETDIST

OFFSETDIST sets the default distance for the OFFSET command. To offset through a point, enter a negative number. The initial default is -1.0000 (for through).

### PELLIPSE

PELLIPSE controls the type of ellipse drawn with the ELLIPSE command.

> 0=Creates a true ellipse object (new for Release 13)

> 1=Creates a polyline representation of an ellipse

### POLYSIDES

POLYSIDES stores the default number of sides to a POLYGON. A valid entry is an integer between 3 and 1024.

### PROJMODE

PROJMODE sets the current Projection mode for TRIM or EXTEND operations. Release 13 allows you to trim or extend objects to other objects in 3D space even if they do not intersect in the same plane or are parallel to the cutting or boundary edges. In a true 3D trim or extend, the objects must intersect in 3D space. If you trim or extend objects projected to the XY plane or current view plane, the trimmed or extended objects might not end exactly at the boundary in 3D space.

> 0=True 3D mode (no projection)

> 1=Project to the XY plane of the current UCS

> 2=Project to the current view plane

### TRACEWID

TRACEWID stores the default width of the TRACE command.

### TRIMMODE

TRIMMODE controls whether AutoCAD trims selected edges for chamfers and fillets.

> 0=Leaves selected edges intact

> 1=Trims selected edges to the endpoints of chamfer lines and fillet arcs

## 13 Menu and Dialog-Box Variables

The *menu variables* and *dialog-box variables* control the behavior or access to information on AutoCAD's Graphical User Interface. You probably will not need to change these variables unless you are developing an application.

### CMDDIA

CMDDIA controls whether the PLOT command issues a series of prompts or uses dialog boxes.

> 0=Prompts for PLOT settings

> 1=Uses dialog boxes for PLOT settings (the default)

### DIASTAT

DIASTAT holds the exit status of the last dialog box. If the dialog box is canceled, DIASTAT is 0. If the dialog box is accepted, DIASTAT is 1.

> 0=Cancel. The last dialog box was canceled.

> 1=OK. The last dialog box was accepted (the default).

### FILEDIA

FILEDIA controls the availability of dialog boxes. If FILEDIA is set to 1, dialog boxes are used. If FILEDIA is set to 0, the Command: prompt is used unless you enter a tilde (~). Then, dialog boxes are used for that prompt or command.

> 0=OFF. Do not use dialog boxes unless they are requested with a
> tilde (~).

> 1=ON. Use dialog boxes if they exist (the default).

> **Note**
>
> The PLOT and Enter Attribute dialog boxes are controlled by independent variables. CMDDIA controls the PLOT dialog box; ATTDIA controls the Enter Attributes dialog box.

### MAXSORT

MAXSORT holds the maximum number of elements that can be in a list if AutoCAD is to sort the list. If the number of elements in the list is greater than MAXSORT, the list is not sorted at all.

**Appendixes**

## MENUCTL

MENUCTL controls screen menu page-swapping in response to keyboard entry. If MENUCTL is off, the screen menu does not change based on keyboard entry. If MENUCTL is on (the default), the screen menu shows the option menus as keyboard entry is made.

> 0=OFF. The screen menu does not switch pages to display options based on keyboard entry.

> 1=ON. The screen menu switches pages to display options based on keyboard entry (the default).

## MENUECHO

MENUECHO controls the echoing of menu commands to the Command: prompt. This is used to clean up the display of menus as they run commands, macros, and AutoLISP expressions. You can enter one of the following values or the sum of some of the values to get a combined effect:

> 0=No suppression (the default).

> 1=Suppresses echoing of all menu items. ^P turns this setting on and off in individual menus.

> 2=Suppresses the display of system prompts and some AutoLISP prompts issued by menus.

> 4=Prevents ^P from turning menu echo on and off.

> 8=Echoes DIESEL input and output for debugging DIESEL code.

---

### Caution

If you set MENUECHO to 3, output from the (prompt) AutoLISP function is not displayed.

---

## MENUNAME

MENUNAME contains the name of the current menu file, as entered when the menu was loaded.

## POPUPS

POPUPS lists the availability of the Advanced User Interface. The Advanced User Interface consists of dialog boxes, pull-down menus, the menu bar, and icon menus. This is useful for applications that must determine the best possible method of user interface.

> 0=OFF. The Advanced User Interface is not available.

> 1=ON. The Advanced User Interface is available (the default).

### SCREENBOXES

SCREENBOXES holds the number of boxes available for menu items in the screen-menu area. If the screen menu has been removed during configuration, SCREENBOXES is set to 0. Some AutoCAD platforms allow the graphics window to be resized, or the screen menu to be reconfigured, during an editing session. Both of these occurrences may cause a change in the size of the screen area and thus SCREENBOXES. The default is 26.

### TABMODE

TABMODE controls the use of tablet mode. When tablet mode is on, the screen-pointing area of the tablet performs like a digitizer rather than a screen-pointing device. The digitizer is calibrated to the scale of the drawing to be digitized so the drawing created in AutoCAD is drawn in true size. When tablet mode is off (the default), the screen area of the digitizer is not scaled and represents the portion of the drawing on the screen.

> 0=OFF. Turns the tablet off (the default).

> 1=ON. Turns the tablet on.

## 14 Screen-Mode Variables

The *screen-mode variables* control the size and access to graphic viewports and the text screen.

### SCREENMODE

SCREENMODE lists the active screen mode or window. The value is one of the following or the sum of some of the options. SCREENMODE is useful when an application needs to determine which screen the user is currently viewing.

> 0=The text screen is being displayed (the default).

> 1=The graphics screen is being displayed.

> 2=There is a dual screen display.

### SCREENSIZE

SCREENSIZE lists the size of the current viewport for the *x*- and *y*-axis in pixels. SCREENSIZE can be used by an application to determine proper scaling of graphic objects drawn with low-level graphic functions such as GRDRAW.

## 15 Point Variables

The *point variables* control the size, orientation, and appearance of point objects.

### PDMODE

PDMODE controls the appearance of points. The value can be any one of the following:

> 0=A dot (the default)
>
> 1=Nothing
>
> 2=A plus (+)
>
> 3=An X
>
> 4=A short vertical line from the point up 90 degrees

You can add any one of the following values to the preceding ones to draw a figure around the point:

> 32=A circle
>
> 64=A square
>
> 96=A circle and a square

### PDSIZE

PDSIZE controls the size of points drawn.

> 0=(the default). The point is drawn at five percent of the graphic area's height.
>
> >0=The point is drawn at the absolute size specified.
>
> <0=The point is a percentage of the viewport height.

> **Note**
>
> If the value of PDSIZE is negative, the point retains its appearance as the viewport is zoomed in and out, provided that the viewport is regenerated. If the viewport does not regenerate, you can enter **regen** to make the points adjust their size according to the new zoom factor.

The Point Style dialog box shows all the available point styles. The top row of points shows the point for the values 0 to 4. The next three rows show the effect of adding 32, 64, and 96 to the point values. The Point Size edit box and the Absolute and Relative radio buttons control the settings for PDSIZE. A positive value for PDSIZE indicates an absolute point size. A negative value for PDSIZE indicates a relative point size.

## 16 UCS Variables

The *UCS variables* control and store information on the User Coordinate System. These variables usually are set by AutoCAD commands, as opposed to direct access by the variable's name or by SETVAR. The values stored in these variables are very important to any drafter, but are particularly useful to those working in 3D. Most of these variables can be set by using the UCS command.

### UCSFOLLOW

UCSFOLLOW controls AutoCAD's automatic display of the PLAN view when the UCS changes. UCSFOLLOW is stored separately for model space and paper space, but in paper space the value is always treated as if it is 0.

> 0=OFF (the default). A change in the UCS does not cause AutoCAD to change the display to the PLAN view for the new UCS.

> 1=ON. A change in the UCS causes AutoCAD to change the display to the PLAN view for the new UCS.

### UCSICON

UCSICON controls the display of the UCS icon. The value can be any of the following values or the sum of the desired options:

> 0=OFF. The UCS icon is not displayed.

> 1=ON. The UCS icon is displayed (the default).

> 2=Origin. If UCSICON is on, the UCS icon is placed on the UCS origin, if possible, in the current display.

Appendixes

### UCSNAME

UCSNAME holds the name of the current UCS. If the UCS is unnamed, the value is "".

### UCSORG

UCSORG holds a World Coordinate System (WCS) point that is the origin of the current UCS.

### UCSXDIR

UCSXDIR holds a WCS point. A vector drawn from the WCS origin to the UCSXDIR points in the X direction of the current UCS.

### UCSYDIR

UCSYDIR holds a WCS point. A vector drawn from the WCS origin to the UCSYDIR points in the Y direction of the current UCS.

### WORLDUCS

WORLDUCS tells whether the current UCS is the same as the WCS.

0=The current UCS is not the same as the WCS.

1=The current UCS is the same as the WCS (the default).

## 17 Undo Variables

The *undo variables* control the behavior of the UNDO command.

### UNDOCTL

UNDOCTL controls how much the UNDO command will undo. The value can be any of the following or the sum of the desired options. The default is 5:

0=OFF. UNDO is disabled.

1=ON. UNDO is enabled.

2=Undo only one command.

4=Each function is considered a single command, no matter how many commands it may contain. For example, a menu item is treated as a single command, even if it performs multiple tasks.

8=The Group option of the UNDO command is currently active.

## UNDOMARKS

UNDOMARKS holds the number of marks placed in the command stream being recorded by UNDO. Marks are placed by using the Mark option of the UNDO command. If the Group option of the UNDO command is in use, the Mark and Back options cannot be used.

## 18 Data and List Variables

The *data variables* and *list variables* store and provide access to information gathered by the inquiry commands. With the exception of LASTPOINT, these variables are all read-only.

## AREA

AREA stores the area value calculated by the last AREA, LIST, or DBLIST command. The value is listed in square drawing units.

## DISTANCE

DISTANCE stores the value calculated by the last DIST command. The value is listed in linear drawing units.

## LASTANGLE

LASTANGLE stores the end angle of the last arc drawn. The *end angle* is relative to the current UCS for the current space (model or paper).

## LASTPOINT

LASTPOINT stores the last point selected. The point is listed in current UCS coordinates for the current space (model or paper). The LASTPOINT is accessed by entering an AT sign (@) at the Command: prompt.

## PERIMETER

PERIMETER stores the perimeter value calculated by the last AREA, LIST, or DBLIST command. The value is listed in linear drawing units.

## 19 Face, Surface, and Polyline Variables

The *face variables*, *surface variables*, and *polyline variables* affect a wide variety of settings, mostly in 3D drawing. Although polylines often are used in 2D drawing, their system variables are included here because polylines often are necessary for the 3D objects that the other variables affect.

## DISPSILH

DISPSILH controls whether a solid or surface model displays the silhouette of an object after a hide, shade, or render.

**Tip**

If you want to establish the coordinates of a specific point in the drawing, use the ID command. LASTPOINT is set to the value returned by ID.

**Appendixes**

0=Off. Displays all facet edges.

1=On. Removes all facet edges, showing the silhouette of the object.

### ISOLINES

ISOLINES system variable is used to control the number of tessellation lines used to visualize curved surfaces in a wireframe. The more tessellation lines on the object, the smoother it appears. As tessellation lines increase, however, rendering, redraw, regen, hide, and shading times all increase. Valid integer values are from 0 to 2047. The default value is 4.

### PFACEVMAX

PFACEVMAX stores the maximum number of vertices per face allowed in a PFACE.

### PLINEGEN

PLINEGEN controls the linetype generation in 2D polylines. If PLINEGEN is set to 0 (the default), each line segment is considered separate when linetypes are applied to the polyline. If PLINEGEN is set to 1, the vertices of the polyline are ignored, and the linetype generation is applied to the entire line from beginning to end.

> 0=OFF (the default). Each vertex-defined line segment is individually considered as linetypes are applied.

> 1=ON. The vertices are ignored, and the entire polyline is considered when linetypes are applied.

---

**Note**

PLINEGEN does not affect polylines with tapered segments.

---

**Tip**
For smoother overall appearance of a linetype on a polyline, set PLINEGEN to 1.

### PLINEWID

PLINEWID sets the default width of a polyline. The default is 0.

### SPLFRAME

SPLFRAME controls the appearance of polylines and meshes. If SPLFRAME is 0 (the default), a splined polyline or smoothed mesh is shown without the original lines that define the polyline or mesh. Invisible edges in 3D faces also are left invisible. If SPLFRAME is 1, the original polyline or mesh is retained when a splined polyline of smoothed mesh is generated. Invisible edges of 3D faces are displayed.

### SPLINESEGS

SPLINESEGS sets the number of line or arc segments used in each curve of a splined 2D or 3D polyline. If SPLINESEGS is negative, the absolute value of SPLINESEGS is used to determine the number of segments, but arcs are used instead of lines, creating a fit curve. If SPLINESEGS is positive, then line segments are used to generate a spline curve.

> **Note**
>
> A negative value for SPLINESEGS does not create a fit curve on 3D polylines. A spline curve is used instead.

### SPLINETYPE

SPLINETYPE sets the type of spline curve applied by the PEDIT command. The value can be one of the following:

    5=Quadratic B-spline

    6=Cubic B-spline (the default)

### SURFTAB1

SURFTAB1 sets the number of tabulated surfaces generated by the RULESURF and TABSURF commands. SURFTAB1 also sets the mesh density along the *m*-axis for the EDGESURF and REVSURF commands.

### SURFTAB2

SURFTAB2 sets the mesh density along the *n*-axis for the EDGESURF and REVSURF commands.

### SURFTYPE

SURFTYPE sets the type of smoothing used by the Smooth option of the PEDIT command when a 3D mesh is selected. The value can be one of the following:

    5=Quadratic B-spline surface

    6=Cubic B-spline surface

    8=Bézier surface

**Tip**
The higher the setting you use for SURFTAB1 and SURFTAB2, the smoother your image is. The lower the setting, the faster your drawing regenerates.

**Appendixes**

> **Note**
>
> Quadratic smoothing requires at least three points in each direction on the 3D surface mesh. Cubic smoothing requires at least four points in each direction on the 3D surface mesh. Bézier smoothing is limited to meshes with no more than 11 points along the m- or n-axis.

### SURFU

SURFU sets the density in the M direction on 3D meshes. A valid entry is an integer from 2 to 200. The default is 6.

### SURFV

SURFV sets the density in the M direction on 3D meshes. A valid entry is an integer from 2 to 200. The default is 6.

**Tip**
The higher the setting you use for SURFU and SURFV, the smoother your image is. The lower the setting, the faster your drawing regenerates.

## 20 Hatching Variables

The *hatching variables* control the behavior of the HATCH and BHATCH commands. This reflects the improvements made in hatching by the introduction of the BHATCH command.

### HPANG

HPANG sets the default hatch-pattern angle.

### HPBOUND

HPBOUND can be used to control the type of object created by the BHATCH and BOUNDARY commands.

    0=Creates a polyline

    1= Creates a region

### HPDOUBLE

HPDOUBLE sets the default for hatch pattern doubling of user-defined hatch patterns. Doubling causes a second set of hatch lines to be drawn at 90 degrees to the original hatch pattern.

    0=Disables hatch pattern doubling

    1=Enables hatch pattern doubling

### HPNAME

HPNAME sets the default hatch-pattern name. To set a default of no pattern name, enter a period (**.**), and HPNAME will be set to "". The name can be up to 34 characters long.

### HPSCALE

HPSCALE sets the default scale factor for hatch patterns. The value must be non-zero.

### HPSPACE

HPSPACE sets the default distance between lines in a user-defined hatch pattern. The value must be non-zero.

## 21 Insert Variables

The *insert variables* control the name and location of inserted objects.

### EXPLMODE

Blocks that contain equal X, Y, and Z scales will explode into their component objects. Blocks that are not equally scaled in the X, Y, and Z scales can also be exploded, but the results might not be as expected. For example, if a block that is not equally scaled contains a circle and is exploded, the circle will explode into ellipses. The EXPLMODE controls whether the EXPLODE command supports blocks that are not equally or uniformly scaled (NUS blocks).

> 0=Does not explode NUS blocks

> 1=Explodes NUS blocks

### INSBASE

INSBASE sets a current UCS 3D point in the current space as the insertion-base point for a drawing file. The default value is the WCS origin 0,0,0.

### INSNAME

INSNAME sets the default block name used by the INSERT and DDINSERT commands. The name cannot exceed 31 characters. Valid characters are letters, digits, and the dollar sign ($), hyphen (-), and underscore (_) characters. The name cannot include any eight-bit characters. Eight-bit characters use the character codes from 127 to 255. On DOS platforms, AutoCAD uses the extended IBM character set (DOS 850 code page). On UNIX and Windows systems, AutoCAD uses the ISO 8859/1 code page. To enter a default of no name, enter a period (.); INSNAME will be set to "". After you enter the name, AutoCAD converts the name to all uppercase.

### SHPNAME

SHPNAME sets the default block name used by the SHAPE command. The name cannot exceed 31 characters. Valid characters are letters, digits, and the dollar sign ($), hyphen (-), and underscore (_) characters. The name cannot include any eight-bit characters. Eight-bit characters use the character codes from 127 to 255. On DOS platforms, AutoCAD uses the extended IBM character set (DOS 850 code page). On UNIX and Windows systems, AutoCAD uses the ISO 8859/1 code page. To enter a default of no name, enter a period (.); SHPNAME will be set to "". After you enter the name, AutoCAD converts the name to all uppercase.

## 22 Xref Variables

The *xref variables* control the behavior of external reference drawings.

### VISRETAIN

VISRETAIN controls the behavior of the external referenced layer settings ON/OFF, Freeze/Thaw, Color, and Linetype. If VISRETAIN is set to 0 (the default), any changes to externally referenced layer settings aren't saved for the external reference file. If VISRETAIN is set to 1, any changes to externally referenced layer settings are saved for the external reference file.

> 1=ON. Changes to external reference layer settings for ON/OFF, Freeze/Thaw, Color, and Linetype are saved in the externally referenced file.

> 0=OFF. Changes to external reference layer settings for ON/OFF, Freeze/Thaw, Color, and Linetype are not saved in the externally referenced file (the default).

### XREFCTL

XREFCTL controls whether external reference log files (XLG) are written. The log file is created and then appended every time the Attach, Detach, and Reload options of the XREF command are used. The log file records the drawing name, the date and time of the operation, and the operation type. The XLG file name will be the same as the drawing.

---

**Caution**

AutoCAD continues to append to a log file once it is created. You should be careful to delete old XLG files or edit existing ones to prevent them from becoming too large.

---

## 23 Attribute Variables

The *attribute variables* control the existence of attributes and their display and editing properties.

### AFLAGS

AFLAGS sets the attribute flag for the ATTDEF and DDATTDEF commands. The value can be one of the following or the sum of any of the desired values.

> 0=No attribute modes are selected (the default).
>
> 1=The attribute value will be invisible.
>
> 2=The attribute value will be constant.
>
> 4=Verify the attribute value by reentering the value.
>
> 8=The attribute value is preset.

### ATTDIA

ATTDIA controls the use of the Enter Attributes dialog box when inserting blocks with attributes.

> 0=OFF. Use the Command: prompt to prompt for attribute values (the default).
>
> 1=ON. Use the Enter Attributes dialog box when inserting blocks with attributes.

### ATTMODE

ATTMODE controls the display of attribute values. The value can be one of the following:

> 0=OFF. All attribute values are invisible.
>
> 1=Normal, (the default). Attribute values are displayed according to their definition.
>
> 2=ON. All attribute values are visible.

### ATTREQ

ATTREQ controls the prompting for attribute values when a block with attributes is inserted.

> 0=OFF. Default values are used for all attributes.

1=ON. You are prompted for values when a block with attributes is inserted (the default).

## 24 Sketching Variables

The *sketching variables* control the behavior of the SKETCH command.

### SKETCHINC

SKETCHINC sets the SKETCH record increment.

> **Note**
>
> If you move the cursor fast enough, you can create sketch segments that are longer than the SKETCH record increment. This will not reset the value of SKETCHINC.

### SKPOLY

SKPOLY controls the use of lines versus polylines when the SKETCH command is in use.

0=OFF. Lines are drawn by the SKETCH command (the default).

1=ON. Polylines are drawn by the SKETCH command.

## 25 View and Viewport Variables

The *view and viewport variables* control the existence, size, and number of views and viewports.

### CVPORT

CVPORT lists the identification number of the current viewport.

### MAXACTVP

MAXACTVP sets the maximum number of viewports to regenerate. The default is 16.

### VIEWCTR

VIEWCTR holds the center point of the current viewport as a current UCS point.

### VIEWSIZE

VIEWSIZE holds the height of the current viewport in drawing units.

### VSMAX

VSMAX holds the upper-right corner of the current viewport's virtual screen. The point is in the current UCS. This point changes as the view is zoomed and regenerated.

### VSMIN

VSMIN holds the lower-left corner of the current viewport's virtual screen. The point is in the current UCS. This point changes as the view is zoomed and regenerated.

## 26 Dview Variables

The *dview variables* control the behavior of the DVIEW command. These variables are all read-only, so they are set by other commands.

### BACKZ

BACKZ holds the distance in drawing units from the target plane to the back clipping plane.

> **Note**
>
> BACKZ will have no effect if VIEWMODE does not include the four-bit code for back plane clipping.

### FRONTZ

FRONTZ holds the distance in drawing units from the target plane to the front clipping plane.

> **Note**
>
> FRONTZ will have no effect if VIEWMODE does not include the two-bit code for front plane clipping and the 16-bit code for front clip.

### LENSLENGTH

LENSLENGTH holds the length of the lens used for perspective viewing with the Distance option of the DVIEW command. The length is expressed in millimeters.

**Tip**

To prevent time-consuming drawing regenerations, avoid zooming beyond the edge of the current virtual screen, as defined by VSMAX and VSMIN.

**Appendixes**

## TARGET

TARGET holds the target point of the current viewport as a current UCS 3D point. The target is the point in the viewport you are looking directly at from the camera point.

## VIEWDIR

VIEWDIR holds the camera point of the current viewport as a current UCS 3D point. The camera is the point in space from which you look at the target point.

## VIEWMODE

VIEWMODE controls the view mode for the current viewport as a result of the DVIEW command. The value can be one of the following or the sum of the desired options.

> 0=OFF. Viewing is normal (the default).
>
> 1=Perspective mode is active.
>
> 2=Front clipping is allowed.
>
> 4=Back clipping is allowed.
>
> 8=The UCS follow mode is on.
>
> 16=The front clip plane is offset the distance in FRONTZ from the target plane rather than at the camera point stored in VIEWDIR.

## VIEWTWIST

VIEWTWIST holds the twist angle for the current viewport. The twist angle enables you to twist the view around the current line of sight from the camera point to the target point. The twist angle is measured in degrees, counterclockwise from 0, which always begins to the right.

**Tip**

If you are more comfortable entering values to the DVIEW and VPOINT commands from the current UCS rather than from the WCS, set WORLDVIEW to 0.

## WORLDVIEW

WORLDVIEW controls the automatic changing of the UCS to the WCS during the DVIEW and VPOINT commands. Both commands expect input to be relative to the current UCS so, by default, the current UCS changes to the WCS for ease of use.

> 0=OFF. The current UCS is not changed to the WCS when the DVIEW or VPOINT commands are issued.
>
> 1=ON. The current UCS is changed to the WCS when the DVIEW or VPOINT commands are issued (the default).

## 27 Shading Variables

The *shading variables* control the appearance of objects rendered with the SHADE command.

### FACETRES

When shading and rendering curved solids, their smoothness is determined by the value of the FACETRES system variable. Raising and lowering the value of FACETRES only affects solid objects. Valid values are from 0.01 to 10.0. A higher value increases the number of facet edges used to display the object.

### SHADEDGE

SHADEDGE controls the appearance of surface edges and faces when using the SHADE command. Valid entries are the following:

> 0=Faces are shaded; edges are not highlighted.
>
> 1=Faces are shaded; edges are drawn in the background color.
>
> 2=Faces are not shaded; edges are drawn in the object color.
>
> 3=Faces are shaded in the object color; edges are drawn in the background color (the default).

### SHADEDIF

SHADEDIF sets the percentage of diffused reflective light versus ambient light in the drawing. Diffused reflective light comes directly from the light source, which is at the camera point. Ambient light has no source, so it lights all surfaces to the same degree. As the diffused reflective light is increased or decreased, the ambient light is decreased or increased so that the light level is maintained at 100 percent.

## 28 Plotting Variables

The *plotting variables* control which plotter is made the default.

### PLOTID

PLOTID sets the current plotter, based on its assigned description. Plotter descriptions are set when the plotter is added to the configuration.

### PLOTTER

PLOTTER sets the current plotter, based on its assigned ID number. Plotter numbers are set when the plotter is added to the configuration. The value can be from 0 to the highest number of plotters currently configured. The maximum number of plotters is 29.

### PLOTROTMODE

PLOTROTMODE controls the orientation of plots.

> 0=Rotates the effective plotting area so that the corner with the Rotation icon aligns with the paper at the lower-left for 0, top-left for 90, top-right for 180, and lower-right for 270.

> 1=Aligns the lower-left corner of the effective plotting area with the lower-left corner of the paper. This is the default.

## 29 Font and Image Variables

*Font and image variables* affect fonts and image import/export capabilities. Release 13 supports Postscript and TrueType fonts. Besides, images can be imported and exported in a wide variety of formats, including PCX, GIF, TIF, and so on.

### FFLIMIT

You can limit the number of PostScript and TrueType fonts in memory by changing the value of FFLIMIT. To avoid filling up memory with fonts, keep the FFLIMIT value low. Valid values are from 0 to 100. If set to 0, there is no limit.

### FONTALT

If you attempt to load a drawing that contains a font your system does not have, AutoCAD automatically substitutes an alternate font. By default this is TXT.SHX. With the FONTALT system variable, you can specify the alternate font to be used when the specified font file cannot be located. If an alternate font is not specified, AutoCAD displays a warning.

### FONTMAP

When AutoCAD cannot find a font specified in your drawing, AutoCAD gives you the option of substituting a different font for it. The FONTMAP system variable specifies the font mapping file to be used when the specified font cannot be located. You can specify a different font mapping table file in the Windows Preferences dialog box.

### PSPROLOG

PSPROLOG sets which prologue section from the ACAD.PSF file is added to your PostScript output when you use PSOUT. Prologue codes are added to customize your PostScript output.

## PSQUALITY

PSQUALITY controls the appearance of PostScript images when they are imported into AutoCAD with the PSIN command.

> 0=Disables PostScript image generation. PostScript images are shown as a box outline.

> Positive=Determines the number of pixels per drawing unit that are used to render the PostScript image. The image will be filled.

> Negative=The absolute value of PSQUALITY determines the number of pixels per drawing unit that are used to render the PostScript image. The image is rendered as an outline only; it will not be filled.

## RASTERPREVIEW

RASTERPREVIEW controls whether drawing preview images are saved with the drawing and sets the format type. This allows an image of the drawing to be displayed in the Preview box.

> 0=BMP only

> 1=BMP and WMF

> 2=WMF only

> 3=No preview image created

## RIBACKG

RIBACKG can be used to change the background color number when importing raster images. Because imported raster files can create large drawing files, RIBACKG can be used to reduce the size of the imported image. This can be done by setting the display background color to the same color that makes up the majority of the raster image. This reduces the size of the imported image because areas of the image equal to the background are not converted to solid objects in the block.

## RIGAMUT

RIGAMUT can be used to reduce the size of imported GIF, TIF, and PCX raster images. This can be done by using RIGAMUT to specify the number of colors GIFIN, PCXIN, and TIFFIN use when they import a color image.

Limiting the number of colors in the imported raster image reduces its size because pixels in the imported image will be grouped together. Common settings for RIGAMUT are 8 and 16. RIGAMUT only specifies the number of colors that will be used to import the image, not the colors themselves. The colors used are the standard AutoCAD shades. For example, setting RIGAMUT to 2 does not produce black-and-white images. It creates black-and-red images because the only colors allowed are 0 (black) and 1 (red).

### RIASPECT

RIASPECT changes the image aspect ratio when you import GIF and TIF raster images. PCX files do not contain an aspect ratio. A raster image is brought in as a 2D solid object, with a specified pixel aspect ratio. A specified pixel aspect ratio is used to prevent circles from appearing as ellipses when the image is transported to different shaped displays. The RIASPECT image aspect ratio can be used to change the aspect ratio of GIF and TIF images. This can be useful if images are appearing on your screen as ellipses instead of circles. The RIASPECT ratio overrides any specification in the GIF or TIF file imported. Although you can specify a scale for the image when it is imported, the raster file will be uniformly scaled.

A useful RIASPECT setting is 0.8333, which is the ratio for importing VGA or MCGA images in $320 \times 200$ mode.

### RIEDGE

RIEDGE controls the edge detection feature when importing GIF, TIF, and PCX raster images. A common use for importing raster images is to use their outline as a guide, and trace over the image using AutoCAD's drafting tools. Because raster images are brought in as a block composed of 2D solid objects, they are normally erased when no longer needed. This is due to their large size, which can create large drawing sizes.

0=Disables edge detection

1–255=Sets the threshold for RIEDGE detection

The GIFFIN, PCXIN, and TIFFIN commands use the value for detecting features in the drawing. If you are going to use a raster image and trace over it, you can use RIEDGE to locate the edges of the features of the image.

### RIGREY

RIGREY imports a GIF, TIF, or PCX image as a grayscale image.

0=Disables grayscale image importing

>0=Converts each pixel in the image to a grayscale value

Importing raster images can create large drawing sizes. You can reduce the size of the drawing database by using RIGREY. Because AutoCAD has few shades of gray, importing an image using RIGREY reduces the size of the image in the drawing database while keeping the details of the imported image intact.

The grayscale value is based on the human eye response function defined for NTSC television (the YIQ color system).

### RITHRESH

RITHRESH can be used to control the brightness of an imported PCX, GIF, or TIF raster image.

> 0=Turns off RITHRESH.

> >0=Rasterin uses a brightness threshold filter. This will allow pixels with a luminance value greater than the RITHRESH value to be high-lighted in the foreground while dropping out darker pixels into the background.

RITHRESH can be used to make a a dark image appear brighter and more distinct. Setting RITHRESH to a value greater than 0 will drop out the darker background, importing only the brighter foreground material.

## 30 File-Name and Saving Variables

The *file-name* and *saving variables* control the file-access feature of AutoCAD. All the variables are read-only, so they are set with other commands.

### DWGNAME

DWGNAME holds the drawing name entered by the user, including any path the user may have entered. If the drawing has not been named, the default value is UNNAMED.

### DWGPREFIX

DWGPREFIX holds the drive and directory prefix for the drawing. This enables you to determine the current working directory.

### DWGTITLED

DWGTITLED lists whether the drawing has been named.

> 0=OFF. The drawing has not been named (the default).

> 1=ON. The drawing has been named.

## DWGWRITE

DWGWRITE holds the value of the read-only feature of the Open Drawing dialog box.

> 0=OFF. Opens the drawing for reading only; no editing is allowed.

> 1=ON. Opens the drawing for reading and writing (the default).

## SAVEFILE

SAVEFILE holds the name of the current file name used by the automatic-save feature. The default is AUTO.SV$.

## SAVENAME

SAVENAME holds the name to which you have saved the drawing. The default is "".

## SAVETIME

SAVETIME sets the length of time, in minutes, between automatic saves of the current drawing to the automatic-save file name stored in SAVEFILE. To disable the automatic-save feature, set SAVETIME to 0. The save-time counter begins after a change to the drawing, and is reset when AutoCAD initiates an automatic save or when the user issues a SAVE, SAVEAS, or QSAVE command.

# 31 Database Variables

The *database variables* control the structure, and thus the search speed, of the drawing database. They also indicate the level of change in the database as a result of editing.

## DBMOD

DBMOD indicates the level of modification to the current drawing. DBMOD will be the sum of following options that are selected:

> 1=The object database has been modified.

> 2=The symbol table has been modified.

> 4=A database variable has been modified.

> 8=A window has been modified.

> 16=A view has been modified.

### TREEDEPTH

TREEDEPTH sets the maximum number of spatial indexes or levels in the graphic tree. AutoCAD indexes objects based on their graphic location in a two-branch tree. One branch is a quad tree for paper space, and the other is a quad (for 2D) or octal (for 3D) tree for model space. The first two characters in TREEDEPTH specify the maximum number of levels in the model-space tree. The second two characters specify the maximum number of levels in the paper-space tree.

The tree performs best when it has more levels because there are fewer objects per level, which speeds searching. Unfortunately, the larger the tree, the more memory it takes, which can cause disk-swapping and negate any speed gains.

Usually you do not need to adjust the tree unless you have very little memory or very few objects compared to the amount of memory. If you have very little memory, you may need to shrink the tree to reduce the amount of memory it takes. If you have lots of memory, you can increase the depth of the tree to increase search speed.

### TREEMAX

TREEMAX sets a limit on the maximum number of nodes or levels in the graphic tree for the current memory configuration.

## 32 User-Assigned Variables

The *user-assigned variables* do not have a default value, and are intended for third-party developers. These variables are used to store numeric and string information about the drawing, which can be used by third-party developers. The user-assigned variables have no direct effect on the drawing.

### USERI1–5

USERI1–5 are five integer variables with no default value. They are saved with the drawing, and are intended for use by third-party developers.

### USERR1–5

USERR1–5 are five real variables with no default value. They are saved with the drawing, and are intended for use by third-party developers.

### USERS1–5

USERS1–5 are five string variables with no default value. They are not saved with the drawing, and are intended for use by third-party developers.

## 33 Macro Variables

The *macro variables* control the behavior of DIESEL expressions in macros.

### MACROTRACE

MACROTRACE controls the display of DIESEL expression evaluations. This is a debugging tool for DIESEL expressions.

> 0=OFF. MACROTRACE is disabled (the default).

> 1=ON. An evaluation of all DIESEL strings is displayed at the Command: prompt.

### MODEMACRO

MODEMACRO controls the display of strings and DIESEL expressions on the status line. You can enter a string or a DIESEL expression.

## 34 Date and Time Variables

The *date and time variables* store information on the dates, times, and durations of an editing session. All the variables are read-only, so they must be set by other commands.

### CDATE

CDATE is the current date and time in calendar format. Calendar format is a real number with the following values:

> YYYYMMDD.HHMMSSmsec

> YYYY=Year

> MM=Month

> DD=Day

> HH=Hour

> MM=Minutes

> SS=Seconds

> msec=milliseconds

### DATE

DATE is the current date and time in Julian-date format. Hours, minutes, and seconds are displayed in decimal format.

### TDCREATE

TDCREATE stores the drawing-creation date as a Julian number.

### TDINDWG

TDINDWG stores the total time that the drawing spends in the drawing editor in numbers of days.

### TDUPDATE

TDUPDATE stores the date and time of the last drawing update as a Julian date.

### TDUSTIMER

TDUSTIMER stores the elapsed time of the current drawing session in number of days.

## 35 Error Variables

The *error variables* give information on on-line program errors and the capability to reset those errors relative to peripheral input/output.

### ERRNO

ERRNO stores the error code produced by on-line applications such as AutoLISP and ADS programs.

### RE-INIT

RE-INIT reinitializes peripherals and the ACAD.PGP file. Valid entries are any of the following, or a sum of the desired options:

> 1=Reinitialize the digitizer port
>
> 2=Reinitialize the plotter port
>
> 4=Reinitialize the digitizer
>
> 8=Reinitialize the display
>
> 16=Reload the ACAD.PGP file

Appendixes

# Appendix D

# Working with Digitizers

This appendix covers the setup, configuration, and use of a digitizing tablet with AutoCAD for Windows. Specific areas of interest include a listing of tablets supported directly by AutoCAD and what you can do about tablets that are not supported by AutoCAD. The steps needed to customize the button portion of the AutoCAD menu are also discussed.

There are many different types of digitizers available on the market today ranging from small desktop tablets to large table-size tablets. A digitizer (tablet or mouse) is one of the most important peripherals you will use to supply information to AutoCAD. The type of information supplied to AutoCAD depends on your use of the digitizer. You can use a tablet to input commands from the overlay menu (the menu that you lay over the tablet), to trace over paper drawings, or simply as a system pointer (a mouse).

## Understanding the Digitizer's Buttons

Figure D.1 shows typical input devices for AutoCAD. These include two- and three-button mice and four- and sixteen-button digitizer pucks. The numbering of the buttons on these figures is an example of the typical button numbering on most devices. The button numbers may vary slightly (refer to your device's documentation) on your input device. Table D.1 lists the default operations performed in AutoCAD when each button is selected. Table D.2 lists operations of the buttons when Shift is pressed in combination with another key (for example, Shift+2). Ctrl and Ctrl+Shift plus button combinations are customizable.

Appendixes

**Fig. D.1**
Examples of
different input
devices.

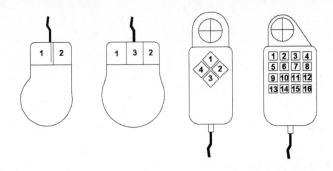

| Table D.1 | Default Button Operations |
|---|---|
| **Button** | **Operation Performed** |
| 1 | Primary Pick Button |
| 2 | Same as Enter on keyboard |
| 3 | Calls the POP0 Floating Menu (Object Snaps) |
| 4 | Two Control+C cancels |
| 5 | Toggles Snap mode on/off |
| 6 | Toggles Ortho mode on/off |
| 7 | Toggles Grid display on/off |
| 8 | Toggles Coordinate display on/off |
| 9 | Toggles Isoplane top/right/left |
| 10 | Toggles Tablet mode on/off |

| Table D.2 | Shift+Digitizer Button Operations |
|---|---|
| **Shift+Button** | **Operation Performed** |
| 1 | Not available |
| 2 | Calls the POP0 Floating Menu (Object Snaps) |
| 3–16 | Customizable |

> **Note**
>
> The exact words used when referring to the digitizer buttons vary a great deal in the many sources of digitizer documentation. Part of this confusion comes from the fact that AutoCAD allows you to program the digitizer buttons starting with the second button. This means that the first button in the customization is the second button on the digitizer, which creates general confusion over where to start counting buttons. For the purposes of documentation, Autodesk counts the Pick button as button one on the digitizer. When referring to customizing the digitizer buttons, Autodesk refers to the second digitizer button (quite sensibly) as either the second digitizer button or the first programmable button. For the purpose of this appendix, the term button one refers to the Pick button and button two refers to the second digitizer button and so on.

# Digitizers Supported by AutoCAD

The first step you have to take when setting up a digitizer is to tell AutoCAD which digitizer you are using. AutoCAD provides you with a list of supported digitizers (see Table D.3). If you are using a tablet or mouse that is not on the list, your tablet or mouse may emulate one that is on the list (often a Summigraphics tablet or Microsoft mouse). If not, you will have to contact the manufacturer of your digitizer to see if it provides current device drivers. Most will provide drivers for Windows, so at a minimum you can use a tablet as a "mouse." Many times the manufacturer will also include AutoCAD DOS and Windows ADI drivers.

Table D.3 lists the digitizers currently supported by AutoCAD and the corresponding dynamic link library files installed during setup. In future releases, some tablets may not be supported; these are marked with an asterisk (*) to indicate they are obsolete.

**Table D.3   Digitizers Supported by AutoCAD**

| Digitizer Model | Driver File |
| --- | --- |
| CalComp®2500 Series tablet | |
| CalComp® 3300 Series tablet | dgcal.dll |
| Hitachi® HDG Series tablet | dgphit.dll |

*(continues)*

| Table D.3 Continued | |
|---|---|
| **Digitizer Model** | **Driver File** |
| Kurta® Tablet IS/ONE* | dgkur1.dll |
| Kurta® Tablet IS/THREE* | |
| Kurta® Tablet XLC | dgkur23.dll |
| Kurta® Tablet XLP | |
| Summagraphics® MM Series tablet | |
| Summagraphics® Microgrid Series I & II | dgpsg.dll |
| System pointing device | |
| Wintab™ compatible tablets | dgwintab.dll |

Notice that one of the supported digitizers in Table D.3 is the system pointing device. The Windows system pointing device is usually a Microsoft or Logitech mouse. If you are using a mouse, choose the system pointer option when configuring your digitizer. AutoCAD uses the pointing device already defined and driven in Windows.

If you are using a tablet, you have two configuration options. The commands and options introduced here are explained later in this appendix:

■ The first tablet configuration combination is not very convenient, but works. You can install a tablet on one port and a mouse on another. Configure Windows to use the mouse as the system pointer. Configure AutoCAD to use the tablet driver for your particular tablet from the list in Table D.3. Use the TABLET command with the Configure (CFG) option to set up the tablet menu and screen pointing areas. After you are finished installing and configuring, you use the mouse in Windows Program Manager, all of your other Windows applications, and for making menu, toolbar, window, and dialog selections in AutoCAD. You use the tablet to pick screen points and select commands from the tablet menu. In effect you make menu, dialog, window, and toolbar selections with one hand and digitize with the other. Technically, you can use the tablet for all AutoCAD functions, but that requires you to move the crosshairs away from your work and to the menus. There is a certain grace and speed in this solution if you are ambidextrous. In the instances where you have to type however, you must either use your toes, grow an extra arm, or let go of the mouse or tablet puck.

■ The second tablet configuration combination offers a much simpler, if not equally entertaining, solution. Most tablet manufacturers provide a Wintab (*Windows tablet*) driver. Install the tablet and load the Wintab driver and then configure Windows to use the Wintab driver as the Windows system pointer. When you use a tablet and a Wintab driver, your tablet behaves like a mouse in all Windows applications. This keeps you from having to have a mouse for all your non-digitizer needs. Configure AutoCAD to use the Wintab compatible tablet option. This option allows you to use the tablet for both digitizing points and for making menu, dialog, window, and toolbar selections. As with any other tablet arrangement, you use the TABLET command and the Configure (CFG) option to set up the menus and screen pointing area on a Wintab tablet. This solution is less confusing, less prone to error of the hardware and software nature, and limits tendonitis to one arm.

---

**Caution**

It is possible to configure Windows to use the Wintab driver as the system pointer and then configure AutoCAD to use the system pointing device. You can use your tablet as you do a mouse but you can't digitize paper drawings, or more importantly, make tablet menu selections.

You also can make the logical mistake of considering the following solution: Install the tablet and use the Wintab driver to allow Windows to use the tablet like a mouse. Configure AutoCAD to use the tablet driver for your tablet from the list in Table D.3. Use the TABLET command with the Configure option to arrange the menu and screen pointer locations and spare yourself having to understand the Wintab driver. This logical solution runs into an equally logical snag, though not obvious to the casual user. As soon as you tell Windows that it can use the tablet as the system pointer, Windows takes control of the port into which the tablet is plugged. The tablet driver you try to use in AutoCAD cannot wrest control of the port from Windows so you can't complete the configuration. Also, in Release 13, Wintab is so improved that configuring a Wintab driver takes no effort.

---

# Configuring the Digitizer

As mentioned earlier, the first step in configuring the digitizer is to select the type of digitizer you have from the list of AutoCAD-supported tablets. One of these choices is the system pointer (which can be a mouse). Selection and setup of the digitizer are accessible through the Configuration menu. There are two ways to access the configuration menu:

- Choose Options, Configure.

  or

- At the Command: prompt, type **config**.

An informational screen that displays your current configuration is displayed first. Press Return as prompted until you are presented with the following Configuration menu:

```
Configuration menu

    0. Exit to drawing editor
    1. Show current configuration
    2. Allow detailed configuration
    3. Configure video display
    4. Configure digitizer
    5. Configure plotter
    6. Configure system console
    7. Configure operating parameters
```

For detailed information on other configurable properties of AutoCAD, including information on digitizers, see the *AutoCAD Installation Guide for Windows*.

> **Note**
>
> AutoCAD asks the basic questions necessary to configure your digitizer to work with AutoCAD. In some cases, your hardware or digitizer software may be set up in an unusual or nonstandard way. When this happens, you may have to specify additional information during configuration. To get all the configuration options for your particular digitizer, select option 2 from the configuration menu. This enables AutoCAD to ask detailed questions during configuration.

From the configuration menu choose option number 4, Configure digitizer. A list of supported digitizers (as listed previously in Table D.3) is displayed. If this isn't the first time you have configured a pointing device (mouse or digitizer), AutoCAD will prompt you with the message that follows, asking you if you want to select a new digitizer.

```
Your current digitizer is: Current System Pointing Device
Do you want to select a different one? <N>
```

For example, you might want to change digitizers if you initially set up AutoCAD to work with the mouse and now want to use a digitizing tablet.

Press N (for no) if you have already configured AutoCAD to use the correct digitizer and do not want to select a new one.

Press Y (for yes) to display the following list of supported devices:

```
Available digitizer:

1. Current System Pointing Device
2. Calcomp 2500 (obsolete) and 3300 Series ADI 4.2 - by
   Autodesk,Inc.
3. Hitachi HICOMSCAN HDG Series ADI 4.2 - by Autodesk, Inc.
4. Kurta IS/ONE, Series I (obsolete) ADI 4.2 - by Autodesk,
   Inc.
5. Kurta XLC, IS/THREE (obsolete) ADI 4.2 - by Autodesk,
   Inc.
6. Kurta XLP, ADI 4.2 - by Autodesk, Inc.
7. Summagraphics MicroGrid v1.1(Series II or later) ADI 4.2
   - by Autodesk, Inc.
8. Summagraphics MM Series v2.0, ADI 4.2 - by Autodesk,
   Inc.
9. Wintab Compatible Digitizer ADI 4.2 - by Autodesk, Inc.
```

If the tablet drivers supplied by the manufacturer (if any) have been installed, you'll see those listed here as well. Notice that all the drivers in the example above are "by Autodesk, Inc." Choose the appropriate device number.

If you choose "Wintab Compatible Digitizer" then the system level Wintab drivers (supplied by the manufacturer) must already be installed. If they are not installed, and you attempt to configure your digitizer as a Wintab device, you are presented with the error message dialog box as shown in figure D.2.

**Fig. D.2**
Wintab error message dialog box displayed when the driver is not installed.

Appendixes

> **Note**
>
> If you're using a mouse, select Current System Pointing Device. AutoCAD for Windows will automatically use the mouse driver already installed and in use under Windows.

For more information on Wintab™-Compatible Digitizers, see the "Wintab Compatible Digitizing Tablets" section later in this chapter, or refer to the AutoCAD installation guide for Windows.

After you have supplied the configuration information for your digitizer, exit the configuration menu and save the settings. This information is saved in the ACAD.CFG file.

Lastly, make sure your preferences are set correctly. From the Preferences dialog box, you can instruct AutoCAD to accept input from your digitizer (or mouse) in Digitizer Only mode or in Digitizer/Mouse. To access the Preferences dialog box, choose Options, Preferences.

If you select Digitizer Only, AutoCAD ignores the input from any mouse that is installed and ignores the tablet when you enter mouse mode areas like the menu or toolbar icons.

If you select Digitizer/Mouse, AutoCAD makes a judgment as to which device or device mode (mouse or tablet) is currently supplying input. For example, if you move the crosshairs to a menu or icon, you are in mouse mode. If you move the crosshairs to the screen, you are in digitizer mode.

The most common selection is Digitizer/Mouse. You would use Digitizer Only if you have a tablet and a mouse going at the same time in AutoCAD and are tracing a drawing on the tablet. Use Digitizer Only to disable the mouse so an accidental bump of the mouse does not move the crosshairs as you trace.

To enable AutoCAD to receive input under both mouse and digitizer modes, make sure that the Digitizer/Mouse mode is selected. After you accept the dialog box, AutoCAD automatically saves the settings to the ACAD.INI file. Figure D.3 shows a typical Preferences dialog box and settings.

> **Note**
>
> If you are configuring AutoCAD to work with a tablet, you'll have to run the TABLET command after configuration is complete. The TABLET command allows you to configure specific elements of the tablet such as the size and location of the tablet menus. The TABLET command is covered later in this appendix in the section "Using a Tablet Overlay Menu."

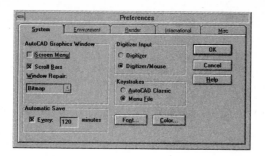

Typical digitizer
input settings in
the Preferences
dialog box.

In review, the steps for setting up a digitizer under AutoCAD for Windows are
as follows:

1. Set up the digitizing tablet. If the tablet has a power cord, plug it in.
   Plug the tablet's serial cable to one of the PC's COM ports.

2. Install the Wintab drivers supplied by the digitizer manufacturer (if not
   already installed). You may need to exit Windows to do this.

3. Configure Windows to use the digitizer.

4. Configure AutoCAD for the digitizer (Wintab Compatible Digitizer as
   an example).

5. Save the configuration and exit back to AutoCAD.

6. Make sure the Digitizer Input option under Preferences is set to
   Digitizer/Mouse.

7. If you have a tablet, use the TABLET command to configure the tablet
   overlay menu, and Fixed and Floating screen pointing areas. This topic
   is covered in more detail in the next sections, "Fixed and Floating
   Screen Pointing Areas" and "Using a Tablet Overlay Menu."

The tablet should be ready for use.

### Note

If your digitizer is a mouse rather than a tablet, follow the same basic steps. Install the
mouse hardware, install the mouse software, configure AutoCAD to use the mouse,
and make sure the Digitizer Input option on the Preferences dialog is set to Digitizer/
Mouse. You don't have to run the TABLET command because a mouse doesn't have
any features to configure.

**Appendixes**

## Fixed and Floating Screen Pointing Areas

For some users, setting up a tablet in Release 12 for Windows that could be used as both a system pointer in Windows, and a system pointing device (mouse, relative mode) and a digitizer (absolute mode) in AutoCAD, was a real nightmare. AutoCAD Release 12 introduced primary and secondary *mole* areas. The actual process of setting up a tablet was quite simple—the trick was figuring out how to do it to begin with. Release 13 has simplified the use of a tablet with Windows and AutoCAD. Now, there are no "mole modes." This has been replaced and improved with "Fixed" and "Floating" screen pointing areas. This section explains the problems inherent in using a tablet with AutoCAD for Windows and how AutoCAD solves these problems. For information on configuring the Fixed and Floating Screen Pointing areas, see the "Using a Tablet Overlay Menu" section later in this chapter.

You can only access pull-down menus, toolbars, dialog boxes, and interact with other Windows applications when you are in a screen area. (It doesn't matter whether the screen area is fixed or floating.) When you are picking commands off the tablet overlay menu you can't be in a screen pointing area (either fixed or floating). To draw objects in AutoCAD you must be in a fixed screen area, a floating screen area, or in a digitizer area if you are tracing a drawing (and have used the TABLET command and On option). While inside a screen pointing area, you can't trace a drawing into AutoCAD, because you cannot calibrate the tablet inside either a floating or fixed screen area (calibrating for tracing is explained later in the section "Using the Digitizer").

The following paragraphs discuss how Autodesk envisions people will use the fixed and floating screen areas with a tablet under AutoCAD for Windows.

AutoCAD users like to interact with other Windows applications and need to access AutoCAD's pull-down menus, toolbars, and dialog boxes. To do this, the digitizer needs to map, not to the AutoCAD drawing window, but to the entire Windows screen (thus including the Windows features and AutoCAD menus). Therefore, the fixed screen area was born. When users install and configure AutoCAD, the fixed screen area covers the entire tablet so users will notice that the entire surface of the tablet maps to their entire monitor. Of course the term "fixed screen area" is a bit of a misnomer because the size and position of the screen area can be changed through the TABLET command and Configure (CFG) option, but after the tablet is configured the fixed area stays fixed in size and location. The entire Windows screen maps to the fixed area. The tablet acts like a mouse whenever the puck is in the fixed screen area. The tablet acts like a digitizer whenever the puck is outside the fixed screen area and on the tablet overlay menus.

A problem with this approach arises when the user wants to digitize drawings into AutoCAD (after calibrating the tablet). The user can't calibrate the tablet for tracing when the fixed screen area exists because the fixed area is mapped to the entire screen already, throwing off the digitizer mapping whenever the puck is inside the fixed area. To solve this, the fixed screen area is turned off whenever Tablet mode is turned ON.

Here is the dilemma. What happens to the poor user who is digitizing a drawing into AutoCAD and wants to access the pull-down menus or toolbar? Because the fixed screen pointing area is off, the user is trapped inside AutoCAD's drawing screen and, without reaching for a real mouse on her desktop, she is out of luck. This is where the floating screen area comes into use. When the user presses F12 (or the button on her puck that she configured for the floating screen area toggle button), the floating screen area comes into existence right under her puck (regardless of its location) and gives her access to the entire monitor just like the fixed screen area did. To return to digitizing the drawing, the user turns off the floating screen area with the F12 key (or the toggle button).

Note that the digitizer acts like a mouse in either the fixed or floating screen areas. Also, it's possible to bring up the floating screen area when TABLET is OFF.

Also, note that at the bottom-right corner of the AutoCAD window are indicators to show whether TABLET is ON or OFF and whether FLOAT (the floating screen area) is ON or OFF.

Users familiar with Release 12's mole areas will be happy with this improvement. They may however, express one additional concern regarding the digitizer button programming. The details on button programming are explained later in this chapter in the section "Customizing the Buttons." This material is presented here for the benefit of Release 12 users who are already familiar with tablets and customizing.

In Release 12, the digitizer buttons are controlled by the Windows system pointer driver when you are in a mole area. The best you can do for programming the Windows system pointer is to assign generic "Left pick," "Right pick," "Middle pick" Windows-style actions to the buttons. You can't assign AutoCAD specific tasks. This means that while in a mole area, your digitizer buttons ignore the button programming in the ACAD.MNU file. The Right, Left, and Middle pick settings allow you to have three buttons behave in a standard manner, but you can't assign any other meaningful tasks to the

**Appendixes**

remainder of the buttons. Because the most logical place for the mole area is directly over the screen area, the number 4 and greater digitizer buttons are essentially useless most of the time.

Release 13 offers a novel and simple solution to this problem. All the button programming is controlled by AutoCAD in the ACAD.MNU file. While your puck is in the fixed screen pointing area, AutoCAD uses the built-in system pointer part of ACAD.MNU (\*\*\*AUX1) to assign Pick and Enter to the first and second buttons. All the other buttons are programmed from the standard pointer area of the ACAD.MNU file (\*\*\*BUTTONS1). Because AutoCAD assigns Pick and Enter to buttons one and two and your other buttons are programmed as usual, your buttons work as expected no matter where the puck is placed on the digitizer. Along with being essentially transparent to the end user, this solution also agrees with the general structure of the ACAD.MNU file so it is logical. Again, the terms introduced in this area are all explained in the following sections.

## Using a Tablet Overlay Menu

AutoCAD provides many different ways to enter commands and command options, one of which is the tablet overlay menu. Commands and options to commands are laid out in logical order. See figure D.4 for an example of the default AutoCAD tablet overlay menu.

To use the tablet menu, you must first configure AutoCAD to accept input from the overlay. Using the TABLET command with the CFG (Configure) option, you can pick key points on the menu which in turn define the various tablet menu areas. In the ACAD.MNU file, these menu sections are labeled as \*\*\*TABLET1 through \*\*\*TABLET4. Each section is customizable, but typically only the \*\*\*TABLET1 section is customized. Each tablet section has a donut at its upper-left, lower-left, and lower-right corners. See figure D.5 (note that this is the standard AutoCAD overlay for a 12 × 12 tablet, and that customized menus for larger tablets may look different). To access the TABLET command do one of the following:

■ Choose <u>O</u>ptions, <u>T</u>ablet, <u>C</u>onfigure.

   or

■ At the Command: prompt type tablet.

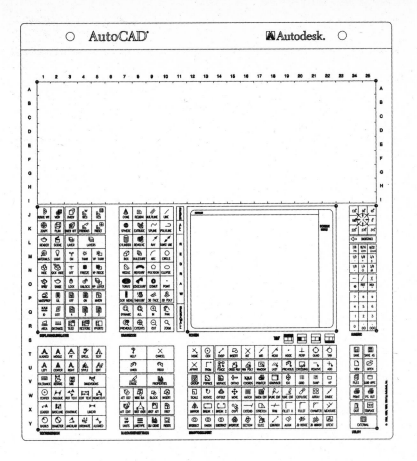

**Fig. D.4**
AutoCAD Release 13 Tablet Overlay Menu.

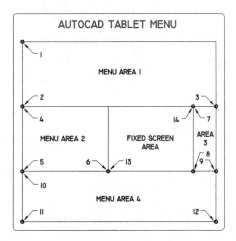

AUTOCAD TABLET MENU

MENU AREA 1

MENU AREA 2

FIXED SCREEN AREA

AREA 3

MENU AREA 4

**Fig. D.5**
The four menu areas, the screen pointing area, and the picking order for tablet configuration.

The steps that follow are used to show the typical responses while configuring your tablet overlay menu using the TABLET command. If you are using a customized tablet menu, your responses will vary. See Table D.4 as needed for information on the number of rows and columns in each tablet area.

1. Start AutoCAD.

2. Choose Options, Tablet, Configure.

3. At the `Option (ON/OFF/CAL/CFG):` prompt, enter **cfg.**

4. When prompted, enter the number of menus desired.

   `Enter number of tablet menus desired (0-4)<0>: 4.`

5. Now pick the upper-left, lower-left, and lower-right corners for menu area number 1 (points 1, 2, and 3 on figure D.5).

6. Notice that at the `Enter the number of columns for menu area 1:1 to 4991 <25>:` prompt, the default is already set to 25 for you. Simply press Enter to accept the default.

7. Accept the default at the `Enter the number of rows for menu area 1:1 to 1839 <9>:` prompt.

8. Continue picking points for menu areas 2, 3, and 4 and accepting the defaults for number of columns and rows. The pick points for menu area 2 are 4, 5, and 6; for menu area 3 they are 7, 8, and 9; and for menu area 4 they are 10, 11, and 12. (See Table D.4.) The values for tablet area 3 are surprisingly large, but they are correct.

| Table D.4   Tablet Areas and Their Sizes | | |
|---|---|---|
| **Defaults** | **Columns** | **Rows** |
| Tablet Area 1 | 25 | 9 |
| Tablet Area 2 | 11 | 9 |
| Tablet Area 3 | 9 | 13 |
| Tablet Area 4 | 25 | 7 |

When you are finished entering the menu areas, you are prompted with:

9. `Do you want to specify the Fixed Screen Pointing Area?<N>:` enter **Y.**

10. Digitize the lower-left and upper-right corners of the screen pointing area (at points 13 and 14).

11. `Do you want to specify the Floating Screen Pointing Area?<Y>:` enter **Y** if you want to specify the size or **N** if you want it to be the same size as the Fixed Screen Pointing area.

12. If you answered Yes, pick again at points 13 and 14.

13. When asked `Would you like to specify a button to toggle the Floating Screen Pointing Area?<N>:` enter **Y** if you would, or **N** to use F12 to toggle (you may still use F12 to toggle even if you designate a toggle button on your puck).

## Wintab™-Compatible Digitizing Tablets

Wintab, much like ADI (Autodesk Device Interface), is an industry-standard API (Application Programmers Interface) for advanced pointing devices such as digitizers. Wintab specifications allow AutoCAD to communicate with digitizers without writing specific drivers for a tablet. If your tablet came with Wintab drivers, AutoCAD will work with it just fine.

Wintab works in three steps. First you must install the Wintab-compatible driver supplied to you from the tablet manufacturer. Without this driver being loaded, Windows and AutoCAD will not be able to communicate with your digitizer (by calls to the Wintab driver, wintab.dll). Second, you configure Windows to use the Wintab driver as the system pointer. Third, you configure AutoCAD as a "Wintab-compatible tablet." This ADI handles communications between AutoCAD and the Wintab driver.

Setting up your digitizer as a Wintab tablet allows you to use your tablet in both absolute and relative modes (digitizer and mouse modes). As an alternative, you can select `System Pointing Device` during configuration but are then limited to using the relative (mouse) mode.

If your tablet manufacturer does not supply Wintab drivers, you will not be able to use your digitizer as a system pointer (mouse) in Windows and as a digitizer/mouse under AutoCAD for Windows. In some cases, digitizers of this nature emulate SummaGraphics tablets and you can use the SummaGraphics Wintab driver. If you are using one of the regular ADI tablet drivers supplied by Autodesk for your tablet (not Wintab), you can still use both the Fixed and Floating Screen Pointing areas. While AutoCAD is running, you can toggle to the Floating Screen Pointing area and interact with other Windows applications. When AutoCAD is inactive, digitizers not using the Windows tablet driver do not function as pointing devices in Windows (system pointer).

## Customizing the Buttons

Whether you are using a two- or three-button mouse or a digitizer with a four- or sixteen-button puck, you can customize what AutoCAD does when certain buttons are pressed. Four sections of the ACAD.MNU (when compiled, ACAD.MNC) control the behavior of the buttons. The sections are called ***BUTTONS1, ***BUTTONS2, ***AUX1, and ***AUX2.

The ***BUTTONS1 and ***BUTTONS2 sections correspond exactly to ***AUX1 and ***AUX2. They use the same format and contain the same information. Which section is used depends on your digitizer. If you have a built-in system pointer (Windows/NT, Macintosh, and SPARCstations), AutoCAD uses the ***AUX1 and ***AUX2 menus. AutoCAD will also use the ***AUX1 and ***AUX2 menus if you are using a tablet and the puck is in a Fixed or Floating Screen Pointing area. The ***BUTTONS1 and ***BUTTONS2 sections are used if you have a separate pointer driver (DOS and Windows). AutoCAD also uses the ***BUTTONS1 and ***BUTTONS2 when you are using a tablet and the puck is outside a screen area (when you are making tablet menu selections or digitizing a drawing).

By default, AutoCAD uses the appropriate ***BUTTONS1 or ***AUX1 section. The ***BUTTONS2 and ***AUX2 sections contain alternative programming for the buttons. To use the alternative programming, you simple press and hold the Shift key while picking a digitizer button.

You can customize all the buttons on your mouse or digitizer puck except the primary pick button. For example, on a mouse, the primary pick button is usually the left button. On a digitizer's puck the pick button is usually the first button (usually button 0 or 1 depending on whether your brand of digitizer starts labeling its buttons with 0 or 1). To customize the buttons you edit the ***BUTTONS and ***AUX sections of your ACAD.MNU file.

The ACAD.MNU file is simply an ASCII text file that can be edited using almost any ASCII text editor, such as EDIT under MS-DOS. Word processing programs such as Microsoft Write or Word for Windows can be used as well, but you must save the edited menu file in text mode only. AutoCAD doesn't know what to do with the control characters used in a program such as Word, and this causes an error. Under Microsoft Windows, the default ASCII text editor is Notepad, but you will most likely not be able to use this to edit ACAD.MNU. The menu file is too large for Notepad, and you'll receive an error message stating this.

Here is a listing of the ACAD.MNU file button menus section. This is the section that you customize regarding the actions that take place with each button on your mouse or puck.

```
//
//  Begin AutoCAD Button Menus
//

***BUTTONS1
;
$p0=*
^C^C
^B
^O
^G
^D
^E
^T

***BUTTONS2
$p0=*


***AUX1
;
$p0=*
^C^C
^B
^O
^G
^D
^E
^T

***AUX2
$p0=*
```

The ***BUTTONS1 and ***AUX1 sections start with the line ; (semicolon), which instructs AutoCAD to issue a carriage return (like hitting the Enter key on the keyboard). This is NOT the first button on the digitizer puck or mouse. Remember, the first button (or primary pick button) can't be customized.

Table D.5 breaks down what each of the lines in the default ***BUTTONS1 and ***AUX1 sections of the menu do.

**Table D.5   Digitizer Buttons and Their Functions**

| Button | Menu Option | Operation Performed |
| --- | --- | --- |
| 2 | ; | Same as Enter on keyboard |
| 3 | $p0=* | Calls the POP0 Floating Menu (Object Snaps) |
| 4 | ^C^C | Two Control+C cancels |

(continues)

| Button | Menu Option | Operation Performed |
|--------|-------------|---------------------|
| 5 | ^B | Toggles Snap mode on/off |
| 6 | ^O | Toggles Ortho mode on/off |
| 7 | ^G | Toggles Grid display on/off |
| 8 | ^D | Toggles Coordinate Display on/off |
| 9 | ^E | Toggles Isoplane Top/Right/Left |
| 10 | ^T | Toggles Tablet mode on/off |

**Table D.5    Continued**

On a 16-button puck there is plenty of room for growth—but even if you do not have a 16-button puck you have some options for customizing AutoCAD. As previously mentioned, the ACAD.MNU file sports a ***BUTTONS2 and ***AUX2 section. The menu options in this section are used when you hold down the Shift key and select a button on your mouse or puck. Besides ***BUTTONS2, you can add a ***BUTTONS3 and ***BUTTONS4 and/or ***AUX3 and ***AUX4 sections. These alternative button sections are activated by holding down the Ctrl and Ctrl+Shift keys and selecting a button. The rule that applies to ***BUTTONS1 still holds true here; there is no customization of the primary pick button.

In general, with a 16-button puck, you may find you have more configuration options than you can keep track of. Be sure to explore other avenues of customization, like adding commands to the ***TABLET1 section of the menu. Those of you with a two- or three-button mouse or a four-button puck may find that having four button sections is very useful. With a two-button mouse you can have as many as four customizable buttons by using Shift+Right button, Ctrl+Right button, and Ctrl+Shift+Right button. With a four-button puck, your options grow to 12.

In the example that follows, you customize the buttons menu by adding the ability to use the REDRAWALL command from one of the buttons. In the first example you add this option to the ***BUTTONS1 menu for a 16-button puck. In the next example, you add REDRAWALL to the ***BUTTONS2 section (for those of you who don't have 16-button pucks).

**Fig. D.6**
An example of a
16-button puck
from Calcomp®.

Customize the menu by following the steps. You should make a backup copy of the ACAD.MNU file before starting this exercise.

16-button puck users follow these steps:

1. Open the ACAD.MNU menu file into the text editor of your choice (for example, Word for Windows, Write (no conversion), or MS-DOS EDIT).

2. Scroll down until you see the section labeled ***BUTTONS1.

3. Add a blank line below ^T and enter the text **_REDRAWALL** (including the (_) underscore) on the blank line.

```
***BUTTONS1
;
$p0=*
^C^C
^B
^O
^G
^D
^E
^T
_REDRAWALL
```

4. Save your changes.

**Appendixes**

> **Note**
>
> If you use a professional word processing package such as Microsoft Word, be sure to save your changes as text only. Some packages refer to this as non-document mode. Some word processors allow you to save as text or text with breaks (meaning a carriage return at the end of each line). If your word processor makes this distinction, use the text file with breaks.

5. Return to AutoCAD and reload the menu using the MENU command. The menu automatically recompiles into ACAD.MNC.

6. Try out your changes by pressing the eleventh button.

Three-button mice and four-button puck users, follow these steps:

1. Open the ACAD.MNU menu file into the text editor of your choice (examples: Word for Windows, Write (no conversion), or MS-DOS EDIT).

2. Scroll down until you see the section labeled ***BUTTONS2.

3. Below the line $p0=* add the line **_REDRAWALL** (including the underscore).

   ```
   ***BUTTONS2
   $p0=*
   _REDRAWALL
   ```

4. Save your changes.

> **Note**
>
> If you use a professional word processing package such as Microsoft Word, be sure to save your changes as text only. Some packages refer to this as non-document mode). Some word processors allow you to save as text or text with breaks (meaning a carriage return at the end of each line). If your word processor makes this distinction, use the text file with breaks.

5. Return to AutoCAD and reload the menu using the MENU command. The menu automatically recompiles into ACAD.MNC.

6. Hold down the Shift key and press the right button on the mouse.

Two-button mouse users, follow these steps:

1. Open the ACAD.MNU menu file into the text editor of your choice (examples: Word for Windows, Write (no conversion), or MS-DOS EDIT).

2. Scroll down until you see the section labeled `***BUTTONS2`.

3. Below the line `$p0=*` add a new buttons section. Label this section `***BUTTONS3` and add the line **_REDRAWALL** (including the underscore).

   ```
   ***BUTTONS2
   $p0=*

   ***BUTTONS3
   _REDRAWALL
   ```

4. Save your changes.

5. Return to AutoCAD and reload the menu using the MENU command. The menu automatically recompiles into ACAD.MNC.

6. Hold down the Ctrl key and press the right button on your mouse.

For those who dabble in customizing AutoCAD, you may have seen the use of a period (.) and/or an underscore (_) in menus. Non-interactive commands (for example, those from the menu, scripts, and so on) have to be preceded by an underscore (_). This is standard practice in the menu files. The underscore tells AutoCAD to translate the command into the native language currently in use. A period (.) tells AutoCAD to use its internal command definition in case someone redefined the command name you are using for their own purposes. In fact, if you look at ACAD.MNU you will see the _REDRAWALL command already used in a different section. The command you should use when customizing is _.REDRAWALL, or just _REDRAWALL.

The previous example on customizing the `***BUTTONS1` menu section to include the .REDRAWALL command is a good real world demonstration but misses an opportunity to drive home the difference between the screen areas (fixed or floating) and the tablet area. The following example does not necessarily demonstrate a customization that would make good sense in everyday use, but as an experiment, it's an excellent demonstration of the difference between the screen and tablet area.

**Appendixes**

> **Note**
>
> For mouse users, this may make interesting reading, but you can't do the example because you do not have fixed/floating/tablet areas.

If you have just started AutoCAD or have not been tracing a drawing on the tablet, Tablet mode is off. If you have not configured your tablet with the TABLET command and CFG option, the digitizer is just one big fixed screen area. If you have configured your tablet with TABLET, the fixed area will correspond to the area you configured.

If you put the _REDRAWALL command in place of the RETURN (;) command rather than after the TABLET ON '^T' command in the ***BUTTONS1 section, and then reload the menu using the MENU command, something interesting happens when you press button two (the one after the pick button) while the puck is in the fixed screen area. You get a Return, not _REDRAWALL. What happened? It is not a bug in AutoCAD as you might first suspect. In fact, AutoCAD is taking its command from the ***AUX1 section of the menu file that specifies a Return or (;) for the first button. As previously mentioned, whenever the digitizer puck is inside a screen area, regardless of whether it is fixed or floating, the digitizer acts like a built-in system mouse that uses the ***AUX menus. The pick button and the very next button are the left and right mouse buttons respectively. All the other buttons do map to the ***BUTTONS1 section of the menu file, so strictly speaking the digitizer is not exactly emulating a mouse.

To continue this example, if the user turns Tablet mode ON by CALibrating the digitizer, button two (the one after the pick button) will now issue the _REDRAWALL command.

# Using the Digitizer

A digitizing tablet can be used in one of three ways:

- As a mouse for selecting points, using pull-down menus, interacting with dialog box options, and so on.

- As an alternative command input device (picking the commands off the tablet menu).

- As a digitizer for tracing paper drawing into AutoCAD.

See Appendix E, "Tracing Existing Drawings," for more information about using the digitizer to trace paper drawings into AutoCAD.

For more information on the TABLET command, see the *AutoCAD Command Reference*.

The largest percentage of digitizers in use are $12 \times 12$ models, therefore this example applies directly to this size of digitizer. To trace paper drawings using your digitizer, follow these steps:

1. Secure the paper drawing onto the tablet. Make sure the drawing does not exceed the active digitizing area of your tablet.

2. Use the TABLET command with the CAL option to calibrate the paper drawing to AutoCAD coordinates. Select points on your paper drawing of which you know the coordinates.

In tablet calibration, more calibration points are not necessarily better than fewer, more accurate points. If you know that your drawing is dimensionally accurate, you should use two points for calibration (orthogonal). If the drawing is skewed in two dimensions (for example, if lines that should be at right-angles are not), use the three-point or affine calibration. For any distortion worse than that, use four or more points for the projective transformation.

While digitizing your paper drawing, you can toggle Tablet mode on and off using the F12 function key. This is provided so that you can use your tablet to pick commands and options off the pull-down and screen menus. Also, you can make Windows selections because the floating screen area responds to your Windows area selections.

After you are finished tracing the paper drawing, turn tablet mode off. If you have any problems and need to reconfigure the tablet overlay menu (if you are using one), see the section "Using an Tablet Overlay Menu" for guidance.

# From Here...

For more information about working with digitizers, see the following appendixes:

■ Appendix B, "Installing and Configuring," explains how to install and configure AutoCAD including information on digitizers.

■ Appendix E, "Tracing Existing Drawings," explains the finer details of using a tablet to trace a drawing.

Appendixes

# Appendix E

# Tracing Existing Drawings

Chances are good that your office has both AutoCAD and manually drafted drawings. The manually drafted drawings were either created before your office switched to CAD, or were produced in departments that use both CAD and manual drafters. This appendix discusses procedures to use if you need to convert a manually drafted drawing to AutoCAD format.

In this appendix, you learn how to digitize a drawing. Digitizing a drawing is the process of converting a paper drawing to digital (AutoCAD) format. There are different methods for digitizing drawings: you can scan the drawings and import the resulting files into AutoCAD, or you can trace the drawings in AutoCAD.

If you only have to make a few conversions, and you have sufficient time, the most convenient way to convert existing drawings is to trace them. As long as you use a digitizer for input, and not a mouse, you can trace drawings using functions in AutoCAD. You don't need any other tools or programs. AutoCAD functions ensure that what you enter into AutoCAD represents the original drawing.

Tracing works well, but it can be time-consuming and tedious. Also, the accuracy of the finished drawing can be less than desired. A great deal depends on the quality and accuracy of the prints you are tracing. If you need an accurate drawing, your time may be better spent drawing the print from start. If you have to put a substantial number of paper drawings into AutoCAD, you'll also want to consider other means. This appendix discusses those other methods preferable to tracing. Scanning the drawings and then using raster-to-vector conversion software to get the drawings into AutoCAD or using a raster file viewing program are discussed.

# Conversion by Tracing

If you only have a few drawings to convert, and they aren't very complex, tracing them provides the most direct and economical way to put them into AutoCAD format. In the tracing process, you perform the following three steps:

- Attach the paper drawing to your digitizer

- Calibrate your digitizer so AutoCAD can accurately interpret what you trace

- Use AutoCAD's object creation commands to trace the drawing

Before you see the process in detail, however, a word about digitizers.

## Large and Small Digitizers

If you have to trace large (D- or E-size) drawings, a D- or E-size digitizer is the most convenient size to use. You can attach and trace the entire sheet to create a single AutoCAD drawing. If you use a smaller digitizer, you have to trace the drawing in sections and stitch the sections together later in AutoCAD to re-create the full drawing.

A larger digitizer offers another advantage. If you have a small digitizer and you use its entire surface for digitizing, you have to reconfigure your digitizer to remove all your tablet menu areas when you want to trace a drawing. Each time you want to stop tracing and go back to using your digitizer as a pointing device, you have to reconfigure your tablet menus. The process is repeated every time you want to trace. With a large digitizer, you can reserve a spot outside of the digitizing area to keep your tablet menu areas permanently configured. You can use the menu areas by simply turning off Tablet mode with the TABLET OFF command. When you want to continue digitizing, use TABLET ON.

Price may be an obstacle to acquiring a large digitizer. Large digitizers typically cost a thousand dollars or more. If you're going to trace only one or two drawings, you may not be able to justify the cost and you probably can make do with a 12" × 12" or 12" × 18" digitizer. If you have to trace many D-size or larger drawings, however, and still can't afford to buy a large digitizer, you may be able to borrow or lease one from another company or an AutoCAD dealer.

Whichever size digitizer you decide to use, the digitizing process itself remains the same. The following sections discuss the digitizing process.

## Attaching a Drawing to the Digitizer

Before you can begin tracing the drawing, you must first attach it to your digitizer. There isn't anything too technically difficult here; taping the drawing to the digitizer with *masking* tape works fine (don't use drafting tape—it isn't sticky enough). Attach the drawing in a way that it won't move while you're digitizing it. The drawing doesn't have to be aligned squarely with the digitizer; AutoCAD can account for that. The drawing should be taut with all the wrinkles, bumps, and folds smoothed out. Many digitizers offer a plastic overlay to protect tablet menus and to help keep digitized drawings smooth and in place while tracing.

## Tablet Calibration: The TABLET Command

After you attach the drawing to your digitizer, but before you can begin tracing, you must use AutoCAD's TABLET command to calibrate the digitizer. Calibration consists of picking points on the taped-down drawing and then giving AutoCAD the *x* and *y* coordinates of those points. AutoCAD calculates the distance between the points, thus establishing the correct drawing scale. AutoCAD requires that you enter at least three sets of points and coordinates for a tablet to be calibrated properly. Then, if you trace a line that is one inch long, AutoCAD knows that it's really one foot, one meter, or one mile long.

To use the TABLET command, follow these steps:

1. Type **tablet** at the AutoCAD Command: prompt. AutoCAD prompts:

   ```
   Option (ON/OFF/CAL/CFG):
   ```

2. Type **cal** (or **ca**) to begin calibration. AutoCAD prompts:

   ```
   Digitize point #1:
   Enter coordinates point #1:
   Digitize point #2:
   Enter coordinates point #2:
   Digitize point #3 (or RETURN to end):
   Enter coordinates point #3:
     .
     .
     .
   ```

Digitize in this context simply means to pick points on the drawing with your digitizer's puck or stylus. Continue to digitize as many points as you want. You shouldn't need to digitize more than four points at various locations on the paper drawing to obtain an accurate calibration.

As you can see from the command prompts, you must already know the "on-the-ground" coordinates of the points you pick. AutoCAD then can accurately record the drawing as you trace it.

**Tip**

The number of points you pick (you must pick at least two) determines the type of transformation AutoCAD uses for calibrating the tablet.

After you pick all the points, AutoCAD continues the calibration process by displaying a statistical table reporting the results of its calculations (see Table E.1).

| Table E.1 Three Calibration Points | | | |
|---|---|---|---|
| **Transformation type:** | **Orthogonal** | **Affine** | **Projective** |
| **Outcome of fit:** | **Success** | **Exact** | **Impossible** |
| RMS Error: | 0.1779 | | |
| Standard deviation: | 0.0674 | | |
| Largest residual: | 0.2277 | | |
| At point: | 1 | | |
| Second-largest residual: | 0.2277 | | |
| At point: | 3 | | |

This information might not mean much to you unless you're a statistician. The following list adds some clarification:

- *Transformation type.* Tablet transformation is the process of equating points on the digitizer with points in the drawing's coordinate system. AutoCAD supports three types of transformations. Which type you choose depends on the condition of the drawing you trace, the number of points you digitize, and whether AutoCAD is successful in fitting your points to that transformation type. The following are the three transformation types:

    **Orthogonal.** The orthogonal type requires that you digitize at least two points. Use it on drawings that you know are drawn accurately—that haven't, for example, been stretched in either the *x* or *y* dimension. If you digitize only two points, AutoCAD selects the orthogonal transformation automatically.

    **Affine.** The affine transformation requires that you digitize at least three points. You can use it on drawings that you know have been stretched in either the *x* or *y* dimension, relative to the other, and where lines that are supposed to be parallel actually are.

**Tip**

If you choose more than four points, AutoCAD may take awhile to calculate the projective transformation. Press Escape at any time to signal AutoCAD to stop calculating and provide the solution based on what it has done.

**Projective.** Requiring four digitized points, the projective transformation projects a perspective view of the drawing's plane onto the digitizer's plane. In effect, projective stretches different parts of the tablet by different amounts, as if you pulled a thin rubber sheet over a three-dimensional object. You should use this transformation if parallel lines on the drawing are not actually parallel, as in a perspective drawing, or if the drawing is inaccurately drawn.

■ *Outcome of fit.* You can see one of the following responses in the Transformation Type columns described previously:

**Exact.** You picked the precise number of points required for the transformation.

**Success.** You picked more than enough points to satisfy the transformation's requirements, and for AutoCAD to successfully fit a transformation.

**Impossible.** AutoCAD couldn't fit the transformation because you didn't specify enough points.

**Failure.** You specified enough points, but AutoCAD couldn't fit a transformation because of a problem with the points. Some of the points are probably collinear or coincident.

**Canceled.** AutoCAD canceled the fit. You only see this response for projective transformations.

AutoCAD displays the statistics in the rest of the table's rows only for a Success outcome of fit transformations. With the exception of the At Point entry, the values are taken by measuring the residual (the difference in distance between the point you picked and the point that AutoCAD recorded). The meanings of these statistics are defined here:

■ *RMS error.* RMS stands for root-mean-square, a statistical measure of how near AutoCAD came to finding a perfect fit to the points you picked. A lower value indicates a closer fit. This value given in the table is an average of all residuals.

■ *Standard deviation.* This is the standard deviation of the residuals. A value close to zero means that the residuals are about equal for each point.

Appendixes

■ *Largest residual/At point.* This is the value of the largest residual and the point at which it occurs (such as the least accurately picked point).

■ *Second-largest residual/At point.* This is the value of the second-largest residual and the point at which it occurs. A large difference between the largest and second-largest residual can indicate that a procedural error occurred during calibration at the point of the largest residual.

If the calibration procedure did not yield at least one Success or Exact Outcome of fit, AutoCAD cancels the command and returns to the Command: prompt. Otherwise, it moves to the next step:

3. After you finish entering points, press Enter to end the process. AutoCAD prompts:

```
Select transformation type...
Orthogonal/Affine/Projective/<Repeat table>:
```

The second line in the prompt shows the full set of possible transformation types. What you actually see may vary; AutoCAD excludes any type for which it did not register either Success or Exact. Choose the type you want AutoCAD to use by typing **o**, **a**, or **p**, or press Enter to see the table again.

After you choose a transformation type, AutoCAD ends the command and turns Tablet mode on, so you can begin tracing the drawing.

## Tracing the Drawing

You can trace the drawing using any of AutoCAD's object creation commands. Use lines or polylines to trace straight segments. Use circles to trace circles, and arcs or polyline arcs for arc segments. Use solids or wide polylines to trace filled objects. Don't trace hatch patterns; you can hatch those areas later with AutoCAD's own hatch patterns. The same applies to text; don't trace it—add any text and dimensions later using AutoCAD's commands. For irregular shapes you can use AutoCAD's SKETCH command.

---

**Caution**

When you use SKETCH, depending on your settings, it's quite easy to create a huge drawing file. Each increment you create records *x*, *y*, and *z* data on the starting and ending points. If you set up SKETCH to use short record increments, it won't take long to fill your hard drive.

---

You may not initially see the crosshairs when Tablet mode is on, or you may see them flash across the screen with only a hairsbreadth move of the digitizer's puck or stylus. This is because you are zoomed into a small area relative to the drawing's scale. You set the scale earlier when you calibrated the digitizer by selecting points and telling AutoCAD the actual coordinates. This behavior can be a bit disconcerting, because you can draw things without seeing the points you are choosing. ZOOM A, and your display clears.

◀ See "Fixed and Floating Screen Pointing Areas," p. 1218

### Note

If it helps, consider that the resulting effect is similar to opening a viewport in paper space. If the zoom factor is set too high in model space you can only see a small portion, or none at all, of your model.

After your tablet has been calibrated, you can use the method of toggling between TABLET MODES, by using the TABLET command's ON and OFF options. When TABLET MODE is ON, you are tracing drawings and sending digitizer coordinates to AutoCAD. When TABLET MODE is OFF, you are selecting commands from your digitizer's tablet menu and sending them on to AutoCAD. The TABLET command prompts are as described below.

Follow these steps to use the tablet for tracing:

1. Type **tablet** at the AutoCAD Command: prompt. AutoCAD prompts:

   Option (ON/OFF/CAL/CFG):

2. Type **on** and press Enter to start tracing.

Follow these steps to use the tablet for menu input:

1. Type **tablet** at the AutoCAD Command: prompt. AutoCAD prompts:

   Option (ON/OFF/CAL/CFG):

2. Type **off** and press Enter to input tablet input commands.

**Tip**
You can toggle between the floating and fixed screen areas using F12 and access tablet commands without turning off the TABLET MODE. Ctrl+T toggles the digitizing mode on or off.

### Note

Turning the Tablet ON and OFF during an AutoCAD editing session does not affect the tablet's calibration after it has been set.

Appendixes

# Conversion by Scanning

As mentioned earlier, tracing works well for a few drawings but it can be time-consuming and tedious. If you have to digitize a lot of drawings, and especially if you must do so in a limited amount of time, you may consider an alternative to tracing: scanning. With scanning, you usually contract with a service bureau to do the work for you because large scanners are very expensive. The scanner produces a raster file, in which the lines, arcs, and circles on the drawing are represented as a series of tiny dots. After the raster files are created, you can proceed in one of two ways:

1. Let the service bureau convert the raster files into vector, format (probably DXF). After you get the DXF files from the service bureau, you can import them into AutoCAD and save them as drawing files quickly and conveniently.

   To finish, these drawings still can require quite a bit of editing. The final output hinges on two factors: the clarity of the print you start with and the quality of the equipment your service bureau uses. Some automatic conversion (vectorizing) software does not put objects on layers nor recognize text, and can intertwine raster objects.

   Carefully question your vendor and look at past samples. Ask a technician to run a test on one of your drawings, then you can see firsthand what you are paying for. For a fee, most service bureaus also will trace the scanned image and clean up the drawing for you. Some programs allow you to trace over a scanned image from within AutoCAD. The end result is a completed drawing file. If you do not have a local dealer who offers these services, you might want to refer to sources such as CompuServe or some of the trade magazines.

2. Take the raster files and, using raster file viewing software, trace them into AutoCAD. Raster viewing software runs inside AutoCAD and lets you view the raster file in the drawing editor.

   There are programs on the market today that allow you to do raster editing, viewing, redlining, and plotting of these files. Softdesk is one company that provides such software with its LFX program and Image Systems scanning software.

   You can snap to raster snap points, and extend and erase rasters as well. You can't manipulate any of the objects with AutoCAD's commands, but you can trace them just as you do when you use your digitizer.

Some of the newest raster viewing software contains routines to auto-matically convert the raster objects into AutoCAD objects. This software is just coming into the marketplace. Your results can vary depending on the quality of the drawings you scan.

In the future, this type of system is sure to be a viable alternative to microfilm and physical drawing archive systems. With computerized databases, network access, and software available to produce hard copy output, the days are surely numbered for drawing vaults and drafters lost for days searching for archived prints.

Appendixes

# Index

## Symbols

installation
AutoCAD, 1104-1109
ACAD.INI file, 1110-1111
backups, 1097-1099
CD installation, 1108
dealer installation, 1095-1096
directories, 1109-1110
hardware requirements, 1096-1097
icons, selecting display icons, 1110
networks, 1125-1139
software requirements, 1096-1097
troubleshooting, 1144-1146
FREECELL, 1103
Win32s, 1103-1104
Installation Options dialog box, 1106
integer variables, 1148
intensity (lights)
ambient light, 952
distant light, 952
point light, 954
spotlights, 955
interfaces (PLOT command), 397-400
international measurements, 1124
International Organization of Standardization, *see* ISO
interoperability, 1046-1047, 1058
intersecting primitive shapes (solid models), 928
INTERSECTION command, 928
INTersection object snap mode, 155
invisible block attributes, 716-717, 728-732
IO.SYS file, 1141
island detection (hatches), 487, 497, 585
ISO (International Organization of Standardization)
linetypes, 193
pen widths (hatch patterns), 490
ISOLINES variable, 1152, 1159, 1190
isometric drawing, 747-748, 753-756

arcs, 751
circles, 751
ellipses, 445
grids, 750
nonisometric objects, 752-753
planes, 748-749, 751
snap, 749
ISOPLANE command, 751
isoplanes, 748-749, 751

# J-K

JIS (Japanese Industrial Standards)
dimensions, 521
prototypes (drawings), 1124
joining
lines, 68
multilines, 616-617
objects
arcs, 278-282
beveled edges, 282-285
corners, 278-282
polylines, 587
primitive shapes (solid models), 922-924
viewports
3D models, 877
model space, 374, 377
joints (multilines), 601, 615, 618, 620-621
justifying text, 470-471
dimensions, 519-520
paragraphs, 1081

keyboards
command-entry, 27-29
accelerator keys, 29
function keys, 28-29
Escape key (canceling object selection), 234
keystroke configuration, 1120
Shift key (selecting objects), 220

# L

languages, *see* programming languages
Last method (object selection), 217, 223-224
LASTANGLE variable, 1152, 1159, 1189

LASTPOINT values, retrieving, 121
LASTPOINT variable, 661-662, 1152, 1159, 1189
LAYER command, 177
Layer Control dialog box, 177, 895
layers, 175-177
associative dimensions, 507
blocks, 691
colors, 686-687, 691
creating, 685-686
linetypes, 686-687, 691
switching, 698-699
colors, 181-184, 466
creating, 178-179
current layer, selecting, 180-181
defaults, 643
deleting, 646
filters, 188-189
freezing, 186
floating viewports (paper space), 895-896
to speed screen regeneration, 335
inserting, 178-179
linetypes, 184-185, 199-201
locking, 186-187
naming, 177-179
purging, 289
renaming, 188, 645
sorting, 179
switching, 628
thawing, 186, 895-896
title blocks, 885
turning on/off, 185, 187-188
unlocking, 186-187
xrefs, 705, 709, 1094
Layers command (Data menu), 177
layouts (3D model viewports), 877-878
LEADER command, 561-566
leaders (dimensions), 507, 561-566, 1075
left justification (text), 470
LENGTHEN command, 274-278, 1088
LENSLENGTH variable, 1152, 1159, 1197
libraries
linetypes, 1071
materials (rendering), 958, 1091
multiline styles, 599

# T

# X-Y-Z